THE PENGUIN DICTIONARY

Jean Chevalier (1906–1993) was a university lecturer in philosophy
and theology before working for UNESCO, where he was Director
of Relations for Member States. He left in 1964 to devote himself to
writing and research. He published many works on topics such as
St Augustine, Descartes, African religion, Sufism, human spirituality
and transcendental meditation.

Alain Gheerbrant was born in Paris in 1920. He is well known as a
poet and traveller, and has published several accounts of his travels,
notably along the Amazon and Orinoco rivers, as well as books on
the ancient civilizations of Central and South America.

John Buchanan-Brown is a long-established translator of French
books ranging from *belles-lettres* to children's literature. He was
General Editor of the three-volume *Cassell's Encyclopedia of World
Literature* and is the editor of John Aubrey's *Brief Lives* for Penguin
Classics.

A Dictionary of Symbols

Jean Chevalier and Alain Gheerbrant

Translated from the French by
John Buchanan-Brown

PENGUIN BOOKS

Published by the Penguin Group
Penguin Books Ltd, 80 Strand, London WC2R 0RL, England
Penguin Putnam Inc., 375 Hudson Street, New York, New York 10014, USA
Penguin Books Australia Ltd, Ringwood, Victoria, Australia
Penguin Books Canada Ltd, 10 Alcorn Avenue, Toronto, Ontario, Canada M4V 3B2
Penguin Books India (P) Ltd, 11 Community Centre, Panchsheel Park, New Delhi – 110 017, India
Penguin Books (NZ) Ltd, Cnr Rosedale and Airborne Roads, Albany, Auckland, New Zealand
Penguin Books (South Africa) (Pty) Ltd, 24 Sturdee Avenue, Rosebank 2196 South Africa

Penguin Books Ltd, Registered Offices: 80 Strand, London WC2R 0RL, England

www.penguin.com

First published in France 1969
Second edition published 1982
This translation of the second edition first published in Great Britain by
Blackwell Publishers 1994
Published in Penguin Books 1996

8

Copyright © Editions Robert Laffont S. A. et Editions Jupiter, Paris, 1982
Translation copyright © John Buchanan-Brown 1994
All rights reserved

The moral right of the translator has been asserted

Printed in England by Clays Ltd, St Ives plc

Contents

Contributors

André Barbault (International Centre for Astrology)
Dominique Bayle (Librarian, Musée de l'Homme, Paris)
Yvonne Caroutch (Buddhism specialist)
Jean Chevalier, dec. 1993 (Philosopher and theologian)
Marguerite Chevalier (Teacher of classical literature)
Marie-Madeleine Davy (Head of research, CNRS, Paris)
Alain Gheerbrant (Travel writer and poet)
Pierre Grison (Art critic)
George Heintz (University of Strasbourg)
Le Roux-Guyonvarc'h (Director of *Ogam*, review of Celtic Studies)
Éva Meyerovich (Researcher, CNRS)
Mohammed Mokri (Professor, University of Tehran)
Henri Pfeiffer (Doctor of Medicine, Professor of Chromatology)
Pierre Prigent (University of Strasbourg, Professor of Protestant Theology)
Jacques de la Rocheterie (Psychotherapist)
Shibata Masumi (University of Kyoto, Japan)
Alexandre Volguine (Director, *Les Cahiers astrologiques*)

A

ablution See WASHING.

abracadabra This charm was used throughout the Middle Ages. 'One only had to write it down in the triangular pattern shown below and wear it round one's neck as a sort of phylactery or charm to be protected from various diseases and to be cured of fever': (PLAD)

ABRACADABRA
ABRACADABR
ABRACADAB
ABRACADA
ABRACAD
ABRACA
ABRAC
ABRA
ABR
AB
A

The word derives from the Hebrew *abreg ad hābra* meaning 'strike dead with thy lightning'. In Hebrew it comprises nine letters. 'Placing aleph on the left side of the triangle – and its ninefold repetition – is the magical element' (MARA p. 48).

By arranging the letters in a reverse triangle, the celestial energies which the charm claims to entrap are directed downwards. Accordingly, the figure should be seen three-dimensionally as a funnel. The magic letters slanting down from the wide mouth to the narrow spout comprise the lines of force of a mighty whirlwind. Woe betide the powers of evil which it strikes since they will vanish for ever from the world above into the ABYSS from which there is no return.

In this sense, the charm, abracadabra, was a response to those same fears which inspired the invention of the AMULET, charm or PENTACLE. It is only one of the many charms based upon a very ancient symbolism and it has been compared with one of the names of Mithras, the Sun-god and saviour who offers sacrifice.

Like amulets, talismans and pentacles, this charm seeks to give the individual a sense of protection through communication with the higher powers and with the mysterious laws which govern the universe.

Abraham The Old Testament patriarch came to the land of Canaan from Mesopotamia during the reign of King Hammurabi early in the second millennium, *c.* 1850 BC. He was a citizen of Ur of the Chaldees until God commanded him to leave his homeland and migrate to an unknown country, to which he would direct him stage by stage. When he reached Canaan, God told him that this was the land ordained for him and for his descendants. Biblical tradition has it that God removed him from a polytheistic society to make him guardian of a monotheistic religion. All the known world had fallen into idolatry, and Haran and Canaan were not exempt from the general corruption. Abraham, however, settled there as a stranger and his faith was preserved from contact with the customs and beliefs of its inhabitants. In reality, a constant struggle must have been needed to keep together the patriarch's family and his dependants. This perpetual reaction against the corrupt environment around it was to become one of the constant features of the history of Israel, and the characteristic of being 'a stranger in a strange land' was to preserve its divine vocation.

Abraham symbolizes the man chosen by God to safeguard the holy faith entrusted to him; the man blessed by God, who lavishes upon him promises of unnumbered descendants and incalculable wealth (the commonly accepted meaning of his name being 'Father of Multitudes'); the man predestined to a universal role as another Adam and the ancestor of the Messiah. Putting all his trust in God's word, he set out for an unknown country; as God promised, the childless husband of a barren wife became the ancestor of countless descendants; when God told him to sacrifice his only son, in apparent contradiction of those promises, Abraham was ready to obey until prevented by the angel. St Paul sums up this faith in a striking phrase, 'who against hope believed in hope'.

From the fact that Abraham is acknowledged as an ancestor by the three great monotheistic religions, Judaism, Christianity and Islam, he symbolizes, too, the spiritual bonds uniting Jew, Christian and Muslim in the brotherhood of Abraham.

On the psychological plane Abraham also symbolizes the need for a complete break away from one's habitual family, social and professional environment if one is to fulfil some extraordinary vocation and to exert an abnormal influence. All those destined to greatness have a penchant for risk and risk-taking. Faith in God can move mountains. Abraham's wisdom incited him to the folly (see SIMPLETON) of taking a gamble on God.

abstinence The idea of purification by giving up the eating of meat is coupled in Christian tradition with that of penance and atonement. Blood symbolizes the sensual urges and is held to be the chief source of sin. Atonement for sin will therefore comprise abstinence from flesh, which is the mainspring of sin itself. Life will be focused upon the springs of spirituality alone, upon relating to the divine, the invisible. In its twofold aspect – purification and atonement – abstinence is seen as one of the ways to the inner life. In this, Christian tradition is at one with the traditions of the East.

In Japan, avoiding the sources of defilement is a means of purification which enables one to gain, as it were, an active purity. This method is the province of the priest rather than that of the lay person. It comprises the observance of certain TABOOS – never to touch a dead body, or to have contact with sickness or mourning. One must also stay at home avoiding all exuberance, song or dance, in short all those activities conducive to defilement. All these practices symbolize the contrast between the visible and the invisible world, as well as the quest for the invisible through introspection.

abyss In both Greek and Latin 'abyss' indicates something which is bottomless, a world of endless depth or height. In apocryphal writings it is a blanket term for all formless states of being. It can be equally well applied to the shapeless Chaos preceding time as to the shadowy Hell of the end of the world. On the psychological plane it corresponds as much to the indeterminacy of childhood as to the undifferentiated state of death and the decomposition of the personality. But it may also indicate the ultimate act of unification, the so-called mystic marriage. The vertical lines are no longer those of descent, but of ascent. The abyss is as much topless as bottomless, one of joy and light as well as of misery and darkness. Historically, however, the sense of the abyss of Hell precedes that of Heaven.

In Sumerian folklore, the home of Enki, the Ruler of the World, floats upon the abyss, while, according to the Akkadians, it was Tiamat, the Mother of All Things, who brought forth monsters at its mouth (SOUN p. 136).

In the Bible, too, the abyss is sometimes imagined as a MONSTER, LEVIATHAN. However, in Psalm 104 the abyss is compared with a garment covering the Earth, while Jehovah 'coverest [him]self with light as with a garment'.

The abyss is to be found in all cosmogonies as the beginning and the end of an evolving universe. Like the monsters of myth, it swallows living beings only to regurgitate them transformed.

The depths of the abyss form an analogy with the kingdom of the dead and hence the worship of the Great Goddess, Mother Earth. Undoubtedly when C. G. Jung connects the symbolism of the abyss to his maternal archetype, the MOTHER who inspires both love and fear, it was upon the basis of this age-old cultural substratum. In dreams pleasant or nightmarish, the abyss conjures up the vast and powerful subconscious and is seen as an invitation to plumb the depths of the soul, to break its bonds and exorcise its ghosts.

acacia The Ark of the Covenant was made of acacia wood plated with gold (Exodus 37: 1–4); Christ's crown of thorns was woven from acacia; and, lastly, a branch of acacia is laid upon the Entered Apprentice's shroud in Masonic ritual to remind him of the acacia planted upon Hiram's grave. These diverse items of folklore show how, in Judeo-Christian thought, this tree, with its hard, virtually incorruptible wood, its terrible thorns and its flowers the colours of blood and milk, has become a solar symbol of rebirth and immortality.

The acacia is symbolically linked with the idea of initiation and the knowledge of secret lore. Something similar may be deduced from the Bambara legend which credits the acacia with the origin of the BULL-ROARER. When the first blacksmith was still a child, as he was carving a mask, 'a chip of acacia wood flew off, humming through the air with the roar of a lion. The child called two of his friends, took the chip of wood, bored a hole through one end, tied a cord to it and whirled it round his head' (SERH p. 121).

The African legend is reminiscent of a still-current Vedic practice. A hole is bored in a disc of acacia wood into which is inserted a fig-wood stick;

this is rotated rapidly and from the friction comes the sacred flame used in sacrifice. Here the acacia stands for the female and the fig for the male principle.

In India Brahmā's attribute of the sacrificial ladle of acacia is analogous (GRAR, GUED, GUES, MALA).

Thus the acacia appears everywhere to be given a religious importance as an adjunct of the godhead in its triumphal, solar aspect.

acanthus The acanthus leaf was widely reproduced in Classical antiquity and in the Middle Ages as a decorative motif, the symbolism deriving essentially from the THORNS which the plant bears.

According to the legend recorded by Vitruvius, the sculptor Callimachus (late fifth century BC) was inspired by the sight of a bunch of acanthus leaves crowning the grave of a young girl to copy them as the decoration for the capital of a column. What can be learned from this legend is that to begin with the acanthus motif was used extensively in funerary architecture to designate the triumphant conquest of the trials of life and death, symbolized by the thorns on the leaf of the plant.

They decorated Corinthian capitals, hearses and the clothes of the great because architects, the dead and heroes had overcome all difficulties in their path. As with thorns in general, the acanthus is also the symbol of virgin soil and of virginity – and that too implies another sort of triumph.

Whoever wears this leaf has overcome the Biblical curse, 'Thorns and thistles shall [the ground] bring forth for thee' (Genesis 3: 18), in the sense that once surmounted, suffering is turned to victory.

acorn The symbolism of the acorn is linked with that of the EGG – plenty, prosperity, fruitfulness. Transferred from the material to the spiritual plane, it may be found at the end of the red cords of the cardinal's hat, on the capitals of columns, in coats of arms and elsewhere. Protruding from its rough-grained cup, it symbolizes birth, emergence from the mother's womb; also in another respect, the virile powers of the PHALLUS; lastly, when paired, it becomes no more than an image of man's sexuality. However, on a spiritual plane, and within a religious context, the acorn symbolizes the power of the spirit and the wholesome virtues of truth, truth which flows from two sources – natural and revealed.

acrobat In every civilization acrobats, circus performers, clowns and jugglers have been held in high regard. Indeed, in Moscow, in a cemetery reserved for the famous, clowns have their marble tombs alongside dancers, writers, philosophers and statesmen of both the old and the new regimes. Acrobats have been a source of inspiration both to literature and to the plastic arts since, although they provide no sharply defined symbolism, yet they can be seen to represent one of the most persistent themes of human imagery and dreams. They may well stand for the joyous freedom of those who are released from the constraints of everyday living (see STUMBLER).

This reversal of the established order, of hidebound attitudes of mind or behaviour – pilloried by the wide-ranging skill of the acrobat – does not necessarily relate to a regressive phase in individual or group development. Of course if acrobats reveal a crisis situation, it is only to suggest the solution

– which must lie in a degree of mobility. The acrobat is therefore seen as the symbol of a critical balance based upon mobility and nonconformism. In this sense he or she is an agent of progress.

Some acrobatic or gymnastic exercises can be linked with those ritual or dance movements which, in defiance of the laws of gravity, either place their performers in the very hands of God or else assume in them a superhuman virtuosity. Acrobats or dancers push freedom from the everyday laws of nature to its human limits and seem to entrust themselves to the power of God alone. It is as if this power worked in them, for them and through them, so that the movements of their bodies should become identified with God the Creator and should bear witness to his presence. Of sacred dance in Ancient Egypt, Henri Wild writes: 'The repeated leaps would grow higher and higher and faster and faster as in the present-day *Zikr* which is, perhaps, a survival of the ancient incantatory dance. In both, the object of the exercise is temporarily to annihilate the individuality of the performer by producing in him or her a state of ecstatic exhaltation which allows the god to possess him or her' (SOUD p. 67). Similarly in Cambodia 'dislocation alone enables the dancer to escape the limits of normal body movement and to encompass those of myth. With elbows pointed out, hands bent back and legs set as though to take flight, hers is no mere show of acrobatics but the imitation of supernatural beings' (SOUD p. 365: see CIRCUMAMBULATION).

The search for identification with the godhead through acrobatic dance comes to its full fruition in Bali and Java in the dances of the *sang hyang dedari*. These little girls, in a state of trance, their bodies completely possessed by a female deity, go through a series of acrobatic dance movements, 'eyes closed and in a somnambulistic state . . . after their heads have been held over a chalice in which incense is burning and after the thick smoke has put them to sleep in two or three minutes' (SOUD p. 391). After Voodoo dancers have undergone preliminary exercises and inhalations, they scatter red-hot cinders on their heads and leap on white-hot coals without suffering burns.

Acrobatics symbolizes taking wing to a superhuman state: it is corporeal ecstasy. Walking on his or her hands, with head down and heels in the air, the acrobat is reminiscent of the figure of the twelfth Tarot, the HANGING MAN. He or she therefore symbolizes the reversal of values in all its initiatory complexity.

Adam Whatever tradition and all its commentators may say – and a whole series of books would be needed to summarize their arguments – Adam still symbolizes the first man, made in the image of God. 'First' implies much more than mere priority in time: Adam is first in the natural order, he is the acme of earthly creation, the highest example of humankind. First, therefore, carries no trace of the primitive, the word bears no hint of the ape-man, planting a milestone in the upward evolutionary march of the species. He is first, too, in the sense that he is accountable to his long line of descendants. His primacy is of the moral, natural and ontological order: Adam is the pattern of mankind: he symbolizes something which lifts us to a level of study beyond that of mere history.

Furthermore, he was created in the image of God. From one symbolic aspect, the phrase may be taken to mean that, just as a masterpiece is in the image of the artist who created it, so Adam is in the image of God. Yet the specific point at which this masterpiece should resemble its Creator resides in succeeding where Deucalion failed, in making manifest the spirit within creation, by giving life to mere matter. What Adam symbolizes is the reality of the spirit – in the image of God, but other than God. From this flow all those other consequent innovations to the universe – conscience, reason, freedom, responsibility, independence – spiritual privileges, but of a spirit made flesh and hence only in the image of God, and not identical with God.

Because Adam attempted to make himself identical with God, he also became the first to sin, with all the consequences that this primacy in sin entailed upon his descendants. In any order of events, the first is always, in some sense, the cause of whatever subsequently occurs within that order. Adam symbolizes Original Sin, perversion of the spirit, misuse of freedom and rejection of all dependence. Now this rejection of all dependence upon the Creator can only result in death, since that dependence is the very condition of life itself. Universally and traditionally whoever attempts to become God's equal falls under some terrible punishment.

At this point, according to Christian tradition, another Adam appeared, Jesus Christ, the second Adam in point of time, but the first, as well, in the mystic sense of the word and, if it may be said, more truly first than the first Adam; historically *primo prior*, since he is the pattern of mankind, by a higher right, first in the natural order and in the order of grace, both these orders reaching their highest fulfilment in him. He was more than the manifestation of the spirit in creation, he was the Word made Flesh – the very Word of God made man, man made God. He was no longer the image, but the reality. Again, it was impossible for him to sin, for the second Adam must confer that grace, holiness and eternal life of which mankind was deprived by the action of the first Adam. Thus the second Adam symbolizes all that was positive in the first and lifts him to the absolute plane of godhead. He symbolizes the antithesis of all that was negative and, for the certainty of death, substitutes the certainty of resurrection. Many a passage in the writings of St Paul emphasizes this antithesis: 'The first man Adam was made a living soul; the last Adam was made a quickening spirit. Howbeit that was not first which is spiritual, but that which is natural; and afterwards that which is spiritual. The first man is of the earth, earthy: the second man is the Lord from heaven' (1 Corinthians 15: 45–7: see also Romans 5: 12–17).

There is a close connection between the first Adam and Christ, the second Adam. Thus the legend tells how Adam died on Friday, 14 Nisan, at the ninth hour, prefiguring the death of Christ. In religious painting Adam's skull is shown at the foot of Christ's cross. According to legend, when Adam was on the point of death, he sent his son, Seth, to Paradise to pluck the fruit of immortality from the Tree of Life. The angel posted to guard Paradise refused to give him the fruit, but presented him with three seeds. After Adam died these seeds sprouted from his mouth and a tree grew which later provided the wood for the Cross. Further evidence for the symbolic links between Adam and Christ may be found in the dialogue with Adam in Dante's *Paradiso*, Canto 26.

Traditional Jewish speculation on the symbolism of the early chapters of Genesis has been subjected to Persian and to neo-Platonic influence. Adam means 'the man of earth created by God from earth' (in Hebrew *'adamah* = 'cultivated soil' or, as others suggest, 'inhabited land'). He was brought to life by the breath of God, but before this, according to the Kabbalah, he was called GOLEM. God created him from the finest clay taken, according to Jewish tradition, from the top of Mount Zion, held to be the centre or navel of the world. This clay stood for the world in its entirety. The Talmud describes the first twelve 'hours' in the first 'day' (or period) of Adam's life: (1) the clay is collected up; (2) the clay becomes a Golem; (3) its limbs are laid out; (4) God breathes a soul into it; (5) Adam stands upright; (6) Adam gives names to all living creatures; (7) he is given EVE; (8) Adam and Eve come together and produce offspring – 'the pair becomes a four'; (9) an embargo is laid upon Adam; (10) Adam and Eve break the embargo; (11) they are condemned; (12) Adam and Eve are driven from Paradise. Each hour tallies with a symbolic stage in life.

The Haggadah does not follow the text of the Old Testament strictly, or rather, it attempts to reconcile the contradictions between the two passages in Genesis, one stating that male and female were created simultaneously (1: 27), and the other (2: 21) that Adam was created first and that Eve was created from one of his ribs. According to the Haggadah, the woman created simultaneously with Adam was LILITH. Adam and Lilith fell out; Cain and Abel quarrelled over which of them was to possess Lilith. It was then that God reduced the first man and the first woman to dust (SCHK pp. 181–4). Then he created man afresh, and having created man split him into male and female.

The first account of the Creation in Genesis suggests that Adam was bisexual and some writers have claimed that he was a HERMAPHRODITE. The *Midrash Bereshit Rabba* states that God made Adam simultaneously male and female. The Kabbalah repeats this and, in any case, gives God the attributes of both King and Queen.

Plato describes man as a spherical entity rotating like a wheel; and here again he was originally hermaphrodite.

In his purest form the first man was Adam Kadmon, according to Kabbalistic tradition (SCHK p. 122), and symbolized God dwelling in man. This was the world of the 'inner' man, only to be revealed by contemplation. The 'first man' was only so called from his nature, being, pre-eminently, 'in the image of God'. Christian commentators, however, rejected the Kabbalistic interpretation and took the words only in the historical sense of 'first man'.

Adam was also:

a synthesis of the created world. Naturally he was taken from the centre and navel of the Earth (Mount Zion), but all the elements were joined together in his creation. God gathered in the dust from which he was fashioned from the four corners of the Earth. Indeed the name Adam is an abbreviation of the elements or the names of the four CARDINAL POINTS from which he was made.

(SCHR p. 181)

Scholem (SCHK p. 184) quotes Lipsius who saw in Adam 'the mythological personification of earth'. He was the 'everlasting symbol, the seal and memorial' of the love of God for the Earth. 'The elements of Earth and Air work as one within Adam and his descendants' (SCHK p. 185).

In other traditions, too, Adam is the symbol of the first man and of the origin of mankind. In Gaul, the progenitor of mankind was represented by Dis Pater (the Latin name for the Celtic god), all Gallic tribes being descended from him.

In Ireland, as in a number of other countries, there are several progenitors or mythic ancestors, the rule being one for each of the five races which invaded Ireland in the five waves of invasion recorded in the *Lebor Gabala* or *Book of Invasions*. The two main progenitors would appear to have been Tuan mac Cairill, who passed through the successive metamorphoses of STAG, BOAR, FALCON and SALMON, and the bard Fintan, high judge of this world because he is wisdom incarnate. Undoubtedly he was the only (just) man spared by the Flood.

Each major historical period had its progenitor who took the role of the new Adam.

In Jungian analysis Adam symbolizes cosmic man, source of all psychic energy, most frequently associated, in the shape of the wise old man, with the archetypal father and ancestor, the image of the old man, of unfathomable wisdom, fruit of long and bitter experience. In dreams he can take the shape of prophet, pope, sage, philosopher, patriarch or pilgrim. The manifestation of the wise old man symbolizes the need to integrate traditional wisdom into the self or perhaps to actualize a latent wisdom. In Jungian thought the second Adam, whose cross, as so many painters depict it, is planted upon the tomb of the first Adam, symbolizes the advent of a fresh human nature on the ashes of the old.

In these three stages of birth, death and resurrection the analyst might discern symbols of the development of the human being on the path of individuation: lack of differentiation in a collective state; separation of the ego, asserting itself in its potential personality; and the realization of that personality by the integration of all its forces in synthetic and dynamic unity.

adze This wood-worker's tool, its handle carved into the shape of a human being and carried over the left shoulder, is the insignia of the sculptor, an important royal attendant in Africa (LAUA p. 129).

In Ancient Egypt it was the instrument used by Anubis to perform the 'miracle of *Opening the Mouth* ... with a magic wand shaped like the URAEUS.' Thanks to this operation – described in the minutest detail in the books of ritual – 'the dead would regain those faculties which they would need to be able to "live" in the other world' (CHAM p. 57). In this instance the adze represents the cutting implement, like the surgeon's scalpel, used to save life.

aegis This weapon of ZEUS (*Iliad* 15) was originally no more than an ordinary goatskin. Next it became the fearful shield forged by Hephaistos (Vulcan) and covered by the skin of the goat Amalthea which had suckled the infant Zeus. Zeus presented it to Apollo and later to Athene (Minerva).

Some describe the aegis of Athene as being a goatskin fringed with snakes' heads and bearing as its boss the fearful face of the Gorgon. It was originally the symbol of sovereignty, and then of the protection or support of the great.

However, unlike the thunderbolt, the aegis was not a weapon designed to strike down. It was an adjunct of psychological warfare, a deterrent used to inspire terror and to urge mortals to place their trust in him who alone deserved it, God Almighty. Originally it was the symbol of storm, the begetter of terror and panic.

'But do thou take in thy hands the tasselled aegis, and shake it fiercely over the Achaean warriors to fright them withal' (Homer, *Iliad* 15: 229–30). Phoebus Apollo held the aegis, that fearful, highly-charged, flashing, hairy object forged by that stout blacksmith, Hephaistos, and given to Zeus to carry and put mortal men to flight. Holding the aegis, he led his men forward:

Now so long as Phoebus Apollo held the aegis moveless in his hands, even so long the missiles of either side reached their mark and the folk kept falling; but when he looked full in the face of the Danaans of swift horses, and shook the aegis, and shouted mightily withal, then he made their hearts to faint within their breasts, and they forgat their furious might . . . for upon them Apollo had sent panic.

(Homer, *Iliad* 15: 218–22, 225–6)

afterbirth   Symbolizes the elemental WATERS and the EARTH from which life sprang and developed. Maoris use the same word, *whenna*, for 'earth' and 'placenta' (ELIT). There is a host of survivals of those rites of birth which involved burying the afterbirth, in other words returning it to its place of origin.

agriculture   Some medieval Irish writers assign divine attributes to artists and craftsmen, classing those who work the land as mere mortals. This betrays the aristocratic and warrior nature of Celtic civilization, which consigned to its own inferiors, or to the peoples which it had conquered or overawed, the task of tilling the land (see CASTE). In medieval Ireland wealth was calculated on the basis not of arable land but of heads of cattle. Prestige belonged to the herdsman rather than the ploughman.

The emblems of agriculture are the cornucopia (see HORN OF PLENTY) or the plough or the spade standing beside a bush or small tree: its patroness is the goddess CERES, crowned with ears of corn; and its ruler, the ZODIAC. Agriculture symbolizes the union of the four elements – Earth and Air, Fire and Water – whose marriage is the prerequisite of all fertility.

Agrarian cults are innumerable, among the earliest expressions of religious sentiment and rich in symbols. Agriculture itself seems always to have held a lowly place in the social scale, while the nomad carried a warrior's prestige. Agriculture corresponds to the WOMB.

air   According to traditional cosmogony, one of the four ELEMENTS. Like Fire, it is male and active, while the other elements, Earth and Water, are held to be passive and female. While the nature of the two latter is considered material, that of Air is spiritual.

The element of Air is linked symbolically with WIND and BREATH. It typifies that rarefied zone between Earth and Heaven, home of what the Chinese call the *k'i*, the breath of universal life. Vāyu, who represents the same principle in Hindu mythology, is depicted riding upon a gazelle and bearing a standard which floats in the breeze and which may be identified with the winnowing FAN. Vāyu is the cosmic breath of life and may be identified with the Word, itself breath. On the more rarefied plane of existence, Vāyu may represent the five vital functions, considered as modalities of *prāna*, the breath of life.

St Martin termed the element Air 'a palpable symbol of invisible life', a 'universal driving force', and a 'purifier', ideas corresponding almost exactly to those of the function of Vāyu who, it should be added, is also considered as a purifier.

In the esoteric teachings of the Ismailis, Air is 'the principle of harmonization and fructification'; it is the intermediary between Fire and Water, the first *lām* of the name of God. It corresponds to the function of the Universal Soul, or *Tali*, which made the Earth fruitful in the beginning and enables shapes and colours to be perceived – which brings us back to the function of 'breath' (CORT, DANA, GUEV, MALA, SAIR).

Air is the proper medium for light, scent, colour, flight and interplanetary vibrations and is the channel of communication between Heaven and Earth. 'Resonance, translucency and fluidity . . . a trilogy, spring from the inner sense of lightening of the self. They are not impressed upon us by the external world.' Someone, once dull and confused, acquires through 'a shift of the imagination, a power which enables him or her to become quick, clear and resonant by obeying the dictates of an airy imagination . . . . Airy freedom speaks, enlightens, flies' (BACS p. 74). The airy being is 'free as air' and so far from being blown away, actually shares the pure and rarefied properties of air.

aircraft 'Nowadays in dreams we often find that the car and the aircraft have taken the place of the monsters and fabulous animals of the distant past' (C. G. Jung).

The aircraft supplements the symbolic attributes of the AUTOMOBILE with that of levitation (see ASCENSION), in the same relationship as that of PEGASUS to the horse. It might therefore be said that its flight expresses a spiritual aspiration, namely individual release of the Earth-bound ego by escape to the purifying reaches of the upper air. That is to say that flight, with the aircraft climbing – the dreamer is very seldom coming in to land – leads to a state of ecstasy on a plane with the orgasm. Hence psychoanalysts frequently give such dreams a sexual connotation, although their analysis is clearly far more complex than this.

The appearance of aircraft in dreams is a recent but frequent phenomenon. Although it is a feature of the modern world, like the bird it would seem to exemplify one of the major aspirations of the human race – flight through the air. In this sense therefore, the aircraft is to Pegasus rather what the automobile is to the horse. The dreamer may find him- or herself either in an aircraft or floating in space. In the first instance the human is freed from the force of gravity which pins him or her to the Earth on which he or she crawls. In the second flight takes the almost magical shape of forces coming from the beyond. It then conjures up the cosmic power of the collective unconscious, in the face of which the conscious ego measures its powerlessness. The aircraft belongs to the province of the Air and is the material aspect of one of the powers of this element. It is the realm of ideas, of thought and of the spirit.

In addition the aircraft may also be identified with the DRAGON or with the THUNDERBOLTS of ZEUS.

When the dreamer sits in an aircraft, then the aircraft assumes an individual symbolism. The personality takes wing into limitless space where it feels completely free, and while remaining within the realm of Earth-Matter it soars towards Heaven-Spirit.

Its speed, its delicate mechanism and its handling difficulties make the aircraft reminiscent of life itself in which each day is a fresh adventure. Airmanship, too, demands capability and self-possession to navigate boundless space.

It restores freedom, independence and speed, allowing the pilot to go wherever he or she pleases freely and almost instantaneously.

Sometimes the dreamer sits in an aircraft piloted by somebody else, an inhibited aspect of oneself. The pilot may also stand for the analyst or even the ego which is effecting the transformation. If the dreamer or the pilot indulges in aerobatics these may perhaps be ostentatious or perilous from the spiritual point of view. They mark indecisiveness or fickleness in the vitality, an overfondness for taking risks and a temptation to take matters to extremes.

To be on board an aircraft when one has no right to be there is a sign that the dreamer has mistakenly followed a course of conduct, subjectively or objectively, which he or she had no right to undertake. It may also suggest favours withheld.

To run out of fuel may indicate a weakness of the libido and perhaps psychic inertia as well.

If an aircraft is so overloaded that it either cannot take off or flies badly, this is because the psychic mechanism is too overloaded with the heavy baggage of illusions, false values, intellectual knowledge, projections, subconscious fixations, pseudo-obligations, anxieties, revulsions, sentimentalism, passion and so on to enable psychic development to begin. We have to throw out ballast to get off the ground.

If the dreamer regards the aircraft purely as a piece of engineering, this will betray, as in the case of the car, a pattern of behaviour too closely governed by the thought process, by the intellect or by the purely mechanical aspects of everyday living or analysis.

Two aircraft colliding or engaged in a dog-fight is indicative of opposing trains of thought clashing in mutual destruction and traumatizing the psyche. It is the clash of opposites.

Aircraft manoeuvring in the sky indicate a perception of spiritual forces or cosmic powers breaking free within our psychic space. When the element is water, they will be seen as fish.

An aircraft crashing to the ground is the indication of too intellectual or too spiritual an attitude of mind, of too utopian a tendency too far removed from the earthly, which shatters when it comes into contact with the material realities of everyday living. The ideal is subjected to the brutal touch of harsh reality. The clash is agonizing. The dreamer, too, may lack a sense of reality (cf. the myth of ICARUS). There is a clash between intellect and instinct. The poles are too far apart. The original personality lacks the bases for its development and collapses. However, if the situation can be accepted, a fresh departure can be made on a new basis which takes the lower world as closely into account as it does the upper world.

Aerial bombardment: the disregarded, lurking subconscious wings its way to the attack like some menacing bombing plane, to impress with the notion of its power. It stands like Zeus wielding his thunderbolts and lightning. It symbolizes the tendency of the subconscious to free itself from conventional constraints, a determination to achieve freedom.

alchemy (see also V.I.T.R.I.O.L.) Alchemy is the art of transmuting metals for the purpose of obtaining GOLD. However, the production of gold for the pleasure it will bring, or even, as in China, of a golden elixir, drunk to prolong physical life, were certainly not the true ends of alchemy. It was in no sense the forerunner of chemistry, but a symbolic activity. 'They believed', states an ancient Chinese writer, 'that it was a matter of turning stones into gold: was this not madness?' To which the Guru Nāgārjuna replied: 'The work may be done through spiritual forces.' But the acquisition of such powers (*siddhi*) can never be considered an end in itself. 'Gold', according to Vedic writers, 'is immortality.' This, in fact, is the objective of the only real transmutation – that of the human self. It is expressly stated that if Liu Hsiang failed to obtain gold it was through lack of spiritual preparation. Li Chao-Kiun could not foresee success without divine intervention and equated fruition of the work with the search for the Isle of the Immortals. Somewhat late in the day, the Chinese gave new meaning to the word by distinguishing inner (spiritual) alchemy, *nei-tan*, from outward (material) alchemy, *wai-tan*, although the latter is but a symbol of the first. In the West, the symbolism was clearly defined by Angelus Silesius: 'Lead becomes changed into gold, doubt vanishes, when with God, I am changed by God into God . . . . It is the heart which is transmuted into the finest gold, Christ, or heavenly grace, being the tincture.'

Nevertheless, and in more general terms, alchemical symbolism is set on the cosmological plane. The two phases of 'coagulation' and 'solution' correspond to the rhythm of the universe – *kalpa* and *pralaya*: of involution and evolution, of inhalation and exhalation of the opposite tendencies of *tamas* and of *sattva*. Alchemy was held to be an extension and acceleration of the natural process of growth. Transmutation of metals was effected in the same way that the 'marriage' of SULPHUR and MERCURY generated minerals in the womb of the Earth, the Earth being the crucible in which the minerals 'ripened' and in which bronze became gold. Furthermore the alchemist's furnace had the same shape (that of the hourglass) as Mount Kun-lun, centre of the Earth, and of the CALABASH, image of the world. Through practising alchemy, the alchemist discovered a space of identical shape within himself – the 'CAVERN' of the heart. Furthermore the Philosopher's Stone was enclosed within the crucible as was the 'World Egg' or the

'Golden Embryo' within the cosmic cave. The calcination of the ingredients within the crucible symbolized in both China and the West the return to primordial Chaos expressed as a return to an embryonic state within the womb. The mouth of the furnace (ATHANOR) was identified with the symbolic perforation in the top of the head (*brahmarandhra*) through which release from the cosmos is effected or, according to the Chinese, the embryo returns to the void.

In the West the 'work' used sulphur and mercury, fire and water, the active and the passive, celestial and terrestrial influences in the correct proportion to produce the 'salt'. In the spiritual alchemy of the Taoists – apparently with heavy borrowing from Tantrism – these are *k'i* and *hsing*, the 'breath' and the 'essence', also identified with Fire and Water ('Fire of the Spirit' and 'Water of Generation', according to *The Secret of the Golden Flower*). They were depicted by the trigrams *li* and *k'an* of the *I-Ching*, fire and water, but still influenced by *Ch'ien* and *K'un*, the active and passive perfections of Heaven and Earth.

Two essential stages in the 'work' were making the White Stone (albedo) and making the Red Stone. In Western, hermetic, terms, they corresponded to the 'Lesser Mysteries' and the 'Greater Mysteries'; but they also corresponded to the Chinese 'Blooming of the Golden Flower', the 'Release of the Embryo' and the attainment of the states of 'True Man' (*tchen-jen*) and 'Transcendent Man' (*chen-jen*); and they corresponded to the 'pre-Adamite Man' and 'Universal Man' of Muslim esoteric doctrine which, moreover, defines the latter as 'Red Sulphur'. What is really at issue is: (a) reaching the 'Centre of the Earth' and attaining a paradisial state; (b) 'Release from the Cosmos' along the World Axis and attaining superhuman states (GRIF, GUED, GUET, GUES, KALT, LECC).

From a different viewpoint, alchemy symbolizes the actual evolution of the person from a state in which the material world predominates to a spiritual state – the transmutation of base metals into gold equates with the transformation of the human being into pure spirit. Alchemy, in fact, involved the practitioner in a knowledge of matter, but it was a knowledge, not a science. It was most generally applied to metals in accordance with a physico-symbolism utterly bewildering to the modern scientist. Both material and spiritual alchemy presupposed a knowledge of the principles governing the traditional order of things and were based far more upon a theory of proportion and interrelation than upon any strict physico-chemical, biological or philosophical analysis of the relationship of the elements. Language and logic partook of symbolism for the alchemist.

The famous *Emerald* TABLE set out in the most hermetic of terms the fundamental axioms of alchemy. Burckhardt summarizes them (BURS) as the classification of opposites on the lines of the basic opposition of male and female, the 'Great Work' being the marriage of the male element, sulphur, with the female element, mercury. All alchemical writers employed a wide variety of metaphors based upon marriage and procreation but this has nothing to do with sexology, it simply acted as a symbolic aid to knowledge.

One of the most interesting alchemical practices was known in the Middle Ages as the 'Royal Art', Burckhardt showing that it was based upon the doctrine of the Fall and had as its objective the restoration of man's original dignity. To find the Philosopher's Stone, therefore, was to attain to the Absolute and to acquire perfect knowledge (gnosis). It was the KING'S HIGH-WAY to the mystic state in which sin was eradicated and the individual became generous, gentle, pious, believing and God-fearing.

The work of the alchemist was governed by four operations, which should also be interpreted symbolically in accordance with the plane on which these transformations or transmutations took place. These comprised the purification of the matter used; its reduction until all that remained was the universal being; its restoration to solid form; and finally a fresh composition controlled by the purest being, on the plane of that new being, of God himself. The second of these operations is variously termed volatilization, sublimation (but not in the modern psychoanalytic sense), combustion, incineration and so on. Other writers hold that there were six operations in the process of transmutation: calcination, identified with the colour black, the destruction of shape, the extinction of lust, the reduction of matter to its primordial state; putrefaction which divided the calcinated elements until they were completely destroyed; solution, corresponding to the colour white, of matter completely purified; distillation, followed by conjunction, corresponding to the colour red, or with the union of opposites, the peaceful co-existence of contrarieties; finally sublimation, corresponding to gold, the colour of the Sun, the fullness of being, heat and light. The various systems and practices, given in more or less detail, may all be summarized in the famous formula *solve et coagula*, which might be translated as 'purify and integrate'. It applied just as strongly to the evolution of the objective universe as it did to the subjective, that of the self on the ladder of perfection.

Alchemical interpretation uses the symbols of its own language as keys to unlock the hidden meaning of folktales, myths and legends, in which it sees the interplay of the ceaseless transmutations of the soul and the ultimate fate of creation. Here is a typical example of the alchemical school of interpretation:

Snow White is the maiden who mines gold. The Seven Dwarfs or gnomes (from the Greek *gnosis*, knowledge) are the seven extensions of mineral matter (the seven metals). Each dwarf partakes of the character of the planet which governs him – Grumpy is saturnine, Dopey is lunar, Happy is venusian and so on. However, it is the saturnine Grumpy who is most helpful to the others and knows what to do whatever happens. Snow White is entrusted to the Green Huntsman, to be put to death. Yet in the end, after appearing to be dead and after having bitten the poisoned apple, the maiden marries the prince of her dreams, who is young and handsome. This Prince Charming is the Philosopher's Mercury (eternal youth is a well-known attribute of Mercury in myth). And after this marriage of Mercury (the Prince) with the Maiden (Snow White) comes the ending of all fairy stories – they lived happily ever after and had lots of children . . . . In fact hermetic multiplication by means of the Philosopher's Stone conforms with the injunction to *be fruitful and multiply* in Genesis.

(Robert Ambelain, *Dans l'ombre des cathédrales*, in TEIR p. 213)

alcohol   Alcohol is the material synthesis of FIRE and WATER. In the words of Bachelard,

Brandy, or *eau-de-vie*, is also *eau-de-feu* or fire-water. It is water which burns the tongue and flames up at the slightest spark. It does not limit itself to dissolving and destroying as does *aqua fortis*. It disappears with what it burns. It is the communion of life and of fire. Alcohol is also an *immediate* food which quickly warms the cockles of the heart.

(BACF p. 83)

Alcohol symbolizes the vital spark struck from the union of the opposite elements of Fire and Water.

It symbolizes both the flame of life and the spark of creative genius. Not only does it stimulate the latent within the spirit, but, as Bachelard observes, it actually creates. 'It incorporates itself, so to speak, within that which is striving to express itself. It becomes evident that alcohol is a creator of language . . . . Bacchus is a beneficent god; by causing our reason to wander he prevents the anchylosis of logic and prepares the way for rational inventiveness' (BACF p. 87).

The ambivalence of alcohol betrays its twofold origin. 'The alcohol of Hoffmann is the alcohol which flames up; it is marked by the wholly qualitative and masculine sign of fire. The alcohol of Poe is the alcohol that submerges and brings forgetfulness and death; it is the wholly quantitative and feminine sign of water' (BACF p. 91).

alligator See CROCODILE.

alloy In Ancient China, alloys occupied an important place in the symbolism deriving from metal-working. The founder's work was only completed when the FIVE colours balanced one another and when the copper and tin were completely fused. An alloy was therefore the image of the perfect sexual union. To assist its achievement, into the crucible were cast the galls of a pair of hares, or even, according to ancient legend, the smith and his wife, as symbols of that union. The tin came from a mountain and the copper from a valley. The wind from the bellows ought to be both *yin* and *yang*. If the wife alone were sacrificed it signified her marriage with the presiding genius of the forge; if the wind from the bellows was only *yin*, it meant that the forge contained the *yang* element (GRAD).

almandine (see also RUBY) A luminescent precious stone, the colour of POMEGRANATE, the almandine was believed to shine in the dark. When set in the eye-sockets of statues, it symbolized clarity of sight and strength of the vital principle and of the will. Set along a dark passageway to guide the steps, it symbolized more accurately eyes which see in the dark or determination which incites to the attainment of an objective.

It was a name given by the Ancients to the ruby as well, because of its colour and its almond shape, and was then confused with the CARBUNCLE, a fabulous gem-stone, its magic powers enthusiastically proclaimed by the German Romantic poets, for whom it symbolized the searing passions which lie buried in the depths of the heart.

almond (Italian: **mandorla**) Because of its husk, the almond is generally taken to symbolize the substance hidden within its accidents; spirituality masked by dogma and ritual; reality concealed by outward appearance; and, according to the secret doctrine, the eternally hidden Truth, Treasure and Fountain. Thus Clement of Alexandria: 'My *Stromates* contain the truth mingled with the dogmas of philosophy, or rather wrapped and enclosed by

them as the edible kernel of the nut is enclosed by its shell.' Or Maḥmūd
Shabistarī: 'The *shariat* is the husk, the *haqīqāt* is its almond . . . . When the
pilgrim has attained moral certainty, the almond is ripe and the husk is red.'
Or again, Abd al-Karim al-Jīlī: 'Throw away the shell and take the kernel;
do not be one of those who ignore the features, but tear away the veil!'

The almond is Christ because his divine nature was hidden in the human,
or in the womb of his virgin mother. It is also, according to Adam of St
Victor, *the mystery of light*, that is to say the end of contemplation, the
secret of inner illumination. The Italian word for almond, mandorla, is
applied to the oval which in the traditional iconography of painting and
sculpture encloses the figures of Christ, Our Lady and the saints as in the
glow of immortality. It shares this mystery of light in another way: it is the
heavenly light which at one and the same time radiates from the dwelling
place of the saints and is the 'veil' of the Beatific Vision. Furthermore it
corresponds to the rainbow, for, according to the Book of Revelation: 'And
he that sat was to look upon like a jasper or a sardine stone: and there was
a rainbow round about the throne, in sight like unto an emerald' (4: 3).

The geometrical shape of the almond associates it with the symbolism
of the LOZENGE, since it is a lozenge with the lateral angles rounded off.
Like the lozenge it symbolizes the union of Heaven and Earth, of the upper
and the lower worlds and, for this reason alone, would be ideally suited to
frame the figures of the saints. It symbolizes the harmonious marriage which
transcends the dualism of matter and spirit, fire and water, Heaven and
Earth.

The Hebrew word for almond, *luz*, expresses perfectly this idea of something hidden, enclosed, inviolable. The same word is also the name of an
underground city (see ALMOND-TREE) and that of the indestructible kernel
of being which carries within itself the seeds of its own resurrection (Chinese,
che-li; Sanskrit, *shārira*). This, in short, is 'the nut of immortality' (BENA,
CORT, GUEM, JILH).

In esoteric tradition the almond symbolizes the secret (a treasure) which
is hidden in some dark place and which must be discovered in order to
nourish the finder. The husk around it is compared with a wall or a gate.
To find the almond or to eat the almond means to discover or to share in
a secret.

In medieval esotericism the almond stood for Our Lady's virginity – the
mystic almond – and she was sometimes depicted surrounded by an elliptical halo.

According to Henri Estienne's *Thesaurus*, 'amandalos' means dark, invisible, of the inner nature.

The figures of saints are often completely enclosed within a mandorla,
frequently divided by three lines to express the Trinity. They have entered
the bosom of the Threefold God, with whom they have become united in
the Beatific Vision.

However, in common parlance to have eaten the almond means to have
had sexual intercourse, since the almond is the vulva, the *yoni*, which the
Upanishads tell us is 'the symbol of the cosmic waters and the stormy whirlpool of the infinite potentialities of existence' (TUCR). The mandorla may
be derived from this old archetypal image.

The fact that medieval esotericism cloaked Our Lady's virginity under the term 'mystic almond' serves to strengthen this theory. The most notable thing about this instance is that in passing from the sacred to the profane, the sacred value of the symbol is in no sense weakened, but rather made all the stronger, as can be seen in so many Sufi poems. For the sexual connotation given to the mandorla makes it the primordial womb, from which Man interfused with God was born into the light of the revelation.

almond-tree The almond is one of the first trees to flower in the Spring and is therefore the sign of the rebirth of nature and of careful watching for the first signs of Spring. It is also the symbol of transience, since its blossom comes out so early that it is susceptible to late frosts. It is the symbol of Attis, born of a virgin who conceived him from an almond.

This legend is perhaps the original of the connection of Our Lady with the almond-tree. However, the symbol depends for its validity upon the meaning of ALMOND itself.

To the Hebrews the almond-tree was the symbol of a new life. It is the first tree to come into flower in the Spring, as the prophet Jeremiah wrote: 'Moreover the word of the Lord came unto me, saying, Jeremiah, what seest thou? And I said, I see a rod of the almond tree. Then said the Lord unto me, Thou hast well seen: for I will hasten my word to perform it' (1: 11–12).

In Jewish folklore, furthermore, it is at the foot of an almond-tree (*luz*) that access can be obtained to the mysterious city of Luz, which is one of the 'Seats of the Immortals'. It is also the name of the town close to which Jacob had his vision and which he named *Beith-el*, or 'House of God'. The connection between the almond-tree and the idea of immortality may be explained yet again by the symbolism of the almond – also called *luz* – (BENA, GUEM). However, if the symbolism of the almond is female, that of the almond-tree is male.

The Greeks compared the milk of the almond as a creative force with the seminal ejaculation of Zeus. Pausanias tells how a dream caused a nocturnal emission. Zeus' seed fell to Earth and from it sprang a hermaphrodite, Agdistis, whom Dionysos castrated. His sexual organs fell to the ground and from them grew an almond-tree. The daughter of the river-god, Sangarius, became pregnant when she placed a fruit from this tree between her breasts.

The theme of these legends is that the almond-tree derives directly from Zeus, through the blood of a hermaphrodite, and that its fruit can unaided make a virgin pregnant, the particular nuance of phallic symbolism being that its powers are exercised independently of sexual intercourse. A folk belief, still current in Europe, has it that the girl who falls asleep under an almond-tree and dreams of her lover will wake up pregnant.

alpha and omega The first and last letters of the Greek alphabet: since they are taken to hold the key to the universe in its entirety locked between these two poles, alpha and omega symbolize the totality of knowledge, of being, of space and of time.

The author of the Book of Revelation ascribes these two letters to 'Jesus Christ, the faithful witness, and the first begotten of the dead, the prince of the kings of the earth . . . . I am Alpha and Omega, the beginning and the ending, saith the Lord, which is and which was, and which is to come, the Almighty' (1: 4, 8). Christ, as the beginning and the end, is a Hellenization of the expression of Isaiah: 'Who hath wrought and done it, calling the generations from the beginning? I the Lord, the first, and the last; I am he' (41: 4) . . . 'I am the first, and I am the last; and beside me there is no God' (44: 6). Revelation 21: 5–8 sets this in more explicit terms.

It should be noted that several other words as well as alpha and omega are used here in a symbolic sense: water, symbol of life, becomes a symbol of the spirit, source of spiritual life; consuming fire, symbol of the torments of hell and of eternal death in God's eyes. Similarly in Revelation 22: 13–15 the words 'tree of life', 'city' and 'gate' are symbols affiliated to 'Alpha and Omega, the First and the Last, the Beginning and the Ending'. These two letters are often set on Christ's CROSS.

More recently Teilhard de Chardin has used these two letters to express a new theory of universal evolution which moves towards the creation of a 'noösphere' through the gradual spiritualization of human beings and human thought. Beginning by condemning a trend in the spirit of the age towards a gradual depersonalization and collectivization of individuals in mass endeavour, he then sets against it his concept of a 'personalizing universe'. The pole omega symbolizes the end of this evolution towards the 'noösphere', the sphere of the spirit towards which all thoughts converge and where the human being will in some sense become deified in Christ.

altar Microcosm and catalyst of holiness, ritual and architectural centre-piece, the altar reproduces on a small scale the entire temple and the universe itself. It is the place in which is the most powerful distillation of holiness, since on or near the altar is the place of sacrifice, that is to say of something which makes holy. For this reason it is raised (*altum*) above its surroundings. In itself it unites the symbolism of the CENTRE of the World: as the threshold of the SPIRAL it implies the gradual spiritualization of the universe. The altar symbolizes the time and place where a person becomes holy or performs something holy.

Amazon The historical existence of warrior women – Amazons or VALKYRIES – is perhaps a survival or a memory of a matriarchal society. Their symbolism, however, is not necessarily linked with any sociological system.

The Amazons were warrior women, with their own system of government, who only coupled with strangers. They raised girl children only, blinding or mutilating their sons. Although legend states that they amputated a breast so as better to handle BOW and LANCE, this is not borne out in art, which depicts the Amazons as beautiful women with both breasts intact. As warriors, huntresses and priestesses they were dedicated to the worship of ARTEMIS (Diana). In Greek mythology they symbolized 'man-killers: women who tried to take the place of men, rivalling them in battle instead of complementing them . . . . This rivalry exhausted woman's basic strengths, the qualities of the lover and the mother, warmth of soul' (DIES p. 207).

The GIRDLE of Hippolyte, Queen of the Amazons, was given to her by
Ares (Mars) 'to symbolize the power which she exercised over her people'
(GRID p. 193). The Ninth Labour of Herakles (Hercules) was to fetch this
girdle. Hippolyte had agreed to give it to him, when a quarrel erupted
between the Amazons and Herakles' followers. Thinking himself betrayed,
Herakles killed Hippolyte. Legend adds that it was Hera who had sparked
the quarrel. With reference to the symbolism of the girdle, to surrender
one's girdle is to surrender one's self, and this is not simply a renunciation
of one's power. For Hippolyte it was to surrender her state of being an
Amazon and to give herself to Herakles. By preventing the surrender of the
girdle, Hera, who stands as the symbol of female normality, showed that
she intended the death rather than the conversion of the virago. This on the
one hand: on the other, she did not want Herakles, whom she had hated
since he was begotten by Zeus of another woman, to enjoy the satisfaction
of obtaining a woman's girdle. The Amazon symbolizes the position of the
woman who behaves like a man but does not manage to be accepted either
by men or by women and does not even succeed herself in living either as
a man or a woman. In the end she embodies the denial of the female nature
and the myth of the impossibility of altering one's real nature to fit an ideal.

G. Lanoe-Villène claims that according to Classical occultism, the Amazons were ranked 'in the metaphysical order, as a symbol of the psychic
stellar powers which encircled the Elysium of the Gods to guard and defend
its approaches'. In this guise 'their girdle is none other than the magic circle
which they make around Elysium and which Herakles was to break by
force of arms. Their horses are the clouds which sweep across the sky in
snowy squadrons' (LANS 1: pp. 77, 84). They loosen their girdles for heroes
and kill the cowardly. Savage protectors of a Paradise, these disconcerting
beings, who offer and deny their bodies, who save and slay, are perhaps
merely the equivocal gates of an unstable Heaven.

amber   In about 600 BC Thales discovered the magnetic properties of amber,
and the word 'electricity' is derived from the Greek name for yellow amber,
'electron'. Amber rosaries and amulets act as condensers of current. As
they themselves become charged, so they take the discharge of excessive
current in those who wear the amulet or handle the beads.

Amber represents the psychic line between individual and cosmic energy,
the individual soul and the universal soul. It symbolizes solar, spiritual and
divine attraction.

A frequent attribute of saints and heroes is a face the colour of amber,
the symbol of Heaven reflected in their persons and in their power of
attraction.

Apollo wept tears of amber when he was banished from Olympus and
fled to the HYPERBOREANS. These tears expressed his homesickness for
Paradise and the subtle chain which still bound him to Elysium.

The Pseudo-Dionysius the Areopagite explains that amber is an attribute
of heavenly beings because 'as being partly like silver, partly like gold, [it]
denotes the incorruptible, as in gold, with unexpanded, and undiminished,
and spotless brilliancy, and the brightness as in silver and a luminous and
celestial radiance' (PSEH p. 48).

There is a popular belief that if a man keeps a piece of amber on him, in no circumstances will he be betrayed by sexual impotence.

ambrosia The food of immortality, together with nectar, jealously reserved for the Olympians. Gods, goddesses and heroes were fed on it and they even went so far as to give it to their horses. Its miraculous qualities included its use as a salve which healed all wounds and as a preservative of corpses from corruption. But woe to the mortal who ate ambrosia uninvited – he or she risked the same punishment as TANTALUS.

The gods of the Veda were not so jealous and the mortal who tasted SOMA or *amrita* was enabled by their means to attain to Heaven.

The person becomes what he eats. Christian mystics were to take up this idea: ambrosia was to become the Eucharist, the body of the Saviour God, 'the true bread of angels'.

amen Symbol of confirmation and affirmation, it is used in the Bible and in the liturgy of both Synagogue and Church. Amen may be set at the beginning or end of a phrase.

In the Book of Revelation (3: 14) Christ is called 'the Amen'.

The word 'amen' approximates to the term AUM, both possessing an identical sense. This affirmation and confirmation contain the Lord himself (VALT), in the role of creative energy.

amethyst Taken from the Greek *amethus(t)os*, 'sober' (literally, not drunk). The amethyst is a jewel of temperance and protects against all forms of INTOXICATION. For this reason, according to orthodox Christian belief, it should be worn by bishops. As shepherd of souls, bearing both spiritual and temporal responsibilities, and unlike the contemplative and the recluse who has abandoned the world, the bishop ought to guard against all intoxication, even spiritual. Traditionally Christian moralists make the amethyst the symbol of humility because of its VIOLET colour.

According to Pliny, the stone protects against enchantment if it is engraved with figures of the Sun and Moon and 'worn round the neck with peacocks' down and swallows' feathers' (BUDA p. 309). It cures the gout and, if placed under the pillow, brings sweet dreams, strengthens the memory and acts as an antidote to poison.

amphora See JAR.

amulet The amulet was believed to possess or to encapsulate a magical power. It embodied what it symbolized – a peculiar relationship between the wearer and the powers which the amulet represented. The amulet 'contains in itself all the . . . forces at work on every level of the cosmos – but actually . . . places the wearer himself at the centre of those forces, increasing his vitality, making him more *real*, and guaranteeing him a happier state after death' (ELIT p. 156).

Egyptian mummies were covered in gold, bronze, stone or faience amulets to preserve the immortality of the dead as they had guarded his or her health, happiness and life on earth. According to their shape and the figures which they represented, these amulets were believed to confer strength, vitality, knowledge, physical enjoyment and so on. The mason's square, the

angle pointing upwards and with a plumb-line dependent from it, provides
a figure with the virtues of an amulet, which is as much a part of Ancient
Egyptian religious art as it is of modern Masonic symbolism – it is the
assurance of perpetual stability. The commonest and the most powerful of
these Egyptian talismans bore the figures of the SCARAB beetle, the EYE, the
GIRDLE of Isis and the ANKH (POSD).

anchor A solid body, its weight holding the ship fast, the anchor was
taken to symbolize firmness, solidity, tranquillity and faithfulness. It holds
firm and steady amid the flux of the elements and comes to symbolize the
stable part of our being, the quality which enables us to keep a clear mind
amid the confusion of sensation and emotion. In this sense it can also act
as a bar or a brake, and doubtless this was its meaning when it was linked
with that symbol of swiftness itself, the dolphin, to illustrate Augustus'
device, *Festina lente* (hasten slowly).

As the seaman's last resort in a storm, the anchor was most frequently
connected with hope, which stands as a support in the troubles of life.
'Which hope we have as an anchor of the soul, both sure and steadfast',
says St Paul (Hebrews 6: 19).

The anchor also symbolizes the war between the liquid and the solid, the
land and the sea. It puts a brake upon life when it becomes too stormy. The
conflict must be resolved, since land and water together promote fruitful
development.

From the mystical viewpoint, this harmonization can never take place in
this world and, as St Paul says, one must anchor one's soul in Christ as the
only way of avoiding spiritual shipwreck. 'My cross and my anchor', say
the mystics, thus strongly affirming their will never to abandon themselves
to the reflux of the natural world devoid of grace, but to anchor themselves
to the source of all grace – the Cross.

anemone The primary symbolism of the anemone is that of transience. It
is the flower of Adonis, who was transformed into a reddish purple anemone
by Venus. Ovid describes the scene (*Metamorphoses*, 10: 731–9): 'So saying, with sweet-scented nectar she sprinkled the blood; and this, imbued
with nectar, swelled as when clear bubbles rise up from yellow mud. With
no longer than an hour's delay a flower sprang up of blood-red hue such as
pomegranates bear which hide their seeds beneath the tenacious rind. But
short-lived is their flower; for the winds from which it takes its name shake
off the flower so delicately clinging and too easily to fall.'

The transient nature of this flower gave it its Greek name, meaning 'wind'.
A version different from Ovid's says that it was born of the wind and
carried away by it. It hints at a love subject to the flux of passion and the
inconstancy of the winds.

Many commentators identify the anemone with the 'lily of the fields' so
frequently mentioned in the Bible. There were no white lilies in Palestine,
but the anemone was widely distributed there. The Song of Solomon alludes to the lilies of the fields and to the lily of the valley which grew among
the thorns and in gardens (2: 1, 2, 5, 13, etc.). When Christ, in the Sermon
on the Mount (Matthew 6: 28–9), speaks of the lily of the fields, he seems
to be referring to the anemone.

The anemone is a flower which stands on its own and with a colour to attract the attention. Its beauty derives from its simplicity and when its crimson petals flutter in the breeze they are like parted lips. Thus the anemone, by seeming to be dependent upon the presence and the breath of the spirit, symbolizes the soul open to spiritual influences. However, in its nocturnal aspect, it can also be the symbol of inviting and transient beauty, so strong is its colour and so weak is a frame unsupported by a soul. A blood-coloured bloom, which the wind brings to flower and which the wind can blow away, the anemone embodies simultaneously the rich profusion of life and its transient nature.

angels Akkadian, Ugaritic, Biblical and other texts mention under different guises beings who act as intermediaries between God and the world. They are either purely spiritual beings, or spirits endowed with ethereal or airy bodies. However, they can only assume a human appearance. They act as God's ministers, his messengers, guardians, steering the course of the stars, giving effect to his laws, protecting his elect and so on, and are ranked in hierarchies of seven orders, nine choirs or three triads. The Pseudo-Dionysius the Areopagite develops the most elaborate and mystical theories about them in his *Celestial Hierarchy*.

Without prejudice to the Roman Catholic belief in the existence of angels, or to the explanations of theologians of other churches, it should, nonetheless, be noted that many writers see the attributes of angels as symbols of a spiritual order.

Others regard angels as symbols of the operations of the godhead or of the relationship of God with his creation. But since opposing ideas converge in symbolism, they can also symbolize human activities sublimated, or unsatisfied or impossible aspirations. To Rilke, in an even wider sense, an angel symbolized 'a being in whom the transformation of the visible into the invisible which we are fulfilling, has already been achieved.' Angels with six wings, the SERAPHIM (literally 'the Fiery Ones') surround the throne of God. 'Each one had six wings: with twain he covered his face [for fear of looking on God], and with twain he covered his feet [a euphemism for his sexual organs], and with twain he did fly' (Isaiah 2: 2). Godhead alone merits such attendants and the angels surrounding the figure of Christ bear witness to his divinity.

Angels also act as warning signs of the divine presence. To the Church Fathers they were 'the court of the King of Heaven, the heaven of heavens'. Some, who linked their beliefs to Aristotelian philosophy, believed that angels guided the movement of the stars, each being assigned to direct one star. Thus one might well enquire if the number of angels did not equal the number of stars. The mighty vault of the Heavens turned at their command and hence, perhaps through the conjunction of the stars or perhaps by more direct means, they influenced 'every plane of material creation' (CHAS p. 14). They are the heralds or agents of divine intervention. According to the Psalmist (18: 9–10), these heavenly beings serve before God's throne: 'He bowed the heavens also, and came down: and darkness was under his feet. And he rode upon a cherub, and did fly: yea, he did fly upon the wings of the wind.'

There is a symbolic and functional equivalence between the messengers of the Celtic Otherworld, who often appear in the guise of SWANS, and of Christianity's angels, depicted with swans' wings, who are in any case so often messengers of the Lord. In the most recent version of the Irish epic, *The Death of Cùchulainn*, there is a significant Christian interpolation – bands of angels, singing a heavenly song, appear to a hero in danger of death as he goes into battle (CELT 7: p. 14; CHAB pp. 67–70).

The heavenly orders of angels are an image of hierarchical structures on Earth. Their mutual relationship should inspire human hierarchies. As Christianity's foremost angelologist, the Pseudo-Dionysius the Areopagite, writes:

We must bear in mind that the more revealing Order of the Principalities, Archangels and Angels presides through each other over the Hierarchies amongst men, in order that the instruction, and conversation, and communion, and union with God may be done in due order, and, in short, that the procession from God vouchedsafe in a manner becoming His goodness to all the Hierarchies, and passing to all in common, may be in a most sacred regularity. Hence the Word of God has assigned our Hierarchy to Angels, naming the distinguished Michael as Ruler of the Jewish people, and others over other nations. For the Most High established borders of nations according to numbers of Angels of God.

(PSEH pp. 34–5)

This statement does not mean that there are necessarily as many angels of God as there are nations of men, simply that there is a mysterious harmony between the number of nations and the number of angels.

This harmony can change as the number of nations changes during the course of history, but it always remains as mysterious if only because the number of angels is itself unknown. The Bible speaks of one thousand times one thousand and of ten thousand times ten thousand – 'thousand thousands ministered unto him, and ten thousand times ten thousand stood before him' (Daniel 7: 10).

But if this is to square the largest numbers which we know, it is, the Pseudo-Dionysius explains,

showing clearly that the ranks of the celestial Beings cannot be numbered by us; for many are the blessed hosts of the celestial minds, surpassing the weak and contracted measurement of our mundane calculation. And being definitely known to the celestial and heavenly intelligence and science among themselves which is given to them in profusion by the supremely Divine and infinitely wise Head, and essential Cause, and connecting Force, and encompassing Term of all created things together.

(PSEH p. 43)

Angels make up God's armies, his court and his household. They transmit his commands and watch over the world. They play an important part in the Bible. Their order is linked by their nearness to the throne of God. The three chief archangels are: Michael (dragon-slayer), Gabriel (messenger and divine instrument) and Raphael (guide to physicians and travellers).

There are various views on angels. According to Justin, one of the principal writers on the cult of angels, despite their spiritual nature, angels have a body analogous with the human. Of course their food bears no relation to that of humans, since it is heavenly. In Justin's eyes the angels' sin was sexual intercourse with mortal women. A child resulting from such a union was a DEMON. The Pseudo-Dionysius makes great play with the part angels play as enlighteners of mankind. Clement of Alexandria describes their function as guardians of peoples and cities.

The Bible makes no mention of guardian angels as such. However, according to Enoch (100: 5), saints and righteous persons have their protectors. St Basil claims that each one of the faithful is helped by an angel who guides his life and is both teacher and protector. The protective role is confirmed by the Bible in the case of Lot (Genesis 19), Ishmael (Genesis 21), and Jacob (Genesis 48). An angel delivered St Peter and St John. In the Middle Ages angels helped in time of peril and of war, during the Crusades and so on.

As a messenger the angel is always the bearer of good tidings to the soul.

anima, animus See SOUL.

animal (see also BIRD; SERPENT; and numerous entries on particular animals) As an archetype, the animal stands for the lowest instinctive levels of the subconscious. Animals are symbols of both physical and spiritual cosmic powers. The signs of the ZODIAC, as typifying cosmic energy, are examples of this. Ancient Egyptian gods were depicted with the heads of animals, and the four Evangelists are symbolized by them, while the Holy Spirit is given the form of a DOVE. Animals touch upon the three levels of the universe – Heaven, Earth and Hell. In Mayan mythology, for example, we can see a CROCODILE, with monstrous gaping jaws, the jaws of some underworld monster, about to swallow the setting sun. In the whole complex mass of symbolism surrounding this word, one must distinguish 'animal' (or 'beast') from 'animals'.

The animal, the beast in us which so embarrasses Judeo-Christian morality, is the fullness of those deep-seated forces which drive us, and first and foremost among them is the libido. Since as far back as the Middle Ages, a French slang term for the penis has been 'the animal', 'the beast', 'the horse', and these terms have sometimes been applied to woman, embodiment of the animal, not to say diabolical, part of man.

The embargo for so long placed upon human nature was first challenged by the Romantics and only lifted by the discovery of psychoanalysis. As Jung still somewhat shamefacedly puts it in *Man and his Symbols*:

The boundless profusion of animal symbolism in the religion and art of all times does not merely emphasize the importance of the symbol; it shows how vital it is for men to integrate into their lives the symbol's psychic content – instinct . . . . But in man the 'animal being' (which lives in him as his instinctual psyche) may become dangerous if it is not recognized and integrated in life . . . . The acceptance of the animal soul is the condition for wholeness and a fully lived life.
(JUNS pp. 238–9)

The symbolism of those animals which mankind has encountered, of which it has observed the individual peculiarities and to which it has given names, sends it back to something very much larger, since it is a phenomenon encompassing the whole of human history and not a moment in our own civilization. The issue is that of totemism, which far from relating to so-called primitive mentalities of so-called archaic states of social evolution, bears witness to a basic and universal tendency in mankind. In discussing Rousseau, Lévi-Strauss summarizes it thus: 'It is because man originally felt himself identical to all those like him (amongst which . . . we must include animals) that he came to acquire the capacity to distinguish *himself* as he distinguished *them*, that is, to use the diversity of species as conceptual support for social differentiation' (LEVT p. 174).

Whether animals are taken singly or as categories (ruminants) or social groups (bees), they correspond to symbolic rather than to allegorical 'characters' because a single meaning will comprehend so many and such complex concepts. Such, to take significant examples drawn from categories of animal, would be birds, creatures of the heavens, or serpents, flesh-eaters with long fangs and gaping jaws, deeply imbued with chthonian or infernal symbolism. Frequent use, in this context, of the metaphor – 'a primary form of discursive thought' (LEVT p. 175) – does not exclude the symbol, for it only illustrates a part, or rather a facet, of the whole. Thus the DOVE, as a symbol of the Holy Spirit, is very far from covering the full range of the symbols transmitted by this bird, indeed it serves merely to broach their study. Without claiming to offer an all-embracing bestiary, this book makes a point of including articles which go into as much detail as possible about those animals which in our opinion are so strongly imbued with symbolism as to retain a permanent value throughout human history (see BULL, DOG, EAGLE, HORSE, LAMB, TORTOISE, etc.).

This interest of humans in animals as the embodiment of their own symbolic and psychic complexes is readily apparent in the current fashion for household pets, which are treated as one of the family rather than as animals. Ancient Egypt offers an even more striking example, since there the treatment of animals verged upon zoölatry. Herodotus states that an Egyptian would let his possessions burn, but would risk his life to save a cat from the blaze. Numberless mummified animals have survived. The pious took great pride in tending the graves of animals, boasting that they had fed the hungry, given drink to the thirsty and clothed the naked and, in addition, had tended sacred ibis, falcons, cats and dogs and had given them ritual burial, anointed with oil and swathed in linen (POSD).

Chinese art is particularly rich in fabulous animals. The earliest examples so far known to us of this world of the imagination are funeral monuments dicovered in Shandong and Henan. It is an art as yet 'uncivilized' by Taoist or Confucian officialdom. The most fabulous creatures, the strangest warlocks, animals with the wierdest shapes all play a major role. Before the Taoist Heavenly Masters took them for their own, these creatures included the solar crow with three claws (Heaven, Earth, Mankind) and the nine-tailed fox (for the nine regions of the empire), as well as such monsters as centaur-like creatures with two human heads and pairs of shoulders, and beasts each with eight human heads on the end of serpentine necks like the hydra of classical Greek mythology.

A low-relief carving from a tomb chamber shows two individuals facing one another, one holding in his hand a sort of chequer-board (emblem of the mythical kings of China), the other a cross (the five CARDINAL POINTS), while both their bodies seem to end in a pair of intertwining dragon's tails.

These carvings date from the period of the Warring Kingdoms (441–221 BC). They were soon to be tamed by the influence of Confucian and Buddhist teachings. Their symbolism was only to reappear in Taoist magical practices and its interpretation was to be coloured by a supernaturalism serving moralistic or such utilitarian purposes as the preparation of the medicine of longevity.

Shintō shrines are guarded by fabulous beasts always standing on either side of the GATEWAY. One of these creatures gapes his jaws, the other keeps them shut. They symbolize the beginning and the end, the limitless powers of the emperor, alpha and omega.

It was long believed that Celtic religion set great store by zoömorphism and totemism. This would have have provided the proof of its great antiquity and of its 'primitive' nature, the next stage in its development being anthropomorphism into a higher conception of the gods on the pattern of the gods of Ancient Greece. But the animal was valid only as a symbol: the boar symbolized the priestly office, the bear that of kingship, the crow belonged to Lug, swans, or birds in general, were messengers of the Otherworld. The horse conveyed the souls of the dead, and so on. There is no substantial evidence of totemism in the Celtic world.

The Turks looked for the qualities of ten animals in their great commanders – the gallantry of the cock, the chastity of the hen, the courage of the lion, the aggression of the boar, the cunning of the fox, the tenacity of the hound, the vigilance of the stork, the prudence of the crow, the fire of the embattled wolf and the plumpness of the *yagru*, an animal which, try as it might, always stayed fat.

(Al Mada' Ini, the ninth-century Arab author, quoted in ROUF p. 233)

Another and slightly earlier Arab writer, in a similar catalogue of the virtues of a warrior, lists the cool and stubborn strength of the wolf, the courage of the bear and the lion, the vengefulness of the yak and the male camel, the chastity of the magpie, the keen sight of the crow, the cunning of the red fox, and the vigilance of the owl. In the symbolic language of the Turkic peoples, the horse is brave, the bull is strong and sheep are weak and timid, while the lion cannot control his rage, the foal is mettlesome and the tiger valiant and brave.

Two quotations will suffice as Old Testament examples: the animals were all shown to Adam; animals as categorized in the Bible seem to be endowed with individuality. According to Philo, the animals named by Adam represent human passions which, like wild beasts, must be brought under control (*Leg. All.* 2: 9–11). Philo surveys the different categories of animal. Of Abraham's sacrifice of a heifer, a she-goat, a ram, a turtle-dove and a young pigeon:

The natures of the aforementioned five animals are related to the parts of the universe. The ox [is related] to the earth, for it ploughs and tills the soil. The goat [is related] to water, the animal being so called from its rushing about or leaping, for water is impetuous; this is attested by the currents of rivers and the effusions of the wide sea and the flowing sea. The ram [is related] to air, since it is very violent and lively, whence the ram is a most useful soul and the most helpful of animals to mankind because it provides them with clothing . . . . But to the birds . . . the whole heaven is equally appropriated, being divided into the circuits of the planets and the fixed stars. And so [Scripture] assigns the dove to the planets. But the turtle-dove [is related] to the fixed stars, for this animal is something of a lover of solitude.

(Quaestiones in Genesim 3: 3)

Pursuing this topic, Philo establishes different analogies between these animals and man, analogies which appear later in Christian art. The ox shows a kinship with the body because of its obedience, the goat relates to the senses which react on impulse. The pigeon, in its perception of the visible world, corresponds to the reason, while the solitude-loving turtle-dove seeks the invisible reality *(Quaestiones in Genesim* 3: 4, etc.; DANP pp. 131–2).

Animals, so frequently recurrent in dreams and works of art, embody partial identifications with man, aspects, images of his complex nature, mirrors of his secret motivations and of subjugated or uncontrolled instincts. Each corresponds to a part of our selves, either integrated or to be integrated into a single harmonious personality.

ankh (see also CROSS, KNOT)   The Egyptian *crux ansata*, or looped tau-cross. This magic knot or cross, known as *Nem Ank*, 'the key of life', was often used in the iconography of opposites. The loop over the tau-cross could stand for the Sun, for Heaven and Earth as the macrocosm and for man as the microcosm. It is generally interpreted as a symbol which expresses the reconciliation of opposites or the integration of active and passive qualities. This is amply confirmed by the fact that, when recumbent, the ankh symbolizes both male and female sexual attributes in precisely the same way as the very realistic Hindu depiction of a HERMAPHRODITE standing on a LOTUS flower. Champdor gives a more traditional interpretation as:

the symbol of the millions of years of the life to come. The loop is the perfect symbol of what has neither beginning nor end and stands for the soul which is eternal because it has sprung from the spiritual essence of the gods. The cross represents the state of trance in which the neophyte struggled or, more precisely, the state of death, the crucifixion of the chosen victim, and in some temples the priests used to lay the neophyte on a bed shaped like the cross . . . . The possessor of the geometric key to the hidden mysteries, of which the symbol was this very looped cross, was able to open the gates of the Kingdom of the Dead and penetrate the hidden meaning of eternal life.

(CHAM p. 22)

Gods, kings and ISIS (almost invariably) are depicted holding the ankh to show that they command the powers of life and death and that they are immortal. The dead also carry it at the time their souls are weighed (see SCALES) or when they are aboard the BOAT of the Sun God, as a sign that they seek this same immortality from the gods. Furthermore the ankh symbolized the spring from which flowed divine virtues and the elixir of immortality. Therefore to hold the ankh was to drink from that well. It was sometimes held upside down by the loop – especially in funeral rites when it suggested the shape of a key and in reality was the key which opened the gateway of the tomb into the Fields of Aalu, the realm of eternity. Sometimes the ankh is placed on the forehead, between the eyes, and then it symbolizes the duty of the adept to keep secret the mystery into which he has been initiated – it is the key which locks these secrets away from the uninitiated. Blessed by the supreme vision, endowed with clairvoyance to pierce the veil of the beyond, he cannot attempt to reveal the mystery without losing it for ever.

The ankh is often set in the same category as the 'GIRDLE of Isis', as a symbol of eternity. This is not because its straight lines may be lengthened in the imagination to infinity, but because they converge upon and meet in a closed loop. This loop symbolizes the inexhaustible essence of the life force identified with Isis, from whom life flows in all its forms. It is therefore carried by all those who wish to share her life. Hence the ankh may be identified with the Tree of Life, with its trunk and foliage.

The significance of the Girdle of Isis is far more complex. Like ropework or plaited hair round the arms and the loop of the cross, it infuses the concept of life and of immortality with the concept of the knots which tie down mortal life on Earth and which must be unravelled to enjoy immortality. 'Free your bonds,' says *The Egyptian Book of the Dead*, 'untie the knots of Nephthys.' And again: 'Shining are those who carry the girdle. Oh! Bearers of the Girdle.' The same meaning is conveyed by the Tibetan Buddhist book called *The Book of the Untying of the Knots*. While the plain looped cross symbolizes divine immortality, sought or attained, the Girdle of Isis makes clear the conditions under which that immortality is obtained – by the untying of knots – dénouement in the true sense of the word.

ankle The slimness of a woman's ankles puts the Chinese in mind of more intimate portions of her anatomy and her potential skill and refinement in the arts of love-making.

Among the Bambara the ankle is called 'the knot of the foot' and carries suggestions of arrival and departure.

For the Ancient Greeks and Romans, the ankle was the part of the body to which the WINGS of such gods as HERMES (Mercury) were fixed. Its meaning was therefore sublimated as the symbol of heightened consciousness.

anniversary See BIRTHDAY.

anointing Anointing symbolizes 'Jehovah's spirit' and through it God diffuses his living light and the divine presence. This is why Jacob, to whom God appeared in a dream, poured OIL upon the stone which he had used for a pillow to show that God had been there (Genesis 28: 16–18). It was in any case a common practice to pour oil on memorial stones. Pouring holy oil upon the head was a sign of consecration, as in the ceremonial consecration of the High Priest or the Anointing, part of the coronation service. Prophets, too, were anointed, Elijah being commanded to anoint Elisha. Psalm 45 proclaims the Incarnate Word as being 'anointed with the oil of gladness' (verse 8). St Paul refers to the unction received by Christians, comparing this with the seal which marks them out from others when the Holy Spirit comes down into their hearts (2 Corinthians 1: 21–2). Extreme Unction is conferred upon the sick and the dying, but the holy oils used in the rite have been consecrated for a specific purpose. There is no symbolic significance in anointing with oil as a matter of hygiene, as for example rubbing the body with scented oils after a bath as is the custom in the East.

anqa (see also SIMURG)   A fabulous bird which shares some of the characteristics of both the GRYPHON and the PHOENIX. From surviving folktales it is apparent that belief in the existence of the anqa is of Arab origin and it is well-known that the Ancient Greeks and Romans believed that the phoenix lived in the deserts of Arabia. With the coming of Islam the role of the anqa became firmly fixed, as Ibn 'Abbās recounts:

One day the Prophet said to us: 'In the first ages of the earth God created a bird of wonderful beauty and gave it every virtue as its share. God created a female in the likeness of the male and called them anqa.' Then he made known these words to Moses son of Imran: 'I have given life to a bird of admirable beauty, male and female I have created it. I have given them all the wild beasts of Jerusalem for their food and I would have you become the familiar of these two birds as proof of the sovereignty I have given you over the Children of Israel.'
                                                                (*Meadows of Gold*)

Belief in the anqa later merged with that in the simurg of the Persians.
    The anqa or simurg came to symbolize mystics winging their way to the godhead. In his wonderful parable, *The Conference of the Birds*, the great Persian mystic poet Farīd al-Dīn Abu Hamid 'Attār (thirteenth century), tells of the spiritual journey of thirty birds (*Si-Morgh* in Persian), representing animal creation, which took them in the end to the divine presence. 'Then,' says 'Attār,

close at hand, the Sun's rays flashed upon them and filled their souls with light. Then these thirty birds, the earthly *si morgh*, gazed upon the spiritual Simurg in the light reflected from their own faces. Busily they gazed at the Simurg until they realized that he was none other than *si morgh*, that is to say that they were themselves the godhead. Thus the mystic only achieves union with the godhead when his own self is annihilated.

    This wonderful bird appears under a different name in the works of such poets as Suhrawardi or Sadr al-Din Shirazi. This is the term *Ququns*, which is also applied to the phoenix, but is no more than a transcription of the Greek *kuknos*, the SWAN. In the *Phaedo* (84–5), Socrates declares that the song of the swan, the bird of Apollo, is never more piercing than when it feels that it is about to die; then it 'sings most and best in its joy that it is to go to the god whose servant it is.' 'This gives us the reason for [the bird's] development into a symbol of the mystical union' (CORN p. 46).
    The home of the simurg is the Mountain of Kāf.
    Under different names, the anqa symbolizes that part of the human being which is summoned to mystic union with the godhead. In that union all differences vanish and the anqa is both creator and spiritual creature.

ant (see also TERMITE)   The ant symbolizes industriousness, the organized community and a prudent foresight which La Fontaine exaggerates to selfish avarice. Quoting Proverbs 6: 6, St Clement of Alexandria writes: 'It is also said: "Go to the ant, thou sluggard; consider her ways, and be wise." For at harvest-time the ant sets aside a plentiful variety of food with which to face the threats of winter' (*Stromata* 1).

Tibetan Buddhists, too, make the ant in the anthill a symbol of an industrious life and an excessive attachment to the good things of this world (EVAB).

In the Talmud the ant teaches honesty; in India it represents the worthlessness of individuals, doomed to obscurity and death unless they try to identify with Brahman, the infinity of littleness suggesting the infinity of the godhead.

The ant plays a very lowly role in Celtic folklore. The only place in which it appears is in the Welsh tale of Culhwch and Olwen. Among the many tasks with which the giant Ysbaddaden Penkawr tested him, Culhwch had to gather a peck of flax seeds. These were all brought to him one by one by the neighbouring ants, all but one, that is. This was carried in just before night fell by a lame ant. The latter symbolizes the diligent and indefatigable servant (LOTM 1: p. 329).

The ant plays an important part in the world structure in the cosmology of the Dogon and Bambara peoples of Mali. In the beginning, in the ritual marriage of Heaven and Earth, the Earth's sexual organ was an anthill. In the final phase of the creation of the world, this anthill became a mouth from which issued language and its material adjunct, the art of weaving, taught to men by the ants (GRIE). They also showed them the traditional pattern of their huts. Fertility rites are still associated with ants and barren women will sit on an anthill and pray to the great god Amma to make them conceive. Men such as blacksmiths, who are endowed with 'powers', use the same spot temporarily to change themselves into such creatures as panthers or hawks (GRIM).

The association of the anthill with the female sexual organs (it is at one and the same time the *mons Veneris* and the vulva) has many practical applications. Thus the Bambara believe that the ant known as the *ndiginew* has ties with streams of water hidden underground. 'So, when planning to sink a well, one cannot choose a better place than the site of an anthill' (ZAHB p. 220). Earth taken from anthills is used ritually by some initiation societies which believe it is connected with the stomach and the digestion, since it symbolizes 'the powers working in the bowels of the Earth and making themselves manifest in springs of water' (ZAHB).

In Morocco live ants used to be given to sufferers from sleeping sickness to swallow (FRAG 8: p. 147).

anteater   This mysterious creature which lives on ants and termites is generally to be feared as a symbol of bad luck. Like the heads of rabbits, hyenas or owls, the anteater is filled with occult power and dangerous emanations (HAMK p. 4) and hence is often forbidden as food.

anthill   See under ANT; TERMITE.

Antigone   Daughter of the incestuous marriage between OEDIPUS and Jocasta. After her father's twofold crime (his murder of his father and his marriage to his mother) was revealed, instead of abandoning him to blindness and despair she accompanied him to the shrine of the EUMENIDES at

Colonos, where he died at peace at last. On her return to Thebes, Antigone disobeyed Creon's orders to leave the body of her brother Polynices unburied by performing the funeral rites over it. She was now condemned to death herself. Buried alive in the family vault, she hanged herself, her betrothed committing suicide on her body and Creon's own wife killing herself in despair.

Psychoanalysis has turned Antigone into a symbol by giving her name to a complex – a girl's fixation on her father, her brother or her family circle to the extent of refusing a personality development towards a love which would shatter these childhood ties. Her death is of symbolic significance – she hangs herself in the family tomb and her betrothed dies.

However, the twentieth-century theatre has resurrected Antigone and raised her from the grave. She has been set on a pedestal as the woman in rebellion against the powers of the state, symbolized by Creon, and as the woman who revolts against the rules and conventions of society in the name of the unwritten laws of her conscience and her love. She is the liberated woman, abandoning in the family vault the corpse of innocence crushed by social custom and constraint. She may be Antigone in revolt, yet however much she rages against the tyrannies of family and society, she still remains psychologically dependent and imprisoned. Antigone must be strong enough and free enough to take full responsibility for her own independence, striking a fresh balance and avoiding withdrawal into the commonplace. Given new life, the legend symbolizes the death and resurrection of Antigone, but an Antigone who has achieved self-realization on a higher plane of development.

antimony An alchemical symbol: 'the sage's matter', 'grey wolf of the philosophers', according to Basil Valentine. Antimony corresponds to the penultimate stage in the search for the Philosopher's Stone. Fulcanelli conceived antimony as 'a chaos, the foster mother of all metals'. It is 'the womb and reef of gold and the seedbed of its tincture' according to Sendivogius (*Lettre philosophique*, translated from the German by Antoine Duval: Paris, 1671).

It was also held to be 'the bastard child of Saturn; passionately loved by Venus'; it was 'the root of metals'. Through its links with Saturn and Mercury, it related to the emerald.

From the psychoanalytic point of view, antimony would symbolize a state very close to perfection in individual development, but the most difficult obstacle to overcome would remain – the final transmutation of lead into gold, the obstacle over which the majority stumbles. It embodies the potential of the supreme impulse, but also of decisive failure. It is as indeterminate as its symbolic colour – grey – and its mythological image of a Diana (Artemis), the perfection of beauty or of ugliness.

anvil The Bakitara, or Banyoro, of the northeast Congo, towards the borders of Sudan, treat the anvil as the BLACKSMITH's bride. It is taken to his hut and greeted by his first wife with the rites appropriate to the homecoming of the second wife. It is ritually sprinkled and ceremonies are performed to ensure it will have many children (CLIM).

The anvil is related to the passive female principle and from it issues the work of the smith, the active male principle. In Great Kabylia the anvil symbolizes water and it is mounted on an ash-wood block. The ash stands for the mountain, 'just as the anvil stands for water. To hammer the anvil is to irrigate the soil' (SERP p. 252). Here again the anvil is seen as a passive fertility symbol. As with lightning, the smith is the active fertilizing principle.

Aphrodite (Venus) The worship of this most seductively beautiful goddess originated in Asia, spread to countless shrines in Greece and centred upon Cythera. Aphrodite sprang from the seed of OURANOS (Uranus, the Heavens), scattered upon the sea when Ouranos was castrated by his son, Cronos – hence the legend of the birth of Aphrodite from sea-spume. She was the wife of the lame god HEPHAISTOS, whom she deceived on many occasions. She symbolizes the irresistible generative force, not in its fruits, but in the passionate desires which it kindles in all living creatures. Thus she is often depicted with an escort of wild animals around her, as in the 'Homeric' Hymn, where the poet first conjures up her power over the gods and then over the beasts:

Even the heart of Zeus, who delights in thunder, is led astray by her; though he is greatest of all . . . . She beguiles his wise heart whensoever she pleases . . . . So she came to many-fountained Ida, the mother of wild creatures . . . . After her came grey wolves fawning on her, and grim-eyed lions, and bears, and fleet leopards, ravenous for deer: and she was glad in heart to see them, and put desire in their hearts, so that they all mated, two together, about the shadowy coombes.

(Homeric Hymns 5: 36–8, 68–74)

This is love in its physical form of lust and sensual pleasure, but not yet love on a specifically human plane. 'On the highest level of the human psyche where love is complemented by a marriage of souls with its symbol as Hera, the wife of Zeus, Aphrodite is the symbol used to express sexual perversion, since pleasure is naturally inseparable from and acts as a spur towards the reproductive act. The demands of nature are then satisfied pervertedly' (DIES p. 166). One may wonder, nevertheless, whether an interpretation of this symbol may not develop along the lines of current research into the exclusively human elements of sexuality. Even theologians, bound by a strict code of morality, are studying the problem of determining whether the sole end of sexuality is reproductive or whether it is not possible to humanize the sexual act independently of its procreative element. The myth of Aphrodite may still remain for a time the image of a perversion, perversion of the enjoyment of life and of lifegiving forces. However, it is not because the intention to create new life is missing from the act of love, but because love itself still remains dehumanized, on an animal level appropriate to the beasts who form the goddess's train. Yet such a development could lead to the reinstatement of Aphrodite as the goddess who sublimates brute appetite by incorporating it into a truly human way of life.

Apocalypse The Apocalypse is first and foremost a revelation which bears upon mysterious realities; next it is prophetic, since these realities are in time to come; last of all it is a vision and the scenes and the numbers are so many symbols.

The language of apocalyptic writing is richly symbolic and the importance of the visions which are described is never in their immediate literal meaning. It can be taken as a rule that every element in this kind of writing has symbolic value – persons, places, animals, actions, parts of the body, numbers and measurements, stars, constellations, colours and garments – and if we are not to misunderstand or distort the writer's message, we must appreciate the imagery at its true value and do our best to translate the symbols back into the ideas which he intended them to convey.

(BIBJ p. 2027)

If one ignores the apocalyptic books themselves which comprise a very common class of literature in the early centuries of the Christian era, the word 'apocalyptic' has also become synonymous with the end of the world, marked by the most terrifying occurrences – gigantic tidal waves, the mountains brought low, the Earth gaping open and the Heavens taking fire in an indescribable fury of sound. Thus the Apocalypse became a symbol of the end of the world.

At the end of the account of the Battle of Moytura, the Celtic death-goddess, the Morrigan, prophesies the end of the world: the order of the seasons will be confounded, mankind will grow corrupt, society will collapse, evil and immorality will flourish. This scenario is taken up again and elaborated in considerable detail in a work known as *The Colloquy of the Two Sages*, written in the mannered and involuted style of the medieval Irish bards. This concept may be likened to the Christian Apocalypse and also to what Strabo records when he reports that the Druids foretold that one day fire and water would rule alone.

As an example of these apocalyptic visions and their interpretation, take the symbol of the Beast.

And I stood upon the sand of the sea, and saw a beast rise up out of the sea, having seven heads and ten horns, and upon his horns ten crowns, and upon his head the name of blasphemy. And the beast which I saw was like unto a leopard, and his feet were as the feet of a bear, and his mouth as the mouth of a lion: and the dragon gave him his power, and his seat, and great authority. And I saw one of his heads as it were wounded to death; and his deadly wound was healed: and all the world wondered after the beast. And they worshipped the dragon which gave power unto the beast: and they worshipped the beast, saying, Who is like unto the beast? who is able to make war with him? And there was given unto him a mouth speaking great things and blasphemies; and power was given unto him to continue forty and two months. And he opened his mouth in blasphemy against God, to blaspheme his name, and his tabernacle, and them that dwell in heaven. And it was given unto him to make war with the saints, and to overcome them: and power was given him over all kindreds, and tongues, and nations.

(Revelation 13: 1–7)

From the historical viewpoint, the wounded Beast suggests the tottering Roman Empire and perhaps Nero's suicide. In more general terms, the Beast stands for the State as persecutor, 'the prime opponent of Christ and his people'. The Beast revived is Anti-Christ of the time to come, the parody and caricature of Christ himself. The Beast's 'seven' heads suggest the innumerable and freshly sprouting heads of the legendary Hydra. The horns symbolize the power of the Beast and the crowns his pseudo-royalty. The

Beast which emerges from the ABYSS will wage war, kill and vanquish (11:
7) and will deceive the whole world (12: 9). The Beast is one of the central
figures of Revelation. It stands for 'the important principle of deception
and blasphemy . . . the demoniac principle of collective delusion', a concomitant of religion throughout human history. After its striking but short-
lived victories in this world, the Beast is doomed to final defeat: it will be
conquered by the LAMB.

Apollo In the *Iliad* (Book I) Phoebus Apollo, 'God of the silver bow',
appears by night and shines like the Moon. Intellectual development and
the interpretation of myth need to be taken into account to recognize in the
Homeric deity the much later Sun-god and to liken his BOW and ARROWS to
the Sun and its beams. Originally he was more closely related to lunar
symbolism. In this context he is described as the god of vengeance, with his
death-dealing arrows, 'Lordly bearer of the silver bow'.

He first manifests himself as the image of violence and unbridled arro-
gance but, as he gathers to himself a range of Nordic, Asiatic and Aegean
attributes, his divine personality becomes more and more complex. It synthesizes within itself so many warring elements which it finally reconciles
into that ideal of wisdom which is regarded as the Greek miracle. Apollo
embodies the balance and harmony of the passions, achieved not by suppressing instinctive impulses but by directing them through the development of awareness towards an ever-increasing spiritualization. He is hailed
in literature as possessor of over two hundred different attributes, which
depict him successively as a RAT-god of primitive agrarian cults; as a quick-
tempered, vengeful warrior; as a ruler of wild beasts, yet at the same time
as the shepherd's friend and the protector of flocks and harvests; as a benefactor of mankind, who heals and purifies, and as the father of the god of
medicine Asclepios (Aesculapius); as 'the seer of Zeus' he founded the oracle
at Delphi (see TRIPOD). He inspired not only seers but poets and painters;
he became the Sun-god, crossing the Heavens in his dazzling chariot. The
Romans identified him with none of their gods. Alone of the deities adopted
by the Republic and the Empire he remained himself, immaculate, unique
and peerless.

Professional etymologists may be suspicious of odd verbal coincidences,
yet they are highly significant in the history of religious thought. The Attic
Greek name 'Apollo' has been compared with its Doric equivalent 'Apello',
the latter suggesting the word 'apella', meaning 'sheepfold'. 'It is easy to
conceive of such a god as having been worshipped by the earliest Greeks,
nomads driving their flocks and herds before them, and also as having in
the Peloponnese identified with himself such pre-Hellenic gods of the flocks
as, for example, the ram-god, Karnos . . . . In any case, Apollo is manifested
as a shepherd in many myths' (SECG pp. 213–14).

Pindar sings of 'Apollo who instills in human hearts love of harmony and
revulsion from civil strife'.

Plato, when describing the duties of the true lawgiver (*Republic* 427b–c),
advises that the basic laws of the Republic should be sought of Apollo:

'[It is] for the Apollo of Delphi [to pronounce] the chief, the fairest and the
first of enactments.'

'What are they?'

'The founding of temples, and sacrifices, and other forms of worship of gods, daemons, and heroes; and likewise the burial of the dead and the services we must render to the dwellers in the world beyond to keep them gracious. For such matters we neither know anything, nor in the founding of our city, if we are wise, shall we entrust them to any other or make use of any other interpreter than the God of our fathers. For this god surely is in such matter for all mankind the interpreter of the religion of their fathers who from his seat in the middle and at the very navel of the earth delivers his interpretation?'

The 'Celtic Apollo' is a Roman creation who does not correspond in all particulars to any native Gallic deity. In fact, the Apolline personality must be split and divided among a number of Celtic gods. The 'Healer' is Dian Cécht (the meaning of this Irish divine name is unclear: perhaps 'prisoner of the gods', while other texts suggest 'the long-handed'). His attribute of eternal youth is embodied in Oenghus, 'the only chosen one', son of the Dagda, or in Mac Oc, 'young son'. Finally, in his shining (but sometimes dark) aspect, he is Lug, the ruler of the Celtic pantheon, by definition the 'Master Craftsman' in the sense of his superiority over all the other gods in knowledge and skill. In so far as it relates to the Celtic Apollo, the Classical legend of the Hyperborean Apollo alludes to the northern origins of Celtic folklore (OGAC 11: pp. 215ff.; 12: pp. 59ff.).

SEVEN is the number of perfection, the number which symbolically unites Heaven and Earth, the male and female principles, light and darkness. It is, moreover, Apollo's number and plays a significant part in all legends relating to him. Apollo was born on the seventh day of the month and lived under this sign. Aeschylus called him 'Noble Seventh God, God of the Seventh Gate (*Seven against Thebes* 800). His chief feasts were always celebrated on the seventh day of the month; his LYRE was seven-stringed; at his birth the sacred SWANS flew singing seven times round the floating island of Asteria which his father Zeus was to anchor and call Delos and where his mother Leto gave him birth. His teachings were embodied in seven sayings attributed to the Seven Sages.

It is unspeakable to reduce this most complex deity to the commonplace of 'youth, wisdom and beauty'; or, to simplify Nietzsche, to set him up as the opposite pole to DIONYSOS, reason opposed to intuition. On the contrary, Apollo symbolizes the defeat of violence, inspired self-control and the marriage of reason and intuition, being the son of a god, Zeus, and through his mother Leto the grandson of a TITAN. His wisdom is acquired, not inherited. All the life forces unite in him to spur him on to find his balance only upon the heights and to lead him from 'the mouth of the vast cavern' (Aeschylus) to 'the heights of heaven' (Plutarch). He symbolizes the acme of spiritualization and is one of the noblest symbols of the ascent of man.

apple(-tree) The apple is employed symbolically in several senses which, however apparently distinct, are in fact interconnected. There are 'The Apple of Discord' awarded by Paris; 'The Golden Apples' from the Garden of the Hesperides, the fruit of immortality; the apple eaten by Adam and Eve; and the apple mentioned in the Song of Solomon, which, according to Origen, is the image of the richness, sweetness and savour of the Word of God. In each case we have a key to knowledge, but one which is on the one hand fruit of the Tree of Life and on the other fruit of the Tree of the Knowledge of Good and Evil, of a unifying knowledge which grants immortality or of a disjunctive knowledge which initiates the Fall. In the language of alchemy, the 'Golden Apple' is a symbol of sulphur.

The Abbé E. Bertrand (quoted in BOUM p. 235) states:

The symbolism of the apple is derived from its core, formed in the shape of a five-pointed star by the compartments which hold the pips.... This is why adepts have made it the fruit of knowledge and of freedom. Thus, the phrase 'to eat the apple' meant to them abuse of the intellect to gain knowledge of evil, abuse of the senses to lust after evil and abuse of freedom to commit evil. However, as is always the case, the mass of the uninitiated mistook the symbol for the reality. Furthermore, the inclusion within the meat of the apple of the PENTAGRAM, the symbol of spiritual man, symbolizes the entanglement of the spirit in the flesh.

Robert Ambelain makes much the same observation in *Dans l'ombre des cathédrales*. 'Contemporary adepts regard the apple as the icon of knowledge. Cut breadthwise it reveals a pentagram, traditional symbol of knowledge, formed by the emplacement of its pips.'

In Celtic folklore, the apple is the fruit of knowledge, magic and prophecy. It also provides miraculous food. The woman from the Otherworld who comes in search of Condle, son of Conn of the Hundred Battles, gives him an apple which provides him with food for a month and never grows less. Among the marvels which the god Lug set the three sons of Tuireann to find, in atonement for the murder of his father Cian, were three apples from the Garden of the Hesperides. Whoever ate of them would never again feel hunger or thirst, sorrow or sickness, nor would the apples grow less. In some Breton folktales, eating an apple is the prelude to a prophecy (OGAC 16: pp. 253–6).

If the apple is a miraculous fruit, the apple-tree itself ('abellio' in Celtic) is an Otherworld tree. It was a branch of an apple-tree which the Otherworld woman who came in search of Bran gave to him before carrying him across the seas. The Isle of Avalon – *Emain Ablach* in Irish, *Ynys Afallach* in Welsh – also known as 'the Orchard', is the mythical resting place of dead kings and heroes. Here, according to Cornish tradition, King Arthur took refuge until the day comes when he will free the Welsh and the Cornish, his compatriots, from the foreign yoke. It is written that Merlin taught under an apple-tree (OGAC 9: pp. 305–9; ETUC 4: pp. 255–74). The Gauls regarded the apple-tree as being as sacred as the oak.

Warding off old age, the fruit is a symbol of renewal and eternal youth.

Gervasius tells how Alexander the Great, in his search for the 'water of life' in India, found some apples which the priests there took to extend their life to four hundred years. In Scandinavian mythology, the apple is the fruit that regenerates and rejuvenates. The gods eat apples and stay young until the *ragna rok*, until the end of the present cycle of the universe.

(ELIT p. 295)

If one follows Paul Diel's analysis, the rounded shape of the apple symbolizes Earth-bound passions or their fulfilment. Divine prohibition was meant to warn mankind against being mastered by those passions which would lead through a species of regression to a materialistic way of life, as opposed to the spiritualized life which is the direction of progressive development. This divine warning makes man aware of these two directions and the necessity of choosing between the way of the Earth-bound passions and that of spirituality. The apple is therefore the symbol of that knowledge and of being placed under the obligation of making a choice.

apron (see FREEMASONRY)   The leather apron is one of the essential Masonic vestments. It is worn by the grade of Apprentice with the bib turned up, and turned down by higher grades. Legacy of the old guilds, the apron suggests, first and foremost, the 'work' which made the wearing of an apron necessary. In Masonic symbolism, the apron, characteristic of the Entered Apprentice, does in fact become 'the emblem of work, reminding the Mason that he should always lead a busy and industrious life'. Others would be reminded of the skins under which Adam and Eve hid their nakedness after the Fall: the apron should be 'white and spotless. By keeping it so, each within his own sphere is able to achieve that degree of perfection to which all Masons aspire.' Others again would see it as 'the symbol of the physical body, the outer covering of flesh which the spirit must assume in order to play its part in the work of the Universal Architect.' Still others would give it a moral significance: 'the masonic apron merely covers the lower parts of the body and above all the lower abdomen . . . seat of the emotions and sexual passions . . . . This means that the upper part of the body, where the spiritual and reasoning faculties reside, should engage in work' and it alone allows 'attainment of peace of soul' which marks the truly accepted Mason (BOUM p. 292).

Neither was it unreasonable to believe that the apron's protective role extended to certain rarefied centres of the being.

Hence arises the triple symbolism of the apron: the person dedicated to work; the adjunct of a working environment; and a protection against the dangers of the workplace.

Aprons of bones have become items of excessive rarity and are frequently substituted in Tibet and Africa by ordinary cloth aprons with paintings of bones in white on a black background. 'The sorcerer's apron of human bones – a trapezium hanging from a cloth belt – is one of the six items of Tantric magical equipment (dagger, sacrificial knife, magic flute, skull-drum, skull chalice and bone apron).' Glowing in the dark, the bone fragments in squares or medallions are sometimes incised with human figures, faces, flowers and so on, and sometimes interspersed with red, green or blue beads in semi-precious stone (TONT p. 18). This apron may very well symbolize either a protection against retaliation by the dead or a demand for the dead to assist in preserving the wearer during the performance of the ritual from harmful or defiling contact. We return once more to the protective role of the apron, but it may well be that the sorcerer by the act of wearing it may intend the apron to make the dead partners in his work and draw upon the magical powers enclosed within their bones. So we revert to the first symbolical power of the apron, its close association with work.

apsara   Reproductions of the temple carvings of Angkor have popularized the attractions of the houris or heavenly dancers, the *apsara*. The etymology

provided by the *Rāmāyana* (*ap*, 'water' + *sara*, 'essence') is indication enough
that we are concerned with symbols rather than with the graceful and
decorative playthings of mythology. They are called 'essence of the waters'
because they are born of the 'welter of the sea' and its wind-blown spume.
As evanescent, they symbolize unformed potential, of which the 'Upper
Waters' are a more general image.

Their secondary role as instruments of love makes them susceptible to
a spiritual metamorphosis which identifies them with the houris of the
Muslim Paradise. As messengers of Kālī, they summon men to the love of
the godhead.

Their comparatively frequent appearance in Buddhist iconography confers upon them the additional role of angels.

In Khmer creation myths, from the *apsara* springs the solar dynasty, thus
they oppose the *nagi*, mother of the lunar dynasty and goddess of the
'Lower Waters'. In India the *apsara* is habitually the goddess of gambling
(CHOO, DANA, KRAA, THIK).

Aquarius (20 January–18 February)   This, the eleventh sign of the ZODIAC,
falls in the middle of the Winter quarter. It symbolizes social cohesiveness,
co-operation, brotherhood and indifference to material objects. Traditionally its 'ruler' was SATURN, with the addition, following its discovery, of
URANUS.

The sign is pictured as an aged sage, of noble appearance, bearing on his
shoulders or under his arms one or two tilted pots from which streams the
water which they contain. However, there is something airy and ethereal
about this stream which shares the characteristic insubstantiality of air as it
does the limpidity and fluidity of water. The environment it suggests is that
of the air flowing around us in waves, the waters of the airy ocean in which
we swim. This airy sign with its watery vibrations testifies to a nourishing
fluid designed to quench the thirst of the soul rather than that of the body.
If the atmosphere of Gemini suggests spiritual communication and that of
Libra the dialogue of the heart, that of Aquarius is of the world of elective
affinities which turns us into beings dwelling in a spiritual community fully
within the universal sphere. The sign has been related to Saturn to the
extent to which that planet liberates the individual from the bonds of instinct
and releases his or her spiritual powers to follow the path of abnegation. It
has been given a second master in Uranus, which recharges the liberated
being in the fire of Promethean power so that it can transcend itself. Opposite
the Herculean Lion stands the Seraphic Water Carrier. The inner substance
of this zodiacal type is fluid, light, ethereal, volatile, limpid, transparently
spiritual and, so to say, angelic. It comprises the gift of indifference to self
together with serenity and self-sacrifice, friendship and concern for others.
In addition there is the Uranian Water Carrier, the Promethean being in
the vanguard of progress, liberation and adventure.

arabesque   Although it may not belong to it exclusively, the arabesque, as
the name implies, is specific to Islamic art, which forbids the depiction of
human or animal forms. It is, in fact, a strict and clear-sighted refinement,
a transcendence of the representational. The arabesque is not a pattern
but a rhythm, an incantation which unendingly repeats the motif, the

'transcription of the mental *dhikr* [liturgical ritual]' (Benoist). Like the latter it enables the practitioner to escape from the constraints of time, and then it becomes an aid to meditation.

The arabesque has its connections, too, with the MAZE, with winding paths designed to lead from the outer margin to a central point (which itself symbolizes the invisible CENTRE of being) and also with the spider's web.

Athough its rhythms are patently different, the depiction in Chinese landscape painting of natural movements by a repeated series of curved brush strokes, is no less a species of arabesque (BURA, BENA).

The arabesque is the great secret of Islamic art. In it, two unvarying elements may be perceived: on the one hand there is the interpretation of flower, leaf and, particularly, of tendril; on the other the ideal exploitation of the line. Of these two principles, the first is patently an exercise of the imagination, the second strictly geometric. From these two processes – *al-ramy* and *al-khayt* – line and the entrelacs develop.

(FARD)

The arabesque corresponds to a religious vision. Islam is iconoclastic and dominated by the Word. 'Islam unfurls the abstract arabesque inset with the verses of its revelation against the Byzantine icon . . . . It is a technical device of Islamic art to avoid idolatry' (BAMC). 'The arabesque is the ultimate refinement of Muslim aspiration . . . . It has no beginning nor end, nor does it claim to such, since it seeks Him, who, according to the Koran (57: 3) is both the Beginning and the Consummation . . . . Tirelessly, but in vain, it steers towards the limitless.'

In addition there are arabesques drawn on no geometric basis and uninspired by any floral motif. These are epigraphic arabesques. 'The language of art is open to a stream of influences which constantly enrich its stock of ornamentation. When it rejects the slavish observance of rules and regulations this secret, undisclosed vocabulary rubs shoulders with extant abstract art, and this the flowing arabesque exemplifies' (FARD).

The arabesque might be termed the symbol of the symbol, hiding when it reveals and revealing when it conceals. As Jacques Berque writes:

A genre which is the prerogative of Islamic art, the arabesque exemplifies the coincidence of two characteristics of a work of art – its character as an object, and as an intersubjective link between the psyche of an individual, the artist, and the collective psyche . . . . The arabesque is a coming together, a complete synthesis of the artist's intentions, the message and medium closely integrated, and their adaptation to a society of whose originality it is so typical as to derive its name. When you go inside a mosque and gaze on one or other of the arabesques on its walls, you do far more than simply stare at them. You listen. An incantation laps around you. If you are a believer you slowly make out the sense of the inscriptions . . . . The whole is also a combination of the written and the chanted word – to the believer a ritual incantation. You are subjected as it were to a cross-fire of the sensual beauty of the arabesque and the impact of the verse from the Koran, that is to say of heavenly illumination.

The onlooker who attempts to decipher the arabesque is provided with 'the sight of a labyrinth or maze . . . . The artist's purpose is simultaneously to conceal and reveal the verse from the Koran and thus to arouse . . . the

combined emotions of truth and beauty which will become pledges of the
world beyond' (BERN).

arbutus   Classical antiquity associated this evergreen shrub with immortality, as in Virgil's description of the funeral rites of Aeneas' ally, Pallas.
'Others in haste plait the wicker-frame of a soft bier with arbute shoots and
oaken twigs, and shroud the high-piled couch with leafy canopy' (*Aeneid*
11: 63–6).

archer(y)   See ARROW; BOW; SAGITTARIUS.

archway   Related to the twofold symbolism of the SQUARE and the CIRCLE;
like the NICHE, it combines the spatial elements of the cube and the CHALICE.
The archway is a triumph over the banalities of the material world. 'The
archway soaring up to its keystone proclaims the lasting triumph of the
upward striving of the unconscious over the clogging flesh . . . .' It also suggests 'the instant and spontaneous stylization of the human form. It borrows
its curves and emphasizes its upward thrust (CHAS p. 269).'

Ares (Mars)   Ares, the god of war, was the son of ZEUS and HERA. Nonetheless, his father calls him 'the most hateful of all the Immortals', his mother
'a lawless madman' and his sister, ATHENE, 'this madman, this embodiment
of evil, this hare-brain'. Showy though his equipment of helmet, breastplate,
shield, spear and sword may be, his exploits were not always so impressive.
Athene defeated him in combat through her keener intelligence; Diomedes'
greater skill enabled him to wound the god in hand-to-hand combat, while
HEPHAISTOS made him a laughing stock when he netted him with APHRODITE.
   Ares symbolizes brute force, intoxicated with its own height, strength,
swiftness, loud voice and capacity to slaughter. It guffaws at the thought of
justice, moderation or humanity. 'He quenches his thirst with the blood
of men', says Aeschylus. And yet this simplistic view is something of a
caricature.
   Without necessarily being a vegetation-god, Ares was also guardian of
the harvest, something which is a duty for the warrior. He was acclaimed
as god of the Spring, less because he promoted the rising of the sap than
because March opens the season when kings go out to war. He was also the
god of youth and especially the guide of young men who leave their homes
to found new cities. Romulus and Remus were to be his sons. In iconography emigrants are often accompanied by the WOODPECKER or the WOLF,
creatures sacred to Ares, while it was a she-wolf which suckled the twins in
a cave on what was to become the Palatine Mount.
   If he is the 'Killer', the 'Guardian' of homes and of young people, he is
also the 'Chastiser' and the 'Avenger' of all crimes, and especially of oath-
breaking, and he is also sometimes honoured as the god of the oath (SECG
p. 248).
   Within the Indo-European triad upon which the work of G. Dumézil has
thrown such light, Ares represents the warrior caste.
   Although the 'Homeric' Hymn to Ares belongs to a much later period,
perhaps as late as the fourth century BC, it points the way to spiritual
development, which would be symbolized by the impetuous Ares were he
able to master his animal passions:

Ares, exceeding in strength . . . doughty in heart . . . father of warlike Victory, ally of Themis, leader of righteous men, sceptred King of manliness . . . hear me helper of men, giver of dauntless youth! Shed down a kindly ray from above upon my life, and strength of war, that I may be able to drive away bitter cowardice from my head and crush down deceitful impulses of my soul. Restrain also the keen fury of my heart which provokes me to tread the ways of blood-curdling strife. Rather, O blessed one, give you me boldness to abide within the harmless laws of peace, avoiding strife and hatred and the violent fiends of death.

In the Celtic world, the duties of the Roman god Mars were wholly if differently complemented at two levels by Nodens (Nuada in Irish), the priest-king of the warrior caste but exercising priestly office, and by Ogmios (Ogma in Irish), 'god of the golden chains', who is the 'champion' (Hercules), master of single combat, of magic and of the black arts. During the Gallo-Roman period when the office of kingship vanished, single combat lost its *raison d'être* and the very nature of Mars himself was changed by Romanization and syncretism, factors which have caused countless mistakes and misattributions (OGAC 17: pp. 175–88).

Aries (21 March–20 April) This zodiacal sign corresponds to the ascent of the Sun, with the passing from cold to warmth and from darkness to light, and is not unrelated to the quest for the Golden Fleece (see also RAM).

It is the first sign of the ZODIAC situated in the thirty degrees immediately following the vernal equinox. Nature wakes from the torpor of Winter and this sign symbolizes first and foremost the thrust of Spring and hence impetus, virility (it is the chief sign of MARS), energy, independence and courage. It is *par excellence* the 'positive' or male sign. Its strong influence is unfavourable to women when it is in the ascendant at the time when a female is born.

The sign of Aries is a symbol intimately connected with the nature of primordial FIRE. It is the cosmic image of the brute force of fire which first manifested itself in an explosion of flame. This is a fire which is simultaneously creator and destroyer, blind and rebellious, disorderly and prolific, generative and sublime; it circulates in all directions from a fixed point. This fiery power is at one with the original gush of life-giving forces, the primal surge of life, with all which such a process possesses in terms of pure animal impulse, shattering, uncontrollable lightning discharge, measureless ecstasy, fiery breath. We are faced with a WORD which re-echoes in RED and GOLD, and in astral affinities with Mars and the Sun. A Word which is essentially aggressive and super-male, which corresponds to a panting, impetuous, tumultuous, bubbling, convulsive nature. Astrology assigns a human character to each sign of the Zodiac, but explains that it is not enough nor even essential to have been born under that particular sign to resemble the character typical to that sign. Thus the Arian type belongs to the choleric (emotional–active–primary) type under modern character classification, with its white-hot vitality, its enthusiasm to live untrammelled in the confusion and intensity of its instincts and violent emotions in a life of action, with all its risks, successes and failures.

ark (see also BASKET)   There are various aspects to the symbolism of the ark and of VOYAGING in general which are linked together. The best known of these is Noah's Ark which sailed on the waters of the Flood, freighted with everything needed to restore the natural cycle. Sanskrit Puranic literature contains a similar account of how Manu, lawgiver to the present cycle, took ship with the Vedas, which are the seeds of the cyclic manifestation, and was saved by the *Matsaya-avatāra*, the god Vishnu in his incarnation as a fish. In fact the Ark floated 'on the face of the waters', exactly like the World Egg – 'like the first seed of life', St Martin writes. The same symbol of the 'seed', the unspoken WORD, which will germinate in some future cycle, recurs in the CONCH and in the Arabic letter *nūn* (a semicircle, the 'ark', with a dot, the 'seed', in the middle). Guénon has drawn attention to the importance of the way in which the RAINBOW complements the Ark by appearing over it as a sign of the 'covenant'. We have here two analogous but opposing symbols – one relative to 'the waters under the earth' and the other to the waters above it – which complement one another to recreate the ring of the unified cycle.

The symbolism of the Ark of the Covenant of the Children of Israel is closer than might be thought to the foregoing. The Israelites set it in the furthest end of the Tabernacle. It held the two tables of the Law, Aaron's Rod and a pot full of the manna on which the people were fed in the wilderness. It was the pledge of God's protection and the Israelites took it with them on their military campaigns. When it was translated with due cere-mony to David's palace, the oxen pulling the cart stumbled, the Ark slipped and the man who put out his hand to steady it was instantly struck dead. You do not lightly touch what is holy, divine or tradition (2 Samuel 16).

The Ark contained the essence of tradition, but developed in the form of the Tables of the Law. According to St Martin it is 'the source of the Powers' of the cycle. Furthermore, a legend claims that it was hidden by Jeremiah on his return from the captivity in Babylon and that it will come to light again to usher in a new age.

In Christian tradition the Ark was one of the richest sources of symbol-ism. Noah's Ark stood as the symbol of the house protected by God pre-serving all living things. The Ark of the Covenant was the symbol of God's presence among his chosen people, a portable sanctuary, the pledge of the covenant between God and his people, and, finally, it was the symbol of the Church. It is clad in the triple symbolic meaning of the New Covenant, which is universal and eternal; of the new presence, which is 'real', and of the new ark of salvation, no longer from the Flood but from sin. It is the Church, the new Ark, available to all for the salvation of the world.

Noah's Ark has been the subject of much speculation, especially among Rabbinical writers. Its pyramidal form conveys a sense of fire or flame. It holds a phallic power. The Ark was built from the immortal wood, *Met*, which is not subject to decay (a pine or acacia). There is a close connection between the dimensions God ordained for Noah's Ark at the time of the Flood and those which were given to Moses for the building of the Ark of the Covenant, the latter being proportionate with the former but on a much smaller scale. Noah's Ark had THREE decks. The importance of that figure is inescapable: it is a symbol of spiritual ascent.

Origen explains the dimensions of Noah's Ark: its length of 300 cubits expresses simultaneously the number one HUNDRED and the number three: the first signifies the fullness of unity, the second the Trinity. Its breadth of fifty cubits is interpreted as the symbol of the Redemption. As to its height, it symbolizes the number ONE, by reason of the unity of God. Origen offers further analogies between the length, breadth and height of the Ark and the length, breadth and depth of the love of God of which St Paul speaks (Ephesians 3: 18). To St Ambrose the Ark also represented the human body in its dimensions and properties, while Isidore of Seville was to point out that 300 cubits equals six times fifty, thus the length is SIX times the breadth and symbolizes the six ages of the world. St Augustine comments on this topic of the Ark that it prefigures the City of God, the Church and Christ's body.

In his treatise *De arca Noe morali et de arca mystica*, Hugh of St Victor takes up Origen's grand ideas once more. The mystic Ark is represented in the human heart. Hugh also compares it with a ship. He scrutinizes in succession the different components of the Ark to give a threefold interpretation of it, literal, moral and allegorical.

The Ark of the Heart is analogous with that most secret place within the Temple where sacrifice was offered, that is to say, with the Holy of Holies. The Ark always retains a mysterious character. Jung finds the image of the mother's breast in it, the sea into which the Sun is swallowed, only to rise again.

It is also the alchemical still in which base metals are transmuted. It is also the Holy GRAIL. The HEART as an ark or a still is a persistent symbol. Man's heart is the vessel in which the human is transmuted into the divine.

The Ark is a symbol of the treasure chest, the treasure being knowledge and life. It is the principle of individual preservation and resurrection. In Sudanese legend Nommo sends the first BLACKSMITH to mankind. He comes down the rainbow bearing an Ark containing one example of every living thing, of each of the minerals and of all the crafts (MYTF p. 239).

arm The arm is the symbol of strength, power, help and protection. It is also the instrument of justice: the secular arm punishes the guilty.

According to the Pseudo-Dionysius the Areopagite, the shoulders, arms and hands represent the power 'of making, striving and accomplishing' (PSEH p. 46). In Egyptian hieroglyphics, the arm is the overall symbol of activity. The Indian god, Brahmā, who presides over manifestation, is depicted with four faces and four arms to show that his activities are omnipresent and all-powerful. Similarly the elephant-headed Ganesha, the god of knowledge, is shown with four arms, while Shiva dances in a halo of innumerable arms.

The arm is one of the means by which kingship makes itself effective in directing policy, balancing interests, allocating office or giving judgement. The priest-king Nuada who had his arm cut off in the first Battle of Mag Tuired could no longer reign and was replaced by the usurper Bres (a FOMORIAN), whose rule was disastrous. When the nobles of Ireland had summoned Bres to surrender the kingship, Nuada was allowed to return to the throne after the healer, Dian Cécht, had fashioned an artificial arm of silver, the royal metal *par excellence*. An Irish carving from the Christian epoch shows Nuada holding in his good hand the arm which he had lost. The essentials of this myth are preserved in part in the legend of St Mela, or Meloir, from Upper Brittany (OGAC 13: pp. 286–9 (pl 56); 16: pp. 233–4; CELT 6: pp. 425ff.).

The arm, and especially the forearm with the hand palm outwards, is held by the Bambara to be an extension of the spirit, while the elbow, the activating joint, is of divine essence. In the simple gesture by which humans put food into their mouths, the forearm, connecting link between mouth and elbow, symbolizes the spirit which mediates between God and man. Hence arises the symbolic importance of the CUBIT which measures the distance between God and man. A Bambara cubit measures TWENTY-TWO finger-breadths, the number corresponding to the total number of categories of created beings, and therefore represents the universe. This is why the Bambara say that the cubit is 'the greatest distance in the world'. This, the distance between man and his Creator, is only filled by the spirit (his arm), because the latter may be measured by twenty-two, the number of the Creation. There is also a Bambara proverb – 'The mouth never manages to bite the elbow' – which evokes the transcendental qualities of the godhead (ZAHB). This symbolism goes on to explain why, when a Bambara puts his arm behind his back, it is a sign that he submits himself to the will of God.

In Christian ritual raising the arms is a sign of imploring heavenly grace and of the readiness of the soul to receive the gifts of God. When writing of the KA of the Ancient Egyptians, André Virel exposes the basic meaning of the gesture:

Raising the arms indicates a passive, receptive state. It is bodily activity yielding to spiritual receptivity. The spread of the arms above the Pharaoh's head is exactly the same as the spread of the horns above the head of a sacred animal. In both cases this embrace governs and signifies the receipt of cosmic powers: the human Heaven takes a share of the universal Heaven.

(VIRI p. 133)

Although forcing prisoners of war or criminals to put up their hands when they surrender is clearly a precautionary measure imposed by the victor to prevent his opponent from using a concealed weapon, deep down it symbolizes an act of submission. The vanquished renounces the means of self-defence, surrenders to the will of the victor and appeals to him for justice or mercy. It is the complete gesture of surrender and hopelessness. Whoever makes it becomes by so doing the passive object of his master's will.

armour See WEAPONS.

arrow In so far as it is a tool or weapon and not simply a sign, the arrow symbolizes

penetration and opening up. The arrow also symbolizes the power of thought to clarify and of the penis to penetrate and fertilize, splitting in order to effect a synthesis . . . . It is also the beam of light which illuminates an enclosed space because an opening has been made for it. It can be a ray of sunlight, itself a fructifying element, with the power of bringing images into focus.

(VIRI p. 194)

Like the LADDER, it is a symbol of intercommunication between Heaven and Earth. Directed downwards, the arrow is an attribute of the power of the godhead, like the vengeful THUNDERBOLT, or fructifying sunshine or RAIN. In the Old Testament those whom God can use to accomplish his works are called 'sons of the quiver'. In its upward flight it is connected with the symbolism of the vertical AXIS. 'The path of its flight, straight through the air, in apparent defiance of the laws of gravity, symbolically throws off Earth-bound limitations' (CHAS p. 162).

Broadly speaking, the arrow is 'the universal symbol of outrunning convention; it is an imaginary release from the confines of space and the laws of gravity; mental anticipation of the acquisition of benefits presently out of reach' (CHAS p. 324).

As opposed to the PITCHFORK, the arrow is the fit symbol of 'breaking down ambivalence, of surmounting obstacles, of objectivity, of decision-making, of working within a time-scale' (VIRI p. 69). It points the direction in which identification is to be found, in the sense that only by differentiation can the person discover his or her identity, individuality and personality. The arrow is a symbol of unification, decision-taking, synthesis (see SAGITTARIUS).

In the Upanishads, the arrow is mainly a symbol of swiftness and of lightning intuition. In European folklore, the arrow – its Latin name, *sagitta*, is derived from the same root as *sagire*, the verb meaning 'to perceive keenly or quickly' – is the symbol of mental alertness and its double is that instantaneous flash of light, LIGHTNING (DURS p. 137).

Symbol, too, of the tooth, the dart, the sharp pointed object which flies through the air to surprise and kill its victim at a distance, the arrow was invoked as a goddess to protect some and strike down others in the *Rig-Veda* (6: 75). While Dante (*Paradiso* 17: 25–7) uses it as a symbol of fate.

The arrow also symbolizes sudden, terrifying death: APOLLO, death-god in the *Iliad*, slays Niobe's children with his arrows.

The arrow striking its predetermined target signifies the outcome of an affair. Although likened to a ray of sunlight, it also takes its place among weapons carved from wood. In this respect C. G. Jung has observed that the fathers of divine heroes are workers in wood, sculptors, wood-cutters, carpenters, like Joseph the foster-father of Jesus Christ. Symbolically the arrow is employed for the fructifying element, an alternative to the sunray. It is also linked with the quiver of the gods and to the BOW of the centaurs. Origen in one of his sermons likens God to an archer.

A twelfth-century Italian illuminated manuscript shows God driving Adam and Eve out of the Garden of Eden with a flight of arrows, much as Apollo in the *Iliad* pursued the Greeks. Other twelfth-century miniatures depict God holding a bow and arrows (JUNL, JUNA, DIDH).

In Japanese folklore bow and arrows together symbolize love. The phallic association is obvious; the arrow strikes deep: the male principle roots itself in the female element. In the mystical sense its meaning is the struggle to achieve union with the godhead.

As images of fate, arrows have been consulted and have symbolized God's answer to man's questions.

Divination by means of arrows, or *belomancy*, was commonly practised in Arab countries. Its mechanics were based upon a process common to all methods of cleromancy (divination by lot) in which objects are used to provide oracles. The mechanics consist of trusting in pure chance to reveal the will or message of the god.

The Arabs developed belomancy to the point at which each arrow was given so precise a meaning as to leave nothing doubtful in the oracle's reply. The earlier sets of arrows with such messages as 'yes', 'no', 'good', 'bad', 'do it', 'do not do it', were supplemented by others bearing detailed and circumstantial instructions, such as 'set out [on your journey]', 'stay at home', 'act at once', 'wait', 'the blood-price must be paid'. Unmarked arrows were given different meanings according to circumstance and after due agreement with those consulting the arrows.

To consult the arrows has become a commonplace of poetic imagery. The poet Wahib maintained that belomancy delivered a lying message while Abū al-'Atāhiyah compares death's dealings with men to the shaking of the arrows (FAHD pp. 184–7).

The accuracy of the arrow's aim and the force of its impact depend on the strength of whoever draws the bow. It is almost as if the arrow has identified with the archer who projects himself and hurls himself upon his prey. Thus the arrows of the gods never miss their mark. Those of Apollo, ARTEMIS and Eros (see LOVE) were always supposed to strike the heart. Thought strikes home like an arrow and rives the soul with a torment which cannot be assuaged.

If love's arrows never miss, they are activated by a lightning glance of the eyes. 'The lover', Alexander of Aphrodisias explains (TERS p. 186), 'simultaneously beholds and desires, and his yearning makes him send out a continuous stream of beams towards the object of his desire. These beams may be likened to a flight of arrows which the lover shoots at his beloved.' However, love, Ovid informs us, uses two types of arrow which always hit their mark: if they are tipped with gold they kindle passion, but if tipped with lead they extinguish it.

Artemis (Diana) Daughter of ZEUS and Leto, twin sister of APOLLO, Artemis, the moody and rancorous virgin, 'for ever untamed', is depicted in mythology as the antithesis of APHRODITE. She cruelly punishes any slight to her dignity, for example by transforming the offender into a stag to be eaten by his own hounds. On the other hand her faithful worshippers, such as Hippolytus, fatal victim of his own chastity, are rewarded with immortality.

'Boisterous Artemis, archer of the golden bow, Bowman's sister' (*Iliad* 20), racing through the forests with her accompanying nymphs and her hounds, ever ready to shoot her arrows, is 'the wild goddess of the woods'. She is at her most merciless with women who yield to the lure of love. She both points the way to chastity and bars the path to pleasure. She was surnamed 'Lady of the Wild Beasts'. As a huntress she slaughtered the stags and does, symbolizing the pleasure and reproduction aspects of sex. When such creatures are young and unsullied she protects them as sacred animals. She protects pregnant women, too, for the sake of the children they are carrying and to whom they will give birth, for, although a virgin, she is also the goddess of childbirth. To punish Agamemnon's offence, she demanded the death of Iphigenia, but at the very altar set a doe in place of the girl, whom she swept up into the clouds to make her her priestess.

'Artemis, protective yet sometimes to be feared, holds equal sway over the human world, presiding over the birth and growth of living creatures.' She was turned into a Moon-goddess, wandering like the Moon and sporting in the mountains, while her twin brother, Apollo, became a Sun-god. Artemis-Selene is connected with the cycle of fertility symbols. Hostile to men, she was to play the part of protectress of woman's life-cycle. Her cult has therefore been considered as deriving from that of the Great MOTHER Goddess of Asia and the Aegean, with its main centres at Ephesus and Delos (SECG pp. 353–65).

The Roman Diana should be identified with an Indo-European sky-god who, according to G. Dumézil, secured the continuity of the human race and provided kings with their successors. Diana was also the protectress of slaves. From about the fifth century BC she became identified with the Greek goddess Artemis.

Some psychoanalysts would see Artemis as symbolizing the jealousy, domination and castration complexes in the mother. Together with her antithesis, Aphrodite, she comprises the total image of womanhood, so deeply divided in itself, in so far as she has failed to reduce the tensions born of the twofold complex within her nature. The wild beasts which accompany Artemis in the chase are those instincts intrinsic to the human condition which must be brought to heel if one is to reach that 'City of the Righteous', according to Homer, so beloved by the goddess.

There is no evidence for a cult of Artemis in the strictest sense in Gaul before the Roman period; but that it became extraordinarily widespread is witnessed by the way in which Church Councils and other ecclesiastical bodies and authorities reacted against it as late as the sixth and seventh centuries AD. It is likely that Diana, symbolizing the virginal and queenly aspects of the oldest Italic mythology, absorbed the cult of a continental Celtic goddess whose name resembled hers and must have been close to the Irish form *Dé Ana*, or 'Goddess Ana', mother of the gods and patron of the arts (CELT 15: p. 358).

artemisia In the Far East artemisia was and still is held to be endowed with purgative qualities. In fact, both in Europe and in China, its virtues have been employed to stimulate menstruation and to expel worms from the intestines, both conditions being different forms of 'impurity'.

At the Tuen Ng Festival (fifth day of Fifth Moon) an infusion of artemisia was drunk. Dolls were made from the plant, shaped like men or tigers, and hung in doorways to purge houses of harmful influences and to prevent their entry. (This custom still survives in places.) Arrows made from artemisia were shot skyward, earthward and to the four cardinal points to destroy ill-omened influences.

An odiferous plant, artemisia was also mingled with the fat of sacrificial victims, since the ascent of aromatic odours was a means of communicating with Heaven (GRAD, GOVM).

Arthur Etymologically the Welsh name Arthur is derived from *artos*, 'bear', via the Old Breton *artoris* of which only the suffix has a Latin origin. Arthur is above all the king and, in the legendary tale of the hunt, his temporal authority comes face to face symbolically with spiritual authority typified by the BOAR. The knightly ideals of the Quest of the Holy GRAIL taken up and elaborated by medieval insular and continental writers reflect the predominance of the warrior caste. As a result, the historical Arthur was metamorphosed into the legendary king mysteriously slumbering on the Isle of Avalon – a localization of the Celtic Otherworld. There he becomes the catalyst for all the small Celtic nations of the Middle Ages, and Bretons and Welsh waited for him to come and free them from the foreign yoke – which he will surely perform before the end of time.

ascension   Christian iconography frequently depicts human ascension, the symbol of the heavenward soaring of the soul after death. The person is generally shown with arms outstretched, as in prayer, and with knees bent under as in adoration. Sometimes he or she is raised above the Earth without any visible means of support, the head haloed by stars; sometimes borne up by WINGS, ANGELS or BIRDS (CHAS p. 322). All these icons represent a positive human response to a spiritual vocation and a motion towards holiness rather than the state of perfection itself. The level of the ascension into space, be it just above the ground or high into the Heavens, corresponds to the level of the inner life and the degree to which the spirit has transcended the material plane of its existence. For example, the Assumption of Our Lady after her Dormition, independently of the historicity of the event, symbolizes the total spiritualization of her being, body and soul.

The ascent of the soul is common to other than Christian traditions. In fact, as Jean Daniélou observes, in both his *Phaedo* and his *Symposium* Plato describes the soul ascending in quest of its native land where it may contemplate ideas in all their purity, and this ascent of the soul is a feature of most writings inspired by Plato, notably those of Maximus Tyrius in the second century AD. On the other hand, Basilides had by then begun to adumbrate the descent of God to mankind. He maintained that revelation came down from on high, Christ revealing the unknown God and coming down to become the centre of history. Nevertheless Christ's coming down was counterbalanced by the soul's going up to God, and this ascent might be seen in the light of a homecoming (RETURN). St Gregory of Nyssa elaborated at some length the metaphor of this ascent as the climbing of a mountain with a regular succession of stages. In this context the transit of the soul through the cosmic spheres should be interpreted symbolically as successive stages of purification. St Augustine understood and described this ascent of the soul through the various cosmic spheres as located, not in the external world, but in the internal world of the soul itself. When he describes his own experience with his mother, St Monica, Augustine mentions the different planes which he traversed – corporeal matter, the sky, the Sun, the Moon, the stars – 'and we still ascend', he goes on to say (*Confessions* 9: 25). Ascension is above all a process of internalization: descent a dissipation of the spirit in the external world.

Other symbols of ascension – TREE, ARROW, MOUNTAIN, and so on – also express the upsoaring of the living being, his or her gradual evolution to a higher plane, thrusting towards Heaven.

The ascension of the shaman is a process of divination or of healing, aimed at saving the sick person whose soul has been stolen by a spirit. Modern psychoanalysis which sees dreams of flying as symbols of the orgasm is at one with medieval Christian belief, which associated night flight with wizards, witches and those possessed by the Devil, and hence with orgiastic cults – the dark side of the symbol.

ashes Ashes derive their symbolism first from the fact that they are pre-eminently a residue – what remains after the fire goes out – hence, anthropocentrically, what remains of the body after life is extinguished.

In spiritual terms what remains is valueless, thus from the eschatological point of view, ashes symbolize the nullity of human life, deriving from its transience.

The old Catholic liturgy for Ash Wednesday was explicit. As the priest marked the worshipper's forehead he intoned *Pulvis es, in pulverem reverteris* ('Dust thou art: to dust thou shalt return'), reminiscent of Abraham's 'Behold now, I have taken upon me to speak unto the Lord, which am but dust and ashes' (Genesis 18: 27). Indeed the symbolic value which Christians give this word goes back via the New to the Old Testament. In India the value is the same. Thus the bodies of yogi and *sadhu* are smeared with ashes as a sign that they have renounced the vanities of this world in imitation of Shiva in his ascetic manifestation, while Christian ascetics sometimes sprinkle ashes on their food. Nevertheless this symbolism is not always so simple and straightforward. Thus Chinese folklore draws a distinction between 'damp ashes' and 'dry ashes'. According to the *Lieh-tzu* (ch. 2), a dream of damp ashes was a presage of death. Nonetheless the ashes of reeds used by Nu-kua to stem the waters of the Flood seem to indicate a conjunction of these elements, rather than the destruction of the one by the other or the result of purging the elements with fire. The 'dead ashes', with which Chuang-tzu compares the heart of the sage, symbolize the extinction of mental activity. The same expression is used afresh in the commentary *T'ai Ch'ing* (GRAD, DANA).

Finally it should not be forgotten that all things associated with death embody the symbolism of the 'eternal RETURN'. This perhaps explains the custom which was long preserved in Christian monasteries of laying out the dying on the ground on which a cross had been traced out in ashes. As is well known, the cross is the universal symbol of the alternation of life and death, which explains why a Christian tradition should find an echo in the religious world of Central America. To the Maya-speaking Quiché, ashes would seem to have had a magical function, linked with germination and the cyclic return of life made manifest. The twin heroes of the *Popol Vuh* turn themselves to ashes before 'coming to life again like the phoenix'. Contemporary Chorti, descendants of the Maya, make a cross of ashes to protect their maize fields against evil spirits and mingle ashes with the seed-corn to inoculate it against rotting, ergot or any other lurking danger to the grain while it lies buried.

Giving ashes a positive value would explain, too, the reason why, in the Christian tradition, they are blessed and used in such rites as, for example, the consecration of a new church.

Finally it is extraordinary that ashes, being pre-eminently associated with the *yang* principle, and hence with the Sun, gold, fire and dryness, should have been employed by the Muisca (Chibcha from Colombia), whose priests used to sprinkle ashes on a mountain top in their rain-making ceremonies.

ash-tree To the Greeks of the time of Hesiod, the ash-tree was the symbol of stability. In the famous myth of the degeneration of mankind, the ash-tree engenders 'the race of bronze, far different from the race of silver, born of the ash-tree, awe-inspiring and mighty'. Ash was the wood used for spear-shafts and is a metaphor for the weapon itself.

In Scandinavian folklore the ash-tree becomes Yggdrasil, the symbol of immortality and the link between the three levels of the cosmos. It was also a giant and a fertility-god.

Germanic peoples considered Yggdrasil as the World Tree. The universe spread out in the shade of its branches, countless creatures sheltered there and from it all living things derived their being. It was eternally green because it drew the power of life and renewal from the spring, Urd. Yggdrasil drew life from its waters and through them gave life to the universe. This spring was guarded by the Norns, or Fates.

The first of the ash-tree's three tap-roots went down to the spring, Urd; the second penetrated to Niflheim, the land of frost, to reach the spring Hvergelmir, from whose waters all the streams on Earth were fed; while the third reached to the land of the Giants and to Mimir, the murmuring fountain of wisdom. The Germanic gods assembled at the foot of Yggdrasil, like the Greek gods on Olympus, to administer justice. Amid all the cosmic upheavals in which one universe was destroyed to give birth to a new, Yggdrasil stood firm, unmoved and unconquered. Not flame, nor frost, nor darkness could uproot it. It was a refuge for those who had escaped the cataclysm to repeople the new world. It is thus the symbol of the indestructible continuity of the life force.

In the Baltic Republics the slow-witted or the simple-minded were called ash-trees. The tree itself was held to be blind to what went on around it, so that it did not know when Spring arrived and its branches remained bare. Then, in Autumn, afraid of making a fool of itself once again, it was the first to shed its leaves at one fell swoop (*Latvi esu Tautas paskas un teikas*, Riga, 1925–37).

According to Pliny and Dioscorides the ash-tree was held to put serpents to flight, exercising a kind of magical influence over them so that if a snake had to choose between slithering under the branches of an ash or through the flames of a fire, it would choose the latter. These authors add that 'an infusion of ash-leaves mixed with wine is a powerful antidote against poison' (LANS 6 Pt 2: pp. 146–7).

As in the Nordic countries, so the ash is a fertility symbol in Great Kabylia. '*Taslent*, the ash, is pre-eminently the tree for women. They should climb its branches to cut leaves as fodder for cows and oxen and on them should be hung certain amulets and especially those charms to attract men's love.' Although it was the first tree to be created, the ash is surpassed by the olive in usefulness. However, this forage-tree is not all sweetness and light; like anything which possesses magical powers, it can be threatening. 'If a man plants an ash-tree, either a male member of his family will die, or else his wife will only produce still-born babies, since all life- and fertility-forces also embody their opposites – the powers of death and sterility' (SERP p. 252).

asphodel This plant of the LILY family with regular, hermaphrodite flowers, was always associated with death by the Greeks and Romans, an Underworld flower dedicated to Hades and Proserpina. Hardly knowing why this should be so, in Classical antiquity an attempt was made to alter or to shorten the name to make it mean 'a field of ashes', or 'the beheaded, that is to say, in mystic terms, those whose head no longer controls their body or commands their will' (LANS 1: p. 166).

Since alcohol can be distilled from it, the asphodel symbolizes loss of consciousness and sensation characteristic of death. Although Classical antiquity – perhaps influenced by the plant's association with death – attributed a pestilential scent to it, the perfume of the asphodel is closely akin to that of jasmine.

ass (donkey) Nowadays the donkey symbolizes obstinate stupidity, but this is only a special and subsidiary aspect of a much more general concept which almost universally makes the ass the emblem of darkness and even of devilish propensities.

In India the ass is the steed of gods, but these are exclusively death-gods, especially Nairrita, warden of the land of the dead, and Kālarātrī, the ill-omened aspect of Devī. The *asura* Dhenuka is manifest in the guise of an ass.

In Ancient Egypt the 'red ass' was one of the most dangerous beings which the soul encountered on its voyage to the Otherworld. Guénon suggests that the creature may be identical with the 'scarlet Beast of the Apocalypse'.

Ismaili esoteric doctrine calls the spreading of ignorance and fraud 'Dajjal's donkey', from its blinkered literal interpretations which inhibit attainment of the inner vision.

A counter-argument is the presence of the ass at the nativity and the part which it played in Christ's entry into Jerusalem. However, Guénon has noted that in the first instance it stands facing the ox, symbolizing the maleficent opposed to the beneficent, while in the second these same forces are shown tamed by the Redeemer. Indeed a quite different significance could be given to the beast which carried Jesus in triumph – in China a white donkey is sometimes the steed of the Immortals.

In fact, on Palm Sunday the beast which Christ rode was a she-ass, and this is significant. In the myth of the false prophet Balaam, the part played by the she-ass was clearly beneficent and Mgr Devoucoux unhesitatingly makes her the symbol of learning and esoteric knowledge, thus showing a complete reversal of the original symbol. From this one might perhaps infer an initiation symbolism in the honours paid to the ass in the medieval Feast of Fools. However, the feast as a whole is imbued with parody and the temporary reversal of accepted values seems so much a part of it as to bring us back to our starting point. As Guénon observes, the feast channels the base instincts of fallen man so as to limit their baleful effects, in other words what current psychoanalysis would term 'catharsis', symbolized by the temporary introduction of an ass into the choir of a church. In theological terms it is effected by reversal and mockery, when a carnival Satanism replaces the she-ass of knowledge with the diabolical donkey (CORT, DEVA, MALA).

Like Satan and like the Beast in the Apocalypse the ass is the symbol of the sexual organs, the libido, human instinct and of life confined to the earthly plane of the senses. The spirit masters matter which sometimes escapes its control, although it ought to be subject to it.

The well-known romance, *The Golden Ass*, or *Metamorphoses*, by Apuleius, tells of the successive changes which transported Lucius from a prostitute's perfumed chamber to rapt contemplation before the statue of Isis. This series of metamorphoses illustrates Lucius' spiritual development. As Jean Beaujeu observes, his transformation into an ass 'expresses in physical terms and in visible shape the punishment of his relapse into sensual pleasure'. The second transformation 'by which his human shape and personality are restored, is not simply a shattering manifestation of the saving powers of Isis, but illustrates the transit through misfortune, mundane pleasure, enslavement to blind fortune into supernatural bliss and the service of an all-powerful, all-provident godhead. It is a true rebirth, the inner rebirth.' Restored to human shape, Lucius can now follow the path of salvation and enter the way of purity which will initiate him into the highest mysteries. Only when he has thrown off the ass and become man once more (and after a series of increasingly severe trials) can he actually embrace knowledge of the godhead.

According to the legend, Apollo changed King Midas' EARS into ass's ears because he preferred the sound of Pan's pipes to the music of the temple of Delphi. In symbolic terms, his choice, and the ass's ears with which he was punished, show him succumbing to the attractions of sensual pleasure rather than seeking the harmony of the spirit and the empire of the soul.

In his description of *The Way to the Underworld*, Pausanias (10: 28–31) states that there was a man called Ocnos sitting beside the sacrificial black rams. He was depicted plaiting a reed rope which a she-ass ate as fast as he plaited it. Pausanias goes on to say that this Ocnos was a hard-working man with a spendthrift wife, who soon wasted all he earned by his hard work. The allusion is obvious, at least so far as the wife is concerned, but her enigmatic husband is not without interest in so far as he complements the symbolism of the account, since 'his name means "hesitation" or "indecision". His presence in this context prompts us to see in him the symbol of weakness, even of fault – of never taking sides and of never bringing his undertakings to a successful conclusion' (Jean Defradas). In this light, the matrimonial scene becomes completely clear.

Renaissance painters depicted a range of psychological states as a donkey – the monk's spiritual disheartenment; moral depression; idleness; bored pleasure-seeking; stupidity; incompetence; obstinacy; foolishly blind obedience (TERS pp. 28–30). Alchemists saw the ass as a three-headed demon, one head being mercury, the others salt and sulphur, the three main constituents of nature, the hidebound being.

The ass was seen as a sacred animal in some religions. It played an important part in the worship of Apollo and asses were sacrificed to him at Delphi. A donkey carried the chest which was used as a cradle for Dionysos and is therefore sacred to him. According to another tradition the sacrifice of asses was of Nordic origin:

Neither by ships nor by land canst thou find the wondrous road to the trysting-place of the Hyperboreans. Yet amongst them, in olden days, Perseus, the leader of the people, shared the banquet on entering their homes and finding them sacrificing famous hecatombs of asses in honour of the god. In the banquets and praises of that people Apollo chiefly rejoiceth, and he laugheth as he looketh on the brute beasts in their rampant lewdness.

(Pindar, Pythian Odes 10: 29–36)

In *The Frogs*, Aristophanes has a slave telling Dionysos, when his master places a burden on his shoulders: 'And I'm the ass with the sacred image on his back.' The scene may be farcical, but the ass carrying the sacred image is a commonplace and is interpreted as the symbol of the king or of temporal power in general.

The wild ass, or ONAGER, symbolizes the eremetical DESERT Fathers, the reason doubtless being that the hoof of the onager is impervious to poison. The jaw-bone of an ass is proverbial for its hardness and it was with this that Samson slew a thousand Philistines.

The ass is under the influence of Saturn, the second Sun, who is the star of Israel. Thus some traditions identify Jehovah with Saturn. This perhaps explains why some satirical caricatures depict a man with an ass's head on a cross, Christ being the Son of the God of Israel.

The she-ass symbolizes humility and her foal self-abasement. Richard of St Victor was to write that humans needed to understand the meaning given to the she-ass in order to become steeped in humility and vile in their own eyes. If Christ deliberately chose a steed of this sort, Richard of St Victor was to say, it was to show the need for humility. Hence he wrote: 'upon whom now rests my spirit, says the Prophet, unless upon the humble, the peaceable and he who trembles at my words [Proverbs 16: 18]. He who practises true humility before God and within his heart, rides upon the she-ass: but he who is attentive to the duties of true self-abasement outwardly and before his neighbour, rides upon her foal.'

Here the she-ass is the symbol of peace, poverty, humility, patience and courage, and is generally exhibited in a favourable light in the Bible. Samuel went to look for the missing she-asses; Balaam was taught by the example of his she-ass, which warned him of the presence of the Angel of the Lord; Joseph set Mary and Jesus on the back of a she-ass to escape Herod's persecutions in Egypt; and on Palm Sunday Christ made his triumphant entry into Jerusalem riding upon a she-ass.

athanor The alchemists' furnace is the symbol of physical, moral or mystical transmutation. Alchemists regarded

the athanor, in which the process of transmutation took place, [as] an egg-shaped matrix, like the world itself, which is a gigantic EGG, the Orphic egg which may be found at the base of all initiatory rites both in Egypt and in Greece. And just as *Ruah Elohim*, the Spirit of the Lord, floats upon the waters,

so ought the spirit of the world, the spirit of life, to float above the waters of
the athanor. The alchemist needed the skill to make this spirit his own.

(GRIM p. 392)

Athene As with her brother APOLLO, throughout Classical antiquity the
image of Athene underwent a steady development towards an ever higher
spirituality. Two of her attributes, the SERPENT and the BIRD, symbolize the
parameters of this development. Age-old Underworld (serpent) goddess from
the Aegean area, she was to acquire a dominant position among the Olympians (bird). A fertility-goddess and goddess of wisdom, she was the virgin
protectress of children, the warrior-goddess who inspired the arts and crafts
of peace. As Marie Delcourt puts it, she was 'a highly enigmatic personality
and undoubtedly the one in all Greek mythology whose inner being remains most closely hidden from us.' This is because our concept of Athene
compresses whole centuries of extremely intense mythological history.

Her birth came like a flash of light across the universe, the dawn of a new
world, an apocalyptic vision. The AXE of bronze forged by Hephaistos struck
and, Pindar chants, 'Athene leapt forth upon the crest of her father's head,
and cried aloud with a mighty shout, while Heaven and Mother Earth
trembled before her.' Her arrival marked a turning-point in the history of
the cosmos and of mankind. A blizzard of gold covered the city of her birth:
snow and gold, purity and wealth, sent from Heaven with a twofold purpose, to fertilize like rain and to illumine like the Sun. This blizzard of gold
is also 'art which begets knowledge and which can grow ever more beautiful
without recourse to lies', in other words to deception or magic. That very
day Apollo, 'the god that bringeth light to man', laid a duty upon man's
countless descendants to 'build for the goddess an altar in the sight of all
men, and, by founding a holy sacrifice, gladden the heart of the Father, and
of the Daughter with the sounding spear (Pindar, *Olympian Odes* 7: 36–8,
39, 42–3).' It is impossible to conceive of an atmosphere so full of light,
'like the manifestation of a goddess emerging from a holy mountain' (SECG,
p. 325).

And yet at certain festivals cakes in the shape of serpents and phalli,
symbols of fertility and plenty, were offered to Athene. In Greece new-
born babies were given a charm in the shape of a serpent, symbol of intuitive wisdom and protective vigilance, in memory of Erichthonius, who was
to become founder of Athens and whom Athene had protected as a baby
by hiding him in a chest with a serpent to watch over and guard him. In a
number of statues Athene is shown wearing belt, skirt and tunic fringed
with hissing serpents, in addition to the shield with the Gorgon's head
ringed with serpents, at which her enemies had only to glance to become
petrified with fear. They symbolize the goddess's fighting spirit and keen
intelligence. She is the virgin armed and defending the heights, in every
sense of the word both material and spiritual, on which she stands.

By setting the Gorgon's head on her shield, she makes it the mirror of
truth. It conquers her enemies by petrifying them with horror at the reflection of their own faces. The loan of this shield to Perseus enabled him to
overcome the frightful Gorgon in the first place. Thus the goddess wins her
victories by her wisdom, her quick-wittedness and by the truth. The spear
which she holds is a weapon of light which cleaves and pierces the clouds
like lightning – a vertical symbol like fire or the AXIS.

The protection which Athene affords to such heroes as HERAKLES
(HERCULES), Achilles, Odysseus and Menelaus 'symbolizes', Pierre Grimal
writes, 'the assistance given by the Spirit to the brute strength and personal
courage of these heroes' (GRID p. 57).

Athene, worshipped as a fertility-goddess and the goddess of victory,
symbolizes, above all, 'psychic creativity . . . meditative synthesis . . . social-
ized intelligence' (VIRI p. 104).

She is the protectress of high places – acropolis, palace or city – and, as
city-goddess, she inspires the arts, is patroness of civil and domestic society,
agriculture and war and is the active working power of the intellect. She is
the goddess of inner stability, of the golden mean. She is 'the divine personage which best expresses the characteristics of Hellenic civilization in war
or peace, ever intelligent and clear-headed, free from mystery and mysticism
and from orgiastic or barbarous worship' (LAVD p. 129).

This observation serves only to corroborate the history of the myth of
Athene and its value as a symbol. It shows the goddess achieving perfection
only after a long period of development, which itself reflects the development of human consciousness. In the course of her mythological history
Athene exhibits more than a touch or two of savagery and barbarism. This
could counter the final image of herself which Athene presents when all the
elements of her rich personality have been welded into one harmonious
whole. She may be scrutinized at each stage in her evolution with the spot-
light focused upon one particular aspect of her character. Or else she may
be surveyed at the highest pitch of Greek consciousness. It would seem that
at that point, like her brother Apollo, she symbolizes 'both aggressive and
harmonizing spiritualization, which are interdependent . . . . They [brother
and sister] symbolize conscious psychic functions inspired by the vision of
the ultimate ideal – absolute truth (ZEUS) and perfect sublimity (HERA).' It
should be observed that in this context both Zeus and Hera, too, are taken
in their highest manifestations. Athene should symbolize especially that
'spiritual aggressiveness' (DIES pp. 97–8) which should be ever on the
alert; since perfection can only be attained by the individual who has become 'one for whom, in the end, eternity fashions the change within him-
or herself.'

Atlantis   Whether its origins be in history or in legend, the drowned continent of Atlantis remains, in the light of what the Egyptians inspired Plato
to write, embedded in human consciousness as the symbol of a sort of
Paradise Lost or ideal city. It was POSEIDON's kingdom, which he inhabited
with the 'children which he had begotten of a mortal woman', and he himself
ordered, embellished and managed the island. It was a great and wonderful
realm and

the wealth [its inhabitants] possessed was so immense that the like had never
been seen before in any royal house nor will ever be easily seen again . . . . They
cropped the land twice a year, making use of the rains from Heaven in the
winter, and the waters that arise from the earth in summer, by conducting the
streams from the trenches.

(Plato, *Critias* 114b, 118e)

Whether these are echoes of an extremely ancient tradition or whether
this is simply some Utopian dream, Plato endows his imaginary Atlantis

with a faultless political and social system. Ten kings share the legislative power:

when darkness came on and the sacrificial fire had died down, all the princes robed themselves in the most beautiful sable vestments, and sate on the ground beside the cinders of the sacramental victims throughout the night, extinguishing all the fire that was round about the sanctuary; and there they gave and received judgement, if any of them accused any of committing any transgression. And when they had given judgement, they wrote the judgements, when it was light, upon a golden tablet, and dedicated them together with their robes as memorials.

(ibid. 120c)

But when their divine nature weakens and the human character comes to the fore, they deservedly incur Zeus' punishment.

Thus Atlantis joins the ranks of the archetypal Eden or Golden Age which is to be found among all civilizations, at either the beginning or the end of human existence. Its originality as a symbol lies in the idea that Paradise comprises the predominance within us of a divine element.

Furthermore Atlantis shows us that, because men connived at the loss of their finest and most precious gifts, in the end they were driven from this Eden, which with its inhabitants was swallowed by the sea. This, surely, suggests that Heaven and Hell are within ourselves.

Aton Egyptian god, whose sole worship was founded by the famous religious reformer, the Pharaoh Akhenaten [Amenhotep IV], whom Daniel Rops has called 'the god-intoxicated king'. He was at one and the same time a tutelary, solar and spiritual deity, bathing all living beings in his light and warmth. His word and his thought had conceived and created the universe. He was depicted as the Sun shooting out his beams as emblems of the life force. He symbolizes this unique force from which all living things proceed.

augury The Celts had their druids, bards and seers, but no specialized body of augurs, since soothsaying was an attribute of the priestly caste as a whole. This is what makes augury in the Celtic regions so original. However, remove this factor and the processes employed do not differ significantly from those used in the Graeco-Roman world – divination by the weather, the flight of birds or the death-throes of a sacrificial animal (LERD p. 53).

In Rome, the College of Augurs is said to have been established soon after the foundation of the city by Numa, its second king. However, taking the auspices from the ritual observation of the flight of birds or the fall of shooting stars and other atmospheric phenomena, which is the specific duty of the augurs, goes back to the remotest antiquity, probably to the time of the Chaldeans. 'The word *augur*', Jean Beaujeu observes,

has the same root as the verb *augere*, to increase. The augurs were the sole authorized interpreters of the will of the gods. In exceptional circumstances, however, recourse would be made to the haruspices, a college of priests who interpreted the will of Heaven from an examination of the intestines of sacrificial animals. The augurs took the auspices in the name of the Republic by studying the flight of BIRDS, watching the behaviour of the sacred HENS and interpreting LIGHTNING flashes. Their reply was a stark yes or no to a precisely

phrased question posed by a magistrate in a strict ritual. There was no appeal
against the augur's decision and his powers were extensive, since he could postpone battles, elections and so on. Another duty of the augurs was the ritual
inauguration of new towns, temples and other places and even of priests.

The augur is generally depicted wearing a red robe, with a crown on his
head, holding his augural STAFF, and standing staring skywards. His staff of
office was the *lituus*, a crook or crozier which he used to mark out the
quarter of the heavens in which the birds would make their flight by drawing a square, on the lines of a temple, in which the bird would be framed.
An augur could never be deprived of his priestly rights, which stamped him
for life. 'Even if the augur is found guilty of the most heinous offences,'
Plutarch writes, 'he can never be stripped of his priesthood in his lifetime.'

As the all-powerful and infallible interpreter of the messages of the gods
written in the skies, the augur symbolizes the predominance of the spiritual
over the rational. He reads the Invisible by means of visible signs in the
Heavens. The human intellect cannot account for the mysterious causes of
success or failure. Other means of investigation are required to ascertain
them. The augur has seen, read and spoken: he must be obeyed. The symbol's validity is unaffected by the collusion, in the days of a declining faith,
between the pronouncements of the augur and the policy of the state.

aum (see also OM)   Set at the beginning and end of all liturgical utterance,
Aum is the first MANTRA and one of the most powerful and most famous
in Hindu tradition. It is the most emphatic symbol of the godhead, which
it expresses externally and actualizes internally in the soul. It is within itself
the epitome of the creative breath, since Vedic tradition would have it that
the universe evolved from cosmic energy set in motion when the demiurge
uttered this first invocation to awaken all things: 'AUM BHUR BHUVAH
SVAH' (Aum! Earth! Atmosphere! Sky!).

Since Aum is the primeval sound, the Word which created the universe,
to utter it releases a considerable charge of energy which is extraordinarily
effective in terms of spiritual transformation. In Hindu thought, the sound
which is both God and the originator of all things endows mantras with
their almost magical properties. The word which gives expression to being
through its sound is at one and the same time that being itself and the
Being from whom all things originate and to which all things return. To
utter the sound of God is to become godlike. According to Vivekānanda
and Vedic tradition, Aum is first and foremost manifestation of the godhead.

The all-embracing significance of the word Aum is strengthened by the
fact that the THREE letters which make it up possess the threefold rhythm
which is of such importance in Indian thought, social structure and cosmogony. These threefold characteristics are to be found, for example, in the
supreme godhead in the shapes of Brahmā, Vishnu and Shiva; in the cosmic
properties of substance, energy and essence; in the three worlds of Earth,
Space and Heaven; and in the division of mankind into three castes – priests,
warriors and artisans – just as each individual comprises body, mind and
soul. This last is similar to the Christian medieval division of *spiritus*, *anima*
and *corpus*.

Indians have studied physiological correspondences with these metaphysical teachings to evolve what is to all intents and purposes a theology of sound. Vivekānanda maintains that the technique of pronouncing the sacred word Aum explains its symbolism:

When we utter a sound we employ breath and tongue and use the larynx and palate as a sounding board. The most natural manifestation of sound is none other than the monosyllable *Aum* which comprises all sounds. Aum is composed of three letters – A, U and M. A is basic sound, the key uttered without there being any contact with any portion of the tongue or palate. It is the least differentiated of any sound and this is why in the *Upanishads* Krishna is made to say: 'In the alphabet, I am the letter A and I am all the parts of every compound word. I am infinite time. I am the god whose face looks in all directions.' The sound of the letter A starts in the buccal cavity; it is guttural. U is breathed out along the whole length of the mouth's sounding board. It represents precisely the forward movement of a force which starts at the root of the tongue and ends at the lips. M corresponds to the final sound in the labial range, since it is produced with closed lips. When correctly pronounced the word Aum epitomizes the whole phenomenon of sound reproduction, as no other word can do. It is therefore the symbol of the whole diversified range of sounds and concentrates within itself the whole potential range of imaginable words.

As the finest utterance of sound, the best expression of breath, Aum is the best manifestation of the godhead. Interfused with every word and every being it works in an endless, universal amd limitless creational movement. It is the subtlest translation of the manifested universe.

Aum has been compared with the Hebrew word *Amen*, taken into the Christian liturgy as the word which ends all prayers and when set to music generally becoming a series of powerful up- and down-beats, swelling and dying away in a final whisper. Some psychologists regard the word and its musical settings as obeying the same archetypal impulse as Aum, and therefore also as symbolizing in the final words of the prayer the breath of the Creator sought in answer to that prayer.

aura By aura is meant the light which emanates from solar beings, that is to say those who are endowed with divine light. This light is termed HALO if it encircles the head alone, mandorla (see under ALMOND) if the whole body. The aura may therefore be compared with a luminous mist and may be of different colours. Sometimes the aura and the halo are confused because of their similarity. Light is always a sign of sanctification by the godhead. Light-centred religions, whose adherents worshipped fire and the Sun, are the origin of that importance which came to be attached to the aura (COLN).

aureole See HALO.

Aurora Borealis A manifestation of the BEYOND; implying the existence of a life after death, it symbolizes a mode of being both bright and yet mysterious at the same time. The Eskimos believe that the phenomenon is caused by the dead playing at ball (KHIE p. 51).

automobile Automobiles occur frequently in contemporary dreams. Either the dreamer him- or herself is in a car or else he or she notices other cars driving past. As with all dream vehicles, the automobile symbolizes the vicissitudes of active psychological development.

If the dreamer is actually in a car, the vehicle acquires a symbolism specific to the dreamer. The car's characteristics, whether luxury model or old banger, express the degree for good or ill to which the individual has adapted to this psychological development. If the dreamer is not at the driving wheel, his or her ego may be dominated by a complex. The nature of that complex is determined by the personality of the driver, who is simply one aspect of the dreamer's personality.

If the dreamer him- or herself is driving, it may be good, bad or even dangerous. Each situation will show the weak, perfect or dangerous way in which the dreamer directs his or her life, whether on the subjective or objective plane. In fact the car's power and delicate mechanism demand that the driver should have excellent self-control and adaptability. Good driving requires control of the impulses, quick reactions and a sense of responsibility – and obedience to the Highway Code, the rules of the game of life, those areas of social convention and behaviour which must, inescapably, be accepted. The good driver suggests independence of the psyche and freedom from inhibition. You can obey the rules without suffering from their constraint, once you acknowledge their social necessity, however absurd they may appear from the rational viewpoint.

To be sitting in a car in which one has no right to be is a sign that the dreamer has mistakenly followed a course of conduct, subjectively or objectively, which he or she had no right to undertake.

To run out of fuel (see AIRCRAFT) may indicate insufficient libido or poor physical condition. Either the strength has been overtaxed or it has not been used to the full.

An overloaded car may be an indication of an overriding obsession or of an attachment to false values which handicap or slow physical or psychological development.

Coachwork and upholstery may reflect the *persona*, the mask or personality projected to others in the hope of making an impression, or for fear of being despised.

If the dreamer sees the car exclusively as a mechanical object, it shows that development is too exclusively the work of thought and intellect and concerned with the nuts and bolts of living and the technicalities of psychoanalysis.

A car running over a child may show that the life force, the development of the personality and external pressures have not taken into account a persistent attachment to childhood and to real psychological values, which can only be integrated into a harmonious development if this is taken at a slower pace. It unveils inner resistance to the laws of motion.

Cars crashing is a painful reminder of the destructive power of internal conflict which should have been allied to the powers of development. The collision of opposites is traumatic.

To crash into some obstacle shows that the conscious ego, too, is colliding with something which blocks the path of its development. What that obstacle is remains to be discovered. It may be external or internal, but it is subjectivized into this shattering crash.

Trucks loaded with useful or valuable cargoes suggest the positive content of the psyche. However, they may also symbolize the fellow-traveller who suddenly turns into an adversary, behind whom one is stuck. This is a highly ambivalent symbol.

The bus is a public service vehicle. It suggests 'the stream of social life on which you are carried' (A. Teillard). Social life, that is, as opposed to isolation, egocentricity, infantilism and excessive introversion. We cannot escape from living in society. Difficulty in boarding the bus or the urge to do so is revealing: 'the individualist feels duty-bound to travel in an over-crowded bus, or else he is forced to do so' (AEPR p. 186). The bus sym-bolizes enforced contact with society during the development of the personality.

awning A symbol of protection granted or received by the person under it. If that person is a king, he grants it to his subjects having received it from Heaven. He is the CENTRE from which it radiates, the centre of the world – hence the use of awnings to display rank and power. A square awning relates to Earth and earthly gifts: a round awning to the gifts of Heaven (see PARASOL).

axe Quick as LIGHTNING, the axe falls and shears. It crashes down and sometimes strikes sparks. Doubtless these make all cultures associate the axe with THUNDER – and hence with RAIN – and make it a fertility symbol. There are many examples of the development of this basic symbol along these lines.

The Maya and contemporary American Indians, the Celts and T'ang Dynasty Chinese all called stone axes 'thunder stone' and all said that they fell from Heaven. Similarly, the Dogon and Bambara from Mali say that THUNDERBOLTS are axes which the water- and fertility-god hurls down to Earth from the sky (DIEB). This is why stone axes are kept in shrines dedicated to this god and used in seasonal rites and rain-making ceremonies. They are also buried at seedtime so that the fertilizing powers with which these stones are endowed may set germination in train.

Since they have the power to bring rain, stone axes have the power to make it stop if it rains too much, or at least that is what another African people, the Azende, claims (EVAS). In a number of legends current among Cambodians and the Montagnards of southern Vietnam, the axe, as the weapon of thunder, is the emblem of power. By opening up and piercing the Earth it symbolizes the latter's fertilization by its marriage with Heaven. An axe cutting into the bark of a tree is a symbol of spiritual penetration, of going to the heart of the mystery, as well as being an implement of release.

Although, in the iconography of Shiva for example, the axe may become a symbol of wrath and destruction, this may remain a positive role, with its destructive powers applied to maleficent influences.

Through a sort of antonym which often occurs in the evolution of a symbol, what divides can also unite. This apparently is the case in an age-old and important Chinese custom which connects the axe with wedding ceremonies. The young man and woman were only allowed to marry, on the principle of exogamy, if they belonged to different families; for more important even than its reproductive function, marriage served to unite such families. In the distant past this alliance came about through diplomatic channels which necessitated the employment of a herald as a sort of go-between. His emblem was the axe with which he stripped the twigs from two logs of wood and tied them into faggots. The motif of the bundle of faggots constantly recurs in wedding hymns.

This ambivalence of function is concretized in the twin-bladed axe which is at one and the same time destroyer and protector. Its symbolism is linked with death–life duality and the duality of opposing and complementary forces and associates the double-headed axe with the CADUCEUS, the VAJRA of the Hindus, Thor's HAMMER and the two natures within the one person of Christ.

What divides is also what separates. Thus the Pseudo-Dionysius the Areopagite, when discussing the attributes of angels, writes: 'The spears and battle-axe denote the dividing of things unlike, and the sharp and energetic and drastic operation of the discriminating powers' (PSEH p. 47).

Separation and discernment are also the powers of differentiation, specifically expressed in Greek mythology when an axe-blow split Zeus' skull and out sprang Athene. To the psychologist, this is 'the intervention of the social environment upon the individuative, introspective consciousness, an external intervention essential to the creation of the individual.'

Mankind's earliest combined weapon and tool, 'the axe is a focus of integration, the manifestation of something permanent, of a stored lightning charge. The word itself seems to have its links with "AXIS", so that the prehistoric axe might be the focus of the world of experience – the axis' (VIRI pp. 105, 180, 245).

Lastly the axe embedded in the tip of a pyramid or of a pointed stone cube, of which seventeenth-century Masonic documents furnish so many examples, has been interpreted in many different ways (BOUM pp. 164–6). In the light of the foregoing, however, it may be understood quite clearly as the opening of the kernel, of the casket, of the secret or of the skies. That is to say, as the final rite of initiation which brings awareness and partakes of enlightenment. The blade of the stone axe has struck a spark.

axis The axis round which the world revolves, links the dominions or hierarchical levels together by their mid-points. If the junction of Heaven and Earth is taken, then it is the precise CENTRE of Earth to the precise centre of Heaven, symbolized by the POLE star. If it is the downward direction, then this axis is the channel down which all heavenly influence flows: if the upward direction, it is the 'Middle Way' (*chong-tao*), or the 'Royal Road' (*wang-tao*). Sometimes it is a matter of linking the three worlds – Heaven, Earth and Underworld – or *Tribhuvana* – Earth, Space and Heaven. This hierarchy itself corresponds to states of being, as the stages in Dante's 'axial' journey so clearly show. Those who have reached the mid-point, that is the edenic or primordial state, may rise along this axis to higher states. Thus Lao-tze is said to have filled the office of 'archivist' – guardian of traditional knowledge from the FOUR corners of the earth – 'at the foot of the COLUMN', the axis joining Heaven and Earth.

In space the World Axis is the polar axis, in time that of the solstices. Its symbolic representations are numberless, but it is seen most often as the

TREE and the MOUNTAIN, but also as LANCE, STAFF, LINGAM, a chariot-pole or axle (if the latter is pictured in the vertical plane the two wheels (see WHEEL) would represent Heaven and Earth), or columns of light or smoke. It is also the GNOMON which casts no shadow at noon at the solstice. The chariot-pole is identified with the gnomon and the charioteer with the pole. This is the role of the *wang*, the king, whose character represents Heaven, mankind and Earth linked through the central axis. The pole extends above the awning of the chariot to symbolize 'release from the cosmos'. In just the same way the top-mast of a sailing ship runs through the crow's-nest. The greasy pole – its equivalent existed in ancient China and in several contemporary ceremonies in the Far East – pushes beyond the ring set at its tip. The column of smoke rises through a hole in the roof of the hut and into the sky. It should be observed further in relation to the ship's mast, that in Vietnam they call the chock in the centre of the keel into which it is stepped, 'the opening of the heart'. Similarly a pole rises above the STUPA or pagoda, bearing rings and sunshades to represent the celestial circles. In the case of the pagoda, the pole is embedded in the ground and around it the whole building interconnects, and with it Buddha is identified as king of the chariot-pole.

In temples such as those at Angkor, the cosmic PILLAR of the *Veda* (*skambha*) is represented by a deep well sunk beneath the central shrine, by the lingam or by the statue of the god within it and, finally, by the pole which soars skywards (Indra's VAJRA, or Shiva's *trishula*). In temples in India the pole runs through an *amalaka* representing 'the Gate of the Sun', in Cambodia most often through a LOTUS flower. However, the *skambha* is in any case identified with Indra himself, and also with Shiva, in the guise of a column or lingam of fire. The *vajra* is an axial symbol since thunderbolts are a manifestation of the working of the gods. During the Hindu festival of Indradhvaja, poles are set up; and here again there is clear identification with Indra. It may be observed that Plato himself envisaged the World Axis as being luminous and made of diamond (the *vajra* is diamond), while Clement of Alexandria writes (*Stromata* 1) that the column of fire which blazed from the Burning Bush was the symbol of divine light which flashed up from Earth through Space to Heaven from the wood of the Cross, through which Christians are able to contemplate it in spirit. Comparison with the axis of the redemptive Cross is widely witnessed and easily explicable through such devices as that of the Carthusians, *Stat crux dum volvitur orbis* (The Cross stands upright while the world revolves), since the Cross is the stable and immobile axis, while all around it is subject to change and decay. The column of light, Clement again assures us, is an abstract image of the godhead. It represents APOLLO: it is a ray of the 'Spiritual Sun'. Manichaeans and Muslim esoterics speak of a 'column of light' which carries the soul back to its beginnings.

The idea of the *Axis Mundi*, the Cosmic Pillar, recurs, from America through Africa and Siberia to Australasia. It exists in Japan where, before their marriage, Izanagi and Izanami revolved in opposite directions around it. Symbols of two complementary and equipoised powers revolving round the axis are the two snakes on the CADUCEUS, the double twist round the Brahman's staff and that of the two *nadi* round the Tantric *sushumna*. The last-named reminds us that Tantrism identifies the axis with the spinal column and that is why Buddha was prevented from turning his head, the axis being firmly fixed.

Within this context can possibly be placed the left- and right-hand columns of the sefirotic tree in the *Kabbalah*, the columns of mercy and of severity surrounding the midmost column. Then there are the Pillars of Hercules (Herakles) which Guénon has shown to be solsticial symbols, since Herakles was a solar hero. From a different angle, columns or pillars are synonymous with support, their architectural function. Thus the 'Pillars of the Church' or the 'Pillars of the Temple', which are sometimes shown as 'cast down', play the same role as the axis as mediators (BURA, BHAB, CADV, CORT, ELIC, ELIY, ELIM, GRAP, GRIR, GUED, GUEM, GUEC, GUET, GUES, HUAV, JACT, KALL, KRAT, SAIR, SCHI, SECA).

The Celts sometimes depicted the World Axis as a column, the *columna solis*. This pillar holding up the sky should be set beside the Tree of Life and the idea of the shrine (*nemeton*). A medieval Welsh manuscript of the twelfth or thirteenth century represents the four Evangelists as the four pillars which support the world, the axis of the New Covenant (OGAC 4: p. 167; ZWIC 1: p. 184).

B

Baal and Baalat God and goddess worshipped by the Semites, Baal as a storm- and fertility-god, Baalat as a fertility- and especially a corn-goddess. The Hebrew prophets, proclaiming Jehovah as a god conceived upon a higher plane, denounced their worship, deep-seated and constantly revived, which 'showed (though in unhealthy and monstrous forms) the religious value of organic life, the elementary forces of blood, sexuality and fecundity' (ELIT p. 4). The worship of Baal came to symbolize the existence or the regular return within all civilizations of a trend towards magnifying the powers of instinct. The worship of Jehovah 'manifested a more perfect holiness, it sanctified life without in any way allowing it to run wild . . . revealed a spiritual economy in which man's life and destiny gained a totally new value; at the same time it made possible a richer religious experience, a communion with God at once purer and more complete' (ibid.).

Babel See TOWER OF BABEL.

Babylon As a symbol, Babylon is the antithesis of Paradise and the Heavenly Jerusalem, although etymologically Babylon means 'the gateway of God'. But although the god to whom that GATE led was for a time sought in the heavens, it degenerated from a spirit into a human, with all man's basest instincts of lust and oppression predominant.

'Babylon', wrote Herodotus, 'is so splendid that no city on earth may be compared with it.' Its walls and its hanging gardens were among the seven wonders of the world, but all was annihilated, because all was based upon temporal values alone. Babylon symbolizes, not magnificence doomed by its beauty, but a vitiated magnificence which is self-condemned because it turns humanity away from its spiritual calling. Babylon symbolizes the fleeting victory of the material world of the senses which, by exaggerating one aspect only, causes personality to disintegrate as a result.

To some medieval Irish writers, Babylon symbolized paganism, and it is there that the FOMORIAN children of Calatin went to learn the arts of magic to kill the hero Cùchulainn. The symbolism differs little from that of the Old Testament writers from which clearly it is borrowed (CELT 7: *passim*).

Bacchantes Bacchantes, or Maenads, were the 'wild, hot-blooded women' inspired by DIONYSOS who gave themselves with such enthusiasm to his worship as to lead sometimes to their madness and death. The principal Greek source is Euripides' tragedy *The Bacchae*, while for the Romans there is Livy's dramatic account (29: 18–19). Their outlandish practices, found round the Mediterranean basin, have been classified as orgiasm or maenadism. Some are even reminiscent of classical medical descriptions of female hysteria:

In so many particulars, the Bacchantes' rage, with its spasms of convulsive movement, the way they bent their bodies backwards, threw back their heads and writhed their necks, are reminiscent of neuropathic symptoms so well described today, which embody a feeling of depersonalization, of the invasion by another personality of the Ego, enthusiasm in the strict classical sense – in other words, possession.

(SECG p. 292)

Bacchantes symbolize intoxication with love and the desire to be interfused with the god of love, as well as 'the irresistible hold which such madness gains and which is like some magic weapon wielded by the god' (JEAD).

Bacchus See DIONYSOS.

badger Athough Buffon may have given the badger the not entirely un-justified reputation of being 'a lazy, suspicious and solitary' beast, the emblem of sleep, in the Far East it bears a completely different character. In Japan the badger is the symbol of cunning and of innocent deception. The Japanese believe that the badger drums on its stomach at the time of the full moon and disguises itself as an aged monk to trick its victims. They use the expression 'old badger' (*furudanuki*) in much the same way as we would call somebody an 'old fox' (applied most notably to the famous Shogun Ieyasu Tokugawa). Figures of potbellied badgers are sometimes set at the entrances of Japanese restaurants, sly emblems of prosperity or of self-satisfaction (OGRJ).

In the *Mabinogion*, Gwawl, Pwyll's rival for the love of Rhiannon, is, during the course of a contest of wildly varying fortunes, shut in a magic sack, which each of Pwyll's followers beats with his staff. This is what the Welsh account calls 'the game of the badger in the bag'. The animal's symbolism is here taken in its negative sense, to extract no clearer definition (MABG p. 24). It would seem that the purpose of the game was to symbolize the punishment inflicted upon the man – the badger in the bag – for the badgerish qualities in him, namely slyness and deceit. He was beaten with staves to beat the badger out of him; to get rid of his ill-will and deceit.

bamboo In Japan, the bamboo, along with the pine and the plum, is one of the three trees of good omen.

Under the influence of Ch'an Buddhism during the Chinese Sung Dynasty, the bamboo was one of the favourite subjects for the painter. Yet to paint it was more than mere art, it was a spiritual exercise. The bamboo's incomparable straightness, its perfect upspringing to the sky, the space between the KNOTS in its stem – an image of *shunyata*, or 'voidness of heart' – symbolize the character and the objectives of the meditative practices of Buddhists and especially of Taoists. Nor should it be forgotten that for some Masters, the rustle of bamboos was the signal of enlightenment. Paintings of bamboos come close to calligraphy as expressions of a living language, but one which can only be approached through intuitive perception.

There are various other aspects of the bamboo. It was used to drive off evil influences, less from any symbolic cause than from the fact that the wood goes off with a sharp crack when placed on the fire. The bamboo clump, the classic barrier, was often depicted as 'the jungle of sinners' through which the TIGER, symbol of the spiritual force of Buddhism, alone can thread its way. A T'ang Dynasty writer identifies the bamboo with the SERPENT, into which, apparently, it can easily change itself with seemingly beneficial effects. The duality of male and female bamboo is a symbol of mutual attachment and conjugal unity. Many writers mention bamboo with three or nine knots: these items suggest a purely numerical symbolism (BELT, CHOO, GROC).

The Bamum and Bamileke have a chip of bamboo which they call a *guis* (laugh) which is their symbol of happiness, the unadorned happiness of life free from illness and care.

In equatorial Africa and in the same latitudes in South America a sliver of fire-hardened bamboo plays the same civilizing influence as the sliver of flint or OBSIDIAN in stone-based cultures, especially in Mexico. It is the instrument of sacrifice and is used especially by medicine men in the rites of CIRCUMCISION.

The nomadic Yanomami of southern Venezuela use the bamboo for the heads of their war arrows, and as knives and fire-sticks. Their neighbours, the Yekuana, related to the Caribs, use it as an instrument of religious music. In their language it is called the *uana* (clarinet) and it should be observed that the chief festival at which this instrument 'talks' is called *ua-uana*; the Demiurge, or culture-hero, invoked at this ceremony is named Uanaji. The full meaning of *uana* for the Yekuana is 'cosmic TREE' or 'Tree of Life', the father of their mythic ancestor, Uanaji, and hence of all the Yekuana. The names of their clans all end with 'uana', such as Dek-uana, Yek-uana.

banana-tree The banana is, of course, not a tree at all but a herbaceous perennial plant, without a woody trunk. Its stalks are very delicate and disappear after fructification. It is for this reason that the Buddha made it the symbol of the weakness and instability of matter which should be of no concern. 'Mental constructions are like a banana-tree' (*Samyutta-nikāya* 3: 142). A classic subject for Chinese painters was the sage contemplating the transience of this world, seated at the foot of a banana-tree.

bandages In the Ancient Egyptian ritual of mummification the corpse was swathed in white linen bandages appropriately tied. These bandages had a twofold significance. They symbolized first of all 'the rivulet of vital fluid winding round the cosmos' and then 'the *robe of light*, resurrection after the sleep of death, a period of incubation and germination' (CHAS p. 77).

banner All organized societies have their own badges in the shape of totems, banners, flags, and standards which are always set at some high point – on a STAFF, or above tents, facades, roofs or palaces.

Generally speaking, standards denote battle flags, being the insignia of military authority, serving as rallying points and being emblems of the commander himself.

Such is their meaning in Hindu iconography, where the banner of victory is a sign of war and consequently of action against maleficent powers. In Taoism, banners are appeals or summonses to spirits, deities or the elements, and simultaneously magical protection. This is because in Ancient China standards were not simply emblems of groups or of their leaders but effectively possessed their genius and properties. The ideogram *wu* denotes both 'banner' and 'being'. Although the banners set in the bushel-baskets of Chinese secret societies are a call to warlike or spiritual action, they are also in fact surrogates for the Ancestors of the lodge. They are supposed to stand for them, and not merely as their emblems, but as their presence protecting the lodge. Banners, too, have symbolic importance in Freemasonry.

Nor should the symbolism of the flag fluttering in the breeze be overlooked. In India it is an attribute of Vāyu, ruler of the element Air. It is associated with the notion of movement and with the phases of breathing. This aspect brings banner symbolism close to that of the FAN (GRAD, GRAC).

'Jehovah nissi', 'the Lord is my banner' (Exodus 17: 15) means 'God is my safeguard.' Banners always played an important part in the lives of Semitic peoples, while in Christian eyes the banner symbolizes the victory won by Christ's resurrection to glory. All processions at Easter and on Ascension Day involve the carrying of banners.

Moving from Christ to the soul, according to Richard of St Victor banners symbolize the arousing (*sublevatio*) of the spirit and its ascension (*elevatio*). The banner is unfurled; the man points it into the air: similarly in contemplation, his spirit points to the good things of Heaven. To hang between Heaven and Earth is to be initiated into the secrets of the godhead.

The protective strength of the symbol is accentuated by the emblem which distinguishes it. The banner of a lord, of a general, of a sovereign, of a saint, of a congregation, of a corporation, of a country and so on protects by virtue of the insignia it bears.

banquet The ritual banquet was a virtually universal phenomenon, frequently consisting of offerings which had been consecrated at an earlier stage. Such is true of Shintōism, while Milarepa attests a similar practice by his *guru*, Marpa. The early Taoists frequently did the same. In Hindu ritual, when the person offering the sacrifice drains the drink-offering he is said to 'drink SOMA at the banquet of the gods', a clear symbol of a share in celestial bliss. In Ancient China the commonly used phrase 'to eat the sacrifice' is connected with a feast held in the Temple of the Ancestors. The *Che-ching* contains the hymns which accompanied the rite, while the *Tso-chuan* states that the 'the feast should serve to enhance virtue.' It was also a rite of alliance and feudal investiture (COOH, GRAD).

Banquets are the symbol of a communal act of worship, especially in the Eucharist. By extension they are a symbol of the 'communion of saints', that is to say of heavenly bliss shared through the same grace and way of life.

In general terms, banquets symbolize membership of a social group, participation in an enterprise, joining in a festival.

The banquet held at the Feast of Samain (1 November) is the only ceremony of this type of proven existence in Ireland. It was held at the royal capital of Tara or, as other epic stories have it, at Emain Macha, the capital of Ulster. The principle was the same in either case: all his vassals were compelled to attend the king. Pork – flesh of the animal which symbolized Lug – was the meat, and to drink there were MEAD and BEER or, more rarely, WINE, the drink of kings and of immortality (OGAC 13: pp. 495ff.).

baptism (see also BATH)   Those who sought out John the Baptist in the desert are described as being 'baptized of him in Jordan, confessing their sins' (Matthew 3: 6). He practised what is known as baptism by immersion, a time-honoured rite, and a symbol of purification and renewal. Baptism was known to the Essenes, but also to other religions apart from Judaism and its sects; in these others it was associated with the rites of passage, particularly of birth and death. Nonetheless, the editors of *The Jerusalem Bible* emphasize in this context what makes John's baptism different from other ritual immersions: 'it is directed to moral, not ritual purification; it takes place once only and for this reason appears as a ceremony of initiation; and it has an eschatological value, in so far as it enrols its recipients among the number of those who professedly and actively prepare themselves for the imminent coming of the Messiah and who are, therefore, the community in anticipation' (BIBJ p. 1613 (3e)). It may be compared with symbolic burial or with initiation through a hole in a rock, a hollow tree or a crack in the ground.

Whatever modifications may have been made in the liturgies of the different Christian denominations, baptismal rites still comprise two actions or phases of remarkable symbolic import – immersion and emersion. Although immersion may now be reduced to sprinkling with water, it bears a wealth of meaning in itself – the sinful creature vanishing in the waters of death, purification by lustration and the revitalization of that creature from the source of life. Emersion reveals the purified being in a state of grace, united with a divine stream of new life.

Some Irish writers mention a druidical baptism about which nothing is known, or even whether it ever existed. It is possible that the use of the term in literature dating from the Christian era is due solely to an accident of liturgical language which enables ritual lustration to be described in analogical terms.

Immersion or sprinkling with pure water is to be encountered in the traditions of several races, associated with the rites of passage, particularly those of birth and death.

Among the Quiché Indians, baptism is interconnected with the archetypal legend of the Twin Gods of Maize. In their funeral customs, too, not only is the corpse ritually washed but the grave is sprinkled with pure water, as much as to say that when the dead person departs for another life, he or she is 'baptized' in the same way as they were when they began this life (GIRP pp. 195–6). The pure water which the corpse receives stands for 'the blood of the gods' and is an assurance of regeneration. This type of baptism therefore forms an initiatory rite of regeneration. Pure WATER, or 'water of life', transformed to 'holy water' plays a role complementary to that of FIRE in rites of purification or regeneration.

In any case, John the Baptist mentions fire in the context of baptism. 'I indeed baptize you with water unto repentance: but he that cometh after me is mightier than I, whose shoes I am not worthy to bear: he shall baptize you with the Holy Ghost, and with fire' (Matthew 3: 11). His *Jerusalem Bible* commentators note that: 'In the O[ld] T[estament] fire, a purifying element more refined and efficacious than water, was already a symbol of God's supreme intervention in history and of his spirit which comes to purify hearts' (BIBJ p. 1613 (3I)). Examples are Isaiah 1: 25 and Zechariah 13: 9: 'I will bring a third part through the fire, and will refine them as silver is refined, and will try them as gold is tried.'

In the early centuries of the Christian era, catechumens who suffered martyrdom before they had been baptized were said to have received 'the baptism of fire'.

To analyse Catholic baptismal ritual is to discover the wealth of symbolism employed in the actions and objects used in administering the sacrament – the laying on of hands, insufflation, signs of the cross, salt which imparts wisdom, opening the mouth and ears, recitation of the Creed, anointing with different exorcistic and eucharistic oils, wearing a white garment and carrying a lighted candle. All the actions of this initiatory rite betray the twofold end of purification and vivification. They also betray the stratified structure of the symbol. First, baptism washes a person clean from the stain of sin and obtains for him or her a supernatural life (passing from death to life). Second, it suggests Christ's death and resurrection: the baptized person makes him- or herself like the Saviour, immersion in water symbolizing entombment, and coming out of the water his rising from the grave. Third, baptism delivers the soul of the baptized from subjection to the Devil and enrols him or her as a soldier of Christ with the seal of the Holy Spirit, since the rite consecrates to the service of the Church. It does not cause some magical transformation, but confers the power to grow in faith and good works in Gospel terms. The whole rite symbolizes and makes real the birth of grace, the inner principle of spiritual perfection, within the soul of the person baptized.

barrel See CASK.

basil The leaves of this plant were held to contain magical powers – they were used in the preparation of a red potion to cure wounds – while its flowers exhale a strong scent. In the central Congo basil leaves are used to project ill luck and as a protection against evil spirits (FOUC). They can be used to cure cuts, scratches and bruises.

basilisk This fabulous SERPENT killed whoever came upon it without seeing it first, by a single glance or by its poisonous breath. It was supposed to be hatched from an egg laid by an aged cock – SEVEN or fourteen years old – a round egg laid on a dung-hill and hatched by a frog or a toad. It was depicted either as a cock with a dragon's tail or as a snake with cock's wings. Its entire symbolism derived from this legend.

It represented kingly power which annihilates all who do not show it due respect; depraved women who corrupt those who fail to recognize them for what they are and cannot in consequence escape their clutches; the mortal dangers of this life of which we have no warning and from which we can only be preserved by the holy power of the angels. 'For he shall give his angels charge over thee, to keep thee in all thy ways .... Thou shalt tread upon the lion and adder [basilisk]: the young lion and the dragon thou shalt trample under feet' (Psalm 91: 11, 13).

Legends state that it is very difficult to capture the basilisk. The only way of doing this successfully is to set a mirror in front of the creature. Then its terrible glance, charged with deadly power, is reflected back upon the basilisk and kills it; or else its poisonous breath rebounds to deal it the death it intended for others. Obviously the basilisk is related to the GORGON, whose single glance caused terror and death. Medusa's head on Athene's shield (see AEGIS) sufficed to destroy the goddess's enemies.

During the Middle Ages it was believed that Christ had crushed the four creatures mentioned by the Psalmist, among them the basilisk. Basilisk was supposed to be used as a medicine and became very valuable when mixed with other ingredients. In alchemy it symbolized the destructive fire which preceded the transmutation of metals.

The basilisk, surely, must always symbolize Death, laying us low with a sudden sweep of his scythe, which flashes like the creature's glance, unless we weigh up our fate in advance and prepare ourselves clear-headedly for it, or as the Psalmist says, place ourselves in the hands of God's angels.

Finally, the basilisk is surely a symbol of the unconscious, to be feared by those who ignore it, dominating those who do not recognize it for what it is to the extent of shattering or destroying their personalities. It needs to be faced and assessed for what it is, or else it will make us one of its victims.

basket (see also ARK, CHALICE)   According to Gardiner's *Egyptian Grammar*, the hieroglyph of the basket conveys the meaning of lordship, mastery, supremacy, of the man who rises above his fellows. A basket is sometimes used as a pedestal or plinth for images of the gods. According to Mariette, this hieroglyph also means 'everything made divine, God and the Universe interfused in one single being'. In Egyptian art and writing, the basket–chalice perhaps suggested wholeness, togetherness under heavenly rule. The dead were sometimes placed in baskets and left to float away on the stream, from which Isis would gather their scattered remains, to knit them together again and place them in another basket, just as she had done with the scattered limbs of Osiris. Apuleius (*Metamorphoses* 11: 11) describes how, in processions in honour of Isis, a basket was carried, in which was hidden 'the secrets of their glorious religion'.

The Buddhist canonical scriptures are the *Tripitaka* – literally 'the triple basket' (*pitaka*); the name conveys the idea of the three powers – Buddha the founder, the Law and the Community.

The basket is also a symbol of the WOMB. Moses and others were found in baskets at the waterside.

When a basket holds fruit or wool, it symbolizes the women's quarters and their housework, as well as fertility. Hence the basket became an attribute of many a goddess, including Diana (Artemis) of Ephesus, whose priestesses wore their hair dressed in the shape of baskets.

bat   Under Mosaic Law, the bat was an unclean beast and became the symbol of idolatry and fear.

In the Far East, the bat is a symbol of good luck because the character which designates it, *fu*, is homophonous with the character which means 'good luck'. In messages of good wishes, a bat is sometimes depicted alongside the character meaning 'longevity'. In Chinese prints, bat and STAG are frequently associated and bats are embroidered on the robe worn by the god of good luck. Five bats depicted quincuncially symbolize the Five

Happinesses (*wu fu*) – wealth, long life, peace, cultivation of virtue (or good health) and a good death.

The bat is especially the symbol of longevity, which is believed to be an attribute of the creature itself because it lives in CAVERNS – passageways to the realm of the Immortals – and in them lives upon life-giving deposits. The Taoist practice of 'fortifying the head', symbolized in art by exaggeratedly large heads, is in imitation of the bat, believed to practise it to the extent that the weight of its brain forces it to roost upside down. Not surprisingly, the bat is itself one of the foods of immortality. In addition, the 'fortification' mentioned above and the consequent acquisition of longevity are frequently linked with erotic practices. Bats are an ingredient in aphrodisiacs, a virtue which Pliny acknowledged to reside in the creature's blood (BELT, CADV, KALL).

Among the Maya, the bat was one of the gods which embodied the powers of the Underworld. The *Popol Vuh* names 'the House of the Bat' as one of the regions which must be traversed to reach the Land of Death. The bat was the ruler of fire; it destroyed life and ate up light and would therefore seem to have been a surrogate for the great Underworld gods, the JAGUAR and the CROCODILE. For the Mexicans, too, it was the death god associated with the north and often depicted in association with gaping jaws or, more rarely, with a sacrificial knife (SELB p. 233). The bat performed the same office for the Tupi-Guarani Indians of Brazil, while the Tupinamba believe that, as a prelude to the end of the world, a bat will swallow the Sun (Claude d'Abbeville, quoted by METT). The Maya made the bat a symbol of death and called it 'he who tears off heads', depicting it with the empty eyes of a skull.

Among the Pueblo Indians, the Zuni regard the bat as the harbinger of rain. In the mythology of the Chami Indians who belong to the Chocó group from the Pacific slopes of the Cordillera Occidental in Colombia, the hero Aribada slew the vampire bat, Inka, so as to acquire its power of putting its victims to sleep. (In fact, when the VAMPIRE tries to suck the blood of a sleeping person, generally from one of the toes, without waking him or her, it is believed to keep its wings beating all the time.) Having acquired this power, Aribada forced his way into the rooms of women and, by waving a pair of handkerchiefs, one red, the other white, was able to pleasure himself without waking them. This relates to the libidinous-erotic powers associated with the bat and previously recorded by Pliny.

In Africa, according to a Fulani initiation tradition, the bat has a dual symbolic significance. In its positive aspect it is the emblem of clear-sightedness, a creature which sees in the dark when all the world is enfolded in night. In its negative aspect it is the emblem of the enemy of light, of the hare-brain who does everything topsy-turvy and who views the universe upside-down, like a man hanging by his heels. The huge ears of the bat considered as a creature of light symbolize hearing which can catch the slightest sound; of the creature of darkness they are hideous growths. As a nocturnal flying mouse, the bat represents a blindness to the most patent truths, and it hangs in accretions of filth and moral deformity. As a creature of the day, it is the emblem of a degree of unity among all living beings through interbreeding, their differences sunk in the hybrid (HAMK p. 59).

In Renaissance iconography as applied to Classical legend, the bat, being the only flying creature to suckle its young, came to symbolize prolific motherhood. It accompanied Diana (Artemis), the many-breasted goddess who, because rather than in spite of the fact that she was a virgin, protected childbirth and infancy.

In alchemical tradition the ambivalence of the HYBRID nature of mouse and bird explains an equally ambivalent symbolism. The bat portrays the hermaphrodite, the winged dragon, devils. Its wings are those of the denizens of Hell. There is a wealth of iconography to illustrate these interpretations.

Again, in some works of art under Germanic influence, the bat symbolizes envy, for just as it 'only flies by night or at dusk, so envy works in the shadows and does not expose itself to the light of day'. Similarly 'the bat is naturally blinded by daylight, just as envious and malevolent persons cannot bear the sight of other people' (TERS p. 90).

Yet again, the bat symbolizes the person who has become bogged down in an intermediate phase of his or her higher development, no longer on a lower plane, and yet unable to reach a higher. The bat is a bird *manqué* and, as Buffon remarked, 'a monstrous creature', quite unlike the blue bird, which remains a creature of the heavens, even at night. 'Something dark and threatening', Bachelard observes,

seems to gather round these night-fliers. Thus many imagine the bat as the incarnation of the clumsy flier, with what Buffon calls 'its uncertain flutterings', silent flight, dark flight, ground-clinging flight, the very antithesis of the Shelleyan trilogy of music, light and space. Doomed forever to beat its wings, the bat can never enjoy the dynamic ease of gliding flight. In fact, as Jules Michelet observes (*L'oiseau* p. 39) it is apparent that Nature tried for a wing and only succeeded in producing a hideous, hairy membrane, which nonetheless performs the office of one .... However, the wing does not make the bird. In Victor Hugo's cosmology of winged creatures, the bat is that accursed being which personifies atheism.

(BACS p. 89)

In this respect the bat would symbolize a person whose spiritual development had been hamstrung, a spiritual failure.

bath (see also WASHING)   The practices, both sacred and profane, of all peoples everywhere and in all ages, bear witness to the well-known cleansing and regenerative properties of the bath. It may be claimed that throughout the world the bath is the prime rite which, as it were, sets the seal upon those milestones in the human life, birth, puberty and death. The symbolism of the bath brings together the meaning behind the act of immersion (see BAPTISM) and the element of WATER.

To the psychoanalyst immersion is an image of the return to the womb. It meets the need for relaxation, sense of security, soothing, going back to one's roots, returning to the womb from which one was born and hence to the source of one's life. By voluntary consent to immersion – which is a kind of burial – one accepts a moment of oblivion, of an abdication of responsibility, of sitting on the sidelines, of EMPTINESS. Hence the countless therapeutic uses of immersion. It breaks the thread of existence as an interval or a gap in the continuum and this automatically gives it an important role in rites of initiation. The best example of these is, perhaps, the ritual for admission to one of the most closely guarded secret societies of witch-doctors in central Africa (Cameroon, Gabon). During the ceremony, the initiate is drugged and buried for twenty-four hours in a watertight pit dug below the bed of a stream in the depths of the rainforest. The symbols (forest = womb; water = mother; and time flowing like a stream) associated with this womblike hiding-place combine in an intricate symbolic network of such potency that those initiated into this secret society to all intents and purposes forget the earlier events of their lives. The regeneration of the initiate acquires the full force of its meaning of death and rebirth. Furthermore, such rites, still practised today although rarely observed, cast a complementary light upon various myths and rites both of Classical antiquity and of other periods in human history. For example, the Greeks ritually immersed the statues of their gods and goddesses such as Hera and Athene in cleansing baths. The initiation of the Nazarenes was preceded by a bath, as was the dubbing of knights in the Middle Ages.

As well as cleansing and regenerating, water also fructifies. Hence the ritual bathing of brides-to-be and the immersion of barren women in lakes or wells or holy springs, a practice recorded in over three thousand years of human history from the Mediterranean Basin to the Far East.

Christianity adopted the cleansing bath for its own ends. John baptized in the Jordan. In Christian baptism, the spiritual and the material are intermingled in the same symbol. When Christ says, 'He that is washed needeth not . . . to wash, . . . but is clean every whit' (John 13: 10), the Greek word used by the Evangelist means both 'clean' and 'pure'. Purity, in the Christian sense of the word, is not a negative quality, but a preparative for a new and fruitful life. The state obtained by baptism is purely a state of life, with no commingling of the state of death, which is sin. Positive purity is not the absence of stain, but life in a pure state.

Despite the host of traditions which imputed a force for good to the bath, a brand of Christian prudishness reversed the symbol and condemned the use of baths as inimical to chastity. Here, however, one should differentiate between cold and hot baths. The latter were considered the pursuit of sensual pleasure and therefore best avoided. This is precisely the point of view advanced by St Jerome (*Epistolae* 45: 5), who regarded the hot bath as an assault on the bather's chastity. In the early years of the Church, Christians readily indulged in mixed bathing. Councils and Church Fathers thundered out against a practice which they deemed immoral. In the Middle Ages bath-houses were held to be nurseries of vice and forbidden to Christians.

Some monks, both Catholic and Orthodox, and the latter were by far the most austere, not only ruled out bathing the body as a whole, but even barred the use of water. Clement of Alexandria had defined four sorts of bath – for pleasure, for warmth, for cleanliness or for reasons of health – and found only the last of these tolerable. He did, however, permit baths for women, provided that they were taken at infrequent intervals. St Augustine proved more tolerant, allowing monks under his rule one hot bath a month.

On the other hand immersion in cold water was often an approved means of self-mortification, the more icy cold the water the better. Thus writers of lives of the saints in the early Christian era and during the Middle Ages copy one another in their descriptions of immersion in icy water as a means of subduing the flesh.

We should also observe that there is a particular alchemical use of the word which applies the term 'bath' to cleansing by fire and not by water, just as martyrs are said to undergo a baptism of fire. Finally, in such treatises as *The Secret of the Golden Flower*, 'bath' is associated with 'fasting in the heart'; 'washing' is the removal of all mental activity to achieve definitive 'emptiness', which ties the symbolic knot and returns us to our starting point.

bean Beans symbolize sunshine in mineral form, the EMBRYO. They suggest SULPHUR imprisoned in matter. Eugène Canseliet observes that in France the bean in the Twelfth Night cake was sometimes replaced by a minute doll (the swimmer), or by a tiny fish (CANA p. 93).

Beans are one of the fruits of the Earth offered in ritual sacrifice at the start of ploughing or during the marriage ceremony. 'Beans symbolize future male children, as many traditions corroborate and explain. According to Pliny, beans were used in the worship of the dead because they held the souls of the departed.' In so far as they were 'symbols of the dead and of their felicity', beans belong to the category of charm known as preservatives. 'In the rites of Spring they symbolized the earliest gift from the Underworld, the first offering of the dead to the living, the sign of their fertility, that is to say of their incarnation. Hence the ban imposed by Orpheus and Pythagoras is comprehensible, for under it eating beans was the equivalent of devouring the head of one's parents, sharing the food of the dead', one of the means whereby they remained within the cycle of reincarnation and made use of the powers residing in matter. However, outside the closed circle of Orphic and Pythagorean initiates, beans were 'the essential element in communion with the Invisible Ones at the time of the rites of Spring' (SERP pp. 143, 158, 171–2).

In short 'beans were the first fruits of the Earth and symbol of the benefits granted by the folk underground' (SERH pp. 92–3).

The 'beanfields' of the Ancient Egyptians derive their name from the same symbolism, being the place where the dead awaited their reincarnation. They thus serve to confirm the symbolic interpretation of the significance of this food-plant.

In Japan, the kidney bean – especially when roasted – had the power of a preservative and was used in exorcism. It drove demons away, shielded against ill fortune and preserved from lightning.

Just before the beginning of Spring, on the evening of 3 February, the Japanese scattered beans on the floor (*mamemaki*), shouting as they did so 'Out with the demons and in with good fortune!' This was to drive demons and evil spirits out of the house. As with the Rice Ceremony, this rite was originally designed to bring fruitfulness to the crop and prosperity to the family.

Bean seedlings seem to have been used as love-charms in Ancient India, because the bean itself resembles a testicle (CHOO, HERS).

bear Throughout the Celtic world the bear was the emblem or symbol of the warrior caste. The common Celtic word for 'bear', *artos* (Irish, *art*; Welsh, *arth*; Breton, *arzh*) is echoed in the name of the mythical King Arthur (*artoris*), or in the Irish male name Mathgen (*matugenos*, 'son of a bear'). It stands in neat opposition to the BOAR, the symbol of the priestly caste. In the Welsh tale of Culhwch and Olwen, Arthur hunts the Twrch Trwyth and its litter. Now this creature was a white boar and their battle – which lasted nine days and nights – represents the struggle between 'Church' and 'State'. In the Irish tale, *The Fate of the Children of Tuireann*, the opposite is the case. Here, rather than a priestly boar ravaging the lands of a sovereign prince, members of the warrior caste murder Cian, father of the god Lug, disguised as a druidical boar. In Gaul (and at Bern, which still keeps its name 'Bear') there was even a goddess, Artio, who still more powerfully underlines the female character of the warrior caste. One may also observe that the Welsh called both the constellations with their polar symbolism, the GREAT BEAR and the Little Bear, *Cerbyd Arthur*, 'Arthur's Wain' (GUES pp. 177–83; CELT 9: pp. 331–2).

Among the Celts, therefore, the bear competed – or associated – with the boar, as temporal power with spiritual authority. In India the same was true of the Kshatriya and the Brahman. This aspect – the bear being slightly *yin* relative to the boar's *yang* – would explain why the she-bear recurs so often. At the other end of the Earth, the bear is regarded as the ancestor of the Ainu. This ancient racial group, inhabiting northern Japan and the island of Hokkaido, believed that the bear was a mountain-god, the ruler of all. They celebrated the Feast of the Bear (*Kaimui omante*) in December. On that day the godhead came down to Earth and was welcomed by mankind, left them different gifts and returned at once to the realm of the gods.

Unlike the foregoing, in China the bear is a male symbol. It heralds the birth of boys and is an expression of *yang*. The bear is in harmony with his home, the mountain, and in conflict with the serpent (*yin*, the equivalent of water). Yu the Great, Regulator of the World, took the shape of a bear in the course of his duties. Again, this is not really a reversal of symbols, still less a relationship setting bear in conflict with she-bear, since the Chinese *wang* combines the two powers, while the duties of the cosmic architect correspond to those of the Kshatriya.

One might add that a bear is the steed of the *yoginī* Ritsamada. In Islamic esoteric tradition the bear is sometimes classed as a wretched, disgusting creature (BELT, CORT, GRAD, GRAR, GUES, MALA).

In Siberia and Alaska the bear is placed in the same category as the Moon, because it vanishes with Winter and returns with Spring. This also shows the animal's links with the annual cycle of vegetation, also controlled by the Moon.

The bear is, in any case, held to be the ancestor of the human race; 'for man, whose life is similar to that of the moon, must have been created out of the very substance or by the magic power of that orb of living reality' (ELIT p. 157). In Canada the Algonquin Indians called the bear 'Grandfather' (MULR p. 229). This last belief appears to have inspired the widespread myth of bears carrying off women, who live a married life with their ravishers.

Among the Koryaks of north-eastern Siberia, the Gilyaks, Tlingits, Tongas and Haidas, a bear . . . is present in the initiation ceremonies, just as it played an important part in the ceremonies of Paleolithic times. The Pomo Indians of Northern California have their candidates initiated by the Grizzly Bear, which 'kills' them and 'makes a hole' in their backs with its claws.

(ELIT p. 175)

In inscriptions from the archaic period in China, one dating from the Shang, the other from the Chou Dynasty, L. C. Hopkins believed he could make out a 'masked shaman dancing dressed in a bear's skin' (quoted in ELIC p. 452).

In the caverns of Europe the mysterious scent of the bear still lingers on. It is thus an emanation of gloom and darkness which in alchemy corresponds to the blackness of matter in its primary state. Darkness allied with the forbidden strengthens the bear's role as the mystagogue.

In Greek mythology, the bear was the companion of ARTEMIS, the goddess of the Moon and focus of bloodthirsty rites, and the goddess often manifested herself in the guise of a bear. This creature of the Moon incorporates one aspect of the dialectic attached to the lunar myth, potentially both aggressor and sufferer, priest and sacrificial victim. In this sense the bear stands in contrast with the HARE, typically representing the aggressive, cruel, sacrificing-priestly side of the myth. Hence the interpretation given by Jungian psychoanalysts.

Like all lunar manifestations of the divine, the bear's relationship is with the instincts. Given its strength, Jung considers it the symbol of the dangerous aspect of the unconscious.

In the underground temples (*kiva*) of the Pueblo Indians, there was a ritual hearth named 'the bear', the animal being associated with the powers of the underworld (H. Lehmann).

The Yakut, in Siberia, believed that the bear was omniscient, 'he remembers everything, and forgets nothing'. The Altaic Tatar believed that he hears 'through the mediation of the Earth', while the Soyot said 'the Earth is the bear's ear'. Most Siberian hunters had a taboo against mentioning the bear by name and instead called it 'the Old Fellow', 'Old Blacky', 'Lord of the Forest' (HARA pp. 281ff.) and often addressed him as 'Grandfather', 'Great Uncle', 'Grandmother' and so on, as if he were one of the family. Certain parts of its body, such as its paws, claws and teeth, were used magically as preservatives. Tungus, Chores and Tatars from Minusinsk nailed a bear's paw close to the door of the house or the entrance of their tent to ward off evil spirits. If they placed one in the cradle, the Yakut believed it would protect their babies. The Telyut believed that the genius of the doorway is dressed in a bear's skin. A bear's claws had therapeutic properties, the Chores believing that it cured enteritis in their herds, the Altaic Tatars that it cured headache. Lastly many Altaic peoples called the bear to witness their oaths; the Yakut made their attestations seated on a bear's skull, while the Tungus chewed his pelt as they said: 'May the bear gobble me up if I am guilty!'

All the hunting tribes of North America and Siberia, and the Lapps, imposed similar taboos, some very severe, upon their womenfolk at the time of the bear-hunt. Thus the Goldi did not even allow them to glance at a bear's head (HARA p. 286). The Lapps forbade them to step on a bear's tracks. As in the far north of Siberia, so around the Thomson River, the Indians never brought a bear's carcass into a tent or through the door of a house, 'because women use the entrance' (ibid. p. 287). According to Uno Harva, all these traditions are evidence of the operation of magical pre-servatives, since a woman ran the risk of attack by the animal's spirit, simply because she was a woman, and he quotes a Finnish song sung on the return from the bear-hunt: 'Take care, poor women, watch for your wombs and the tiny fruit inside them!' (HARA p. 288).

Like all large carnivores, the bear shares the symbolism of the chthonian unconscious. A lunar creature and therefore nocturnal, it originates in the inner landscapes of the Earth Mother. It is therefore all too easy to under-stand why so many Altaic peoples regarded the bear as their ancestor. This gives point to Harva's observation (HARA p. 322) that: 'Sternberg men-tions the existence in the Amur Valley of several tribes which derive their ancestry from a tiger or a bear, because their ancestor dreamed he had sexual intercourse with one or other of these creatures.'

Until recently there were graveyards for bears in Siberia.

In alchemical terms, the bear corresponds to instincts and to the primary phases of development. Its colour is BLACK, the same as that of primary matter. Powerful, violent, dangerous, uncontrolled, like some primal force, the bear is traditionally the emblem of cruelty, blood-thirstiness and brutal-ity. And yet there is another side to the symbol. The bear can to a degree be tamed: it can be made to dance and do tricks. It can be allured by honey, for which it is a glutton. What a contrast the bear provides in its simple-minded clumsiness with the thistledown flight of the bee whose nectar he drinks and that of the dancer whose steps he copies. All in all the bear symbolizes elemental forces, susceptible of evolutionary progress, but also liable to awesome regressions.

beard   Symbol of manhood, bravery and wisdom.

The Vedic god Indra, Zeus (Jupiter), Poseidon (Neptune), Hephaistos (Vulcan) and other gods, heroes, kings and philosophers have nearly always been depicted with beards. The same is true of the Jewish and Christian god. In Ancient Egypt, ruling queens were shown with beards to emphasize that their power was equal to that of kings. In Classical antiquity, beardless youths and women who gave proof of courage and of wisdom were given imitation beards.

In Celtic legend, the women asked the young hero Cùchulainn to stick a beard on his chin and in *The Cattle Raid of Cooley*, the Irish warriors refused to do battle with the Ulster hero, Cùchulainn, because he was beard-less. Faced by their refusal, he was forced magically to make himself a false beard out of grass (WINI p. 309). Frankish warriors were bearded and in the Middle Ages the Nine Worthies wore golden beards as a sign of their prowess and prestige.

Leviticus 19: 27 enjoins the Children of Israel 'not to round the corners of your heads, neither shalt thou mar the corners of thy beard.'

Great importance was attached to the beard by Semitic peoples. Not only was it a sign of manhood, but it was also considered an ornament to a man's face. It was therefore tended scrupulously and often scented. Accordingly, it was a sign of madness (1 Kings 21) when its owner left it tangled and neglected. Eastern practice (1 Kings 20: 9) was to kiss the beard as a token of respect. To shave the beard of an enemy or a stranger was to inflict a deadly insult on them. The victim would hide until his beard had grown again, to avoid mockery. The only occasion on which shaving the beard was permitted was as a sign of mourning or sorrow, and in the second case the beard was sometimes simply covered. Lepers had to wear a veil over their beards. In spite of this, priests in Ancient Egypt shaved beards, heads and body hair and Moses decreed that when the Levites were ordained to the priesthood they should be completely shaved (Numbers 8: 7).

Although the Ancient Egyptians shaved, 'from the outset,' François Daumas writes (DAUE p. 582), 'their gods were marked out by wearing a long and slender imitation beard. It was plaited and secured to the ears by wires running down the sides of the face. Kings shared this privilege with the gods.' The tip curved forwards and this imitation beard was very like those still worn today by the dignitaries of some central African tribes. (See also PIGTAIL; PLAIT.)

bed (see also PROCRUSTES)   Symbol of the regenerative effects of sleep and love, the bed is also a place of death. Birth, marriage and death make the bed a focus of particular care and even of veneration, since it is a centre devoted to the mysteries of life, of life in its basic and not in its higher states of development.

The marriage-bed was dedicated to the ancestral genii – hence the term 'genial bed'. The bed shares the twofold significance of the Earth – it both gives and receives life. It may be classified among the group of symbols of horizontality.

Under the marriage-bed the Dogon scatter grains of seed-corn and above it they hang a pall. The husband is deemed to act like the genius of the waters, irrigating with his life-giving semen the grains of seed-corn within his wife. The bed thus demonstrates the link between marital sex and the work of the land. However, their ancestor plays his part, too, and that is why the married couple sleep under the pall (MYTF p. 249).

Both marriage-bed and death-bed are mentioned in the Bible. Thus Reuben was dishonoured for having defiled his father's bed (Genesis 49: 4), while Jacob, lying on his death-bed, sits up and hangs his feet over the side so as to speak with his sons and, 'when he had made an end . . . he gathered up his feet into the bed, and yielded up the ghost' (Genesis 48: 2; 49: 33).

In Christian tradition, the bed does not simply signify a place of rest in which people lie to enact the basic functions of life, according to time-honoured custom. For Origen it symbolized the body. Thus, when Christ healed the paralytic he ordered him to take up his bed, that is to say to make use of a body strengthened by divine power. The bed may denote the body of the sinner cleansed and restored by grace.

bee   Numbers, organization, unwearied toil and discipline would all make the bee no more than another ANT – the symbol of the masses doomed to endure their fate – were it not that it has wings and a song and distils immortal HONEY from the delicate scent of flowers. This is enough to add a powerful spiritual dimension to the bee's purely material symbolism. Working in their HIVE, a home buzzing with activity and which is naturally equated with the airiness of the artist's studio rather than with the gloom of the factory, bees collectively ensure the survival of their species. Yet taken as individuals, a universal quickening power between Heaven and Earth, they come to symbolize the vital principal and to incarnate the soul. Hence it is this dual dimension – collective and individual, material and spiritual – which enriches their symbolism as a whole wherever it occurs. In his commentary on Proverbs 6: 8 ('Consider the bee and see how she labours'), Clement of Alexandria adds 'for the bee draws the nectar from a whole field of flowers to make a single drop of honey' (*Stromata* 1). Theocleptus of Philadelphia advises: 'Imitate the sagacity of bees' and sets them as a pattern for the spiritual life of monastic communities.

The Nosaïris, leaders of a heretical Muslim sect in Syria, regard Ali, 'Lion of Allah', as the 'Prince of Bees', these according to one tradition being angels, or, according to another, believers, since 'true believers are like bees which choose the fairest flowers' (HUAN p. 62).

In the metaphorical language of the Bektashi Order of Dervishes, the bee stands for the Dervish and the honey for divine reality (*haq*), the goal of his search (BIRD p. 255). Similarly some Indian writers compare the bee with the soul sucking the intoxicating pollen of knowledge.

A popular character in the fables of the Sudanese and the tribes which inhabit the bend of the Niger, the bee had become a symbol of royalty in Chaldea long before Napoleon adopted it for his empire. The Ancient Egyptians provide evidence that the royal or imperial symbolism of the bee is a solar one by associating it with lightning and by relating that bees were born of the tears of the sun-god, Ra, dropping to earth.

As a symbol of the soul, the bee was sometimes associated in Greek religion with Demeter, when it could either represent the soul descending to the Underworld, or else its materialization on leaving the body. The belief is re-echoed in Kashmir, Bengal and in many Amerindian traditions in South America, as well as in central Asia and Siberia. Lastly Plato declares that the souls of the righteous are reincarnated as bees.

Emblem of the soul and of the Word, for the Hebrew word for 'bee' (*dbure*) comes from the same root as that for 'word' (*dbr*), it is natural that the bee should play a part in initiation and in liturgy. At Eleusis and at Ephesus the priestesses bore the names of bees. Virgil has proclaimed their virtues.

Bees may be seen depicted on tombs as emblems of the afterlife – for the bee became the symbol of resurrection. The three-month winter season, when bees seem to vanish since they do not come out of their hives, was compared with the three days when, after the Crucifixion, Christ's body vanished, only to reappear once more at the Resurrection.

In addition the bee is the symbol of eloquence, poetry and the mind. The legend that bees touched their lips as they lay in the cradle, which was told of Pindar and Plato, was revived for St Ambrose, on whose lips they are said to have walked and into whose mouth they are said to have gone. Medieval Christianity, too, kept alive Virgil's theory that bees embody a spark of the divine intelligence. This imparts symbolic property to the buzz, really the 'song' of the bee.

The so-called Gelasian Sacramentary alludes to the extraordinary qualities possessed by bees which ravish nectar without harming flowers. They
do not give birth in the normal way, but produce their young from their lips
just as Christ proceeded from the Father's mouth.

Its honey and its sting makes the bee an emblem of Christ, the one of his
mildness and mercy, the other of his role in the Last Judgement. Medieval
writers often evoke this emblem, while to Bernard of Clairvaux, the bee
symbolized the Holy Spirit. The Celts refreshed themselves with honey-
sweetened wine and with MEAD. In Ireland bees, which produced the honey
from which mead, the drink of immortality, was produced, were given the
firm protection of the law. A Middle Welsh legal document states that 'the
noble nature of the bees derives from Paradise and it is because of man's
sinfulness that they come thence. God has anointed them with His grace
and because of this no Mass can be celebrated without candles.' The text
may be late and written under Christian influence, but it does bear witness
to an age-old tradition, traces of which still persist in Welsh (*cwyraidd* from
cwyr (wax) means 'finished', 'perfect'), while in Irish Gaelic *céir-bheach*
(literally 'bee's-wax') is another word for 'perfection'. Thus, in common
with so many other peoples, for the Celts symbolism of the bee was imbued
with notions of wisdom and the immortality of the soul (CHAB pp. 857ff.;
REVC 47: pp. 164–5).

The sum of the characteristics taken from all cultural traditions indicates
that the bee was regarded everywhere as a choleric creature, that is a creature endowed with the element of Fire. It symbolized the priestesses of the
Temple and the Sibyls of Delphi, the pure souls of the initiates, the Spirit
and the Word. The bee cleansed with fire and nourished with honey; its
sting burned and its glittering form cast light. On the social plane the bee
symbolized the ruler, be he king or emperor, not simply endowed with
courage and warlike ardour but ruling with order and in prosperity, as lord
of an orderly and prosperous realm. The bee thus shows its kinship with
those culture-heroes who imposed civilization and order by wisdom as well
as by force of arms.

beer   Beer brewed by Gobniu, smith of the gods, was called 'the drink of
kings', while Medb, the name of the Queen of Connaught, who personified
the Lordship of Ireland, also had the connotation of drunkenness. Enormous amounts of beer were drunk by the warrior caste at major festivals
and especially at Samain, celebrated on 1 November. At the end of his
reign and in the ashes of his palace, the old king, deposed because of age
or for his abuse of power, used to be drowned in a vat of beer or, after the
introduction of Christianity, in a butt of WINE. In contrast with MEAD, which
was reserved for the priestly caste, beer, the royal drink, was apparently a
privilege of the warrior (OGAC 14: pp. 474ff.).

Apocryphal writings confirm the Welsh legend of how Ceraint the
Drunken, son of King Berwyn (*berwi* = boil), was the first to brew beer with
malt (*brag*). With the malt he boiled wild flowers and honey and while the
brew was simmering a wild boar let fall a drop of foam from its jaws and
made it ferment. Although there is no equivalent legend surviving in Irish
mythology, it should be noted that consumption of pork (or rather of BOAR's

flesh) was on a par with the consumption of beer at all the ritual feasting at the festival of Samain (the Celtic New Year) and in the myths of the Other-world. Since the pig (or wild boar) was the animal which symbolized Lug and beer was the warrior caste's drink of immortality, it is hardly suprising that the creature which is the god's symbol should come to instil the seed of life in the brew, in the form of its own spittle (DUMB pp. 5–15).

Banana-beer (*pombe*) seems to play a similar role as the drink of immor-tality among the warrior caste in the rigidly hierarchical society of the Tutsi of Rwanda (central Africa).

In tropical America beers made from maize (*chica* in the Andean cordillera) and manioc (Amazonia) had and even today still have an import-ant ritual function, their use being prescribed in all rites of passage (see the description of the initiation ceremonies of the Piaroas in GHEO). Sometimes beer is the sole nourishment of the elders, or wise men. Its symbolism is undoubtedly connected with that of FERMENTATION. It is to the initiate who has accepted the responsibilities of the involutional stage of life, what MILK is to his opposite, the baby, unaccountable as it begins its development.

In Ancient Egypt beer was a national drink as well as a drink of immort-ality, prized by the living and the dead and by the gods.

Behemoth   De Plancy comments:

Because it was written in the Book of Job (40: 15) that Behemoth 'eateth grass as an ox', the Rabbis turned him into a miraculous ox reserved for the banquet of their Messiah. This ox, they said, was so huge that every day it cropped the grass of the thousand massive mountains on which it had been fattening since the world began. It never left these thousand mountains and the grass which it ate during the day grew again during the night for food the next day . . . . The Jews look forward to the banquet at which it will be the main course. They swear their oaths by the ox Behemoth.

(COLD p. 86)

Of course this ox is really a HIPPOPOTAMUS, and although it may eat the grass of a thousand mountains, it does not live among the mountains but among the water-lilies and reeds of rivers and marshes. It symbolizes the ANIMAL, the brute force of the beast. Only in a far later tradition did Behe-moth come to symbolize the vast stock of food of which the revellers were to partake at solemn or mythical banquets.

bell   The symbolism of the bell is governed by the different perceptions of the sound which it makes. In India, for example, it symbolizes hearing and what hearing perceives, sound, which is the echo of some primordial vibration. For this reason the vast majority of 'sounds' during yogic experi-ences are 'sounds of bells'. In the Islamic world the 'reverberation of the bell' is the delicate sound of Koranic revelation, the reverberation of the power of God in the living world. To hear the 'noise of the bell' is to dissolve the limitations of one's existence in time. In something of the same way the Pali Buddhist canon assimilates heavenly 'voices' to the 'sound of a golden bell'.

In China the sound of the bell is placed in the same category as that of thunder and, as is so often the case, is associated with that of the DRUM. The music of bells, however, is a princely music and a standard of universal harmony.

The small bells hung from the roofs of pagodas have the purpose of making audible the 'sound' of Buddhist law. However, the ringing of bells and of handbells has a universal power of exorcism and purification. It wards off evil influences or at least warns of their approach.

A very special symbolism attaches to the Tibetan handbell or *tilpu* (Sanskrit *ghantā*). By contrast with VAJRA (thunderbolt), the bell symbolizes the world of the senses as opposed to the 'diamond' realm; it symbolizes the world of illusion, typified by the bell's fleeting sound. The bell is also Wisdom as opposed to Law, the passive female element, while *vajra* is the active male element. This is expressed by sexual symbolism, and also by the initiate wearing a gold ring (*vajra*) on the right hand and a silver ring (*tilpu*) on the left (DAVL, ELIY, MALA).

As opposed to thunderbolts, handbells

also symbolize the virtues of womanhood and the Teachings . . . . The handle is usually shaped like an eight-branched bolt of lightning cut in half. Often used ritually and in magic, it frequently bears the Sanskrit greeting of 'The Jewel in the Lotus' (*Om Mani Padme Aum*, sometimes abbreviated to *Om Aum*) or else some magic spell. It is often decorated with the Prayer Wheel, a ring of lotus petals, lions, gods and so on.

(TONT p. 3)

It undoubtedly symbolizes the divine command to study the Law, obedience to the word of God and, at all events, intercommunication between Heaven and Earth.

The position of its clapper suggests the position of all which hangs between Heaven and Earth, and by this very fact it establishes a relationship between them. But the handbell also possesses the power to communicate with the Underworld.

A magic handbell can be used to summon the spirits of the dead. It is cast from an alloy of tin, iron, gold, copper and quicksilver, and on the base should be inscribed the name 'Tetragrammaton'; above this are the names of the ruling spirits of the seven planets, above them the name 'Adonaï', and on the holding-ring, the name of Jesus. According to Girardius Pervilues, to make it work it has to be

wrapped in a fragment of green taffeta and kept therein until whosoever is to undertake the mighty mystery has the means and the ability to take the said bell to a graveyard and there set it in a grave and leave it for the space of seven days. So long as the bell retains its covering of graveyard earth, the emanations and the sympathies which it contains will never leave it. They will give the bell the lasting quality and requisite virtue, whenever you ring it to that end.

(GRIA p. 177)

Bellerophon   After a succession of heroic deeds, and in particular his victory over the CHIMERA which was won with the aid of his winged horse, PEGASUS, Bellerophon tried to seize the throne of Zeus. The gods in council symbolize 'the law which confines man's aims and ambitions within just bounds', while Bellerophon's attempt typifies man's vanity developed into 'a perverted desire to dominate, cloaked in the form of the highest degree of daring' (DIES pp. 83–90). Defeated, Bellerophon was confined in Hell with other ambitious figures such as IXION. Yet, unlike Ixion, his ambitions bore no trace of sexuality, but were rather those of the man whose warlike deeds of heroism have intoxicated him to the point at which they fill him with the lust for sovereign power. He symbolizes overweening ambition in the soldier, or military power attempting to seize civil rule and become the overriding authority.

bellows The bellows naturally represents breathing, through its function and by its rhythm. It is a tool which produces BREATH, symbol of life and especially of spiritual life.

The symbol of the cosmic bellows is a constant element of Taoist (Daoist) thought. Its best-known expression is in the *Tao Te-Ching* (ch. 5): 'The space between heaven and earth is like the bellows in a forge. When empty it does not subside: when full it constantly exhales.' It has, the *Huai Nan-tzu* explains, 'the heavens for lid and the earth for base.' This intermediate area is the same as the atmosphere (*Bhuvas*) of Hindu tradition, and the realm of breath (*k'i*) in that of the Tao. The region in which the Primal Virtue holds sway, its rhythm is the rhythm of life itself and it gives birth to 'ten thousand beings' (LIOT).

belt See GIRDLE.

betel Its dictionary definition is 'the leaf of a plant [the betel-vine or -pepper] which is wrapped round a few parings of the areca nut and a little shell lime and chewed by the natives of India and neighbouring countries as a masticatory.' Its users will, as occasion arises, also add tobacco and different spices.

In Vietnam, betel has always played a major part in betrothal and marriage ceremonies. Betel, in fact, symbolizes love and conjugal fidelity, and sometimes a quid of betel may be used in a love potion. The symbolism may derive from the actual 'marriage' of the ingredients of betel, but it is vindicated by a very lovely legend which narrates how a young man was transformed into an areca palm and his wife into a betel-pepper which wreathed her vine round his trunk, the nut-tree and the pepper thereafter being called after the couple, *lang* and *trâu*.

In another legend an evil priest is turned into a POT full of the corrosive lime into which betel-chewers dip their spoons.

Even in present-day Vietnam time is measured for practical purposes by the three or four minutes which a quid of betel lasts.

In addition to its supposed hygienic and medicinal qualities, betel is regarded in India as an aphrodisiac. The *tāmbūla*, the betel-box, is an attribute of Devī according to the *Agni-Purana*. It is often of cylindrical shape with a pointed lid, and this may derive from phallic symbolism (HUAN, LEBC, MALA, VUOB).

bethel A word of Semitic origin, meaning 'House of God', applied essentially to sacred STONES venerated especially by Arabs of the pre-Islamic period as manifestations of the divine presence. They were one of the receptacles of the power of God. Jacob's head was pillowed upon a stone when he had the dream which revealed to him the destiny allotted to his descendants by the power of God (Genesis 28: 11–19). He then set up the stone as a memorial, to which the Children of Israel came in crowds as pilgrims. The LADDER which the patriarch dreamed was reared upon that stone symbolized communication between Heaven and Earth, God and man. Joshua, too, raised a stone as a memorial of the covenant of Jehovah with his people (Joshua 24: 26–7). It was the seal of spiritual communion. Such stones were manifestations of divine action, kinds of theophany and, since they marked sites of worship, they easily themselves became objects of idolatrous worship. They had therefore to be destroyed in accordance with the injunction given to Moses (Leviticus 26: 1; Numbers 33: 52).

The OMPHALOS of Delphi, which the Greeks regarded as the NAVEL of the world, was, according to Pausanias (10: 16, 2) a white stone believed to lie in the centre of the earth. According to a tradition reported by Varro, the omphalos covered the tomb of the sacred serpent of Delphi, the PYTHO. As the navel, this stone guaranteed 'by its symbolism a new birth and reintegrated conscience'. It was the abode of a superhuman presence and 'from the simple elementary hierophany represented by boulders and rocks – which *strike* men's minds by their solidity, steadfastness and majesty – to the symbolism of *omphaloi* and meteorites, religious stones invariably *signify* something greater than man' (ELIT pp. 232, 234).

A somewhat dubious etymology derives the name of the god Hermes from *hermai*, tall stones planted at the roadside to represent 'a presence, to embody a power and to guard and make fertile the field'. They were topped by a head and were to become images of the god who had lent them his name. The mind of man had crowned the stone with divinity. The worship of Apollo derived from that of standing stones, which were always one of the distinctive emblems of the god.

Enough bethels have survived to the present in Celtic countries for their MENHIRS to be considered so many local *omphaloi*, CENTRES of their worlds. The principal bethel in Ireland, denounced in all the lives of the saints, was Cromm Cruaich, the chief idol surrounded by twelve others. St Patrick himself destroyed its worship, striking them so firmly with his crozier that the stones were swallowed up by the earth. On the bethel at Kermaria (Morbihan, France) was carved a swastika (CELT 1: pp. 173ff.).

The sacred stone at Heliopolis in Ancient Egypt was named Benben. This bethel represented the primordial hill, the dune on which the god Atum stood when he created the first man and woman. The first rays of sunlight fell upon this hill and upon the stone, Benben, and it was here that the phoenix used to settle. There is some reminiscence of Benben in both obelisk and pyramid, and there is some connection between this primitive stone and both omphalos and phallic worship. Serge Sauneron and Jean Yoyotte (SOUN pp. 82–3) both observe that 'there are good grounds for explaining the meaning of the noun *benben* from the root *bn*, to spurt. In fact it would be useful in the study of Egyptian cosmogonies to reappraise the many Egyptian words containing *bn* or *bnbn*, which relate to the spurting of water, the rising of the Sun or to the act of procreation.'

Beyond The Beyond is the mysterious realm to which all mortals go after their death. It differs from the **Otherworld**, which is a world adjoining or often duplicating our own, in the sense that its inhabitants are free to come and go between the two. They can even invite mortals in, while none returns from the Beyond. The Beyond is sometimes localized as an 'evil' world lying under some mound or hillock.

By its very definition the Otherworld is a world of gods as opposed to the world of men, terrestrial beings who on their death depart for the Beyond. The Otherworld is free from the constraints of time and space. Those who know it well are immortal and can gain it whenever they wish and wherever they may be. It is what the Irish call, in blanket terms, *sid*, or, as it is spelled today, *sidh*, from a noun with the etymological meaning of 'peace'. Above all it is a holy world, with which human beings cannot communicate except at certain times (festivals) and in certain places (consecrated sites or *omphaloi*). When Christians came to transcribe the pagan Irish legends with their descriptions of the marvellous, they muddled the Otherworld with the Beyond and with the biblical Garden of Eden, so that the distinction between the Beyond and the Otherworld was lost. It is for this reason, too, that a *sid* is sometimes located under an Irish hill or lake (OGAC 28: pp. 136ff.).

bicycle Bicycles often make their appearance in contemporary dreams. They suggest three characteristics.

1 As a means of transport bicycles differ from other vehicles, in that they owe their motion to their riders whereas others depend upon an outside force for their motion. Forward progress is determined solely and exclusively of any other source of energy by the rider's personal and individual efforts.
2 Balance can only be maintained by forward motion, just as in the development of the external or inner life.
3 Only one person at a time can ride a bicycle – tandems are a separate subject.

Since the machine itself symbolizes evolutionary progress, dreamers 'mount' their unconscious and develop through their own inner resources without 'losing the pedals' by inertia, neurosis or infantilism. They can count upon themselves as independent people, assuming the appropriate personality and unbeholden to anyone else in their development.

On rare occasions in dreams the bicycle is an indicator of real or psychological isolation brought about by excessive introversion, egocentricity or an individualism which inhibits social integration. It corresponds to a need for normal independence.

bindu *Bindu* (Sanskrit: drop, symbol of the absolute; Tibetan *Thi-gle*) is materialized by the central point of the VAJRA. It is the image of measureless unity in the shape of the final point of integration, as well as being the point of departure for all deep meditation. This 'flaming droplet' comprises 'an infinite space flashing with the light of innumerable Suns' (EYTA). The *bindu* also conveys the meaning of 'bud' and of 'seed'. It is a man's semen inwardly transformed. It marks the point at which internal and external space divide and at which they return to become the One. It is also the 'Lord Almighty', effulgent and dwelling within a higher CHAKRA. It is associated with the sky-blue light of the Wisdom of the Dharmadhatu, pure element of consciousness which emanates from the heart of Vairocana, the Dhyani-Buddha in the centre of the MANDALA. It proceeds from the infinite VOID, as the spirit which resides in all things.

This speck of light, as bright as a star, is fashioned by the marriage of *prana*, the breath of life, with the essence of our spirit and with the 'conscious principle'. Its aspect is called Bliss, its nature is light and its essence, void (Lama Guendun).

birch The birch is, above all, the sacred tree of the peoples of Siberia, among whom it takes on all the attributes of the *Axis Mundi* (see AXIS, TREE). Like the cosmic PILLAR, it is cut with seven or nine notches as symbols of the heavenly orders. During shamanistic initiation ceremonies, it is set in the centre of the circular yurt (tent), directly below the smoke-hole which represents the 'Gate of Heaven' or the 'Sun', through which the shaman becomes detached from the cosmos along the axis of the Pole Star (see DOME).

The birch is sometimes connected with the Moon and even with both Moon and Sun. In the latter event it is dual-natured, both father and mother, male and female. The birch plays a protective role, or rather it is the means by which heavenly influences 'come down'. Hence the notion of duality which is essentially that of manifestation (ELIC, ELIM, SOUL). The birch symbolizes the path by which energy comes down from Heaven and human aspirations rise up in return.

The tree was regarded as sacred in eastern Europe and central Asia, and in Russia in particular it symbolized Spring and the Maiden. (A famous group of Russian songs and dances performed exclusively by girls is called 'The Birch Tree'.) Selkup hunters hung the figures of guardian spirits from the sacrificial birch near their homes.

There is no very clear indication of the symbolism of the birch in the Celtic world, but it was most probably funerary. The Welsh poem, *The Battle of the Trees* (Kat Godeu), describes a battle, or rather a massacre, and then somewhat enigmatically remarks 'the top of the birch tree covered us with leaves; he changed and transformed our withered state.' This is perhaps an allusion to the custom of covering the bodies of the slain with birch branches (OGAC 5: p. 115). But it may also mean that the birch works the changes which prepare the dead for their new lives.

Pliny believed that the birch came originally from Gaul. It was, he wrote, 'a cause of terror, as supplying the magistrates' rods of office; it is also easily bent to make hoops and likewise the ribs of small baskets.' He added that it was 'the most auspicious tree for supplying wedding torches' (*Natural History* 16: 30). In both instances the birch is closely linked with human life as a guardian symbol in life as in death.

bird (see also ANQA; BUSTARD; COCK; CRANE; CROW; CUCKOO; DOVE; DUCK; EAGLE; FALCON; GROUSE; HOMA; HOOPOE; KINGFISHER; KITE; LARK; MACAW; MAGPIE; NIGHTINGALE; NIGHTJAR; ORIOLE; OWL; PARTRIDGE; PEACOCK; PELICAN; PHEASANT; PHOENIX; PIGEON; QUAIL; ROC; SIMURG; SPARROWHAWK; STORK; SWALLOW; SWAN; VULTURE; WAGTAIL; WINGS) The flight of birds leads them, naturally, to serve as symbols of the links between Heaven and Earth. In Greek, the word itself could be used as a synonym for forewarning and for a message from Heaven. In Taoism, they carry the same meaning, while the Immortals take on the shapes of birds to signify their 'lightness' and their freedom from terrestrial 'heaviness'. Those who offer sacrifice, or ritual dancers, are often described in the Brahmanas as 'birds flying skywards'. From the same point of view, the bird represents the SOUL escaping from the body or, to a lesser degree, the intellect – 'intelligence', according to the *Rig-Veda*, 'is the swiftest of winged creatures'. Cave paintings from Altamira and Lascaux showing bird-men may be taken in a similar sense, either as the flight of the soul or the 'spirit-flight' of the shaman.

The bird stands in opposition to the SERPENT as a symbol of Heaven as opposed to Earth.

Again, in a more generalized sense, birds symbolize spiritual states, angels and higher forms of being. The innumerable blue birds in Chinese literature of the Han period are fairies, Immortals and heavenly messengers. Birds, both in the West and in India, perch in order of seniority upon the branches of the World Tree. In the Upanishads they are two in number. One eats the fruit of the tree, while the other looks on without eating. They are symbols, respectively, of the active individual soul (*jīvātmā*) and of the Universal Spirit (*ātman*), which is pure knowledge. In reality they are not separate and for this reason they are sometimes depicted as a single bird with two heads. In Islam birds are more especially symbols of angels. The 'language of birds' of which the Koran speaks is that of angels – spiritual knowledge. Po-yi, who assisted the Jade Emperor in his great task of regulating the world, learned the language of birds and perhaps by this means was able to subdue the Bird-Barbarians. Birds as travellers – such as those described by Farīd al-Dīn 'Attār or in Ibn Sīna's (Avicenna's) *Visionary Recital* – are souls involved in an initiatory quest. In addition Guénon notes the instance of the auspices (see AUGURY) of the Romans, since divination from the flight and song of birds may, in some way, be held to be an understanding of the 'language of birds' and hence of the language of Heaven.

It is often the case that the very lightness of birds carries with it a negative aspect, and St John of the Cross saw them as symbols of the 'workings of the imagination', especially in terms of their volatility, flitting hither and thither without aim or purpose: what Buddhism would call 'distraction' or, worse, 'diversion'.

It is in this sense, perhaps, that the Taoists invested the Barbarians with the shape of birds, to indicate their violent, uncontrollable, primordial wilfulness. In China the symbol for Chaos is a red and yellow bird, like a fireball, featureless but with six feet and four wings, able to sing and dance, but unable to eat or to breathe. Incidentally the Ancient Chinese believed that when a bird destroyed its nest it was a sign of trouble and disorder in the empire.

In the East, reference should be made to the Hindu symbol of the *Kinnara*, half-man, half-bird, playing the zither, and especially associated with such kingly or solar personnages as Vishnu, Sūraya or the Buddha (AUBT, BENA, COOH, DANA, ELIY, ELIM, GRAP, GUEV, GUES, LECC, MALA).

The earliest Vedic texts show that birds – as a generalized unspecific term – were held to be symbols of the friendship of the gods towards mankind. It was a bird which went to fetch SOMA (ambrosia) from an inaccessible mountain-top to feed mankind. By attacking the serpents, birds gave the Aryans victory over the barbarians who stood in their way. Later epic poetry was to extol the faithfulness of the bird Jatayu, which gave its life trying to stop the demon, Rāvana, from carrying off Sītā. The mystical interpretation of this story, which many Hindus believe, sees the friendship of the gods in the guise of a bird striving to preserve the soul from the diabolical assaults of the spirit of evil. The stronger the belief in the gods as winged beings (like angels in the Bible), the more birds are seen as being in some way living symbols of divine freedom, liberated from such earthly constraints as heaviness; weightlessness is seen pre-eminently as a divine attribute. As for the bird's nest, this virtually inaccessible retreat in the tree-tops was regarded as a symbol of Paradise, a dwelling-place in the heights of Heaven which the soul would only reach if it were able to cast off the trammels of the flesh and take WING there. Hence came the idea that the soul itself was a bird, the Upanishads defining it as a migratory bird (Sanskrit *Hamsa*: cf. German *Gans*, 'goose'), in accordance with the belief that the soul migrates from body to body until its final flight to the nest where it is safe from the perils of transmigration. This last is so powerful a symbol that the story goes that some hundred years ago Rāmakrishna fell into a trance when he saw a completely white migratory bird emerge from a black cloud.

In the Celtic world, birds were in general regarded as the assistants or the messengers of the gods and of the Otherworld, whether they were swans in Ireland, cranes and herons in Gaul or geese in Britain, as well as crows, wrens and chickens. The Ulates hunted birds in their chariots and there are scattered literary references to eating duck. This, however, would seem to have been infrequent and the Celtic world as a whole held birds in profound veneration. The Welsh goddess Rhiannon ('Great Queen'), according to a brief passage in the *Mabinogion* ('Pwyll Prince of Dyved'), is said to have possessed birds which sang so sweetly that they awoke the dead and put the living to sleep (death). Romano-Gallic sculptures depict a bird-divinity, to which monuments were consecrated in France at Alésia (Côte-d'Or) and Compiègne (Oise) and at Martigny and Avenches in Switzerland. This reminds us of the birds which Germanic mythology associates with Wotan (Odin) (OGAC 18: pp. 146–7; *Genava* 1941: 119–86).

In the Koran, the word 'bird' is often synonymous with 'fate' and this is the literal meaning of the word in *sura* 17: 13, 'And every man's fate we have fastened about his neck.'

In Muslim tradition 'green bird' is an epithet applied to a number of saints, and the Archangel Gabriel has a pair of green wings. Souls of martyrs fly to Paradise as green birds (Koran 2: 262).

It is a common belief that birds have a language. The Koran (27: 16) states that King Solomon knew this language. *Mantic al-Tair* (*The Conference of the Birds*), the famous work of Farīd al-Dīn 'Attār (*c.* 1119–1230), a classic of Persian literature, uses this theme to describe the events of a mystical journey in search of the godhead (see ANQA, SIMURG).

Both in poetry and in the Koran (2: 262; 3: 43; 67: 19) birds are used as symbols of the immortality of the soul. The soul is likened to a falcon, summoned by the beat of the Master's drum, to a bird imprisoned in a cage of clay and so on. As in most other traditions, Islamic mysticism often compares 'spiritual birth' with the hatching of the spiritual body which breaks its earthly matrix like a bird cracking the shell of its egg.

Birds, symbols of the soul, play the role of intermediaries between Heaven and Earth.

The sign of the bustard, symbol of the marriage of souls, of fertility and of the descent of souls into the material world . . . is common to many Berber tribes of Marabouts. The Tuareg of Aïr, south of Hoggar, have their shields charged with a pair of *shin* (bustard's feet). Symbolism of the same type is to be found in the Far East, in the crow's foot of the Celtic world, on the robes of Uralo-Altaic shamans and even in the caves of Lascaux.

(SERH pp. 74–5)

On the other side of the globe Hopi Indians also attribute to birds the magical power of communicating with the gods. They are often depicted with their heads surrounded by clouds, symbols of the rain which is one of the gifts of the gods who make the soil fertile, and haloed with a broken circle, which represents creation and life as well as the opening of the GATE, the symbol of communication.

With respect to divination from birds, Ibn Khaldūn declared that it was a matter of having the ability

to express the unknown, awoken in certain persons by the sight of a bird flying or an animal passing, and of spiritual concentration after its disappearance. It is a faculty of the soul which through the intellect, prompts a swift grasp of things seen or heard, which provides the substance of a forewarning. It is a faculty which assumes a strong and vivid imagination . . . .

The two branches of Arab ornithomancy rely upon the interpretation of the flight of birds and their calls.

(FAHN pp. 206–7)

In Kurdistan, both the Yezidi and the Ahl-i-Haqq (Followers of the Truth) regard the symbol of the bird as originating with the spiritual world. Thus the Yezidi depict God, at the time when waters covered the Earth, as a bird perched in a TREE with its roots in the air. The cosmogony of the Ahl-i-Haqq is very similar. At a time before the creation of Heaven and Earth, God is represented as a bird with golden wings. This is reminiscent of Genesis 1: 2, which describes the Spirit of God moving, like a bird, over the face of the waters (MOKC).

Birds are a constant motif of African art, especially on masks. Birds 'symbolize strength and life and are often fertility symbols. Sometimes, as with the plumed crane among the Bambara, the power of speech is attributed to birds. A common motif on pottery is a battle between birds and snakes, an emblem of the battle between life and death' (MVEA p. 129).

The Yakut believe that after death the souls of both good and evil fly up to Heaven in the shape of birds. Apparently the soul-bird roosts in the branches of the World Tree, an almost universal mythic image (ELIC p. 206).

Similarly in Ancient Egypt the dead person's soul was depicted by a bird with either a man's or a woman's head, as were gods and goddesses visiting the Earth. The oldest religions of the Middle East had long borne witness to the concept of the soul as a bird and, consequently, to the identification of the dead person with a bird. The *Book of the Dead* describes the dead person as a falcon on the wing, and in Mesopotamia the dead are depicted as birds. The myth seems even older than this. On prehistoric monuments in both Europe and Asia, the Cosmic Tree is depicted with two birds in its branches. Apart from their cosmological significance, these birds may also have symbolized the ancestral soul. In fact, it should not be forgotten that, in central Asian, Siberian and Indonesian mythology, the birds roosting in the branches of the World Tree symbolize human souls. Because shamans were believed to be able to change themselves into birds in their 'spirit' state, they could fly to the World Tree and bring back the soul-bird (ELIC pp. 480–1).

The earliest evidence of the belief in the soul-bird is undoubtedly provided by the myth of the phoenix. This purple-hued fire-bird – that is, a creature composed of the life-force – symbolized the soul to the Ancient Egyptians. The phoenix, the sublimated counterpart of the eagle, perched on the top of the Cosmic Tree, with the serpent at its foot, symbolized the successful conclusion of the alchemist's 'work' (DURS p. 135).

As in the case of BUTTERFLIES, so small birds do not simply symbolize the souls of the dead, souls in general freed from their earthly bonds and flying back to their heavenly home, but specifically children's souls. This is particularly true of the Uralo-Altaic peoples of central Asia (HARA). Among the Goldi it was believed that 'should a pregnant woman dream of birds, and should she be able to tell the sex of the bird, she will know if the child she carries will be a boy or a girl' (HARA p. 120).

Nocturnal birds are often equated with ghosts and with the souls of the dead who come to wail by night around their old homes. Their calls terrify whole villages of Semang Negritos since, according to Semang tradition, the dead return to their families to kill their relatives since they hate being alone.

The Buryat of Siberia believed that eagle-owls hunt the souls of women who have died in childbirth and who return to persecute the living (HARA p. 263). The Yakut nailed the head of an eagle-owl above the doors of their byres to protect their livestock (ibid. p. 284). In the Altai, the shamans who always metamorphosed into birds often decorated their cloaks with eagle-owls' feathers. According to Harva (ibid. p. 341) in bygone days they were fully robed to look like eagle-owls. The folk belief in the Altai is that eagle-owls drive away evil spirits. 'In many areas, when children fall ill, it still remains the custom to catch an eagle-owl and keep it, having in mind that the bird will drive away the evil spirits which are attacking the baby. When the Yogul celebrate a bear feast, one of them is disguised as an eagle-owl with the task of keeping away the dead bear's soul' (HARA p. 349).

Esoteric tradition has sketched a whole series of correspondences between birds, colours and psychic compulsions. The four main colours are represented by the crow, a BLACK bird which symbolizes intelligence; by the BLUE and GREEN peacock, representing the yearnings of the affections; by the WHITE swan, symbol of the libido which engenders physical and, through the Word, spiritual life; and by the scarlet (see RED) phoenix, symbolizing immortality and the supreme godhead. Countless variations produce a regular chart of correspondences (LOEC pp. 150–2). For example, love both sacred and profane can be represented by doves, APHRODITE's birds, by pigeons and by ducks; sublimation of the soul by doves (again), eagles and by the simurg; crows and swans act as mediators between Heaven and Earth, and are guides and messengers (a strange and significant alliance between black and white); vultures and the phoenix conduct the souls of the dead; eagles, falcons and macaws stand for solar and celestial qualities, victory in battle, succesful hunting and rich harvests; while nocturnal birds represent lunar and chthonian qualities.

In dreams birds are one of the symbols of the personality of the dreamer.

birthday Birthdays symbolize important stages in the cycle of existence; anniversaries give true meaning to the 'circling years'.

In Japan the birthdays of individuals (*Sanga*) are celebrated with due solemnity, of especial importance being:

- fortieth birthday: *shoro* ('the beginning of old age'), since Confucius said: 'When I was forty I did not wander';
- sixty-first birthday: *kanreki*, the completion of the sixty-year cycle; on this birthday, the celebrant wears a RED cap and a red kimono and is congratulated by everybody for having become 'a new-born baby once more';
- seventieth birthday: *koki* ('rare age'), so called because the great Chinese poet Tu Fu said that it was a privilege for a person to reach the age of seventy.
- seventy-seventh birthday: *kiju*, long and happy life;
- eighty-eighth birthday: *beiju*, the rice birthday.

These last two birthdays gain their names from the similarity of the Japanese ideograms for 'joy' and 'rice' with those for the numbers seventy-seven and eighty-eight.

We can compare these special birthdays with wedding anniversaries, which combine the symbols of remembrance and marriage with those of increasingly valuable, substantial and rare objects:

paper (1 year);
wood (5 years);
iron (10 years);
silver (25 years);
gold (50 years);
diamond (60 years).

bison Since it was the main source of food and leather, the hunting tribes of North American Indians regarded the bison as a symbol of prosperity and plenty. Even after the species was virtually wiped out, the function of the symbol remained. It even recurs among settled agricultural tribes when it is associated with the ear of MAIZE (Pawnee *Hako* ceremony).

bite The teeth are ramparts; in relation to the human being they are like the walls of a castle, and on the symbolic plane they are the citadel which

92

protects the spirit. The mark which teeth leave on the flesh is like the imprint of something disembodied – intention, love, passion. They are the seal set upon the determination to possess.

In dreams a bite may symbolize operational shock (TEIR p. 174), while to C. G. Jung it is the symbol of dangerous aggressive instincts.

For the latter the symbolism of the bite carries most weight, for the former, that of the mark left by the bite. In any case it is a successful or failed attempt to take possession.

black (colour) Antithesis of WHITE, black is its equal in terms of absolute colour. Like white it can be set at either end of the chromatic scale as a boundary to both warm and cold colours. Depending on its mattness or its glossiness, black can become the absence or the sum, the negation or the synthesis, of colour.

Symbolically, black is most often seen in its cold and negative aspect. As the antithesis of all colour it is associated with primeval darkness and primal, formless matter. In this sense it is reminiscent of the significance of neutral, empty white and balances it in such analogous symbolic images as the horses of Death, which are sometimes black and sometimes white. However, neutral, chthonian white is associated in pictures of the world with the east–west AXIS, the axis of departure and change, while black is connected with the north–south axis, the axis of absolute transcendence and of the poles. North or south is considered as black, depending upon the direction in which peoples locate their Underworld. Thus the north is black to the Aztecs, Algonquin Indians and the Chinese, the south to the Maya, and is the Nadir, that is the base upon which the World Axis stands, to the Pueblo Indians.

When so set beneath the world, black expresses absolute passivity, a state of unchanging and complete death, sandwiched between the two 'white nights' during which night becomes day and day becomes night. Black is therefore the colour of mourning and is unlike white by being far more overwhelming. To wear white as a sign of mourning has something Messianic about it. It shows a loss that will be filled and it marks a temporary void. It is mourning worn for gods and kings whose rebirth is inevitable. To wear black, it could be said, is to mourn hopelessly in a sign of irrevocable loss and of a plunge into a nothingness from which there is no return. When the Zoroastrian equivalents of Adam and Eve had been seduced by Ahriman and driven from Paradise, they dressed in black. Black is the colour of guilt and also the colour of the renunciation of the vanities of this world, hence for both Christians and Muslims a black cloak is a proclamation of their faith. The black cloaks of the Whirling Dervishes, the Mevlevi, is emblematic of the gravestone. When the initiate takes the cloak off before beginning his gyratory dance, he is seen to be wearing white, symbol of his rebirth in the godhead, the True Reality after the trumpets have sounded the Last Judgement. In Ancient Egypt 'according to Horapollon, a black DOVE was the hieroglyph for the woman who remained a widow until her own death' (PORS p. 175). This black dove may be considered as Eros frustrated and life denied. From Greek epic to the medieval romance of Tristan, the dire fate of ships with black sails is a commonplace.

However, the chthonian world lying beneath the crust of apparent reality is also the womb of the Earth in which the regeneration of the world of sunlight takes place. 'In the West, black is the colour of mourning, yet originally it was the symbol of fertility, in Ancient Egypt, for example, and in north Africa, being the colour of rich earth and of rain-clouds' (SERH p. 96). If it is as black as the ocean depths, it is because the Underworld contains the treasury of hidden life and because it is the storehouse of all things. Homer describes the sea as wine-dark. The great fertility goddesses, ancient Earth mothers, were often black by virtue of their chthonian origins. Black Madonnas are thus renewals of black Isises, Demeters, Cybeles and Aphrodites. According to Portal (PORS), Orpheus said: 'I shall hymn the Mother of Gods and Men, Night, original of all created things, and we shall call her Venus.' This blackness cloaks the cosmic womb where the RED of blood and fire, symbols of the vital force, work in the darkness of gestation. Hence the frequent juxtaposition of red and black on the north–south axis or, what amounts to the same thing, the fact that red and black seem to be substitutes the one for the other, as Soustelle observed in connection with the Aztec world-picture (SOUM). Hence, too, the depiction on a Greek vase described by Portal, of the Dioscuri riding a pair of horses, one black and the other red, while on another vase described by the same author, Camillus, the Etruscans' chief conductor of the dead, has a red body, but black wings, boots and tunic.

The colours of the thirteenth Tarot, DEATH, are significant. The death which the initiate undergoes as the preparation for a true birth reaps the world of apparent reality – a world of perishable illusions – with a red scythe, while the world itself is depicted in black. The weapon of death represents the vital force and its victim, nothingness. By scything an illusory life the thirteenth Tarot prepares the way to real life. Numerical symbolism corroborates colour symbolism. THIRTEEN follows TWELVE, the number of the completed cycle, introducing a fresh start and initiating a renewal.

In the (Old French) language of heraldry, black is called *sable*: the modern French meaning 'sand' expresses its affinity with barren earth, always depicted in YELLOW ochre, sometimes employed as a substitute for black. Some American Indian tribes depict the cold and wintry north as this same earthy or sandy yellow, and the same is true of Tibetans and Kalmucks. Sable symbolizes 'prudence, wisdom and perseverance in sorrow and affliction' (PORS p. 177). The same symbolism is revealed in the famous line from the Song of Solomon, 'Daughters of Jerusalem, I am black but comely', which, according to Old Testament commentators, symbolizes 'a severe trial'. This may not be so, since warm, glossy black, the outflow of red, is the sum of colour. Muslim mystics consider that it becomes above all else the light of the godhead. The founder of the order of Whirling Dervishes, Mevlana Jalāl-al-Dīn Rūmī, compares the inner stages through which the Sufi progresses towards beatitude with a LADDER of colours. This begins at white, the symbol of the book of Koranic law; white, inactive, because the Dervish has yet to start to travel along the path of perfection; white, the foot of that staircase which ends with red and then finally black. Black, to Mevlana's mind, was the absolute colour, the point to which all colours lead, like so many stairs, to reach the highest level of beatitude when the godhead manifests itself to the initiate and ravishes him. Here again glossy black is the exact equivalent of shining white. Undoubtedly the glossy blackness of the sacred stone in the Ka'ba at Mecca can be interpreted in the same way. It recurs in Africa, in Gabon, in the deep patina with reddish tints which glows on the statues guarding the shrines in which the skulls of the ancestors are preserved.

Beyond the sacred, this same glossy black, with reddish tints, is a characteristic of the coursers of Russian folklore, symbolizing youthful strength and ardour.

The marriage of black and white is a sacred marriage and its issue is mid-grey, the quality in the chromatic sphere of the mid-point, that is of mankind.

In the Far East, the duality of black and white is, generally speaking, that of light and shade, day and night, knowledge and ignorance, *yin* and *yang*, Heaven and Earth. In Hinduism it is the duality of the tendencies of *tamas* (downward moving and diffusive) and of *sattva* (upward moving and cohesive), or again, those of the *shudra* caste and of the Brahman (white, in general terms, being the colour of the priesthood). All the same, Shiva (*tamas*) is white, while Vishnu (*sattva*) is black, a contradiction which literary sources explain as the interdependence of opposites, and above all by the fact that the external manifestation of the principle of whiteness is seen as black – and vice versa – since it is reversed by its reflection in the 'mirror' of the waters.

Generally speaking, in Hindu, Chinese and Japanese symbolism, black is the colour of the universal substance (*prakrti*), of *materia prima*, of primordial formlessness, of Chaos at the beginning of time, of the lower waters, of the north and of death, as well as of the hermeticists' *nigredo* (although it may not always be the opposite of white but, for example in China, of red or of yellow). In this sense black indubitably has the aspect of darkness and impurity. Yet, conversely, it is a higher symbol of non-manifestation and of primordial 'virginity' and it is this sense which links it with the symbolism of medieval Black Madonnas, as well as with Kālī, black because she returns to the state of formlessness and of diffused shapes and colours. In the *Bhagavad Gītā*, it is apparently the immortal, Krishna, who is 'dark', while Arjuna, the mortal, is 'white'; cut-out figures of the Universal Self and the individual ego. Here, in any case, we are back to the symbolism of Vishnu and Shiva. The Hindu initiate sits upon a skin with black and white fur, a further symbol of manifestation and non-manifestation. From the same viewpoint, Guénon has observed the substantial symbolism of the 'black faces' of Ethiopians, the 'black heads' of Chaldeans and also of Chinese (*kien-cheu*), as well as the *Kemi*, or 'black earth', of the Egyptians, all these expressions undoubtedly containing a sense of the 'central and primordial', the manifestation which shines out from the centre being seen as 'white' as light itself.

For, in fact, the Chinese *hei* suggests both the colour black and sin and repentance, the face being ritually blackened as a sign of self-abasement to ask pardon for evil-doing. Similarly, *malkūt* is the second *hé* of the Tetragrammaton. A wretched outcast, the letter shrinks from its normal size until it becomes a tiny black dot suggestive of the letter *yod*, the smallest in the Hebrew alphabet.

Alchemical 'work' began with black, a death and return to formless chaos, leading on to the white and finally to the red of spiritual freedom. Taoist symbolic embryology drew the 'principle of humidity' from the blackness of the 'abyss' (*k'an*), to marry it to the 'principle of fire' to cause the 'Golden Flower' to blossom: the colour of gold is white (CHOO, DANA, ELIF, GRIF, GUEC, GUES, HERS, MAST).

Psychoanalysts would view black in dreams by day or night as well as in the sense perceptions of the waking state, as an absence of all light and colour. Black sucks in colour and does not return it. Above all, it suggests chaos, nothingness, night sky, night shadows on the ground, evil, anguish, sorrow, the unconscious and death.

However, black is also 'good ground' which receives the 'seed' which the Gospels tell us 'must die'. The soil of graveyards thus becomes the place where the dead rest until they are ready to rise again. For this reason the rites of Pluto, God of the Underworld, included the sacrifice of black animals wearing fillets in the same colour. Such sacrifice could only be celebrated in darkness and the victim's head had to be twisted towards the ground.

Black also evokes vast abysses and ocean depths, and this is the reason why black bulls were sacrificed to Poseidon (Neptune) in Classical antiquity.

In so far as black suggests nothingness and chaos, that is to say confusion and disorder, it is the darkness before time began which, in all religions, preceded creation itself. Genesis tells us that before light existed 'the earth was without form, and void: and darkness was upon the face of the deep' (1: 2). In Classical mythology, the primordial state of the world was Chaos. Chaos bore Night, who married her brother Erebus and bore him a son, Aether. Thus the light of creation – Aether – begins to pierce Chaos and Night. However, in the meantime Night had borne not only Sleep and Death, but all the miseries which afflict mankind – poverty, sickness, old age and so on. Yet despite the pains produced by darkness, the Greeks surnamed Night *Euphrone* or 'Mother of Good Counsel' and 'Night brings good counsel' is proverbial in many languages. This is because, in fact, it is the night which enables us to make headway by making use of the warnings given to us in dreams, as both the Bible (Job 33: 14–16) and the Koran (*sūra* 42) advise.

If black is associated with the idea of evil, that is to say with all which contradicts or delays the development of God's plans, it is because black suggests what the Hindus term Ignorance (Jung's 'shadow') or the devilish Serpent-Dragon of mythology, which must be vanquished within the individual to ensure his or her transformation, but which constantly betrays the individual. Thus – very occasionally – medieval artists depicted Judas, the Betrayer, with a black halo.

Black, as the colour of melancholy, pessimism, sorrow and misfortune, is applied in everyday language in such terms as *black magic*, *black books*, *blackmail*, *black market*, *black mass* and so on. The Romans distinguished unlucky days with a black stone and different disasters have stigmatized Mondays, Fridays and Saturdays as 'Black'.

Black as the colour of death is all too apparent in mourning clothes and in the vestments worn by the celebrant at masses for the dead or on Good Friday.

Lastly black is classed among the Devil's colours, its combination with red suggesting smoke and flame. Satan is called the Prince of Darkness and Jesus himself, when tempted by the Devil, is sometimes depicted in black, as though covered with the black veil of temptation.

In the doctrine of the universal soul, black stands for opacity, density and weight. Thus a load coloured black will seem heavier than one coloured white. Nevertheless it must be said that this gloomy list of associations with the colour black is not wholly negative. As well as being the image of death, earth, burial and the mystics' 'dark night of the soul', black is also connected with the promise of the renewal of life, just as darkness holds the promise of dawn and Winter of Spring. Furthermore, we know that in the majority of ancient mystery religions, the initiate had to undergo certain ordeals by night or experience rituals performed underground in darkness. Similarly today monks and nuns in enclosed orders are dead to the world.

Black is the equivalent of the Chinese *yin*, feminine, intuitive, earthy and maternal. As already observed, mother-goddesses such as Diana of Ephesus, the Hindu Kālī or Isis are depicted as black, while Black Madonnas have been venerated throughout Europe. A black stone symbolized the Magna Mater on the Palatine Hill, while at Mecca, the Ka'ba, emblem of the Anima Mundi, comprises a cube of black stone.

Along the same lines, the horseman of the Apocalypse who rides a black horse carries a pair of scales to weigh out, in time of dearth, the wheat, barley, oil and wine harvested from soil made fertile by Great Mother Earth.

The appearance in dreams of black animals, of Blacks or of people with dark complexions reveals that we are in touch with our own intuitive, primitive universe and that we have to enlighten and tame it and channel its forces towards higher aims.

black (pigmentation)   Clearly the symbolism of the Black varies according to time and place. The Renaissance Venetian and the Virginia planter will have a very different picture from that of a twentieth-century Léopold Sédar Senghor. Any comment refers only to an historical psychological attribute and to the residue it may have left in the Western subconscious.

The salient fact is that all value judgements must be excluded, leaving the bare bones of the interpretation. In the mental images of an age, the Black is associated with a primitive stage of human development when barbarity was triumphant, but loyalty, too; capricious blood-letting, but kindness as well; in other words, with a state in which opposites existed as a series of sudden changes, not balanced by a uniform state of tension. Jung considered 'black' to be the dark side of the personality and one of the first stages to be passed, while 'white' was the end to which perfection developed. In this he was in accord with the theories of the alchemists, for whom the 'Great Work' orginated from 'blackness'. 'Black' would thus mark the initial stage of evolutionary progress or, inversely, the final stage of a regression. The identification of the Black with Rousseau's or Bernardin de St-Pierre's 'noble savage', and the eighteenth-century fashion for Negro pages, are noteworthy. Their symbolism shares to some degree that of the DWARF and BUFFOON.

Another picture of the Black was vulgarized by the famous novel, *Uncle Tom's Cabin*, in which he becomes the symbol of the slave, ill-treated and tortured by pitiless owners who exploit him, but whom he forgives in the spirit of religion. It is unnecessary to emphasize the unconscious racism of such images, so patent are they to any observer.

Black Moon   See under MOON (PLANET).

Black Sun   See under SUN.

blacksmith   Of all the trades connected with METAL-working, that of black-smith is most significant in terms of both the weight and ambivalence of the symbols which are implicit in it. The smithy itself contains elements which are cosmogonic and creative as well as diabolical and destructive, and is also associated with rites of initiation.

The first 'blacksmith' was the Vedic *Bramanaspati*, who 'hammered out' or rather 'cast' the world, the work of his smithy being the creation of being from a state of non-being. Casting metal ('cast the universe and refashion it' equates with the alchemists' *solve et coagula*) is a basic concept of Taoism. 'Heaven and Earth are the great furnace, transformation the great metal-founder', Chuang Tzu wrote (ch. 6). The Montagnard tribes of southern Vietnam believe that the work of creation was a blacksmith's work. 'Bung took a small hammer and hammered out the Earth; then he took a short hammer and beat out the Sky. The Earth (*Tian*) married the Sky (*Tum*).' Humans, or at least their bones and joints, are sometimes hammered out. The primeval blacksmith, however, is not the creator, but his assistant, his instrument, the maker of the god's tools or the organizer of the created world. Thus Tvashtri forged Indra's weapon, the THUNDERBOLT, just as HEPHAISTOS (Vulcan) forged those of Zeus, Ptah those of Horus, the DWARFS Thor's hammer and the NIGHTJAR Könas's axe. The weapon, or cosmogonic tool, is most often LIGHTNING or the thunderbolt, symbols of celestial activity. Furthermore, the symbolism of the smithy is often linked with words or songs which introduce us not only to the part which the craft plays in rites of initiation, but also to the creative action of the Word.

Nevertheless, the blacksmith's symbolic share in the work of creation carries with it the serious danger of negation, of diabolic parody in forbidden activity. Furthermore, since metal is drawn from the bowels of the earth, the smithy relates to subterranean fire and smiths are sometimes monsters or identified with the guardians of buried treasure. They therefore embody an aspect which inspires fear and may rightly be termed 'infernal'. Their trade connects them with sorcery and magic and this is why they are often more or less excluded from society and why their labours are usually surrounded by ritual purification, sexual TABOOS and exorcisms.

On the other hand, in different civilizations the smith plays an important part as the revealer of heavenly secrets, the rain-maker and the healer of the sick. He is sometimes the chief's or the king's equal and understudies the organizer of the world – after all, Genghis Khan was supposed to have been a blacksmith once. However, this aspect of the craft is linked with the rites of initiation. The Chinese say that the smithy converses with Heaven. Control of fire summons rain, the marriage of fire and water which is the alchemists' 'Great Work'. When the Taoist poet Hi K'ang took up the work of the smithy – and, significantly, set it beneath a WILLOW-tree in the middle of the courtyard of his house – it was no leisure activity but a means of communicating with Heaven from the foot of the World Axis.

CAIN may have been the first blacksmith: Tubalcain undoubtedly was one. In Genesis 4: 22 he is called 'an instructer of every artificer in brass and iron'. His Chinese equivalent is the Yellow Emperor, Huang Ti, patron of smiths, alchemists and Taoists. His rival, Ch'e Yu, was himself a smith, but provoked disorder. Both aspects of the symbolism are here present and with them the earliest evidences of initiation societies. Ch'e Yu forges weapons, instruments of death and destruction: Huang Ti casts the three-legged copper cauldron which earns him immortality. On the other hand the forging of swords is itself a craft for the initiate and successful tempering of metal is a marriage of fire and water, *yin* and *yang*, a perfect recreation of primordial unity. Its exact equivalent is the alchemists' 'work', a marriage of being and breath, of the trigrams *li* and *k'an*, of mercury and sulphur, of Heaven and Earth. In fact it is a return to the innocence of Eden, the acquisition of immortality (DAMS, ELIF, GRAD, GUER, KALL, MAST, SILI).

Gobniu the smith plays his part in the Old Irish mythological tale, *The Battle of Moytura*. Helped by worker gods, he forges the weapons with which the Irish vanquish the Fomorians, a lower order of Underworld powers. While in no sense cast in an unfavourable light, he nevertheless remains a minor figure in the Celtic pantheon. Caesar does not mention him in his list of their five principal gods. As the gods' Brewer, he is also responsible for producing their beer (see FERMENTATION) (REVC 12: pp. 94–6).

In African cultures the smith bears a somewhat enigmatic character, standing as the central figure at the heart of the problems posed by these civilizations.

In the first place he is the craftsman who fashions the iron tools needed by both hunters and farmers: the working life of the tribe depends upon his activities.

Then he is the only person able to 'carve the statues of the ancestors and spirits who are the mainstays of their worship': he therefore plays a part in religious life.

He also has the social role of 'peace-maker and intermediary, not only between members of his tribe, but also between the worlds of the living and the dead'. He is sometimes associated with the Demiurge as the one who brought down knowledge of crops and crafts; he is the leader of initiation societies.

Because the smith is endowed with a semi-religious character, he arouses in others a degree of uncertainty and ambivalence towards him. He is at one and the same time despised and feared and reverenced, holding very different positions within the tribal hierarchy. He lives either at a distance from the village or in a specially reserved quarter, together with his wife, a potter, who makes the pipes for the bellows of his forge.

The art of iron-working is sometimes regarded as a royal or priestly secret. Smiths have been known to fill high political office, especially among the Tuareg whose chiefs choose smiths as their chief ministers.

In the Dogon cosmogony, the smith is one of the eight Nommo (spirits). He fractured his bones and his joints when he came crashing down to earth with the chest containing all crafts, all seeds and shoots and the ancestors of all human beings and animals. Hence he is often depicted as being lame (see LAMENESS) like Hephaistos in Greek and Roman mythology (LAUA pp. 121, 124, 126, 181).

All in all, the smith is regarded as the symbol of the Demiurge. However, while he may be able to forge the cosmos, he is not God. Endowed with superhuman power, he can use it against both gods and men and for this reason he inspires the same dread as a magus of the black arts. His powers are essentially ambivalent and can be just as maleficent as they are beneficent. Hence he inspires everywhere a reverential dread.

blessing Blessing symbolizes a transfer of power. To bless really means to sanctify, to make holy through the WORD, that is to say, to approach holiness, the highest form of cosmic energy.

blindfold When placed over the eyes it symbolizes BLINDNESS. Themis, Goddess of Justice, wears a blindfold to show that she favours none and knows neither party whom she judges. Similarly Eros: to show that LOVE strikes blindly.

The Goddess of Fortune is also blindfold, since wealth is distributed by chance.

In the Middle Ages the emblematic figure of the Synagogue was blindfold to symbolize its blindness.

In esoteric tradition, to be blindfold has the sense of inner withdrawal and contemplation. Eyes are shut, closed to greed and idle curiosity.

The linen blindfold worn by nuns symbolizes that blindness to the vanities of this world which they ought to feel and, more positively, an attitude of meditation and spiritual contemplation.

The symbolism of the blindfold used in Masonic ritual is so obvious that it is barely worth mentioning. The eyes of the initiate are covered by the outside world, and once this blindfold is removed it symbolizes the acquisition of light or spiritual illumination. Sons of Masons are blindfold with a translucent material since they do not come straight from outer darkness, but from an environment which has received flashes of the knowledge of the initiated (BOUM).

blindness (see also CYCLOPS) For some, blindness means ignorance of the real state of things, denial of the obvious and hence madness, stupidity and irresponsibility. To others, the blind are those who ignore the deceitful shows of this world, and thanks to this are privileged to know its secret reality, too deeply buried to be discerned by ordinary humanity. The blind share the godhead, they are inspired: poets, wonder-workers, 'seers'. Such, in short, are the two aspects, blessed and cursed, positive and negative, of the symbolism of blindness; and all traditions, myths and customs waver between them. This means that blindness, which is often a punishment of the gods, bears some relation to the ordeals of initiation (see also BLIND-FOLD). Similarly folklore is full of blind musicians, bards and singers treated as inspired beings.

This is no doubt the reason why sculptors portrayed Homer as a blind man and tradition made blindness the symbol of the wandering poet, the rhapsodist, bard, trouvère and troubadour. Yet here again we keep within the bounds of allegory. Old men are also depicted as blind: in their case blindness symbolizes the wisdom of old age. Prophets are usually blind as well, as if their eyes needed to be closed to physical light for them to perceive the light of the godhead. Their blindness was sometimes a punishment inflicted by the gods, when these seers had abused their gift of clairvoyance to gaze upon goddesses in their nakedness or otherwise to offend the immortals, or else to reveal the secrets of the arcane. Tiresias was blinded by Athene for watching her bathing. OEDIPUS tore out his eyes of his own accord in expiation of his twofold crime. Tobit became blind while asleep, but had his sight restored when his son Tobias, instructed by the Archangel Raphael, applied the gall of a fish to his eyelids. Samson offended Jehovah and was blinded, and so on. The gods blinded or drove mad those whom they wished to destroy or – sometimes – to save. However, when it was the gods' pleasure to restore sight to the guilty, they became Masters of Light. This most notably is the meaning of the miracles in which Jesus restored sight to the blind. Such miracles were attributed to Indra, Athene and others.

The Celts generally considered that blindness debarred a candidate from the priesthood or the ranks of the seers. However, by reverse initiation, a number of mythological Irish characters endowed with clairvoyance were blind. When their sight was restored they lost the gift of prophecy (OGAC 13: pp. 331ff.). Perhaps inner vision is only permitted or granted if the sight of fleeting external things is renounced. Hindu ascetics believe they can obtain spiritual insight by staring into the burning glare of the sun until they lose their sight. The blind man evokes the image of someone who 'sees' something from another world with other eyes. He is regarded less as handicapped than as from a different world.

blood (see also FIRE; GREEN; RED)   Blood symbolizes all the integral qualities of fire and the heat and vitality inherent in the SUN. With these qualities is linked all that is lovely, noble, generous and high-minded. Blood also shares some of the symbolism of the colour red.

Blood is universally held to be the medium of life and is sometimes taken for the principle of procreation. According to Chaldean traditions it was the blood of the godhead mingled with earth that brought beings to life. In many myths, blood gives birth to flowers (ANEMONE) and even to metals. In Ancient Cambodia, blood spilled in jousting or sacrifice was believed to bring fertility, plenty and good fortune: it was also the presage of rain. The arrows which Chu Sin shot at the celestial WATER-SKIN, made it rain blood. The blood – mingled with water – which flowed from Christ's wounds was collected in the Holy Grail and became the 'draught of immortality' *par excellence*. This is so *a fortiori* in the Christian dogma of transubstantiation. Use of symbolism of the same order should be noted in the oaths of BLOOD-BROTHERHOOD in antiquity and in Chinese secret societies.

Blood also corresponds to vital and bodily heat, as opposed to light, which corresponds to breath and spirit. Hence blood, as the corporeal principle, is the channel of the passions (CADV, ELIF, GUEM, GUES, PORA, SAIR).

Some peoples consider blood to be the medium of the soul, which, according to Fraser, is why in ritual sacrifice great care is taken to prevent the blood of the victim from spilling on the ground (Solomon Islands rites described in FRAG 1: p. 358). In New Zealand any object which receives the minutest drop of a high chief's blood is endowed with a sacred character by that fact. This is another instance of the symbolism of communion in blood or the bond of enfeoffment through a blood-oath.

Some of the myths of the Uralo-Altaic peoples of central Asia relating to the end of the world give a striking instance of the association of celestial blood and fire. In one of these myths (of the Yurak from the Obdorsk area) the world ends in fire because a sacred tree dies and, as it falls, spills its blood which changes into fire as it flows over the ground. The Tatars of the Altai believe that a hero sent from God Almighty to fight the Devil will spill his blood over all the Earth and that this blood will change into fire. In a ninth-century German poem and in a Russian *Revelation* of the Pseudo-Methodius, it is the blood of Elijah, shed in his battle with Anti-Christ, which turns to fire and swallows up the world (HARA pp. 99–100).

blood-brotherhood BLOOD being the medium of life and its generative ingredient, a 'blood-oath' is a ritual covenant which produces actual consanguinity. It comprises the drawing of some drops of blood from the limbs of each of the sworn brothers, which is then given to them to drink. Such a rite was practised by some eastern European guilds and, it is alleged, by the Knights Templar. It was, however, particularly prevalent in the Far East. *The Book of Lieh Tzu* (ch. 5) places such a ceremony in the remote past. It bound together in the Peach Orchard the celebrated heroes of the Three Kingdoms, Lieu Pi, Kuan Yu and Chang Fei, and provided the pattern for Chinese secret societies, whose members practise an identical ritual to this day. Until a comparatively recent period the blood-oath was deeply respected in Vietnam, particularly by the Pham Môn, a breakaway sect from Caodaism. It existed in Cambodia during the Angkor period and is still practised by the Montagnard tribes in northern and southern Vietnam. It is clearly an oath of the Kshatriyas, the warrior caste. As we have said, it makes brotherhood effective in a very real sense. Among secret societies, blood mixed with WINE became the draught of immortality and a symbol of knowledge; drinking from the same cup simultaneously established an indissoluble covenant and imparted longevity. 'The brethren drank the blood of the Hong mingled with wine: they will reach the age of one hundred and ninety-nine.' It should be added that in Chinese marriages bride and groom still exchange blood, obviously with the same intention.

Another covenant in the shedding of blood may be found in Exodus 24: 5–8 (CADV, GRAD, GRIL).

In Ireland the normal form which an oath took was *tongu do dia toinges mo thuath* ('I swear by the gods by whom my tribe swears') and there are countless examples of its use. However, the only god to sponsor oaths was the Dagda, god of friendship and alliances, according to the author of *The Courtship of Etain*. The elements would intervene as sureties on behalf of whoever called upon them to punish perjury. The High King Loegaire entered Leinster at the head of an army to collect a tax which he had sworn he would repeal and was duly punished by the elements which he had taken as sureties for his oath. He died between two mountains, victim of the Sun, the wind and all the other natural elements. Conchobar, King of Ulster, swore by Earth, sky and sea. When the Gauls signed their treaty with Alexander the Great in the fourth century BC and swore to observe it, they, too, called upon Earth, sky and sea as witnesses.

Inherently an oath is a covenant with the cosmos, to which the oath-maker turns as surety for his word. When he pledges his word he enrols it in an order of things which is greater than he and he takes responsibility for breaking up that order if his word is broken. Upon him will fall the punishment due for such a crime. An oath may be seen as the symbol of an accord with whatever being, divine, cosmic or human, who has been invoked as surety.

blot(ch) The Swiss psychiatrist Rorschach designed a famous projective test using blots of black or coloured inks. The blots themselves were shape-less; their significance proceeded from the interpretations placed upon them by patients when questioned, the latter projecting their own personalities into what the blots suggested to them. Their symbolic quality varied as widely as the character, cultural level, obsessions, idiosyncracies and so on of the patient concerned. What he or she says they see is the symbol. The blot itself merely plays the part of an inductor of symbols. The same role could be played by clouds, puddles in the roadway, patterns on a wall, damp-stains.

Over and above the part it plays as an inductor, which makes it highly multivalent in symbols, the blot is itself the symbol of something abnormal, shameful and irregular when it occurs on human skin. By its very nature such a blotch is something monstrous and unnatural. Whether it be caused by the ageing process which causes decay, or is the result of an accident, the blotch is a sign of the contingency of being, whose perfection, if ever attained, is only fleeting. The blotch is the mark of weakness and death and pro-claims that all things pass away like smoke.

blue Blue is the deepest colour; unimpeded, the gaze plumbs infinity, the colour forever escaping it. Blue is the most insubstantial of colours; it seldom occurs in the natural world except as a translucency, that is to say as an accumulation of emptiness, the void of the Heavens, of the depths of the sea, of crystal or diamond. Emptiness is austere, pure and frosty. Blue is the coldest of colours and, in its absolute quality, the purest, apart from the total void of matt WHITE. From these fundamental qualities blue's symbolic applications derive.

Apply the colour blue to an object and it will reduce, cut open and destroy its shape. Paint the surface of a wall blue and it is no longer a wall. Movement and sound, like shapes, disappear into blue, sink and vanish like a bird in the sky. Insubstantial in itself, blue disembodies whatever becomes caught in it. It is the road to infinity on which the real is changed to the imaginary. It is, after all, the colour of the bird of happiness, that blue bird which is always so near and yet so far. To penetrate the blue is rather like Alice passing to the other side of the looking-glass. Light blue is the colour of meditation and, as it darkens naturally, it becomes the colour of dreams.

Conscious thought yields little by little to the unconscious, just as the light of day gradually becomes the light of night, midnight blue.

The realm, or rather climate, of the unreal – or of the surreal – blue stands still and resolves within itself those contradictions and alternations of fortune – day following night – which modulate human life. Indifferent and unafraid, centred solely upon itself, blue is not of this world: it evokes the idea of eternity, calm, lofty, superhuman, inhuman even. To a painter like Kandinsky, its movement is at one and the same time one which distances itself from mankind, a movement directed solely towards its own centre but one which, nevertheless, draws the individual towards the infinite and awakens a yearning for purity and a hunger for what surpasses nature. Its substantial metaphysical significance can be appreciated, as well as the limitations on its clinical use. Blue surroundings calm and soothe but, unlike GREEN, they do not stimulate, since they provide merely an escape from the real world, an escape which in the long run may lead to depression. According to Kandinsky the depth of green provides a feeling of earthy restfulness and self-content, while blue has a solemn supraterrestrial gravity. This gravity evokes the idea of death. The walls of Ancient Egyptian tombs, on which painted scenes of the weighing of souls stood out in ochre, were generally given a sky-blue background. The Egyptians are also supposed to have considered blue to be the colour of truth. Truth, death and gods go together and this is why sky-blue is the threshold which separates mankind from its rulers, from the Beyond, from Fate.

Juxtaposed with RED or YELLOW ochre, blue displays the sacred marriage or rivalry of Heaven and Earth. With nothing to break the flat monotony of the steppes of central Asia, earth and sky have lain face to face since time began and their marriage has preluded the birth of every hero of the steppes. The legend is still current that Genghis Khan, who founded the great Mongol dynasty, was born of the coupling of a blue WOLF with a yellow doe. The blue wolf is none other than Er Töshtük, the hero of Kirghizian courtly verse, clad in blue steel and bearing a blue shield and a blue lance (BORA). Mongolo-Turkic literature is full of blue lions and tigers and these are the manifestations of the power of Tangri, 'Father' of the Altaic tribes who is throned above the mountains and the sky and who became Allah when the Turks were converted to Islam.

In the war between Earth and Heaven, blue and white were allied against red and green as Christian iconography corroborates, especially in depictions of St George and the dragon. At Byzantium the four factions which confronted each other at the chariot races in the Hippodrome were the Reds and Greens on one side and the Whites and Blues on the other. There is every reason to believe that these games in New Rome were invested with as great a religious and cosmic significance as the games of hand-ball celebrated during the same period in Central America. Both staged a sacred drama which symbolized the rivalry of the immanent and the transcendent, of Heaven and Earth. French history provides real and bloody battles between opposing sides who still wore the same emblematic colours in the name of the Divine Right of Kings and the Rights of Man which they claimed to embody. The royalist Chouans wore blue and the Revolutionaries red, and these are still the colours of party politics throughout the world.

Blue and white, the colours of Our Lady, express a detachment from the things of this world and the flight of the liberated soul towards God, that is to say towards the GOLD which comes to meet the virginal white as it ascends into the blue of Heaven. Belief in the hereafter gives positive validity to the associations of blue and white with children's funerals. Under the age of puberty they are not yet fully developed human beings in the sense of not being fully developed sexually and are not fully of this world for that reason. Hence they more readily answer the blue call of Our Lady.

Then the zodiacal sign of Virgo corresponds to harvest time when the evolution of Spring has given way to the involution of autumn. Like the colour blue, Virgo is a centripetal sign and it will strip the Earth of its cloak of greenery, bare it and dry it up. When the time comes round for the Feast of the Assumption of the Virgin Mary (15 August) to be celebrated under a cloudless sky, the golden Sun will turn to an unquenchable fire to devour the ripened fruits of the Earth. To the Aztec mind, this azure was TUR-QUOISE blue, the colour of the Sun, which they named 'Prince of the Turquoise' (Chalchihuitl). It was the sign of drought, famine and death, yet Chalchihuitl was also the blue-green stone, the turquoise, which ornamented the skirts of the goddess of rebirth. When an Aztec prince died, one of these stones replaced his heart before his body was cremated, just as in Egypt, before mummification, the dead Pharaoh's heart was replaced by a scarab beetle carved from EMERALD. In some parts of Poland the custom of painting the houses of brides-to-be blue still survives.

In Hindu tradition, the southern face of Mount Meru is of SAPPHIRE and, when it reflects the light, it tinges the atmosphere with blue. In Jewish tradition, Luz (see ALMOND- TREE), the home of the immortals, is also called the 'Blue City'.

For Tibetan Buddhists, blue is the colour of *vairocana* (transcendent wisdom) and of potentiality, and at the same time of emptiness, for which the vastness of the blue sky is perhaps an image. The blue light of the *dharmadhātu* (law or primordial conscience) is of dazzling strength, but it is what opens the way of liberation.

Blue is the colour of the *yang* (see YIN AND YANG) and of the geomantic dragon, and hence is beneficent. *Huan* (blue), the colour of the darkling distant sky, suggests, as previously noted, the realm of the Immortals, but also, if interpreted in accordance with the *Tao Te Ching* (ch. 1), the non-manifested. The original pictogram would relate to the unreeling of the thread of a double cocoon, reminiscent of the symbolism of the SPIRAL.

There is no specific word in Celtic languages for blue (*glas* in Breton, Welsh and Irish Gaelic means 'blue' or 'green' or even 'grey', according to context), and when a distinction is essential, alternatives or synonyms are used. In social systems blue is the colour of the worker–producer function; however, in Middle Irish and Welsh literature it no longer seems to have possessed functional qualities comparable with those of white and red. Caesar, nevertheless, records the phenomenon of Breton women stripping themselves naked and painting their bodies blue for certain religious ceremonies. An Irish mythical ancestor, *Goedel Glas* ('Goidel the Blue') was the inventor of the Gaelic language (on a par with Hebrew) (OGAC 7: pp. 193–4).

boar The symbolism of the boar is of great antiquity. It is found throughout most of the Indo-European world and, in some aspects, beyond it as well. The myth is part of the HYPERBOREAN tradition in which the boar represents spiritual authority. This may arise because, like the druid and the Brahman, the boar retires to a solitary life in the forest, or because it has the faculty of uprooting the TRUFFLE, that mysterious fungus which according to ancient legends was produced by lightning, or, lastly, because the boar feeds upon acorns, fruit of a sacred tree, the OAK. The BEAR stands in opposition to the boar as a symbol of temporal power. In Gaul and in Greece, the boar was hunted and killed, emblem of the spiritual hounded down by the temporal.

In China, too, the boar was the emblem of the Miao, the bear of the Hia. The Miao belong to a very ancient version of Chinese folklore. The boar is taken, or driven, away by a warrior, Yi the Archer. Herakles (Hercules) takes the Erymanthian boar; Meleager, helped by Theseus and Atalanta, hunts the Calydonian boar. Here, quite clearly, is a species of cyclical symbolism, one reign giving place to another, one *kalpa* to the next. Hindus classify the present cycle as that of the 'White Boar'.

The boar is endowed with 'Hyperborean', and hence with primordial, characteristics. It represents the avatar (incarnation) in which Vishnu raised the Earth to the surface of the waters and set it in order. Vishnu, again, takes the shape of a boar (*Varāha*) rooting in the earth to find the foot of the column of fire, which is no less than Shiva's lingam, while *hamsa-Brahmā* seeks its tip in the sky. Thus the Earth was generally seen as the attribute of Varāha (Vishnu), under whose hand or protection it could well be regarded as a primitive Holy Land.

Another aspect is apparent in Japan where the wild pig or boar, Inonshishi, is the last of the animals of the Zodiac. Emblematic of courage and even of rashness, a boar is used as their steed by the war-*kami* (deities). Small statues of boars stand outside Shintō shrines dedicated to Wakenokiyomaro. The war-god himself, Usa-hachiman, is sometimes depicted on a boar.

Although the boar is set at the hub of the Buddhist Wheel of Existence, it is in the shape of a black animal, the symbol of ignorance and of the passions. It is sometimes called a PIG and it is under this designation that its negative symbolism should be regarded for, just as the boar is the symbol of all that is noble, so the pig is the symbol of all that is base. The wild pig symbolizes unrestrained debauchery and brutality (BHAB, DANA, GOVM, GRAD, GUES, MALA, OGRJ, PALL, VARG).

The 'Diamond SOW' plays an important part in the *Vajrayāna*. It is an attribute of that *Vajra varahi* (Dordje Phagmo) which manifests a female aspect of the Awakening. She is frequently depicted coloured scarlet and with a tiny sow's head, like a growth, over her right ear. This deity is associated with the cycle of Hevajra, whose co-adjutator she may be, as well as with that of Samvara, and should be likened to a realization of EMPTINESS and to the delicate central channel (*sushumma*) into which respirations are collected in order to liberate Joy.

The boar was a common motif on Gaulish battle standards, especially on those carved on the triumphal arch at Orange (France) and upon Gaulish coins. There are many examples of boars in votive bronzes or relief carvings

in stone. Nevertheless the animal has nothing to do with the warrior caste
except as the symbol of the priestly caste to which it stood in opposition.
Like the druid, the boar was closely connected with the forest, feeding on
acorns, while the wild sow, symbolically surrounded by her nine piglets,
rooted in the ground at the foot of the apple, the tree of immortality.
Since the Celts' herds of pigs lived more or less in the wild, the pig and the
wild boar were often undifferentiated, and since the boar was the animal
dedicated to Lug, pork was the sacrificial food at the festival of Samain
(1 November). A number of legends tell of the feasts in the Otherworld at
which there is a magic pig, always perfectly cooked and never growing less.
Mercury is given the surname, *Moccus*, ('pig') in a Gallo-Roman inscription
from Langres (France). The *Twrch Trwyth* (Irish: *triath*, 'king') with which
Arthur did battle symbolizes the power of the priesthood in conflict with
that of the king at a time of spiritual decline. Lug's father, Cian, changed
himself into a 'druidic pig' to escape his pursuers. However, he died in his
human shape.

Nowhere in Irish literature, not even when under Christian influence, is
the boar anything but a symbol of good. Here the Celtic world stands in
sharp contrast with the tendency of the rest of Christendom. Here the boar
symbolizes the Devil – whether one equates it with swinish lust and gluttony or with its rashness (comparable with the storm of passion), or again
with the devastation which it causes by its headlong rush through crops,
orchards and vineyards. By the association of ideas, however, one is reminded of the instance when Dürer replaces the ox and ass of the Christmas crib with a lion and a boar. (CHAB pp. 173–5; OGAC 5: pp. 309–12;
MABG pp. 130ff.; STOG p. 34)

boat (see also SHIP)   The boat is the symbol of VOYAGING, or of a crossing
made either by the living or by the dead.

Aside from the custom of exposing the dead in canoes, there are in Indonesia,
and also, in part, in Melanesia, three important categories of magico-religious
practice that involve the use (real or imaginary) of a ritual boat: (1) the boat for
the expulsion of demons and sicknesses; (2) the boat in which the Indonesian
shaman 'travels through the air' in search of the patient's soul; (3) the 'boat of
the spirits', which carries the souls of the dead to the beyond.

(ELIC p. 356)

All civilizations have their boat of the dead. The belief that the dead
accompany the Sun in 'boats of the sun' is widespread throughout Oceania
(Frobenius, quoted in ELIT p. 137).

In Irish epic literature there is very little mention of boats as such, but in
mythological literature they are the symbols and the means of reaching the
Otherworld (OGAC 16: pp. 231ff.).

In Ancient Egyptian art and literature the dead were described as sailing
through the twelve regions of the Underworld in a sacred boat. It sails
through dangers by the thousand, serpents, demons and evil spirits with
long knives. As in the case of the weighing of the soul (see SCALES), its
depiction contains constant hierarchical, ritual elements, enriched by occasional variations. In the centre of the picture the solar boat rides on the
waves. Amidships stands the Sun-god, Ra, the dead person kneeling in

worship before him. At bow and stern Isis and Nephthys raise their left arms as if to point the way, while their right hands hold the *crux ansata*, the ANKH, symbol of the eternal life which awaits the voyager. On the far left of the picture, the JACKAL-headed god, Anubis, 'guide along the roads', follows the dead person as he makes for the boat bearing his own entrails in an urn.

Like the spinal column, the entrails were endowed with a particularly sacred character. They had a magic power and without it the dead person could not retain his personality or his consciousness . . . . Therefore every dead person had to be especially upon the alert in case they were stolen by one of those evil spirits which swarmed in the Beyond and were always on the hunt for magic power.

(CHAM p. 52)

At all events they haunted the waterways of the Underworld along which the boat sailed towards the dead person's final home in brightness and light – unless, that is, it was shipwrecked on the way. Sometimes the sole crew of the boat was a pig. This was the Devourer, waiting to take the damned to a hell of lamentation, ruled by cruelly taloned torturers.

Sometimes the boat was towed along the bank by a long rope which took the shape of 'a live serpent, symbol of the god who chased the enemies of light from before the face of Ra' (CHAM p. 70). At other times the serpent Apophis, the awesome incarnation of Set, was to be seen in the water attempting to capsize the boat. Apophis, dragon-like, breathed fire and raised the waves in an endeavour to snatch the dead person's terror-stricken soul. If the boat withstood these attacks, having avoided rocks, hell-gates and monsters with gaping jaws, it would sail out into the light of the rising Sun, before Khepri, the golden SCARAB beetle, and the justified soul would enjoy the bliss of eternal life. Sometimes the scarab would be standing in the boat bearing the Sun in its pincers like the promise of immortality. One may imagine how this prodigal wealth of imagery can lend itself as easily as Greek mythology to psychoanalysis, premissed upon the underground voyage of the solar boat being an exploration of the unconscious. At the end of the voyage the justified soul can sing: 'The bonds are loosened. I have thrown down all the evil which was upon me. O mighty Osiris, I am born again! Behold me, I am born again!' (quoted by CHAM p. 156).

Bachelard looks upon the boat which bears the soul to this rebirth as 'a rediscovery of the cradle'. It suggests similarities with the bosom and the womb. The 'first' boat was perhaps the coffin. 'If Death were the first sailor . . . the coffin, according to such a mythological hypothesis, would not be the last boat. It would be the first boat. Death would not be the last voyage. It would be the first voyage. For some deep dreamers it would be the first true voyage' (BACE p. 100).

However, Bachelard observes, the boat of the dead arouses the awareness of sin, just as shipwreck suggests the idea of punishment: 'Charon's boat always steers towards Hell. Nobody pilots the boat of happiness. Thus Charon's boat has become a symbol which will remain firmly connected with the immutable misfortune of mankind' (BACE p. 108).

If this present life is viewed as a dangerous voyage, then the boat presents a symbol of security. Amida is generally depicted by Japanese artists with a boat-shaped halo, to remind the faithful that he is a ferryman and that his compassion will carry them over the ocean of misery which is life in this world and attachment to this life. This Buddhist personage, perhaps, 'pilots the boat of happiness'.

In Christian tradition the Church is the boat in which the faithful embark to overcome the perils of this world and the storms of the passions. In this context Noah's ARK springs to mind as the prefiguration of the Church. 'It is pleasant', Pascal was to say, 'to be aboard a storm-tossed vessel in the knowledge that she will not sink.'

Bodhisattva A Sanskrit word (Tibetan: *Diang tchoub sempa*) meaning 'an enlightened being who acts bravely'. The Bodhisattva is the ideal being who, through compassion to humankind, will become an adept of the *Mahāyāna* (Great Vehicle) as well as of the *Vajrayāna* (Diamond Vehicle). As distinguished from the *arhat* (saint) who achieves deliverance through personal asceticism without thought of others, the Bodhisattva who has mastered his own ego devotes his enlightenment to the good of his fellows. On the threshold of NIRVANA, his deep wisdom and infinite compassion forbid him to renounce the world into which he will be reborn. 'Although his enlightenment delivers him from SAMSARA, he manifests it continuously for the good of all beings' (KALE). Chenrezi (Avalokitesvara), ever shining with light and compassion, is the typical Bodhisattva. The practice of reciting his mantra, *Om mani padme hum*, 'transforms all impure appearances sounds and thoughts into the pure aspects which correspond to them' (Kalu Rimpoche). *Thankas* (Tibetan painted fabrics) often depict the Bodhisattva of Compassion, Chenrezi, rising from a lunar disk on a white LOTUS and irradiating his fivefold ray of light. He has four arms: one pair of hands is clasped, the other holds a crystal rosary and a white lotus. His head is crowned by Eupame (Amitābha), the Buddha of Infinite Light. Chenrezi is often depicted with a thousand arms ready to help the countless beings who are in distress. In the palm of each hand is the open eye of wisdom. His eleven faces derive from one of his meditations upon human suffering. Its intensity, coupled with the immensity of his task, split his head open. Amitābha formed it anew with ten other heads so that he could carry out his work in all directions, adding his own head, orange-tinted, above the rest. The dark blue face below it bears a savagely angry expression, showing the violence the Bodhisattva sometimes employs against the forces of evil (KALE).

There is also a female Bodhisattva, Kurukulla, originating from western India, where a mountain bears her name. She is identified with Venus as the protector of lovers and as the goddess of submission. The *Tara* of the *Vajrayāna* is one of her peaceful manifestations. Her name means 'she who permits transition', like the morning star crossing the heavens to become the evening star which watches over the fate of mankind and allows humans to pass through the darkness. This female Bodhisattva of the *Vajrayāna*, known also as 'the Great Deliverer', does not represent an external being but an aspect of the transmuted ego. Like most of the deities of Tibetan Tantric Buddhism, she symbolizes a victory over the ego, that is to say over the inner turmoil which prompts the use of energy for selfish ends. The female personification of wisdom, she holds Amitābha, the Buddha of Infinite Light, in her close embrace while he, with a fearless gesture, blesses all beings.

Although the *Taras* present the appearance of peacefulness, Kurukulla is an angry, scarlet goddess, miraculous emanation of Emptiness, who dances upon the corpses of the dead, bends her bow, like Eros, and brandishes the war axe without which deliverance is impossible. She is pure energy, ringed in fire, which gains the heights of ecstasy in love. Her most fervent worshippers dispense her favours. 'Here aspirations towards deliverance are mingled with and overshadowed by magical and amorous designs' (TUCK).

bonds See CHAIN.

bone The symbolism of bones follows two main lines of development. In the first place the bones are the framework of the body and its essential and relatively permanent element. Second, bones contain marrow, as the shell contains the almond. In the first instance bones are the symbol of resoluteness, strength and virtue (St Martin). In this context it is worth quoting the 'bone of my bones' of Genesis 2: 23. Bones are the essential and somehow primordial element of the being. This is why the shell of the nut of immortality, the *luz* (see ALMOND) or the *che-li*, is very hard bone. Shamans meditating over skeletons are in some sense returning to a primordial state with the perishable parts of the body stripped bare. The use in India and Tibet of human bones for making sacred weapons and musical instruments is in no sense alien to ideas of asceticism, of surmounting the notions of life and death and of access to immortality.

If the *luz* – which is an almond – is depicted as a bone it is not simply because the revival of 'dried bones' suggests the glorious resurrection, but because it contains the seed of that resurrection as the bone contains marrow. As Rabelais so famously phrased it 'break the bone and suck the substancific marrow!' (ELIM, GUEM, SAIR).

The Bambara see the bones, comprising 'the most durable, not to say imperishable part of the human body, the inner frame of the visible exterior, as symbolizing the essential element, the essence of creation' (ZAHB). Yo, the First Spirit, who existed before the creation of the world, is 'the great creator of marrow in the bones'. The hub of the four points of the compass, from which the word of creation (Faro) spiralled out, is called 'the bone in the middle of the world' (DIEB).

SKULL-worship is probably a residue of this belief, which is still held by hunting tribes. Since the bones comprise the least perishable part of the body, they represent the physical manifestation of life and the continuance of the species.

Some peoples believed that the most important 'soul' was contained within the bones. Hence the reverence they had for them. The Mongolo-Turkic peoples of the Altai, and similarly the Finno-Ugrians, always honoured the bones of game, particularly of big game animals, putting their skeletons together again after eating their flesh and being scrupulously careful not to break a bone. The Lapps 'believe that if the bones of a bear are carefully preserved, the animal will come to life again and allow itself to be hunted and killed once more' (HARA pp. 303–4, quoting Wiklund). Travellers and ethnographers have reported from both Lapland and Siberia many instances of the 'funeral' of a bear or else of the display of its reconstructed skeleton, the funeral ceremonies being similar to those observed for humans.

After killing and butchering a bear, the Orok used to take all its bones into the forest and lay them out 'so that they looked like the animal when it was whole' (HARA p. 300). The Tungus used to lay out the skeletons of bears on platforms in the forest, facing west towards the land of the dead, just as they would do for a human. Over the years, in the taiga the honours rendered to the whole skeleton became reserved only for the creature's skull. 'Thus the Karaga hang the skull in a tree. They refrain from eating the brains to avoid breaking the bone.' The Sagay, Kalar, Karghinz, Tubalar, Telengit and Soyot perform similar ceremonies. The skull so exposed acquires magical properties: 'the Soyot believed that each passer-by who greeted the skull would be protected from all harm caused by other bears.' Uno Harva quotes evidence by Maak showing how a ritual concerned with the preservation of species – or indeed with life itself – can by an evolutionary process gradually become a preservative for the human species in the face of other animal species. Mounting animal heads as trophies illustrates this phenomenon. In fact, during his travels Maak had noted how when the Yakut and Tungus returned from a bear hunt, they would take the animal's bones into the forest to reconstruct its skeleton, with the exception of the skull. This they would hang 'near their encampment as a sign of victory.' Harva also quotes evidence from Lehtisalo that 'the forest Yurak set this skull in a shelter close to the track, but they collect the other bones to bury them or throw them into the water.'

Fishing and hunting customs confirm that the bones of the prey are honoured by returning them to the wild to assure the continuance of the species. Among the Lapps, 'the first fish to be caught are killed without a single bone being broken. That is to say the flesh is so skilfully removed that none is broken. These bones are then returned to the same lake or stretch of water from which the fish was taken' (Nippgen, quoted in ROUF p. 40). In her work on the hunting rituals of the Siberian peoples, Mme Lot-Falck states that bones are essential to an animal's resurrection. When bones are not returned to the wild, as in the case of the Lapp fishermen, they are burned. J. de Plan Carpin had already noted that 'when they kill animals for food, they do not break any of their bones, but burn them in the fire.' As J.-P. Roux observes, this describes a custom which ensured that the animal would go to Heaven, cleansed and, so to say, purified by the flames. Heaven being the primordial reservoir of life, the cycle of the animal's life remained unbroken. In the complex symbolism from which such customs derive may lie the origins of the myth of the PHOENIX, which to the Ancient Egyptians symbolized the soul. This fabulous bird was held to be reddish purple, the colour of the vital force, as its name shows. This is derived from 'Phoenician', the people who discovered the properties of purple dye.

Ancient Greece provides evidence of offering the gods the bones of sacrificial animals covered in their fat. These bones were then burned upon the altar so that the animal could ascend to Heaven where it would be reborn (see Hesiod *Theogony* 555–60).

Among the myths which Bley collected in New Britain at the beginning of this century, are those which tell of heroes restored to life after their bones had been laid together, covered with leaves (generally banana leaves) and magic passes made over them (BLES pp. 424, 425, 429).

There was a belief among the hunters of the Caucasus that any game they caught had previously been killed and eaten at the court of Adagwa the Deaf, god of the chase. It was said that after their meal the god, his children and his servants would put the bones of the animals which they had eaten back into their skins to bring them to life so that in their turn they might become the food of men. If one of the bones was broken, it would be replaced by a twig (DIRK, from the Georgian journal *Krebuli*: 1898–9). Germanic mythology displays the same reverence for bones as receptacles of the life force. The god Thor, as the guest of a peasant, killed, skinned and boiled his goats. However, before the meal, he told his host's sons to place the bones in the animals' skins lying near the fire-side. The next morning he took his hammer, blessed the skins and the goats were restored to life. One of the animals, however, was lame through the fault of one of the peasant's sons, who had cracked a thighbone to suck the marrow. Thor became furiously angry and carried off his host's children in punishment for their disobedience (MANG p. 212).

book That the book is the symbol of knowledge and wisdom is true, but commonplace. On a higher level, books are symbols of the universe. 'The Universe is one vast book', wrote Mohyddin ibn-Arabī. Rosicrucianism also employs the phrase *Liber Mundi*. However, the 'Book of Life' in the Book of Revelation is set in the midst of Paradise and may be identified with the Tree of Life. The leaves of the tree, like the letters in the book, represent not only the totality of all created beings but also the totality of God's decrees.

The Romans consulted the *Sibylline Books* in time of crisis in the hope of finding a divine answer to their problems. In Ancient Egypt, the *Book of the Dead* was a collection of sacred charms buried with the dead in their tombs, to provide them with the correct replies when called to judgement and to guard them on their journey through the Underworld and bring them safely to the light of the eternal Sun – 'The Chapters of Going Forth by Day'. In all these instances books were regarded as symbols of the divine secret which is only to be revealed to the initiate.

The universe may be a book, but the book is revelation and hence, by extension, manifestation. The *Liber Mundi* is, at the same time, both the divine message and the archetype of various books of revelation which merely define and translate it into intelligible language. Islamic mystics sometimes draw a distinction between a 'macrocosmic' and a 'microcosmic' aspect of books and draw up lists of correspondences between them. The first aspect is, in fact, the *Liber Mundi*, the manifestation which stems from its principle, cosmic intelligence. The second is individual intelligence, residing in the heart.

In some versions of *The Quest of the Holy Grail*, the book is identified with the CHALICE. The symbolism is unmistakable. The quest for the Grail is the search for the 'Missing Word', highest wisdom which has become inaccessible to common humanity (CORT, GUEM, GUEC, GUES, SCHC).

A closed book symbolizes virgin matter; when it is open, the matter has been fertilized. Closed, the book keeps its secret. Open, its contents may be understood by whoever reads it. Thus the heart may be compared with a book: open, it exposes its thoughts and feelings; closed, it hides them.

For alchemists (see ALCHEMY),

'the work' was expressed symbolically by a book. Sometimes it was open, sometimes closed, according to whether [the primary matter] had been worked or only extracted from the mine. Sometimes when the book is closed – showing that the matter is in its raw mineral state – it is not unusual to see it sealed with seven ties. These are the emblems of the seven successive operations required to open it, each one breaking one of the seals which lock the book. Such is the Great Book of Nature, whose leaves contain revelations of the secrets of profane knowledge and sacred mysteries.

(FULC p. 193)

bosom   See BREAST.

bottle   'What does it matter what shape the bottle is, so long as we can get drunk.' Once again common sense unerringly puts its finger upon what gives the symbol its peculiar character. The quality of the bottle is metonymic and resides in what it contains, fleeting but valuable though it may be, and which the bottle or flask alone can hold because, unlike all other vessels, it is hermetically sealed. Hence bottles reveal what is secret or – its mirror image – what is sacred. They hold elixirs and philtres, whether elixirs of long life or, in more down-to-earth terms, brandy. Both are as intoxicating as esoteric knowledge. These are two levels of the same symbol which, as so many legends and stories bear witness, also makes of bottles prisons for 'spirits'. These are evil or otherwise, depending upon the light in which they are regarded. After all, Lesage's mischievous and clairvoyant 'Devil on Sticks' came out of a bottle, just like any drunkard's mumblings.

The symbolism of bottles may alter with their shape and contents, and these are innumerable. However, basically bottles 'come from the ARK and carry an olive-branch'. They symbolize knowledge, and knowledge which brings peace and salvation. The SHIP and ark are vessels of secret knowledge and revelations of things to come. The poet Alfred de Vigny used the bottle thrown into the sea from a sinking ship as the symbol of human knowledge, exposed to all the storms of life but containing the riches of a divine elixir, worth infinitely more than all the gold, diamonds and pearls in the world.

bough   See BRANCH; GOLDEN BOUGH.

bow   Archery is a classic example of a ternary structure, as much in the elements involved – bow, bow-string and arrow – as in the successive stages which it displays: tension, relaxation and ejaculation. That is to say that the sexual symbolism in this instance shows particularly clearly how indissoluble its links are with war and the chase. In rigidly hierarchical societies the symbolism of the bow embraces both the act of procreation and the search for perfection. This is evident from its role in the life of the warrior, mainly in the Japanese tradition, as well as in spiritual life; Shiva's bow, like that of the zodiacal Archer (SAGITTARIUS), displays the way of the sublimation of desire. From the arousal of the libido to the search for sanctity, primordial energy and psychic energy – which Indian tradition locates respectively in the sacrum (first CHAKRA) and at the top of the skull (seventh *chakra*) – may be seen united in the same symbol.

Archery is at one and the same time the office of the king and the hunter and a spiritual exercise. The bow is universally the weapon of royalty and also of the warrior, the *Kshatriya*; hence it is associated with initiation into that caste. The bow constantly recurs in the imagery of the Purānas, where it is expressly the emblem of kingship. It is Arjuna's weapon, and the battles of the *Bhagavad Gītā* are battles between bowmen. Archery is one of the essential disciplines of Japanese *Bushido*. Together with chariot driving, it is chief among the Chinese liberal arts, since it proves the worth of a prince and makes manifest his virtues. The warrior whose heart is pure will immediately hit the bull. His ARROW is fated to strike the enemy and bring down the emblematic beast. The second of these actions is designed to bring order to the world, the first to destroy the ill-omened powers of darkness. This is why the bow – and particularly the bow of peach-wood and arrows of WORMWOOD or thorn – is a weapon of war. It is also an instrument of exorcism, expelling or destroying malign forces by shooting arrows to the four points of the compass and upwards to the Heavens and downwards to the Earth. Shintöism has a number of purification rituals which involve shooting arrows. In the *Rāmāyana*, Parashurāma's offering of arrows partakes of a sacrificial character.

The arrow may be identified with the flash or bolt of LIGHTNING . . . . Apollo's arrow was a Sun-ray with the same function as Indra's THUNDERBOLT (VAJRA). The solar emperor, Yao, shot his arrows at the Sun, but when unworthy monarchs shoot their arrows into the sky, they come back at them as lightning bolts. In Ancient China they used to shoot serpents or red fire-arrows, clear symbols of lightning. In the same way, the arrows of North American Indians bore a red zig-zag to represent lightning. Like lightning or the Sun-ray, the arrow is the flash of light which pierces the night of ignorance, and is therefore a symbol of knowledge. (This is true of the 'Dragon-slayer's' arrow in the Vedas, which, from the same viewpoint, has a phallic significance to which reference will be made later.) Similarly the Upanishads turn the monosyllable 'OM' into an arrow shot by the human bow through ignorance to strike supreme illumination. Om, again, is the bow which shoots the arrow of the ego towards its target, Brahman, to which it is united. This symbolism was particularly prevalent in the Far East and is still current in Japan. The *Book of Lieh Tzu* quotes many an instance of the random shot which hits its mark simply because both mark and shot were unintentional. This is the Taoist spiritual attitude of 'non-doing'. Furthermore the effectiveness of the shooting is such that the arrows form an unbroken stream between bow and target. Apart from the notion of continuity between subject and object, this implies the effectiveness of the connection which the king establishes in shooting skywards, the stream of arrows being identified with the World Axis.

'Who shoots?' asks a Japanese treatise on archery. 'Something shoots' which is not 'I', but the perfect identification of Me with the 'non-doing'action of Heaven. 'What is the mark?' Confucius had already said that the archer

who misses the mark should seek the cause of failure within himself. Yet
he himself is also the mark. The Chinese ideogram *chong*, meaning 'centre',
depicts a target pierced by an arrow. What the arrow hits is the 'centre' of
the person, the Self. A person prepared to name that mark would call it
Buddha, because in fact it symbolizes the attainment of the state of Buddha, or as we have already noted, of Brahman. The same spiritual discipline
is to be found in Islam, where the bow is identified with divine power and
the arrow with its function of destroying evil and ignorance. At all events,
to hit the mark, which is spiritual perfection or union with the godhead,
implies that the arrow will pierce the 'darkness' of the individual's faults
and imperfections.

On another plane, the Buddhist Wheel of Life depicts a man struck in the
eye by an arrow, symbol of the sensations (*vedanā*) aroused by the impact
upon the senses of their object. The symbolism of sensation recurs in India.
As the emblem of Vishnu, the bow symbolizes *tamas*, his destructive, 'dis-
integrating' aspect, which is at the basis of sense-perception. Kāma, the god
of love, is depicted with five arrows, which are the five senses. This is reminiscent of the use of bow and arrows by Eros. Arrows are emblematic of Shiva,
who is in any case armed with a bow resembling a RAINBOW. His arrow is
to be identified with the five-sided LINGAM. Now the lingam is also light.
Thus the arrow is associated with the number FIVE and is also by derivation
a symbol of Parvatī, not only the incarnation of the five *tattva*, or elemental
principles, but also, it is true, the sheath of Shiva's phallic arrow. The destructive 'tendency' should also remind us, too, that the word *guna* originally
meant 'bow-string' (COOH, COOA, DANA, EPET, GOVM, GRAD,
GRAC, GRAF, GUEC, GUES, HEHS, HERS, HERZ, KALL, MALA).

The bow represents 'the tension from which our desires spring', desires
linked with our subconscious. Love, the Sun, God all possess quiver, bow
and arrows. The underlying significance of the arrow is always male. It
penetrates. When they wield their bows, Love, Sun and God all play a
fecundating role. Thus the bow and arrows are symbols of love and life-
producing tension everywhere from Japan to Ancient Greece and to the
shamanist sorcerers of the Altai. Behind all this symbolism is to be found
the concept of dynamic tension, defined by Heraclitus as the expression
of the vital force, both material and spiritual. Apollo's bow and arrows are
solar energy, with its rays and purifying and generative powers. In Job 29:
19–20, the symbol means strength: 'My root was spread out by the waters,
and the dew lay all night upon my branch. My glory was fresh in me, and
my bow was renewed in my hand.'

A very close comparison would make the bow set in the hand of Shiva,
like the lingam, the emblem of the power of the god. Odysseus' bow symbolized the sole authority exercised by a king. None of the suitors was able
to bend it; he alone succeeded and slew them all.

When it shoots upwards, the bow can also be the symbol of the sublimation of desire. This it would seem is the case of the zodiacal sign SAGITTARIUS,
which shows the archer pointing his arrows skywards. 'Among the ancient
Samoyed, the drum was called the musical bow, the bow of harmony, symbol
of the covenant between the two worlds, but the hunting bow as well which
shoots the shaman like an arrow towards Heaven' (SERH p. 149).

In the Vedas, the bow is the symbol of warlike power, even of military superiority: it is also the weapon which conquers the Heavens. The poems contain a wealth of symbols and evoke the shock of battle, albeit in spiritual warfare:

With the bow let us win cows, with the bow let us win the contest and violent battles with the bow. The bow ruins the enemy's pleasure; with the bow let us conquer all the corners of the world. She comes all the way up to your ear like a woman who wishes to say something, embracing her dear friend; humming like a woman, the bowstring stretched tight on the bow carries you safely across the battle.

(VEDR)

In Vedic tradition the bowstring symbolizes the power which makes the bow effective. That power is, however, invisible and of an almost immaterial nature, deriving neither from weight, hardness nor sharpness, but from tension. It is, as it were, female.

Lastly the bow is the symbol of fate. As a rainbow, it displays the will of God himself in religious mysticism. To the ancient inhabitants of Delphi, to the Children of Israel and to primitive peoples, the bow symbolized spiritual authority and the ultimate power of decision making. It was the attribute of shepherds of their people, sovereign high priests and all those who hold their power from the gods. A king or a god who is more powerful than his rivals breaks the bows of his enemies. The enemy cannot impose his rule upon him.

Joseph is a fruitful bough, even a fruitful bough by a well; whose branches run over the wall: The archers have sorely grieved him, and shot at him, and hated him: But his bow abode in strength, and the arms of his hands were made strong by the mighty God of Jacob; (from thence is the shepherd, the stone of Israel:) Even by the God of thy father, who shall help thee.

(Genesis 49: 22–5)

Apollo enforced his rule upon Olympus whenever he wished, just as Jehovah smote the enemies of his Chosen People. The 'Homeric' Hymn in Apollo's honour exalts his power in these words: 'I will remember and not be unmindful of Apollo who shoots afar. As he goes through the house of Zeus, the gods tremble before him and all spring up from their seats when he draws near, as he bends his bright bow' (Hymn to the Delian Apollo 1–5).

Humans have every reason to bow to his commands. He is an archer and master of their fate. In the *Iliad*, Homer calls him 'death-shooting God . . . Apollo with the fateful arrow'. Whoever is the target of his winged arrows is doomed.

Similarly, Anubis, the jackal-headed god of Ancient Egypt, whose task it was to judge the living and the dead, was often depicted drawing the bow in an attitude symbolizing the chain of circumstance and the fate which cannot be avoided. There is no appeal against fate; even the Underworld obeys its laws, and free choice sets in motion a chain of consequences which cannot be reversed. As Mephistopheles remarks in Goethe's *Faust, Part I*: 'Our initial action is that of free men: we are slaves to our second.'

bowels The Ancient Egyptians believed that the bowels possessed magical powers. During the ritual of embalming, the intestines were carefully removed from the dead person's corpse and preserved in a jar. This jar is shown deposited in the magic BOAT which is depicted making the voyage to the Beyond. Demons and monsters made every effort to seize the jar and with it the magical powers which it contained (see also EXCREMENT).

box (see also COFFER) The box is interpreted as a female symbol of the unconscious and the maternal. It always holds a secret, enclosing and keeping from the world something precious, fragile or awesome. The box protects, but at the risk of stifling.

PANDORA'S box – or jar – remains the symbol of what must not be opened:

> For ere this the tribes of men lived on earth remote and free from ills and hard toil and heavy sicknesses which bring the Fates upon men; for in misery men grow old quickly. But [Pandora] took off the great lid of the jar with her hands and scattered all these, and her thought caused sorrow and mischief to men. Only Hope remained there in an unbreakable home within under the rim of the great jar, and did not fly out at the door; for ere that, the lid of the jar stopped her, by the will of Aegis-holding Zeus who gathers the clouds. But the other countless plagues wander amongst men; for earth is full of evils and the sea is full. Of themselves diseases come upon man continually by day and by night, bringing mischief to mortals silently; for wise Zeus took away speech from them. So there is no way to escape the will of Zeus.
>
> (Hesiod, *Works and Days* 90–106)

The box, at the bottom of which Hope remains, is the unconscious, with all its potentialities for the unexpected, the excessive, the destructive or the positive if it is left to its own devices. Paul Diel links this symbol with a highly charged imagination which invests the unknown object hidden in the box with the power to realize our heart's desire, a power which is totally illusory and the source of all our woes!

The box may be set on a par with those caskets which so often recur in tales and legends. The first two contain happiness and riches, the third, storm, ruin and death. The three caskets correspond to three stages in human life, two fortunate, one unfortunate. In sum, whether a box be plain or richly decorated, its symbolic worth lies in what it contains, while to open a box is always to take a risk (LOEF).

box-wood In Classical antiquity the box was sacred to Hades and Cybele, and it was and remains a symbol of burial and, at the same time, of immortality, because it is an evergreen. This interpretation is consonant with the use of branches of box-wood in Nordic countries on Palm Sunday, in place of the PALMS preferred in warmer climates, and with the fact that their branches are used to decorate graves.

Furthermore, because box-wood is hard and close-grained it symbolizes resolve and perseverance, and hence its use in making mallets for Masonic lodges (DEVA, ROMM). Because of its hardness, in Classical times it was used in the manufacture of rods, tops, combs, flutes and, especially, writing tablets. These were coated with wax and provided a solid base for the stylus.

The Gauls made the box a god, symbol of eternity. On the other hand, because it had been categorized as one of the trees dedicated to the gods of the Underworld, it was commonly looked upon as a symbol of sterility. For this reason the Ancients were careful never to lay it upon the altars of Venus, the widely worshipped goddess of love, for fear that such an offering would destroy their virility. This was merely a superstition and I believe, to the contrary, in the principle that trees which kept their foliage green during the winter must originally have been dedicated to Aphrodite, for green was a colour which was always specifically attributed to her.

(LANS B p. 222)

It is hardly surprising that the same tree should be dedicated to Aphrodite, Cybele and Hades and should at one and the same time symbolize love, fertility and death, if it represents the life-cycle.

branch In Christian tradition the waving of branches is the accompaniment of a triumphal procession, as the antiphon, *Occurrunt turbae cum floribus*, in the Palm Sunday procession confirms. 'The multitude goes out to meet our Redeemer with flowers and palms, and pay the homage due to a triumphant conqueror: nations proclaim the Son of God; and their voices rend the skies in the praise of Christ: Hosanna in the highest.' It was an Eastern tradition to greet heroes and great men by waving green branches, symbolizing their deathless glory. Thus Christ made his last entry into Jerusalem riding upon a she-ASS, the crowds believing that this was the triumph of the Messiah. A few days later he was crucified. However, the Catholic ritual for Palm Sunday has perfectly internalized this triumph, as the prayer of Blessing the Palms makes clear: 'Bless, we beseech thee, O Lord, these branches of palm and olive: and grant that the bodily service with which thy people honour thee today may be perfected spiritually by the utmost devotion, by victory over the enemy, and by the ardent love of works of mercy.' The victory here celebrated is nothing less than the inner victory over sin, gained through love and ensuring eternal salvation. It is decisive and final victory. The symbolism of the branch has reached its ultimate expression.

It had already been prefigured in the olive branch which the dove carried in its beak as a sign that the Flood was over. 'And the dove came in to [Noah] in the evening: and, lo, in her mouth was an olive leaf pluckt off' (Genesis 8: 11). It was a message of pardon, of peace regained and of salvation. The green bough symbolized the victory of life and love.

In medieval art, the branch is an attribute sometimes of logic, sometimes of chastity and sometimes of the rebirth of Spring.

A green bough with flames coming from it symbolized the endurance of a hopeless love. An example of this may be seen in one of the rooms of the Palazzo Vecchio in Florence. Vasari describes it as 'a stock of green wood spouting flames from the places from which the branches have been trimmed. It bears the word *semper* ('always') . . . and was the device which Giuliano de' Medici wore on his jousting-helmet. It meant that although all hope had been hacked from his love, it remained no less fresh, fiery and enduring.'

Giuliano's nephew Piero de' Medici altered this device to read *In viridi teneras exurit flamma medullas* ('the flame burns the soft marrow in the green wood'). However, this only makes more clear the meaning of its predecessor, 'that of a love so passionate that it burns green wood or so enduring that it survives loss of hope hacked off like the branches of the tree' (TERS p. 320).

In Irish, the same word, *craeb* or *croeb*, is used for both 'branch' and 'magic WAND'. In literature, this branch with such potent magic powers as the ability to wipe away all memories of sadness with the mysterious music which comes from it, is often the branch of an apple-tree. Now, the fruit of the apple-tree confers immortality (OGAC 14: pp. 339–40). The branch is both symbol and instrument of a cosmic music and soloist in the music of the spheres.

brass See BRONZE.

bread Bread is plainly the symbol of basic nourishment. Although it may be true that 'man does not live by bread alone', bread is the name given to his spiritual nourishment, to Christ in the Eucharist, the 'bread of life'. This is the 'sacred bread of eternal life' of which the Catholic liturgy speaks. 'Blessed', wrote St Clement of Alexandria, 'are they who feed those who hunger for righteousness by the distribution of the Bread.'

The 'shew bread' of the Children of Israel bore a similar meaning. Unleavened bread – of which the host is still made – 'symbolizes', St Martin wrote, 'at one and the same time sorrow for deprivation, preparation for purification and a reminder of man's origins.'

Traditionally *Beith-el* (BETHEL), the 'House of God', the STONE set up by Jacob, became *Beith-lehem*, ('House of Bread'). The House of Stone is changed into the House of Bread, that is to say, the symbolic presence of God is changed into the physical presence of God as spiritual food, and not as material food as the Tempter in the Gospels suggested.

Bread – in the Eucharist – traditionally relates to the active life and WINE to the spiritual, bread to the 'Lesser' and wine to the 'Greater Mysteries'; bearing out the point noted by Schuon, that the miracle of the feeding of the five thousand by multiplication of the bread is of a quantitative order, while the miracle of the wine at the marriage feast at Cana is of a qualitative order.

The symbolism of yeast is displayed in Gospel writings under two aspects. On the one hand it is the active principle in baking bread and is therefore a symbol of spiritual transformation. Its absence – and this comes back to unleavened bread – carries with it the idea of purity and sacrifice (GUEM, SAIR, SCHG).

breast The symbol of protection and of measure(ment) (see WEIGHTS AND MEASURES).

Werner Wolf observes that, for the Children of Israel, the word *bath* meant both 'girl' and 'a liquid measure'; while the word *amah* meant 'girl' and 'a measurement of length' (WOLB p. 235).

The breast is connected with the female principle, that is to say with measure in its sense of restriction, since measurement is restricted to the object measured. This is in contradistinction to the male principle, which is limitless and measureless. The right breast symbolizes the Sun, the left the Moon.

But above all breasts are symbols of motherhood, comfort, security and plenty. They are connected with fertility and with MILK, the first nourishment, and associated with pictures of intimacy, giving and protection. Upturned chalices, like the sky they distill life, yet, like all symbols of motherhood, they are also the reservoirs and promise of regeneration. Returning to the bosom of the Earth, like all deaths, marks the prelude to a new birth.

The place where the righteous take their rest is called Abraham's Bosom, where those that are admitted await the grace of the first resurrection. All funeral liturgies evoke the repose of the souls in Abraham's Bosom, where there is 'no pain, suffering nor sighs'. Despite this, the term seemed very vague and hard to interpret and even such Fathers of the Church as Augustine (*Confessions* 1: 9) and Gregory of Nazianzus (*Sermons* 7: 17) admit their lack of comprehension.

According to the Pseudo-Dionysius the Areopagite the breasts of angels symbolize 'the invincible and protective faculty of the life-giving distribution as being placed above the heart' (PSEH p. 46). The breast (chest) is a symbol of protection.

Furthermore he makes the breast (rib-cage) the seat of wrath, not in the bad sense of the term but in the sense of that surge of courage inspired by the battle against evil.

To bare the breast has often been judged a sexual invitation, a symbol of sensuality or of a woman's physical endowments. Caesar records this of the Gallic women of Avaricum, begging the Roman soldiers for mercy. This was, however, no more than a gesture of humiliation and pleading and was of secondary importance compared with that of stretching out the hands (*passis manibus*). The latter is all that Caesar records of a similar situation at the surrender of Bratuspantium, a fortress of the Bellovaci (OGAC 18: pp. 369–72).

breast-bone The lower portion of the breast-BONE is one of the four CEN-TRES allotted by the Bambara to the human microcosm and is called 'the heart's skull' by them. It controls those parts of the body between the base of the skull and the diaphragm, that is, the upper limbs, heart and lungs. A pot which stands for this 'centre' is placed on the altar of the Kore initiation society; it contains a fragment of unidentified resinous matter known as 'the spirit's arm-bone', symbolizing the essence of the divine spirit associated with the upper limbs. That the breast-bone acts as a 'CROSSROADS' is emphasized by the fact that in the pot there are also two twigs in the shape of a cross, conjuring up the primeval crossroads from which all life and all knowledge originated. These two twigs symbolize the heart and lungs. These are the crossroads of the Word, which by their means takes physical shape from out of air, as a result of impulses despatched by the brain. This precise location also controls the area of breast- collar- and shoulder-bones and the trapeziuses, which the Bambara regard as the foundation or support of the neck and hence of knowledge itself. This area is depicted as a LOZENGE, emphasizing the womblike function of the brain.

Internally the end of the breast-bone corresponds to the 'ropes' which control the ventral organs, their equivalents in the macrocosm being the invisible channels along which the life force circulates between Heaven and Earth.

breastplate See HELMET; SHIELD.

breath   Breath is universally regarded as a principle of life; it is only in extensions of the symbol that one tradition differs from the other. 'The Spirit of God which brooded upon the face of the [primeval] waters' in the Book of Genesis was *ruah*, 'breath'. This is also the primary meaning of the Muslim term *Er-Ruh* ('spirit'); and *Hamsa*, the swan which incubated the Vedic cosmic egg, was also 'breath'. Under the entry RESPIRATION attention is drawn to the two phases of breathing, the *yang* and *yin* which were evolution and involution, manifestation and latency, *kalpa* and *pralaya*. Taoists of the Han Dynasty believed that in the beginning there were nine 'breaths' which gradually came together and entwined themselves to constitute physical space. The intermediate space between Heaven and Earth is filled with a 'breath' (*k'i*) in which mortals live 'like fish in the water'. This same intermediate or 'subtle' realm is in Indian belief the domain of *Vāyu*, the wind and breath of life. *Vāyu* is the THREAD (*sūtra*) which joins the two worlds together and is also *ātman*, the Universal Spirit, which is, literally, 'breath'.

The structure of the microcosm is identical to that of the macrocosm; therefore just as the universe is knitted together by Vāyu, so is the individual by breaths. These are five in number – *prāna*, *apāna*, *vyāna*, *udāna* and *samāna* – and these regulate the vital functions and not just the rhythm of breathing. In fact, the practice in Yoga of *prānāyāma* (breath-control), which has its Chinese equivalents, is applied not only to physical breathing, but also to 'subtle' respiration, of which the first is merely an image. 'Circulation of breath' associated with Tantric *kundalinī* or with the Taoist doctrine of the Embryo obviously does not relate to air, since this would be absurd in physiological terms, but to controlled and transubstantiated vital energy. Mastery of *prāna* involves control of both mental and seminal energy (*manas* and *vīrya*). In Chinese terms, *k'i* ('breath' as well as 'spirit') 'marries' *hsin* ('essence' or 'strength') to beget the Embryo of Immortality (AVAS, GRIF, GUES, ELIF, MAST, SAIR, SILI).

At another level of the symbol, the breath (*ruah*) from Jehovah's nostrils is the sign of the exercise of his powers of creation. It divided the waters and possessed the properties of a torrent. Breath and the speech afford one another mutual assistance, the one supporting the emission of the other. Jehovah's *ruah* is the breath which issues from his lips, creating and sustaining life. Hence the Psalmist: 'Thou hidest thy face, they are troubled; thou takest away their breath, they die, and return to dust. Thou sendest forth thy spirit [or 'breath'], they are created; and thou renewest the face of the earth' (Psalm 104: 29–30).

According to the account of the creation of man given in the Book of Genesis, Jehovah breathed the breath of life into Adam's nostrils, and what had before been lifeless was animated by a living soul (*nephesh*). Anatolian Shi'ites use the term *nefes* to describe their hymns of invocation. There is an identical meaning behind Job's words: 'The spirit [*ruah*] of God hath made me, and the breath of the Almighty hath given me life' (33: 4).

The breath of life given by God to mortals is imperishable. 'Then shall the dust return to the earth as it was: and the spirit shall return unto God who gave it' (Ecclesiastes 12: 7). The flesh perishes when the breath is taken away.

In all major traditions, the word 'breath' conveys the same meaning, whether it be *pneuma*, or *spiritus* (GUIB). The Hebrew word *ruah* is regularly translated as 'spirit' and corresponds to the Greek *pneuma* and the Latin *spiritus*, all three meaning the breath passing through the mouth or nostrils. This breath possesses mysterious activating powers and was compared with the wind (Proverbs 30: 4; Ecclesiastes 1: 6; 1 Kings 19: 11).

Jehovah's breath is life-giving (Genesis 6: 3); it changes physically and materially, as well as spiritually, the person who receives it. Whether it was Othniel (Judges 3: 10), Jephtha (Judges 11: 29) or Gideon (Judges 6: 34), each became a hero through the breath of God. The most typical example is provided by Samson (Judges 13: 25; 14: 6) who, once he had received the breath of God, went out and tore a lion to pieces and slaughtered ten thousand Philistines with the jaw-bone of an ass (Judges 14: 14).

The divine breath inspired prophecy, even in King Saul (1 Samuel 10: 9), and Hosea (9: 7) calls a prophet 'a spiritual man'. There are many Old Testament references to the HAND of God, the word in this context conveying the meaning of 'spirit'. While the spirit of God can work temporarily in individuals, it may also reside there permanently, as in Moses (Numbers 11: 17, 25), Joshua (Numbers 27: 18), David, Elijah, Elisha and others. According to Isaiah (11: 2) the breath or spirit of God means 'wisdom and understanding . . . counsel and might . . . knowledge and fear of the Lord.'

It should be observed that in most instances when used in the Old Testament the noun *ruah* is feminine. Now in Hebrew the feminine gender denotes some impersonal being or thing. Although the word *ruah* means 'spirit', it is sometimes used to denote 'speech'. However, this spirit or breath is a manifestation of the one God and not an attribute of the godhead (P. van Imschoot in *Bible et Vie Chrétienne* (May–July 1957), pp. 7–24).

The Celts believed that the breath possessed magic properties. In the tale of the siege of Druin Damhghaire, the druid Mog Ruith on several occasions employs 'druid's breath', which was both symbolic of and instrumental in the power of the druids. On the first occasion he breathed on the threatening circle of warriors around him, making them all look like him, with the result that they slaughtered one another and he was able to make his escape. On the second, he breathed upon a hill which evil druids, his enemies, had raised by magic and which provided his foes with a dominating position. The whole thing collapsed in ruins. On the third occasion Mog Ruith breathed upon his enemies and turned them to stone (see WIND).

Jung has recorded the practices of Zulu wizards who cured the sick by 'breathing into the person's ear through a bull's horn, so as to drive the evil spirits out of the body'. In scenes of the Creation through the breath of God, Christian iconography depicts that breath as a glittering spray, like a spray of spittle, able to cure disease and raise from the dead and instill life. Human breath, on the other hand, is thick with filth and threatens to defile whatever it touches. In the cult of Svantovit, the all-powerful Slav god, the priest who alone had the right to enter the temple, would sweep it out on the eve of his festival, 'taking care not to breath while inside. So every time he needed to exhale his breath he would have to dash outside so that the god remained untouched by human breath and therefore undefiled' (MYTF p. 92).

brick In Akkadian creation myths, the creator himself, Marduk, is credited with the invention of the brick. In the orderly succession of things, bricks stand immediately after the appearance of Earth and Water and the birth of life, and just before the building of houses and towns. 'He created trees .... He set down a brick and fashioned a brick-mould. He built a house and founded a town' (SOUN pp. 146–7).

The brick-god was named Kulla. He had been formed from a handful of mud taken from the primordial river, Apsu. He superintended the restoration of temples.

Setting aside their practical and historical employment, or rather because of them, bricks here symbolize mankind's adoption of a settled way of life and the beginnings of urbanization in house, temple and city. Such a social revolution required divine intervention in a new act of creation. Bricks are therefore the gift of the gods. They are the symbol of man, settled in his own house, upon his own land, with his family around him, structuring the life of his village or town and the places of worship in them. Bricks brought him the security of a dwelling, a way of life and a society, and the protection of the gods. They also imposed restraint; for bricks are rules, measure and uniformity, giving him a closed society, the opposite to the open society of the nomad.

bridge The symbolism of bridges, as structures enabling one to pass from one side of something to the other, is one of the most widespread. The transition may be from Earth to Heaven, from the human to the suprahuman state, from contingency to immortality, 'from the world of the senses to the world beyond the senses' (Guénon) and so on. Various eastern European legends make great play with successions of metal bridges which have to be crossed on horseback, as Sir Lancelot crossed 'The Bridge of the Sword'. For the Zoroastrians, the 'Bridge of the Separator', *Chinvat*, was hard to cross, being broad for the righteous but 'as thin as the blade of a razor for the impious'. Sometimes these narrow, knife-edged bridges are reduced to a single shivering length of creeper. Similar symbols occur in the ancient East, in the *Apocalypse of Paul* and in the Upanishads. The journey of initiation into Chinese secret societies is also made across bridges. The *kuokiao* (bridge) has to be crossed, be it a 'golden bridge', represented by a piece of white cloth, or a 'copper and iron bridge', with its alchemical echoes, iron and copper corresponding to black and red, water and fire, north and south, *yin* and *yang*. This bridge, it may be added, is sometimes represented by a sword.

Two points stand out: the symbolism of passage, and the dangerous nature of this transition, which is that of any 'journey' of initiation. Passing from Earth to Heaven identifies the bridge with the RAINBOW, that bridge which Zeus flung between the two worlds and down which came the lovely Iris, the bearer of glad tidings. The relationship is particularly clear in the case of the hump-backed bridges of the Far East. Thus those leading to Shintō shrines are images of the celestial bridge which leads to the world of the gods and can only be crossed after the performance of ritual purification. They are also identified with the World AXIS in its various aspects and especially that of the LADDER. In that case the bridge must be looked upon as 'vertical'.

It is particularly noteworthy that the title of 'Pontiff' which is applied to the Pope derives from the title borne by members of an Ancient Roman college of priests, *pontifex*, meaning 'bridge-builder'. The Pontiff is simultaneously the builder of the bridge and the bridge itself, being the mediator between Earth and Heaven. Nichiren says of the Buddha, that he is 'the great Bridge ... for all living beings' enabling them to 'cross the CROSS-ROADS of the Six Ways.' The *Chāndogya Upanishad* teaches that the true bridge is the Self 'which links these two worlds and prevents their drifting apart. As you cross this bridge night becomes day, for this world of Immensity is nothing less than Light' (DANA, GUEM, GUET, GUES, HERS, RENB, SCHI).

In the Mabinogion of *Branwen, Daughter of Llyr*, the Welsh armies invade Ireland in order to avenge the evil lot imposed upon Branwen by her husband Matholwch, King of Ireland. They are halted by the Shannon, a magical river across which there is no bridge and on which no ship can sail. King Bran therefore lies across the river from bank to bank and the armies march over his body. The Welsh tale attributed to this mythical incident the origin of the saying 'The chief should be a bridge'. It recurs in the mouth of King Arthur who, as king, is the perfect intermediary, and therefore the bridge between Earth and Heaven. The symbolism is akin to that of the Roman *pontifices*. The 'Bridge of the Sword' as slender and as sharp as its blade, which provides so dangerous a crossing in the Arthurian *Lancelot* or *Li conte de la charette*, symbolizes the passing from one state of being to a higher state.

Muslim tradition, collected in the Hadīth, describes the Sirāt, or 'crossing of the Bridge' which spans Hell and leads to Paradise. Thinner than a hair and sharper than a sword, this bridge bears a name which recalls the figure in the Koran who points sometimes to 'the way to Hell'and sometimes to the straight path followed by true believers.

Only the elect cross it, the damned either slip or are hauled off it before they can reach Paradise and are hurled down into Hell .... There is a persistent belief that the elect will cross the bridge at a rate, faster or slower, proportionate to the worth of their deeds or the strength of their faith .... Some cross the bridge in one hundred, others in a thousand years, according to the purity of their lives, but none who has seen the Lord is in danger of falling into Hell.

Other traditions assert that the bridge has seven arches, each corresponding to one of the seven duties, 'of faith, of prayer, of alms-giving, of fasting, of making the pilgrimage to Mecca, of observing ritual purity and of filial piety. Whoever fails any one of them is cast into Hell' (Dominique Sourdel in SOUJ pp. 188, 189, 199, 200). All these traditions corroborate the symbolism of the bridge as a place of passage and of trial, but give it a moral, ritual and religious dimension. Taking this analysis deeper, it might be said that bridges symbolize the transition between two inner states or between two conflicting sets of desires. They may also show the solution to a confrontational situation. The crossing must be made: avoidance solves nothing.

Legends of 'the Devil's Bridge' have very wide currency, with examples throughout Europe. It is as if their very name is a sort of admission of the grave difficulty in building such works of art and a tribute to their beauty and durability. It is as if the architects and engineers, incapable of succeeding on their own, were forced to have recourse to all Satan's cunning. These 'Devil's Bridges' are enmeshed in story and superstition in which sometimes God and sometimes Satan, and their respective worshippers, are duped. The Devil is promised the soul of the first person to cross the bridge. This is his due, for otherwise he would have worked for nothing for mankind. Yet he is tricked out of it by countless ruses. There was another superstition that the first person to cross the bridge would die within the year. At all events legends show the anxiety aroused by passage over a difficult and dangerous place and corroborate the general symbolism of bridges and their meaning in dreams. They are a danger to be overcome, but also a decision to be taken. Bridges set men and women on a narrow path in which they meet the unavoidable obligation to choose – and that choice is salvation or damnation.

brimstone See SULPHUR.

bronze Symbolically the values of both bronze and brass are identical, both being alloys of copper; in the case of brass, with zinc, and of bronze with tin and silver. Being children, symbolically speaking, of a marriage of opposites, since copper is associated with the Sun and with FIRE and the other metals with the Moon and WATER, the two aspects of this metal's symbolism are in violent conflict and it is as a whole ambivalent. Given the metal's high degree of resonance, it is first a voice – on the one hand the voice of the cannon and on the other that of the bell – and however unlike the one may be from the other, both are powerful and terrible.

According to Greek tradition the inventor of bronze-working was Cinyras, the first king of Cyprus, who probably came from Byblos (GRID, 93).

According to Hesiod, the Race of Bronze was 'terrible' and 'powerful'. One of its last earthly representatives must have been Talos, a figure of Cretan legend, part human, part machine, a sort of robot, believed to have been fashioned from bronze either by HEPHAISTOS or by King Minos' engineer and architect, DAEDALUS. This bronze Talos was an awesome being. Minos entrusted him with the task of preventing strangers from landing in Crete or its inhabitants from leaving the island. He would hurl enormous boulders at any vessel which approached or, what was even worse, heat his body red-hot, chase, catch and burn his victims to death by clasping them to his chest. It was to avoid him that Daedalus took to the air when he escaped from the island. However, and this proved crucial, 'Talos was invulnerable except for one place in his body. At the bottom of his leg there was a tiny vein, closed by a pin .... Medea, with her spells, succeeded in opening this vein and Talos died' (GRID p. 435). It is interesting to observe that just as Achilles was invulnerable save for his heel, so this creature's vulnerable point was at the bottom of its leg. This is an indicator of psychic and moral weakness. It is strange that the energy which powered this bronze robot should have drained through this channel once the witch had opened it. One might venture to suggest that Talos symbolizes debased energy, purely material, applied to evil ends and completely controlled by magic spells, whether these spells be those of the knowledge and arts of a Hephaistos, a Daedalus or a Medea.

Bronze was a sacred metal, used to make the instruments of worship from antiquity to Buddhism and Christianity. The Brazen Serpent was carried like a standard by the Children of Israel (Numbers 21: 9), who had only to glance at this figure to be saved from death from the bite of the fiery serpent. It was later to be displayed in the Temple as a symbol of God's protection. There, too, was the altar of sacrifice with four brazen horns which gave sanctuary to the criminal who clasped them. The vessels which tinkled in the wind in Zeus' wood at Dodona were of bronze, as were Hephaistos' palace and temple doors, the roof of the Temple of Vesta and the earliest statue of Ceres at Rome. So were the vessels used to pour sacred libations. The Ancient Egyptians thought of the vault of Heaven as being of bronze and *The Book of the Dead* speaks of going 'towards Heaven, across the firmament of bronze'. The Ancient Romans used a bronze razor to shave the heads of their priests and a bronze plough-share to mark the boundaries of a camp or a new town. This tough metal was the symbol of incorruptibility and immortality as well as of unswerving justice. If the vault of Heaven was believed to be of bronze, this was both because it was as impenetrable as this metal and because the metal itself was associated with the most transcendent powers of the sky-gods, those whose voices boomed out like thunder filling mankind with awe and fear.

The quite extraordinary resonance of this alloy caused Fama, the Roman goddess of fame, to choose it as the material from which her palace was built on a mountain peak. This again reveals the ambivalence of the symbol, for Fame's palace 'was always open and both re-echoed and amplified whatever was spoken near it. Here the goddess lived, surrounded by Credulity, Error, False Joy, Terror, Sedition and False Rumour, and from her palace she looked down upon the whole world' (GRID p. 157).

There is similar ambivalence in the legend of the HIND with brazen hoofs and in that of Empedocles' sandal, also brazen. In both cases it may well be that the metal symbolizes separation from the worldly state and from corruption. If Mount Etna, into the crater of which the philosopher threw himself, vomited up his bronze sandal, Classical antiquity believed that Empedocles' teachings remained incorruptible on earth, immortal among men, while their author was admitted to immortality by the company of the gods. The hind's brazen hoofs are ambivalent. On the one hand they might mean that thanks to this hard and holy metal the creature was kept apart from earthly corruption, on the other that the hind, naturally light-footed and pure, was weighed down by earthly desires. On the one hand you have the sublimation and on the other the corruption of its natural character, for such is the bipolar nature of the symbol. A less complicated view might be that it emphasizes the headlong dash of the tireless hind to escape the pursuit of its hunters, the unending and holy flight of the virgin and the untamed.

Early Irish literature contains many references to bronze in the context of weapons, jewellery and utensils. However, a problem is set by the word *findruine* or 'white bronze', since it is not clear whether the word describes brass or electrum (a gold and silver alloy), and it may well be that the Irish applied it indiscriminately to both.

brooch Medieval Irish literature describes in minutest detail the *delg* or brooch, a piece of personal jewellery of bronze, silver or, sometimes, of gold, ornamented with enamel or precious stones, which glittered upon the breast of the hero whose cloak it held. Despite this, it would seem that brooches, almost always described as priceless jewels, were merely symbols of the luxurious dress of the warrior caste. The vast numbers discovered in France and in the British Isles, and indeed throughout the ancient Celtic world, are clearly pieces of costume jewellery of gold, silver and bronze, elaborately patterned with masks, spirals, leaf motifs, human heads, triskeles, swastikas and so on, and studded with amber, coral and enamel. They are most often found in graves and in pairs.

It was more usually the object depicted on the brooch which had a meaning and this would be passed on as a spell or power to the wearer. Sometimes the brooch was regarded in some sense as a symbol of protection, and by extension of virginity and faithfulness. Thus twelve brooches held together the scarf in which Penelope draped herself like a cloak or *peplos*.

In Great Kabylia, brooches symbolize woman (SERP pp. 251–2) and, by extension, fertility. It might be legitimate to wonder whether the brooch which wounded Cùchulainn was not the love of a woman and whether brooches, with their sharp pins, are not symbols of love which can join together and yet wound two persons.

broom (plant) In some parts of the world it is the symbol of the north (see CARDINAL POINTS) and of the office of kingship. It is alleged that the flowers of broom or gorse are the origins of the heraldic *fleur-de-lys* or of the GOLDEN BOUGH (see also MISTLETOE). Obviously this symbolism is inexplicable in terms of botanical origin. Branches of broom in flower were used at funerals to cover the corpse.

broom(stick) Although it is to outward appearance a humble piece of household equipment, the broom is for all that a sign and symbol of sacred power. In ancient shrines and temples, sweeping was itself an act of worship, since only those with clean hands could clear the floor of all those elements which had entered from the outside world to defile it. Similarly in north African agricultural civilizations, the broom 'used to sweep the threshing-floor' is a cult object. Again, during the first few days of mourning, the house should not be swept to avoid 'prosperity being driven out of doors' or 'offence to the soul of the departed' (SERP p. 148). Similarly, in Brittany the house should not be swept after dark since this will 'drive the luck away' and the movements of the broom hurt the souls who 'walk' (COLD p. 76).

Brooms which drive out the dust and dirt can, in fact, hurt and put to flight those invisible house guests, the spirits which protect hearth and home. Equally important, too, are the materials from which brooms are made. At the time of their great Spring festival, Kabyle women gather bunches of flowering thorn. This will be made into lucky brooms which 'will not drive good fortune out of the house or accidentally strike against invisible guests' (SERP p. 164). However, if the broom reverses its role it becomes an instrument of sorcery and in every land WITCHES mount their broomsticks, go up the chimney and ride to their SABBATHS. These broomsticks may, perhaps, be phallic symbols, but they are also and especially symbols of the powers which the broom has failed to drive out but which gain control of it and use it as they please.

broth Broth is especially suggestive of boiling and bubbling, rather than the end-product of the process.

In Ancient China 'Jade Broth' was the saliva and its methodical swallowing was a recipe for immortality.

Broth, that nicely balanced mixture of substance and flavour, was a symbol of universal harmony (*ho*) and of the *yin* and the *yang*, always bearing in mind that it is produced by the interaction of fire and liquid.

There seem, too, to have been rituals of ordeal, purification and communion which involved the eating of broth. For example a broth of ARTEMISIA was supposed to have the power of purifying (GRAD, MAST).

According to *The Madness of Cùchulainn*, at the coronation of a High King of Ireland, a bard (*file*) would drink the broth and eat his fill of the flesh of the bull slaughtered for the ritual feast. He would then sleep and dream of the man to be elected king. According to other sources, the process was repeated during the course of the coronation, but with the new king and a horse. The reign formally opened when the elected king had bathed in the broth of the ritually slaughtered animal, drunk his fill of the broth and both he and his subjects had eaten the flesh.

Broth is a channel of that strength or regeneration which is expected of the new king. The bathing and the broth play exactly the same part as bathing and eating the marrow of an animal play in the regeneration of several heroes of the Ulster Cycle (OGAC 15: pp. 123–37, 245–55).

In Vedic India, broth was the means of celestial regeneration and return to cosmic oneness. For this purpose the five broths (FIVE being the number of totality) which accompanied the sacrifice of a goat were five sorts of rice gruel.

brown Brown is a colour somewhere between russet and black, and shading from ochre to dark earth colour. Above all, brown is the colour of earth, of ploughed land and soil. It calls to mind dead leaves, autumn and melancholy. It degrades and bastardizes pure colours.

For both the Ancient Romans and the Catholic Church, brown was the symbol of humility (*humus*, earth) and of poverty, a motive for some religious orders to wear brown homespun.

In Ireland brown (*donn*) was a substitute for BLACK and shared all its Underworld and warlike symbolism.

Brown has connections with EXCREMENT. Sadists have a predilection for brown – for example Hitler's Brownshirts – which would appear to confirm Freud's observations upon the anal complex aroused by this colour.

Brunhild A VALKYRIE, a virgin who remained hidden behind an impregnable curtain of flame and who was only to yield to the hero preordained by the gods. She slew whoever attempted to seduce her.

Some critics believe that 'the sleeping virgin freed by a shining warrior symbolizes the dormant Earth woken to life by the Sun' (LBDP).

Undoubtedly at a deeper level Brunhild represents the marvellous and unattainable focus of an inordinate passion. The subject of this passion dies because he is unable to satisfy it through being unable to pass through the necessary ordeals. He who believes he can obtain the object of his desire by trickery and by avoiding the trials before him, only achieves something second-rate, which is not the object of his desire and which does not answer his expectations. Brunhild has also been compared with ARTEMIS (Diana) and with the AMAZONS, those virgin warriors whose one ambition was to outshine men in war and the chase.

Wagner saw Brunhild as 'the heroine ... who channels the divine into the human and the ultimate epitome of the earthly in the heavenly.' She was the Valkyrie who renounced the Paradise of gods and heroes to live among mankind so that she could enjoy love. She disobeyed her father, the god WOTAN. However, this love in the end lifted her above her human condition and restored her to Paradise once more. She symbolizes the renunciation of personal advantage for the sake of love and the redemptive power of such a sacrifice.

By her divine birth she represents an aspect of the godhead: by her human marriage she represents an aspect of humanity. She is the dual knowledge of Heaven and of Earth, of strength and weakness, joy and sorrow, life and death, of which the secret is hidden in love. Her manifestation and her deeds, dominated by a search for love, deliver mankind from the tyranny of wealth and power.

bubble Air- or soap-bubbles symbolize a created object which is light-weight, spontaneous and short-lived and which suddenly bursts to leave no other trace of its existence than the transient and arbitrary volume of a little air.

Similarly Buddhists make them emblems of *anitya,* the transience of the world of illusion. 'Whoever', states the *Dhammapada*, 'looks upon the world as upon an air-bubble, can look beyond the kingdom of death.' Another *sūtra* affirms that 'the occurrences of this life are no more than dreams, phantasies, air-bubbles, shadows, glittering dew, a lightning flash.' This is no doubt the source from which *The Secret of the Golden Flower* teaches 'that in the sight of the Tao, Heaven and Earth are but an air-bubble and a shadow' (GRIF).

Bucentaur A fabulous creature of Greek mythology, half man and half bull, a CENTAUR which, instead of having the body of a horse, had that of a BULL with a human head. Its symbolism is the same as that of the centaur with the differences which a bull's body implies. The centaur symbolizes the basic duality of human nature, material–spiritual, instinctive–rational. However, the horse symbolizes the powers of instinct, the bull those of procreation. Herakles' (Hercules') battle with the centaurs is the archetype of every struggle against the dominance of instinct and against oppression and obsession in all its forms. It is reminiscent of that between Theseus and the MINOTAUR.

The gilded Venetian state galley in which the Doge embarked each Ascension Day to celebrate the marriage of Venice with the sea, was called the Bucentaur. Doubtless the vessel had a figurehead carved in the shape of a bucentaur to symbolize the wealth which the city gained from her mastery of the sea. The sea was the fertile strength of the bull, which the human head of Venice was able to control.

Bucephalus The name given to the charger of Alexander the Great. The horse was untameable, would allow none but its master to ride him, was afraid of its own shadow and would only gallop towards the Sun. It would kneel before Alexander and no amount of galloping could quench his fire. It was killed during a bloody battle and the King built a town around its tomb. Bucephalus symbolizes the servant of a single master whom he serves with deathless devotion and whose ambitions he shares, perhaps the more deeply of the two, and even incites. Like Bucephalus, restive or bucking at the sight of his own shadow, Alexander could not live in the shadow of his father, Philip of Macedon. Aristotle's pupil needed horizons wider than those of the petty kingdom of his birth. He needed a blaze of glory and, just as Bucephalus would only be ridden towards the Sun, so his incredible expedition across Persia and to the borders of India led him towards the sunrise. Creature of the Sun, all his fire was kept for great adventures and he shines out like a star in the sky.

buckle The buckle shares the symbolism of the GIRDLE, the KNOT and the CHAIN. Self-defence is implied when the buckle is tightened; freedom when the buckle is undone. It proffers or gives what it implies.

Like the OUROBOROS, the buckle chews its own tail, completes a journey which takes it back to its starting-point, acquiring cyclical powers and symbolizing the eternal homecoming when ALPHA AND OMEGA constantly lead back from one to the other. The buckle evokes fate.

buffalo See under OX.

buffoon (see also CLOWN) In a number of places in Irish literature buffoons are equated with druids. There is a homonymic relationship in Irish between *drui* ('druid') and *druth*, or *druith* ('buffoon'), but this would seem to be a clear case of parody (OGAC 18: pp. 109–11).

A parody, granted, but a highly significant parody, a parody of the personality, the ego, which reveals the dual nature of each person and his or her ridiculous aspect. The character of the buffoon is always present in royal occasions, in triumphal processions and in stage plays. This character is the opposite facet of reality, which our attainments make us forget and which it recalls to our notice. Characteristically buffoons will deliver commonplaces in tones of high seriousness and serious statements as if they were jokes. They embody ironic awareness. Their obedience mocks authority by its very exaggeration and they will cringe as they enumerate all your faults and failings. Behind the comic facade, one becomes aware of the tortured conscience. Properly understood and accepted as the DOUBLE of one's self, the buffoon becomes a factor in balanced development: balanced, especially when buffoonery catches you off balance, because then you are forced to seek inner harmony at a higher level of integration. The buffoon is not just a comic character, but expresses the inner personality in all its many facets and hidden discrepancies.

Sometimes the buffoon is condemned to death for high treason against society and executed or sacrificed as a SCAPEGOAT. In fact history shows us the buffoon as the associate of the sacrificial victim. This indicates a moral weakness or a spiritual involution on the part of the executioner. Society or the individual is incapable of assuming full responsibility for its actions and makes a sacrificial victim of that part of itself which embarrasses it.

Some of the phenomena of racism are in this respect typical, whether

relating to Blacks, Yellows, Whites, Redskins or Jews. There is a tendency
to dress up the oppressed race as buffoons, without realizing that it is a part
of one's self which one denies in trying to reject the interloper. The natural
reaction to buffoons is, in fact, to dissociate oneself from them. However,
you will not get rid of them by violence nor by piling mockery upon them.
All they stand for must be integrated into a new, more comprehensive,
more humane order of being. The buffoon cast out or condemned symbolizes a check to higher development.

building Hindu tradition attributes a treatise on architecture to Brahmā
and, in fact, he is depicted as an architect in his aspect of Vishvakarma,
carrying axe and measuring rod (*mānadanda*), the 'golden reed' of the
Book of Revelation. From this viewpoint, building may be regarded as
the very symbol of universal manifestation. From an opposite angle it is the
same – all building renewing the work of creation. Whatever the building,
it is always set, in some sense, in the CENTRE of the world and lends itself
to the dual symbolism of the return to the centre and of the transit from
Earth to Heaven. Symbolism of this order serves as the basis of FREEMASONRY,
which originated among the medieval builders' guilds and has kept their
language and emblems (compasses, square, plumb-line, mallet, trowel). The
will of the godhead, known as the Great Architect of the Universe, conjures
precisely Vishvakarma. The Great Architect's plan gives a universal dimension to the individual's spiritual objectives.

Building trades – among others – have been able to provide the basis of
such a schema, by virtue of a traditional symbolism which applied spiritual
principles to contingent activities. Building and shaping the stone are creating order out of chaos, harmonizing raw matter in accordance with divine
laws. Simultaneously the soul is shaped to the divine pattern, raised like the
House of God (BETHEL). The science of geometry is made holy.

It is rather significant that, throughout the world, building is accompanied
by ritual, often sacrificial practices directed to incorporating into the structure the essence or life of the victim so sacrificed. (In India this was the
Universal Essence (*purusha*), originally a human sacrifice.) Concomitantly,
as in Japan, the objective was to purify the site and to appease the wrath
of the local *kami*; to protect oneself from accidents and, as in Vietnam, to
ensure long life to the building and protect it from fire. In no case does
the deeper meaning of this imitation of cosmogony appear to have been
disregarded.

Now let us instance two applications of the symbolism of building on a
quite different plane.

The Buddha regarded the elimination of mental 'buildings' as essential to
the achievement of Deliverance. 'Now I have seen you, builder of the house,
never again shall you build for me . . . . My heart is delivered from all building, I have achieved the elimination of thirst' (*Dhammapada* 154). During
the course of Deliverance, 'detachment from the cosmos', the 'roof of the
house' shatters to pieces.

The *Secret of the Golden Flower* – oddly in tune with St Simeon the New
Theologian – makes building the symbol of the rigorous method which
should be applied to spiritual experimentation (BURA, DANA, GUES,
HERS, SCHP).

bull (see also COW) Bulls arouse visions of irresistible strength and vitality. They not only evoke male impulsiveness, but also the terrifying MINOTAUR which guarded the Labyrinth (see MAZE). They are epitomized in the savage, bellowing Rudra of the *Rig-Veda*, whose free-flowing sperm fertilized the world. Most heavenly bulls fall into this category, especially the Babylonian Enlil.

As a symbol of the powers of creation, the bull was an emblem of the god El, often fashioned as a small bronze figure to be set on the end of a staff or rod as a portable standard, on the lines of the GOLDEN CALF. In their most primitive forms these emblems occur as early as the third millennium BC. The Hebrew patriarchs carried the worship of El to Palestine. It was proscribed by Moses but survived until the reign of David, as statues of the sacred bull, dating from that period and influenced by Egyptian art, confirm. Bulls are featured on the ceremonial slate palette of King Narmer (now in the Cairo Museum) and on the battle-standard of Mari (from eastern Syria); and their statuettes have been found on the plateaux of central Anatolia.

In Greek mythology, bulls symbolized the unleashing of uncontrolled violence. They were animals sacred to POSEIDON, god of the sea and of storms, and to Dionysos, god of male fertility. Hesiod (*Theogony* 832) describes the bull 'bellowing aloud in proud ungovernable fury'. ZEUS took the form of a gleaming white bull to seduce Europa. He came gently up to the girl and knelt at her feet. She stroked the beast and sat on its back. At once he carried her off, launching himself into the air and over the sea. Landing in Crete, they mated and legend says that three children were born to them.

Bulls, or rather cattle in general, symbolized sky-gods in Indo-Mediterranean religion because of the similarity between their tireless and uncontrolled fertility and that of the sky-god OURANOS (Uranus). Indra, the Vedic god, is also likened to the bull, while his equivalents in Persia and the Middle East are in addition compared with rams and he-goats. They are so many 'symbols of the male and combative spirit and of the elementary forces of the blood' (Benveniste-Renou, quoted in ELIT p. 86). There are Vedic hymns in honour of the cow as a divinity, which, in this context, should be taken to be applicable to cattle in general.

Indra the bull is the fecundating power of heat and is related to the complex symbolism of fertility – horn, sky, water, lightning, rain and so on. Autran observes that in Akkadian, 'to break the horn' is 'to break the power'. However, that power need not be broken, it can be sublimated. The bull may be the emblem of Indra, but it is also the emblem of Shiva, when it is pure white and stately, its hump reminiscent of a snowy mountain. It represents sexual energy, but when Shiva bestrides it, he tames and transforms this energy to spiritual ends and for the purposes of Yoga. Nandi, Shiva's bull, symbolizes justice and strength. It symbolizes *dharma*, the cosmic order, and for that reason is called 'unfathomable'.

Vrishabha, the Vedic bull, also carries the manifestation of the world and, standing motionless at its hub, sets the cosmic wheel turning. By virtue of this analogy, Buddhist legend claims the place of the Vedic bull for its hero. The bull, it is said, at the end of each of the four ages, withdraws one of its hooves from the ground. When all are free the foundations of the world will be destroyed. The Sioux cast the primordial BISON in the same part. Among the Altaic peoples and in Islamic tradition the bull belongs to the cycle of animals which, like the TORTOISE, bear the world upon their backs. The bull is sometimes placed in an intermediate position. Thus, in ascending order, the tortoise bears a rock, the rock bears a bull and the bull bears the Earth on its back. Sometimes still more creatures intervene. In different civilizations, different animals, such as elephants, play the same part. In Solomon's temple, twelve bulls held up the sea of bronze cast to hold water for lustration, three facing each of the cardinal points (2 Kings 7: 25).

Many Turkic and Tatar tribes regard bulls as incarnations of the powers of the Underworld and believe they carry the weight of the world upon their backs or their horns (HARA).

The symbolism of the bull is also tied to that of storms, rain and the Moon.

From a very early period (c. 2400 BC) bulls and THUNDERBOLTS were conjoined as symbols of the sky-gods. Archaic cultures identified the bellowing of the bull with hurricanes and thunder (hence the Aborigines' BULL-ROARER), both being manifestations of the powers of fertility.

The triad thunder–storm–rain was sometimes held, for example by Eskimos, Bushmen and Peruvian Indians, as a manifestation of the sacred nature of the Moon. Menghin demonstrated a link between Aurignacian female figures (carrying a horn in their hands) and the crescent Moon. In the Neolithic period, cult figures of bovine and related species are common and always found in connection with the worship of the Great Mother (the Moon). Leroi-Gourhan's researches (LERP, LERR) have shown by detailed comparison of late (Aurignacian and Magdalenian) Paleolithic cave painting that there is an unchanging order of precedence in the arrangement of the animals, whether they are depicted at Lascaux or Altamira, or in the cave paintings in Russia or the Caucasus. In this arrangement, the central place is always filled by a pairing of either horse and bull, or horse and bison. One can well imagine what broad new vistas this observation has opened in the study of symbolic thought and its part in the genesis of mankind.

Mediterranean and Middle Eastern lunar deities were depicted in the shape of bulls and endowed with taurine attributes. Thus the Chaldean Moon-god of Ur was styled 'the mighty, the young bull of the sky' or 'the mighty, the young bull with powerful horns', while in Egypt, the Moon-god was 'the bull of the stars' (ELIT pp. 79, 89, 90, 91–6). The Moon-god, Osiris, was depicted as a bull. Sin, the Mesopotamian Moon-god, also assumed the shape of a bull. Venus dwells by night in the sign of TAURUS (the Bull) and the Moon is there in its ascendant. In Persia, the Moon was Gaocithra 'who preserves the bull's sperm' for, according to ancient myth, the primordial bull deposited its sperm in this star of night (KRAM p. 87).

Among Mongols and Yakuts in central Asia and Siberia one can meet with a belief in a water bull, lurking at the bottom of lakes and presaging storms by its bellowing (HARA p. 279).

Bulls are thus held to be lunar animals and connected with darkness. Shiva's 'perfect horn' is the crescent Moon. This identification occurred at a very early period, as evidence from Ancient Egypt and Babylon shows. Nonetheless the bull is also attributed to Mithras, a Sun-god, when it symbolizes the death and resurrection of the god. However, here too the bull preserves the lunar aspect of death.

The first letter of the Hebrew alphabet, '*aleph*, which means "bull", is the symbol of the moon in its first week and also the name of the sign of the zodiac where the moon's mansions begin' (ELIT p. 178). Many letters of the alphabet, hieroglyphs and ideograms are simultaneously associated with the phases of the Moon and with the bull's horns, the latter often compared with the crescent Moon.

In the second century AD a cult was introduced to Italy from Asia Minor which enriched the subterranean rites of Cybele with a practice hitherto unknown in Rome – the 'taurobolium'. This was initiation through baptism in blood, described by Jean Beaujeu. The devotee

who wished to participate went down into a trench especially dug for that purpose and covered over with a board pierced with holes. A bull had its throat cut with a sacred spear immediately above and its blood splashed down through the holes and over the devotee's entire body. Whoever underwent this sprinkling with blood was *renatus in aeternum*, reborn to eternal life. The energy and vitality of the bull, commonly held with the lion to be the strongest of all animals, would regenerate the body, and perhaps the soul, of the participant.

The blood of the bull spattering upon the priest of the mysteries was believed to confer upon him, by dual symbolism, the physical strength of the bull and above all to endow him, under a higher form, with the immortal life of the spirit.

The worship of Mithras came originally from Persia and included the sacrifice of bulls, with a similar significance but in a slightly different ritual and doctrinal setting. The Roman legions carried throughout the Empire the worship of the saviour, the invincible conqueror, the god to whom a rock gave birth on 25 December, when the days begin to grow longer, 'the day on which the rebirth of the Sun, Natalis Solis, was celebrated . . . . The central deed in Mithras' life was the sacrifice of the primordial bull, the first living creature created by Ahura Mazdā. Having subdued and led the bull to his cave, on the orders of the Sun, Mithras cut its throat. From its blood, marrow and seed, plant and animal life sprang up despite the efforts of Ahriman's accomplices, the serpent and the scorpion, to prevent them. Innumerable Mithraic emblems carry the ascension of Mithras and the sacrifice of the bull, the two scenes symbolizing the struggle of the powers of good against the spirits of evil, a struggle in which all the faithful should constantly join with all their strength, and attainment of the realms of eternal light assured to the souls of the righteous through the intercession of Mithras the Almighty' (BEAG).

It is perhaps to apply too generous a law of interpretation to regard, as Krappe does, the sacrifice of the bull as the penetration of the female by the male principle, of water by fire, of the Moon by the Sun and, hence, to explain it as a fertility symbol. What the cult of Mithras reflects is less a fertility symbol than that of the cyclic recurrence of death and resurrection and thus of the unity and permanence of the vital principle.

Death is inseparable from life and there is a death aspect to the bull. To the Ancient Egyptians the bull bearing a solar disk between its horns was at one and the same time a symbol of fertility and a funeral-god associated with Osiris and his resurrections. The funeral rites of the bull itself were celebrated with due pomp at Memphis and offerings were brought from all quarters of Egypt, 'but scarcely had Apis vanished than he was reincarnated in another bull, to be recognized from his fellows by the black markings on face, neck and back of his pure white hide.'

The Tatars of the Altai Mountains depicted the lord of the Underworld sometimes seated in a black boat without oars and sometimes seated facing backwards on a black bull (HARA p. 244). He held either a snake or a Moon-shaped axe in his hand and black bulls or cows were sacrificed to him.

Throughout almost the whole of Asia, black bulls are associated with death. In India and Indonesia it was customary to cremate the bodies of princes in bull-shaped coffins. Ancient Egyptian wall-paintings show Osiris' body carried on the back of a black bull.

The Celts do not seem to see the bull's symbolic qualities as purely those of virility and it is not clear whether their original significance should be sought in the bull's duality with or sexual opposition to the cow. In fact, in Ireland the bull is especially prominent in warlike metaphor. A hero or king of outstanding warlike qualities is often called 'a bull in battle'. On the other hand bulls were victims of what in Ireland were termed 'bull feasts', the preliminary stage in the election of kings, as recounted in *The Madness of Cùchulainn*. A bull was sacrificed and a bard ate and drank his fill of the broth and flesh of the animal. He went to sleep and dreamed of the royal candidate whom the assembly of nobles was to choose. The second stage in the ritual (involving the king-elect) had a horse as its sacrificial victim. The bull is thus paired in opposition to the horse, but is as warlike as the latter. The sacrifice of white bulls which Pliny reports (*Natural History* 16: 249) when describing the culling of mistletoe, was an ancient royal rite which had lost its meaning in Gaul after the loss of all political independence following the Roman conquest. Like the horse, the bull is a beast royal. The tetrarchs of Galatia bore the title of Deiotaros, 'Divine Bull', because they were kings, and not because they were priests as is sometimes incorrectly supposed. This context takes us back to the binary role of horse–bull in Paleolithic art, which we have already discussed.

Bulls are most certainly primordial creatures. In the tale of *The Cattle Raid of Cooley*, a white bull and a brown bull fight to the death. One represents Ulster and the other Connaught, and to possess them is the possession of supremacy in war – all the more so because the animals are endowed with human speech and reason. They are in fact the last of a series of animal metamorphoses undergone by the swineherds of the kings of the north and the south of Ireland. Celtic iconography from Gaul includes a bull with three cranes (probably the equivalents of swans in the British Isles) and a bull with three horns. The latter is probably an ancient warlike symbol of which the meaning was lost in Gallo-Roman times. The third horn may well represent what in Ireland was called the *lon laith* or 'hero's moon', a sort of halo of blood which spouted from the crown of a warrior's head in the heat of battle. Incidentally it may be observed that the name of 'bison' has survived in France in Vesontio, the old name of Besançon (CHAB pp. 54–65; OGAC 10: pp. 285ff.; 15: pp. 123ff., 245ff.).

The bull is a mass of ambivalences and ambiguities. Fire and water: he is lunar in his association with fertility rites, solar through the fire in his blood and the jetting of his seed. On a royal tomb in Ur stood a bull with a golden head (Sun and fire) and jaws of lapis-lazuli (Moon and water). He is both celestial and chthonian. In fact cattle, like dogs, can feature sometimes in chthonian and sometimes in celestial manifestations. Often their colour provides the clue to their precise symbolism. Thus some of the Altaic peoples depict the marriage of Heaven and Earth as the dun ox, a manifestation of the female and Earth, in contrast with the white horse, embodying the male powers of Heaven (ROUF pp. 343ff.).

In China, the horns on the head of Chen-nung, inventor of agriculture, recall the ox or bull, but those of Ch'i-You may positively be identified with the bull. Again Huang Ti is opposed to them both. The bull is a spirit of the wind. Ch'i-You, with his horned head and cloven hooves, thanks to wind (and rain) battles with Huang Ti who fights him not only with water-dragons but with drought as well. Ch'i-You abets cosmic disorder and is defeated by Huang Ti, whose emblem is the owl.

The OX, symbolic antithesis of the bull, underlines this complexity, for the ox, too, is associated with agrarian religions. However, he becomes the symbol of the sacrifice of the bull's procreative powers, underlining by contrast their unique quality. By suppressing that power, the ox only makes it the more valuable, just as chastity underlines the importance of sexuality. The celestial principle shows its strength in the absolute affirmation or renunciation of its powers. When free, it fertilizes; chaste and restrained, it emphasizes equally clearly that without it there can be no fertility, at least in that order and on that level of being. It is the counter-proof of the same truth. Sublimation of the life force gives rise to fertility of another order, that of the spiritual life.

In the Jungian analysis of symbolism the sacrifice of the bull 'can be seen as a symbol of the triumph of man's spiritual nature over his animality' (JUNS p. 147). The bull is uncontrolled force, upon which the developed personality gradually exerts its influence. Infatuation with the bull-ring may perhaps be explained, according to some analysts, as the secret and inarticulate wish to kill the beast within. However, what happens is substitution. The sacrifice of the beast externally absolves from the need of internal sacrifice or, through the intervention of the torero, provides the illusion of personal triumph.

Some analysts, too, regard the bull as the dominant father figure, like some OURANUS (Uranus) whom his son CRONOS determined to castrate. This is another form of the OEDIPUS complex; killing the bull is suppressing the father.

According to Paul Diel's ethico-biological interpretation, bulls with their brute strength symbolize tyranny: 'They breathe the flames of destruction. The attribute of *brazen* complementing the symbol *hoof* is a frequent image in Greek mythology which is used to characterize the soul-state. When attributed to bulls, brazen hooves symbolize the dominant trait of the tendency towards tyranny, ferocity and hardening of soul' (DIES p. 176).

Hephaistos had forged a mighty pair of ferocious bulls with brazen hooves, which breathed fire and seemed untameable. To win the GOLDEN FLEECE, Jason had to yoke them unaided. This task symbolized the hero's duty to curb the violence of his passions before acquiring this symbol of spiritual perfection, that is to say he had to have sublimated his instincts.

bulla An ornament worn as a medallion by young Romans; it was offered to the gods when the *praetexta* (the child's dress) was laid aside on reaching manhood or at the time of marriage. Fashioned by welding together two circular concave sheets of anything from gold to glass, the *bulla* contained magic spells and acted as a preservative. It is the symbol of the guardian spirit which the the wearer wished to conciliate and decorated the victorious commander at his triumph.

From it is derived the name of Papal Bull, which from the second century onwards was applied to documents emanating from the Roman Curia and sealed with round lead seals in the shape of *bullae*. 'Bull' was also applied to royal enactments. In this context the symbolism derives from its spherical shape, displaying astral perfection, sovereignty and independence.

bull-roarer A musical instrument made of a piece of wood attached to the end of a cord and whirled round to produce a roaring sound suggestive of THUNDER, or, as the name implies, the bellowing of a BULL. Universally regarded as sacred and used in initiation ceremonies, its deep and mysterious booming sound in the depths of the night suggests 'god is coming' (ELIT p. 41). The bull-roarer is the voice of the spirits and sometimes of the mythic ancestors and is associated with the complex symbolism of the storm and its attributes – thunder, LIGHTNING and RAIN. It is simultaneously an expession of the wrath of the gods, that is to say an unleashing of primordial celestial and of male procreative powers, associated with the lunar level of symbol.

The Apache medicine man used the bull-roarer to make himself invulnerable and to foretell the future (Bourke, *The Medicine-men of the Apaches* in ELIC). When young women of the Aranda Aborigine tribe in Australia hear the bull-roarer, they cry: 'What pricked me? Oh! That man was my husband!' and they feel a sharp pain in their genitals.

Like most cult instruments through which the voices of the gods are heard, for ritual reasons the bull-roarer is only handled by men and, among the Amerindians of the Orinoco (Piaroa, Maku and Puinave), women are even forbidden to look upon it.

There is evidence of its employment in sexual orgies in Ancient Greece. In Australia it is the voice of the Ancestor and of thunder.

When ancient beliefs have disappeared and rituals have lost their meaning, the bull-roarer becomes a child's toy.

bundle The enigmatic phrase, 'the bundle of life' (*seror hahayim* in Hebrew) occurs only once in this context in the Bible, in 1 Samuel 25: 29: 'Yet a man is risen up to pursue thee, and to seek thy soul: but the soul of my lord shall be bound in the bundle of life with the Lord thy God; and the souls of thy enemies, them he shall sling out, as out of the middle of a sling.'

'Bundle' describes the place where life is preserved, with a clear sense of salvation (see Ecclesiasticus 6: 16).

This figuration is close to that of the Book of Life evinced in Psalm 69: 28 (cf. Isaiah 4: 3; Daniel 12: 1; Enoch 47: 3; Revelation 3: 5 and 20: 12). For a person's name to be written in this book is the equivalent of salvation: for it to be blotted out, of damnation (DORH p. 52).

A recent archaeological discovery has cast a direct light upon the precise meaning of the phrase. A cuneiform tablet excavated from the Mesopotamian site of Nuzu (Yorghan-tepe near Kirkuk) uses the same term (root: s-r-r) to describe the activity of casting accounts, in this case an inventory of livestock (EISB). The Bible retains this quality of accountancy when using it, often to describe the act of putting money into a purse or bag (see Genesis 42: 35; Proverbs 7: 20; Haggai 1: 6) or some other valuable item into a bundle (see Song of Solomon 1: 13: 'a bundle of myrrh').

The term has also been related to the practice of keeping written scrolls in a jar, a practice confirmed by the discoveries at Qumran of the famous Dead Sea Scrolls (VUIO). Isaiah (8: 16) undoubtedly refers to this practice, from which it may be presumed that from an early age the teachings of the prophets were handed down, at least in part, through written tradition.

The juridical aspect of this action is clearly emphasized by other references to the insertion and recording of the sins of the people (Hosea 13: 12) or of the individual (Job 14: 17). In this context it is a matter of recording a person's deeds, which will bear witness for or against them at the Day of Judgement (CAZJ).

However, this ethical motif remains subsidiary to the basic meaning of the symbol, which remains that of the protection and salvation which God provides. This aspect is of very long standing – from Biblical times to our own day – sustained by religious writings and funeral epitaphs.

To the first category belongs a hymn from Qumran in which the author expresses his absolute trust in God during a time of persecution, saying: 'I give Thee thanks, O Adonai, for thou hast placed my soul in the [bundle] of life and protected me from the snares of the Pit' (DUPE p. 221).

Meanwhile a wealth of Jewish epitaphs, especially from north Germany, bear witness to the survival to the present day of the theme of trust in God extending beyond the confines of human existence (JACT pp. 185–6).

bush In the Old Testament, the 'Burning Bush' symbolizes the presence of God. Exodus 3: 2, paints the picture of the bush from the midst of which God appeared to Moses and 'the bush burned with fire, and the bush was not consumed.' In Judges 9: 8–15, there is the fable of the trees consulting to elect a king and choosing the bramble-bush. It replied: 'If in truth ye anoint me king over you, then come and put your trust in my shadow: and if not, let fire come out of the bramble, and devour the cedars of Lebanon.'

In Celtic tradition there is very little difference in the symbolism of the bush and the TREE, and this is especially noteworthy in the Middle Welsh poem *Cad Goddeu* ('The Battle of the Trees'). The word *goddeu* can mean both 'tree' and 'thought', which confirms the symbolic equivalence of 'wood', 'bush' and 'knowledge' (OGAC 5: p. 119).

Symbols are completely amoral and, like malicious imps, enjoy superimposing antithesis upon thesis to shocking, not to say scandalous effect, unless an all-embracing view is adopted. And this is true of 'bushes' and 'burning bushes' which are held to conceal a treasure in their thickets. This in French erotic literature is just as likely to be a woman's sexual organs as the presence of God. In both cases it is most certainly burning, so powerful and rapacious is the desire it provokes. It is also fascinating to recall that in medieval liturgical writing, 'Burning Bush' is used metaphorically to describe Our Lady, the Mother of God, manifesting the presence of God, her burning love and her revelation.

bushel The British dry measure of capacity equals 36.4 litres. In China the standard dry measure is the *teu* (Vietnamese *dau*), holding only 10.31 litres nowadays and slightly more than the British 'peck' of 9.1 litres. The *teu* is of great antiquity and was standardized in Han times because the Taoist organizations of that period levied a 'celestial tax' of five *teu* of rice. Hence bushels (the containers) became the emblems of Taoism for those who were not members of the sect.

Essentially the symbolic employment of the bushel is the achievement of the secret societies which stem from the *T'ien-ti-huei*, or Society of Heaven and Earth. In the centre of its lodge, in a space called 'The City of Willows', stood a bushel full of red rice. Since the City of Willows epitomized the lodge as a whole, the *teu* represented the city and became a substitute for it; and in any case the ideograms *mu-yang cheng* (City of Willows) were written on the bushel itself. As they lifted the bushel, new initiates expressly stated: 'We raise the City of Willows to destroy *Ts'ing* and to restore *Ming*.' Now, *Ming* was not merely the name of an Imperial dynasty, but had the primary meaning of 'light'. To bring back the light by raising the bushel corresponds in an odd way to a symbol which is familiar to Europeans: if it is not *hidden under the bushel*, the light is at least contained in it.

The emblem of ingathering, 'ARK of the covenant' and receptacle of the basic symbols, the *teu* held RICE, the 'food of immortality'. It contains it 'through the power of *ming*', that is 'by the strength of light' or of knowledge.

Furthermore, *teu* is the name of the GREAT BEAR. Now the Great Bear is enthroned in the middle of the heavens like the sovereign in the heart of the Empire and rules the march of the seasons and the course of the world. If the *teu* is the Great Bear, the four main doors of the lodge correspond to the four seasons. Lying directly on the vertical line of the celestial pole, the bushel is the point upon which the activities of the celestials are exerted. Its place in the City of Willows is precisely that of the LINGAM in the *cella* of a Hindu temple, the receptacle of light in the 'cavern of the heart' (FAVS, GUET, GRIL, MAST, SCHL, WARH).

One of the sons of the Irish god, Dian Cécht (who may be identified with Apollo in his aspect of the healer), was called *Miach*, 'bushel'. His father killed him because he had grafted onto the one-armed king, Nuada, a live arm instead of the artificial silver arm fashioned by Dian Cécht. Airmed, Dian Cécht's daughter, arranged the 360 plants which had sprung up from her brother Miach's grave according to their virtues. However, Dian Cécht brought them to such confusion that nobody could use them. Miach (bushel) symbolizes the measure of cosmic balance, and Dian Cécht kills his son because knowledge of the virtues of plants should be kept secret. He puts it 'under the bushel' (OGAC 16: p. 223 n. 4; ETUC 398 (1966), pp. 272–9).

bustard The cock bird of this large ground-running species often has two or three hens with him and in Africa symbolizes the polygamous family. Because it is a ground-runner and seldom takes wing, it is proverbial of the child which never leaves its mother's apron-strings and never grows up. On the other hand, hunters find it very hard to catch. Proverbially able to run rings round its hunters, it has given rise to their saying: 'You can't catch me, I'm a bustard!'

As a night bird it symbolizes the changeful world. The delicate crest of feathers which crown the cock are merely ephemeral ornaments. The world is like this bird which stands on one leg, flaps its wings and can never be caught and held. As a day bird, it suggests the prey which can never be taken, over which men quarrel and fight and for which they do murder in the end. 'Better', says the Fulani proverb, 'to leave this world without regrets since it trips and crushes those who try to master it' (HAMK pp. 14, 62).

In Africa the sign for the bustard is either a single ∨ or double ✕ claw-print. In marriage, the bustard may be the symbol of 'the union of souls and of fertility, and of the interpenetration of matter by the soul'. If the sign of the bustard is traced in the ashes round the bed of a dead person, 'this is because the soul has at last been delivered and taken wing.' The bustard's double claw-print emphasizes its role of mediator between Heaven and Earth. It also stands for 'TREES with leaves which bud in the upper world and roots which draw nourishment from the Underworld.' Lastly, this migratory bird may symbolize 'the questing human soul' (SERH pp. 74–6).

butter (see also FAT) The Celtic words for butter (*imb* in Irish: *amann* in Breton) are related to the Indo-European roots meaning 'unguent' and 'unction', from which it may be inferred that this is a word which has lost a great deal of its original religious quality. Apparently in magical practices butter was a substitute for HONEY and beeswax, since traces of its use have been found in Brittany.

In the past, butter, which had magical properties similar to those of beeswax, was used to trap the intangible. When somebody died of cancer, a pat of butter was left at the bed-side and, on the return of the funeral party, it was buried, being deemed to have caught the disease. Furthermore there was a proverbial saying that honey attracted souls, which is yet another way of expressing the same property.

(OGAC 4: extra fasc. 20)

A marginal note in an eighth-century manuscript from St Gall states that the Irish invoked the blacksmith Gobniu to keep their butter sweet (OGAC 4: p. 262), since it was held to have caught and retained the life force.

Butter became known to and appreciated by Mediterranean civilizations at a comparatively late period, Pliny mentioning it as 'a delicious dish eaten by the Barbarians'. However, the opposite was the case in India where, from the remotest Vedic past, butter had qualities of holiness and was invoked in hymns as a primordial godhead.

That is the secret name of butter: 'tongue of the gods', 'navel of immortality'. We will proclaim the name of butter; we will sustain it in this sacrifice by bowing low . . . . Like whirlpools in the current of a river, the young streams of butter surge forth and swell with waves, overtaking the wind like a chestnut racehorse that breaks through the sides of the track . . . . The streams of butter . . . touch the fuel-sticks, and Agni joyously woos them.

(VEDR pp. 126–7)

In this as in many other hymns, butter is an essential element in sacrifice, being the prescriptive substance for offering. As the navel of immortality, it is emblematic of the life stream. Spread on fire, it makes it crackle and restores Agni himself to life.

As a concentration of the life force, butter symbolizes strength in general, that of the cosmos, the soul, of gods and men and as it splutters in the sacrificial flames it is held to reinvigorate them all. Every blessing, both material and spiritual, will flow out over the world like liquefied butter and with increased strength. In so far as butter is cast upon the flames in a ritual gesture, it is suggestive of prayer. It is, again like prayer, a source of holy vigour working in the spirits of the faithful and fit to rouse the universe.

butterfly By its grace and airy lightness, the Japanese make the butterfly an emblem of womanhood. Two butterflies, however, represent marital happiness. Their airy lightness is rarefied, for butterflies are wandering spirits and to see them presages a visitor or a death in the family.

Another facet of butterfly symbolism is based upon its metamorphoses. Its chrysalis is the egg which contains the potentiality of being and the butterfly which emerges from it is the symbol of resurrection, or one might rather say of rising from the grave. The myth of PSYCHE employs symbolism of this order and she is depicted with butterfly wings. It recurs in the myth of the Immortal Gardener, Yuan-k'o, whose lovely wife taught the secret of the silk-worm and may perhaps have herself been a silk-worm.

It may seem paradoxical that in the Sino-Vietnamese world the butterfly should serve as the expression of a wish for long life. This arises from the homophony, two ideograms being pronounced *t'ie*, the one meaning 'butterfly' and the other 'great age' or 'seventy-year-old'. Furthermore, the butterfly is sometimes associated with the chrysanthemum to symbolize autumn (DURV, GUEM, KALL, OGRJ).

In the *Tochmarc Etaine* or *Courtship of Etain*, a tale from the Irish mythological cycle, the goddess, who symbolizes kingly power and who is married to the god Midir, is changed into a puddle of water through the jealousy of Midir's first wife. Shortly afterwards, however, from the puddle is born a worm which becomes a splendid butterfly. Although the Irish writer sometimes calls it a fly, the symbolism is eminently favourable. The gods Midir and later Oenghus sheltered and guarded it.

And that worm became a purple fly. It was the size of a man's head and it was the most beautiful fly in all the world. The sound of its voice and the hum of its wings were sweeter than bagpipe, harp or horn. Its eyes glittered like precious jewels in the darkness. Its scent and perfume took away hunger and thirst from whoever it fluttered around. The dewdrops which fell from its wings cured all pain, sickness and plague from whoever it visited.

The symbolism is that of the butterfly and that of the soul freed from its covering of flesh, as in Christian symbolism (CHAB pp. 847–51), to become both blessed and a blessing.

To the Aztecs the butterfly symbolized the soul or the breath of life exhaled by the dying. A butterfly fluttering among the flowers represented the soul of the warrior who had fallen on the battlefield (KRIR p. 43). Dead warriors accompanied the Sun on the first half of his visible journey, until midday. They then descended to earth in the shapes of hummingbirds or butterflies (KRIR p. 61).

All these interpretations probably stem from the similarity between the flickering brightness of flame and the fluttering, coloured wings of the butterfly. Thus the Aztec fire-god wore a pectoral ornament called 'the OBSIDIAN butterfly'. Like flint, obsidian is a fire-stone and its use for the blades of sacrificial knives is well known. In 'the House of Eagles' or Warriors' Temple, the Sun was depicted as a butterfly.

Symbol of daylight and the solar fire – and hence of the warrior's SOUL – the butterfly for the Mexicans was also a symbol of the 'Black Sun' which passed through the Underworlds during its nightly journey. It was thus a symbol of hidden chthonian fire and associated with ideas of sacrifice, death and resurrection. In Aztec carving, the butterfly became an alternative for the hand as the emblem of the figure FIVE, the number of the centre of the Earth (SOUC).

A Baluba and Lulua fable from Kasai (central Zaire) demonstrates the analogy of butterfly to soul and the shading of symbol into image. The cycle of human life and death follows that of the butterfly, they say. In childhood a person is a tiny caterpillar, in maturity a large caterpillar and in old age becomes a chrysalis. The grave is the cocoon from which the person's soul emerges and flies away in the shape of a butterfly. That the butterfly then lays eggs is an expression of human reincarnation (FOUA). Similarly contemporary psychoanalysis sees the butterfly as a symbol of rebirth.

In Classical antiquity it was a common belief that the soul left the body in the shape of a butterfly. In Pompeian wall paintings, Psyche is depicted as a little girl with butterfly-wings (GRID). This belief recurs among some Turkic tribes in central Asia, who have felt Persian influence and who believe that the dead return in the shape of MOTHS (HARA p. 254).

C

Cabeiri The Cabeiri were phallic genii, worshipped with special rites at Lemnos (SEGC p. 266, n. 89). According to Grimal (GRID p. 70), they were 'mysterious divinities whose chief shrine was at Samothrace, but who were worshipped throughout the Mediterranean area and even, Herodotus tells us, at Memphis in Egypt.' Their numbers are variously given as three, four or seven and sometimes they are said to be the children of HEPHAISTOS and at other times are associated with Demeter, Persephone, Hades or Hermes, and in Rome with the Capitoline Triad of Jupiter, Minerva and Mercury. Their peculiarity was that they could not be named with impunity. They formed part of the retinue of Rhea, the wife of Cronos and mother of the third generation of gods. Because they were her servants, they were confused with the Corybantes and Curetes. Because they were held, at a later period, to protect sailors, they were identified with the Dioscuri. However, their mystery still remains insoluble and, seldom invoked as they were, the Cabeiri's place in mythology is as equivocal genii. Undoubtedly they corresponded with the most secret and hidden aspect of the godhead, the never-to-be-revealed mystery of divine energy. This, perhaps, is why they were made to symbolize unknown spiritual powers, those energies contained within gods and men like a reserve of strength which can neither be calculated nor spoken of, and which it is dangerous to unleash, in the fashion of the Sorcerer's Apprentice.

caduceus One of the most ancient of symbols, represented in an engraving on the goblet of Gudea, King of Lagash, in 2600 BC, and on those stone slabs known in India as *nāgakala*. The patterns and meanings of the caduceus are much more varied than is generally thought, but they are not necessarily mutually exclusive.

The caduceus, the emblem of HERMES (Mercury), is a wand around which two SERPENTS are threaded in opposite directions. It thus holds the balance between the two symbolical aspects of the creature, left and right, light and dark. Symbolically the serpent has a dual aspect, both beneficent and maleficent, presented in opposition and equilibrium in the caduceus. This balance and polarity are the especial attributes of the cosmic stream which is represented in more general terms in the double SPIRAL. The legend of the caduceus associates it with primordial Chaos (two serpents fighting) and their eventual wreathing round the wand actualizes the equilibrium of opposing tendencies around the world AXIS. This has sometimes resulted in the caduceus being called a symbol of peace. Hermes was the messenger of the gods and also guided humans through their changes of being. The latter, as Guénon observes, neatly relates to the ascending and descending streams represented by the two serpents.

The twofold binding round the Brahman's staff manifests the same symbolism as does that of the two *nādi* around the Tantric *sūshumna* and by their twice circumambulating the cosmic pillar before Izanagi and Izanami consummated their marriage. An even better example is that of Fu-hsi and Nu-kua, their serpent-tails intertwined as they exchange their attributes of COMPASS and SQUARE (BURN, GUET, GUES, SAIR, SCHI).

Another interpretation stresses the symbolism of fertility. The caduceus comprises two serpents coupling on an erect PHALLUS. It would seem to be one of the most ancient of Indo-European images, found in association with various rites in both ancient and modern India, as the emblem of Hermes in Greek mythology and then transferred to Mercury by the Romans. In the words of Jung's disciple Henderson, this spiritualized phallus of Hermes, conductor of souls, 'penetrates from the known into the unknown world, seeking a spiritual message of deliverance and healing' (JUNS p. 156). The caduceus is known worldwide today as the symbol of medical science.

However, the caduceus only acquired its full meaning when the Ancient Greeks placed a pair of wings on the serpents. From then on the symbol became a synthesis of the chthonian world below and that of the sky above, transcending its origins. It is somewhat reminiscent of Chinese winged DRAGONS and depictions of the Aztec god, Quetzalcoatl, who gave himself up to sacrifice, was born again and went up to Heaven in the shape of a plumed serpent.

'The magic WAND for which the caduceus stands and which is commonly represented by a rod round which a pair of serpents are wreathed, suggests the worship of TREES and of the Earth, foster-mother of the serpent, of great antiquity around the shores of the Aegean' (SECG p. 278). In fact:

the Hindu caduceus is associated with the sacred tree .... The Mesopotamian caduceus displays a central rod. It seems in all likelihood to have been a reminiscence of the tree .... Hermes' caduceus (and, of course, Aesculapius' snake-wreathed staff) may justly be regarded as symbols of the tree, associated with the dwelling of, or a substitute for the godhead. Although that wand may have subsequently acquired a different meaning, prophetic or healing powers, it still remains the symbol of the powers of the tree-god.

(BOUA p. 166)

Quoting Athenagoras and Macrobius in support, Court de Gébelin regards the rod as symbolizing the equator, the pair of wings as time and the two serpents, male and female, 'as the Sun and Moon which, in the course of a year, travel through the ecliptic on which they are sometimes separated and sometimes come together.' This interpretation is consistent with the view of Hermes as the father of astronomy and agriculture (BOUA p. 168). Alchemists are equally ready with their own explanation of the caduceus.

It is the sceptre of Hermes, the god of alchemy. It was presented by Apollo in exchange for the lyre which Hermes invented, and comprises a wand of gold enwreathed by two serpents. To the alchemist these represent the two opposing principles which have to be reconciled, be they sulphur and mercury, fixed and volatile, wet and dry or hot and cold. This is effected by the unifying gold of the rod of the caduceus, which is seen as expressing the basic dualism which is the well-spring of alchemical thought and must be sucked back into the oneness of the Philosopher's Stone.

(VANA pp. 18–19)

This explanation introduces the concept of the caduceus as a symbol of equilibrium achieved by the integration of opposing forces, represented by the confrontation of the two snakes over which Hermes stood in judgement. Their conflict may symbolize the inner struggle between opposing forces of the physical or ethical order which undermine a person's health or moral stability. Thus the Romans, for example, regarded the caduceus as an emblem of moral stability and good behaviour. 'The rod represented strength, the two serpents prudence, the wings diligence and the helmet highmindedness.' Nevertheless this interpretation hardly rises above the level of the emblematic. The caduceus also unites the four natural elements and their symbolic qualities. The rod corresponds to Earth, the wings to Air and the serpents to Fire and Water. However, it is not simply their snaking movement, like the waves of the sea or the flicker of flames, which identifies serpents with water and fire, but their very nature. Their poisonous bite is fiery, their fluid movement almost liquid, making them the source of both life and death. According to esoteric Buddhist doctrine and, in particular, to Tantric teachings, the rod of the caduceus corresponds to the World AXIS and the serpents to *kundalinī*, the power which lies coiled at the base of the spine and which rises through successive CHAKRA to the apex of the fontanelle, a symbol of that pure energy which drives a person's inner development. In fact, the essential nature of the caduceus is defined by its very structure and the synthesis of the elements of which it is composed. It evokes the dynamic equilibrium of opposing forces which come together to constitute higher and stronger static forms and active structures. The duality of serpents and wings displays the ultimate condition of strength and self-mastery which may be achieved as much by instinct (serpents) as on a spiritual level (wings) (CIRD pp. 34–6).

However, the caduceus remains the symbol of human ambiguity and complexity and of the infinite potential of human development. Hermes' attribute comprises a wand or golden rod round which two serpents are symmetrically wreathed in a figure of eight. Hermes, says Homer (*Iliad* 24: 343–4), 'took the wand wherewith he lulls to sleep the eyes of whom he will, while others again he awakens even out of slumber.'

The wand may be an echo of the original worship of Hermes in an agrarian cult and of the magical powers which he controlled. Again, the two serpents re-echo the chthonian character which the god originally bore and his power to go down to Hades, to despatch his victims thither as well as to return whenever he pleased and to restore to the light of day some of those held imprisoned there. Pausanias records the existence of the worship of a white Hermes and a black Hermes, the dual aspects of this god, the one a sky-god, the other an Underworld deity, the one life-giving, the other death-dealing. The serpents on the caduceus indicate this ambiguity which is in itself a human characteristic.

Lastly we come to Paul Diel's explanation of the caduceus. His interpretation of its symbolism is inspired by his ethico-biological philosophy and based upon the myth which accords the caduceus as an attribute to Asclepios (Aesculapius), the first physician and future god of medicine, because he was able to use poisons to cure diseases and restore the dead to life. The entire life-cycle of medicine is condensed into the myth of Asclepios and comprised within the caduceus, for true cure and true resurrection apply to the soul. The serpents entwine around the staff – symbolizing the Tree of Life – to show egotism tamed and brought under control, their venom transformed to healing, the corruption of the life force brought back to its proper channel. Health 'is right proportion, harmonization of desire (the serpents' symmetrical coils), control of emotional stimuli, the need for spiritualization and sublimation [which] not only rule the health of the soul, [but] determine the health of the body as well' (DIES p. 233). Such an interpretation would make the caduceus the especial symbol of psycho-somatic balance.

Cain Whatever historical interpretations may be made of the Old Testament story (Genesis 4: 1–24), they are in no sense affected by the symbolic meaning which may be drawn from the same material. In other words, to discern symbols in the actions charted in this chapter of Genesis, is not thereby to exclude the possibility that those actions actually occurred, it is merely to give them an extra dimension which takes them beyond time and place. And even if the events never took place in precisely the way described in the Old Testament, their symbolism endures. Luc Estang (*Le jour de Caïn*, Paris, 1967) shows an extraordinary insight into the symbolic qualities of this old story.

According to the Book of Genesis itself, Cain was the first person to be born of man and woman; he was the first to till the land; he was the first whose sacrifice was rejected by God; he was the first murderer, and he was the first person to reveal the existence of death, for until he killed his brother, nobody had looked upon a corpse. Cain was the first 'wanderer' in search of fertile land and the first to build a town. He was also the man upon whom God 'set a mark ... lest any finding him should kill him'. He was also the first person who 'went out from the presence of the Lord', journeying endlessly towards the rising Sun.

The cycle of his life is of unparallelled greatness, since it is that of a man thrown upon his own resources, accepting all the risks of life and all the consequences of his own actions. Cain is the symbol of human responsibility.

His name means 'possession', because his mother said 'I have gotten a man from the Lord', because he was the first human birth. However, the possession of which he dreamed was possession of the Earth and above all, possession of his own self 'so as to possess all the rest. You have borne me in accordance with the will and with the help of God [he tells his mother]. I soon realized that he would not lift a finger to help me and that I had to rely upon myself alone. Remember this, you others, that the fire and the fury, the strength and the obstinacy for which you admire me, were things which I had to win for myself' (Luc Estang p. 88).

To be truly lord of the work of his hands, he tried to crown God's Earth with the fruits of man's labour. 'I dreamed of reconciling God with his earth' (p. 84). He tried to build a town which would show man's labours more clearly than the tilling of the soil. 'I saw the city as another sort of ploughing, sowing and harvesting. What am I saying? It was to raise the Earth above itself, yes, to lift it upright in the image of man, by man who would in so doing establish his own kingship .... Its walls would have enclosed the space in which I expected nothing of him [God]' (pp. 112–13). The town serves as the prologue of the atheism to come.

But God would not accept the sacrifices of this tiller of the soil and planner of cities. Why? Cain could not agree to be 'least-loved by God'. He had been ready to accept any sacrifice 'if only he had offered the slightest sign of acceptance. An unlovely creature, I needed love more than anything else. With this it would have been easy to please him. Without it, I became the hardened criminal, when one look would have made me relent' (p. 41).

Furthermore, God did not reward all his backbreaking toil. '"Let it be clearly understood," Cain said, "I didn't complain because Abel had all the advantages, but because I had none .... God remained indifferent to my exhaustion, blind to my sacrifice and deaf to my prayers"' (pp. 82, 92). And so he rebelled. Not for himself alone, but for 'all of you'. For all of you who do not accept the mystery of predestination which divides the human race into the saved and the damned, for all of you who do not understand 'the scorn which God feels for earthly greatness, and the favour which he shows to the humble'. This was the divine order against which he rebelled when he slit 'God's favourite' Abel's throat with a sliver of flint. Yet perhaps the secret of Cain's attitude towards God lies in the fact that his offering was not complete. He held back a part of his labours, not realizing that that portion, too, was owed to God. Then, in jealousy of his brother, in pride in his own achievements, in rebellion against God, he committed murder and dispensed with God.

From henceforth he was doomed to wander towards a future which he had perpetually to create. 'We are going into the empty spaces of mankind which mankind in its countless numbers will inhabit. Our guide will be the ever-fresh dawning of the day .... By never finding a resting place, we shall be everywhere. Our wanderings will measure out the world and at the same time build it up' (p. 125). He goes on to find 'man's future free from Jehovah's presence' (p. 126).

But he was forced to kill his brother, another aspect of his own self, and advance the hour of death. To gain his own freedom he was forced to resort to crime. Death 'is simply being forced to fall into a sleep from which there is no waking' (p. 24). He thrust it cruelly under the eyes of the first mother. 'That ancient bugbear, that lurking punishment, now you stand revealed! Under Abel's features we can see that you have the features of us all and that you reduce us all to the level of brutes' (p. 25). Adam and Eve saw death as the final fruit of the Tree of the Knowledge of Good and Evil. Standing before Abel's corpse, Adam cried out 'Here and now we suck the juice of the fruit of knowledge, and more than ever it is bitter to the taste' (p. 53). But he told Eve, 'We infected Abel's body with the germs of death' (p. 55). Utterly rejecting this, Eve replied, 'What purpose then to pass on life! Oh! It is as if he had torn a hole in my side: my children will now go on killing one another until the end of time' (p. 74). But Cain's wife, Temech, defended her husband: 'Let life be the winner, even at the price of death' (p. 57).

It is true that death was bound to arrive, since it was the punishment of the sin of disobedience. Cain's real sin was that he 'anticipated Jehovah's plans. He added a fresh sin to the sin of which death was the punishment' (p. 77). He brought death into the world.

From now on, on Cain's forehead, and on Everyman's forehead, the rest of mankind may read 'Danger! Keep out!' However, beneath the warning should be discerned the protective sign that this is one of God's creatures, the mark of one of the sons of Adam rather than the brand of infamy. ' "The mark of the outcast protects me", Cain says. "Yes, God has done me the kindness of making my crime put fear into those who would avenge it, because their expiation of a crime against me would be seven times heavier. Mercy at too heavy a cost!" ' (p. 50). Now, according to Cain, the only threat man has to face from God is his absence. And yet he must face the threat which he poses through his human nature – as Cain's relentless wife Temech reminds him. 'Your own presence Cain! From henceforth Cain will be present in every generation of mankind.' When he gazes into the mirror of his conscience Everyman will see the features of a Cain. As Adam remarks, 'My son Cain is that other portion of my self which endlessly casts its shadow before. You who follow after him must realize that you are the swarms of my dreams' (p. 126).

Were one straining after a similar symbol in Greek tradition, the myth of PROMETHEUS might come to mind. He attempted to take possession of a divine power on behalf of mankind and to free it from complete dependence by endowing mankind with fire, the element which was to change the future, whether as spiritual or material fire. Like Prometheus, Cain is the symbol of the man who claims his share in the work of creation.

calabash (see also GOURD)   The Dogon, whose dominant symbolism is lunar, regard the calabash as a female, solar symbol. It is a substitute for the 'earthenware pot', the womb of the Sun, around which the red copper spiral winds eight times as the symbol of light, the Word, water, semen and the principle of fertility. The mythic ram, the Sun's eldest son, bears between its horns a calabash, painted red with *sa*-oil, which is none other than the womb of the Sun. The ram, which represents the principle of earth and water, fertilizes the womb-like calabash with a phallus which stands erect on its forehead (GRID). The water-god, Nommo, the mighty Demiurge of Dogon cosmogony, sometimes manifests himself on Earth in the shape of a calabash. The family of plants associated with the calabash-tree are linked to ideas of space, distance and intercourse. 'The calabash is the image of man's entire body and of the world in its fullness' (DIED).

calendar   To give a history of Egyptian, Greek, Aztec, Roman, Masonic, French Revolutionary, Chinese, Muslim, Gregorian, Positivist or any other calendars, would be beyond the scope of this book. The nub of the matter is that mankind has tried to establish points of reference in relation to the regular recurrence of observable natural phenomena as time fled ever before them. Thus the first calendars were lunar, since the phases of the Moon are shorter and easier to observe than the solar cycle. To compile a calendar is something reassuring, organizing time in the same way as dykes are built to control the flow of rivers. They convey the feeling of mastering what cannot be escaped. Calendars offer the means of recording the stages of one's own inner or external development and of being able to celebrate at fixed times human intercourse either with the gods, with the universe or with the dead. Looking at the calendar conveys the suggestion of a perpetual fresh start. The calendar is the symbol of death and resurrection, as well as the comprehensible order which rules the passing of time. It regulates this movement, as these examples show.

The Egyptian calendar 'was undoubtedly the calendar best suited to its environment'. It comprised a year of 365 days, divided into twelve months each of thirty days with five epagomenal or extra days at the end of each year. It perfectly suited a country which has no Spring, since the months formed three seasons, each of four months, 'flood-time, Winter and Summer'. Months were subdivided into three 'decads', each of ten days, the first day being a holiday in honour of the dead.

There was, however, no leap year, hence a gradual retardation on the solar year. Day and night were split into twenty-four hours, which astronomers in the Hellenistic age were to subdivide into sixty minutes, according to a sexagesimal system which originated in Ancient Babylon (POSD p. 34). The rising of Sothis (Sirius), sacred to Isis, marked the start of the civil year, 'Sothis being regarded as the ruler of the 36 constellations which successively governed 36 decads' (PIED p. 520).

The earliest Jewish calendar – copied from the one used by the Phoenicians – was lunar, *Yerah* (month) being derived from *Yereah* (Moon). The calendar used during Old Testament times was solar. We know (1 Kings 4: 7) that Solomon had at his command twelve officials who had each to undertake one month's service. Although the solar calendar was used before their Exile, during their Captivity the Jews would have become familiar with the Chaldean solar–lunar calendar, which computed the months by the phases of the Moon and the year and the seasons by the movements of the Sun.

The Maya used two calendars, a solar calendar for a civil year of 365 days (*haab*), and another for the religious year of 260 days (*tzolkin*), that is thirteen months each of twenty days. The god THIRTEEN – a sacred number – was the god of time, of birth and death. The latter calendar, based upon folk beliefs, recorded birthdays and the major events of life. The civil calendar comprised eighteen months, each of twenty days, plus an extra month of five days. These five days were considered most inauspicious. They were the bridge between or the staircase rising from the old to the new year. With two calendars running parallel, dates calculated on two planes of existence, the secular and religious, had to be made to tally. Cycles were composed based on the correspondences between the two calendars and were so complex and so accurate that the same date or juxtaposition could only recur once in 374,440 years, symbol both of the immutable and of the eternal homecoming.

calumet The Plains Indians' sacred pipe – of peace or of war – typifies primordial man, standing at the CENTRE, and hence on the World AXIS, and by prayer welding the powers of the Underworld with those of the all-powerful sky-god. To him that prayer rises in the material shape of tobacco smoke, which is none other than BREATH, that is, the soul. The calumet therefore symbolizes the strength and power of primordial man, a microcosm invulnerable and immortal through his being in the likeness of the macrocosm which he embodies. All the literature on the calumet (Sioux,

Osage, etc.) describes it as if it were a human being, each of its parts being given the name of a part of the human body (ALEC pp. 4–6).

To bring his life, outward and inward, into harmony with that of all nature is in essence the meaning of the sacred fume which arises from the pipe whose bowl is an altar and whose stem is the breath's passage . . . .
    The savage sends its first fruits, or first puffs, to the great Waconda, or Master of Life, to the Sun which gives them light, and to the Earth and Water by which they are nourished; then they direct a puff to each point of the compass.

They then direct three puffs one after the other, to the ZENITH, to the ground and to the Sun.
    The calumet ensures strength and invulnerability:

There was nothing more mysterious nor more remarkable. So much honor is not rendered to the crowns and sceptres of kings as they render to the calumet. It seems to be the god of peace and war, the arbiter of life and death. It is enough to carry it with one and show it in order to journey with assurance in the midst of enemies, who in the height of combat lower their arms when it is displayed.

    Alexander states that the RED-painted pipe of war is looked upon as the calumet of the Sun.
    'Its fuller symbolism is very clearly that of a sacred, or "medicine" emblem, to be employed wherever the issue was serious or fateful.' The Dakota legend of the gift of maize to mankind states explicitly that 'This pipe is related to the heavens . . . . The pipe is itself, in some deeply indefinable sense, a mystic token of man's union with nature.' In our opinion it would be more correct to say that it is a sign of the marriage of nature with the supreme deity through man, who stands as the channel of sacred communication. The latter is embodied in the SMOKE produced by fire from tobacco – the sacred marriage of vegetable creation (Moon) with fire (Sun) – and rising to Heaven thanks to the breath of the priest. In this sense performance of the ritual is truly a prayer and even 'the pipe itself may constitute a man's prayer . . . . Central in the universe is man; central in man is his mind's thought and his heart's aspiration. The pipe of peace was the emblem of each' (ALEC pp. 23–4).
    According to the alchemist Jābir (Geber) smoke symbolizes the soul which has left the body (*De alchemia*, Strassburg, 1529).

camel The camel is generally taken as the symbol of sobriety . . . and of awkward nature. It is the attribute of temperance and often the emblem of Asia, because of the countless caravan routes across that continent.
    Leviticus (9: 4) held the camel to be an unclean beast, but the Jews also held to be unclean those animals which the Gentiles dedicated to their false gods, as well as those which were deemed unpleasing to God because man found them repugnant.
    The camel is depicted – very seldom it is true – in Hindu iconography as the emblem of malevolent *yoginī*, in relation to death.
    But above all else the camel is the animal which enables its rider to cross the DESERT and thanks to which he or she can reach the hidden centre of the divine essence. Companion in the desert, the camel is the vehicle which

moves from oasis to oasis. The Three Wise Men are depicted riding on camels to the crib at Bethlehem. This is why many early writers – notably Honorius of Autun – try to establish dubious etymological links between *camelus* (camel) and *camilli*, youths of noble birth who served the throne and altar, and also provided a channel for transmitting hermetic philosophy (DEVA, MALA).

The *Zohar* mentions 'flying camels', similar to DRAGONS and winged SERPENTS, who seem to have guarded the Earthly Paradise and which are also mentioned in the Ancient Persian holy book, the Avesta.

In central Asia the camel is the symbol, not of an awkward nature, but of self-conceit. 'Because the camel considered itself so great, it destroyed the army' is a Buryat proverb (HARA p. 145).

camphor   In Hindu terminology camphor designates pure WHITE – Shiva is 'as white as camphor'. The power of sublimation possessed by the substance compounds this notion with one of smoothness. In his *Risālat*, Ibn al-Walid describes 'a body of great nobility' as having the whiteness and the smoothness of camphor.

Cancer (22 June–22 July)   The fourth sign of the ZODIAC, falling immediately after the Summer solstice, when the days begin to grow shorter. It is expressed hieroglyphically as a pair of SPIRALS. These convey the change in the direction of the Sun's movement, hitherto in the ascendant but now in the descendant, and represent schematically the fluctuations of life. It is a lunar sign, signifying self-withdrawal, sensitivity, shyness and perseverance.

With Cancer rises a world of WATERS and the sign itself is a symbol of the primordial ocean, of deep and peaceful pools, of rippling springs as well as of mother's milk and plant-sap. The crayfish or CRAB which embodies the sign is a creature of the waters, dwelling inside its protective shell. With the spirit of the waters is closely identified a quality of intimacy, of inwardness, of internality, which reminds us that the beginnings and prefigurations of rebirth in seed, egg, embryo or bud are wrapped in shell, womb, bark or sheath, designed to preserve the power of resurrection enclosed within their protection. In fact this fourth sign may be identified with Jung's maternal archetype and all the qualities which this implies: the large enfolding, sheltering, preserving, nourishing, protecting and fostering of what is small. Principle of the generation and conservation of life which comprises everything from the womb to Mother Earth herself: the depths, the abyss, wells, caverns, caves, pouches, pots, shelters, houses, towns . . . to that great sanctuary of mankind, the Mother Goddess, the sign is associated with the pallid, earth-lit Moon, itself the planetary symbol of the womb-principle, of the subconscious universal soul, of the dim light of the vegetable kingdom and of the life force still uncontrolled by reason. In the music of the spheres, Cancer's score, when the bars do not call for rest, imitate the murmurous melody of the dusk, or the dreamy song of the twilight. The Cancerian personality evolves through the sensitivity of the child's soul in a maternal environment as well as through the growth of the imagination in a world of romantic, fantastic and lyrical subjectivity, memories and dreams.

Cancer also plays the part of intermediary, marking as it does the middle of the year, linking what is to what will be, the threshold of reincarnation, the way from ZENITH to nadir. Those influenced by this sign enjoy strong and hidden powers potentially favourable to future incarnations.

candle Candles symbolize light. Their wick melts the wax and thus the wax shares the flame, emblem of the flesh and the spirit.

By ancient custom virgins carried lighted candles in each hand. In countless religious rites candles retain their phallic symbolism – the reverse aspect of the symbolism of the soul and of immortality. In Catholic ritual there is the Paschal Candle and the tall candle set beside the coffin in the funeral ceremonies for a pope. In the twelfth century Guillielmus Durandus explained this usage by saying that virgins carried candles to show that they were ready to receive the Bridegroom, like the Wise Virgins in the Gospel (Matthew 25: 1–13). He also points out the further symbol in the carrying of candles: virgins seeking to be like the Light of the World. The symbolism of light has always played an important part in Christian thought (METC p. 198).

This ritual may have been borrowed from Classical marriage ceremonies in which the bride was led in solemn, TORCH-lit procession to the home of her husband to be. Bride and groom also carried torches. This custom is retained in Greece and among most Orthodox communities.

In Ancient Greece candles were offered to the gods of the Underworld as well as to those of fertility.

Pope Paul VI, in an audience to nuns on 2 February 1973, gave a modern twist to the language of the books of ritual. Candles, he said, symbolized 'the pure and primal source of light' by which nuns should be enlightened.

Unwavering and gentle, they are images of purity and innocence. They burn and give light and typify a life wholly devoted to a burning, total and unique love . . . . Lastly, candles are doomed silently to burn away just as your lives are consumed in the inevitable struggles of hearts which have renounced the world, in self-sacrifice like that of Christ on the Cross, and in the joys and pains of love which will not end with death but which will shine for ever in the everlasting encounter with the Divine Bridegroom.

candlestick Symbol of spiritual illumination, of the seed of life and of salvation.

Its cosmic symbolism supports its religious symbolism. 'It has as many branches', Flavius Josephus writes of the SEVEN-branched candlestick, 'as there are planets, together with the Sun.' While Philo of Alexandria states that it is 'an earthly imitation of its archetype, the celestial sphere.'

The candlestick of the Children of Israel was the same as the Babylonian Tree of Light. According to Exodus (25: 31–2), 'of pure gold: of beaten work shall the candlestick be made . . . . And six branches shall come out of the sides of it; three branches of the candlestick out of the one side and three branches of the candlestick out of the other side.' The two series of three embody duality. 'Three bowls made like unto almonds . . . in one branch; and three bowls made like almonds in the other branch' (25: 33). The candlestick thus represents an ALMOND-TREE, that is to say 'the golden nut', a common motif in different cultures.

The seven-branched candlestick or *Menorah* undoubtedly stood in Zerubbabel's Temple. Zechariah (4: 1–14) describes it in prophetic terms, leading one to suspect that its symbolism was based upon the stars, the seven planets and the seven Heavens. The seven lamps which it bears are, to Zechariah, the eyes of God, seven being the perfect number, and they watch over the whole Earth. Later Jewish writers, such as Philo of Alexandria and Flavius Josephus, as well as some of the older rabbinical commentators, underline the symbolism explicitly. To Philo (*Life of Moses* 2: 105) the candlestick was the Heavens with the planetary system, in the centre of which blazed the Sun; the central shaft represented the Sun, with three planets on either side of it. It therefore symbolized the Logos, the Light of the World.

The passage in Zechariah also describes the candlestick as being flanked by two olive-trees which provided a direct supply of the oil needed for the lamps. It is therefore reasonable to suggest that the seven-branched candlestick perhaps derived directly from a sacred tree. Graeco-Roman parallels and depictions of the candlestick – admittedly of a later date – in which the branches are shown bearing leaves would seem to support this hypothesis.

To Zechariah, however, the two branches of the flanking olive-trees are the golden pipes which supply the oil, or power. Joshua represents the spiritual, and the temporal is embodied in Zerubbabel, both having been anointed, the first as a priest and the second as king, and both with parts to play in the work of salvation.

As a symbol of the godhead and of the light with which he endows mankind, the *Menorah* was often used as a decorative motif, albeit rich in meaning, upon grave-stones and the walls of synagogues.

In the Book of Revelation, there are, it is true, seven candlesticks, but no mention of their possessing seven branches. They symbolize the Seven Churches (1: 20).

In the early Christian era candlesticks represented 'the Sun in his chariot with seven-rayed nimbus, surrounded by the twelve signs of the Zodiac and flanked at the corners by the figures of the seasons' (Jean Daniélou, *Symbolisme cosmique et mouvements religieux*, Musée Guimet, Paris, 1953, p. 63).

To Clement of Alexandria the seven-branched golden candlestick represented 'the movements of the seven bright stars which make their regular motions across the heavens' (*Stromata* 5: 6, 34, 8). He also relates the candlestick symbolically to Christ's cross, not simply from its shape but because the candlestick recalls the cross as a source of enlightenment. Lastly the candlestick recalls the seven Archangels (Jean Daniélou, 'Aux sources de l'ésotérisme judéo-chrétien', in *Umanesimo e esoterismo*, Padua, 1960, p. 40).

In Celtic tradition a courageous warrior was normally praised as 'a candlestick of valour' (or else as 'Bodb's candlestick'). The metaphor is clearly based upon the refulgent brilliance of the famous warrior. In the same way a great warrior's lance is sometimes described as a 'kingly candlestick' (WINI 5: p. 373).

canopy See AWNING.

cape The cape, the poncho or the chasuble, any circular garment or vestment with a hole in the middle, suggests the DOME, tent or round hut with a hole in the roof to let out the smoke. It exhibits 'a celestial and ascendant symbolism'. The priest, robed in such a chasuble or cape, 'is set, ritually, at the centre of the universe, identified with the World AXIS, the cape being the celestial tent, and with his head in the beyond, the dwelling of the God whose earthly representative he is' (CHAS p. 380).

Capricorn (21 December–19 January) The tenth sign of the ZODIAC; it begins at the Winter solstice, the 'GATEWAY of the gods', when the apparent death of nature corresponds with the flood-tide of the spirit; at the time when humans, freed from seasonal labour, allow their ingenuity full play. Symbol of the end of a cycle, indeed, but more truly the symbol of the beginning of a fresh cycle, in the Far East it is the first sign of the Zodiac. SATURN is its ruler and it is emblematic of patience, perseverance, prudence, industriousness, achievement and a sense of duty.

To the northern hemisphere, Capricorn symbolizes the icy grandeur of Winter, stripped bare, indrawn and concentrated. It is like midnight on Christmas Eve, the peak of cold and darkness, the crucial time for the seed buried deep in the soil and awaiting the distant harvest. Earth is the element which sets it all in motion and it is in the depths of the wintery ground that the slow and painful work of vegetable growth begins. To this notion of beginning, the idea of end is dialectically linked: the idea of destination, aim, conceived as a peak or mid-point on Earth. The sign is depicted either as a fabulous animal, half-GOAT, half-DOLPHIN, or as a goat, that sure-footed creature drawn to the mountain-tops. It is ruled by Saturn, himself associated with all that is hard, harsh, dark and gloomy. He is the remorseless god of time who crystallizes in human hearts their loftiest ambitions – when he does not doom them to their loss or renunciation. A Capricornian nature bears the marks of this cold, silent and still universe. It is built upon an original movement of self-withdrawal and concentration. Externally this character appears lifeless and often dulled to grey sobriety and self-effacement. However, life retreats to the depths of being and it is the slow upsurge of these deep forces, often long ignored by the person him- or herself, which permits the affirmation of personal qualities by the full exercise of self-control. This self-command is the fruit of long training of the will, exercised to demonstrate mastery of instinct and feeling. Hence these chilly qualities predominate, that is unless self-realization receives a check which diverts it to taciturnity, pessimism or melancholia.

The symbolic representation of the goat's body and FISH's tail betrays the ambivalent nature of the Capricornian, exposed to two tendencies, the heights or the depths, the mountains or the seas of life. This character possesses inverse potentiality, extravert or introvert, and can only find a precarious balance in the perpetual tension between opposing tendencies.

car See AUTOMOBILE.

carbuncle See ALMANDINE; RUBY.

cardinal points They represent the FOUR directions of two-dimensional space – north, south, east and west. A third dimension is provided upwards by the line of ZENITH–nadir, and an internal dimension by the CENTRE. Very many beliefs about the origins of life, the dwelling-places of the gods and of the dead and the cycle of evolution gather around the cross made by the intersection of these two axes, north–south, east–west, which, together with the AXIS of the zenith and the nadir comprise the complete sphere of cosmic space, and, symbolically, human destiny. In symbolism, space is the framework within which the world born of Chaos takes shape and where all its forces are released.

The symbolism of the cardinal points was of enormous importance to the Ancient Mexicans, as Soustelle has emphasized (SOUM).

The north is 'the side which lies on the Sun's right hand'. It is the country of 'the NINE plains' of the Underworld. It is the land on either side of life, since the living come from it and the dead return to it. It is a land of cold, hunger, darkness and drought. It is the home of the EAGLE, the symbol of war, because, above all other, it is the land of hunting and of fighting. This is where the 'flint' years are located and among its emblems is depicted the sacrificial knife with its OBSIDIAN or flint blade, often decorated with eagles' feathers. Tezcatlipoca, God of the north, symbolizes night sky and night wind. The north is also the home of the Moon and the Milky Way. Its colour is BLACK (RED for the Maya).

The south is 'the side which lies on the Sun's left hand'. In Nahuatl, 'the side of the THORNS. In certain situations, the emperor and the priests took agave-thorns and stuck them into their calves to draw blood to offer to the gods.' It is the land of fire and of the great god Huitzilopochtli, the midday Sun deified. Its emblem is the MACAW, solar bird *par excellence*, and it rules the 'rabbit' years. Very clearly the north and south complement one another. This is shown not only by the presence in the south of the rabbit, a typically lunar emblem, while the Moon itself was located in the north (SOUA), but also by the fact that the south was the dwelling of Mictlantecuhtli, the death-god, while the land of the dead lay in the north. This is because Mictlantecuhtli deals death and the red of the blood of sacrifice leads on to darkness, as the flint blade plunges into the breast of the warrior offered as victim. The symbols of north and south were sometimes superimposed upon one another and their attributes inverted among the different peoples of Central America. Parallel thinking sees an agreement between opposites. The south is opposite to the north, but the south leads towards the north on the principle of cyclical discontinuity. This is the foundation of the process of the concatenation of death with rebirth in rites of initiation. The Mexicans clearly seem to have regarded the directional cross as symbolizing, along its two axes, the two mysteries of the passage from life to death (south–north axis), and from death to life (west–east axis), as may be seen by examining the symbolism of the two other cardinal points.

East is the land of birth, or of rebirth, of the Sun and of VENUS. It is identified with every manifestation of renewal, with the sprouting of MAIZE, with youth, with feasting, song and love.

East is the home of the rain-god, Tlaloc, and there lies his garden, all greenery and waters. It is 'the house of green feathers', the home of the 'green reed' years and of the Amerindian PHOENIX, the sacred bird, the quetzal, which gave its long green feathers to Quetzalcoatl. Under this sign he was reborn, in the shape of the rising Sun, after he had offered himself in sacrifice in the west. However, GREEN takes second place as the colour which symbolizes this point, since east's colour was originally the red of fresh blood and the vital force, of the rising Sun and of the morning star, Venus. Thus, as Soustelle observes, within this sign solar symbolism is superimposed upon that of water and the vegetable kingdom. However, one should remember that Amerindian solar symbolism was expressed under a multiplicity of forms. The noonday Sun and the night Sun are symbols of parallel complexes, in opposition to that of the rising Sun.

West is the land of evening, of old age, of the descending passage of the Sun, and the place where he vanishes 'into his house'. The 'house' years live here. It is 'the women's side', the waning side, in which Venus vanishes, like the Sun. Here Quetzalcoatl offered himself in sacrifice to be reborn in the east. It was called 'the land of mists'; it was the gateway of the mysterious, of the immanent and of the beyond. However, mists suggest the idea of RAIN and hence of fertility and fecundity. Thus the mother-goddesses dwell in the west, where they have their garden, complementing that of the rain-god, Tlaloc, in the east. It was also the home of the maize-god, who was to make himself manifest in the east. Lastly, here too lived the flower-goddess and 'the Fishes of Chalchiuhtlicue', or of Precious Water or of Precious Stone, which are the sum of the complex symbolism which brings together the blue-green water of EMERALD and of JADE, the fertilizing rain and the celestial seed, and the fresh blood, offered to the Sun for his rebirth.

Thus opposites are brought together and even contained, the one in the other, as strongly on the east–west as on the north–south axis. These two axes comprise a cross on the centre of which – and this mid-point is none other than mankind's place – the double duality is superimposed and resolved. The north–south axis symbolizes the transcendental countries and their powers – of both sky and Underworld – from which everything comes and to which everything returns. This is the axis of potentiality. Against it is set the west–east axis, of manifestation, of the immanent godhead and of humanity. From east to west and from west to east, like a pulse-beat, the cycle of initiation welds life and death together. However, the eternal homecoming, at the end of this axis, would never be achieved without the existence of the invisible countries of north and south. Thus the CROSS is manifestly the primordial symbol without which nothing could exist. As Soustelle has written, 'the cross is the symbol of the world in its totality.'

African tradition is no less evocative. In Dogon cosmogony, each of the cardinal points is associated with a constellation or star and a class of being in the following way:

north: the Pleiades; human beings and fishes;
south: Orion's Belt; domestic animals;
east: Venus; birds;
west: an unidentifiable 'star with a long tail'; wild animals, plants and insects (GRIE).

The Bambara have the following associations:

east: the colour white; land of the dead;
west: land of 'the sunset people'; source of custom and of all goodness and loveliness;

north: identified with the seventh Heaven, a far distant country, the dwelling of the great god Faro, lord of the word and the waters, who created the world in its present form; by extension, the north is the home of all kingship;

south: peopled by evil beings whom Faro was forced to destroy at the beginning of time, because they had stolen speech from him; the home of pollution (DIEB).

Like the Dogon, the Bambara divide all living things into four categories corresponding to the cardinal points, as follows:

north: water creatures – fish, crocodiles and frogs;
south: plants;
east: wild and domestic animals;
west: birds (DIEB).

The Baluba and Lulua from Kasai (Congo) imagine the world as an upright cross, the horizontal arms dividing west, home of the evil spirits, from east, home of good spirits and site of Paradise or 'the village of sweet bananas'. The west is identified with the interior of the Earth through which the souls of the wicked tumble into 'the pit of red earth', and, in fact, its colour is red. East and Paradise are set under the sign of the colour white (FOUA). (Note the opposition of RED and WHITE.) The centre of this cross, the place to which the souls of the dead are brought to judgement, lies at the fork of the Milky Way. The earthly, or human, plane lies below: above in the upper Heaven dwells the Supreme Deity surrounded by his assessors (ibid.).

Altaic peoples generally believed that the 'World Mountain' which rises from the 'NAVEL of the World' with a peak which touches the Pole Star, lies in the north. Here, too, on its peak is the dwelling or golden throne of the Supreme Deity. For this reason the devotees of some religions faced north when they wished to adore the sky-god. This is the practice of the Mende and of central Asian Buddhists (HARA).

The image of the World Mountain reached the Kalmuk via central Asian Lamaism, and they pictured each side as lying towards one of the cardinal points. Each had its own appropriate colour: south was blue; west red; north yellow and east white (HARA p. 49). Around the mountain float four continents, one for each of the cardinal points, and these are depicted as islands in the sea. The inhabitants of these continents differ from the one another, above all in the shapes of their faces. Those who inhabit the southern continent have oval faces, those in the northern, square, those in the western, round, while those in the eastern continent have faces shaped like the crescent Moon. The continents themselves are exactly of the same shape. 'This astonishing vision of the world holds sway in Tibet and, with insignificant differences, in all Buddhist countries' (HARA p. 50).

Lamaistic Kalmuk also depict the cardinal points as animal heads: an elephant for the east, an ox for the south, a horse for the west and a lion for the north or, to be more precise, the northwest.

The Chinese on the other hand associate the east with a blue dragon, the south with a red bird, the west with a white tiger and the north with a black

tortoise. According to Sioux myth, 'the gods dwell on a mountain-top looking out over the four quarters of the world. At each of the gates of Heaven
there stands a guard: a butterfly on the west, a bear on the east, a stag on
the north and a beaver on the south' (HARA p. 64). According to the
Book of Revelation (4: 7) the throne of God was guarded by four beasts,
'the first . . . like a lion, and the second . . . like a calf, and the third . . . had
a face as a man, and the fourth . . . was like a flying eagle.'

The Transbaikal Tungus believed that God created the first pair of human beings from iron which he took from the east, fire which he took from
the south, water which he took from the west and earth which he took from
the north. Since each of these materials was used to fashion a separate constituent of the human body, this myth serves to create correspondences
between the cardinal points, the elements and the human body on the following pattern: north – earth – flesh and bones; west – water – blood; east
– air and iron – heart; south – fire – body heat. According to the Franciscan
friar, Ruysbroek (whom the French King, St Louis IX, sent as his envoy to
the Mongols in the thirteenth century) when the Mongols made their libations, they poured the contents of their goblets to the four cardinal points
– to the south in honour of fire, to the east in honour of air, to the west in
honour of water and to the north in honour of the dead.

The Hindu world image locates the heavenly home of demons in the
northeast (HARA p. 119).

The position of the GREAT BEAR in relation to the cardinal points marks
the seasons for central Asian peoples. 'When the Great Bear's tail points
east, Spring rules the whole world; when it points south, then it is Summer-
time; when it points west, then it is Autumn. But when it points north then
Winter rules the whole world.' The Siberian Goldi regard east as the direction of the living and west as that of the dead (HARA pp. 128, 234).
Ruysbroek noted that the entrances of Mongol tents faced south; that the
men sat on the western side of the tent, the women on the eastern and that
the place of the master of the house was at the far end, that is to say, to the
north (HARA p. 261).

The early Christians regarded the west–east axis as that of the Devil and
God, of Hell and Heaven, as is apparent in a description of the ritual of
baptism left to us by the Pseudo-Dionysius the Areopagite. Deacons loosed
the girdle and removed the catechumen's garments. The priest set him
facing west, his arms raised as a sign of cursing these regions of darkness,
and 'he [the priest] thrice commands him to breathe scorn on Satan, and
further, to profess the words of renunciation . . . then [the priest] turns him
to the east, after . . . he has looked up to heaven and extended his hands
thitherward, he commands him to be subject to Christ' (PSEH p. 55).

carrion crow See under RAVEN.

carp In the Far East the fish is an omen of good fortune and is therefore
frequently employed when paying compliments. Since its longevity is so
well-known, it becomes the emblem of good wishes for a long life. The carp
is the steed and messenger of the Immortals, which they use to rise up into
the sky (carp's leap) and in the stomach of which messages or seals are to
be found. It is a simple matter for the carp to become a winged DRAGON. To

protect a house from fire, a model of a carp should be set on the roof-top.
In Vietnam it is the carp which conducts the household-god to the celestial
regions shortly before New Year's Day and it is also the carp which guards
homes at the mid-Autumn festival against the misdeeds of the Golden Carp,
the evil spirit of popular mythology.

In China, but more especially in Japan, the carp symbolizes courage and
endurance, because it swims against the river's flow and, allegedly, up cata-
racts. As a symbol of virility, it is the emblem of young men, and on their
festival paper carps are set on the tips of poles or on the roof-tops of houses
(CHOO, DURV, HERS, KALL, OGRJ). The carp is also the symbol of
intellectual supremacy and the gift of a carp to a student is an augury of
success in examinations.

In Japan they say that, unlike other fish which try to wriggle away, the
carp lies still on the chopping-block. This is the way in which humans should
ideally face inevitable death.

To the Bambara, carp symbolize the vulva. After circumcision, their girls
sing: 'Carp, Mother Carp, she went to wash her face and there in front of
her something appeared. It was like a red ribbon or a red tuft', alluding to
the clitoris (ZAHB). The carp is an augury of fecundity on both the spiritual and material planes.

carpet   While carpets in the West are regarded as prized items of furniture, in the East they are 'important elements of personal, family and tribal
life. Their patterns are not in any sense matters of chance but evolve from
a climate of feelings and beliefs which are often thousands of years old'
(GENT). These patterns carry traces of magical powers: the LOZENGE and
the octagon with curlicues or small TRIANGLES jutting from its sides may well
stand for the SCORPIONS and tarantulas against which they were designed to
be guardians.

Motifs which are also both magical and symbolic include the following.
CAMELS are the wealth of the Bedouin and hence their image is a pledge of
happiness and riches for the weaver and the owner of the carpet. DOGS drive
all undesirables, sorcerers and such personified diseases as smallpox from
the house in which the carpet is spread, while PEACOCKS are sacred birds in
both Persia and China and the DOVE symbolizes love and peace. The TREE
of Life and the CYPRESS are symbols of eternity, the POMEGRANATE in flower
symbolizes the Sun and its mass of seeds are symbols of wealth and plenty.
The violet is a symbol of good luck.

In so far as the colours of carpets are concerned, YELLOW and GOLD are
symbols of rank and power, appropriate to palaces and mosques; WHITE –
the colour of purity, light and peace – was until the times of the Umayyads
the colour of the standard of the Arabs; RED – the banner of the Seljuk and
Ottoman dynasties – is for good fortune and happiness; BLACK – the colour
adopted by the Abbasids when they rose in revolt agains the Umayyads –
is for destruction and rebellion; GREEN for rebirth and resurrection, the
colour worn by those who dwell in Paradise, the colour of the followers of
Ali (Shi'ites) and, from the fourteenth century onwards, of all the descendants of the Prophet and of pilgrims to Mecca; sky-BLUE, adopted by the
Byzantine emperors and, although the colour of mourning throughout the

East, the national colour of Iran; purple (or deep or light violet) the distinctive colour of monarchs, chosen by Constantine for the LABARUM, and influential throughout the East; the heraldic colour, *vert*, the green associated with the Prophet and frequently used for prayer mats which, consequently, must never be crumpled, but always rolled after use.

On carpets, weavers' marks may be turned into decorative motifs and also possess magical powers. Thus the mark of a comb, but one with five teeth, symbolizes the Hand of Fatima, a preservative against the evil eye.

In some parts of Morocco, when a stranger comes into a house in which there is a fine new carpet (*zarbīya*) the woman who has woven it burns a tuft of wool from its border as a charm against the evil eye, while the Ait Warain do the same when they take a new carpet to sell in the market.

The lower classes observe certain rituals with carpets when a person dies. Thus, in Fez, the carpets from the floor of the dead person's house must be taken out and replaced by mats from the mosque. They are left in the house for three days including the day of death (WERS pp. 429, 468, 540).

A prayer mat exactly defines a *templum*, a place made holy and set apart from the profane world. Muslim saints, such as Sidi Ouali Dada at Algiers, are sometimes depicted sailing upon prayer mats drawn by fishes (DERS p. 184).

As an aesthetic symbol, the carpet often gives expression to the idea of the GARDEN, inseparable from the notion of Paradise. In its patterns may be seen real or mythical flowers, trees, beasts and birds.

The medium does not allow of too realistic a copy . . . so that the formal and universal characteristics displayed by these carpets are those of a garden of the mind, no one particular garden, but the abiding pleasure which gardens confer. Thus in the Islamic age, a carpet-weaver wrote in a poem that his cool garden always displayed the blossoms of Spring, never to be battered by autumnal gales or Winter storms.

(ENCI 4: p. 47)

This is a form of mental sleight-of-hand by means of the carpet, to enjoy the delights of Spring in the depths of Winter.

The carpet sums up the symbolism of the HOUSE, in its sacred nature and the yearning for the joys of Paradise which it contains.

cart See CHARIOT.

cask The symbolism of the cask is linked with that of the JAR, WELL and HORN OF PLENTY, as well as that of the WINE which it holds. It suggests the idea of wealth and pleasure.

Although later legend places the Danaids in Hell, eternally pouring water into bottomless casks, they were, in fact, nymphs of springs and wells. Many paintings and sculptures survive of *hydrophori* (water-carriers) pouring water into casks or pitchers. This symbol could be linked with that of Sisyphus as ceaseless repetition of the same activity but, in this instance, what is displayed is the insatiable force of human desire. According to the legend, all except one of the Danaids, whose husband had respected her virginity, had murdered their bridegrooms on their wedding night and had great difficulty in finding new husbands. This, we think, is the symbolic meaning of their legend.

Apart from being a symbol of the indestructible character of natural desire, there is a further symbol of Greek morality. To decline a natural act in normal and legitimate circumstances, is to doom oneself to endless folly and abortive action, to a punishment which matches the crime. The bottomless cask thus means the opposite to the cask filled with wine, or rather the symbolism of the cask is the same, but the meaning drawn from it is opposite.

casket Caskets, sometimes described as 'golden caskets', symbolize in both the *Atharva-Veda* and the Upanishads the head or, less precisely, that mysterious 'inner void' which surrounds and protects from all aggression that priceless treasure, the Self. 'In that golden casket, with three spokes and three containers, dwells a prodigy, the *ātman*' (*Atharva-Veda* 10: 2).

caste The Hindu caste system is not, as is generally supposed, simply a typical phenomenon of Aryan social organization and the means of imposing a hierarchical structure. It is also an expression of the division of office which applies, symbolically and with equal force, to the actions of the gods and to the existence both of society as a whole and of its individual members. Indeed the complexity of human nature makes each person a miniature of society. In this light the caste principle acquires a universal validity. Spiritual or intellectual activities correspond with priestly office; management, legislation and strength with the kingly; production and exchange of goods with the commercial, mercantile and agricultural; humble duties with the servile. Spiritual authority, temporal power, wealth production and servile toil are all essential duties which comprise the activities of the individual and of the society to which he or she belongs. If the social world is patterned upon the divine world, the inner world of the human being is patterned upon society. From these concepts a wealth of symbols has developed.

The *Rig-Veda* declares that Purusha (primeval man) provided the FOUR *varna*. From his mouth (organ of speech) came the Brahman (priestly class); from his arms (organs of strength) came the Kshatriya (royal and warrior class); from his thighs (organs of effort) came the Vaishya (merchant class); while the servile class, the Shudra, were born from the soles of his feet.

This fourfold division affected town planning, each class having one of the cardinal regions of the city set aside for it. The Brahmans took the north, the warriors the south, the merchants the east and the servants the west. Each caste, too, had its specific season. The Brahmans had the months of lengthening daylight from the Winter solstice to the vernal equinox; the warriors the Spring, 'the season when kings go forth to battle'; the merchants the Summer, season of ripening crops and trading voyages; while the servants had the Autumn, the season of reaping and harvesting when the days shorten from the autumnal equinox to the darkness of the Winter solstice.

This fourfold division of castes was also displayed in the four arms of Ganesha, in so far as he was lord of the universe and of all the duties entailed thereby. Some see it again in the four Vedas, or in the four paths of knowledge, each specifically adapted to the generally perceived capacities of a particular caste. It has been identified, too, with the four colours (in India and among the Maya: white, red, yellow and black); with the four elements; with the four essences of Sadashiva or of Vishnu; and with the four ages of the world – Golden Age (primacy of the Brahman or of spiritual activity), Silver Age (supremacy of the warrior), Bronze Age (dominance of trade), Iron Age (tyranny of mob rule).

Analysts would admit that these social, historic and cosmic divisions correspond to tendencies, structural levels and developmental phases which are to be met in the inner life of all human beings. Thus they symbolize psychic functions. As a symbol at least – despite the change of historic circumstance – caste remains real and abiding (DANA, GUES, MALA, SCHC).

castle The castle, fortress or stronghold is the near-universal symbol of humanity's inner refuge, the CAVERN of the heart, that place of privileged intercourse between the soul and its God, or the Absolute. The Psalmist compares God himself with such a stronghold: 'But I will sing of thy power; yea, I will sing aloud of thy mercy in the morning; for thou hast been my defence and refuge in the day of my trouble' (Psalm 59: 16).

In Psalm 60: 9, we read: 'Who will bring me into the strong city?' And in Theoleptus of Philadelphia: 'Strive to make your way into the innermost fortress of the soul, into the house of Christ.' And again in Meister Eckhart's *Sermons*: 'There is within the soul a castle into which not even the gaze of the Triune God can penetrate', because it is the castle of pure Oneness.

The Arabs call the constellations of the Zodiac *borj* (stronghold), as does the *ta'wil* (esotericism), in so far as they 'shelter souls from damnation'.

In the *Bhagavad Gītā* (5: 13), the 'castle with nine gates' is a metaphor for the body of the yogi, closed to feelings for and attachments to the outside world, and therefore safeguarding his inner spiritual concentration.

Lastly, the Taoist treatise, *The Secret of the Golden Flower*, recommends the fortification and defence of the Primeval Castle, which is the home of the *hsing*, the Spirit or, in Zen terminology, the natural self (CORT, ECKT, PHIL, GRIF, SEGI).

Just as in stories and in dreams, castles are usually set either upon hilltops, or in forest glades. They are strongly built and hard to come at. They convey the feeling of security, as do houses in general, but at a far higher level. They are symbols of protection.

Yet their locations in some measure set them apart in the middle of fields, woods or hill country. What they immure is isolated from the rest of the world and assumes an aura of remoteness which makes it as desirable as it is inaccessible. Thus castles are placed among the symbols of transcendence and the Heavenly Jerusalem is depicted in paintings as a castle bristling with towers and turrets and set upon a mountain peak.

The funerary temples which the Pharaohs built beside their tombs were called 'castles of millions of years'. Just like the royal tombs, they were destined to stand for ever and to link the fate of human grandeur with that of the gods (POSD).

Spiritual transcendence is the castle's protection. Castles are deemed to shelter some mysterious and intangible force. They appear in enchanted forests and mountains, themselves laden with the power of holiness, and magically vanish like mirages on the approach of some knight errant. Or else castles shelter beautiful young maidens or Prince Charmings, the former to be awakened from their sleep by a visiting lover, the latter to welcome some ravishingly beautiful female pilgrim. The castle symbolizes the realization of the heart's desire.

The 'black castle' is the castle of utter failure, of unsatisfied desire. It is an image of Hell and of a hopelessly immovable and irrevocable fate. It is a castle without a drawbridge, empty but for the lonely soul who wanders forever within its gloomy walls.

The 'white castle' is, on the contrary, a symbol of achievement, of destiny perfectly fulfilled and of spiritual perfection. Between the black and the white, at intervals, stand the other castles of the soul described by the mystics, as successive resting-places along the path of sanctification. The castle of illumination, on the mountain peak, merging with the sky itself, is where the soul will for ever be united with its God and will fully and mutually enjoy that untarnishable presence.

The 'castle in darkness' is not necessarily the 'black castle', but symbolizes the unconscious, bewilderment or unfocused desire. The 'lighted castle', which is again not the same as the 'white castle', symbolizes awareness, desire aroused and intentions put in hand.

cat The symbolism of the cat varies widely from beast of good to beast of evil omen, explicable simply in terms of the combination of the gentle and the sinister in the creature's appearance. In Japan, cats are held to be beasts of ill omen, allegedly capable of killing women and assuming their appearance. Jingoro's famous peaceful cat, at Nikko, would seem to have had no more than decorative value. In the Buddhist world, cats, along with snakes, are blamed for being the only creatures left unmoved by the death of the Buddha, something which might be considered from another angle as a sign of higher wisdom.

In India, statues of ascetic cats are to be found depicting the 'beatitude of the animal kingdom' (Kramrisch). On the other hand the cat is also the steed (and an aspect) of the *yoginī* Vidāli. Ancient China was generally inclined to view the cat as a beast of good omen and in rustic dances its gait was copied, as was that of the LEOPARD (Granet).

Even today, in Cambodia, a cat is carried round in a cage from house to house, with songs and processions to pray for rain. Every villager pours water over the cat and its howls are supposed to awaken Indra, giver of fecundating rain-showers. This, given the symbolism of rain, may be interpreted in different ways. The cat is therefore associated with drought and prompts a notion of primordial Chaos and of the *materia prima*, unfertilized by the 'waters above'.

It is also interesting to observe that the Kabbalah is at one with Buddhism in associating the cat with the SERPENT as an emblem of 'sin and the misuse of the good things of this world' (Devoucoux). Cats are sometimes depicted in this guise at the feet of Christ.

Popular caricature in Vietnam used to portray cats as emblems of mandarins, the exact equivalent of the description of rapacious government officials as 'fat cats' (DEVA, GRAR, OGRJ, DURV, KRAA, PORA).

In Ancient Egypt, the cat-goddess, Bastet, was worshipped as the guardian and benefactress of mankind. Painters and sculptors often depict her, knife in paw, decapitating the serpent Apophis, the 'Dragon of Darkness' and personification of the enemies of the Sun who try to sink his sacred boat on its voyage through the Underworld. In this respect cats are symbols of their own natural strength and agility, which a tutelary deity places at the service of mankind to enable it to overcome its hidden enemies.

Celtic tradition views the cat in a far less favourable light than the DOG or the lynx. Apparently the creature was regarded with a degree of mistrust. Cenn Chaitt, 'Cat's Head', was the surname of the usurper, Cairpre, who seized the kingship and brought ruin upon Ireland. In *The Voyage of Maelduin*, a mythical cat punishes one of his foster-brothers who tries to steal a golden torque from a deserted castle in which the crew had feasted. The thief was turned to ashes by the flames which darted from the eyes of a little cat, which then went unconcernedly on with its games. At Tara, King Nuada's porter, too, had a cat's eye which proved most awkward when he tried to go to sleep, for the eye would open when birds called or mice squeaked at night. Lastly, in Wales, one of the three plagues of Anglesey, according to the Triads of the Islands of Britain, was a cat littered by the mythical sow Henwen ('Old White'). The swineherd cast it into the sea but unfortunately it was saved and reared by people unaware of its nature. It is tempting to ask, however, whether all these stories might be referring to wild cats rather than to the domestic species (MEDI 10: pp. 35–6; OGAC 16: pp. 233–4; BROT pp. 46–8).

Islamic tradition regards the cat more favourably, unless it is black. 'Legend relates that when rats disturbed the passengers on the Ark, Noah stroked the lion's face, making it sneeze and spit out a pair of cats. This is why the creature looks like a lion.' Cats have *baraka*. A completely black cat has magical properties: its flesh cures the bewitched, and if a woman during her periods carries a black cat's spleen it will stop her menstruation. Its blood is used to write powerful charms. It has SEVEN lives and jinn often appear in the guise of cats. In Persia, if you tease a black cat you risk harming yourself, since you are mistreating your own *hemzād* (a genius born at the same instant as the person to keep him or her company), which has taken this shape (MASP p. 359). Other sources maintain that black cats are jinn which must be greeted politely when they come into a room at night (WERS pp. 308–9).

Many traditions hold black cats to be symbols of darkness and of death.

Cats are sometimes viewed as servants of the Underworld. The Nias in Sumatra believe that to reach Heaven, the dead cross a bridge below which is the abyss of Hell. A guard with shield and lance stands at the gates of Heaven with a cat to help him throw the souls of the guilty into the waters of Hell (ELIC p. 260).

To the North American Pawnee Indians, the wild cat is the symbol of cunning, forethought and ingenuity: 'it watches in crafty consideration until it can achieve its ends.' For this reason it was a sacred animal which could only be killed for religious reasons with a set ritual.

From cunning and ingenuity we progress to clairvoyance, and it is for this reason that in Central Africa so many 'medicine bags' are made of wild cat's skin (FOUC).

catalpa   In Ancient China the catalpa was the tree corresponding to Summer and the south – the trees for the other CARDINAL POINTS were acacia, chestnut and thuja. Thus the southerly altar to the Earth ought to have a catalpa tree planted beside it.

Furthermore the name of the catalpa (*cheu*) is homophonous with the ideogram for 'son'. Thus the tree symbolizes the paternal home and filial piety, as the *Che-ching* shows. When the Emperor Wu dreamed that catalpas sprouted in the courtyard of his concubine Wei Cheu-fu, he concluded that Heaven willed him to beget a male line upon her (GRAR, LECC).

catastrophe   In literature and in dreams catastrophes symbolize violent change, sought or suffered. In their more obvious negative aspect, they indicate destruction, loss, separation, broken relationships, setbacks and the death of part of the self or its environment. The very force of the catastrophe, however, conceals its positive and far more important aspect, that of a new and different life, a rebirth, metamorphosis of the psyche or social change. These can be consciously sought, can spring from the unconscious or can arise in the course of events. Catastrophes give birth to their opposites or disclose the wish for or the manifestation of a new order of things.

Symbolically the meaning of the catastrophic change is linked with the elemental form in which it appears to the imagination – as AIR for air-crashes, WATER for floods, FIRE for fires and EARTH for earthquakes. The determining element is itself a symbol which may help to specify the meaning of the generic symbol of the catastrophe, that is to say the domain in which the catastrophe and its subsequent reawakening may occur.

caterpillar   Caterpillars suffer from a twofold prejudice against them – they are larvae (the name the Romans gave to evil spirits) and they are crawling creatures, emblems of greed and ugliness.

Nonetheless the *Brhadaranyaka Upanishad* makes them symbols of transmigration because of the way in which they move from one leaf to another and because their life-cycle of larva, chrysalis and butterfly is like life passing from a bodily to another manifestation. However, as Coomaraswami, following Shankara, observes, the caterpillar does not represent an individual essence in the course of transmigration, since that essence is not distinct from the Universal Self (*ātman*), but, so to speak, a part of that Self – with all the inadequacy which such a description entails – swathed in those activities which postpone what is to come. The symbolism of the caterpillar displays the whole doctrine of transmigration without providing in itself a clear explanation of it (COOH).

caul   The membrane which sometimes covers a baby's head at birth is regarded as a sign of good luck. It is also the sign of the spiritual order which manifests itself in different guises for adults. The spirit is invisible and nothing can harm it. Covering implies both invisibility and the spirit. To wrap somebody in a cloak is at one and the same time to make that person invisible and to shelter him or her from misfortune (JUNM). Similarly a caul is an affirmation of spirituality and its safeguard: it doubly protects the invisible.

cauldron Cauldrons are 'large metal vessels for heating, boiling or cooking'. Their main use is for making BROTHS or stews, but they also produce diabolical or magic potions, hence the Devil's or witches' cauldrons of legend. Among the Celts, the cauldron corresponded to the HORN OF PLENTY, JAR or VASE of other cultures and it was their 'cauldron of plenty' which not only provided an inexhaustible supply of food but was also the symbol of limitless knowledge.

In Celtic literature three types of cauldron are to be found. One is the cauldron which belongs to the god–druid, the Dagda. This is the cauldron of plenty which leaves none unsatisfied. The second is the cauldron of rebirth into which, according to the Mabinogi of Branwen, the dead were cast to come alive the following day. A third type of cauldron was sacrificial. It was filled with wine or beer and in it the king of the old year was drowned while his palace was burned about him, on the last day of the last feast of Samain of his reign. Here we have three variations on the same divine talisman, the ancestor and prototype of the GRAIL. The Bern scholia (ninth century), although late, almost certainly preserve lost originals and are evidence of the practice in Gaul of ritually drowning a man in a half-tun in honour of Teutates (OGAC 10: pp. 381ff.; 12: pp. 349ff.).

It should be noted that the Dagda's cauldron of plenty, since it belonged to 'the Lord of Great Knowledge', not only held enough to feed all mankind bodily, but knowledge of all arts and sciences. It may also be added that Kerriwen, goddess of poets, smiths and physicians, also owned a cauldron which was a source of inspiration and of magical powers.

The majority of mythical and magic cauldrons in Celtic tradition find

parallels in other Indo-Aryan mythologies . . . [being] found at the bottom of the sea or of lakes. The traditional city of the magic cauldron in Ireland, Murias, gets its name from *muir*, the sea. There is magic power in water; cauldrons, kettles, chalices, are all receptacles of this magic force which is often symbolized by some divine liquor such as ambrosia or 'living water'; they confer immortality or eternal youth, or they change whoever owns [or bathes in] them into a hero or a god, etc.

(ELIT pp. 206–7)

Cauldrons are Chinese *ting* vases, ritual vases in which not only offerings but also the guilty were boiled – as a form of execution – and those on trial – as a form of ordeal. The ideogram *ting* and the hexagram of the *I Ching* which it designates, expressly depict the cauldron. According to the *I Ching*, the cauldron is the symbol of good fortune and prosperity, replicating the idea of the cauldron of plenty. There follow a number of partial interpretations in the shape of proverbs which involve the choice of good or evil (by overturning the cauldron) and the success or failure of the cookery, which may be seen as reflections of the 'Great Work' of alchemy. 'When the cauldron breaks a leg, the Lord's broth is spilled.' The first three-legged cauldron was cast by Shang Ti and from it he gained the powers of divination, of controlling the cycle of the seasons and finally of immortality. Three-legged cauldrons appeared simultaneously with the Sages: they vanished when men ceased to be virtuous. Yu the Great, founder of the Empire, cast nine cauldrons with metal brought from the nine regions. Five were *yang* and four were *yin*, and they symbolized the uniting of the nine regions at their CENTRE, and hence the whole world. They moved about of their own accord, boiled without any fire and were filled through the influence of the Celestial Powers. Under the decadent Chou Dynasty, the three-legged cauldrons took refuge under water, and their virtues and knowledge were lost. The first emperor, Ch'in Shih Huang Ti, tried to recover one from the River Sseu, but was prevented by a DRAGON. His virtue was insufficient to obtain a cauldron.

Inner alchemy (*Nei Tan*) uses the human body as the three-legged cauldron in which the elixir of immortality is brewed. Or, to be more precise, the cauldron corresponds to the trigram *k'uen*, Earth, the passive principle, the receptacle, at one and the same time the 'field of cinnabar' (*hia tant'ien*) and the 'foundation' of alchemical symbolism (ELIF, GRAD, GRAP, KALL, KALT, LECC, LIOT).

Magic cauldrons, with symbolism closely related to that of the MORTAR, play important parts in Uralo-Altaic tribal myth and epic and in those of all shamanistic Asia. Many heroes, some real and others legendary, were named *Kazan* ('Cauldron'). It is the name of a Turkic tribe and was frequently applied to towns and cities, such as Kazan, capital of the Tatars of the Golden Horde, Kazan of the Volga Tatars and so on. The Tara and Baraba Turks' giant, Sïmir-Kazan or Salir-Kazan, seems to have been lord of the lowest deeps and, in some versions of the story, he wrestles with the hero Ak-Köbök ('White Foam'). In the Kirghiz epic, *Er Töshtük*, the hero is forced by the 'Blue Giant', Lord of the Underworld, to go in search of the magic cauldron with forty handles:

a living cauldron, endowed with a soul, and so blood-thirsty that it eats all those who dare come near it. According to the traditions of the wise, it was the opinion of the Sages that one of the handles of this cauldron was a blood-sucking dragon, another contained the seven plagues with which God will set the whole world ablaze, while yet another stands erect in such mad fury that whoever encounter it think they have met Death himself.

(BORA p. 200)

In the event, Tchal-Kuryuk, the hero's horse (itself a magician) saves its master from this ordeal by diving to the bottom of the lake in the Land of No Return to attack and overcome the Magic Cauldron.

Cauldrons are recurrent elements in Greek legend. 'Boiling in a cauldron was a magical rite designed to confer upon whoever submitted to the ordeal a variety of faculties, first and foremost being immortality.' Here we clearly have a myth of initiation which explains and interprets the dangers threatening children and young people and is hence utterly consonant with primitive practice (H. Jeanmaire in SECG p. 295). Nevertheless, other Greek legends represent passing into the cauldron as a sort of ordeal to determine the divine nature of the person so subjected. 'Thetis, for her part, anxious to know whether the children which she had borne to Peleus were mortal, dipped them into a bowl or cauldron full of water in which they drowned, or according to another source into boiling water in which they naturally met with no better fate. Lastly, there was Medea who boiled old Pelias in a cauldron on the specious pretext that she was restoring him to youth' (ibid. p. 308). The cauldron represents the means and the place of restoring strength, regeneration and even of restoring to life, in other words of profound biological change. However, the symbol is ambivalent and the cauldron may also be the prelude to birth as a new being after death and cooking.

cavern As the archetype of the maternal WOMB, caverns feature in myths of origin, rebirth and initiation from many cultures. Under the heading 'cavern' are included 'cave' and 'grotto', although they are not precisely synonymous. It implies a place, roofed with rock or earth, at any depth in earth or mountainside, more or less dark, often lying at the end of a long passageway, and without direct daylight. Lairs of robbers or wild animals are excluded, since their significance is no more than a corruption of the symbol.

In Greek initiatory tradition the cavern represents the world. Servius, in his commentary on Virgil's *Eclogues* 3: 105, writes: 'The cavern through which Ceres descended to the Underworld in search of her daughter has been called the world.' To Plato this world was a place of ignorance, suffering and punishment, in which human souls were chained and imprisoned by the Gods as if in a cavern. In his *Republic* (7: 514a, b), he writes:

Picture men dwelling in a sort of subterranean cavern with a long entrance open to the light on its entire width. Conceive them as having their legs and necks fettered from childhood, so that they remain in the same spot, able to look forward only, and prevented by the fetters from turning their heads. Picture further the light from a fire burning higher up and at a distance behind them.

This, says Plato, is mankind's condition in this world. The cavern is its image. The shadowy light which flickers upon its walls comes from an invisible sun, but it points the way the soul must follow in search of the good and true. Upward ascent and meditation upon what is above stand for the path the soul must follow to ascend to the seat of the intellect. In Plato the symbolism of the cave carries not merely cosmic, but ethical or moral significance as well. The cavern and its shadow- or puppet-show represent this busy world from which the soul must escape to contemplate the real world of ideas.

At the start of many initiation rites, the candidate enters a cavern or pit. This is 'the return to the womb', as defined by Mircea Eliade, in material form. This was especially true of the Eleusinian rites (MAGE p. 286), in which symbolic logic was strictly translated into action. Candidates were placed, bound, in the cave from which they had to escape to reach the light of day. Prior to this, in the religious ceremonies prescribed by Zoroaster, a cave represented the world (MAGE p. 287).

Zoroaster was the first to dedicate a natural grotto, watered by springs and thick with foliage and flowers, to Mithras. This cave represented the shape of the world which Mithras had created .... Inspired by these beliefs, the Pythagoreans, and after them, Plato, called the world a cavern or grotto. In fact, according to Empedocles, the powers which guide souls say, 'We have come into this grotto covered by a roof'.

(Porphyry, *Concerning the Nymphs' Grotto* 6–9)

Plotinus remarks of this symbolism, that 'Plato's cave, like Empedocles' grotto, I believe, stands for this world of ours in which progress towards knowledge is deliverance of the soul from its bonds and its escape from the cave' (*Enneads* 4: 8, 1). A more mystical view holds that it is Dionysos who is, at one and the same time, the guardian of the cavern and the one who frees the prisoner by breaking his chains. 'Since the candidate is another Dionysos, it is he himself who confines himself to prison in the first place and who frees himself in the end. That is to say, as both Plato and Pythagoras regarded the matter, the soul is held prisoner by its own passions and freed by the Nous, that is, by the power of the mind' (MAGE pp. 290–1).

Thus Greek tradition may be seen closely to link metaphysical with moral symbolism, the harmonious development of the ego being patterned upon cosmic harmony.

Opposed, however, to this interpretation stands another symbolic aspect of the cavern. This is its terrifying aspect, the cave being a gloomy pit, an underground region with boundaries which cannot be seen, a fearful ABYSS in which MONSTERS dwell or from which they arise. It is a symbol of the unconscious and its often unexpected dangers. In fact, the cave of Trophonius, so famous in Classical antiquity, is one of the most perfect symbols of the unconscious. Trophonius, ruler of a petty kingdom and famed as an architect, built with the aid of his brother, Agamedes, the temple of Apollo at Delphi. Subsequently, when King Hyrieus commissioned them to build his treasury, they dug a secret passage to it so that they could steal his riches. Their theft was discovered: Hyrieus set a trap and Agamedes was caught. Unable to free him and anxious not to be incriminated when his brother's face was recognized, Trophonius cut off his head to carry it away with him. However, he was at once swallowed into the bowels of the earth. Years later when people came to consult the Pythian oracle to find the way to end a terrible drought, the priestess told them to ask Trophonius who lived, she said, in a cave in the depths of the woods. The royal architect provided a satisfactory answer and thereafter his oracle was much consulted, but only after the most frightening ordeals. A series of underground passageways and grottoes led to the entrance to a cavern which opened into a cold, black, yawning chasm. The enquirer climbed into it down a ladder which brought him to another chasm with a very narrow entrance. Squeezing through, feet first, he was dashed headlong down to the floor of the grotto. He would emerge eventually feet first, thrust as rapidly upwards by some invisible means. Through all this he would clutch honey cakes in both hands, to prevent him touching the machinery and enabling him to appease the serpents swarming in the cavern. His stay in the grotto could last a day and a night. Unbelievers never saw the light of day again: believers sometimes heard the oracle. When they returned above ground once more, they were seated in the Chair of Memory and recalled the terrible experiences which they had endured and by which they were marked for the rest of their lives. Sad and serious persons were proverbially said 'to have consulted the Oracle of Trophonius'.

The Trophonius complex (killing a brother to conceal one's guilt) is that of persons who deny the truth of their past to stifle their feelings of guilt. The past, however, is so deeply engraved upon the depth of their being that it cannot be so easily erased. The past continues to torment them in different guises (serpents, etc.), until the moment when they are prepared to expose it to the light of day, bringing it out of the cavern and recognizing it for their own. The cavern represents the inward ego and more especially the primal ego, buried in the depths of the unconscious. Despite the clear differences between them, Trophonius' fratricide is similar to CAIN's killing of Abel. The immemorial stain of murder haunts the unconscious and is depicted in the image of the cavern.

The cavern may also be considered as a gigantic reservoir of energy, but of Earth-born, not of celestial energy. Thus it has played and still plays an important part in magical practices. As an underground temple it preserves

memories of the Ice Age, truly the second birth of mankind. It is auspicious for the rites of initiation, of mock-burial, and for the transfer to individuals of magical powers. It symbolizes the hidden life which lies between childbirth and the rites of puberty. It placed early man in touch with Earth-bound forces of death and fertility (the gods who dwelt in the centre of the Earth).

(AMAG p. 150)

Historians of magic add that 'the roughly circular shape of the cavern, its depth underground and the twists and turns of the passageways leading to it – reminiscent of human entrails – have always made it the preferred site for magical practices.' In this respect caverns perform functions analogous with those of TEMPLES or TOWERS in concentrating magical or supernatural forces, except that these forces are Earth-born, proceeding from 'the stars of the lower depths' (AMAG p. 151), and directed towards those other stars of the lower depths which kindle the hearts of humankind.

In the Middle East, the cavern, like the womb, is the symbol of birth and rebirth. There is a particularly striking fourteenth-century Turkish legend which tells how, 'on the borders of China, on the Black Mountain, streams flooded a cave and filled a pit, shaped like a human being, with mud. The cave acted like a kiln and nine months later the heat of the sun brought the figure to life.' This was the first man, Ay-Atam, 'my Moon-Father' (ROUF p. 286). For FORTY years this man lived by himself until a fresh flood brought another human being into existence. This time the sun did not complete its task and this imperfect creature became a woman. From their marriage forty children were born. They married and had children of their own. When Ay-Atam and his wife died, their eldest son buried them in the pit in the cavern in the hope that this would bring them back to life.

In the Far East, apart from some relatively unimportant variations, the cavern is interpreted as a symbol of the world, the place of birth and initiation, image of the CENTRE and the HEART.

Image of the cosmos, its floor corresponds to the Earth and its roof to the sky. The Thais, amongst others, in fact regard the sky as the roof of a cave. 'The House of Men' of the Ancient Chinese was a cave which included a central pole, substitute for the World AXIS and the KING'S HIGHWAY. The monarch had to climb this pole to 'be suckled by the Heavens' – the stalactites on the cave-roof – thus showing proof of his heavenly lineage and his identification with the Way. The cavern – whether symbolically or the actual home of cave-dwellers – had a hole in the middle of the roof to allow smoke to escape, light to come in and to give passage to the spirits of the dead and of the shamans. This was the 'Sun Gate' or 'Cosmic Eye' (see

DOME) through which 'detachment from the cosmos' took place. Incidentally, it should be observed that both the alchemist's furnace and the human
skull have 'openings' in the top, and both may be likened to the cavern.
Taoist symbolic anthropology is quite explicit on this point, identifying the
skull with Mount Kun-Lun, the centre of the world. There is a secret cave
in which a return to the primal state occurs before detachment from the
cosmos.

This, in fact, suggests all the essentials of the symbolism of caverns and,
first and foremost, their association with MOUNTAINS. As Seckel has observed, the cavern is epitomized in traditional Indian architecture in the
rock-temple, hollowed out of a mountainside. In its turn the temple contains a STUPA. A cavity containing relics is cut out of this stupa-mountain.
The *cella* of the rock-temple is patently regarded as a cavern. According to
a Thai legend from northern Vietnam, the waters of the world pour into a
cavern at the foot of the cosmic mountain and emerge from its peak to form
the celestial river. The Immortal, Han-Chou, made his way one day into a
mountain cave and emerged at the peak in a celestial palace. These facts
show that the cavern lies on the axis running through the mountain and
identifies that axis with the World Axis.

In the case of Indo-Khmer rock-temples, the *cella* is quite literally
transpierced by this axis. It points upwards to the heavens and downwards
in a narrow well-shaft sunk in the ground. When it holds a LINGAM, the
latter stands overtly on the line of the axis. It is interesting to observe that
the OMPHALOS at Delphi stood on the tomb of the serpent Pytho and on the
chasm down which the waters of Deucalion's Flood had poured.

Guénon has remarked that if the conventional sign for a mountain is an
equilateral TRIANGLE, the cavern should be marked by a smaller triangle
within it, its apex pointing downwards. This would express simultaneously
the changed perspective of cyclical downturn which changes manifest truth
to hidden truth, and the symbol of the heart. For it represents at one and
the same time the spiritual centre of the macrocosm, growing progressively
'darker' – which may well have been true from the time of Stone Age caverns
– and the spiritual centre of the microcosm, that of the world and that of
mankind. In the Upanishads, the 'cavern of the heart' contains ether, the
individual soul, and even ātman, the spirit of the universe.

The characteristic 'centrality' of the cavern makes it a place of birth and
of regeneration – and of initiation, too, since initiation is a 'new birth'
preceded by the ordeal of the MAZE which generally provides the approach
to the cavern itself. It is a 'womb' similar to the alchemist's furnace. Many
peoples – and most notably American Indians – believed that mankind was
born of embryos which matured within underground caverns. In Asia, the
belief was that they came from GOURDS, for gourds are caverns, too, and
grew in caverns where they were gathered by the Immortals. *K'iao* is both
womb and cavern: mankind is born from it and returns to it. Ancient Chinese
emperors were shut into an underground cave before ascending to Heaven
at the start of the new year.

Thus to enter a cavern is to return to one's beginnings and thence to
'ascend to Heaven', 'to fly from the cosmos'. This is why the Chinese Immortals were to be found so often in caverns, why Lao-tzu was born in a

cave and why the Immortal Liu T'ong-pin is 'Lord of the Cavern'. The same ideogram, *tong*, is used for 'cavern' and also for 'penetration', in the sense of understanding hidden matters. Furthermore the Sages taught – and here we see the interiorization of the meaning of these legends – that the cavern of the Immortals should not only be sought on the mountain tops but in the body itself, beneath Mount Kun-Lun, which is the crown of the head. The *cella* of a Hindu temple is called *garbhagrha* or 'womb-house'. Luz, the abode of immortality in Jewish tradition, is an underground city. Typically, Jesus was born in a rock-cut stable from which the light of Redemption and the Word shone out; the dazzling rays of Amaterasu emanated from the mouth of a cave in the rocks, as did those of the Vedic *go*, or 'cows'; the rites of the Sun-god Mithras were often celebrated underground; and, in Chinese tradition, the Sun rose from *Ch'ong-sang*, 'the hollow mulberry tree'. The idea of light enclosed within the cavern is expressed in a number of different ways. St John of the Cross's 'stony caverns' are those sacred mysteries which can only be attained in the spiritual marriage. Abū Ya'qūb's 'cavern' is the primordial cavern, the cycle of concealment and revelation while, according to Islamic esotericism, *ta'wil* is a return to the 'innermost' matter.

It will have been noted that, in many ways, caverns are passageways from Earth to Heaven. It should therefore be added that, if Jesus was born in a cave, he was also buried in one, whence he descended into Hell before his ascension into Heaven. Furthermore, caverns are also passageways from Heaven to Earth down which the Chinese believed the Celestials passed. This playing the part of half-way house undoubtedly explains why in Celtic tradition, especially, Purgatory was located in a cavern and why Plato's cave should itself be a kind of Purgatory where light is only seen by reflection and beings by their shadows, as they wait for their souls to be changed and to ascend to contemplate the Ideal face to face.

Lastly the subterranean nature of the cavern is open to a number of less important interpretations. It shelters miners, it is the home of the gnomes who guard buried treasure and are dangerous psychic entities often linked with the unlucky aspect of metal-working. In Ancient Greece the Dactyls were both BLACKSMITHS and priests of CYBELE, the goddess of caverns. Caverns were frequently the place of monsters and robbers and, clearer indication still, the very gates of the Underworld (this is particularly true of Chinese tradition). It should be further noted that although caverns lead down to Hell and although the dead were buried there as the first stage of their journey beyond the grave, 'descending into Hell' is universally held to be the prelude to rebirth. This reveals the two aspects common to all major symbols, the positive and the negative.

Dream images of caverns are generally associated with other images of similar import. Caverns symbolize the locale of identity formation, that is to say the process of psychological internalization through which the individual reaches maturity and achieves a fixed identity. To do this, that person must absorb the collective world implanted in the self, at the risk of unbalancing it, and integrate those acquisitions with his or her own powers in such a way as to create his or her own personality, a personality adapted to the constantly changing world. The regulation of the inner ego is concurrent with the regulation of its relationship with the external world. From this angle, the cavern symbolizes subjectivity coming to grips with the problems of differentiation.

cedar The cedar of Lebanon, the best-known variety, has because of its sheer size become the emblem of grandeur, strength and survival. However, its natural properties have made it even more the symbol of incorruptibility. The second-century philosopher and theologian, Origen, brings this out most clearly in his commentary on the Song of Solomon 1: 17, 'The cedar is not subject to decay, therefore to make "the beams of our house . . . of cedar" is to preserve the soul from corruption.'

Consequently, like all conifers (see TREE), the cedar is a symbol of immortality (VARG).

The Ancient Egyptians used cedar in ship-building, for coffins and for sculpture; the Jews in Solomon's reign used it for the woodwork of the Temple in Jerusalem. There are Greek and Roman cedar-wood statues. The Romans also used its resinous wood to make scented torches, and carved statues of their gods and ancestors from it, regarding it as sacred. The Celts embalmed the heads of their noblest enemies with cedar-resin, replacing it, in some instances, with gold which, as all evidence shows, carried the same significance for them. Christ is sometimes depicted in the heart of a cedar.

cellar Cellars are enclosed rooms in which wine or food is stored. In Old Testament times the flat-roofed Jewish houses had no lofts. Cool rooms, out of the sunlight, were sometimes dug below ground level and used as cellars for wine and food. Cellars could also be described as 'treasure chambers' or 'storehouses'. Such a one was used in the First Temple to hold tithes and similar rooms are mentioned in connection with the Second Temple (2 Esdras 13: 12–13; Malachi 3: 10), to which the Children of Israel had to bear their offerings.

On the spiritual plane the word 'cellar' carries a precise mystical meaning. St Bernard of Clairvaux was to say that the Holy Spirit draws the soul into the cellar so that it shall take stock of its riches. Thus 'cellar' corresponds to 'self-knowledge'. The soul which knows itself manages to show charity to others and will not keep for itself the benefits which it has received. Christ governs the soul from within and his Holy Spirit encourages it to share its spiritual resources. St Bernard compares the cellar with a second Heaven. In mystical terms, 'cellar' is also a term for the secret room to which the soul must gain admittance in order to refresh itself by taking stock of the graces which it has received. It savours the wine stored in the cellar and tastes its spiritual food. Cellar here has the meaning of inwardness, of the secret room.

In Islam, too, the cellar in which is stored the wine of divine knowledge symbolizes the secret chamber to which the mystic withdraws so as to unite himself with his God.

centaur A monstrous creature of Greek mythology, with a human head, arms and torso and the body and legs of a HORSE. Centaurs, male and female, lived on mountains and in forests, fed on raw flesh, could not drink wine without getting drunk, went about in herds and were very prone, if male, to rape mortal women. They represent man's animal nature (DIES p. 134).

According to legend they were divided into two families. The descendants of Ixion's encounter with a cloud represented blind, ignorant, brute force: on the other hand the children of Philyra and Cronos, of whom Chiron was the most famous, represent strength and nobility in the service of right. A highly skilled physician and friend of Herakles (Hercules), Chiron fought at the hero's side in the battle which set them against the other centaurs. Wounded in error by one of Herakles' poisoned arrows and longing for death, he offered his own immortality to Prometheus so as to find rest. There are undoubtedly few myths which teach so clearly the battle between instinct and reason.

Iconographically, centaurs are generally depicted with an expression of sorrow on their faces. They symbolize lust, with all the brute violence which can reduce mankind to the level of beasts unless it is counterbalanced by spiritual strength. They are a striking image of the twofold nature of mankind – half god and half beast (TERS p. 64). They are the antithesis of the HORSEMAN, who tames and masters the elemental forces, while the centaurs, with the exception of Chiron and his brothers, are ruled by wild, untrammelled instinct. They are also an image of the unconscious, an unconscious which gains mastery of the personality, subjecting it to its own impulses and eliminating inner conflict.

centre With the CIRCLE, the CROSS and the SQUARE, the centre is one of the four fundamental symbols (CHAS p. 22).

Above all the centre is the beginning of all things and absolute reality. The centre of centres can be none other than God. Nicholas of Cusa states that 'the poles of the spheres meet together with the centre which is God. He is both circumference and centre, who is both everywhere and nowhere.' One is immediately reminded of Pascal quoting Hermes Trismegistus: 'God is a sphere whose centre is everywhere and circumference nowhere.' This means that his presence is boundless and universal and that it is therefore at the invisible centre of being, unaffected by time or space.

If the centre may be conceived as Nicholas of Cusa's meeting of opposites, it may also be seen as the reservoir of dynamic intensity. It is the spot at which opposing forces accumulate and co-exist, the place where energy is at its most concentrated. It is the balance of opposing forces.

In symbolism, the centre should never be thought of merely as some fixed point. It is a storehouse from which flow the movements of the one towards the many, the inner towards the outer, the immanent towards the manifest, the eternal towards the temporal and all the processes of emanation and divergence, and, being the place from which they originated, to which are directed all processes of return and convergence to a oneness.

Mircea Eliade (ELIT p. 375) observes that, in general terms,

the symbolism in question expresses itself in three connected and complementary things: 1. The 'sacred mountain' where heaven and earth meet, stands at the centre of the world; 2. Every temple or palace, and by extension, every sacred town and royal residence, is assimilated to a 'sacred mountain' and thus becomes a centre; 3. The temple or sacred city, in turn, as the place through which the Axis Mundi passes, is held to be a point of junction between heaven, earth and hell.

Again, the Tree of Life grows in the centre of the world. It should be remembered that the images of the centre and of the AXIS are correlative in symbolic dynamism and only differ according to the angle from which they are observed. Look down upon its summit and a COLUMN is no more than a central point, when viewed from horizontal distance, it stands perpendicular and is an axis. Thus the Holy of Holies, which always tries to stand upon an elevation, is at one and the same time the centre and the axis of the world, and hence a spot set apart for the manifestation of the godhead.

The centre of the world often takes the form of something elevated – a MOUNTAIN, HILL, TREE, OMPHALOS or STONE – but it should be noted that while the centre of the Earth is unique in Heaven it is not so on Earth. Every race – one might almost say every individual – has its own centre of the world, its own viewing point, its own magnetic POLE. This may be conceived as the point at which the the collective or individual will intersects with the superhuman power which is capable of satisfying it, be it a desire for knowledge, love or action. Where this desire and that power intersect is the centre of the world. No race is without its holy mountain which it regards as the centre of its world.

This notion of centre is also closely connected with that of a channel of communication. In fact the centre is called the NAVEL of the world. It is extraordinary to observe in African carvings the way in which the navel is often given the dimensions of a long tube, making it larger even than the penis. The navel is the centre from which life originates. The Greeks regarded the omphalos (navel-stone) of Delphi as the centre of the world. The Samaritans' holy mountain, Garizim, was the Earth's navel, while Mount Tabor derives its name from *tabur* meaning 'navel'. The centre has as strong a spiritual as a physical meaning. Mystical food flows as strongly from the centre as does the biological food of the mother's blood.

The centre also symbolizes law and social organization. We speak of the central power which organizes the state. At a higher level it organizes the universe, physical evolution and the ascent of the spirit. In this symbol 'may be perceived the underlying and dynamic opposition of unorganized and chaotic TOHU-BOHU into which obsolete or vanquished forms sink and from which new forms arise, and the organized cosmos ascending towards the light, organized life and ultimately spiritual genesis' (CHAS p. 166).

In what may be termed its horizontal radiations, the centre may be seen as an image of the world, a microcosm containing within itself all the potentiality of the universe; and in its vertical radiations, as a place of passage, a shrine of initiation, the pathway between celestial, terrestrial and infernal levels, the boundary to be crossed and, consequently, the breaking point. The crucial centre is the place of highest concentration, the place where decisions are taken, the dividing line.

In Gaul the idea of the centre is enshrined in the place-name *Mediolanum*, from which is derived, among some fifty other known examples, the name of the northern Italian city, Milan, originally in Cisalpine Gaul. The name apparently means 'centre of perfection' as well as 'central plain'. In his *De bello gallico*, Caesar mentions a 'holy place' in the forests between the Rivers Loire and Seine where the druids assembled to choose their chief. In Ireland the county of Meath (*Midhe*: 'centre') was created by taking portions of each of the four original provinces. It was the site of national and religious festivals and its capital, Tara, was the seat of the High Kings of Ireland. The centre was the link which ensured the unity of the four different parts (CELT 1: pp. 159ff.).

In Central American civilizations, the centre of the cross formed by the four CARDINAL POINTS corresponds to the 'fifth Sun' and hence to the present world. In the *Codex Borgia* it is depicted surrounded by the four gods who correspond to the four first suns, painted in the four fundamental colours – red, black, white and blue – and joined together by blood-red lines. The central figure is that of Quetzalcoatl, god of the rising Sun. Other illustrations in this codex depict a multicoloured Tree of Life growing in the centre, and perched on the tree the quetzal bird. The Aztecs regarded FIVE as the number of the centre, allotted frequently by tradition to the human personality.

Cruciform signatures, or seals with a centre shaped like a circle or lozenge, signify universal sovereignty. Charlemagne's is not unique in this respect. 'The four consonants in his name, *Karolus*, were written as the four cardinal points, while the vowels were grouped in a lozenge in the centre. This arrangement of a ruling centre and of cardinal points which simultaneously co-ordinate and obey, is a feature of the signatures of all the Carolingian emperors' (CHAS p. 443). A name, sign or DOT at the centre of a figure displays the pivotal role upon which all rests and depends, of the person so symbolized.

Cerberus Son of the serpentine ECHIDNA and TYPHON, Cerberus was a monstrous, many-headed dog (the number of heads varied from three to one hundred), with a dragon's tail and a back bristling with serpents' heads. He barred the way to the Underworld to the living and prevented the dead from escaping from it. Orpheus tamed him with the music of his lyre and Herakles (Hercules) dragged him off by brute force. Yet his nature became all the more terrifying on his return from Earth to the Underworld.

As the 'Hound of Hades' he symbolizes the terrors of death felt by those who dread Hell and the hell within each human individual. It should be observed that it was with no weapon other than his own strength that Herakles succeeded temporarily in taming him and that it was by the spiritual effect of his music that Orpheus calmed him, again temporarily. These two instances strongly support the neo-Platonic interpretation of Cerberus as an in-dwelling daemon, the spirit of evil. This spirit can only be tamed above ground, that is to say by a sudden – and ascensional – change of environment and by the individual's spiritual strength. To conquer, one has to rely upon oneself.

Ceres See DEMETER.

chain Chains symbolize the bonds which link Heaven and Earth and, in more general terms, tie together two extremes or two beings. Plato alludes to a ROPE of light encircling the universe. The aim of this golden chain might well be to link Heaven with Earth.

He speaks of 'iron and adamantine chains' (*Gorgias* 509a), and these are the logical steps of an argument or thesis. By such chains Socrates linked human happiness with the practice of justice, his reasoning having the brilliance of diamonds and the strength of steel. According to Homer, a golden chain hangs down from the vault of Heaven to the Earth. Zeus with his thunders assembled the gods on the highest peak of Olympus, demanded their complete submission to his supreme power and, to prove his omnipotence, addressed them:

Nay, come, make trial, ye gods, that ye all may know. Make ye fast from heaven a chain of gold, and lay ye hold thereof, all ye gods and all goddesses; yet could ye not drag to earth from out of heaven Zeus the counsellor most high, not though ye laboured sore. But whenso I were minded to draw of a ready heart, then with earth itself should I draw you and with sea withal; and the rope should I thereafter bind about a peak of Olympus and all those things should hang in space. By so much am I above gods and above men.

(*Iliad* 8: 18–28)

The Pseudo-Dionysius the Areopagite applies the same argument to the nature of prayer (PSEN p. 26). The infinitely luminous golden chain is regarded as going from Earth to Heaven and, in order to make his point more clearly, the writer likens it to a rope mooring a boat to a rock. Pull on the rope and the rock does not move, but the boat floats shorewards. Homer's golden chain was constantly used and commented upon.

The astral cord is, of course, akin to the golden chain. Its task is to bind the spirit to the psyche; that is to say to bind *nous* (or reason) to the soul (*animus–anima*). Plato alludes to it in his treatise on Socrates' *daimon*. In this connection Mircea Eliade observes that similar themes were elaborated by neo-Platonists, basing themselves upon Plato's theory of men as puppets of the gods and the golden rope of reason ('Mythes et symboles de la corde', in ERAJ 29 (1960)). Mircea Eliade was to go on to say that such an image could be related to parapsychology, since according to some studies in it, there were individuals capable of visualizing and of feeling this rope or wire linking their physical body to their 'subtle' body.

A chain ran to the ears of his listeners from the tongue of the Celtic god Ogmios, the Irish Ogma, symbolizing the hold which the god of speech exercised upon his hearers through his eloquence. Generally speaking chains are symbols of chains of communication and command and, consequently, of marriage, the family, the city, the nation and of all collective or communal activity. We speak of making a human chain. In the sociopsychological context, chains symbolize the need to adapt to communal life and the ability to integrate with the group. They mark a stage in personal development or involution and nothing is harder, from the psychological point of view, than to realize that the bonds of society are indispensable and to feel this, no longer as a heavy chain riveted upon one by external forces, but as a spontaneous act of acceptance.

This sense of binding is, like the NET, a symbol of kingship. Dumézil emphasizes that 'Varuna is supremely the master of *māyā*, of magic influence. The bonds of Varuna are magic as is his sovereignty itself; they are the symbol of those mystical powers held by the chief which are called: justice, administration, royal and public security, all powers' (quoted by

ELIT p. 70). By these bonds the god underwrites bargains and preserves intact the network of human obligation. He alone can loosen them and is thus generally depicted holding a rope.

In the Bible the power of binding symbolizes the force of justice. Christ said to Peter: 'whatsoever thou shalt bind on earth shall be bound in heaven' (Matthew 16: 19). On this the *Jerusalem Bible* commentators remark:

'bind' and 'loose' are technical rabbinical terms; primarily they have a disciplinary reference; one is 'bound' (condemned) to or 'loosed' (absolved) from excommunication. Their secondary usage is connected with doctrinal or juridical decisions: an opinion is 'bound' (forbidden) or 'loosed' (allowed).

Thus all obligations are comprehended in these words, not simply those which derive from juridical acts but also those which proceed from an inward acceptance, like faith. In the latter case bonds no longer symbolize only those imposed by force, but also those willingly assumed by the different parties which feel united among themselves. The symbolism is stood upon its head: liberty and bondage are no longer at opposite ends of the spectrum; the binding chain has become free acceptance. Within the context of the Gospels, bonds are related to the powers of the KEYS and to the GATES of Hell or of the Kingdom of Heaven. Obedience to the bond opens the gates of the Kingdom, its betrayal leads to the gates of Hell.

chain of office   See NECKLACE.

chair   The chair is universally recognized as a symbol of authority. To remain seated while others stand is to demonstrate your superiority, while to offer somebody a chair is to recognize his or her authority or prestige, either as a person or as a representative of that authority. In academic circles professorial authority is dignified by the Chair in that particular branch of learning, while in the church the bishop's sphere of authority is known as his see, from the Latin *sedes*, meaning 'chair'. Thus the Holy See is the symbol of the divine authority with which the Pope is invested as Sovereign Pontiff. A raised chair confirms superiority.

chakra   A Sanskrit word meaning 'WHEEL' and applied to the hidden meeting points of the *nādīs* or channels of the 'subtle' body, along which, according to Hindu physiology, vital energy flows. This mystical physiology sets these energy centres at intervals up the spinal column to the top of the head, and they could be described as 'generators of etheric matter' (*avas*). From the base of the spine (the *mūladhāra*), *kundalinī*, a static form of creative energy, may be roused. Hindu Tantrism numbers FIVE of these energy centres with a sixth, a higher cerebral centre, known as the *sahasrāra*, or 'thousand-petalled lotus'. Tibetan Tantric Buddhists reckon five *chakra* or *khorlos*, located in the perineum, navel, heart, throat and brain. They correspond respectively to Earth, Water, Fire, Air and Ether; to the four cardinal points and the centre, or summit; to the five families of Dhyani-Buddhas; to the five seed sounds; and to the five sections of the stupa, or *chörten.*

chalice (see also BASKET)   There are two essential aspects to the extensive symbolism of the chalice, that of a vessel of plenty and that of a vessel holding the draught of immortality.

In the first instance chalices are often compared with the breast filled with mother's milk. A Gallo-Roman dedicatory inscription to the goddess Flora, from Autun in France, identifies the 'chalice from which flows grace' with the 'breast from which flows the milk which nourishes the city' (Devoucoux). In the case of the Hindu Mahā-Lakshmi there is the same symbolism and the same identification, although in this instance 'milk' is SOMA. This brings us back to the notion of the draught of immortality (see SAP). The chalice in which the soma is offered is likened to the crescent Moon, whose light is traditionally compared with the colour of milk.

The more generalized symbolism of the chalice has been applied to the medieval GRAIL, the vessel in which Christ's blood was received which contains simultaneously – although at bottom they are identical – secret lore temporarily lost and the draught of immortality. The chalice holds blood – the principle of life – and is therefore homologous with the heart and consequently with the CENTRE. The heart is a vessel. Etymologically the Grail is both a 'vessel' and a 'book', thus confirming the twofold meaning of what it contains – revelation and life. There is a tradition that it was carved from the EMERALD which fell from Lucifer's forehead, and this again relates to the Shivaite and Buddhist urnā, the 'third eye' associated with the sense of eternity (Guénon). Now, as the Zen Master Dōgen writes, when a gem is polished, it becomes a vessel and the content of that vessel is the scintillation exposed by the polishing, just as illumination finds root in the heart through spiritual concentration.

The Grail is also known as 'the Vessel', symbol of the ship and of the ARK which holds the seeds of cyclical rebirth and of lost tradition. It is noticeable that the crescent Moon, which equates to the chalice, is also a BOAT.

The symbolism of the Tantric skull-cup is very similar to that of the Grail. It holds blood (or sometimes tea or alcohol) and is another expression of immortality or of knowledge purchased at the cost of death to this present state of existence, hence the rebirth of the initiate into a superhuman state.

Some Western alchemical writings advise the use of skull-cups in achieving the 'Great Work' and this clearly reveals a similar symbolism. On the other hand Chinese alchemists, failing in their initial attempts to distil the elixir of life, made the vessels and cups, clearly destined to contain the food and drink of immortality, from the gold obtained from their furnaces.

Eucharistic chalices containing the Body and Blood of Christ display a symbolism similar to that of the Grail, for Jesus said: 'Unless you eat of my flesh and drink of my blood ye shall not have eternal life.' The communion rite for which they are used, and which makes real its potentiality for sacrifice and beatific union, belongs to many traditions and particularly to those of Ancient China. (This is taking into account only the externals of these rituals and not their dogmatic significance.) Although predominantly a rite of binding together in, as it were, a BLOOD-BROTHERHOOD, it is also a symbol of immortality. Drinking from the same cup is a common practice in Far Eastern wedding ceremonies, while in Ancient China it was the custom to drink from the two halves of the same calabash (see GOURD).

The cup is also a cosmic symbol. The World EGG is split to form two cups facing one another, the upper one, in the image of a DOME, being the sky. These two halves provided caps for the Dioscuri.

The Vedic sacrifice of the 'division into four chalices shining like the day of the unique chalice of Tvashtri' by the three Ribhus describes the cosmic work of expanding the manifestation from the centre to the four cardinal points. Conversely, the Buddha made one bowl out of the four begging-bowls brought to him from the four cardinal points by the four Maharajas. He restored the quaternary cosmos to its original unity (DANA, DAVL, DEVA, ELIF, GOVM, GRAD, GUEM, GUES, MALA, SILI).

In Japan to exchange cups (*Sakazuki o Kawasu*) is a symbol of faithfulness. It forms part of the wedding ceremony. Gangsters exchange cups when they drink with a new recruit and, by extension, so does the manager when he engages a new subordinate.

In the Celtic world, a chalice filled with wine or with some other intoxicant such as beer or mead which a maiden handed to the king elect, was a symbol of sovereignty, and this is very plain in the famous tale of the *Baile an Scail*, 'Town of Heroes'. The King of Ireland, Conn, watches as a maiden of wondrous beauty hands him the chalice in the presence of the god, Lug, who prophesies that his descendants will reign for many a generation. In Christian tradition the chalice becomes confused with the Dagda's CAULDRON, with the result that the Holy Grail continues the role of the chalice of sovereignty and inherits that of the Dagda's cauldron.

The cup employed both for ritual libation and for profane feasting has been the foundation of a fully developed symbolism in both Christian and Jewish tradition.

The 'cup of salvation' which the Psalmist takes and offers to the Lord (Psalm 116: 13) is both a material object used in a ritual act of worship and a symbol of thanksgiving, as is the Eucharistic chalice (meaning 'cup of thanksgiving') or 'cup of blessing' (1 Corinthians 10: 16).

However, in the Bible the main stress is upon the cup as symbol of human destiny, individuals being allotted their fate by God as though receiving a cup or its contents. In these circumstances the cup may overflow with blessings (Psalm 23: 5) or be filled with 'snares, fire and brimstone' (Psalm 11: 6), this being 'the cup of the wine of the fierceness of [God's] wrath' (Revelation 16: 19). This is why the instrument which God employs against an individual, a people or a city may be compared with a cup (Jeremiah 51: 7; Zechariah 12: 2). When Jesus speaks of the cup which he must drink (Matthew 20: 22ff.) and which he asks his Father to let pass from him (Matthew 26: 39), it is not simply his death to which he refers, but to the destiny which God has offered him and which he accepts in full knowledge of the divine purpose.

In Muslim mystical writings cups generally symbolize the HEART, understood as intuition or the most sensitive point in the soul.

Since the initiate (*ārif*) is himself a microcosm, his heart is often compared with the chalice which belonged to Jamshid, in which this legendary king of Persia was supposed to have been able to view the entire universe.

The 'Secrets of Hamza' recount how one of the companions of Muhammad's uncle, the Emir Hamza, travelled to Adam's tomb on the island of Serendib (Sri Lanka). Here Adam himself presented him with a magic cup which enabled him to assume whatever shape he pleased. This, surely, is the symbol of the power to become whatever one wishes through the intimacy of one's knowledge of it.

In the Muslim Paradise the saints enjoy the special privilege of the 'cup of love' or the 'wine of gladness'.

After their long journey, the saints leave their staves at the door and are ushered in to drink the wine, poured into the chalice by angelic cup-bearers. Then by candlelight they are greeted by a mysterious being who suddenly appears in the guise of a young man of lofty beauty and they bow down before this shrine of the divine essence.

(MASL pp. 109–10)

The chalice is the symbol of the prelude to communion in worship and in love.

The chalice symbolizes not merely the content, but the essence of revelation. It is related that when the Prophet reached Jerusalem on his night-long journey, he entered the Temple.

'When I came out,' he said, 'Gabriel came to me bearing a cup of wine and another full of clotted milk. I chose the latter. Gabriel said to me "You have chosen *Fitra*, that is natural man, as first conceived, uninfluenced by Christian baptism or Mosaic Law."' Tradition adds: 'I was told [after he had drunk the milk], "If you had taken the wine, your followers would have fallen into error."'

(HAYI p. 286)

In another version, when Muhammad reached Jerusalem, he was welcomed by all the prophets and offered three chalices, the one full of milk, the other of wine and the third of water. He chose the milk, 'since, had he chosen water, it would have presaged the ruin (*gariqa*) of him and his followers, wine their falling into error (*gawiya*), while milk foretold their following the right path (*hudiya*).'

This allegory may be interpreted in two ways. The first, pre-Islamic, takes milk as the symbol of herdsmen and wine as that of farmers, water being their joint symbol. The second, Islamic, takes them for the three monotheistic faiths: Judaism, in which water plays both a destructive role (the Flood) and one of salvation (the Crossing of the Red Sea); Christianity, in which wine plays a transcendent part; and Islam, which gives victory to the values of the nomadic life by returning to the uncontaminated faith of Abraham. For, in dream symbolism, MILK stands for natural religion and knowledge.

(FAHN pp. 206–7)

chameleon   The traditions of the Pygmies of the Ituri River in Zaire lend the supreme sky-god, Arebati, the attributes of thunder, lightning and the chameleon. The last is the Demiurge, creator of mankind, and therefore sacred.

If Pygmies come across one, they carefully remove it from their path for fear of attracting thunder and lightning. Since the chameleon climbs to the tops of the highest trees, it is the closest to God . . . . One day a chameleon heard a rustling and a muttering in a tree-trunk. It split the tree and out flowed a mass of water which divided and spread over all the Earth. This was the first water in the world. With the water emerged a pair of human beings, a woman named Otu ('Blood') and a youth named Mupe . . . . Their eldest child was father of the Pygmy race and their second of the Black race . . . . The tree from which they sprang was the father of all trees. The chameleon made it bear fruit and from this fruit came fresh species to which the chameleon gave their names.

In this way he named all kinds of animals except the goat, which came straight down from Heaven. The part of go-between played by the chameleon between mankind and the sky-gods seems to have been recognized in antiquity in Europe. 'The head and gullet of a chameleon burned with oak give command of thunder and rain.' Through the chameleon, the Sun was able to communicate with mankind.

Since the chameleon 'has been given every colour', the Dogon associate it with the RAINBOW, the path from Earth to Heaven.

The Ela of Upper Volta regard it as a fertility symbol and hence employ ashes of the chameleon to prepare magical and medicinal powders (NICO).

In African civilizations, the solar role played by the chameleon is illustrated in Dahomeyan shrines by the figures of the Supreme Deity – Lisa (Fon) or Orisha (Yoruba) in the Voodoo pantheon – as a chameleon with the Sun in its mouth (GRID, MAUG). This is somewhat akin to the Ancient Egyptian SCARAB.

According to other traditions, the chameleon was one of the first living creatures.

It first appeared before the Earth had completely emerged from the primal waters. Because it had learned to walk in the mud, the chameleon adopted that slow and apparently lazy gait. And this was the reason for the arrival of Death. What happened was that Uculunculu (a Demiurge and the first man) entrusted the Chameleon with the message for mankind that they would not die. But the Chameleon lingered on the way and in his annoyance Uculunculu sent the LIZARD with the message that they would die and the lizard got there first.

(MYTF p. 233)

Death is therefore the result of the chameleon's laziness and stupidity.

In the legends of the Kaydara, the chameleon is endowed with SEVEN qualities, as many symbols as are revealed to the initiate.

1   It changes colour whenever it wishes. On the positive side this is to be sociable, tactful and able to engage in pleasant conversation with anybody and to adapt oneself to any circumstance and to any social environment. Negatively it is to be hypocritical, changeable, swayed by sordid interest and base intrigue. It is also to lack originality and individuality. It is to spend one's life in the anteroom courting the mighty.
2   Coiled in its belly is a long, sticky tongue which enables it to take its prey from a distance without having to pounce upon it. If it misses its aim, it simply retracts its tongue. This is carefully concealed greed, persuasive talk which deprives the hearer of all means of resisting its arguments. It is the art of escaping from every dilemma, of deceiving with sweet talk, the ability to lie and wait patiently in ambush, the better to surprise one's victims.
3   It steps carefully, one foot after the other, unhurriedly. The wise man is circumspect and never rushes headlong into anything. He balances its importance and its risks without a spark of generosity and without taking the slightest risk. He spies out the land and makes sure before advancing a step or venturing advice or making a decision.

4 It does not need to turn round to see what lies about it. Slightly bending
   its head, it lets its eye revolve in its socket and sweep the horizon. It is
   the crafty watcher, impervious to external influence as it gathers in every
   scrap of information.
5 Its body is slender-flanked, soft-skinned but lithe and dexterous.
6 It has a spiny ridge along its back. In a positive sense, this may be taken
   as an assurance against any surprise; negatively, as empty vainglory.
7 It has a prehensile tail. Hypocrite and coward, it steals other' goods
   behind their backs and without the least appearance of ill intent. This
   is a trap set to obtain an advantage in a manner which could not be
   foreseen (HAMK p. 56).

Thus, even in Africa, the symbolic significance of the chameleon may
be seen to shift from the cosmic to the ethical and psychological plane,
marking a similar shift in the points of interest and observation. From the
Demiurge which fails in its task of making man immortal, to the creature
whose physical characteristics and habits illustrate the teachings of the initiator, the chameleon exhibits a startling bipolarity, positive and negative,
which brings together its strengths and weaknesses.

Chaos In Classical antiquity Chaos was the 'personification of the primeval void, before the work of creation, at a time before the elements of the
world had been set in order' (GRID p. 88). This is an idea very similar to
that expressed by Genesis 1: 2: 'And the earth was without form, and void:
and darkness was upon the face of the deep. And the Spirit of God moved
upon the face of the waters.' 'Darkness . . . upon the face of the deep' possesses a negative quality and is as much a symbol of lack of differentiation
and non-existence, as of a complete range of potentialities including those
in opposition to each other. Both Jewish and Christian commentators have
seen in this verse a revelation of creation arising from nothingness.

In Ancient Egyptian cosmogony, Chaos was 'a force in the shapeless and
unformed world . . . which surrounded the created world as the sea surrounded the earth.' It had existed before creation and co-existed with it,
apparently enclosing it like a vast and everlasting reservoir of forces (MORR
pp. 48–9) in which all created things would be dissolved at the end of time.
It would seem that primeval Chaos was known as *Nun*, father of gods, of
the Sun, of mankind and of all things, conceived of as the primal water from
which even Ra himself arose, 'the god who is greater and mightier than his
creator' (ibid. pp. 225, 229).

In Chinese tradition, Chaos was that uniform space which existed before
the 'division into four horizons', which is the same as the creation of the
world. This division marks the attainment of differentiation and the potentiality of orientation. It is the basis of cosmic order, since to become dis-
oriented is to return to Chaos. The only means of escape is active thought
which cleaves a passage through the primeval element (SOUN).

The FOMORIANS, those dark malevolent creatures, stand for the Chaos
from which sprang the Celtic world. However, in distinction to all other
races, their home was Ireland. They were never migrants, but true abori-
ginals. Nonetheless, both life and knowledge sprang from Chaos, and
Delbaeth ('Shape') was father to both gods and Fomorians. The gods are

thus all brothers and sisters, while Dana, or Ana ('Art') was mother of the gods. Despite this she remained a virgin (Brigit, equivalent to the classical Minerva, was daughter of the Dagda, while remaining the virgin mother of the three primordial gods). Elatha ('Knowledge') coupled with Eri ('Ireland') to give birth to the usurping king, Bres. The gods of the Tuatha Dé Danann ('Children of Dana') had to fight the great Battle of Mag Tuired, with the all-skilful Lug to lead them, before they succeeded in gaining mastery over Chaos (OGAC 17: pp. 399–400; 18: pp. 365–99). These battles are reminiscent of the war between the gods and the giants in Greek mythology.

Modern psychoanalysis sees Chaos merely 'as a symbolic term . . . . Chaos symbolizes the human spirit put to flight in face of the mystery of being' (DIES p. 110). Chaos precedes even the formation of the unconscious. It is the equivalent of proto-matter, of the undifferentiated, the shapeless and the state of utter passivity to which Platonic and Pythagorean tradition refers.

chariot In the symbolism of the chariot, clear distinctions must be drawn between the vehicle itself, its driver (see CHARIOTEER) and the team which draws it.

In China it was a symbol of the world. Its square floor (*tavu*) represents the world; its circular awning (*kai*) the sky; while between them runs a pole which represents the World AXIS. The pole rises head-high and stands for an intermediary between Heaven and Earth. In India the symbolism of the chariot is closely related to this, the body (*kosha*) of the cosmic chariot corresponding to the space separating Heaven and Earth (*antariksha*). But in this case it is the axle (*aksha*) which represents the World Axis and the two WHEELS which are Heaven and Earth, joined and yet kept apart by this axis.

Chariots are often associated with the Sun, especially in India and in the worship of Mithras, Cybele and Attis, where they symbolize its path across the sky. The passage of Mithras' chariot plays the subsidiary part of the Demiurge, as does that of Attis. However, chariot – or rather cart, as in Charles's Wain – is one of the names of the Great and Little Bear. These are polar constellations and therefore central and motionless. The shaft of Charles's Wain – also known as the handle of the Big Dipper – points in succession to the four ascendants and therefore determines the four seasons. Ssu Ma Ch'ien describes it as 'moving in the midst of things' while *The Secret of the Golden Flower* explains that it sets the manifest world revolving round it.

The chariot also symbolized to both Indians and Platonists the ego. The chariot does not exist except as an assembly of its component parts, and if these parts are considered individually then the chariot ceases to exist. The chariot is therefore, like the ego, a conventional term. Buddhism, too, made ample use of this symbol, especially in the *Milindapañha*.

However, Buddhism lays greater stress upon the way in which the chariot is driven than upon the chariot itself. In the *Rig-Veda* Agni or *prāna* ('breath') or *ātman* ('the ego') or even *buddhi* ('intellect') was 'master of the chariot'. In Buddhism this was the Buddha or *atta* ('the ego') or *dharma* ('the Law'). The CHARIOTEER is the spirit and his team the senses, and these the charioteer must control by reference to his knowledge of the 'master'.

In Zen Buddhism 'the chariot of the White Ox' is the name given to Buddha's spiritual vehicle, by contrast with the chariots drawn by goats, stags and oxen, vehicles of the *shravaka*, Pratyeka-Buddha and Bodhisattva which cannot provide the means of supreme knowledge.

It should also be observed that in Ancient China, chariot driving was, along with archery, a means whereby princes could demonstrate their skill and virtue. Ability to drive a chariot was, as we should say nowadays, to measure up to steering the ship of state (AVAS, COOH, ELIF, GRAD).

In his commentary upon the Scriptures and in particular upon the book of Ezekiel, the Pseudo-Dionysius the Areopagite (PSEO) remarked early in the Christian era that chariots were images of the harmonious equality which brought together spirits of a similar order.

From prehistoric times the chariot of the Sun symbolized the path it makes, curving across the sky from east to west. The chariot was successively that of Apollo, Mithras and Attis as each was identified with the Sun-god. Anything associated with these ancient solar cults had to be rooted out from among the Children of Israel. 'And [Josias] took away the horses that the kings of Judah had given to the sun, at the entering of the house of the Lord . . . and burned the chariots of the sun with fire' (2 Kings 23: 11).

All religions in the ancient world were acquainted with

a chariot driven with a tremendous din (the chariot of Zeus or of the Sun) and with an omnipotent Charioteer steering this chariot across the boundless tract of Heaven . . . . Several attributes were required to complete this image of a supernatural equipage which bestowed all good and evil, all prosperity and disaster upon mankind. Lightning was represented by a WHIP handled by Zeus or by a flail in the hands of the Spartan Dioscuri . . . . The original myth of the chariot of thunder was modified by some peoples into a sled or a galloping horse'.

(LOEF pp. 27–8)

The heavenly chariot of cloud and thunder speeds unfettered and free wherever it will, unlike the chariot of the Sun which must follow a set course. The former suggests the fickleness of the gods rather than their majestic control of the universe. It points rather to the phase of cosmic and spiritual development represented by Ouranos (Uranus) rather than Zeus (or Jove).

These images have been taken up and prettified in fairy stories and although their very sweetness cloys, they do preserve the idea of the chariot as a symbol of both good and evil fortune coming down in equal measure from Heaven. In his story 'The Hind in the Forest', Perrault tells us that the fairies have two sorts of chariot:

one used to bring good fortune and the other when they work evil. Each individual fairy had her own chariot made of a different material: one was of ebony drawn by white doves; others were of ivory drawn by small crows; others again were of cedar or bamboo. In these they travelled on peaceful and kindly missions. But when they were angry, they would harness winged dragons or serpents which spat fire or shot it from their eyes and with these they could travel from one end of the Earth to the other in less time than it takes to say good-night or good morning.

(LOEF p. 31)

In widely propagated Vedic tradition, the chariot is regarded as 'the vehicle of the soul in a state of travail: it carries that soul for the duration of its incarnation' (LOEF p. 60). Modern psychoanalysis would correct the 'substantialist' or at least 'separatist' dualism of this interpretation by the concept of an energy centre under tensions which must be resolved. This would relate to the underlying meaning of these mythic chariots, but by identifying the vehicle and its passenger as 'vehicles of determined cosmic forces'. These cosmic forces originate in the planets and act upon Earth and its inhabitants in set and different ways. Cybele's chariots affect the harvests; those of Venus, love; and those of Mars, war (LOEF p. 61).

The chariot of fire is as much a universal symbol as the chariot of the Sun or the winged chariot of the soul. Elijah, carried up to Heaven in a whirlwind, was generally depicted in a chariot. 'Whenever a person is depicted sweeping aloft towards the realm of the immortals in a chariot of fire it symbolizes the spiritual being, destroying on the way his or her physical body to obtain an extraordinarily swift ascension' (LOEF p. 63).

The animals harnessed to chariots give an individual flavour to this general symbolism, although sometimes what was intended as an adjunct tends to set in the shade what it was intended to enhance. Eagles are harnessed to Zeus' chariot; peacocks to Juno's; horses to Apollo's; unicorns to Athene's; goats to Dionysos'; swans or doves to Aphrodite's; storks to Hermes'; stags to Artemis'; dogs to Hephaistos'; wolves to Ares'; dragons to Ceres', and lions to Cybele's.

However, symbol slides into allegory when an ass draws the chariot of idleness or peace-making; cocks that of vigilance; black oxen that of death; bats that of night; winged horses the chariot of the dawn; elephants the chariot of fame; mules that of poverty; birds of prey that of greed; and calves the chariot of the Spring (TERS pp. 71–89).

In the TAROT, the Chariot is the seventh major arcanum. In it stands the LOVER from the sixth arcanum. He is slightly aged and crowned with gold to show 'that he has mastered his ambivalences and thus acquired the unity which favours all those who have resolved their conflicts. On his shoulders two faces in profile (a double projection) bear witness to the opposition which he has overcome. Indeed, it is because he has surmounted it that he is in the Chariot, in other words, he has progressed' (VIRI p. 77). He holds a SCEPTRE and stands beneath a flesh-coloured awning held up by four columns, two red and two blue, set at the four corners of the chariot. He wears a red kilt belted in yellow below a blue breastplate, on which a triple builder's square emphasizes the task of building which he must accomplish in the three worlds, natural, human and divine. One of his sleeves is red, the other yellow. The horses which draw his chariot both look in the same direction, but one is blue and the other red and they appear to be pulling in opposite directions since each has its outer foreleg raised. Between them are the initial letters 'S M' which may mean Sa Majesté ('His Majesty') or, if taken alchemically, SULPHUR and MERCURY, the basic elements of the Great Work. Commentators here recall the legend of Alexander, who mounted a chariot drawn by two gigantic birds or by two gryphons, to discover whether Heaven and Earth met together; or else the chariot of fire which took up the prophet Elijah. Some interpret this card as 'success, triumph, careful diplomacy' (Wirth); 'expertise, the need to find out' (Tereschenko); 'surrendering one's advantages, scandal' (Bost). 'In astrology it corresponds to the Seventh House, that of social life' (Virel).

On the psychological plane, the seventh card is that of the man who has overcome opposition and by strength of will brought together contrary tendencies. We are now in the sphere of personal action set in space and time. Calamity has been avoided; the man has chosen, he has taken himself in hand and is the triumphant master of his fate, pushing on perhaps oblivious of the fact that if he does not steer for the POPE (IV) he risks running upon the WHEEL OF FORTUNE (X), perhaps prefigured by the side view of the wheels of his chariot.

charioteer In the Classical age, the charioteer at the games or in the Hippodrome, although generally a slave, was sometimes so skilled a servant that his master erected a statue in his honour. Thus the Charioteer of Delphi is the statue of a victor, dressed in a long tunic and holding the reins in his right hand. He is the very symbol of calm, self-control and mastery of the passions. He reduces the manifold around and within by well-directed will-power to unity.

He is reason confronting the fiery HORSES of our instincts and passions with firmness and watchfulness allied to supple adaptability. He has only to move a finger to bring a horse back into line, just as reason restores balance and good sense. Yet without the fire of the horses, or passions, he could do nothing. The charioteer is the one to control the team of the divided soul, pulling in opposite directions, and his calm, relaxed seriousness symbolizes inner balance achieved by the tension between opposing forces. The hand holding the reins perfectly symbolizes the KNOT which draws together spiritual and physical strength. This symbolism is akin to the Platonic myth of the winged chariot (*Phaedrus* 246a–e).

In traditional images of the CHARIOT, there are always grounds for distinguishing between the vehicle and its driver, be he the Charioteer of Delphi, Arjuna's companion, or the human soul of Plato's *Phaedrus*. The chariot, sometimes identified with a second person, such as the archer in the case of Arjuna, stands for the body of cosmic and spiritual forces which he has to drive. If this is applied to the human condition, as in Plato's dialogue, it amounts to this: the chariot, or its personified double, 'stands for humanity's physical nature, its appetites, its dual instinct for self-preservation and for self-destruction, its baser passions and the physical control which it exerts upon what is matter.' To these might be added all the forces of the unconscious. 'The Charioteer for his part represents man's spiritual nature . . . . He controls the direction of his team' (LOEF p. 58).

In addition he symbolizes the conscience. Chariots and their drivers therefore form single human beings seen under all their different aspects and in more or less dynamic conflict situations.

chequer-board This pattern of geometrical shapes, SQUARES, diamonds, lozenges and so on, used for example for draughts, CHESS and the game of goose, is a figure of the visible world, woven from light and darkness, in which the balance is maintained as *yin* follows *yang*. In its basic form the chequer-board is the simple square MANDALA, the symbol of Shiva the transformer, and equivalent also to the Chinese YIN–YANG. The standard chequer-board comprises SIXTY-FOUR squares (sixty-four being the number of the realization of cosmic unity) and is the *vastu purusha mandala* which provides the pattern for TEMPLE-building, setting universal rhythms and crystallizing cosmic cycles. The chequer-board is thus 'the battlefield of cosmic forces' (Burckhardt), a field which is also the Earth (square) bounded by the four CARDINAL POINTS. Of course, since the mandala is the symbol of life itself, the warring tendencies concerned can also be transposed to man's inner life.

Symbolizing the opposing powers which battle against one another in a life-and-death struggle within both the universe and the human individual, its pattern is especially suitable for a board game. It encapsulates the conflict situation. The arrangement of squares is a signal that battle is about to commence. That battle may be between reason and instinct, design and chance, of one set of factors against another, or of the different potentialities of a single life. The chequer-board thus symbolizes the arena in which such conflicts and battles take place.

cherry   For the Japanese samurai, the cherry was the symbol of the warrior's calling and of the fate for which he must prepare himself.

Crushing the red flesh of the cherry to reach the hard stone is, in other words, to sacrifice flesh and blood to attain the corner-stone of the human personality. The samurai took the cherry-blossom turned towards the rising Sun as his emblem and symbol of the dedication of his life. His scabbard was decorated with cherries, another symbol of the search for the invisible in the inner life, on a par with the V.I.T.R.I.O.L. of adepts in the West.

(SERH p. 161)

The blossoming of the cherry-tree is one of the most highly esteemed sights which nature provides in Japan. In fact it is one of the most touching exhibitions of pure beauty which there are; but the feelings which it inspires are not purely and simply aesthetic, given that Japanese flowering cherries bear no fruit.

The blossom of the *sakura* is a symbol of purity and this is the reason why it is the emblem of *bushido*, the warrior's code. In marriage ceremonies an infusion of cherry-blossom is substituted for tea and in this instance it is the symbol of good luck.

It should also be noted that the blossoming of the commonest variety of *sakura* takes place at the Spring equinox, a public holiday and a time of rejoicing and of religious ceremonies invoking protection for the crops and a plentiful harvest. In fact the blossoming of the cherry prefigures the flowering of the rice and, by its abundance and duration, was held to foreshadow the wealth of the harvest to come. In any case the cherry-blossom is clearly regarded as an image of prosperity and earthly bliss; and these, in fact, although the connection may not be immediately obvious, are the same as prefigurations of eternal happiness (HERS).

The fragile, swiftly fading cherry-blossom, all too soon scattered by the wind, in Japan also symbolizes the perfect death, with indifference to the good things of this world and the precariousness of human existence.

If I were asked to define the spirit of Japan, I would call it the blossom of the mountain cherry scattering its scent in the morning sun.

(Motoori Norinaga: 1730–1801)

cherubim   Angelology became highly developed in Ancient Persia and in Assyria and Babylon, and the Hebrew word *cherubim* corresponds to the Babylonian *Kāribu* which was used to describe genii, half-human and half-animal, which stood on watch at the gates of temples and palaces, guardians of buried treasure, like the dragons posted at the gates of Chinese palaces. When the Ark of the Covenant was being made, the Lord instructed Moses:

And thou shalt make two cherubims of gold, of beaten work shalt thou make them, in the two ends of the mercy seat. And make one cherub on the one end and one cherub on the other end: even of the mercy seat shall ye make the cherubims on the two ends thereof. And the cherubims shall stretch forth their wings on high, covering the mercy seat with their wings, and their faces shall look one to another; toward the mercy seat shall the faces of the cherubims be. And thou shalt put the mercy seat above upon the ark; and in the ark thou shalt put the testimony that I shall give thee.

(Exodus 25: 18–21)

The commentary in the *Jerusalem Bible*, after referring to numerous other instances, adds 'because of their position on the Ark of the Covenant, Jehovah was later said to be seated upon the cherubim. They overshadowed the Ark in Solomon's temple. Ezekiel described them as drawing God's chariot and the Psalmist (18: 10) could write that God "rode upon a cherub, and did fly: yea, he did fly upon the wings of the wind."'

Two thousand years later these golden statues came to display 'an out-pouring of wisdom', apparently because, after the destruction of Solomon's Temple, cherubim came to symbolize heavenly beings. Subsequently, as in Egypt, ANGELS were depicted covered with wings and eyes, symbols of omnipresence and of omniscience. It should, however, be observed that this symbolic role in no way affects the nature of the cherub, a golden statue or a pure spirit.

Cherubim belong to a superior order in the angelic hierarchy, between THRONES and SERAPHIM seated 'immediately around God, with nearness superior to all ... there is not another ... nearer to the earliest illuminations of the Godhead [receiving] the first-wrought Divine manifestations and perfections.' A characteristic of the cherubim's conformity with God is their 'fullness of knowledge and stream of wisdom . . . . But the appellation of the Cherubim denotes their knowledge and their vision of God, and their readiness to receive the highest vision of light' (PSEH pp. 27–8).

chess   (see also CHEQUER-BOARD)   The game of chess originated in India and its symbolism is clearly linked to the strategy of war and is applied to the warrior caste (Kshatriya). What takes place is a battle between black pieces and white pieces, between light and darkness, between Titans (*asura*) and gods (*deva*). The game of Stones (Go) between Heaven and King Wu-yi, was a battle between the OWL and the PHEASANT and the stakes in the game, as always, were the mastery of the world.

The game is essentially a test of discipline and intelligence and the player's skill partakes of the Universal Mind (*virāj*) of which the *vastu-mandala* (see CHEQUER-BOARD) is another symbol. One of the arts of the Kshatriya is world dominance through sharing in the *virāj*: this is the 'royal art' (BURA, BURE, GRAD, GUES).

In all the Celtic languages the game of chess (Irish: *idchell*; Welsh *gwyddwyll*; Breton *gwezboell*) means literally 'intelligence of the wood' and, according to some sources, was played by the king for one third of the day. His opponent was always some prince or high dignitary and never a person of humble birth. The play was for high stakes. Thus the King of Ireland saw the god Midir carry off his wife, Etain, after losing a game during which he had foolishly failed to specify the stake. In fact, in the Celtic world, the game of chess symbolizes the intellectual side of kingly activity (OGAC 18: pp. 323–4) and its purposes have nothing to do with the moral order.

chestnut   In Ancient China the sweet chestnut corresponded with west and Autumn. It was planted on the altar of the Earth facing in that direction (see CATALPA). Traditionally it was the symbol of foresight, its nuts being used as a Winter food (GRAR).

chevron   Whether single or multiple, the chevron, shaped like a wave, crest alternating with trough, suggests the movement of water. The rising wave also represents the capital A, the first letter of the alphabet. Both these images point in the same symbolic direction: WATER is the primordial element of all things and the letter A is the beginning of all WRITING. On some sleeves a chevron indictes the first rung in the ladder of command. Although often overlaid by decoration, on different cosmogonic, cultural and social planes, the chevron carries a sense of an unfinished movement. 'Movement is the very essence of life', Griaule wrote, and at all levels (GRIE). Every beginning is heavy with the seeds of its own development. Water makes the Earth fruitful. The first letter (a vowel) vivifies language. Authority fructifies society. But, like every other symbol, its significance can be turned against itself in a process of perversion: water can flood and destroy, words can deceive and authority can be used to oppress and ruin. According to Freud, repetition of the chevron, the A inverted to a V like the teeth of a saw, is, like all repetitive phenomena, akin to the death-wish. However, the number of saw-teeth can complicate the meaning. EIGHT, for example, would indicate the acquisition of or a direction towards a new life and hence death and rebirth – like so many of the basic symbols, a rhythmic succession of advances and pauses.

In terms of practical use, the chevron is a symbol of stability, worth, competence and experience, the very basis of authority. Yet its symbolic meaning is unimpaired, since rank, distinction and fresh beginnings presuppose preparation, testing, birth, a past and a previous existence.

Nevertheless, both in architecture and in heraldry, the single chevron, pointing upwards, is essentially a representation of a balance achieved, just as the Freemason's COMPASSES.

child   Childhood symbolizes innocence, which is the state anterior to Original Sin and hence a paradisal state. This is symbolized in many traditions by a return to the WOMB; childhood is closely akin to it. The child is the symbol of natural simplicity, of spontaneity, and this is the meaning given to the word by Taoists. 'Despite your great age, you have the gloss of childhood' (*Chuang Tzu* ch. 6). Children are spontaneous, unaggressive, self-contained, without forethought or afterthought (*Chuang Tzu* ch. 23, commenting on Lao-tzu 55). Hindu tradition employs the same symbolism and terms childhood *bālya*, a state precisely analogous to that in the Christian parable of the Kingdom of Heaven, before the acquisition of the knowledge of good and evil (GUEV, GUEC).

The idea of childhood is a constant in Gospel teaching and among a substantial proportion of Christian mystics. For example, St Theresa of Lisieux's 'little way' of the child recalls Christ's words: 'Except ye be converted, and become as little children, ye shall not enter into the kingdom of heaven' (Matthew 18: 3). Or: 'Whosoever shall not receive the kingdom of God as a little child shall in no wise enter therein' (Luke 18: 18).

Furthermore, in Christian tradition ANGELS are often depicted as children as a sign of their innocence and purity. In the development of the human psyche, puerile or infantile attitudes – which should in no way be confused with the child symbol – mark periods of regression. On the other hand the image of a child may indicate a conquest of some anxiety or complex and the attainment of inner peace and self-confidence.

Freemasons are called 'Widow's children'. Some interpret this particular widow as ISIS searching for her husband's dismembered limbs, others as the architect Hiram's mother, others again as a personification of ever-fruitful Nature. The phrase is indicative of the bond which unites Masons; whether it is light, energy, strength or nature, they are sons of light, energy and so on.

(BOUM pp. 280–3)

childbirth (death in)   The Aztecs believed that women who died in childbirth rejoined the warriors who had been killed in battle or died in sacrifice. At noon they took over from them the task of accompanying the Sun on the second stage of his daily journey (SOUP). Together they made up the dialectic pairing of evolution and involution. By assuming the 'declining' aspect of this duality, of light sinking into darkness, they shared in the perilous manifestation of the holy. Soustelle explains that 'sometimes they were to be seen at dusk on Earth at CROSSROADS. They terrified those whom they met and struck them down with epilepsy or paralysis', that is with holy sicknesses. A woman who died giving birth to a child took on a holy significance in all cultures, akin to the human sacrifice which ensures not simply that life will go on, but that the tribe, nation or family will survive with it.

Chimera   A HYBRID monster with a LION's head, a GOAT's body and a DRAGON's tail, begotten by Typhon on Echidna, whose sisters were the GORGONS and who was brought forth from the bowels of the Earth. The Chimera was crushed by BELLEROPHON a hero identified with lightning, mounted upon the winged horse, PEGASUS. Their battle is a common theme in works of art and upon coinage, especially that of Corinth. All these elements foreshadow a highly complex symbol embodying mental pictures drawn from the depths of the unconscious and perhaps representing tendencies so strongly repressed that they become a source of suffering. Whoever surrendered to the Chimera was seduced and destroyed and the creature could not be fought face to face. It had to be hunted down and destroyed in its very lair. From the very first, poets and sociologists have regarded the

Chimera simply as an image of rushing torrents, as unpredictable as goats, as destructive as lions and as winding as snakes. They cannot be kept to their channels by dykes, but must be brought under control by cunning, blocking them at their source and altering their course.

According to Paul Diel (DIES p. 83), the Chimera is a disease of the psyche, characterized by a fertile and unrestrained imagination. It displays 'the perils of exalting the imagination'. The snake's or dragon's tail represents the way in which vainglory perverts the spirit; the goat's body sexual fickleness and perversion; the lion's head a tendency to dominate which spoils all social relationships. This complex symbol might equally well be embodied in 'the disastrous reign of a perverted, tyrannous or weak ruler' as in a monster devastating the countryside.

chimney   The chimney is the symbol of the mysterious channels of communication with the beings in the Heavens. It is the channel used by witches when they go to their Sabbaths (GRIA p. 54) and it is used by Father Christmas when he comes with his presents. It is akin to the smoke-hole in the nomad's tent or the hut of more settled peoples, as well as to the DOME of a temple or the fontanelle in the human SKULL. Its symbolism relates to that of the World AXIS down which come celestial influxes and up which souls rise from the Earth. It links the two worlds. The smoke which rises through it is a witness that the house breathes, and is therefore alive, and when the doors and windows are shut the winds of Heaven enfold the house and sing down the chimney (see also CENTRE).

The chimney is also the channel for the 'BREATH' which keeps the hearth alive, fanning the flame, drawing the fire and maintaining the life of the family or social group. On these terms it shares the symbolism of FIRE and HEAT. It is also the symbol of the bonds of society. It was in the chimney corner that bygone customs were recalled and old stories were told on Winter evenings.

choice   See CROSSROADS.

chisel   Like all edged tools (see AXE; PLOUGH) the chisel embodies the active (male) cosmic principle, piercing and changing the nature of the passive (female) principle, in the same way as the sculptor's chisel changes the nature of the stone. This symbolism has been used in rites of initiation into crafts and traces of it may still be found in Freemasonry. The chisel is lightning, agent of the will of Heaven, piercing matter. It is the 'ray of the intellect' piercing the individual spirit. It is the power to cut open, dissect, separate and classify, the first operation of the spirit which only passes judgement on the basis of comparison.

However, although it may be an agent, it is itself acted upon. It is only active in respect of the material upon which it works, but is passive in respect of the HAMMER or HAND which themselves represent the active will. This, as is so often the case, constitutes a reversal, on the plane of manifestation, of the order of first principles, on the level of which will cannot precede knowledge.

The alterations to the nature of the raw material effected by the chisel (and the hammer) were nevertheless regarded by the *Chuang Tzu* (ch. 11) as symbols of unlawful attacks upon the natural instincts and derogations of the natural law governing mankind.

The chisel (*tanka*), often confused with the axe, clearly has the same significance when it is depicted as an attribute of the Hindu gods (BURA, MALA, ROMM).

Christ So far from casting doubts upon the historical Jesus or the dogma of the Word made Flesh, but rather basing themselves upon them, some writers have regarded Christ as the synthesis of the basic symbols of the universe – Heaven and Earth through his two natures, divine and human; Fire and Air by his descent into Hell and his ascension into Heaven; the tomb and the resurrection; the CROSS; the Gospel BOOK of life; the axis and centre of the world; the sacrificial Lamb; the almighty King and ruler of the world; Golgotha, the mountain of the world; the ladder of salvation – all symbols of verticality, of light, of the centre, of the axis and so on (CHAS pp. 444ff.). Church architecture – the church being both Christ's image and his dwelling-place – as well as that of monastic houses, also displays a synthesis of symbols. Christ enjoys the unique privilege of acting both as the intermediary and as the two extremes, to be brought together ('I am the way, the truth and the life'). Endowing the symbol with all its historic strength and all its ontological and semantic reality, it may be said that, for Christians, Christ is the king of symbols.

On the other hand, in the black side of the symbol, in Calvary, in his Passion and Crucifixion, he displays the consequences of sin, lust and the perversion of human nature. For those who reject notions of sin, compassion and sacrifice, Christ embodies the rejection of nature and the vital impulse. He is the anti-Dionysos. He overturns all human qualities. The Church, Nietzsche wrote in *Antichrist*, has become an opponent of all that is good in life, of 'all which raises man's feelings of power, of the urge to power and of power itself.'

chrysalis It symbolizes the place where transformations take place and is related to the SECRET ROOM in which the rites of initiation are performed, to the transforming WOMB, to the TUNNEL, and so on. The chrysalis is more than a mere protective shell and represents that pre-eminently fleeting state between two stages of being, the time of 'ripening'. It implies the renunciation of a past and the acceptance of a new state as a condition of development. A chrysalis is as mysterious and as fragile as an adolescence rich in promise but unpredictable in performance, and hence inspiring respect, care and protection. It is this formation of something unpredictable which makes it a biological symbol of emersion, or emergence.

chrysanthemum The way the petals of this flower expand in ordered rays makes it essentially a solar symbol and hence associated with notions of longevity and even of immortality. This explains why the chrysanthemum should be the emblem of the Japanese Imperial family. Japanese heraldry gives it sixteen petals, superimposing upon the solar image that of the compass-card. From the centre of this the Emperor rules, epitomizing the dimensions of space.

From Japan to China and Vietnam the chrysanthemum has through various homophonies been given the role of intermediary between Heaven and Earth and been associated, not simply with notions of longevity and immortality, but additionally with those of fullness and completeness. It has therefore become a symbol of perfection and hence a delight to behold.

As in Europe, so in Asia it is above all the Autumn flower and Autumn is the time of ease after the labours of the harvest. For this reason the philosopher Chu Tun-i regarded it as 'of all flowers, the one which hides itself and flees the world'. The T'ang Dynasty poet, So-Chong Tu, made it the symbol of Taoism's simplicity and natural, but restrained, spontaneity, which when all is said and done is not very different (DURV, KALL).

chthonian   Chthonos was the Greek name for Earth, mother of the Titans, the abode of the living and the dead. It is 'below' as opposed to 'above', and stands for the inward, dark side of the Earth.

The description of chthonian is given to such fabulous creatures as dragons and to such real ones as SERPENTS, originating in the Underworld, their natures often inspiring dread and their beings linked with notions of germination and death. They symbolize the threatening side – whether the danger is internal or external – in the struggle between the forces of death and of life, always so closely interwoven. They surface in those crucial moments which precede some decisive event, in the shape of unforeseen difficulties, weakness and fear, the very reverse of feelings of confidence, strength and optimism. The chthonian aspect of the unconscious embraces everything which creates fear by its buried nature, its unexpectedness, its suddenness, violence and virtually irresistible strength. It must, however, be emphasized that this aspect should be identified with part only and not with the unconscious as a whole. The chthonian is the nocturnal aspect of the bride, MOTHER or CAVERN.

Church   The symbol of the Church takes a number of different shapes. As a female figure she often stands in contrast with the female figure of the Synagogue, which is blindfold to indicate spiritual blindness. The Christmas hymn, *Laetabundus*, states the reason. Isaiah foretold the birth of Christ; the Synagogue recalls this but still remains blind (*numquam tamen desinit esse caeca*). The Church is also symbolized by a VINE, BOAT, and TOWER. 'She is often compared with Our Lady and is also known as the Bride of Christ. Christian commentators upon the Song of Solomon have substituted the Church for Israel there. As Israel was the Church of the Old Testament, so the Church is the Israel of the New Testament.'

The Church frequently recurs in the visions of St Hildegard of Bingen (twelfth century). The saint will, for example, say: 'I saw the figure of a vast woman, like a city. On her head she wore a wonderful crown. Down her arms streamed rays of glory from Heaven to Earth. Her womb was like a thousand-meshed-net with crowds of people going in and out.'

In another vision the Church was like the head and shoulders of a woman set upon a tower fashioned from a single block of white stone. Three windows were cut into the walls of the tower and they were decorated with precious stones and surrounded by golden flames. These flames symbolized the Holy Spirit which the Church received at Pentecost. The gifts of the Holy Spirit continued to be showered upon the Church and every Christian benefited by them. Those who had been confirmed were represented by small groups of two or three tiny figures, some in bright colours, others in dark. They stand for different approaches, some being filled with a bright light, others with a dimmer light, since some disregard the Holy Spirit; and these little figures represent different spiritual states (DAVR pp. 227–8).

The apocryphal *Shepherd* of Hermas describes the Church by means of his visions. In the first he sees her as a venerable old woman; gradually the signs of age peel away and in the fourth vision she is like a bride, symbolizing those whom God has chosen. That the woman appeared old was because the Church was among the first of created beings.

The Christian Church symbolizes the image of the world. In the words of St Peter Damien, '*Ecclesia enim figuram mundi gerit.*'

Guillaume Durand, Bishop of Mende (thirteenth century), in his *Ration ale divinorum officiorum*, writes that the Church symbolizes Jerusalem, the heavenly church, the kingdom of the elect, the microcosm of the human soul (GROM p. 80).

To St Ailred of Rievaulx, the Church meant the People of God, embracing all just persons from Abel to the last just man (*Sermones de tempore et de sanctis* 10).

The Church is also held to be the Bride of Christ and the Mother of Christians and, as such, shares the symbolism of motherhood.

cinnabar Cinnabar is red sulphide of mercury, a mineral in which are to be found the two basic elements of alchemy in both East and West – SULPHUR and MERCURY. The ancient shape of the ideogram *tan*, which is used for its Chinese name, depicted cinnabar in the alchemist's furnace, while another ancient version suggested human transformation by its medicinal use, for cinnabar was pre-eminently the drug of immortality. This is as much because it is itself RED (a lucky colour and the colour of blood) as because it turns the body red, that is to say that it simultaneously rejuvenates the complexion and gives it the sheen of the Sun. It should also be observed that consumption of cinnabar was not exclusive to China, but practised in both India and Europe, where it was recommended by Paracelsus.

It should also be noted that the symbolism of cinnabar does not derive from its saline qualities, a combination of *yin* and *yang* and a neutralization of their reciprocal effects, since Chinese alchemy set little store by sulphur. Its aim was to obtain *yang* in its pure form, while cinnabar, although identified with the ovule, was substantially *yin* (VANG). This was achieved by successive calcinations which resulted in the freeing of mercury. The alternation of cinnabar and mercury is the symbol of death and rebirth or of perpetual regeneration, in the same way as the PHOENIX is reborn from the flames.

The symbolism of cinnabar is set on two planes:

as an alchemical operation symbolically achieving rebirth;
as a medicinal ingestion of the substance, which was held to confer physical immortality.

There is a clear difference of degree between these two concepts and Chinese writers quite correctly award the palm to the first, longevity in the body being itself a consequence of it (ELIF, GRIF, KALL, WIEG).

cinnamon The bark from this lauraceous tree was among the spices imported into Europe from the East and is a traditional 'fortifying' drug in Chinese pharmacy. For this reason it was employed in those Taoist practices which were intended to purify the body 'by abstention from cereals'.

Cinnamon was, in fact, the staple diet of the Immortals and especially of the illustrious P'ongchu, who lived for 888 years. Because cinnamon partakes of the nature of *yang* it nourishes the vital principle, the *sing*. There was a preparation of wine and cinnamon, one drop of which would give the body the colour of gold, that is to say would change it into pure *yang*. According to the *Pao-pu Tzu*, cinnamon should be eaten mingled with tortoise brains, since tortoises nourish the *yin* (being associated with the element of Water), while cinnamon nourishes the *yang*. Their conjunction, in harmony with the rhythm of the universe, enables one to become part of it, to 'walk on water' and, in the end, to attain to immortality.

In the context of the preparation of immortality drugs, cinnamon (or cassia, or LAUREL) is sometimes held to be the tree of the Moon under which the HARE prepares her simples.

Finally, by simple homophony, cinnamon (*chouei*) is the symbol of nobility and honours (BELT, DURV, SOUL).

circle (see also GIRDLE; SQUARE (RECTANGLE); WHEEL) . According to de Champeaux and Sterckx, the second of the four fundamental symbols (with the CENTRE, CROSS and square):

> In the first place the circle is an expanded DOT and shares its perfection. Furthermore the circle and the dot share certain symbolic properties, namely, perfection, completeness and freedom from distinction or separation . . . . While the primeval dot symbolizes immanent perfection, the circle may also symbolize the results of creation, in other words, the universe in so far as it may be distinguished from its First Cause. Concentric circles represent states of being and the orders of creation. All of them comprise the universal manifestation of the sole and non-manifest Being. In all this, the circle has been regarded in its undivided completeness . . . . Circular motion is perfect, immutable, without beginning or end or variation. From this it is a short step to make it a symbol of time. Time may be defined as a continuous and invariable succession of identical instants . . . . The circle may also symbolize the circular and unchanging motion of the Heavens.
>
> (CHAS p. 24)

At another level of interpretation, the Heavens themselves become the symbol of the invisible, transcendent world of the spirit. However, in a more direct sense, the circle symbolizes cosmic Heaven and, in particular, its relation to Earth. In this context 'the circle symbolizes the dynamic instrumentality of Heaven within the cosmos, its causality, exemplarity and providentiality. In this respect it is another of the symbols of the godhead brooding over his creation and originating, ruling and regulating its existence' (CHAS p. 28).

Philosophers and theologians would consider 'the circle as symbolizing the godhead viewed not only as immutable, but also as a goodness broadcast in the creation, subsistence and consummation of all things, or what Christian tradition would term the ALPHA AND OMEGA' (CHAS p. 29).

By means of the symbolism of the centre and concentric circles, the Pseudo-Dionysius the Areopagite, as philosopher and mystic, defined the relationship of the created being to its First Cause, all things dividing and multiplying as they move away from the oneness of the centre. On the other hand,

at the centre of the circle all the radii are brought together in a single unity and this point holds within itself all the radii united to one another and to the one origin from which they proceeded. And in the centre they are perfectly united, but at a short distance from it they are separated, and the greater their distance from the centre, the greater their separation, and in short, the nearer they are to the centre, the more they are united to it and to one another, and the further from the centre, the further they are apart from one another.

(PSEN p. 58)

Here the symbol betrays its social as much as its mystical import.

Zen Buddhism often employs drawings of concentric circles to symbolize the stages of inner perfection and the progressive harmonization of the spirit.

The circle is the sign of primordial unity and of the Heavens. As such it is indicative of instrumentality and of cyclic movement. It is the development and manifestation of the central point. 'All the points on the circumference of a circle are to be found at its centre, from which they originate and to which they return', Proclus wrote. For Plotinus, the centre was 'the progenitor of the circle', while Angelus Silesius held that 'the circle was contained within its centre.' The fourteenth-century German Dominican mystic, Heinrich Suso, made the same comparison between God and Creation.

Circles provide an image of celestial cycles, especially planetary cycles and the annual cycle represented in the ZODIAC. They characterize the tendency to expansion (*rajas*) and are therefore signs of harmony. This is why so many architectural standards are based upon divisions of the circle. 'Why', asked Plotinus, 'is the movement of the Heavens circular?' And he answered himself: 'Because they imitate the Intelligence.' The symbolism of the Zodiac may also be found in other similar radiations from a solar centre, such as the twelve Indian Aditya, the Knights of the Round Table and the Dalai Lama's 'circular' Council.

The primal shape being less the circle than the SPHERE of the World EGG, the circle is however the CHALICE, or projection of the sphere. Thus the Earthly Paradise was circular. The passage from circle to square, as in the MANDALA, for example, is that of spatial crystallization to the NIRVANA and primal indeterminacy, or what the Chinese term the passage from Earth to Heaven. This is confirmed by Western and Christian symbolism.

The symbolism of the circle is not, however, always quite so straightforward, for celestial immutability is also expressed in the square and terrestrial mutability in the circle. These two aspects are used in traditional Hindu architecture, which may be said to be based upon the transformation of the circle into the square and the square into the circle. Moreover, the shrines of nomadic peoples are in the shape of circles, symbols of the quickening powers, while settled societies build their temples in the shape of a square (BURA, BENA, DANA, GUEM, GUEC, GUER, GUES, KRAT, SECA).

In combination with the square, the shape of the circle suggests ideas of movement and of changes in status or level.

The human psyche unprompted sees the shapes of square and circle conjoined as a dynamic image of a dialectic between the transcendent Heavens, to which mankind naturally aspires, and the Earth, mankind's present situation. Here, thanks to the conjunction of these signs, there comes the realization that from henceforth human beings must make the passage from the one to the other.

(CHAS p. 131)

The diagram of the square surmounted or elongated horizontally by the arc, or fragment of a circle, and also the CUBE and DOME, the structure as common to Muslim as to Romanesque art, express this dialectic of Heaven and Earth, of perfect and imperfect, in material terms. This complex shape causes a break in rhythm and level and invites the discovery of a fresh balance through movement and change. It thus might symbolize aspirations towards a higher world or a more elevated plane of existence. It has become the classic image of the triumphal arch, through which only the victorious hero is allowed to pass. On the intellectual plane, that hero is the genius who has solved a problem; on the spiritual, the saint who has triumphed over his baser instincts. Each within his own order has achieved a plane of life which more closely shares that of the godhead in respect of his power, wisdom or holiness.

The circle drawn within the square is 'a familiar symbol to Kabbalists. It represents the spark of divine fire concealed in matter and quickening it with the fire of life' (GRIA p. 234).

The circle is also the symbol of time, the turning wheel. From the very earliest times the circle was used to express fullness and perfection, to embrace time itself in order to measure more accurately its passing. It was used in this way by the Babylonians, who divided it into 360°, subdivided into six segments each of 60°. Its name, *shar*, meant the universe or cosmos. Babylonian religious speculation derived from the circle the notion of infinite, cyclical and universal time, transmitted to the Ancient Greeks in the image of the OUROBOROS, the serpent biting its own tail. In Christian iconography the circle symbolizes eternity, while three overlapping circles represent the Trinity of Father, Son and Holy Spirit.

To North American Indians, too, 'the circle is the symbol of time, for the daytime, the night-time, and the moon time are circles above the world, and the year time is a circle around the border of the world' (ALEC p. 8).

In the Celtic world circles had magical functions and qualities. To stop the Irish army invading Ulster, Cùchulainn carved a message in ogam letters on a disc of wood. He nailed the disc to a pillar, and the inscription imposed upon those who read it the obligation to pass no further without accepting the challenge of single combat. The circle thus symbolized a magical boundary which could not be crossed. The circle had more practical religious applications. According to the lives of the saints, the chief Irish idol – Cromm Cruaich, or the stone of Fal – stood in the middle of a circle of twelve other smaller stones. In Gaul there were circular Gallo-Roman temples within squares, for example at Périgueux (Dordogne) and Allonne (Sarthe), and these represented the interrelation of Heaven (the circle) with Earth (the square). When the Gallic chieftain, Vercingetorix, surrendered to Julius

Caesar, he rode his horse in a great circle round him. The circle has a twofold symbolism – it is both celestial and magical (see ENCLOSURE) (WINI 5: p. 69; CELT 1: pp. 159–84).

In so far as Jewish and Christian traditions are concerned, the circle is not found in Old Testament buildings, it originates in Byzantium. On the architectural plane, it precedes the dome. Some medieval churches, especially those associated with the Knights Templar, were built circular in imitation of the Holy Sepulchre at Jerusalem. Basilican apses are semi-circular.

Architects were still able to copy Classical monuments and Byzantine designs. The Holy Sepulchre at Jerusalem was an attempt to conjure up the great vault of the universe which in human beings is symbolized by the brain-pan. Honorius of Autun returns to this twofold division when writing of cruciform and round churches. He employs everyday terms and the symbolic meaning which they carry.

The circle expresses the exhalation of the godhead. It has neither beginning nor end, it is continuous and omnidirectional. Were the exhalation to cease, the world would be absorbed once again into itself. The conventional sign for the Sun and for GOLD is a circle. The circular plane is connected with fire worship, hero cults and the godhead. Roundness has a universal meaning symbolized in the globe. The roundness of the universe and of the human head are pointers to perfection.

Gothic churches display an image of man, but above all they present the symbol of the perfect man, that is to say of Jesus Christ. (It should also be observed that the word 'Jesus' in Hebrew letters means 'Man'.) The Word made flesh and taking on human nature assumes a human form. Through the Incarnation he unites his divinity with our humanity, joins Earth to Heaven and casts into the circle a square shape which corresponds with mankind's shape or, better still, inscribes the square within the circle of godhead. However, this is not the end of the story, for the square is the emblem of strength. The vision of the FOUR beasts and the four kings (Daniel 7: 1–28) enforces acceptance of this view. However, through the Redemption, Christ shattered the square and broke it in pieces, for he was a banished monarch. All that was left of the square was the CROSS. Thus Christ set his human nature in the very centre of his divine nature, and the human being of the square, through the Incarnation and Redemption themselves, took his place in the circle. In other words, the human was joined to the divine, time to eternity, the visible to the invisible and the heavenly to the earthly.

Modern writers readily speak of the Church built in imitation of Christ crucified. This is only partly correct: all human nature was crucified, since the human figure symbolizes the cross and carries the meaning of the cardinal axes.

Thus temples have always been built in the human image. Christian temples are the effect of inserting the quadrature of the cardinal axes within the circle. The plan of the Hindu temple displayed in the *Vāstu-Purusha Mandala* is also a square shape, expressing the quaternary division of the great circle which symbolizes the solar cycle (DAVS pp. 190–2; HAUM pp. 3–4; BURH p. 364). It would seem as if all religious architecture has recourse to these basic configurations.

In Islamic tradition circular shapes are considered the most perfect of all. Thus poets say that the circle formed by the lips is the most beautiful shape of all, since it is completely round.

'Because it is completely sef-contained, has no beginning or end, is finished and perfect, the circle is the symbol of the Absolute.' The problem was to pass from the square to the circle, 'given that the place where the faithful met was a square chamber, but only the dome was worthy to display the measureless greatness of God.' At Mecca the black cube of the Ka'ba stands in the middle of a white circular space and the pilgrims move in procession round it 'describing a circle of unbroken prayer around the black cube' (BAMC p. 120). It is customary to make a CIRCUMAMBULATION of the tombs of saints, of mosques and of places where animals have been sacrificed at the moment when a child has been named and so on (WERS pp. 441, 462–4).

Small roses or multi-petalled rose-like flowers, so frequent a motif in Middle Eastern embroideries, ornamentation, charms and architecture, featured as frequently in pre-Islamic civilizations. If they may be considered as being more specifically designed as preservatives against the evil eye, it is surely permissible to see beneath the apparent image of the flower, the figure of a wheel and a symbol of life and the length of earthly existence. In Lower Mesopotamia, 0 was the perfect number, expressing wholeness, the universe. When separated into degrees it represented time. 'The representation of the wheel originates with the circle and the notion of time and derives from them, and evokes the image of the revolution which corresponds with the idea of a period of time. (Hebrew etymology derives the word for "circuit", a circular revolution, from the root of the verb "to turn" and similarly the word for human procreation is derived from the root of the verb "to turn in a circle".) The symbolism of the circle embraces both that of eternity and that of a perpetual series of fresh beginnings' (RUTE p. 333).

The revolving dome of the heavens and the celestial wheel are common currency in Persian literature. They imply the sense of fate. Thus Omar Khayyām writes: 'Since the Wheel of Heaven has never turned at the bidding of the wise, what matter if there be seven or eight heavens?'

The round dance of the Mevlevi, or Whirling Dervishes, was inspired by cosmic symbolism. They copy the circular motion of the planets round the Sun, all gyratory motion, as well as the search for God, symbolized by the Sun. Their founder Jalāl-al-Dīn Muhammad Rūmī, commonly called Maulavī, greatest of the Sufi poets, celebrated this circumambulation of the soul in his monumental work, the *Mathnavi*. 'I have revolved with the nine fathers [planets] in every Heaven', he wrote. 'Year in year out I have turned with the stars.'

The neo-Platonic comparison of God with a circle of which the centre is everywhere, was a theme adopted by all Sufis and especially by Sheikh Mahmūd Shabistarī in his *Gulshan-i Rāz* (*The Secret Rose Garden*). Rūmī, meanwhile, contrasts the material circumference of the physical world with the Circle of Absolute Being. He also states that if a grain of dust were dissected, in it would be found the Sun and the planets circling it: could an atomic physicist have said more?

Furthermore the throne of God is said to be set upon a circle, the 'farthest horizon' round which Muhammad made his way in the course of his Mi'rīj (see LADDER) in 'two bow-shots'. 'Muslim ecstasy therefore consists in a circumambulation of the inaccessible throne of God' (MASH pp. 849–50).

Circles also stand for the different levels of meaning of a word. The first circle symbolizes its literal meaning, the second its allegorical and the third its mystic sense.

The *Tauhīd* (acknowledgement and proclamation of the unity of God) was depicted by Hallāj as three concentric circles. The first comprised God's external actions, and the second and third their marks and consequences. These are the two concentric circles of created things. The central point is the *Tauhīd* itself, knowledge which is, at bottom, the knowledge of non-knowledge (MASH p. 850).

Jung has demonstrated that the symbol of the circle is an archetypal image of the totality of the psyche, symbol of the ego, while the square is the symbol of terrestrial matter, of the body and of reality (JUNS pp. 240–9).

In so far as it is a shape which embraces like the closed circuit, the circle is a symbol of protection, a protection assured to all that lies within its embrace. The circle is therefore magically employed as a defensive line around cities, temples and tombs to prevent the entry of enemies, disembodied souls or evil spirits. Wrestlers drew a circle round their bodies before engaging in a bout.

For individuals the protective circle takes the form of a RING, bracelet, NECKLACE, GIRDLE or CROWN.

The talisman- or amulet-ring, the magic circle worn like a PENTACLE on the finger, was used at all periods and by all peoples. Its specific purpose was to afford immediate protection to the magician's most sensitive points, the fingers of the hand, the natural means whereby magical effluxes were both transmitted and received, and hence exceedingly vulnerable.

(MARA p. 342)

These circles were not simply ornamental, but acted as 'stabilizers, maintaining cohesion between soul and body . . . . This symbolism, perhaps, explains why in ancient times warriors wore so many bracelets. Perhaps they were the gifts of all those who wished them to return safe and sound, soul securely enwrapped in body' (LOEC p. 164).

This same symbolic quality would explain why rings and bracelets were either taken from or denied to those whose souls could leave their bodies or ascend to the godhead, like the dead or mystics. However, in the second instance another symbolic quality could take precedence. The ring also symbolizes voluntary attachment or irrevocable surrender. For this reason nuns wear wedding rings. When there is a conflict between different symbolic qualities, the one selected reveals the especial importance attached to it. However, the quality overshadowed in this particular instance continues no less strongly to exist.

circumambulation Few rites are as universally practised as that of circumambulation. The Old Testament Jews circumambulated the altar (Psalm 26: 6, once recited by the celebrant in the Canon of the Mass) and Muslims go in procession round the Ka'ba at Mecca, continuing what is actually a pre-Islamic rite. Buddhists circumambulate their STUPAS (like the Buddha and the Bodhi-tree); Bön-po and Lamaistic Tibetans circumambulate temples and *chörten*, as do Cambodians a new house or an altar; kings circumambulate their capitals when they take possession of them, bishops do the same when they consecrate churches and priests when they incense the altar. Circumambulation was widely practised in India and in China by the Emperor in the Forbidden City. It is known to central Asian and Siberian tribesmen, and according to Japanese mythology, the primeval pair only coupled after circumambulating the celestial pillar.

It should be observed that although Izanami and Izanagi moved in an anti-clockwise direction before they met, most circumambulation is clockwise, following the apparent movement of the Sun in the northern hemisphere. This is the case in India, Tibet and Cambodia. In other instances the movement is anti-clockwise, just as the stars revolve around the POLE. This is the case with Islam, Bön-po and, exceptionally for Hinduism, at Angkor Wat.

It is apparent that although circumambulation is sometimes no more than a ritual of homage – which may, of course, have originally had symbolic meaning – it possesses above all else cosmic quality. The (solar) *pradakshinā* sometimes takes place at sunrise, since it is the cycle of light. When the Chinese Emperor went in procession round the Forbidden City, he halted at the twelve gates, corresponding to the twelve suns (*aditya*) and to the twelve signs of the Zodiac. At Mecca pilgrims make seven circuits corresponding to the number of the celestial spheres. In Siberia these circuits are three, seven or nine in number, corresponding to the number of worlds, of planets or of celestial orders. In addition it should be observed that in the Japanese myth the male *kami* (deity) revolves in one direction and the female *kami* in the other. This would be still more significant were the basic sources not in conflict over the direction of each.

Clearly, to employ the course of the stars aims to secure the harmony of the world by ensuring that the microcosm moves in harmony with the macrocosm. The universe is concentrated in the temple or holy place which represents the CENTRE. To circumambulate this holy place is to restore the circumference to its centre.

Temples are also World Axes on which the WHEEL of existence revolves until it is stopped by Enlightenment, and then circumference and centre become one. The terraces of the temple at Borobudur in Java, rising in ever smaller concentric circles towards the invisible Buddha at the summit, are the most striking example of a progressive concentric movement towards the discovery of the self or one's true nature.

Angkor presents both directions, *pradakshinā* and *prasavya*, celestial and terrestrial paths, the way of life and the way of death, *kalpa* and *pralaya*. In Tantrism the 'right-hand path' corresponds to the east and to Spring, while the 'left-hand path' corresponds to the west and Autumn. These are the contra-flowing currents of cosmic energy. Admittedly Angkor Wat is a funerary temple, but it is the only one which faces the setting Sun and is also one of the few temples in the group dedicated to Vishnu. *Prasavya* may be regarded as a Vishnic rhythm since its involutions do not lead to Nothingness, but to Vishnu the Preserver, the principle which re-establishes rhythm and absorbs shape. On the other hand, *pradakshinā* is Shiva's rhythm, evolving centrifugally, that of current manifestation regulated by the reigning sovereign who is there at the centre of space and time as Shiva's surrogate (BURA, GRIS, GUET, HERJ, SOUP, SOUD).

In Celtic tradition clockwise (solar) circumambulation was generally employed as a sign of friendly intention: the opposite implied hostility, enmity or blood-lust. When he returned from his first expedition on the frontiers of Ulster the seven-year-old hero Cùchulainn drove his chariot so that its left side was towards Emain Macha, the capital of the province. The King, Conchobar, at once took the necessary precautions.

In the Whirling Dervishes' *samā'*, their round dance takes on simultaneously cosmic and mystic significance. The twofold maelstrom of dance and shrilling flutes tends to suggest the revolution of the stars and to inspire spiritual ecstasy. Eva Meyerovitch explains:

Each movement of their dance has its special symbolic meaning. The sheikh standing motionless in the middle represents the pole, the point at which the temporal and the eternal intersect and through which grace passes and descends on the dancers. The circle is split in the middle into two semicircles, one representing the arch of involution or descent of the soul into matter; the other of its ascent again into light.

circumcision (see also CLITORIS)   In Polynesia, as among the Jews, circumcision is a repetition of the cutting of the umbilical cord at birth and symbolizes a new birth or rather a new stage of life.

In so far as it is practised by class it becomes a sign of obedience and faithfulness. In so far as it is practised as a means of distinguishing those who have undergone it from other peoples, it is a sign of community.

It is highly probable that circumcision existed from time immemorial among the Jews and related peoples. In the days of Jeremiah, other tribes descended from Abraham practised it (Jeremiah 9: 24–5), as did the Egyptians, or certain sections of them. It was known to be current among the Arabs well before Islam and is still practised by many races. These races circumcise – and have always circumcised – boys when they reach puberty. The Old Testament carefully records that Ishmael was circumcised at the age of thirteen (Genesis 17: 25).

It would seem that this rite was not employed by Phoenicians, Assyrians or Babylonians. The closer the Jews entered into contact with these peoples, the more circumcision became the mark of nationality and became more heavily charged with religious significance, especially when the Jews were exiled to Babylon. It was probably at this time that the rule was established that boys should be circumcised at a week old (Leviticus 12: 3; Genesis 17: 12; 21: 4). Circumcision then became the sign, it might also be said the sacrament, of the covenant between God and his people. In the Hellenistic period, circumcision was the pretext for persecution and resistance.

During the early years of the Christian Church, there was bitter controversy over whether Gentile converts should be circumcised. God himself gave the answer, baptism not circumcision was the seal (Acts 10: 4, 48; 11: 1–18; 15: 5–12).

(BIBM)

citron   The fruit is used to prepare oil of bergamot and its crystallized peel is highly prized in the Far East where it is known as 'the Buddha's Hand'

and is a symbol of longevity. Because of the homophony of the ideograms
fo and *fu* with *fu* (good fortune), the citron is also a symbol of good luck.

Like most fruit with large numbers of seeds (see also GOURD; ORANGE;
POMEGRANATE), it is also a fertility symbol. In Indian iconography it is a
specific attribute of Sadā-Shiva, and is an emblem of his powers of creation.

Moses commanded that boughs of citron, palm and WILLOW should be
woven together to form the booths at the Feast of Tabernacles. The Jews
regarded the citron as a holy tree: its fruit was exempt from the tithe and
was carried by those entering the Temple.

In the Middle Ages the citron was used for magical practices (DURV,
MALA).

city The building of towns and cities was originally attributed to Cain
(Genesis 4: 17) and is a sign of the settlement of nomadic tribes, the fruits
of a genuine cyclical crystallization (see TILE). This is the reason why towns
were traditionally built in SQUARES, symbols of stability, while nomad tents
or encampments are most frequently round, symbols of movement (see
CIRCLE). For the same reason the Earthly Paradise was round and expressed
the symbolism of vegetation, while the Heavenly JERUSALEM, at the end of
the cycle, is square and mineral.

Cities founded in the centre of the Earth reflect the celestial order and
receive its influences. They are also, and for the same reason, images of
spiritual CENTRES. Thus primal Heliopolis, 'city of the Sun'; Salem, 'City of
Peace'; and Luz, the 'ALMOND-TREE', which Jacob named BETHEL, 'House
of God'. The name 'Heliopolis' is naturally suggestive of zodiacal symbolism,
nor should it be forgotten that the Heavenly Jerusalem has TWELVE gates
(three opening to each of the CARDINAL POINTS). They clearly correspond to
the twelve signs of the ZODIAC as well as to the Twelve Tribes of Israel.
Such duodenary division was practised in Roman towns and, less obviously,
in Hindu cities. The role played by astrology in the founding of cities becomes apparent. They reflect the movement of the Sun and of the fixed
stars and their plan often coincides with the positions of the GREAT BEAR.
In Rome as in China, in India as in Angkor Wat, the town plan was fixed
with the aid of the GNOMON. Since the town was the centre, the gnomon had
to cast no shadow at mid-summer. The geomancer's role is also apparent,
since the site of the city had to be established at a convergence of winds and
waters, of earth currents, and in accordance, too, with light and dark.

Towns are generally square and orientated. In India the four orientations
correspond to the four castes. In Rome, and equally with Angkor, with
Peking and with all countries which have felt Chinese influence, the four
GATES at the cardinal points are joined by two streets at right-angles to one
another, making the plan of the city similar to Shiva's simple fourfold
MANDALA. When developed into the mandala with sixty-four zones, you
have the plan of Ayodhyā, the City of the Gods. Such an arrangement
made the capital city the centre and epitome of the empire. From it flowed
the four cardinal points, to it flowed their four regions. In these four directions the virtues of the monarch flowed to the ends of the Earth. Through
its gates vassals came to pay homage and evil influences were expelled. In
China the city was the centre of a series of concentric squares, reminiscent

of the triple enclosures of the Celts and Greeks, as well as of the temples at Angkor. According to Plato, the capital of Atlantis was similarly arranged, but in a series of concentric circles, the circle being the symbol of celestial perfection.

In the centre of Ayodhyā stands the Brahmapura, the dwelling of Brahmā; in the centre of the mandala is the Brahmāsthana; in the midst of the Heavenly Jerusalem dwells the Lamb. The word *ching*, used in Chinese for 'capital', also has the meaning of 'pivot'. In the centre of Angkorian cities stood the 'MOUNTAIN', an image of Mount Meru, centre and axis of the world. The external walls are homologous with the mountain ranges which enclose the world. On this temple-mountain stood the royal lingam – just as the Chinese Emperor was enthroned in the centre of his pivot-capital. Indeed Pātaliputra was supposed to have been built upon the very site of Meru, while Kash, the mythical ancestor of the city of Benares, is homologous with the crown of the head, the point through which humans enter into communication with the Heavens. The 'Divine City' (*Brahmapura*) is one of the epithets of the heart, the centre of being in which *purusha* dwells. Nor is the symbolism employed by the Zen patriarch Hui Neng very different when he speaks of the body as being a town, its senses the gates and the king who dwells there the self, the *hsing*, or 'true nature' (BURA, BENA, COEA, DANA, GIUP, GRAD, GRAC, GRAP, GRIR, GRIC, GUER, GUES, HOUD, HUAV, NGUA).

Medieval thinkers saw humanity as a pilgrim between two cities and life as a pilgrimage from the city below to the city above. 'The city above is the City of the Saints. Here on Earth, mankind, pilgrims by grace and citizens by election of the city above, journey on to the kingdom' (DAVS p. 32).

Contemporary psychoanalysis regards the city as one of the symbols of the MOTHER in her dual aspect of protectress and controller. In general the city is akin to the female principle.

Just as a city contains its inhabitants, so the mother contains her children within herself. This is why goddesses were depicted wearing mural crowns. In the Old Testament towns are described as if they were persons and, furthermore, this theme is repeated in the New Testament, the Epistle to the Galatians providing a prime example. 'But Jerusalem which is above is free, which is mother of us all. For it is written, Rejoice, thou barren that bearest not; break forth and cry' (Galatians 4: 26–7). The City above engenders through the spirit, the City below through the flesh, but both are women and mothers. The symbolism of the city is most strongly elaborated in the Book of Revelation (JUNM pp. 213–17).

Babylon the Great, the symbolic name for Rome, a city with a million inhabitants at that time when her Empire had reached its peak, is here described as the antithesis, the reverse of the Heavenly Jerusalem.

And there came one of the seven angels which had the seven vials, and talked with me, saying unto me, Come hither; I will shew unto thee the judgement of the great whore .... And the woman was arrayed in purple and scarlet colour, and decked with gold and precious stones and pearls, having a golden cup in her hand full of abominations and filthiness of her fornication: And upon her forehead was a name written, MYSTERY, BABYLON THE GREAT, THE MOTHER OF HARLOTS AND ABOMINATIONS OF THE EARTH. And

I saw the woman drunken with the blood of the saints and with the blood of the martyrs of Jesus.

(Revelation 17: 1, 4–6)

Rome on her seven hills was *the* city of those days. Yet she was the inverted symbol of the city, the anti-city in other words, the corrupted and corrupting mother who, instead of bringing life and blessings brought death and a curse.

clavicle The clavicle, or collar-bone, is regarded by the Dogon of Mali as a granary containing EIGHT grains associated with the four elements, the four cardinal points and, as well, with the eight mythic ancestors from whom the Dogon are descended. They regard these bones, together with the skull, as the first formed by the foetus, since they support the skeleton as a whole. Such is the importance given to clavicles by the Dogon that they place them among the five elements constituting the human personality, along with the body, the twin male and female souls, the light which these souls shed in the darkness, and the life force which they look upon as a fluid associated with blood. Similar beliefs are to be found among other riverine tribes along the Niger. Thus the Bozo, a fishing tribe next to the Dogon, consider that the collar-bones hold the symbols of the eight families of fishes. The fertilizing powers of these bones constrain the Dogon to preserve the collar-bones of animals, which they grind and mix with their seed-corn in order to increase their harvests (DIED, GRID).

The clavicle or collar-bone should not be confused with the clavicle (literally 'little key') of the alchemists in the context of the clavicle of Solomon. This monarch, whose wealth and luxury is described in detail in the Old Testament, so struck the imagination of Eastern peoples that they have continued to list the minutest aspects of his glory. Since God granted him wisdom, they have endowed him with omnipotence over this world and especially over evil spirits. They have also credited him with compiling the celebrated *Clavicle of Solomon*, of which every wizard should carry a copy written in his own hand, and without which he cannot conjure up evil spirits. The clavicle of Solomon is the key to magic.

clay Symbol of shapeless matter. Moulding clay therefore symbolizes the act of creation and displays a male desire to make something. It is easy to understand why children should enjoy working with clay and its educative value. However, the dual symbolism of the shapeless matter absorbing water and the way in which the fingers penetrate the clay also gives it a very strong sexual significance (BACE pp. 142, 146).

clitoris Symbolizes the male element in women. The Bambara and Dogon from Mali believe that every human is born with two souls, one of each sex. The clitoris contains the male soul of the woman. Hence the origin of clitorodectomy, which confirms the sexual status of the woman by removing the ambivalent organ. The clitoris excised becomes a SCORPION (GRIH). In men, the female soul resides in the FORESKIN. CIRCUMCISION corresponds to clitorodectomy in defining and confirming the sexual status of the male.

cloak A cloak (*brat*) was one of the royal attributes of the gods of Ireland. In the story *Tochmarc Etaine* (The Courtship of Etain), the god of the

Otherworld, Midir, demands in compensation for the loss of an eye in a brawl, a chariot, a cloak and the most beautiful maiden in Ireland as his bride. The cloak is doubtless that of Manannán (another name for Midir). This was a cloak of invisibility (like Siegfried's *tarnkappe* in the *Nibelungenlied*) and of forgetfulness. In the story *Serglige ConCulaind* (The Madness of Cùchulainn), the god shakes his cloak between his wife Fand ('swallow') and the hero Cùchulainn, whose mistress she had become, to prevent them ever meeting again (OGAC 10: p. 295; CELT p. 15) and it made her invisible. The god Lug wore a similar cloak which enabled him to pass through the entire Irish army without being seen when he came to aid his son.

In Celtic tradition the men from the 'great world to the east' told the Dagda that 'whoever wraps himself in the cloak acquires the air, shape and face of whomsoever he wishes, so long as he wears it.' This is a symbol of the changes wrought by human trickery and the different personalities which humans can assume.

When monks or nuns withdraw from the world, take the habit and make their final vows, they cover themselves in a cloak or cape. This action symbolizes a withdrawal into oneself or into God, the corresponding separation from the world and its temptations and the renunciation of the desires of the flesh. To put on the cloak is to show that you have chosen Wisdom (the philosopher's cloak), or that you have a rank, office or role of which the cloak is an emblem.

Cloaks, by process of identification, symbolize their wearers and to give away one's cloak is to surrender oneself. When St Martin gave half his cloak to a beggar, there was more to the act than the material gift: it symbolized the charity which inspired the saint. The cloak which Elijah bequeathed to Elisha meant that the disciple continued the spiritual tradition which he had received from his master and benefited from all his gifts. Similarly Sufi masters cover their disciples with their cloaks when they bestow upon them their teachings and their powers. (See also CLOTHING; TUNIC; KHIRKA.)

cloister De Champeaux compares the cloister with the Heavenly JERUSALEM: 'In the space where four paths meet, is a well, a tree, a column', to mark the navel or centre of the world. Through it passes the World Axis, that 'spiritual LADDER with its foot in the darkness below' (CHAS p. 152). The cloister is also a cosmic centre in respect of the three levels of the universe: of the Underworld by virtue of the well; of the surface of the globe; and of the celestial world through the tree, rose-bush, column or cross. Furthermore its square or rectangular shape, open to the vault of heaven, is the image of the marriage of Earth and Heaven. The cloister is the symbol of intimacy with the godhead.

clothing See DRESS.

cloud Clouds symbolically embrace various aspects, chiefly those relating to their confused and ill-defined nature and to their qualities as instruments of apotheosis and epiphany (see MIST).

The Sanskrit word for 'cloud' (*ghana*) was applied to the primal Embryo (*Hiranyagarbha* or *jīva-ghana*), *ghana* here being a compact and undifferentiated element. In Islamic esotericism, the cloud (*al'-amā*) is the primordial,

unknowable state of Allah before his manifestation. Even in his manifestation and in temporal existence, 'cloudiness' is a notion too commonplace to need emphasis. It cloaks the flashes of light which sometimes pierce human darkness, writes de Saint-Martin, 'because our senses would be unable to bear their brightness'.

The Koran describes the epiphany of Allah 'in the shadow of a cloud', but not like the Eternal Father of classical iconography. Esotericism interprets the 'cloud' as the 'wall' which separates two cosmic levels. In Ancient China, WHITE or coloured clouds would come down upon the mounds on which acceptable sacrifices had been offered. They rose from the tombs of the Immortals who themselves ascended into Heaven upon clouds. RED clouds were particularly favourable signs: one of these emanated from Lao-Tzu. It was upon a miraculous red and YELLOW cloud – the colours of cosmic differentiation – that, in the legend of the *Hong*, the monks escaped from the blazing monastery of Chao-lin. All these signs were so important that the Emperor Huang Ti 'governed all things, thanks to the clouds'.

In Chinese tradition, clouds indicate the transformation which sages have to undergo to 'annihilate' themselves in accordance with the esoteric teachings of the jade DISC. 'Clouds dissolving in the ether will not simply be achievements of the *habokis*, but a symbol of the sacrifices which the sage must make when he renounces his perishable being to gain eternity.' In this connection Liliane Brion-Guerry quotes one of the thoughts of Chuang Tzu: 'Disciples, make yourselves exactly like the limitless ether, free yourself from your senses, dissolve your souls, annihilate yourselves and surrender your temporal soul.'

So far as rain-clouds are concerned, these are related to manifestations of heavenly 'activity'. Their symbolism connects with all the well-springs of fertility – RAIN itself, prophetic revelation and theophany. In Greek mythology, Nephele was the magic cloud fashioned by Zeus in the likeness of Hera to divert the lustful attentions of IXION and from their coupling the centaurs were begotten. Helen, of whom Paris became enamoured and who caused the Trojan War, was no more than a cloudy phantom conjured up by Proteus. Clouds, in Orphic belief, perhaps echoed by Aristophanes in his comedy of that title, were connected with the symbolism of WATER and consequently with that of fertility. Personified, they were the daughters of Ocean and lived upon islands or close to springs. Clouds are symbols of a metamorphosis observed, not in any one of its stages, but in its fulfilment (GRIL, GUEV, JILH, KALL, LECC, SAIR, SCHC).

clown Traditionally the clown is the image of the murdered king. He symbolizes the reversal of the role of kingship in speech, stance and attributes. Irreverence and absurdity are substituted for majesty, total lack of authority for sovereignty, laughter for awe, defeat for victory, blows received for blows given, ridicule for the most sacred ceremonies, mockery for death. He is, as it were, the other side of the coin of kingship, its walking parody. (See also BUFFOON; DWARF.)

club The club is generally regarded as being connected with brute and primitive force. It was Herakles' (Hercules') weapon.

But in Vishnu's hands it has another significance, being the symbol of

primal knowledge and of the power of knowledge. At the same time it is
identified with the goddess Kālī, who, according to the *Krishna-Upanishad*,
is 'the force of time which destroys all that stands in its way.' In other
instances she is the power of action or of 'dispersion' (DANA).

In Celtic tradition, the club was the chief attribute of the Dagda. According to the *Yellow Book of Lecan* (fifteenth century) one end of it was soft
and the other exceedingly hard. One end killed the living: the other raised
the dead to life. The Dagda proved the truth of this by experience, killing
his enemies and restoring his friends to life, and by this means became king
of Ireland. This is an example of the bipolarity of symbols. Indo-European
mythology contains many similar instances – Herakles' club, Thor's HAM-
MER, the *vazra* of the Indo-Iranian god Mihr, the VAJRA or THUNDERBOLT of
Indra in the Vedas and the thunderbolt wielded by Zeus in the roles of god
of lightning and awe-inspiring judge. Moses' miracle-working rod also had
this dual power of working good or evil, opening and closing the waters of
the Red Sea, making the fountain spring from the rock and turning itself
into a serpent. Achilles' spear had the twofold power to wound and to heal.

The symbolic quality of the club is akin to that of lightning – single
essence, dual power – but with opposite effects.

When the Dagda himself did not carry his club, it took eight men to drag
it along the ground and, according to the *Cath Maighe Tuireadh* or *Battle
of Mag Tuired*, the furrow which it left was deep enough to mark the
boundary of a province. (Incidentally, there is an interesting link between
the Irish word for club (*lorg*) and that for furrow (*lerg*).) The generalized
symbolic meaning of the club is undoubtedly very similar to that given to
lightning in Roman mythology – it deals both life (lightning is one of the
fertility symbols) and death, according to circumstance. However, it is
worth adding an observation in respect of the club as a symbol of boundaries, namely that the Dagda was also the god of friendship and treaty-
making and in these matters of equity and judgement his club also played
its part.

Finally the intrinsic qualities of the Dagda's club may be compared with
those of the weapons of other gods and heroes such as Lug and Cùchulainn.
The wounds which they inflicted were incurable unless the owner of the
weapon were himself willing to heal them. In this way the Morrigan, the
war-goddess whom Cùchulainn had seriously wounded, tricked the young
hero into healing her. Clubs, however, were not always warlike and death-
dealing. The Welsh tale of the Lady of the Fountain describes a giant with
one foot, one eye in the middle of his forehead and an iron club, living on
a mound in a forest glade. He was lord of the wild beasts. With his iron club
he struck a stag on the forehead and the creature's braying brought together thousands of animals (OGAC 12: pp. 360–3; MABG p. 154).

From the psychological and ethical point of view, the club is the symbol
of force which dominates by crushing opposition. If it is covered with hide,
as were the clubs of a number of mythic beings, it means crushing by brute
strength. In the hands of villain or hero it may 'show either destruction due
to perversion or its punishment by the law. In the hands of a villain, the
club symbolizes the destructive power of perversion; in the hands of a hero
it becomes the symbol of the destruction of that perversion' (DIES p. 184).

In the perversion which destroys and the destruction of perversion may be seen the ambivalence present in all symbols of power.

cobra See NAGA; SERPENT; URAEUS.

cock The cock is a universal solar symbol because its crowing heralds the dawn. In India, for this reason, it is an attribute of Skandha, personification of solar energy. It plays an important part in Japan because its crowing, associated with the songs of the gods, summoned Amaterasu, Goddess of the Sun, from the cave in which she had hidden herself; this shows a correspondence with the dawn and with the manifestation of light. This is why splendid cocks strut around the grounds of major Shintō temples and why sacred cocks are reared at the Ise Jingū temples. Based upon a somewhat dubious homophony, the *torii* of Shintō temples are sometimes thought originally to have been roosts for these cocks.

The quality of courage which the Japanese attribute to cocks is echoed in other countries in the Far East where the cock plays an especially beneficent role. This is due in the first place to the homophony between the Chinese ideogram for cock (*ki*) and that which means 'of good omen', 'favourable'. Secondly its appearance and general behaviour make it a fit symbol of the 'five virtues': of the civil virtues, because its comb makes it look like a mandarin; of the martial virtues because of its spurs; of courage because of its behaviour in battle (in countries where cock-fighting is highly regarded); of kindness because of the way in which it shares its food with its hens; and of confidence because of the accuracy with which it announces the dawn.

Furthermore, because it heralds the coming of daylight, the cock counteracts the evil influences of darkness. It drives them from the house if care is taken to paint its effigy on the door. In Vietnam a boiled cock's claw is still seen as an image of the microcosm and used in fortune telling.

Tibetan Buddhists have always regarded the cock as a particularly unlucky symbol. It is depicted in the centre of the Wheel of Life, alongside the hog and the serpent as one of the 'three poisons'. It signifies lust, attachment to material things, covetousness and 'thirst'. It will be remembered that in Europe, too, the cock is sometimes regarded as an image of anger and of the explosion of inordinate and frustrated desire (DURV, GOVM, HUAV, PALL).

In Greek tradition 'the Cretan cock-god, Velchanos, was assimilated to Zeus' (SECG p. 10). There was a cock standing beside Leto when she gave birth to Apollo and Artemis, begotten by Zeus. Thus the bird was sacred to both Zeus and Leto and to Apollo and Artemis, that is to say to solar gods and to lunar goddesses. In his *Golden Verses*, Pythagoras consequently advises that cocks should be cared for and not sacrificed, because they are dedicated to the Sun and the Moon.

As a symbol of dawning light, the cock is nonetheless the especial attribute of Apollo, the hero of the dawning day.

Despite the advice attributed to Pythagoras, cocks were offered in sacrifice to Apollo's son, Asclepios (Aesculapius), the god of healing. Before his death, Socrates reminded Crito that they owed a cock to Asclepios. Undoubtedly this betrays the role attributed to the cock of psychopomp, acting as herald and guiding the dead person's soul to the Otherworld, where it would awaken to a fresh day, the equivalent of rebirth. Therefore Apollo's son was precisely the god who, by his healing powers, had brought the dead to life, prefiguring rebirth in Heaven. For the same reason the cock was the emblem of Attis, the oriental Sun-god, who died and came to life again. The role of psychopomp explains why the cock was an attribute of Hermes (Mercury), the messenger who travels the three levels of the cosmos, from the Underworld to the Heavens. Before he was deified, Asclepios was a healing hero, and therefore cocks were supposed to cure disease. (See also HEN.)

Alongside the horse and the hound, cocks were among the psychopompous animals sacrificed to the dead by the Ancient Germans in their funeral rites (KOPP p. 287).

In the rituals of certain Altaic tribes connected with purification and the expulsion of spirits after a death, the dead person was represented by a cock tethered to the death-bed; the shaman then drove it out (HARA p. 229).

In Norse tradition the cock is also the symbol of soldierly vigilance. It scans the horizon from the topmost branches of the ash, Yggdrasil, to warn the gods when their perpetual foes, the giants, are preparing to attack (MYTF pp. 12, 44). However, the ash, a cosmic tree, is the source of life and so the cock keeping watch from its summit, like the cock on top of the weather-vane on a church, may be regarded as the guard and protector of life.

The Pueblo Indians are another group which associates the cock with the sun. 'My grandfather cautioned me that chickens are the chosen pets of the Sun god. "The crowing of the cocks in the morning is important", he said. "The Sun god put them here to wake up the people. He rings a little bell telling the roosters when to announce the coming dawn. They crow four times before daylight"' (TALS p. 62). This example also emphasizes the symbolic function of the number FIVE. The cock crowed four times, but the Sun did not come up until he had crowed for the fifth time, five being the number of the centre and of manifestation.

In Africa a Fulani legend associates the cock with secrecy. The appearance, behaviour and changes of shape of the cock correspond to the different forms which secrets take. Thus a cock in a hut is like a secret told to nobody; a cock (metamorphosed into a ram) in a yard is like a secret told to relatives or close friends; a cock (in the guise of a bull) in the streets is like a secret told to everybody and a cock (metamorphosed into a fire) is like a secret told to an enemy and causing ruin and desolation (HAMK p. 68). The Azande see its foreknowledge of the dawn as tainting it with suspicion of witchcraft (EVAS).

Sudanese peoples of Mali relate the cock's foot to the symbolism of the CROSS-ROADS. According to Zahan (ZAHB p. 232) the shape of the cock's foot, in conjunction with the bird's behaviour patterns, explain why these Sudanese tribespeople should entertain this notion of the crossroads and display simultaneously symbols of the centre, of uncertainty when faced by the choice of three roads, and of the spiral, that is of rotation around a point or an axis. In fact, the cock, with a crow which heralds the daily rotation of the Sun and the alternation of light and darkness, becomes 'to a certain extent the equivalent of the rotation of the Sun around the Earth and consequently any depiction of the bird's foot is a sign of the universe in its rotary movement .... The quality of the cock as a sacrificial victim rests on these premises. To sacrifice this bird is to sacrifice a substitute for the world' (ibid.).

Like the EAGLE and the LAMB, the cock is also a symbol of Christ. It emphasizes, however, his solar symbolism – light and resurrection.

To Job, the cock was the symbol of God-given intelligence and the ibis the symbol of wisdom. Both birds had been granted the gift of foreknowledge, the ibis unfailingly heralding the flooding of the Nile and the cock the dawning of the day. Like the Messiah, the cock announces that darkness has vanished and light has come. Thus the bird is set on church spires and cathedral towers and this positioning on the highest points of holy buildings may suggest the supremacy in human life of the spiritual. It may also suggest the heavenly origins of the inner light which brings salvation and the watchfulness of the soul to catch the first gleams of the spirit dawning in the closing shades of night. According to Durand, the cock on the church steeple may well originate from a Zoroastrian assimilation of the Sun to the cock which heralds daybreak. The Talmud makes the cock a master of courtesy because he announces his Lord the Sun with a fanfare of crowing.

In Islam the cock has enjoyed a veneration far above all other creatures. The Prophet himself used to say: 'The white cock is my friend: he is the enemy of the enemies of God.' Its crow announces the presence of the Angel.

The prohibition on cursing the cock which calls to prayer is also attributed to the Prophet.

He is supposed to have said that among God's creatures there was a cock whose comb is below the throne, whose claws grip the world below and whose wings beat the air. When two thirds of the night are over and only one third remains, he flaps his wings and calls: 'Praise the most holy king, worthy of praise and holiness, sole and unique!' At this moment all the birds flap their wings and all the cocks crow.

(FAHN p. 505)

The cock is often combined with the serpent, and this is especially true of Hermes and Asclepios. In dream analysis, both serpent and cock are interpreted as symbols of time. 'They belong to the god Aesculapius [Asclepios] who was in all probability an incarnation of inner psychic life, for he it was who sent dreams' (TEIR p. 160). They mark a phase in inner development: the integration of chthonian forces on the level of a personal life in which spiritual and material tend to balance out in harmonious unity.

To alchemists the cock symbolizes the three stages through which the 'work' must pass, through his BLACK claws, to his WHITE feathers and his RED comb. 'The matter for the work starts to become black through putrefaction and then white as ozoth or philosopher's dew purifies it. Finally, when it is perfectly set, it turns red .... The philosopher's urn was called the home of the cock' (PERD pp. 397–8). The philosopher's urn was the 'original and root of all teaching'. It was water and 'the reservoir of all tinctures'. These phrases should be understood in their hermetic sense, as the accumulation of all hidden knowledge.

As a Masonic symbol the cock is both the sign of vigilance and of the enlightenment which comes from initiation.

coffer (see also BOX)   Two elements provide the bases for the symbolism of the coffer: the act of depositing some material or spiritual treasure in it, and the act of opening the coffer in what may be the equivalent of a revelation.

Depositing something in a coffer is on a par with the Tables of the Law in the Jewish ARK of the Covenant; with Amaterasu's mirror in Ise's coffer; with Kuvera's treasure in his JARS; with Fate in PANDORA's chest, as well as with the rice of immortality and the various symbolic objects in the *teu* (see BUSHEL) of Chinese secret societies. What is deposited in the coffer is the treasure of tradition, the means of its revelation and transmission to Heaven. This is perhaps the reason why the Chinese emperors placed their petitions to the Lord of Heaven in sealed coffers on the summit of T'ai Shan. The coffer is in fact the container of the divine presence, analogous to the tabernacle.

Although ancestor worship has fallen into disuse in the Far East, the family register is still kept in a coffer. At the same time the region of the Nine Obscurities or of the Nine Springs, in which the spirits of the ancestors dwell, is compared with a 'jade coffer' in which they were 'deposited' to await a 'rebirth' or 'release'. In Ancient Egypt the cyclical burial of OSIRIS was marked by the manufacture of coffers shaped like the crescent Moon.

In Arabic the same word, *tābūt*, is used for the Ark of the Covenant and the BASKET in which Moses was set adrift on the Nile. It should also be observed that Hiruko, the first-born of the marriage of Izanagi and Izanami, was set adrift on the waters in a reed basket. The opening of the basket containing the infant Moses is, in fact, a divine revelation, the annunciation of a new traditional epoch, of a fresh 'coming'. However, unlawfully to open a coffer is fraught with danger. When the rebellious Genji seized the imperial coffer and tried to open it they were blinded and driven mad by the blaze of the Mirror.

Divine revelation can never be rashly made. The coffer may not be opened until the time that fate ordains, and then only by whoever lawfully possesses the key (GRAR, HERS, HERJ, MAST, SOUL, VALH).

coins   Two aspects of coinage must be borne in mind: the purely metaphorical use of the notion of coinage and the symbolism and role of coins as such.

The first is to be found in many Christian writers. St Clement of Alexandria uses the notion of true and counterfeit coinage in the context of perceiving those events and actions which conform with the Spirit, using the Faith as the criterion of truth as the money-changer uses the touchstone (*Stromata* 2). A late and anonymous Eastern writer, perhaps taking his cue from this, stresses in this context the use of the touchstone – provided by the early Fathers – and of the 'money-changers', who are their qualified commentators. Angelus Silesius uses the symbol of coinage frequently as an image of the soul, the soul being impressed with the mark of God as coinage is impressed with that of the king. In fact he compares the soul with the old English coin, the rose-noble, since the rose is the symbol of Christ and also conjures up the notion of the Rosy Cross (Rosicrucianism).

Coins were particularly significant in China and especially the *cash*, a round coin with a square hole in the middle. It is an image of the supreme Triad – the space intermediate between Heaven (round) and Earth (square) being filled by the superscription of the Emperor, son of Heaven and Earth and representative of Universal Man. Secret societies used cashes symbolically in sets of three, hence the name, 'Three Cash Society', given to some branches of the T'ien-ti Huei, their superscription being that of the society, *huei* (society) being substituted for (*jen*) Man in this depiction of the Triad.

A no less important aspect of coin symbolism is the fineness of the coinage. Hence any debasement, in the light of the foregoing, could be seen as a debasement of the truth. In fact debasement of the coinage is a charge which has been levied against many kings, especially Henry VIII. As we have seen in the case of Chinese coins, and the same is true of Gaulish ones as well, ancient coinage bore symbols and hence was charged with spiritual influences. A spiritual authority therefore existed to regulate the fineness of coinage and such regulatory power might well have rested in the hands of the Templars. Hence, Guénon suggests, the link between the two crimes of the French king, Philippe le Bel, the seizure of the Italian merchants' property (1291) and the suppression of the Templars (1307).

A similar tradition of the debasement of the coinage is attached to the Chinese Emperor Wu. To have it approved, the coinage had to be wagered against pieces of the hide of a ritual white stag marked with the symbols of the Triad, that is to say it had at least to be given the outward appearance of traditional fineness.

A great many Gaulish coins bear symbols, figures or signs – heads, horses, boars, horsemen, trees, etc. – of which the power and significance are in all probability religious and traditional. However, numismatic researches into type, chronology and provenance are still insufficiently advanced to admit any chance of determining accurately their symbolism. So often there is a danger of seeing as a traditonal Celtic symbol what is no more than the distortion of a foreign (Greek) numismatic motif. The earliest Celtic civilization avoided using coinage, with all the involved economic problems which come in its train, and the first Gaulish coins to be struck were copies of Philip of Macedon's stater. According to Caesar, the Bretons used iron ingots or lumps of gold or copper. A wealth of coinage confirms this. However, it was only very late and under Saxon influence in the ninth and tenth centuries that the Irish replaced cattle, the archaic exchange mechanism (cf. Latin: *pecunia*), with metal coinage (OGAC).

In any case a purely quantitative notion of coinage clearly demonstrates that its symbolism has been forgotten; and counterfeiting coins shows its degeneration into mere emblem and effigy (PHIL, GUER, GRAD, GUET, GUEA).

cola Many ornamental motifs in Black Africa have been inspired by the cola-pod, four of them often being set end to end in the shape of a CROSS. Because of its bitter taste, in tradition the cola symbolizes the trials of life. 'However, because it symbolizes the trials of life, the cola is also the symbol of firm friendship and of faithfulness. In the betrothal ceremony the engaged couple share a cola nut and offer it to their relatives, announcing in so doing their agreement to live together' (MVEA p. 64).

collar See NECKLACE.

collar-bone See CLAVICLE.

colossus The most famous colossal statues of gods and kings are to be found in Egypt, America, Asia, and on Easter Island. Of these the most celebrated are the statues of Amenhotep III at Thebes, and of Ramses II at Memphis, Thebes and Abu Simbel. Giant figures of stone, or cliff statues carved from the face of the rock itself, these colossi are as detailed as figurines or life-size statues and needed architects and engineers as well as sculptors to realize them. The superhuman scale of these portaits of the Pharaohs symbolized the supranormal powers with which they were endowed. Rising against the vastness of the desert, the mountains or the sky, they pointed the way to the infinite and absolute from which the grandeur of this royal power derived. They also emphasized 'the unchangeable and superhuman nature' of princes. 'They were, indeed, visible manifestations of the King-god and were given names like "Amenhotep Sun of the Rulers", "Ramses Mont in the Two Lands" .... The common people, especially the soldiers, paid particular honour to these dynastic divinities whose crowned faces rose above the sacred enclosures' (POSD p. 49).

colour (see also BLACK; BLUE; BROWN; GREEN; GREY; MOTLEY; ORANGE; RED; VIOLET; YELLOW) The prime characteristic of the symbolism of colour is its universality. This is not merely geographic, but applies to all levels of being and knowledge and to cosmology, psychology, mysticism and so on. Interpretations may differ and red, for example, might receive interpretations which vary with the cultural environment, yet colour remains always and everywhere the mainstay of symbolic thought. The seven colours of the RAINBOW – in which the eye can distinguish 700 shades – have, for example, been made to correspond to the seven notes of the musical scale, the seven Heavens, the seven planets, the seven days of the week and so on. Some colours symbolize the elements – red and orange, Fire; yellow or white, Air; green, Water; black or brown, Earth. They also symbolize space: blue, vertical space, with light blue at the summit (the sky) and dark blue at the foot. Red symbolizes horizontal space, lighter to the east and darker to the west. Other colour symbolism includes black for time and white for eternity; and for all the concomitants of time, the alternation of light and dark, of strength and weakness and of sleeping and waking. Lastly opposing colours, such as black and white, symbolize the intrinsic duality of being. A parti-coloured item of dress; two animals facing one another or back to back, or two dancers, one black the other white; all these coloured images betray the duel of strength which occurs at all levels of existence, from the cosmos to the deepest internal level of the human being, with black representing the forces of darkness, negative and introvert, and white the forces of light, positive and extrovert.

It should not, however, be forgotten that darkness, as Jung has so strongly emphasized, is the place of germination and that black is the colour of origination, beginning, impregnation, occultation, the period during which seeds germinate before they burst into life and light. Perhaps this is the meaning of Black Madonnas and of such goddesses of CAVERNS and of germination as Diana of Ephesus, with both light and dark aspects.

In several cosmogonies colours display a cosmic symbolism and mediate as divinities. For example they play an important part in the Navaho story of the creation of the Sun. 'The Navaho had already partially separated light into its several colours. Next to the floor was white, indicating dawn, upon the white blue was spread for morning, and on the blue, yellow for sunset, and next was black, representing night' (ALEC p. 13). Earlier in the story, white had been involved in the form of pearls and blue used in the form of turquoise.

According to the same sources (ALEC p. 85; MULR p. 278) the cosmic colour symbolism of the Pueblo Indians is as follows: yellow-maize = north; blue = west; red = south; white = east; speckled = above; black = below; varicoloured = the place where the cooking-fire is lit, the centre of the world. For the Prairie Indians red = west; blue = north; green = east; yellow = south (ALEC p. 145). The Andaman Islanders believe that humans possess a red soul and a black spirit. Good proceeds from the spirit and evil from the soul (SCHP p. 165). According to Herodotus the seven walls of the city of Ecbatana were painted in the colours of the seven planets, the whole conceived as a microcosm.

In some European agrarian traditions the last sheaf from the harvest is given a black face with red lips, originally the magical and symbolic colours of the female sexual organs (ELIT p. 357). The Indian Spring festival of Holi degenerates into a mass orgy. Groups of men and boys run through the streets sprinkling passers-by with powdered colours and reddened water, red being the primary, vital and generative colour (ibid.).

Like most American Indians, the Aztecs had only one word for both blue and green. For them blue or blue-green stones held a dual symbolism. On the one hand there was the solar symbolism associated with the turquoise, a fire- and Sun-stone, the emblem of drought and famine: on the other the lunar symbolism of the blue-green *chalchiuitl* stone, the emblem of rain and fertility and a pledge of rebirth inserted in place of a heart into the corpses of the dead. It was the very colour of the plumed serpent with the blue-green feathers of the quetzal, symbol of Spring, and of the *chalciuitl* fish.

Many North American Indians associated a sacred colour with each of the six cosmic sectors. The north was yellow, the west blue, the south red, the east white, the zenith multicoloured and the nadir black (MYTF pp. 177–9).

Among the Maya four colours, one assigned to each of the genii of the cardinal points, ruled the Earth and inspired mankind with feelings like the scattering of seed. North, the first tree, the first man, promise and hope correspond to white; west, the hidden invisible centre, mother, night, misfortune and death, to black; east, honey, greed for wealth and power to red; and maize and south and fertile soil to yellow.

The Alakaluf of Tierra del Fuego believe that mankind occupies the centre of an imaginary sphere of which the four axes are represented by four symbolic colours: blue for the sky and north; green for the earth and south; red for the rising Sun and east; and yellow for rocks, that is to say for the rocky mountains among which the Sun sleeps, the western abode of thunder and of the dead (Alexander quoted by Breton in AMAG).

Colours are also possessed of a quasi-biological and ethical symbolism.

In Ancient Egyptian art, for example, symbolic qualities often determined colour. Black was 'the sign of resurrection from the dead and eternal life'; it was the colour 'of the bitumen in which the mummy is soaked', and the colour of the gods Anubis and of Min, the first of whom introduced the dead to the Otherworld and the second of whom was lord of generation and harvest. Black OSIRIS was sometimes tinged with green because it was the colour of 'vegetation, youth and health. The skin of Amon, god of the air, was painted pure blue. Yellow was gold, the colour of the flesh of the immortals. White, too, was joyful and lucky . . . . Red was, at best, awesome violence; at worst perversion and wickedness.' Red was an accursed colour, the colour of Set and of all that was harmful. Scribes would dip their reeds in red ink 'to write words of ill omen', such as the names Apophis, the snake-demon of misfortune, or of Set, the god of evil, the TYPHON of the Nile (POSD p. 121).

Colour symbolism can also be highly charged with a religious quality. In Christian tradition, colour has a share in created and uncreated light. The Scriptures and the Fathers cannot too highly praise the grandeur and beauty of light. The Word of God is termed 'light from light'. As a result, Christian artists are among those most sensitive to the reflection of the godhead which is

the luminous structure of the universe. Both in miniature painting and in stained glass, the beauty of the colours employed is extraordinary . . . . Interpreting colour derives from the standards of Classical antiquity and is reminiscent of Ancient Egyptian painting. Colour symbolizes an ascensional power in the play of light and shade which is such a feature of Gothic churches, where shade is not the opposite of light, but is its companion, the better to enhance and to aid in its blossoming . . . . There is an enhanced solar presence not only in the church, but in the liturgy which proclaims the magic of the day.

(DAVS pp. 159–60)

Despite this, St Bernard, striving against the seductive force of natural beauty upon those who did not relate it directly to God, recommended monochrome in Cistercian buildings and a chapter of the Order directed that, in manuscripts, initial letters should be of one colour only and without floral decoration. Nevertheless, Suger ground sapphires to obtain blue for his stained glass. However, it was not enough to admire colour for its beauty, its meaning needed to be understood and colours used to raise the beholder to the light of the Creator (ibid. pp. 174, 211). Without making it an absolute rule, Christian art came to attribute white to the Father, blue to the Son and red to the Holy Spirit; green to Hope, white to Faith and red to Charity, black to penance and white to chastity.

Philo of Alexandria regarded four colours as encapsulating the universe, by symbolizing the four ELEMENTS of which it was made – white for Earth, green for Water, violet for Air and red for Fire. Religious vestments containing these four colours symbolize the totality of the elements of which the world is made and thus associate the totality of the universe in the action of the ritual.

In Black Africa, colour is an equally religious symbol, charged with meaning and with power. Different colours are so many ways of getting to know the one and acting upon the other. They are endowed with magical properties.

White is the colour of the dead. Its ritual significance goes further still: the colour of the dead is used to drive death away. An enormous power of healing is attributed to it. In initiation rites, white is often the colour of the first phase, the struggle with death . . . . Yellow ochre is a neutral colour used for painting floors because it is the colour of earth or of dead leaves . . . . Red is the colour of blood, the colour of life . . . . Young mothers, young initiates and mature men are all decorated in red, covered with *nkula* and gleaming with oil in seasonal rites. Black, the colour of night, is the colour of ordeal, suffering and mystery. It may hide a watchful enemy . . . green is a colour seldom used on its own, green leaves are worn by initiates at the phase of life's triumph.

(MVEA p. 32)

Islamic tradition is especially rich in colour symbolism, it, too, tinged with magical beliefs.

Black animals are regarded as unlucky. Black dogs bring deaths in the family: black hens are used in witchcraft. Black is used as a charm against the evil eye and as a means to influence the weather on principles of homeopathic magic.

White, the colour of light and sunshine, on the other hand, is lucky. A magical quality is attributed to milk, due in large part to its colour. When betrothals are celebrated at Fez, milk is drunk to make life 'white' and, in rural weddings, the bride is spattered with milk. Flour, wool and white eggs are all lucky, as is the whiteness of silver. When somebody is sick and a spell is read over him or her or a charm given, the doctor or scribe must be paid either in silver or with something white.

Green is also lucky: it symbolizes plant life. To give somebody something green, especially in the morning, is to bring that person good luck. Grass is thrown towards the new Moon to ensure that the month is happy or 'green'. Vegetation, which water, the source of life, causes to grow, is believed to affect the dead, transmitting vital energy to them (WERS 2: p. 532). In some parts of Morocco the floors of tombs are lined with palm- or myrtle-leaves.

Yellow, the colour of gold and of the sun, possesses magical properties. Saffron owes its prophylactic qualities to its colour.

However, colours raise us to another level of symbolism. Mystics see a rising scale of colours as representing the manifestation of Absolute Light in ecstasy. Thus according to Jalāl-al-Dīn Muhammad Rūmī one rises through blue, red, yellow, white, green and pale blue until one reaches colourless light. The rungs of another LADDER are white (the colour of Islam), yellow (the colour of the true believer), dark blue (the colour of a blessing), green (the colour of peace), azure (colour of intuitive conviction), red (colour of Gnosis) to black (the colour of the divine essence, that is to say, colour in its true meaning since it embraces all colours and in it all colours are indistinguishable) (NICM p. 265).

Rūmī, again, regarded red and green as symbolizing divine grace, bringing the soul a message of hope when it was in darkness. Red derives from the Sun and on that score is the best of colours.

According to the methods employed by the Naqshbandī masters in the *dhikr* (remembrance of God) the subtle centres of the human being are visualized by associating them with the colours with which they correspond. Thus 'the light of the heart [is] yellow; that of the spirit, red; the light of the subtle centre, known as the secret, is white. The centre known as the hidden is black, while the most hidden has a green light' (PHIL pp. 323ff.).

Abd al-Qadir Jīlānī, in his treatise on the perfect man (al-Insānū'l Kāmil), proclaims that mystics have seen seven heavens rising above the spheres of Earth, Water, Air and Fire and that they can thus interpret them for those who dwell on Earth:

1 The Heaven of the Moon is so subtle that it cannot be seen. Created from the nature of the Spirit, it is the home of Adam. Its colour is whiter than silver.
2 The Heaven of Mercury, home of certain angels and created from the nature of thought. Its colour is grey.
3 The Heaven of Venus, created from the nature of the imagination, the abode of the World of Likenesses. Its colour is yellow.
4 The Heaven of the Sun, created from the light of the heart. Its colour is yellow and glittering gold.
5 The Heaven of Mars, ruled by Azrael, the Angel of Death, created from the light of judgement. Its colour is red.
6 The Heaven of Jupiter, created from the light of meditation. Here dwell the angels whose chief is Michael. Its colour is blue.
7 The Heaven of Saturn, created from the light of the First Intelligence. Its colour is black.

(NICM pp. 12ff.)

The same author describes the seven earthly limbos with their corresponding colours:

1 The Land of Souls, created whiter than milk, but turning to the colour of dust when Adam trod it after the Fall, that is, all except an area in the North where the people of the Invisible World dwell.
2 The Land of Devotions, inhabited by jinn who believe in God. Its colour is emerald green.
3 The Land of Nature, inhabited by infidel jinn. Its colour is saffron yellow.
4 The Land of Lust, inhabited by devils. Its colour is blood red.
5 The Land of Greed (arzu'l-tughyān), inhabited by devils. Its colour is indigo blue.
6 The Land of Impiety (arzu'l-ilhād). Its colour is black as night.
7 The Land of Poverty (arzu'l-shaqawā) is the land of Hell.

(NICM pp. 124–5)

From the seven Heavens and the seven Earths we move on to the inner man and to the seven colours of the organs of subtle psychology. According to the fourteenth-century writer, Alāoddwa Semanani:

The characteristic coloration of the light, which acts as a veil concealing each of the subtle centres, reveals to the pilgrim the stage which he has reached in his growth or in his spiritual journey.
The light of the body (the Adam of your being) is smokey grey deepening to black; that of your living soul (the Noah of your being) is blue; that of your

heart (Abraham) is red; that of the conscience (Moses) is white; that of the spirit (David) is yellow; that of the secret (Jesus) is gleaming black; and that of the divine centre (Muhammad) is shining green, for that is the colour most appropriate to the mystery of mysteries.

(Corbin, 'L'intériorisation du sens en herméneutique soufie iranienne', in ERAJ 26 (1958))

Colours have acquired a political significance as well in the Islamic world. With the Abbasids, black became one of the emblems of the Caliphate and of the State in general. Black banners became the symbol of the revolt of the Abbasids.

According to al-Bukhārī and to Muslim, the Prophet wore a black turban on the day he entered Mecca, while his personal standard, known as Al-'ikab, was said by some to be black, while other traditions claim it to have been green.

There is a saying that Arabs only wear a black turban when they have a duty of vengeance to execute.

Black was the Persian mourning colour and its use has survived in Islam. The North African historian, Makkari, states that among the ancient Spanish Muslims, white was the colour of mourning, while among the 'Easterners' it was black.

Black is thus associated with notions of mourning, of vengeance and of revolt.

The Caliph wore a black cloak and a tall headdress of the same colour. Those who entered his palace had to be dressed in black and high dignitaries went to the mosque black-clad. Robes of honour were black, as were the wardrobe of an important personage and the upholstery and hangings of his audience chamber. The veil of the Ka'ba is black. The wearing of white garments was ordered as a punishment.

As black was the the emblem of the Abbasids, their opponents, the 'Alids, adopted green. At the beginning of his reign the Caliph Ma'mūn, who favoured the 'Alids, forbade the use of black.

White became the emblem of the Umayyad cause and chroniclers traced the progress of their revolt by the expression 'whitening'. Gradually white came to be the sign of all opposition groups and the Carmathians marched under a white banner. By extension, the term 'white' was applied to any religion opposed to Islam and the religion of the rebels was called 'the white religion'.

The phrase 'Black and White' was used to describe all the subjects of the empire, both loyal and rebellious.

Rebels in Persia were sometimes called 'Reds', but this arises from a different order of ideas. From pre-Islamic times Persians and foreigners in general were called Reds, in contrast with Arabs, the Blacks. Hence their expression for everybody, 'Red and Black'.

Psychologists have distinguished warm from cold colours. The former (red, orange and yellow) enhance the processes of adaptation and of stimulation by their powers of stimulus and arousal. The latter (blue, indigo and violet) enhance the processes of antagonism and relapse by their powers of sedation and relaxation. This has been applied to a whole range of flats, offices and factories. The colours arouse what they symbolize.

There are good grounds for taking colour tonality into account as well. Bright, light colours produce a more positive effect but, uncontrolled, may produce over-stimulation. Dull, matt colours produce a more deeply interiorized effect, but that may become negative.

Dreaming in colour is a significant expression of the unconscious. It represents a certain soul-state in the dreamer and betrays different tendencies of psychic pulsation. According to Jung, in analysis colour may be conceived as expressing the main human psychic functions – thought, emotion, intuition and sensation.

Blue is the colour of the sky and of the spirit; on the psychic plane it is the colour of thought.

Red is the colour of blood, of passion and emotion.

Yellow is the colour of sunlight, of gold and of intuition.

Green is the colour of nature and of growth; from the psychological point of view it is indicative of the function of sensation (function of reality) and of the relationship between dreams and reality (TEIR p. 64).

De la Rocheterie observes that sometimes

an object or an area in a dream attracts notice by the brightness of its coloration, as if to underline the importance of the message being conveyed by the unconscious to the conscious. Dreams seldom shine throughout with such striking colours. If that is the case, the contents of the unconscious are lived at a high intensity of emotion. But these feelings may be extremely varied since, just as colour originates from variations in light waves, so the quality of the feeling varies with the tone of the colour.

In Masonic symbolism, 'white corresponds to Wisdom, Grace and Victory; red to Intelligence, Discipline and Glory; while blue corresponds to the Crown, Beauty and the Foundation; and, lastly, black to Malkut and the Kingdom.' Blue is also the colour of Heaven, the Temple and the Starry Vault.

Masons also wore ribbons in their hats, on their canes and in their buttonholes. Stone-cutters of the Lodge of Liberty wore green and blue ribbons in their right button-hole, while Cabinet-makers of the same Lodge wore green, blue and white ribbons in the left button-hole.

Masons of the French Rite wore a blue scarf, those of the Scottish a blue scarf fringed with red. 'The two colours in the ribbon', Henri Jullien remarks, 'may be considered as an expression of the two forms, positive and negative, of terrestrial energy and universal magnetism . . . . According to Frederick Portal, red and blue are images of love and wisdom.' 'Red', observes Jules Boucher, 'makes the senses aware of an irradiation, an extension of spiritual feeling' (BOUM pp. 140, 206, 304–6).

Alchemy also had its colour scale. In ascending order, black was associated with matter, with the arcane, with sin and with penitence; grey with the Earth; white with mercury, innocence, enlightenment and happiness; red with sulphur, blood, passion and sublimation; blue with the sky; and gold with the 'Great Work'.

column In architecture, the column and pillar are the essential supporting elements, the AXIS which links the various levels of the building. Columns ensure its stability and to undermine them is to threaten the entire structure.

This is why they are taken as the sum of the whole and they therefore symbolize the strength of a structure, be it architectural, social or personal. By pulling down the columns of their temple, Samson, the Philistines' prisoner, destroyed his enemies and, although sharing their fate, gave his own people victory (Judges 16: 25–30).

The column, together with its normal accessories of base and capital, symbolizes the TREE of Life, the base being its roots, the shaft its trunk and the capital its branches. The Ancient Greeks appear to have given the column a sexual connotation, if this is the significance of occasionally depicting Demeter (Ceres) with a column and a dolphin, symbolizing the sea and its fertility. The notion of verticality which predominates in this aspect of the symbol may also be applied to the spinal column. This would make the spine the symbol of self-assertion and would give their full significance to the customs of prostration or of bowing before superiors or some holy object or image.

The Ancient Egyptians often represented Osiris in the shape of a pillar, known as a *jed*. The god stands like a column, arms crossed on his chest and in his hands the insignia of kingship, the sceptre and flail. On his head, like four spinal vertebrae, he wears the double crown, the horns of Amon and the two URAEI. This piling of one on top of the other would seem to symbolize the passage of the vital fluid, the BREATH of life, down the spinal column, while the fire-serpent crowning the whole would seem reminiscent of the Hindu *kundalinī*. In this instance the column is a channel rather than a support and serves to 'warm once again and return to life through the warmth of Isis.' It can, however, be interpreted differently as symbolizing 'the enduring quality of the soul, stability, the magical liquid which is Osiris's spinal column' (CHAM pp. 46, 74). Nonetheless, the idea that the column is the channel for the divine principle of light and life persists and also that it is through this that the magical powers of the vital fluid pass.

The Ancient Egyptians were also familiar with figures superimposed one above the other, as in India and Black Africa, to form a sort of cosmic pillar. For example, one of the Anhai papyri (reproduced CHAM p. 133) shows Nun, god of the Primeval Waters, rising from the abyss, hands raised above his head and carrying the boat of the Sun, in the middle of which stands the sun-beetle, Khepri, surrounded by seven gods. The scarab-beetle is upright, bearing in his two forefeet a yellow disc symbolizing the universe or, more especially, the lower world. At the top of the picture are two figures apparently coming down from Heaven head first. Thus the three levels of the cosmos are depicted in what are predominantly columnar terms to express both ascending and descending movement. This might well symbolize the evolution of manifest being.

Architecturally, however, columns are what give the buildings they support life and all which this implies. In any case columns took their shape from trees. 'In most cases Egyptian columns were copies in stone of supports made from plants, either trunks or bundles of stems, which were formerly used to hold up the ceilings of wood and clay buildings .... At the top was a capital which emerged from five horizontal ties which theoretically held together the bundle of stems of which they were composed' (POSD p. 50).

Egyptian columns generally borrow their shape from the palm tree or papyrus complete with their fluting and veining. These 'symbolic themes' of the column 'express vitality infused into or circulated through a building'. The relative dimensions of a column vary 'according to the requirements of the symbols to be expressed'. For example, the capital of a column will be made quite disproportionate to represent the heads of the goddess Hathor, or else the plant-shaped abaci will be similarly treated if they are to represent a god dancing, etc. (DAUE p. 588). In this instance the architectonic role of the column seems to have been subordinated to its representational function. However, in both instances it retains its symbolic properties.

In Celtic tradition, too, the column, or pillar, symbolizes the World Axis and this notion, fairly close to that of the Tree of Life, is reflected in linguistic metaphor which compares heroes and warriors with pillars of battle. The earliest Irish mythological text – a combination of Genesis and the Book of Revelation – is called *Cath Maighe Tuireadh*, which may be literally translated as 'Battle of the Plain of the Pillars'. This may be taken either as a reference to megalithic standing stones or to battling heroes. Cùchulainn, for example, bound himself with his GIRDLE to a pillar so that he would die on his feet, as did the bards (*file*) who were present at the first Battle of Mag Tuired against the Firbolg. Conall Cernach avenged the death of Cùchulainn by killing his murderer, Lugaid, and setting his head upon a pillar. *The Cattle Raid of Cooley* tells how Cùchulainn cut off the heads of twelve enemies and set each on the top of a pillar (MENHIR), with the thirteenth, that of their chief, in the middle, on the plan of the 'chiefest idol in Ireland', Cromm Cruaich, a standing stone surrounded by twelve smaller stones. The central pillar symbolizes the centre of the world, the wellspring and channel of life (OGAC 28: p. 350; WINI 5: p. 418).

A very ancient Welsh poem compares the four evangelists with the columns which hold up the world. This concept probably underlies the four columns accompanying the giant serpent-footed horseman, a common subject of Gaulish iconography (REVC 12: pp. 52–103; MYVA p. 29A; Friedrich Hertlein, *Die Juppitergigantensäulen*, Stuttgart, 1910).

However, columns or pillars, in so far as they contain alphabets, may also be symbols of the supports of knowledge.

In a mystical Celto-Iberian sense, however, the Pillars [of HERAKLES: see below] are alphabetical abstractions. 'Marwnad Ercwlf', an ancient Welsh poem in the *Red Book of Hergest*, treats of the Celtic Herakles – whom the Irish called 'Ogma Sunface' and Lucian 'Ogmios' . . . – and records how Ercwlf raised 'four columns of equal height capped with red gold', apparently the four columns of five letters each, which formed the twenty-lettered Bardic alphabet known as the Boibel-Loth . . . . It seems that, about the year 400 BC, this new alphabet, the Greek letter-names of which referred to Celestial Herakles' journey in the sun-chalice, his death on Mount Oeta, and his powers as city-founder and judge . . ., displaced the Beth-Luis-Nion tree-alphabet, the letter names of which referred to the murderous sacrifice of CRONOS by the wild women (GRAM p. 132, 3).

Classical art did not restrict the column to a purely architectonic role. It was employed as votive and triumphal columns girdled with relief sculptures or incised and gilded inscriptions which commemorated the glorious deeds of the hero concerned. Trajan's Column, raised to the Emperor's glory, depicts in low relief 115 of the most notable incidents in his military campaigns, spiralling from base to summit. Such columns symbolize the involvement of Heaven with Earth, suggesting both gratitude of man to god and deification of some famous men. They display the power of God in man and the power of man under God's influence. Columns symbolize the power which ensures victory and the permanence of its effects.

In the 'Homeric' Hymns, columns sustain and therefore encapsulate both the Olympian order and the power of the godhead.

The 'Pillars of Hercules (Herakles)' were supposed to have been raised by the hero at the end of his expedition to North Africa – the Libya of the Ancients – when he reached Tingis (modern Tangiers) and after he had slaughtered a host of monsters. One of these pillars stood in Africa – the Jebel Zatout, a mountain above Ceuta – the other was Mount Calpe (the Rock of Gibraltar) in Europe. In fact, they were destined less to mark geographical boundaries and to separate continents than to narrow the passage between them so as better to separate the Mediterranean Basin from the Atlantic Ocean and thus prevent sharks and other marine monsters from passing the Straits of Gibraltar. This was a frontier defence which was not to be crossed. Other 'columns' of Herakles have been recorded, on the North Sea and Breton coasts, on the Black Sea and along the coasts of India. In these cases, columns would symbolize the limits beyond which a god could no longer exercise his powers of protection and beyond which a person ought not to venture.

While columns thus mark boundaries, they generally frame GATE ways and mark the passage from one world to another.

And yet it was the ambition of princes to cross these thresholds. Such certainly was the case of the Emperor Charles V, who took as his device *Plus Ultra* to show that his Empire had crossed the boundaries of the Ancient World and extended his power 'far beyond the Straits of Gibraltar' (TERS p. 108).

Judeo-Christian traditions share his symbolism in its cosmic and spiritual connotation. Columns involve the heavenly with the earthly, as trees of life, cosmic trees, or trees of the world. The Bahir makes this very plain when it states that a column joins the last *sefirah*, that is, the Earth, with the sixth, known as Heaven. In medieval symbolism the column, which sustains life and underpins the world, suggests the power of the Lord to shake the columns of the world.

Such images reflect their contemporary traditions of cosmology – 'The earth reposes on columns and when the Lord shakes them, it causes earthquakes' – and of eschatology – the end of the world will come when its columns are overthrown.

Columns are sometimes used with the connotation of theophany. 'On the subject of light: the Easter liturgy evokes the symbol of the Pillar of Fire which led the Children of Israel through the Wilderness. A column of light always sets apart those souls who love God and whose purity allows light divine to shine through them' (DAVS p. 237).

The pillars of Solomon's own house and his TEMPLE have given rise to countless theories. First, two different sets of pillars are involved.

The columns of the great hall of Solomon's house which was used for

royal entrances, as a guard-room and as a vast anteroom to the royal apart-
ments and the throne room, were of CEDAR, which, it will be recalled, is the
symbol of incorruptibility and immortality (1 Kings 7: 2–6).

The other set of columns, two in number, were the work of Hiram. 'For
he cast two pillars of brass . . . . And he set up the pillars in the porch of
the temple: and he set up the right pillar, and called the name thereof
Jachin: and he set up the left pillar, and called the name thereof Boaz . . . .
So was the work of the pillars finished' (1 Kings 7: 15, 21, 22). The symbolism of brass (BRONZE) is well-known. It is a sacred metal, sign of the
indissoluble compact between Earth and Heaven and the pledge of the
everlasting stability of this covenant. The name given to the right-hand
pillar (Jachin) in Hebrew suggests precisely this idea of solidity and stability
while that of the left-hand pillar (Boaz) suggests that of strength. According
to Crampon, 'The two words together mean, therefore, that God has in
his strength firmly established the temple and the worship of which it is the
centre.'

Such other writers as Oswald Wirth have discovered sexual connotations
in the names of the pillars, the right-hand expressing the active or male
principle, the left, the passive or female principle. This interpretation, which
associates them with the reproductive organs, may well be corroborated by
the sexual symbolism of the POMEGRANATE: 'And the chapiters upon the two
pillars had pomegranates . . . two hundred in rows round about' (1 Kings 7:
20).

The pillar of cloud by day and the pillar of fire by night which guided the
Children of Israel across the Wilderness (Exodus 13: 21–2) symbolized the
presence of God. This was an active presence which, historically, guided his
chosen people safely on their way and, mystically, pointed their souls along
the paths of perfection.

In its connotation of the involvement of Heaven with Earth, the column
may under certain circumstances be a sacrificial stone. The animal was
sacrificed on its top, in its heavenly part. Following ritual consecration,
ritual purification took place round the base of the column. Laws were
carved on the face of the pillar and oaths sworn before it. It was the axis
of the holy or the holy axis of society, as Plato so admirably makes plain
when describing the customs of Atlantis (*Critias* 119d–120b).

The Chinese set the Pillars of Heaven round the edges of the Earth, but
their number was unsettled (eight, four or one) as was their location (MYTF
p. 126).

The Uralo-Altaic peoples believed that one or more columns supported
the sky. They worshipped in sacred groves in which stood the Tree of Life,
which may well have been a symbol of the pillar which supported the sky
and was the pivot on which the Heavens moved in their round,

thus accounting for the position of the stars changing at different times of day
and night. A BLACKSMITH of miraculous skill had made it and it needed to be
kept in good condition, otherwise the universe was in danger of collapse, which
would dash the sky in pieces on the face of the Earth. The POLE Star was
supposed to be set on the top of the sacred pillar around which the heavens
turned.

(MYTF p. 109)

The centre-pole of Samoyed Yurak tents was the emblem of the pillar which holds up the sky and the focus of certain shamanic rituals, especially after the death of any of the inhabitants of that tent. It was up this pillar that the shaman could rise to the heavens. The smoke-hole then became the hole in the sky through which the magician could enter Heaven in search of the spirits who dwelt there (MYTF p. 109).

Aboriginal Australian rituals which enact creation myths employ a post as the axis and centre around which the world order was built. Break this column and the world will come to an end, the floodwaters of pain will flow in and all will return to primeval Chaos. The pillar thus symbolizes the principles upon which society is organized.

This example provides an admirable illustration at one and the same time of the cosmic function of the ritual post and of its soteriological role. On the one hand the ritual post is a copy of the pillar which Numbakula used when he ordered the universe and, on the other, it is the means whereby the Achilpa are enabled to communicate with the heavenly kingdom. Now, human life is only possible because of this permanent link with heaven. The Achilpa's 'world' can only and really become 'their' world in so far as it replicates the Cosmos ordered and sanctified by Numbakula. Life is impossible without a vertical axis which ensures an 'opening' into the transcendent and, at the same time, enables them to take their spiritual bearings. In other words, life is incompatible with Chaos and once contact with the transcendent is lost and the whole system of orientation destabilized, life in this world becomes impossible – and the Achilpa accept death.

(SOUM p. 476)

The traditions of Freemasonry contain similar symbolism. It is common knowledge that it is based upon Solomon's Temple and accordingly all Lodges display a Temple where, facing the Blazing Delta, two columns, one marked J for Jachin and the other B for Boaz, play an essential part. Column J is painted red for its male, active, fiery qualities, while column B is painted white for its passive, female, airy virtues. Furthermore, the former is associated with the Sun, the latter with the Moon. In their ceremonial, the Apprentices stand in line at the foot of column J, Masons beside column B and Master Masons in the room in the middle.

All in all the symbolism of the column and pillar is akin to that of the World Axis and the Tree of Life. It expresses the relationship between the different levels of the universe and of the ego, and is a channel between them and cosmic, vital and spiritual energy and a source from which such energies flow.

comb Although the comb may generally be regarded as nothing more than a utilitarian or decorative item, in Japanese mythology it plays an extremely important, if highly complicated, part. The most interesting aspect would seem to be that when not combing the hair, but simply stuck in it, the comb was a means of communication with, or identification by, supernatural forces. The teeth of the comb stood for the rays of heavenly light penetrating into the person's being through the CROWN of the head.

Again, the comb is what holds together the hair, that is, the components of the individual's personality seen as strength, nobility and capacity for spiritual elevation. A comb picked up by chance may change the finder's individuality. In the tales of *Nihon-gi*, combs also seem to play a protective role, which their transformation into BAMBOO-clumps does not define precisely. Bamboo-thickets, however, sometimes carry the same significance as impenetrable jungle (HERS). The comb, to which it is likened, may act as a protective barricade and its teeth may be regarded as daggers.

comet In both Ancient Mexico and Ancient Peru, the passage of comets was observed by priests and soothsayers. They were held to foretell misfortune and to be heralds of national disasters, such as famine, defeat in war and the imminent death of kings. Both Aztec and Inca tradition records the appearance of a comet to warn Montezuma and the Inca Huayna Capac of the arrival of the Spaniards and the fall of their empires.

In Mexico comets were called 'flaming serpents' or 'smoking stars'.

Similar beliefs are held by the Bantu of the Kasai River (a tributary of the Congo), who regard the appearance of a comet as a signal of deep misfortune or of events which seriously threaten their communities (FOUG).

A comet was seen before the murder of Julius Caesar.

compasses In pictorial terms – and, to some extent, generally speaking – compasses are regarded as emblems of the exact sciences and of the strict rules of mathematics, in contrast with free-ranging imaginative poetry. The notion of precision and rules in any case lies at the base of the Chinese *kuei*.

Nonetheless, in both Western and Ancient Chinese esotericism compasses – generally combined with the Mason's SQUARE – were important cosmological symbols in so far as the one was used to measure and describe a CIRCLE and the other to draw a square. It was an axiom of French medieval lawyers 'that in the square and compasses resides the perfection of the square and circle.'

A fine drawing by William Blake, 'The Ancient of Days Measuring Time', depicts him seated in the solar disk and stretching a vast pair of compasses earthwards. Coomaraswamy and Guénon have compared this symbol of measurement – or determination – with the 'bounds of Heaven and Earth' of which the Vedas speak and have drawn attention to the part played by the celestial architect, Vishvakarma, as well as to the 'Great Architect of the Universe' of the Freemasons.

Dante praised God the Architect as 'He who turn'd his compass' (*Paradiso* 19: 40).

Compasses have been interpreted as images of thought, drawing or following the circles of the world. By tracing images of movement while being themselves mobile, compasses have become the symbol of that constructive dynamism which is an attribute of creative work.

Compasses, with one arm stationary and the other returning to its point of departure, have also come to symbolize the cycle of existence. 'However far and however long you travel, you will always return to your point of departure, like compasses with one arm fast in the centre and the other travelling round the circumference. However far it turns, it will never reach any other point than that from which it started' (Sohrawardi, *L'Archange empourpré*, CORE 2: p. 248).

In both Europe and China, square and compasses suggest, respectively, Earth and Heaven. The Master Mason 'between square and compasses' plays precisely the same role of 'intermediary' as does the Taoist *jen*. In the West, square and compasses are attributed respectively to the two halves, female and male of the Hermetic REBIS (hermaphrodite), corresponding to Sun and Moon, and in China to Fu-hi and Nu-kua, the male and female aspects of manifestation. However, when Fu-hi and Nu-kua are wedded, their attributes are reversed or, more accurately, exchanged. It is the graphic representation of 'sacred marriage', a reconstituted synthesis of *yin* and *yang* in which the *yin* figure bears the *yang* attributes and *vice versa*. Similarly, in any representation of the T'ai Chi, the *yang* half requires a touch of *yin* and the *yin* a touch of *yang*.

More prosaically, the phrase 'square and compasses' (*kuei-kin*) is applied to sound morality, good order and in fact to the complementary harmony of celestial and earthly, female and male principles.

It will also be observed that in conformity with the symbolism of the square and the circle, compasses relate especially to the determination of time, and squares to that of space, as the Chinese ideogram *kin* indicates, the ancient square being used to measure area.

In the Middle Ages, square and compasses were emblems of most of the Guilds, Guénon remarking that in France only shoemakers and bakers were forbidden to use them (GRAD, GRAP, GUER, GUET, GUEO).

In Masonic tradition the angle between the two arms of the compasses is an indicator of the potential and the grades of knowledge.

Forty-five degrees is the equivalent of the eighth, sixty of the sixth and ninety of the fourth. By restricting the angle of opening to ninety degrees, Masons show that there are limits to knowledge which man should not pass. Ninety degrees is the angle of the square and the square, as we know, is the equivalent of matter, while the compasses are symbols of the spirit and of its power over matter. An angle of opening of forty-five degrees shows that this control is not fully exercised, while at ninety degrees the two powers are exactly balanced and the compasses have become a true square.

(BOUM p. 7)

The relative positioning of compasses to square also symbolizes the different situations of the Mason in respect of spiritual and material forces. If the square is set over the compasses, matter controls spirit; if the compasses are placed over the square, this indicates spiritual control; and lastly, if the angle of opening of the compasses coincides with the right angle of the square, this is harmonization on the highest plane between spiritual and material (BOUM p. 6).

In traditional iconography the compasses are regarded as symbols of prudence, justice, temperance and truth, virtues which are all based upon the spirit of moderation. They have also become the emblem of geometry, of astronomy (and of the Muse Urania, who is its personification), of architecture and of geography, and always because they are a measuring instrument used especially to determine relationships between objects. Since Saturn, who was originally an agrarian god, numbered land-surveying among his duties, compasses were one of his attributes. Saturn is also the god of time, a lame, miserable, taciturn being, his mind always 'searching for the unknown, for the philosopher's stone and for the secret of the quintessence' and compasses have therefore become the symbol of melancholy (TERS pp. 109–12).

conch The conch is the SHELL from which Greek mythology relates that
APHRODITE (Venus) was born. This made it an attribute of the Tritons.

There are two aspects of the shell's symbolism: its relationship with the
primeval waters and its use as a musical instrument, or rather as a noise-
producer. It is audible over great distances and induces terror, hence the
use of the conch in ancient warfare. The opening of the *Bhagavad Gītā*
echoes with the ghastly blaring of 'awesome sound, confounding Earth and
Heaven and riving the hearts of Dhritarāshtra's allies'. In this context, with
the cosmos on the brink of destruction, the rending of the spirit certainly
plays a part in preparation for the spiritual experience expressed in the
poem as *karma*, or action. Brahmans, Tibetan lamas and even Maoris still
use the conch ceremonially, perhaps in an identical role, perhaps because,
as we shall discuss later, it suggests the primal sound (OM). The Tibetan
conch is used in association with other instruments precisely to produce
mental confusion and annihilation as a preparation to inner perception of
the 'natural sound of Truth'. In any case, the noise of the conch is inwardly
perceived in some Yoga exercises. In funeral ceremonies, a conch accompanies the effigy of the deceased to indicate the functions of sound and
hearing, so important in *bardo*.

Since it is sea-born, the conch is associated with the element of WATER
and hence is an attribute of Varuna, Lord of the Waters. In this instance,
as also when it features among the eight treasures (*nidhi*) of King Chakravartī or of Shrī, it is associated with the LOTUS. This attribution undoubtedly
partakes of universal domination because of the sound which the conch
produces. It is also connected with water and the Moon (the lotus, on the
other hand, possessing a solar nature), the conch being white, the colour of
the full Moon. In China, a huge shell was used 'to draw the waters of the
Moon', or 'celestial dew', and also the *yin* element; *yang*, fire, was drawn
from the Sun by means of a metal mirror.

Furthermore, the conch has echoes of the pearl-oyster and of the PEARL
which it contains. In this case the conch means the ear, which it resembles,
the organ of hearing and the means of intellectual perception, while the
pearl becomes speech or the Word. According to Burckhardt this is the
significance of the conch depicted in Islamic art in some prayer niches. It
should also be observed that in *The Secret Rose Garden*, Shabistarī writes:
'The shell is the spoken word: the pearl is the heart's knowledge.' In this
context the shell symbolizes concentration upon the Word.

In India, the conch is pre-eminently an attribute of Vishnu, the conserving
principle in manifestation. Both sound and pearl are 'conserved' within the
shell. The conch is itself Lakshmi, too, Vishnu's *shakti*, wealth and beauty.
There is evidence from Cambodia to support the view that the conch explains the shape of the *sālagrāma*, the counterpart of the lingam in the
worship of Shiva. Furthermore, in India the conch is sometimes regarded as
the complement of the THUNDERBOLT (VAJRA), although in Tibet this complementary role is played by the BELL. The conch is therefore the relatively
passive and receptive aspect of a principle of which the *vajra* is the active
aspect. In Buddhism these are right understanding and right purpose.

One of the Upanishads makes Vishnu's conch the emblem of the five
Elements, being 'born' of them and yet being at one and the same time

their original. These elements individualize the notion of the ego and personal awareness (*ahamkāra*). Hence the conch denotes the origin of the 'appearance', a fact corroborated by its relationship with the primeval waters and its SPIRAL growth from a central point. It is said, furthermore, that the conch encloses the *veda* during periods of *pralaya* between two cycles of 'appearance'. Hence it holds the seed and potential evolution of future cycles. This seed is also the primal sound, the monosyllable 'om'. Some traditions group together the three elements of the monosyllable as a spiral (the conch), a point (the seed which it holds) and a straight line (the development of the potential contained within the shell). It is the symbol of distant voyages and of massive developments both inward and outward (BURA, CORT, BHAB).

Like all shells, the conch draws its characteristics from its archetype – Moon and water, gestation and fertility. The Maya believed it bore the burgeoning Earth on the back of the monstrous CROCODILE which emerged from the cosmic waters at the beginning of time. The conch is associated with chthonian gods and especially with the JAGUAR, the great god of the Underworld who, like the great crocodile, bears the Earth on his back. By extension, then, the conch symbolizes the Underworld and its deities (THOH).

condor In the myths of all Andean peoples, the condor appears as an avatar (manifestation) of the SUN. It is depicted as such as far apart as Tiahuanaco (Bolivia) and Chavin de Huantar (Peru) as well as on Paracas, Nazca, Huayla and other pottery (MEJP).

cone Although this geometrical shape shares the symbolism of the CIRCLE and the TRIANGLE, there is little precise or authoritative definition of its significance in tradition. The cone may well have been the symbol of Astarte, the Canaanite love- and fertility-goddess, corresponding to the Assyrian Ishtar and the Greek Aphrodite. The cone might perhaps represent the vagina as an image of femininity. It is also related to Moon-worship.

Frazer has likened its symbolism, too, to that of the PYRAMID and it might well suggest that of the TOWER and ZIGGURAT. It provides an image of ascension, of development from the material to the spiritual, of the gradual spiritualization of the world, of a return to Oneness and of personalization.

confession In *The Book of the Dead* and other Ancient Egyptian literary texts there are plenty of examples of 'confessions'. In nearly every case they take a negative form, listing the sins which the deceased has *not* committed. The interrogation to which he or she submitted at the weighing of souls (see SCALES) was not designed to elicit admissions of or remorse for guilt. 'Far from it: it principally comprised declarations by the deceased that he or she had not committed certain offences against contemporary morality, certain breaches of the ritual laws and even certain crimes. It was followed by other declarations affirming the fulfilment of certain moral duties.' It was as though the deceased were asking the judges: 'Please don't expose the evil in me to the god whom you serve.' Underlying this is a very profound and sane concept: the deceased wishes to preserve only those actions of which his or her conscience approves. What is rejected no longer belongs completely to his or her personality, but relates to a part of the self which he or she does not ask to survive.

The Ancient Egyptian concept does not, however, rule out magic. Although confessing only to good deeds, it is by this means that the good is made real; denial of evil destroys evil.

The deceased person's declarations are uttered in the same spirit of magic. By mentioning only innocence and right conduct, they act as a spell with the power to achieve salvation. The same is true of the iconography [of the weighing of the soul]: by showing only the heart and the *ma'at* [divine order] in balance, it effects the desired equivalence between the one and the other.

(MORR p. 177)

Confession symbolizes positive intention of the deceased, the eternal image of him- or herself which he or she wishes to leave to gods and men, a moral last will and testament.

In the Old Testament, however, it is confession of sin committed which frees the sinner and not the reminder of his or her good deeds. 'He that covereth his sins shall not prosper: but whoso confesseth and forsaketh them shall have mercy (Proverbs 28: 13).'

It is not completely unknown for the sinner to protest his or her faithfulness to the Lord, but generally the sin has to be acknowledged, publicly confessed and expiated by sacrifice:

And it shall be, when he shall be guilty in one of these things [concealment of knowledge, touching an unclean thing, etc.], that he shall confess that he hath sinned in that thing: And he shall bring his trespass offering unto the Lord for his sin which he hath sinned, a female from the flock, a lamb or a kid of the goats, for a sin offering; and the priest shall make an atonement for him concerning his sin.

(Leviticus 5: 5–6)

Numbers 5: 7 prescribes, in addition to confession and sacrificial atonement, the duty of making restitution (to the priest when it is impossible to do so to the injured party).

Christian confession has kept such various elements as acknowledgement, restitution, sacrifice and forgiveness by God which it inherited from Judaism, adding, in perhaps more explicit terms, the intention not to sin again as a very condition of that forgiveness. Sin is a tie, spiritual bondage, and confession, in its full sense, is an untying of those bonds since to absolve means to unloose. Christ gave St Peter the power to bind and to loose, that is to say to preserve the bonds of sin or to break them. Here confession symbolizes the intention to free oneself from sin and evil.

Aztecs had the right, once in their lives, to confess their sins. This washed them of their faults in this life and the life to come, before gods and before men. This confession was made to 'the goddess of lechery and unlawful love', Tlazolteotl, also, and for that reason, known as 'she who eats filth (sin)' (SOUA p. 199). She was the goddess who inspired the most perverted lusts and who forgave them, displaying thereby what is so typical of symbolic concepts – the association of opposites (see CONTRARIETY and, for example, EXCREMENT, OBSIDIAN).

conflict Since it results from forces, whether internal or external, pulling in opposite directions, and capable of reaching crisis-point, conflict symbolizes the potential for passing from one extreme to the other and of reversing a tendency towards good or evil – freedom or slavery, sorrow or joy, sickness or health, war or peace, ignorance or wisdom, revenge or forgiveness, separation or reconciliation, depression or elation, guilt or innocence and so on. Its image is the CROSSROADS. Conflict is the symbol of reality and, at the same time, of moral instability due to circumstances or to the personality, as well as to the psychic incoherence, either individual or collective, of those involved.

confluence The symbolism of confluence is related to that of conjoining and the concordance of opposites and is to be found in many myths and images. It bears the meaning of unity restored after division, synthesis after disjunction, the marriage of Heaven and Earth and the resolution of an inhibitive complex.

In Ancient China confluences played an especially important role, ceremonies being performed where the River Lo flowed into the Yellow River and where the Ts'in joined the Wei. Granet maintains that the notion of coming together and of WATERS mingling inspires jousting and sexual rites. To be precise, it is the symbol of exogamy. The Spring rituals recorded in the *Shih-ching* were intended to drive away evil influences, the chief of them being barrenness, the mingling of waters being an example of natural fertilization. The *Tao Te Ching* (ch. 61) associates the notion of the confluence with that of the 'female aspect of the Empire', of receptivity and, if one dare say it, of passive productivity. To play a subordinate part in this context is to set oneself at a point of irresistible convergence, that is, by definition at the CENTRE.

The notion of confluence was equally strongly felt in India where, for example, the junction of the Ganges and the Jumna is celebrated in literature and by pilgrimage to Allahabad. Nor should it be forgotten that Gangā and Yamunā (Jumna) (see RIVER) were the matching companions of Varuna, but that the first was fair and the second dark; that the first was associated with Shiva and the second with Vishnu; and that, lastly, the king of holy rivers married the daughter of the Sun.

The mouths of rivers were also especially holy places since they overpoweringly suggest the return to the primeval undifferentiated state (see SEA). In any case Chuang Tzu maintains that the 'flowing together' of opposites bears the same meaning as their return to the First Cause.

Lastly Coomaraswamy translates as 'confluence' the Buddhist SAMSARA, the delusive 'flux' of phenomena which carry us willy-nilly in the continuous chain of cause and effect (COOH, GRAF, GRAD, SOUP).

constellations Before it ever became the cerebral subject of spherical mathematics, the starry vault was the well-spring of astral mythology. This never claimed the objectivity of astronomy since it was not so much the perception of the heavenly object for its own sake as for the vision of self perceived through it. Nowadays it is known that myths were not brought to Earth after being 'read' in the sky, but emitted from the heart of mankind to inhabit the vaults of Heaven by a process of unconscious 'projection'.

This made Bachelard declare that 'The ZODIAC is the Rorschach Test of the infancy of mankind.' Upon this tapestry of the firmament, embroidered with the thousand and one secrets of human nature, the souls of peoples have scattered a world of objects, such as triangles, trestles, sextants, cups, compasses, scales, lyres or arrows, of specific items such as hair, masts or ships' sails, of such creatures as bees, dogs, crows, chameleons, giraffes, lions or serpents, of such mythic beings as unicorns, dragons, hydras, centaurs or winged horses. Hermeticists assure us that these deified representations confirm our inner reality. They are primitive images of psychic forces projected long ago into Heaven, but still alive to this day in the hearts of mankind and present in its mythologic projections.

As far back as the twelfth century BC constellations bore the same names which they carry today. They were not placed at random in the Heavens. In his *De macrocosmo*, Robert Fludd follows many others in his insistence upon the symbolism of the constellations. The Venerable Bede, the first English encyclopedist, a distant ancestor of reformers of the Julian Calendar and an astrologer, was only too well aware that astrology was the living and seductive expression of Classical paganism and that to teach it was to introduce a Trojan Horse into a monastery. His attempt to Christianize astrology never sought to change the outline of the constellations and his fruitless attempt to substitute for the pagan names of constellations and signs those drawn from the Old and New Testaments would seem to have encountered opposition even from his friends and disciples. He recommended that the Zodiac should be baptized with the names of the twelve Apostles, Aries being called St Peter, Taurus St Andrew and so on. The constellation Lyra was to be called Christ's Crib; Andromeda, the Holy Sepulchre; the Great Dog, David; Hercules, the Three Kings and so on.

Inspired by Bede's example, many others attempted to give the starry skies a Christian baptism, not simply at the level of astrology, but at that of astronomy as well. There is, however, a vast difference between their points of view, and it is this. The astrologer believes that the name Mars, for example, has not been given to that planet by chance but because its influence corresponds exactly with the character of that god. Indeed, for some, the mythological story of Mars is a poetical transposition of the planet's astrological qualities, easily verifiable through drawing horoscopes. On the other hand, to the astronomer, the name could have been given to any planet in our solar system independent of any grounds of this kind. Bede's attempt was, however, far more astrological than astronomic, since he did not distribute his Christian names haphazardly but took care to place the astral influence of each star-sign under a character or Biblical incident appropriate to it. Some of these Christian equivalents are traditional and were not of Bede's invention. Thus, for example, the Children of Israel always associated the constellation Orion with Nimrod, the 'mighty hunter', generally identified with the Babylonian god Marduk.

From antiquity until the eighteenth century European astrologers – and Oriental astrologers to this day – felt duty-bound to use the constellations and fixed stars in conjunction with the signs of the Zodiac. Contemporary Hindu astrologers employ a system based upon an adjustment of the zodiacal constellations. With a few rare exceptions, twentieth-century Western astrologers, when preparing horoscopes, fail to take into account the influence of the constellations.

In Chinese symbolism, constellations form a fundamental element, being the third element of interpretation and affecting the relationship of the first two. The first is the active principle, the power of light called YANG; the second the passive principle or power of darkness, called YIN. It will be observed that the role of these two principles in the interpretation of symbols is in fact primal. A constellation represents the whole body of relationships and links between all differences and all worlds: small wonder, then, that it soon became the Imperial emblem.

For the symbolism of the individual constellations of the Zodiac see ARIES; TAURUS; GEMINI; CANCER; LEO; VIRGO; LIBRA; SCORPIO; SAGITTARIUS; CAPRICORN; AQUARIUS; PISCES.

continent Land-masses hold symbolic meanings which are as much linked with cultural stereotypes as with real-life experience. Europe holds different meanings for the European who lives there, for the American who originated from it, for the African who is freeing himself from its influence, for the Pacific islander, and so on. Stereotypes of the continents have not remained purely and simply products of cultures born of more or less accurate knowledge, more or less lively feelings and more or less clear awareness. They have sunk into the unconscious with so strong an emotional charge as will emerge in dreams or in spontaneous reactions, often linked with unconscious racism. At this point a continent will no longer represent one of the Earth's five land-masses, but will symbolize a world of images, emotions and desires. For example, Dr Verne has clearly shown in the analysis of one of his patients' dreams that she did not regard Asia as a memory of, goal of or desire for intercontinental travel, but as a symbol of 'the return to something holy, to the world of the absolute, the mystery of out of the body experience, the way towards the oneness which bears the message of the true and real'. Asia had become an inner continent, like Africa, Oceania or Europe. These continents and what they symbolize will differ from person to person. This inner dimension may fasten upon any place, be it town or locality; what is important is to know what it means to each individual, what images, feelings, emotions and prejudices it carries, since these comprise the subjective truth of the symbol. Geography generates as much geosociology and geoculture as it does geopolitics.

contrariety This is one of the classic shapes of internal antagonism within the same subject or between different subjects. Such terms as 'contradictory', 'contrary', 'different', 'divergent', 'distinct', 'other', 'complementary' or 'relative' are used to describe a form of antagonism which is more or less exclusive of the other, more or less inclusive of it or co-existent with it, more or less determining or determined and simultaneously homogeneous and heterogeneous. The most advanced modern sciences of physics and biology acknowledge the simultaneous presence of opposite forces within every being or manifestation of energy. Hence the new logic, which is no longer that of mutual exclusivity. These sciences concur with the abiding intuition of symbolic interpretation which has always seen a bipolarity in every symbol: its dark and bright faces, its positive and negative aspects, its variability and its constancy in different lights and in different circumstances.

'To walk when all the world lies sleeping' is an initiatory adage meaning that one should systematically go against all conventional rules in order to set oneself apart from the rest of the group, because one is seeking the other face, the reverse side of things (HAMK p. 23). Similar attitudes may be found in Zen Buddhism and in the 'hunters' of the White Whale.

The analysis of a multiplicity of symbols will produce that 'conjunction of opposites' which is one of the basic principles of symbolism.

copper   Red copper plays a leading role in the symbolic cosmogony of the Dogon of Mali. It represents the fundamental element, WATER, the vital principle of all things; and also light, which radiates from the copper helix wrapped round the Sun; speech, another channel of fertility; and sperm, which covers the walls of the womb.

As the symbol of water, copper is also the symbol of plant life. Hence, as with the Aztecs, so with the Dogon, the colours RED and GREEN are of equal potency, both expressing the life force.

Copper-coloured sunbeams are the paths along which water travels and this is why they can only be seen when they pierce the clouds in dank mists or in storms. They are called 'copper-water'. However, they only change to real copper deep down underground, 'too far below for men to see them'. In the Dogon tribal area there is a mountain especially rich in copper ore and called 'Mount Copper-water'. The souls of the dead are supposed to go there to collect their supply of copper, in other words, water, before they make their long journey towards the land of the dead, lying to the south. Since copper is water, those who wear copper ornaments avoid walking on the banks of rivers for fear of drowning (GRIH, GRIS, GRIE).

Similar beliefs exist among the Dogon's neighbours, the Bambara who, like them, believe in a demiurge who is lord both of water and of speech. This almighty god, Faro, controls the world in its present shape and is also lord of the seven metals, among which are numbered red and YELLOW copper, the former male, the latter female. Copper comes from the fifth Heaven, the red heaven of blood, fire, war and divine justice. It comes down to Earth as LIGHTNING and digs its way into the ground with stone axes (THUNDERBOLTS). It represents speech in its divine essence; it is 'the sound of Faro', the god wrapping himself in the helical copper earrings which the Bambara wear, in order to enter the eardrum. In the ground, copper corresponds to the 'second waters', the red waters reflecting the fifth Heaven, in which Faro drowns the guilty. Like the Dogon water-god, Faro is depicted as having a human torso and a fish's tail, but with this difference, the tail is red copper, not green. Faro wears two necklaces which enable him to overhear everything said by human beings. His copper necklace tells him their everyday conversation, while his GOLD necklace tells him their 'hidden words of power', gold in some way being a concentration of red copper (DIEB).

In Russian beliefs, copper has always been associated with the colour green. The 'Mistress of the Copper Mountain' (Ural) has green eyes and wears a malachite dress. She sometimes appears in the shape of a green lizard and malachite is supposed to display 'all the beauties of the Earth'. Like gold, copper is associated with the mythic SERPENT. You may meet the Mistress of the Copper Mountain on the night of the snake-festival (25 September), but such an encounter is fatal. Whoever sees her is doomed to die of longing.

coral As an undersea tree, coral shares the symbolism of the TREE (World AXIS) and of deep WATER (origin of the world). Its red colour makes it akin to blood: its shape is twisted. All these marks make it a symbol of the BOWELS.

According to the Greek legend, coral sprang from drops of blood spilled by Medusa, one of the GORGONS. That is to say, that when Perseus cut off Medusa's head, the head itself became coral while Pegasus was born from the spouting blood. This agrees with the internal dialectic of symbols if it is remembered that Medusa's head had the power of turning to stone whoever gazed on it.

The symbolism of coral is based as much upon its colour as upon its rare property of combining in its own nature the three animal, vegetable and mineral kingdoms.

In Classical antiquity coral was used as an amulet, a preservative against the evil eye. It was also believed to act as a coagulant to stop bleeding and to preserve against lightning.

Middle Irish literature uses red coral (called *partaing*, a word of doubtful derivation, perhaps from *particus*) in similes of woman's beauty, and chiefly her lips. In the Celtic world it does not apparently share the martial symbolism of the colour red, although there is archaeological evidence for the use of coral to decorate helmets and shields during the Second Iron Age. Thereafter, supplies of coral failed and Celts substituted a red enamel of their own invention.

Central European goldsmiths frequently employed coral in its natural shapes from the sixteenth to the eighteenth centuries when, in combination with precious metals, it gave rise to all sorts of monsters and mythical beings, the creatures of an innate imagination and fantasy.

cornucopia See HORN OF PLENTY.

cosmogony The story of the CREATION of the world is a wealth of symbols. Every religion and every cultural level has its own theories and its own myths about the origins of the universe and the birth of the world. Existence suddenly springing out of nothingness, or the sudden appearance of the cosmos, cannot be susceptible to historical study because it was, by definition, unwitnessed. The only reality which can be grasped is the result of that creation, the creature and not the act of creation itself. If all birth is holy, how much more so absolute birth. Its description can only take the shape of a MYTH springing from human imagination, or of a revelation by the Creator himself. However, these myths are forced by their mode of expression to set within a time-frame what, by the very nature of existence, escapes the bounds of time. They are compelled to force the superhuman into a human mould. They cannot fail to be deceptive and yet they are not devoid of meaning and of truth. They tell us about mankind and its conceptualization of the explosion of life. Cosmogonies express a universal

feeling of transcendence, that is to say an attribution of the cosmos to a
being or to beings outside the cosmos. This is, however, simply to change
one problem, that of origins, for another, that of transcendence. This is why
they may be said to talk essentially the inner language of symbols and this
cannot be rationally nor unequivocally translated.

Some cosmogonies begin, not with nothingness, but with CHAOS. Earth,
Water and darkness have pre-existed from all eternity, but a power intervenes to produce order and light. The problem here is less one of origins
than of the originating principle. More often than not this principle is
identified with BREATH, with the spirit or with the WORD. This, however, is
not the place to analyse all these cosmogonies, suffice to say that from the
general point of view they correspond to a human plan of action. They
provide the pattern which mankind can follow to imagine how its energies
may be deployed and to attempt to bring its own schemes to fruition. 'Cosmogony', Mircea Eliade writes,

is the perfect pattern for whatever requires 'doing'. This is not just because the
Cosmos is the ideal archetype both of all creative situations and of all created
things, but also because the Cosmos is the work of God. Hence it is made holy
in its very structure. By extension, all that is perfect, complete, harmonious or
fruitful, in short, all that is 'cosmosized', all that is like a cosmos, is holy. To do
something well, to craft, to build, to create, construct, fashion, shape, form, all
simply mean that something has been brought into existence, has been given
life and, in the last resort, made to resemble that pre-eminently harmonious
organism, the Cosmos. Therefore the Cosmos, let it be said once more, is the
pattern created by the gods, their masterpiece.

(SOUD pp. 474-5)

On the other hand, Jung observes that all cosmogonies imply some idea
of sacrifice. Shaping material is sharing in primeval energy to change it.
This cannot be done without a struggle. Cosmogonies always contain battles between gods, or between giants, gigantic upheavals in which gods and
heroes are dismembered, crush and kill one another, raise great mountain
ranges or pour oceans into the abyss. Life and order only arise from chaos
and death. These contrarieties are TWINS or the two faces, bright and dark
of all contingent being. Destruction is the foundation of all progress. Change
is simultaneously birth and death. The general law that sacrifice regenerates
is another aspect of cosmogony. Often in cruel, barbarous or monstrous
shape it illustrates and symbolizes this law of energy.

covenant The word 'covenant' (Hebrew: *berith*) has the sense of a contract or still more of a compact made in respect of a person or group of
persons. Both senses of the word are to be found in the Greek *diatheke* and
syntheke and in the Latin *foedus* and *testamentum* – hence Old and New
Testament for Old and New Covenant. The Old Covenant is applied to the
undertaking which God gave to Abraham; this was preceded by the covenant between God and Noah after the Flood, of which the external sign
was the RAINBOW, just as the Passover LAMB was to be the sign of the covenant with Moses. It may be said of the covenant sealed by the sign of the
rainbow that it was a divine revelation which corresponded by its nature
with the covenant with Noah. The continuance of this covenant did not

depend upon the faithfulness of an individual or of a people, God kept his compact regardless of the attitudes of the other parties. Israel knew this and this is why God was asked to remember his covenant.

In his analysis of the meaning of the Covenant, Jean Daniélou (DANA p. 38) makes the point that the covenant is symbolized by the division of a sacrificial victim. The Lord commanded Abraham to take a heifer, a goat, a ram, a turtle-dove and a pigeon and to cut them in half. Between the severed carcasses ran a flame of fire, the sign of the covenant which unites what was divided and which shares in the same blood. In the New Covenant, the victim was to be Christ and the sign the Eucharist. In this way covenant followed covenant, not destroying its predecessors but taking on their obligations.

cow (see also BULL) Generally speaking cows, as milk-producers, are symbols of Mother Earth. In Ancient Egypt the cow Ahet was the origin of all manifestations and mother of the Sun. In the Osirian mysteries the god's body was enclosed within a wooden cow and was reborn through its gestation. The Ahat amulet depicting the head of the sacred cow with a solar disk between its horns was used to transmit 'warmth' into mummified bodies. This custom arose from the belief that when the Sun, Ra, dropped for the first time below the horizon, the cow-goddess sent fiery beings to succour him until morning so that he did not lose his heat (MARA p. 79). Wallis-Budge (BUDA p. 149) on the other hand notes that the custom of women in the most primitive tribes in the Nile Valley was to wear an amulet depicting the goddess Hathor in the shape either of a cow's head or of a woman with long flat ears like a cow's, in order to ensure their own fertility.

In the Ancient Egyptian pantheon the figure of Hathor sums up all these different aspects of the symbol of the cow. She was fertility, wealth, rebirth, the Mother, heavenly mother of the Sun, 'young calf of the pure mouth', and also wife of the Sun, 'bull of his own mother'. She was nurse of the King of Egypt; she was the very essence of rebirth and the hope of survival since she was 'ruler and indeed the body of the sky, the living soul of trees' (POSD p. 117). She was in all those places which the Greeks regarded as 'cities of Aphrodite'. She was a charming young woman, the smiling 'goddess of joy, music and dance'. It is easy to see why the hopes which were realized each Spring on Earth should be projected into the Otherworld and that she should have become, both at Memphis and at Thebes, on the right bank of the Nile, 'mistress of the mountains of the dead'. The Mesopotamians' 'Great Mother' or 'Great Cow' was also to all appearances a fertility-goddess.

In Sumer, depiction of the symbol which associates the cow with the MOON, with the HORN and with plenty is even more sharply defined. Here the Moon was decorated with a pair of cow's horns, while the cow itself was depicted as a crescent Moon. The starry night is 'dominated by the mighty Bull whose fertile cow is the Full Moon, and whose herd is the Milky Way.' In some contexts it would seem as if the Sumerians had conceived the strange picture of moonlight as a jet of the Moon Cow's milk.

'Among the Ancient Germans the milch-cow, Audumla, was the first companion of Ymir, the first giant, born like him from melted ice. She was

the ancestress of all living things and the symbol of fertility.... Like
Audumla, Ymir existed before the gods' (MYTF p. 40).

This same symbolism extends to all Indo-European peoples and has
retained its full force in India. Hence the veneration paid to this animal,
nowhere more eloquently expressed than in the Vedas where it plays a
divine and cosmic role as archetype of maternal fecundity. Cows are CLOUDS
swollen with fertilizing RAIN which falls to Earth when the spirits of the
wind – who are the souls of the dead – kill the heavenly animal. They eat
it, only to bring it to life again in its own skin which they have first flayed.
A symbol of the cloud containing the WATERS of Heaven, the cow which is
dismembered in Heaven is made whole upon Earth thanks to the rich crops
provided by the rain. Cows therefore play a part similar to the role of the
GOAT and the RAM in innumerable other mythologies of peoples and tribes
from Scandinavia to the River Niger.

In addition to acting as the container – or well-spring – of the waters of
Heaven, cows often were given the task of guiding the souls of the dead, as
Vedic tradition bears witness. Cows were brought to the bedsides of the
dying who, with their last reserves of strength, clutched the creature's tail.
The corpse was then taken to the funeral pyre on a cart drawn by cows and
followed by a black cow. The latter was sacrificed, its flesh laid on the
corpse and both laid on the pyre, carefully wrapped in the victim's hide.
The pyre was lighted and the mourners chanted a hymn begging the cow
to rise up with the deceased along the Milky Way to the kingdom of the
blessed (MANG pp. 49–50).

There were variations in this ritual, the cow which was to conduct the
dead person's soul being sometimes tethered to his left foot and at others
being replaced by an unspotted goat. The cow would be sacrificed at the
foot of the funeral pyre and the best pieces ritually laid upon the corpse,
with the kidneys sometimes placed in the hands of the deceased, while the
mourners chanted.

It should be emphasized at this point how strongly the animal's colouring,
its 'coat', defines some aspect or other of the symbol. For this black cow –
undoubtedly an avatar (incarnation) of the 'hidden cow' of the Vedas, which
corresponds to primeval dawn – may also be found in the *Tao Te Ching*
(ch. 6) as an epithet for the 'mysterious woman', the Female Principle, the
'origin of Heaven and Earth'. Again in the Vedas, the 'spotted milch-cow'
is a symbol of the original HERMAPHRODITE, while the white cow – the all-
embracing embodiment of the symbol – is, like the black cow, related to
sacrificial fire (*agnihotra*). But *agnihotra* is also sacrifice of the WORD and
'cows' are the sacred formulae of the Vedas. Perhaps it is an echo of the
Upanishads which makes some Zen Buddhist scriptures closely associate
the cow with the gradual process which leads to Enlightenment. However,
the ascetic is no longer the 'cow-herd', the *gopāla*, worshipper of Krishna,
nor is the cow itself light, as it sometimes is in Hinduism. It represents
human nature and its potentiality for enlightenment and is depicted in the
'Ten pictures of the Taming of the Cow' as passing by stages from black to
white. When the 'white cow' itself vanished, the human being had escaped
the limitations of individual being (DANA, HERV, LIOT, MALA, SILI,
SOUN, SOUL).

cowrie   More than that of any other sea-SHELL, the shape of the cowrie calls to mind a woman's sexual organs, whence its symbolism, associated with notions of fertility, wealth and good fortune. From Malaysia, from which they originate, cowrie-shells were for centuries articles of a lively trade first in the Far East and then in Black Africa, where they were widely used as small change. However they provided both artistic inspiration and use in propitiatory and other forms of magic, mainly in Africa, where they continue to be used as bodily ornaments and lucky charms. 'Their use in art is unlimited – masks, dance costumes, necklaces and hair-styles are all decorated with cowrie-shells .... Like money they arouse all the passions' (MVEA p. 63).

coyote   A cunning and unlucky creature, which, in the cosmogonic legends of the Californian Indians, hinders the activities of the heroes responsible for the creation and is itself responsible for all that is evil entering it (KRIE p. 73). It stands in exactly the same relation to the hero (the silver FOX) as does the bad TWIN to the good twin in Iroquois cosmogony. Notably, it was responsible for the creation of Winter and of death (KRIR pp. 314–16).

crab   Like so many other water creatures the crab, paradoxically, is linked in myth with drought and the Moon. In China it is associated with the myth of Nu Chou, who was burned up by the Sun. Crabs were the food of the Spirits of Drought. Their growth was linked with the phases of the Moon. In Thailand they were among a number of WATER-creatures used in RAIN-making ceremonies and were believed to accompany the guardian of 'the Waters' end' at the mouth of the cosmic cavern.

In India the crab is the emblem of the zodiacal sign of CANCER, which corresponds with the Summer solstice and marks the star of the Sun's descendant. In some parts of China it is also called *Pao-pu Tzu*, the sign of the fifth hour of the day. Both cases establish links between the crab and the solar cycle. The crab is a lucky symbol for Cambodians and to dream of catching a crab is to see all one's wishes fulfilled.

According to T'ang literary sources, crabs were sometimes called *koei* (crafty or mischievous), no doubt from their sideways walk. One may quote, simply as a reminder, the trivial symbolism of the 'basket of crabs' (BELT, GRAD, GUES, MASR, PORA), associated with its sideways scuttling and greedy claws.

Bengali Munda tradition makes the crab, after the tortoise, to be the first demiurge despatched by the Sun, supreme deity and husband of the Moon, to fetch the Earth up from the bottom of the sea (ELIT p. 130).

According to a myth from the Andaman Islands, the first man drowned in a creek while hunting. He changed himself into a water-creature and capsized the boat in which his woman had set out in search of him. She, too, drowned and went down to join him, changed into a crab (SCHP p. 162).

The crab is an avatar (incarnation) of transcendent vital forces, originating, more often than not, in the Underworld, but sometimes in the sky. The red crab of Melanesia which revealed magic to mankind is one example of the latter, while the mythic crab on the ocean bed which causes storms when it moves, is a typically chthonian figure and relates this creature to such important animals which carry the Earth on their backs as the tortoise, crocodile and elephant.

Crabs are lunar symbols. From classical antiquity their images have been associated with that of the Moon and, together with the lobster, it is depicted on the trump card, 'the MOON', in the Tarot pack, 'because these creatures, just like the Moon, sometimes move forwards and sometimes backwards' (RIJT p. 180).

In Africa, some Machica statues are decorated with a crab, symbolizing evil or the spirit of evil.

cradle Whether it is carved from a tree-trunk in Ancient Roman style, or is a plain wicker BASKET, a cradle is a symbol of the mother's breast and is its complement. Soft and warm, it is an essential element in the protection of the baby and it abides as a memory of one's beginnings, stimulating an unconscious yearning for a return to the WOMB, while its rocking motion is associated with a sense of total security. It is as strongly associated with travel, and this is why the cradle is shaped like a boat or the gondola of an airship. It is a womb which floats the air or sails the seas and which instills security as it travels the world.

crane In the West, the crane is generally regarded as a symbol of clumsiness and stupidity, doubtless from the bird's awkward, one-legged stance. In China, however, a far different conclusion was reached. The legendary crane which belonged to the philosopher Leonicus Thomaeus and which was commemorated by Buffon, suggests that constant of Far Eastern symbolism, longevity, and, above all, unrivalled faithfulness. Even more significant was the Crane Dance performed by Theseus after his escape from the Labyrinth and of which parallels existed in China. Cranes being migratory birds, the dance undoubtedly relates to the cyclical aspect of the ordeal of the Labyrinth. In Ancient China the Crane Dance suggested the power of flight and consequently of reaching the Isle of the Immortals. Humans on stilts copied the dance. Indeed, the crane may, like the tortoise, be the symbol of longevity, but it is supremely the Taoist symbol of immortality. The Japanese believed that cranes (*zuru*) lived for thousands of years and old people were often given as presents paintings or prints of cranes, tortoises and pine-trees, all three symbols of longevity. According to Ancient Egyptian tradition, during the reign of the son of Manes a two-headed crane was seen over the Nile and this was taken as presaging an era of prosperity.

Cranes were supposed to live a thousand years and to practise a breathing technique which was something to be copied. Their WHITE feathers were symbols of purity, while their CINNABAR-red heads showed the endurance of their vital forces, concentrations of *yang*. Furthermore, cranes were the customary steeds of the Immortals and their eggs were used to prepare drugs to confer immortality. The annual return of the crane was a symbol of regeneration, and this is why it was associated with PLUM-blossom as an emblem of Spring. Its cinnabar crest associates it with the alchemist's FURNACE and specifically with its fire. Indeed the Pi-fang bird, resembling a one-legged crane, is a fire-spirit. It foretells outbreaks of fire (see STORK).

In India, cranes were seen in a completely different light and doubtless from some idiosyncracy in their behaviour were symbols of treachery. The crane-headed goddess, Balgalā-mukhī, is the deceiver, the embodiment of sadistic and destructive instincts (CHRC, DANA, BELT, GRAD, KALL).

In the traditions of their initiation ceremonies the Bambara regard the crested crane as being at the birth of speech. Their secret doctrine declares: 'The beginning of all beginning of the word was the crested crane. The bird said: I speak.' The crested crane, it is explained 'combines in its plumage, its call and its mating dance the three basic characteristics of the word – beauty [it is supposed to be the most beautiful of birds], sound [it is held to be the only bird which inflects its call] and movement [its mating dance is an unforgettable sight].' This is why mankind is supposed to have learned to speak by copying it. But the real reason why this bird is so highly regarded is that Africans are convinced that it is aware of its own gifts – and indeed it looks as though it is – and that it possesses self-knowledge. It is therefore by reason of being the symbol of self-contemplation that the crested crane was at the birth of the Word of God and of the knowledge which mankind has of God. Their implicit, intuitive reasoning is as follows, that man never knew the 'word' relating to God until he knew himself. This presupposes that knowledge of God derives from self-knowledge. Such would seem to be the deep symbolism of the crested crane (THOM).

In the Celtic world, wading birds, of which cranes and HERONS were the main representatives, were sometimes deliberately contrasted with SWANS, and this nearly always in a bad light and as creatures to be guarded against. However, in some parts of Germany the crane played a religious role. Alive or in effigy it was sacred to a god who fulfilled much the same duties as Hermes, the messenger.

creation Creation symbolizes the end of CHAOS through the introduction into the universe of a degree of shape, of order and of hierarchy. Pascal says: 'Invention may simply be characterized as order.'

Invention is the perception of a new order and of new relationships between different basic elements, while creation is realization of this order through the infusion of energy. Without summarizing the many different cosmogonies, they all describe the work of a creator either preceding or following Chaos. Chaos is only the first phase: an elemental and undifferentiated mass which the spirit penetrates by giving it shape. Creation, in the strict sense of *a nihilo*, is the act which brings this chaos into existence. As it evolves, time begins, but the creative action is itself outside time. In the wider sense, the act of creation is energy which rearranges the first shapeless data – creation being the effects of that energy. In some cosmogonies this world precedes creation and the latter is conceived as a First Cause giving separate shape to things, or as an energy which awakens shapes locked in the primeval magma.

Traditional hieroglyphics, attributed to the Ancient Egyptians, depict the main aspects of creation as FOUR geometric figures: the SPIRAL, to indicate cosmic energy breathed in by the creating spirit; the squared spiral, to indicate that energy at work in the heart of the universe; as shapeless a mass as possible, like some shadowy CLOUD, to indicate primeval Chaos;

and a SQUARE, representing the orderly world, firmly based upon the four CARDINAL POINTS.

After the act of creation, a distinction is generally drawn between the two forces, one immanent in matter, the other transcendent. The former is matter itself suffused with creative energy and tending spontaneously to produce constantly differentiated shapes. The latter is creative energy continuing its work and sustaining it in being, the world being conceived as a continuous creation.

No Celtic mythological source describes the creation of the world directly. However, often enough it is a matter of some primordial being, god, hero or heroine, who clears the first field or fields, causes lakes to well up and rivers to flow and simultaneously bears or fathers a host of descendants. Thus Ireland underwent five mythic invasions and each time fresh fields, new lakes and fresh rivers came into existence bearing the names of their creators. Chaos was annihilated, making it possible for mankind to settle, stock to be raised, hunting to take place and finally a culture to be established. Slight as it is, the symbolism of this aspect is akin to that of WATER and the PLAIN. To the underlying notions of the creation of the world may be linked the theme of the Battle of Mag Tuired between the gods, the Tuatha Dé Danann representing the ordered, hierarchical society of gods and men, and the FOMORIANS, an image of Chaos and the world before Genesis (LEBI).

cremation Cremation is the symbol of total sublimation, destroying what is inferior to cut a path towards what is superior. In mythology, tradition and even in ALCHEMY, passing through the FURNACE determines the rise to a higher plane of existence.

The *Scholiae Bernenses* may be treating myth as historical record when they mention a Celtic rite of sacrificial cremation. 'They appease Jupiter Taranis in the following manner. They burn a certain number of men in a wooden cage.' This is confirmed by Caesar in his *De bello gallico*. 'Others have great willow baskets in human shape which they fill with living men. These they set alight and the men perish in the flames.' Nothing similar is known from Irish sources except for the myth of the iron house which was heated until it was red-hot and in which the Ulates were treacherously locked in the tale, *The Drunkenness of the Ulates*. There is a similar myth of Branwen the daughter of Llyr in the Welsh *Mabinogion* (OGAC 7: pp. 34, 35; CELT 2: *passim*).

The symbolism of sublimation and of purification displays an equally strong 'ascensional' character and this should not be ignored. This is what accounts for the fundamental meaning of cremation in so many funeral rites – the immortal soul purged by FIRE of its enveloping flesh flies heavenwards – as well as all forms of prayer and invocation in which a message is freed and launched towards the godhead by means of fire. In this context one should compare the ceremonies of the CALUMET of the North American Indians in which SMOKE rises up to carry to the gods a message from mankind; the Buddhist rite by which prayers, generally written on expensive paper, silk or even silver and gold, are burned; or the burning of *sapek* paper money: rites in which invocation, prayers and offerings are sure to reach the godhead because they have been purged of matter and reduced to their absolute spiritual reality by virtue of fire. This may be confirmed visually since Indian tobacco like Buddhist prayers dissolves in smoke.

Analytic interpretation of the myth confirms the general symbolic meaning of cremation – what inhibits elevation be it internal or external is burned. If these barriers which are burned are internal, an inner perfection is the result: if external antagonisms are destroyed then external forces are strengthened. Similarly with sacrifices: external sacrifice achieves only ritual purification: internal sacrifice – burning one's own incubi – personal purity.

crescent The crescent is one of the shapes which best characterizes the phases of the Moon and is the symbol both of changing shape and of return to the same shape. It is associated with the symbolism of the female, passive and 'watery' principle.

Classical antiquity identified ARTEMIS (Diana) with the Moon and often depicted this 'goddess of the night, glory of the stars, protectress of forests' either holding a crescent Moon or wearing one in her hair. Lucina, a Roman goddess whom Cicero identifies with Diana, presided at childbirth. She, too, wore a crescent Moon in her hair. Since she was goddess of chastity as well, the crescent Moon symbolized both birth and chastity, with the dual aspect, light and dark, of the latter. It should also be observed that Our Lady is often compared with the Moon in Christian litanies and, in Christian iconography, is depicted as standing upon a crescent Moon.

In various Muslim countries, the crescent Moon is accompanied by a STAR and is apparently the image of PARADISE. Even in the depths of the Maghreb, the tombs of the saints come in shapes which are lent a wealth of symbolic value. Among these symbols the crescent Moon is to be found. 'Their square foundations symbolize Earth and the body; their domes – sometimes, as in the M'zab, elongated into a cone – represent the passive aspect of the soul; on the summit the star and crescent embody the triple flame of the spirit' (SERH p. 73). René Guénon considers that the crescent shares in the symbolism of the CHALICE as well.

It is also a symbol of resurrection to Muslims:

Although it comes close to it, the crescent is not a finished shape, unlike the closed CIRCLE. Muslim theologians say that the crescent is both open and closed, both expansion and contraction. At the very moment when they close upon one another, the horns stop and reveal an opening. Similarly mankind is not imprisoned in the perfection of God's plan . . . . The sign of the crescent is pre-eminently regarded as an emblem of resurrection. Just as it seems to close in and stifle, so an outlet appears giving on to free and boundless space. Thus death would seem to close upon mankind, but the latter is born again in another and infinite dimension. That is why the sign of the crescent is set upon tombs. In the symbolism of the Arabic alphabet, the letter 'n', shaped exactly like a crescent as the arc of a circle with a dot above it, is also the letter of resurrection. Prayers for the dead are written in verses which chiefly rhyme with the letter 'n'. The letter is pronounced *nun* in Arabic and this also means 'fish'.
(BAMC p. 135)

Again, in a parable in the Koran, the fish is a symbol of eternal life.

The crescent was the emblem of the Ottoman Turks and, after the Crusades, was adopted by most Muslim countries, many of which still bear this sign on their national flags (Pakistan, United Arab Republic, Tunisia, Turkey and so on). Initially infrequent, this growing use has gradually regained a symbolic quality similar to that of the Cross of Christendom. 'Thus the Islamic equivalent of the Red Cross is generally the Red Crescent' (RODL).

cricket The cricket, which lays its eggs in the soil, lives underground as a larva and emerges to change into the imago, was to the Chinese the three-fold symbol of life, death and resurrection. Just as they regarded its presence by the hearth as a promise of good fortune, so did the peoples of the Mediterranean civilizations. However, what sets the Chinese apart is the fact that they specially bred singing crickets which they kept near them in little golden cages or in less elaborate boxes, even going so far as to arrange fights between crickets (BEUA pp. 93–8).

crocodile The crocodile, which carries the Earth on its back, is a divinity of darkness and the Moon, whose greed is like that of the NIGHT which each evening devours the Sun. From civilization to civilization and from age to age the crocodile exhibits a high proportion of the countless links in that basic symbolic chain which belongs to the controlling forces of death and rebirth. The crocodile may be a formidable figure, but this is because, like all expressions of the power of fate, what he displays is inevitable – darkness falling so that daylight may return, death striking so that life may be reborn.

While the West emphasizes the creature's greed and makes it the symbol of treachery and hypocrisy, in Chinese mythology the crocodile was the inventor of singing and the drum and therefore plays some part in the rhythm and harmony of the world. The same source mentions a crocodile which produced a flash of light. Cambodian legends, too, associate crocodiles with the glitter of jewels and diamonds. In these instances its symbolism is linked with that of LIGHTNING, traditionally associated with that of RAIN.

For the crocodile relates naturally to WATER, perhaps because it was its creator, perhaps because it was its ruler. In India it is the steed of the Mantra Vam, the seminal word of Water. Iconographically the distinction is not always drawn between it and the MAKARA, the steed of Varuna, 'Lord of the Waters'. In popular legend and belief in Cambodia, the King of Earth and Water is not the NAGA of Angkor, but its exact homophone and homologue, the *nak*, or crocodile. The Cambodian Kron Pali, the *asura* Bali, 'Lord of the Earth', was a crocodile.

The 'crocodile banner', used in Cambodian funeral ceremonies, may also be compared with the legend of Kron Pali. At all events it reminds us that Pali rules the Underworld and this in turn must be compared with the attribution by the Ancient Egyptians of the crocodile to Set – the Greek TYPHON – 'symbol of darkness and death'. Crocodiles are in any case associated with the kingdom of the dead in many Asian countries (DANA, GRAD, GUES, PORA, SOUN).

The Pueblo-Mixtec and the Aztecs believed that a crocodile which lived in the primeval ocean gave birth to the Earth, and in the Codex Borgia, the crocodile is depicted as the symbol of Earth (KRIR p. 62). In one of the manuscripts of the *Chilam Balam*, 'the Crocodile of the House of Running Waters' is one of the names given to the Celestial DRAGON which will disgorge the flood at the end of the world.

In a Maya version of the creation myth, the great primeval crocodile bears the Earth in a CONCH-shell on its back.

A chthonian deity, the crocodile seems often to have replaced the JAGUAR as lord of the Underworld. As such, it was often associated with WATER-LILIES.

When the lunar aspect predominates, the crocodile becomes a symbol of abundance, often depicted in Maya glyptics with the sign 'u' – the sign for the Moon – over its head, or else sprouting water-lilies or maize shoots. In other instances, plants sprout from its nose composed of shells. In Maya mythology the crocodile, like the Aztec jaguar, stands guard at the ends of the four roads and in this instance it is often two-headed and may be replaced by SERPENTS or LIZARDS (THOH). In Maya glyptics the association of crocodiles with gaping jaws further emphasizes their relationship with the jaguar, the jaws of Earth which devour the Sun. The connection of crocodiles and jaws is associated throughout the world with their role in intitiation.

In many South American Indian myths the crocodile is also seen as a substitute for the jaguar as an embodiment of the powers of the Underworld. Its opponent is generally the turtle (LEVC). The crocodile, and its complement the jaguar, parallels the complementary relationships of fire and water, of which they are the avatars (embodiments) or masters.

The ancestor-crocodile of the fourth and most recent social class among the Melanesians also has a serpent as surrogate (MALM).

The deep significance of the crocodile in rites of initiation is nowhere better illustrated than by the Poro Society of Liberia. When summoned to celebrate the rites (of circumcision) by which they become adults, boys vanish into retreat in the forest for anything up to four years. During this period they are said to have died, eaten by the Poro or 'crocodile-spirit'. They are then regarded as passing through a new period of gestation at the end of which – and if, as is sometimes the case, they have not really died in the interim – they are 'cast out' by the Poro, minus their foreskins. They are then said to have been born a second time, bearing the scars which are the Poro's teeth-marks. This is somewhat reminiscent of the *vagina dentata* and Bruno Bettelheim, in discussing this custom, mentions a patient of Dr Abraham who compared the vagina with a crocodile's jaws, 'evidence that in our day Westerners can produce similar fantasies' (BETB p. 140).

In Ancient Egyptian mythology, the crocodile Sobek, who stood greedily watching the weighing of souls, was called 'the Devourer'. He would swallow the souls who were unable to plead their cause and who would become mere EXCREMENT in his bowels. When driving flocks and herds across fords, recourse was had to many different magical practices to escape crocodiles which were even celebrated, no doubt in mockery, in song as the 'beauties of the stream'. Temples were dedicated to the crocodile which even had a city in the lake region, Crocodilopolis, named after it. 'Who didst rise from the primordial waters', the crocodile was invoked as 'bull of bulls, great male being', a fertility-god who was simultaneously aquatic, chthonian and solar. In fact, he was pictured rising from the waters like the Sun at morning and eating the fishes which were considered the Sun's enemies. Sacred crocodiles were tamed and hung with jewels (POSD).

On the other hand, in other regions of Egypt, crocodiles were looked upon as monsters. Hieroglyphs betray this difference of feeling and belief and at the same time explain it in part. The crocodile's eyes stand for the dawn; his jaws for murder, and his tail for darkness and death.

Plutarch (*De Iside et Osiride* 75) regarded the crocodile as a symbol of the godhead, but the reasons which he offers are some of the feeblest in all sacred hermeneutics.

In the Old Testament the crocodile, in the guise of LEVIATHAN, is described as one of the monsters of primeval CHAOS (Job 40: 25; 41: 26).

In any case this is the image which predominates in dreams, at least so far as Westerners are concerned. 'In so far as its meaning goes, the crocodile is closely akin to the dragon, but it enshrines a life which is far older still, far less feeling and capable of destroying human life without a qualm. It is a negative symbol, for it expressess the dark and aggressive attitude of the collective unconscious' (AEPR p. 275).

Its role as intermediary between Earth and Water makes the crocodile a symbol of fundamental contradictions. It wallows in the mud which nourishes a wealth of plant life and is a fertility symbol. However, it darts from the water and the reeds to devour and destroy and in this context becomes a devil of malignancy, the symbol of natural viciousness. In fertility and in cruelty it is the image of death and assumes the office of conductor of souls, the dead in Ancient Egypt being sometimes depicted as crocodiles. It has a family resemblance to prehistoric dinosaurs and legendary dragons and in this respect is lord of the mysteries of life and death, the great initiator, symbol of hidden knowledge, light which sometimes blinds and sometimes is in eclipse.

Cronos (see also SATURN; OURANOS)   Cronos, youngest of the TITANS, brought the first generation of gods to an end by castrating his father, Ouranos (Uranus). To prevent himself from being dethroned by his children in his turn, as his parents had predicted, he ate them as soon as they were born. Rhea, who was both his wife and sister, fled to Crete to give birth to ZEUS and in place of the child, gave Cronos a stone to eat. On reaching manhood, Zeus gave his father a drug which made him disgorge all the children he had eaten and with their help he bound him in chains, mutilated him and inaugurated a second generation of gods.

Cronos was often confused with Time (Chronos), of which Classical mythologists made him the embodiment. As so often happens, although such explanations may be based upon a play on words, they do contain a grain of truth. Although Cronos may not be identical with Chronos, he played the same role as time – as well as generating, he destroyed. He devoured his own offspring. By castrating Ouranos he dried up the wells of life, but by impregnating Rhea made himself such a well. He symbolizes a hungry greed for life, a longing which cannot be satisfied. Furthermore, with him there begins the realization of the passing of time and, more precisely, 'of the passage of time between the wish and its fulfilment' (DIES p. 115). He also symbolizes the fear aroused by thoughts of an heir, a successor, or a replacement – the Cronos Complex, the opposite to the OEDIPUS Complex.

Robert Graves believed that Classical identification of Cronos with Chronos was not simply a matter of word-play.

The later Greeks read 'Cronus' as *Chronos*, 'Father Time' with his relentless sickle. But he is pictured in the company of a crow, like Apollo, Asclepius, Saturn, and the early British god Bran; and *cronos* probably means 'crow', like the Latin *cornix* and the Greek *corōne*. The crow [see RAVEN] was an oracular bird, supposed to house the soul of the sacred king after his sacrifice.

(GRAM 6: 2)

This theory would liken the castration of Cronos to a sacrificial rite, while the mutilated god, turned into a bird, would consequently symbolize the sublimation of the instincts.

Graves also relates Hesiod's account of the myth to the struggles between the pre-Hellenic inhabitants of Greece with the Hellenic invaders from the north. During that period, castration was currently practised. The castration of Ouranos, like that of Cronos, in the context of contemporary history and society 'is not necessarily metaphorical if some of the invaders had originated in East Africa where, to this day, Galla warriors carry a miniature sickle into battle to castrate their enemies; there are close affinities between East African religious rites and those of early Greece' (GRAM 6: 1).

'In Orphic religious tradition, Cronos was depicted as freed from his chains, reconciled with Zeus and living in the Isles of the Blessed. It is this reconciliation with Zeus, in which Cronos is regarded as the good king, the first to rule over Heaven and Earth, which has produced legends of a Golden Age' (GRID p. 105a). However, it was only after his ordeal and his castration that Cronos, like the Roman Saturn later, was to play the part of the good king of a legendary country in a legendary time. When mankind became evil, with its races of bronze and iron, Cronos left them and retired to Heaven. Nevertheless, Hesiod's version is somewhat different since it is before his misfortunes that Cronos rules over the Golden Age so idyllically depicted in the *Works and Days*.

However, at whatever stage Cronos ruled during a Golden Age, whether it was before or after his castration, the quality of the symbol remains unaltered. Cronos is the ruler unable to adapt to social development and change in life-style. While he may well desire his subjects' peace and prosperity in a Golden Age, he must be sole ruler, rejecting all thought of a successor and knowing no social structure but the one of his choice. In order to be transformed, society must rebel and Cronos either be castrated by his son or return to Heaven. In other words, either he is expelled or he refuses to obey any structure other than the one which he has chosen and conceived. He is the complete picture of blind and stubborn conservatism. He, in his turn, is defeated and, if his memory is linked with that of a Golden Age, it is because the latter occupies an ideal slot in the passage of time into which is packed the realization of all dreams and when time itself must of necessity stand still. It is a contradiction of the meaning of time, a halt to the inexorable advance of evolution, a stop to death. Cronos is the perfect ruler of this perfect period of stagnation. Of course this Paradise is self-sufficient, it ought to be satisfactory and nobody should want to leave it. However, fresh individuals arrive with their potential for innovation and confrontation and with their own temptations to develop their power and freedom to the full. This Cronos cannot allow and it dooms him to inevitable defeat. He loses his power, in other words, is castrated.

Plutarch in his *De defectu oraculorum* 18, describes the mysterious islands of the HYPERBOREANS where Cronos sleeps, guarded by Briareus. He is imprisoned upon an island and sleep is the chain which binds him, while around him cluster the spirits who are his servants and slaves. Cronos bound or asleep symbolizes the non-existence or suspension of time and this Greek myth may be related to Celtic concepts of eternity and the Otherworld (LERD pp. 145–7; *Mélanges Grénier* 2: pp. 1052–62).

cross There is evidence of the cross as a symbol from the remotest ages, in Egypt, China and in Crete, where a cross dating from the fifteenth century BC has been discovered. The cross (according to CHAS) is the third of the four basic symbols – the others being the CENTRE, the CIRCLE and the SQUARE – and provides a link between the other three. By the intersection of two right angles at the centre, it opens the latter to the external world; when drawn within a circle, it divides it into four segments; and it gives birth to the square and the TRIANGLE when its four ends are joined by right-angles. From these simple factors a highly complex symbolism derives, and they have fathered a language which is both universal and extremely rich. Like the square, the cross symbolizes Earth, but it expresses aspects of intervention, dynamism and the rarefied. The cross in large part shares the same symbolism as the number FOUR, and in particular what relates to an interplay of relationships within the number four and the square. The cross is above all other symbols the one which creates a totality (CHAS p. 365).

The cross, placed on the lines of the four CARDINAL POINTS, is in the first place the foundation of all symbols of orientation on every plane of human existence.

Total human orientation predicates . . . a triple concord: the orientation of the physical being in respect of the self; spatial orientation in respect of the terrestrial cardinal points; and lastly temporal orientation in respect of the celestial cardinal points. Spatial orientation hinges upon the east–west AXIS, marked by the rising and setting of the Sun. Temporal orientation hinges upon the axis around which the world rotates and is both an upward and downward and a north–south axis. When humans are in harmony with both physical and spatial orientation they are in tune with the immanent terrestrial world and, when in harmony with all three, with the transcendent world, outside time, through and beyond their earthly environment.

(CHAS p. 27)

There is no better precis of the linked and manifold meanings of the cross. Such a synthesis may be confirmed at all cultural levels and flourishes in so many different variations and ramifications.

In China the number of the cross is FIVE.

Chinese symbolism . . . teaches us once again never to overlook the essential relationship between the four sides of a square and the four arms of a cross with the centre or the point at which the arms of the cross intersect . . . . The centre of the square and the centre of the circle coincide and what they have in common becomes the great CROSSROADS of the imagination.

(CHAS p. 31)

Consequently:

the cross performs a function of synthesis and measurement. In it Heaven and Earth are conjoined . . . in it time and space are intermingled. The cross is the

unbroken UMBILICAL CORD of the cosmos, linking it to the centre from which it sprang. Of all symbols the cross is the most universal and all-embracing. It symbolizes intervention, mediation, the natural and permanent structure of the universe and communication between Heaven and Earth and Earth and Heaven.
(CHAS pp. 31–2)

The cross is the major channel of communication. It limits, prescribes and measures out holy ground, such as TEMPLES; it delineates town squares; it crosses fields and burial-grounds, and where its two arms meet it marks out crossroads. At such central points ALTARS, STONES or poles are erected. Although centripetal, its powers are centrifugal: it 'makes explict the mystery of the centre. It is diffusion, emanation, but also concentration, ingathering' (CHAS p. 365).

The cross also possesses the qualities of an ascensional symbol. A medieval German riddle-book asks which is the TREE of which the roots are in Hell and the top at the throne of God and which enfolds the world in its branches: and answers that it is the Cross. In Eastern legends, the cross is the BRIDGE or LADDER by which human souls climb towards God. 'In some versions the cross has seven notches in it like the cosmic trees representing the seven Heavens' (ELIT p. 294).

Christian tradition has lavishly enriched the symbolism of the cross by making it the visual epitome of the Saviour's Passion and Redemption. The Cross symbolizes the Crucified, Christ, the Saviour, the Word, the second person of the Trinity. The Cross is more than a representation of Jesus Christ, it is identified with his life on Earth and even with his physical body. The Church once celebrated the feasts of the Finding and the Exaltation of the Holy Cross, and such hymns as 'O Crux, spes unica' were sung in its honour. It, too, had its own story. Fashioned from the tree which Seth planted on Adam's grave, after Christ's death its fragments were scattered throughout the world and caused miracle to follow miracle. And it will be seen again, carried by Christ, at the Last Judgement. There is scarcely a symbol more full of life.

Christian iconography has used the Cross to express not simply the sufferings of the Messiah, but also his presence, for where the Cross is, there is the crucified. Four main types of cross are to be distinguished: the tau-cross in the shape of a T (as in the mystic cross (i) p. 252); the cross with a single cross-beam; one with two beams; and one with three beams.

The different meanings which symbolism gives them are not individually absolute nor mutually self-exclusive. One is not true and the others false. Each expresses a facet of living experience interpreted as a symbol.

The tau-cross would appear to symbolize the serpent nailed to the stake, death overcome by sacrifice. Even in Old Testament times it was endowed with mysterious meaning. It was because the wood for the sacrificial fire which Isaac carried on his shoulders gave him that shape that he was spared, when the angel held back Abraham's arm as he was about to sacrifice his son.

The cross with one cross-beam is the Cross of the New Testament. Its four arms symbolize the four ELEMENTS vitiated in human nature, the whole of mankind gathered to Christ from the four quarters of the globe, and the virtues of the human soul. The foot of the Cross buried in the earth signifies

a)

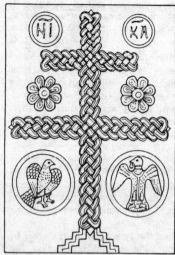

CROSS: An eleventh-century sculpture of a Greek cross with two bars (Athens)

b)

CROSS: An eleventh-century sculpture of a Greek cross with two bars (Athens)

c)

CROSS: An early-Christian sculpture of a Greek cross taken from a sarcophagus

d)

CROSS: An early-Christian sculpture of a Greek cross taken from a sarcophagus

e)

CROSS: A fourth-century sculpture of a star-shaped Greek cross with six equal branches (Thessaloniki)

f)

CROSS: An early-Christian sculpture of a Greek cross taken from a sarcophagus

g)

CROSS: An early-Christian fresco depicting the Four Gospels (Catacombs)

h)

CROSS: A fourth-century sculpture of a Greek cross with six unequal branches (Thessaloniki)

i)

j)

CROSS: A Florentine woodcut of a
cross with human occupants (1491)

CROSS: An early-Christian seal
engraved with a mystical cross

faith based upon firm foundations; the upper end of the Cross, hope rising
heavenward; the cross-beam, love shown even to one's enemies; and the
whole length of the Cross, perseverance to the very end. The Greek cross
has arms of equal length and may be drawn within a square, while the
vertical and horizontal beams of the Latin cross are of unequal length, like
a man standing upright with his arms outstretched, and can only be drawn
within a rectangle. One is idealistic, the other realistic. 'The Greeks transformed the instrument of punishment into an ornament' (DIDH 1: p. 376).
The ground plan of both Orthodox and Catholic churches is usually in the
shape of a cross, Greek oriented to the east, Latin to the west, but there are
exceptions to this.

The upper beam of the cross with two cross-beams appears to represent
Pilate's mocking superscription, *Jesus of Nazareth, King of the Jews*, while
the lower beam is that to which Christ's hands were nailed. This is what is
known as the Cross of Lorraine, although in fact it was originally Greek
and examples are more often to be found in Greece.

The cross has become a symbol of church hierarchy, like the TIARA, the
cardinal's hat and the mitre. Since the fifteenth century the Pope alone has
been entitled to the cross with three beams, although for many years now
he has used a plain one-beamed cross: archbishops have been assigned that
with two and bishops the plain cross.

Equally, a distinction is drawn between the Cross of the Passion and the
Cross of the Resurrection. The first recalls Christ's sufferings and death, the
second his victory over death. This is why the Cross bears a banner or flame
and resembles a standard or LABARUM which Christ brandishes as he rises
from the tomb and 'the shaft of which, instead of being sharpened into a

spear or pike, terminates in a cross . . . . We no longer have a tree, as in the Cross of the Passion, but a staff . . . . It is the cross of suffering transfigured' (DIDH 1: p. 386). One might go so far as to call it a sceptre: it is an instrument of torture transformed.

In drawings of Greek crosses with double beams (a and b) may be seen in Greek the initial letters of the name Jesus Christ and also the word 'NIKE', meaning 'victory'. At the foot of one of the crosses illustrated stand a FALCON with wings closed and an EAGLE with wings outspread; at the foot of the other, two PEACOCKS with tail-feathers displayed. One of the crosses is plaited with woven ribbons, while the other comprises interlacing ribbons: in both this signifies the union of the two natures, human and divine, in the Incarnate Word.

Other typical crosses (c and f) bear the first two letters of Christos (Christ's name in Greek), the Chi-Rho, the Rho (P) dividing the Chi (X) like a vertical axis. Note, too, the A and Ω, ALPHA AND OMEGA, signifying that Christ is the beginning and the end of the development of creation. Other monograms include the initials of Iesus Christos, where the upright of the Iota (I) replaces the Rho as the axis. Example (d) is set in a circle like a mystic WHEEL, others appear in squares. The latter relate to Christ's life on Earth, the former conjure up his heavenly and divine being.

The power of this symbolism in the early Church shines out of the mystic cross carved in stone which is reproduced here (i).

A Christian seal . . . is engraved with a cross in the form of a TAU (T); the CHI (X) crosses the shaft of the TAU which is rounded above into a RHO (P). The name of Christ and the figure of his cross are comprised in these lines. Christ the Son of God is the commencement and the end of all; the A and Ω, the beginning and end of intellectual signs, and, by extension, of intelligence itself, and lastly of the human soul, accompany the cross, on the right hand and on the left. The cross has crushed and conquered Satan the old serpent; a serpent, therefore, unrolls and entwines himself around the foot of the cross. The enemy of the human race seeks above all things to destroy the soul, which is represented under the form of a dove; but the dove, although menaced by the serpent, looks steadfastly at the cross, whence she derives her strength, and by which she is rendered safe from the poison of Satan. The word SALUS written below the ground on which the cross and doves are standing, is the song of triumph poured forth by faithful Christians in honour of Jesus and the cross.

(DIDH 1: 395–6)

Its continuing development in the world of symbols turned the Cross into the Paradise of the Elect, and a 1491 illustrated edition of Dante depicts the Cross set in a starry sky and filled with the blessed in adoration (*Paradiso* 14). The Cross has now become the symbol of eternal glory, of glory acquired by sacrifice and culminating in ecstatic bliss (j).

In Jewish and Christian traditions, the sign of the cross belongs to primitive initiation ceremonies. The Christian cross is prefigured in the Old Testament by the doorposts and lintels of the Children of Israel being marked with the blood of the Passover lamb in the sign of the cross. The lamb itself was roasted on two spits crosswise to each other.

The cross encapsulates the creation and has a cosmic meaning. This is why, when writing of Christ and his crucifixion, St Irenaeus should remark:

'He came among us in visible shape to what was his and he was made flesh and nailed to the Cross in a manner whereby he took the Universe to himself' (*Adversus haereses* 5: 18, 3).

Thus the Cross became the pole of the world, as St Cyril of Jerusalem states: 'God stretched out his arms upon the Cross to embrace the furthest bounds of Earth and this is why the hill of Golgotha became the pole of the world' (*Catechesis* 13: 28). St Gregory of Nyssa was to speak of the crucifixion as a cosmic happening (*Oratio de resurrectione*) and Lactantius was to write: 'God, in his suffering, opened his arms and embraced the circle of the world' (*Divinae institutiones* 4: 26, 36). Medieval writers took up from the Fathers the theme of the cosmic Cross which St Augustine had also developed in *De Genesi ad litteram* 8: 4–5.

The cross is present in the natural world. A man with his arms outstretched symbolizes the cross, as do birds flying, the ship with its mast and the ploughman's tools. Thus, in his *Apologia* 1: 55, St Justin lists all that bears the image of the cross. His list of hidden crosses, *cruces dissimulatae*, includes ploughs, anchors, tridents, ships' masts and yards, swastikas.

The cross becomes one of the basic themes of the Old Testament. It is the Tree of Life (Genesis 2: 9), Wisdom (Proverbs 3: 18), the wood of Noah's Ark, the rod with which Moses struck water from the rock, the pole on which the brazen serpent hung or the tree planted beside running water. In its turn the Tree of Life symbolizes the wood of the cross, hence the expression used by the Latin Church *sacramentum ligni vitae* (sacrament of the wood of life). Barnabé lists all the prefigurations of the cross in the Old Testament.

One ought, however, always to draw a distinction between the cross, the instrument of torture on which Christ suffered, and the glorious Cross which should be viewed in an eschatological sense. The glorious Cross, the Cross of the Second Coming which will be seen before Christ returns, is the sign of the Son of Man, sign of the Risen Christ.

In the theology of redemption, again, the Cross is the symbol of the ransom demanded by justice and of the hook which caught the Devil.

A whole tradition demands the need for a ransom paid to the Devil, based upon a scheme of justice. The latter is implicit as the work of redemption unfolds. The sacrifice of the Cross was necessary and, in consequence, so was the death of Christ, so that mankind could be freed from the consequences of sin. Hence the frequent use of the word 'ransom'. The Cross would therefore be seen as a sort of hook which stopped the Devil's mouth and prevented him from continuing his work.

(J. Rivière, Le dogme de la rédemption, Paris, 1948,
pp. 231ff., in DAVS pp. 225–6)

St Bonaventure, too, likens Christ's Cross to the Tree of Life. 'The Cross is a tree of beauty, consecrated by the blood of Christ, it is full of all fruits' (GOUL p. 293).

There is an old belief that the wood of the True Cross restored the dead to life. It owed this privilege to the fact that the Cross was fashioned from the wood of the Tree of Life which stood in the Garden of Eden.

In any explanation of the Celtic cross one must return to the symbolism of the cross in general. However, since the Celtic cross is drawn within a circle from which its arms protrude, it joins the symbolism of the circle with that of the cross. One might add the symbolism of the centre as well, since a roundel is set at the geometric centre of the cross and in the middle of its arms in many archaic examples. During the course of the earliest periods of Irish art, crosses were drawn completely within the circle and devoid of any decoration. In the next development the arms protude slightly beyond the circle. In the final phase, crosses are much larger and completely covered with incised and pierced decoration. In Irish crosses it is possible to see the Christianization of Celtic symbols. The four arms display the division of the four elements – Air, Earth, Fire and Water – with their traditional humours – hot, dry, moist and cold. They coincide with the division of Ireland into four provinces, with a fifth in the middle made up of land taken from each of the other four. There were also the Four Masters, traditional annalists who correspond to the four Evangelists, and St Patrick's surname, *Coithrige*, 'Servant of the Four'. The two axes of the cross call to mind once more the flow of time and the four cardinal points, and the circle the cycles of manifestation. However, the centre, in which time and space cease to exist and there is no change of any sort, is a place of passage or communication between this world and the Otherworld. It is a navel-stone (see OMPHALOS), a breaking-point of time and space. The close correspondence between ancient Celtic concepts and esoteric Christian data lead one to believe that for the Irish of the Carolingian era, the cross-in-a-circle represented a close and perfect synthesis of Christianity with Celtic tradition (GUES p. 185; GUEC *passim*).

Although in Asia the cross does not bear that wealth of mysticism which it carries in the Christian world, it is nonetheless extremely important. These few lines would be quite insufficient to comprehend the vast symbolism of the cross upon which whole books have been written. Fundamentally, however, that symbolism is based upon the fact that the cross comprises an intersection of two directional lines which may be viewed in different ways, either in themselves, or in that they meet at a centre, or that they branch out from that centre. The vertical axis may be viewed as a line linking together a whole hierarchy of orders or planes of being, the horizontal axis as the expansion of being to a predetermined degree. Additionally the vertical axis may represent *purusha*, the active celestial component; and the horizontal axis may represent the surface of the waters, upon which the component acts and which corresponds to *prakrti*, the passive universal substance. The two axes are also those of the equinoxes and solstices or their intersection with the polar axis. This gives a three-dimensional cross which determines the six directions of space.

The directional cross which divides the circle into four segments is the intermediary between the circle and the square, Heaven and Earth, and is therefore the symbol of the intermediate world and also of Universal Man in the Chinese Triad. According to de St-Martin, it is the emblem of the centre, of fire, of the intellect and of the First Cause. The centre of the cross, the point at which divergent directions converge and where balance is achieved, effectively corresponds to 'the void in the centre', with the 'non-active action at the centre', the Doctrine of the Mean (*Chung Yung*). In view of the fact that a cross within a circle is effectively a wheel, the cross is also the symbol of radiation from the centre, be it solar or divine. Because it signifies the whole of space, in China the cross represents the figure TEN, which contains all the one-digit numbers (Wieger).

A central, vertical cross is another symbol of the world axis, expressed by an orb surmounted by a polar cross, an imperial symbol which alchemists identified with the furnace of regeneration.

Nor should the cruciform plan of Christian churches and Hindu temples be forgotten. There the apse corresponds with the head, the transepts with the arms, the nave with the body and legs and the high altar (or LINGAM) with the heart.

Abū Ya'qūb Sejestānī attached a very special esoteric meaning to the symbolism of the cross, identifing its four arms with the four words of the Shahada, or Muslim profession of faith (BURA, CORT, GUEC, SAIR).

The Ancient Egyptian looped cross is fully described under the heading ANKH.

African art provides many examples of cruciform motifs made up either by straight lines or in the shape of manioc leaves, and these contain a wealth of meaning. In the first place, the cross has cosmic significance, as its totality, since it indicates the cardinal points. When there is a circle at the end of each of its arms, it symbolizes the Sun and its daily course, while the Bamum symbol for a king was a cross with arcs at the end of the arms. As the crossroads, it depicts the paths of life and death and is the image of human fate (MVEA p. 106). The milk-whisk of the Fulani is cruciform and should they accidentaly spill any milk, they dip their fingers in the drops of the pool and make the sign of the cross with it on their bodies (HAMK p. 25).

Bantu tribes from Kasai (Congo, Lulua, Baluba) think of the world as an arrangement of cross and SPIRAL. The vertical axis of this cross links the Earth (the human dwelling-place and also, in its chthonian manifestation, that of the souls of the dead) and the Highest Heaven, where the Supreme Deity resides. He himself sits at the centre of a cross on the arms of which dwell the Four Spirits, higher beings who are his judges. The horizontal axis links the world of the good spirits (in the east) with that of the evil spirits (in the west). The centre of this primeval cross is at the crossroads of the Milky Way where, having crossed a bridge, the souls of the dead are judged and then despatched according to their deserts either to the left or right (west or east). Spirits and souls proceed from one to another of these four primeval levels in a spiral path.

This archetypal structure dictates the architectural arrangement of huts and meeting-places as well as the hierarchical relationship between individual members of a family or group. Thus within the family kraal the husband's hut stands at the centre of a cross, on the arms of which are set in order of seniority, north, south, east and west, the huts of his four wives. Similarly in the forest clearings where the secret societies meet, the four senior initiates take their places round a central point which is the position of the invisible, all-powerful chief, this central point being where the arms of a cross intersect and equally from where a spiral begins (FOUA, FOUC). A cross tattooed on the skin or worn in wood or metal symbolizes both the cardinal points and the four paths across the universe leading to the dwellings of the

Spirits (sky or north), humans (downwards or south), good souls (east) and evil souls (west).

'The cross', Guénon wrote, 'is above all the symbol of space encompassed in its totality.... As a symbol, the cross is a marriage of opposites ... which must be compared with the *kua* [marriage of *yang* and *yin*] as well as with the TETRAKTYS of the Pythagoreans.' This symbolism is particularly strongly felt in Ancient Mexican mythic tradition. The cross was the symbol of the world in its totality and of the central thread which bound the years together. 'When the ancient scribes attempted to depict the world, they set four blank spaces round a central point in the shape of a Greek or Maltese cross.' Better still, Mexican mythology provides, as it were, a full range of symbolic colours under this sign of the cross. First, in the centre, the fire-god Xiuhtechutli sits beside the universal hearth. Being a place of synthesis, this centre has a dual aspect, ominous and fortunate. Then, in the Codex Borgia, this central point is depicted as a multicoloured tree, and again there can be little doubt about the dual nature of its verticality since on its top sits a quetzal, bird of the east, while the tree itself springs from an Earth-goddess, symbol of the west. Furthermore, this cosmic tree is flanked on one side by the great god Quetzalcoatl, the god who offered himself in sacrifice upon a pyre to give life to the Sun, and on the other side by Macuilxochitl, god of the dawn, of Spring and of sports, music, dancing and love (DURS pp. 354–5).

The American Indian regarded the Latin cross as much the Tree of Life as did the European, sometimes depicted in its simple geometrical shape, and at others with its arms as branches or foliage, as in the case of the famous Palenque cross (ALEC p. 37).

In the Codex Ferjérváry-Mayer, each of the cardinal points is depicted as a cross surmounted by a bird.

In some codices the Tree of Life is shaped like a Cross of Lorraine, bearing upon its horizontal arms seven flowers clearly representing the god of the fields. In other examples the sevenfold deity is represented by six flowers and the Sun-bird in the middle of the sky.

At the end of his study of the significance of the cardinal points to the Ancient Mexicans, Soustelle was able to state that 'the cross is the symbol of the world in its totality.'

crossroads The importance of the crossroads as a symbol is universal. It is connected with the essence of the crossroads itself, two paths intersecting to create the CENTRE of the world, and the true centre of the world for whoever stands where they meet. Being the place of all places for revelations and manifestations, crossroads are haunted by spirits, generally terrifying, which it is in the interest of human beings to propitiate. Whatever the tradition, it was the custom to set up at crossroads obelisks, altars, stones, chapels and inscriptions, since they are places where people stop to think. They are also places where one passes from one world to another, from one life to another and from life to death.

At crossroads in the Peruvian Andes the votive STONES left by travellers have built up into real PYRAMIDS and the tradition still survives. A similar practice seems to have been observed in Siberia. Again, the Aztecs believed that it was at crossroads, and of course at dusk, that the spirits of women who had died in childbirth appeared. Malignant ghosts, 'they terrified and struck with epilepsy or paralysis all whom they met.'

In Africa, and particularly in areas of forest and savannah, crossroads are invested with the importance of holy places. Whenever Fulani pastoralists meet in a clearing where two tracks cross, they give it a name and the place is made holy by a well-defined ritual. The caravan master, the initiate, makes contact with the spirits of the place, either in dreams or else by means of specific herbs. Depending upon how closely thronged with spirits the place may be, it will become a camp or meeting-place for several days. Such animals as an ox, a sheep or a speckled goat will be sacrificed and meaning will be drawn from the cries and flight of birds, especially those of doves, for they are the messengers of the gods and their hearts are free from malice.

The Bambara from Mali make offerings of tools, raw cotton, cloth and so on at crossroads to the Soba spirits who regularly meddle with human fate. The same is true of Baluba, Lulua and other Bantu tribes in the Kasai.

Although crossroads are pre-eminently places of passage, they are also places where, cloaked in anonymity, one may dispose of such residual, negative and unusable powers as are dangerous to the community. This is where the Bambara throw the rubbish from the village since it is charged with a power of uncleanness which the spirits alone can either neutralize or change to positive power. For the same reason the Bambara place the possessions of the dead at crossroads. The spirits of the crossroads are believed to absorb the powers of which the Bambara rid themselves in this way and which provide the spirits with 'a sort of food for which they pay human beings with gifts purged of all uncleanness'. The protection of these spirits is invoked on occasions important in communal life and particularly at seedtime. Among the Bambara, again, it is the old men – that is, those who have least to fear from the spirits – who abandon new-born babies of doubtful legitimacy at crossroads. Abnormal, and especially hydrocephalous, births are buried there and anything soiled by those undergoing the rites of CIRCUMCISION. (In their seclusion and being neither boys nor yet men, they make anything which they touch unclean.) J.-P. Lebeuf has observed similar beliefs among the Likuba and Likuala of central Africa who dispose of rubbish charged with a dangerous power at crossroads.

The crossroads of the Otherworld are no less important or to be feared. Bantu tribes from the Kasai believe that at the crossroads of the Milky Way the gods judge the souls of the dead, sending some eastwards to Heaven and some westwards to Hell, midway between the world on Earth and the transcendent world in the sky.

There are many practical applications of this symbolism: earth from crossroads is used in ordeals and divination. Again it is at crossroads that Lulua and Baluba women, responsible for working the fields, place the first-fruits of the harvest. If the village is threatened by famine, the entire population goes to the nearest crossroads in procession to lay offerings of food and old household utensils for the souls of their ancestors. Again, after weaning a child and coming to the end of the ban on sexual intercourse imposed during nursing, women sacrifice a white hen to the souls of dead children at crossroads.

The Senufo, too, believe that the rubbish heaps at crossroads are holy places 'haunted at night by the spirits who protect the family'. They place such votive offerings there as egg-shells, bones of animals sacrificed to the spirits and chicken-feathers mingled with blood. By their choice of ex-voto, the Senufo clearly show that they believe a regenerative power resides in the combination of crossroads and rubbish heap.

Holas quotes Itmann for the belief in the Cameroons that crossroads are closely associated with fertility spirits. In Guinea there is evidence that many tribes – Yakuba, Toma, Guere, Kissi, for example – place offerings at crossroads.

Dennet records the existence among the Yoruba in Nigeria of depictions of the god Olirimeri with a human body and four heads, known in Abomey as 'he who looks to the four points of the compass'.

To the Bambara, crossroads embody 'the central point, the first state of the godhead before the creation. With his own essence the creator at the beginning of all things set the boundaries of space and gave order to creation by tracing the intersection of the four ways.'

These traditions were carried to the Americas by African slaves. In Voodoo ceremonies the first god to be invoked – Legba or Atibon Legba to the Fon from Dahomey (now Benin); Esu Elegbara in Haiti; Exu to the Yoruba in Nigeria or in Brazil – is considered the messenger or intermediary between mankind and the other gods. He is called 'the crossroads man' in Brazil, because 'Exu is wherever two paths cross and it was he who taught mankind the art of divination.' In Cuba, as Eleggua (Lydia Cabrera) and in Haiti, just as in Africa, he appears at doorways, for 'he opens and closes the ways'. In Haiti he is lord of roads and crossroads and guards all entrances. He presides over Voodoo ritual. Like all symbolic figures, Legba has a dark and bright side, the former being typified by the statuette known as 'Legba-aovi' ('Bad Luck-legba'), set up at some crossroads in the forests in the Fon country in Dahomey. The death of parents may be a consequence of meeting him.

Crossroads are encounters with fate. OEDIPUS met and killed his father, Laios, at a crossroads and set his destiny in motion. And yet it was at the end of a long journey, undertaken solely to escape his fate, that fate caught up with him at a crossroads.

Within each person is a crossroads at which the cross-currents of the personality meet and wrestle. APHRODITE is known for her triple aspect – sky-, sea- and Underworld-goddess. She may be a chaste, a fruitful or a lascivious goddess, and it was at crossroads that she became the goddess of casual and illicit sex. (Curiously enough the word 'trivial' is derived from the Latin for 'crossroads' – *trivium*.) Aphrodite, Goddess of the Crossroads, who lingers there, symbolizes casual sex and identifies with the goat astride which the sculptor Scopas depicted her.

The Ancient Romans observed the worship of the Lares of the Crossroads simply to avoid the ill luck which they might encounter there. They came to crossroads with their offerings in order to propitiate the local gods and gain protection for the homes clustering along the roads which met there, for the neighbouring crops and for villages and cities. Where they did not build shrines, they erected altars and set benches nearby for rest and meditation.

In Rome itself, the festival of the Lares Compitales (*compitum* is another word for 'crossroads') was held in January, the month of Janus, god of the gates. It was so important to the citizens that Augustus absorbed it into the Imperial cult, setting his statue alongside that of the Lares at the crossroads, in token of his role as protector of the fate of all.

In India, too, invocations were set for safe passage at crossroads. The Vedic marriage ritual provided a hymn to be sung by the wedding procession when the ox-drawn cart carrying the young couple from the bride's home to her new house passed a crossroads (*Rig-Veda*, *Grhyasutra* 1: 6).

HECATE was the somewhat nebulous deity, of uncertain origin, with a boundless sphere of activity and identified with Artemis, Demeter, Apollo and other gods and godesses, known to Geek mythology as 'the Goddess of the Crossroads'. This functional title was doubtless given to her in token of her generally accepted role as mistress of the three worlds – Heaven, Earth and the Underworld. She had a triple body, three faces and a triple role as the provider of all good things to mankind, the source of all fame and wisdom and the most skilled practitioner of magic and spells. Her statue, in the shape of a woman with three bodies or three heads, was erected at crossroads or at the meeting of paths in forest clearings, and there travellers left their offerings. She presided over birth, preserved life and determined when it should end. She is paralleled in Zoroastrian worship by a triple goddess with three faces and three functions. In Syracuse the festival of Hecate lasted three days. Offerings of food were placed at crossroads in small pots bearing her image and these the poor ate in her name. The remains were thrown away with sprigs of thyme, hence the name *oxythymia* applied to crossroads. Hecate was goddess of night and darkness, and since she also ruled the Underworld, her rites were also celebrated in CAVERNS. Dogs were offered to her, especially in propitiatory sacrifices. She would often appear to WITCHes and warlocks in the shape of a mare, a she-wolf or a bitch. The Greeks also attributed to her special powers of conjuring up ghosts, phantoms and hallucinations of the imagination. The gigantic phantoms which appeared during her festivals were called 'Hecates', and naturally it was her priests or sorcerers who were most adept at conjuring them up. Benefactress or bugbear, the goddess with three faces epitomizes the unknown which the crossroads symbolizes. This aspect of the crossroads is enshrined, too, in the statues of HERMES which were set up there. Hermes was the conductor of souls and, according to Jung, symbolizes the activities of God as intermediary between the different worlds. His was the task of guiding the souls of the dead along the underground ways of Hell. Jung also regards crossroads as maternal symbols and as symbols of the marriage of opposites, and an epitome of all marriages. Hence their characteristic ambivalence, now appearing salutory, now baleful.

Throughout Europe witches and warlocks gather at crossroads or upon baneful mountain tops to conduct their sabbaths.

The Christian world must surely have erected so many crosses, Calvaries, statues of Our Lady and of the saints, shrines and chapels where, in some countries, candles burn perpetually, to offer sacrifice in atonement, prayer and supplication. This is the salutary side of the crossroads, a place of enlightenment where good spirits, fairy-godmothers, Our Lady and the saints appear.

To summarize: whatever the civilization, to reach the crossroads is to come face to face with the unknown and, since the natural human reaction to the unknown is one of fear, the primary aspect of the symbol is anxiety. In dreams it betrays the wish for an important, solemn and, in some sense, holy, meeting. It may also show that a parting of the ways has been reached and that one must take a new and decisive direction in one's affairs. The symbolism of all traditions teaches that it seems to be necessary to pause at the crossroads, as if a moment's thought, spiritual retreat or even sacrifice has to be offered before setting off along a fresh path.

Crossroads are also places where one meets 'the enemy', either within or without. It is a favourite place for ambush and travellers must be carefully on their guard. The triple Hecate and Hermes, conductor of souls, stand at the crossroads, because this is the place where we must make, by ourselves and within ourselves, the inevitable choice between Earth, Heaven and Hell. The real hazards of living are encountered in the inner life and there, at the crossroads, the only person you ever meet is yourself. You may have sought a positive response, but all you have in prospect are fresh paths, new trials and fresh developments. The crossroads is not the end, it is merely a pause and an invitation to go on. You only linger there so as to react for good or ill upon others, or if you yourself realize that you cannot make a choice. It then becomes a place of meditation and waiting, not of activity. It is, however, also a place of hope. The way there may have been long and rough, but a fresh crossroads affords the opportunity of choosing a smooth path. But there is no going back once the choice has been made. To emphasize the full force of the symbol there are tales in which the crossroads themeselves vanish after the hero has passed through them and the problems of choice have been resolved (SOUM, ALEC, DIEB, FOUA, FOUG, LEBM, HOLS, DENY, ZAHB, MARV, METV, MAUG).

crow See RAVEN.

crowbar The symbolism of the crowbar is of the same nature as that of the CHISEL and, similarly, it is part of the mason's equipment. In so far as it sets in motion the passive principle, inert matter, the crowbar is the active principle. However, its action is the result of the will of whoever activates it and to whom it is itself passive. Thus, as has been observed of the chisel, will takes precedence over knowledge:

Like the chisel, the crowbar is a passive intermediary. Its active power depends upon the strength of whoever employs it. Of itself it is inert. It is therefore related to knowledge which only becomes initiatory when its owner is fit for initiation, that is to say, is capable of understanding. The crowbar then becomes a fertilizing power . . . and a dangerous one, and this is why it should never be displayed unless controlled by the RULE, the LEVEL and the PLUMB LINE.

(BOUM p. 21)

The crowbar merely symbolizes the force of an implement set in motion and controlled by a higher power and the quality of its use can only be measured by the quality of what it is employed to raise.

crown Three factors supply the bases of the crown's symbolism. Being set on the crown of the head gives it an overriding significance. It not only shares the qualities of the head – the summit of the body – but also the qualities of whatever surmounts the head itself, a gift coming from on high. It sets the seal of transcendence upon the character of any accomplishment. Its circular shape is indicative of perfection and of its sharing in the heavenly nature of which the CIRCLE is the symbol. It marries, in the person crowned, what is above and what is below, but in so doing marks the bounds which in any other person divide the celestial from the terrestrial, the human from the divine. As a reward of virtue, crowns are promises of eternal life on the pattern of that of the gods. Finally, the very material, be it vegetable or mineral, from which the crown is made defines by the fact that it is dedicated to this or that god or goddesss, the nature of the heroic deed accomplished and that of the prize awarded by assimilation with Ares (Mars), Apollo, Dionysos, or whichever. At the same time it reveals the supraterrestrial powers entrapped and used to achieve the deed rewarded. From this it may be seen how crowns symbolize rank, power, kingship and the attainment of higher powers and status. When a crown is topped by a DOME it asserts absolute sovereignty.

There is a certain similarity in the Latin words for 'crown' (*corona*) and 'HORN' (*cornu*) and both express the same sense of elevation, power and enlightenment. Both are raised above the head and both are the emblems of power and of light. In ancient times crowns were decorated with spikes – like horns – to represent beams of light. This may well be the symbolic significance of Christ's Crown of Thorns and was certainly that of the cobras' heads borne on the foreheads by Ancient Egyptian gods and Pharaohs. In Kabbalistic symbolism the crown (*Kether*), which expresses the Absolute and the state of Non-Being (*Ayn Soph*), is placed at the top of the Tree of the Sefirot. Alchemical iconography depicts the spirits of the planets receiving their light, in the shape of crowns, from the hand of their king, the Sun. All crowns share the dazzle and symbolism of the solar crown.

In Ancient Egypt only gods and Pharaohs wore crowns. As rulers of both Upper and Lower Egypt, the Pharaohs bore the double crown (*pschent*) comprising the white mitre of Upper Egypt set in the red crown of the Delta. The sacred headdress of Osiris was known as the *atew*. It consisted of

a white mitre, a pair of ostrich FEATHERS, RAMS' horns and the URAEUS and was sometimes adorned with other ornaments. Each of these elements was a hieroglyph since, in Ancient Egypt, every object was symbolic. The white mitre expresses the notion of light, the ostrich feather is the emblem of truth, the rams' horns suggest procreative heat.

(PIED p. 75)

These royal and divine crowns became objects of worship, ' "Great of Magic" . . . . "Initiates into the mystery of the Two Uraei" . . . had their own cult [and were] considered by the Egyptians as beings full of power' (POSD p. 56).

Tibetan priests wear crowns with five portraits on them when they prepare the holy water for the sacrifice to the 'Eight Terrible Gods', a ritual
aimed at driving evil spirits away. Similar crowns are known in Mongolia,
Nepal and Bali.

Each panel depicts a network of ideas corresponding to the five Dhyāna-
Buddhas, or Buddhas of meditation:

GREEN, north, freedom from fear;
RED, west, meditation;
BLUE, east, bearing witness;
WHITE, centre, teaching;
YELLOW, south, charity. (TONT p. 6)

This crown both symbolizes and concentrates the internal and external
forces which ensure the cosmic – and ethical – qualities of the sacrifice by
associating in it the five Buddhas and the material universe – the four
CARDINAL POINTS, their centre and their five colours.

Both in yoga and in Islam, too, the crown of the head is the point through
which the soul escapes the confines of the body to ascend to superhuman
states. In Hindu fashion, it is the *sahasrōra padma*, the thousand-leaved
LOTUS (GUEV, GUES, WARK).

From earliest ages a protective quality was attributed to crowns. They
acquired this quality from the material from which they were made, flowers, foliage, precious metals and gems, and from their circular shape which
made them kin to the symbolism of Heaven.

In Ancient Greece and Rome, crowns were signs of consecration to the
gods, and at sacrifices both priest and victim were crowned. 'The gods
disregard those who stand before them uncrowned', wrote a Greek Archaic
poet. Statues of the gods were crowned, generally with the leaves of the
trees or fruits of the plant sacred to them, oak for Zeus, laurel (bay) for
Apollo, myrtle for Aphrodite, wheat for Ceres. To attract the protection
of the gods, the corpses of the dead were crowned, as were the living
upon important occasions. Crowns tend to identify their wearer with the
godhead and are symbols of assimilation. They trap celestial forces, being
shaped like Heaven, and the power of the god with whom their material
identifies them (LAVD pp. 302–3). A mural crown decorated the brows
of such gods, goddesses and heroes as Cybele, goddess of the Earth and
harvest.

Crowns such as the Dantesque circles in the *Divine Comedy* were to
represent the abode of the Blessed or the dead, or the spiritual status of
initiates. The Orphic Tables put these words into the mouth of a soul
addressing Persephone: 'I have escaped the mournful cycle of pain and on
swift feet reached the crown I longed for.' While another initiate, according
to Plutarch, 'set free and walking unconstrained, celebrates the mysteries,
a crown upon his head' (see SECG pp. 120, 169). One version of the legend
of Ariadne and Theseus claims that it was a crown of light which guided
him to the centre of the Labyrinth and, having killed the Minotaur, out
again; and that this crown of light was given to him by Ariadne who, in
turn, had received it as a betrothal gift from Dionysos. It symbolizes the
inner light which enlightens the soul of the person who has been victorious

in some spiritual battle. Jung was to regard the radiant crown as the pre-eminent symbol of the highest level of spiritual development.

In Central American iconography crowns only appear as attributes of agrarian gods (GIRP p. 80).

The Indian crown of feathers, the golden crown and the HALO all 'represent an attempt to identify with the Sun-god and, in consequence, an extraordinary acquisition of power' (LOEC pp. 50–1).

As the meaning of the symbol became cheapened, this crown of feathers was reduced to mere fancy-dress or fairground decoration, or else to serving 'as the attribute of America in any allegorical representation of the continents of the world' (TERS p. 131).

In Jewish and Christian writings the image of the crown has been associated with the following very different modes of presentation.

(1) The royal or priestly crown: in all civilizations the crown is the attribute of kingship. Nonetheless, the Jewish faith sometimes identified the golden diadem worn by the High Priest (Exodus 28: 36–8) with a crown (see Ecclesiasticus 45: 12).

Since God is the ruler of all things, he is able to crown persons and peoples with his blessings (Ezekiel 16: 12; Isaiah 62: 3). The prophets went so far as to claim that Israel was the crown of God, that is to say the sign of his omnipotent working on behalf of mankind. Its symbolic content widened and the crown naturally came to denote greatness, happiness and victory. It was an easy step from there to eschatological or transcendent victory. Thus at Qumran, *The Manual of Discipline* (4: 7ff.) promised the faithful a crown of glory after the final victory. The Book of Revelation must be read in this context. The four-and-twenty Elders (Revelation 4: 4–10) who represent in Heaven the Church of God, wear crowns which they set down before the Throne of God. Christ appears as sovereign, crowned like God himself (Revelation 14: 14).

(2) The crown awarded to victorious athletes in the Games: the early Church took this theme from secular life and transposed it into a religious and spiritual key. Sustained effort is implicit in the Christian life of faith, as the individual strains with all the powers at his command towards a goal (1 Corinthians 9: 24–7). Victory and the crown which is its prize are not, however, identified with living an exemplary moral life, but with the eternal salvation granted to the person who has taken seriously the meaning of the Gospel and whose life's sole aim has been to live up to that message. Hence the eschatological tone so prevalent in the image of the crown (James 1: 12; 1 Peter 4: 5). This is why the crown of life can be called a crown of immortality (Revelation 2: 10). When St Polycarp was martyred in the arena he truly gained the prize – eternal life.

Using the symbol involves generalization and completely losing sight of its original links with athletic games. Thus *The Ascension of Isaiah* (9: 7) speaks of crowns kept in the seventh Heaven for the friends of the Beloved (the Messiah).

(3) This extended meaning enables the crown to be likened to the garland which was given to initiates of the mystery cults. The worshipper of Mithras

who was promoted to the rank of 'soldier' was rewarded with a crown and cried out: 'Mithras is my crown!' The same applied in the mysteries of Isis (see Apuleius, *The Golden Ass*).

At this point it is legitimate to suggest that the image of the crown symbolizes the Christian initiation of BAPTISM. The majority of scholars acknowledge the baptismal nature of *The Odes of Solomon* and it contains a number of references which may be understood in this sense. Ode 1: 'They have woven me a crown of Truth' and Ode 20: 7–8: 'Clothe thyself in the grace of the Lord, return to Paradise and wreathe thyself a crown from his tree and set it on thy head.'

It will be observed that in these quotations the image of the crown is indissolubly linked with that of PARADISE and the TREE of Life from which the crown is made. Similarly, in his *Catecheses*, St Cyril of Jerusalem writes: 'You catechumens wreathe spiritual flowers into heavenly crowns.'

Mandaean liturgies bear witness to a ritual coronation celebrated by the newly baptized person.

To explain the references in *The Odes of Solomon*, recourse may be had to one final motif in the theme of the crown. It is well known that the gift of a nuptial crown forms an essential part of Eastern marriage ceremonies (Song of Solomon 3: 11).

Since the *Odes* do not disdain to speak of the spiritual marriage of the soul with Christ, it is legitimate to ask whether the symbol of the crown cannot be widened in this sense.

(4) In fact this sense is confirmed by medieval ceremonies connected with the final vows taken by a nun, for they were borrowed from the sacrament of marriage. 'The principal symbols were the veil, the ring and the crown.' The veil symbolized the nun's intention and plea to be preserved from all defilement through love only of eternal goodness; the ring symbolized her attachment to the Faith, and was 'the sign of the Holy Spirit, that you may be called the Bride of Christ.'

Finally the bishop set a crown on the nun's head saying: 'Receive the sign of Christ upon your head, so that you may become his bride and, if you remain in that state, you will be crowned for all eternity.'

These symbols are clearly traditional. Because of its solar origins, the crown symbolizes royal, or rather divine, power. The symbol of the crown is in any case extremely ancient. Jewish priests used to wear crowns of flowers when they went in procession on the Feast of Tabernacles. Later the crown was to symbolize the presence of Christ, for he is as a crown on the heads of the elect.

(DAVS pp. 24ff.)

This use of crowns in baptismal ceremonies displays a new birth in Christ, and it is by and through Christ that the nun assumed a new name when she made her final vows (DAVS pp. 239–40).

Later, the crown was used to indicate all degrees of superiority, however slight or short-lived they might be, and to reward some outstanding deed or attainment. The image retained only a pale shadow of the memory of its symbolic quality and was only the outward sign of success or of rank. It is depicted in various shapes and forms on the brows of victorious generals, of geniuses, the learned, poets, or in allegories of victory, war, peace, learning, oratory, philosophy, theology, astrology, fortune, virtue, wisdom and honour. Crowns even decorated the brows of the vices, such as Pride, if they were pre-eminent, or, according to taste, of Gluttony and Lust. We have shown how a crown of feathers represented America; a crown was also the attribute of Europa and of Europe, since the nymph of that name was seen as 'superior to the rest' and the continent of that name remained 'superior to the rest of the world and was as if its queen'. But the crown was also an attribute of Africa, the continent 'with its head ringed in radiant flames' (TERS pp. 125-33).

crozier The crozier is the symbol of the faith of which the bishop is the interpreter. Shaped like a hook, semi-circle or open circle, it signifies the opening upon Earth of the powers of Heaven, the transmission of God's blessings and the power to create and re-create living beings. A bishop's or abbot's crozier is the emblem of their pastoral jurisdiction and is therefore a symbol, too, of authority, of an authority which originates in Heaven. It is akin to the shepherd's crook, the hooked STAFF which enables him to return the strayed lamb to the flock.

cruentation Cruentation is the outflowing of blood through a wound before or after death. The *scholia* in a ninth-century manuscript of Lucan at Bern, which draw upon now lost sources, mention cruentation as a method of sacrificing to Esus-Mars. 'Esus-Mars is propitiated in this way. A man is hung upon a tree until his limbs are flaccid from loss of blood.' But the evidence of this method of sacrificing is unique and only corroborated in part by a single Germanic parallel. The *Inglingasaga* explains that Odin is the god of the HANGING MAN and the *Havamal* tells how he hung for nine days and nights on a tree consecrated to himself. But there is no mention of cruentation, nor are there any references to it from insular Celtic sources (OGAC 7: pp. 34-5; 10: pp. 3ff.).

Cruentation was used as an ordeal and a means to discover murderers. The seeping or spurting of blood was a confirmation of truth, confirming that the sacrifice had been accepted or that a true confession of crime had been extorted.

crutch This 'staff with a cross-piece at the head' (Chambers) which the old or the infirm use to help them to walk, has always possessed a meaning of assistance or support. Crutches therefore reveal weakness, but this weakness may be genuine or assumed. If genuine, it is that of the old, worn out by age, and in this sense the crutch often forms an attribute of images of Saturn, god of time. When assumed, it is that of witches, robbers and pirates, who put on an air of weakness the better to conceal their maleficent powers. This is very similar to the meaning attached to the FOOT as a symbol of the soul: its physical infirmity being an external sign of spiritual weakness.

And yet crutches can have a positive significance. They enable us to go forward, symbolizing the will which refuses to accept a given situation without attempting to alter it. They are symbols, too, of faith – when we think of the crutches cast aside by the sick miraculously healed in the Gospels – and of the spiritual light which guides stumbling footsteps or makes good a physical handicap.

crystal Crystal is a foetus, born from the rocks in the ground. Indian mineralogy distinguishes it from the DIAMOND by its embryological development, crystal being a diamond which has not reached its full time (ELIM, ELIF).

Its transparency is one of the best examples of a marriage of opposites. Although crystal is composed of matter, it allows the eye to see through it as though it were immaterial.

It represents a level intermediate between the visible and the invisible. It is the symbol of divination, wisdom and of the hidden powers granted to mankind. Heroes in both Eastern and Western romance encounter crystal palaces as they emerge from gloomy forests in their quest for the royal talisman. An identical belief links the *juringa* quartz of the Australian Aborigine initiates with the Holy GRAIL of Western chivalry, carved from a mystical EMERALD.

(SERH pp. 102–3)

Nor would it be foolhardy to compare this view with that of Australasian, Oceanic or even of North American shamanism. The latter regarded rock crystal as 'light-stones', splinters from the Heavenly Throne, and instruments of the shaman's clairvoyance. The Dyak shamans in Borneo use different magical objects to uncover the soul of a sick person and the most important of these are quartz crystals which they call *bata ilau*, 'light-stones'. At Dobu in the D'Entrecasteaux Islands (Papua New Guinea) 'in his crystal the healer sees the person, living or dead, who has brought on the illness' (ELIC p. 363). In Australia, rock crystals, which play an important part in the initiation of medicine men, are thought to originate from the sky. They are often held to be splinters from the throne of the celestial Supreme Being. 'What is significant for us is . . . that Australian and other medicine men in some obscure way connect their powers with the presence of these rock crystals in their own bodies' (ELIC p. 139). The Negritos of Malacca hold the same beliefs. Dyak and Semang shamans have 'light-stones' which not only reflect all that affects the sick person's soul, but also where it has strayed. The Negrito medicine man also sees the illness 'in the crystals'. These crystals are believed to be the homes of Cenoi, spirits which show him the disease (ELIC p. 339; SCHP p. 154).

Closely related to the rainbow-SERPENT, crystals have the power of ascending into Heaven. There is the same symbolism among American Indians who consider crystal as a sacred substance, originating in the sky and possessing the powers of clairvoyance, wisdom and flight.

Transparent or translucent stones like rock crystal, quartz, OBSIDIAN or Southern diorite were traditionally used by the Prairie Indians as talismans and as a means of producing visions, since they heightened the trance state for perception of the invisible. The Navaho believed that it was the rock crystal which first caused the Sun to cast its light upon the world (ALEC p. 14). Mayan priests read the future in splinters of rock crystal steeped in a goblet of mead because 'it aroused the consciousness' (KRIR p. 105).

For Christians, light striking crystal is the traditional image of the Immaculate Conception. 'Mary is crystal, her son heavenly light which passes through leaving the whole intact' (Angelus Silesius). Again, before ever they became the stock-in-trade of fortune-tellers, crystal balls were venerated by the Scots who called them 'victory stones'.

According to most Irish literary sources, messengers from the Celtic Otherworld came in the shape of birds. However, when they came by sea, they used glass or crystal boats. Apparently these materials symbolized a technical perfection beyond all human endeavour (ZEIP 17: pp. 193–205). Perhaps, too, the transparency of the crystal boat symbolized the immateriality of the messenger and the spiritual nature of his mission. Elves, like Cinderella, had slippers of glass or crystal.

cube Being a three-dimensional SQUARE, the cube bears the same relation to volume as the square does to plane surfaces. It symbolizes the material universe and the four ELEMENTS. It has been regarded as the symbol of stability because it provides a firm foundation and, for this reason, it is often found at the base of THRONES.

Cubes have been regarded in a mystical sense as 'symbols of wisdom, truth and moral perfection' (PORC p. 55). They are models of the New Jerusalem, foretold in the Book of Revelation, equal in all its dimensions. The Ka'ba, the Muslim Holy of Holies in Mecca, stands in the Great Mosque and, as its name in Arabic expressly states, is a cube. It enshrines the famous 'Black Stone' which is held to have been given to Abraham by the Archangel Gabriel. It is interesting to observe that the first Ka'ba – the present building was rebuilt in the tenth century after a fire – stood at the fountain-head of revealed religion since it was traditionally supposed to have been built by Adam and then rebuilt by Abraham and Ishmael after the Flood. It follows that the cube has been regarded as a symbol of perfection from the dawn of our civilization. It is an image of eternity for its solid, rather than its spiritual qualities.

When coupled with the SPHERE, the two together symbolize the totality of the heavenly and the earthly, the finite and the infinite, the created and the uncreated, this world and the world above.

cubit As a measuring-rod, used mainly in Ancient Egypt, it symbolized order, justice and truth. The ibis-headed god Thoth, the lawgiver and patron of scribes, is depicted holding a cubit. (See ARM.)

cuckoo The French regard the cuckoo as a symbol of jealousy, an emotion which it provokes, and also of parasitism, because it lays its eggs in the nests of other birds. This is also a sign of laziness, since it is believed to be incapable of building a nest of its own.

The bird is sometimes found as an emblem of Hera (JUNO). Zeus seduced Hera by 'fluttering towards her and nestling in her bossom in the shape of a cuckoo, the herald of the Spring' (SECG p. 176). On the basis of this legend there has been an attempt to make the cuckoo 'a symbol of the spirit of God injected by the lightning into the rain-clouds' (LANS 3: p. 98), the rain-clouds standing for the goddess.

In Japan, its dawn appearance makes it a messenger of the kingdom of the night, its morning flight accompanying the disappearance of darkness.

Among Siberian peoples, Sun and Moon are sometimes depicted as a pair of cuckoos. The relationship of the bird with Spring and the awakening of nature aids the shaman and brings the dead back to life. Among other peoples in the same region, the cuckoo presides over the administration of justice (SOUL, OGRJ).

In Africa, doubtless because it excites their instincts to fever-pitch and awakens their sexual urges, the call of the cuckoo in the heat of the day is believed to drive livestock mad (SERP p. 157).

In Vedic tradition the cuckoo would seem to symbolize the human soul before and after incarnation, the body being like the strange nest in which the soul is laid (LANS 3: p. 99).

According to the folktale, the first sound of the cuckoo's voice in Spring may foretell riches, provided the hearer has money in his or her purse.

cup   See CHALICE.

curl   The curl is a symbol of identification. 'One single curl from Medusa's locks, was enough to rout an attacking army' (GRID p. 168a), being the equivalent of the terrible Gorgon herself. Ancient Egyptian poets compare the crescent moon with a curl of HAIR. Khonsu of Thebes was called 'Lord of the Curl', and his curl was enough to identify him (SOUL pp. 20, 62). The circular shape of the curl is not without context: it encloses the signified within the signifying. Ordinary hair, hanging straight, would not have this property.

curtain   See FIERY CURTAIN; VEIL.

cuttle-fish   The cuttle-fish or squid would seem to be a curious candidate for the first master of FIRE in a myth recorded by G. Frazer (FRAF) from the Nootka Indians of Vancouver. The deer stole it from him and gave it to mankind. The myth explains that at that time the cuttle-fish lived both on land and in the sea.

Cybele (see also DEMETER)   Earth-goddess, sky-daughter, wife of Saturn and mother of Jupiter, Juno, Neptune and Pluto, Cybele symbolizes energy entombed in the Earth. She engendered the deities of the four ELEMENTS and was the primeval, chthonian source of all fertility.

Her chariot was drawn by lions, signifying her mastery, control and direction of the vital force. She was sometimes crowned with a seven-pointed star or a crescent Moon, signs of her power over the cycles of living growth on Earth. She was first worshipped in the shape of the black STONE, her symbol, which the Romans carried off from Pessinus to Rome *c.* 205 BC. 'Then further she contains the means to raise up bright corn and fruitful trees for the races of mankind, the means to produce rivers and leaves and fruitful pastures for the mountain-ranging brood of wild beasts. Therefore she alone is called great Mother of the gods, and Mother of the wild beasts, and maker of our bodies' (Lucretius, *De rerum natura* 2: 594–99).

In the third century BC her worship was introduced to Rome from Phrygia as that of the Mother of the Gods and reached its peak in Imperial times. Cybele was the Mother Goddess, the Magna Mater, the Asiatic Great Mother whose worship from the earliest times and in all places is inextricably involved with fertility rites. Sometimes she was seated under a TREE, sometimes escorted by lions, sometimes wreathed with flowers. The Ancient

Greek goddesses Gaia and Rhea, who played her part in Hellenic religious ritual, long fought against the introduction of the orgiastic worship of the Asiatic goddess. Her twin symbols, the LION and the TABOR, were originally Asiatic. A 'Homeric' Hymn thus describes 'the Mother of all gods and men. She is well-pleased with the sound of rattles and of timbrels, with the voice of flutes and the outcry of wolves and bright-eyed lions, with echoing hills and wooded coombes.'

In the decline of the Roman Empire her worship was associated with that of Attis, the god who died and came to life again, in a cult overlaid by sexual perversion, ritual castration and the bloody sacrifice of the taurobolium (see BULL). In almost hallucinatory style she came to symbolize the rhythms of death and fertility, or rather of fertility through death. A complete theology of 'mother worship' evolved around the goddess in a 'mixture of barbarism, sensuality and mysticism' (LAVD pp. 639–42).

Cyclops (see also ONE-EYED)   The Cyclopes had one eye set in the middle of their foreheads. They were masters of THUNDER, LIGHTNING and THUNDER-BOLTS, resembled volcanoes in their sudden eruptions of violence and were symbols of brute force at the service of Zeus. However, when they roused the anger of APOLLO, he slew them.

If, in human terms, two eyes marks a normal degree of awareness and three a superhuman clairvoyance, then one eye indicates a low and basic level of the powers of the understanding. One eye in the middle of the forehead betrays either the ebbing of the intellect, or its burgeoning, or a loss of apprehension of certain dimensions and relationships.

In Christian tradition the Devil is often depicted with one eye in the middle of his face, symbolizing the domination of the dark powers of the instincts and passions. Left to their own devices and without spiritual direction, they cannot but play a destructive role in the universe and in the human person. In Greek tradition the Cyclopses were a primitive or regressive force, characteristically volcanic, which could only be subdued by a solar god, Apollo. The Cyclops was the focus of two traditions: that of the BLACKSMITH, the servant of Zeus and HEPHAISTOS, making the gods' thunderbolts; and that of the savage MONSTER, of superhuman strength, lurking in CAVERNS, from which it only emerged to hunt its prey. To these legendary creatures the so-called 'cyclopean' architectural remains are attributed, and especially those at Mycenae where stone building blocks of up to 800 tons were employed.

There are no Cyclopses, properly speaking, in Celtic mythology, instead there is a whole series of dark beings with only one eye, one arm, or one leg and who are afflicted in addition with gigantic size and bodily deformity. They symbolize the dark or Titanic side of creation and for that reason Irish legend identifies them with evil and infernal forces. Nevertheless, they maintained constant bonds of kinship with the heavenly or 'bright' deities. Some of them may serve as examples, such as the Irish Balor, who had one eye which by a single glance could paralyse whole armies. The god Lug killed him with a sling-shot. His Welsh equivalent, Ysbaddaden Penkawr, had the same physical peculiarities and was also the father of a daughter whom Culhwch, the counterpart of Lug, asked for in marriage. To sum up, the Cyclops evokes the force or violence of the elements, of brute strength unleashed and uncontrolled by reason. He is an example of the 'odd', that is to say of the subversion of order since, as is well known, all human order is based upon the 'even', the image of balance (see ONE-LEGGED).

cypress The cypress was regarded as a sacred TREE by many different peoples. Thanks to its longevity and evergreen leaves the cypress-thuja was called the Tree of Life.

The Ancient Greeks and Romans associated it with the Underworld deities. It was the tree of the regions below, linked with the worship of Pluto, god of the Underworld and, for this reason, planted in graveyards.

It owed its place as the funereal tree round the whole Mediterranean Basin to the common symbolism of the conifer, its incorruptible resin and evergreen leaves suggesting immortality and resurrection. 'Winter frosts only emphasize the powers of resistance possessed by the cypress, from which they cannot take its leaves' (*Chuang Tzu* ch. 28). In Ancient China it was believed that longevity could be obtained by eating cypress seeds, because they were rich in *yang* substances. To rub the heels with cypress resin enabled one to walk on water, since it made the body light. Jade and gold could be found by the light of burning cypress resin, they being *yang* substances and symbols of immortality.

Origen makes the cypress an emblem of the spiritual virtues since 'cypress emits a sweet smell', the odour of sanctity.

In Japan, a variety of cypress, *hinoki*, is one of the woods most commonly in use in Shintō worship. Apart from its employment in the manufacture of such objects as the *shaku* (sceptre) carried by their priests, it is particularly noticeable that the ritual fire is lighted by rubbing together two *hinoki* sticks. The wood is also used in temple building, as at Ise. Undoubtedly it embodies notions of incorruptibility and of purity.

Again as a symbol of immortality, the cypress (together with the PINE) plays its part in the lodges of Chinese secret societies, standing at the entrance of the 'City of Willows' or the 'Circle of Heaven and Earth'. Confucius says that the Yin planted cypress beside their altars to the Earth (DUSC, HERS, SCHL).

D

Daedalus Daedalus together with HERMES symbolizes ingenuity, but in his case the accent is upon technical rather than commercial skill. He built the labyrinth (see MAZE) in which people lost themselves, and the artificial WINGS with which ICARUS was enabled to escape by flight, but which ultimately brought his destruction. As the builder of the labyrinth, symbol of the subconscious, he might well, in contemporary terms, stand for the misuse of technology and for 'intellectual perversion, the power of thought deprived of its affective function so as to lose clarity and become quixotic and trapped in its own creation, the subconscious' (DIES p. 47). However, his achievements may just as well be conscious and motivated by an ambition which, because it is uncontrolled, leads to disaster. The legendary Daedalus is a symbol of the technocrat, of the sorcerer's apprentice with an engineering degree. He does not know the limitations of his powers, although he represents 'practical intelligence and skill in execution' (DEVD p. 143) and is 'the archetypal thruster, by turns architect, sculptor and mechanical inventor' (GRID p. 118). The living statues which he is supposed to have invented remind us of Leonardo da Vinci's automata: like his successor, Daedalus had as little luck with the princes whom he served.

dakini Female emanations of the Buddhas, heavenly messengers, guardians of secret teachings and the principal inspiration of the yogi, *dakini* symbolize female energy – sometimes destructive but more often creative – linked to transcendental knowledge and complete receptivity, like dancers in boundless space. *Dakini* (Tibetan: *Khandro*) frequently escort the deities depicted in the iconography of the Diamond Vehicle. They were originally shamanistic WITCHES and fairies, subsequently absorbed into Tibetan Buddhism. The 'language of the Dakinis' describes the intimate sense of the terms employed in Tantric literature. The yogi who succeed in 'cosmicizing' their bodies must also experience the destruction of language as an indispensable part of their spiritual training. It shatters the worldly universe and replaces it with a universe with levels which may be transformed and integrated. This is not simply to conceal from the uninitiated the Great Secret – *bodhisattva*, mental enlightenment, semen – but the yogi is called upon to penetrate, both through language and the making of a new and paradoxical language, to that level upon which semen may be transformed into thought and vice versa.

dance Dance is celebration and dance is language, a language beyond words. The courtship dances of birds display this. It is beyond words for, when words fail, up surges the dance. This fever, which can take hold of all beings and drive them to the pitch of frenzy, can only be a manifestation of the Spirit of Life. Often explosive, its aim is to throw off every vestige of the dual nature of temporal things to rediscover at a bound the primeval Oneness. Then body and soul, creator and creation, visible and invisible meet and anneal timelessly in a unique ecstasy. The dance proclaims and celebrates its identification with the imperishable.

Such was David's dance before the Ark of the Covenant or the dance which carried off in a rapture of endless whirling Maulavī (Jalāl-al-Dīn Muhammad Rūmī), founder of the order of Whirling Dervishes and one of the greatest lyric poets of all time. Such are all the primary dances, dances which may be described as sacred. However, the same is true in everyday life of dance of all descriptions, disco or ballet, choreographed or improvised, solo or group, in which, as best they can, humans seek freedom in ecstasy, be it restricted to the body or set on a higher plane – always supposing that there are degrees, forms and levels of ecstasy.

The arrangement and rhythm of the dance are the rungs of the LADDER which provides this escape. This cannot be better illustrated than by the shamans, who on their own admission use dancing in time to the beat of their DRUM to achieve their ascension into the spirit world. Whether it was in the mystery religions of Ancient Greece, in African Orisha and Voodoo, in Siberian or North American shamanism or in the freest of contemporary dance, mankind throughout has expressed in dancing the need to throw aside the bonds of the perishable. The most mundane of dancing lovers differ not a jot in intention from those who join in the innumerable ritual rain dances, the ordeal of the Sun Dance of the Prairie Indians or the funeral dances of Ancient China. All try the soul and aim to strengthen it and to guide it along the invisible path which leads from the perishable to the imperishable. For if dancing is ordeal by fire and prayer, it is also theatre.

There are thousands of examples, like the spirit-possession dances of Haitian Voodoo, which show that this essentially symbolic, theatrical element possesses curative properties. This doubtless is the reason why modern medicine has discovered – or rediscovered – therapeutic qualities in dancing which the so-called animist religions have always employed.

In India, Shiva-natarāja's *tandava* was the prototype of the cosmic dance. Confined within a CIRCLE of FIRE, this dance symbolized creation or propitiation, destruction or preservation. It also symbolized the discipline of yoga. Furthermore, in Tantric Buddhism, Buddha Amoghasiddhi, lord of the current of life, the creator and the intellect, is known as the 'Lord of the Dance'.

Indian religious dancing brings into play every portion of the body in movement which symbolizes precise spiritual states. Hands, fingernails even, eyeballs, nose, lips, arms, legs, feet and thighs all move in a swirl of silk and colours and sometimes in a state of semi-nakedness.

All these images display and invoke a kind of fusion in the same aesthetic, emotional, erotic, religious or mystic motion, like the return to the Sole Being from whom all things emanate and to whom all things return in the ceaseless ebb and flow of the life force.

Chinese tradition, linking dance to the rhythm of numbers, held that it allowed the universe to operate. It tamed wild animals and established the harmony of Heaven and Earth. By dancing, Yu the Great brought to an end the flood caused by an excess of *yin*. The ideogram *wu*, which expresses non-manifestation or destruction, may, according to some critics, have had the original meaning of 'dance'.

Of all places in the world dancing takes its most extravert form in Africa. As Father Mveng observes, it is 'the most dramatic example of cultural display, for it is the only one in which human beings, breaking the mould of the natural world, can seek not merely freedom, but freedom from their natural limitations.' This is why, he maintains, dancing is the only mystical expression of African religion (MVEA p. 81).

In Ancient Egypt, where dances were as numerous as they were elaborate, 'if we can believe Lucian some mimes "translated into expressive movements the most mysterious tenets of their religion, the myths of Apis and Osiris, the transformations of gods into animals, and above all their love affairs"' (POSD p. 57).

Daruma (Bodhidharma)   In Japan he is the symbol of patience and tenacity, popularized in countless small figurines.

Dharma was the first 'Father' of the Zen school, bringing its teachings from India to China in the sixth century AD. According to legend, he sat cross-legged in meditation facing a wall for nine years. This is why he has become the symbol of patience.

His image is to be found throughout Japan in different shapes and forms. One of these shows him seated with a rounded surface substituted for his legs. As a result, whenever the figurine is pushed over it always rights itself, thus illustrating the Japanese proverb that one can fall over seven times and still get up on the eighth.

The origins of this type of figurine are unknown, but they are found worldwide and represent unfailing patience as much as unwearied perseverance.

date-palm   The date-palm was the Assyro-Babylonians' sacred TREE. In the Old Testament it is a symbol of the just man, enriched by the blessings of God. ('The righteous shall flourish like the palm tree' (Psalm 91: 12).)

In Ancient Egypt it was used as a model for architectural COLUMNS, suggesting the Tree of Life and the World AXIS.

Da'wah (call, invocation)   We are concerned with a highly secret method of incantation, but one still regarded as legitimate in Muslim tradition, based upon a complete symbolic theology of LETTERS OF THE ALPHABET. The tables in the *Jawāhiru'-Khamsah*, a treatise by Sheikh Abūl-Muwwayid of Gujerat, set out the correspondences which provide the key to this doctrine. Minutely detailed rules govern the diet to be observed and the ablutions to be performed by the exorcist who practises it or by the mystic who uses it to inspire his meditations. Both should also follow a strict code of morality. The entire system is based upon a supposed relationship between the letters of the Arabic alphabet, the attributes of the godhead, numbers, the four elements, the seven planets and the twelve signs of the Zodiac. Each component of a given series must have correspondences in parallel series. During the incantation appropriate perfumes are burned.

The Da'wah is perhaps the most extensive network of symbolic correspondences. Whoever has mastered it might well possess an almost godlike power over the universe. Whoever knows the secret of letters holds the keys of creation. The Da'wah might also be regarded as symbolizing what contemporary logic understands by a complex system or complex thought. (See appendix on p. 1175.)

dawn For every civilization, 'rosy-fingered' Dawn is the joyful symbol of awakening to a fresh day. Dawn is forever young, never ageing, never dying, she follows her destiny and sees generation succeed generation. There she is every morning, symbol of infinite potentiality and sign of infinite promise. She begins the world afresh and freely offers it to us. Dawn heralds and makes ready the fullness of HARVEST as youth heralds and makes ready that of adulthood. Dawn is the symbol of LIGHT, the promise of fullness and a wellspring of hope in every being.

Insular Celtic literary sources preserve traces of an ancient myth of the dawn, similar to that of Usas in the Vedas, in the legend of Boann and the Dagda and in the Welsh legend of Rhiannon ('Great Queen'). The child of the Sky (the Dagda) and the Dawn (or the Earth) is the Day. Welsh literature regularly uses 'in the youth of the day' as a metaphor for 'dawn' (CELT 15: p. 328).

Dawn, with all its wealth of Judeo-Christian traditional symbolism, is the sign of God's power in the heavens and heralds his victory over the world of darkness, the world of the wicked.

In Islamic mystical poetry, Dawn denotes 'a state of spiritual tension in which the primal event occurs'. The poet feels called upon to become 'fellow-witness and fellow-creator of the beginning of things'. He is filled with 'an intense metaphysical emotion which sometimes takes the shape of anguish . . . and sometimes that of ecstasy' (Daryusch Shayegan in HPBA pp. 126–7).

day The first comparison to be made with the day is that of a regular succession of events – birth, growth, maturity and decline. If some point in the sky above is taken for reference – the eastern horizon, for example, since this is the most important aspect of any horoscope and is termed the 'ascendant' by astrologers – in twenty-four hours this reference point will see the passing of all the degrees of the ZODIAC, while the Moon makes its circuit of the sky in slightly less than twenty-eight days – 27.32, to be precise – and the Sun a whole year. In its monthly course, the Moon would seem to copy the day: it grows larger, reaches its fullness, shrinks and passes into a phase of darkness. The seasons of the year seem, too, to repeat upon a larger scale the divisions of the day: Spring is morning; Summer, noon; Autumn, sunset; and Winter, darkness. As far back as the third millennium BC Sumerian literary sources show how comparisons were made between a day, a lunar month and a year.

The same concept as Ezekiel's 'For I have laid upon thee the years of their iniquity, according to the number of the days' (4: 5), is to be found not only among the Babylonians, but in the Vedas and in Chinese tradition as well. To an astrologer, these are not vague comparisons or poetic similes, but astronomical interactions which must be taken into account when casting a horoscope and upon which datable forecasts are chiefly based. The configurations produced in respect of the position of the stars on the twentieth day after birth, together with those in the twentieth lunar month, correspond with events occurring in the twentieth year of the subject's life, and so on. These comparisons are the very basis of what are termed 'astrological directions' which are classified, in order of importance, primary, secondary and tertiary. The 'primary directions' are favoured by French astrologers, the 'secondary' (1 day = 1 year) have been employed by astrologers in the English-speaking world since the seventeenth century, while the 'tertiary' (1 lunar month = 1 year), although first studied by the American Benjamine and the Frenchman Maurice Froger, have been particular favourites of the Germans for the last twenty years.

Jewish thinkers have represented the CREATION as being carried out over six days: the significance of the SEVENTH day being that it represented eternal life. The six days' creation set out in Genesis has been a favourite topic for countless Jewish and Christian commentators.

In the *Ascension of Isaiah*, freed from the bondage of the flesh, the soul undertakes a journey which corresponds to the six days of the creation of the world, the seventh day symbolizing the rest which God took. The soul had thus to pass through seven Heavens. It experienced the creation of the self through the different creations of God and the succession of days. Each day symbolized a stage of spiritual ascension.

Other rabbinical commentators interpret the seventh day not as the day upon which God rested after his work of creation – since God cannot feel weariness – but as the moment when God of his own volition ceased to intervene in the world, the moment when he handed government of and responsibility for the universe to mankind. This was so that by undertaking the task he might bring it to completion, humanize it and make it worthy to receive in due course its Creator, who would then dwell with his creation. Correspondingly by being given this task of joint creation, mankind becomes worthy to live with its God. Thus the seventh day represents the time for specifically human activity, when mankind is left to its own devices, the time for creation and cultivation as opposed to the natural world, created in six days and given to mankind as a field for its own activity. By contrast, the eighth day will be one of renewal, when Creator and creature will be made one again in a universe of perfect harmony.

day-lily The day-lily is a symbol of fleeting beauty by reason of its splendid yet short-lived blossoming. In China it is called *huan*, and has the virtue of dispelling care (BELT).

death Death marks the absolute conclusion of some positive thing, such as a human being, an animal, a plant, a friendship, an engagement, peace or an age.

In so far as it is a symbol, death is the impermanent and perishable aspect of living. It points to what must vanish in the inevitable evolution of material things and is akin to the symbolism of EARTH. However, it also ushers in the unknown worlds of Heaven and Hell, thus demonstrating its ambivalence, like Earth, and setting it, in some respects, upon the same plane as rites of passage. Death is the harbinger of revelation. All rites of initiation include a death-phase preceding a new life. In this sense, death has psychological properties, in that it liberates from negative and regressive forces, dematerializes and sets free the ascensional powers of the spirit. Although Death may be the daughter of Night and the sister of Sleep, like her mother and brother she is endowed with powers of regeneration. If the person struck down by death lives only on the material and animal plane, he or she sinks into Hell: on the other hand, if that person lives at a spiritual level, Death unlocks the GATES of the realm of light. Mystics are in agreement with doctors and psychologists in observing that within every being at all levels of existence life and death co-exist. In other words, that there is a tension between countervailing forces. Perhaps death at one level may be the condition for life at another, higher level.

Dis Pater, mentioned by Caesar in his *De bello Gallico*, and from whom all the Gauls claimed descent, was primarily a death-god as well as being the father of the tribe. The former was the dark side of the Supreme Deity, otherwise known as Ogmios (Ogme in Ireland). The Ankou, the allegory of death in Britanny, carries on the tradition of the conductor of the dead from the medieval Dance of Death and, despite Christianization, that of Ogmios (OGAC 3: p. 168; 15: p. 258).

This does not stop the mystery of death from being regarded traditionally as an agony and depicted as something terrifying. Taken to its logical conclusion, however, this is more resistance to change into an unknown existence than dread of being absorbed once again into nothingness.

The Ancient Greeks embodied the destructive powers of death in Eurynomos, an Underworld spirit 'whose task it was to devour the flesh of the dead and to leave only their bones . . . . Painted dark blue, like a blow-fly, he bared his teeth, and the throne on which he sat was covered with a VULTURE's skin' (Pausanias, *Description of Greece* 10: 28–31).

Life-giving and, correspondingly, death-dealing powers were invested in the gods. Second only to Zeus, these death-dealers were Athene, Apollo, Artemis (Diana), Ares (Mars), Hades (Pluto), Hecate and Persephone. Death was personified in Thanatos, son of Night and brother of Sleep, 'unpredictable, unfeeling and pitiless' (LAVD pp. 656–64). In Classical iconography, death may be depicted by a tomb; by a being armed with a SCYTHE; by a divinity with its jaws clamped upon a human being; by a winged spirit; by two youths, one BLACK, the other WHITE; by a HORSEMAN, a SKELETON, a dance of death; by a SERPENT or indeed any animal, such as a HORSE or a DOG, which performs the duties of conductor of souls.

The general symbolism of death may also be seen in the thirteenth major arcanum of the TAROT. It bears no name, as if its number was in itself significant enough and its makers were too afraid to mention it. The number THIRTEEN carried a maleficent significance throughout the Christian Middle Ages as it had already done in Classical antiquity, since it symbolizes 'the cyclic course of human activity . . . the passage to another state of being and, hence, of death' (ALLN pp. 358–60).

Death – or the Reaper – embodies an important development, grief, the transformation of beings and things, change, inescapable destiny and, according to Wirth, disillusionment, detachment, stoicism, loss of confidence and pessimism. Jean Vassel states (ETUT 278: p. 282) that Death constitutes a break in the series of Tarot picture cards and those that follow it are

the higher arcana. As a result, the first twelve may be made to correspond
to the 'lesser mysteries' and the twelve which follow to the 'greater mysteries', since it is obvious that the succeeding cards have a more 'celestial'
character than those which preceded them. Like the JUGGLER, in astrology
Death corresponds to the first house in the horoscope.

The Tarot card depicts a skeleton armed with a scythe, and speaks for
itself. The figure is completely flesh-coloured and not golden, and one foot
is deep in the soil. In its left hand it carries a scythe, the handle YELLOW and
the blade RED, the colour of fire and blood. 'Is this to warn us that the death
depicted here is not death of the physical body, but the destruction which
threatens our spiritual existence, if initiation does not save us from annihilation?' (RIJT p. 214).

The soil is BLACK: BLUE and yellow plants grow in it. Beneath the skeleton's foot there is a woman's head and beside the scythe-blade that of a
man crowned. Three hands, a foot and two bones are scattered here and
there.

The faces preserve their expressions, as if they were still alive. The one on the
right wears a kingly crown, symbol of the kingship of the will and the intelligence which none abdicates in death. The features of the face on the left preserve their feminine beauty, because love does not die and the soul retains its
power beyond the grave. The hands sticking out of the ground, ready for action,
proclaim that the Work cannot be interrupted while the feet . . . are prepared to
set ideas in motion . . . nothing ceases: everything moves on!
                                                                (WIRT pp. 190–1)

This is because death has more than one meaning. It frees from trouble
and care; it is not an end in itself; it opens the gates to the realm of the
spirit, true life: *mors janua vitae* (Death is the Gate of Life). In its esoteric
sense, death symbolizes the profound change effected in a person by initiation. 'The uninitiate must die to be reborn in the higher life conferred
by initiation. Unless he or she dies to a state of imperfection, the way of
progress by initiation is barred' (WIRT p. 188). Similarly, in ALCHEMY, the
matter which will provide the substance of the Philosopher's Stone is sealed
within a closed receptacle, deprived of all external contact, and must die
and putrefy. Thus the thirteenth card of the Tarot symbolizes death in the
sense of renewal and rebirth given to it by initiation. Following upon the
mystical HANGING MAN, abandoned in total surrender, who regains his strength
by contact with the Earth, Death reminds us that we must go beyond and
that it is the essential ingredient of progress and of life.

decan(ate)   An important division of the astrological ZODIAC into THIRTY-
SIX parts. As its name shows, each decanate comprises ten degrees and
there are three to each sign. Classical tradition attributed their discovery to
the Ancient Egyptians and they did, in fact, use decanates to determine the
hours of darkness.

They had drawn up tables of these constellations and when one appeared on
the horizon they were able to tell what the time was . . . . During a period of
about ten days the same decan was visible on the horizon. The 36 decans, each

of which presided over 10 day periods of the Egyptian year, were believed to be protective geniuses. Later they figured prominently in Hellenistic astrology.
(POSD p. 58)

Archeological evidence goes back to the tenth Dynasty – mid-third millennium BC – but often defies identification with definite stars and signs, since there were at least four different sets of symbols for them. Kassite documents of around the middle of the second millennium BC bear witness to this division of the sky into thirty-six sectors in Mesopotamia.

It is impossible to give here the different symbolic images employed by the Ancient Egyptians and depicted upon sarcophagi, temple walls and tombs. However, from those times until the present day, each of these decanates has been represented by a symbol, has a particular significance and stands in affinity to a particular planet. Below, these decanates are listed according to their contemporary employment in India, as given by Cyrus D. F. Abayakoon.

Aries 1st Decanate: A brave man in armour, brandishing a sword in his right hand, signifying boldness, courage, strength and lack of humility: governed by Mars;
2nd Decanate: A man in vestments like a priest, indicative of nobility, greatness, power and high authority; the Sun;
3rd Decanate: A maiden seated on a stool and playing her lute; represents delicate skill in the crafts, gentleness, grace, cheerfulness and beauty; Venus.
Taurus 1st Decanate: A book and a young man ploughing the land, indicative of tilling, seed-time, building, in-dwelling, agricultural knowledge, science and especially the science of geometry; Mercury;
2nd Decanate: A tall man, wearing a belt and holding a key in his right hand; signifies power, nobility, rank and command of others; the Moon;
3rd Decanate: An old man supported by a crutch, with one arm hanging down and a wooden leg; represents poverty, slavery, madness, privation and lowliness; Saturn.
Gemini 1st Decanate: A youth wearing a belt; harbinger of writing, giving or receiving money, the search for or knowledge of unprofitable matters; Jupiter;
2nd Decanate: A man with an axe cutting wood; signifies burdens, pressure, toil and gaining possession of wealth by hard work or dishonesty; Mars;
3rd Decanate: A man with a falcon on his right hand and a net in his left; indicates forgetfulness, scorn, cheerfulness and listening to idle chatter; the Sun.
Cancer 1st Decanate: A beautiful maiden holding a flower in her hand; signifies joy, discrimination, kindness, courtesy and the qualities which attract men's love; Venus;
2nd Decanate: A man and a woman seated at table with a great pile of money in front of them; expressive of sexual enjoyment, wealth and plenty; Mercury;
3rd Decanate: A huntsman blowing his horn, with his hound at his heels and a spear over his shoulder; illustrative of hunting, the pursuit of fugitives, obtaining wealth through warfare, quarrels and arguments; the Moon.

Leo 1st Decanate: A man mounted on a lion with a feather in his hat; indicative of cruelty, malevolence, violence and the accomplishment of great deeds, boldness and greed; Saturn;

2nd Decanate: A man with a falcon on his wrist; indicative of love, society, integration, loyalty to one's friends, and the avoidance of quarrels; Jupiter;

3rd Decanate: A man brandishing a sword above his head with one hand and holding a shield in the other; signifies quarrels, arguments, poverty, ignorance and triumph over the poor and lowly by force of arms and through playing upon their ignorance, wars; Mars.

Virgo 1st Decanate: A man placing money in a chest; indicates seed-time, ploughing, farming, peopling the Earth, the piling up of wealth and the filling of barns; the Sun;

2nd Decanate: Two men, one holding a purse; symbol of profit, acquisition, greedy accumulation, of being miserly and raising oneself through force; Venus;

3rd Decanate: A broken-down old man leaning on a staff; suggests old age, weakness, laziness, loss of limbs though sickness, and the destruction of woodland and the unpeopling of places; Mercury.

Libra 1st Decanate: A student with an open book in front of him; illustrative of justice, righteousness, truth, help given to the weak against the strong and the wicked, as well as help to the poor and unfortunate; the Moon;

2nd Decanate: An old man in a long gown, seated in a chair; foretells gluttony, sodomy, song and enjoyment, indulgence in evil pleasures; Saturn;

3rd Decanate: A young man holding a chalice; suggests peace, plenty and the good, tranquil and secure life; Jupiter.

Scorpio 1st Decanate: Two men fighting and gripping one another by the hair; symbolizes struggle, sorrow, trickery, treachery, destruction and malevolence; Mars;

2nd Decanate: A man sitting on a stool with two dogs beside him fighting; signifies insults, betrayals, the creation of discord and the pursuit of bitter feuds; the Sun;

3rd Decanate: Two women pulling one another's hair, one of them beating the other over the head with a stick; war, drunkenness, fornication, anger and pride; Venus.

Sagittarius 1st Decanate: A man armed with an axe; signifies boldness, freedom and war; Mercury;

2nd Decanate: A weeping man sitting on a stool; suggests fear, grief, disappointment and timidity; the Moon;

3rd Decanate: A man with a feather in his hat, holding a stick with his finger-tips; indicates obstinacy and a closed mind, inability to deny oneself, a proneness to evil, contention and horrible things; Saturn.

Capricorn 1st Decanate: A man journeying on foot; sign of foresight, toil, joy, profit and loss, weakness and baseness; Jupiter;

2nd Decanate: A man trying to catch a flying bird; the pursuit of the unattainable; Mars;

3rd Decanate: A man sitting at a table counting his money; depicts covetousness, management of one's wealth, of not being self-sufficient and of being suspicious; the Sun.

Aquarius 1st Decanate: A woman sitting on a rock spinning; suggests an anxious temperament, pursuit of sordid gain, never being able to relax, toil, injury, poverty and slyness; Venus;

2nd Decanate: An attractive, well-dressed woman seated on a stool; signifies beauty, understanding, modesty, sound morals, good manners and freedom; Mercury;

3rd Decanate: A man with his hands on his hips and an envious look in his eye; indicative of betrayal and insult; the Moon.

Pisces 1st Decanate: A traveller with a pack on his back; suggests richness of thought, travel, change of location, the pursuit of wealth and the means of livelihood; Saturn;

2nd Decanate: An old man pointing to the sky with his finger; illustrates self-praise, the spirit of greatness, the pursuit and intervention in other people's business for the highest and noblest of motives; Jupiter;

3rd Decanate: A youth hugging a lovely woman; depicts fornication, petting and sexual pleasures and love of peace and quiet; Mars.

It is impossible to set a date upon this series of symbols which is virtually unknown in Europe, but it is undoubtedly extremely ancient. When casting a horoscope, especial regard is paid to those decanates which contain the ascendant, the Sun or the Moon, by relating their significance to other astrological factors.

decapitation In various primitive religions, decapitation derived from ritual and belief. Since the HEAD was the home of the spirit, it needed to be preserved or destroyed, according to whether it belonged to a friend or to an enemy.

The Celts in the British Isles as well as on the continent used to cut off the heads of the enemies whom they had killed in single combat. This custom had a religious basis for, if the god of medicine, Dian Cécht, were to be believed, restoration to life or cure were possible so long as the essential organs – brain, spinal marrow and cerebral membrane – were intact. The heads thus cut off were kept as battle trophies and, whole or in part, treated for this purpose. One Irish literary source mentions tongues and another brains mixed with clay and rolled into balls for games. Livy records that after the Cisalpine Gauls defeated the consul Postumius, his SKULL was carried with high ceremony to their chief temple, mounted in precious metal and used as a ritual CHALICE (OGAC 10: pp. 130, 139ff., 286; 11: 4).

Similar customs are recorded all over the world, from the celebrated shrunken skulls of the Jivaro Indians of Ecuador to the skull-sculptures of the Pacific. The Bamum of Cameroon, it may be observed, cut off the heads of enemies killed in battle, but only preserved the lower jaws of these trophies. Among the various uses to which they were put was to decorate the rims of the CALABASHES used ceremonially to serve palm-wine at the court of Fumban.

deer (see also GAZELLE; HIND; STAG) Eating deer (*venado*) is taboo to the Panche Indians of Colombia since they believe that after death human souls pass into the bodies of these creatures.

The Aztecs sometimes depicted the first deified woman, the mother of the Twin Heroes, called the serpent-woman, as a two-headed deer which dropped from the sky and was used as a fetish in war (SOUM).

In Mayan hieroglyphics, the dying deer is a symbol of drought (THOH).

In several ancient Mexican codices, including the Codex Borgia, deer are depicted carrying the Sun (BEYM).

To most of the tribes peopling the steppes of central Asia the deer was a conductor of souls. The robes of the shamans were often made from deerskin and some shamans wore on their heads or their backs iron copies of deer's or stag's antlers (HARA).

deformity (see also BLINDNESS; CYCLOPS; DWARF; ONE-ARMED; ONE-EYED) Those malign or dark beings which Irish literature calls Fomorians are without exception described as being deformed, having either naturally or by counter-initiation, only one eye, one leg or one arm, and these limbs are often of monstrous size or back-to-front. All beings, therefore, suffering from physical blemish or deformity – mutilation, whole or partial blindness – may be judged as belonging to the powers of darkness and therefore endowed with magical powers (OGAC 18: pp. 37–394).

The removal or absence of anything which contributes to the body's wholeness or symmetry, although it may not necessarily be a deformity, involves a return from human 'duality' to 'oneness', is connected with the symbolism of the sacred nature of RIGHT AND LEFT and is more fully treated under ONE-LEGGED and MUTILATION.

All deformities are signs of mysteries which may be either benign or malign. Like all anomalies, the first emotion they arouse may be one of repugnance, but this is a ground or a sign of being favoured, by the concealment of something very precious which requires great pains if it is to be acquired. This explains the mingled fear and respect in which African society holds the feeble-minded, the halt and, especially, the blind, the latter being judged able to see beyond the outward appearance of things.

(HAMK p. 32)

To understand the anomaly, one must overstep the normal bounds of judgement. In so doing one gains a deeper knowledge of the mysteries of being and of life.

It is a commonplace that the blind are often regarded as 'seers' in the sense of being 'second-sighted' or clairvoyant. In the same way, deaf people may be regarded as being 'clair-audiant'.

Deformity makes its victim the benign or malign intercessor between the known and the unknown, the dark and the bright side of nature, this world and the beyond. This ambiguous role is given to the hunchback on so many occasions in folktales.

Finally, it should be observed that a number of sexological studies and enquiries provides evidence that some deformities or infirmities, such as a club-foot or the complete or partial paralysis of a limb, are charged with strong erogenous powers.

degree It would appear as if in the beginning the whole of astrology was expressed in pictorial symbols which were open to more than one interpretation. Before the specific influence of each factor had been written down, picture had preceded logical formulation, symbols always being both more meaningful and universal and thus more correct. As far as the ZODIAC is concerned, the entry DECANATE lists the symbols and the significance which Hindu astrologers currently attach to each third of a sign. However, each zodiacal degree is represented by a symbol and governed by a PLANET as well.

The symbols of the decanates and those of the degrees combine to form the *Sphaera Barbarica* mentioned by Nigidius Figulus, Firmicus Maternus and many others. It is traditionally claimed that in antiquity this *Sphaera Barbarica* was given physical shape in vast buildings like Ozymandias' Golden Circle mentioned by Diodorus Siculus (2: 7) (its name should be compared with that of 'the golden keys' given to the *Volasfera*); like the 360 towers of Babylon, each 8.3m wide and set 44m apart; or the 360 stelae, altars or idols surrounding the Ka'ba of pre-Islamic Mecca. In Muslim countries the 360 degrees of the Zodiac are regarded as the 360 expressions on the face of Allah, each one different.

(For contemporary lists of the 360 symbols of the Zodiac see: 'Charubel', *The Degrees of the Zodiac Symbolized*, London, 1898; 'Janduz', *Les 360° du Zodiaque symbolisés*, Paris, 1938; and Marc Edmund Jones, *The Sabian Symbols in Astrology*, New York, 1953.)

Demeter (Ceres) (see also CYBELE) Fertility-goddess, Earth-mother-goddess, Mother Earth herself, her worship is lost in the mists of antiquity and shrouded in the deepest mystery. She was central to the initiatory and mystery rites at Eleusis, which celebrated eternal renewal, the cycle of death and rebirth, probably in the sense of the progressive spiritualization of matter. She bore PERSEPHONE, her only daughter, who was ravished by Hades and became queen of the Underworld. Her agonized search for her daughter, which took her down to Hell, itself provided the theme for many moving poems in Classical antiquity. In art, mother and daughter are depicted as being joined in equal affection. They were jointly invoked by worshippers seeking to ensure the survival of souls in the kingdom of the dead.

Demeter endowed Triptolemus, son of the King of Eleusis, with an EAR OF CORN. Triptolemus journeyed worldwide to teach mankind agriculture. Plants, however, are just as subject to the laws of death and rebirth: 'if the grain die not'. Before it germinates and sprouts, the seed must spend months under ground, just as Persephone spent six Winter months with Hades in the Underworld and six Spring and Summer months with her mother in the sunshine of Olympus.

Through her connections with her daughter, an Underworld goddess, and with Triptolemus, who taught the cultivation of corn, Demeter is revealed as the goddess of the alternation of life and death which underlies the cycle of plant- and all other life-forms. She thus shares the symbolism of the Earth Mother. However, her Earth differs from the cosmogonic element of Gaia and Rhea in that she symbolizes cultivated Earth, the soil which produces corn and rich HARVESTS of all sorts (GRID p. 120; DIES p. 122).

Thus Demeter symbolizes a vital phase in evolution, the passage from wild crops to cultivated crops, from the savage to the civilized state. If sexual symbols were interposed in the rites of initiation into the great

Eleusinian Mysteries, it was apparently not so much to evoke the fertility
of sexual intercourse as to assure the initiate of rebirth into LIGHT and bliss
in the Beyond. 'Blessed among men', says the 'Homeric' Hymn to Demeter,
'are those who behold these mysteries.'

In Paul Diel's psychoanalytic interpretation (DIES p. 197), Persephone,
Demeter's daughter, is seen as 'the pre-eminent symbol of unconscious
repression', while the hidden meaning of the Eleusinian Mysteries would
comprise 'a descent into the subconscious in order to set free the suppressed desire (in order to reach the truth with regard to oneself) which
may well be one's very highest achievement.' Demeter, who gave to mankind BREAD, the symbol of spiritual nourishment, would give it the true
meaning of life, the 'sublimation and spiritualization of earthly desire', in
other words, 'freedom from all emotional excess', as well as from all inhibitions. Thus Demeter establishes her claim as the 'symbol of justifiable
earthly desire, receiving satisfaction thanks to the artful work of the servant-
intellect which, while it tills the land, remains open to the call of the spirit.'
Demeter, a fertile spiritual and material influence, is inferior to a spirit such
as Hera, wife of Zeus (DIES p. 122). She is not the light, but the path to
the light, or the torch which lights that path.

demon (see also DEVIL) In Greek thought demons, or rather *daimones*,
were divine or godlike beings with their own special powers. A particular
person's *daimon* was also identified with the divine will and in consequence
with the fate of that person. Later the word came to be used of minor gods,
and finally of evil spirits.

According to another line of thought, daimons were the souls of the
dead, protective or malign spirits which acted as intermediaries between
the immortal gods and living, but mortal men. Each person had his or her
own GENIUS, which acted as a secret adviser by way of sudden intuitions
rather than by the thought process. They were in some sense the person's
inner source of inspiration.

Daimons symbolize a higher than normal degree of enlightenment which
enables their owners to see farther and more clearly, and in a way which
defies explanation. They allow the rules of logic to be set aside in the name
of transcendent enlightenment which belongs not just to the order of knowledge but to that of fate.

Unlike the inner daimon which is, as it were, a symbol of the special
relationship of its owner with a higher consciousness and which sometimes
plays the part of a guardian angel, many primitive peoples regard demons
as a distinct species. Their numbers cannot be counted and they hover
everywhere for better or worse. Such peoples, as for example those in
Indonesia, see

the universe peopled with visible and invisible beings – living plants, the spirits
of animals in human shape and those of humans in animals, demons dwelling
in the seven depths of the Underworld and gods and nymphs filling the seven
Heavens above, all able to mingle through the seven levels of the human world
and in man himself, the microcosm within the macrocosm, all confounded in
one moving polymorphous mass.

(SOUD pp. 403–4)

In Christian demonology, according to the Pseudo-Dionysius the Areopagite, demons are ANGELS who have betrayed their nature, but who were neither originally nor naturally evil. 'But neither are daimones evil by nature. For if they are evil by nature they are neither from the Good, nor do they exist in the nature of things, nor, again, did they change from good, if they are always evil by nature . . . . Hence the race of daimones is not evil in so far as it is according to nature, but in so far as it is not' (PSEN pp. 48–9). They are shown to be enemies of the natural world and opponents of whatever is.

desert There are two essential symbolical meanings to the word 'desert'. It is the primordial undifferentiated state; or it is a superficially sterile crust under which Reality must be sought.

It is hardly surprising that this symbolism should be employed by Islam, but generally, it would seem, in the latter sense. Thus Abd al-Qadir al-Jīlānī wrote: 'Outside His abode the flock wanders in the desert. What impassable barriers stretch before the caravan which moves towards It.' It will be noticed how this search for the Essence is reminiscent of the search for the Promised Land by the Children of Israel across the Sinai Desert and the Quest of the Holy GRAIL.

In Ismaili esotericism the 'desert' is the external being, the body, the world, the letter, blindly traversed in oblivion of the divine Being concealed beneath these outward appearances. According to St Matthew (12: 43) the desert is the abode of unclean spirits. The opposite view is taken by Richard of St Victor: the desert is the heart, the place where the ascetic life may be interiorized. The contradiction is more apparent than real, since Christ was tempted in the wilderness and such Desert Fathers as St Anthony underwent the attacks of DEMONS there. Nor are the heart's Desert Fathers more likely to escape: their desert is that of lusts and diabolical imaginings exorcized.

Shankara used the symbolism of the desert (*marū*) rather in the first sense, to mean primordial and undifferentiated uniformity beyond which nothing exists except as illusion, rather like a mirage. For Master Eckhart 'the desert where God alone is king' is an undifferentiated state, rediscovered by spiritual effort, identical in this respect with the 'SEA' of Buddhist symbolism. Angelus Silesius says 'the Deity is the desert' and even 'I must rise still higher above God in a desert', in other words, until I attain the undifferentiated state of the First Cause (CORT, ECKT, JILH).

At the risk of seeming paradoxical, the symbol of the desert is one of the most fertile to be found in the Bible.

Sterile, uninhabited land: mankind sees the desert as meaning the world deprived of God's presence. It has been regarded as the abode of unclean spirits (Matthew 12: 43; Luke 8: 29), as the place of punishment for the Children of Israel (Deuteronomy 29: 5), and where Jesus was tempted (Mark 1: 12ff.).

Nevertheless, the writers of the Bible could not conceive of circumstances mightier than their God. That is why, if we go back to the passages quoted above, the sojourn of the Children of Israel in the Wilderness was regarded by the prophets (for example Hosea 2: 16; 13: 5ff.) as a time when the

people had to place themselves completely in the grace of God (see MANNA).
Even Jesus, when he had overcome temptation, had ANGELS to minister to
him in the desert (Mark 1: 13).

This is why, in the primitive Church, monks retired to the desert as hermits (the Greek for 'solitary' is *eremos*), there to confront their own nature
and that of the world with the help of God alone. The symbolic undertones
of the word are particularly appropriate in this context, because it was not
long before it was no longer believed essential to retire to an actual desert
in order to lead an eremitical life.

Because the passage of the Children of Israel through the Wilderness had
been a striking manifestation of the power of God, the Jews ardently awaited
the time when similar circumstances would herald their final salvation. Thus
the historian Flavius Josephus (*Jewish Wars* 2: 259–61) records how a prophet
drew enthusiastic crowds into the desert in clear anticipation of God's final
intervention in human affairs (Acts 21: 38). After the capture of Jerusalem,
when the destruction of the Temple visibly ended the hopes of Jewish
nationalism, a mass movement made one plea to the Roman invaders – the
vanquished asked leave to withdraw to the wilderness. There, no doubt,
they would be better placed to await final salvation from their God. Such
currents of contemporary thought must be seen behind the warning of the
Evangelist: 'Wherefore if they shall say unto you, Behold he [the Messiah]
is in the desert; go not forth' (Matthew 24: 26). Finally, it was clearly not
due to chance that St John the Baptist preached the imminent coming of
the long-awaited Messiah in the desert (Matthew 3: 1; and parallels). Since
the wilderness is made for revelation, it favours the endeavours of false as
strongly as that of true prophets.

Revelation 12: 10, 14 must be understood within the context of a second
Exodus which duplicates the conditions of the first. The Woman, that is the
People of God, is persecuted by the Dragon and flees to the wilderness
where God provides her with miraculous food.

The opposing aspects of the symbol are particularly striking. Setting
aside its image of solitude, the desert, without God, is barrenness: with God
it is fruitfulness, but fruitfulness due to God alone. The desert displays the
supremacy of grace. In the spiritual order nothing exists without it: all exists
through it and through it alone.

Devil (see also DEMON)

The myth of the Devil is closely akin to the myths of the DRAGON, the SERPENT
and the guardian at the door [see MONSTER] and to the symbolism of closing off
and of setting fixed limits. To pass those limits is to become either damned or
saved, the Devil's victim, or the elect of God. It is either the Fall or the Ascension. The notion of God comprehends that of the opening of a hidden CENTRE
of grace, light and revelation.

(VIRI p. 791)

The Devil symbolizes all those forces which disturb, cloud or weaken
human consciousness and cause it to regress to indeterminacy and ambivalence. He is the centre of darkness, as God is the centre of light, blazing in
the Underworld as God shines in Heaven.

The Devil is the symbol of evil. It matters little whether he is the fine gentleman or the grotesque of the capitals of cathedral pillars, whether he wears the GOAT's or the CAMEL's head, cloven hooves, horns or shaggy hair, he has a multitude of shapes at his disposal, yet always remains the Tempter and the Tormentor. His fall from grace is symbolized by his debasement into animal shape. The Devil's entire purpose is to deprive humans of the grace of God and to make them yield to his control. The fallen angel, his wings clipped, wills the clipping of the spiritual wings of all beings. He is the synthesis of all those powers which lead to the disintegration of the personality. By contrast, CHRIST's role is to snatch humanity from the Devil's clutches through the mystery of the Crucifixion. Christ's CROSS sets mankind free; that is to say, by the grace of God it restores to human beings the freedom, which the Devil's tyranny had taken from them, to dispose of their own selves.

With TEMPERANCE on one side and the TOWER on the other, the fifteenth major arcanum of the TAROT provides a meditation upon the Devil. 'It expresses the conjunction of the powers of nature and of the four natural elements (Earth, Air, Fire and Water) with which human life is interwoven. These are the desire to slake one's passions at no matter what cost, cares, hyperactivity, the use of illicit means and weakness yielding to oppressive influences' (Wirth). 'In astrology it corresponds to the third house of the horoscope and somehow stands for qualities opposite to those of the EMPRESS. Instead of the carefully controlled mastery of external powers, the Devil stands for a regression into disorder, discord and dissolution, not simply upon the physical plane, but on a moral and metaphysical level, too' (André Virel).

Standing half-naked upon a flesh-coloured orb half-buried in a pedestal or in a red anvil of six plates set one above the other, the Devil, his androgynous qualities heavily emphasized, has blue and BAT-like wings, blue breeches held up by a red belt curving below his navel and with fingers and toes clawed like those of an ape. His right arm is raised. In his left he holds, by its blade and pointing towards the ground, a sword which lacks both hilt and guard. His head-dress is a peculiar yellow combination of a pair of crescent Moons facing one another and the antlers of a stag of five points. To his pedestal is fixed a ring through which a rope passes, either end knotted round the throat of a pair of identical imps, both stark naked, one male the other female, although they, too, are sometimes hermaphrodites. Each has a long tail touching the ground. Their toes are clawed and their hands are behind their backs, while on their heads they wear red caps from which sprout a pair of black antlers, two sparks of fire or two horns. The ground is yellow, the upper portion streaked with black lines, but below the feet of the two imps, it is as black as that over which passes the SCYTHE of DEATH, the thirteenth arcanum.

The entire atmosphere is that of the domain of Hell, where brute beast and human are no longer differentiated. The Devil rules the occult powers and his parody of God, the 'Ape of God', stands as a warning of the perils incurred by those who seek to use those powers for their own purposes by diverting them from their appointed ends.

The seeker after hidden knowledge and occult power must keep his balance like the JUGGLER, or, like the hero in the CHARIOT, hold in check the adverse tendencies of the abyss, like the HERMIT gain inner peace or, like the HANGING MAN, unselfishly victorious broadcast the fruits of his knowledge. Otherwise he will fall victim to the untrammelled, flowing currents which he has raised or projected and which he cannot control. When dealing with the occult one has either to succeed in mastering it or resign oneself to being its slave. There is no standing on level terms with the Powers of Annihilation, one is either victor over or vanquished by them.

(RIJT p. 250)

Nevertheless these powers are esssential to the balance of nature itself. Lucifer, bearer of light, alone could become the Prince of Darkness, and when the cards of the Tarot are arranged in two lines, the eighth arcanum dominates the fifteenth, 'the odd, triangular number, the dynamic and creative agent' (ALLN p. 362), so as to remind us that the Devil himself remains bound by the universal law of JUSTICE.

On the psychological plane the Devil demonstrates the servitude which awaits the person who is the blind slave of instinct, emphasizing, however, at the same time the fundamental importance of the libido. Without it, full human development is impossible; while to escape the fall of the TOWER (sixteenth arcanum), a person will have needed to be able to confront these terrifying powers in a dynamic fashion.

Devourer (*t'ao-t'i*)   In Granet's writings in particular, this word is used to translate the Chinese ideogram *t'ao-t'i*. In the present context it may also be applied to those representations carrying very much the same significance which in India and other Hindu areas are known as *kāla-mukha* or *kīrtimukha*. In both instances, the words in question are applied to frightening MONSTERS which often, but not always, lack their lower jaws, perhaps a dim memory of the animal skins worn by the shaman. Chang dynasty bronzes are decorated with *t'ao-t'i* but, it is claimed, they had already been used on Hia cauldrons. They were one of the four evil influences which Chouen exiled to the four points of the compass. The *t'ao-t'i* was a man-eating monster, part OWL and part RAM, but perhaps also depicted sometimes as a stylized double DRAGON.

The *kāla* was at one and the same time LION and sea monster. It was Rahu, the DEMON who devours the Sun during eclipses. Kāla is Time, the devourer of life, and is a title of Yama, lord of the dead who, in his Tibetan shape of Shinje, devours the living contents of the Wheel of Life. Nevertheless, while Yama may be Mrityu (death), his origins were solar and he was the creator of the living. The Javanese *kālamakara* itself shares these solar characteristics, while the *t'ao-t'i* is sometimes depicted upon MIRRORS, themselves Suns.

It can therefore be seen that the Devourer is both destruction and creation, death and life, whence may be derived the symbol of the two dragons facing one another. Kāla may devour, but he also produces wreaths of foliage, MAKARA and, at Angkor, NAGA. This is why the monster's jaws stay gaping wide and why the QUAIL may be delivered from the jaws of the WOLF. If it is not to be brought to a halt for good, the movement of the cosmos must be one of ebb and flow. It is significant that, like the *kālamukha*, the *t'ao-t'i* should be most commonly depicted upon door-posts. While the doorway may be that of death, it is also that of deliverance. Death is not destruction but transformation. Life, an emanation of the First Cause, returns to the First Cause. The quail may be swallowed, but it is not destroyed, entering the CAVERN which is the antechamber of Heaven. The *kālamukha* is the universal rhythm of manifestation, comforting yet frightening at one and the same time, now ebbing, now flowing, expansion and contraction, *kalpa* and *pralaya*. The face of glory is the face of the Sun through which release from the cosmos may be effected. It is also the face of God, abstract and concrete, hidden and revealed, the eternal and awesome play of cosmic illusion (BURA, CHRC, COOS, CORA, COMD, DANA, SWAC).

dew   Generally speaking the symbolism of dew is closely akin to that of RAIN, but its influence is of a more subtle order. As the expression of heavenly blessing, it is essentially life-giving grace. 'The waters which spring from the heart,' wrote Callixtus II Xanthopoulos, 'fill the entire inner being with divine dew.' 'The pearly dew of the noble godhead' of which Angelus Silesius writes has a similar significance, but suggests the redeeming BLOOD of Christ. Now, in medieval iconography, the blood, which falls drop by drop from the Centurion's spear, is also the heavenly dew, the symbol of redemption and rebirth, which recurs in Hermetic writings and also in the Jewish Kabbalah, where it is an emanation of the Tree of Life. Apparently there was a 'tree of sweet dew' on Mount Kun-Lun, the Chinese centre of the Earth.

Pliny calls dew 'the sweat of Heaven, the spittle of the stars'. In Indian sacred scriptures it is 'the symbol of the word of God' (PORS p. 219). The Song of Moses (Deuteronomy 32) opens with the evocation: 'My doctrine shall drop as the rain, my speech shall distil as the dew, as the small rain upon the tender herb, and as the showers upon the grass.' Dew is a symbol of regeneration: 'Awake and sing, ye that dwell in dust: for thy dew is as the dew of herbs, and the earth shall cast out the dead' (Isaiah 26: 19).

The Catholic Advent liturgy takes up the theme: 'Drop down, ye heavens, from above, and let the skies pour down righteousness' (Isaiah 45: 8). In this context the soil is to be prepared for salvation.

If the heavenly dew of the Jews restored life to dry bones, the lunar dew of the Chinese cleared the vision and allowed the attainment of immortality. The Immortals on the island of Ho-chu feed upon air and dew, according to Lao-Tzu. The dew is drawn from the Moon in a huge shell (*ta kiue*). It was gathered by such mortals as the Han Emperor, Wu, in a jade CHALICE, to be mixed with powdered JADE.

In China, too, dew was associated with the princely power of the *yang*, sometimes in opposition to the *yin* influence of rain. The down-dropping of 'gentle dew', according to Lao-Tzu (ch. 32), is the sign of the peaceful marriage of Heaven and Earth. Dew is also born of a perfect harmony struck on a four-stringed lute.

On the other hand, in Buddhist terms, the 'world of dew' is that of appearances, and is a sign of the ephemeral nature of material things and of the brevity of life (BURA, PHIL, GRAD, GRAP, GRAR, GUEM, GUEC, GUET, GUES, HEHS, KALL, LECC).

The Ancient Greeks associated dew with fertility myths, DIONYSOS embodying the fertilizing dew of Heaven. Texts from Ras Shamrah place Astarte in contact with the sea as with a fertilizing dew, and the same is true of APHRODITE. It should be emphasized that these are love-gods and goddesses.

The importance of dew in so many rituals and magic spells arises from the fact that it resolves the confrontation between the upper and the lower, the heavenly and the terrestrial waters. Dew is pure WATER, precious water, pre-eminently primeval water, a distillation of the generative powers of the watery principle. The Fon of Dahomey (now Benin) call it 'Mother-Water' and in the Voodoo pantheon, the deified watery element materializes in the shape of drops of dew preserved in a CALABASH. In Bambara mythology the primal waters first appeared on Earth in the shape of dew. The spider, the Ashanti Demiurge, first created the Sun, Moon and stars and divided night from day and next created dew (TEGH p. 56), Harry Tegnaeus concluding: 'thus this concept of dew should be related to that of vegetation and fertility.'

Similarly North American Indians believed that 'The Great Dew Eagle' regenerated the soil blasted by evil spirits.

diamond   Its outstanding material attributes of hardness, translucence and brightness have made the diamond a pre-eminent symbol of perfection, although its reputation has not been universally beneficent.

Indian traditional mineralogy maintained that it was born in the Earth in an embryonic shape, and that CRYSTAL represented an intermediate state in its development, the diamond being 'mature' and the crystal 'immature'. The diamond was the peak of development, notionally that of perfect fulfilment, which Indian alchemists themselves employed symbolically by associating the diamond with immortality – in other words, by identifying it with the Philosopher's Stone.

The diamond's hardness and its ability to score and cut were particularly emphasized by Tantric Buddhists, for whom the VAJRA (diamond or THUNDERBOLT) was the symbol of immutable and all-conquering spiritual force. Etymologically the equivalent Tibetan word, *dordje*, gives it the meaning of 'Queen of Stones'. It symbolizes light, brightness, the cutting edge of Enlightenment, the void and the indeterminate. Yet again, it is 'true nature', identical with 'the Buddha's nature; for what neither waxes nor wanes is the Diamond', the Zen patriarch Hui Neng taught. Mircea Eliade quotes a passage in Tantric literature which sets down expressly the equation *shunyāta* = vajra.

Immutability is above all an 'axial' characteristic, and this is why the Buddha's throne, set at the foot of the Bodhi-tree, is a diamond throne. This, too, is why Plato describes the World AXIS as being made of diamond. Harbouring a dazzling brilliance, it shares the symbolism of the CENTRE. (See under STONE for the comparison made between 'cornerstone' and 'diamond', the German word *Eckstein* being possible for either.)

In Tibetan iconography the *dordje* (diamond sceptre) stands opposed to the BELL (*tilpu*) as the 'diamond' world (potentiality and immanence) stands in contrast to the phenomenal world ('the mother's womb'), the active principle to the passive and wisdom to method (ELIY, GOVM, GUES, HOUD, SECA).

In Western tradition the diamond is the symbol of universal sovereignty, of incorruptibility and absolute truth.

According to Pliny it is a universal talisman and preservative against all poisons and diseases. It drives away evil spirits and nightmares. Dipped in wine or water it preserves the drinker from apoplexy, gout and jaundice (BUDA).

In western European tradition, diamonds drive off wild animals, ghosts, sorcerers and all the terrors of the night. Russian tradition ascribes to them the powers of controlling lust and encouraging chastity (MARA p. 272). In France, too, the diamond was supposed to banish anger 'and to strengthen the bonds of marriage, which led to its being called the jewel of reconciliation' (PLAD p. 214). 'It contains innocence, wisdom and faithfulness .... In the language of iconography, the diamond is the symbol of constancy, strength and other heroic virtues' (PLAD pp. 53, 54).

Folktales add that one diamond begets another – the ancestral origin of self-begotten wisdom. The shape of the raw diamond must be compared with the belief which regards the CUBE as another symbol of truth, wisdom and moral perfection.

The device of the Medici family bore a diamond which stood as the symbol of divine love. This interpretation was based upon a pun – *diamante* = *dio* (God) + *amante* (loving).

'Cosimo de' Medici took for his device three interlaced rings, each mounting a diamond ... Pietro, his son, adopted his father's device, modifying it according to the laws of heraldry, placing a diamond ring in the talons of a falcon, with the motto *Semper*. This meant that he vowed to God eternal love and faith, proof against all doubt. To the ring Lorenzo the Magnificent added three feathers, white, green and red, with the intention of showing that in loving God, the three virtues appropriate to those three colours blossomed in him – faith, white; hope, green; and charity, red – with the motto *semper* below' (TERS p. 147).

The Medici diamond has also been interpreted as a symbol of the wisdom inherent in that family and of its triumph over itself and others. When Botticelli depicted Minerva (ATHENE) taming a CENTAUR, he decorated the goddess's dress with a diamond ring.

In Renaissance art the diamond also symbolizes equanimity, courage in the face of adversity, the power to free the spirit from every fear, integrity of character and good faith.

Diana See ARTEMIS.

Dionysos (Bacchus) It is an oversimplification to make this god simply the symbol of zestful, sexual passion. The personality of Dionysos, the divine youth or twice-born god, is infinitely complex, as the many names given to him show, although it is true that the earliest, 'Raging' or 'Breaker in Pieces', derive from the 'wild shouts of the orgy' (SECG p. 285).

He was the son of Zeus and of Semele, originally either a Phrygian mother-goddess or a mortal woman, daughter of Cadmus and of Harmony. Wishing to entertain her divine lover in all his glory, she was consumed by LIGHTNING.

Abstracted from the lightning-blasted body of his mother, the unborn Dionysos completed his term in his father's THIGH. This is the clear echo of a simple nature-myth: Mother Earth, impregnated by the lightning of the sky-god, bears a young god whose essence mingles with the life which springs from Earth's entrails . . . . Creating the fable of the double birth served two purposes. It preserved the lightning-flash which originally symbolized the coupling of Earth and Heaven and it increased the prestige of the new god by deriving his descent from Zeus himself.

(SECG ibid.)

This double birth, implying as it does double gestation, re-echoes the classic pattern of initiation – birth, death and rebirth. Zeus' thigh – a hollow like the hollow TREE – gave symbolically to the initiatory powers possessed by Dionysos the exceptional strength which, again symbolically, lay within the thighs of the father of the gods.

He married Ariadne, originally an 'Aegean vegetation- or more specifically a tree-goddess'. Their marriage provided the theme for much Dionysiac art, the scene often symbolizing the union of the god with the initiate into his mysteries. According to Jean Beaujeu:

These motifs were so frequently repeated and so widely disseminated as to lose a great deal of their significance, since it was not because the purchaser had been initiated into or attached to the cult that he bought or commissioned from an artist or a studio a Dionysiac subject. On the other hand there are instances – and the whole group of paintings depicting the principal scenes of an initiation, on the walls of the main room in the Villa of the Mysteries at Pompeii, is one – which display a definite purpose and a genuine devotion.

Dionysos may be seen clasped by Ariadne and yielding to her in ecstasy. His wife, Ariadne, and his mother, Semele, are images of the salvation freely wrought by Dionysos' love (JEAD p. 345).

As a vegetation-god of vine, wine, fruit and seasonal renewal, Plutarch's 'Lord of the Trees', it is he who, Hesiod tells us, 'scatters joy in profusion'. As 'genius of SAP and budding shoots', Dionysos controls human and animal fertility. In any case, he bears the name of Phallenos and a phallic procession was the high point of many of his festivals. (In the Villa of the Mysteries there is one among many examples of wall paintings of initiations depicting the 'unveiling' of the PHALLUS.) In Dionysiac legends and worship such prolific beasts as GOATS and BULLS often occur, bulls and goats being his favourite sacrificial victims, in earlier times torn to pieces by his worshippers in a bloody communion (SECG p. 290).

Both the social effects of his worship and the forms which it took provide some justification for calling him the god of liberation, of the destruction of inhibitions and TABOOS, the god of unbridled licence. 'The purpose of Dionysiac purification', says Boyancé, 'was to give ultimate expression to that from which the soul needed to be freed.'

Because he saved his mother Semele from the Underworld when she was blasted by Zeus' lightning and guided her to the abode of the Immortals, Dionysos was also regarded as a chthonian god, who initiated and guided souls and freed them from the Underworld. Aristophanes has depicted, under the name of Iacchos (see SHOUT), an infernal Dionysos who leads the dance of his initiates, dances of the dead in the meadows of the Underworld.

However, the part which he played in the Eleusinian Mysteries reveals his passage through the depths of the Earth as a phase of germination and as a pledge of fecundity. 'All things growing upon Earth ultimately originate in the depths of the Underworld' (SECG p. 294). His descent into that Underworld, whether in search of his mother or to make it his temporary abode, would therefore symbolize the round of the seasons, Winter and Summer, death and resurrection. Once again this displays the structural pattern of gods who die and are brought back to life common to religions and mysteries which flourished throughout the Greco-Roman world at the beginning of the Christian era.

In a more deeply religious sense, despite its perversities and even through their medium, the cult of Dionysus bears witness to the tremendous effort made by human beings to break the barriers which separate them from the divine and to set their souls free from the trammels of Earth. Sexual excess and giving full rein to the irrational were rather clumsy efforts to grasp the superhuman. As paradoxical as this may seem, if we consider his myth in its entirety, Dionysos symbolizes the attempt to spiritualize life-forms, from the plant to the ecstatic, since he is the tree- and goat-god, the god of religious enthusiasm and the mystic marriage. In his myth he synthesizes a whole cycle of evolution.

Before his time, as has been said, there were two worlds, the human and the divine, and two races, that of gods and that of mortals. Humans were to accept the risk of alienation in the hope of transfiguration.

Every devotee of Dionysos hoped to escape from the body through ecstasy and, at the highest pitch of fervour, to achieve intimate union with the god by whom he or she was temporarily possessed . . . . The worship of Dionysos was a major source of Greek spirituality in helping to define and to propagate the notion of the soul . . . . Thanks to the Dionysiac movement, the notion dawned of a soul related to the godhead and, in one sense, more real than the body itself.

(SECG pp. 291, 300)

Since he had led his mother (the Earth) from the Underworld to Olympus, it was legitimate to believe that he meant to open the doors of immortality to all the children of Earth. That at least is one of the meanings and vectors of the Dionysos symbol.

In psychoanalysis – and as a reminder of the main primitive aspects of the god – Dionysos symbolizes the shattering of inhibitions, repressions and regressions. He is a Nietzschean figure of the life force confronting Apollonian restraint.

He symbolizes those dark forces which well up from the unconscious. He is the god who presides over the outbursts inspired by intoxication in all its forms, that of the drunkard or of the crowd gripped by music or dance, and even that of the very madness with which he afflicts those who have not paid him due honour. He endowed mankind with the gifts of the natural world and, in particular, with that of the vine. He is a god of many shapes, creator of illusions and worker of miracles.

(Defradas in BEAG)

He would, therefore, symbolize the forces which bring the destruction of the personality, his 'orgies' promoting regression to life-forms reflecting primordial chaos and the drowning of the conscious in the lava of the unconscious. His appearance in dreams denotes very severe psychic tension and the imminence of breakdown. The ambivalence of his symbol may be perceived as a Dionysiac liberation which may lead either to spiritualization or to materialization, a factor causing the personality either to develop or to regress. Deep down, he symbolizes the life force which tends to break free of all bounds and restraint.

disc In Hindu iconography, the disc is one of the attributes of Vishnu. It is a particularly deadly weapon. In the *Harivamsa*, Shiva tells Krishna: 'Lay down the disc which you have grasped, the irresistible, indestructible disc which terrifies your enemy in battle.'

But the disc 'which delights the eye' is also a solar symbol – in this respect it is hard to distinguish it from the WHEEL (CHAKRA) – and this is why it is an attribute of the Aditya, who are Suns. It is in any case the colour of the Sun. In the classic depiction of Vishnu, it stands for the 'sattvic' tendency and is expressly associated with the symbolism of the disc as a deadly weapon, as well as with the Sun which kills as it gives light (BHAB, DANA, MALA).

The word for 'disc' (*kenten* or *kantena*) occurs in a number of Gaulish inscriptions. Literary sources are insufficient to make clear the precise symbolism of the disc for the Celts, but in all probability it was related to that of the CIRCLE, the wheel and the RING (OGAC 10: pp. 30ff.). It might also mean the sky.

In China the sacred disc is the symbol of celestial perfection. The JADE disc with a hole in the middle (*pi*) represents Heaven itself.

In Ancient Egyptian paintings eight blue discs are sometimes to be seen in two columns each of four set one above the other, on a blue background, symbolizing the depths of space and the infinite extent of the heavens.

The winged disc, so frequently used in symbolism, represents the trajectory of the Sun and, successively and by extension, flight, sublimation and transfiguration.

disguise See MASK.

distaff (see also SPINDLE) The Palladium, the magical statue of ATHENE which guaranteed the safety of the city which paid worship to the goddess, depicted her holding in her right hand a spear, symbolizing her warlike virtues, and in her left a distaff and spindle, symbols of the domestic arts and manual skills.

As in the case of the Fates, the distaff is akin to the spindle as a symbol of day succeeding day, the thread of life ending when the distaff is bare. It is the reckoning of time which passes beyond recall.

Without the spindle, the distaff, a short length of reed, has a phallic and sexual significance. It not only stands for the male sexual organ, but also for the thread binding one generation to the next.

Elsewhere, the distaff is 'the emblem of the virginal female sexual organ', notably in Perrault's tale 'L'Adroite Princesse' in which two sisters break their 'distaffs' as a result of the ardour of a Prince Charming. The third preserves hers 'intact' (LOEF pp. 176–80). The distaff thus symbolizes 'the dawn and beginning of love' – sexual initiation.

dodecahedron A solid convex geometrical shape with TWELVE pentagonal sides which also exists in a star shape with twelve points. Etruscan and Gaulish sites have produced some thirty of these objects cast in bronze with circular holes in their sides and their trihedral angles guarded by tiny balls. They date from the early years of the Christian era and may have been buried towards the end of the third or beginning of the fourth century AD.

The dodecahedron derives its meaning from the Pythagorean symbolism of numbers and from Platonic idealism. Like the idea, the number expresses intelligible truths which, although beyond the range of sense, are eternal types or models of things of this world, the latter being no more than a more or less adequate representation of the eternal perfection embodied in these numbers and ideas.

The dodecahedron stems from the PENTAGRAM – twelve pentagrams, one side of each touching one side of the other and linked by a SPIRAL, if they are placed together and joined in space produce a solid dodecahedron. Matila C. Ghyka considers this passing from the second to the third dimension via the pentagram to be 'the ideal archetype of dynamic growth' (GHYN 1: p. 46).

The dodecahedron expresses the most perfect synthesis in the series of the five great regular polyhedrons deriving successively from numbers. It should be remembered that in geometrical symbolism the tetrahedron (a four-sided triangular PYRAMID) represents Fire; the octahedron, Air; the icosahedron (a solid body with TWENTY plane faces formed by equilateral triangles), Water; the CUBE, earth. The dodecahedron, for its part, undertakes the task of expressing the whole universe. For this reason, traditions stemming from Pythagoreanism have endowed it with the most remarkable qualities on the mathematical, material and mystical planes. 'The dodecahedron is not merely the image of the Cosmos, it is its number, formula and Idea. The abode of the Blessed Spirits adopts this shape. It is the profound reality of the Cosmos and its very essence. Without straining language, one may say it is the Cosmos itself' (Léonard Saint-Michel, *Lettres d'humanité* 10: p. 101). The ancient artefacts which have been unearthed served to support this symbolic quality, each being 'a tiny microcosm, resembling the Macrocosm in every detail as expressed by the analogous rules of traditional magic; symbols similar in the geometric sense of the word, identical in essence, transubstantiating, if one may use the word, the real and living Universe under the accidents of a mere dodecahedron' (ibid.).

It is hardly surprising, then, that these mysterious objects should have been employed in magical practices. There is a constant temptation to pass from knowledge to power and both magic and divination are normal perversions of the perception of the symbol. The long-lived and hidden properties of the symbol, which ought to lead the soul to a mystical view of nature, are perverted for the purposes of domination. Nor is it improbable, either, that this symbol of the cosmos was used for the purposes of worship and became an idol.

Wherever the Celts settled a certain number of bronze dodecahedrons have been discovered. They have holes pierced in their planes and their angles are tipped with tiny balls. Their weight varies between 35 and 1100 grams and there has been considerable controversy over their use, but there can be little doubt now that this was religious. It seems highly probable that they represented Heaven, or the universe, and undoubtedly were used as dice in the rituals of divination by lots. Furthermore, they provide remarkable evidence of the coincidence of Celtic and Pythagorean thought (OGAC 7: pp. 302–5).

Since these dodecahedrons have been found in some numbers in Gaul, some writers have related them to the serpents' EGGS which Pliny the Elder mentions and which were 'highly regarded throughout Gaul'. These eggs were fashioned by twining and knotting snakes into a ball and they were endowed with all sorts of benign virtues. They were used by the druids. Camille Jullian equates them with fossilized sea-urchins. Léonard Saint-Michel relates them rather to dodecahedrons with their trihedral angles topped by tiny balls, now plain, but which might originally have been made to resemble the heads of entwined snakes. Whatever their identification, the kinship of serpent's egg and dodecahedron owes nothing to chance: both symbolize the development of the universe.

'A geometric symbol of especial potency, the dodecahedron built upon the Golden Number (and with the exception of the pentagram famed for its beneficent powers) is the shape which is richest in eurhythmic, cosmogonic and metaphysical teaching.' In fact it evokes the development of the physico-chemical into the vital and of the physiological into the spiritual, and in these the history and meaning of the universe are epitomized.

dog   There cannot be a mythology which does not associate a dog, be it as Anubis, T'ien k'uan, CERBERUS, Xolotl or Garm, with death, Hell, the Underworld or with those invisible realms ruled by the deities of Earth or Moon. At first glance, therefore, the extremely complex symbolism of the dog seems linked to the threefold elements EARTH, WATER and MOON, with their recognized hidden and female significance, all connected with the basics of growth, sexuality and divination, as much in terms of the uncon-scious as of the subconscious.

Evidence of the primary mythic role played by the dog, that of psychopomp, is worldwide. Having been man's companion in the light of living day, the dog becomes his guide through the darkness of death. At every stage of Western cultural history the dog has featured among such powerful psychopomps as Anubis, Cerberus, Thoth, HECATE, or HERMES. But dogs are universal phenomena and make their appearance in every culture in different forms which serve only to enrich this primary symbolism.

The dog-headed deities, so common in Ancient Egyptian art, had the duty of 'imprisoning and destroying the enemies of light' and of standing guard at the GATES of holy places.

The Ancient Germans had a terrifying hound, Garm, which guarded the entrance to Niflheim, the realm of the dead, a land of frost and darkness.

The Ancient Mexicans bred a special dog to accompany and guide the dead in the beyond. With the body was buried 'a lion-coloured dog – in other words a dog with fur the colour of the Sun – to accompany the dead person just as the dog-god, Xolotl, had accompanied the Sun during his journey under the Earth' (GIRP p. 161; SOUA). In other instances the dog would be sacrificed on its master's grave to help him to cross, at the end of his long journey, the nine rivers (SOUA) which barred access to 'the eternal house of the dead, Chocomemictlan, the Ninth Hell' (ALEC p. 202).

Even today the Lacandon Indians of Guatemala set four figures of dogs, made from palm-leaves, at the four corners of their graves.

The THIRTEENTH and final constellation in the Ancient Mexican ZODIAC was the constellation of the Dog. It induces not only notions of death, of the end and of the Underworld (BEYM), but also of initiation and of rebirth, for, in the words of the French poet, Gérard de Nerval, 'the thirteenth comes full cycle and is first again.' And this example affords a clearer understanding of some details in the funeral rites of shamanistic peoples in Siberia on the opposite side of the world to Central America. Thus among the Goldi, a man was always buried with his dog, while, among a tribe of horsemen, the dead man's HORSE was sacrificed and its flesh given to the dogs and birds which would guide the dead man to the realms of Heaven and Hell (HARA).

The dead, the old and the sick in Persia and Bactria were thrown to the dogs. In Bombay, Parsees would place a dog close to a dying person so that human and animal stared into one another's eyes. On the mythical bridge, Chinvat, where the souls of the dead are judged by the pure and impure gods, the dogs which guard the bridge beside the pure gods guide the righteous to Paradise (MANG p. 52n).

However, dogs, so familiar with the invisible, do more than merely guide the dead. They also act as intermediaries between the two worlds and as spokesmen for the living to question the dead and the Underworld deities of their land.

Thus the Bantu who live along the Kasai, a tributary of the Congo River, have been observed to use a method of divination by hypnosis. In it, the witch-doctor's 'customer', linked to the former by a thread, goes down into a pit in which, under hypnosis, he gains contact with the spirits thanks to the presence at his side of a dog and a HEN (FOUC). In this region the appearance of a dog in dreams is a warning that the dreamer is the victim of sorcery. Finally, and perhaps most strikingly, these same observers have recorded the following custom employed by the Bantu to solve the problem of the unexplained death of any villager. The chief hangs the dead person's dog on a tree, covering it with a LEOPARD's skin, doubtless with the aim of heightening its aggressive instincts. The flesh of the animal so sacrificed is shared among all the villagers, who are obliged to eat it all except for the head. The chief keeps the latter and, having smeared it with chalk (see WHITE) questions it in these words: 'You, dog, and you, leopard, look closely round! You dog, pick up the scent of the death which laid this man low! You see souls, you see sorcerers, make no mistake about the person who caused this man's death!'

When, some time later, one of the villagers who has eaten the dog's flesh falls ill, the dog will have pointed out the guilty party.

However, this very gift of second sight and the familiarity of dogs with death and the invisible powers of darkness may on the contrary rouse suspicions of the black arts. Evans-Pritchard (EVAS) has recorded an instance among the Azande of southern Sudan in which trial by ordeal fixed the responsibility for unexplained deaths upon the dogs suspected of them.

Here, too, there is a correspondence between African and Siberian custom. At Telyut funeral feasts, the dogs were given the dead man's share of the food after these words have been spoken: 'When you were alive, you yourself could eat: now that you are dead, your soul eats!' (HARA p. 227)

Elsewhere Banyowski has described a shaman's robes made of tanned dogskin, showing the powers of divination attributed to this animal. The same belief recurs in West Africa, on the former Slave Coast. Bernard Maupoil (MAUG p. 199) has recorded how one of his informants from Porto Novo told him that to strengthen the powers of the ROSARY which he used in divination, he had buried it for several days in the belly of a dog sacrificed for that purpose.

To the Iroquois the dog was both messenger and intercessor and traditionally, at their New Year festivals, a white dog was sacrificed. 'This sacrifice formed the centre-piece of the festival. Effectively the dog was a messenger who hastened off to Heaven bearing the prayers of mankind' (KRIR p. 267).

Although dogs descend to the Underworld, more often they are its guardians, while its rulers are dog-headed. Innumerable examples might be added to those which have been mentioned above. In Greek mythology, the goddess of darkness, Hecate, could sometimes take the shape of a mare or of a bitch. She haunted CROSSROADS, a pack of hell-hounds at her heels (ROYR). Similarly, when the shamans of the Altai Mountains recounted their Orphic journeys, they told of their encounters with dogs at the gates of the home of the Lord of the Underworld (ELIC p. 203). The tenth day of the Aztec soothsaying calendar was the day of the dog. Its patron was the god of the Underworld and it was in the tenth Heaven that the deities of darkness dwelt.

The association of dog, chthonian deities and human sacrifice comes out most clearly in a pre-Inca Peruvian myth recorded by Francisco de Avila in his chronicle (AVIH) compiled in the early years of the Spanish conquest. According to this myth, the beginning of 'new times' – probably corresponding with the mythical beginnings of the agrarian cycle – were marked by the triumph of the sky-god, lord of the waters and fire of Heaven, over the Underworld-god, lord of the fires below the ground. Having lured his rival into a deep Andean valley, and thus reduced him to impotence, the sky-god decided that 'since he had fed on human flesh, from henceforth he should feed upon the flesh of dogs.' This is the reason, Father de Avila deduced, why the Yunca, who worshipped the defeated deity, still ate dogs' flesh to that day.

Like Hermes, the dog is a conductor of souls, and also possesses healing powers when the need arises. In Greek mythology, the dog is one of the attributes of Asclepios, the Roman Aesculapius, the hero and god of healing (GRID).

Lastly, with its knowledge of the visible and invisible sides of human life, the dog is often held up as a culture-hero, most often as the master or conqueror of fire, as well as being a mythic ancestor. This enhances its symbolism with a sexual significance.

Thus the Bambara liken the dog to the penis, which they euphemistically term 'the dog'. According to Zahan (ZAHB), this comes about through the comparison which they make between the 'anger' of the penis – its erection – when confronted by the vulva, and the dog's barking at the approach of strangers. It may also arise from 'inordinate male sexual appetite which can only be compared with the dog's greed for food' (ZAHB p. 70).

Mongolo-Turkic myths take note of women made pregnant by LIGHT. They often go on to say that after the latter had gone in to the woman it left her in the shape of a yellow dog. This relates to some extent with the Aztec 'lion-coloured dog', a patently solar emblem.

Dogs and wolves were, in any case, founders of a number of Mongol and Turkic dynasties, which tends to widen the scope of Amerindian myths and to corroborate them. Thus, the Alaskan Dene tribe believe that the human race sprang from secret sexual relations between a woman and a dog (KRIE p. 62). Aztec tradition told how the dog-god, Xolotl, stole from the Underworld the BONES from which the gods were to create a fresh human race (METB).

As a mythic ancestor, the dog was often to be seen in the spots on the face of the Moon, and just like other lunar animals such as the HARE, the FOX, etc., was often considered a slightly rakish ancestor and hero. In Melanesia he was ancestor of one of the four social classes studied by Malinowski (MALM). The Roman she-wolf should be compared with the countless other members of the dog family which were culture-heroes, always linked with the institution of the agrarian cycle.

However, in these traditions the dog most frequently appears in the guise of the hero who discovered fire, the spark of fire often preceding or being confounded with the spark of life. Thus the Chiluk from the White Nile and all the tribes of the Upper Nile believe that the dog stole fire from the serpent, the rainbow, the sky-gods or the Great Spirit himself, and took it away on the tip of its tail (GRAF). As the dog ran past the hearth, the tip of its tail caught alight and, yelping with pain, it set on fire the bush – from which men had only to take it. The Fali of northern Cameroon associate the dog with the black monkey, the avatar (embodiment) of the BLACKSMITH who stole fire (LEBF), while their neighbours, the Prodovko, believe that the dog brought mankind their two most precious possessions – fire and millet. Again, the Ibo, Ijo and other peoples of southeastern Nigeria believe that the dog stole fire from Heaven to give to mankind (TEGH p. 88). In South America *canis vetulus* was not the conqueror of fire but its original owner. The TWIN heroes, taking the shapes of SNAIL and FISH, stole it from him (FRAF). In North America the symbolic similarity between fire and the sexual act is inherent in other myths which show the dog as the hero who obtained fire. Thus to the Sia and the Navajo of New Mexico, the Karok, the Gallinomero, the Achomawi and the Maidu of California, the COYOTE, the great hero of the prairies, either discovers fire by friction, or else steals it and carries it off in his EARS, or else organizes a relay race, thanks to which mankind steals fire from the gods (FRAF).

Myths from the Pacific region underline still more emphatically the sexual undertones always linked with the conquest of fire. In New Guinea, several tribes believe that the dog stole fire from its first owner, the RAT, and in this case it is chthonian fire. The Motu-Motu and the Ozokaiva from Papua New Guinea are convinced that the dog is lord of fire since it always sleeps close to the hearth and growls when you try to drive it away. However, a myth which Frazer recorded, this time in New Britain, demonstrates most strikingly the link between dog, fire and sexuality. It tells us how, long ago, a male secret society was the only group which knew how to make fire by rubbing two sticks together. A dog watched them and took his discovery to women in this fashion. He painted his TAIL in the colours of the men's society and began to rub a log of wood on which a woman was sitting until it burst into flame. Thereupon the woman began to cry and said to the dog: 'You have dishonoured me and now you must marry me.'

The Murut of North Borneo believe the dog to be both their mythic ancestor and a culture-hero. The eldest child of the incestuous union of a man and his sister, sole survivors of the FLOOD, the dog taught the new race of mankind all the new arts and crafts, among them that of making fire. Once again, this is an explanation of the beginnings of the agrarian cycle. Their neighbours, the Dyak, believe that in the aftermath of the flood, the dog showed the woman the secret of fire by rubbing his tail against a creeper. Finally, according to a myth from the Caroline Islands, fire was given to the woman by the THUNDER-god who appeared to her in the shape of a dog. This last example clearly shows the oscillation of the symbol between sky and Underworld and takes us back to Central America. The Maya, as we have seen, believed that the dog guided the Sun on his journey underground and hence represented the Black Sun, while to the Aztecs, the dog was the synthesis and very symbol of fire.

In the Celtic world the dog, or hound, was associated with the warrior caste. In contrast with the Greco-Roman world, the hound was used as an object of laudatory comparison and metaphor. The name of their greatest hero, Cùchulainn, means 'Hound of Culann' and we know that all Celts, both insular and continental, trained dogs for war and hunting. To compare a hero with a hound was to do him honour and to pay tribute to his valour in battle. There is a complete absence of the pejorative and there does not seem to have been a hell-hound like Cerberus. The maleficent hound is only to be found in folklore, probably under the influence of Christianity. In Brittany, the Black Dog of the Monts d'Arrée represents the damned. The chief taboo placed upon Cùchulainn was against eating hound's flesh. The witches who doomed him to death, offered it to him and made him eat it when he was going out to battle (OGAC 11: pp. 213–15; CELT 7: *passim*).

Some aspects of the symbolism of the dog which have been described above – culture-hero, mythic ancestor, symbol of sexual potency (and hence of everlastingness), seducer, lacking chastity, overflowing with vitality like nature in the Spring, or fruit of unlawful marriage – represent the bright side of the dog as symbol. Equal attention should be paid to its dark side, and the most convincing illustration of this is implacable prejudice against the animal in Muslim society.

Islam has created in the dog the image of all that is utterly vile in creation. According to Shabistarī, to be attached to the things of this world is to become identified with the corpse-eater, the dog. The dog is the symbol of greed and of gluttony. Dogs and ANGELS cannot live together. However,

Islamic tradition states that dogs have fifty-two characteristics, half of them holy and half of them evil. Thus dogs keep watch, are patient and do not bite their masters. On the other hand they bark at scribes, etc. Their faithfulness is praised: 'If a man has no brothers, the dogs are his brethren. The heart of a dog is like the heart of its master.'

Dogs are also regarded as unclean. Jinn often appeared in the shape of black dogs. Dogs howling near a house presage death and their flesh is used as a preservative against barrenness, ill-luck, etc. In Tangier, a puppy's or a kitten's flesh is eaten as a preservative against witchcraft. Unlike other dogs, the greyhound is not regarded as unclean but, on the contrary, to be endowed with *baraka*. It protects its owner against the evil eye. Syrian Muslims believe that angels never enter a house in which there is a dog (WERS 2: p. 303). According to tradition, the Prophet Muhammad proclaimed that any utensil from which a dog had drunk should be cleansed SEVEN times, the first time with earth. He is supposed to have prohibited the killing of all dogs except black dogs with two white patches above the eyes, such dogs being the evil one. Killing a dog makes the person unclean. It is also said that it is as bad as killing seven men, from the belief that dogs have seven lives. The name of the dog which watched over the Seven Sleepers in their cave (Koran 18) is used in charms.

Muslims, nevertheless, distinguish between the 'unclean' run of ordinary dogs and the greyhound, its noble appearance making it a 'pure' creature. Dante's 'envoy', the *veltro*, was a greyhound, a dog depicted by Dürer and one identified with the harbinger of Christ's Second Coming. St Dominic's emblem is a dog spitting fire and members of the order which he founded are called *Domini-can[e]s* ('Hounds of the Lord') who with their voices protect the House of God or are heralds of his Word. In the Far East the symbolism of the dog is fundamentally ambivalent: benign, because dogs are man's close companions and vigilant protectors of his home; malign, because they are closely related to wolves and jackals and regarded as contemptible, unclean beasts. These aspects are not confined to specific geographical limits but spread everywhere.

Very similar feelings are prevalent in Tibet, where dogs are emblems of sensual appetites and sexuality, but at the same time of jealousy as well. The Buddha taught that whoever lived like a dog, would become a dog when the body decayed after death (*Majjhima-nikāya* 387).

In Japan dogs are generally regarded favourably and, as faithful companions, their figures protect children and assist women in childbirth. In China they are no less faithful companions of the Immortals even in their apotheosis. When the Great Venerable appeared on Mount T'ai She in the days of the Han emperor, Wu, he had a yellow dog on a leash. Han-tzu's dog turned red, like the Celestial Dog, sprouted wings and gained immortality. The alchemist Wei Po-yang ascended into Heaven with his dog. The dog is the ancestor and emblem of some tribes, and perhaps even of the Chinese themselves since P'an-ku may have been a dog.

The Celestial Dog (*T'ien-k'uan*) is storm and meteor; he provides the crash of thunder and the flash of lightning and is as red as fire. Although he is foe to the demon OWL, he is the herald of war. As protection against the owl, dogs are always made to bark by pinching their ears. According to some ancient traditions the Chinese also depicted CHAOS in the shape of a huge shaggy dog. It had eyes, but was blind; ears, but was deaf; and it was alive, despite lacking the FIVE internal organs.

Another typically Chinese symbol was that of 'straw dogs' (cf. *Tao Te Ching* ch. 5). Kaltenmark suggests that they may originally have been shamanistic, while Wieger describes them as acting 'as filters against spells' which were destroyed after use. The symbol employed by Chuang Tzu depends precisely upon the ephemeral existence of an object which is cast aside, trampled under foot and burned after it has performed its office (ch. 14). He concludes that what has ceased to be useful must be destroyed in case it should become harmful. Lao-Tzu takes straw dogs as symbols of the ephemeral nature of the things of this world which the sage renounces (CORT, GRAD, KALT, OGRJ, LECC, SCHC, WIET). According to Chuang Tzu, in *Celestial Fate*, 'Before being offered, straw dogs were kept in chests wrapped in fine linen. After being offered to the dead, they were burned, for, had they been kept for further use, each member of the dead man's family would have suffered from nightmares.'

Central Asia provides myths which might be described as intermediate, 'missing links' for understanding how the dog gradually came to be regarded as unclean, accursed and stained with the indelible mark of original sin.

Some Tatar tribes believed that, at the Creation, God entrusted man to the protection of the dog to guard him against the assault of the Evil One. However, the dog allowed the 'enemy' to bribe him and thereby became the 'He' responsible for the fall of man. The Yakut believed that it was images which God entrusted to the dog's protection. Having let the devil befoul them, the dog was punished by being given its present shape by God. The same theme is taken up, with variations, by the peoples related to the Finns and living along the Volga (HARA). They all share this important detail: the dog was originally naked and was given its coat by the Evil One as a reward for its treachery. This treachery took the physical shape of fur, and the dog's activities as an intermediary gradually made it an unclean and untouchable animal. Worse still, it brought sickness to mankind and that inner foulness which, like the dog's fur, was born of the Devil's spittle. Thus the dog was responsible for death, the ultimate outcome of these disasters and of these befoulings and slaverings. The Buryat, for their part, say that God cursed the false dog in these terms: 'You shall always go hungry; you shall gnaw bones and eat the scraps of man's food and he shall whip and beat you' (HARA p. 85).

At this nadir of its malign aspect the symbol of the dog coincides with that of the SCAPEGOAT.

Harva regards these Asiatic myths as being tinged with Iranian dualism and in this context reminds us that a dog, the creature of Ahura Mazda, played a dominant part in the ancient Persian religion by driving away evil spirits. Once again the symbol oscillates within the myth. As Jean-Paul Roux remarks, this duality, the property of the symbol of the dog in the thought of Asian peoples, for whom it was at one and the same time a guardian and benign spirit and the object of God's curse, makes it the pre-eminent example of the 'fallen angel' (ROUF p. 83).

To sum up, the dog forms an ambiguous symbol and no civilization has ever decided upon one or the other of its opposing aspects. However, in this context it is striking to remember that alchemists and 'philosophers' used the analogy of the dog devoured by the wolf for the purification of GOLD by ANTIMONY, the penultimate stage of the 'Great Work'. Now dog and wolf are none other than the two aspects of the symbol in question, which undoubtedly is resolved in this esoteric image as well as being given its deepest significance. Simultaneously dog and wolf, the sage – or saint – purifies himself by devouring himself; in other words, by an act of self-sacrifice he finally reaches the last stage of spiritual self-mastery.

dogwood The ritual of the Fetiales, a Roman college of priests charged with the task of declaring war, involved going to the border 'carrying an iron-tipped spear or a javelin of dogwood with a hardened tip' and challenging the enemy (Livy 1: 32). This ceremony corresponds to an ancient magical practice which antedates the use of iron. The choice of Bloody Dogwood for the weapon to be hurled into the enemy's country, would symbolize the bloody death which would fall upon that enemy. However, in the Far East dogwood stands for the life-giving power of BLOOD and its benign influences.

dolmen See BETHEL; DOME; MENHIR; STONE.

dolphin The symbolism of the dolphin is linked with that of WATER and METAMORPHOSIS.

The pirates who tied Dionysos to the mast of their ship, got drunk, fell overboard and were changed into dolphins. Dolphins became symbols of the power of regeneration. They are also emblems of divination, wisdom and prudence and their images stood beside APOLLO'S TRIPOD at Delphi. These qualities, in conjunction with their speed through the water, made them master voyagers and, like Poseidon, they were often depicted with TRIDENT or ANCHOR.

In pre-Hellenic Crete dolphins were given divine honours. Apollo took the form of a dolphin, according to the 'Homeric' Hymn, to reach the banks of the Crisa on his way to Delphi.

Greek art often depicted men riding dolphins. This sacred creature undoubtedly played a part in funeral rites, in which it was regarded as a conductor of souls. 'The Cretans believed that the dead withdrew to the ends of the Earth, to the Isles of the Blessed, and that dolphins carried them on their backs to their homes beyond the tomb' (Defradas). Plutarch has told the story of Arion's voyage, when dolphins saved him from the sailors who threatened to murder him and then escorted him on his way, carrying him on their backs. Arion dived into the sea:

But before his body was entirely submerged, dolphins swam beneath him, and he was borne upward, full of doubt and uncertainty and confusion at first. But when he began to feel at ease ... the many dolphins gathering around him in a friendly way ... there came into his thoughts, as he said, not so much a feeling of fear in the face of death, or a desire to live, as a proud longing to be saved that he might be shown to be a man loved by the gods and that he might gain a sure opinion regarding them.

(*Banquet of the Seven Sages* 17–18)

His account contains a wealth of symbols which present no difficulty of interpretation. Arion passes from this violent and anxious world to immortal salvation thanks to the mediation of the dolphins. It is hardly surprising that CHRIST the Saviour was subsequently depicted as a dolphin. On a more ethical and psychological level the account depicts the passage from a state of nervous stress and imagined terrors to the quietude of spiritual enlightenment and contemplation by meditating upon goodness (the life-saving dive, the ease and benign appearance of the dolphins and so on). Three stages in spiritual development are described: the predominance of the emotions and of the imagination; the interposition of goodness, love or devotion; enlightenment in the glow of inner peace.

The legend to which reference was made at the beginning of this article corroborates the interpretation of the dolphin as a symbol of conversion. Dionysos had hired a boat to take him to Naxos, when he noticed that the crew was steering towards Asia, undoubtedly to sell him into slavery. Thereupon 'he transformed their oars into serpents, filled their ship with ivy and caused the music of invisible flutes to be played. Wreathed in vines the ship lost way, the sailors went mad, jumped overboard and were turned into dolphins. This explains why dolphins are friends to humans and try to save them from shipwreck – they are reformed pirates' (GRID p. 127).

dome   The dome is universally regarded as a representation of the vault of Heaven, and thus a domed building is an image of the world. The dome is commonly set upon FOUR pillars (see COLUMN) or upon a structure with a SQUARE ground-plan. This relates directly to the Chinese symbolism of the sky as 'covering' and the Earth as 'supporting', while the sky is seen as 'round' and the Earth as 'square'.

Dolmens, Mycenean tombs and the many rock-temples from India to Korea possess this generalized significance of representing the cosmic dome. The Montagnards of southern Vietnam see the sky as a hemispherical BASKET set upon a flat, circular DISC. This, surely, is very similar to the Chinese image of the TORTOISE, the symbolism of the rounded upper and the flat under shells being exactly the same. The Egyptians depicted the sky as the goddess, Nut, supporting herself on fingers and toes with her body arched. Byzantine domes, Buddhist STUPAS and Muslim *qubba* all possess the same quality.

When the Prophet Muhammad ascended into Heaven, he describes it as a mother-of-pearl dome supported by four pillars. The dome is the Universal Spirit 'enveloping' the world and the pillars are the four corners of the cosmic CUBE, its spiritual and material components. The 'Throne of Divine Light', according to an Arabic writer, 'is like a dome above the ANGELS and this world.' Sometimes the cosmos – as in the notable case of the Dome of the Rock Mosque at Jerusalem – is octagonal in shape, but this is a case of the square being developed by doubling its spatial locations (see EIGHT).

The meaning behind the Byzantine dome, on which is represented Christos Pantocrator, is the same and the similarity is heightened with the realization that it is sometimes 'supported' by representations of the four Evangelists. The Buddhist stupa is often set on a square base and its dominion over quaternary space is confirmed by the gates set at the four CARDINAL POINTS.

Coomaraswamy has observed that the groins which meet at the top of a dome – and which are identical to the curved poles of a Mongolian yurt – represent 'the concentration of psychic powers at their source' provided by the eye of the dome, the 'GATEWAY of the Sun'. It might be said, conversely, that the groins represent the rays of sunlight enveloping the Earth.

From this gateway at the top of the dome rises actually or metaphorically the World AXIS. In the case of stupas, it is always actualized in the POLE rising above them. In central Asia it is the column of smoke rising from the central hearth up into the sky, in Siberia it is the trunk of the BIRCH-TREE protruding from the tent and, more generally speaking, it is also the tip of the PARASOL or of the pole holding the AWNING over the chariot and also, in its own way, rising above a 'dome'. The central HOLE, sometimes identified with the Pole Star, is essentially the Sun, 'the eye of the world'. To emerge through it is 'to ascend in Agni's train', to 'become detached from the cosmos' (see CAVERN) or to escape the phenomenal world. The *Dhammapada* tells how Moggalāna 'broke through the dome and took to the air'. When the Buddha had attained enlightenment he said that 'the roof-ridge shattered in pieces'. Again, the eye of the dome is in this instance the 'opening' in the CROWN of the head – itself similar to the VAULT – the *brahmarandhra* through which escapes the soul of the sage delivered from temporal conditions or, according to *The Secret of the Golden Flower*, the 'subtle' body born of the embryo of immortality (BURA, COOH, ELIM, GUES).

donkey See ASS.

door(way) See GATE(WAY).

dot The dot, or point, symbolizes the residual state after the removal of volume, the CENTRE, the source, the principle of emanation and the termination of return. It denotes the creative force and the end of all things.

According to Clement of Alexandria, if the properties and dimensions of a body are removed, there remains 'a point with a precise location'. If that location is removed, primeval unity is achieved (*Stromata* 5: 2). Similarly in the symbolism of the Jewish Kabbalah, when the 'hidden dot' appears it becomes the letter *iod*. In Hindu and Tibetan teaching, the dot (BINDU) is once again the 'fleck' or 'seed' of manifestation.

The manifestation itself is a spatial expansion of the dot. The dot is therefore the point at which the arms of a CROSS intersect. As the source of that expansion, it is itself non-dimensional and unconstrained by the laws of space. 'The dot', Angelus Silesius wrote, 'contained the CIRCLE.' Leibniz drew a distinction between the 'metaphysical point' (primordial unity) and the 'mathematical point', the spatial description of the former, a point 'with a precise location'. On the other hand the dot is the resolution of opposing tendencies, the 'changeless mean' of the Chinese, 'the void in the centre' of the cosmic WHEEL, the 'pivot of the norm' and 'the still centre of the circle' as Chuang Tzu terms it (ch. 2), balance and harmony. It is the source of meditation and the goal of spiritual integration.

In the YANTRA, the bindu is the point at which the upper angles of the two triangles representing Shiva and Shakti meet: it is undifferentiated Brahman. In the MANTRA, it is the diacritical dot (*anusvāra*) which accompanies *nāda*, the primal sound. The bindu is a minute circle, but the 'void' and the state of potentiality implicit in it are precisely symbolized by the void within the circle. The dot is also the letter of the sacred monosyllable OM, the seed within the CONCH. In any case it is the completely formless principle from which all beings and all matter originated (AVAS, ELIY, GOVM, GUEC, VALA).

In African art, dot-shaped decoration generally represents some actual thing – grains of millet, stars and so on. These dots are separate or in groups, when they form the rough patterns of circles, squares and diamonds. In African hunting country, for example, three dots in close proximity within a triangle or square may sometimes stand for the hunter, his dog and his quarry. In savannah country, white dots on a dark ground may suggest 'fires lit at night, their twinkling like the twinkling of the stars' (MVEA p. 95).

double In every culture artists have depicted double-headed creatures, SERPENTS, DRAGONS, BIRDS, LIONS, BEARS and so on. This is due neither to mere love of ornamentation nor to some Manichean influence: the creatures so depicted all have a bipolarity, both benign and malign, and this is described in their individual entries in this dictionary. It is very likely that it is this double aspect of the live creature which is suggested by its depiction with two heads. For example, the lion's strength symbolizes both sovereign power and a consumimg lust, whether it be for justice or for the exercise of absolute authority in a bloodthirsty tyrant. Similarly, ribbons or wreaths depicted round a person's head may symbolize, if they form a closed CIRCLE, confinement in difficulty and misfortune, but if broken, release. Sometimes duplication serves merely to reinforce and redouble the meaning attached to one of the POLES of the symbol.

Traditional religions generally thought of the soul as being the double of its living owner, able to leave the body at death, in dreams or through magical practices, and to return to the same or some other body. Mankind thus provided its own self-portrait in duplicate. In any case, instances of hysterical or schizophrenic duplication of personality are well known to psychotherapy.

German Romanticism endowed this notion of a person's double (Doppelgänger) 'with tragic and fatal overtones . . . . It may sometimes be our complement, but is more often the foe with whom we are lured to fight . . . . In some ancient traditions, meeting one's double is an unlucky occurrence, and is sometimes even a presage of death' (BRIR II p. 120).

dove Throughout Judeo-Christian symbolism the dove – which culminates in the New Testament by representing the Holy Spirit – is basically a symbol of purity, simplicity and even, as when it brings the OLIVE-branch back to Noah's Ark, of peace, harmony and re-found happiness. As with most depictions of winged creatures in the same cultural environment, it might be said that the dove stands for the sublimation of the instincts and, specifically, of the erotic instincts (DURS p. 135).

The pagan context, with its different sense of values so far as purity was concerned, associated it rather than contrasted it with physical love, so that the dove, APHRODITE's bird, represented the pledge of love which the lover offered the object of his desire.

Such views, which differ in appearance only, resulted in the dove standing for that imperishable part of the human being, in other words the vital principle or soul. In this context some Greek funerary urns depict a dove 'drinking from a vase which symbolizes the fount of memory' (LAVD p. 258). This image is transferred to Christian iconography; a depiction of the martyrdom of St Polycarp, for example, shows a dove emerging from the saint's body after death.

All this symbolism stems from the bird's grace and beauty, its spotless WHITE feathers and gentle cooing. This would explain why 'dove' is one of the most universally current metaphors for woman, from everyday slang to the highest flights of literature. Jean Daniélou quotes St Gregory of Nyssa as saying that the closer the soul approaches the light, the lovelier it becomes and, in the light, takes the shape of a dove. And the lover calls his beloved 'my soul'. Lastly, it should be noted that doves are extremely social birds, which further strengthens the ever-positive powers of the bird as symbol.

According to George Catlin, the Prairie Indians regarded the turtle dove as the messenger of the cycle of rebirth, bearing a sprig of WILLOW leaves in its beak. In this respect it may be compared with Noah's dove.

Christian tradition made the bird the symbol of faithful marriage.

dragon Basically dragons are seen as strict guardians or as symbols of evil and of diabolical tendencies. They guard buried treasure, and as such are enemies which must be defeated if the treasure is to be won. In the West, dragons guarded the GOLDEN FLEECE and the Garden of the HESPERIDES; in China, in the story of the T'ang, they guarded the PEARL; while the legend of Siegfried confirms that the treasure which the dragon guarded was that of immortality.

In fact the dragon may be identified with the SERPENT as a diabolical symbol and Origen confirms this identification in his commentary on Psalm 74 (see LEVIATHAN). The breaking of 'the heads of serpents . . . [and] . . . of leviathan in pieces' is Christ's victory over evil. In addition to the well-known portrayals of St Michael or St George, Christ himself is sometimes pictured crushing the dragon under foot. The Zen patriarch Hui Neng, too, made dragons and serpents emblems of evil and of hatred. When the unshakable Fudo-Myoo of Japanese Buddhism overcame the dragon, in so doing he overcame ignorance and darkness.

These negative aspects, however, are neither the only nor the most important ones, for dragon symbolism is ambivalent. This is in any case made plain by Far Eastern iconography depicting a pair of dragons facing one another, and more especially by European and Islamic hermeticism where this confrontation is depicted upon lines similar to those of the CADUCEUS. This is the neutralization of opposing tendencies, of alchemical sulphur and mercury; while immanent, undeveloped nature is portrayed in the OURO-BOROS, the dragon biting its own tail. Even in the Far East the dragon possesses different aspects, in that it is simultaneously a creature of WATER, of EARTH – even of the Underworld – and of the sky. This makes it akin to Quetzalcoatl, the Aztec plumed serpent. Unsuccessful efforts have been made to distinguish the *long* dragon of the waters from the *kui* dragon of the earth. In Japan, four dragon species were popularly distinguished: celestial, rain, terrestrial or aquatic and chthonian.

In fact, this is simply a matter of four aspects of a single symbol, the symbol of what Grousset calls 'the active First Cause and Demiurge; divine force and spiritual vigour.' The dragon is, in any case, a celestial symbol, of the life force and power of manifestation, ejaculating the primeval waters or the world-EGG. It is thus an image of the creating Word. The dragon is the cloud which thickens overhead before dropping its fertilizing showers. It is the *k'ien* principle, the source of Heaven and maker of RAIN, its six lines six harnessed dragons. Again, the *I Ching* tells us, dragon's blood is black and yellow, the primal colours of Heaven and Earth. The six strokes of the hexagram, *k'ien*, traditionally depict the six stages of manifestation, from the 'hidden dragon', potentiality, immanent and inactive, to the 'swooping dragon' which returns to the First Cause, through the dragon 'in the fields', 'visible', 'leaping' and 'flying'.

Hindu teaching identifies the dragon with the First Cause, with Agni or with Prajāpati. The 'dragon-slayer' is the celebrant who offers sacrifice to appease the divine powers and who identifies with those powers. The 'dragon' produces SOMA, the beverage of immortality, and is the soma offered in sacrifice. Chuang Tzu taught that the power of the dragon is a mysterious thing. It is the resolution of opposites. This is why, he said, Confucius dwelt in Lao-Tzu, the very personification of the dragon. In any case, while dragon-soma may confer immortality, Chinese dragons take you to it, since they are the winged steeds of the Immortals, too. They carry them up to Heaven. Huang-ti, who had used dragons to overcome temptation to evil, ascended into Heaven on a dragon's back. However, he was himself a dragon, as was the primeval sovereign, Fu-hi, who received the Ho-t'u. Thanks to a dragon, Yu the Great was able to set the world to rights by draining off the over-abundant waters. The dragon was sent to him from Heaven and 'opened the way' (*k'ai tao*) for him.

It was quite natural for the dragon, a celestial, creative and law-giving power, to become the symbol of the Emperor. It is, however, remarkable that this symbolism applied not only in China but among the Celts, and that a Hebrew writer speaks of the Celestial Dragon as 'a king seated upon his throne'. Dragons being, in fact, associated with lightning – they spit FIRE – and with fertility – they make rain – thus symbolize the duties of kings and the rhythm of existence which ensures order and prosperity. This is why they became an imperial emblem. For the same reason their pictures were displayed: 'in time of drought, they made an image of the Yin-dragon and then it began to rain' (GRAD 1: p. 361). The dragon was a manifestation of the omnipotence of the Emperors of China; 'the dragon's face' meant 'the emperor's face'; 'the dragon's pace' was the majestic walk of the head of state; 'the dragon's pearl' – which it was believed to keep in its throat – was the indisputable prestige of the head of state's words, the perfection of his thoughts and commands. 'You do not argue with the dragon's pearl', Chairman Mao was to state.

Although the aquatic aspects of dragon symbolism remain of prime importance, since dragons live in the water and cause springs to bubble up, and while the 'Dragon-King' is a king of the NAGA (which further identifies dragons with serpents), the dragon is above all linked to rain-making and to lightning, both manifestations of celestial activity. Uniting Earth and Water as it does, the dragon is a symbol of the rain of Heaven which makes the soil fruitful. 'Dragon-dances', displays of appropriately coloured dragons, enabled mankind to receive Heaven's blessing in the form of rain. Consequently, dragons were signs of good omen and their appearance was the culmination of prosperous reigns. Sometimes from their jaws hung foliage, the symbol of germination, and wherever the dragon-dance was performed, the watchers fed the 'dragon' with greenstuff. Thunder is inseparable from rain and its link with dragons derives from the notion of the active First Cause, the Demiurge. Huang-ti, who was a dragon, was also the genius of thunder. In Cambodia it was believed that the water dragon possessed a jewel which glittered like lightning, whose flashing brought on the rain.

The upsurge of the thunder-cloud, which is that of the *yang*, of life, of plant-growth and of the cycle of regeneration, is embodied in the appearance of the constellation of the Dragon, which corresponds to Spring, the east and the colour GREEN. The Dragon rises with the vernal and sets at the Autumn equinox, heralded by the positions of the stars *kio* and *ta-kio*, the 'Dragon's Horns', the bright stars Spica in the constellation Virgo and Arcturus in Boötes. The employment of the dragon motif in the decoration of Eastern GATEWAYS also endows it with cyclical symbolism, but this is more characteristically solstitial. In astronomy, the head and tail of the Dragon are nodes in the lunar orbit, the points at which eclipses occur, hence the Chinese symbolism of the dragon devouring the Moon and the Arabic symbol of the Dragon's tail as the 'realm of Darkness'. This brings us to the dark side of dragon symbolism, but its ambivalence is constant. As the sign of thunder and the Spring and of celestial activity, the dragon is *yang*; but *yin* as ruler of the realm of the waters. It is *yang* in so far as it is identified with such solar animals as the horse or the lion and with swords: *yin* in so far as it changes into a fish or is identified with the serpent. It is *yang* as a geomantic principle; *yin* as the alchemical principle of mercury. (BELT, BURA, BHAB, CHAT, CHOO, COOH, COMD, CORT, DURV, ELIY, ELIF, EPEM, GRAD, GRAP, GRAR, GROC, GUEV, GUET, GUES, HOUD, KALL, LECC, LIOT, MATM, OGRJ, PORA, SECA, SOUL, SOUN, SOYS)

The emblem of Wales is a red dragon. In the *Mabinogion* the tale of Lludd and Llewelys describes the struggle between the red dragon and the white dragon, the latter symbolizing the invading Saxons. In the end both dragons, made drunk with mead, were buried in the centre of the island of Britain, at Oxford, in a stone coffin. So long as they remain undiscovered the island will suffer no invasion (CELT 6: pp. 451–2; CHAB pp. 391–401). The coffined dragons are symbols of hidden and chained powers, the two faces of a veiled being. The white dragon carries the pallid colours of death, the red dragon those of anger and violence. The burial together of both dragons signifies that their fates have become interfused. Anger may have calmed, but the dragons could rise together. They remain a threat, a potential force ready to launch itself at any new invader.

The image of the WHALE vomiting the Prophet Jonah may be associated with dragon symbolism, since dragons are creatures which swallow, transfigure and vomit up their prey. 'The image, based upon a solar myth, depicts the hero swallowed by the dragon. Overcoming the monster, the hero acquires eternal youth. His journey to the Underworld completed, he returns from the realm of the dead and his night-time prison in the sea' (DAVS p. 225). Jungian analysis has taken advantage both of the myth itself, which clinical experience shows recurs in dreams, and of its traditional interpretation.

A familiar type is that of Jonah and the whale, in which the hero is swallowed by a sea monster that carries him on a night sea journey from west to east, thus symbolizing the supposed transit of the sun from sunset to dawn. The hero goes into darkness, which represents a kind of death . . . . The battle between the hero and the dragon . . . shows more clearly the archetypal theme of the ego's triumph over regressive trends. For most people the dark or negative side of the personality remains unconscious. The hero, on the contrary, must realize that the shadow exists and that he can draw strength from it. He must come to terms with its destructive powers if he is to become sufficiently terrible to overcome the dragon: i.e. the ego can triumph, it must master and assimilate the shadow.
(J. L. Henderson in JUNS pp. 120–1)

Henderson also quotes in this context Faust's acceptance of Mephistopheles' challenge, the challenge of life, the challenge of the unconscious. Through it and through what he has believed to be the pursuit of evil, Faust sees salvation on the horizon.

The battles of St George or of St Michael with the dragon, so common a subject for artists, illustrate the perpetual struggle of good with evil. In a wide variety of shapes and forms it pervades every culture and every religion, not excepting dialectical materialism in the guise of the class struggle.

dream   This entry relates simply to dreams as channels for and makers of symbols. It also displays the complex, representational, emotional and vectorial nature of symbols as well as the difficulties in interpreting them accurately. The bulk of this article may be applied to symbols as a whole and to each symbol separately, all symbols owing something to dreams and vice versa.

As a proportion of a lifetime
The most recent scientific research suggests that by the age of sixty a person will have dreamed during sleep for a minimum of five years. If sleep occupies one third of a person's life, about twenty-five per cent of that person's sleep will have been spent dreaming. Dreams therefore fill about one twelfth of most people's lives. In addition there are waking dreams and daydreams to swell that already impressive proportion.

Now, dreams, as Frédéric Gaussen has so aptly put it, 'are symbols of the individual's experience, so deeply lodged in the depths of consciousness that they elude their own creators, and we view them as the most secret and uninhibited expression of our very selves.' For at least two hours every night we live in this dream-world of symbols. What a vast source of information this would be about human nature in general and our own in particular if we were able to remember them and to interpret them correctly!

As Freud remarked, 'the interpretation of dreams is the royal road to knowledge of the soul.' Thus from the very earliest ages 'keys' to the interpretation of dreams have proliferated; nowadays psychoanalysis has taken their
place.

As phenomena

Just as with symbols, so there has been a considerable development in ideas
on dreams, but this is not the place for a history of them. However, even
today there is considerable professional disagreement, Freudians seeing
dreams as expressions or even as fulfilment of repressed wishes (FRER
p. 123), while for Jungians they are 'spontaneous and symbolic autopresenta-
tions of the current state of the dreamer's unconscious' (JUNH p. 228).
Sutter, however, more baldly describes dreams as 'psychological phenomena occurring during sleep and comprising a series of images which unfold
in more or less connected dramatic form' (PORP p. 365).

Dreams thus elude the dreamer's volition and responsibility by the very
fact that this nocturnal play-script is spontaneous and uncontrolled. This is
why the dreamer experiences the dream as though it were real and not
confined to his imagination. Consciousness of reality is wiped out, the dreamer's identity alienated and dissolved. Chuang Chou no longer knows whether
it is Chou who dreamed that he was a butterfly or a butterfly which dreamed
that it was Chou. 'If a labourer were certain to dream every night for twelve
hours at a time that he was a king,' Pascal wrote, 'I believe that he would
be almost as happy as a king who dreamed every night for twelve hours at
a time that he was a labourer.' Conflating Jungian thought, Roland Cahen
writes:

Dreams express that innate mental activity which thinks, feels and receives
impressions, and engages in speculation on the fringes of our everyday activities
at all levels, from the most carnal to the most spiritual, without our being aware
of it. By revealing the psychic undercurrents and the requirements of a life-
programme written at the deepest level of being, dreams express the individual's most cherished aspirations and, incidentally, become an infinitely valuable
source of all orders of information.

(RSHU p. 104)

Classification

The Ancient Egyptians respected dreams above all for their premonitory
qualities. 'God made dreams to show men the way to follow when they
could not see into the future', a book of wisdom states. In their temples,
priests and scribes would interpret dreams according to a set of keys handed
down from generation to generation. Oniromancy, or divination by dreams,
was universally practised.

The Negritos of the Andaman Islands believe that dreams are created
by the SOUL, which they regard as a malign part of a human being. It
escapes through the nose and performs the acts which the person experiences in the dream-state.

All North American Indians regard dreams as the final and decisive proof
of anything under dispute.

Dreams inspire sacred song, they determine the choice of priests and endow
the shaman with his powers. Knowledge of healing, the names to be given to

children and taboos all equally derive from them. Dreams dictate the composition of war- and hunting-parties, death-sentences and reprieves. They alone provide the keys to the mysteries of life and death.

Lastly dreams 'corroborate tradition and provide the seal of legitimacy and authority' (MULR p. 247).

The Bantu living along the Kasai, a tributary of the Congo River, believe that some dreams are brought back by souls which separate from their living bodies and gossip with the souls of the dead (FOUC p. 66). These dreams may either serve as warnings to the dreamer or comprise genuine messages from the dead to the living and therefore concern the community as a whole.

There are countless different sorts of dream and there have been as many attempts to classify them. For the convenience of study, however, psychologists, ethnologists and parapsychologists have divided night dreams into certain categories:

1 *prophetic or didactic:* more or less open warning about some critical occurrence, past, present or to come; these dreams are often believed to derive from some heavenly power;
2 *initiatory:* shamanistic or Buddhist (Tibetan Bardo-Todol school), endowed with magical powers and conducing to an introduction into another world by means of knowledge imparted to or a journey undertaken in the imagination;
3 *telepathic:* putting the dreamer in touch with the thoughts and feelings of individuals or groups at a distance;
4 *visionary:* transporting the dreamer into what Corbin terms the 'imaginal' world and presupposing the existence within the individual of a level of consciousness and of 'forces which have perhaps become atrophied in our Western civilization', forces for the existence of which Corbin has found evidence among the Persian mystics; this is neither a premonition, nor a journey, but a vision;
5 *warning:* these hunt out and bring one possibility in a thousand to the fore;
6 *mythological:* which recreate some major archetype and echo some basic universal anxiety.

Functions
Dreams are as essential to physical and mental balance as sleep, fresh air and a healthy diet. By turns they tighten and relax the psyche and fulfil a vital function; only death or madness bring dreaming to a complete stop. Dreams serve as a release mechanism for impulses repressed during the day, they enable problems to emerge and, in giving them play, offer solutions to them. Like memory, their selective function comforts conscious life. However, dreams play yet another part of quite different depth.

Dreams are some of the best channels of information on the psychic status of the dreamer. They provide an existential balance sheet in living symbols, a picture of the dreamer that is frequently unsuspected, and revelations of the ego and the self. However, just as with symbols, so dreams conceal these messages under images of beings separate from the dreamer. The processes of identification work uncontrolled in dreams. The dreamer projects him- or herself into the image of another being and by identification with the other becomes alienated, being able to assume shapes which have to all appearances nothing in common with the dreamer's self, being male or female, plant or animal, planet or vehicle and so on. One of the parts which dream analysis plays is that of uncovering these identifications and of discovering their causes and their objectives. It must reconstruct the subject's real identity by revealing the causes of alienation.

Analysis
Analysis of dream symbols is founded upon a threefold study: of the content of the dream (the images and parts they perform); of the structure of the dream (the type of pattern provided by these images as a whole); and of the meaning of the dream (its direction, outcome and intent). The principles governing the interpretation of the analysis may in any case be applied to all symbols, over and above those of dreams, and especially to any with mythic content. Dreams may be regarded as personalized mythology.

Interpretation
To decipher a symbol or a dream does not simply depend upon intellectual curiosity. Dreams raise the relationship between the conscious and the unconscious to a higher level and improve their channels of communication. Thus, for this reason alone, dream or symbol analysis is on the psychological plane a method of personality integration. A more enlightened and better balanced being tends to replace the person torn apart by desires, aspirations and doubts, with no understanding of self. As Professor Meier, quoted by Roland Cahen, remarks: 'The synthesis of conscious with unconscious psychic activity is the very essence of creative mental work.'

dress Clothes are the external symbols of spiritual potency, the outward and visible shape of the inner being. Despite this, the symbol may become a simple sign which destroys the reality when dress is mere uniform unconnected with personality. For example, the current liking of priests and officers for lay dress and plain clothes in place of clerical dress or uniform may doubtless be explained in terms of social development, but it may conveniently be observed that this fact is a sign of desacralization and loss of meaning of the symbol. If dress no longer displays a relationship of a symbolic nature with the underlying character of priest or soldier, it would in fact be far better to get rid of it altogether and for the people concerned to be reduced to the dead level of mediocrity. Dress indicates membership of a body with a specific character, be it the church, army, navy or the law, and to cast off its particular dress is in some sense to deny membership of that body.

It is rather too easy to say that 'the habit does not make the monk' or, as Chuang Tzu remarked, the mandarin. Indeed, and this is not something which should be ignored, the purpose of the monastic habit may well have been to conceal individual physical differences. In the past, in the Orthodox Church as in religious orders, taking the habit could stand in all respects as a form of second baptism, with effects which were not purely external. Buddhist monastic dress suggests complete withdrawal from the world, the dust and rags picked up haphazardly along the road. A Zen patriarch is invested by transmission of a robe, his *kāsaya*. They might not owe it to their learning, but educated Chinese told the world that 'by their round caps they understood heavenly things; by their square slippers they understood earthly things, and by their tinkling earrings they understood how to achieve harmony everywhere' (Chuang Tzu: ch. 21). If dress exteriorizes office or status, it is sometimes their symbol and helps to confer both the one and the other.

The Sufi master gives his KHIRKA to the person he admits to his community.

The vestments of Jewish priests were reminders of the correspondences between micro- and macrocosms, and their fringes of the grace raining down. Use of priestly vestments is widespread, but it is to be observed that this hieraticism is also applied to lay clothing. In this context the priestly vestment above all others is the PILGRIM's dress, often a WHITE robe, as in Islam for both Sunni and Shi'ite and in Japan for both Buddhist and Shintō. The pilgrim has to change from everyday dress into a special garment, which sacralizes him. This is 'putting off the old man' and 'putting on the new man' spoken of by St Paul, purification as a preliminary to 'passage'. Before initiation into Chinese secret societies the candidate, too, puts on a white garment. This calls to mind the 'wedding garment' mentioned in the Gospels (Matthew 22: 11–14).

In China the Imperial robe had a round collar and a square hem, which therefore made its wearer an intermediary between Heaven and Earth, CIRCLES symbolizing Heaven and SQUARES Earth. When discussing the hexagram *k'uen* (Earth; passive First Cause), the *I Ching* links it with the 'undergarment' denoted by the same ideogram, which was yellow, the colour of earth. The *Li-ki* attached the highest importance to the symbolism of this garment, which prescribed the noble carriage and qualities of its wearer. It was fashioned from TWELVE strips like the year from twelve months (harmony); its sleeves were round (graceful movement); the stitching at the back was straight (rectitude) and the lower hem was horizontal (peace of heart). 'When dress is as it should be, the bodily carriage will be correct, the facial expression calm and gentle, in conformity with rule, prescript and order' (BURA, GRAC, GUET, SCHP, SOOL, SOUP, VALI).

The shaman's robe contains an equally great wealth of symbolism. 'In Ancient Uralo-Altaic cultures, the shaman's CLOAK was decorated with a three-branched emblem known as the mark of the bustard, a symbol of communication between the worlds of death and resurrection.' In Western popular art the wizard's pointed hat, his magic wand and cloak ornamented with stars recall the shaman's kaftan, a 'robe with long sleeves decorated with iron rings and the figures of mythical beasts', and the different items in his wardrobe. Wearing wings upon his shoulders signified that he was the 'intermediary between the two worlds' (SERH p. 139). 'North African peasants wear a burnous of seven separate pieces of cloth stitched together, symbolizing the seven parts of the human being.... Throughout time and place,' Jean Servier concludes, having given countless examples, 'whether clothing is made of thread, beaten bark or skin, its wearer through symbols finds the place which he believes he should fill in this world, clothed in light' (SERH p. 257).

Even in Old Testament times choice of dress could indicate the underlying character of the wearer. Thus in Daniel's vision (7: 9), he describes God as the Ancient of Days, seated upon a heavenly throne and dressed in white, the colour of light. The prophet Isaiah gives thanks to the God who has saved and justified him by saying that he has 'clothed [him] with the garments of salvation [and] covered [him] with the robe of righteousness.' Dress is no external attribute, foreign to the nature of its wearer, but on the contrary is an expression of the inherent and essential truth of his character.

White, shining or glistening garments enable angels to be identified immediately (Matthew 28: 3; Luke 24: 4). In the Transfiguration, Jesus' garments became gleaming with a supernatural, heavenly and divine whiteness (Mark 9: 3ff.). It should be seen as a manifestation of the glory of the Resurrection in advance of the event; the gospel account of it betrays the literary influence of other accounts of the manifestation of the godhead.

When, according to legend (2 Enoch 22: 8ff.), Enoch was taken up into Heaven, the Lord commanded him to remove his earthly garments and to put on glorious robes. In so doing he assumed the character of the new world into which he had been taken.

In this context it is legitimate to enquire whether the dress of the Essenes should be regarded merely as a symbol of purity, or rather as the sign that members of this sect belonged to the new covenant with the angelic world, a belief expressly stated in their writings.

As both Christian and Jewish writers testify, since the salvation of mankind in some sense numbered humans among the heavenly host, it is hardly surprising that around the beginning of the Christian era we should repeatedly find the image of clothing as a symbol of the eternal lot promised to the elect and to true believers. The author of *The Ascension of Isaiah* (8: 14–16; 9: 9ff.) knew that such garments awaited each of the faithful in Heaven. 1 Enoch 62: 15ff. thus describes the resurrection of the elect: 'They shall put on robes of glory. And such shall be your garments; garments of life from the Lord of Spirits.'

In the Book of Revelation (6: 11; 9: 14ff.) martyrs received hereafter the final reward (of white robes) promised to all Christians (2: 10; 3: 11).

A difficult passage from St Paul should be understood in the light of the foregoing: 'For in this we groan, earnestly desiring to be clothed upon with our house which is from heaven. If so be that being clothed we shall not be found naked. For we that are in this tabernacle do groan, being burdened: not for that we would be unclothed, but clothed upon, that mortality might be swallowed up of life' (1 Corinthians 5: 2–4). The clothing to which the apostle aspires is clearly the final manifestation of his salvation. To be found naked would be seen as being rejected by Christ. Nevertheless, St Paul superimposes a second symbol upon this traditional symbol. Salvation is a second garment added to and transforming the first garment, which must accordingly only designate the body.

This is the germ of a symbol which Gnostics were to develop to an extraordinary pitch. At its best it may be seen in 'The Hymn of the Soul' in *The Acts of Thomas*. The king's son (elect; of divine nature) departs into Egypt (into a world which is evil because it is material). He soon forgets who he is and exchanges his royal robes (signs of his divine origins) for the squalid garments of the Egyptians (sign of his soiling by the phenomenal world). He only casts them aside in disgust when there appears before him a marvellous royal robe, made to fit him perfectly in his father's court. In this robe he was to recognize himself for who he was, that essential being beyond deceptive appearance.

There can be no better example of the symbolism of dress in its most highly worked Gnostic guise – dress as symbol of the very essence of the human being.

Reverting to Christian symbolism, the employment of the image of clothing should be observed in a baptismal context in *The Odes of Solomon* 21: 3: 'I have cast darkness aside and put on light'; while St Paul says 'Let us cast aside the works of darkness and put upon us the whole armour of light.' Again, Christ is said to have 'put on human nature' while the Christian 'puts on Jesus Christ'. It may also be recalled that ancient liturgies provide evidence that in baptism the neophyte was clothed in a white garment, symbolizing the purity which was received simultaneously with salvation, of which the newly baptized person received the reward. In addition, numerous Mandaean sources could be quoted to show that they regarded baptism itself as the divine gift of a robe of glory.

Dress is something unique to mankind, since no other creature wears it, and is one of the first signs of consciousness of nakedness, of self-consciousness and of moral consciousness. It is also revealing of certain aspects of the personality and in particular of that part of it open to influence (fashions) and of its wish to exert influence. Uniforms or certain items of dress – helmets, caps, ties and so on – show membership of a specific group, entrusted with specific duties or possessed of particular abilities.

In Islamic tradition, the ritual changing of garment marks the passage from one world to another. An emir, for example, will not dress in the same way in his own country as he would in a Western luxury hotel, unless he were travelling in his rank. However, some garments proclaim an even more fundamental change, such as the monastic habit which denotes the passage from the everyday world to the religious world. In his journey from the land of Abraham to the Heavenly Malakūt, the mystic pilgrim passes through twelve worlds, twelve 'veils of light', and thus changes clothes, these symbolizing the necessary inner disposition, the 'garments of the soul', stage by stage until he achieves enlightenment in Paradise. 'The Tale of the White Cloud' provides examples in the Islamic tradition. Similarly, the ritual employed in Mithraic mysteries displays 'clothing in different garments appropriate to the specific level of mystical ascension' (CORE 4: p. 341).

drinking bout (see also ALCOHOL) Drinking bouts were rites held in high esteem in Ancient China where, like BANQUETS, they had the property of a covenant and were the expression of a sense of community. The void in the calendar between successive years, when the year itself was reborn, was filled by drinking bouts for seven or twelve nights. Their objective was to renew the life force before the beginning of the annual cycle and the awakening of nature which the bouts themselves aimed to encourage. The rites and their concomitant concerns were not, in any case, peculiar to the Chinese.

The Montagnards of southern Vietnam believe that to dream of a drinking

DROUGHT

bout is a presage of rain. Customarily they drink from a common jar and this rite is supposed to promote fertility (DAMS, DAUB, GRAD, GRAC).

Drinking bouts were ritual and compulsory during Celtic festivals and particularly at the festival of Samain in which the community as a whole was involved. After the feast, MEAD and BEER was drunk and there are many friendly literary references to these drinking bouts and to the INTOXICATION which ensued. This was as true of Wales as it was of the rest of the Celtic world. In Gaul, where they eagerly drank what the Ancients termed 'pure' WINE, that is, wine of high alcoholic content, these love feasts must often have ended disastrously. The Irish took the precaution of disarming the participants at the start of proceedings, but this did not entirely prevent quarrels and brawls. It would appear that sacred drunkenness was rare. It did, however, exist, not as a means of divination but of contact with the Otherworld, the person concerned acting as a passive channel under the influence of the godhead (see ORGY) (OGAC 4: pp. 216ff.; 13: pp. 481ff.).

drought Dryness is one of the four fundamental qualities of the elements (see STAR OF DAVID) and characterizes FIRE. Drought is one of the disasters which the gods unleash to punish mankind for its sins.

The Old Testament is replete with this threat (Isaiah 50: 2; Haggai 1: 9–12). Wise men and prophets ceaselessly reiterate it: 'Fire, and hail, and famine, and death, all these were created for vengeance' (Ecclesiasticus 39: 29).

Drought is also one of the plagues of the Book of Revelation. 'And the sixth angel poured out his vial upon the waters of the great river Euphrates; and the water thereof was dried up; that the way of the kings of the east might be prepared' (16: 12). The 'kings of the east' were the kings of Parthia, the terror of the Roman world. In this context they also symbolize all the monstrous powers of spiritual perversion which will cause world war, the origin of most horrible suffering for mankind. Drought forms both the prologue and epilogue of disaster – it is death by fire.

However, drought – and this is its positive aspect – is sometimes an instrument of divine aid and favour. 'Art thou not it which hath dried the sea, the waters of the great deep; that which hath made the depths of the sea a way for the ransomed to pass over?' (Isaiah 51: 10). In this context 'the great deep' means not only the Red Sea through which the Children of Israel passed on their journey to the Promised Land, but also primeval CHAOS regulated by the Creator, the Ocean which enfolds the world. The passage might also be applied to all the miracles which the Creator wrought by fire. In a spiritual and psychological sense, the great deep might also describe the human soul and one of its stages along the upward path of mystical experience, the transitory period of spiritual aridity. The verse from Isaiah is most applicable.

In mystical theology, aridity describes a testing time when the soul loses contact with God, feels no elation, suffers a mental paralysis and lacks light, warmth, touch and any sign of God's presence. It is temptation in the wilderness, spiritual death agony, when faith itself seems to have dried up. However, it is during this period when dryness reaches it highest pitch, that its incandescent quality is displayed, that its fire opens the way to the immortal life of union with the divine and that the true path to that union

is revealed. Far from indicating absence of love, aridity harbours the fires
of passion: its opposite, WATER, is the soul's death.

But there is also a negative aspect to this. For those whose minds are set
upon earthly rather than upon heavenly fire, drought is the symbol of barrenness. For whoever seeks earthly consolation instead of surrendering to
the burning fire of Heaven is truly barren.

druid Etymologically the word 'druid' is the same as 'knowledge' –
dru[u]id-, 'the very wise' – and there is a primary semantic equivalence
with the words for 'WOOD' and 'TREE' (*-vid*). However, trees are symbols of
power and power and knowledge rightfully belonged to the druids. This
summarizes the similar etymology which Pliny employed to associate the
word 'druid' with the Greek for OAK-tree, *drus*. Despite the reluctance of
both Classical and some modern writers, who would see them solely as
philosophers, druids must be considered as corresponding strictly to Indian
Brahmans. They were priests and their teachings were essentially metaphysical. In fact, alone in Western Europe they comprised an organized and
hierarchical priestly caste, as priests who offered sacrifice, seers and satirists, prophets or specialists in the physical sciences. As trusted counsellors,
druids could be more than priests – in the Christian era druids were supplanted by confessors and domestic chaplains. Seers and poets could be
judges and historians, although they were satirists first and foremost. Prophets
were also physicians. But there was no restriction upon plurality of office.
While Ireland provides many descriptive nouns (mainly concerned with
divination and satire), from Gaul the only one applied to the *gutuater* (druid)
is that of 'invoker'. Druids ruled, stood above all human society and were
the dominant political power. As in Gaul, so in Ireland druids took precedence over kings in voicing their opinions. They managed elections to the
throne and determined the choice of candidate or candidates for kingship.
They also influenced the entire warrior caste by a closely interlocking system of taboos and obligations, both individual and collective, bringing them
to heel when the need arose by a well-honed arsenal of magic. Since the
priestly caste was the mirror image of the family of the gods, the druids
symbolized the Celtic pantheon in its nature and its duties. Free from all
obligations, they were able to adopt both the role of priest and that of
warrior, something corresponding to an exceedingly archaic aspect of tradition. The Aeduan druid, Diviciacus, commanded a body of horsemen,
and the Irish druid, Cathbad, wielded the sword. However, the leading role
played by druids was that of managing the relationship of humans with the
gods of the Otherworld at the great yearly festivals. This, too, is the main
reason why they preferred to restrict themselves to their priestly duties.
When the men of Munster offered the kingship to the druid, Mog Ruith, he
accepted their rich gifts but declined the honour for himself and all his
descendants. There are far fewer remains of druidism in Britain, although
it should be remembered that according to Caesar, the Gallic druids, and
according to written legend, those from Ireland, went to Britain to complete their studies, the only concrete evidence for this being Tacitus' account of the destruction by a Roman army of a shrine on Anglesey in the
first century AD. However, the priestly caste in Britain did not survive the

introduction of Christianity, which preceded the evangelization of Ireland. The intellectual inheritance of druidism passed to the bards who did not, in Ireland, belong to the priestly caste. All modern groups which claim their foundation in druidism have been created *ex nihilo* and are worthless in the traditional sense (OGAC 12: pp. 49–58, 209–34, 349–82, 475–86; 18: pp. 105–14, 161–2).

drum   The drumbeat is associated with the utterance of the primal SOUND, with the beginning of manifestation and more generally with the rhythm of the universe. Such is the part it plays as an attribute of Shiva (*damaru*) or of the Buddhist DAKINI. In the second instance, the rhythm is linked to the spreading of the *dharma*, in the context of which the Buddha spoke of the 'drum of immortality'. The *damaru* is shaped like an HOUR-GLASS and the point shared by the opposing cones is the BINDU, the seed of manifestation, from which cyclical rhythms evolve and radiate.

   In Ancient China drums were associated with the Sun's passage across the sky and, relatedly, to the Winter solstice. This solstice is the start of the Sun's ascensional phase and the beginning of the growth of *yang*. This is why drums were beaten during thunder-storms. The same viewpoint associated drums with WATER, the element of the north and of the Winter solstice, with the heavenly WATER-SKIN, with THUNDER, the smithy, and with OWLS, these last named being symbols linked to the Summer solstice, the high point of the dominant *yang*. In fact in Laos ritual drumming called down the blessing of Heaven in the shape of beneficent rain. However, the wood used and the time at which the drum was made, as well as the ritual employed in drumming, produced either benign or malign effects, the influences raised not being uniformly favourable. Similarly African drums summon the down-pouring of heavenly favours.

   Very naturally the use of war-drums is also associated with thunder and LIGHTNING in their destructive aspects. Consequently in India it is associated with Indra (DANA, FRAL, GOVM, GRAD, GRAC).

   Drums are symbols of psychological warfare, breaking down the enemy's resistance from within. They were held to be sacred or at any rate to embody a sacred power. They rumbled like thunder. They were anointed, invoked and received offerings.

   Drums not only beat the alarm and the attack, they were the very voices of the tutelary powers from which the riches of the soil sprang. As with Ares and Mars in Greek and Roman tradition, the drum was attributed to the war-god, Indra, who is simultaneously the tutelary god of harvests.

   Magic drums were used by shamans in the Altai region in religious ceremonies. They repeated the primal sound of creation and induced ecstasy. They seemed to stand for two worlds divided by a horizontal line. Sometimes a Tree of Life crossed this line. The upper world was heavenly and tranquil or a world of the dance: the lower world seemed that of warring men, of hunting and feasting. Drums were probably used in initiations and provided the rhythm of rites of passage which brought men into a safe place, stronger, happier and closer to the heavenly powers. The drum was like a spirit-boat, ferrying from the visible to the invisible world. It may be associated with the symbols of mediation between Heaven and Earth.

The shaman shaped his drum from a branch of the Cosmic Tree during an initiatory dream. Therefore, every time he used his drum the shaman made contact with the World AXIS and this allowed him to enter the world of the gods. With its decoration of symbolic figures, his drum became for him and for him alone a microcosm. It was the shaman's horse which bore him off on his mystical journeys. It beat the rhythm of the shaman's magic seances and was truly an instrument of ecstasy and possession.

(MYTF p. 108)

The Lapps, too, used drums for divination. 'The Ancient Samoyed called the drum a "BOW". It was a musical bow, a harmonious bow, symbol of the covenant between the two worlds, but a hunting bow as well, which shot the shaman like an ARROW into the sky' (SERH p. 149).

The Quiché Indians of Guatemala used the drum as the symbolic representation of thunder, of the power of death and of fertility (GIRP p. 27).

In eastern and central Sudan a god brought animals and the seeds of all plants to mankind in a drum. It is a fertility symbol and the seed of all seeds.

Far more than this, in Africa drums are associated with every event in human life. Drums are the deep echo of existence.

Known to specialists in Black Africa as 'the pre-eminent African musical instrument', the drum is in the full sense of the word 'the *Logos*, identified with the human condition of which it is the means of expression' (MVEA p. 80). However, in all cultures drums are the manifestation of the (male) powers of Heaven or of the (female) powers of the Underworld and, in the latter case, are associated with the symbolism of the CAVERN, cave and WOMB. As they say, the beat of the drum 'hits you in the guts'.

duck (drake)   In the Far East the duck or, strictly speaking, the pair of Mandarin ducks (*oshidori* in Japanese) is the symbol of marriage and of conjugal felicity, including, sometimes, that of the life force. The reason for this is that duck and drake always swim in company. This symbol is a frequent motif of high art, as in the prints of Hiroshige or the fifteenth-century paintings of Li Yi-ho, as well as of popular art, where it is found on greetings cards. There are many legends to confirm the explanation of this symbol. A picture of a pair of ducks is hung in the bridal chamber (OGRJ, DURV).

In America the Plains Indians regarded ducks 'as faultless guides as much at home on water as in the air', hence the use of ducks' feathers in certain religious ceremonies.

There is no mention of ducks in Welsh or Irish mythological or epic literature. They have been confused with SWANS despite differences of size and coloration. It would, therefore, be hard to attribute any particular symbolism to them. Nevertheless duck-shaped objects belonging to the La Tène culture have been found (CHAB pp. 553–5). One would tend to interpret these images from the Celtic world as if they were swans.

dung-beetle   In Ireland the symbolism of this creature is wholly malign. In the Ulster Cycle a chieftain is known as Dubthach of the Dung-beetle's Tongue (*Dubthach Doel Tenga*) because of his proneness to slander, the metaphor being based on the insect's colour. In the tale of 'The Death of the Children of Tuireann' there is an account of how a dung-beetle gnawed the side of King Nuada, whom the three physician sons of Dian Cécht (APOLLO) had come to cure (OGAC 16: pp. 233–4; CHAB pp. 900–7). The dung-beetle gnawing the king's side may be understood in material terms as a leprosy or in spiritual terms as a besetting sin. The sons of the Celtic Apollo were as much healers of souls as of bodies. (See also SCARAB.)

Durgā Goddess paid particular honours at the temple of Kālighat, at Calcutta. To some she is simply 'a goddess of terror to whom goats are sacrificed; but for a few initiated *Shāktas* Durgā is the manifestation of cosmic life in constant and violent regeneration' (ELIT p. 7). She therefore partakes of a twofold symbolic quality of apparently opposite meanings. They may, however, be reconciled, the intensity of the life force being both regenerative and destructive, while the sacred MOTHER both gives life and devours it.

dust As a symbol of the power of creation, dust is compared with sperm and with the pollen of flowers.

According to Genesis, not only was ADAM created from the dust of the earth, but Abraham was promised that his 'seed shall be as the dust of the earth and . . . [shall] spread abroad to the west, and to the east, and to the north, and to the south' (Genesis 28: 14).

On the other hand dust is sometimes a sign of death. The Children of Israel cast dust on their heads in token of mourning (Joshua 7: 6), while Psalm 22: 15 refers to 'the dust of death'.

To shake the dust from one's sandals was a formal act symbolizing a complete abandonment of one's past, an absolute break and a renunciation of all that which the dust stood for, country, family, friends and so on.

dwarf Genii of Earth and soil, born from the worms which the ancient Germans believed gnawed the corpse of the giant Ymir, in the tradition of the peoples of northern Europe, dwarfs are often the fairies' companions. But if fairies seem etherial, dwarfs are associated with CAVERNS and mountain caves in which they hide their smithies. Here the ELVES help them to forge such marvellous swords as Durendal or Gungnir, Odin's magic spear which nothing could turn from its mark. In Brittany, the chief dwarf, Gwioi, guarded the mystic urn which would become the Holy Grail. Like the CABEIRI of the Phoenicians and the Greeks, dwarfs were associated with the gods of the Underworld. Coming from it and remaining linked to it, they symbolize those dark forces which are within us and which can so easily take monstrous shape.

Their freedom of speech and gesture in the company of kings, ladies and grandees personify the uncontrolled outbursts of the unconscious. Dwarfs were regarded as irresponsible and invulnerable, but were heard with a smile as though they were not quite of this world. The smile might sometimes be a trifle forced, since dwarfs never minced their words but spoke the naked truth. Their image was then somewhat akin to that of the fool or BUFFOON. However, with a full share of the mischievousness of the unconscious went a logic beyond the bounds of reason, and they were endowed with all the strength of instinct and intuition. Their small size enabled them to overhear the most closely guarded secrets and they became creatures of mystery. Their pointed remarks had more than a hint of clairvoyance, pin-pricks deflating self-satisfaction. Augustus raised a statue in memory of his dwarf with diamonds for its eyes, since he had been all-seeing, all-hearing and all-feeling, and had kept it all to himself. Some critics link the symbol-ism of dwarfs with that of guardians of buried treasure or of secrets. How-ever, according to tradition, dwarfs are talkative guardians, even if they generally express themselves in riddles. Although they may appear to have renounced love, they remain closely tied to nature, whose secrets they know. Thus they may act as guides and counsellors. They share the powers of the soil and may be regarded as ancient Earth-gods. They have been endowed with magic qualities like genii or DEMONS (SOUD p. 79).

This kinship with demons has been due to their small size and a degree of DEFORMITY. In this case dwarfs no longer symbolize the unconscious, but an unnatural birth, a *lusus Naturae*. The latter might all too easily be im-puted to sin if the deformity were not caused deliberately by potentates; for in the decline of the Roman Empire, very ancient recipes were used to create dwarfs and human monsters. Dwarfs are also images of perverted lusts. Companies of dwarfs even came into fashion in the Renaissance and were often treated like domestic pets. This suggests that they became sub-stitutes for the unconscious, which was pampered to keep it lying dormant, or else kept and toyed with as if it was something which existed outside of the self.

History records the names of many dwarfs famed for their extraordinary qualities as orators or thinkers. Licinius Calvus successfully engaged Cicero in the Roman courts, while Alypius of Alexandria was famed for his know-ledge and wisdom. 'He thanked God for having burdened his soul with only the smallest proportion of corruptible flesh.'

E

eagle King of the BIRDS, deputy or messenger of the highest heavenly godhead and of the FIRE of Heaven, the Sun, at which it alone dares stare without burning its eyes, the eagle is so important a symbol that there is no written or pictorial image, historic or mythic, in European or any other civilization, in which it is not the companion, when it is not the representative of the highest gods and the greatest heroes. The eagle is the attribute of ZEUS (JUPITER) and of CHRIST, the imperial emblem of the Caesars and of Napoleon, while on the North American prairie as well as in Siberia, Japan, China and Africa, shamans, priests and seers in common with kings and great commanders have borrowed the attributes of the eagle in order to share its powers. The eagle, too, is the primitive and collective symbol of the father and of all father-figures. However, the universal distribution of the image takes nothing from the wealth and complexity of the symbol which it expresses. This article endeavours to develop these qualities by juxtaposing examples drawn from different sources.

King of the birds
The eagle is the crowning glory of bird symbolism, which is that of higher spiritual states and hence of ANGELS as Biblical tradition so often bears witness. 'They four . . . had the face of an eagle . . . and their wings were stretched upward; two wings of every one were joined one to another, and two covered their bodies . . . whither the spirit was to go, they went' (Ezekiel 1: 10–12). These images express transcendence and, even if we increase the eagle's noblest attributes, there is nothing to match them. While in the Book of Revelation (4: 7) 'And the fourth beast was like a flying eagle.'

The Pseudo-Dionysius the Areopagite explains why eagles stand for angels since: 'The representation of the Eagle [depicts] the kingly, and soaring, and swift in flight, and quickness, and wariness, and agility, and cleverness in search of the nourishment which makes strong; and the unimpeded, straight, and unflinching gaze towards the bounteous and brilliant splendour of the Divine rays of the sun, with the robust endurance of its visual powers' (PSEH p. 48).

The eagle staring at the Sun is once again the symbol of the direct perception of mental enlightenment. 'Fearlessly the eagle looks the sun in the face,' wrote Angelus Silesius, 'as you can stare at eternal brightness if your heart is pure.' The eagle is thus a symbol of contemplation, which is why it became an attribute of St John the Evangelist. In some medieval works of art the eagle is identified with Christ, expressing thereby his Ascension and his kingship. This latter interpretation is to transpose the symbol of Imperial Rome, which was also to be that of the Holy Roman Empire.

Lastly, the Psalms make the eagle a symbol of spiritual renewal like the
PHOENIX.

Bird of the Sun
In Arctic and northern Asiatic mythology the eagle is a substitute for the
Sun (ELIT p. 130). The same is true in American Indian mythology and
conspicuously among the Plains Indians. Hence it is easy to understand why
an eagle's feather and a pipe made of an eagle's bone were indispensable
adjuncts for whoever underwent the ordeal of the Sun Dance. In Japan and
among the Aztecs there was similar identification. In Japan, the *kami*'s
messenger or supporter was an eagle known as 'the Eagle of the Sun'.

When they depicted the universe, the Zuni Indians set an eagle and a Sun
at the fifth cardinal point, the ZENITH, THE sixth point being the nadir and
the seventh the centre, man's place (CAZD pp. 256–7). By setting the eagle
upon the World AXIS, their beliefs coincided with those of the Ancient
Greeks. The latter held that eagles, setting out from the ends of the Earth,
wheeled directly over the navel-stone (see OMPHALOS) at Delphi. They thus
followed the course of the Sun from its rising to its zenith, the latter coinciding with the World Axis. By taking its place with the supreme sky-god,
the eagle stood in the Indian pantheon as it stood beside Zeus, lord of
lightning and the thunderbolt.

Its outspread wings, Alexander observes, suggest jagged flashes of LIGHT-
NING as well as the shape of the CROSS. In these two images – eagle-as-
lightning and eagle-as-cross – Alexander sees the symbols of two civilizations,
that of hunters and that of farmers. He also maintains that the eagle sky-
god, a manifestation of the thunder-bird, was originally the main emblem
of the civilizations of nomadic hunters, warriors and conquerors, just as the
Mexican leafy cross, stylized shoots of dicotyledonous maize, was the main
emblem of agrarian civilizations. At the very beginning of Indian culture
the former embodied the north (cold and male polarity), while the latter
characterized the south (red, moist, heat and female polarity). Nor should
it be forgotten, in this context and in relation to what has gone before, that
north and zenith, south and nadir are akin as above and before, behind and
below.

However, with the passage of time the two civilizations united and the
two symbols which had originally been antagonistic were superimposed, the
one on the other, and fused together. 'It is odd that the simple cruciform
of the Roman pattern became eventually, even for the red men of the Plains,
the symbol for the spread-winged hawk or eagle as well as for the
dicotyledon of the maize plant, earth-emergent – and this natively and
without any influence from Europe' (ALEC pp. 90–1). Generally speaking,
the thunder-bird – Ashur's and Zeus' eagle – as time passes and civilizations mingle also becomes Lord of Fertility and the Earth, symbolized by
the Cross (ibid.).

One might venture to suggest that, in the marriage of these two cultural
stages, the powers of sky and Underworld come into equilibrium. A study
of feudal iconography would tend to support this hypothesis by the frequent association of eagle and LION, whether in conjunction or in opposition. This is reminiscent of the Aztecs, whose two great warrior guilds were

those of the Eagle and the JAGUAR (MYTF p. 193). Again, the Aztecs believed that the Eagle of the Sun fed on the hearts of warriors offered in sacrifice. The latter were known as 'people of the eagle'. The symbolic qualities of warriors killed in battle and men sacrificed to the Eagle of the Sun were the same: they fed the Sun and accompanied him on his journey.

The symbolic association of eagle and jaguar recurs in the description of the Aztec emperor's ceremonial throne. Its seat was of eagle's feathers, its back of jaguar's skin (SOUA). Many other instances might be given of the association of eagle and jaguar in both North and South America.

Another manifestation of the duality Heaven–Earth is seen in the opposition of eagle–SERPENT mentioned in the Vedas, with the mythical bird, the GARUDA, which was originally an eagle. A solar bird, 'blazing like fire', it was Vishnu's steed and his nature, too, was solar. The Garuda was *nāgāri*, 'foe of serpents', or *nāgāntaka*, 'destroyer of serpents'. The duality, eagle–serpent, signifies universally that of Heaven and Earth, or the struggle of angel with demon. In Cambodia the Garuda is the emblem of the kings of the solar line, the NĀGA that of the sovereigns of the lunar line. The Garuda, again, is the 'winged Word', the threefold Veda, a symbol of the Word, just as the eagle is in Christian iconography.

Finally, the Garuda is the symbol of strength, courage and penetration, as is the eagle, by reason of the sharpness of its sight (CORM, DANA, HERS, MALA).

Endowed with these powers of Sun and sky, which it manifests in the strength of its wings, the eagle quite naturally became a tutelary bird, an initiator and psychopomp which guided the shaman's soul across invisible space. American and Asian tradition constantly and mutually reinforce and corroborate this factor, be it only in the identical use of eagles' feathers in shamanistic practices on both continents. Thus in Siberia 'the shaman dances for a long time, falls to the ground unconscious, and his soul is carried to the sky in a boat drawn by eagles' (ELIC p. 349); while in North America the Pavitso place upon the head of a sick person a stick with an eagle's feather in the end, obtained from a shaman, in the belief that the disease will be carried away like the shaman, borne aloft by the eagle in spirit-flight. In the same cultural context there is the fundamental belief that an eagle perches on the topmost branch of the Cosmic TREE to watch and cure all the ailments in its branches (KRAM p. 266; ELIC pp. 272–3). A great she-eagle played the part of initiator and psychopomp, saving the hero, Töshtük, from the world below to bear him to the world above, she alone being able to fly from one world to the other. Twice she swallowed the dying hero, to 'renew his body' in her belly and regurgitate him alive. Such powerful images of initiation display the force of regeneration through absorption.

In an apocryphal Welsh tale, parallelled by the Irish story of Tuan mac Cairill and a passage in the tale of Culhwch and Olwen, the eagle is one of the 'ancient things'. The eagle was one of those primal initiatory creatures, like the thrush, the OWL, the STAG and the SALMON. The only other occurrence of eagles in Celtic mythology is when Llew is wounded by the lover of his adulterous wife, Blodeuwedd, and changed into an eagle; however, they appear frequently on Gaulish coins. In Ireland the FALCON would seem to have taken the eagle's place (CHAB pp. 71–91; MABG pp. 77–80).

Uno Harva records a Siberian myth which associates the archetypal father-figure with the figures of initiator and conductor of dead souls, by giving the eagle the role of culture-hero and father of shamanism. The Almighty sent an eagle to help mankind when it was tormented by evil spirits which brought disease and death. Mankind could not understand what the eagle was saying. God therefore commanded the eagle to give mankind the gift of shamanism. The eagle flew down once more and made a woman pregnant. She gave birth to a child who became the first shaman (HARA p. 318).

Western tradition, too, endows the eagle with extraordinary powers which remove it from earthly constraints. Thus, although mortal, eagles possess the power of regaining their youth by exposing themselves to the Sun and, when their plumage catches fire, diving into a pool of clear water. This may be compared with the rites of initiation and the practices of ALCHEMY, which include passing through fire and water. Its keen eyesight makes the eagle a seer as well as a psychopomp. Even in the heyday of Christianity eagles were believed to carry the souls of the dead upon their wings and return them to God. Their downward stoop symbolized the downpouring of light upon the Earth.

Medieval mystics often invoked the eagle to evoke the vision of God and compared prayer with the eagle's soaring flight into the sunlight.

It was an easy step from clairvoyance to augury and divination. Augury in Classical Mediterranean civilizations was the art of interpreting the will of the gods in the flight of eagles. 'Like the Germano-Celtic RAVEN, the Roman eagle was essentially a messenger of the will of heaven' (DURS p. 134).

Pindar says that the King of Birds roosts on Zeus' sceptre and makes his will known to mankind. Before setting out to beg Achilles for the body of Hector, Priam poured a libation to Zeus. He prayed the god to 'send a bird of omen, even the swift messenger that is to thy self the dearest of birds and is mightiest in strength . . . . And he appeared to them on the right, darting across the city. And at sight of him they waxed glad, and the hearts in the breasts of all were cheered' (*Iliad* 24: 308–21). On the other hand, an eagle flying on the left was an evil omen, reminding us yet again of the symbolism of RIGHT AND LEFT.

In Persian tradition the eagle was a bird of augury but, just as in Ireland, it was often confounded with other birds of prey and especially with the falcon. By the period of the Medes and Persians it had come to symbolize victory. According to Xenophon (*Cyropaedia* 2: 4), when the armies of Cyrus (560–529 BC) came to the aid of Cyaxares, King of Media, in his war with the Assyrians, an eagle flew over the Persian troops and this was taken as a favourable omen. Even Aeschylus (*Persae* 205ff.) describes how the Greek defeat of the Persians was predicted to Atossa in a dream of an eagle chasing a falcon.

Herodotus (3: 76) recounts that just as Darius and the seven Persian nobles were hesitating as to whether to march on the palace of the usurper, Gaumata, they saw seven pairs of falcons chasing two pairs of vultures and tearing the feathers from them. This they took as an omen favourable to the success of their enterprise and they set out to attack the palace.

The royal standard of the Persian Achaemenidae depicted an eagle with golden wings standing on a spear-point (*Cyropaedia* 7: 1), which was intended to signify the victorious and warlike power of the Persians. In his *Shāh-Nāme*, Firdausī, too, describes the standard of ancient Persia as bearing an eagle. However, what is most closely associated with the symbol is the notion of *varana* ('divine power and light of glory') in Zoroastrianism, the pre-Islamic religion of Persia.

In the Avesta (*Zāmyād-yasht: yasht* 19 § 34–8) *varana* is symbolized as an eagle or a falcon. When the legendary king of Persia, Jamshid (Yama) – according to the Avesta, the first King of Kings, although Firdausī calls him third – told a lie, the *varana* dwelling in him left his body in the visible shape of a falcon (*vāraghna*). The king immediately perceived that he had lost all his miraculous powers. He was defeated by his enemies and lost his throne.

The symbolism of the eagle was unaffected by the rise of Islam: in many a tale one magician proves his superiority over another by changing himself into an eagle.

The old druggists attributed supernatural powers to this bird and prescribed a draught of eagle's blood to induce virility and courage and claimed that eagle's droppings mixed with a type of alcoholic drink known as *sīkī* would cure barrenness in women (MOKC pp. 23–43). Within living memory, the nomadic Turkish Yürük set the eagle midway between the fish and the sheep as representing the three ages of man – youth, maturity and old age.

In dreams and Eastern divination eagles symbolized powerful kings, while kings presaged misfortune. The symbolic quality is preserved in folklore. In 'The Secrets of Hamza', King Anūshiravān (Chosroes I) dreamed that he saw a flock of ravens flying towards him from the Khyber. The leading bird snatched off his crown. At the same instant three royal eagles which had flown from Mecca fell upon the raven, took the crown away and returned it to Chosroes. His vizier, Būzarjomehr, interpreted the dream as foretelling that one of the king's enemies would be defeated by the Emir Hamza, his squire 'Amr, and Moqbel, his archer. The title of royal eagle is often used to designate these three, who are also called *sāheb-qarān*, 'Lords of the Age', their victories over the infidel earning them the right to be compared with royal eagles.

Bird of ill omen
As with all symbols, the eagle has its dark, malign and sinister (left-hand) side. This is the exaggeration of its qualities, the perversion of its strength and its inordinate self-exaltation. The duality of the symbol was long apparent to the Pawnee Indians. Fletcher (FLEH) noted that they believed the female brown eagle to be associated with night, the Moon, north and the Mother of All Things, the terrifying and generous temptress, while the male white eagle belonged to daylight, the Sun, the south and to the Father of All Things, who might also take a domineering and tyrannical shape.

In dreams the eagle, like the lion, embodies lofty thoughts and its significance is almost always positive. It symbolizes the 'sudden impulse', 'devouring spiritual passion', but its characteristic as a bird of prey which carries its victims off to eyries from which they cannot escape, makes it the symbol of an undeviating and devouring thirst for power as well.

If this is applied to Christian tradition, this same reversal of image leads from Christ to Anti-Christ. In this context, the eagle becomes the symbol of pride and of oppression, the cruel and greedy bird of prey.

Two-headed eagle

This symbol was not unknown to the Ancient Mexicans. Excellent examples are provided by the Codex Nuttal, where Beyer maintains it embodies a vegetation-god, since it is in fact accompanied by depictions of plants and SHELLS.

It is well known that in the ancient civilizations of Asia Minor, the two-headed eagle symbolized supreme power. In the shamanistic traditions of central Asia, a two-headed eagle is often shown perched on the top of the COLUMN of the world, set in the centre of a village. The Dolgan call it the 'master-bird' and believe that the column on which it is set will 'never fall', being a copy of the very column set before the home of the Supreme Deity and called that 'which never grows old or falls' (HARA pp. 35-6).

According to Frazer, this symbol was originally Hittite, revived by the Seljuk Turks in the Middle Ages, borrowed from them by Europeans at the time of the Crusades and, through this route, incorporated into the arms of Imperial Austria and Russia (FRAG 5: p. 133n).

The duplication of head is less an expression of the dual nature or the many separate portions of the empire, than a reinforcement, by doubling it, of the symbolism of the eagle itself – a more than royal authority of the truly imperial king of kings. Similarly creatures so often depicted in art either back-to-back or face-to-face carry their symbolic qualities to the highest pitch.

ear The most notable piece of symbolism associated with ears is that which in the myth of Vaishvanara, relates them to Cosmic Intelligence. His ears corresponded to spatial direction. This is all the more remarkable if one calls to mind the importance which contemporary medicine attaches to the semi-circular canals of the human ear.

Under WINNOWING-BASKET, the very special role played by Ganesha's ears has been noted. His ears were as large as winnowing-baskets and, as a result, performed the same function.

In China the most remarkable symbolism is that concerning long ears, signs of wisdom and longevity, Lao-Tzu having ears seven inches long and being, in any case, surnamed 'Long Ears'. The same was true of a number of other famous – and long-lived – personages, such as Wu-chuang, Yuang-chou and Chou Chun-mi, whose prodigious feats made him the legendary hero of secret societies.

It should be observed at this point that we should remember the symbolic role played by the faculty of hearing, such as in the Hindu mental image of inaudible sounds which are echoes of the primal vibration, and the mysterious Taoist mental image of 'the light of the ear'. For the symbolism, see under SOUND (GUEV, KALL).

In Africa ears are always symbols of animal nature. To the Dogon and Bambara of Mali the ear is a twofold sexual symbol, the external ear being a penis and the auditory duct a vagina. This explains the comparison of words with sperm, both being verbal equivalents of the fertilizing water poured out by the Supreme Deity. A man's words are as essential to making a woman pregnant as his seminal fluid. The male word flows in at the ear, as sperm flows in at the vagina, to go spiralling down into the womb and make it fruitful.

In the Fon myth which Maupoil (MAUG p. 517) collected in Dahomey (now Benin), when the creator-god, Mawu, first made woman, he set her sexual organs where her ears are now.

This sexual symbolism even recurs in the history of primitive Christianity. 'A heretic called Aelian', Rémy de Gourmont writes (GOUL p. 315),

was condemned by the Council of Nicea for having stated that 'the Word entered by Mary's ear'. Despite this, the Church, reluctant to enter too deeply into a study of the matter, did not make this a question of dogma and allowed Enodius to take up Aelian's theory and the Salzburg Missal to borrow a pair of the poet's verses: 'Gaude, Virgo mater Christi / Quae per aurem concepisti' (Rejoice, Virgin Mother of Christ, who conceived through the ear).

'The Maronite Breviary', adds Rémy de Gourmont, 'still contains an antiphon in which the words "Verbum Patris per aurem Benedictae intravit" [The Word of the Father entered through the ear of the Blessed Virgin] may be read.' However, a sexual interpretation deliberately ignores a very different meaning in this context. The ear symbolizes obedience to the Word of God. Because Mary heard, in the full sense of understanding and accepting the message of the Archangel, she freely conceived the Messiah. Here, the ear is the organ of understanding.

Ear-piercing is a very ancient form of pledging and assignment. In the Old Testament, voluntary servitude is formalized by taking 'an aul, and [thrusting] it through [thy manservant's] ear unto the door, and he shall be thy servant for ever. And also unto thy maidservant thou shalt do likewise' (Deuteronomy 15: 17).

In the Middle East, the Bektashi order of Dervishes, who take vows of celibacy, also pierce one ear and in it wear the EARRING by which they may be recognized. The European traditional practice of sailors piercing one ear and wearing a ring in it to signify their 'engagement' to the sea doubtless originates from the same source.

One of the druidical spells recorded by Irish literary sources is the *briamon smethraige* – its meaning is obscure – which was directed at the ears, the druid rubbing the ear of the person mentioned in the spell and causing his or her death. Not only did the druid isolate the person from the rest of humanity, as the Irish commentator thinks, but he caused his or her death by stopping them from communicating with anyone else and completely preventing the person under the spell from receiving any enlightenment. In several lives of Irish and British saints, the ear was also used for symbolic suckling, of a spiritual quality, given to their favourite disciples by certain saints. In the allegory of Eloquence in Albrecht Dürer's *Kunstbuch*, the persons who follow Ogmios are linked to him by chains which run from the god's tongue to his worshippers' ears. A small bronze in the museum at Besançon shows a god with stag's ears seated in the lotus position (OGAC 9: pp. 187–94; 12: pl. 27; LERD pp. 87–8).

The ear is the symbol of the receptive, passive aspect of communication, as distinct from its active transmissive side. At Pozan, in Burma, there is a very ancient statue of the Buddha receiving enlightenment through his ears, while St Paul's *fides ex auditu* explains that the faith handed down by oral tradition is received through hearing. The ear stands in this context as the womb, or at least as the channel of spiritual life.

According to Greek legend, King Midas' asses' ears were also emblems of stupidity. However, analysis of the legend uncovers rather more. By his preference for Pan's pipes to Apollo's lyre, Midas chose between what the two gods symbolized – the attractions of sensual pleasure rather than the harmony of reason. His asses' ears signify the stupidity which was the direct result of his perverted desire. Furthermore, he tried to hide his deformity, thus piling folly and vanity on top of his lust. 'King Midas, symbol of the platitudinous and commonplace, despite his refusal to recognize it, was the most pitifully duped of mortal men' (DIES p. 132).

ear of corn   To the Plains Indians, 'the ear of corn ... represents the supernatural power that dwells in H'Uraru, the earth which brings forth the food that sustains life; so [they] speak of the ear of corn as h'Atira, mother breathing forth life. The power in the earth which enables it to bring forth comes from above; for that reason [they] paint the ear of corn BLUE' (ALEC p. 106).

In agrarian civilizations the ear of corn – of WHEAT in the Eleusinian Mysteries; of MAIZE in those of North American Indians – was the son, born of the sacred marriage of Heaven and Earth. To resolve this basic dualism is the reason why, by synthesis, the sacred ear of maize simultaneously bore the female colour of earth – RED – and the male colour of heaven – blue. 'The feminine ear of corn is capped with the blue of the masculine sky' (ALEC p. 129).

Renaissance artists used the ear of corn as the attribute of Summer and of harvest-time; of Ceres the goddess of agriculture (see DEMETER) who gave mankind corn and who was usually depicted holding a bunch of ears of corn; and of Charity and Plenty who pour forth grain, and the food for which it stands, in profusion (TERS pp. 158–9). The ear of corn was also the emblem of the Sun-god OSIRIS who died and was reborn and who, in Ancient Egypt, symbolized the natural cycle of death and rebirth. The ear contains the grain which dies either to provide nourishment or the seed which will sprout.

In general the ear is the symbol of growth and fertility, both food and seed. It marks the stage of ripeness, both in animal plant life as much as in psychic development. It is the blossoming of every potentiality in the personality; the image of ejaculation.

earring   Earrings would appear to have been worn in all cultural areas, and examples have survived from Mycenae, Athens, Rome and so on. In North Africa they carry an especial and originally sexual significance. Jean Servier records 'their mention in a rogational prayer used by the Beni-Snus'. Its literal translation is 'May God bedew her earrings!' The obscene implication is 'May God bedew the lips of her vulva.' The sexual symbolism of earrings is plainly demonstrated by the women of the Aurès region of

Algeria who from puberty to the menopause wear earrings called *Töbularwah*, literally 'soul-carriers'. Old women wear earrings fashioned from a plain silver ring with horn or amber ornament. By linking this jewel with female fertility, it comes in the end to personify the 'RAIN-bride' (SERP p. 188; SERH p. 94). Servier also observes that these practices are akin to ritual scarring, of which they would appear to be a 'symbolic form, like piercing the nose or upper lip and stitching up the ear.'

Be this as it may, the sexual symbolism of the earring (French: *boucle*) agrees with the etymology of its Latin source, its literal meaning being 'little mouth'.

Earth Symbolically Earth is contrasted with Heaven as the passive with the active principle; the female with the male aspect of manifestation; darkness with light; *yin* with *yang*; *tamas* (heaviness) with *sattva* (lightness); density, fixity and concentration with rarity, mobility and dissipation.

According to the *I Ching*, it is the HEXAGRAM *k'uen*, passive perfection, receptacle for the action of the active principle, *k'ien*. Earth is the support, while Heaven is the cover. From Earth all beings receive their birth, for she is woman and MOTHER, but she is completely submissive to the active principle, Heaven. All female creatures share the nature of Earth. In a positive sense her qualities are those of gentleness, submissiveness and quiet and lasting firmness of purpose. To them should be added humility, derived etymologically from *humus* ('soil'), to which she bends and from which mankind was fashioned. The primitive ideogram *t'u* signifies the production of beings by the Earth.

Earth is *prakrti*, the 'original producer', primal CHAOS, original matter, separated, according to Genesis, from the WATERS; brought to their surface by Vishnu's wild BOAR; kneaded together by the heroes of Shintō; material from which the Creator, Nu-Kua to the Chinese, fashioned human beings. The Earth is a virgin penetrated by hoe or PLOUGH, impregnated by water or by BLOOD, Heaven's SEMEN. Universally, the Earth is a WOMB engendering springs of water, minerals and metals.

The Earth is SQUARE – especially to the Chinese – within the bounds of the FOUR points of the compass. Thus the Chinese Empire was a square divided into smaller squares, with the square Forbidden City standing for its centre, while the Chinese universe comprised a series of squares within one another (CORT, ELIF, GRAD, GUEM, GUES).

The Earth symbolizes motherhood – Mother Earth – giving life and receiving it back. Throwing himself on the ground, Job cries out: 'naked I came out of my mother's womb, and naked shall I return thither' (Job 1: 21), identifying Mother Earth with the womb.

In Vedic religion, Earth also symbolizes the mother, fount of being and of life and protecting it against all the powers of annihilation. The Vedic funeral rituals included the recital of verses at the moment when the urn containing the ashes of the dead person was placed in the ground: 'Creep away to this broad, vast earth, the mother that is kind and gentle . . . . Soft as wool to anyone who makes offerings; let her guard you from the lap of Destruction. Open up, earth; do not crush him . . . . Earth, wrap him up as a mother wraps a son in the edge of her skirt' (VEDR p. 53).

Some African tribes have the custom of 'eating earth', a symbol of identification. The man offering sacrifice tastes it: the pregnant woman swallows
it. Fire springs from earth which is eaten: 'the womb is set alight', as they
say (HAMK). In their notions of the basic sacred marriage of Heaven and
Earth, the Dogon conceive of the Earth as a woman lying on her back with
her head to the north and her heels to the south, her womb being an anthill
and her clitoris a TERMITE's nest (GRIE).

Identified with the mother, Earth is the symbol of fertility and regeneration. 'She gave birth to all things, nourished them and then took from them
the fertile seed once more' (Aeschylus, *Choephori* 127–8). According to
Hesiod (*Theogony* 126ff.), she (Gaia) even gave birth to Heaven (OURANOS)
who then had to impregnate her to give birth to all the gods. The latter
copied this first sacred marriage to produce mankind and animal creation,
the Earth thus being the source of all life and in consequence being given
the title of 'Great Mother'.

Symbolic burials exist, on a par with baptismal immersion, as curative or
strengthening rituals, or as part of rites of initiation (see CAVERN). The idea
is always the same – regeneration by contact with the Earth, death in one
life-form to be reborn in another.

This may be demonstrated in the myth of Antaeus who was invulnerable
so long as he was in contact with his mother, the Earth. To overcome the
giant, HERAKLES (Hercules) had to lift him onto his shoulders and then to
squeeze him with all his strength until he had stifled him. Making contact
with the Earth by wallowing on the ground, in the sand or on the rocks
symbolizes the need to allow Earth-forces to penetrate the skin, to suckle
from the breast of Mother Earth not through the mouth but from every
pore, in short to recharge the being with energy. Apparently medical opinion
recommends mud-baths, especially for healing the blood vessels and improv-
ing the circulation.

Lying curled up on the ground as if trying to return to the womb of the
Earth corresponds symbolically to passing through the sleep of death to an
awakening, being reborn reinvigorated and standing upright. Wallowing on
the ground provides an image of death and resurrection, but to remain
supine is the first step towards degeneracy.

The Waters were also at the beginning of the world and they are distinguished from Earth in that they preceded the ordering of the Cosmos, while
Earth produced all living things. The Waters stand for undifferentiated mass;
Earth for the seeds of those differences. Aquatic cycles embrace longer
periods of time than telluric cycles in the general development of the Cosmos.

In literature, woman and plough-land are often identified – seeded furrows, ploughing and sexual penetration, giving birth and harvesting, gathering fruit and giving suck, ploughshare and male phallus. Both in Asia and
in Africa there is a body of belief that a barren woman risks making her
husband's lands barren and that for this reason he may divorce her. Pregnant women, on the other hand, make the harvest all the richer if they plant
the seed, being a source of fertility. 'Your wives are like fields for you'
(Koran 11: 223). It was in the Spring and in a thrice-ploughed fallow that
Iasion copulated with DEMETER (*Odyssey* 5: 125–7).

The Aztecs conceived of the Earth-goddess under two opposing aspects.

On the one hand she is the Bountiful Mother, allowing mankind to live from the plants she bears: on the other she demands the bodies of the dead for her own nourishment and is, in this sense, a destroyer (ALEC p. 78).

The Maya hieroglyphic for Earth was the Moon-goddess, mistress of the cycles of fertility. The old Maya Moon–Earth goddess had a primal function, being mistress of the number ONE. In other words, she commanded birth, the origin of all things and the beginning of manifestation (THOH).

The Earth was believed to be carried on the backs of different creatures. In Japan it was a gigantic FISH; in India, a TORTOISE; in Central and South America, a SERPENT; in Egypt, a SCARAB; in south-east Asia, an ELEPHANT; and so on. Earthquakes were explained as being due to sudden movements by the creature carrying the Earth, corresponding to different stages in its development.

Jews and Christians call Palestine 'the Holy Land', but obviously different traditions have the same name for different places. Such different names as 'Land of the Saints', 'Land of the Blessed', 'Land of Immortality' and so on, are applied to places that bear the same significance for various traditions. In all cases we are dealing with spiritual centres corresponding to what each tradition regards as the centre of the Earth, which is itself an echo of the the primeval Centre or Earthly Paradise. With this may be compared 'the Promised Land', the goal of a quest which was also on a spiritual plane; and again 'the Black Land' (Kemet), the Ancient Egyptians' name for Egypt, with undoubtedly primeval characteristics. The Promised Land is what Dante calls one of the spiritual poles, like Canaan for the Children of Israel, Ithaca for Odysseus and the Heavenly Jerusalem for Christians. Plato's 'Pure Land' corresponds to what we should think of as 'the Holy Land'. In the specific case of Amida worship, the 'Pure Land' (Japanese: *Jōdo*; also called 'Land of Retribution' or *Hōdo* by Shinran) is Amida's Paradise in the West and again, by definition, a 'Land of the Blessed'.

However, the land of the journey's end may well be the same as that of its beginning. The latter never loses its sacred character. Thus, when a group tries to achieve spiritual regeneration, it undertakes a sort of return to the earth from which it sprang. 'A sacred place is what it is because of the permanent nature of the hierophany that first consecrated it. That is why one Bolivian tribe, when they feel the need to renew their energy and vitality, go back to the place supposed to have been the cradle of their ancestors' (Lévy-Bruhl, *L'expérience mystique* pp. 188–9, quoted in ELIT p. 368). Pilgrimages to Mount Zion, Golgotha and other places are similar.

Like Latin, Irish had two words for 'earth'. *Talamh* corresponds to *tellus*, meaning Earth as an element by contrast with Air or Water, while *tir* corresponds to *terra*, meaning earth or land as a geographical location. Druids had power over the element Earth. Before the Battle of Mag Tuired, one of the druids among the Tuatha Dé Danann promised Lug that he would hurl a mountain on top of the Fomorians and that he would set the twelve chief mountains in Ireland at his service. In Celtic mythology the Earth is personified by Tailtiu, who is not Lug's wife, but his foster-mother. Her festival was observed on 1 August. Again, the Earth was one of the pledges of a Celtic oath, which may be compared with the oath which the angel

Amnael swore to Isis. 'I swear to you by Heaven and Earth, by light and darkness, by Earth, Fire, Water and Air, by the heights of Heaven and the depths of Earth and Hell, by Hermes and by Anubis, by the howlings of Kerkoros, by the ferry-boat and ferryman of Acheron, by the three Fates, by the Whips and by the Sword . . .' (*Collections des anciens alchimistes grecs*, Paris, 1887, pp. 29–30).

Paul Diel has sketched a whole psychogeography of symbols in which the flat surface of the Earth stands for mankind as conscious beings; the Underworld with its demons, monsters or malevolent deities represents the subconscious; while the highest peaks which approach closest to Heaven are images of super-consciousness. 'The whole Earth thus becomes a symbol of the consciousness and its state of conflict and a symbol of the will and its potential for sublimation or perversion. It is the ring in which human consciousness fights its battles' (DIES p. 37).

east–west If the east is so often contrasted with the west as spirituality with materialism, wisdom with instability, the contemplative with the active life or the metaphysical with the psychological (or with the logical), it is for deeply underlying but no less real or exclusive reasons which, with the contemporary Westernization of Eastern ruling classes, have become matters more of theory than of practice. Nevertheless the symbol endures in defiance of mere geography.

There are, in any case, other reasons for this duality, the chief being the fact that the Sun rises in the east and sets in the west – *ex oriente lux* (light comes from the east). Journeys like those of Christian Rosenkreuz to the East are quests for enlightenment. The symbolism of the east is especially cherished by Sufis, who regard the west as relating to the body and the east to the Universal Soul; the west to externals and to the letter, the east to esotericism and spiritual knowledge; the west to matter and the east to 'shape' which, in Hindu terms, would be expressed by the duality *prakrti–purusha*, or again by *tamas–sattva*.

The east is the source of light. In China it corresponds to Spring and to the *ch'en*, the 'thunderclap' which is the source of the pre-eminence of the *yang*, while the west corresponds to Autumn, to the *tuei*, the 'CLOUD', standing WATER, marshes, images of undifferentiated matter, source of the pre-eminence of the *yin*. Sufi journeys start with a 'western exile' which is a return to primal matter, purification, alchemical 'separation', a step required before reintegration into the eastern source of spiritual knowledge. A Buddhist legend places the Buddha Amitabha in the west, where he welcomes the souls of the dead. About the times of the vernal and autumnal equinoxes (around 18 March and 20 September) when the Sun sets most exactly in the west, many ceremonies take place which kindle in the faithful a belief in the Beyond (*Higan* means 'shores of the Beyond') and in the Heaven of Amitabha.

It will be remembered that the entrances of most Hindu temples – and notably all those at Angkor – face the rising Sun. The exception is the temple of Angkor Wat, which is a funerary temple and faces west. East–west is that especial modality which we have described, the duality of life and death, of contemplation and action (CORT, CORA, GRIF).

In Sufi mysticism, east and west lose their geographic meaning to take on a metaphysical and spiritual sense. By contrast with the spiritual East, the West is a world of darkness, materialism, immorality, decadence and dissolution. 'From the higher sphere,' Suhrawardi confesses in his account of his western exile, 'I tumbled into the pit of Hell, among unbelievers and was held prisoner in the land of the West.'

Celtic attitudes to the CARDINAL POINTS have this peculiarity, that the same word is used for 'north' and 'left', and for 'south' and 'right', but this in no sense implies that the north, from which Celtic traditions take their source and origin, should in any sense be of evil omen. In Irish, *ichtar* conveys both the sense of 'below' and 'north', while *tuas* is 'above' and 'south' by reference to the position of the Sun at its ZENITH. Close etymological study has shown that the Irish word for 'left', *tuath*, is of similar but comparatively recent Christian, origin. In fact we are concerned with the name for 'north', derived from that for the word 'tribe' (*tuath*), since the Irish gods came from the north and the POLE is the source of Irish tradition. The SID is in the west, not because the Otherworld is malign, but because monks localized it and confused it with the BEYOND and because one of the pre-Christian literary themes to be most swiftly Christianized was that of the *immrama*, or Wonder Voyage. Throughout Celtic literature, independent of country of origin or of date, dextrorotation, clockwise movement, is beneficent while anti-clockwise movement is of ill omen (see RIGHT AND LEFT). Queen Medb's charioteer drove his chariot in a clockwise direction to call up forewarnings of evil, but when Cùchulainn returned from his first border foray, in his rage he turned his chariot anti-clockwise towards Emain Macha, the capital of Ulster. The kings of Ireland always made their progresses clockwise, following the path of the Sun, and the Troménie of Locronan in Brittany is still made in the same direction (OGAC 18: pp. 311–23).

ebony Ebony is characterized by its BLACK colour and Masonic gavels are painted black to make them look like ebony. The fact that the wood is hard, is not enough to justify the practice symbolically (see BOX-WOOD).

Ebony was once believed to act as a preservative against fear and was thus used to make cradles (BOUM p. 14).

Pluto, King of the Underworld, was seated upon an ebony throne. In this instance the symbolism of ebony, like that of black, would be linked with that of Hell and passing through darkness.

Echidne She was the MONSTER with a woman's body ending in a SERPENT's tail, identified with the viper. The wife of TYPHON, she bore him monsters such as CERBERUS, the hound of the Underworld, the Nemean lion, the CHIMERA, etc.

In his general analysis of incest, C. G. Jung has made Echidne stand for the MOTHER, 'a beautiful maiden above, a hideous serpent below. This double creature corresponds to the picture of the mother; above, the human, lovely and attractive half; below, the horrible animal half, converted into a fear animal through the incest prohibition' (JUNL p. 113). She gives birth only to monsters and especially to 'Orthrus, the dog of the monstrous Geryon who was killed by Hercules [Herakles]. With this dog, her son, Echidne, in incestuous intercourse, produced the Sphinx. These materials will suffice to characterize that amount of libido which led to the Sphinx symbol' (JUNL p. 134). Echidne is a symbol of 'the Whore of Babylon', the libido which burns and consumes the flesh. She is the mother of the vulture which tore Prometheus' liver. She is the fire of Hell, lust which is roused and can never be satiated. She is also the tempting siren whom Odysseus refused to hear.

echo The Maya made echoes an attribute of the great Underworld-god, the JAGUAR. Hence they were associated with mountains, wild animals, especially with the tapir, and with warning DRUMS (THOH).

According to the Greek legend, the nymph, Echo, thwarted in her infatuation for NARCISSUS, scorned and despairing, sought refuge in caves and forests and, in the end, was changed into a rock which repeated every sound. According to other legends, she had distracted Hera's attention while the latter's husband, Zeus, was pursuing her sisters, and was punished by becoming 'a person who can never speak first, can never be silent when spoken to and can only repeat the last words which she has heard' (Ovid, *Metamorphoses* 3). The subject of many other legends, Echo can be seen as the symbol of regression and passivity, which may only be passing phases preceding transformation. She also calls to mind ideas of DOUBLES, shadows and GOLEM.

eclipse An eclipse, in so far as it indicates the disappearance or accidental concealment of light, is universally regarded as something dramatic, a sign of ill omen, heralding disaster. This was the case in Ancient Egypt, in China and, although apparently hardly compatible with the teachings of the Prophet, in Arab lands as well. Only, it would seem, in Cambodia did the circumstances surrounding the eclipse determine whether it should be interpreted favourably or unfavourably. Muslims have prescribed prayers and Buddhists ceremonies to be employed at eclipses. These are often compared with death, since it is the PLANET or STAR which seems to die, believed to have been swallowed by some monster. In India this is *Rahū*, who is also *kāla*, the DEVOURER, while in China 'eclipse' and 'eat' are expressed by the same ideogram (*ch'u*), since the Moon was believed to have been eaten by a toad.

However, the Ancient Chinese further believed that this cosmic disorder was caused by disorder in the microcosm, that is to say in that of their emperors or the latters' wives. It was the dominance of the *yang* (male; light) by the *yin* (female; darkness). It was therefore necessary – and this was a widely-shared view – for assistance to be given to the planet or star which was in danger or which had gone astray. Cosmic order was restored by restoring order on Earth – by drawing up the imperial vassals in a SQUARE, for example – or by shooting arrows into the air. This may have been done to attack the monster devouring the Sun or Moon, or perhaps, as Granet suggests, as an offering; or perhaps, as a rather unsatisfactory recent theory suggests, to attack the Moon (*yin*) eclipsing the Sun (*yang*).

Generally speaking, eclipses were regarded as heralding the cataclysmic events which bring a cycle to an end and which demand intervention and reparation aimed at preparing the way for a fresh cycle – the freeing of the star or planet swallowed by the monster (GRAD, GRAP, SOUL).

From Ancient Peru come four explanations of eclipses, which were in any event considered of ill omen, an eclipse of the Sun foretelling the arrival of the Spaniards and the fall of the Inca Empire. (1)In the oldest belief, it was a JAGUAR or SERPENT which swallowed the Sun or Moon; (2) the latter were sick and died; (3) the Sun hid his face out of anger with mankind; (4) a sacred marriage of Sun and Moon had taken place, the Moon having seduced and dominated the Sun, rather as in China the *yin* might impose itself upon the *yang*.

eel Eels are akin to SERPENTS in shape and, by their habitat, aquatic symbols. In Ancient Egypt they were the emblems of the *Harsomtus* of Dendera, the rising Sun, symbol of primordial manifestation emerging from the WATERS.

In Japan the eel is a well-known creature, regarded as a messenger of the gods and associated iconographically with the TORTOISE (OGRJ).

An eel features in one incident in Irish mythology. The war-goddess, Bobd, disappointed that her love for Cùchulainn was not returned by the hero, changed herself into an eel and wound herself around his legs when he was fighting his enemies in a ford. Cùchulainn roughly tore her loose and hurled her against the rocks (WINI p. 315).

At a lower level eels combine the symbolism of serpents and water.

egg If the egg is regarded as holding the SEED from which manifestation will spring, it is a universal and self-explanatory symbol. The idea that the Earth hatched from an egg is common to Celts, Greeks, Egyptians, Phoenicians, Canaanites, Tibetans, Hindus, Vietnamese, Chinese, to the peoples of Siberia and Indonesia and to many more besides. Nevertheless, the fashion in which the manifestation occurs takes several different forms. There is the Celtic 'SERPENT's egg', represented by the fossil SEA-URCHIN, the egg vomited by the Egyptian Kneph and even the Chinese DRAGON, each standing for the production of manifestation by the WORD. Elsewhere the first man hatches from an egg, as is the case of Prajāpati and of P'an-ku. Later Chinese heroes are hatched from eggs incubated by the Sun or after their mother has swallowed some bird's egg. More often, again, the Cosmic Egg rises to the surface of the primeval waters, where it is incubated – in Hindu belief by the GOOSE, Hamsa, which is the Spirit or BREATH of God – and splits into two halves to give birth to Heaven and Earth. This is the polarization of the HERMAPHRODITE. Thus the Hindu Brahmānda split into two hemispheres, one of silver, the other of gold; the Dioscuri sprang from Leda's egg, each of the twins wearing a hemispherical cap; Chinese YIN–YANG, a polarization of Primal Oneness, offers the same symbolism with its two halves, one black, the other white. The Shintō primal egg split in the same way into two halves, the lighter becoming Heaven and the heavier, Earth. Ibn al-Walid's notion is closely akin to these, his Earth being thick like the yolk of an egg, his Heaven thin, like the white surrounding it.

The general symbolism which links the egg with the CREATION of the world and with its gradual differentiation, deserves detailed description. The egg is a primeval reality containing within itself the germs of a multiplicity of beings. The Ancient Egyptians believed that the activities of a Demiurge caused a hillock to emerge from Nun, personification of the primeval ocean, 'water in its absolute state containing the seeds of creation in a suspended state', and that on this hillock an egg was hatched. From this egg – the noun is feminine in Egyptian – sprang the god who brought order out of CHAOS by giving birth to differentiated beings. The god Khnum, born of the ocean and the primeval egg, in his turn, like a potter, shaped eggs, EMBRYOS or seeds of life. He was 'he who moulds flesh and blood'. However, various cosmogonies were current in Ancient Egypt. In Hermopolis it was believed that the primal egg was none other than Qerehet, 'protectress of the life force of the human race'. In other traditions the part of the egg was played by the primeval LOTUS which opened in the Nile Delta marshes to reveal the Sun, although the Sun itself others held to have sprung from 'the mysterious seed enclosed within the Mother Egg' (SOUN pp. 22–62).

In Canaanite tradition, 'at the beginning of the world Mochus set the air in place. The air begot Ulōmos [the Infinite] and Ulōmos begat the Cosmic Egg and Chansōr [the craftsman-god]. Chansōr split the Cosmic Egg in two and formed the Earth and the Heavens from the two halves' (SOUN p. 183).

In Hindu tradition, according to the *Chāndogya Upanishad* (3: 19) the egg sprang from Non-being and gave birth to the elements.

In the beginning there was only Non-being. It was Being. It grew and changed into an egg. It remained for a whole year and then it split open. Two pieces of its shell could be seen, one of silver, the other of gold. The silver became Earth: the gold, Heaven. The outer membrane became the mountains: the inner, clouds and mist. The veins became the rivers and the liquid, the ocean.

(SOUN p. 354)

Although in Tibetan teaching the egg is not primeval, it is at the head of a long line of descendants. 'From the essence of the five primordial elements came a huge egg', and from this egg came a white lake, ten categories of being and other eggs from which sprang limbs, the five senses, men and women, descendants enough.

In Chinese tradition, before Heaven and Earth began to separate, Chaos itself resembled an enormous hen's egg. After 18,000 years – the numerical symbol for an infinite length of time – the Chaos-egg broke open, its heavier elements forming the Earth (*yin*) and its lighter and purer elements the Heavens (*yang*). Every day the space between them widened and after another 18,000 years, P'an-Ku measured the distance. On the other hand, according to the Huen-t'ien theory, the world is conceived as a vast egg, standing upright upon its broader end. The sky and stars are the inside of the upper portion of its shell; Earth is the yolk floating in the midst of the primeval ocean which fills the bottom of the egg. The seasons are the outcome of periodic storms in this ocean.

The focal ornament of the great Inca temple of Coricancha, at Cuzco, was an oval gold plate flanked by figures of the Sun and Moon. Lehman-Nitsche believes this is the representation of the supreme godhead of the Incas, Huiracocha, as the Cosmic Egg. In support of his theory he cites a number of cosmological myths collected in Peru by the early Spanish chroniclers, including the following. The hero–creator asked his father, the Sun, to create people to inhabit the Earth. The former sent three eggs down to earth. From the first – a golden egg – sprang nobles; from the second – a silver egg – sprang women; and from the third – a copper egg – sprang peasants. A variant tells how the same three eggs fell down to Earth after the FLOOD.

The name Huiracocha appears to be an abbreviation of Kon-Tiksi-Huira-Kocha, meaning 'God of the lava sea' or '. . . of the molten fire within the Earth'. Huiracocha was, in fact, lord of the volcanoes.

The myth of the Cosmic Egg recurs among the Dogon and Bambara in Mali. The Dogon hieroglyphic for 'the universal life force' ♀ depicts the Cosmic Egg on top of a cross showing the four cardinal points, while at the base there is another egg, opening below, and this is the womb of the Earth, the 'female pot' (GRIS). The Bambara regard the Cosmic Egg as Spirit. It is the Primal Spirit springing from the centre of the 'sounding vibration' through the latter's rotation. Thus this egg is shaped, concentrated and gradually separates from the vibration; it then swells, emits a humming sound, hangs in space under its own power, rising and cracking to scatter the twenty-two basic elements which had taken shape within it and which would set in train the orderly creation of twenty-two different life forms (DIEB).

The egg is the image of the universe and of perfection according to the cosmogonic notions of the Likuba and Likuala of the Congo, as recorded by Lebeuf. The yolk represents female moisture and the white, male sperm. The shell, separated from them by a membrane, represents the Sun, which sprang from the Cosmic Egg and 'would have burned up the Earth had the Creator not changed the membrane into moist atmosphere'. The Likuba and the Likuala also say that 'men should try to be like eggs.'

In the Finnish epic, the *Kalevala*, before time began the Virgin, goddess of the waters, exposed her knee above the surface of the primal deep. On it the duck, Ruler of the Air, laid seven eggs, six of gold and one of iron. The Virgin dived down and the eggs broke, the shell becoming the firmament, the yolk the Sun and the white the Moon; speckled pieces of shell became stars and white pieces, clouds; and time began. This is an example of the representation of the egg as a source of light.

There is no separate evidence from the Celtic world of the symbolism of eggs since that symbolism is comprised within that of the fossil sea-urchin, the Cosmic Egg which contains the seeds of every potentiality.

Within the structures of all these cosmogonies the egg plays the part of what Mircea Eliade (quoted in SOUN p. 480), calls a 'stereotype image of the whole'. However, generally speaking eggs follow on from Chaos as a first principle of order. The whole range of differentiation derives from the egg rather than from the undifferentiated magma which is the beginning of things. Although the egg may not be first, absolutely, it nevertheless symbolizes the seed of the first differentiations. The Primal and Cosmic Egg are one, but within itself this one contains both Heaven and Earth and the upper and the lower waters: within its unique totality it carries all manifold potentialities.

The egg may also be regarded as one of the symbols of the seasonal renewal of nature, whence arise the traditions of Easter eggs and of coloured eggs in so many countries. They illustrate 'the myth of periodic creation'. Mircea Eliade takes exception to any empirical or rationalistic interpretation of the egg looked upon as a seed: . . . the symbol embodied in the egg [drawn from the mystical and ritual gatherings from many religions] bears not so much upon birth as upon *rebirth* modelled on the creation of the world . . . . The egg strengthens and assists the resurrection which, again, is not a birth, but a 'return', a 'repetition'.

(ELIT pp. 414–15)

However, it can be argued that these two interpretations are not mutually exclusive, as Mircea Eliade would seem to think. Clearly eggs symbolize rebirth and repetition: it is equally apparent from the oldest literary sources that in the beginning the egg was the primeval seed or reality. If there is a rationalist structure, it is rather to be seen in a concept inspired by a cosmogonic model which may be repeated. This does not exclude the egg from symbolizing a biological cycle as well.

Clay eggs, for example, found in burials in Russia and in Sweden have been interpreted as emblems of immortality and symbols of resurrection. It is not in the least surprising that the same image should share so many different properties. In graves in Boeotia, too, there have been found figures of Dionysos holding an egg as a sign and promise of a return to life. Hence it can be seen why those who taught the goal of escape from an endless cycle of reincarnation and condemned the desire for periodical return to life should forbid the eating of eggs. This prohibition is to be found, for example, in Orphic tradition, but is conceived in far different terms from those of the Buddhist ascetic. The latter try to break all the chains which link them with this world and their goal is the extinction of all desire. The Orphics, on the other hand, tended to accentuate desire, but to direct it towards a spiritual transfiguration. To that end it behoved them to avoid above all 'contact with anything which symbolized a relationship with the world of decay and death'. Now, by the customs which they rejected, eggs were offered to the dead as food and as pledges of their rebirth. Since Orphic rules aimed to free the soul from all that fastened it to Earth so that it could return, purified, to the God whence it had come, they had to prohibit this symbol of rebirth on Earth. Eggs bound the soul to the cycle of rebirth from which it sought to escape. The very existence of this ban corroborates the belief in the near-magical qualities of eggs, through their basic significance as the beginnings of life on Earth.

Eggs also share in the symbolic qualites of quietude like the home, the nest, the shell or the mother's womb (BACE pp. 51–130). However, the interior of the egg is as much a battleground of freedom and constraint as the womb itself. The living being seeks to escape a cloying security, the hatchling to break the cosy warmth of the eggshell. Like the mother, the egg might become the symbol of the hidden conflicts which lurk within all human beings; between the hunger for home-loving comfort and the challenge of confrontation and risk, as well as between intro- and extroversion. The Psychic Egg, like the Cosmogonic Egg, contains both Heaven and Earth, the seeds of all good and evil, as well as the laws of rebirth and fulfilment of personality. The student feels shut in by his universe, the university, and longs to escape by breaking the shell: he must accept the challenge in order to live.

The alchemical tradition of the Philosopher's Egg embodies the idea of the seed, but in this case it is the seed of spiritual life. It is the 'universal hearth':

within its shell it contains the elements of life, just as the hermetically sealed flask contains the matter of the work. Whatever the shape of the flask . . . it had to be incubated like an egg so that the matter within it was transmuted. The heat for this incubation was provide by the ATHANOR, or alchemists' furnace. . . . The matter might then be distilled to provide an elixir or transmuted into silver or gold. . . . From the products of this matter . . . ought to spring the Philosopher's Child, in other words gold, or wisdom.

(VANA p. 19)

An anonymous alchemical manuscript quoted by Monod-Herzen (MONA pp. 63–4) speaks of the Philosopher's Egg in these terms: 'This is how the ancients described the egg: some called it the copper stone or the Armenian stone; others the brain stone; others the stone which is no stone; others the Egyptian stone, and others again the image of the world.' The athanor was traditionally compared with the Cosmic Egg, the egg symbolizing the home, place and object of all transmutation.

Egg symbolism is displayed less directly in such images as those of ovoid STONES (as well as in that of CYBELE), the dung-ball pushed by the SCARAB beetle and the hemispheric portion of the STUPA, which is, in fact, called the *anda* (egg). Both the dung-ball and the stupa hold a germ or seed of life. In this sense eggs may be compared with such other symbols as CONCHES, CAVERNS, HEARTS and NAVELS as centres of the world and points from which space, time and living things evolve.

Both the laying and the hatching of eggs contain aspects of symbolism which deserve to be noticed. Buddhist contemplatives consider the broody hen to be the symbol of spiritual concentration and of its spiritually fruitful powers. Chuang Tzu compares purely externalized, theoretical teaching with addled or unfertilized eggs. When the schoolmen questioned which came first, the chicken or the egg, Angelus Silesius replied, 'The chicken was in the egg and the egg was in the chicken.' Duality is potentially contained within unity, and is resolved in unity.

To end on a more prosaic note, but without departing too far from the foregoing, it should be observed that eggs are sometimes regarded as symbols of prosperity. If the A-kha, from northern Laos, dream that a hen lays a clutch of eggs, they interpret it as a promise of imminent wealth.

Egypt In Old Testament tradition, Egypt symbolized the land of bondage, the land from which came temptations to idolatry or threats of invasion, by contrast with the Promised Land. And yet, at the beginning of the New Testament, there is the Flight into Egypt, as if Herod's Palestine surpassed in wickedness the Egypt of the Pharaohs of old. The Holy Family, however, soon returned to Galilee. In these traditions may be seen the symbol of flight, of escape from a life of servitude to the senses or to foreign power and the journey towards a higher and a freer existence.

The Ancient Egyptians themselves called their land 'Black and Red'. Red described the Saharan side of the country, its scorched and barren wastes; black, its Nilotic side, the long valley lying on either side of the river which made it fertile. The Nile blackened it with its floods and shaded it with its wealth of vegetation. Egypt thus symbolized the marriage of opposites – the barrenness of the desert with the fruitfulness of the valley.

It also symbolized another pair of opposites 'an open crossroads and an isolated oasis' (POSD p. 76). It was the crossroads where four worlds converged – the Sahara, Black Africa, the Asian Middle East and the semi-European Mediterranean. It was an oasis, isolated by sea and desert and thus able to enjoy three thousand years of autonomous and almost unchanging civilization.

eight Universally eight is the number of cosmic balance. With the addition of the intermediate points, it is the number of the CARDINAL POINTS and the number of the pointers on the weather-vane of the Tower of the Winds in Athens. It is often the number of spokes in a wheel, in the rowels of Celtic bits and in the Buddhist Wheel of the Law. There are eight petals on the LOTUS and eight paths in the Way, eight TRIGRAMS in the *I Ching* and eight pillars in the Temple of Heaven. There are also eight angels which support the Throne of Heaven and it is also the number – in what precise form is not known – of the Mirror of Amaterasu. As the pillars of the Temple of Heaven, the angelic supporters and the octagonal plan of the LINGAM would indicate, the number eight and the octagon have also the quality of intermediation between the SQUARE and the CIRCLE, between Heaven and Earth, and are therefore linked with the intermediate world.

In Hindu art and architecture the symbolism of ogdoads is given ample scope. Vishnu has eight arms, corresponding to the eight Guardians of space; the planets (*grahas*) grouped round the Sun are eight in number, as are the shapes (*mūrti*) taken by Shiva and incorporated in the eight lingams set round a central lingam in two of the Angkor group of temples. In the Bayon of Angkor Thom the statue of the Buddha stands in the centre of a lotus-blossom of eight radiating chapels, the arrangement ensuring that the duties of Shiva are performed along with those of the king, or *chakravartī*, who is the person who turns the Wheel in the very centre of the Universe.

This symbolism of central equilibrium, which is also that of justice, it should again be observed, recurs in Pythagorean and Gnostic ogdoads (groups of eight) (BHAB, BENA, GRIC, GUES, HERS).

Another aspect of the symbol is reflected in the fact that, from a very remote age, Japan has been called by its inhabitants 'Great-Eight-Islands', meaning that it is composed of a countless number of islets. Eight is a number often to be met with in the oldest Shintō sacred writings in this sense of multiplicity and has become a sacred number. However, eight is not an indefinite or dissipated multiplicity, but a multiplicity which constitutes the entity expressed by eight.

An example from our own day is the National Centre for Spiritual Education built at Yokahama in 1932. It is on an octagonal plan and contains within it the statues of eight world sages – Shakyamuni, Confucius, Socrates, Jesus Christ, the seventh-century Prince Shōtoku, the ninth-century Japanese Kōbō Daishi and the thirteenth-century Japanese priests Shinran and Nichiren. The octagonal ground plan was not chosen because of the eight world sages, nor was the number of sages a limiting factor, the shape of the building and the number of sages signified infinite wisdom in countless shapes at the centre of all spiritual endeavour, all education and all research.

In African belief eight is the number which completes the grand total. This is certainly true of the Dogon, to whom the number which is the key to creation is not FOUR, but eight, because of its quality of being twice four. As we know, in Dogon thought all that is unadulterated, in other words, that is fair and balanced, is double.

Thus there are eight hero–creators and eight human families sprung from eight primal ancestors of whom four were predominantly male and four female, although all possessed both sets of sexual organs. The seventh ancestor was the lord of speech, but the eighth was speech itself. The Word is therefore symbolized by the number eight, which also comprehends water, semen and the whole range of fertilizing powers. Word and semen wreathe eight times round the womb to impregnate it, just as the spiral of red copper, another substitute for primeval water, encircles eight times the pot of the Sun to give light to the world. Lastly, man is himself the figure eight in his skeleton, reinforced by the eight joints of his limbs (GRIE). These joints are of primary importance since from them comes the man's semen.

Man, the image of the macrocosm, is controlled by the number eight not only in the mechanics of procreation and in his bodily structure, but also in the creation and ordering of everything upon which his continuing survival depends. Thus the seeds of the plants which he grows were brought down to Earth in the collar-bones of his eight ancestors and these eight primordial seeds were planted in eight fields set at the cardinal points around the village.

Lastly, the Dogon sacralization of the number eight overlaps with that of seasonal renewal, eight being the number of the Genius and of the Ancestor – the oldest ancestor – who offered himself in sacrifice in order to ensure the regeneration of the human race once it was firmly established on Earth (GRIE, DIED). Only after this sacrifice was the Earth purified and made fruitful by the first rain, the first fields were sown and the first sounds of metalwork came from the smithy to the north of the village.

The Quechua myth which tells of the origins of the Inca dynasty also mentions eight ancestors, four brothers and four sisters.

Christian tradition, like the Dogon, makes eight the number of fulfilment and completeness. According to St Augustine, all the activities of this life relate to the number four, while THREE governs those of the SOUL. After SEVEN, comes eight which seals the eternal life of the righteous and the damnation of the wicked.

As for the Eighth Day, following the six days of creation and the seventh day of rest, this is the symbol of resurrection and of transfiguration and heralds the age of eternity which is to come. It comprises not only Christ's resurrection but that of the human race. If the number seven is especially the number of the Old Testament, eight corresponds with the New. It foretells the bliss of the life to come in another world.

Finally we should remind ourselves that the mathematical symbol for infinity (∞) is like an eight on its side and that the eighth Tarot is JUSTICE, symbol of final summing-up and of balance, matching perfectly the Dogon four plus four equals eight.

Electra According to Greek myth, she was the daughter of Zeus by Harmony. For the most part, however, Electra is best known through Greek tragedy as the daughter of Agamemnon and Clytemnestra. After Agamemnon had been murdered by Aegisthus, Clytemnestra's lover, Electra was consumed by the desire to avenge her father through the killing of her mother. In psychoanalysis, the Electra complex is the female equivalent of the Oedipus complex. In fact, Electra was not to kill Clytemnestra herself, but to push her brother Orestes to do so and to help him thrust home the dagger. After a phase of emotional fixation upon her mother as a child, the adolescent girl transfers this fixation to her father and becomes jealous of her mother. Alternatively, should her father remain unresponsive, she will either develop a degree of masculinity in order to seduce her mother or reject marriage and drift into homosexuality. In any case Electra symbolizes passionate love for parents going so far as to equate them in death. In this equality in the grave, in the demand for justice against injustice, Electra becomes once more at one with the symbol of the myth and restores the Harmony ordained by Fate.

elements The Chinese theory of the five elements would appear to date from the second millennium BC and was promulgated in a short treatise, the *Hong-Fan*, which is generally regarded as the oldest work of Chinese philosophy.

The five elements are: WATER, FIRE, WOOD, METAL and EARTH, which the Chinese made to correspond to the first five NUMBERS, 1–5.

These elements corresponded to other things both in time and space, as follows:

Water corresponded to the nadir, Winter and north (positioned at the bottom of the map);
Fire: the zenith, Summer and south;
Wood: Spring and east;
Metal: Autumn and west;
Earth, at the CENTRE, lent its aid to all the CARDINAL POINTS and SEASONS.

The Chinese also made each element correspond to an animal, an internal organ, a colour, a taste, a plant, a mode on the pentatonic musical scale and a planet. This led them to claim that everything which existed upon Earth was governed by an element (see table 1).

Naturally it was unthinkable that the elements could act independently of the YIN–YANG.

These five elements reacted upon one another, either in mutual creation or in mutual destruction. The principle of classification and correspondence answered the need to harmonize human life and the cosmic order. The task of the *yin* and the *yang* was to energize the antithetical aspects of the cosmic order, in other words, the elements of which it was composed, and it is patent that the theory of the five elements could not be conceived independently of them.

The Greeks, in common with most other traditions, set the number of elements at FOUR: Water, Fire, Air and Earth. However, they were not individually incommutable but, on the contrary, transmuted the one into

Table 1: The Chinese system of elements

Element	Water	Fire	Wood	Metal	Earth
Number	1	2	3	4	5
Taste	salt	bitter	acid	pungent	sweet
Human character	serious	methodical	learned	friendly	holy
Sky-sign	rain	*yang*	hot	cold	wind
Vegetable	yellow millet	bean	wheat	oil-seed	white millet
Domestic animal	pig	hen	sheep	dog	ox
Musical note	*Yu*	*Chue*	*Chih*	*Shang*	*Kung*
Bodily organ	kidneys	lungs	spleen	liver	heart
Colour	black	red	green	white	yellow
Body element	blood	breath	bones	nails	muscles
Emotion	anger	pleasure	joy	sorrow	love

the other (Plato, *Timaeus* 56ff.). They even proceeded the one from the other in a succession so strict that it partook of a mathematical progression. In the *Timaeus*, the theory of the elements is linked to that of numbers and ideas as well as to that of forms which lies at the heart of Platonic dialectic. Each of these elements subdivides into varieties according to the proportion of participation and mixture. Thus three sorts of Fire were to be distinguished – burning flame, light and the incandescent particles of fire. A fifth element, Ether, was associated sometimes with Air and sometimes with Fire.

These elements have their correspondences in symbolism based upon the psychoanalysis of imagery. Each is conducive to a reality other than itself. Gaston Bachelard's work in this area has been extraordinarily fruitful, showing, as it does, that the image of Air is the basis of all ascensional psychology and that in itself it comprises its own contrarieties of rising and falling (BACA). It also shows how the four elements correspond to the four 'humours', Water with the phlegmatic, Earth the melancholic, Air the sanguine and Fire the choleric (BACF).

The four elements are the basis of what Bachelard calls 'material image-making, the amazing urge to penetrate which ignores the attractions of external shapes to think, dream and dwell in matter, or else – and this amounts to the same thing – to materialize the imaginary. . . . Physiologically, even more than anatomically, the imagination is governed by the four elements' (BACS pp. 14–15). He regards the four elements as 'the hormones of the imagination. They stimulate the activity of groups of images. They assist in the internal assimilation of reality dissolved into its various forms. They are the means whereby those major syntheses take place which provide the imaginary with a more ordered character. Air, especially, is the psychic growth hormone' (ibid. p. 19). Jungian analysis has adopted the traditional distinction between the active, male principles of Air and Fire and the passive, female principles of Water and Earth. The different combinations of these elements and their interrelationships symbolize the complexity and infinite diversity of beings or of manifestation, as does their ceaseless development from one pattern to another, as one or another element predominates. On the inner and spiritual level, psychic development is what is suggested by the conductive valency which is the property of each element. Fire is often regarded as the motivating element which energizes, transforms and produces the three states of matter, solid (Earth), liquid (Water) and gaseous (Air), developing the one from the other. Fire symbolizes the active element in all development.

By regarding the elements as symbols, astrology is linked to the teachings of the great Classical philosophers, Pythagoras, Empedocles, Plato, Aristotle and others. According to this, the different phenomena of life amount to the manifestation of those elements which govern the essence of the powers of nature. Nature herself accomplishes her task of creation or destruction by means of the elements of Water, Air, Fire and Earth. Each of these latter rises from a combination of two primary principles. Water derives from the Cold and Moist principles; Air from the Damp and Hot; Fire from the Hot and Dry; and Earth from the Dry and Cold. Each represents a state, whether liquid, gaseous, igneous or solid, and each is identified with a given group of life situations. This identification is conceived as developing and proceeding in a cycle which begins with the first element (Water) and ends with the last (Earth), having passed through the intermediate stages of Air and Fire. We thus have a fourfold order of nature, of humours and stages in human life: Winter, Spring, Summer and Autumn; from midnight to dawn, from dawn to midday, from midday to sunset and from sunset to midnight; phlegmatic, sanguine, melancholy and choleric; childhood, adolescence, maturity and old age; budding, flowering, fruiting and decaying. On such universally accepted qualities are based the practices of ALCHEMY and astrology and the rules of esotericism.

Masonic symbolism has drawn up a table of correspondences between the elements and the main grades of Masonic initiation (see table 2). In this, Jules Boucher observes, 'the candidate first leaves Earth behind and is then successively purified by Air, by Water and by Fire. By stages he sets himself free from material life, philosophy and religion to reach Absolute Initiation at last' (BOUM p. 45).

Table 2: The Masonic system of elements

Element	Human adjunct	Level
Fire	spirit	initiation
Water	soul	religion
Air	mind	philosophy
Earth	body	physical life

Boucher draws comparisons with the astrologer's traditional table of values: 'the element of Fire corresponds to ardour and enthusiasm; Water to sensitivity and emotionalism; Air to intellectual power; and Earth to materialism' (ibid. p. 44). The correspondences between the elements and the signs of the Zodiac are as follows:

Fire: Aries, Leo, Sagittarius;
Water: Cancer, Scorpio, Pisces;

Air: Gemini, Libra, Aquarius;
Earth: Taurus, Virgo, Capricorn.

It is interesting to observe in this context that Muslim mystic tradition in Sufism links the four degrees of initiatory development to the four elements in a relationship which is the complete opposite of the foregoing.

1 Since the phenomenal world is completely illusory and lacks all substance, it is the element Air.
2 The person who sets out on the way of perfection (*tarīqa*) must therefore begin by burning all the images of that illusory reality (Fire).
3 Through this begins apprehension of the godhead and of the unique reality, first in its most volatile and intangible form (Water).
4 The seeker is finally absorbed within that unique reality, the *Haqq*, the godhead which is the one truly solid substance (Earth).

The four elements are traditionally represented by the patterns shown below, with decorative variations on the central theme.

Water   9999   or else   6666 (waves)
Air   ∿∿∿∿∿∿∿ (clouds)
Fire   /\/\/\/\/\/\/\/\/\ (lightning)
Earth   ⎍⎍⎍⎍⎍⎍⎍⎍⎍ (squares)

The TRIANGLES and SQUARES associated with Fire and Earth echo the symbolism of the numbers THREE and FOUR and are especially helpful in explaining why a male quality should be associated with the number three and a female with the number four. In this connection one should remember the association of the penis with lightning which Geza Roheim has emphasized (GEZH).

elephant   While in Western eyes the elephant is the picture of overweight clumsiness, the Asian image is very different.

Elephants were ridden by kings and first and foremost by Indra, Lord of the Heavens. They therefore symbolize the power of kingship, Shiva being titled 'the Elephant' in the exercise of his kingly office. Since the effects of settled kingship are peace and prosperity, whoever invokes the power of the elephant (*mātangi*) is given their heart's desire. In many regions, and particularly in the monsoon countries, the gift they desire is rain, which is one of Heaven's blessings. In Thailand, Laos and Cambodia the white elephant grants rainfall and plentiful harvests. For Indra is also the storm-god and his elephant wears a rich jewel – the lightning – on its forehead.

The elephant is also a symbol, not of excessive weight, but of unchanging stability. Yoga attributes it to the chakra *mūlādhāra*, where consequently the elephant corresponds to the element Earth and the colour ochre. It was also a companion of the Boddhisattva Akshobhya, the Changeless One. Elephants are also to be found on some Tantric mandalas, set either at the gates of the CARDINAL POINTS, or at points beside them. At Angkor they are to be seen on the eastern Mebon and especially on the Bakong. Their significance is that of the dominion of the CENTRE of kingship extending to the FOUR corners of the Earth. The presence of elephants, among other symbols, next to Vāsudeva – Vishnu as Lord of the Three Worlds – would seem to indicate his sovereignty over the terrestrial globe.

Elephants also call up the image of GANESHA, the symbol of knowledge. His human body is still the microcosm or manifestation, while his elephant's head is the macrocosm, the non-manifestation. If this interpretation is accepted, the elephant is the beginning and the end, and this applies both to the evolution of the world manifested at the sound of the syllable *om* (and therefore of the non-manifested), and also of the yogi's inner creation. Ga-ja, the elephant, is ALPHA AND OMEGA.

Elephant symbolism is a common feature of Buddhist thinking. Queen Maya conceived the Buddha as an elephant calf. It would seem to play an unexpectedly 'angelic' part, were one not already aware that elephants were instruments of heavenly intervention and blessing. An elephant is some-times depicted on its own to signify the Buddha's conception. When set on the top of a pillar, it evokes enlightenment. This echoes Ganesha as the symbol of knowledge. Lastly, and this is very significant, the Boddhisattva Samantabhadra rides an elephant in a display of the power of knowledge. Incidentally, brute strength is exhibited in the episode of the mad elephant, Nālagiri (GOVM, GROI, KRAT).

Like BULLS, TORTOISES, CROCODILES and other animals in India and Tibet, elephants are also cast in the role of animals which hold up the world and carry the universe upon their backs. Because they were believed to support the cosmos, they are the caryatids in the architecture of many ancient monu-ments. The elephant was also regarded as a cosmic animal because it was itself in the shape of the cosmos – four pillars holding up a SPHERE.

In Africa, Baulé beliefs make elephants the symbol of strength, prosper-ity, long life and wisdom. To the Ekoi they symbolize violence and ugliness. From them, the Ibo of southeastern Nigeria borrowed the worship and religious organization of the Ekkpe. But in their case the elephant symbol barely rises above the level of metaphor.

It is also at this level that it is employed as an attribute of kingly power, in consideration of their massive bodies, or as symbols of the monarch who avoids foolish and rash action, in consideration of the elephant's vigilance and wariness. If one were to believe Pliny and Aelian, elephants are also symbols of piety, since they reported that at the time of the new Moon they could be seen gazing up at the planet, softly waving freshly plucked branches as though praying to the Moon-goddess for her favour and blessing. According to Aristotle, the cow elephant's pregnancy lasts two years and during that time the bull neither attempts sex with her nor with any other cow. The elephant may thus be seen as the symbol of chastity; while a seventeenth-century engraving depicts modesty, in the guise of an elephant fighting a wild boar, symbolizing lust (TERS pp. 153–5).

eleven In African esoteric tradition, this number is especially holy, to the extent that some would regard it as one of the principal keys to Black occultism. It is linked to the mysteries of fertility. Women have eleven body-openings: men only NINE. SEMEN is believed to take eleven days to reach its goal and fertilize the ovum. The child which is born receives through its mother's body-openings eleven divine powers. This tradition employs eleven in a favourable sense and in the direction of the notion of the renewal of the life-cycle and of the transmission of the life force. However, the contrary is more generally in evidence in other cultural contexts.

TEN symbolizes a complete cycle and by adding to its fullness, eleven is the sign of excess, extravagance and exaggeration, in whatever category you like, promiscuity, violence, biased judgement. The number heralds potential conflict. Its ambivalence resides in the fact that the excess which it signifies may either mark the beginnings of a renewal or the collapse and breakdown of the number ten, a fault in the universe. It is this latter sense that made St Augustine say that 'the number eleven is the blazon of sin'. Its disturbing activities may be compared with the unbalancing and overenlargement of one of the pillars of the universe (the number ten), a definition of disorder, disease and sin.

Generally speaking, the number is that of 'individual initiative, but of an initiative exercised without relation to cosmic harmony, and therefore more often than not of a malign character.' Eleven is, therefore, the symbol of internal conflict, 'of discord, rebellion, aberration, law-breaking, . . . human sin, . . . and of the revolt of the angels' (ALLN pp. 321–2).

The number eleven, which would seem to have been one of the keys of the *Divine Comedy*, also derives its symbolism from being the sum of the numbers FIVE and SIX, these being the microcosm and the macrocosm, or Heaven and Earth. In China, eleven was the number which 'in its totality (*ch'eng*) comprised the way of Heaven and Earth.' It was the number of the *Tao*.

On the other hand, the Bambara consider it to be the number of discord and conflict. The eleventh stage in their story of the creation was the rebellion of the air-god, Teliko, against the authority of the Creator, the water-god, Faro.

In the lodges of Chinese secret societies eleven flags are set in the rice-basket in two lines of five plus one flag, in memory, it is said, of the two series of five founders who came together as one (GRAP, GUED, GUET).

elixir The elixir of immortality which recurs in tradition symbolizes a transmuted state of consciousness. Whatever heights this may reach, the elixir assures its lasting effects (ALLA p. 154).

In its negative aspect, the elixir may confer the lasting continuation of unconsciousness. Such was the elixir of forgetfulness which the Druids of Ulster gave the hero Cùchulainn at the request of Emer, his wife, so that he would lose all remembrance of Fand, the lovely wife of the sea-god. King Conn of the Hundred Battles ordered one of his druids to give a similar draught to his son Condle, so that the latter would forget the Lady of the SID who had stolen his love. However, the power of the lady from the Otherworld was too strong for the druid. Unfortunately nothing is known of the ingredients of the elixir of forgetfulness and one can only assume that it was some decoction of plant juices (OGAC 10: p. 310).

elves Norse in origin, these airy spirits delight to dance in the meadows at night. While appearing to invite mortals to join them, in reality they cause their death.

Although they are spirits of AIR, they spring from EARTH and WATER, are charming, fickle, small, floating, cloudy and terrifying (see DWARF). They symbolize the powers of darkness and the Underworld which cause mortals, and especially adolescents, to die of fright. Adults are too dim-sighted, too thick-skinned, to see them, as young people do, lurking in the mists. They are like the swirling fog of burgeoning passions and of the first dreams of love. They fascinate and enchant young hearts and ingenuous minds. The White Lady is Queen of the Elves.

Some scholars regard the elves' round dances as ways of concentrating the energy emanating from the universe. From it they derive their powers of enchantment and their ability to pass through the GATES which separate the three levels of the universe and, especially, the world of the living from that of the dead. They react upon the imagination, heightening the sensibility in dreams and apparitions, and drag into their dance whoever they have attracted by their beauty. They symbolize the unconscious powers of desire transformed into attractive images and their seductive power tends to inhibit judgement and self-control.

ember Symbol of hidden power and of occult forces, solar energy stolen by the Earth is stored within it: the ember is a reservoir of HEAT. A burning ember displays the spiritual or physical power contained within it; it provides warmth and light without exploding into flame. It is the perfect image of a fiery nature which is completely self-controlled. A dead black ember displays only its potentiality; it needs a spark or touch of FIRE to reveal its true nature. It will then realize its alchemical transmutation from black to red. It is dead and, if it remains black, cannot take fire by itself.

embryo The embryo symbolizes potentiality and the state of non-manifestation, as well as the sum of all possible existences. While these may not always be upon the cosmic level, they are generally related to it.

The idea of an embryo of the phenomenal world is especially clearly displayed in Hindu mythology. Hiranyagarbha, the golden embryo of the Vedas, is the principle of life floating on the primordial WATERS, the 'SEED of Cosmic Light' (GUES). In a more immediate sense Mother Earth carries embryonic forms within herself. Europeans in the Middle Ages, as well as the Chinese and Babylonians, all believed that minerals 'ripened' in the Earth. This ripening was completed in the metallurgist's hearth or the alchemist's crucible as the embryo ripens in the mother's WOMB. Indians believed that diamonds were crystals which had ripened in the womb of the Earth and in northern Vietnam they believed that, if bronze was ripened in the same way, it became gold.

In any case the relationship between the symbolism of Hiranyagarbha and the matter in the alchemist's crucible will have been noted, for the latter, too, was a 'golden embryo'. From it sprang what Angelus Silesius called 'the Philosopher's child', in other words, the Philopher's Stone. The same order of symbolism evolves in the Tantric alchemy of the Taoists. From the inward marriage of being and BREATH (*hsing* and *k'i*) springs 'the

Mysterious Embryo. The Mysterious Embryo ripens and gives birth to a body (*T'ai-siching*).' The same ideas are expressed in *The Secret of the Golden Flower* and confirmed by the advice of the *Huiming Ching*: 'Do not look outside yourself for the Primordial Embryo.' For, as will be shown later, a return to the embryonic state is synonymous with attaining the paradisal or primeval state. This is why the alchemico-tantric embryo is the seed of immortality.

Hiranyagarbha was fire and is sometimes identified with Agni. The seed of light was seen in his mother's womb and this was believed of the Buddha, of the Ancient Egyptian Sun-god and even of Christ. One of the constant comparisons of the Bible is that of the Messiah with the seed, while St Paul writes of his converts as 'My little children, of whom I travail in birth again until Christ be born in you' (Galatians 4: 19).

The return to the embryonic state, so dear to the alchemists, finds expression yet again in the Taoist technique of *t'ai hsi*, or embryonic breathing. Its object was to return to the primordial state and thus obtain immortality by imitating the closed-circuit breathing of the foetus. Furthermore, and as a means of assisting their rebirth, many peoples, and notably the Tibetans and Andean Amerindians, lay their dead out in the foetal position. The practice, too, of identifying the candidate for initiation with an embryo ready for a new birth is widespread. A precise application is provided in the Brāhmanas.

Embryo symbolism should be compared with that of the seed of light contained within the heart, like Hiranyagarbha in the World EGG. This is sometimes represented iconographically by the Hebrew letter *iod*, as well as by that of *luz*, or the kernel of immortality (see ALMOND-TREE) which holds within itself the complete range of potentiality of individual rebirth.

Ismaili esoterics readily describe the formation of the prophetic body in foetal terms. 'Moses and Imams of his time and their great men were as an embryo', says Ibn al-Walid (COOH, CORT, DANA, ELIY, GRAP, MAST, SILI).

emerald The green and translucent emerald is the stone of GREEN light, which endows it simultaneously with an esoteric significance and with regenerative powers.

Central Americans regarded the emerald, which they associated with RAIN, BLOOD and all the symbols of the lunar cycle, as a pledge of fertility. The Aztecs called it *quetzalitzli* and associated it with the quetzal, the bird with long green plumage which was a symbol of the seasonal renewal of Spring. Emeralds were thereby linked with the east and with everything connected with the worship of the hero-god, Quetzalcoatl (SOUA). Emeralds were distinguished from green JADE in that, unlike the latter, they were unconnected with the bloodthirsty ritual offerings to the high gods Huitzilopochtli and Tlaloc, personifications of the Sun at noon and the no less pitiless tropical storm. Their benign influence was also felt in Europe where, if Portal is to be believed, 'superstition long attributed to the emerald the miraculous quality of easing childbirth' (PORS p. 214). By extension, it might well have had those aphrodisiacal qualities which Rabelais claims for it.

Alchemists regarded the emerald as the stone of Mercury (Hermes), messenger of the gods and great conductor of the souls of the dead. They also called emeralds 'Maydew, but that Maydew was itself merely a symbol of mercurial dew, from the fused metal at the moment when it was transmuted into vapour in the still' (GOUL p. 203). Having the property of penetrating the thickest darkness, the jewel gave its name to the famous *Emerald Table*, attributed to Apollonius of Tyana, which included *The Secrets of Creation* and *The Science of the Causes of All Things* (MONA). Hermetic tradition also maintained that an emerald fell from Lucifer's forehead when he was cast down from Heaven.

The Christian lapidary associated it in its maleficent aspect with the most dangerous inhabitants of Hell.

Medieval folklore, however, endowed the emerald with all its beneficent powers with which, of course, a little wizardry was mingled. The emerald was a mysterious stone – and therefore dangerous to those ignorant of its powers – but was almost universally regarded as a powerful talisman. Although Hell-born, it could turn itself against the inhabitants of the infernal regions, whose secrets it knew. This is why, in India, it was said that the mere sight of an emerald so frightened the viper or cobra that its eyes dropped out of its head (BUDA p. 313). According to Jérôme Cardan, if bound on the left arm, it acted as a preservative against witchcraft (MARA p. 273). According to a medieval manuscipt in Oxford, it set prisoners free, provided that it had first been consecrated, that is separated from its malign powers. In St John's vision, the Ancient of Days appeared, seated on his throne like 'a jasper and a sardine stone: and there was a rainbow round about the throne, in sight like unto an emerald' (Revelation 4: 3). The Holy GRAIL was a chalice carved from an enormous emerald.

As the stone of occult knowledge, the emerald partakes, as do all symbolic objects, of lucky and unlucky aspects which, in religions of good and evil, are translated into benign and malign. An excellent example of this may be seen in the equestrian statue of St George in the Treasury at Munich. This precious item of Baroque jewellery shows the saint, dressed in sapphire (heavenly blue) and riding a solar white horse, spearing an emerald dragon. This is an example of Christian tradition drawing a distinction between properties connected with the Heavens and with the Underworld, designating the first as good and the second as evil. In it the blue of the sapphire confronts the green of the emerald, the latter symbolizing the BLACK arts. Nevertheless, Christian tradition retains the ambivalent symbolism of the emerald, since it is also the Papal jewel. Certain Egyptian and Etruscan beliefs survived into medieval Christendom, namely, that if an emerald was placed upon the tongue it enabled the person concerned to summon evil spirits and converse with them. It was also recognized as being able to heal some diseases, and especially those of the sight, by touch. It was the jewel of clairvoyance as well as of fertility and immortality. The Ancient Romans attributed the emerald to VENUS: in India it was believed to impart immortality.

An elemental manifestation of power, the emerald is essentially an expression of the seasonal renewal of nature and therefore of the Earth's positive forces. In this sense it is a symbol of Spring, of the manifestation of life and of evolution, as opposed to the deathly, regressive forces of Winter. The stone was regarded as moist, watery and lunar as opposed to dry, fiery and solar. It was therefore in opposition to the sapphire. However, it could also act against other malign chthonian influences homeopathically rather than allopathically.

Emperor, the   The Emperor, the fourth TAROT, 'symbolizes precisely what it depicts – empire, dominion, rule, power, success, control and intellectual supremacy in both temporal and physical spheres' (RIJT p. 231).

The Emperor sits upon a flesh-coloured throne, holding his sceptre and dressed in a BLUE tunic and hose. However, over the tunic he wears a RED jacket and his feet, hair and beard are WHITE. In strict uniformity with the third Tarot, the EMPRESS, he, too, has a shield bearing an EAGLE, but this time the eagle is at the foot of the card, leaning against the throne, 'head and wings turned in the opposite direction to those of the Empress's eagle, to ensure the balance of forces through the confrontation of opposites' (MARD p. 308). The Emperor is the first Tarot character to wear red on blue (see POPE, NECESSITY, FOOL). For him, action is the goal of intelligence, and wisdom is useless unless allied with strength. Through their marriage, their energy interpenetrates this world, of which he is the unchallenged ruler. Another symbol of this concentration of power is the position of his legs. They are crossed as a defence against evil influences and simultaneously to husband the powers of good.

This fourth Tarot, also called the CUBE Stone, stands for order, protection, intelligent and constructive work, solidity, good counsel, tradition and authority or, in an adverse sense, obstinate opposition, hostile prejudice, tyranny and the excercise of absolute power. It corresponds to the fourth house of a horoscope. The TRIANGLES which the Emperor wears on his head symbolize the bounds of space, in other words, universal sovereignty. Red, the predominant colour, suggests FIRE, conquering, transforming instrumentality.

(André Virel)

At the psychological level, the Emperor calls for self-possession to bend circumstances to the urge for power. One of his hands holds a SCEPTRE and the other grips his belt, displaying his authority and his readiness to defend it. In short, he is the Demiurge who created both humankind and the world.

Empress, the   On the heels of the JUGGLER, who manifests the world's diversity in its unity, and of the Female POPE, who calls on us to penetrate its secrets, the Empress, the third TAROT, symbolizes sovereign intellect which provides the strength and 'motive power by which all living things enjoy life' (RIJT p. 230), the celestial VENUS of the Greeks.

Seated upon her flesh-coloured throne, she faces us, white-haired, wearing a BLUE tunic over a RED robe, as if she needed to wrap herself in blue the better to grasp the occult forces and as if all her burning, passionate instrumentality, the red background to her crown, needed to be sublimated. Her right hand holds a shield against her side. It bears an EAGLE, coloured YELLOW like her girdle, necklace, pointed crown (reminiscent of the Zodiac), and sceptre, a colour which symbolizes the spiritual powers which govern the world over which she reigns. Her sceptre is topped by an orb and cross, the alchemical sign for ANTIMONY, signifying 'the intellectual soul, ascensional or spiritualizing influences, the spirit freeing itself from the material, evolution and redemption' (WIRT p. 95).

The Empress has been compared with Isis or with the Cosmic Mother. 'She represents universal fertility' (Enel); 'overt or concealed emotional instrumentality' (Bost); 'comprehension, intelligence and discrimination, or else pretentiousness and lack of refinement' (Wirth). In astrology this Tarot corresponds with the third house of the horoscope.

Thus all aspects of the Empress emphasize her resplendent powers. However, there are two sides to her, and her power may as easily be perverted to the seductions of vain glory as rise to the peaks of the highest sublimation. She symbolizes all the wealth of the female nature, idealism, gentleness, persuasiveness, but also all its weaknesses. Her means of action do not appeal directly to the spirit but to the emotions and are based more upon attraction than upon reason. She reminds us in this context of Ernest Hello's remark: 'One should always aim at the head to be sure of hitting no lower than the heart.'

emptiness (see also VOID) Emptiness takes material shape in the central DOT of the VAJRA and at the still centre of the CROSS and SWASTIKA, the changeless principle at the centre of the wheeling universe, the point which is no point, from which all flows and to which all returns.

Emptiness (*shunyata* in Sanskrit; *tong-pa-ni* in Tibetan), as a notion inseparable from *vajrayāna*, is infinite brightness, linked to the creative void, complete receptivity, perfect enlightenment, the disappearance of the ego, as well as to boundless space, the interdependence of all phenomena, an inconceivable degree of truthfulness, with beings and objects completely drained of their own essence. Reality is only a bait. 'Apart from the mere appearance resulting from the chance juxtaposition of related elements, in itself reality comprises nothing' (KALE).

Emptiness therefore designates a state of mind based upon the renunciation of what one believed to be real, beyond all comprehension or lack of comprehension. This revelation of the essential mind of the Spirit, Prajñāpāramitā, the perfection of wisdom, is devoid of feeling unless it be the feeling of deep compassion for all living things.

Northern Buddhism lists eighteen types of emptiness, including amongst them the Emptiness of Non-thought, of Immateriality and of Nonsubstantiality of Reality. Vajrayogini is one of the manifestations of emptiness, as are the Cosmic Tent and the Mirror of Great Wisdom, which reflects shape in void and void in shape, the temporal in the timeless and the finite in the infinite.

Kashmiri worshippers of Shiva distinguish seven types of emptiness and Mahayana Buddhists twenty-seven, but the ultimate goal of tradition, Eastern or Western, is to achieve awareness of emptiness and then emptiness of awareness. 'In awareness all things reside', said the Buddha. This brings us back to the *dharma-kāya* or body of emptiness in the *vajrayāna*, in which, like the Classical UNICORN's horn, all potentiality resides. By contrast with annihilation, emptiness may be compared with a series of numbers starting, not from a positive or negative digit, but from zero.

enclosure In the Celtic world the concept of the enclosure was akin to that of the CIRCLE. At the heart, is a specific place which may be shut off in a number of ways, by walls, ditches or stockades. Archeology has records of circular, rectanguar and square enclosures from the early historic to the Gallo-Roman periods. Round enclosures are, however, rare since circles are images of Heaven.

An Irish chronicle records that, when the god Lug came to Tara, he beat the High King, Nuada, at a game of chess and placed his winnings in 'Lug's enclosure' (*cro Logo*). The reference was in all probability to a cattle-yard and the word *cro* has no very precise symbolical meaning.

The idea of a 'sacred enclosure' is much better expressed in the word *Fal*, which not only bears the meaning of 'hedge' or 'wall' and by homophony 'sovereignty' and 'power', but also 'prince' and 'land'. The notion of sovereignty being inseparable from physical ownership of land, the land itself is seen as a global image of the world and the sacred enclosure as an image of the land as a whole. One of the names for Ireland is *Mag Fail* (Plain of Fal). The roots of the words meaning 'power' and 'enclosure' are homophones.

Tara itself was surrounded by a triple enclosure and in this may be seen a symbolic representation of the THREE worlds. The triple enclosure may also correspond to the three orders of druidical priesthood – seers, bards and druids. Diodorus Siculus (5: 27) reports that the Celts deposited great masses of gold and silver in their sacred enclosures which they dedicated to the gods and which none dared touch (CELT 7: *passim*; GUES pp. 99–104). The enclosure was thus the symbol of the HOLY OF HOLIES, a forbidden place which none but the initiate might enter.

In contemporary psychoanalytic theories, the enclosure symbolizes the inner being. Medieval mystics called it 'the soul's cell', a holy place which the godhead could visit and in which it might dwell. The spiritual man retired to this fortress of silence to defend himself against all external assaults of the senses or of the cares of the world, and it was in it that his power lay and from it that he drew his strength. The enclosure symbolizes the sphere of intimacy surrounding a person over which they have complete control and to which only the chosen few are admitted.

enlightenment Symbol of a condition experienced by candidates during rites of initiation. The known pattern of these rites involves death, a journey to the spirit world and a rebirth. For this reason initiates of the secret societies of the Kasai (Middle Congo) are known as *Mutabala*, the 'Enlightened Ones' (FOUC). Buddha means 'the Enlightened'.

en-sof A Hebrew word much used in the Kabbalah, *en-sof* has the meaning of 'the Infinite', the being who cannot be conceived of by thought, in other words, the *Deus absconditus*, the hidden deity.

Erinnyes The Greek name for the Furies, Underworld DEMONS, like Harpies and GORGONS, which took the shapes of dogs and serpents. They were instruments of divine vengeance upon the sinful, whom they pursued, filling their hearts with terror. Classical antiquity identified them with the conscience. Interiorized, they symbolize remorse, guilt feelings, and the self-destruction of anyone who surrenders to the feeling of having committed an unforgivable sin. Like the Fates (Moirae), they were originally 'guardians of the laws of nature and of the natural order both physical and moral', and in consequence they punished 'all those who exceeded their rights at the expense of others, be they gods or mortals.' It was only later that they became specifically 'the deities who avenged crime' (LAVD p. 391).

This development corresponds to that of the conscience, which first bans and prohibits and then condemns and destroys. The Erinnyes could become the EUMENIDES, benign and fostering deities, when reason, symbolized by Athene, had brought the sickly but appeased conscience to a more measured understanding of human action.

ermine   Carnivore with spotlessly white fur which, as a trimming to robes or mozettas, symbolizes innocence and purity of behaviour, teaching and administration of justice.

Aelian (2: 37) wrote that if an ermine fell into a puddle it went rigid and died (quoted in TERS p. 211). This is the origin of the symbolical significance of the creature which is so often to be found in the devices of kings – 'Death before Dishonour'. The ermine thus signifies moral purity and this is the meaning of ermine trimmings on the robes and mozettas of high governmental, ecclesiastical and academic dignitaries.

Eros   See LOVE.

eroticism   The Song of Solomon has familiarized us with love symbolism and with the use to which such Christian mystics as St Bernard and St John of the Cross have put it. The love of the spouse for the beloved has been interpreted as the love of Jehovah for Israel, of Christ for the Church or of God for the soul. Closer, literally, to the Eros (LOVE) of the Greeks, were such writings as the erotic hymns of St Hieroteus quoted by the Pseudo-Dionysius the Areopagite and interpreted by him as signifying an underlying power of unification and conjoining, a translation in intellectual terms of the mystics' marriage. In any case, the Upanishads display symbolism of the same order, present to a still greater degree in the writings of Muslim mystics.

Throughout the world coitus is a repetition of the first sacred marriage, the coupling of Earth and Heaven from which all living things took their birth. 'When this mutual interpenetration takes place,' says the *I Ching*, 'there is harmony between Heaven and Earth and all things are produced.' Sexual intercourse is a sign of harmony, of the conjunction of opposites and, of course, of fertility. At many times and in many places, especially in Ancient China and, until quite recently, in Thailand, ritual copulation marked the renewal of nature at the Spring equinox and promoted fecundation.

Nevertheless, the best-known erotic symbolism is that of Shakti-ism, Tantrism and also the Taoist 'methods of prolonging life'. Interpretation of the most important point which they have in common has been subjected to the grossest misunderstanding through being taken literally. Of course the cosmic and ritual symbolism of sexual intercourse was familiar in India and the Chinese practices of the bed-chamber were not simply emblematic, but the former were sublimated to the point at which they became wholly a pure image of the spirit, while the latter were considered aberrant by the most reliable sources. All marriage melts into that between Shiva and the SHAKTI, itself a recreation of the primal state of androgyny, since the *shakti* is indistinguishable from Shiva. It is the marriage of Sun and Moon, of Fire and Water. In ritual sexual intercourse the *yoginī* is not simply the image of the *prakrti* or the *shakti*, she is the *prakrti* or the *shakti*, just as the yogi who couples with her is, in fact, in pursuit of his own reintegration. The iconography repeated in the *maihuna* displays the marriage not of beings but of the universal Essence and Substance themselves, or in Tibetan Buddhism, of Wisdom and Discipline. In Yoga, the marriage of opposing principles takes place in each of the 'subtle' bodily energy centres (CHAKRAS) and because this involves male and female elements within the individual it is expressed in terms of INCEST.

Yet another aspect, but one which serves to define more clearly and upon a lower level the notion of inner integration and unification, is the 'sublimation' of SEMEN, linked with breath-control, which is an essential source of energy in Yoga. The same process – which may perhaps originate in the same source – is described in the Taoist *Secret of the Golden Flower*, which states that erotic practices erroneously attributed to some of the Immortals as a means they used to restore their virility, should be interpreted as sublimation. Although it may, in fact, be accepted that the best of them sought rejuvenation in this way, there is abundant literary evidence to show that many failed to understand the symbolism and, as a result of taking the literal meaning, were sunk in the grossest aberrations – but obviously we are no longer dealing with 'Immortals'. Inner alchemy itself employs sexual symbolism, since 'the embryo of immortality' is generated by Heaven's penetration of Earth, the marriage of semen and sulphur, which is that of Fire and Water (AVAS, COOH, DANA, ELIF, GOVM, MAST).

Aside from any symbolic interpretation, Ancient Egyptian art included the erotic. Men and women were indicated by depicting their appropriate sexual organs and their marriage by the intersection of two hieroglyphs. The subjects of their erotic art – gods copulating, among them Osiris with Isis, scenes of sexual abandon, phallic idols, statuettes of prostitutes – comprise 'the earliest indications of sexual malaise' (POSD p. 260). Condemnation and prohibitions were equally evident. Eroticism cannot but betray a sexual urge, or even obsession, and yet at the same time it displays the almost irresistible power of the life force, in pornographic obscenity no less than in works of higher refinement and in relationships which attain the highest levels of intimacy and spirituality. Eroticism may also be distinguished from pornography by its aesthetic character and, sometimes, by its mystic symbolism.

It may, nevertheless, be emphasized that currently fashionable Western pornography bears witness, willy-nilly, to a current of reaction to the hypocrisy which restricted discussion of sex throughout the nineteenth and during the first half of the twentieth centuries when an industrial civilization was developing. Pornography is, in this sense, a symbol turned upside-down. It answers refinement of speech that conceals coarseness of feeling, by a coarseness of speech which may not necessarily correspond to feelings any less coarse.

eternity Eternity symbolizes whatever is limitless in terms of duration.

Accordingly, Boethius (*De consolatione* 5: Prosa 6) describes eternity as 'the complete and unqualified possession of life without limitation', repeating the definitions of earlier philosophers. Thus Plotinus (*Enneads* 3: 7) regarded eternity as a 'life which endures in its identity, ever-present to itself in its totality'. Discussing eternity, St Bonaventura was to write (*Quaestiones disputatae, De mysterio Trinitatis qu.* 5, *art.* 1: 7–8) that the simplicity and invisibility which are properties of the worlds of the 'CENTRE', also belong to eternity; while Dante was to allude to the point at which all seasons were present (*Paradiso* 17: 18). Eternity is a life-act of infinite intensity.

Eternity represents the infinitude of time free from all limiting contingencies and is the assertion of being in the negation of time. The Irish, like any other people, had no means of making comprehensible an idea like this, inaccessible to the human intellect. They got over the difficulty by symbolically setting human time in a fixed, regular and changeless cycle, against which humanity is powerless, alongside divine time with its elastic boundaries and in which several centuries may pass in the space of a year or vice-versa. They broke the cycle by adding a unit. Thus 'a year and a day' or 'a day and a night' became symbols of eternity (OGAC 18: pp. 148–50). This addition of a unit conveyed the 'evolution' of shared conditions of submission to time.

Many forms have been devised to suggest eternity, among them goddesses holding Sun and Moon or sceptre and HORN OF PLENTY, or sitting on a globe surrounded by stars, or wearing a girdle of stars. Eternity generally carries with it the notion of a state of bliss. Because of their legendary longevity, ELEPHANTS, STAGS, the PHOENIX and DRAGONS also symbolize eternity; as also, because of their shapes, do coiled SERPENTS and the serpent eating its tail (see OUROBOROS).

Eternity is the absence or appeasement of conflict and the resolution of differences upon both cosmic and spiritual planes. It is the perfect integration of the being with its First Cause; it is the absolute and permanent intensity of life, freed from all vicissitude and change and in particular from that of time. The human yearning for eternity reflects a ceaseless struggle with time and, perhaps still more, longing for life so intense that it will for ever conquer death. Eternity no more resides in stillness than it does in the whirlwind; it is in the intensity of the act.

Eumenides (see also ERINNYES) Legendary figures schematically contrasted with the Erinnyes and representing the spirit of understanding, forgiveness, projection and sublimation, in contrast with the spirit of revenge, delight in torture and torment, the punishment of all breaches of conduct. These opposing and interrelated images embody two tendencies of the erring soul, poised between sorrow and remorse. 'The Erinnyes symbolize repressed culpability, which becomes destructive, and the torments of remorse. The Eumenides stand for that same culpability, but acknowledged and sublimated, so as to produce a sense of sorrow which sets the victim free' (DIES p. 162).

The Erinnyes were pitiless, the Eumenides benign. Even in Classical antiquity these were the same genii, who protected the social order, and especially the family, avenged crime and were the enemies of anarchy. They were called Erinnyes or Furies when their anger was unleashed and Eumenides when an attempt was made to appease their wrath by appealing to their kindness. This latter attitude, however, presupposed an inner conversion which was itself a return to order.

Eve It is unnecessary to allude to the story of the creation of woman and her temptation by the serpent in the Garden of Eden except to recall the essentials of the many significations for which she stands.

According to patristic tradition, ADAM and Eve before the Fall were clothed in the garment of incorruptibility, their baser appetites were governed by reason and, according to St Augustine, they had experiential knowledge of God, who had spoken and revealed himself to them (*De Genesi ad litt.* 8: 18). Free from all care, they could indulge in contemplation. Such bliss was to end with the Fall and the chief culprit was to be Eve, whose role was to tempt Adam.

What should be the meaning of Eve? According to Genesis, she was extracted from Adam's side while he was sleeping; a sleep which St Augustine was to describe as being comparable with an ecstasy (ibid. 9: 19) and from this arose the belief of woman's subordination to man. Eve was regarded as the first woman, the first wife and the mother of nations. On the spiritual plane she symbolizes the female element in the male, in the sense employed by Origen, that the inner man comprises soul and spirit since 'it is said that the spirit is male and the soul may be termed female' (*Sermons on Genesis* 4: 15). From their accord sprang their sons, as righteous thoughts and good intentions may be termed.

Eve signifies human sensitivity and the irrational element in the individual. Given that only this part of the soul had succumbed to temptation, the consequences need not have been fatal. The Fall was caused by the consent of the spirit, in other words of Adam. Adam and Eve's quarrel, their falling out and Adam's placing of the blame upon Eve, arose from the enmity which henceforth divided soul and spirit. Man in his entire being sinned, since soul and spirit consented to sin. In this sin, the first step was taken by the soul (Eve) and ratified by the spirit (Adam). The Tempter (the SERPENT) could not achieve his purpose by a direct attack upon the spirit, he had to employ the soul as intermediary.

To relate the Fall to the inner spiritual plane is singularly enlightening, since to debase it to giving consent to sexual intercourse is to destroy all its meaning and significance.

Such an attitude was not one which would be preserved by the early Fathers and by their commentators. More often than not Eve was to stand for woman, the flesh and lust, while Adam represented man and the spirit. This was not so much an error as a partial understanding of the myth of Adam and Eve.

When Tertullian exclaimed 'Do you not know that you are Eve ... and that God's judgement still lies upon your sex?' (*De cultu feminarum* 1: 1), he was blinded by his hatred of women. The curses which the Fathers so often called down on women's heads were inspired by this entirely external and strictly literal interpretation of the facts. Hence a modern writer interestingly suggests that 'Tradition has barely glanced at the topic of Eve as the female within the male, despite its current interest. It has often been regarded as a moral allegory of no interest to the theologian except as a substantial component of Augustinian and medieval anthropology' (PLAE).

Nevertheless there are examples of writers who accept this symbolism. Thus Plotinus retained the meaning of inner spirituality. It was exploited by St Ambrose (*De Paradiso* 2: 11) and made explicit by St Augustine himself in a striking passage in which he describes the act of knowing:

This act of knowing is like the creation of woman from man's side, of which the goal was to signify marriage. Each person should therefore strictly control that part which is in submission to him and become as it were conjugal within him so that the flesh does not work against the spirit but remains submissive to it . . . such being the work of perfect wisdom (*De Genesi contra Manichaeos* 2: 12, 16).

(PLAE)

The word 'conjugal' is the one which should hold our attention. If man's inner structure is 'conjugal' it predicates a marriage between two separate elements. It should be noted here that, when the train of argument followed by St Augustine in his discussion of the act of knowing forces him to display this conjunction and to define it, he compares it with the creation of Eve and with the marriage of the pair, Adam and Eve. Now, in Hebrew thought, as evidenced by the Old Testament, 'to know' carries the meaning of sexual intercourse, and thus Adam 'knew' Eve. In almost the same sense St Ambrose had written 'Let none judge it misplaced to regard Adam and Eve as standing for soul and body' (*In Lucam* 4: 66). Hence the marriage of soul and body, of flesh and spirit on an inner plane, symbolizes the marriage of male and female. If the ends of marriage are the procreation of children, then the marriage of spirit and flesh brings with it a fitting end product, that of 'good works'.

Medieval writers were to be influenced by the Pauline division of Adam = Spirit, Eve = Flesh and the statement that 'Adam was not deceived, but the woman' (1 Timothy 2: 14). In their commentaries upon the symbolism of Adam and Eve they very seldom quoted St Augustine's subtle theories. Peter Lombard was to assemble textual references to Adam and Eve and to be satisfied merely with paraphrasing them (*Collectanea in Epistolas ad Corinthos*). Richard of St Victor went one better by suggesting the symbolism of Adam and Eve upon different levels, speaking not only of spirit and soul, but of intelligence and emotionality, of knowledge and of love.

Lastly it should not be forgotten that the name of this archetype of woman is a palindrome. This is no accident. It symbolizes the fact that 'woman, like the ANGELS in Plotinus' theory of divine manifestation, unlike men, possess a double nature . . . creators of an intelligence and simultaneously its physical containers' (DURI p. 37).

excrement   Regarded as a reservoir of strength, excrement symbolizes a holy product of human biology, indwelling in the human being and to some extent capable of being recovered after it leaves the human body. Thus what should, to all appearances, be endowed with the most minimal of properties might, in fact, be the most richly charged with them. In so many traditions the significance of GOLD is linked to that of excrement and some dowsers even claim that they emit the same vibrations.

The association of excrement and filth with the notion of sin was to be found among the Aztecs. Their pantheon included Tlazolteotl, the goddess of physical love, fertility and the confessional. Her name would seem to mean 'Eater of Excrement' or 'Goddess of Filth', because she ate up sins (SOUP).

In Black Africa special rituals surround rubbish, which is regarded as being charged with forces transmitted to it by humans. The Bambara in Mali first burn it and then throw the ashes into the River Niger as an offering to Faro, the god who regulates the universe. He is then believed to purify and regenerate these forces and to give them back in the shape of the rain which waters the Earth (DIEB). Jean-Paul Lebeuf has recorded similar beliefs among the Likuba and Likuala of the Congo (LEBM). The Fali of Northern Cameroon, and also the Bateke in the Congo, believe 'that the souls of the dead choose to live in rubbish heaps, from which they pass into the bodies of women going about their household tasks' (LEBF p. 326n).

This symbolism is the source of the esoteric signification of excrement and consequently of the significance of the ritual eating of excrement. Excrement is regarded as being charged with a substantial part of the life force of the creature, human or animal, from which it has dropped. According to Zahan (ZAHB p. 168) it effects 'a type of synthesis between the eater and what he eats'. Hence its life-giving powers and the frequent use of excrement in the traditional medical lore of so many peoples.

Ritually the eater of excrement is a person who takes the place of the godhead, able to bring to life again the residual powers of the creature or of the food contained in the excrement. Among the Bambara, the society of initiates which practises the eating of excrement is appropriately that of the 'Vultures', representing 'childhood', the first of the four stages of spiritual life which follow the stages of physical life. The initiate 'ingurgitates the deep and hidden forces of the universe. The riper these droppings are and the more maggotty, the more highly are they prized, for these are proofs of the life force within them. By eating them, "vultures" . . . become part of the universe through coprophagy' (ZAHB p. 169).

This 'dark side' classification of excrement which explains the initiatory powers endowed in VULTURES, HYENA and other carrion-eaters, is clearly in evidence among the Dogon and Bambara. One of his earliest informants told Griaule (GRIE): 'What is eaten is sunlight: excrement is darkness.' This echoes the alchemical significance of gold. In Dogon and Bambara thought, gold is in fact a sublimation of its 'younger brother', red copper (GRIE), while red copper itself is the excrement of Nommo, the controlling spirit of the universe.

The Bambara regard the excrement of Faro, the 'regulator' who plays the same role as the Dogon's Nommo, as the waste matter from the creation of the world and the First Cause from which all living creatures sprang (ZAHB p. 227). This should be compared with the fact that the Bambara associate the colour RED, the symbol of the life force, with corpses and with flies, the same word being used for both colour and insect.

The same thought process makes many American Indian myths credit carrion and rotting corpses with being the melting-pot or WOMB from which life is reborn. Thus the Cashinaua believe that the first human beings in the present world came out after the Flood in the shape of maggots which had bred in the bodies of the giants which had formed the earlier race of men (METS). In place of the maggot, the mushroom can be set as a symbol of regeneration, since it, too, appears to spring from decomposing matter. One may then compare with the foregoing the belief of the Orok, a Tugus tribe from Siberia, that after death the human soul flies towards the Moon in the shape of a butterfly and is reincarnated on Earth in the shape of a MUSHROOM (FOUD).

Among those excrements regarded as signs of plenty and employed ritually to obtain that plenty, mention should be made of those of the 'rainbow' SERPENT in Dahomey (now Benin) (MAUG).

Excrement is only very occasionally mentioned in Celtic literature, and then it would seem to have been the symbol of the most sovereign contempt. The only account of its use in the Irish Heroic Age occurs in a work known as *Aided Cùroi* (The Death of Cùroi). After a battle, the spoils were particularly unfairly divided and although Cùroi, King of Leinster, had given the Ulates very valuable help, he received nothing. To get his revenge, he defeated the young Cùchulainn in single combat, shaved his scalp, threw him to the ground and rubbed his head in cow-dung. Cùchulainn, in his turn, to avenge the insult seduced Cùroi's wife, Blahnat ('Little Flower') and made her his accomplice in his enemy's murder (OGAC 10: pp. 399–400).

It is open to question as to whether in this instance Cùroi proved his own ignorance in plastering his opponent's head with excrement. Believing that he was defiling him, unwittingly he gave him fresh strength to a degree that Cùchulainn, despite his defeat, seduced the victor's wife and involved her in Cùroi's murder. Although nowhere else in Celtic literature is there any mention except in this story, here is to be found the traditional interpretation which regards excrement as a concentration of those biological powers needed for regeneration. Cow-dung, especially, and at least in Kabylia, is the prime ingredient of all charms used magically to affect lactation (SERP).

eye It is only natural that the eye, the organ of visual perception, should almost universally be taken as a symbol of intellectual perception. It is essential to study in succession the bodily eye, in its function as a recipient of LIGHT; the 'third' eye – set in Shiva's forehead; and, lastly, the 'eye of the HEART', recipient of spiritual enlightenment.

Eskimos call shamans and seers 'the people with eyes'. In both the *Bhagavad Gītā* and the Upanishads, the two eyes are identified with those two luminaries, the Sun and the Moon. They are the two eyes of Vaishvanara. Similarly, in Taoism the Sun and Moon are the two eyes of P'an-ku or of Lao-kun and of Izanagi in Shintō. Traditionally the right eye (the Sun) corresponds to the active and the future while the left eye (the Moon) corresponds to the passive and the past. To resolve this duality requires the passage from a perception which distinguishes to a perception which unites and synthesizes. The Chinese ideogram *ming* (light) is the synthesis of the ideograms for the Sun and the Moon. The ritual of a secret society states 'My eyes are images of the ideogram *ming*.'

Unifying perception is the function of the 'third eye', the eye in Shiva's forehead. If the two bodily eyes correspond to the Sun and the Moon, the third eye corresponds to FIRE. Its glance reduces everything to ashes. In other words, simultaneity, its expression of a non-dimensional present, destroys manifestation. This is the 'Eye of Wisdom' (*prajnāchaksus*) or Buddhist 'Eye of Dharma' (*dharmachaksus*) which is set on the bounds of unity and multiplicity, of emptiness and non-emptiness, and is therefore able to apprehend them simultaneously. It is, in fact, an organ of inward vision and, as such, an exteriorization of the 'eye of the heart'. This unitive vision is expressed in Islam by the 'breaking of the barriers of the two eyes' of the letter *ha*, its two curlicues being symbols of duality and division. The third eye is indicative of a superhuman state, one in which clairvoyance has achieved its perfection as well, at a higher level, as a share in the properties of the Sun.

Dualistic vision is also a form of mental perception. 'The soul', Angelus Silesius wrote, 'has two eyes: one is fixed on time, the other on eternity.' According to the Victorines, one is love and the other the rational function. Once again there is the concept of the inner vision being required to unify these dualities. Both Plato and St Clement of Alexandria maintained that the 'eye of the soul' is not only unique but immobile. It is therefore only capable of global and synthesizing perception. Plotinus, St Augustine, St Paul, St John Climacus, Philotheus of Sinai, Elias the Ecdosite and St Gregory of Nazianzus all use the term 'eye of the heart' or 'eye of the spirit'; and again, it is one of the constants of Muslim spirituality (*Ayn-el-Qalb*) where it is employed by most of the Sufis and especially by al-Hallāj. Schuon has found a similar concept among the Sioux. The eye of the heart is man 'seeing' God, but it is also God 'seeing' man. It is the instrument of the unification of God with the soul and of the First Cause with the manifestation.

A single, unlidded eye is in any case a symbol of the Divine Essence and of Divine Knowledge, and when depicted in this sense within a TRIANGLE it is both a Christian and a Masonic symbol; it is to be found in the Armenian *trinacria*. In Vietnam the Cao-Dai religion adopted it in some sort, making it 'the stamp which sealed the heavenly investiture of the Elect'. The single eye of the CYCLOPS, on the other hand, is indicative of a subhuman condition, as is Argus' multiplicity of a hundred eyes, scattered all over his body and never all closing together. This signifies a personal absorption in the external world and watchfulness permanently directed towards the outside.

When the human eye is regarded as a symbol of knowledge and of supernatural perception, it is sometimes endowed with surprising qualities. The inhabitants of Tierra del Fuego believed that it leaves the body, without separating from it, and of its own accord steers towards the object which it has perceived. The Taoist Immortals had square pupils to their eyes. 'Opening the eyes' was a rite of revealing knowledge and of initiation. In India holy images had their eyes 'opened' with the aim of bringing them to life. The eyes of MASKS were opened. In Vietnam a newly-built junk has its 'lights opened' when two large eyes are painted on its bows.

The Eye of God which beholds all things is represented by the Sun. It is 'the eye of the world', a title which corresponds to Agni and which is also applied to the Buddha. The eye of the world is also the opening at the top of a DOME, the 'Sun Gate', which is God embracing the entire cosmos with one glance, as well as the obligatory way of release from the cosmos.

The correspondence between the eye and fire relates to the comtemplative role of Amitābha, his throne being supported by PEACOCKS, their tail-feathers sprinkled with eyes.

It will be observed, too, that the eye is sometimes used as a symbol of the sum of external perception and not simply of sight (BENA, CADV, COEA, COOH, CORT, DANA, ELIM, PHIL, GOVM, GRIF, GUEV, GUES, MAST, MUTT, SCHC, SUSZ).

In Ancient Egypt the *ujat* (painted eye) was a sacred symbol to be found on nearly every work of art. It was regarded as 'the fount of a magic fluid, purifying eye-light' (CHAM p. 120). The place of the FALCON in Ancient Egyptian art and religious literature is also well-known; 'the Ancient Egyptians had been struck by the strange mark to be found under the falcon's eye, an eye which sees everything. Around the Eye of Horus developed a whole symbolism of universal fertility' (POSD p. 85).

The Sun-god, Ra, was endowed with a burning eye, a symbol of his fiery nature, and was represented by the URAEUS, a cobra with staring eyes poised to strike.

Ancient Egyptian coffins are often decorated with a pair of eyes, which were believed to allow the dead person to 'look at the outside world through the painted eyes without moving himself' (POSD p. 251).

Throughout Ancient Egyptian tradition, the eye retained its solar, fiery nature, as a source of light, knowledge and fertility. It is a concept which the third-century AD Alexandrian Neoplatonist philosopher, Plotinus, takes up and stands on its head. He maintained that the eye of the human intellect could not gaze into the light of the Sun (the Supreme Spirit) without sharing the nature of the Sun-Spirit.

In Muslim tradition the word *'ayn*, meaning 'eye', may also be applied to a specific entity, a fountain or an essence. Mystics and theologians often use the term to indicate the universal nature of a particular thing. Mystics and philosophers, influenced by Neoplatonism, maintained that universals exist eternally in the Spirit of God, these eternal ideas corresponding to Plato's Ideas or Archetypes and being like eyes.

Mystics regard the physical world as a dream, the real world and true reality reside in the One God. God is the only true and ultimate fountain from which all things flow. The word *'ayn* (eye) is therefore used in its double meaning of 'real' and 'fountain' to convey the sense of the supra-existent and deepest Essence of God. Avicenna gives the word this meaning when he writes of those who made their way deep into the very *'ayn*, the contemplation of the depths of the divine nature.

Lastly attention should be drawn to the term *'ayn ul-yaquīn*, one of the levels of knowledge and perhaps used in the sense of 'intuition' in both accepted meanings of the word: in its pre-rational sense of intuitive comprehension of the first principles of philosophy and in its post-rational sense of the intuitive comprehension of mystical truth beyond the powers of reasoning (ENCI). Arabic and Persian elegiac poetry employs a multiplicity of metaphors to associate the eye with notions of magic, of danger and of intoxication. The 'eye of beauty' is said to be 'drunk', or 'half-drunk, but not with wine'; it 'hunts' or 'traps lions'; it is 'thirsty for blood' or 'murderous', but it is also 'a chalice, a narcissus, a gazelle, a sea-shell' (HUAS pp. 28–31).

The term 'evil eye' is widespread in the Muslim world and symbolizes taking power over someone or something through envy or with evil intent. The evil eye is said to cause half the deaths among mankind and to empty houses and fill graves. Old women and young brides have especially dangerous eyes, while small children, women in child-bed, young wives, horses, dogs, milk and corn are especially susceptible to their effects.

The possessor of the evil eye is called *ma'iān* in Arabic. 'When the *ma'iān* looks longingly at some [person or thing which pleases him],' writes Qast'allāmi, 'it causes injury to what he looks at. The problem is to know whether or not his eye discharges some invisible substance at the object of his gaze, like the poison which squirts from the viper's eye. The question remains unsettled and is only a matter of probability.'

The eyes of such creatures as vipers and geckos are to be feared. The evil eye can destroy livestock. 'I take refuge in the shadow of God against the harm which the envious can cause when possessed by envy.' The Prophet said: 'The *'ayn* is a reality.'

There are means of defence against the evil eye such as veils, geometrical designs, objects which glitter, burning sweet scents, red-hot iron, salt, alum, horns, the crescent shape, and the Hand of Fatima. Horse-shoes are also preservatives against the evil eye, apparently because of their shape, material and use concentrating the magical powers of such various symbols as HORN, CRESCENT, HAND as well of those of the HORSE, a domestic and once-sacred animal.

North European tradition tells of the one-eyed King of Connaught, Eochaid, who gave that eye to the evil druid, Aithirne of Ulster. When he went to a spring to purify himself, God restored both his eyes as a reward for his generosity. The god Midir lost an eye in a brawl and his blindness disqualified him from further rule. Those responsible, Oenghus and his father the Dagda (APOLLO and JUPITER) therefore summoned Dian Cécht (an aspect of Apollo the Healer) who restored to the sufferer the sight of his eye. By law Dian Cécht had the right to a reward and he claimed a chariot, a cloak, and the most beautiful maiden in Ireland, Etain (the embodiment of kingship). Oenghus' mother, Boann, as a punishment for her adultery with the Dagda, lost an eye, an arm and a leg in the waters of the well of Segais to which she had gone to purify herself. In this context the eye may be regarded as a symbol of the rule of conscience. The sin, be it anger, violence or adultery, blinds its perpetrator and blindness debars from rule, while generosity or an admission of guilt make their authors clear-sighted.

In a different context, the eye is the symbolic equivalent of the Sun and the Irish *sul*, 'eye', corresponds to the Brythonic word for 'Sun'. In Welsh the Sun is metaphorically termed 'the eye of day' (*ilygad y dydd*). Many Gaulish coins carry the head of a hero with an exaggeratedly large eye. A single Gallo-Roman inscription gives Apollo the surname *Amarcolitanus*, 'Apollo of the long eye', and the description 'of the long eye' (*imlebur inachind*) is often to be found in Irish literary sources. On the other hand, the solitary eye of the subhuman species of FOMORIANS was malign. Balor's eye could paralyse an entire army and needed a prop to lift its lid, as did the eye of the Welsh Ysbaddaden Penkawr. Queen Medb turned the sons of Caltin into wizards by counter-initiatory mutilation. She put out their left eyes (see ONE-EYED), and all the wizards to be met with in Celtic legend are blind in the left eye. Total BLINDNESS is a sign or symbol of clairvoyance, and druids and seers are sometimes blind (OGAC 4: pp. 209–16, 222; 12: p. 200; 13: pp. 331–42; CELT 7: *passim*).

Sight, for the Bambara, is the sense which epitomizes and replaces all the others. Of all the sense organs, sight is the only one which allows perception to partake of the nature of wholeness (ZAHB). The image which the eye perceives is real and the eye captures and preserves an actual duplicate of it. During sexual intercourse 'the wife is joined to her husband through her eyes as well as through her sexual organs' (DIEB). The Bambara say that 'sight is desire; the eye is the wish' and, lastly, that 'a man's world' is 'his eye'. Also, metaphorically, the eye is able to correspond to notions of beauty, of the world, of the universe or of life (ibid.).

The importance given to the sense of sight in central Africa is emphasized by the frequent use made of animal or of human eyes by witch-doctors in the magical potions which they prepare for ordeals. In the Kasai region, Baluba and Lulua witch-doctors use the eyes and muzzle of the victim's dog to track down the wizard responsible for a suspicious death (FOUC). In Gabon the Panther-men make a point of tearing out their victims' eyes.

In Masonic tradition, the eye symbolizes 'on the material plane, the visible Sun, source of Life and Light; on the intermediate or astral plane, the Word, Logos or Creative First Cause; on the spiritual or divine plane, the Great Architect of the Universe' (BOUM p. 91).

F

face Incomplete and fleeting though it may be, the face is an unveiling, like the unveiling of the Mystica in Pompeian wall-paintings. Nobody has ever had a direct sight of his or her own face, it can only be seen with the help of a MIRROR. Faces are not for their owners, but for others and for God. Faces are silent words. The face is the most vital part of the body and the most sensitive since in it are located the organs of sense. Whether we like it or not, it is the part of oneself which one reveals to the world at large. It is the ego laid bare in part and far more revealing than the rest of the body. Furthermore, Max Picard remarks,

the individual dare not look into the face of another without a tremor, since above all, the face is there to be gazed at by God. To gaze upon a human face is as though one were attempting to govern the Almighty.... Only in a climate of love can a human face retain the properties with which God created it in his own image. Unless encircled by love, the human face becomes set and whoever gazes upon it sees only the lifeless flesh and bone of which the face is made instead of the true face and whatever conclusions the observer draws from the face are falsified.

(PICV)

To understand a face requires deliberation, patience, respect and, with them, love. To study a face without loving it is to debase it, to destroy it, to murder it and to subject it to vivisection. The face is the symbol of the divinity in each human being, a divinity erased or manifest, lost or rediscovered.

Symbol of the mysterious, the face is like an invisible door to which the key has been lost. The Holy Shroud of Turin was the object of an extraordinary adoration because it was believed to reflect the face of Christ. Father Le Guillou calls Christianity 'the religion of faces'. Olivier Clément writes: 'God is made manifest in a Face of which the light grows brighter as from generation to generation the faces of ordinary people are transfigured.' A whole theology and way of mystic life might be developed from the face.

The face symbolizes human evolution out of darkness and into light. It is their degree of brightness which will mark the difference between the Devil's and the angel's face. The Devil's forehead is seamed with horizontal lines and shaded by its sprouting horns. When the face expresses no inner life, it is no more than 'an artificial limb . . . a rubber mask.'

The Hebrew always uses the plural (*pānīm*) for the human face on which thoughts and feelings are written. Turned to the light, it may glow with its brightness. God's face is identical with his essence, and this is why it is impossible to gaze upon it. Hence God's words in the Old Testament, 'Thou canst not see my face: for there shall no man see my face and live' (Exodus 33: 20); while St John wrote, 'No man hath seen God at any time' (1 John 4: 12). When Moses cried 'I beseech thee show me thy glory' (Exodus 33: 18), his appeal expressed his longing to contemplate the divine essence. Nevertheless, St Augustine suggests that ecstasy – in so far as it is an image of death – allows of some apprehension of God, as was the case of Moses upon Mount Sinai and of St Paul taken up into the third heaven. Such a vision anticipates the state of bliss. Seeing God face to face is reserved for eternal life. Mystics often pray God to reveal his face to them. The face is the symbol of God's very being, or of the human personality whose manifestation it is. This was the reason why it was regarded as sacrilege to stare upon the face of the Emperor, especially when, as in China, his nature was divine.

Since the face stood for the individual as a whole, to Celts 'face-price' measured the compensation paid by one individual to another and the phrase 'so many faces' was used like the term 'so many souls'. It was upon the face that the tenth-century Welsh laws of Hywel Dda and the Irish legal treatise, the *Senchus Mor*, set the price of settlement or indemnity to be paid to the family of a murder-victim or to an injured party. The 'face-price' was also the dowry paid by the husband to the wife before the marriage could be consummated, like the Germanic *Morgengabe*. Welsh laws sometimes mention the gift in damages of a gold plaque or plate the size of a face and the thickness of a finger (see MASK). 'Loss of face' is well known in Chinese and Muslim tradition. This is another aspect of the same symbolism.

faggot In Ancient China faggots (*sin*) were the symbol of fleeting human nature, successively bound together by life and unloosed by death. FIRE is the spirit (*chen*) which spreads from one faggot to the next without ever going out. Chuang Tzu repeats this teaching, which he regarded as very ancient, and his commentator adds 'the state of life is the bundle of faggots tied together: the state of death when they are loosed.' And later: 'Fire is to the faggot what the spirit is to the body.' If in folktale and legend WITCHES are often depicted carrying a bundle of faggots, it is undoubtedly because of this symbolic comparison of the flame of the faggot and the spirit. Occult knowledge and power are deceptively hidden beneath poverty and rags just as the faggot of dead wood conceals the riches of the spirit and the energy of fire. The lives of the Sufi saints linger lovingly on the picture of the mystic who attained a state of sanctity by gathering faggots for his community's kitchens over a period of FORTY years.

fairy As the mistresses of magic, fairies symbolize the paranormal powers of the spirit or the extraordinary capacities of the imagination. They can effect the most amazing transformations and in a flash satisfy or disappoint the most extravagant whims. Perhaps they represent the human power to create in the imagination what can never be realized in the actual world.

Irish fairies are predominantly *banshee*, to whom fairies in other Celtic lands are more or less closely related. Originally, fairies, confused with women, were messengers from the Otherworld. They travelled in the guise of BIRDS, for preference as SWANS. However, after the arrival of Christianity this function was no longer understood and those who copied out the pagan legends turned them into lovelorn women coming in search of their heart's desire. By definition the *banshee* is a being endowed with magic, free from three-dimensional contingency, and the APPLE or BRANCH which she offers has miraculous properties. The most powerful druid could not detain the person whom she summoned, and when she left him temporarily, her chosen lover would fall into a decline (OGAC 18: pp. 136–43).

Shakespeare (*Romeo and Juliet* I. iv. 53ff.) describes Queen Mab in a way which marvellously illustrates the fairies' ambivalence and their capacity for malice which can turn them into witches. In fact, the palaces which fairies conjure up to sparkle in the darkness vanish as suddenly and leave no more than a memory of the deception. In psychological development fairies may be classed among the processes of adaptation to the real world and acceptance of the true self with all its limitations. The fairies are a resource for overweening ambition or a compensation for frustrated endeavours. Their WANDS and their RINGS are the emblems of their powers: they tie or unloose the bonds of psychosis.

It is beyond dispute that the fairies of European folklore were none other originally than the Roman Parcae, themselves Latin versions of the Greek Moirae, the Fata, or Fates. (*Fairy* derives from the French *fée*, itself deriving from the Latin *fata*.) Like the Fates, fairies are generally to be found in groups of THREE, drawing the THREAD from the DISTAFF, spinning it on the WHEEL and when the time is ripe cutting it with their SCISSORS. Perhaps they were originally the tutelary goddesses of the fields. The triple rhythm so characteristic of their activities is that of life itself – childhood, maturity and old age; or birth, life and death – which astrology translates as evolution, culmination and involution. According to age-old Breton tradition, when a child is born, a table is laid with three places and a lavish meal provided in an isolated room, to win the fairies' favour. The fairies, too, carry the souls of still-born babies up to Heaven and help them counter Satan's evil spells.

To understand fairy symbolism, one has to dig deeper than Parcae or Moirae, and go back to the Keres, Underworld deities in Greek mythology, rather like the VALKYRIES, who carry off the dying from the battle-field but who, according to the *Iliad*, seem also to have determined the hero's fate or destiny by offering him a choice upon which would depend, for good or ill, the outcome of his journey.

This fairy family-tree shows them to have been emanations of the Earth Mother. However, the current of history, operating, as is so frequently instanced in these pages, in the 'ascensional' mode, gradually raised them from the bowels of the Earth to its surface where, by moonlight, they became water- and vegetation-spirits. However, the places in which they reveal themselves clearly show from where they came. In fact, they appear most frequently on MOUNTAINS, beside chasms and torrents, on countless fairy rings or in the depths of woods and FORESTS, beside cliffs and caves, or else beside babbling brooks or WELLS and SPRINGS. They are associated with a triple rhythm which upon close examination turns out in fact to be fourfold. Musically this might be termed three-four time, three beats and a rest, which in fact represents the phases of the Moon and the rhythm of the seasons. The Moon is visible for three of these phases, but disappears during its fourth when it is said to be 'dead'. Similarly life, in its vegetable form, waxes when it comes out of the ground in Spring, is at its full in Summer, wanes during Autumn and vanishes during Winter, a time of silence and of death. If fairy lore is closely examined, it will be seen that its anonymous authors have not disregarded this 'fourth time'. This is the period of breakdown when the effects of the fairy's transformation into human shape wear off. The fairy shares in the supernatural because her life is continuous, not discontinuous like ours and like that of every other earthly living thing. It is quite natural, then, that fairies should remain invisible during the dead season when they do not appear. And yet their lives go on, but in a different shape, like them related, in its essence, to continuous eternal life. This is the reason why MELUSINE would leave her husband every Saturday, telling him not to look for her and to keep her secret. In this fourth phase, she had, in fact, to abandon her human shape to adopt that of a SERPENT which, as one knows, is the animal manifestation of eternal life. Melusine alternated between woman and serpent, just as the serpent sloughs its skin to renew itself indefinitely. This is the time, in human terms, corresponding to silence and death. Again, fairies only ever reveal themselves intermittently, appearing only to vanish, although they themselves exist permanently. As much might be said of the manifestations of the unconscious.

falcon In Ancient Egypt, where its strength and beauty made it prince of birds, the falcon symbolized the principle of LIGHT. It was the embodiment, among other deities, of Horus, god of etherial space, whose two EYES were the Sun and the Moon and who took the shape of a falcon or of a falcon-headed man. 'The Egyptians had been struck by the strange mark to be seen under the falcon's eye, an eye which sees everything. Around the Eye of Horus developed a whole symbolism of universal fertility' (POSD p. 85). The falcon was also the attribute of the god Ra, symbol of the rising Sun, who is sometimes depicted with head surmounted, not by that of a falcon, but by the solar disc encircled by a cobra, which symbolizes FIRE.

The Peruvian Incas used the falcon as a solar emblem and symbol. Means quotes the chronicler Sarmiento's statement that all the Incas, from Manco Capac, founder of the dynasty, onwards, had a double or spiritual 'brother', like a guardian angel. It was represented in the shape of a falcon which they called Inti, the Sun (MEAA).

In a myth of the Yunca Indians of Peru, the creation-heroes were born in the shape of falcons from five eggs laid on a mountain, before they assumed human shape. In another version, the heroes' mother bore them as a result of sexual intercourse with the falcon-ostrich-god (LEHC).

In the Irish tale of the adventures of Tuan mac Cairill, the falcon was one of the successive shapes through which this primordial character passed. It therefore corresponds to the EAGLE in the Welsh mythological tale of the Ancient Worlds. However, the importance attached to falcons in the tenth-century Welsh Laws of Hywel Dda would be due rather to the development of the sport of falconry (CHAB pp. 443–57).

In the Middle Ages, falcons are sometimes depicted tearing hares in pieces. If hares symbolize lasciviousness, as many interpret it, falcons in this case would signify the conquest of lust (CIRD p. 134). Generally speaking, however, this is the victory of the solar, bright male principle over the lunar, dark female principle.

Indeed, the falcon, in the symbolic category of the solar, celestial, male and bright, is an ascensional symbol on every level, material, intellectual and moral. It signifies superiority and conquest, either acquired or in process of attainment. 'When', wrote Horapollon, 'the Egyptians wished to depict a god, height, abasement, superiority, nobility or victory, they drew a falcon' (TERS p. 162).

Falcons are sometimes depicted hooded. They then symbolize that hope in the light which is nourished by those who live in darkness. They are images of prisoners, of spiritual ardour stifled, of light hidden under a bushel and of esoteric knowledge. This is doubtless why many Renaissance printers adopted the emblem of the hooded falcon with the device *Post tenebras spero lucem* (After darkness I hope for light) (TERS p. 163). The same symbolism inspired the Boswell family crest of the hooded falcon and the device *Vraye foy* (True faith).

fan In Hindu iconography the fan is an attribute of Vishnu. Because it stirs the flame, it is a symbol of ritual sacrifice, and for this reason is also an attribute of Agni. The standard of Vāyu, god of the wind, might itself be identified with the fan.

It is also the emblem of kingship in Africa and in Asia and similarly, in the Far East, of the powers of the emperor or the mandarin. Fans have been compared with the *flabella* (fly-flaps or small fans) of the Ancient Romans and *flabella* continued in use in the early Church during the celebration of the Mass. Fans of ostrich feathers decorate the Papal throne, the *sedia gestatoria*, during solemn ceremonies in St Peter's in Rome.

In the famous novel *Si Yu-ki*, fans are mentioned which not only kindle fire, but also put it out and, in addition, raise wind and rain. Taoists seem to have related fans to birds, as instruments of bodily liberation and as symbols of flight to the land of the Immortals. Thus, when Kiai-zu T'ui returned to Earth as a fan-seller, he may perhaps be understood as providing either a recipe for immortality or the symbol of what he had himself attained, while the fan belonging to the Immortal, Chung-li K'iuan, generally regarded as the badge of a mandarin, may be viewed in the same light.

Nor can there be any doubt that fans were used as a screen against evil influences, and this is why in Japan they are sometimes decorated with a three-coloured *mitsu tomoye*, the triple version of the YIN–YANG which in China has the same protective qualities (DANA, KALL, MALA).

The Chinese would have beeen ill-advised to fan themselves with their hands. Since such gestures were likely to attract evil spirits, they used fans.

fat Scraps of animal fat were used in many of their ceremonies as symbols of plenty by North American Indians (ALEC, FLEH).

In Black Africa the oil of the karite nut in the Sudan and of the palm in equatorial Africa play a similar part in sacrifice as well as in all rites connected with birth and pregnancy. Thus, in Bantu areas, the young married couple will rub their bodies with palm-oil as an aid to conception. In this instance the symbolism of the colour RED reinforces that of all fat or oily substances and their association with wealth.

On the third day after the birth of a child both the Yakut and the Buryat throw butter on to a fire lighted for that purpose in the yurt in which the birth has taken place (HARA p. 126). When the Torgut bride-to-be enters her future husband's dwelling, she bows three times to the hearth and offers him fat or butter. 'Among the Telyuts it is her companions who pour onto his hearth enough butter for the flames to leap up to the smoke-hole and the same ritual is observed at each new Moon. With the Tatars of the Altai Mountains, the husband-to-be's relatives put horse-fat on the fire while the bride-to-be's hair is unloosed' (HARA p. 166).

Animal fat, as a symbol of wealth and plenty, is something essentially precious to hunting tribes because they believe that it embodies the special powers of the animal concerned. Thus some New Guinea tribes explain the supernatural power of their witch-doctors to fly through the air to wherever they wish, by their first eating 'the fat of a bird which flies strongly. Witch-doctors do so with the intention that the fat which they eat will transfer to their bodies the powers of flight possessed by the bird' (Wirz, *Die Marind-anim von hollandisch Sud-Neu-Guinea*, quoted by LEVM p. 232).

In Vedic and subsequently in all central Asian rituals connected with human life it was BUTTER which underpinned the whole of the same complex symbolism (VEDR pp. 126–8).

father As a symbol of procreation, ownership, domination and courage, the father is an inhibiting and, in psychoanalytic terms, a castrating figure. He stands for all figures of authority in education, employment, the armed forces, the law, and for God himself. The role of the father is regarded as one which discourages attempts at independence and exercises an influence which impoverishes, constrains, undermines, renders impotent and makes submissive. The father stands for awareness, as opposed to instinctive impulse, spontaneous enthusiasms and the unconscious; he is the old authoritative order opposed to the fresh forces of change.

Paul Ricoeur, in his book *De l'interprétation* (Paris, 1966), attributes the symbolic wealth of the father-figure, specifically 'to its potentiality for transcendence. Symbolically the father ranks less as a progenitor equal to the mother than as a law-giver' (p. 520). He is the fountain of social order. Like God and Heaven, he is an image of regular, wise and righteous transcendence. In accordance with the inversion which is the rule in symbolism, the original progenitor changes into the God who is to come. The father is at one and the same time both past and future. His function as progenitor becomes one of regenerator, birth a rebirth in every analogous accepted sense of the term. His influence may then be related to that exercised by the hero or by the ideal. Not only does the individual wish to have or to possess a father of his own, but fatherhood is a role to which he aspires or whose properties he wishes to acquire. Such a development embodies the suppression of the 'other' father and the acquisition of 'self' fatherhood (see OEDIPUS, PERSEUS). Such identification with the father involves a two-way movement of (his) death and (my) rebirth. The father therefore always remains the image of transcendence who cannot be accepted uncritically and only by mutual affection in adulthood.

In Celtic tradition the notion of 'the father of mankind' finds expression in the surname of its god, the Dagda Eochaid Ollathair, 'Almighty Father'. He may thus be compared with the Dis Pater mentioned by Caesar, from whom the Gauls all claimed descent. The Father of Mankind stands above and beyond primeval man. He is the first god, the Absolute Being, father of the living and lord of the dead, exercising both the bright and dark aspects of godhead. He does not himself procreate, but is responsible for procreation. His essence represents something unique, while his manifestation is twofold (OGAC 12: p. 359).

feather In Shamanism, the symbolic function of feathers is linked with the ritual of ascent into Heaven and hence with second sight and divination.

On the other hand, in many civilizations feathers are associated with lunar symbolism and represent the growth of plant life. This is true of Central America, where to Aztec and Maya they had a similar symbolic function to HAIR, GRASS and RAIN. Similarly during the Great Feather Dance, the Iroquois offered ceaseless thanks to their twin culture-heroes for everything which sprang up to bless mankind, fruit and waters, animals and trees, sun and vine-shoots, darkness and moonlight, stars and the givers-of-life (beans, maize and pumpkins, which they called 'the Three Sister Goddesses') (KRIE p. 128; MULR p. 268).

The twofold symbolism of feathers as ascensional forces and as plant growth recurs in the use by the Zuni (Pueblo) Indians during their solsticial festivals of 'prayer-sticks' with bunches of feathers attached to their upper ends. These staves (STAFF) are set up in maize-fields, or in flower-vases, and in all holy places on mountain peaks and beside springs as offerings to the ancestors, the Sun and the Moon. 'The fluttering of the bunches of feathers on the end of the sticks,' Muller explains (MULR p. 281), 'wafts their prayers to the gods': in other words, to Heaven. In his autobiography (TALS p. 44), the Hopi (Pueblo) Indian chief Don C. Talayesva describes the first time he saw as a child the votive offering of feathers at the important festival of the Winter solstice, as follows:

A few days later, at sunrise, my mother took me to the eastern edge of the mesa [plateau] with everybody else in the village to place prayer feathers on the shrines. These sacrifices bore messages to the gods in order to bring good luck. The people placed feathers in the ceilings of their houses and in all the kivas [temples]. They tied them to the ladders to prevent accidents, to the tails of burrows [donkeys] to give them strength, to goats, sheep, dogs, and cats to make them be fertile, and to the chicken houses to get more eggs.... This was also the safest day for mothers to cut their children's hair without harm from evil spirits or Two Hearts.

This example clearly shows the association of feathers/hair/fertility linked to the symbolism of ascension, since the prayers and feathers go up to Heaven, from which the fructifying rain will fall.

Elucidating the myths of Australasia and New Guinea, Lévy-Bruhl explains (LEVM p. 238) that:

feathers are an appurtenance of BIRDS, their skin and body. Thus they are the bird's self. To dress in feathers, to suck or eat them, is therefore to become one with the bird and, if in possession of the requisite magical powers, a sure means of transforming oneself into a bird.... For the same reason feathers have a specific magical power. They are used as flights for ARROWS. They are often employed as personal adornment. The first people to stick feathers in their hair doubtless flattered themselves with the belief that they were transmitting some of this power to themselves.

In fact feathers are symbols of the power of AIR, of freedom from the force of gravity. A crown of feathers worn by kings and princes is a reminder of the Sun's rays and of the HALO kept for the elect. Coronation ceremonies are related to rites of identification with the Sun-god or with those of delegation of heavenly power. The plumes which surmount the AWNINGS over sovereigns and Popes, rising from the pillars supporting the FOUR corners, signify that supreme authority, derived from Heaven, stretches to the four corners of their kingdoms or of the world itself. That authority brings with it a duty to administer justice. If, as was the case with the Ancient Egyptians, the feather is a symbol of justice, it is perhaps because, when set on the SCALES, its minuscule weight is enough to upset their just balance (see OSTRICH).

Some critics regard feathers as a symbol of sacrifice. Worldwide, when chickens or HENS were offered in sacrifice to the gods, only the feathers were left around the altar. They bore witness to the proper performance of the rite (see REED; SERPENT).

Female Pope, the See under POPE.

Feminine, the Eternal The closing words of Goethe's *Faust* Part II are 'the Eternal Feminine', what attracts man to transcendency. The feminine represents sublimated desire. Margarete hears the voice saying: 'Come, take flight to the higher spheres. If he guesses your fate he will follow you.' And the mystic chorus proclaims: 'The Eternal Feminine draws us to the heights.'

Dante's Beatrice is an example of this type of guide. Prophetically Nicolas Berdiaeff wrote of a society to come in which:

woman will play a major role . . . Being more closely linked than man to the world-soul and to primal elemental forces, it is through her that he will enter into communion with them. . . . As the women in the Gospels, so women are predestined to be bearers of precious ointment. . . . It is not liberated woman, nor woman adopting male characteristics, but the Eternal Feminine which will have a major part to play in the future period of history.

(BNMA pp. 162–3)

In the phrase 'the Eternal Feminine' Pierre Teilhard de Chardin saw the name of love itself as the major cosmic force. It is the meeting of a human aspiration towards trancendency with a natural instinct from which appear (1) the most commonly experienced mark of the domination of individuals by an extraordinarily broad vital current; (2) to a certain extent the source of all affective potentiality; (3) and lastly an energy especially favourable to self-development, to the enrichment of the self in so many increasingly spiritualized ways and to the contemplation of such manifold objects, and notably of God himself.

Our Lady, the Virgin Mary, is its most perfect embodiment. 'The genuine and pure Feminine is, above all, a chaste and bright Energy, which brings with it courage, idealism and happiness = the Blessed Virgin Mary . . . the

Pearl of the Cosmos . . . the true DEMETER.' The feminine symbolizes 'the aspect of being which draws together and unifies' (LUEF pp. 12, 41).

For Jung the feminine personified the aspect of the unconscious which he termed the *anima.*

The anima is the personification of all feminine psychological tendencies in a man's psyche, such as vague feelings and moods, prophetic hunches, receptiveness to the irrational, capacity for personal love, feeling for nature, and – last but not least – his relation to the unconscious. It is no mere chance that in olden times priestesses (like the Greek SIBYL) were used to fathom the divine will and make connection with the gods.

The anima may also symbolize

an unreal dream of love, happiness, and maternal warmth (her nest) – a dream that lures men away from reality. . . . Another way in which the negative anima in a man's personality can be revealed is in waspish, poisonous, effeminate remarks by which he devalues everything. Remarks of this sort always contain a cheap twisting of the truth and are in a subtle way destructive. There are legends throughout the world in which a [beautiful woman] . . . appears. She . . . has weapons hidden in her body or a secret poison with which she kills her lovers during their first night together. In this guise the anima is as cold and reckless as certain uncanny aspects of nature itself.

(JUNS pp. 177, 178–9)

In Islamic poetry the eternal feminine through its physical attractions symbolizes Divine Beauty.

fennel Fennel is the symbol of spiritual rejuvenation. Devotees of the cult of the ancient Phrygian Dionysos, Sabazius, carried fennel leaves. According to Pliny, fennel had the virtue of clearing the sight and, furthermore, it was by eating fennel that serpents acquired the miraculous power of periodic rejuvenation.

fermentation The word *kumu* (to ferment) in the Bambara language 'designates all processes whereby a substance, or even a thing, is transformed into a bitter-tasting and effervescent state, which enables it to obtain an ascendancy over anyone who partakes of it' (ZAHB p. 167). Hence fermented drinks are images of an effervescence of knowledge which enables the spirit to surmount its normal limitations and to attain through intuition or in dreams a knowledge of the deepest secrets of nature and of the universe. This explains the ritual drinking of fermented liquors such as BEER made from millet, manioc, bananas or maize in Africa and in the Americas and, generally speaking, in all agricultural societies.

In this context it is interesting to emphasize that the great agrarian god of the Aztecs, Tlaloc, lord of the fertilizing RAIN, of THUNDER and LIGHTNING, 'the fiery rain', is sometimes represented by an overflowing jar of *pulque* (beer made from agave sap). The god's name even means 'Pulque from the Earth' (BEYM).

On the other hand, equal emphasis should be given to the fact that the symbolism of fermentation is related to that of decomposition and decay (see EXCREMENT). A myth of the Amazonian Tukuna Indians is in this respect significant, because it associates the qualities of beer (fermentation) with those of WORMS in giving the recipe of an elixir of immortality. We shall only quote the portion relevant to this context. Because she fed on tree-fungus (symbol of life reborn from decay), his betrothed rejected the tortoise (male) who, after numerous adventures, smashed the jars of manioc-beer provided for a feast. 'The beer, which was full of worms, spilled onto the ground and was licked up by ants and other creatures that shed their skin: and that explains why they never grow old' (LEVC p. 158).

In alchemy, fermentation is associated with the notion of transmutation. It is transformation, organic 'ripening', the prelude to regeneration, the passage from a state of death to one of life. Alchemists believed that metals and jewels fermented in the soil.

The idea of fermentation invokes that of seasonal renewal and places where fermentation occurs naturally are magic places haunted by the spirits of the dead (see CROSSROADS). This explains the custom during the festivities of Christmas and the Epiphany, in the Russian region of Kurak, of burning dung in farmyards to warm the dead in the Otherworld.

Fermentation, regarded as an essential manifestation of life triumphant, along with the symbolic qualities conferred upon it, was equally present throughout Jewish history and tradition. This is exemplified by the association of repentance with unleavened, or unfermented, bread, which is to BREAD made with yeast what ASHES are to FIRE, implying an element of mourning or penance, in short, a castrational element.

The host in the Eucharist, made from unleavened dough, symbolizes food which does not 'ferment' the passions, but which is of a wholly spiritual order.

fetish Symbol of divine energy encapsulated, ready and usable. 'Natural fetishes owe their magic properties to the forces which dwell in them and which come to them from the natural world in the shape of shells, pebbles, pieces of wood, excrement ... etc. Carvings permeated with this power become the fetishes which somebody who is endowed with supernatural powers – the *nganga,* or witch-doctor – can activate.' STATUETTES are thus to be seen as the mere adjuncts, or, if you like, conductors, of magic power (LAUA p. 279).

field See PLAIN.

fiery curtain Symbolizes the passage from a former existence, the old man, to a new state of existence, the new man. As metal requires a fusion, in other words passage through FIRE and WATER, to effect its transmutation, so human beings must pass through fire and water if they are to be transformed and become imperishable. The fiery curtain is the dividing line between the perishable and the imperishable. By passing through it, the human being effects a mutation and the imperfect becomes the perfect.

fig-tree Together with the OLIVE-TREE and the VINE, the fig is one of the trees which are symbols of plenty. However, it, too, has its negative aspect. When withered it becomes a TREE of evil and, in Christian symbolism, stands for the Synagogue, which became barren through its failure to acknowledge the Messiah of the New Covenant. It may also stand for any Church of which the branches have withered away through heresy.

The fig-tree symbolizes religious knowledge. In Ancient Egypt it was given a significance in rites of initiation and the early Christian hermits ate figs by choice.

This symbol recurs in both Old and New Testaments. When Adam and Eve saw that they were naked (Genesis 3: 7) 'they sewed fig leaves together and made themselves APRONS.' While, when Jesus curses the fig-tree (Matthew 21: 19–22; Mark 11: 12ff.), one ought, perhaps, to comment that he is cursing the knowledge which it contains or fails to contain. Jesus was also to say to Nathaniel (John 1: 48): 'When thou wast under the fig tree, I saw thee.' Nathaniel was an intellectual.

In Islamic esotericism fig and olive are associated to signify the duality of different natures.

In Eastern Asia, the fig-tree plays an extremely important part. Here it is a specific variety of fig cast in this role, the imposing *ficus benghalensis*, or banyan tree. This is the everlasting fig-tree of the Upanishads and the *Bhagavad Gītā*, the 'World Tree' which links Earth to Heaven. In Buddhism it plays a similar role. The peepul at the foot of which the Buddha received Enlightenment, the Bodhi Tree, is identical with the World AXIS. Furthermore, in primitive iconography it symbolizes the Buddha himself and the Buddha, in various guises, becomes one with the Axis.

Throughout southeast Asia banyans are homes for countless spirits. They are a symbol of power and of life, of procreation to the Sre and of longevity to the Rongao and Sedang (CORT, DAMS, GUEV). They also symbolize immortality and higher knowledge and were the trees under which the Buddha preferred to sit when he taught his disciples.

Like the WILLOW-TREE, the fig symbolizes immortality rather than longevity to the Chinese, since they believe that immortality cannot be conceived except in spiritual and intellectual terms.

In Indo-Mediterranean tradition, the fig was a sacred tree often associated with fertility rites. In Dravidian thought (BOUA p. 18) 'it owed its powers of fecundation to its milky SAP, because the milky sap was of the same essence as *rasa*', that particle of universal energy contained within the element of Water. *Rasa* may be likened to 'the waters below the firmament' of Genesis 1: 7. Milky sap is also the fluid of life, *ojas*, which calls the child in the womb into being. Countless rites of sympathetic magic bear witness to the symbolic importance of trees with milky sap, and hence arises the Dravidian custom recorded by Boulnois of hanging a calf's placenta, wrapped in straw, from the boughs of a banyan-tree in order that the cow should give milk and calve again in future. Throughout India the banyan is held sacred to Vishnu and Shiva. Its worship is associated with that of SERPENTS, the association of tree and serpent being pre-eminent in calling into existence the powers of fruitfulness.

'In modern India the fig-leaf plays the same part as the vine-leaf in Greek and Roman art as a cache-sexe. This is, perhaps, not entirely devoid of all symbolic meaning' (BOUA p. 72). The Ancient Romans believed that Romulus and Remus were born under a fig-tree and Pausanias states that worship was long paid to the deified twins in the Comitium under a fig which grew from the stump of the original tree. In India similar beliefs were held regarding Vishnu, while in Greece the fig was sacred to Dionysos.

The high holiness with which the fig and other trees with milky sap were held by both Dravidians in India and the ancient inhabitants of Crete, recurs in Black Africa. Boulnois has recorded the belief of the Kotoko in Chad that 'to dig up a *yagale* fig-tree will cause sterility', while Kotoko women 'slit the bark of this fig-tree and take the sap to increase their own lactation.' The fig is also held sacred among many central African Bantu tribes (BOUA p. 113).

In north Africa the fruit is 'the symbol of fertility imparted by the dead'. The word itself 'became synonymous with the testicles, although currently the name of the season of fig harvest, *krif* (Autumn), is used conversationally.' At this level of comparison, this is barely to go beyond allegory and analogy. Jean Servier achieves the level of symbolism when he adds: 'Stuffed with countless SEEDS, the fruit is a fertility symbol and, as such, an offering to be deposited upon rocks, beside hot springs and the shrines of guardian spirits and the Invisibles. It is an offering which travellers in need may share, because it is the gift of the Invisible' (SERP pp. 38, 143).

finger The Dogon regard the index finger as the finger of life and the middle, or long finger, as the finger of death. The long finger is the only visible portion of the dead person's body, all the rest being carefully bundled into a ritual shroud. The Dogon say that it is 'by help of this finger that the dead speak with the living' (GRIS). However, the index finger (with the numerological value of SEVEN) is also the master of speech and the long finger (with a value of EIGHT) is speech itself (GRIE).

To the Bambara the THUMB is the symbol of power and their chiefs wear on their thumbs a ring decorated with the sign of the THUNDERBOLT, so that when they give an order and gesticulate they threaten their hearer with lightning (DIEB). By contrast with the thumb, symbolizing social power, the little finger is still regarded by the Bambara, who call it 'the other fingers' son', as possessing the *nyama*, or life force, of the other fingers. It is used in divination and in the casting of lots (DIEB). In addition they believe that the thumb is not only the embodiment of physical, but also of mental strength (ZAHB). Being 'an extension of the instrumentality of the soul, it also stands for work.'

The Dogon assign the numbers THREE and SIX to the thumb (GRIE), giving it a triply male quality, since three is the sign of masculinity. The index is the finger of judgement, decision, balance and of silence, in other words of self-mastery. The long finger symbolizes self-assurance, while the ring and little fingers are linked to the functions of sexual desire and appetite, the symbolism of the ring finger being more sharply sexual and of the little finger more esoteric. The latter is the finger of secret desires, occult powers and divination.

Father Dupeyrat has recorded the custom of the women of a Papuan tribe who cut off a finger-joint in mourning for the death of a husband. Alfred Métraux (METM) records the same custom among Indians in the Parana Delta in Brazil.

In the system of planetary correspondences with the microcosm, traditional astrology assigned the thumb to Venus, the index finger to Jupiter, the long finger to Saturn, the ring finger to the Sun and the little finger to Mercury (GRIA).

fire Hindu religious teaching, which gave it fundamental importance, contains most of the symbolical aspects of fire. Agni, Indra and Sūrya are, respectively, the fires of the terrestrial, intermediate and celestial worlds, in other words ordinary fire, LIGHTNING and the Sun. In addition, there are two other fires, Vaishvanara, which penetrates and absorbs, and the fire – another aspect of Agni – which destroys. Ritual fire itself – a further aspect of Agni – was conceived as having five aspects.

According to the *I Ching*, fire corresponds to south, the colour RED, Summer and the HEART. This last correspondence is constant, perhaps because fire symbolizes the passions (and especially those of love and hate), perhaps because it symbolizes the spirit (the 'spiritual fire' which is also the BREATH and the trigram *li*) or that intuitive knowledge mentioned by the *Bhagavad Gītā* (4: 10, 27). The supernatural significance of fire embraces both lost souls – represented by will-o'-the-wisps – and the Divine Spirit. The *Bhagavad Gītā* (4: 25) says that Brahman and fire are identical.

Fire is the essential symbol of the godhead in Zoroastrianism. Guardianship of the sacred fire stretches from Ancient Rome to Angkor: the symbol of purifying and regenerating fire is common from the Americas to Japan. On Easter Eve the Roman Catholic liturgy celebrates the 'new fire': in Shintō ritual this falls at the New Year. The Holy Spirit came down as 'tongues of fire' at Pentecost. Some legends tell how Christ – and his saints – brought the dead to life by passing their bodies through the fires of a BLACKSMITH's furnace. From the part played by the latter, it is a natural step to that of his relative the alchemist who 'forges' immortality in the fire of his FURNACE or, in China, in the inner crucible, located perhaps in the solar plexus or the *manipura-chakra*, to which Yoga assigns the sign of fire. Furthermore, Taoists enter the fire to free themselves from the burdens of the flesh, an apotheosis which may well remind us of that of Elijah in the CHARIOT of fire. They enter the fire 'without being burned' and within it, we are assured, they are able to call down heavenly blessings in the shape of rain, reminiscent of the 'fire which burns not' of Western hermeticism, which is an ablution or alchemical purification symbolized by the SALAMANDER. Among these instances of fire as a purifier should be numbered its use in Ancient China, along with bathing and fumigation, in ritual enthronements. And, of course, fire has been used as an ordeal worldwide.

The Buddha replaced the sacrificial fires of Hinduism with inner fire, which is simultaneously knowledge which penetrates, enlightenment and destruction of the outer shell. 'I kindle the flame within myself .... My heart is the hearth, the flame is the taming of self' (*Samyutta-nikāya* 1: 169). Similarly the Upanishads give the assurance that to burn externally is not to burn, hence the Yoga symbol of the burning *kundalinī* and the 'inner fire' of Tibetan Tantrism. This last system, with respect to the five 'subtle' centres, makes fire correspond to the heart. Again, in India, *taijasa*, a state of being corresponding to the dream or 'subtle' state, derives from *tējas*, or fire. It is at least interesting to observe that Abū Ya'qūb Sejestānī regarded a function of fire to be the transformation of matter to a 'subtle' state by destroying its material shell. The apparently childish Chinese alchemical formula, that water married to fire engenders steam, readily expresses symbolism of the same nature. According to a Fulani initiatory tradition 'fire comes from Heaven, because it goes up; water comes from Earth because it comes down as rain' (HAMK). Its birth is earthly, but its destiny is heavenly.

The destructive aspect of fire implies a negative aspect and to be 'Lord of the Fire' is a function of the Devil. It will be observed that the fire of the blacksmith's forge is simultaneously the fire of Heaven and the flames of Hell, the instrument both of the Demiurge and of the Devil. The Fall is that of Lucifer, 'Bearer of the Light' of Heaven, cast down into the flames of Hell, into a fire which burns without consuming, but can never regenerate (AVAS, BHAB, COOH, GOVM, HERS, SAIR).

The only information on Celtic traditions of fire as a ritual element and symbol comes indirectly or via the lives of the saints. In Ireland the only written references are to the Feast of Beltaine ('Bel Fires') on 1 May, the beginning of Summer. The druids lit huge bonfires through which the live-stock was driven to preserve it from disease. At Uisnech, in the centre of the country, St Patrick replaced the druids' bonfires with his own, as a sign that Christianity would triumph in the end. In his *De bello gallico*, Caesar, too, mentions the huge willow MANIKINS into which the Gauls thrust men and animals and which they then set alight. The Gaulish phenomenon is obscure and still awaits full analysis, but in Ireland the symbolism is patently solar. This was a pagan Easter (CELT p. 173; OGAC 14: pp. 181–3).

A characteristic of countless agrarian cults is purification by fire, generally in rites of passage. In fact they symbolize the burning of the fields 'which then put on a fresh cloak of living green' (GUES).

In the *Popol-Vuh*, the Hero Twins, the maize-gods, die upon a pyre lit by their enemies, offering no defence, only to be reborn in the green sprouts of maize.

Their myth is perpetuated in the rite of New Fire, still celebrated by the Chorti at the equinox, when the fields are burned for the sowing. At this time, the Chorti 'light a huge pyre on which they burn the hearts of birds and other creatures' (GUES). The Indians thus symbolically repeat the burning of the maize-god Twins, birds' hearts symbolizing the divine spirit.

In rites of initiation, of death and rebirth, Fire is associated with its chief rival Water. Thus, after their burning, the Twins of the *Popol-Vuh* were reborn from the river into which their ashes had been thrown. Later, the two Maya-Quiché heroes become the new Sun and the new Moon, achieving a fresh differentiation of the opposing principles of Fire and Water which had presided over their death and rebirth.

Thus purification by fire complements purification by water on both the microcosmic level in rites of initiation and, on the macrocosmic level, in alternating myths of floods and great fires or droughts.

Codices give as emblems for the Aztecs' 'old god' of fire, Huehueteotl, a tuft of FEATHERS surmounted by a blue bird, a pectoral ornament shaped like a BUTTERFLY and a dog. On his headband are a pair of interlocking isosceles TRIANGLES, one pointing up, the other down (SEJF). Sahagun says that the god dwells 'among the water-pools, among the flowers which form walls and battlements, wrapped in clouds of water.' Thus earthly, chthonian fire stood for the Aztecs for that deep-seated power which allowed the marriage of opposites and the ascension – Séjourné calls it the sublimation

– of water into clouds, in other words, the transformation of impure, earthly water, into heavenly water, divine and pure. Fire is, therefore, the prime motive force in the cycle of regeneration. The upward-pointing triangle, the emblem of kingship, is the hieroglyphic of evolutionary power. The downward-pointing triangle, according to Séjourné, stands for Tlaloc, the great sky-god, lord of thunder, lightning (fire from the sky) and rain. The 'burnt water' hieroglyphic associated with him comprises the marriage of opposites which takes place in the bosom of the Earth (see JAGUAR; MACAW).

The Bambara regard chthonian fire as representing human wisdom and ouranian fire, divine. In their society, the religious takes priority over the secular, hence the dependence of the human upon the divine (ZHAB).

Some ritual cremations stemmed from the belief that fire was a vehicle or messenger between the worlds of the living and the dead. Thus the Telyut went in procession to their burial-grounds at certain memorial festivals of the dead and lit two fires, one at the head and one at the foot of the grave. They placed items of food especially kept for the purpose in the first of these fires, the fire undertaking to transmit the offering to the dead person (HARA p. 228).

The sexual significance of fire is linked worldwide with the first technique of obtaining fire by up and down friction, the image of the sexual act (ELIF). According to Dieterlen, spiritualization of fire would have arisen from obtaining fire by striking a spark. Mircea Eliade concurs. Fire obtained by friction 'is either of divine origin or "demoniac" (for, according to certain primitive beliefs, it is engendered magically in the genital organ of the sorceress)' (ELIF p. 40). Durand notes that the sexualization of fire is emphasized by the many legends which locate the natural seat of fire in the tail of an animal (DURS pp. 360–1).

Bachelard considers that:

The love act is the first scientific hypothesis about the objective reproduction of fire ... before being son of wood, fire is the son of man.... The method of rubbing then appears as the *natural* method. Once again it is natural because man accedes to it *through his own nature*. In actual fact fire was detected within ourselves before it was snatched from the gods. ... Does not the life of the fire, made up entirely of sparks and sudden flickerings, remind us of the life of the ant heap? ... At the slightest incident, the ants can be seen swarming tumultuously out of their underground dwelling: similarly, at the slightest shock to the piece of phosphorus, the igneous animalculae can be seen to collect and come forth with luminous appearance.

(BACF pp. 23, 25, 32, 44)

Like Bachelard, Durand (DURS pp. 180–3) distinguishes two directions or 'psychic constellations' in the symbolism of fire depending upon whether, as already noted, it has been obtained by friction or by striking. In the latter case it is related to LIGHTNING and arrows and possesses the qualities of purification and enlightenment. It is the igneous extension of LIGHT. In Sanskrit the same word means both 'pure' and 'fire'. This spiritualizing fire is associated with cremation ceremonies, the Sun, fire which elevates and sublimates and all fire which communicates 'an intention to purify and enlighten'. It stands in opposition to the 'sexual' fire obtained by friction, just as the purifying flame stands in opposition to 'the procreative matriarchal hearth' and, as the exaltation of heavenly light, is distinct from an agrarian fertility rite. From this viewpoint, the symbolism of fire marks 'the most important stage in the intellectualization' of the cosmos and 'distances the human condition further and further from its animal nature.' By extending the symbol in this direction, 'fire would become what Burnouf calls that living and thinking god whom the Aryan religions of Asia named Agni and Athor and the Christians, Christ' (DURS p. 182). Although unrelated, a certain similarity of form brings fire and BIRDS close together as celestial symbols.

It is now easy to understand why fire should be the best and least imperfect image of God. This, as the Pseudo-Dionysius the Areopagite explained, was why

the Word of God prefers the sacred representations of fire in preference to almost any other. You will find it, then, representing not only wheels of fire, but also living creatures of fire; and men flashing like lightning; and placing around the heavenly Beings themselves heaps of coals of fire; and rivers of flame flowing with irresistible force. But also it says that the thrones are of fire; and that the most exalted CHERUBIM glows with fire, it shows from their appellation; and it attributes the characteristic and energy of fire to them; and everywhere, above and below, it prefers pre-eminently the representation by image of fire. I think, then, the similitude of fire denotes the likeness of Divine minds to God, in the highest degree, for the holy theologians frequently describe the super-essential and formless being by *fire*, as having many likenesses, if I may be permitted to say so, of the Divine character, in things visible.

(PSEH pp. 44–5)

As the Sun through its rays symbolizes the act of making fertile, or pure, and of enlightenment, so does the fire through its flames. However, it does display a negative aspect. Its smoke blinds and stifles and the fires of love, punishment and war burn, devour and destroy. When Paul Diel interprets fire psychoanalytically, he regards terrestrial fire as symbolizing the intellect, that is to say consciousness in all its ambivalence:

Flames rising skywards depict impulses towards spiritualization. In its developing form, the intellect is subservient to the spirit. But the flame may flicker and thus fire may come to symbolize the intellect oblivious of the spirit. [It should be remembered that in this context 'spirit' means 'super-consciousness'.] Unlike the flame which casts light, the fire which smokes and devours symbolizes an imagination inflamed ... the subconscious ... the hole in the ground ... hellfire ... the intellect in rebellion, in short, all forms of psychic regression.

From this viewpoint, in that it burns up and consumes, fire is as strongly a symbol of purification and regeneration. Once more we have the positive aspect of destruction and a fresh reversal of the symbol. Water, too, purifies and regenerates, but fire is distinct from it, in that it symbolizes 'purification through understanding to the highest degree of spirituality, by enlightenment and by the truth. Water symbolizes purification of desires until they reach their most sublime in goodness' (DIES pp. 37–8).

firefly In China, fireflies are traditionally the companions of poor students, providing them with light for their night-time studies.

The Montagnards of southern Vietnam believe that the souls of ordinary people take the shapes of SPIDERS, while those of heroes appear in the form of fireflies (DANS).

In Japan they celebrate a firefly festival.

first fruits Gifts to mark the start of a fresh cycle go back to the remotest antiquity. They are similar to those seasonal rituals designed to obtain the protection of gods, kings and influential people in general. In this sense it is a sacrifice of what is to hand in the hope of future abundance.

Descended from these are presents to mark the start of any fresh cycle, such as New Year or Christmas, birthdays, new business ventures, launching of ships, books or new products, first use of anything new.

fish Of course fish are symbols of WATER, the element in which they live. They are carved on the bases of Khmer monuments to show that their foundations are in the 'waters under the earth', the Underworld. In this context they may be regarded as sharing the 'chaotic' character of their element, whence arises their 'uncleanness'. This is the reason given by de St-Martin who also notes that their heads cannot be distinguished from their bodies. Yet, although Leviticus excludes fish from sacrificial animals, it allows them, alone of aquatic creatures, to be eaten.

As a symbol of water and the creature on which Varuna rides, fish are associated with cyclical birth or rebirth. Manifestation occurs upon the 'face of the waters'. Fish are at one and the same time saviours and instruments of revelation. A fish (*matsya*) was one of Vishnu's avatars (incarnations); it saved Manu, lawgiver of the present cycle, from the FLOOD and then brought him the Vedas, in other words revealed to him the whole of sacred knowledge. CHRIST himself is often depicted as a fisherman, Christians being fish since the waters of BAPTISM are their natural element, and he himself is symbolized by a fish. Thus he is the Fish which guides the Ark of the Church, just as the *Matsya-avatāra* guided the ark of Manu. In Kashmir, Matsyendranāth, whose name undoubtedly should be translated as 'The Fisherman' and identified with the *Bodhisattva* Avalokitesvara, is said to have had Yoga revealed to him when he was transformed into a fish.

Sacred fish in Ancient Egypt, the Phoenician god, Dagon, and the Mesopotamian, Oannes, bear witness to identity of symbol, especially the last named who was specifically regarded as 'the Revealer'. Oannes, indeed, has been regarded as a prefiguration of Christ. In Ancient Greece, with the legend of Amphion's rescue by a DOLPHIN, the theme of the dolphin-as-saviour was a commonplace. Dolphins were associated with the worship of APOLLO and gave Delphi its name.

Fish are, in any case, symbols of life and fertility because of their extraordinary powers of reproduction and the vast number of eggs which they lay. This is a symbol which, of course, can be transferred to the spiritual plane. In Far Eastern iconography fish are paired and thus become symbols of marriage (DANA, DURV, ELIY, CHAE, GUES, MUTT, SAIR). Muslims also associate fish with notions of fertility. Rain-making charms are known, shaped like fish, and they are also associated with prosperity, since to dream of eating fish is considered lucky.

'In the iconography of Indo-European races, fish, emblem of water, are a symbol of fertility and wisdom. Hidden in the Ocean's depths, they are charged with the sacred powers of the ABYSS. Lurking in lakes or swimming in streams, they bring rain, water and flood and thus regulate the Earth's fertility' (PHIU p. 140).

Fish are a symbol of the Central American Indian MAIZE-god. Hentze (HENL) believes they are phallic symbols and Breuil has found them among Magdalenian bone-carvings. The Sanskrit name for the love-god was 'he who has the Fish for a Symbol', while fish were attributes of the love-goddesses worshipped in Syria. Aximander explains that in Ancient Asia Minor fish were forbidden as food because they were the parents of mankind. They are often associated with rhomboid shapes (see LOZENGE), especially on Babylonian cylinders. Marcel Griaule records that the name given to the Bozo circumcision knife is 'the knife which cuts the fish' (GRIB).

In China fishes were a symbol of luck and when accompanied by CRANES (longevity), together they symbolized happiness and good luck.

In Ancient Egypt fresh or dried fish was a staple article of food, but it was forbidden to 'all persons connected with religion', priests or kings. According to legend, 'the gods of Busiris were then supposed to change themselves into chromis-fish' and this demanded a total abstinence from fish-eating. A goddess was called 'the Chief of the Fishes' and this was a name given to the female dolphin. Despite many variants in both legend and ritual practice, fishes were generally ambiguous creatures and

silent and mysterious . . . hidden but glistening under the green Nile, were for ever taking part in fierce dramas. So every day in the creek at the end of the world a chromis with fins edged with pink and an *abdju*-fish of blue lapis took shape mysteriously and acting as pilots to Ra's boat reported the approach of the monster Apophis.

(POSD p. 91)

The chromis-amulet was a lucky and protective charm.

Christianity has made wide use of fish symbolism, some applications being specific to it, others obviously to be excluded. The Greek word for 'fish' (*ichthus*) was in fact taken by Christians as an ideogram, each of the five Greek letters being taken as the initial letters of the words *Iesu Christos Theou Uios Soter* (Jesus Christ God's Son Saviour). Hence the large number of symbolic representations of fish in early Christian monuments, particularly funeral monuments.

Nevertheless, although in most cases the symbolism remains strictly Christological, it is given a slightly different emphasis. Since fish was also a food eaten by the risen Christ (Luke 24: 42), it became a symbol of the Eucharistic feast and is often depicted alongside the bread.

Lastly, because fishes live in water, the symbolism may sometimes be pursued along baptismal lines. Reborn in the waters of baptism, the Christian may be compared with a little fish in the image of Christ himself (Tertullian, *De baptismate* 1).

The fish has provided Christian artists with a wealth of iconography. Carrying a ship upon its back, it symbolizes Christ and his Church; lying upon a plate with a basket of bread upon it, it stands for the Eucharist; while in the Catacombs it is Christ himself.

fishing Myth, ritual and art contain a wealth of fishing scenes, with sailors casting their NETS and hauling fish out of the water.

In Ancient Egypt fishing was responsible for restoring Osiris to his original shape. Similarly 'the Moon, which was an eye torn from Horus, was found in a fishing net; the hands severed from the god were discovered in a fishing basket.' Jean Yoyotte speculates whether the Theban tomb-painting of a fishing scene 'does not perhaps represent fishing for eternal happiness' (POSD p. 93).

'Fisher of Men', the title given to St Peter in the Gospels, designated somebody who was to save mankind from damnation, the Saviour's apostle, the agent of conversion. Here fishing is a symbol of preaching and the apostolate: souls for conversion are the fish to be caught.

Fishing, in the psychoanalytic sense, is a type of recall process of abstracting elements from the unconscious under no logical or predetermined plan, but by allowing spontaneous forces to operate and then collecting their chance results. The unconscious may, in this context, be likened to any stretch of water, river, lake or SEA, in which are hidden riches which recall and psychoanalysis will bring to the surface like a fisherman with his net.

five The number five derives its symbolism in the first place from the fact that it is the sum of the first even and odd number $(2 + 3 = 5)$ and secondly because it is at the CENTRE of the first NINE numbers. It is a sign of marriage (the Pythagorean 'nuptial' number) as well as being the number of the centre, of harmony and of balance. It is therefore the number governing sacred marriages between the principles of Heaven (2) and the Earth Mother (3).

Furthermore, it is the symbol of the human being, which, with arms outstretched in the shape of a CROSS, appears to comprise five parts, two arms, two legs and head and body, the latter sheltering the heart. It is also a symbol of the universe, its two axes, vertical and horizontal, passing through the same centre; of order and perfection; and, lastly, of the will of God, which can only desire order and perfection (CHAS pp. 243–4).

It also stands for the phenomenal world in its entirety – the five senses and the forms of matter amenable to sense-perception.

Pythagorean pentagonal harmony has left its mark upon the architecture of medieval cathedrals. Hermetic symbolism set the five-pointed STAR and the five-petalled FLOWER in the centre of a cross comprising the four ELEMENTS. This is the quintessence or ether. Five bears the same relation to SIX as the microcosm to the macrocosm, the individual to Universal Man.

In China, too, five was the number of the centre. It was to be found in the middle hut of Lo-chu. In the beginning the ideogram *wu* (five) was no more than the cross comprising the FOUR elements plus the centre. At a later stage two parallel lines were added – Heaven and Earth – between which *yin* and *yang* produce the five active elements. Ancient writers also maintained that 'under Heaven, the universal laws are five in number'. There were five colours, five flavours, five musical tones, five metals, five internal organs, five planets, five cardinal points, five spatial regions and, of course, five senses as well. Five is the number of Earth being the sum of the four cardinal regions and of the centre, the phenomenal world. But five is also the sum of two and three, Earth and Heaven in their own natures, of the marriage of *yin* and *yang*, of *T'ien* and *T'i*. Five is also the basic number of secret societies. It is the marriage symbolized by the five colours of the rainbow. Five is also the number of the heart.

In Hindu symbolism five, once again, is the conjunction of two (the female number) with three (the male number). It is the principle of life, the number of Shiva the Transformer. The star-shaped PENTAGON – another symbol of Shiva – was regarded as an ordinary pentagon ringed by five triangles of fiery rays which were LINGAMS. Shiva who, as Lord of the Universe is also master of the five regions, is sometimes depicted with five faces and, in Cambodia especially, was worshipped in the shape of five LINGAMS. Notwithstanding, his fifth face, which looks upwards, was identified with the AXIS and generally remained featureless (BENA, BHAB, DANA, GRAP, GUEC, GUET, LIOT, KRAA).

The Japanese Buddhist Shingon sect also distinguishes five cardinal points (four points of the compass and the centre), five elements (Earth, Water, Fire, wind and space), five colours and the five qualities of knowledge which the supreme Buddha possessed and which the devotee of Shingon esotericism must try to acquire progressively to reach the level of enlightenment. Five, in this context, proves to be the number of integrated perfection.

The provinces of Ireland numbered five, the four traditional provinces of Ulad (Ulster), Connacht (Connaught), Lagin (Leinster), Mumu (Munster) and a fifth central province Midhe (Meath) comprising portions of land taken from the four other provinces. The Middle Irish word for 'province' is *coiced*, literally 'a fifth'. Five is also the number of the deities at the heart of the Celtic pantheon, that is a supreme, multi-skilled deity Lug ('the shining one') which Romanization assimilated to Mercury, and four other deities, all of whose aspects he transcended – the Dagda ('the good god') assimilated to Jupiter; Ogma (the champion) and Nuada (the king), to Mars; Dian Cécht (the physician) and Mac Og (the young man), to Apollo; and Brigit (the shining mother of the gods, of the arts and crafts and of Gobniu, the blacksmith), to Minerva. This arrangement is confirmed by Caesar who, in his *De bello gallico*, lists Mercury, Jupiter, Mars, Apollo and Minerva. However, the Roman names for gods given by the Roman author do not designate deities as such, but rather their functions, and this explains the twofold assimilation in some cases. Five would thus be the symbol of totality – the totality of the land of Ireland and of the Celtic pantheon, but a totality obtained by a centre which gathers in and integrates the other four and in which these four parts take a share.

Throughout the bulk of medieval Irish literature, fifty or its threefold multiplication, one hundred and fifty (*tri coicait*, literally 'three fifties') is a conventional number meaning or symbolizing infinity. Numeration seldom extends beyond it, but the Celtic system of numeration is archaic and clumsy even in current forms of the languages.

In Central America five was a sacred number and during the agrarian period was the symbolic number of the maize-god. In both Maya manuscripts and Maya sculpture he is often depicted as an open HAND. According to Girard (GIRP p. 198) the sacralization of the number five was linked to the process of maize-cultivation, the first shoots appearing five days after the seed is planted. Following their initiatory death, the maize-god Twins were brought to life again by the waters of the river into which their ashes had been cast five days before (*Popol-Vuh*). The myth describes how they first appeared in the shape of FISH, afterwards as half men, half fish, before becoming shining solar youths. The Maya hieroglyphic for five generally takes the form of a hand, but may sometimes be encountered in the shape of a fish. The modern descendants of the Maya, the Chorti, still associate five with maize and fish. In the later stages of their legend, the Twins separated as the Sun-god and the Moon-god. It was the Moon-god who retained five for his symbolic number, hence the similarity with the fish, a lunar symbol.

The Chorti, too, set the period of childhood as one of five years, on the analogy of human growth with that of maize. The maize-god is the patron of children who have not attained the age of reason, that is to say, those who are under five years of age (GIRP p. 210).

The Maya believed that God drew up the dead person by a ROPE, which was his or her soul, five days after death, just as the maize-seed ends its gestation period and sprouts from the soil, drawn up by God, five days after sowing. The maize-shoot, too, is called 'rope' or 'soul'.

According to Mexican tradition, Quetzalcoatl remained four days in the Underworld before his rebirth on the fifth day (GIRP pp. 200–1). The Maya solar hieroglyphic comprises five circles, the maize-god being a solar god as well.

Five was also the Maya symbol of perfection (THOH) and the fifth day belonged to their Earth-gods. Thompson most emphatically adds that it was also the day of the serpent which sent the rain.

The succession of four Suns in Aztec tradition stands for the creation of a world which, with the fourth Sun, was immanent but not yet manifest. Only the appearance of the fifth Sun, the sign of the present age, completed the manifestation. As we have seen, each of these Suns – and ages – corresponded to one of the four cardinal points. The fifth Sun corresponds to the centre or middle of the CROSS which they form. The dawning of that centre is the awakening of consciousness. Five is therefore the number which symbolizes human–world–consciousness. The Aztecs assigned the central Sun to the god Xiuhtecuhtli, lord of FIRE, sometimes represented by a butterfly (SOUM).

The Aztec god Five (young maize) was lord of the dance and of music. This Apollonian function associated him with love, Spring, dawn and all sports. The same god, called 'the Singer', was the Huitchol morning star.

Returning to the interpretation given to the number five by the Ancient Mexicans, we find Soustelle (SOUC) clearly showing the ambivalent nature of this number. Five, he remarks, is the number of the present world – preceded by four abortive creations – and of the centre of the cross formed by the four cardinal points. Hence it symbolizes fire, but in both senses of the word. On the one hand there is solar fire, so that the number is linked to LIGHT, the day and the triumph of life. On the other, there is the chthonian, earthly, underground fire, linking five with darkness and the journey of the 'Black Sun' through the Underworld. In his successive metamorphoses, the hero Quetzalcoatl twice embodied the idea of sacrificial rebirth, identified on the one hand by the Sun and on the other by the planet VENUS, which both vanish into the west, the realm of darkness, to reappear – reborn – with the dawn in the east. In his role of 'Lord of the House of the Dawn', reborn in the shape of Venus, the morning star, Quetzalcoatl is depicted in Mexican manuscripts as a personage bearing on his face the figure five in the form of dots disposed in a quincunx. Hence, as Soustelle explains, five has an esoteric significance 'among the priestly and warrior castes, as sacrifice, or rather as self-sacrifice and resurrection'. As a solar hieroglyphic, it embodies the notion of the triumph of the Sun and of life, but underpinning this are those sacrifices of warriors whose blood fed the Sun, making possible its daily return and hence making life itself possible. Similarly the centre of the world, represented by the number five, is also the hieroglyphic for the earthquake, the Last Judgement and the end of the world, when evil spirits will descend upon the centre from the four quarters of the Earth to annihilate the human race. The centre of the world is thus the central crossroads and, like all CROSSROADS, is a place for the production of terrifying apparitions.

It should be remembered that it was at crossroads, five times a year, that women who died in childbirth appeared, women who, like the warriors killed in battle or in sacrifice, were the deified companions of the Sun in his daily course, oddly reminiscent, as will be seen, of Dogon notions of the number. Lastly, and again underlining the unlucky aspect of the symbol, it should be remembered that five, being the middle of the 'dark' series (9) is in opposition to SEVEN, the middle of the 'bright' series (13). The fifth lord of darkness, Mictlantecuhtli, Lord of Death, is in opposition to the smiling goddess, Chicomecoatl, seventh of the THIRTEEN deities of light. On his back he wears a solar sign, but it is the Sun of the dead – the Black Sun – which journeys underground during the night. Thus, Soustelle concludes, to the Mexicans the number five symbolized 'the passing by death from one life to another and the indissoluble marriage of the dark with the bright side of the universe.'

Father Francisco de Avila's valuable account (AVIH) demonstrates the major role played by the number five in the beliefs of the Ancient Peruvians. 'All things providing nourishment sprouted five days after sowing' and the dead would come to life again five days after death, which was the reason why their bodies were exposed rather than interred. 'On the fifth day their spirits could be seen emerging in the shape of a little fly.' A flood which lasted five days and an eclipse of the Sun which plunged the world into darkness for another five days both occur in myths relating to the end of earlier ages. 'Then the mountain peaks crashed together and mortars and grinding-stones started to crush humans.' The god Paryacaca, lord of the waters and the lightning, was born from five eggs in the shape of five kites. He is one in five. He makes the rain fall from five different places at once and darts the lightning from the five quarters of the sky.

The notion of five successive races of human beings, our own being the fifth, recurs in Hesiod's *Works and Days*. This cosmological poet believed the Earth to have been inhabited successively by men of the Golden Age, men of the Silver Age, demi-gods and men of the Bronze Age – they perished in the Trojan War – before the arrival of our own generation, the men of the Iron Age. In the Golden Age, men were 'pure spirits dwelling on earth . . . guardians of mortal men . . . givers of wealth' (121–5). Their successors in the Silver Age were guilty of the unbounded folly of refusing to render worship to the Immortals and were buried by Zeus. 'But when earth had covered this generation also, they are called blessed spirits of the underworld by men, and, though they are of second order, yet honour attends them also' (140–2). The men of the Bronze Age were guilty, too, not of the Satanic pride of their predecessors, but of the excess of their own terrifying strength. 'These were destroyed by their own hands and passed to the dank house of chill Hades, and left no name' (152–4). As for the divine race of the demi-gods, they dwell 'untouched by sorrow in the islands of the blessed along the shore of deep-swirling' Ocean (170–1), that is to say, far off in the west near the Garden of the Gods guarded by the Hesperides. This makes Greek tradition oddly akin to the Aztec tradition of five Suns or five ages.

The Dogon and Bambara of Mali think of ONE as being unique, not as a symbol of completion and perfection, but as synonymous with the unnatural, since it is the number of primal CHAOS, while two is the number of cosmic order. Hence five, made up by the association of four, the female symbol, with one, is itself a symbol of the unfulfilled, of uncleanness, discord, instability and of unfinished creation. From this, it follows that five is most generally regarded as an unlucky number and is associated with the most severe setbacks – including still-birth – and with death. Despite this, it may also be regarded as a lucky symbol, since the Bambara in fact speak of a fifth world – to come – which will be a perfect world, not springing, like the present world, from the association of one and four, but of three and two (DIEB).

St Hildegard of Bingen evolved a complex theory of the number five as a symbol of man. 'Man's height from the crown of his head to the soles of his feet may be divided into five equal parts. Again, his breadth from the finger-tips of each hand when they are outstretched, may also be divided into five equal parts. Reckoning five equal measurements both of length and breadth, man can be depicted within a perfect SQUARE' (DAVS p. 170). Five squares lengthwise and five squares breadthwise, intersecting at the chest, make a cross within this square. If Earth is symbolized by a square, man is either a cross within the world or the world is his cross.

Aside from the five equal parts both lengthwise and breadthwise, man possesses

five senses and five extremities (head, hands and feet). Plutarch uses this number to designate the succession of species. A similar notion may be found in Genesis where it is written that the fishes and the fowls of the air were created on the fifth day. . . . Even numbers signify the womb, for they are female, while odd numbers are male. The association of the one with the other is androgynous . . . Thus PENTAGRAMS are emblems of the MICROCOSM and of the HERMAPHRODITE. In Medieval miniatures microcosmic man is often depicted with legs and arms outstretched, the better to display the five points of the pentagram.

(DAVS p. 171)

Five therefore controls human bodily structure.

Five is a lucky number and favourite of Muslims. They have the pentagram of the five senses and of marriage. Five is the number of the hours of
prayer and the types of goods upon which tithes are payable; there are five
elements in the *hajj* (pilgrimage) (and five days at Arafat), five types of
fasting, five motives for ablution, five dispensations for Friday; there is a
fifth of treasure or booty, five generations for a tribal feud, five camels for
the *diya* and five *takbīr* or formulae of prayer: God is Great! There were
five witnesses to the *Mubāhala* (treaty) and five keys to the Koranic mystery (Koran 6: 59; 31: 34). There are also five fingers in 'the Hand of Fatima'
(MASA p. 163).

To counteract the evil, the five fingers of the right hand are stretched out
while you utter the spell: 'Five in your eye!' or 'Five on your eye!' In Fez
you say 'Five and fifteen' to avoid the danger caused by excessively admiring something or somebody. The number five has thus become a charm in
itself. Thursday, the fifth day of the week, is under the sign of effective
protection.

Five, Allendy states (ALLN p. 121), 'is the number of physical and objective being. Both psychoanalysis and Maya tradition are at one here, as
are Eastern traditions, in making five the sign of manifested life. As an odd
number it expresses an action rather than a state. The Quinary is the number
of created being and individuality.' In this sense, it is noteworthy that man's
shape may be drawn in a pentagram of which the centre is his genitals. This
pentagram is the original of the Chinese ideogram *jen*, meaning 'man'. If
a man lies with arms and legs outstretched, his genitals being the centre,
the upper part of his body equals the lower part. Each of those parts provides a radius for a circle drawn from that centre. Once again, five symbolizes manifestation of man in the full maturity of his physical and spiritual
development.

flag See BANNER.

flagellation Symbolizes those actions required to put to flight the powers
or DEMONS which inhibit material fertility or spiritual development. The
WHIP was employed as a means of correction on all subjects of princes, kings
and Pharaohs thoughout the East, but especially on slaves, mechanics, peasants and soldiers, as well as disobedient children. Since it was a degrading
punishment, flagellation was kept for slaves.

There were also ritual flagellations, pale surrogates of human sacrifice
although they could be severe enough to draw blood; or simulated
flagellations to drive off the evil spirits who interfered with hunting, harvesting or fertility. Barren women were beaten with straps made from goat's
leather and, according to Plutarch, slaves were beaten to the cry of 'Famine, begone!'

Religious ascetics of all sects have flagellated their bodies until the blood
ran as a penitential act or to drive off temptation.

Flagellation is intended to destroy symbolically and in practice everything which may create disorder in a society or in an individual and which
upsets or inhibits their normal smooth running.

flame (see also FIRE) In all traditions the flame is a symbol of spiritual purification, enlightenment and love. It is the image of the spirit and of transcendence, the soul of fire.

In its 'dark' and pejorative sense, of flame put to wrong uses, it is the torch of discord, the burning breath of rebellion, the devouring spark of envy, the devouring fire of lust and the murderous flash of the exploding shell.

flamen A Roman priest attached to the cult of various deities, the chief being the Indo-European active triad, JUPITER, MARS and Quirinus. Etymologically the word is akin to the root of 'brahman' and, according to Jean Bayet, expresses 'a mysterious power of enlargement by prayer or ritual presence.' The flamen is a symbol of the spiritual flame in the individual and in society.

flamingo When, in the Upanishads, a fatherless boy with heroic sincerity asks to be initiated as a Brahman, his master first of all makes him a cowherd, entrusting him with four hundred thin and sickly beasts. When his herd amounts to a thousand head, a bull tells him: 'Drive us back to your master's house and I will teach you a quarter of the Brahman's lore.' He then teaches him about the regions of space. Fire teaches him another quarter, that of the infinity of worlds, and then the flamingo teaches him 'in four sixteenths' the Brahman's portion of the lore of LIGHT. Lastly, the grebe explains the meaning (*Chāndogya Upanishad* 4: 4). Thus that great pink bird, the flamingo, initiates him into light and is to be seen as one of the symbols of the soul migrating from darkness to light.

flesh The word flesh has, over the ages, developed a meaning which has become increasingly internalized. The flesh is often regarded in terms of St Jerome beating his body with a stone or of the temptations of St Anthony. It is seen as a diabolical force dwelling in the human body, the DEVIL incarnate.

In the Old Testament the flesh was depicted, in contrast with the spirit, as naturally weak and short-lived, human nature comprising flesh and the spirit of God (*pneuma*). In the New Testament flesh is associated with BLOOD to show CHRIST's human nature, while the enmity between spirit and flesh displays the void between Nature and Grace (John 3: 5–6). The flesh is not simply impervious to spiritual values, it is prone to sin. St Paul shows how the flesh is so subject. To give oneself up to the flesh means that one actively, not simply passively, allows the seeds of corruption to enter oneself. The individual is caught between the flesh and the spirit and torn between two driving forces, desiring good, but unable to attain to it (Romans 7: 14; 8: 8; Galatians 5: 13; 6: 8). St Paul's is a departure from Jewish tradition; the terminology is different and the terms themselves bear a different meaning. The flesh carries moral overtones which it never possessed hitherto. It is no longer a matter of the physical body or the physical nature of the individual, but of human nature which has lost its righteousness through Original Sin. The flesh clogs, whence the constant need to wrestle with the disorders which it constantly produces.

St Paul's teachings were bound to attract the attention of the Church

Fathers who, in accordance with the forcefulness or moderation of their own temperaments either exaggerated or played down the apostle's views in their commentaries. Jerome and Tertullian belong among the former group, Augustine and Ambrose among the latter. The flesh was regarded as the enemy of the spirit and would be judged as such, an untamed and untameable beast, constantly in revolt. When trying to express the weight of the flesh, St Gregory of Nazianzus compares it with a lump of lead. According to St Ambrose, God does not dwell in the carnally minded but in those who detach themselves from the flesh and become like the ANGELS who do not experience the trials and servitude of the flesh. Free from earthly concerns, they belong completely to the reality of God.

Gnosticism, Montanism and Manicheanism had exaggerated the enmity of flesh and spirit. Some of the Fathers, in their efforts to combat these different heresies, fell into the errors which they sought to refute. The teachings of Stoicism, in particular, were to exert a profound influence upon the war declared between flesh and spirit.

From this reservoir twelfth-century monasticism drew its sharpest epithets. By a close reading of Cassian, it rediscovered those elements of Stoicism and Neoplatonism which he had borrowed and which provided themes for meditating upon the power and wickedness of the flesh when its propensities were given full rein. The lives of the Desert Fathers, monastic Rules and the writings of the great reformers were to provide the evidence to show what examples to imitate and what practices to follow in religious life. As ascetics, monks would have the goal of attaining to the freedom which derives from grace and from a spirit regulated by God, a freedom which would entail a weakening of the demands of the flesh. Hence the importance given to VIRGINITY, which had acquired from the earliest years of the Church a degree of excellence which placed it next in esteem to martyrdom and, furthermore, led to its being regarded as an acceptable substitute for the latter.

The flesh is the well-spring of many vices in the sense in which St John speaks of 'the lust of the flesh, and the lust of the eyes, and the pride of life' (1 John 2: 16). This is why the flesh is associated with the world and the Devil.

According to William of St Thierry the flesh should be treated soberly, since its lusts are contrary to the intentions of the spirit. Nevertheless, the flesh blossoms again when the spirit is refashioned in God's image. Sometimes the flesh precedes the spirit which guides it, and takes delight in what nourishes the spirit, so that its submission to the spirit becomes natural. A spiritual person, using the flesh in a spiritual fashion, deserves to discover that the submission of the flesh has become, as it were, spontaneous and natural (DAVS pp. 44, 82, 264).

To St Bernard of Clairvaux, the flesh was the prime foe of the SOUL. Corrupt from birth, it seemed vitiated by its evil habits and darkened the inward vision. He told his novices to leave the flesh outside the monastery gates; the spirit alone was granted admission to the cloisters within. 'For how much longer will this wretched, obstinate flesh, in its blind, mindless, utter folly, seek its fleeting imperfect consolations?' he thundered in the sixth of his Advent sermons. Yet, although the flesh could become the faithful companion of the spirit, it continued to arouse the mistrust of Christian thinkers. Humanism only diminished this distrust by lowering the barriers between spirit and flesh and by emphasizing the indissoluble unity of human nature.

Although Hildebert of Lavardin might regard the flesh as a 'foul ensnarement', it is obvious that to free oneself from it demands a dynamism of which few would admit themselves capable. Prayer, humility, compassion and a longing for God's kingdom are powerful aids to that attainment of peace of heart which results from complete control of the flesh. Step by step the flesh becomes holy and shares in the enlightenment of the spirit. Thus the soul gains a foretaste of heavenly bliss as it continues on its earthly pilgrimage. For the flesh is not tinged only by the colours of darkness inherited from Platonist dualism and exacerbated by Manicheanism. The flesh is also endowed with a quality of intimacy, not simply physical, but spiritual as well, an intimacy which embraces the whole of individual being. Feelings of love or hate can pierce the flesh – in common parlance, 'gut feelings'. Thus the flesh comes to designate the most deeply rooted principle of the human personality, the seat of the HEART, when the latter is understood as being the principle of action. 'I will take away the stony heart out of your flesh, and I will give you an heart of flesh' (Ezekiel 36: 26). Christianity even carries the promise of 'the resurrection of the body', demonstrating that the individual will be reborn as a whole being. Christ himself was 'the Word made Flesh', making Paul Valéry declare that no other religion has set the flesh on so high a plane.

flight In such myths as those of ICARUS or in dreams, flight is an expression of the desire for sublimation and the search for internal harmony and the resolution of conflict. Such dreams are most common among neurotics who have little capacity to realize by their own abilities their longing to enhance their status. Flight symbolizes in dreams the inability to fly. The stronger that desire, the more the incapability will develop as anxiety and the vain hopes which inspired it change to feelings of guilt. The dream of flying ends in the nightmare of falling. It gives 'symbolic expression to real life, to real setbacks, and is the unavoidable consequence of a wrong attitude to the real world' (DIES p. 51). The image of flying is an unreal substitute for the action which ought to be taken. Not knowing what it is, or being unwilling or unable to take it, we look to the dream to realize it by outstripping it. There are grounds, nevertheless, for seeing in the desire or dream of flight not only the desire for independent action, but also the symbol of ascension on the level of thought or morality; but it is an ascension which is more imaginary and erratic than proportionate to real needs or capabilities.

From the psychoanalytic aspect of the symbol, it is odd to think that space flight and projected interplanetary travel – despite the heroism and genius which they demand – may hide the inability of the industrial nations to solve the human problems of economic and social development. Not knowing how to use their vast resources, or unable or unwilling to apply their almost limitless potential to the benefit of mankind as a whole, they take flight beyond the boundaries of Earth. It betrays a collective psychology in which the will to confirm one's power in the sky compensates for the feeling of powerlessness upon Earth. There is something infantile in this monstrous growth of science: it bears witness to a social structure unfitted to solve problems of its own creation. It is as if it were incapable of assuming responsibility for the control of its own destiny. It revives the myth of Icarus and simply flies from itself when it believes it takes to the skies. (See also WINGS.)

flint   See OBSIDIAN.

flock   See HERD.

flood   To recognize the symbolic significance which floods have taken in tradition and myth is not to deny their occurrence as historical events. Of all natural disasters, floods stand out by their lack of finality. They are 'pre-eminently the sign of growth and regeneration. A flood destroys simply because the "forms" are old and worn out, but it is always followed by a new humanity and a new history' (ELIT p. 160). This suggests 'the idea of humanity returning to the water whence it had come, and the establishment of a new era and a new humanity' (ibid. p. 210). This may be likened to the sinking of whole continents beneath the waves, like the geographical myth, or even, perhaps, to the reality of ATLANTIS. Floods are often linked to human sinfulness, be it moral or ritual, actual sin or failure to obey rules and regulations. Like BAPTISM, floods purify and regenerate and are like vast collective baptisms determined, not by human conscience but by a higher and almighty one. Floods display

what human life may be worth to a 'mind' other than a human mind: from the 'point of view' of water, human life is something fragile that must periodically be engulfed, because it is the fate of all forms to be dissolved in order to reappear. If 'forms' are not regenerated by being periodically dissolved in water, they will crumble, exhaust their powers of creativity and finally die away. Mankind would eventually be completely deformed by 'wickedness' and 'sin'; emptied of its seeds of life and creative powers, humanity would waste away, weakened and sterile. Instead of permitting this slow regression into sub-human forms, the flood effects an instantaneous dissolution in water, in which sins are purified and from which new, regenerate humanity will be born.

(ELIT p. 211)

The Biblical Flood was adapted within the context of Irish creation mythology to symbolize the boundary between prehistory and history. Only primordial man, Fintan, escaped it. He reached Ireland 'on the back of a wave' and slept for several centuries upon a sandy beach before imparting to the wise men of Ireland all the traditional lore of which he had been the guardian.

flour   Since it is the result of sifting to remove the bran, an exercise in purification, flour symbolizes essential food obtained by choice and discernment. This notion is to be found in the *Rig-Veda*, where speech is described as issuing from the thoughts of the Wise like flour from the SIEVE.

flower (see also CHRYSANTHEMUM; DAY-LILY; HELIOTROPE; IRIS; LOTUS; ORCHID; ROSE; SUNFLOWER)   Although every flower may possess, secondarily, its own specific symbolism, for all that, flowers generally are symbols of the passive

principle. The calix of a flower, like the CHALICE, is the receptacle of heavenly instrumentality, among the symbols of which DEW and RAIN should be
mentioned. Furthermore the way flowers grow up out of EARTH and WATER
(see LOTUS) symbolizes manifestation rising out of these passive elements.

St John of the Cross makes flowers the image of the virtues of the soul,
spiritual perfection being the bouquet into which they are gathered. In his
Heinrich von Ofterdingen, Novalis regards flowers as the symbol of the love
and harmony characteristic of primeval nature. They become identified with
the symbolism of childhood and to some degree with that of the paradisal
state of innocence.

The Tantric–Taoist symbolism of *The Secret of the Golden Flower* is also
that of the attainment of a spiritual state. The 'flowering' is a result of
internal alchemy, of the marriage of essence (*hsin*) with breath (*k'i*), of FIRE
and water. The Flower is to be identified with the Elixir of Life: the flowering is a return to the CENTRE, to unity and the primal state.

In Hindu ritual, the flower (*pushpa*) corresponds to the element Ether.

Setting aside the methods and spiritual attitudes which are among its
essentials, the Japanese art of flower arranging (*ikebana*) involves a symbolism all of its own. Flowers are regarded, effectively, as the pattern of
the evolution of a manifestation, of art which arises of its own accord,
uncontrived and yet perfect, as well as being an emblem of the cycle of
plant life, and an abridgement of the cycle of life itself and of its fleeting
nature. The arrangements themselves are conceived upon a ternary plan,
the upper spray representing Heaven, the central one Man and the lower
one, Earth. They thus give expression to the rhythm of the universal triad
in which Man is the intermediary between Heaven and Earth. This pattern
includes all that lives. Just as the three natural forces should harmonize to
form the universe, so the sprays should balance effortlessly in space. Such
has been the true art of *ikebana* since the fourteenth century: there is,
however, a complex or 'flowing' method in which the sprays hang downwards. This method of flower arranging aims to give expression to the
decline of life and the flow of all things into the ABYSS. For this reason, the
tips of the sprays must bend downwards ever more sharply. *Ikebana* may
just as easily give expression to ancestral tradition or to feelings of joy and
sorrow as it does to the cosmic order. Between the eighth and fourteenth
centuries another school (*rikka*) had as its objective the arrangement of
flowers in an upright pose; the upward flow of the flower was to symbolize
fidelity to God, the Emperor, the husband or the wife and so on. The
masters of the art of *rikka* observed that initially the arrangements are as
stiff and intransigent as the faith of the novice.

If the styles of these arrangements are categorized as 'formal', 'semi-
formal' and 'informal', it will clearly be seen that the ideas to which they
give expression are never themselves really 'formal'. They may thus be
compared with the flower which the Buddha presented to Mahākashyapa
and which replaced all speech and teaching, being the whole cycle of life in
miniature, an image of the perfection to be attained, of spontaneous enlightenment and even an expression of the inexpressible (AVAS, DANA,
GRIF, GUES, HERF, OGRJ).

Evidence as to flower symbolism in the Celtic world is extremely scanty.

It existed, since colour and shape are sometimes compared with those of flowers, but nothing can be stated for certain. Women bearing the name 'flower' included the Welsh Blodeuwedd and the Irish Blathnat. The former was created from a great mass of flowers by magic to be the bride of the god Llew, whom she betrayed with a neighbouring lord. The latter was the wife of Cùroi, 'King of the World', whom she betrayed for love of Cùchulainn (OGAC 10: pp. 399–402).

In this context, flowers would appear to have been symbols of fickleness, not of the adaptability proper to women, but the essential fickleness of something in a constant state of evolution; and especially of the fleeting nature of beauty itself.

This is the significance of the basket of flowers which Lan Ts'ai Ho is often shown carrying. They set in stronger relief his immortality against the fleeting brevity of life, of beauty and of pleasure.

To the Maya the frangipani was a symbol of fornication. It might have represented the Sun as an aspect of the belief in the basic sacred marriage between Sun and Moon. It may equally have meant 'monkey'. It bears the lunar number of FIVE petals, but its hieroglyphic often only shows it with FOUR, four being a solar number (THOH).

Aztec civilization cultivated ornamental garden flowers, not simply as a pleasure for gods and men and a source of inspiration for artists and poets, but the flowers themselves characterized many of their hieroglyphics and symbolized the phases of cosmogonic history. Mexican art, too, is rich with flowers, which would seem to have manifested the infinite variety of the universe and the abundance and wealth of the gifts of the gods. However, this very generalized symbolism was specifically connected with the regular passage of time and with the cosmogonic ages. It gave expression to specific phases in the relationships between gods and men. The flower was, as it were, the yardstick of these relations.

Flowers were associated analogically with BUTTERFLIES and like them often stood for the souls of the dead.

Thus Greek mythological tradition has it that Persephone, to become Queen of the Underworld, was carried off by Hades from the meadows of Sicily, where she was happily gathering flowers with her companions (GRID).

In fact, flowers often stand as archetypal figures of the soul and as spiritual centres. Their precise meaning is determined by their colour, which discloses their psychic bearing. YELLOW gives a solar symbolism; RED, sanguine; BLUE, unreal and dream-like. But the shades of psychic meaning are endless.

The allegorical use of flowers is endless, too, and they are numbered among the attributes of Spring, the dawn, youth, oratory, virtue and so on (TERS pp. 190–3).

fly   To the Njinji tribes, the Bamileke and the Bamum, the fly 'is the symbol of unity . . . In this kingdom of tiny winged insects, unity is strength. A solitary fly is defenceless' (MVEA p. 26).

Flies were sacred creatures to the Ancient Greeks and both Zeus and Apollo bore names which related to flies; perhaps they evoked the turmoil of Olympian life or the omnipresence of the gods.

Their ceaseless buzzing, whirling around and stinging make flies unbearable. They breed from corruption and decay, carry the germs of the foulest diseases and breach all defences against them. They symbolize a ceaseless quest. It was in this sense that an ancient Syrian deity, Beelzebub, whose name meant 'Lord of the Flies', became 'Prince of DEMONS'.

On the other hand flies represent pseudo men-of-action, feverishly busy, useless and importunate like the fly in the fable of the Fly and the Coach, which demanded its wages after having merely watched the others work.

foetus See EMBRYO.

Fomorians Deformed, dark and malign beings of Celtic mythology, who symbolize the counteragents of initiation and psychic development.

font The symbolism of the font used in BAPTISM is akin to that of the CAULDRON in Celtic mythology. It is the BATH which purifies and reinvigorates, it is rebirth as a new being or elevation to a higher order. The font is one of the countless images which correspond to those rites of passage and intiation which raise the individual to a higher plane of existence. Fonts are generally set upon a central pillar which acts as a plinth and which symbolizes the World AXIS around which changing existences revolve. In other instances it rests upon four COLUMNS, recalling the four CARDINAL POINTS and the totality of the universe, or the FOUR Evangelists and the totality of revelation. Fonts are symbols of regeneration.

Fool, the (see also SIMPLETON; TWENTY-TWO; ZERO)   This is the most mysterious, enthralling and hence the most disturbing card in the TAROT. Unlike the other major arcana, numbered from ONE (the JUGGLER) to TWENTY-ONE (the WORLD), the Fool has no number. He is outside the pack, that is the human city, beyond the walls. He walks leaning upon a golden staff, a jester's cap of the same colour on his head, his breeches are torn and, although he is apparently oblivious of the fact, behind him a dog is pulling the cloth and baring his buttocks. Safe behind the walls of his city, the observer concludes that he is a fool. The Hermetic philosopher, however, will mutter that this is a Master, when he notices that the limp bundle which he carries on the end of a stick over his shoulder is WHITE, the colour of secrets and initiation, and that his feet are shod in RED and pace firmly over real ground, not an imaginary base. His pouch is empty but it is pink, like his thighs and the dog which tries to get its teeth into them – symbols of animal nature and of possessions, to none of which he pays heed. By contrast, the STAFF on which he leans is GOLD, the colour of knowledge and of transcendental truth, as is the ground over which he strides, his shoulders and the cap on his head. Most important of all, he walks unhesitatingly, he goes forward.

Some writers call this card Zero, others, Twenty-two. Twenty-one forms a complete cycle, so twenty-two can only mean a return to zero, like a meter. Whether twenty-two or zero, in the symbolism of numbers the Fool denotes the boundaries of speech and what lies beyond computation. This is none other than EMPTINESS, presence overtaken to become absence, ultimate knowledge which becomes ignorance, or culture, which is supposed to be what remains when all else is forgotten. The Fool is not nothingness, but rather the emptiness of the Sufic *fanā'*, when no possessions are needed, the individual's consciousness becoming that of the world and of its totality in human and physical terms. From it the individual has cut his or her way in order to go still further forward. If emptiness it be, it is the gap separating the completed cycle from the cycle to come. Chaboche observes that ELEVEN and its multiples are 'advancing Suns' (FRCH p. 165). And so it is with the Fool; be he zero or twenty-two, he goes forward, conspicuously solar, across the virgin soil of knowledge beyond the city of men.

foot, footprint, footstep   The legends are well-known: that of the Buddha at his birth measuring out the universe by taking SEVEN steps in each of the quarters of space; or that of Vishnu doing the same thing with THREE strides, the first corresponding to the Earth, the second to the intermediate world and the third to Heaven, and also, as is sometimes said, to dawn, noon and sunset. In East Asia innumerable *Vishnupada* and *Buddhapada* and even the occasional *Shivapada* are worshipped. They are the footprints of God, of the BODHISATTVA upon human earth. Similarly Christ's footprints are shown on the Mount of Olives, those of the Immortal P'ong-chu on Mount Tao-ying and those of Muhammad at Mecca and in several of the great mosques. The mother of the Millet Prince Hu-chi gave birth to him because she stepped in the footprint of the Celestial Emperor. 'Pilgrims' footprints' are to be found round many shrines. 'In making his mark, the pilgrim is not saying "I was here", but stating "here I am and here I stay", as the occasional inscriptions found in them bear witness when they express the desire to remain in the presence of the godhead' (SOUP p. 59).

And yet it is said of the Buddha and the great Buddhist saints that they are out of reach, untrackable. Here we come to the universal symbolism of the footprint which is the track which the hunter follows in life and the spiritual huntsman in symbol. But these tracks only take us to 'the GATEWAY of the Sun', to the bounds of the cosmos. Beyond that they vanish, since the godhead, SERPENT-like, loses his feet at the beginning and at the end. Within the context of a hierarchical order of spiritual states, the footprint of the higher state is lost in the foot of the vertical AXIS and hence in the central state which is that of the 'True Man' of Chinese tradition (*chen-jen*). It is therefore impossible to discern the footprint in question unless in that central state.

In the myth of Vaishvanara, it is easy to explain why feet correspond to Earth, with which they made contact in bodily manifestation. Furthermore, when the Buddha is represented aniconically (i.e. not in human or animal form), the footprints, too, correspond to the Earth, the throne to the intermediate world and the parasol to Heaven (BAHB, COOH, GUEV, SOUJ). In more down-to-earth fashion, the foot also symbolizes a sense of reality, as when we say somebody 'has their feet firmly on the ground'.

Because it is the point of balance when walking, the Dogon regard the foot first and foremost as the symbol of stability, giving expression to notions of chieftancy, of kingship and of power. But underlying this is also the notion of 'beginnings', the Bambara saying that the foot is the first limb which the foetus puts forth (ZAHB p. 51). But the foot also points to the end, since walking begins and ends with movement of the feet, so they are symbols not simply of power but of coming and going, akin to the symbolism of the KEY, itself an expression of the idea of rule.

In so far as they are the 'beginning', the feet may be contrasted with the HEAD, which is the end of the body. Although, as Zahan notes, the Bambara observe that this 'beginning' is forgotten, neglected and misused, they teach that 'the head is powerless without the feet'; this, as Zahan concludes, is a way of emphasizing 'that man's divine nature is dependent upon his human nature' (ZAHB).

The human foot leaves its mark upon the paths which, for good or ill, are chosen by the exercise of free will. Conversely, the foot bears the marks of the path taken, for good or ill. This explains ritual WASHING of the feet as a rite of purification. During the initiation ceremonies of the Bektāshī dervishes, the spiritual leader pronounces these words as he washes the candidates' feet: 'The God of Mercy and Compassion sets us under the obligation of washing you each time from the pollution left by the paths of error and rebellion along which you have walked' (HUAS p. 183).

Angels' feet are winged to show their agility and their ceaseless and speeding flight towards the godhead (according to the Pseudo-Dionysius the Areopagite). Thus HERMES (Mercury) had wings on his heels.

Both Jungian and Freudian analysts would see phallic significance in the foot, while footwear would be a feminine symbol since the foot has to fit inside it. American investigators have placed the foot fifth in ranking order of sexual attractiveness after eyes, hair, the body as a whole and the buttocks. These results are, however, highly controversial, since, as Professor Hesnard has so rightly pointed out (HAVE pp. 40–1):

The normal male is sexually and physically attracted to the woman of his desires by a structure (*Gestalt*) and not by any commonplace aggregate of its parts. That is to say he is attracted by the whole, by a totality in which each part exists for the lover only to the extent that its specific quality contributes to the significance of the entire personality, both physical and psychic. . . . Erotic preferences for the foot fall into line with a structuralization of woman and involves elements which are linked to fixations, to the subject's actual experience, perhaps occurring in childhood, which have been retained by the unconscious through lack of erotic maturity.

Restif de la Bretonne had a foot fetish and footwear provided him with powerful sexual stimulation. If not the fountain, the foot seems at least to be one of the poles of sexual attraction. Feet are an erotic symbol of mixed power, strongest at opposite social extremes, among the least and the most highly cultivated.

The discovery of its feet plays an important part in a child's psychological development.

To stroke somebody else's feet, especially if they are well formed, can become a real passion for some children and many adults admit to the survival of the same impulse which seems to cause them to feel intense pleasure. The interest which some mothers take in their children's toes and to which they give expression with a violent and barely credible passion, is frequent and contains a substantial sexual factor in it.

(HAVE p. 40)

A male whose sexual development has followed a normal pattern will find that the phallic significance of the foot will tend to lessen as he gains an objective view of the functions proper to each of his limbs and bodily organs.

According to Paul Diel, the foot is also a symbol of the strength of the soul, since it is the basis of the upright stance characteristic of human beings. Vulnerability in (Achilles), injury to (HEPHAISTOS) or any deformity of the foot betrays a weakness of the soul (see ONE-LEGGED). (See also SHOES; SLIPPER).

ford Throughout Celtic literature, fords are the approved arena for single combat and it was in fords that Cùchulainn killed most of the warriors whom the Irish sent against him. Fords were therefore above all meeting-places and boundary-points. Many place-names in Ireland include the word 'ford', first and foremost the capital of the Republic, Dublin, *Baile Atha Cliath*, 'Town by the Ford of Hurdles' (WINI 5: *passim*).

Archeological excavations have often unearthed weapons on sites of fords in Ancient Gaul. This would tend to prove that the Irish custom of single combat at fords existed among the continental Celts and Bretons and was related to that of passage and travel. Inscriptions from the Roman period provide evidence of a goddess called Ritona who may be regarded as being the patroness or presiding deity of combat in fords. The Irish hero Cùchulainn was fighting in a ford when the war-goddess changed herself into an eel and wrapped herself round his legs (LOUP p. 186).

Fords symbolize the struggle to gain possession of a narrow passage, from one world to another or from one inner state to another. They bring together the symbolism of WATER (the place of rebirth) and of opposite banks (places of confrontation, crossing and dangerous passages).

foreskin The Bambara and Dogon of Mali believe that each individual is born with two souls of opposite sex. The foreskin is the female soul in material shape in the man, hence the practice of CIRCUMCISION, which removes this original ambivalence and confirms the male in his sexual polarization. According to their myths, the foreskins of the circumcised are transformed into 'sun-lizards', the Heavens possessing female properties for the Dogon and Bambara (GRIE).

forest In many parts of the world and especially in the Celtic world, forests constituted truly natural shrines. Such were the forests of Broceliand and the Dodona of the Ancient Greeks. In India, the *sannyāsin* and the Buddhist hermit retire to the forests. 'Forests are sweet,' we read in the *Dhammapada*, 'when the world does not enter them. There the saint may find his REST.'

In Japan the TORII mark not so much the entrance to a temple as to a natural shrine which is more often than not a PINE-forest. In China, a MOUNTAIN-top capped by forest is generally the site of a temple.

The forest which truly forms the mountain's HAIR is its source of strength, since it allows the mountain to call down RAIN, in other words and in every sense of the term, the blessings of Heaven. The Jade Emperor Yu cut down TREES in order to attack mountains. Feeling insulted at having been greeted on Mount Kiang by a storm, Chin Che Huangti had all the trees felled in revenge. On this, as on other occasions, the First Emperor was probably unaware of the favourable symbolism of this welcome (GRAD, SCHP).

In the early period there was a strict semantic equivalence between the Celtic forest and the shrine, or *nemeton*. As a symbol of life, the tree may be regarded as a link or intermediary between the Earth into which its roots delve and the vault of Heaven which its topmost branches brush. In Gaul, stone temples were only erected under the Roman influence and after the Roman conquest (OGAC 12: pp. 185–97).

Contemporary psychoanalysts regard the darkness of the forest and the deep roots of its trees as symbolizing the unconscious. The terrors of the forest, like all panic terrors, are inspired, Jung believed, by fear of what the unconscious may reveal.

fortress See CASTLE.

Fortune In Ancient Rome, Fortune was the goddess who symbolized the capricious and arbitrary forces which control human life. She was inexorable, not from malevolence or hatred but through apparent indifference to the consequences of her whims or of chance. She was depicted with a rudder, since she was the steerswoman of life, but was also depicted as a blind goddess.

Later she was assimilated to ISIS and Tyche and became the goddess of luck, the HORN OF PLENTY her attribute. She promoted fertility, prosperity and victory, and an increasing number of temples were built in her honour.

forty Forty is the number of waiting, of preparation, of testing and of punishment. This first aspect is undoubtedly the least understood and the most important. It might be said that the writers of the Bible set milestones along the way of salvation by endowing major events with this number. It is thus characteristic of God's intervention in human affairs and indeed the one is the mark of the other. Like Saul, David reigned for forty years (2 Samuel 5: 4) and Solomon likewise (1 Kings 11: 42). The covenant with Noah followed the Flood which lasted forty days; Moses was summoned by God at the age of forty and remained for forty days on the top of Mount Sinai. Jesus preached for forty months and the risen Christ appeared to his disciples during the forty days preceding his Ascension (Acts 1: 3).

The emphasis is just as often placed upon testing or punishment. The faithless Children of Israel were condemned to wander for forty years in the Wilderness (Numbers 32: 13). Sinful mankind was punished by forty days of rain (Genesis 7: 4). Jesus, standing for the new race of mankind, was taken to the Temple forty days after his birth, emerged victorious from a Temptation which lasted forty days (Matthew 4: 2) and rose from the dead forty hours after being placed in the tomb.

According to Allendy (ALLN p. 385), the number forty marks 'the completion of a cycle'. This cycle, however, does not end simply to resume the same pattern, but ends in a radical change or a passage to a fresh level of activity or of living. Thus both the Buddha and the Prophet Muhammad began their mission at the age of forty while Lent, the period of preparation for the Resurrection at Easter, lasts for forty days.

In Black Africa, and particularly among the Fulani, funerals last for forty nights when a bull is over twenty-one or a man over 105. For the supreme initiation of the Kamo, the Bambara offer in sacrifice forty cowries, forty horses and forty head of cattle. The expression 'twice forty' means a hundred (HAMK p. 23), or the virtually uncountable.

The number plays an important part in the death rituals of many different peoples. It is in fact the number of days needed to ensure that the corpse is free of all living matter, however subtle, that is to say of all his or her SOULS. Since, according to these beliefs, the dead person is not completely dead until this length of time has passed, the fortieth day is that on which the final mourning taboos are lifted. The same period of time also applies to women after childbirth. It is also when rites of purification are performed, the dead person's relatives only then being freed from all obligations to the deceased.

It is also the length of time which must elapse before the body is disinterred, the bones cleansed and set in their final resting-place by those peoples who practice the custom of secondary burial, notably among the Indian tribes of equatorial America. Among Altaic peoples it was the day on which the widow pronounced the ritual words, 'Now I leave you', which made her free to take a second husband. On this day, too, the yurt was purified (HARA pp. 227–8). The custom of 'placing in quarantine' (from the Italian word *quarantina*, 'forty days' arises from the belief that forty symbolizes a cycle of being or of non-being.

forty-nine Being SEVEN squared, this number carries the same cyclic significance for Lamaism as does the number FORTY for Jews, Christians and Muslims (HARA p. 233). It is the length of time needed by the soul of a dead person to reach its new abode. It is the ending of a journey.

fountain See SPRING.

four The symbolic meanings of the number four are linked to those of the CROSS and the SQUARE. 'Almost from prehistoric times, the number four was employed to signify what was solid, what could be touched and felt. Its relationship to the cross made it an outstanding symbol of wholeness and universality, a symbol which drew all to itself.' Where lines of latitude and longitude intersect, they divide the Earth into four portions. Throughout the world kings and chieftains have been called 'Lord of the Four Seas' ... 'Lord of the Four Suns' ... 'Lord of the Four Quarters of the Earth' ... by which is understood the extent of their powers both territorially and in terms of total control of their subjects' doings (CHAS p. 31).

There are four CARDINAL POINTS, four WINDS, four COLUMNS of the Universe, four phases of the Moon, four seasons, four ELEMENTS, four humours, four letters in the name of God (JHVH or YHVH) and of the first man (ADAM), four arms to the cross, four Evangelists and so on. The Pythagorean TETRAKTYS is the product of the sum of the first four numbers (1 + 2 + 3 + 4). Four symbolizes the earthly, the totality of the created and the revealed.

This totality of created things is at the same time the totality of all that perishes, and it is strange that, in Japanese, the same word, *shi*, means both 'four' and 'death'. However, the Japanese take great care to avoid using the word, replacing it in everyday conversation by *yo* or *yon*.

In the Vedas, four is a sacred number, they themselves being divided into four parts – hymns, spells, chants and sacrificial formulae. Human beings are themselves composed of SIXTEEN parts (four squared) according to the *Chāndogya Upanishad*, as is the spell for SOMA (comprising sixteen chants). This also applies to the instruction concerning the Brahman, which is divided into four quarters corresponding to the four domains of the universe, the regions of space, worlds, lights and senses. When the disciple knows the four quarters of the Brahman, or four times four-sixteenths, he possesses all the knowledge of his Master. Once again, then, four, together with its multiples and divisors, is seen to be the symbol of totality.

In the Bible, and especially in the Book of Revelation, four also suggests this notion of universality, the four living creatures being the totality of all living beings in the world of light (they are covered with eyes). The four HORSEMEN carry the four great plagues, the COLOURS of their horses corresponding to the colours of the cardinal points and those of the day, to show the universality of their action within space and time. White is east and dawn; red, south and noon; grey, west and dusk; black, north and night. The four destroying angels standing at the four corners of the Earth (Revelation 7: 1); the four rivers of Paradise (Genesis 2: 10ff.); the four walls of the Heavenly Jerusalem, facing the four points of the compass; the four camps for the twelve tribes of Israel (Numbers 2); the four emblems of the tribes, one for each group of three, lion, man, bull and eagle; the four letters of the name of God, YHVH, each one according to Jewish tradition corresponding to one of these emblems – Y with man, H with lion, V with bull and the second H with eagle; the four Evangelists – there could not, St Irenaeus says, have been more nor less – and each of these emblems of the tribes of Israel attributed to one of the four Evangelists and agreeing, in a most peculiar way, with the characteristics of the Gospel concerned – the lion to St Mark, the man to St Matthew, the bull (or ox) to St Luke and the eagle to St John; these creatures, furthermore, corresponding with the cardinal constellations in the signs of the ZODIAC – TAURUS (bull), LEO (lion), Aquila (eagle) and AQUARIUS (man); all these groups of four symbolize a totality (CHAS p. 429).

In Ezekiel's vision (Ezekiel 1: 4ff.), dating from around 593 BC, this extraordinary symbolism may already be seen.

And I looked, and, behold . . . out of the midst thereof came the likeness of four living creatures. And this was their appearance; they had the likeness of a man. And every one had four faces, and every one had four wings. And as for the likeness of their faces, they four had the face of a man, and the face of a lion, on the right side: and they four had the face of an ox on the left side; they four also had the face of an eagle.

Commentators detect the symbol of Jehovah's power of movement and spiritual ubiquity, not being tied only to the Temple in Jerusalem, but assuring his presence among the faithful wherever their place of exile. The *Jerusalem Bible* commentators also observe that the strange creatures of Ezekiel's vision are reminiscent of the Assyrian *karibu* (a name akin to that of the great winged creatures over the ark, *see* Ex[odus] 25: 18), creatures with a human head, the body of a lion, the hooves of a bull and the wings of an eagle; their effigies stood guard outside the palaces of Babylon. These servants of the gods are here shown harnessed to the chariot of the God of Israel, a vivid illustration of Yahweh's transcendence.

They also held up

a throne, as the appearance of a sapphire stone; and upon the likeness of the throne was the likeness as the appearance of a man above upon it. And I saw as the colour of amber, as the appearance of fire round about within it, from the appearance of his loins even upward, and from the appearance of his loins even downward, I saw as it were the appearance of fire, and it had brightness round about. As the appearance of the bow that is in the cloud in the day of rain, so was the appearance of the brightness round about. This was the appearance of the likeness of the glory of the Lord.

(Ezekiel 1: 26–8)

No better idea of God's transcendental superiority can be suggested than by this climb up the stairway of Heaven in terms of all these quaternaries.

Although more generally applied to the phenomenal world, four is again the number characteristic of the Universe in its totality. In the Old Testament both Jeremiah (49: 36) and Ezekiel (37: 9) speak of the four winds, while two visions in Daniel (chapters 2 and 7) distinguish four great periods of time embracing the whole of human history.

The number four plays a distinctive part in North American Indian philosophy and thought. It is 'conceived as a principle of organization, and in some sense as a potency' (ALEC p. 164). Space is divided into four regions, time measured in four units (day, night, moon and year); plants have four parts (root, stem, flower and fruit); there are four different animal species, those which crawl, those which fly, those which move on four feet and those which move on two; the four heavenly bodies are the sky, the Sun, the Moon and the stars and there are four winds which move in a circle round the Earth. Human life is divided into four 'hills', childhood, youth, maturity and old age; there are four basic qualities in man – courage, endurance, generosity and faithfulness – and four in woman – skill, hospitality, faithfulness and fruitfulness – and so on.

Four is also the number of completion. 'We have now made four times four circuits of the lodge . . . Four times four means completeness. Now all the forces above and below, male and female, have been remembered and called upon to be with us' (from the Pawnee Hako ceremony, in ALEC p. 120). On the metaphysical plane, Wakantanka, the Great Mystery, is a 'Quaternity [of] the God-Chief, the God-Spirit, the God-Creator and the God-Executive' (ALEC p. 166). Each of these gods is himself a quaternity of two opposing dyads.

Calling to mind that Pythagoras' disciples, too, made the tetrad the key to a numerical symbolism which was capable of giving structure to the mechanism of the world, Alexander regards the Dakota Indian pantheon as 'New World Pythagoreanism'.

In the Maya-Quiché tradition of the *Popol-Vuh,* there were four successive creations, corresponding to the four Suns and the four ages. Definitive humans only appeared in the last of these ages as Maize-Man (GIRP).

Full initiation into the Algonquin Indians' medicine men's lodge passed through four degrees corresponding to the symbol of a quadripartite universe. The Great Manitu who presided over the fourth degree was represented by a series of quaternary symbols, among them a cross upon a four-sided pillar, each face of the pillar painted in a cosmic çolour.

In Zuni Pueblo Indian cosmogony, based upon a primal sacred marriage of Heaven and Earth, Earth was called 'fourfold Earth-Mother, the container'. This confirms the worldwide symbolic quality of the number four as that of passive matter. Like the Earth, four does not create, but contains all that is created subsequently. Its property is potentiality. While four is the number of Earth, by extrapolation it may be applied to the supreme godhead, in that as the ALPHA AND OMEGA containing all things, he entrusts to Demiurges the task of creation and of bringing to life what is within him.

In addition to the four elements and the four quarters of the Earth which Pueblo Indians believed were ruled by the four rain-gods and the Maya by the four tigers or JAGUARS which guarded the village crops, the Zuni also believed that underground there were four CAVERNS, the 'four wombs of the Earth-Mother'. From the lowest level and the thickest darkness in the world, came mankind, thanks to the deeds of the divine Twins, the Ayahuta warriors, created by the Sun and sent by him to look for mankind. To reach light, men had to pass through the world of soot, the world of sulphur, the world of mist and the world of wings (H. Lehman).

The chronicler Poma de Ayala similarly states the Peruvian belief in the four mythic ages which preceded the creation of man in his present form.

To sum up, four may be seen as the sign of potentiality awaiting the manifestation which occurs with the number FIVE.

The Dogon of Mali regard four as the number of womanhood and, by extension, of the SUN, and symbol of the primeval womb. The fertilized womb, represented as an egg with an opening in the base, an earthly replica of the intact Cosmic Egg, has the numerical value of four (top, two sides and opening in the bottom) (GRIS). The FORESKIN is also called 'four' since it is regarded as a man's female soul and this is the reason for male circumcision.

The Dogon regard one as falsehood and uncleanness. Purity is that accuracy which demands that all created things should be two in one, the twinning achieved by the association of opposing principles (see under SOUL). It is for this reason that four becomes the symbol of creation in the guise of its double, EIGHT. At the beginning of time there were eight families of mankind, animals, plants and so on. However, the Dogon and Bambara regard perfection as the number SEVEN, since it brings together two opposing principles or sexes, four for the female principle and three for the male (DIEB).

Among the characteristic cultural features of West African coastal tribes living between the mouths of the Senegal and Congo Rivers, are the converse sexual connotations of the numbers three and four, four being a male symbol and three a female (FROA). Such inversion is, however, exceptional.

According to Sufi tradition and that of ancient Turkish congregations of Dervishes, four, the number of the elements, is the number of GATES through

which the adept has to pass on his mystic way. With each of these gates one
of the elements is associated, in the following order of progression: Air,
Fire, Water, Earth. Their symbolism may be interpreted as follows: at the
first gate (the Shariat), the neophyte who only knows 'the Book', that is to
say the letter of religion, is left in the Air, that is, in a void. He is fired when
he passes the threshold of initiation, represented by the second gate, which
is that of the Way (*tarīqa*), in other words his acceptance of the rule of the
order of his choice, those who have passed this second gate sometimes
being called hermits (*zahitler*). The third gate reveals mystic knowledge to
the man, who becomes posseded of gnosis (*ārif*); it corresponds to the
element of Water. Lastly, the man who reaches God and becomes rooted
in him as in the Sole Reality (*haqq*) passes through the fourth and last
gateway of Haqiqat into the densest element of Earth. These elect are
called the Lovers. The progression from Air to Earth is the exact opposite
of mystic development as normally envisaged by European minds; and yet
the Way of Perfection of an Ibn Mansur el Alladj or a Jalāl-al-Dīn
Muhammad Rūmī is not so far from that of St Teresa of Avila or of St John
of the Cross. However, Sufi teachings, more clearly perhaps than Christian
mysticism, postulate that what we term reality is only a reflection – and
therefore unreal – of the one, transcendental and divine reality, hidden
behind the veil of duality which separates the unbeliever from God and
therefore places him in a state of sin (BIRD pp. 95ff.). It should be observed that only one of these gateways, the second, is associated with the
purifying and transforming symbolism of fire and encompasses an initiatory
threshold. The stages of mystical ascension, properly so-called, are therefore only three – *tarīqa*, *ma'rifa* and *haqīqāt*. This brings the doctrine very
close to the three degrees of perfection recognized by the Neoplatonists of
Alexandria – virtue, wisdom and ecstasy. 'The first degree corresponded to
the perfection of social life and was attained by the practice of the moral
virtues; mental contemplation acquired the second; and religious exaltation
the highest degree' (MONA p. 53). Such notions were the common property of pagans, such as Plotinus, and Christians, such as St Clement of
Alexandria.

These four stages or gateways of spiritual perfection may be compared
with the quaternary development of the *anima* according to Jung's theories.
The analyst takes as archetypal figures 'Eve, which represents purely instinctual and biological relations. . . . Faust's Helen . . . personifies a romantic and aesthetic level that is, however, still characterized by sexual
elements. . . . The Virgin Mary – a figure who raises love (*eros*) to the heights
of spiritual devotion.' And finally the Shulamite in the Song of Solomon
'symbolized by Sapientia, wisdom transcending even the most holy and
the most pure' (JUNS p. 185). According to Marie-Louise von Franz, the
Mona Lisa would also represent this fourth and final stage in the development of the *anima*. All the same, it is patently obvious how the spiritual-
istic conception of the Jungian school differs from traditional mystical
hierarchies.

Be that as it may, the whole system of Jungian thought is based upon the
fundamental importance which he attached to the number four and he
regarded quaternity as 'the archetypal basis of the human psyche' (JACC

p. 139), that is to say 'the totality of conscious and unconscious psychic processes' (JUNT). His entire analysis of psychological types rests upon his theory of the four basic functions of the conscious, thought, feeling, intuition and sensation. In this instance the psychoanalyst displays an attitude of mind which appears to have remained a human constant since the Stone Age. It runs from the crossed arms of the four cardinal points, a basic in all cosmogonies, through initiatory rituals and the theories of the alchemists, for whom quaternity was a fundamental axiom in the completion of the Great Work and the quest for the Philosopher's Stone.

four hundred See HUNDRED; TWENTY.

fox 'Semper peccator, semper justus' (ever sinning, ever righteous), so Germaine Dieterlen sums up the verdict of African folk wisdom upon this creature and adds: 'Independent, yet liking company; busy and inventive, yet destructive, too; bold but cowardly; alert and cunning but equally careless, [the fox] embodies the contradictions inherent in human nature' (GRIP p. 52). The most archaic beliefs about foxes have survived in North America and in Siberia. The Indians of central California regarded the silver fox as a culture-hero, while in Siberia the crafty messenger from Hell, who lured the legendary hero underground, was often depicted in the shape of a black fox (HARA). The latter probably had the powers of a conductor of souls, as Celtic tradition also confirms. In several Breton folktales a young man or a young prince sets out in quest of a charm to cure his sick father and succeeds where his two elder brothers have failed. Having spent all his money on the funeral expenses of some stranger, he soon meets a white fox which helps him in his quest with its advice. Once the search is over, the fox reveals that he is the soul of the dead person buried by the young man's charity; and then he vanishes. Foxes also feature in Scottish folk-songs.

In Japan the fox is a fertility symbol and companion of Inari, the god of plenty, with whom the animal is so closely identified as occasionally to become the focus of worship. As the etymology of his name shows, Inari is the Shintō god of the larder and of the cultivation of mulberry trees for silkworms. Not only does he protect the larder, but even now shopkeepers and businessmen keep a little altar in their homes consecrated to the fox, so that he will watch over their affairs. At the entrance to temples dedicated to Inari, numbers of effigies of foxes are set in pairs facing one another. One will have the key of the rice-store in his mouth, the other a bowl representing the spirit of the larder. The creature itself is called Kitsune, and popular superstition blames it for cases of hysteria and demonic possession. Inari is thus used in its religious and beneficent sense; Kitsune in its common and maleficent connotation.

The association of foxes with fertility-gods no doubt arises from the vigour and strength of their appetites, and these have given them an almost worldwide reputation of being Don Juans and even, as we shall see, female Don Juans. Van Gulik observes that in China in the Ch'u Kingdom 'foxes were believed to possess plenty of vital force because they live in earths and are therefore close to the generative powers of Earth itself. In consequence foxes were thought to enjoy longevity' (VANG p. 267).

Throughout the Far East, this aspect of fox symbolism takes shape in a

number of different beliefs. It is sometimes held that foxes possess the elixir
of life, or else that they are the cause of a demonic possession which can
be cured only by the war-god, Kuan-ti. However, exorcistic powers also
belong to the Taoist Heavenly Master who shuts foxes in jars. Having
achieved longevity, the animal may become the fabled Heavenly Fox with
Nine Tails. In Ancient China the Fox with Nine Tails lived in the Green
Country of the South; it was a man-eating monster which could, however,
protect from witchcraft (HERS, MASR, MAST, OGRJ).

Mention has already been made of the amorous reputation of foxes,
which were long held – and in some parts of the Far East are still believed
– to play the part of *succubi* and, more especially, of *incubi*. The belief that
they changed themselves into young men to seduce women, but more frequently into women to seduce men, made folk wisdom conclude 'that a fox
which seduced a woman could cause little harm to a man, but that the real
damage was done by women who could enchant like foxes.'

In its lasciviousness the fox is symbolically akin to the rabbit, and indeed
some Amerindian myths attribute the rabbit which can be seen in a pattern
of Moon-craters to an affair between a sky-fox and the Moon (GARC).

Providing, as it does, a mirror image of the contradictions in the human
character, the fox might be considered the double of human consciousness.
The Chinese maintain that foxes are the only creatures to greet the sunrise,
prostrating themselves by kneeling on their hindlegs, clasping their fore-
paws and stretching them out in front. The fox which has done this over a
period of years then becomes able to change its shape and live among
mankind without being noticed – once again a mirror image of so many
foxy characters in the world.

frangipani   See under FLOWER.

Freemasonry   Masonic symbols are mentioned, as the occasion arises, in
the articles ACACIA, COLUMN, COMPASSES, G, HIRAM, TRIANGLE, etc. The Tracing Boards reproduced here enable the symbolism of the Brotherhood to
be shown in abridged and concise fashion.

At the beginning of a Lodge meeting, a SQUARE carpet, called the Tracing
Board, is spread over the floor upon the Chequered Pavement in which the
alternation of black and white slabs symbolizes the way in which positive
and negative, the two cosmic principles, complement one another. At the
close of the meeting the Tracing Board is removed in a ritual which balances its laying. Originally the Tracing Board was actually traced upon the
floor at the opening of each meeting and rubbed out when it ended. Each
Masonic degree has a Board appropriate to it, but here we shall touch only
upon the basic initiatory foundations of Freemasonry. These, in any case,
contain all the symbols of the Brotherhood and of its three degrees, Entered Apprentice, Fellowcraft and Master Mason. The Tracing Board gathers into an organized schema the symbols peculiar to each degree and
provides Masons with a conspectus in graphic form of Masonic esotericism.

Here are some of the differences between the Tracing Board of the En-
tered Apprentice and that of the Fellowcraft Mason, which is illustrated.
The overall layout is the same, but on the Fellowcraft Mason's Tracing
Board there are two spheres on top of the columns J∴ and B∴ where the

Tracing Board: Fellowcraft's Lodge

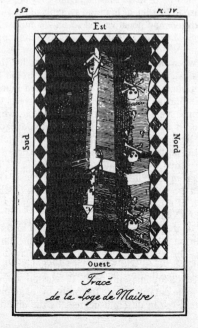

Tracing Board: Master Mason's Lodge

Entered Apprentice's columns have pomegranates; there are FIVE (and
sometimes SEVEN) steps leading to Solomon's Porch instead of THREE; the
symbol of the Blazing Star marked in the centre with the letter G is to be
seen; the three windows open outwards; and the pointed stone CUBE is also
there. On the Fellowcraft Mason's Tracing Board all the symbols of the
Mason's work are methodically arranged – the tools by whose aid, operating in initiatory fashion upon himself, the Mason will turn himself slowly
but surely into a stone no longer raw but fit to be incorporated into that
great human and cosmic Building which must be constructed here on Earth.
Traditionally, speculative Freemasonry claims to be heir to the working
masons of the Middle Ages, that is to say to the initiatory heritage of the
cathedral builders.

The really basic symbols of Freemasonry are borrowed from the builder's
craft and underpin a psychological and spiritual development. They include
HAMMER and CHISEL, tools with which the apprentice will dress the raw stone;
SQUARE and COMPASSES, LEVEL, PLUMB LINE and RULE. So far as the pointed
STONE cube is concerned, its symbolism applies to the structure of reality
itself. It is the quaternary of the four traditional elements, AIR, WATER, FIRE
and EARTH, surmounted by the divine ternary. It also provides an example
of a figurative representation of the quintessence, regarded by alchemists as
the fifth element, created by a synthesis of the other four. Architectural
symbolism is enriched by that of the Old Testament. The porch, up to
which the steps lead, is Solomon's Porch, while the two columns, J∴ (Jachin)
and B∴ (Boaz), male and female, are those which tradition says stood on
either side of the Porch. In all Masonic Halls they are depicted at the West
end and they are to be seen as material symbols of the two polarities – male
and female, positive and negative and so on – continually in confrontation
in the phenomenal world. This struggle and essential opposition is symbolized by the Chequered Pavement, which shows how inseparable is the confrontation between the two cosmic polarities. As for the Blazing Star, or
PENTAGRAM, its five points may well take it back to the Pythagoreans who,
like the Freemasons, regarded five as their sacred number. It will be observed that the Blazing Star faces east, which suggests that it may well be
a HERMAPHRODITE symbol. In fact, the Blazing Star, which in various religious traditions is associated with the female godhead, for example the
association of the pentagram with Our Lady, might well stand as an ideal
expression of the perfect conjunction between two opposing polarities, their
confrontation turned to fusion and unity. The letter G inscribed upon the
Star has been given such different meanings as 'gnosis' (knowledge), 'God',
'geometry' and 'generation', the last named being possible as an interpretation for each of the degrees, because of the conjunction of positive and
negative, in the Columns J∴ and B∴.

At the top of the Tracing Board the SUN and MOON are to be seen, a
recurrence, but on a higher plane, of the complementarity of the two cosmic principles. This might remind us of the part played in Freemasonry by
the solar and lunar cycles which rule all earthly life, the former being predominantly active. Freemasonry is to be classed among those initiation
societies with male polarity, hence the problems of admitting women to the
Masonic Mystery felt in different degrees by the different Grand Lodges.

There is a twofold significance in the substitution of two SPHERES for the two pomegranates on the tops of the columns J∴ and B∴. It may well both symbolize a growing control of the passions and, since one sphere is terrestrial and the other celestial, embody the fields of the Mason's activities.

The Tracing Board is bordered by a length of ROPE ending in tassels and knotted in a special way in love-KNOTS. They symbolize the bonds which unite all members of the Brotherhood, those living, those who have passed to the Eternal Orient and those of generations unborn. The knots, which are shaped like the mathematical symbol for infinity ∞, might well symbolize the nature of the Mason's task, always unfinished, always to be resumed.

The Master Mason's Tracing Board depicts the coffin of Hiram, the legendary builder of Solomon's Temple, lying on the Chequered Pavement, its slabs lozenge-shaped, rather than square as hitherto. The coffin is covered by a pall embroidered with silver tears and decorated with a Latin cross as well as with six sets of human skulls and cross-bones. The head of the coffin, inscribed with the letter G, lies to the west and the foot, on which rest square and compasses, to the east, the left of the Tracing Board corresponding to the north, the right to the south. It is worth remembering in this context that in so many traditions the Land of the Dead lies to the West. The CROSS is a patent symbol of sacrifice. The acacia branch lying on the middle of the coffin is a reminder of the legend of Hiram, typical of those initiation legends in which symbols of the new life and of resurrection replace those of death. Hiram is the hero and initiate who, by accepting the complete sacrifice of himself as an individual, attains thereby to a state of liberation in which he is enabled to work for the cause to which he is devoted and which overrides individual concerns. The cross is, therefore, not simply a funeral symbol but also a symbol of complete human liberation, the twofold blossoming of the spirit, horizontally and vertically; in other words, to the four cardinal points on the one hand and along the AXIS from ZENITH to nadir on the other. Similarly the Masonic temple is placed in correspondence to the world in its wholeness and to the six spatial coordinates. The cross-bones under the skulls form a saltire (diagonal), a symbol of life and of perfection. As regards the LOZENGES on the floor, they are none other than a combination of right-angle and inverted TRIANGLES (the earthly and the divine) and display the Resurrection ruling the upper and lower realms of reality.

frog Frogs were employed in many symbolic guises, but chiefly in relation to their natural element – WATER. In Ancient China, frogs were used, or imitated, as RAIN-makers. They figured upon bronze DRUMS because they recall the THUNDER and summon the rain. Frogs – sometimes confused with TOADS – are lunar creatures, corresponding to the *yin* element of water. At the equinoxes, the QUAIL, a FIRE (*yang*) bird, was believed to change into a frog, a water (*yin*) creature, and then turn back into a quail, in accordance with the basic rhythm of the seasons. However – and these different viewpoints are not unrelated – in India, the Great Frog (*Mahamandūka*) was said to hold up the Universe and was a symbol of unenlightened, undifferentiated matter. This is why the sixty-four-square MANDALA is sometimes called 'the frog'; this is the mandala which is said to be the corpse of a conquered *asura*.

Even in the West frogs have been regarded as a resurrection symbol because of the changes in their life-cycle. The Montagnards of southern Vietnam believe that they, like SPIDERS, are a shape taken by souls in their travels, while the body sleeps. To harm a frog, therefore, is to risk hurting the owner of the soul in question.

Elijah the Ecdicus made frogs a symbol of those fragmentary and disjointed thoughts which distract contemplatives still too firmly attached to the material concerns of this world. His viewpoint finds an echo in the Vietnamese seizing upon the frog's ceaseless and mindless croaking, which they have made the symbol in countless metaphors of dull and stereotyped teaching (BURE, DAMS, DURV, PHIL, PORA).

The Vedas portray frogs as embodiments of the Earth made fertile by the first Spring rains, croaking their thanksgiving to Heaven for the promise of rich harvests made to Earth. Their drunkenness is mentioned and they are compared with 'brahmins who speak around a full bowl of soma' and 'the officiating priests [who] come forth heated and sweating'. They are Mother-Earth's choristers and priests and the hymn to the frogs in the *Rig-Veda* ends: 'By giving hundreds of cows, the frogs have prolonged life in a thousand Soma-pressings' (VEDR pp. 233–4).

During the months of Winter drought, the Earth is silent and sterile. The sudden chorus of frogs is the manifestation of renewal fulfilled, the sign of nature's yearly reawakening.

The Japanese believe that the frog attracts good fortune by its habit of sitting panting. They also say that however far you may take it, a frog always returns to its point of departure. The Japanese word *kaeru* also means 'to return'. Some people carry lucky charms in the shape of frogs, known as 'stand-ins', meaning, in other words, that if their owners encounter dangerous situations the frogs will take their places.

In the Ancient Egyptian ogdoad, or group of EIGHT, which comprises four pairs of elemental forces which existed before the creation of the world, frogs are coupled with SERPENTS: 'Obscure forces in a world still not organised . . . creatures self-created in the primaeval waters' (POSD p. 194).

fruit The symbol of abundance, spilling from the fertility-goddess's HORN OF PLENTY, or from the bowls of banqueting gods. Because of the SEEDS, stones or pips which fruit contains, Guénon compares it with the World EGG, a symbol of the beginning of things. In literature fruits have been endowed with symbolic meanings (see APPLE(-TREE); FIG-TREE; POMEGRANATE) which make them expressions of sexual desire or else of the yearning for immortality or for wealth.

Fudo In esoteric Shingon Buddhism, Fudo symbolizes decision-making energy and especially that used in choosing the life of compassion. He is the chief of the Five Great Kings (*Vidyārājas*), each of whom has a double aspect, his 'angry' or 'compassionate' face, but these are two aspects of one and the same being and might even be termed two channels of one and the same feeling, since the terrifying figures which correspond to the 'angry' face act only against the powers of evil. Fudo is more often than not portrayed in BLUE-BLACK – and sometimes in RED and YELLOW – as a burly youth.

His face is strained, his lips pulled back to show pointed teeth, one eye is staring, the other squinting, all indicates intense effort. In his right hand he holds a SWORD and in his left a noose, to symbolize the destruction of obstacles and the depriving of the forces of evil of their power to harm. He sits or stands upon a diamond-hard rock, symbol of resoluteness. Behind him is a halo of flames, symbol of purification.

(MYTF p. 168)

This image of Fudo might just as easily be universalized, on the assumption that all the virtues are connected, to represent the strength required in the exercise of prudence, temperance and justice, to mention only the cardinal virtues. In Buddhism, it is the strength needed to acquire and retain compassion, which is not a gift of nature. It is hardly necessary to state that this strength may be exerted as strongly against internal as external enemies.

furnace The symbolism of the furnace derives from the rituals connected with METAL-working and the crafts using FIRE. Smelting, enamel-work, pottery and the alchemists' Great Work are either marriages of *yin* and *yang*, of Fire and Water or of Earth and Heaven, or else returns to the WOMB, regression to an embryonic state for the purposes of rebirth. Furnaces are the crucible in which that marriage is consummated, the mother's womb in which the rebirth gestates. The old European enamel-workers called their furnaces 'the mother's womb' and from China examples are known of sacrifices of wife or of husband and wife to the god of the furnace, to assist smelting operations.

The Chinese alchemist's furnace was shaped like an hourglass or like a CALABASH, the image of the cosmos, or like Mount Kun-Lun, the centre of the world. In it matter died to be reborn in sublimated form. Similarly, many European legends have for their theme the rejuvenation of the old or the healing of the sick by their being placed in a furnace. Although there are times when a miracle is required to save the victims of this operation from the hazards to which the BLACKSMITH's imprudence has exposed them, the symbolism remains the same.

G

G One of the Masonic symbols to be found on the Tracing Board of the Fellowcraft Mason is the letter G in the centre of the Blazing Star (see FREEMASONRY). It presence is explained as being the initial of some such word as 'glory', 'grandeur', 'geometry' and so on, but this is scarcely satisfactory. However, English Masons regard the letter as the initial of 'God' and Guénon has observed that this may have come about through the phonetic assimilation of the Hebrew *iod*, symbol of the divine principle. It is also claimed as the initial of Geometry, the science of the Great Architect of the Universe, but such an interpretation only acquires full force of meaning if for the Roman 'G' we substitute the Greek 'Γ', gamma, shaped like a Mason's square. The swastika is formed by the conjunction of four gammas and indicates the four positions of the Great Bear, the tempo of the year and of the day. Sometimes a plumbline joins the letter G with the centre of a swastika and then the letter G may be regarded as a surrogate for the Great Bear and hence as a representation of the celestial pole (BOUM, GUET, GUES). It symbolizes a centre of direction or enlightenment.

gall See under LIVER.

games Basically games are a symbol of struggle, against death (funeral games), against the elements (country games), against hostile powers (war games) and against the individual's fears, weaknesses, doubts and so on. Even when they are pure rejoicing, they bring the glow of victory at least to the cheeks of the winner. Whether fighting or risk-taking, play-acting or obsessed, games are a universe in themselves in which the individual has to find his place whether he likes it or not. Games, Caillois believes, not only comprise the specific activities which give them their names but also the whole mass of images, symbols and implements needed in the game itself or in the operations of a complex structure (CAIJ). As in everyday life, games associate within a predetermined setting notions of wholeness, of rules and of freedom. The different patterns emerging from a game are so many models of real life. Games tend to replace anarchic relationships with a degree of order and to make the transition from a state of nature to a state of civilization, from the unpremeditated to the predetermined. However, games allow the depths of the unpremeditated and the most private reactions to external constraint to come to the surface in obedience to their rules.

From their beginning games were, like all human activities, linked with the sacred. Even the most profane, the most spontaneous, the least directed towards any conscious end all stem from this. The Ancient Greeks and Romans, for example, had 'periodical ceremonies which accompanied certain religious festivals, during which athletes, musicians and declaimers competed with each other' (DEVD pp. 211–12). Each city organized its own games, associated with some festival, and allied city-states joined in communal games. Games may thus be regarded as a social ritual which, acting like a symbol, gave expression to and bonded more closely the unity of the group, while sporting competition externalized and resolved conflicts within the group.

These great public games acquired the highest degree of sociopsychological importance.

Around them crystallised national sentiment and a civic sense. They became for the inhabitants of the same city and the children of the same race ... the bond that reminded them of their common interests and their common origin. They had influence on public as well as private life; they not only inculcated in everyone the idea that physical education should be encouraged by training young people in the palaestra, they also gave an opportunity to scattered members of the same ethnic family to fulfill themselves in the pursuit of an ideal that distinguished them from the Barbarians. The celebration of this ideal put a temporary stop to the rivalries and hostilities between cities.

(DEVD p. 214)

While the games were taking place, truces were proclaimed, capital and other legal punishments were in abeyance and all was peace.

These games were generally consecrated to the gods under whose protection lay the cities, confederations or alliances which staged them. The Olympic Games were dedicated to the King of the Gods, Zeus, the Pythian to Apollo and the Isthmian to Poseidon. The only woman admitted to the Panhellenic Games at Olympia was the priestess of DEMETER, for whom a place of honour was reserved. This honour paid to the goddess of fertility leads one to regard these games as a symbol of the struggle between the powers of life and death, a symbol of the growth of the seed which sprouts and dies. The division between victor and vanquished expressed by synthesis the cosmic and biological struggle over which Demeter presided and which was displayed in the eternal return of the cycle of seedtime and harvest.

In Ireland, games, or *cles*, were sporting and warlike performances through which the hero was able to surprise, bewilder or dazzle his opponents. The more 'ploys' which he mastered, the greater his chances of becoming famous. Cùchulainn, for example, mastered scores of different ploys – the salmon-leap, the thunder-game, the trick of the spear-point and so on – occasionally defensive, more often offensive. Thus Cùchulainn could, with a single sword-stroke, shave an opponent without so much as grazing his skin, or cut the grass from under his feet without his noticing anything but its fall. He had learned all these tricks when serving his apprenticeship as a warrior with the two Queens of Scotland, Scathach and Aife. The latter even bore him a son and taught him the cunning use of the *ge bulga*, the notched spear, which saved him two or three times when he was faced by more skilled opponents. War-games symbolized individual skill and training for single combat; Celts had not the least notion of tactical training on the Roman pattern, and their games stemmed directly from initiation rites (REVC 29: pp. 109–52).

The Ancient Germans readily employed games as methods of divination, especially on the eve of battle. They used them to consult their gods who, for their part, were addicted to the game of backgammon.

Some games and toys possessed a wealth of symbolism now lost. Caillois suggests (CAIJ) a link between the greasy pole and myths of the conquest of Heaven, while hopscotch in all likelihood stood for the maze in which the initiate strayed at first. In the Far East, kites represented the external soul of their owners, free to wander the heights of Heaven while remaining magically (and really by their strings) linked to their owner on Earth. In Korea kites were used to carry away the people's sins like a scapegoat. Although these games and playthings may have lost their sacred character, they continue today to be just as valid objects, since they play a highly important social and psychological part as symbols both of conflict and of the learning process.

In north Africa, funeral games, both ritual and competitive, follow the funeral sacrifices, feasts and processions. They are like the sudden release or explosion of energy concentrated under pressure. They mark the end of a period of time set aside as holy and a return to everyday living. The games are designed to disperse an atmosphere of holiness, so intense that it has become oppressive, by unleashing utterly different feelings and re-establishing the normal pattern of existence. According to Jean Servier, these games 'scatter the accumulation of holiness . . . which pilgrims would find dangerous to carry home.'

The games also possess magical qualities. By grouping the competitors into two camps, they in fact set two principles or two polarities in opposition, and the triumph of one or the other is bound to ensure a boon such as rain or the blessing of the dead person and of his ancestors. 'East camp and west camp . . . opposing clans from the same village . . . the dry male principle, or the moist female principle from whose marriage the world is shaped, just as Mankind is formed from vegetative and subtle souls.'

The games take the most varied forms, from harmless social games to the cold-blooded horseman's courage of the *fantaziya*. The latter are held for preference with the change of the season and to a degree symbolize the warring of the elements and of plant life against them. 'All these games exude a feeling of competitiveness, of a struggle between two powers magically polarized along the east–west axis, one standing for dryness the other for moisture. This contest, emphasizing the opposition of the two elements essential to the world, is the necessary prelude to their marriage, in other words to making the world fruitful' (SERP pp. 63–7, 196–203).

The games may also assume the quality and aspect of an offering. Competitors rival one another in skill and endurance, even, at times, to the point of blood-letting, in order that this effusion of strength, of fatigue, of sweat and of tears should honour the invisible powers to whom they are offered and thus appease them, turn them and win their favour. Whether consciously or unconsciously, games are to be regarded as one of the ways in which mankind engages in dialogue with the invisible. Even playing with dolls, for example, is linked among the Berbers to fertility rites, the only rites which children may perform. It is their way of copying the behaviour of adults and of associating themselves with the major sacred rites which initiation will later reveal to them (SERH p. 95).

Psychoanalysis detects in games the transfer of psychic energy either between the two players or through endowing the toys – dolls, model trains and so on – with a life of their own. Games supercharge the imagination and activate emotionality. However pointless the game may be, it remains nonetheless weighted with significance and consequence. 'To play with something implies a surrender to the plaything, the player endowing, to some extent, the object with which he plays with his own libido. As a result the game becomes a magical activity which brings to life. . . . To play is to build a bridge between the imaginary and the real through the magic workings of the libido. To play is, therefore, a rite of passage and prepares the way for adaptation to reality. This is why games played by primitive peoples or by children so easily become serious and sometimes tragic' (ADLJ pp. 102–3).

Children's games and the private games of grown-ups, of which so many examples are known from China, India, Egypt, Greece, Rome and elsewhere, are in their way, and deep down, copies of public games. Although on the surface they may seem shallow and undirected, this should not disguise their basic confrontation symbolism. Games are at the heart of human relationships and are highly efficient teachers.

Groos has rightly called children's games 'an act of spontaneous personality development, being instinctive and unconscious preparations for future real-life activities.' Games reflect 'the child's relationship not only with its own internal world but with the persons and happenings of the external world' (ADLJ p. 103).

Psychodrama, the brilliant invention of Moreno, uses for its methods the formative, educational and even therapeutic properties of games and the cluster of images which they generate. The psychodramatist's task is to release the springs of spontaneity so that patients, while remaining themselves, adapt to all the roles life demands they play. Instead of being preconditioned by their past, they are seemingly free, their own creativity endowed with a massive power of expansion. If adaptation is one of the secrets of sociability, it will be seen how well suited psychodrama is to reintegrate a person into social life, to set him or her more at ease and to make that person far more attractive. Psychodrama is found to be a synthesis of social and affective symbols which it sets in motion of their own accord, and they tend to counterbalance one another and thus to ease the passage from games to real life. They break down and dissolve, in play, the complexes which, had they remained latent, would have brought on conflicts, but which, once overcome, encourage adaptation and progress.

Esoteric teaching has laid bare a whole lore of initiation in such different games as the TAROT, dice, dominoes and CHESS, to mention only a few. Tarot is richest in symbols and has been given a separate article, with further articles on each of the twenty-two major arcana. So far as dice are concerned, for example, it has been maintained that the six sides of these small cubes and the six dots marked on them are symbols of the world manifested in its six aspects – mineral, vegetable, animal, human, psychic and divine. The six faces of these cubes may be arranged in the shape of a cross, the horizontal arm comprising the animal, the psychic and the human and the vertical arm, the divine, the psychic, the vegetable and the mineral (BOUM p. 163).

Games exhibit the most varied aspects in accordance with the concerns of each age. They are not only an opportunity for relaxation, but can be initiatory, educational, mimetic or competitive. They draw their inspiration from the demands of everyday life and they develop faculties of social adaptation. The success of computer games in this latter part of the twentieth century ushers in a new form of intelligence which grasps more readily the triumphs of technology than the subtleties of speech. The most popular games symbolize the chief concerns of any given age, such as Monopoly, business games, Trivial Pursuit and the Rubik Cube. They reflect their age and herald an era of electronics, mathematics, mechanics and automation.

gammadion See SQUARE (MASON'S); SWASTIKA.

Ganesha Son of Shiva, worshipped throughout India, often in the form of a statuette of a human being with an elephant's head, tusks (one or both of which are broken) and huge trunk, an enormously fat belly and grotesque body seated upon the tiniest of steeds – a mouse! This discordant mixture of grotesque and solemn, of the ponderous and the lightweight, the sagging belly seated upon a mouse or a flower, all these contradictions stand for Māyā, Manifestation, of which Ganesha is an expression of the principle, with all his ventures in the shifting and illogical phenomenal world of fleeting reality. He conjures up the full potential of life and all its manifestations, however ludicrous, in space and time.

garden (see also PARADISE) Gardens are a symbol of the Earthly Paradise, of the Cosmos of which it is the centre, of the Heavenly Paradise of which it is a prefiguration and of those spiritual states which correspond to the enjoyment of that Paradise.

Genesis tells us that the Earthly Paradise was the Garden of Eden and that Adam was set by God in this garden. This would correspond to the dominance of plant life at the beginning of a cyclical period, while the Heavenly Jerusalem, which will mark its close, will be a city. Ancient Roman gardens might be described as recollections of Paradise Lost, but they were also epitomes of the world, as, in our own day, are world-famous Japanese and Persian gardens. In the Far East, gardens are not merely miniature worlds, but nature restored to its original state and invitations to human beings to restore their original natures, too. 'How pleasant', wrote the Chinese poet, Chang Chi, 'to stroll in a garden! I orbit the infinite.' East Asia, too, had its Gardens of Eden. Mount Kun-Lun, centre of the world and gateway to Heaven, was decorated with hanging gardens – more than an echo of Babylon – from which flowed the fountain of immortality, while the circular garden, shaped like Eden, surrounding the Forbidden City, had a strongly paradisal character, a copy of Kun-Lun at the centre of the Empire.

Monastic cloisters and enclosed Muslim gardens with a fountain in the middle are images of Paradise. As Abū Ya'qūb Sejestānī observes, *jannīt* (Paradise) is the equivalent of the Persian word for 'a garden full of fruit trees, sweetly scented plants and streams of running water . . . In like manner the knowledge of higher things and the gifts imparted by the Intelligence and the Soul are the garden of the clear-sighted inner eye.' When Muslims speak of these gardens, which are states of bliss, they call Allah 'The Gardener'. St John of the Cross wrote that God himself was a garden, the Bride so calling him because of the blissful dwelling she had in him. She entered this garden whenever she was transported into God.

A Kabbalistic tradition also regarded Paradise as a garden ravaged by some of those who entered it. In this context, *Pardes* is the domain of higher knowledge, the four consonants in the word corresponding to the four rivers which flowed from Eden and the four senses canonized by Holy Scripture. The ravages in the garden consisted of cutting the plants, that is to say, separating the growth from the principle which gave it birth (CORT, GUER, GUES, MAST, STEJ, BURA).

The Ancient Egyptians were gardening enthusiasts and depicted gardens with pools and banks of FLOWERS on the walls and floors of their palaces. Each flower had its own language. Mandragora berries were symbols of love, while the open petals of the lotus suggested the solar wheel and the lotus roots, entangled in the waters, the birth of the world.

The wedding feast of Zeus and Hera was held in the wonderful and mythical Garden of the HESPERIDES, a symbol of the eternal cycle of fertility. However, Ancient Greek gardens were a luxury, of which they discovered the attractions during the Asiatic conquests of Alexander the Great. The Romans carried garden design to ever greater heights of sophistication, combining buildings, statues, stairways, springs, grottoes, wells and fountains with the colourful charm of plants grown to rules imposed by man. 'What fairer sight is there than rows of trees planted in ranks which present straight lines to the eye from whatever angle they be viewed' (Quintilian, *Institutio Oratoria* 8: iii, 9). The Quincunx, or Garden of Cyrus, in particular, displayed a symbol of man's power to tame Nature. On a higher plane, gardens may be regarded as symbols of civilization as opposed to raw nature, of the considered as opposed to the unpremeditated, of order as opposed to disorder and of the conscious as opposed to the unconscious.

However, it was in Persia that the garden partook of metaphysical and moral significance, in addition to the cosmic significance it had already enjoyed in Japan. Love of gardens is a cornerstone of the Persian world vision and two famous collections of poetry are called respectively 'The Rose-Garden' (Gulistan) and 'The Orchard' (Bustan). Gardens were a source of musical inspiration and, constantly, of literary simile, the beloved being likened to cypress, rose, jasmine and so on. Major poets asked to be buried in gardens, which are related thematically to oases and ISLANDS: cool, shady places of refuge. They were carried into the design of Persian 'garden' rugs (see CARPET), their surface divided into squares by the straight lines of canals with fish swimming in them. These squares are themselves filled with flowers and shrubs (BODT pp. 142ff.).

The typical Sassanid park was arranged as a CROSS, its four arms meeting at right angles, with the palace in the centre. This corresponded to the cosmological notion of a universe divided into FOUR quarters and watered by four rivers flowing from the Earthly Paradise. Typical Persian gardens on this rectangular plan are also related to the ancient ground-plan of cities. In some versions of this quadripartite cosmology a mountain was set in its centre. This is imitated in a number of both Persian gardens and Indian

Mogul gardens as well. Persian gardens were always surrounded by walls to preserve their privacy, and they were never scentless. A whole range of symbols are based upon the PERFUME of flowers. The scent of jasmine is the scent of kings; that of roses, of the beloved. The scent of *saman*, a species of white jasmine, is like the scent of one's own children. The narcissus is the scent of youth, the blue lotus that of power and wealth and so on.

Craftsmen specialized in creating miniature gardens. Princes had gold and silver trees made for them with leaves and fruits of precious stones. At Karakorum, Mangu Khan (*c.* 1250) had a silver tree with so capacious a trunk that a man could hide inside it; round it four golden serpents were twined and at its foot four silver lions sat dispensing white mare's milk. Once again the symbolism of the four quarters of the world and the four rivers of Paradise recurs. The garden is a dream-world to take you out of the real world.

Jalāl-al-Dīn Muhammad Rūmī regarded the beauty of flowers as a sign to remind the soul of its immortality since, in its ascension, it had experienced every level of being and knew what it was to live as a plant.

Both the ultimate reality and heavenly bliss are interpreted by the Koran (18: 55 etc.) in terms of a garden, a home beyond the grave preserved for the Elect where they will be close to the throne of God. Paradise is a garden, gardens a paradise.

Amerindian civilization also conceived of gardens as epitomes of the universe. The Aztec pleasure gardens, however, combined the traditional function of the private garden with those of the botanical garden and the zoo. There they preserved not only plants, but all species of bird and wild beast, with a staff of 600 men to tend them. In addition they housed human specimens of dwarfs, albinos and those born with different degrees of physical deformity.

In dreams, gardens are often regarded as agreeable expressions of pure desire free from all anxiety. They are places 'of growth and for the cultivation of vital internal phenomena.'

There the cycle of seasonal change occurs within a strictly regulated pattern ... and life in all its abundance is displayed in the most miraculous of ways. The garden wall protects the internal forces which flourish within it .... Entrance to the garden is only through a narrow gateway. The dreamer is often forced to circle the walls in search of the gate. This expresses visually a long psychic development which has arrived at internal richness .... When a tall tree or a fountain stands in the centre of the garden, the garden may be an allegory of the self.... Frequently the garden stands, in the male psyche, for the female sexual organs. However, behind the whole allegory of the tiny Garden of Eden ... religious mystical verse carries far more than the expression of mere love and its embodiment, it searches for and enthusiastically lauds the inner depths of the soul.

(AEPR pp. 282–3)

garlic   Central European tradition prescribes a bunch of garlic nailed to the bed-head or a wreath of garlic flowers as a remedy against vampires. Earlier, Pliny had observed that garlic drove away serpents and was a pre-servative against madness. In Siberia, the Buryat believed that the smell of garlic was a warning of the presence of the souls of women who had died in childbirth and who now came to persecute the living (HARA).

In Borneo, the Batak endow garlic with the power of recovering souls which have become lost (FRAG 3: p. 46). Frazer also records the former custom of the inhabitants of Draguignan in southeastern France of roasting cloves of garlic on the bonfires lit in every street on St John the Baptist's day. These cloves were then shared out among all the households (FRAG 10: p. 193).

Classical Antiquity acknowledges that garlic had certain virtues and traces of this belief are still to be found in modern Greek folklore. Thus, during the festivals of the Thesmophoria (sacred to Demeter) and the Scirophoria (sacred to Athene), women chewed garlic, since the plant was reputed to make easier the sexual abstinence imposed during these festivals (DARS). The Ancient Greeks in any case loathed garlic. However, the most persistent belief current in the Mediterranean basin and extending as far as India, was that garlic was a preservative against the evil eye. This is the reason for the bunches of garlic tied up with red thread to be found in Sicily, Italy, Greece and India. In Greece, saying the word 'garlic' brings ill luck (HASE).

The protagonist in the rites of Spring, Dionysiac ceremonies still celebrated in Thrace and recently analysed by the ethnographer, Katerina J. Kakouri, carries a string of garlic in a ritual which includes the ordeal of fire-walking (KAKD p. 41).

Even today, shepherds in the Carpathians rub their hands with garlic which has been blessed before they milk a ewe for the first time. This is to protect the flock against snake-bite (KOPK p. 434).

All these practices demonstrate the belief that garlic is a preservative against evil influences or dangerous attacks.

The Ancient Egyptians made garlic what was probably an anti-serpent god, because of its smell. In Rome, those who had just eaten garlic were forbidden to enter the temple of Cybele, and Horace pours out his harshest invective against garlic in one of his epodes. However, because it was part of the rations of the Roman legionary, garlic became a symbol of the soldier's life.

Garuda   The creature upon which Vishnu rides is depicted as a bird of prey with a human head, three eyes and an eagle's beak. As 'cousin and enemy' of the NAGA, the Garuda is often shown tearing serpents with its beak and crunching them in its talons. The serpents which it kills are often given human heads and shoulders in place of their snake's head. Tibetans generally depict the Garuda with a savage expression on its face and it is sometimes represented as being in the power of the King of Hell (TONT p. 19). The war of birds and snakes is a constant motif of Asian iconography and may be seen as the battle of life with death, of good with evil, of the chthonian with the celestial powers, or as the image of the twofold aspect of Vishnu who kills and restores to life, destroys and rebuilds. Perhaps analysts would see in the human-headed snake crushed by the bird an image of the unconscious stifled by rationality or of desires repressed by moral inhibitions.

gate(way)   Gateways symbolize the scene of passing from one state to another, from one world to another, from the known to the unknown, from light to darkness. Doors open upon the mysterious, but they have a dynamic psychological quality for they not only indicate a threshold but invite us to cross it. It is an invitation to a voyage into the beyond.

The passage to which they invite us is more often than not, in the symbolic sense of the term, a passage from the realm of the profane to that of the sacred. This is embodied in the doorways of cathedrals, Hindu *torana*, the gateways of Khmer cities and temples, Japanese TORII, etc.

The gates of Chinese cities were set at the four points of the compass. Through them evil influences were expelled, good influences drawn in, strangers received, the virtues of the Emperor disseminated to the four corners of the empire and the hours of the day and the seasons of the year regulated. The four main gates of Angkor Thom display the gleaming face of Lokeshvara, Lord of the Universe, to the four points of the compass, but they also give access from these four directions to the CENTRE of the world. The doors of churches and porticos of temples allow the pilgrim to enter and approach the very *cella*, the Holy of Holies or the Real Presence of God. In themselves they sum up the symbolism of the sanctuary, which is the gate of Heaven. Temple gates are often provided with such terrifying guardians as fabulous animals, the *dvārapāla* of Asian temples, and even of Tantric mandala, or the armed guards outside the lodges of secret societies. They are there to perform two tasks: to bar entry to the sacred enclosure to maleficent and unclean forces and to protect the entrance of worthy candidates. The latter 'enter in through the gates into the city' (Revelation 22: 14); the former are 'cast into outer darkness'.

The symbolism of the guardians clearly derives from initiation (= entrance), which may be interpreted as crossing the threshold. JANUS, the Roman god of initiation into the mysteries, held the keys of the 'Doors of the Solstices', that is of the ascendant and descendant phases of the annual solar cycle. These were the 'Gateway of the Gods' and the 'Gateway of Men' opening onto the two roads of which Janus, like Ganesha in India, was the master – *pitri-yana* and *dēva-yana* in Hindu tradition, the roads of the Ancestors and of the Gods. The two gates are also *janua coeli* and *janua inferni*, the Gates of Heaven and Hell.

As the articles CAVERN and DOME demonstrate, the transit from Earth to Heaven is made through 'the gateway of the Sun', which symbolizes release from the cosmos beyond the constraints of the human condition. This is the eye of the dome or the smoke-hole of the tent through which passes the World Axis. It is also the crown of the head and most of all the 'strait' gate which leads to the Kingdom of Heaven, notionally expressed by the rope or camel passing through the eye of a needle.

Another image of the gateway is the Hindu *torana*, associated with the DEVOURER (*kala*). In this instance, the gateway is the monster's MOUTH, the image of the passage from life to death, but also from death to liberation, the twofold cyclical current of expansion and reintegration, *kalpa* and *pralaya*. In Khmer art, the *kala* disgorges a pair of sea-monsters (MAKARA), one on either side, and they in turn vomit out what becomes the lintel of the doorway, which is thus akin to a RAINBOW, indirect confirmation of passage from Earth to the abode of the gods.

The cosmic manifestation which we have just discussed is again expressed in China by the ideogram of the door. According to the *Chi-Chu*, the trigram *k'un* (Earth; passive principle) is the closed door, while the trigram *Ch'ien* (Heaven; active principle) is the door which opens – manifestation. The alternate opening and closing of the door expresses the rhythm of the universe. It is also the alternation of *yang* and *yin*. However, in this instance the doors would seem to be equinoctial rather than solsticial (*yang* emerges under the sign *Ch'en* which corresponds to Spring). Following this line of thought, the opening and closing of the Gates of Heaven (*Tao* 6 and 10) are related to human respiration, which is a recognized image for this alternation. In Taoist methods (*Tao* 52), 'shutting the doors' is holding the breath and annihilating sense perception.

When he observed how the hinge remained immobile while the door itself moved, Master Eckhart made the latter the symbol of external man, the former of internal man unaffected by external movement because of his central, axial position (BURA, BENA, COEA, GRAD, GRAP, GUES, ELIY, HERS, COOS, SCHI, SECA).

In Jewish and Christian tradition doors and gates play a vastly important role since they open the way to revelation and they become reflections of the harmony of the universe. Pilgrims and worshippers coming to cathedral doorways were met by Old Testament and Apocalyptic themes, Christ in majesty and the Last Judgement. Suger used to tell visitors to St-Denis that they ought to admire the beauty of the finished work rather than the material from which the door was made. He added that the beauty which enlightens the soul should direct it towards the light of which Christ is the true door (*Christus janua vera*).

Christ in glory may be carved on the tympanum of cathedral doorways, but it is he who, by the mystery of the Redemption, is the true doorway which gives entrance to the Kingdom of Heaven. 'I am the door: by me if any man enter in, he shall be saved' (John 10: 9). 'Christ', wrote St Clement of Alexandria, quoting a Gnostic source, 'is the gate of righteousness, since it is said (Psalm 118: 19–20): "Open to me the gates of righteousness: I will go into them, and I will praise the Lord: This gate of the Lord, into which the righteous shall enter."'

The symbol of the gateway is a recurrent theme of medieval authors, Hugues of Fouilloy, for example, writing that Jerusalem has gates through which we enter the church and attain to eternal life. Our Lady, too, is called 'Gate of Heaven' and is sometimes depicted in medieval iconography in the guise of a closed door (VALC p. 146).

Doorways play a major role in medieval architecture. Burckhardt emphasizes the importance of the doorway and niche in combination and maintains that the niche is an image, in miniature, of the world cavern. It corresponds, in his view, to the church chancel and becomes the site of the epiphany of the godhead since it conforms with the symbolism of the Gates of Heaven. These allow the passage of a two-way traffic, the entry of souls ascending into the Kingdom of God, while through the gates God's word comes down to Earth. Crossing a threshold is altering a level, an environment, a centre or a way of life (BURI pp. 168, 233; DAVR pp. 204–5).

Doorways also have eschatological significance. As places of passage and particularly of entry, they naturally become symbols of the imminence and potentiality of entry into a higher reality – and, conversely, of the diffusion of heavenly blessings upon Earth. Thus Christ's Second Coming is foretold and described in terms of a traveller knocking at the door, as in Revelation 3: 20 when Christ says: 'Behold, I stand at the door, and knock: if any man hear my voice, and open the door, I will come in to him, and will sup with him, and he with me.' The image is taken from the Song of Solomon (5: 2), of which Judaism confirms the Passover symbolism. Jewish tradition expected final liberation and the coming of the Messiah to occur at the Passover and often gave expression to this time of waiting in the symbol of the door (Josephus, *Jewish Antiquities* 18: 29). In his *Jewish War* (6: 290ff.) he tells how the gates of the Temple were to be opened in the middle of Passover night and, when miraculous signs occurred during the feast of the Passover and especially when one of the Temple gates opened of its own accord, the people concluded that God had opened the Gate of Blessing – that is, that the final, Messianic process had started. The primitive Church, as heir to this tradition, expected Christ's Second Coming on Easter Eve and kept vigil, listening for the sound of his knocking on the gates of the world.

The Bible also speaks of the 'gates' (Genesis 28: 17) or 'doors' (Psalm 78: 23) which God opens to make himself manifest (Revelation 4: 1) or to shower his blessings upon mankind (Malachi 3: 10). Conversely, the opening of the gates, such as those of the ideal Temple in the eschatological New Jerusalem (Isaiah 60: 11), symbolizes the free access of the Chosen People to God's grace.

The Gates of the Grave (Isaiah 38: 10) or the Gates of Hell (Matthew 16: 18) symbolize the awesome power of the abyss, from which none can escape, but of which Christ proclaimed his conquest. His are its keys (Revelation 3: 7).

Now it is far easier to understand why 'door' or 'gate' should have been used as the symbolic designation of Christ himself (John 10: 1–10), he being the one door through which the sheep could enter the sheepfold, that is, the kingdom of the elect.

The carved door of a Senufo shrine in the village of Towara, in Africa, is the equivalent of a lesson in visual images, but in images which are to be understood not by what they offer the eyes but for what they symbolize to the spirit. The door is a symbol of the development of the cosmos. In its centre is carved a circular disc and around it, in a vast square, figures of animals and of human beings, those in the upper half being carved head downwards. Above the square are line carvings in relief of six figures, one of whom is a horseman; and below the square are a walking man, a leopard, what is probably a rhinoceros, a bird with wings displayed and a serpent poised to strike. Jean Laude interprets the carvings as follows:

The door dividing the holy place [the inner sanctuary] from the outer world, displays an epitome of the creation, a cosmogony, to the living. The persons depicted are genii [intermediaries between the created world and the invisible powers which created it] ... The dimensions of the figures depicted are non-figurative [the horseman's head is larger than the horse; proportion is based not upon physical size but upon hierarchical order] ... The universe is conceived as an outward expansion from a central nucleus, from which beings and things irradiate.

(LAUA pp. 307–9)

Doors lend themselves to a number of esoteric interpretations, alchemists regarding them 'as the same thing as the key, an entry to or means of operating throughout the course of the "work"' (PERD p. 396). The door is the communication of the hidden implement, the secret tool.

Freemasons set the door of the Temple between two columns, 'the facade surmounted by a triangular pediment above which are a pair of compasses, their tips pointing heavenwards.'

The Temple door should be very low. When the uninitiated enter the Temple they should be forced to bend down, not as a sign of humiliation, but to show how hard it is to pass from the world of the uninitiated to that of the adept. ... This enforced action may also make the candidate remember that when he dies to his old life, he will be reborn to a new life which he should enter like a new-born baby coming into the world.

(BOUM p. 182)

Plantagenet also observes: 'The gates of the Temple are known as the Western Gates, which should remind us that it is beyond its threshold that the sun sets, in other words, where the Light is extinguished. Beyond is the realm of darkness, the world of the uninitiated.'

gazelle (see also DEER; STAG)   This graceful creature has always been marked out by its swiftness and its light-footedness, its beauty and its keen-sightedness, and these are the qualities which have been taken for symbolic use.

Thus Indian tradition associates the gazelle with Vāyu, Lord of the Wind and of the element Air, as well as with the *yoginī* Vayuvegā ('Swift as the Wind'). It is also the symbol of Ishvara (to whom the traditional dance, the *mudra mrigacīrsha* (gazelle's head), is related). In Tantrism, gazelles correspond to the element of Air, which is that of the innermost heart (*anāhatachakra*).

In depicting the Buddha's first sermon, Buddhist iconography often shows gazelles kneeling beside his throne, or on either side of the Wheel of the Law, in the Deer Park at Sarnath, near Benares.

Semites, on the other hand, seem to have been especially impressed by the creature's beauty and particularly by its eyes. The Houris of the Muslim Paradise have 'eyes of gazelles'. In the Song of Solomon (2: 9) 'gazelle' might be substituted for the Authorized Version's 'my beloved is like a roe' (GOVM, JACA, MALA).

Origen derived the animal's name from the Greek word 'to see', on grounds of homophony, and made the gazelle the symbol of keen sight and, hence, of the contemplative life. Christian tradition dwelt upon the fact that gazelles are very keen-sighted. William of St Thierry followed St Bernard of Clairvaux in his commentary upon the Song of Solomon by observing that gazelles possess keen eyesight and that this is why the Soul-Bride asks the Beloved to sharpen his inner vision and to be swift-spirited in order to understand.

Lastly, countless works of art depict gazelles as the victims of predators, generally lions, which couple with them before tearing out their throats. Analysts readily regard these as images of the self-destructive tendency of the unconscious, symbolized by the predator, in respect of the spiritual ideal, represented by the gazelle. It is as if the latter were crushed by the weight of animality and her bright eyes misted under the assault of passion.

gem The study of the symbolism of this word cannot be separated from that of the word JEWELLERY. The shade of meaning that distinguishes them undoubtedly arises from the fact that the gem is pure stone, directly produced by the chthonian womb of Earth, and therefore comprises that precious manifestation of the unfathomable collective unconscious; while jewellery, the work of human hands, gives these stones glory and fame by cutting, polishing and setting them. To obtain an all-embracing approach to the symbolism of the gem, such individual entries as CRYSTAL, DIAMOND, JADE, PEARL, STONE should be consulted, although admittedly each provides only a facet of the symbol as a whole. This entry examines some aspects of this symbolism taken from Middle and Far Eastern traditions which, it is agreed, have always paid avid attention to gems.

In Muslim esotericism the *al-jawhar alfard* (the jewel beyond price) conveys a sense of the Intellect or incorruptible essence of being. The Buddha's glittering *urnā* was a gem, while from the EMERALD which Lucifer wore on his forehead and lost when he was cast down from Heaven, angels are supposed to have carved the Holy Grail. Both are assuredly symbols, too, of either exalted or debased intellect. Emeralds were long believed to enhance sight and to restore memory, derivatives of the same order of symbolism. They were used at the oracle of Jupiter-Ammon and were worshipped in pre-Inca Peru. The table of Hermes Trismegistus was an emerald table.

At Jerusalem, gems were set on the High Priest's breastplate as symbols of truth. They are also symbols of spiritual perfection, since Muhammad is called 'a precious gem among gems'.

In India, one of Vishnu's attributes was a gem. It was 'Ocean's treasure', 'born of the waves', but it had undergone all the stages of the ascent of matter. It symbolized ātman, the Universal Spirit, in its bright and shining manifestations. In some contexts there are groups of five gems corresponding to the five elements – for example, sapphire = Earth; pearl = Water; *kaustubha* = Fire; cat's eye = Air; topaz = Ether. The *kaustubha* forms the centre-piece, its birth from the waves resulting from the churning of the Sea of Milk and thus relating it to the symbolism of immortality.

In addition to the mirror and the sword, the emblems of the Japanese imperial dynasty include famous gems expressly symbolizing the power of domination. Granet observes that their shape is akin to that of a half T'ai-ki (see YIN–YANG), and must have some relation to the phases of the Moon.

Jizo Bosatsu, patron of the dead in Buddhist tradition, has powers to prolong life. He is depicted seated, holding in his right hand a ringed staff and in his left the gem which satisfies all desires.

A gem's virtues are not always inherent in its nature or its shape, but sometimes can only operate when it is in the hands of its rightful owner. This was true of the jade slab mentioned in the *Tzo Chuang*, which became mere stone in the hands of commoners, but regained its properties in those of the king. Dōgen used the symbol of the glitter immanent in the gem and only made manifest by polishing, when he taught that the virtues inherent in the individual were only revealed by spiritual training.

According to Tantric physiology the *manipītha* (altar studded with gems) in the *manidvīpa* (island of gems) is located in the *sahasrārapadma* (lotus with a thousand petals) on the crown of the head. The 'altar' is that of Ishtadevatā, the deity adored within; and the 'isle of gems' is the highest state of consciousness. 'The jewel in the lotus' in any case evokes Avalokitesvara's great mantra, *Om mani padmi om*, at the heart of Tibetan spirituality. A generally accepted interpretation makes its six syllables correspond to the six *loka*, the six kingdoms of the phenomenal world, and to the six segments of the Wheel of Life.

In Buddhist terms, the *triratna* (triple gem) is the synthesis of teaching – Buddha, Dharma, Sangha; or Buddha, Law, Assemblage (AVAS, DEVA, GOVM, JILH, MALA, PORA, RENB, ROMM).

Gemini (21 May–21 June) Generally speaking, the symbol of duality in outward appearance and even in identity. They are the image of all internal and external opposites, conflicting or complementary, relative or absolute, which are resolved in creative tension, the Gemini phase ending with the start of Summer.

The third sign of the ZODIAC, it immediately precedes the Summer solstice and is the principal sign of Mercury. It is predominantly the sign of human contact, interplay, communication and the interfaces of the social environment; and of polarity, even including sexual polarity. Some Zodiacs do not employ the usual image of two children holding hands, but depict the sign as a man and a woman or even, in the case of a Coptic Zodiac, as a pair of lovers (see also TWINS).

genius In most ancient traditions and under a variety of different names, a 'genius' was believed to be the companion of every human being, as double, demon, guardian angel, counsellor, intuition or supra-rational voice of conscience.

The genius symbolizes the flash of enlightenment which, uncontrolled, engenders the deepest and strongest of convictions. Immanent in every individual, physical or moral, the genius symbolizes the spiritual being (GRID p. 165) (see DEMON). Jean Beaujeu wrote that:

Every individual had a Genius whose precise nature and significance are open to argument. Rather, however, than being an embodiment of the fertility principle (*qui gignit* = who engenders), it would seem that the Genius was, in Dumézil's words, the human personality made divine. However, it may also be regarded as a double of the ego and even as a separate being which guards the ego. ... Subsequently such groups as the Roman Senate, the Roman people, cities and army units were fitted out with a more or less symbolical Genius and in the end even the gods themselves had one each.

It was to require a long development of the consciousness before 'genii' could be regarded as aspects of the individual human personality and of the internal tensions of impulses, tendencies and ideals.

In Ancient Egypt, 'genii' seem to have existed separately from humans both in this world and in the beyond. Distinctions were made between 'good demons', the 'protectors of Osiris' which guarded temples and tombs and the 'evil spirits . . . forces of chaos, hybrid creatures, headless men and monstrous animals . . . a whole army of mysterious creatures . . . discontented spirits returning from beyond the tomb . . . incubi, sleepwalkers, epileptics and drowned people . . . come to torture the living . . . who attempt to bar the way to the afterlife' (POSD pp. 60–1).

In Dogon tradition, the Nommo, eight little people, represent the eight genii who were the ancestors of mankind. They are often carved as the legs of thrones, chairs or stools. Their limbs and bodies need to be supple 'as befits the genii of water, essentially protective spirits, in dry savannah country'. They revealed to mankind the laws which the gods had given to regulate human activity. Rejection of their commands brings serious trouble and disorder, since they have set permanent standards governing the inter-reaction between all living things, and especially between human beings. They are regarded as archetypal of the social order imposed by God. These genii are often the subjects of African sculpture. 'As intermediaries with the invisible world (ruled by the supreme deity, the Mother of the Universe) . . . these STATUETTES accompany sacrificial rites and especially those of divination' (LAUA pp. 137, 181, 309).

geomancy It is incorrect to describe the true traditional cosmological science which survives today as the study of 'wind and water' (the Chinese *feng-shui*) as geomancy – divination by means of the soil.

Inherited from the Stone Age and known to Celts, Classical Rome and Byzantine Greeks, this symbolic science was anciently employed in China as *hin-fa*, 'the art of shapes and locations' (LIOC). This sought to determine the influences which would allow humans to live in harmony with their natural surroundings and, consequently, in harmony with Heaven. Geomancy was used to fix the ground-plans of cities and of fortresses – in colonial times the fortifications of Hanoi, plotted by French military engineers, were altered in accordance with geomantic data. It was also used to determine the location and orientation of houses and tombs, and even the rules of tactics and of strategy. The conjunction of lucky influences, of which geomancy seeks to take advantage, is that of YIN AND YANG, manifest not so much in air and water currents as in those of the life forces which may be detected flowing through the soil by means of the geomancer's compass. These opposing forces are given the names of Green (or Blue) Dragon and White Tiger, names also borne by the elements in the alchemists' Great Work. Furthermore, the locations thus chosen must harmonize with the position of the stars in the sky, and the whole success of the operation depends equally upon the personal qualities of the person undertaking it. The aesthetics of landscaping are at one and the same time the consequences of cosmic harmony and of the qualities of the person able to understand and to interpret it.

In Cambodia, geomancy depends upon the ability of the practitioner to discover the position of the *nak*, the Underworld CROCODILE identical with the Balinese *asura*, whose duties are the same as those of the DRAGON (CHOO, GRAP, HUAV, LIOT, PORA).

geometry (see also CIRCLE; CONE; CROSS; PYRAMID; SPHERE; SPIRAL; SQUARE (RECTANGLE); TRIANGLE)   Geometrical figures at all cultural levels are heavily weighted with significance. This is especially true of those aniconic religions, such as Judaism and Islam, which from fear of idolatry are sworn foes of the depiction of living beings.

The famous tomb door from Kefer Yesef, in Palestine, and now in the Louvre in Paris, richly exemplifies geometric symbolism. According to Rutten (*Arts et styles du moyen-orient ancien*, Paris, 1950, p. 170), the vertical band dividing the panel, decorated with six rings with triangular buckles at either end, resembles a girdle, a fertility symbol. To the right of this band, three motifs are set one above the other. At the top there is a rosette, at the bottom a helix and between them six squares bonded together. Rosette and helix form a pair, the rosette being associated with Apollo in his solar aspect (as in a low-relief carving from Doueir in Phoenicia), while the helix is an emblem of lunar Artemis. Between these two types of circle, are six magic squares. Their NUMBER is emblematic of the interposition between the First Cause and its manifestation and, since the world was created in six days, they stand for creation. Taken in conjunction, these figures could symbolize the marriage of the Sun and Moon, the two forces which control the passage of earthly time, in other words, cosmic evolution in time and space. On the left side of this tomb door, three other elements are vertically juxtaposed. At the top is the nine-branched candlestick, part of the Temple

Geometry: Roman-period tomb-door found at Kefer Yesef (Paris: Louvre)

furniture at Jerusalem. In the centre there is a geometrical floral motif in a hexagon (see OCTAGON), itself enclosed within a circle. This latter symbolizes both the cyclical revolution of earthly time (the polygon) and infinite duration, eternity and universality (the circle). At the foot there is a sort of coffer supposedly holding the books of the Law and surmounted by a conch or cockle-shell. (From the synagogue at Dura-Europus comes a similar design which could have provided Islam with a pattern for the *mihrāb* in the mosque.) The coffer containing the holy book of the Law – represented by the lozenge with a dot in the centre – welds together notions of Heaven and Earth. The triangle pointing upwards could, in the context of Neoplatonist influence, signify the return of the creature, rising through the revolutions of time and through the graces imparted by the Law, to its heavenly creator. The two inverted triangles, acting as buckles to the six-ringed girdle, would then acquire the meaning of the creative force which makes fruitful the universe, and of the ascension of the creature towards the eternal, thus emphasizing the twofold movement, ascending and descending.

The famous royal door with the two elephants at Baoulé in the Ivory Coast is equally rich in geometrical symbols, especially triangles (emblem of the divine triad) and lozenges (the female symbol) (LAUA p. 310).

ghost Celtic folklore is full of ghosts, driven by both good and evil intentions. Generally speaking, it is unhealthy to meet a ghost. The most spectacular spectres in the repertory of Breton legend are the *kannerezed-noz* or nocturnal washer-women, women or girls who wash the shrouds of those fated to die. Almost inevitably they cause the deaths of those who encounter them upon the road. They correspond to the banshees of Irish folklore and the *banshidhe* of medieval writers, which Christianity consigned to the category of evil spirits. In modern Breton folklore, the *skarz-prenn*, the stick used to clean the ploughshare, is believed to have the power of driving off ghosts (OGAC 3: p. 124).

Among those unquiet spirits which return to Earth to trouble the living are the souls of young women who have died in childbirth. This belief was current among the Aztecs and recurred in Siberia where the Buryat believed that these ghosts 'grasp children by throat on which their fingers leave bluish marks' or else 'cause a dangerous form of gastric catarrh to those who eat food which they have touched'. As a protection against this type of ghost they used the skin of the eagle-owl which, they believed, hunted it by night. These ghosts are characterized by a smell of garlic (HARA p. 263). Mongolo-Turkic peoples were just as afraid of the ghosts of the unburied dead.

The image of the ghost embodies, and in a sense symbolizes, the fears of beings who dwell in another world. The ghost returning may perhaps also be an apparition of the ego, of the unknown ego, springing out of the unconscious, inspiring an almost panic fear and being thrust back into darkness. The ghost might well be the reality which is disowned, feared and rejected. The analyst would regard all this as the return of the repressed off-scourings of the unconscious.

giant Earth (Gaia) gave birth to the Giants in order to avenge the Titans, whom Zeus had imprisoned in Tartarus. They were chthonian beings, by their vast physical bulk and their spiritual poverty symbolizing the predominance of forces arising from the Earth. They were the commonplace on a vast scale. Images of all that is unrestrained, existing solely to gratify their own physical and animal instincts, echoes of the dinosaurs which once ruled the Earth, they took up the battle of the Titans. 'They were huge creatures. Their strength was invincible and their appearance terrifying. They had shaggy hair, bristling beards and their legs were serpents' bodies' (GRID p. 164).

One of the most remarkable features of mythology is that the Giants could only be overcome by the joint efforts of a god and a man. Zeus required Herakles (Hercules) – before the latter became immortal – to dispose of Porphyrion. The god laid him low with his thunderbolt and the hero finished him off with his arrows. Apollo blinded Ephialtes in the left eye, but needed Herakles to complete the killing by shooting the giant in the right eye. All the gods who fought the Giants, Athene, Dionysos, Aphrodite, Poseidon and so on, entrusted a human with the task of finally exterminating the monsters. The scope of this myth cannot be overemphasized.

In the struggle against Earth-born animal instincts, the divine has as much need of human assistance as the human has of divine. The development of life in the direction of increasing spiritualization is the real battle of giants. The myth, however, involves human effort to overcome innate involutionary and regressive tendencies, without relying solely upon the assistance of the higher powers. The myth of the Giants is a summons to human heroism. Giants stand for all those things which the individual must overcome to allow full freedom and the development of personality.

Celtic mythology contains a fair number of giants, but their gigantic size is not a characteristic of the Otherworld but of the FOMORIANS, or lower powers. One of the most notable Fomorian chieftains was Balor, who could paralyse whole armies with a glance of his eye. His Welsh equivalent in the *Tale of Culhwch and Olwen* was Ysbaddaden Penkawr (OGAC 14: pp. 482–3).

ginger A colour which is a mixture of red and yellow, a muddy red. It suggests flames, but instead of the clear blaze of heavenly love (red) it characterizes unclean fires which burn below the surface, Hell-fires. It is a chthonian colour.

In Ancient Egypt, the god of lust, the destroyer Set–Typhon, was depicted with ginger hair, and Plutarch relates that at some of the god's feasts, ginger-haired men were rolled in the dirt. Traditionally Judas Iscariot had ginger hair and beard.

In short, ginger suggests the consuming flames of Hell, the delirium of lust, the passion of greed, the hidden fires which consume the physical and spiritual being.

ginseng The best-known drug in the Far Eastern pharmacopeia, its qualites are related to two properties, the human appearance of its root (somewhat similar to the mandrake) and its therapeutic power of harmonizing. This is why the effects of ginseng upon the human organism have been compared with royal or divine action. Ginseng is, nevertheless, primarily the food of the *yang* and consequently a symbol of virility and of immortality. It is 'the godlike plant' as well as being 'the root of life' (BEAM, THAS).

girdle Girdles are primarily garments and, if such accounts of the creation as are given in the Old Testament are to be believed, the very first garments of all; this seems to be consonant with what ethnographers have observed. This is what marks out the girdle's symbolic field, in sharp distinction from that of the BUCKLE. Buckles derive from the cosmic, girdles from the human. Knotted round the waist at birth, it bonds the part to the whole and binds the individual. This sums up its symbolic ambivalence: bonding, it gives assurance, comfort, strength and power; binding expresses the consequent submission and dependence which this entails, and hence, willy-nilly, the restriction upon the individual's freedom.

As an embodiment of a contract, oath or vow undertaken, the girdle often partakes of a sacral or initiatory quality. In material terms it becomes a visible and sometimes proud emblem of the strength and powers invested in its wearer. Into this category fall the various coloured judo belts, the sashes of officers and civic dignitaries and the countless votive, initiatory or ceremonial girdles which belong to the rites and traditions of all peoples.

Thus, in Indian initiatory rites investiture with the girdle was of great significance. After making his offerings, the master stood on the northern edge of the hearth, facing east, with the boy on the eastern edge, facing west. The master then took the girdle, winding it three times round the boy's waist, from left to right. Each time he encircled the waist, the master prayed that the girdle would protect from evil spells, purify the wearer and give him strength. In this instance the girdle itself became the symbol of the qualities it was supposed to impart.

In his prayers, the master addressed the girdle as 'friendly goddess' and attributed its power to its 'breathings', respiration having spiritual and divine significance. The knots in the girdle remind us of the Ancient Egyptian 'Girdle of Isis', itself an emblem of life and a symbol of protection, purity, strength and immortality.

In the Bible, too, the girdle is a symbol of strict attachment and constant assiduity, with the double meaning of attachment as a blessing (Psalm 76: 11) and tenacity as a curse (Psalm 109: 18–19): 'As he clothed himself with cursing like as with his garment, so let it come into his bowels like water, and like oil into his bones. Let it be unto him as the garment which covereth him, and for a girdle wherewith he is girded constantly.'

The Children of Israel used to celebrate the Passover with their loins girt about as the Lord had commanded.

The traveller wears a girdle in the sense that he or she is ready to meet any danger. The components of that girdle display the vocation of the wearer and, whether it reveals lowliness or power, it always indicates a choice and is a concrete example of the power of choosing. This is why, when Christ said to St Peter (John 21: 10), 'When thou wast young, thou girdest thyself, and walkedst wither thou wouldest: but when thou shalt be old, thou shalt stretch forth thy hands, and another shall gird thee, and carry thee whither thou wouldest not', he meant that when Peter was young he chose his own fate and that later he would answer the summons of his vocation.

Girdles defend the wearer from evil spirits in the same way that the walls which girdle cities protect them from their enemies.

'To gird up the loins for a journey or for any determined course of physical action was regarded in antiquity as proof of energy and consequently as rejection of ease and sloth. It was at the same time a mark of chaste conduct and of purity of heart . . . and this is why St Gregory made the girdle a symbol of chastity' (AUBS 2: pp. 150ff.). It is in this sense, too, and in its association with continence, that we should interpret in the Christian tradition the girdle worn by the celebrant at Mass or the leather or rope girdle which the religious wear round their waists. In this context, however, the symbol goes far deeper since, in the Bible, the loins symbolize not only power and strength (Psalms 17, 28, 40), but justice as well (Isaiah 11: 5). This will give greater insight into the reasons why some monastic Rules, such as those of St Basil, prescribe that monks shall sleep fully dressed and with their loins girded. The Pseudo-Dionysius the Areopagite corroborates this important aspect of the symbol and his interpretation of it is, in a sense, both materialistic and spiritualized when he writes that celestial minds are clothed in a robe and a girdle which should be interpreted symbolically. 'But the girdles signify their guard over their productive powers, and their own collected habit to be turned to Oneness with it, and to encircle it with good order by being drawn around itself by an unbroken identity' (PSEH pp. 46–7). In this context the symbol of the girdle widens, as Christian art confirms, to include the fruitfulness of the spirit which comes from mental concentration, as well as that permanence of identity which is one of the major aspects of faithfulness. To be unfaithful is to change one's identity: to be fruitful is to multiply one's identity.

Countless examples might be quoted of the close relationship at all levels of the words 'girdle', 'chastity' and 'fruitfulness'. Thus, in the Middle Ages, when widows renounced their rights to their late husband's estate, they would lay their girdles on his grave; and Church councils condemned as magical those miraculous girdles which were supposed to ease the pains of childbirth. All this symbolism makes the belt in which the traveller placed his money and from which he hung his weapons akin to that of the HORN OF PLENTY.

If fastening a girdle is fulfilling a vow, loosing it will mean breaking that vow. Traditionally, Islam speaks of the Christian who abjures his faith to become a Muslim as snapping his girdle. To lay aside one's sash is to renounce one's duties if one is an official or civic functionary, to lay down one's arms and surrender if one is an officer. When the sash is not voluntarily taken off, but torn away and pulled off by somebody else, it is degradation, impairment and violation of office. In Classical antiquity, to say that a girl had unloosed her girdle implied her sexual surrender. Hence it is apparent that, unlike the chastity belt which the lord and master imposed upon a passive wearer, the 'girdle of virginity' was something that a girl wore with pride until her husband unloosed it on their wedding-night. 'This girdle', Festus tells us, 'was woven from lamb's wool and signified that, just as the woollen threads were woven together, so the husband was bound by a girdle and strict tie to his wife. The husband unloosed the girdle, bound with the . . . Herculean knot as a presage that he would be as fortunate in the numbers of his children as was Hercules who sired seventy.'

Girdle of Isis See ANKH.

glove The clichés for giving and accepting a challenge – throwing down or
picking up the gauntlet – are survivals from the age of chivalry. The wearing of gloves as part of the Catholic liturgy, as well as the wearing of white
gloves by Freemasons, is a symbol of purity, preventing unwitting and direct
contact with anything unclean.

Boucher, noting that 'magnetism really does emanate from the finger-
tips', believes that 'white gloves allow only magnetism transformed into
benign influences to filter out. At a Masonic lodge meeting where all those
present wear white gloves, there is a very special atmosphere of peace, calm
and stillness' (BOUM p. 313).

Gloves are also emblems of investiture, and their colour and shape, as for
example those worn by bishops when they celebrate Mass, display their
function. Gloves are the especial mark of the nobility and were worn for
preference upon the left hand. The gauntlet with the leather covering the
wrist and upon which a falcon could perch was an emblem of the rights of
the chase.

By removing one's gloves in somebody's presence, one acknowledged
their superiority and paid them homage by disarming oneself before them.

glow-worm See FIREFLY.

gnome According to the Kabbalah gnomes were genii, short in stature,
who lived underground and possessed treasures of precious metals and
jewels. Their legend travelled from the Near East to Scandinavia and to
Central America. They came to symbolize the invisible being who by inspiration, intuition, imagination or in dream makes visible things which are
invisible. They exist within the human soul as flashes of knowledge, enlightenment or revelation. They are, as it were, the hidden soul of things, whether
organic or not, and when they leave them those things die, become lifeless
and shadowy. Gnomes are fickle and can swiftly change from loving to
hating a person. Slowly gnomes grew in the imagination into ugly, misshapen, malign and evil DWARFS. On the other hand their womenfolk, although even smaller, were dazzlingly beautiful and wore long pointed
slippers, one ruby, the other emerald. The pair, or the gnome duplicated as
a male and female complex, symbolizes the conjunction in all beings of the
beautiful and the ugly, good and evil, dark and light. Undoubtedly they are
images of complex and fleeting states of consciousness in which knowledge
co-exists with ignorance, moral wealth with moral poverty. They are examples of the conjunction of opposites and of knowledge held in secret or
hidden.

The symbol has no connection with gnomic poetry except a common
derivation from the Greek *gignōskein*, 'to perceive'.

gnomon An instrument used in antiquity for measuring the variations in
the length and height of an object by means of the movement of the shadow
cast by a stylus (the pointed implement used for writing on wax tablets)
upon a screen. For example it follows the movement of the Sun and consequently marks the hours which can be shown on a sun-dial. The gnomon
was known to the Chinese, the Ancient Egyptians and to the Indians of

Central America. It originated the earliest astronomical discoveries. The gnomon symbolizes all instruments which enable their users to delve into the secrets of time and space and to acquire knowledge by casting images of movement and position and translating them into numbers (see COMPASSES).

goat (see also SCAPEGOAT)   Like the RAM, the he-goat symbolizes the powers of procreation, the life force, the libido and fertility, but at times this becomes the likeness of opposites since the ram is a solar creature of the day while the goat, more often than not, is a lunar creature of the night. The goat is also the animal of tragedy since, for reasons beyond our reach, the creature has given its name to an art form. Tragedy means, in Greek, 'goat-song', and it was originally the hymn sung ritually during the sacrifice of a goat at Dionysiac festivals. Dionysos was the god to whom goats were especially sacred and who made them his chosen victims (Euripides, *Bacchae* 667). It should not be forgotten that sacrifice involves a whole process of identification, Dionysos himself being metamorphosed into a goat when Typhon attacked Olympus and the gods fled in panic. Dionysos escaped to Egypt, reaching a land in which shrines had been built to a goat-god whom the Greeks called Pan. In them, the temple slaves prostituted their bodies to goats in ritual identification with the procreative forces of nature and with the powerful drive of the life force. Like rams, hares and sparrows, the goat was sacred to Aphrodite and was ridden by the goddess. It was also used as a steed by Dionysos and Pan, who sometimes dressed in its skin.

The Old Testament, too, acknowledges the sacrificial qualities of the goat, the Mosaic offering in expiation of sin, disobedience and uncleanness among the Children of Israel. 'Then shall he kill the goat of the sin offering, that is for the people, and bring his blood within the vail, and do with that blood as he did with the blood of the bullock, and sprinkle it upon the mercy seat, and before the mercy seat' (Leviticus 16: 15).

Hence it is hardly surprising that through complete misunderstanding of the symbol and misdirection of the instincts which it signified, the goat should be made a traditional image of lust. This is the tragedy. Horace (*Epodes* 10: 23) describes as 'lustful' or 'lascivious' the goat which he intends to sacrifice to the storm-gods, as if libido was to be identified with sexual excess and procreative powers with violence. In this context, the goat, a smelly animal, comes to symbolize an abomination, a reprobate or, as de St-Martin says, 'corruption and iniquity'. An unclean beast, obsessed by the sex drive, the goat is reduced to an emblem of the accursed, a sign which was to come into its own during the Middle Ages. The Devil, the sex-god, was then displayed in the guise of a goat and in books of piety, his presence, like that of the goat, was said to be betrayed by his strong, rank smell.

Religious iconography set goats on the left hand at the Last Judgement to represent the wicked awaiting damnation and sometimes showed a he-goat at the head of a flock of she-goats. Here they may represent the powerful who through their wealth or reputation lead the weak astray. According to Grillot de Givry, the goat-headed Satan of Christian iconography is 'the god Mendes, of Egypt in its decline, a mixture of faun, satyr and goatlike Pan, with the tendency to become the pattern of all factors militating against the divine' (GRIA pp. 66–7). Witches used to ride goats, like broomsticks, to their Sabbaths.

In Ireland some of the lower orders of ugly, misshapen beings, related in a general way to the FOMORIANS, were given the blanket description of *goborchind*, or 'goat-heads'.

In the end the malign or dark aspect of the symbol so dominated as to make goats the image of

the male in such a state of constant sexual excitement that it would require three times four-score women to sate him. The goat is the man who dishonours his patriarchal beard with sodomy and wastes the precious seeds of life. The animal is the image of the unfortunate man whose inability to control his vicious courses makes him pitiful, the disgusting creature from whom one should run, holding one's nose.

Medieval terror and sexual taboos could not, however, utterly erase the positive aspects of the symbol, as countless folk traditions go to show. In Mediterranean tradition, as recorded both by Pliny and by recent research, goat's blood is believed to possess extraordinary powers, especially its miraculous ability to temper steel. Furthermore, goats represent those fetish creatures which absorb disease and evil influences and take on their backs all the misfortunes which threaten a village. Every village has its he-goat acting as its guardian. Nobody beats or torments it since it acts as a lightning conductor and intercepts all the bad luck before it can strike. Its efficiency is gauged by the length of its beard and the rankness of its smell. Another he-goat is always kept in reserve in case the first should die.

In Africa, a Fulani legend displays the twin polarities of the he-goat symbol, of procreative force and protective power.

Being covered by long hair, goats are emblems of virility but, because their whole bodies are so covered, they are emblems of malevolence and hence they become images of lust. The African legend of Kaydara describes how a bearded he-goat 'kept circling a tree-stump, ceaselessly mounting it, backing down and mounting it again. And each time it mounted the stump, the goat ejaculated, just as if it had been mounting a she-goat and, despite the flood of semen which it discharged, it could not satisfy its sexual appetites' (see HAIR; HORN). This legend explains that among the categories of living things, the he-goat sometimes represents an attempt to marry animal and plant, just as coral is intermediate between plant and animal and bats link birds and mammals.

However, by contrast with Christian Europe, Vedic India sufficiently counterbalanced the negative aspect of the symbol by identifying the he-goat, a sacrificial animal, with the fire-god, Agni. Goats were therefore seen as symbols of the fire of procreation, the sacrificial fire from which a new and holy life was born. A he-goat was also used by Agni, Lord of Fire, as a steed. Hence it became a solar creature which, like the she-goat, was endowed with the three basic qualities, or *guna*.

Because the same Sanskrit word for she-goat also meant 'not-born', the she-goat became the symbol of immanent primeval matter. She was the Mother of the World, Prakrti. The three colours attributed to her – red, white and black – corresponded to the three *guna*, or primordial qualities – *sattva, rajas* and *tamas* (DANA).

Some Ancient Chinese peoples related the she-goat to the lightning-god, who used the skull of a sacrificial she-goat as his anvil. The same relation between lightning and she-goats is to be found in Tibet. In short the she-goat stands as a means whereby the blessings of Heaven are conveyed to Earth, and especially blessings on farmers and herdsmen.

In Germanic belief, the she-goat, Heidrun, fed off the leaves of the ash, Yggdrasil, and supplied Odin's warriors with her milk.

To the Ancient Greeks, the she-goat symbolized LIGHTNING and the star of that name in the constellation Auriga, like Amalthea, the she-goat which suckled Zeus, heralded storms and rain.

The notional association of the she-goat with a divine manifestation is very ancient. According to Diodorus Siculus it was the behaviour of some she-goats which directed the attention of the men of Delphi to the spot where smoke was coming from the bowels of the Earth. The fumes made the animals dizzy and they appeared to dance. Fascinated, the men realized that the fumes seeping from the ground were a manifestation of the divine and they founded an oracle on the spot.

The Lord appeared to Moses on Mount Sinai in thunder and lightning. In memory of this manifestation, the covering of the tabernacle was woven from goat-hair.

Syrians and some Romans wore a garment woven from goat-hair and known as the *cilicium* when they offered prayer, as a symbol of their union with the godhead. The Christian use of the hair-shirt carries the same overtones, the aim being to mortify the flesh through penance and thus to free the living soul intent upon surrendering wholly to God. There are also echoes of this in the rough homespun of the monastic habit.

In this context it should also be observed that the derivation of the word *sufi* generally accepted in the Middle East is from *suf*, the goat-hair cloth from which was made the ritual garment of dervishes belonging to those mystic Muslim brotherhoods with especially strict rules.

The Orphic mystagogues compared the soul of the initiate with a kid fallen into its mother's milk, that is to say living on the food of neophytes to acquire the immortality of divine life. In Dionysiac orgies the Bacchantes were dressed in the skins of slaughtered kids and Dionysos, in his mystical trance, is sometimes depicted as a kid, new-born to the divine life. The infant Zeus was suckled by the she-goat Amalthea, who was transformed into a nymph, then into a fostering goddess and lastly into a daughter of the Sun.

All these traditions regard the she-goat as the symbol of the wet-nurse and initiator in both the material and mystical senses of the words. However, from her Latin name comes our adjective 'capricious' and she is therefore an embodiment of the unpredictable way in which the gods bestow their gifts. The he-goat, regarded by some as a god and by others as a devil, is truly a tragic creature, symbolizing the strength of the life force, its bounty and the ease with which it can be perverted.

goblet There is very little difference between goblets and CHALICES and, in general symbolic terms, they are identical. One of the most heavily

Christianized Irish tales, *Altrom Tighe Da Medar*, 'The Food of the House with Two Goblets', is the story of the gods Manannan and Oenghus, and how they brought from India, the land of righteousness, two sacred cows and with them the two goblets from which they intended to drink their milk. For a whole month this milk formed the sole food of a girl, Eithne – allegorically representing Ireland – who had been humiliated by one of the inhabitants of the SID and who, until her conversion to Christianity, was no longer willing to eat the food of the pagan gods (ZEIP 18: pp. 189–229).

The symbolism of the goblet is linked to its liquid contents. In the Irish tale, milk is the sacred food, provided by the fountain of all life, for such is the cow according to the Vedic and Hindu beliefs which inspired the story. Eithne has been humiliated and will only take this god-given drink because she has dedicated her life almost completely to spiritual ends and it is her soul which she feeds. The episode symbolizes the sublimation of desire. Communion with the blood of Christ in the chalice might be seen in the same light, if strictly in terms of transposition. In itself the goblet would symbolize the material means which aid humans in their spiritual ascent.

God The symbols of the godhead are chiefly those of father, judge, almighty, sovereign. Because the study of God (theology) is linked to that of pure being (ontology), these two terms have often been confused and each of them taken for the symbol of the other in the imperfect extent of our knowledge of them. 'God' might be a convenient term to use for what we do not know about perfect being and 'being' a convenient term for what we do not know about God. This is in fact what God himself has called himself: 'I am that I am' (Exodus 3: 14).

Roman Catholics believe that:

All that which exists is related to subsistent being [God] and is relative to it, but [God] itself is not, by virtue of the fact that it is pre-existent and is in itself existence. This is why it is not of necessity related to existing things and is, in respect of them, independent, separated and hence 'ab-solute'. Divine independence is therefore to be seen as the real nub of this ontological argument. Any valid statement on the nature of God presupposes that one has reached this essential point. . . . It is here that we meet with the tendency of each being to encroach beyond the boundaries and specific conditions of his or her own domain or again the need to anchor oneself in the absolute of which the plenitude knows no limits – what we in fact find in subsistent being.

(ENCF 1: p. 332)

Polytheists give separate individuality to each of the manifestations of the Absolute, since they regard them as distinct and separate beings. God is, and symbolizes, the monad, to which all manifestations tend, and life, in which all living is fulfilled. Even atheism, at least in some shapes, is not a denial of all ideas of God. All ideas, limited and imperfect as they are, if not denials, are at least the negative path of theology and of the mystics. It might then be objected that, although God cannot be encompassed by the power of thought, some thoughts act as vectors to direct the spirit towards God.

All that exists in nature, which is visible to the eyes and sensible to the touch, is part and parcel of pure being, just as all the mysteries of life and of grace are to believers part and parcel of the very nature of God. Contingent being by its very reality is a symbol of pure being and of God, the elect being promised that they shall see face to face what they now see in a glass darkly. Individuals in this world, whose sense-perceptions are taken as reliable evidence, are, truth to tell, enigmas, since we do not know one aspect of the relationship by which they exist. However, it is towards this hidden aspect that the spirit, as by a symbol, is directed by what it knows of pure being. It is hardly surprising, then, that in its efforts to solve this puzzle, mankind here on Earth should have created God in so many different images and should have endowed their ideas of God with the knowledge which they had obtained of themselves and of the phenomenal world (see CREATION). Smitten by feelings of powerlessness and dependence, mankind projected its fears and desires upon a superior Being able to satisfy and protect them.

Strabo (3: 4, 16) related that every month at full Moon the Celtiberians danced before the doors of their houses in homage to a nameless god. Although it is reasonable to conceive of a god the mention of whose name was taboo, yet it is preferable to regard this as a metaphysical concept, similar perhaps to the Irish 'gods' and 'non-gods'. The god who cannot be named is 'non-being', and this is the reason for his anonymity. The Aztecs, too, worshipped an unknown god.

St Paul mentions the Greek notion of the unknown God (Acts 17: 23ff.), interpreted as a presentiment of the existence of the One, good and transcendent God. 'Non-being' and 'unknown' might well designate some being immeasurably different from the being we know and which human language expresses.

From the bulk of Irish literary sources and countless Gallo-Roman sculptures it has generally been concluded that the Celts were polytheists and practised a primitive form of nature worship. But this is to look at accidentals. The structure of their pantheon makes one think that theirs may have been a monotheism, not so remote from Christianity. Each of their chief deities possessed several aspects described by a variety of names, and each in themselves comprised an aspect of the great all-knowing deity who transcended all the rest. The godhead proceeded from a single being to a plurality of beings and the determinate ruled the indeterminate. But once the teachings of the druids were lost, such a concept was forgotten, and this explains the vague and nebulous attraction of the Gallo-Roman pantheon (OGAC 12: p. 335).

gohei See PAPER.

gold Gold, traditionally regarded as the most precious of all metals, is the perfect metal. The Chinese employ the same ideogram, *kin*, for both metal and gold. It flashes like light and in India is allegedly called 'mineral light'. Its nature is fiery, solar and royal, even divine. Some peoples believed that the gods' flesh was made of gold, as did the Ancient Egyptians of their Pharaohs, too. Images of the Buddha are gilded as a sign of enlightenment and of absolute perfection. The backgrounds of Byzantine icons are gilded – as is sometimes the case with Buddhist paintings – as a reflection of heavenly light.

In many places, and especially in the Far East, gold was believed to be the offspring of Earth. The ancient ideogram, *kin*, suggests Earth-born nuggets. Gold was held to be either the product, after long gestation, of an embryo or else the result of the perfecting of base metals. It was the child of Nature's desires. Alchemy was restricted to completing or accelerating the natural process of transmutation: it did not originate fresh matter. Naturally the aim of true alchemists was not to obtain precious metal for, although Nagarjūna maintained that clay might be transmuted into gold, Sri Rāmakrishna was well aware that gold and clay are one and the same. The Chinese symbolic colour for gold is white, not yellow, the latter corresponding with Earth. Transmutation is a form of redemption. Changing lead into gold, Angelus Silesius would say, is transforming man into God through God. Such were the mystical objectives of spiritual alchemy.

Gold and light are generally symbols of knowledge, basic *yang*. The Brahmanas tell us that gold is immortality. Taken literally this meant that in both China and in India the medicine of immortality was prepared with gold as its base. The man who followed such a course of treatment would find his hair turning black again and fresh teeth sprouting ... but above all he would become a 'true man' (*chen-jen*). However, it was through knowledge, rather than by medicine its physical symbol, that earthly immortality was to be attained.

In this context it is as well to be reminded that traditionally the primordial age was the Golden Age and that the ages of silver, bronze and iron which followed it mark the descending stages in the cycle.

The Aztecs associated gold with the Earth's 'new skin' at the start of the Spring rains and before it became green once more. It was a symbol of the seasonal cycle of natural renewal and for this reason Xipe Totec, the Flayed God of Spring rains and renewal, was also the goldsmiths' god. The victims sacrificed to this bloodthirsty deity were flayed and his priests dressed themselves in their skins, painted yellow like gold leaf (SOUA).

According to the chronicle written by Guzman Poma de Ayala, the inhabitants of Chincha-Suyu in the northwestern portion of the Inca Empire buried their dead with a coca leaf and pieces of gold and silver in their mouths. Undoubtedly this re-echoes the symbolic qualities of YIN AND YANG in gold and silver.

From the Urals comes evidence of an association of gold with the mythic SERPENT. The Great World Serpent, the Mighty Crawler, is lord of gold. He is sometimes seen in the shape of a snake with a golden crown, sometimes as a black-eyed, black-haired man with very swarthy skin, dressed in yellow (Bajov). 'Wherever he goes, gold springs up in his footprints, but if he is provoked he can take it away.' Everything, even fire, freezes as he passes by; except in Winter, when he brings warmth and thaws the snow. This characteristically chthonian association illustrates the widespread belief that gold, the precious metal above all others, is Earth's most closely guarded secret.

Throughout West Africa gold is 'the royal metal which is one of the basic myths, long before any monetary value was placed upon it.' Different proverbs show the reasons for this:

Gold neither rusts nor becomes soiled; it is the only metal to become cotton while remaining iron; from an ounce of gold you can make a thread as thin as a hair and long enough to encircle a whole village; gold is the tree of knowledge and the throne of wisdom, but if you shake the tree for knowledge, it will fall and crush you; be Fortune's horseman not its horse; gold, by its purity and incorruptibility, is the metal above all others of hidden knowledge.

Gold is to be found beneath ELEVEN layers of earth and other different minerals. If it is well used, that is to say in the search for knowledge, it brings happiness, otherwise it causes its owner disaster. It is an ambivalent metal, possessing once again that primeval dualism. It is the key to many doors, but also the weight or burden which can crush limbs or break necks. It is as hard to use it properly as it is to obtain it (HAMK p. 29).

Dogon and Bambara regard gold as the quintessence of red COPPER, the latter the primordial vibration in material shape, the spirit of God, speech and water, the fertilizing word.

This primeval and cosmic spiritual meaning attached to the yellow metal is re-echoed and explained in the myth of the Rainbow Serpent. Dan, this serpent, which chews its own tail (see OUROBOROS), the symbol of continuity, is coiled round the Earth to prevent it falling in pieces. He is the SPIRAL and primordial movement of creation, carrying the stars in their courses, and is also Lord of Gold and gold itself. He is the Rainbow Serpent, servant of the universe, who does nothing of his own volition, but without whom nothing can be done. In this respect the notions of the Fon coincide with those of the Dogon, and Dan, the golden spiral, the path of Sun and stars, becomes the *alter ego* of the red copper spiral, which gave expression to the primordial vibration and is coiled around the Dogon Sun. Since, however, gold is the quintessence of red copper, in the building of the cosmos it became the first principle of its stability and, hence, of human security and, by extension, of human happiness. On these grounds, and by his solar and spiritual qualities, Damballah became the Haitian god of wealth and gold, the symbol of material riches, themselves the symbolic principle of spiritual riches. Here is the recurrence in the notions of African peoples of the hidden and alchemical meaning of gold as conceived in traditional European and Asian thought.

The Bambara also regard gold as the symbol of the fire of purification and enlightenment. The word *sanuya*, which may be translated as 'purity', is derived from the root *sanu*, meaning 'gold' (ZAHB). Their fundamental deity, the monitor lizard Faro, who regulates the world and who is Lord of the Word, is depicted as wearing two collars, one of copper, the other of gold. The former tells him everything that is said in everyday conversation, the latter 'secrets and words of power' (DIEB). This 'dark' function of gold, symbol of hidden knowledge, coincides with the meaning which alchemists attached to the metal. Gold was produced by 'digesting' 'bright' or external qualities, and enshrines the ambivalence of notions of the sacred, by making holy the residue of the digestion, excrement and filth. In this context one should emphasize that among the Bambara there is a group of initiates, known as the Kore Dugaw or Vultures, who give public displays of coprophagy and are called 'possessors of real gold' and 'the richest men in the world' (ZAHB p. 178). Dowsers claim that gold and EXCREMENT produce similar vibrations.

In Greek tradition, gold suggests the SUN and the range of symbolism belonging to it – fertility, wealth, dominion, a centre of warmth, love and generosity, the fire of light, knowledge and radiance. The GOLDEN FLEECE imparted a higher level of solar symbolism to the animal which wore it, such as the ram. (This already represented the physical powers of procreation and now acquired those on a spiritual plane as well. The Golden Fleece became the badge of the master and mystagogue.)

Gold is a weapon of light and golden knives alone were employed in sacrifices to the sky-gods. Similarly, the druids cut mistletoe only with a golden sickle. The Sun-god, Apollo, was clothed and armed with gold – tunic, buckles, lyre, bow, quiver and sandals.

Hermes, initiate, conductor of souls, messenger of the gods and god of traders, was also the god of robbers, thus signifying the ambivalence of gold. However, the Ancients regarded the latter title borne by the god 'as a symbol of mysteries withdrawn from common sight, the priests stealing away the gold, a symbol of light, from the gaze of the uninitiated' (PORS p. 78).

As we have already observed, the Ancient Egyptians regarded gold as the Sun's flesh and, by extension, that of their deities and Pharaohs. 'The goddess Hathor was believed to be the incarnation of gold . . . Gold conferred divine survival . . . By an extension of this belief gold became of great importance in funerary symbolism' (POSD p. 111).

Lastly, but still in accordance with the identification of gold with sunlight, gold is one of the symbols of Jesus, the Light, the Sun and the Dayspring. 'It may be readily understood why Christian artists have depicted Christ as golden-haired like Apollo and have set a halo on his head' (PORS p. 73).

But gold is an ambivalent treasure. The colour gold and the pure metal gold may be solar symbols, but 'minted gold is a symbol of perversion and the exaltation of unclean desire' (DIES p. 172), the spiritual degraded to the level of the material, the immortal to the mortal.

Golden Bough The Golden Bough is akin to that universal symbol of rebirth and immortality, the green branch. The Golden Bough was a branch of MISTLETOE, the plant's pale green leaves turning gold with the turn of the year, and thus its plucking coincided with the New Year.

The druids took their name from the combination of two roots *dru* and *vid*, which have the meaning of strength and wisdom or knowledge respectively and which were represented by OAK and mistletoe in the tree-alphabet. Druids were therefore mistletoe and oak, wisdom joined with strength, or priestly authority backed by temporal power. This conjunction of mistletoe and oak shows that the two qualities remained indistinct within the individual. Guénon, incidentally, has observed that this symbolism is precisely upon a par with that of the Egyptian sphinx, human head and lion's body, symbols of wisdom and strength (GUES, GUEA).

Although Greco-Roman tradition provided no precedent for the Golden Bough, Virgil set such a bough in the hands of Aeneas for his descent into the Underworld. 'A bough, golden in leaf and pliant in stem, held consecrate to nether Juno; this is all the grove hides, and shadows veil in the dim valleys. But 'tis not given to pass beneath the earth's hidden places, save to him who has plucked from the tree the golden-tressed fruitage' (*Aeneid* VI: 136–41). Guided by a pair of doves, Aeneas set off in search of the tree with the Golden Bough in the heart of the woods and suddenly saw it in a deep ravine.

Once equipped with this precious bough he was able to descend into the Underworld. Commenting upon these passages in the *Aeneid*, Jean Beaujeu observes that:

the mythology of mistletoe was scarce in Italy but abundant in Celtic and Germanic lands. The mistletoe was endowed with magic powers; it was the key to the Underworld, drove away evil spirits, conferred immortality and was impervious to fire, a detail which would endear it to Romans. The incident is so structured as if Virgil had adapted a theme from his birthplace – the Po Valley had been occupied by the Celts for several centuries – and Romanized it by the dedication of the bough to Proserpina.

Mistletoe was gathered in accordance with strict ritual. The bough could not be cut by iron, the use of iron being forbidden in most religious rites since it was believed to drive spirits away. Iron would, therefore, have removed its magic powers from the mistletoe bough, and the druids accordingly gathered it with a golden sickle.

The Golden Bough is a symbol of that light which enables us to explore unscathed the dark caverns of the Underworld and not to lose our souls. It is strength, wisdom and knowledge.

Golden Calf It is the idol of wealth, the god of material goods set up in place of the god of the spirit.

The expression originates in the Old Testament story (Exodus 32: 1–10) of how in Moses' absence the Children of Israel persuaded his brother, Aaron the High Priest, to make them 'gods that shall go before us'. Aaron accordingly fashioned a calf out of the golden earrings contributed by the people, thus incurring the Lord's wrath.

The Golden Calf consequently symbolizes the constantly recurring temptation to deify the lust for material things, be they wealth, sensual pleasure or power.

It was probably also one of the idols of Baal (see BAAL AND BAALAT) which the prophets denounced throughout the history of Israel (1 Kings 12: 18) and of mankind itself.

Golden Fleece Jung maintains that the legend of the Golden Fleece symbolizes attainment of what reason regards as the impossible. It brings two symbols together, that of innocence, portrayed by the RAM's fleece, and that of glory, represented by the GOLD. It is thus akin to all myths involving the quest for a treasure, either material or spiritual, like the quest of the Holy Grail.

Jason, the hero of the Golden Fleece, is categorized by Paul Diel as an opponent of degeneration into the commonplace. The glory which he seeks is that of attaining truth (the gold) and spiritual purity (the fleece). Like all treasure, the fleece is guarded by a MONSTER, in this case by a DRAGON, which has first to be overcome. This dragon is the perversion of the desire for glory and the 'uncleanly enhancement of lusts'. It symbolizes Jason's 'own perversion. Had the dragon been heroically slain, it would have become the symbol of true liberation.' Jason, however, merely puts the dragon to sleep with a draught prepared by the witch, Medea. He is defeated by his own internal dragon. Jason remains subservient to Medea who blackens his name with her crimes. Jason compromises with what stands in direct opposition to his own mission and despises the spirit and purity of soul. Thus he drains his heroic enterprise of all its meaning and simultaneously destroys both his exploit and his ideal.

Jason is a symbol of the idealist who fails to realize that some means are incompatible with the ends for which they are employed, and who allows himself to be perverted by the methods which he uses. His ship, the Argo, 'is the symbol of youthful promise, of apparently heroic deeds on which his glory was based. Jason wished to rest in the shadow of that glory, thinking it enough to justify his life as a whole. When it fell into decay, the Argo, symbol of the heroic hopes of his youth, become in the end the symbol of the wreck of his life. It punished him for his surrender to the commonplace' (DIES pp. 171–82).

golden-haired   The gods, goddesses and heroes of Classical antiquity were golden-haired. Even Dionysos, described as brown-haired in the 'Homeric' hymn, soon became what Euripides calls 'a handsome young man with black eyes and golden hair'. GOLD is the colour which symbolizes the psychic powers which emanate from the godhead, and the Old Testament confirms such an interpretation. King David's hair was reddish gold (1 Samuel 16: 12) and Christ is so depicted in countless works of art.

The Celts regarded golden hair not simply as a sign of male or female beauty, but as a mark of royalty. Nevertheless, like Dionysos, the hero Cùchulainn was not completely golden-haired, but had some brown hair, too, and it is generally mentioned in any description of him. The same criteria applied in Wales, but was not universal. Derdriu, one of the loveliest girls in Ireland, had brown hair. Classical authors state that the Gauls bleached their hair with soda.

The regard paid to golden hair derives fom the fact that it is the colour of the sun, of baked bread and of ripe corn. It is a manifestation of heat and ripeness, while brown hair is rather a sign of immanent subterranean warmth and of internal ripeness (see BROWN; YELLOW).

Golem   In Jewish Kabbalistic legend, the Golem was a sort of human robot, a man created by magic or artificial means in competition with God's creation of Adam. The creation of the Golem was accomplished by copying the divine act of creation and might be considered to be in conflict with it. The Golem was dumb.

Scholem has observed that in German and Yiddish nineteenth-century literature, many Romantic writers regarded the Golem as a symbol of their own conflicting and destructive emotions. In Gustav Meyrink's eerie novel, the Golem is depicted as a symbolic image of the way of redemption. Based as much upon Hindu concepts as upon Jewish traditions, this figure stands for the collective soul of the ghetto in physical shape, with a full share of the dark side of the phantasmagoric. It is also in part the double of the hero, who is a painter striving for his own personal redemption. He cleanses messianically the Golem, who is his own unredeemed self.

At one stage of his creation, and before God had given breath and speech, Adam was no more than a shapeless Golem. In a second- or third-century Midrash 'Adam is described not only as a golem, but as a golem of cosmic size and strength, to whom, while he was still in this speechless and inanimate shape, God showed all future generations to the end of time. The juxtaposition of these two motifs, between which there is an obvious relationship of tension, if not of contradiction, is exceedingly strange' (SCHS p. 161).

This legendary creature from the Kabbalah has taken a number of different shapes.

The sorcerer who wanted to create a Golem would imitate God's creation of Adam as told in Genesis, and mould from RED clay the statue of a human being of roughly the size of a ten-year-old boy. He would then write on its forehead the Hebrew word meaning 'Life'. The Golem would immediately become endowed with breath, movement and speech, just like any human being. He would become the sorcerer's obedient servant and could be given the hardest tasks to do without fear of his becoming exhausted.

(LERM p. 42)

Unfortunately these artificial creatures would grow very fast and reach the size of giants. The sorcerer would then write on their foreheads the Hebrew word meaning 'Death' and the giant would then collapse in a heap of lifeless clay. However, the reckless sorcerer might sometimes be crushed by this mass of clay. If the giant kept the word 'Life' the worst disasters might ensue, because the Golem was, of its own volition, capable only of committing evil, although a Kabbalist might control its powers for good as strongly as for ill. Golems were sometimes substituted for real men and women or else were given such animal shapes as those of lions, tigers or serpents.

The Golem symbolizes human creativity aping God by creating a being in its own image, but only making a servile creature with a propensity to evil, a slave to its own passions. True life proceeds from God alone. In a more internalized sense, the Golem is no more than an image of its creator, or rather an image of one of his passions, which swells until he is in danger of being crushed under it. Lastly, its significance is that of the creation which passes out of the control of its creator. It demonstrates that humanity is no more than a sorcerer's apprentice and that Mephistopheles was right when he remarked that initial action was an exercise of free will, but that the subsequent act enslaved.

goose In Chinese literature or painting all allusions to geese are to the wild goose, and the same is true of DUCK. The symbolic primacy of the wild over the domestic animal goes back to the dawn of history. Thus in the beginning the goose, which has now become a symbol of marital fidelity, was a sign and an emblem when presented to a girl by a young man that she should lower the defences of her sexual modesty like wild creatures at the advent of the Spring.

The wild goose is the frequent theme of poems in the *Shih-ching*, or

'Book of Odes', a collection of popular and religious verse of which the oldest examples would appear to date from the beginning of the seventh century BC. The migration of geese from one region to another, like human movement from one place to another, was shown to be full of pitfalls. In later literature, references to 'wild geese weeping' allude to refugees and those forced from their homes.

When the Pharaohs were identified with the Sun, their souls were depicted in the shape of the goose, since the goose 'was the Sun as it emerged from the primeval egg' (CHAM p. 118).

As in China, so in Ancient Egypt geese were regarded as messengers between Heaven and Earth. Among the ceremonies attendant upon the proclamation of a new Pharaoh, four wild geese were released to the four corners of the Earth. '"Hasten towards the south and tell the gods of the south that pharaoh 'X' has taken the Double Crown." The formula was repeated for each of the cardinal points' (POSD p. 219).

In north Africa it is still customary to sacrifice a goose (as a solar creature) in the critical period of the turn of the year (SERH p. 332).

In Ancient Rome, too, the sacred geese kept around the temple of Juno were given the duty of raising the alarm. They were believed to be able to sense danger and give warning of it. They especially distinguished themselves in 390 BC when their cackling warned of an attempt by the besieging Gauls to storm the Capitol in a night attack.

Radlov records that in the Altai Mountains after the ritual sacrifice of a horse, the shaman ascends on the back of a goose in pursuit of its soul. Frequently the shaman uses a goose rather than a horse to ride back from the Underworld after visiting the King of the Dead (ELIC pp. 190–203; HARA p. 368).

Both insular and continental Celtic tradition equated the goose with the SWAN, the words for the respective birds not always being clearly distinguished. Regarded as the messenger of the Otherworld, the goose, like the hare and the hen, was forbidden food for the Bretons. Caesar records this fact (*De bello gallico* 5: 12), adding that these creatures were raised 'as pets' (*voluptatis causa*), without knowing the real reason (CHAB pp. 554–5). (See also BIRD.)

Gorgons Medusa, Euryale and Stheno, three monstrous sisters with hissing serpents instead of hair, boar's tusks instead of teeth, hands of brass and wings of gold; they symbolize 'the enemy to be encountered. Their monstrous psychological deformity is due to perversion of their social, sexual and spiritual drives.' Euryale would represent the sexual, Stheno the social and Medusa would symbolize the most important of all these drives, the spiritual and evolutionary, perverted to 'self-satisfied sloth'. 'The guilt complex arising from self-centred enhancement of desire' can only be overcome by recourse to 'harmony and the golden mean', symbolized by the Gorgons or ERINNYES hounding their victims to the entrance of the temple of Apollo, god of harmony, which acts as a sanctuary.

Whoever gazed on Medusa's face was turned to stone, perhaps because it reflected an image of personal guilt. However, acknowledgement of sin, in sound self-knowledge, may be perverted to an unhealthy degree, producing such scrupulousness of conscience as inhibits action. Paul Diel so wisely observes:

Confession can be, and nearly always is, a specific type of enhancement of the imagination, an exaggerated expression of sorrow. Exaggeration of guilt inhibits attempts to atone. It serves only to provide the guilty party with a self-centred image of him- or herself, in the complexity of his or her subconscious life, believed to be unique and of exceptional depth. . . . It is not enough to reveal guilt, the sight of it must be endured in an objective fashion, with a balance between emotion and inhibition, neither overdramatizing or minimizing. Confession itself should be free from egocentricity and guilt-complexes. . . . Medusa symbolizes the deformed image of the ego.

(DIES pp. 93–7)

– which produces stony horror instead of enlightened judgement.

gourd (see also CALABASH) The gourd provides an excellent example of the ambivalence of symbols. Although their different varieties, pumpkins for example, are emblems of stupidity to Western eyes, some African initiates eat their seeds as symbols of intelligence. It is however true that the gourd remains after its seeds have been removed.

Because of its countless seeds, the gourd has become on the same grounds and for the same reasons as citron, orange and water-melon, a symbol of plenty and of fertility. Most of the tribespeople of northern Laos and the Laotians themselves were born from gourds growing on the creeper which is the World Axis. However, those real horns of plenty, the celestial gourds of the Thai, not only contained every race of mankind and every species of rice, but books of hidden lore as well. As a source of life, the gourd was also a symbol of rebirth, and this is why Taoists made it a symbol and a food of immortality. With the help of a gourd, the mythic ancestor of the Chinese, P'an-Ku, escaped the flood. In any case, P'an-Ku may himself have been a gourd. Gourds grow in the isles of the Immortals, but they also help in the journey there, and to Heaven as well. Furthermore, it is plain why their seeds should be eaten as the food of immortality at the Spring equinox, since this is the time of seasonal renewal and the beginning of the ascendancy of the *yang* (see YIN–YANG). Equally plain is the reason for hanging calabashes in the entrance porticos of the lodges of Chinese secret societies, since they are a sign of spiritual regeneration and of access to the dwellings of the Immortals.

Miraculous gourds are also to be found in CAVERNS, but they themselves are cavernous and consequently share their cosmic symbolism. The 'Heaven shaped like a gourd' which the sage found within himself is 'the cavern of the heart'. The microcosm shaped like a gourd is also the double sphere or the two cones which meet at their apices, shapes similar to that of the alchemist's crucible and to Mount Kun-Lun. Both are basically calabashes and, like the calabash, the receptacle of the elixir of life.

It should also be observed that in Ancient China, the loving cup ritually drunk at wedding ceremonies took the form of two halves of a calabash, quite clearly embodying the notion of the two differentiated halves of primordial Oneness. In Vietnamese 'gourd' is a word used to describe the shape of the Earth. Again, it would seem wasted effort to find further reasons for making the gourd a symbol of longevity, since when it is dried and used as a calabash its enduring qualities are self-explanatory (CADV, FRAL, KALL).

The Bambara regard the gourd as a symbol of the Cosmic EGG, of the gestatory process and of the mother's womb in which the manifestation of life takes place. The Bambara call the child's umbilical cord its 'gourd stalk'.

The gourd also represents the intelligible aspect of existence. After Jonah had preached to the inhabitants of Nineveh as the Lord had commanded, he became sad and anxious, since God's attitude dismayed him. He felt that he was living in a world deprived of natural law and hence one which had become chaotic. God caused the gourd to spring up to shade the prophet's head. The sight of the gourd filled Jonah with great joy. But on the next day, at dawn, God sent a worm which attacked the gourd and it withered away. When the Sun rose, God sent a burning east wind and Jonah fainted. And then the prophet became enraged and announced that he would rather die than remain alive. Hence the dialogue between God and Jonah (Jonah 4). God's reactions cannot be foreseen. The divine dynamism, carrying with it apparently contradictory decisions, countermanded orders and changes of mind, also finds expression in Jeremiah (18: 6–10). Nothing can be forecast and mankind suffers from this insecurity and this lack of logic, or rather from a logic of which it cannot decipher the secrets. The sudden growth and death of the gourd are symbols of this. Human logic cannot grasp the incoherence of things and the absurdity of events; but they are amenable to a different logic. What happened to the gourd suggests to mankind that it should not trust to its dialectic alone, since there is another superior to it.

grafting   In the Middle East, grafting has always embodied a symbolic and ritual aspect because it is a method of artificially fertilizing plant species. It is believed only to be effective if it corresponds to a predetermined conjunction of Sun and Moon and it is also linked with the sexual activities of the person performing the grafting. In general terms, it has sexual significance. It constitutes an intervention in the natural order of generation and is the equivalent, in some cases at least, of unnatural sexual intercourse. It was for this reason that the Children of Israel were forbidden to eat grafted fruit. The problems of grafting are all linked with the power – and the right – which human beings have to modify plant life and the means and the parameters which they should employ in exercising that power and right (EPEM).

Modern science and medicine has widened the scope of grafting from plant to animal life, through organ transplants, artificial insemination and *in vitro* fertilization. Consequently the symbolic scope of these operations has been altered, too. Grafting is no longer regarded as being against nature, but as working with nature, even if outside the powers possessed naturally. It would therefore symbolize the acquisition by mankind of the powers of the Demiurge, restricted nonetheless to exchanges within the same species, the continuation of which it helps to ensure. Genetic engineering at a level at which one species were changed into another would pose a different set of problems and would charge the symbol with a different meaning. In this case it would probably acquire overtones of maleficence, since this would be an attack upon the natural order and balance of nature and upon properties which might be truly termed 'specific'.

Grail In medieval European literature the Holy Grail is the heir, if not the direct descendant, of two talismans in pre-Christian Celtic religion – the CAULDRON of the Dagda and the CHALICE of kingship. This would explain why this miraculous object should often be a deep platter carried by a virgin. In the traditions surrounding the Knights of the Round Table, it had the power of providing each of them with his favourite dish and is in this respect linked to the symbolism of the HORN OF PLENTY. Amongst its countless powers, and apart from those of giving food (the gift of life) and radiating light (spiritual enlightenment), it possessed that of granting invincibility (Julius Evola in BOUM p. 53).

Setting aside the more or less crazy explanations, the Grail has given rise to many different interpretations corresponding to the plane of reality on which the critic concerned was standing. Albert Béguin summarizes their essentials as follows:

The Grail represents at one and the same time and in substance, Christ who died for mankind, the cup used at the Last Supper (that is the divine grace with which Christ endowed his disciples) and lastly the chalice used in the Mass and holding the real blood of Christ. The table upon which the vessel rests is thus, in terms of these three levels, respectively the stone of the Holy Sepulchre, the table around which the Twelve Apostles sat and, lastly, the altar on which the Mass is celebrated every day. These three realities, the Crucifixion, the Last Supper and the Eucharist, are indivisible and the ceremony of the Holy Grail is their manifestation, providing in the communion a knowledge of Christ's person and a share in his redemptive sacrifice.

(BEGG p. 18)

This is not unrelated to Jung's psychoanalytic explanation, since he regarded the Grail as symbolizing 'the inner wholeness for which men have always been searching' (JUNS p. 215).

However, the quest of the Holy Grail demanded a state of internal life rarely to be found. External activities debar the searcher from the contemplation required and divert his longings. The Grail is close at hand, and yet it cannot be seen. This is the tragedy of blindness in the face of spiritual realities, all the more intense because of the most sincerely held belief that they are the object of one's quest. However, more attention is paid to the material than to the spiritual demands of the quest. On the spiritual plane, which is the important one, the quest of the inaccessible Grail symbolizes the spiritual risks and the demands of internalization which alone can open the gates of the Heavenly Jerusalem where the divine chalice stands in the light of its own radiance. Human perfection is the price of victory, which is achieved not with lance-thrust like a worldly prize, but by a fundamental transformation of heart and soul. To attain to the translucence of Galahad, 'Christ's living image', one has to outstrip both Lancelot and Percival.

grasshopper Its silence during the night and its shrilling during the heat of the day make the grasshopper the symbol of the complementary pairing of light and darkness. In Ancient Greece, the insect was sacred to Apollo.

Grasshoppers have become attributes of bad poets whose inspiration is inconstant, and La Fontaine also made them images of careless lack of foresight.

grave See TOMB.

Great Bear When the bear stood for the warrior caste in opposition to the wild boar of the priesthood, it was sometimes depicted in its feminine aspect. This was the case in the myth of Atalanta, who had been fostered by a she-bear and hunted the Calydonian boar. The same is true of our two polar CONSTELLATIONS. The Great Bear was once represented by a boar, and its transfer to the bear is a sign of the defeat of the priesthood and of the ascendancy of the temporal arm.

In Hindu tradition, the Great Bear (*sapta-riksha*) is the abode of the seven Rishi, symbols of wisdom and primordial tradition. The constellation is thus both the home of the Immortals and the CENTRE or ARK in which traditional knowledge is preserved.

In China, the Great Bear was originally known as the Scales and then as the Bushel (*tu*). As it turns on the centre of the sky, the handle of the Bushel shows successively the four divisions of the day and the four seasons of the year. According to Ssu Ma Ch'ien, 'the Bushel is the Ruler's chariot. It sets in motion at the centre; it governs the four corners of the Earth; it separates *yin* from *yang*; it determines the four seasons; it balances the five elements; it fixes the divisions of space and time and settles different accounts.' It should be observed that this is precisely the role of the Emperor in the Forbidden City, at the centre of the world. The Forbidden City (like the *tu* of the secret societies) is in a vertical line with the Great Bear and is its microcosmic representation. *The Secret of the Golden Flower* states that 'the pole of the Great Wain makes the whole manifestation turn about' its centre. The Pole Star, which was originally a star in the Great Bear (*tu-mu*), is the *T'ien-ki*, the 'roof-ridge of heaven'. It is the dwelling-place of T'ai-I, the Supreme One. This is why the Great Bear was used as an aid in modes of spiritual concentration aimed at retention of the One. The constellation then comes into vertical line with the person who has attained a central state and descends upon the crown of the individual's head. In different ceremonies T'ai-I is invoked by unfurling flags on which the seven stars of the Great Bear are depicted.

According to Ssu Ma Ch'ien, the seven stars correspond to the seven Rulers, an echo, indeed, of the seven Rishi, but also of the seven bodily orifices and the seven orifices in the heart. Thus the heart, the centre of the human microcosm, is regarded as its Great Bear. The Lord T'ai-I is said to hold in his left hand 'the seven stars of the handle of the Bushel and in his right, the net of the northern constellation [the Pole Star]'. This is akin to Christ of the Second Coming who 'had in his right hand seven stars' (Revelation 1: 16). Both these symbols hold notions of immortality, as doubtless did the Chinese custom of painting seven stars on coffins. The extension of these different interpretations at a popular level made the Great Bear the dwelling place of Pi-tu, Ruler of Fate, who gave his name to the constellation itself.

Lastly it should be observed that the Montagnards of southern Vietnam regard the Great Bear as a celestial archetype. It provides a pattern for boat-building, which returns us by a roundabout route to the notion of VOYAGING and of the primeval ark (CHAT, DAMS, GRAP, GRIF, GUET, GUES, LECC, MAST, SOOL).

According to Lehmann-Nitsche, the constellation, depicted upon the walls of the great Temple of Coricancha at Cuzco, stood in the eyes of the Inca of Peru for the rain- and thunder-god.

In Celtic legend, the Great Bear was known as Arthur's Wain.

green Green is a COLOUR combination of blue and yellow, but takes part with RED in the symbolic interplay of alternations. Roses blossom between green leaves.

Set midway between the inaccessible absolutes of the blue of Heaven and the red of Hell, green, with its middling quality, mediates between heat and cold and high and low. It is a comforting, refreshing, human colour. After Winter strips bare and freezes the Earth which supports human beings, convincing them of their loneliness and vulnerability, Spring comes to clothe the Earth once more in green, bringing hope and making it again the nurse of the human race. Green is warm. The coming of Spring is heralded by the thawing of the ice and falling of fructifying rain.

Green is the colour of plant life rising afresh from the regenerating and cleansing WATERS to which baptism owes all its symbolic meaning. Green is the colour of the awakening of the primeval waters: green is the colour of the awakening of life. Vishnu, who bears the weight of the world, is depicted as a tortoise with a green face; and, according to Fulcanelli, the Indian goddess representing alchemical matter, born from the sea of milk, had a green body, precisely as had Phidias' statue of Venus.

Had a painting of Neptune come down to us, he would have been depicted in a sea-green or celadon garment, as was the custom to paint the Nereids. Lastly, all things connected with the sea-gods, down to the very animals offered to them in sacrifice, wore fillets of sea-green. It is in accordance with this maxim that poets endow rivers with sea-green hair. Generally speaking nymphs, whose name is derived from water (*nympha, lympha*), are depicted in green in Classical paintings.

(Winckelmann in PORS pp. 206–7)

Green is the colour of water, as red is the colour of fire, and this is why humanity has always instinctively felt a relationship between these two colours on a par with human life and being. Green is linked to thunder. In China, it corresponds to the trigram *ch'en*, the 'arousing' (of manifestation as well as of nature in Springtime), thunder and the beginning of the ascension of the *yang*. It also corresponds to the element, Wood. Green is the colour of hope, of strength and of longevity (oddly enough, of acidity, too). It is the colour of immortality, with its worldwide symbol of the green bough.

Life ascends from red and blossoms in green. The Bambara, Dogon and Mossi regard green as a secondary colour, the offspring of red (ZAHC). This configuration is often regarded as representing the complementarity of the sexes. Man makes woman pregnant: woman nourishes man. Red is a male colour: green, a female colour. In Chinese thought they are *yin* and *yang*, one male, impulsive, centrifugal and red; the other female, reflective, centripetal and green. To balance the one against the other is the secret of the balance between mankind and nature.

By contrast with this Eastern dialectic, our Western societies, based upon the cult of male dominance, have always given priority to the creative spark, whether struck from the loins or brain of man. It is what the Spaniards term *chispa* and is the foundation of an ethical system. It is, however, counterpoised by the Oedipus complex, that is to say by the cult of mother fixation. In essence the man, as son and lover, returns to the mother as though to an oasis after a wild ride through the desert. She is the haven of peace, refreshment and recovery. This factor is the basis of a whole therapeutic system using green which, whether or not it knows it, is based upon a return to the WOMB. In the Middle Ages physicians wore a green robe, allegedly because they used herbs and simples. Nowadays this has been replaced by dark red, which intuitively expresses belief in the secrets of the art of medicine. Green has, however, remained the colour of pharmacists who actually dispense drugs. Drug manufacturers have cannily revived an old belief by giving words like 'chlorophyll' and 'vitamins' the mythic qualities of panaceas in their advertisements. Green is the colour of environmentalists, who press their case politically through Green Parties. Urbanized society, too, seems to need a periodic return to the green of the countryside. It would seem to make this a mother-substitute. A quotation by Durand from the diary of a schizophrenic would seem to bear this out. 'As I became better,' he wrote, 'I felt myself slipping into a wonderfully peaceful state. My whole room was green. I felt as if I was in the depths of some pool. It was though I was back in my mother's body. I was in Heaven, in my mother's womb' (DURS p. 249).

While green has always been the colour of the theological virtue of Hope, Christianity itself evolved in temperate climates where greenery and water are commonplace. It was very different for Islam, whose traditions flowered like mirages over vast, hostile, burning desert and steppe. Islam's standard is green and that colour is the Muslim's emblem of salvation. It is the symbol of the most highly prized riches, both material and spiritual – first and foremost the family. The Prophet's cloak is supposed to have been green and under it his direct descendants – his daughter Fatima, his son-in-law Ali and their children, Hassan and Hussein – would take refuge in time of danger. This is why they are called 'the four under the cloak', that is also to say the four pillars upon which Muhammad built Islam.

After desert nomads have said their last evening prayer, at night, they recount the wonderful tales of Khidr, Khisr or Al Kadir, the Green Man. Khisr is the patron of travellers and embodies divine providence. Traditionally he is supposed to have built his house 'on the very edge of the world, where the heavenly and the earthly oceans meet'. He therefore stands for that mean in human relations, midway between the High and the Low. Whoever meets Khisr should not question him, but should do whatever he advises, however far-fetched it may seem. Khisr, like all true initiates, points the way of truth in words which may sometimes appear ridiculous on the surface. In this sense Khisr is closely related to Andersen's 'Travelling Companion' and, like him, disappears once his task is over. His origins are obscure. Some say he was the son of Adam, the first of the prophets, and that he salvaged his father's body from the Flood. Others say that he was born in a cave – the womb of the Earth itself – was suckled and raised by wild animals and entered the service of a king who could not reasonably be any other than God or his Spirit. He is sometimes confused with St George and more often with Elijah – confirmation of the kinship of green with red, of water with fire. The story goes that, as he was travelling through the desert one day, carrying a dried fish, he came across a spring. He dipped the fish into the water and it immediately came to life again. Khisr realized that he had found the fountain of life. He dived in and became immortal and his cloak turned green. He is often associated with the primordial ocean and is said to live on an island in the middle of the sea. Consequently he has become the patron of seamen, Syrian sailors calling upon him when caught in a storm. In India, where he is worshipped under the name of Khawaja Khidr, he is depicted seated upon a fish and is identified with the river-gods. However, he is of necessity ruler over plants as well as over streams. Some Arab writers say that he 'is seated upon a white fur which turns green' and a commentator adds that this fur 'is the Earth'. The Sufi say that he also aids mankind against 'drowning and fire, kings and evil jinn, serpents and scorpions'. He is thus clearly a mediator, reconciler of opposites who settles fundamental divisions to make safe the road along which mankind travels. In Islam green is still the colour of knowledge, like that of the Prophet. The saints in Paradise wear green.

In its benign aspect, green acquires a mythic quality of the green pastures, the Eden of childhood affection, green as the infancy of the world and as the eternal youth promised to the Elect. Before it was given to Ireland, Green Erin was the name of the island of the blessed in the Celtic world. The German mystics Mechtilde of Magdeburg and Angelus Silesius associate green and white with the Epiphany and with Christlike qualities, the green of justice complementing the white of innocence.

The Heraldic tincture, or colour, for green is known as *vert* in English, but *sinople* in French. According to a fifteenth-century writer quoted by the lexicographer Littré, 'the blazon means woods, meadows, fields and greenery, that is to say, civility, love, joy and abundance' (PORS). Anselm in his *Palais de l'honneur* (quoted in PORS pp. 215–16) wrote that: 'Archbishops bear a hat *sinople*, with green tassels interlaced . . . bishops too bear a hat *sinople*, because having been ordained as shepherds to Christian folk, this tincture denotes good pasturage where wise shepherds bring their flocks to feed and it is the symbol of the sound doctrine of these prelates.'

These marvellous virtues of green suggest that this colour hides a secret and that it symbolizes deep and hidden knowledge of nature and of fate. 'Sinople' is derived from the Low Latin word *sinopis*, which originally meant the reddish brown soil (or the pigment made from it) which came from the Black Sea port of Sinope. In the fourteenth century, for reasons unknown, it acquired the meaning of green while still retaining that of red. It is perhaps for this very reason that those anonymous lawgivers who drew up the rules of the language of heraldry chose *sinople* for 'green'. The hidden qualities of green derive from the fact that it contains red, so that, to borrow the esoteric language of alchemists, the fertility of all 'works' arises from the fact that the fiery principle – the hot, male principle – impregnates the cold, moist, female principle. In all mythologies the green deities of annual renewal spend the Winter in the Underworld where they are regenerated by chthonian red. As a result, they are externally green but internally red, and their rule extends over both worlds. 'Green' Osiris was torn to pieces and cast into the Nile. He was brought to life again by the magic of 'Red' Isis. He is the Great Initiate, because he knows the secrets of death and resurrection; and thus he presides on Earth over Spring and the rebirth of nature and, in the Underworld, over the judgement of souls. Persephone came back to Earth with the first buds of Spring, but in the Autumn she returned to the Underworld to which she was eternally bound because she had eaten a pomegranate seed. This pomegranate seed was her heart, a spark of the fire in the bowels of the Earth which governs all regeneration. It was green Persephone's internal red. The Aztec myth of the goddess Xochiquetzal, who, like Persephone, was carried off to the Underworld during Winter, bears a disturbing similarity to the Greek myth. She vanished into the 'Garden of the West', that is, into the land of the dead, to reappear in the Spring, when she presided over the birth of the flowers. In manuscripts she may be recognized 'by her twin plumes of green feathers, the *omoquetzalli*, which serve for her headdress' (SOUM p. 40). In Aztec thought, green was also the *chalchihuitl*, or green precious stones which decorated the skirts worn by the water-goddess, while red was the *chalchihuatl*, the 'precious water', as they called the blood which spurted from the hearts of the human victims sacrificed each morning to the Sun by his priests to strengthen him for his battle against the powers of darkness and to assure his rebirth (ibid.).

In traditions relating to the deities of love the same complementarity between red and green necessarily exists. Aphrodite, born from the sea-spray, is shared between the demands of the two male principles – her husband Hephaistos, chthonian fire, and her lover Ares, fire from the sky. And when Hephaistos catches the lovers in his net, it is the sea-god Poseidon who springs to Aphrodite's defence.

Doubtless for this very reason medieval painters depicted the Cross in green, since it was the instrument whereby the human race was regenerated through Christ's sacrifice. In Byzantium, the colour green was symbolized by the monogram of Christ the Redeemer formed by the initial letters of the Greek word for 'green'. Hence the occult significance acquired by green light. The Ancient Egyptians feared cats with green eyes and imposed the death penalty upon all those guilty of killing these creatures. In Orphic tradition, green is the light of the spirit which, at the beginning of time, made fruitful the primordial waters, hitherto shrouded in darkness. Alchemists believe that the light of the EMERALD pierces the most closely guarded secrets. In this context the ambivalence of the 'beam of green light' may be appreciated. It may be capable of piercing all things, but it brings death as well as life, since at this point the qualities of the symbol may be reversed. In contrast with the fresh green of the buds of Spring, there is the green of slime and putrefaction: there is a death-green as well as a life-green. The greenish complexion of the sick is in contrast with the green skin of the apple and, although green frogs and caterpillars are pleasant and amusing,

the CROCODILE's gaping green jaws are nightmarish, the gates of Hell opening wide to swallow light and life. Green, like all female symbols, has its
dark, malign aspect. Although emeralds are Papal jewels, they were also
the jewels of Lucifer, before his fall from Heaven. Although green, as the
mean, might be the symbol of reason – the grey-eyed goddess Minerva – in
the Middle Ages it became the symbol of madness and the tincture of fools.
Such ambivalence is typical of all chthonian symbols. In a window in Chartres
Cathedral, Satan is depicted 'with green skin and huge green eyes' (PORS
p. 213). Contemporary science fiction quite naturally describes aliens from
other planets, the reverse of the human race, in terms of devils or little
green men. Sometimes they are endowed with green blood, which instinctively assumes a sacrilegious quality, like bloodshed, such is the instinctive
dislike of the human race for revealing what should be hidden and hiding
what should be revealed.

In their attempts to reconcile opposites, the alchemists went far beyond
the scope even of contemporary imagination. They described their 'secret
fire, a living and radiant spirit' as a green, translucent crystal, as malleable
as wax, saying that 'this was what nature used under the Earth for whatever
art created, since art should be bound to copy nature' (YGEA pp. 103–7).
This was the fire which reconciled opposites and was described as being
'dry, but causing rain; moist, but always causing drought'.

Lastly, all hermetic teachings hold that the secret of secrets, the life force
itself, is to be seen as blood contained within a green vessel. Western alchemists called it 'the blood of the Green Lion, which is not ordinary gold, but
Philosopher's Gold' (YGEA p. 96). In Chinese philosophy and medicine
this becomes the no-less-mysterious 'dragon's blood'. This is the GRAIL, too,
a vessel of emerald or of green crystal, and hence of the purest sort of
green, which holds the blood of God-made-Flesh. In it coalesce all those
notions of love and of sacrifice which condition the regeneration expressed
by the radiant greenness of the vessel, in which dawn and dusk, death and
rebirth come together and strike a balance. Undoubtedly in this myth the
Middle Ages were inspired by the most hermetic of New Testament writings. St John (Revelation 4: 3) describes his vision of God Almighty, which,
like that of Ezekiel, was a manifestation of light, without face or form: 'And
he that sat was to look upon like a jasper and a sardine stone: and there was
a rainbow round about the throne, in sight like unto an emerald.' In all
probability the Grail derives from this 'vision of emerald', the female jewel
which embraces and holds, a vessel containing the divine light. The very
essence, as it were, of godhead is two-in-one, both jasper green and deep,
dark, cornelian red (the red of the 'sardine [sardonyx] stone').

When they came to consider these two basic aspects of green, as the
colour of womanhood and of the natural world, modern media and market-
ing experts concluded after tests and surveys 'that green was the most tranquil of all colours', a colour unacquainted with joy or sadness or passion,
'an undemanding colour'. 'Were colours to be patterned like society, green
would be the middle classes', a static group, 'measuring its efforts and
counting its money' (FANO p. 22). As the needle flickers between day and
night, germination and putrefaction, it stops at the zero mark on the scales,
for green's tranquillity is that of neutrality. This suggests the green which

Angelus Silesius, as has already been observed, associated with justice. However, these same advertising consultants explain that the green in question is pure green, and that any admixture, however slight, of another colour shatters its neutrality.

The language of symbols, lively but coded as it is, is made to open doors to reflection rather than to lock them. It expresses our feelings and thoughts in infinitely complex ways, and provides a kind of access to them that is different from that afforded by applied psychology, which answers very finite ends. Very often the deep message conveyed by this language can only be read by experience; giving rise to quite unexpected dialogue between one age or one civilization and another. Aztec healers used the following spell to cure chest complaints: 'I am the Priest, I am the Lord of Enchantments, I seek the green pain, I seek the tawny pain' (SOUA p. 227). Many centuries later, Vincent Van Gogh was to discuss his painting 'Café de nuit' in a letter to his brother Théo of 8 September 1888: 'With green and red I have tried to give expression to the terrible passions of the human heart.' St John the Evangelist, the Aztec priest and Van Gogh have only one quality in common – they were inspired.

Green retains a strange and complex character derived from its twin polarity – the green of the bud and of decay, life and death. It is the image of the depths and of Fate.

grey Composed equally of black and white, grey is a Christian symbol of the resurrection of the dead, medieval artists depicting Christ with a grey cloak at the Last Judgement (PORS p. 305).

Grey is the colour of ashes and of mist. The Children of Israel covered their heads with ashes to give expression to the poignancy of their grief and Europeans dressed in ash-grey for half-mourning. The grey of misty weather sometimes gives a feeling of sadness, melancholy and boredom, while when dreams are enshrouded in a certain greyness, they are drawn from the depths of the unconscious and need to be clarified and brought into the open by a heightened level of consciousness.

In COLOUR genetics it would seem that grey is the first colour to be perceived and that it remains at the centre of the human colour-sphere. The new-born baby lives in a grey world, the same grey which we see when our eyes are closed, even in complete darkness (*das physiologische Augengrau*). From the point at which a child's eyes are fully open, it becomes more densely surrounded by more and more different colours and, during the first three years of its life, it becomes aware of the world of colour. Because it is used to grey, it identifies with grey, and grey becomes the centre of its colour-world and its reference point. It realizes that all it sees is colour. The predominance of colour explains mimicry in the animal and camouflage in the human worlds.

Human beings are grey in the middle of the world of colour, which may stand by analogy for the celestial sphere in the chromatic sphere. Human beings are the product of opposite sexes and, if they stand in the grey centre between the opposing colours which make up a harmonious chromatic sphere, all the pairs of colour-opposites will be in perfect balance. The imperfect image of this chromatic sphere may be given material form by physical action.

Human beings have always been trying to give physical shape to the absolute colours which they perceive in dreams. They colour their surroundings and even their skin. They need colours and colour-opposites because they are the central grey between the opposing colours, yellow and blue, red and green, black and white, the passage from one to the other of these countless pairs of colour-opposites always leading through a grey mid-point.

Aware of being in the centre of a world of colour, of an ideal and perfect chromatic sphere in which real and imaginary colours are in perfect balance, human beings feel that they are in the centre of a very powerful colour force-field; in the centre of a three-dimensional space composed of pairs of colour-opposites, and at the same time in the middle of another space, like the first, but without equilibrium, where all the colours in a homogeneous colour-sphere are evenly divided. This combination of two spheres is alive, because there is a heart-beat, and that heart-beat is the human being in the centre of the midmost grey.

Thanks to the four absolute tones, this world of colour can be oriented. The four basic tonalities are known as absolute yellow, absolute green, absolute blue and absolute red. These four tones remain absolute and their yellow, green, blue and red aspects do not depend upon intensity of light. The tonality of all other colours varies with the density of light. The four absolute tones correspond to the four cardinal points. Human beings assign to each point a colour which will depend upon human circumstances.

Each basic tonality predominates over countless related colours which are warmer or colder than itself. All colours tending towards yellow, red, and their intermediary, orange, show an inclination towards warmth; all colours tending towards blue and green and their intermediary, sea-green, have an inclination towards cold. Human beings feel that orange is the pole which attracts warm, and sea-green the pole which attracts cold tendencies.

Mauve is popular with the young, being unaffected by warmth or cold. Boys identify with this lack of differentiation. Yellow-lake, a greenish yellow, the colour-opposite of mauve, attracts many girls, who identify with it in the same way.

The attitudes of human beings in the grey centre alter with their character and way of life. In the circular field containing the twelve major tonalities, the four absolute tones and their intermediaries, there is a perceptible echo of the Zodiac. Each will unconsciously turn towards the chromatic section to which he or she belongs, towards his or her favourite colour. Groups, and even whole peoples, react in conformity with this and take up attitudes similar to the central grey. Colour becomes significant to the individual, the people or perhaps to humanity as a whole in an irrational and quite unforeseeable fashion.

grouse In the Spring the mating instinct takes blind and burning possession of the Black Grouse, which calls and displays on a communal area called the *lek*, dancing round the hen birds and issuing its bubbling call. The grouse is the symbol of uncontrolled passion and of a love which challenges death. 'The measure of love is to love without measure', said St Augustine, but he was speaking of the love of God. The grouse's love impels the bird to disregard the fear of any predator creeping up upon its raptures; it symbolizes, too, the ecstasy of nothingness, the bitter lust for annihilation which accompanies a passion blind to all else besides. However, the passion which kills is also the passion which brings life to the highest pitch of intensity. The image of the grouse calling and displaying is that of life and death entwined.

gryphon A fabulous beast, with the beak and wings of an eagle and the body of a lion, which in medieval allegory shared the symbolism of both LION and EAGLE. Although this would seem merely to double its solar characteristics, in fact the gryphon shared those of both Earth and Heaven, which made it a symbol of the two natures – human and divine – of Christ. It also echoed the twin qualities of the godhead, strength and wisdom.

If a comparison is made between the distinctive symbolism of eagle and of lion, it will be seen that the gryphon unites the terrestrial strength of the lion with the celestial energies of the eagle. The gryphon may therefore be classed broadly speaking among the symbols of the powers of salvation.

To the Children of Israel, the gryphon would seem to have been the symbol of Persia, where it was a common motif, and consequently of its state religion, Zoroastrianism, the teaching of the Magi, based upon the fundamental principles of Good and Evil.

A gryphon is also depicted on the balustrade of a stupa at Sanchi where it stands for *adrishta*, the invisible. The twofold solar symbolism of lion and bird is particularly in evidence here, but nonetheless remains close to that of lion and lioness as steeds and symbols of Shakti (BURA, DEVA, KRAA).

The gryphon, however, bears a sinister significance in another Christian tradition, perhaps later than the one already mentioned. 'Its hybrid nature deprives it of the freedom of the eagle and of the nobility of the lion.... It rather stands for strength and cruelty. In Christian symbolism, it is an image of the Devil, to the extent that theological writers used the expression *hestisequi* as a synonym for Satan. In lay terms, however, it represented superior force and imminent danger' (Gevaert, quoted in DROD p. 90).

The Ancient Greeks identified gryphons with the MONSTERS which guarded treasure in the country of the Hyperboreans. They watched over Dionysos' *krater* of wine and they hunted the gold-seekers in the mountains. Apollo rode a gryphon. They symbolized strength and vigilance, as well as the obstacles to be overcome in reaching the goal.

guardian See DRAGON; GENIUS; HERO; MONSTER.

gull Frazer records a myth of the Lilloet Indians, of British Columbia, telling how the Gull was the first owner of daylight, which it kept locked up in a box for its own use. The raven, noted as a Demiurge in northwestern American cultures, managed by trickery to break open the box and steal the daylight for the use of mankind. The same myth goes on to explain how the Raven organized an expedition to the land of the fishes using the Gull's canoe (Sun-boat) to steal fire.

H

Hades See HELL.

hair (see also HEADDRESS) Like nails or limbs, hair was believed to preserve an intimate connection with its owner even when it ceased to be part
of him or of her. It symbolized its owner's virtues by concentrating their
qualities spiritually, and retained a 'sympathetic' link. Hence arose the cult
of venerating the relics of the saints – and especially of a lock of their hair
– a cult which not only comprised the act of veneration, but the desire to
share their particular qualities. Somewhat akin to this is the custom in many
families of keeping locks of hair and children's milk teeth. Such practices
are more than the preservation of mementos: they betray the desire for the
survival of the person from whose head the hair is taken.

More often than not hair represents certain male qualities or powers such
as strength and virility, as in the Old Testament myth of Samson. Hair may
even act as a surrogate for its owner, as when T'ang the Victorious offered
himself as a sacrifice for the prosperity of his people by cutting off his hair
and finger-nails, biologically speaking the equivalents of hair. To bring to
a successful conclusion the Great Work of smelting sword-blades, Chang-
tziang and his wife Mo-ye offered themselves as a sacrifice to their forge by
throwing their hair and finger-nails into the furnace. Similar occurrences
are recorded in Western alchemy. In Vietnam, hair which falls or is caught
in the comb is not thrown away, for it can have a magical influence upon
the fate of its owner.

Maximum virility coincides with the strongest growth of hair. In China,
a shaved scalp was a mutilation on a par with emasculation and it debarred
the person from the exercise of some offices. Cutting the hair corresponded
not simply to sacrifice, but to surrender, a renunciation willy-nilly of qualities, prerogatives and, in the last resort, of the individual's personality.
An echo of this may be found not only in the terrible practice of scalping
by North American Indians, but in the nearly universal fact that entry into
the monastic life involves cutting the hair (remember Sakyamuni). The Vietnamese make all sorts of judgements about a person's fate and character
from the way in which his or her hair grows, and have created a sort of
system of divination by means of the hair.

The style and cut of the hair has always been a means of determining not
only personality, but also social or spiritual status, whether individually or
collectively. The way the hair was dressed was of enormous importance to
the Japanese *samurai*. When the Franks adopted the custom of cutting the
hair, only kings and princes retained the privilege of long hair as an emblem
of power. In Asia, cutting the hair or altering the style in which it was worn

was often a means of group domination, as when the Manchu invaders of China imposed the pigtail upon its inhabitants.

Dishevelled hair, as a ritual accompaniment, produced its own set of symbols in China, where it is still a sign of mourning. This is a survival of its ancient meaning of a sign of submission. Some of the Immortals had dishevelled hair, as did those who practised a Taoist method of concentration to 'preserve the Monad'. Those who took part in some ancient ritual dances had dishevelled hair, as did sorcerers and candidates for admission to the lodges of some secret societies. It would have seemed generally speaking to have been a renunciation of the rules and conventions governing the fate of individuals and of those those ruling everyday life and the social order.

In Hindu iconography dishevelled hair is more often than not a characteristic of the demon gods, as it is of GORGONS and TYPHON in Greek mythology. It is, however, a characteristic of Shiva as well, being related to the wind, Vāyu, and to Ganga, the River Ganges, the manifestation of the former, flowing down from the peak of a tangled mass of hair. The texture of the universe is woven from Shiva's hair, identified with spatial orientation.

Hair radiating from the crown of the head is also an image of the Sun's beams. Generally speaking, hair shares a relationship with Heaven. In China, cutting one's hair or felling the trees on a mountain peak, which came to the same thing, stopped rainfall. On a different level, the part should be observed which is played by the Muslim's tuft of hair and by the top-knot (*sikhā*) of Hindu deities. In both cases they are signs of potential or actual connections with the realm of the superhuman, and by-passing individuality and escaping from the cosmos.

Classical iconography depicted Diana of the Ephesians as wearing her hair in a circle, like a wall with towers, as befitted her role as the goddess of and guardian deity of cities. Similarly the Earth-goddess, Cybele, dressed her hair like a crenellated mural crown for, according to Ovid (*Fasti* 4: 220) 'she was the first to give the cities of Phrygia their TOWERS.' Virgil (*Aeneid* 6: 785) wrote that she, 'turret-crowned, rides in her car through the Phrygian cities' (TERS p. 130).

The Ancient Greeks cut their hair as a sign of mourning, while the Romans let it grow.

The devotees of Isis and Serapis shaved their heads. Catholic priests were once distinguished by their tonsure and monks by shaving the skull. Perhaps the tonsure on the crown of the head may be compared with the opening in the top of a DOME which is supposed to allow the temple or the individual to open itself to the inflowing of heavenly enlightenment and power. The monk's head was shaved, except for a more or less wide ring of hair. This would consecrate him to perfection and to solar radiance, transported to a spiritual plane and symbolized by the CROWN. It would also mark his separation from the world and his fidelity to tradition.

Although it is nowhere specifically stated in Celtic tradition that long hair was a symbol or mark of virility, in Welsh and Irish literature long hair is a royal or aristocratic status symbol. Common folk and slaves have short hair and when somebody important is mentioned, a description of his golden or brown hair is seldom omitted. In Roman times, long hair was the distinguishing mark of the independent Gauls. Unlike the Roman province of Gallia Narbonensis, independent Gaul was known as Gallia Comata ('Hairy Gaul') or Gallia Braccata ('Breeches-wearing Gaul'). 'The Treviri too rejoiced that the troops were moved; so did the Ligurians with their hair now cropped, though once they excelled all the long-haired land in the locks that fell in beauty over their necks' (Lucan, *Pharsalia* 1: 441–3). In the Treviri, the Roman poet symbolizes the Gauls who had remained free and independent, and in the Ligurians the Gauls who had lost both long hair and liberty, but had also abandoned their native barbarism. In any case the Celts took great care of their hair, combing and plaiting it and, according to some Classical writers, dyeing it. Silius Italicus (*Punica* 4: 200) describes how one of the Gauls dedicated his hair to Mars. When Christianity first spread to Ireland, the priestly tonsure was a mark of great humility. The tonsure of Celtic Christendom long corresponded to that attributed to the god Lug by all literary sources (WINI 5: pp. 733ff.; ZWIC 1: pp. 47–8, 60).

The hair is a link making it one of the magical symbols of annexation or even of identification. A rain-maker from the Lower Zambezi was possessed by two spirits, one of a lion and the other of a leopard. In order to prevent these spirits from leaving him he never cut his hair or drank alcohol (FRAG 3: pp. 259–60). Frazer also emphasizes how often the hair of kings, priests and others was placed under a taboo against its being cut.

Elsewhere, hair remained uncut during wars, a journey or as a consequence of a vow. The Ancient Egyptians allowed their hair to grow when they travelled. Many different peoples, among them some of the tribes in Papua New Guinea, allow hair, beard and moustaches to grow as a sign of mourning. Comtemporary history, in Fidel Castro's *Barbudos*, provides a striking example of the same practice in consequence of a vow. Castro's followers had sworn not to shave or cut their hair until they had liberated Cuba from Batista's tyranny.

Hair may be considered as the dwelling place of the soul or as one of a person's souls. In Celebes and Sumatra, a child's hair is allowed to grow to avoid the danger of destroying the soul living in it. In some parts of Germany, people used to believe that a child's hair should not be cut until it had passed its first birthday, for fear of bringing bad luck (FRAG 3: pp. 258ff.).

Countless different peoples mark the first time a child's hair is cut with considerable ceremony and a wealth of propitiatory activities aimed at driving off evil spirits. In fact, they feel the child to be particularly vulnerable to evil influences at this time, since with its first haircut it is being deprived of a portion of its life force. This is especially true of the Hopi Indians of Arizona (see TALS), who make this a communal event taking place once only in the year at the time of the celebration of the Winter solstice. The first time the hair of the Inca crown prince was cut coincided with his weaning at the age of two. He was then given his name 'and this was the occasion of a great feast at which all the king's relatives gathered at court' (GARC p. 90).

This association is patent evidence of the link between hair and the life force. The king-to-be is given a name and therefore becomes an individual at the same time as he loses his baby-hair, linking him with his prenatal existence. This boils down to saying that in this ceremony his own life force takes up the torch handed on to him by his mother's. That it took place when he was weaned serves to confirm this interpretation.

The notion of the life force brings with it that of the soul and of fate. Thus when Don Talayesva describes the marriage customs of the Hopi, he explains that the female relatives of the bridal pair first washed their hair and then, as at his own wedding, 'they poured the [yucca] suds into one bowl, put our heads together, mixed our hair and twisted it into one strand to unite us for life' (TALS p. 217).

Persian poetry takes up the same theme when it compares flowing locks of hair with the bowstring which runs between the two tips of the bow, an image of the link binding together two beings who love one another. Curls symbolize the seal of engagement which lovers swear never to break.

Hair is also linked in symbolic thought with grass, the Earth's hair, and hence with plant life. Agricultural societies see its growth as an image of that of the plants which feed them, hence its importance and the care which all so-called primitive peoples give to the hair. The idea of growth is connected with that of ascension. The Heavens pour down the rain which makes the Earth fruitful and plants to rise up skywards from it. Thus, in propitiatory rites, hair is often associated with FEATHERS, messengers of mankind to the sky-gods.

Hair is one of woman's main weapons and therefore the fact of its being concealed or displayed, plaited or hanging loose, is often the sign of a woman's availability, surrender or modesty. In Christian art, St Mary Magdalene is always depicted with long, flowing hair, a sign of her surrender to God rather than an echo of her former sinful state. In Russia, the married woman used to cover her hair and there was a proverb that a girl could enjoy her freedom so long as her head was bare. The sense of sexual provocativeness connected with a woman's hair is also behind the Christian tradition that a woman may not enter a church bare-headed. This would be to lay claim not only to natural freedom but to moral freedom as well. In Russia, girls wore their hair in a single plait as a sign of virginity, while married women wore it in two plaits.

To comb somebody's hair is a mark of respect and of welcome, as is, for many peoples such as Russians or Dravidians in India, delousing the hair. On the other hand, to allow somebody to comb your hair is a sign of love, trust and intimacy. To spend a long time combing somebody's hair is to cradle, soothe or caress that person, hence the occurrence of magic COMBS in so many folktales. From this probably derived a custom among Russian students of not combing their hair the night before their exams, in case they forgot what they had been taught.

All Christian ecclesiastical practices relating to the hair convey a number of different symbols. Thus hermits let their hair grow, following the example of the Nazarenes who never used razor or scissors. Their hair was long and tangled and in the Middle Ages hermits would sometimes allow their hair to be cut once a year. Hair was not considered as an adornment. On the other hand, all those who entered the religious life, both men and women, had their heads shaved as a sign of repentance.

To have one's hair cut by an old man could carry with it the sense of dependence, of making oneself, as it were, his ward. Since wearing one's hair long was regarded as a sign of one's strength, cutting it carried with it the quality of a loss of power.

So far as the laity was concerned, women never wore their hair short except when doing penance. Penitents of both sexes were encouraged to cut their hair. Contemporary shaving of the heads of guilty men and women is perhaps an unconscious echo of this practice. St Clement of Alexandria, Tertullian and other early Fathers refused women the right to dye their hair or to wear wigs. These bans were inspired by penitence to counter the wiles of female seduction. It should be observed that the importance attached to the hair was so great that any breach of these rules could entail the barring of the guilty party from entry into a church and even from Christian burial. When youths had their hair cut, it was to the accompaniment of prayer, and medieval sacramentaries contain collects for this occasion.

Body hair symbolizes virility and is benign if it grows only upon parts of the body such as a man's chest, chin, arms or legs, but malign if it covers the entire body like the god Pan (see GOAT). Plentiful hair is a manifestation of plant life and is sensory and instinctual.

In the *Iliad* (Book 3), cutting the hair of an animal which is going to be sacrificed signifies that it is 'doomed to death'. It is the preliminary rite of purification.

hairpin When Chinese scholars discussed female beauty a metaphor which they applied to a pretty woman was 'a wooden hairpin and a homespun skirt', their symbols of a natural beauty which had no need of the artificial aids so often used by women. It was a phrase used to express feminine elegance in its purest shape.

The phrase itself originates from a traditional Chinese queen of beauty – Hsi-Chi. She lived in the fifth century BC and could often be seen doing her laundry on the banks of the Yun-Chi River. This Venus of the Middle Kingdom inspired the great poet of the T'ang period, Wang-Wei, to write: 'At dawn she was no more than a girl on the banks of the Yun-Chi: at night she became Queen of the Kingdom of Wu.'

Memories of this lovely lady linger in the proverb: 'Hsee-Chee creeps into lovers' eyes.'

The philosopher Cheng-Tien-hsi has tried to turn her into a symbol of democratic philosophy, since she changed from the wooden hairpin and the homespun skirt worn for household tasks into robes of royal state for the evening. This, however, does not simply enshrine the elegance or demo-cratic habits of Chinese women, it symbolizes their dual role – servants going about their household duties during the day and queens in the sports of love at night.

halcyon This legendary and symbolic bird has been variously described as a sort of swallow, a seagull or else as a beautiful but sorrowful, fabulous bird. According to a Greek legend, Halcyone, or Alcyone, was the daughter of Aeolus, King of the Winds, and married Ceyx, son of the Morning Star. Their happiness was so perfect that they likened themselves to Zeus and Hera and thus drew down upon themselves the vengeance of the gods. They were changed into birds, and their nests, being built upon the sea shore, were constantly broken into pieces by the waves (GRID). Such were the origins of their plaintive calls. Zeus, however, took pity upon them and, for seven days before and for seven days after the Winter solstice, calmed the seas; and in this period the halcyon could rear its young. This is the ground for its symbolizing peace and quiet – halcyon days – but it is a peace and quiet which should be snatched at once, for it is short-lived.

As sea-birds sacred to the sea-goddess Thetis, who was one of the Nereids, the children of the wind and the rising Sun, halcyons belong to sky and sea, to air and water. On these grounds they symbolize both material and spiritual fruitfulness, but one threatened by the jealousy of the gods and of the elements. The dangers which they represent are those of self-satisfaction and of attributing to oneself the happiness which only the gods can grant. This blindness in the midst of bliss lays one open to the most terrible punishment.

Later legend assimilated Halcyone to Isis and made her skim through the air above the wave-crests in search of her husband, son of the Morning Star, as Osiris was the rising Sun. Ovid (*Metamorphoses* 11: 732–43) describes, in terms reminiscent of the Egyptian myth, how the wife, changed into a bird, discovered her husband's body floating in the sea.

halo The halo, or nimbus, is a solar image which possesses much the same significance as the CROWN and specifically the kingly crown. It is displayed by a radiance around the head and sometimes around the whole body (see mandorla under ALMOND). This originally solar radiance is a sign of holiness, of sanctity and of the divine. It is a manifestation in specific form of the AURA.

An elliptical halo above or a circular halo around the head are signs of spiritual enlightenment. It is a prefiguration of the resurrection of the dead, an anticipation of the transformation of the body into glory (COLN).

Haloes are not the property of saints only, but also of kings, emperors and of animals, in so far as the latter symbolize sacred persons. When the lamb or phoenix are depicted as symbols of Christ, they are given a halo.

Christian use of the halo dates back to the catacombs. The early Church copied the pagan Roman practice of surrounding the heads of their gods and emperors with a halo (COLN).

The tonsure of priests and monks is related to the halo in so far as it is shaped like a crown, is a sign of their exclusive devotion to matters spiritual and is the opening for the soul.

In Byzantine art, circular haloes were kept for those who, having lived saintly lives here on Earth, had died and gone to Heaven. Living personages were granted the privilege of a square halo, an echo of the universal symbolism of the CIRCLE (Heaven) and of the SQUARE (Earth).

'The halo is a universal means of displaying personal qualities in that part of the body judged to be the noblest – the head. By means of the halo, the head appears enlarged and radiant. The heavenly and spiritual part of the person wearing a halo has taken the dominant role and become a complete and unified personality in the upper reaches of the body' (CHAS p. 270). Just as the wheel represents the Sun's beams, so the halo stands for the irradiation of supernatural light. It marks the diffusion and the expansion beyond its physical bounds of that centre of spiritual energy believed to reside in the soul or head of the saint wearing the halo.

hammer In some respects both hammers and mallets are images of evil and of brute force. However, the symbolic converse of this interpretation is their identification with celestial instrumentality and the manufacture of the thunderbolt.

The weapon of the Norse storm-god, Thor, was a hammer which had been forged by the dwarf, Sindri. It was also the tool used by the lame god of smithies, HEPHAISTOS (Vulcan). When identified with the VAJRA (THUNDERBOLT), it was both creator and destroyer, the instrument of life and death. It is the symbol of Hephaistos and of initiation into metal-working (CABEIRI), the hammer standing for the shaping instrumentality of the Demiurge. When the hammer strikes the chisel, it is spiritual will-power activating the faculty of knowing which carves out ideas and concepts and stimulates detailed knowledge.

In some societies, ritually smelted hammers are effective against disease, enemies and thieves. Their role is one of active magical protection. In Hindu iconography – at all events when it is an attribute of Ghantākarma – the hammer destroys disease (BURA, DEVA, ELIF, MALA, VARG).

In Japanese mythology the hammer is a magical implement with which Daikoku, god of wealth and happiness, strikes gold from the Earth.

The hammer of the Gaulish god, Sucellos (probably 'Good Smiter'), must be regarded as a substitute for or as a continental form of the Irish Dagda's CLUB. Due to later misunderstandings, particularly those of recent date, he has been regarded as the god of coopers, thus depriving the god and his hammer of all symbolic significance. In fact, however, like the club, the hammer stands in Celtic fashion for the god's powers of creation and orderly regulation.

Sucellos' hammer and the Dagda's club should be related to the Breton *mell benniget* ('the Holy Mallet'), either a round stone or a hammer with a heavy stone head. As late as the nineteenth century this was still laid on the forehead of the dying to ease their passing and release their souls. Following a pagan Roman tradition, the Dean of the Sacred College strikes the forehead of the Pope with a hammer made of ivory or precious metal as a preliminary to proclaiming his death.

In northern Europe hammers occur in countless Runic inscriptions, rock-carvings and grave-stones and it would appear that they were intended to preserve the dead person against the attacks of his enemies. Hammers were carried in marriage ceremonies to drive evil spirits away from the bridal couple and as promises of fertility for the bride. Clearly this is related to the solar symbolism of the thunderbolt.

In Lithuania traces have been discovered of the worship of an iron hammer of enormous size. When Jerome of Prague asked the priests of the cult what its significance was, they answered:

Once upon a time the Sun disappeared for several months. A mighty king had made him his prisoner and had shut him up in a castle which could not be stormed. However, the signs of the Zodiac came to the help of the Sun. They shattered the tower with an enormous hammer, set the Sun free and restored him to mankind. The implement through which sunlight was restored to mankind, therefore, is worthy of veneration.

(MYTF 55, p. 103)

In this myth the hammer symbolizes thunder rumbling in a thick mass of CLOUD before storm and rain clear the sky and the Sun shines again. It is more likely to symbolize thunder than lightning. According to another Lithuanian legend, iron hammers are the implements with which those gods who watch over mankind break the depths of snow and ice in Springtime. The images of masses of clouds are the same as those of thick blankets of ice and snow covering Earth and sea and are offered as examples of the divine powers possessed by the hammer if it is to shatter the one and sweep away the other.

In Masonic symbolism 'the hammer is the symbol of the active and persistent powers of the intellect directing the thoughts and animating the meditation of the man who searches for the truth in the silence of his own conscience.' Seen from this viewpoint, it cannot be separated from the chisel, standing for discernment, for without the latter's intervention, effort would be both dangerous and wasted. The hammer may also 'represent the executive action of the will. It is the emblem of authority wielded in the right hand, the active side of the body, and in a relationship with active energy and the moral determination from which flows practical achievement' (BOUM p. 11). It is the symbol of the authority of the Worshipful Master at Lodge meetings.

hand The hand expresses ideas of action, as well as those of power and dominion. In Far Eastern languages such expressions as 'setting one's hand to' or 'taking one's hand from' still have the meaning of starting or of ending a piece of work. Nevertheless, some Taoist writings, such as *The Secret of the Golden Flower*, impart an alchemical meaning of 'coagulation' or of 'dissolution' to these words, the first phrase corresponding to the effort of spiritual concentration, the second to 'non-intervention' and to the free development of inward experience in a microcosm released from the fetters of space and time. It should also be borne in mind that the word 'manifestation' derives from the same root as *manus*, the Latin word for 'hand'. What is manifest can be held in or grasped by the hand.

The hand is an emblem of royalty, an instrument of command and a sign of dominion. Justice is a kingly quality and the 'Hand of Justice', a sceptre tipped by a hand, was one of the medieval insignia of the French kings. Traditionally, God's left hand is concerned with justice and his right hand with mercy, corresponding to the Kabbalistic teaching of the 'hand of punishment' and the 'right hand' of the Shekinah (see RIGHT AND LEFT). The right hand is the hand which blesses and is an emblem of priestly authority just as the hand of justice is of kingly power. Although it is not the invariable rule, in China the right generally corresponds with action and the left with non-action and wisdom (*Tao Te Ching* 31). This polarity may, furthermore, be regarded as the basis of Hindu and Buddhist *mudrā*.

In the canons of Buddhism the 'closed hand' is the symbol of dissimulation, secrecy and hermeticism. The Buddha's hand 'is in no wise closed'

(*Dīgha-nikāya* 2: 100), that is to say that there are no hidden points in his teaching.

However, in both Buddhism and in Hinduism, the basic symbolism is that of the *mudrā*, poses with the hand, of which the most important are listed below. Hindu iconography makes special use of:

abhaya-mudrā ('absence of fear'): hand raised with all fingers extended and palm facing forwards; attributed to Kālī, the destructive power of time, who is herself beyond fear and delivers from it those who invoke her;
varada-mudrā ('giving'): hand pointing downwards with fingers extended and palm facing forwards; Kālī who destroys the transient elements in the universe and who is thus the fountain of happiness;
tarjanī-mudrā ('threat'): fist clenched and index finger pointing upwards.

In addition, there are esoteric *mudrā*, such as the *swastika mudrā*, as well as large numbers of ritual *mudrā*, some of which are employed in classical theatre and dance.

The *abhaya-* and *varada-mudrā* (also called *dāna* or 'gift') are also used in Buddhist ritual. They stand respectively for spiritual appeasement and the gift of the Three Jewels of Knowledge, the first being generally performed with the right hand, the second with the left. To them should be added:

anjali-mudrā (gesture of adoration and of prayer): hands joined in the well-known attitude;
bhumisparsha-mudrā (taking Earth to witness): hand pointing downwards with fingers touching the ground and back of the hand facing outwards; this is either the Buddha taking the Earth as witness of his Buddhism or a reference to the unshakeable and immovable;
dhyāna-mudrā (gesture of meditation): open hands, palms uppermost, resting one on the other;
dharmachakra-mudrā (the Wheel of the Law, a preaching gesture): generally the right hand faces outwards, the left inwards, the index fingers and thumbs of both touching one another;
vitarka-mudrā (the gesture of controversy or dissertation): similar to the *abhaya*, but with the index or middle finger touching the tip of the thumb. There are numbers of variations on these poses.

The Mahāyāna assigns certain mudrā to certain Buddhas or Bodhisattvas and these gestures are frequently prescribed. In the Javanese *Borobudur* as well as Japanese *mandala*, Akshobhya (East) performs the *bhumisparsha-mudrā*; Ratnasambhava (South) the *varada-mudrā*; Amitābha (West) the *dhyāna-mudrā*; Amoghasiddhi (North) the *abhaya-mudrā*; and Vairocana (the Centre) either the *vitarka-* or the *dharmachakra-mudrā*.

The symbolism of the *mudrā* is not simply that of gesture if it is true that the word means both bodily and spiritual attitudes which the movement expresses and develops (BURA, BENA, CADV, COOI, DANA, GOVM, GROI, GUEM, JACA, MALA, SECA).

The dances of southern Asia have been called 'hand-dances'. It is not simply the hand movements which are highly significant, but their position relative to the rest of the body and even the position of the fingers relative to one another. The same is true of the plastic arts of painting and sculpture, where the relative positions of hand and fingers symbolize internal states. The chief *mudrā* have been described, but there are others. For example, hands with palms resting on the knees express concentrated meditation, while in Japan the 'Embryo of Great Compassion', expressing affective concentration, is formed by bending the fingers into a triangular formation with the thumb, and the 'Diamond Plane', the penetration into knowledge, by pointing the index finger of the left hand upwards and inserting it into the clenched right fist. The Japanese Shingon sect represent the attitude of thought as a seated Bodhisattva, bent head supported by the right hand, with the left hand holding the right ankle lying across the knee of the left leg which hangs free.

All civilizations, with a greater or lesser degree of subtlety, employ this language of hands and gestures or poses. In Africa, placing the left hand with fingers bent in the right is a sign of humble submission; in Ancient Rome, having the hand covered by the sleeve was a mark of respect and acknowledgement of servitude; and so on.

In the Celtic world, the symbolism of the hand is linked with that of the arm and it is impossible to distinguish clearly between the two. In any case, the Irish word *lam* ('hand') is often used to mean the whole arm. What Caesar in his *Gallic Wars* calls *passis manibus*, that is, arms raised with the palms of the hands facing forwards, was a supplicatory gesture. It was employed by Gaulish women several times during these wars – at Avaricum and Bratuspantium, at least – sometimes baring their breasts at the same time. The hand also had a magic quality. When King Nuada lost his right arm he could rule no longer, since in the Celtic world it was unimaginable for a king to be endowed only with dangerous powers, his remaining hand being the left. Apart from a few hands depicted on Gaulish currency, there is no literary or iconographic evidence for the 'Hand of Justice', that symbol of the other aspect of the royal function of preserving the balance of society. However, Celtic kings were also judges and the good king was the one who pronounced equitable sentences. Calatin's children, who were by definition FOMORIANS, in other words malign creatures of darkness, had only one eye, one hand and one foot each, because they had been subjected to counter-initiatory mutilation. As the legend of the red hand in the arms of Ulster shows, the hand was employed in formally taking possession. A motif in the cross of Muiredach at Monasterbuice in County Louth is the carving of a left hand within four concentric circles. Lastly, the hand was used in invocation. The British queen Boudicca invoked the war-goddess Andraste by raising a hand to Heaven (Dio Cassius 60: 11, 6); and the druids on the Isle of Anglesey (Mona) raised their hands to Heaven when they prayed and rained curses and spells down on the invading Romans (Tacitus, *Annals* 14: 30; OGAC 18: p. 373; ETUC pp. 109–23).

In pre-Columbian Central America, an open hand, often with the thumb sticking up, is often depicted both in hieroglyphics and in low-relief carvings. Its primary, numerical meaning is FIVE, and it is the symbol of the god of the fifth day. However, he was an Underworld deity and this is why the hand became the symbol of death in Mexican art. In fact, hands are often to be met with in association with death's heads, hearts, bleeding feet, scorpions and sacrificial knives with flint or OBSIDIAN blades. This knife is called, in the Yucatec language, 'the Hand of God'. In Mayan hieroglyphics, JADE, the symbol of blood, is depicted by a hand (THOH).

In connection with the association of the hand with human sacrifice, Thomson emphasizes that during sacrifices to Xipe Totec, the priest would dress in the skin flayed from the human victims. However, since he was unable to slip on the fingers, the flayed skins were cut off at the wrist so that the priest's own hands could be seen in shocking contrast with his sinister costume. This visual detail could, therefore, suffice to make the hand the symbol of the whole and perfect the rite of substitution belonging to the sacrifice.

In both Old Testament and Christian traditions the hand is the symbol of power and of supremacy. To be touched by the hand of God was to receive the manifestation of his spirit. When the hand of God laid hold of a man, the latter received into himself divine strength. Thus God's hand touched Jeremiah upon the lips before he was sent out to preach. Elijah upon Mount Carmel saw a slight cloud rising from the sea and felt the hand of the Lord upon him. Faithful to the Covenant, Abraham refused to accept bribes and, when the King of Sodom offered him wealth, 'lifted his hand unto the Lord', not solely to beseech his protection but because it was the Lord alone who possessed Earth and Heaven. The Midrash lays emphasis upon Abraham's attitude towards his son, Ishmael, whom he sent away 'empty-handed' – without rights or inheritance.

When the Old Testament alludes to the hand of God, the significance of the symbol is that of God in the wholeness of his power and instrumentality. The hand of God creates and protects, but if God's will is thwarted, it also destroys. It is important to distinguish between the right hand, the hand of blessing, and the left hand, the hand of cursing. The hand of God is often depicted emerging from a cloud which hides his body. To display its divine nature, it is often surrounded by a cruciform halo. To fall into the hands of God or of some man means to be at his mercy, to be raised up or annihilated by him.

The hand is sometimes compared with the eye – it sees. Psychoanalysis has made this interpretation its own, regarding the appearance in dreams of a hand as being the same as that of an eye.

St Gregory of Nyssa regarded human hands as being linked to sight and to knowledge since, ultimately, they were designed for communication. In his treatise on the creation of mankind he wrote that:

a man's hands are of especial use to him in communication. Whoever regards use of the hands as one of the properties of natural reason is not deceived. All agree, and it is easy to see, that hands allow us to display our words in writing. It is, in fact, one of the marks of a rational being to express thoughts in writing and, in some sense, to talk through the hands which give a permanent form to sounds and gestures.

To place one's hands in those of another is to surrender one's freedom, or rather to resign one's claims to it by entrusting it to that person, and to lay down one's power. Two examples of this may be given. The act of homage in feudal times involved the *immixtio manuum* when the vassal, generally kneeling, bareheaded and unarmed, placed his hands in those of his overlord, who gripped them. In the ritual act of homage there is on the part of the vassal a radiation of self and its reception by the overlord. The obligations which ensued were reciprocal.

There is something similar in the final vows of a nun or the ordination of a priest, the *Rituale* laying down the ceremonial in which the nun or priest clasps their hands togethes and places them in those of the bishop. The significance of this re-echoes Christ's last words: 'Father, into your hands I commend my spirit.'

The laying on of hands expresses the transfer of energy or power. Thus, early in the second century, the Christian community in Rome included a number of women who had renounced marriage and wished to profess the vocation of virginity. They made their request to a bishop to lay his hands on them to obtain formal consecration of their vows. For fear that this laying on of hands might be confused with that used in ordination to the priesthood, it was subsequently forbidden. This shows the importance attaching to this ritual action and the depth of its significance, factors confirmed by *The Apostolic Tradition* of St Hippolytus (early third century). In his treatise *De virginibus*, St Ambrose tells the story of the girl who wished to dedicate her life to God. Her parents, however, wanted her to marry. To thwart their wishes, she stood beside the altar, took the priest's right hand, placed it upon her head and asked him to say a blessing over her. She was thereafter regarded as linked to and endowed with divine power.

Lastly, the hand is a symbol of 'action that differentiates. Its significance is akin to that of the ARROW and echoes the name of the Archer, Chiron [*cheir* = hand (Greek)], whose ideogram is an arrow' (VIRI p. 193). The hand is, as it were, an exclusively human synthesis of male and female. It is passive in what it contains; active in what it holds. It employs weapons and tools and extends its activities through their instrumentality. However, it differentiates man from all animals and serves to differentiate the objects which it touches or shapes.

Even when it is the sign of taking possession of something or of confirming the powers of someone, as hand of justice, hand taking seisin of land or goods, or hand given in marriage, it sets its owner apart either in the performance of his or her duties or in some new office.

Hanging Man, the   Having as its ancestor the HERMIT and its descendant the DEVIL (ninth and fifteenth TAROTS), equivalents on the spiritual plane of the two women in the LOVER (sixth Tarot), the twelfth Tarot, of which the complementary card is the WHEEL OF FORTUNE, displays a Hanging Man, very much resembling the JUGGLER in looks.

A young man is suspended from a dark green gallows by one foot. On either side stands a yellow tree with six red wounds, corresponding to the number of branches lopped from it. Each of these trees stands upon a little green mound on which a plant with four leaves also grows. The Hanging Man's hair and slippers are blue, as is the upper half of his coat, with red half-sleeves and yellow skirts, both decorated with a horizontal crescent, and fastened by nine buttons, six above and three below the belt. The buttons are white, as are the collar, the belt and the portion of the coat to which they are sewn.

The Hanging Man has his hands behind his back at waist level and his right leg is bent back behind the other at knee level. The Hanging Man, alias 'the Sacrifice' or 'the Victim'

stands for imposed or voluntary expiation; renunciation [Poinsot] . . . payment of debts, punishment, mob-hatred and treachery [Rolt-Wheeler] . . . psychic slavery and the enlightenment which brings freedom, bonds of all sorts, guilty thoughts, remorse, the desire to throw off a yoke [Terestchenko] . . . disinterestedness, self-forgetfulness, apostleship, philanthropy, good intentions unfulfilled, promises unkept, unrequited love [Wirth].

In the early eighteenth-century French Tarot, this card was not called the Hanging Man, but 'Prudence', advice to be borne in mind when considering the different meanings of this Tarot. In astrology it corresponds to the Twelfth House.

At first sight, this Tarot would seem to be one of defeat and utter impotence, and yet the Hanging Man's arms and legs form a sort of cross within a triangle, and this is the alchemical sign for the completion of the Great Work. One can only say, yet again, that it is essential to delve beneath the surface. In the first place, one might wonder whether the Hanging Man is not the victim of magically induced slavery. The two ends of the rope, reminiscent of a pair of tiny wings, do not really bind his foot and one might question how it is in fact tied. This is because the Hanging Man, in this context, symbolizes all those who are so obsessed by a passion, so utterly enslaved body and soul by an idea or a feeling, that they are quite unconscious of their servitude.

'All', wrote Van Rijnberk, 'who are influenced by an ingrained way of thinking, relate to the Hanging Man.' He added: 'Similarly, all those influenced by an overriding moral prejudice, for or against whatever it may be, fall into the category of the un-free, tied head downwards to the gallows of their prejudices' (RIJT p. 242).

There is, however, another level to the Hanging Man. His seeming stillness and pose are signs of complete submission, the promise and assurance of an accretion of greater esoteric and spiritual powers – chthonian rejuvenation. The Hanging Man has relinquished enhancement of the powers within him, standing aside the better to ingest cosmic influences. The twelve red scars of the lopped branches are reminders of the signs of the Zodiac. However, the strongest sign of all is his head, with a mound on either side, apparently burying itself in the ground which is swept by his hair, blue, the colour of the occult powers. One is reminded of the giant Antaeus who grew stronger every time he touched the ground, or of the Yoga position, standing on the head, supported by the forearms flat on the ground so as to obtain greater mental concentration by the regenerative strength of the forces circulating upward from Earth to Heaven. The Hanging Man firmly brings a cycle to an end, man turning upside down to bury his head in the ground, it might be said to restore his mental being from the Earth from which he was fashioned.

As a symbol of purification by the reversal of the normal order of things, the Hanging Man is thus the mystic *par excellence.* It is from this angle that Wirth regards the twelfth Tarot as the card which begins a series of passive initiation, by contrast with the first eleven which belong to the category of active initiation 'based upon the culture and the use of the energy available to the individual from within him- or herself' (WIRT p. 182).

hare In that tapestry which serves as the backcloth to deep dream-states and on which the archetypes of the world of symbols are depicted, it is essential to bear in mind the vast importance of animals connected with the Moon, if we are to understand the significance of those countless mysterious hares and rabbits, familiar and often awkward companions of the moonlight of the imagination. They haunt mythology, belief and folklore. They are all alike, even in their contradictions, just as all images of the Moon are alike and, like the Moon, hares and rabbits are linked to that oldest of deities, the Earth Mother, to the symbolism of water which makes fruitful and regenerates, of plants and of the constant renewal of life in all its shapes. This is the world of that great mystery of life renewed through death. The spirit, a creature of the day, comes into collision with it, prey to desire and fear at the sight of creatures which necessarily hold ambivalent meanings for the spirit.

Hares and rabbits are lunar creatures because they sleep during the day and come out to play at night; because, like the Moon, they are able to appear and vanish with the silence and speed of shadows; and lastly, because they are proverbially prolific.

Sometimes the Moon even becomes a hare, or at the very least the hare is regarded as a manifestation of the Moon's powers. The Aztecs believed that the marks on the Moon's face were caused by a rabbit which a god had hurled at it, the sexual significance of this image being readily apparent. In Europe, Asia and Africa, these marks are hares or rabbits, or even a Great Rabbit.

When not the Moon herself, the hare or rabbit is her accomplice or close relative. They cannot be her husband, since this would require that they be of an opposite nature, but they are her brothers or lovers and, in this instance, there is something incestuous about the relationship, a type of left-handed holiness. In the Aztec calendar, the years of the rabbit were governed by the planet Venus, in their cosmogony the elder brother of the Sun, who committed adultery with his sister-in-law, the Moon (THOH). As the *Popol-Vuh* shows, the Maya-Quiché believed that when the Moon-goddess was in danger she was helped and saved by a Hero-Rabbit. The Codex Borgia illustrates this belief by bringing together, in the same hieroglyphic, drawings of a rabbit and of a water-pot, representing the Moon (GIRP pp. 189–90). By saving the Moon, the Rabbit saved the principle of cyclical renewal of life which, on Earth, controls the continuity of plant, animal and human species.

Rabbits – or more frequently, hares – thus become culture-heroes, Demiurges or mythic ancestors. Such was Menebuch, the Great Hare, of the Algonquin Ojibwa and Sioux Winebago Indians. Possessing the secret of the elements of life – a quality accorded to this animal in Ancient Egyptian hieroglyphics – it placed its knowledge at the service of mankind.

'Menebuch came down to earth in the guise of a hare and allowed his uncles and aunts, that is to say, the human race, to live as they do to this day. He taught them manual skills. He fought monsters from the depths of the waters. After the Flood, he made the Earth anew and, when he went away, he left it in the state in which it is today' (MULR p. 253). It is because he shares in the unknowable and the unattainable while still remaining mankind's familiar friend and neighbour on Earth, that the mythic hare or rabbit is an intercessor and go-between between this world and the transcendent realities of the Otherworld. Menebuch is the only link between mankind and the invisible Great Manitou, the all-powerful sky-god who, like Jehovah, embodies the archetypal Father-figure (KRIE p. 61). Menebuch is, therefore, a Hero-Son, whom Gilbert Durand regards as being akin to Christ. 'Like some Indians, African and American Blacks regard the Moon as a hare, an animal both hero and martyr, symbolically akin to the Christian lamb, a gentle, inoffensive creature, emblem of the lunar Messiah, and of the son, in contrast with the conquering and solar warrior' (DURS p. 339). After the Algonquin had been converted to Christianity, they effectively transformed Menebuch into Jesus Christ. Radin sees this as an archetypal expression of the second stage in the concept of the Hero, succeeding the Trickster, closely related to the JUGGLER of the Tarot, whose motivation is purely instinctive or infantile (JUNS pp. 112ff.). 'Menebuch,' Radin explains, 'the culture-hero, is a weak yet struggling figure, ready to sacrifice childishness for the sake of further development' (JUNS p. 118).

Ancient Egyptian mythology corroborates this induction by clothing the great initiate, Osiris, in the shape of a hare, which was torn to pieces and thrown into the waters of the Nile to ensure the seasonal cycle of renewal. Today, the Shi'ite peasants of Anatolia explain the taboo on eating hare's flesh by saying that the creature is a reincarnation of Ali. They regard Ali as the true intercessor between Allah and all True Believers, for whom this saintly hero sacrificed his two sons. This would emphasize and explain the hermetic saying of the Bektāshī Dervishes: 'Muhammad is the chamber and Ali is the doorway.' One might also instance the appearance in India of the Sheshajātaka, or Bodhisattva in the shape of a hare, which sacrificed itself by leaping into the flames.

The hare which, like the Moon, dies in order to be reborn, became thereby the Taoist's maker of the medicine of immortality and is depicted working under a FIG-TREE, pounding herbs in a MORTAR. Chinese smiths used hare's gall when smelting sword-blades. It was believed to impart strength and durability to the steel for the very same reasons which led the Burmese to regard the creature as the ancestor of the lunar dynasty.

The ambivalent symbolism of the hare is often to be seen in images and beliefs so deeply tinged by these two aspects of its symbol – the lucky and the unlucky, the left and the right – that it is hard to distinguish them. Thus, the Chinese said that the doe became pregnant by looking at the Moon, and Yang Chu wrote that 'girls nearly always behave like doe-rabbits gazing at the Moon' (VANG p. 286). Hence the Chinese belief that, if moonlight falls on a pregnant woman, her child will be born with a hare-lip. This touches upon the widespread and varied sexual significance which brings together hares, rabbits and the Moon. In Cambodia, when hares mated or gave birth it was supposed to bring fertilizing rainfall, but the Moon, being *yin*, was also its provider. Aztec farmers believed that what protected their harvests was not a rabbit-god, but four hundred rabbits, four hundred expressing the idea of the uncountable, or rather inexhaustible plenty. However, these familiar little rustic gods were also lords of idleness and drunkenness, two vices severely punished by Aztec law. The same ambivalence recurs in the significance attached by fortune-tellers to calendar years of the rabbit. These could be both lucky or unlucky since 'the rabbit hops from one side to the other' (SOUP, THOH).

Whatever is linked to ideas of plenty, of rampant growth and of the proliferation of living things or material possessions, also carries with it the seeds of unchastity, wastefulness, lust and excess. Thus at any given moment in the history of civilizations, the spirit will rise in rebellion against symbols of elemental life, which it will attempt to control and to channel. In fact, the spirit fears that these forces, naturally active and positive in the infancy of mankind and of the world, may subsequently destroy the very things which they have created. In what may be termed 'the Age of Reason', people turn against animist worship. It is at this point that hares are placed under a taboo. Deuteronomy and Leviticus damn them as unclean and forbidden food. Nearer home, the Celts in Ireland and Brittany, according to Caesar, 'raised hares as pets, but never ate their flesh'. Similar taboos were to be found among Baltic peoples, throughout Asia and as far afield as China. Looking back to Menebuch and the Trickster, the hare may thus be conceived as symbolically associated with puberty, without the excuses of childhood but producing its first-fruits. In the bestiary of lunar creatures, MONKEYS and FOXES are nearest neighbours to rabbits and hares. All were the companions of HECATE, protector of children, but haunting crossroads and inventor of witchcraft.

Harlequin   The name of an Italian *commedia dell'arte* character, traditionally dressed in a patchwork costume of triangular, multicoloured bits of cloth. He wears a black mask over his eyes and carries a wooden sword stuck in his belt. He embodies in youth the funny fellow, playing spiteful practical jokes and yet childish and capricious despite his cunning. The last characteristic is emphasized by his motley costume. He incarnates the undecided, inconsistent person who lacks character, ideas and principles. His sword is only made of wood and his face is masked, while his clothes are a mere patchwork. That they are in a CHEQUER-BOARD pattern suggests a confrontational situation, that of the person who has failed to achieve individualization, personalization or detachment from desires, schemes and potential courses of action.

harp   The pre-eminent traditional musical instrument, in contrast with such wind instruments as the bagpipes or percussion instruments such as the drum.   Harp-strings were generally made of cat-gut and, although many different sorts of harp are known, they fall, broadly speaking, into two categories – the hand-harp, a sort of zither, and the great ceremonial harp. In Norse lands it was with the harp that the gods or their messengers played a tune which irresistibly lulled its hearers to sleep and occasionally risked ushering them into the Beyond (OCUI 3: pp. 212–409; OGAC 18: pp. 326–9).

The harp links Heaven with Earth. The heroes of the Eddas asked to be burned with their harps beside them on their funeral pyres for they would lead them to the Otherworld. This role of instructor of the soul was not only filled after death, for during the hero's earthly life his harp would symbolize the tensions between carnal instincts, embodied in the wooden frame and the cat-gut strings, and spiritual aspirations, embodied in the vibrations of those same strings. The latter were only tuneful if they proceeded from a well-controlled tension between all the individual's drives, that ordered dynamism itself symbolizing balanced personality and self-mastery.

The famous Ancient Egyptian 'Harper's Song' exalts the quest for earthly happiness in a life of which the sole certainty is death at its end and nothing less sure than the individual's fate beyond the grave. The harpist strikes the strings and sings 'Cast care far away from you and think only of pleasure until the time comes for you to go to the land of silence' (POSD p. 17). In this context the sound of the harp symbolizes the quest for happiness, of which human beings know only the fragile assurances of this world.

harpies Evil spirits or winged monsters with the bodies of birds, the heads of women, sharp claws and a foul smell, which tormented souls with their ceaseless vexations and spite. Their name means 'snatchers' and they were generally reckoned to be three in number – 'Squall', 'Swift Flyer' and 'Dark' – their names suggestive of black, speeding storm clouds. Only Zetes and Calais, sons of the North Wind, Boreas, could drive them away (GRID p. 175). They were diabolical particles of cosmic energy, supplying the Underworld with the souls of those who died before their time.

They symbolize the vicious passions, the obsessive torments inspired by lust, as well as the feelings of guilt once they have been satisfied. They may be likened to the ERINNYES, but the latter stood for punishment, while the Harpies embodied vicious disposition and the provoking of evil-doing. The wind, which alone can drive them away, is the breath of the spirit.

harvest There is little point in lingering over the metaphorical uses of this word in the Bible; they are as readily comprehensible as ever they were – reaping what one sows (Proverbs 22: 8), or the harvest as an image of all work (Matthew 9: 37) and so on.

It is far more interesting to abstract the symbolic content of the image. 'The harvest is the end of the world', St Matthew writes (13: 39) and goes on to explain that this is the context of the Last Judgement. Thus God proclaims that he is about to take his seat as judge: 'Put ye in the sickle, for the harvest is ripe' (Joel 3: 13). The prophet goes on to use the parallel image of the vintage.

Nevertheless, a number of New Testament passages enable the rational explanation to be excluded. It is not a matter of the individual's actions, as he or she grows and reaches maturity, being simply harvested and assessed by a passive judge as with a pair of scales. The Parable of the Wheat and the Tares (Matthew 23: 24–30, 36–43) imparts a hint of mystery to the harvest as Last Judgement, God in his patience reserving its final verdict to himself. However, the ultimate criterion applying that to the harvest will be the essential quality of the fruit borne by the individual. It is a question of whether that person has sown and borne fruit for his fleshly appetites or whether for goodness and for the spirit, that is, for the will of God and his kingdom (Galatians 6: 7–10). It is for this reason that the outcome of the harvest does not always follow logic. Those that have sown in tears shall reap in joy (Psalm 126: 5).

hat See under HEADDRESS.

hazel The tree and the nut which it bears played an important part in the symbolism of Germanic and Norse peoples. Idun, the North German goddess of life and of fertility, was freed from captivity by Loki, who changed himself into a falcon and carried her off in the shape of a hazel-nut (MANG p. 25). In an Irish tale, a noblewoman walks in a hazel-grove to seek the advice of the gods for a cure for her barrenness. Hazel-nuts often played their part in wedding ceremonies. In Hanover tradition enjoined the crowd to shout 'Nuts! Nuts!' at the groom, while the bride was to hand out hazel-nuts on the third day after her wedding to show that the marriage had been consummated (ibid.). The custom of the Little Russians from Volhynia was for the mother-in-law at the marriage-feast to throw nuts and oats over her son-in-law's head. Lastly, in Germany, the phrase 'to crack nuts' was a euphemism for sexual intercourse.

It would seem, then, that the tree of fertility often became the tree of debauchery. In some parts of Germany, folk-songs contrast the hazel with the pine, the tree of constancy.

Thus medieval practices enlighten us as to the reason why magicians and dowsers of precious metals chose hazel for their WANDS. Since metals 'ripened' in the womb of Mother Earth and, like spring-water, were expressions of her inexhaustible fertility, they caused a sympathetic reaction in a hazel-wand. Mannhardt records that in Normandy 'they used to strike a cow three times with a hazel-stick to make her give milk.' He then quotes from evidence given at a witchcraft trial in Hesse in 1596 'that on Walpurgis Night the said witch did strike the cow with the Devil's wand so that the said cow would give milk for a whole year.' Thus the hazel, the fertility-tree, gradually became the tree of unchastity, of lust and lastly of the Devil. In Celtic custom the nut-tree was often the place where magic rites were performed, while Germanic mythology makes the hazel an attribute of the god Thor.

head Generally speaking, the head symbolizes the driving force of the active principle, including the powers of government, legislation and enlightenment. It also symbolizes the manifestation of spirit, in contrast with the body which symbolizes the manifestation of matter. The spherical shape of the human head, according to Plato, likens it to a universe (see SPHERE). The head is a microcosm. All these meanings converge in the the symbolism of the One, of perfection, the Sun and the godhead.

In the Celtic world, the head was the focus of practices and beliefs which differed in detail, but possessed an overall homogeneity. The most important custom was warlike: the Gauls used to cut off the heads of their conquered enemies, tie them to the necks of their horses and bear them home in triumph. These trophies were carefully preserved, in cedar-oil if need be (Diodorus Siculus 5: 29, 5; Strabo 4: 4, 5). The decapitated head is a regular motif of Gallic coinage and in the Gallic and Gallo-Roman plastic arts. Irish custom was identical with Gallic and insular heroic literature contains countless examples of the warrior carrying off the head of the enemy he has killed in single combat. The head would thus symbolize the enemy's strength and warlike virtues that his conqueror had acquired, and decapitation would also ensure the death of the enemy. According to Celtic notions, death did not occur until the cerebral membranes were destroyed. The heads taken by the warriors of Ulster were preserved at the court of King Conchobar in a special building, the 'Red Branch'. This is the counterpart, in myth, of the shrine at Entremont in what was southern Gaul. The followers of the Welsh king, Bran, brought his head back from Ireland, where they had been defeated, and buried it on the Gwynrryn, 'the White Hill', in London. So long as it remains buried, the island of Britain will remain free from invasion (OGAC 8: pp. 300–16; 10: pp. 129–54). Similarly, when the Romans were digging the foundations for a temple to Jupiter and discovered a skull of unusual size in the ground, the soothsayers interpreted this as a sign of the future greatness of Rome, which would become head of the world (GRID p. 328).

All mythologies contain many-headed creatures, animals, men, spirits, gods and goddesses. Each of these heads is a manifestation peculiar to its owner. For example, a three-headed god expresses three aspects of his power. The NAGA, a seven-headed serpent, on the other hand, expresses the symbolism of that NUMBER, together with the symbolism peculiar to itself (fertility), as infinite fertility. Symbolic arithmetic combines with the symbolism peculiar to the many-headed creature. The three heads of the goddess of the crossroads, HECATE, or of CERBERUS, the guard-dog of the Underworld, relate to the relationship of goddess and dog with the three worlds. JANUS had two faces so that he could look forwards and backwards, into the past and into the future. The Ancient Egyptian god, Amon-Ra, was often depicted with a green body and four ram's heads. According to Champollion they symbolized the four elements, the soul of the cosmos. Horapollon (quoted in LANS 6: pp. 1–28) states that 'in Egypt the coupling of two heads, the one male the other female, was a symbol of protection against evil spirits.'

Indra is a god with three heads because he rules the three worlds, just as Agni's three fires denote the three lights which shine in the three worlds. An endless list of examples might be given, but the principle of their interpretation remains the same – the meaning of the number has to be combined with that of the many-headed creature depicted.

In Christian iconography there are many examples of saints carrying their own heads, like the statue in Notre Dame of the first Bishop of Paris, the martyr St Denis. Both his legend, and its depiction, symbolize the belief that the executioner has been unable to deprive his victim of life, that St Denis continues to live and move spiritually and that through the spirit he masters the power of death. The victim's spirit, symbolized by his or her head, not only lives, but continues to be carried on Earth by those who share the same faith as it was by the martyr.

headdress This is a word which can mean both what one puts on one's head, and also the way in which the head, or rather its hair, is dressed. Hence it shares the full symbolical significance attaching to HAIR.

All forms of hair-dressing have been used to provide headdresses of short or long hair, curled hair, plaits or flowing locks (exposed or covered depending upon the demands of age or of ceremonial) and wigs. Both men and women have regarded headdress as so important because the way in which the hair was dressed provided the means of trapping, controlling and making use of the life force contained within the hair. Copying its shape was a means of approaching the axis or centre of life, either the beam or the solar disc. Thus hair- or head-dressing could become a distinguishing mark of profession, caste, rank, age or of the ideal and even of unconscious tendencies.

In Ancient Egypt the long plait which children wore over the right temple eventually became the hieroglyphic for the word 'child' (POSD p. 116), while the priests shaved their heads in reaction against the fantastic and over-elaborate headdresses worn during the imperial period and as a sign of obedience and fidelity to tradition. To wear a special headdress is to state a difference, to distinguish a particular rank or dignity and to choose a particular path. Ceremonial headdress will be different from others and he or she who wears it will tend to partake of a magic power like that imparted by CROWN or diadem. According to its shape – square, pointed, round, tall or flat – it will symbolize harmony with Earth, aspiration towards Heaven or the accretion to its wearer of heavenly powers. It is one of the images of the deep personality.

In a particular part of Algeria a sacred headdress, the *barrita*, is linked to the ritual of ploughing the first furrow. Kept completely hidden, it is only brought out once a year and may only be seen 'by the old man charged with the task of ploughing the first furrow'. He places it upon 'the right horn of the plough-ox' as he sets out for the field before day-break and, 'when he reaches the place where he will plough the first furrow, he faces east, sets the sacred headdress on his head and pronounces a blessing' (SERP pp. 126–7).

The name given to this headdress is that of crown or diadem and it is undoubtedly 'a sort of mitre or cap, either made of metal or embroidered, but in any event closed' (SERP p. 128). In this instance it is associated with symbols of fertility.

At Masonic lodge meetings, the Worshipful Master keeps his hat on, sitting with his head covered as 'a sign of his prerogatives and superior status' (BOUM p. 278). Whether or not this custom is retained for practical reasons, the symbolism of the hat is unaffected. The role which it plays would seem to correspond to that of the crown, a sign of power and kingship, and this was even more true in the days when the hat concerned was a tricorn (see HORN).

It has been claimed that wearing a hat could mean that the part played by the hair as recipient of celestial influences was at an end and even that the ultimate goal of the initiatory quest had been reached. However, reaching that goal does not stop – rather it intensifies – its mediatory function. The tips of the three-cornered hat, like the spikes on a crown and like the hair itself, are conceived as images of the Sun's rays (BOUM).

As a head-covering, the hat also symbolizes the head and thought. It is, once again, a symbol of the identity. As such it comes into its own in Meyrink's novel *The Golem*, in which the hero has the thoughts and undertakes the schemes of the owner of whatever hat he wears. As Jung says, to change one's hat is to change one's ideas and view of the world. To wear a different hat is to assume a different set of responsibilities.

heart Being the organ in the CENTRE of the human body, the heart corresponds in the broadest of terms with notions of centricity. Although the West may have made it the seat of the feelings, all traditional civilizations, in contrast, place within it intellect and intuition. This is perhaps because the centre of the personality has been displaced from intellectuality to affectivity; and yet Pascal remarked that 'great thoughts come from the heart.' One might also say that in traditional cultures knowledge embraces a far wider range, not excluding affective properties.

In fact, the heart is the living centre of the human being in so far as it ensures that the blood circulates. This is why it is taken as the symbol of the intellectual functions but not, of course, of their physical location. This localization existed in Ancient Greece and it was important in India, where the heart was regarded as the *Brahmapura* or abode of Brahmā. In Islam the heart is called 'the throne of God'. If, too, in the Christian vocabulary the heart is said to contain 'the Kingdom of God', this is because this centre of individuality, to which the personality returns in its spiritual pilgrimage, embodies the primordial state and hence the place of God's instrumentality. Angelus Silesius calls the heart the temple and altar of God, which can contain him in his entirety. Again, in the *Huang-ti ni Ching*, we read that the heart is a royal organ; it represents the king; it is the home of the spirit. If the cruciform church is to be identified with Christ's body, then the altar is sited in the place of the heart. The Holy of Holies was said to be the heart of the Temple at Jerusalem, which was itself the heart of Zion, which, like all religious centres, was the heart of the world.

In the cardiac cycle the periods of contraction (systole) and expansion (diastole) make the heart a symbol, too, of the similar movements of the universe. This is why the heart is *Prajāpati*. It is Brahmā in his creative role, originator of the cycles of the ages. According to St Clement of Alexandria, God, the heart of the world, manifests himself in the six directions of space. Similarly Allah is 'the Heart of hearts and Spirit of spirits'.

Because it is at the centre, the Chinese drew a correspondence between the heart, the element Earth and the number FIVE. However, by reason of its nature – since it is the Sun – they also attributed it to the element Fire. The *Su-wen* comments that the heart 'lifts itself up to the principle of light'. The light of the spirit, the light of intellectual intuition, enlightenment, shines forth in 'the cavern of the heart'. Sufis call the organ of these perceptions *Ayn el-Qalb*, 'the Eye of the Heart', and similar phrases occur in a number of Christian writers, particularly in St Augustine.

The *Ni-Ching* states that the heart is king and this is corroborated by the Ismaili dictum that 'the task of the heart is to rule.' The Taoist Master Lu-tzu taught that the heart was the lord of the breath, and this may be explained simply by the similarity between the rhythm of the cardiac and respiratory cycles, identified as cosmic symbols in their tasks. Plutarch, however, employs the same image of the Sun spreading its light as the heart diffuses the breath. In Taoism, too, breath (*k'i*) is light; it is spirit. Lu-tzu concentrates the spirit between the eyebrows, precisely where Yoga sites the *ajnā-chakra*, and transfers to it in some ways the tasks of the heart. This is why this 'finger-breadth space' is called 'the celestial heart' (*t'iensin*).

Ancient Egyptian hieroglyphics used a vase to stand for the heart. The heart also bears a relationship with the Grail, the chalice which contained Christ's blood. One should in any case note that the inverted triangle not only has the same configuration as a chalice, but is also a symbol for the heart. Furthermore, a chalice holding the beverage of immortality must of necessity belong to the heart of the world (BENA, CHAT, CORT, DANA, GRIF, GUEV, GUEM, GUEI, GUES, JILH, LIOT, SAIR, SCHC).

The heart played a fundamental part in Ancient Egyptian religion. 'According to the Memphite cosmogony the god Ptah conceived of the world in his heart before bringing it into existence with his creative utterance' (POSD p. 119). However, it was primarily the centre of every individual's life, will and intellect. When the souls of the dead were weighed, it was the heart, the only internal organ left in the mummy, which was placed in the pan of the scales, while that essential talisman, the scarab of the heart, had engraved upon it the magic spell which would prevent the heart from bearing witness against the dead person at Osiris' judgement seat. In the life of a disciple of one of the sages it is written, 'A man's heart is his own god and my heart is content with my deeds.' Similarly, a funeral stele now in the Louvre identifies the heart with the conscience: 'It is my heart which has made me do these deeds, since it was my guide in the business of living. It was an excellent witness on my behalf . . . I excelled because it made me do what I did . . . It is a judgement of the god which dwells in the bodies of all beings.' Every individual's most ardent desire is that expressed by the blessing of Paheri of El-Kab: 'May you pass through eternity in peace of heart and in the grace of the god that is within you' (DAUE p. 331). Thus the heart within us is the symbol of the presence of the godhead and of our awareness of that presence.

In Classical antiquity the symbolic meaning of the heart was ill-defined. One tradition relates that by eating the still-beating heart of Zagreus, whom the Titans had torn to pieces, Zeus brought his son to life again in the shape of Dionysos, who was born to him by Semele (GRID pp. 221a, 477b). This would seem to be the only legend in which hearts play a part; the part is that of the vital principle and the principle of personality, since Zagreus' heart was reborn in the shape of Dionysos.

In the Celtic world there is a remarkable interconnection between the words for 'centre' (Breton: *kreiz*; Welsh: *craidd*; Irish: *cridhe*) and those for 'heart'. These three words are related to the Indo-European root-word *krd* ('heart', 'centre', 'middle') from which are derived the Latin, Greek, Armenian, Germanic and Slav words for 'heart'. In Irish literature, when a person

dies burdened with sadness their hearts are sometimes described as 'breaking within their breasts' (OGAC 5: p. 339). The heart obviously symbolizes
the life-centre.

In Old Testament tradition the heart symbolized the inner personality
and its emotional life, and was the seat of wisdom and understanding. The
heart was to the internal personality what the body was to the external. The
principle of evil was located in the heart and the individual was always in
danger of following the promptings of his or her evil heart. This perversion
of the heart derived from flesh and blood. When commenting upon the
words 'to love with one's whole heart', Babua ben Asher (late eighteenth
century) was to say that the heart was the first part of the body to be
created and the last to die, and that hence the phrase 'with one's whole
heart' meant until one's last breath (VAJA p. 237).

The heart plays a major role in Jewish tradition. *Sim lev* is to set one's
heart upon something, to pay close attention, while meditation is described
as 'speaking to one's heart'.

According to the Midrash, the human 'heart of stone' must become a
'heart of flesh and blood'. The 'wise in heart' possess the spirit of wisdom
(BARH).

In the Old Testament, for every ten times that the word 'heart' is used
for the bodily organ, there will be a thousand instances of its employment
in a metaphorical sense. Memory and imagination derive from the heart,
as does vigilance, hence the phrase: 'I sleep, but my heart wakes.' The heart
plays a central part in the life of the spirit: it thinks, makes decisions, outlines
plans and accepts responsibilities. To 'ravish' somebody's heart is to make
them lose self-control (Song of Solomon 4: 9).

The heart is associated with the spirit and sometimes the words are confounded because of the identical sense in which they are used, hence the
expressions: 'A new heart also will I give you, and a new spirit will I put
within you' (Ezekiel 36: 26); and 'a broken spirit: a broken and a contrite
heart' (Psalm 51: 17). The heart is always more closely linked to the spirit
than to the soul.

In Islamic tradition, the heart (*qalb*) does not stand for the organ of the
emotions, but for that of contemplation and of the spiritual life. 'It is the point
at which spirit is infused into matter . . . it is the essence of the individual,
a parcel of flesh of which the beat is the regulatory mechanism of life itself.
It is the hidden and secret abode (*sirr*) of consciousness' (MASH p. 477).

It is held to consist of successive layers – 'Alā al Dawlah lists seven – and
their colours may be seen when in a state of ecstasy. Within the *nafs*, or
material soul, the *sirr* comprises 'latent personality, implicit consciousness,
deep subconscious, the secret cell walled against all creatures, virgin and
inviolate' (MASH p. 486). (This should be compared with Master Eckhart's
spark, the foundation of the soul.)

> The spiritual organ which the Sufi call the heart (*qalb*) is barely distinguishable
> from the spirit (*rūh*). Jīlī says that, when the Koran talks of the divine spirit
> breathed into Adam, it is referring to his heart.   (NICM p. 113)

This same mystic speaks of the heart as being 'eternal light and sublime
consciousness (*sirr*) revealed in the quintessence of created beings, so that

by this means God might contemplate Mankind. It is the Throne of God (*al-'Arsh*) and his temple in the human being . . . the centre of divine consciousness and the circumference of the circle of all that is.'

The Koran says that the heart of the believer is between two fingers of the All-Merciful One and a sacred tradition puts into God's mouth the words: 'Heaven and Earth do not hold me, but I am contained within the heart of my servant.' The Names and Attributes of God comprise the true nature of the heart. 'The heart stands for the presence of the Spirit in its twofold aspect of Knowing and Being, for it is at one and the same time the organ of intuition [*al-kashf* = unveiling; see VEIL] and the point of identification (*wajd*) with Being (*al-wujād*) and it is that intangible point where the created being encounters God' (BURD p. 118).

Sufi mystics also regard the heart as 'the Throne of Mercy'. The love of which it is the abode, in fact, makes manifest God's love. The loving heart is a manifestation of the godhead, the mirror of the invisible world and of God himself.

Ibn al-'Arabī regarded the mystic's heart as something absolutely pliable and receptive. This is why it clothes itself in whatever shape God reveals himself, just as wax receives the impression of the seal. There is a similarity between the root of the word *qalb* (heart) – QLB – and the QBL of *qābil*, meaning to receive, to stand opposite; to be passive or receptive (BURD p. 152).

In the ninth century, Tirmidhi, as a mystic psychologist, expounded the theory of the 'knowledge of hearts' and states explicitly that the word *qalb* denotes both the organ which controls thought and physical organs of the body (MASL p. 293).

In Muslim psychology 'the heart prompts thoughts which are most deeply concealed, most secret and most true, it is the foundation of the human intellect.'

The notion of spiritual birth is associated with the symbol of the heart. 'Hearts in their secrecy are a solitary virgin', says al-Hallāj. Sufi mystics are known as 'men of the heart'. Spiritual vision is likened to 'the heart's eye'. 'I have seen my Lord in the heart's eye', to quote al-Hallāj again.

Even the Koran uses the heart as a synonym for knowledge. When relating Muhammad's vision (53: 11) it says: 'The heart does not deny what it has seen', and in a different context (22: 45), 'their eyes are not blind, but the hearts in their breasts cannot see.'

The Caribs of Venezuela and the Guyanas have one word for both soul and heart; the Tucano (Amazon Basin) one word for heart, soul and pulse; while the Wuitoto (southern Colombia) use the same word for heart, chest, memory and thought (METB).

The Pueblo Indians of Arizona believed children to be 'produced from the semen of a man's spinal cord and the blood from a woman's heart' (TALS p. 259).

Contemporary folklore has made the heart as much a symbol of profane love and of charity as of divine love, friendship and righteousness (TERS pp. 102–3).

Guénon observes (GUES p. 224) that the heart is shaped like an inverted triangle. Like all symbols which embody this shape, the heart should be related 'to the passive or female principle of universal manifestation . . . while [the symbols] which are shaped like upright triangles are related to the active or male principle.' It will be recalled that in India one of the chief symbols of Shakti, the female element in existence, and also the symbol of the primal Waters, is an inverted triangle.

hearth The symbol of community, of home, of marriage between man and woman, of love and of the conjunction of fire with its container. In so far as it is a solar centre which gathers living things to itself through the light and heat which it emits – and because it is also the place where food is cooked – the hearth is the centre of life, of life given, received and passed on. Every form of society has held the hearth in honour and it has become the shrine from which God's protection is invoked, where God is worshipped and where sacred statues are kept.

'The Maya-Quiché believe that the light of the hearth-fire gives expression to the manifestation of the spirit of the godhead, just as candles stand for the souls of the dead' (GRIP p. 81).

In countless traditions, the family's hearth plays the same role as the CENTRE or navel of the world. It then often becomes the sacrificial altar, as is the case with the Buryat who hang coloured ribbons at each of the four cardinal points around it, and the same notion occurs in India. Among such Siberian tribes as the Yakut, offerings were made at the hearth to the gods and, to adopt the words of Prikonski, in this context the fire became a doorway (HARA p. 171).

heat Heat is associated physically with light, as love is associated with intuitive knowledge and organic life with the instrumentality of the spirit. According to Plutarch, heat and light were set in motion by the Sun, just as were the intellectual and vital principles, blood and breath, by the heart. This has a slight notional similarity with Tantrism. In depicting the Sun, its heat is shown by wavy lines, its light by straight lines.

Heat is a cosmic power which, according to the *Rig-Veda*, allowed the One to be born from primordial Chaos. The incubation of the World Egg has often been compared with that of the hen's egg, life being equally present in both, as *The Secret of the Golden Flower* observes, 'through the powers of heat'. This is, in any case, merely a symbol of the concentration of the spirit within the heart to give birth to 'the embryo of immortality'. In this respect heat is the principle of rebirth and regeneration, as well as of communication, playing this part at all sacrificial feasts and at all banquets and celebrations. Thus Jung makes it an image of the libido. Its action is all the swifter and more effective if the recipient, through natural sympathy, is more open to its influence. 'Again, the heat of fire transmits itself chiefly to things that are more receptive, and yielding, and conducive to assimilation to itself' (PSEH p. 40).

In Yoga, heat is *tapas,* which also means ascetic discipline. The acquisition of internal fire is sometimes taken literally. In Shamanism and also in Tibetan *g'Tummo,* this takes the form of an extraordinary resistance to external cold. These are, however, subsidiary manifestations since *tapas* is the heat internalized, the flames of the spirit and the destruction by fire of sense-perceptions and of the limitation on the individual's existence. Furthermore, in Tantrism the element Fire corresponds to the *anahāta-chakra*, the centre of the heart. Some Buddhist schools practise meditation on the element Heat (*tejodhātu*); however, the feeling of heat is particularly associated with the raising of energy in Kundalinī Yoga and is readily compared with a blazing fire. Some writers maintain that this heat is a consequence of 'raising' and sublimating sexual energy. This is what *The Secret of the Golden Flower* calls the 'kindling power' of the breath of the 'pre-existent Heaven'. The *Pāli* Buddhist canon itself links the acquisition of heat with the control of respiration.

At a different level, heat is identified with the 'anger' of initiation into warrior castes, linked to the acquisition of some psycho-physical 'power'. As is often the case, such an acquisition carries its own dangers with it. In any case 'anger' and 'heat' may also spring from satanic influences which it is as well to exorcize. *Shānti* (peace) is literally putting out 'fire'.

It should also be observed that in Ancient China fire and heat were associated with drought and rain-making and also, as is universally the case, with the colour red. The ideogram *ch'e* also gives the meaning of drought. It is literally 'man's fire', which would link it with the meaning of anger (AVAS, CORM, ELIC, ELIY, ELIF, GOVM, GRIF, GUES, KALL).

In the Celtic world, heat is often related to a HERO's or an individual's warlike valour. Irish heroic literature mentions several warriors, and especially Cùchulainn, who melted the snow for thirty feet around them. Since heat and warlike frenzy go together, this is probably the reason why the Ancient Celts fought stark naked, as Classical authors so often record.

Heaven (sky)   The almost universal symbol expressing the belief in

a celestial divine being, who created the universe and guarantees the fecundity of the earth (by pouring rain down upon it). These beings are endowed with infinite foreknowledge and wisdom; moral laws and often tribal ritual as well were established by them during a brief visit to the earth; they watch to see that their laws are obeyed, and lightning strikes all who infringe them.
(ELIT p. 38)

Heaven is a direct manifestation of transcendence, power, sacrality and everlastingness which no Earth-dweller can attain.

The mere fact of being high, of being high up, means being powerful (in the religious sense), and being as such filled with the sacred.... The transcendence of God is directly revealed in the inaccessibility, infinity, eternity and creative power (rain) of the sky. The whole nature of the sky is an inexhaustible hierophany. Consequently, anything that happens among the STARS or in the upper areas of the atmosphere – the rhythmic revolution of the stars, chasing CLOUDS, storms, THUNDERBOLTS, meteors, RAINBOWS – is a moment in that hierophany.
(ELIT pp. 39, 40)

As the power which ruled the cosmic order, Heaven was regarded as the father of kings and earthly rulers. In China, the emperor was called the 'Son of Heaven'. The passage from transcendence to sovereignty falls into a classic pattern, heaven–god the creator–sovereign, as does its counterpart, empire–Son of God–benefactor–king. The heavenly hierarchy provides a pattern for earthly hierarchies. The uppermost becomes the master; the giver of gifts takes upon himself the right to rule; service becomes slavery. The inscription which Genghis Khan engraved upon his seal is well-known: 'One God in Heaven and the Khan on Earth. Seal of the Master of the World.' In practice, however, the opposite may well become true, in accordance with the process of perversion which all symbols undergo. The master may still be called a benefactor, yet bring ruin to others; father, yet slaughter his subjects; heavenly, yet wallow in vice. This corruption does not, however, in any sense diminish the original strength of the symbol.

Heaven is the complex symbol of the sacred nature of the cosmic order, both revealed, in the regular, wheeling motion of the stars, and hidden, in the idea of invisible orders of being that are superior to the phenomenal world: the transcendent divine and the immanent human orders.

Heaven is often represented by figures of bells, inverted CHALICES, DOMES, PARASOLS, sunshades, awnings, doves, an umbrella turning upon its own axis, or by the human heart.

Heaven is the universal symbol of superhuman powers, which may be either well-intentioned or to be feared. The Chinese ideogram for heaven (t'ien) stands for what is above the human head. It is unfathomable space, the sphere of universal rhythms and great stars and, hence, the source of light and perhaps the guardian of the secrets of fate as well. Heaven is the abode of the gods and sometimes denotes the power of the godhead itself. It is also the abode of the Blessed. There are often thought to be SEVEN (or NINE) heavens, a theme running from Buddhism to Islam and from Ancient China to Dante. Clearly this involves a hierarchy of spiritual states which must be ascended one by one.

In a different light, both Heaven and Earth result from primeval polarization, Heaven being the uppper half of the World EGG. This is especially true of its representation in the *Chāndogya Upanishad* and in Hindu architecture. Even when the symbolism is not explicitly stated, the notion of a link in the beginning between Heaven and Earth, which was later broken, is almost universal. This polarization is especially clearly expressed in China. Heaven is the active male principle in contrast with passive, female Earth. In discussing the hexagram *ch'ien* (Heaven), the *I Ching* states that 'Heaven in its instrumentality is the supreme power.' Hence, Heaven is not the supreme First Cause, but the positive pole of its manifestation. 'Heaven is the instrument of the First Cause', wrote Chuang Tzu. The First Cause is the pinnacle of Heaven (*Ch'ien-Chi*).

All beings are produced by the action of Heaven upon Earth. The penetration of Earth by Heaven is therefore seen as though it were sexual intercourse, its fruits either Man, son of Heaven and Earth, or, in the special symbolism of internal alchemy, the embryo of immortality. The myth of the marriage of Heaven and Earth is current, via Greece, Egypt and Black Africa, from Asia to the Americas. The phrase 'Son of Heaven and Earth' is as much part of the Orphic Mysteries as of Chinese literature. The true Son of Heaven and Earth, he whom the *I Ching* describes as their equal and 'consequently not in conflict with them', is the true man', and, specifically, the emperor. The ideogram *wang*, which denotes him (see JADE; KING) gives precise expression to this mediation, which is also mentioned in

The Emerald Table of Hermes – 'He ascends from Earth to Heaven, and descends once more from Heaven to Earth.'

Chinese ALCHEMY, as we have noted in the article on it, transports Heaven to within the human microcosm. Muslim esotericism arrives at the same destination although by a different route, Abū Ya'qūb writing that Heaven is within the soul, rather than the reverse. This is an aspect of spiritual astrology well worth investigation (CORT, ELIM, GRIF, GUED, LIOT, MAST).

Unlike the Chinese, Ancient Egyptian tradition believed Heaven to be a female principle and source of all manifestation. In fact, Heaven was depicted as the goddess Nut, her body arched across the sky. She is carved on a Thirtieth Dynasty sarcophagus, arched like a Gothic doorway, her hands touching the ground to the east, her feet to the west. Within the doorway there is painted a world-map showing the different countries, the Underworld and its gods and the Sun irradiating all. This goddess bending in a half circle along which the Sun moves, encloses the complete cosmos and its three levels. As a personification of the celestial space encompassing the Universe, Nut was called the 'Mother of Gods and Men' and she was depicted upon countless sarcophagi. A papyrus now in the Louvre makes her speak like a loving mother to the dead person, promising to protect him in his coffin, and she is also depicted in a sycamore-tree pouring upon souls the heavenly water which will regenerate them (POSD). She was held to have married the Earth, the god Geb, and higher than the stars and planets, to have given birth to the Sun, the god Ra. Heaven married Earth and the Sun was born.

In Old Testament tradition, Heaven was identified with the godhead, chroniclers and prophets studiously avoiding mention of the name of God. Thus 'Heaven' is used in place of 'the God of Heaven', which was the term current during the Persian period, and 2 Maccabees 2: 21 attributes to Heaven the special blessings of Jehovah.

In the New Testament the *Jerusalem Bible* commentators on Matthew 3: 2 remark that he uses the phrase 'kingdom of heaven is at hand' 'instead of "the kingdom of God". The phrase is peculiar to Matthew and reflects the Jewish scruple which substituted the metaphor for the divine name.' When he repeats it (4: 7) it shows that 'the sovereignty of God over the chosen people, and through them over the world, is at the heart of Jesus' teaching.'

In the Book of Revelation, Heaven is God's dwelling, a symbolic method of denoting the distinction between the creator and his creation. Hence Heaven becomes part of the systematic relationship between God and mankind. When this relationship changes, as, for example, after the Incarnation of the Redeemer, then the whole system is altered and one can speak of a new Heaven. Thus the author of Revelation is enabled to write (21: 1, 2, 5): 'And I saw a new heaven and a new earth: for the first heaven and the first earth had passed away ... And I ... saw the holy city, new Jerusalem, coming down from God out of heaven ... And he that sat upon the throne said, Behold I make all things new.' In this context, the new Heaven symbolizes the universal renewal which ushers in the age of the Messiah. The relationship between God and his creation is utterly transformed.

In Celtic symbolism, Heaven plays no decisive role, since it is neither the abode nor the seat of the gods. Although a distinction is drawn between the religious sense of Heaven and that of the heavens (sky) there is no evidence that the pre-Christian Celts either drew such a distinction or, indeed, that it was necessary. Generally speaking they seem to have regarded the heavens as a vault, and hence their fear that the sky would fall upon their heads and the habit of the Irish to call the elements to witness their oaths (OGAC 12: pp. 185–97).

During the historic age (c. 1000 AD) the Mexicans believed in nine heavens, symbolized in their temple-building by the nine steps in their pyramids. They also believed in nine Underworlds. 'The Aztecs replaced this step-cosmology with one of strata, distinguishing thirteen heavens and nine Underworlds' (KRIR p. 60).

Each of the twelve heavens of the Algonquin Indians was inhabited by a Manitou, the twelfth being the home of the all-powerful Creator, the Great Manitou (MULR p. 237).

According to the *Historia de los Mexicanos por sus pinturas* (quoted in SOUM), the thirteen Aztec heavens may be characterized as follows:

1 Land of the Stars;
2 Land of the Tzitzimime (skeleton-like monsters who will be unleashed upon the world when the Sun dies);
3 Land of the 400 Guardians of the Heavens;
4 Land of the Birds which come down to Earth (undoubtedly the souls of the elect);
5 Land of the Fiery Serpents (meteors and comets);
6 Land of the Four Winds;
7 Land of Dust [?];
8 Land of the Gods.

The ninth to thirteenth Heavens are the homes of the Great Gods, the Sun dwelling in the twelfth Heaven and the powers of darkness in the tenth. The primordial divine couple live in the thirteenth and last Heaven. The thirteenth Heaven is also the land from which babies come and to which still-born babies return. In it grows a 'milk-tree' (SOUM).

The Bambara believe in seven heavens rising one above the other:

• the first Heaven is unclean;
• the second Heaven is clean, partly purified, and is the abode of human souls and of those of animals;
• the third, or black, Heaven is the resting place of the spirits who act as intermediaries between mankind and the gods;
• the fourth Heaven is the 'mirror' held to the first three. In it Faro, the Demiurge, lord of water and the word who regulates the present order of the universe, keeps his accounts. He keeps watch upon the doings of his creation in his mirror;
• the fifth Heaven is red. This is the Heaven of divine justice in which Faro pronounces sentence upon those who have infringed his commandments. It is also the Heaven of war and battle. It is a land of blood, fire and pestilential hot winds. The Bambara offer propitiatory sacrifice to

it before engaging in battle. This fifth Heaven is a land of drought and the abode of the spirits who try to stop the rain falling. They are assailed by the Kwore, spirits riding winged horses who live in the third Heaven (DIEB). Their battles create thunder and lightning;

- the sixth Heaven is the Heaven of sleep. The secrets of the universe are kept here. The souls of men and spirits come here to be purified and to be given in dreams the commands of the god, Faro;
- the seventh Heaven is the kingdom of the god Faro, where he stores the water which he pours down on Earth in the shape of fructifying and purifying rain.

In the world-picture of the Uralo-Altaic peoples there are sometimes seven and sometimes nine Heavens. These different heavenly strata are embodied in the notches cut in the stake or sacred birch-tree through which the shaman gives material form to the successive stages of his ascension. 'In many places they sometimes mention Heaven as having twelve, sixteen or even seventeen strata' (JEAD p. 41, quoting Katanov and Radloff). The Pole Star plays an especial part in this celestial system. According to Anokhin it constitutes the fifth obstacle in the shaman's upward path and consequently corresponds to the fifth Heaven (ibid. p. 39). According to Bogoraz, the Chukchi imagine that 'the opening in the sky providing a passage from one world to another lies close to the Pole Star' (ibid. p. 41). 'All worlds', Bogoraz adds, 'are linked the one to the other by openings lying close to the Pole Star. Shamans and spirits use them when passing from one world to another. Different legends tell how heroes, mounted upon eagles or storm-birds, are also able to pass through them.'

The Tatars of the Altai region and the Telyut set the Moon in the sixth heaven and the Sun in the seventh.

They also locate the Paradise of the Blessed in the third Heaven, the abode of Jajyk-Khan, 'Prince of the Flood', the deity who guards mankind and mediates between them and the Supreme Godhead. The third Heaven also provides souls for children in the womb: Jajyk sends them down to Earth (HARA p. 96).

An Uighur book, the *Kudatku Bilik*, written *c.* 1069, sets the seven stars in the following order, starting at the highest Heaven: Saturn, Jupiter, Mars, Sun, Venus, Mercury and Moon (HARA p. 116). This arrangement has always been that followed by European astrologers and occultists.

According to Uno Harva, this arrangement of Heaven in nine strata is undeniably a later notion than its arrangement in seven, 'not only among Turkic races, but among the other Asiatic peoples where this configuration occurs' (HARA p. 43). Hara argues that the last generation of Mithras-worshippers, about the time of Julian the Apostate, began to speak of nine Heavens. Tenth-century sources reveal that the Sabaeans had organized their temple priesthood in accordance with the nine stellar circles. The nine planets, each corresponding to a metal, are mentioned in a Hindu legal compendium, the *Yaajnavalkya*, which Bousset explains as deriving from a late Persian source.

In Dante's Paradise there are above the seven planetary circles, eighth, the Heaven of the fixed stars and, ninth, the *primum mobile*. The idea of

nine Heavens circulated so widely in the Middle Ages that it reached the
Norse lands and traces of it may be found in Finnish magic spells.

Heaven is also a symbol of awareness. The word is often used to mean
'the absolute of human aspiration, like the achievement of a quest, like the
place where the human spirit may come to perfection, as if Heaven were
the spirit of the universe. . . . It is understandable that the thunderbolt –
splitting the heavens with its lightning – should be so fitting a symbol of that
opening of the spirit which is the onset of awareness' (VIRI p. 108).

Hecate   Goddess of the dead but, unlike PERSEPHONE, the bride of Hades,
a goddess

who presides over necromancers' spells and the summoning up of the dead. She
is invoked by witches and is depicted brandishing a torch and accompanied by
mares, bitches and she-wolves. Her powers are terrifying, especially at night and
under the treacherous light of the Moon with which she is identified. She was
often depicted as a woman with three bodies or else as three women backed
against a column. . . . She was worshipped at CROSSROADS especially, where her
statues were erected.

(DEVD p. 224)

As a lunar and chthonian goddess, she was linked to fertility rites, but she
displays two contrasting aspects. One is benevolent and benign – she presides at seedtime and childbirth; she protects sailors; she grants prosperity,
eloquence, victory, plentiful harvests to the farmer and rich catches to the
fisherman; and she is the guide along the path of Orphic purification. On
the other side of the coin is her terrifying and infernal aspect. She is 'the
goddess of ghosts and night-terrors . . . of phantoms and fearful monsters
. . . she is the witch *par excellence*', mistress of sorcery. She is only conjured
up by incantation, by love charms or by death philtres (LAVD p. 497).

The goddess lends herself to symbolic interpretation at various levels
both because of her legend and because of the way in which she is depicted,
with three bodies and with three heads. As a Moon-goddess she could
represent the three phases of the lunar cycle – waxing, waning and disap-
pearing – and the three corresponding phases of the life-cycle. As an Underworld-goddess she might draw together the three levels of the universe –
Hell, Earth and Heaven. In this context she might well be venerated as
goddess of the crossroads, since every decision taken at such crossroads
demands taking new directions, not only horizontally along the plane of the
Earth's surface, but, at a deeper level, a vertical direction to one or other
of the levels of life selected. Lastly, the dark goddess of ghosts and witches,
she might symbolize the unconscious in which beasts and monsters swarm.
This is not just the living hell of the psychotic, but a reservoir of energy to
be brought under control, just as Chaos was brought to cosmic order under
the influence of the spirit.

hedgehog   This creature, which occupied so prominent a place in ancient
Irish mythology, plays a corresponding role in many of the myths of central
Asia. The Buryat regarded the hedgehog as the inventor of fire (the porcupine is cast in the same part by the Kikuyu of East Africa (FRAF)); it
was the trusted counsellor of mankind which, thanks to it, recovered the Sun
and Moon when they were once lost. The hedgehog was also credited with

the invention of agriculture (HARA p. 131). In short it is a culture-hero linked to the period when the wandering Turko-Mongol nomads adopted a sedentary life-style. The rash which the pricking of his spines causes is no doubt the source of his fiery, solar and, hence, civilizing symbolism.

Medieval iconography made hedgehogs symbols of greed and gluttony, no doubt from the habit attributed to them of rolling on fallen figs, grapes and apples and returning, spines laden with fruit, to hide in some hollow tree and amass this wealth and use it to feed their young.

heel The Semang believe that at death the soul leaves the body through the heel (ELIC p. 281).

Achilles was vulnerable in the heel. Scorpions and snakes most often bite the heel. The heel is, as it were, the foundation-stone of the human being with the characteristically upright stance. Once the heel is affected, the person falls down. In the logic of the imagination, then, there is no contradiction for the entry-point of death to be also the final exit-point of the soul.

heliotrope This plant symbolizes either the Sun in its daily course or the movement of light radiating from the Sun. It first adorned the brows of Roman emperors and of the kings of eastern Europe and of Asia and was then used in Christian iconography as a characteristic of the persons of the Trinity, Our Lady, angels, prophets, apostles and saints.

This solar plant is depicted in a glass-painting of St Remy at Rheims, 'two heliotrope stalks springing from the haloes round the heads of Our Lady and of St John, weeping at the foot of the Cross' (DAVS p. 220). The property possessed by this flower of turning to follow the Sun's course symbolizes the attitude of the lover or of the soul, continually turning eyes and thoughts towards the beloved; and it symbolizes perfection, always stretched out to the contemplative presence which seeks to unite with it.

Thus the heliotrope next comes to symbolize prayer. A flower which grows alone, according to Proclus, 'it sings the praise of the leader of the divine order to which it belongs, spiritual praises, and praise which can be apprehended by reason, touch and feeling.' Proclus regarded the sky-blue heliotrope as praying because it always turned, in token of its fidelity, to look towards its Lord.

According to Greek legend, Clytie was first loved and then abandoned for another by the Sun. She could not be consoled, died of grief and was changed into a heliotrope, the flower which always follows the Sun as if it were the lover she had lost. She symbolizes the inability to overcome one's emotions and receptiveness to the influence of the beloved.

Its delicate perfume makes it a symbol, too, of intoxication, with mysticism as much as with love or glory.

Hell (Hades) Ancient beliefs – Egyptian, Greek and Roman – differed widely and existed simultaneously, and only the most important of these will be mentioned in this article.

Hades – the 'Unseen One', although the etymology is shaky – was the Greek god of the dead. Since nobody dared mention his name for fear of arousing his anger, he was surnamed Pluto ('Rich One'), a grisly joke rather than a euphemism, by reference to the wealth lying below the Earth's surface, where the kingdom of the dead was located. The joke became somewhat macabre when Pluto was depicted holding a horn of plenty. Nevertheless, the Underworld is, symbolically, the site of mineral wealth, metamorphoses, transitions from death to life and germination (see also CAVERN).

After the Olympian gods had defeated the Titans, the universe was divided between the three sons of Cronos and Rhea. Zeus received Heaven; Poseidon the sea; and Hades the Underworld, Hell or Tartarus. He was a pitiless ruler, as cruel as his niece and bride, Persephone, who never let any of his subjects go. His name was given to his kingdom and Hades became the symbol of Hell. It, too, partook of his character, being a place which was invisible, from which, except for those who believed in reincarnation, there was no escape, sunk in cold and darkness and haunted by demons and monsters who tormented the dead (GRID). In Ancient Egypt, for instance, the tomb of Rameses IV at Thebes provides an early example of Hell symbolized by caverns filled with the damned. However, not all those who died became the victims of Hades, the elect – heroes, wise men and initiates – were granted a dwelling-place far from the darkness of Hell, in the Fortunate Islands or the Elysian Fields, where light and happiness were lavished upon them.

Analysing Hell from the ethical and psychological angle, Paul Diel remarks:

A personified figure stands for each function of the psyche and the intrapsychic actions of sublimation or perversion are expressed in the interaction of these personifications. The spirit is called Zeus; Apollo, the harmonization of desire; Pallas Athene, intuitive inspiration; Hades, repression; and so on. The essential desire – developmental drive – is represented by the hero, and the confrontational situation of the psyche by battles with the monsters of perversion.

(DIES p. 40)

From this viewpoint, Hell is a state in which the psyche has fallen victim to these monsters, either through failure in its attempts to repress them into the unconscious or through voluntary identification with them in conscious perversion.

Some Middle Breton religious writings mention Hell as being *an ifern yen*, an 'icy hell'. This term is so at variance with accepted norms that it must be regarded as an echo of ancient Celtic notions relative to non-being.

Aztec cosmology set Hell in the north, the land of darkness called 'the Land of the Nine Plains', or nine Hells. Apart from deified heroes, warriors who had been killed either in battle or in sacrifice, women who had died in childbirth and stillborn babies, all human beings returned to the Hells from which they had come, led by a dog as conductor of souls. Having passed through the first eight Hells, they reached the ninth and last into which they plunged and were annihilated (SOUP).

The God of Hell was the fifth of the nine Lords of Darkness. His place is therefore at the precise middle of the night and we might call him 'Midnight Lord'. On his back he carried the Black Sun (see under SUN) and his symbolic creatures were the spider and the owl.

The Turkic peoples of the Altai approached the spirits of the dead by travelling from west to east, that is, in the opposite direction to the path of the Sun, the latter symbolizing the forward motion of the life force (HARA).

Travelling to meet light head-on, instead of following in its path, symbolizes regression into darkness.

Christian tradition pairs LIGHT and darkness as symbols of the two opposites, Heaven and Hell. Earlier, Plutarch had described Tartarus as being deprived of light. If, therefore, light is to be identified with God and with life, Hell denotes deprivation of God and of life.

'Nothing less than the mortal sin in which the damned have died, is the essential nature of Hell' (ENCF p. 470). This is the loss of God's presence and, since no other apparent good can delude the soul separated from the body and from sensory reality, this is absolute misfortune, radical deprivation and 'mysterious and unfathomable torment'. For the individual this is total, final, and irreversible disaster. It is no longer for the damned to turn once more to God; hardened in sin, they must bear their punishment for ever.

helmet (see also CAUL; HEADDRESS; HOOD)   Helmets are symbols of invisibility, invulnerability and power.

Hades' helmet, often depicted as a Phrygian cap, made him invisible, even to the other gods, when he wore it (*Iliad* 5: 841; Plato, *Republic* 10: 612b). Hades, on somewhat doubtful grounds, has long been held to mean 'the Unseen One'. The Cyclops gave him the helmet so that he could join victorious battle against the Titans. Athene, according to the *Iliad*, wore this precious helmet when she came to the help of Diomedes in his battle with Ares. Other gods and heroes wore similar head-pieces in their battles. Like the pointed hats or hoods worn by DWARFS or wizards, the helmet protects its wearer by making him or her invisible.

Even when it does not confer this ultimate privilege, helmets at least are manifestations of power. Such, for example, was Agamemnon's helmet described by Homer (*Iliad* 11: 42–3) as having two crests, four bosses and horse-hair plumes which fluttered in the wind. This is very like the helmets worn by Napoleon's cuirassiers, with the long horse-hair plumes which billowed out in threatening black clouds when they charged.

The symbolism of helmets is akin to the symbolism of the HEAD which they protect. It may be said in this context that they hide as well as guard the thoughts. The helmet is a symbol of elevation, but also of dissimulation when the vizor is closed. The more or less elaborately decorated crest discloses the creative imagination and ambitions of the head which wears it.

However, the fact that the helmet is an especial attribute of Hades, King of Hell, who keeps a jealous eye upon the dead, gives rise to all sorts of other plausible interpretations. It may, perhaps, be that the desire to escape the gaze of others may only be satisfied in death. The helmet of Hades might also signify Death, the invisible one continually prowling round us. Again, like Gyges' RING, the helmet's desires and dreams might conceal the ambition to possess supreme power or the position of the gods who see everything while remaining unseen. Or else, as Paul Diel (DIES p. 147) suggests – and none of these theories excludes the rest – a helmet of invisibility worn by the lord of the punishments of Hell, might well be a symbol of the unconscious. It could denote our attempts to hide something from ourselves, or even to hide our selves from ourselves. The emblem possessed by this symbol of power would be reversed so that it expressed only the powerlessness of the individual to achieve complete self-expression. Invisibility would then be reduced to a means of avoiding spiritual struggle with the self.

hem In the wider realm of dress symbolism, and particularly within the context of the ancient Middle East, there is one term which deserves especial attention. It is the 'hem of a garment', that garment, generally speaking, being the cloak. The term is backed by two groups of evidence, meaning, symbolically, two totally different things, according to whether the hem of the garment is clasped or cut off.

This ambivalent topic is related to the well documented identification of dress with its wearer, for the basic meaning of the motif is that of the power of the individual, regarded as a negative or positive attribute according to the verb governing and therefore determining its meaning.

The term 'to clasp the hem of a garment' occurs in an Aramaic inscription carved upon the statue of King Panamnu (seventh century BC) found at Zenjīrli. 'In his wisdom and in his fidelity he clasps the hem of the garment of his Lord, the King of Assyria . . .' This precisely translates the stock phrase already known in Babylon and Assyria, and clearly proves the relationship between the King and the King of Assyria to be that of vassal and overlord.

In fact the same set phrases occur a thousand years earlier, again in a political context, among the royal archives of Mari (6: 26): 'Clasp the hem of Zimri-Lim's [King of Mari] garment and obey his commands.'

However, among these same documents is another letter providing an extremely interesting variation on this symbolic theme. In this case two persons are described as joining the hems of their garments together as part of a treaty-making ceremony. 'My brother has joined the hem [made a treaty] with the Man [King] of Babylon.'

What sets these two similar actions apart is highly instructive. While at Zenjīrli – and in parallel Akkadian sources – it is clear that the Aramaic king was submitting to his Assyrian overlord in a very one-sided peace treaty, the last-quoted document from Mari, on the other hand, displays the ritual of political alliance between equal partners.

The act of clasping the hem of someone's garment must have originated in the juridico-political ritual of treaty-making. It was to enjoy a wider currency and finally – and especially within the sphere of religion – it came to express a particular devotion to a god who was conceived of as king and overlord. This is the form it took in a prayer by the mother of the sixth-century BC king, Nabonides: 'I clasp the hem [of the cloak] of Sin, king of the gods, while night and day my ears are open to his call.'

There is undoubtedly an echo of this in the New Testament account of the cure of the woman with an issue of blood by Jesus, worshipped in this instance as Messiah and Saviour: 'And, behold, a woman, which was diseased . . . came behind him and touched the hem of his garment. For

she said within herself, If I may but touch his garment, I shall be whole'
(Matthew 9: 20-1).

Cutting off the hem of a garment was part of the solemn ceremony of
divorce under Sumerian law, when the husband cut off the hem of the
guilty wife's dress. In Assyro-Babylonian law, right down to the Cappadocian
period, the custom was preserved of cutting off the hem (*sissiktum*) of the
accused person's robe.

The meaning of all this is quite clear, if it is borne in mind that the
garment – or rather its hem, the part standing for the whole in the familiar
process of symbolic intensification – characterizes and symbolizes the wearer's total personality. To cut off the hem, therefore, is the same as to gain
absolute power over that person from then on, that power being the power
of life and death.

This juridical act, often supplemented by cutting off part at least of the
person's hair as well, provides a satisfactory basis for explaining a series of
letters from the royal archives of Mari, one of which (13: 112) contains the
following phrase: 'Now, therefore, I have sent my lord [the king] the hem
of his garment and a lock of his hair.'

Lastly, this casts a fresh light upon the symbolic background of David's
accession to the throne of Israel (1 Samuel 24: 4-16). David had surprised
Saul in a cave in the Judean desert and 'cut off the skirt of Saul's robe
privily', but spared his life. It is very hard to determine the meaning of this
passage, but it would appear – in the light of the documents already quoted
– that this act was more than merely making the king look ridiculous. By
doing what he did, David took Saul into his power, hence the remorse
which he felt afterwards. However, he had also acquired the means of
demonstrating this power in material shape, first to Saul and then, if need
be, to the people as a whole. Thus he succeeded in ending Saul's persecution of him, since the latter now had to come to terms with David, before
finally yielding the kingship to him.

The symbol of the hem of the garment, on the one hand part of the
symbolism of vassalage or political alliance and on the other of absolute
legal domination, provides a faithful picture of the magico-religious mentality of this oriental society, structured both by concrete reality and by conditioned and symbolic thought.

hen Hens play the part of conductors of souls in the initiatory rites and
ceremonies of divination of the Bantu tribes in the Congo Basin. Thus Dr
Fourche records that in the rites of initiating a female shaman of the Lulua,
after the candidate has emerged from the trench in which she has endured
the ordeal of death and rebirth, she is not regarded as having been completely initiated until one of her sisters has hung a hen from her neck. 'This
is the bait which she will use from henceforth, having the power to go into
the bush and with it lure the souls of dead mediums, bring them back and
install them in the trees consecrated to them' (FOUG). In many characteristically Orphic rites hens appear to be associated with dogs.

The widespread custom in Black Africa of sacrificing a hen in order to
get in touch with the dead derives from the same symbolism. (See also
COCK.)

Hephaistos (Vulcan) The lame son of Zeus and Hera, despised by his parents and married to the most beautiful of the goddesses, APHRODITE. She was unfaithful to him with his brother, Ares, and with many other gods and mortals. He was, however, beloved by Charis, grace incarnate, and by other very beautiful women and he never lacked the companionship of charming women.

Lord of the arts associated with fire, he ruled the busy world of BLACK-SMITHS, workers in precious metals and their craftsmen. He was to be seen panting and sweating over his anvil, on which he hammered and forged the weapons of gods and heroes; glittering shields; jewellery, brooches, brace-lets and necklaces for goddesses and lovely mortal women; and cunning locks, wheeled tripods and robots.

'Within the circle of the Olympian gods, Hephaistos was lord of the element of Fire and of metals' (GRID p. 185). In battle, his weapons were flames, molten metal or red-hot bars of iron. 'As the god of metal-working, he ruled the volcanoes which were his workshops and in which he laboured with the Cyclops to assist him. . . . He was to the gods what Daedalus was to mankind – an inventor to whom no technical miracle was an impossibil-ity' (GRID p. 186).

Three legends from different periods illustrate the part attributed to Homer's 'renowned craftsman'. It was he who helped give birth to Athene, by breaking open, with his double-headed axe, Zeus' skull in which she was shut. It was he who, on Zeus' orders, nailed Prometheus to the side of Mount Caucasus. Lastly it was he who moulded from mud the body of Pandora, the first woman.

These characteristics enable us to disentangle symbol from myth. Weak and lame in both legs (see LAMENESS), Hephaistos displays a twofold spir-itual weakness. He is quite content with the technical perfection of what he makes; its moral qualities and the uses to which it is put are matters of complete indifference to him. He chained Prometheus to the rock; he made a mockery of Aphrodite and Ares; and he trapped his own mother on a throne of gold. On the other hand he endowed his creations with a magic power which gave him a hold over whoever used them. He is the technician who abuses his creative powers to impose his wishes in spheres other than those which are rightfully his. He captivates living beauty with his master-pieces in metalwork, and the magic of his technical achievements makes a successful lover of this piece of physical deformity. He is akin to those gods of the Hindus and Celts who bind their victims but 'with this difference and superiority, in that his powers enable him to set in motion what was without motion, as well as to immobilize the living and moving, and to give life and movement to what was inanimate as easily as to bind with unbreakable chains' (SECG p. 256). Hephaistos constantly sought to compensate for being 'a huge panting bulk, halting the while, but beneath him his slender legs moved nimbly', as Homer describes him (*Iliad* 18: 410–11). Although he paid for his knowledge with his physical deformity – in accordance with a law so often to be found in myths – he took vengeance for such defects by his success as both craftsman and lover. However, by concentrating upon technical know-how, he lost the art of being.

He ensured the victory of Fire over Water, but not the harmony of the elements. Through 'the lightning stroke of his irresistible strength' he is 'the fiery element itself. Yet his hobbling walk ... was regarded as a symbol of his twofold nature, both celestial and terrestrial, or as an embodiment of the flickering aspect of flames' (SECG p. 257). It is, however, to Hephaistos' honour that an Orphic hymn can beseech the god to 'tranform into the heat of life ... all that is flame in the universe.' This is doubtless the highest meaning of his symbol – amoral Demiurge transformed as inspired apostle. He was identified with the Ancient Egyptian god of craftsmen, Ptah.

Herakles (Hercules) His labours, exploits and adventures are a high-point of mythological story-telling and have made Herakles the best known of the heroes. The Pythia gave him his name, 'Glory of Hera', and it denotes what might be called his life-vocation, to glorify Zeus' wife, the greatest of the goddesses. However, the figure which emerges from this wealth of legend is a cross between the fair-ground strongman and Don Quixote. Nevertheless, one constant theme emerges from this luxuriant growth of ragbag literary material. If one sets the obstacles over which he triumphed upon a moral and psychological plane, Herakles becomes 'the idealized representative of combative strength; the symbol of the victory of the human soul – and of its high price – over its own weaknesses' (DIES p. 216).

Later tradition placed great emphasis upon the sufferings of the hero from the TUNIC poisoned by Nessus' blood, his death on the funeral pyre and his apotheosis, when he was admitted amongst the gods and wedded to Hebe, goddess of youth.

In the final phase of his mythological development, famed through Hera who had never ceased to persecute him, Herakles embodied 'the Hellenic ideal of manhood ... which could only be found in Heaven – Earth being unable to supply its living peer – and which could only find a worthy mate in the goddess of eternal youth' (Kern).

His whole legend is epitomized in the 'Homeric' hymn in his honour: 'Herakles [was] the son of Zeus and much the mightiest of men on earth ... Once he used to wander over unmeasured tracts of land and sea ... and himself did many deeds of violence and endured many; but now he lives happily in the glorious home of snowy Olympus, and has neat-ankled Hebe for his wife.'

The role of the Classical Herakles was taken in Ireland by Cùchulainn, son of the god Lug, as Herakles was the son of Zeus. The fame and popularity of the Celtic HERO accounts for the wide diffusion of the worship of Hercules (the Latin form of Herakles) throughout Gaul during the Roman period. Greek authors claimed that Hercules had travelled the Celtic world and when in Gaul had fathered Keltos and Galatos, but the detail they provide is fragmentary. The Celtic Hercules symbolizes pure strength alone, and shares the magical aspect of the warrior's role.

herbs Herbs are a symbol of all that cures and brings back to life, since they restore health, virility and fertility. 'To Christians, medicinal herbs owed their efficacity to the fact that they were first found on Calvary. To the ancients, herbs owed their curative properties to having been discovered *first* by the gods' (ELIT p. 298). According to Mircea Eliade, simples derive their properties from a celestial archetype which is a manifestation of the Cosmic Tree. The mythical place of their discovery or of their birth was always a centre, like Calvary, mentioned above.

Through the properties attributed to them, simples display the belief that all healing must derive from some gift of the godhead, as does all which concerns life.

Generally speaking, herbs are often the means whereby deities of fertility make themselves visible. Herbs ease childbirth, increase the procreative powers and ensure fecundity and wealth. Such were the reasons for going so far as to recommend animal sacrifice to plants.

One of the Breton names for 'herb', *louzaouenn*, still retains in the plural the ancient meaning of 'medicine'. Primitive Celtic physic made great use of medicinal herbs and the tradition originates from myth, since herbs were the foundation of the curative properties of the Fountain of Health (*Slante*) of the Tuatha Dé Danann, in the story of the battle of Mag Tuired, spells being merely a secondary means. The symbolism of herbs is linked with that of fountains (see SPRING) (OGAC 11: p. 279; 12: p. 59; 16: p. 233).

herd Herds symbolize the herd instinct. The individual is to the collective what the animal is to the herd. The more able the individual is to live alone, separate from party or group, the more he or she is self-sufficient and thus enabled to become a person, ceasing to be a mere individual. The individual within the group or herd needs to feel surrounded by other individuals. Their presence is reassuring, in the same way that the sheep is frightened when it is on its own. The herd comprises a mass, a totality from which no separate creature or human stands out. If an animal or an individual takes the lead in a herd or group, this leader remains linked to the rest and inspired by their presence. Heroes, sages and saints possess a personal destiny, no longer belonging to the herd, but being completely independent.

Every community, however, is not a herd. Herds are animal forms of groups and mean a regression for humans. Integration into a human community is, on the contrary, progress and one of the most difficult stages in the development of the personality. The herd then symbolizes a perversion of mankind's social vocation as well as the perversion of society's humanizing vocation.

herdsman See SHEPHERD.

hermaphrodite In the beginning the hermaphrodite was merely an aspect or anthropomorphic representation of the Cosmic EGG. It occurs at the beginning of all cosmogonies and at the end of all eschatologies. The fullness of fundamental Oneness stands at the alpha as well as at the omega of the world and of manifested being, when opposites are fused together, either because they are still only potentialities or else because they have achieved their final reconciliation and integration. Mircea Eliade quotes countless examples drawn from the religions of the Norse lands and Ancient Greece, Egypt, Persia, China and India. It is the norm that when this image of primordial Oneness is applied to mankind, it should be expressed in sexual terms, often as primeval innocence or virtuousness, or as a Golden

Age to be regained. Sufi mysticism makes this very plain – the dualism of the phenomenal world in which we live is false and deceiving and comprises a state of sinfulness. There is only one way of salvation, by fusing with divine reality, that is returning to a fundamental state of Oneness. Such is the meaning of the sobbing of the reed flute plucked from the bosom of the Earth in the proem of the famous *Mathnavī* of Jalāl-al-Dīn Muhammad Rūmī Maulavī.

Primordial separation which created cosmically, that is, differentiated, light and darkness, Heaven and Earth, is also the separation of YIN AND YANG which created, in addition to those fundamental opposites, heat and cold and male and female. They are the Japanese Izanagi and Izanami, originally interfused in the egg of Chaos, as well as the Egyptian Ptah and the Akkadian Tiamat. According to the *Rig-Veda*, the hermaphrodite was the pied milch-cow which was also the bull with plentiful semen. ONE produces TWO according to Taoism and thus the primordial Adam was in no sense male, but hermaphrodite, becoming Adam and Eve.

Indeed hermaphrodites are often depicted as twin beings, each possessing the attributes of the two sexes and on the point of separation. This is a particularly important factor in explaining the cosmogonic significance of Indian erotic sculpture. Thus Shiva, a hermaphrodite deity since he is identified with the formless First Cause of manifestation, is often depicted tightly clasping Shakti, his own power, depicted as a female deity.

Further traces of hermaphroditism are to be discerned in Adonis, Dionysos, Cybele and Castor and Pollux, the last-named echoing Izanagi and Izanami. Such examples could be quoted for ever, for, in the last resort – as Ancient Greek theogony most amply proves – all deities were bisexual, which meant that they did not need a mate to bear children. Ritual hermaphroditism, as Mircea Eliade emphasizes, represents the totality of the united magico-religious forces of both sexes (ELIM pp. 134–5; DELH p. 29).

As a sign of totality, the hermaphrodite is as apparent at the end of time as at its beginning. In the eschatological vision of salvation, the individual is regenerated into a wholeness in which difference between the sexes no longer exists. This echoes the 'mystic marriage' of so many traditional literary sources and thus re-echoes the image of Shiva with his Shakti.

And yet this belief that after death humans must be integrated once more in their original Oneness, of which there is such universal evidence, is accompanied by an overriding need in this world to differentiate completely between the sexes. This is because, and here the most ancient beliefs are at one with the most modern biological discoveries, no human being is ever born completely polarized sexually. The Bambara maintain that 'it is a basic rule of creation that every human being is both physically and in spiritual principles simultaneously male and female' (DIEB).

This explains the commonest forms of male and female circumcision which are designed once and for all to place the child in the gender to which it seems to belong, since the clitoris is regarded as a survival in woman of the penis and the foreskin as a survival of the vulva in man. This is the meaning of the Chinese sacred marriage between Fu-Hsi and Nu-Kua, by the junction of their serpent tails and, what is more significant, by their exchange of attributes. The same is true of the alchemists' REBIS, who is also Sun and

Moon, Heaven and Earth, essentially one, phenomenally two, sulphur and mercury.

Hindu symbols relate not only to the primordial hermaphrodite, but also to the final return to that undifferentiated state of Oneness. Such reintegration is the goal of Yoga. The Chinese phoenix, symbol of regeneration, was hermaphrodite. The marriage of semen and breath to produce the Embryo of Immortality takes place within the yogi's own body. Return to the primeval state and liberation from cosmic contingency are the result of the resolution of opposites and achievement of primordial Oneness. The Chinese alchemists used to say that this was melting together *ming* and *sing*, the two polarities of being.

In his *Symposium* (189e), Plato introduces the myth of the hermaphrodite. 'For "man–woman" was then a unity in form no less than in name, composed of both sexes and sharing equally in male and female.' Echoes of this myth recur in some *midrashim* relating to Adam's condition of hermaphroditism or, again, in the teachings of the Christian Gnostics in which hermaphroditism was presented as the primeval state which had to be regained. Furthermore, in one tradition, men and women in their primitive state possessed one body between them with two faces. God separated them and gave each of them a back. Thereafter they began a differentiated existence. To say – as in the myth of the Book of Genesis – that Eve was taken from Adam's side means that in the beginning all human beings were undifferentiated.

The goal of human life is to become one. Origen and St Gregory of Nyssa discerned an hermaphrodite being in this first man created in the image of God. The deification to which mankind is invited causes him to regain the hermaphroditism lost by a differentiated Adam, but restored thanks to a second glorified Adam. Several passages in the New Testament relate to this oneness.

Having emphasized that hermaphroditism is one of the characteristics of spiritual perfection in the Pauline Epistles and St John's Gospel, Mircea Eliade suggests that, in fact, to become 'male and female' or to be 'neither male nor female' are blanket terms in which language attempts to describe *metanoia*, conversion, the complete reversal of all properties. It is as much a paradox to be 'male and female', as to become a little child, to be born again or to pass through the 'strait gate' (ELIM p. 132).

Masculine and feminine are only one of a multitude of opposites that need to become interfused once more.

The reality of hermaphroditism should be studied in minerals and plants for, in the eyes of alchemists, they, too, are separated into male and female. All that separates must be broken down through the marriage of Heaven and Earth and through human power, which should be exercised upon the cosmos in its totality.

Hermes (Mercury) Hermes is one of the symbols of the power of the working and creative mind. He presided over trade. Although his attributes of winged sandals showed his powers of flight and his ability to move rapidly, these advantages were restricted to a somewhat utilitarian level and very liable to corruption. Hermes also carried the sense of 'intellectual perversion, being the protector of thieves' (DIES pp. 46–7). This type of misapplied intelligence is to be found among all classes of fraudsters with their intellectual sleight of hand.

He invented the lyre by stretching the guts of bulls which he had sacrificed across the shell of a dead tortoise. This was the first lyre which Apollo used – he had heard the sounds of its music coming from the cave in which Hermes had hidden himself. He next invented the flute, which he gave to Apollo in exchange for lessons in divination and magic and a golden CADUCEUS. Zeus was impressed by his skill and chose Hermes to be his especial messenger to the gods of the Underworld, Hades and Persephone. He is often depicted with a lamb on his shoulders, hence his name 'Criophoros'. Undoubtedly Hermes was originally an agrarian deity, the tutelary god of shepherds, but he was also the god who guided souls to the domains of the dead. This function gave him his title, Hermes Psychopompos, Conductor of Souls. In this context he might symbolize the Good Shepherd. He acted, in a sense, as mediator between the godhead and mankind.

As the god of travellers, Hermes was especially worshipped at CROSS-ROADS, where his statues were erected to drive off ghosts and robbers. Boundary stones – known as *hermai* – were dedicated to him.

However, he was above all a messenger and, as a bearer of good news, was sometimes given the name of Evangelist. Hermes symbolizes the channels of communication between Heaven and Earth, mediation and those offices which can as easily be corrupted into simony and money-grubbing as they can raise the individual to holiness. He makes safe for the traveller the roads between the Underworld, Earth and Heaven.

The functions of his Roman counterpart, Mercury, were undertaken in Ireland by the all-skilful god Lug. (He gave his name – Lugdunum – to many towns, including Lyon and Leyden, as well as to Carlisle – Luguballium.) His duties and abilities transcended those of all the other gods and he was simultaneously druid, satiric poet, physician, magician, craftsman and so on. In that great mythic account of the Battle of Mag Tuired, it was he who overcame the Fomorians, not so much by his great skill at arms as by his magic. Although widespread traces of the worship of Mercury, apparently in the Roman name and on the pattern of Roman practice, have been found in Gaul, it must nevertheless be said that there is a lack of congruence in the theological, Roman and Celtic fields. The Celtic Mercury (Lug) was no merchant and traveller and, in his *Gallic Wars*, Caesar calls him 'inventor of all arts and crafts', which corresponds with his Irish surname, *samildanach*, 'all-skilled'. With the Dagda (Zeus–Jupiter) and Ogmios (Ares–Mars) he makes up a basic triad, and surnames are often interchangeable between its members. In 1514 Dürer chose to portray Hermes in his *Kunstbuch* as god of eloquence in the guise of the Celtic Ogmios; and in the introduction to his *De mysteriis*, Iamblichus explained (1: 1) that the god of eloquence is common to all priests. In these circumstances it would seem as if the symbolism of the Celtic Mercury were universal.

The symbolism of Hermes also draws its inspiration from that of the Ancient Egyptian god, Thoth, the supreme deity Ra's lieutenant, messenger, enlightener, judge of the human conscience, guide and mediator. He embodies the revelation to mankind of wisdom and the way of eternal life.

He is the word which, to the degree to which they are open to it, penetrates to the very depths of people's consciousness.

Hermes is, consequently, the fourfold god, tetramorphic, god of the four winds of Heaven, god with four faces. These attributes carry a twofold meaning. Objectively they stand for the whole body of knowledge garnered from the four quarters of the Earth and from all levels of existence (a world information bureau). Subjectively, he also stands for the innumerable ways in which his messages are received, for the many different faces or interpretations given to his words in the minds of individuals all equally convinced that they alone have heard him correctly. He is simultaneously the god of hermetics and hermeneutics, of the mystery and of its unravelling.

Hermit, the The LOVER on the sixth TAROT, who became the triumphant driver of the CHARIOT, first collided with JUSTICE, who reminded him that strict balance is the very law of the universe and that nothing must be thrown out of true. Then, to resolve this fresh ambivalence, he chose the path suggested to him by the Hermit, the ninth Tarot. This slightly bent, wise old man leans upon the STAFF which symbolizes both the length of his pilgrimage and his weapons against the injustice or error which he encounters on his way. His red robe, with wide white sleeves, is covered by a long blue cloak lined with yellow and with a red hood with a yellow tassel. In his right hand he holds by a white ring a six-panelled LANTERN, of which only three panels are visible. Two of them are yellow and one red. Of course, this lantern reminds us of the one which Diogenes carried at midday as he searched for a wise man in the streets of Athens and found only fools. However, like the lamp of Hermes Trismegistus, it also symbolizes the veiled light of wisdom, the light which the Hermit shrouds with his initiate's blue cloak. It must remain an inward light and cannot be used to blind or dazzle those for whom it is not destined. The Sage's path is that of prudence and the Hermit, 'secret master, works invisibly to mould the future as it comes into being' (WIRT p. 165). Detached from the world and from its passions, the Hermit is pre-eminently the hermetic philosopher; and the way in which his name is written with a capital 'H' emphasizes beyond argument his symbolic links with HERMES, the all-powerful lord of the pure and the initiate.

hero As the child of the mating of god or goddess with mortal woman or man, the hero symbolizes the marriage of heavenly and earthly powers. Although he may possess supernatural strength until his death, he does not naturally enjoy the immortality of the gods. He is rather a fallen god or a mortal with god-like powers. Nonetheless, heroes such as HERAKLES (Hercules) or Pollux may acquire immortality and they may also rise from their graves to defend against its enemies the city which has placed itself under their protection. The prototype of the deified Greek hero was Herakles.

Hero-cults were exceedingly rare in Ancient Egypt. Kings were divine because they were held to be sons of Ra, the Sun god, and their mortuary temples were places of worship after their death. Similarly, a few court officials such as the great architect, Imhotep, received divine honours after their deaths and had chapels built for their worship. At the time of the

Roman conquest, there was a comparatively recent belief that death by drowning in the Nile, the river-god, introduced the victim into the company of the gods. Hadrian's favourite, Antinoüs, drowned in the Nile and was accordingly deified, a town being built upon the river-bank where his body was found (POSD p. 59).

In Ireland the prototype of the Celtic hero was Cùchulainn who, while still a child, accomplished the most extraordinary warlike feats. He was quite capable of holding the frontiers of Ulster single-handed for several months against the united armies of the other four provinces of Ireland. This hero, whose birth, deeds and death loom so large in mythological and heroic cycles, was the son of the god Lug. However, on the earthly plane he had been begotten by King Conchobar, acting as a surrogate for the god, on his own sister, Dechtire. Subsequently he was entrusted to his putative father, Sualtam, who had married Dechtire. Cùchulainn was thus thrice conceived and since he had three fathers was called 'child of the three years'. His Classical equivalent was Herakles, whom he resembles in a number of details – physical strength, beauty, skill and intelligence. However, he epitomizes a different concept of war since he, in the Celtic mode, stands for the essential character of the warrior in its purest form, at bottom comprising most often personal courage, sometimes cunning, but never concerted military action. In fact, in the Irish heroic cycle war is no more than a series of single combats, preceded each time by a challenge thrown down by one or other of the two opponents. The same is true on the continent of battles between the Gauls and the Romans, as Livy records in the cases of Manlius Torquatus and Valerius Corvinus. The warrior is adept at insult and invective or terrifies or paralyses his enemy by facial contortion and skill at arms. It is the hero's property to be endowed with uncommon physical strength, extraordinary skill – Cùchulainn had mastered a wide range of warlike ploys – and courage to face any odds. Sometimes – and this was the case with Cùchulainn – he might be granted intellectual abilities as a bonus. A true Irish hero obeyed the rules of a rudimentary law of chivalry. Cùchulainn never killed unarmed men, swineherds, servants, women or children. Single combat was, however, the strict rule – Celtic legend is devoid of any idea of military strategy – taking place, generally speaking, in a ford until one or other of the combatants was killed and then decapitated by the victor. The best-known instance of this is when Cùchulainn, single-handed, held off Queen Medb's whole army. The hero was bound to accept any challenge. A hero's other employment was as a surrogate for the king, who had to be present upon the field of battle without taking part in it (OGAC 12: pp. 209–34).

In battle the hero was in a state of warlike frenzy (*ferg*), a magical and religious phrase for the heroic excess which found it hard to distinguish friend from foe. When the young Cùchulainn returned from his first expedition on the borders of Ulster, King Conchobar was forced to send fifty naked maidens with his queen at their head to meet him. Taking advantage of his bashfulness, they seized Cùchulainn and plunged him into three vats of ice-cold water. The first one shattered, the second boiled over and the third was left with its water warmed.

There is a link between the word for the HEAT generated by a warrior (*lath*) and its homophone, which is applied to sexual excitement. The heat generated by Cùchulainn and the heroes of Ulster in their warlike frenzy melted the snow for thirty paces round each of them. This is the reason why Celtic champions fought stark naked.

Like their divine archetype Ogmios, and as a result of the normal direction of their passions – warlike properties being essentially feminine – heroes had the right to the magical side of knowledge. Cùchulainn could inscribe spells in Ogham on wooden strips, and warriors were sometimes prophets or seers. This is in line with what Nicander of Colophon records – Gauls spending the night beside the graves of heroes to obtain oracles. The warrior, however, had no right to priesthood or to kingship, standing for and symbolizing pure strength devoid of intelligence and riven by passion and therefore needing to be directed by spiritual authority. Cùchulainn may have been 'King of the Warriors of Ireland', but his was an honorific title; and when he stepped on the Stone of Fal to receive the reward of true kingship, instead of crying out as it did when each king of Ireland trod upon it, the stone remained dumb. The hero broke it in pieces in his rage (OGAC 17: pp. 175–88).

The hero symbolizes 'the developmental drive (the basic desire), the confrontational situation of the human soul in its battle with the monsters of perversion' (DIES p. 40). The hero, too, should be adorned with the attributes of the Sun, its light and heat having vanquished the darkness and chill of death. The hero's challenge, according to Bergson, lies at the heart of unrestricted normality and, on the spiritual level, is the motive for creative development. Jung was to identify the hero with spiritual power among symbols of the libido. A hero's first victory is that which he gains over himself.

heron The white heron is the Toltec hieroglyphic for Atzlan, the primeval island Atlantis. With stork and ibis, the heron is a snake-killer, and all three are therefore regarded as anti-Satanic creatures, fighting evil, and consequently as symbols of Christ. This opposition of heron and SERPENT, like that of Fire and Water, recurs in Cambodian folk-beliefs. The appearance of a heron foretells drought and when it perches on a house, it heralds fire.

In Ancient Egypt the PHOENIX, the symbol of the solar cycle and of resurrection, may well have been the purple heron. The stance of these birds, erect and motionless on one leg, naturally conjures up the notion of contemplation (BELT, CORM, GUEM, PORA, SOUM).

The symbolism of the heron is the same as that of other wading birds in Ancient Irish literature. It most often occurs in a metaphor used to describe the warlike grimaces of the hero Cùchulainn. This hero made one of his eyes pop out like 'a cauldron in which a yearling calf could be cooked' and the other sink so deep into its socket that a heron's beak could not reach it (CHAB pp. 579–82).

In European and African tradition the heron symbolizes not only the indiscretion of somebody who pokes his nose into other people's business, but the vigilance which may so easily degenerate into busybody-ness. In ancient occultism, herons passed for symbols of divine knowledge, no doubt because of their sharp penetrating bills.

Hesperides   The Hesperides were the daughters of Atlas and Hesperis and lived in a GARDEN, its entrance guarded by a dragon, in which golden APPLES grew. Herakles (Hercules) vanquished the dragon and seized the garden and its treasures. Myths depict the existence of a sort of PARADISE, which is the goal of human longing, and of the potentiality of immortality in the golden apples; the dragon denotes the appalling difficulties in gaining access to this Paradise; and Herakles, the hero who overcomes all obstacles. The whole comprises a collection of symbols of the human struggle to attain the spiritualization which will ensure immortality.

The legend relates that Atlas taught Herakles astronomy, while the dragon gave his name to a constellation and Herakles was identified with the Sun.

hexagon   See OCTAGON.

hexagram (star-shape)   This figure, composed of two superimposed equilateral triangles, one being inverted so that together they form a six-pointed star, is one of the most widely used symbols. In India it is called the *yantra*, and among Jews, Christians and Muslims it is known as Solomon's Seal or as the STAR OF DAVID or Shield of David. It is also to be found in Central American hieroglyphics. It represents, in hermetic philosophy, the synthesis of evolutional and involutional forces through the interpenetration of the two ternaries. Indian tradition regards it as standing for the marriage of Shiva and Shakti, in other words, the fundamental sacred marriage. In terms of the Jungian school of psychology, 'it expresses the union of opposites – the union of the personal, temporal world of the ego with the non-personal timeless world of the non-ego. Ultimately, this union is the fulfilment and goal of all religions. It is the union of the soul with God' (JUNS p. 240).

hexagram (in the *I Ching*)   These very different figures to the above are typically Chinese symbols, gathered in a book, the *I Ching*, or *Book of Changes*, apparently the only book to escape burning when, in the third century BC, Chin Che Hung-ti ordered the destruction of philosophical writings. Maspero considers that the *I Ching* is as early as the eighth or seventh century BC. Hexagrams are figures made up of six lines each. These lines may be continuous (———) or discontinuous (– –), and represent a *tao*, or universal source of all things.

Any continuous line (———) forming part of a hexagram symbolizes the Sun, heat, instrumentality, the male element, odd numbers and *yang* (see YIN AND YANG); any discontinuous line (– –), cold, passivity, the female element, even numbers and *yin*. There are sixty-four hexagrams, the first being:

that is to say formed exclusively of continuous lines and therefore pure *yang*, representing the father, strength and the Sun; and the second:

```
         - -
         - -
         - -
         - -
         - -
```

comprising discontinuous lines, and therefore pure *yin*, symbolizing the mother, passivity and the Moon.

The other sixty-two symbols are made up in unequal proportions of continuous and discontinuous lines, with the exception of symbol number 11, representing prosperity, honour and the generous heart:

```
         - -
         - -
         - -
        ─────
        ─────
        ─────
```

and of symbol number 12, standing for confrontation, misfortune and mischief:

```
        ─────
        ─────
        ─────
         - -
         - -
         - -
```

From what we know of Ancient Chinese attitudes, they believed that universal order was constituted by a balance between the two elemental principles, *yang* and *yin*, or rather by their 'changes'. The symbolical formation of hexagrams provided the basic elements of a philosophy of the Universe, a logical classification of existing things and even a means of grasping their essence through rearranging each line of the hexagram, which itself symbolized a *tao* or state regulating the universe and the beings in it.

Hexagrams are symbols set out as geometrical figures, drawn from ideal and eternal archetypes. Their readers are enabled to conduct a form of psychoanalysis based, not upon the subjective interpretation of the analyst, but upon the numerical combinations of the lines. The Ancient Chinese maintained that by their knowledge of the *I Ching*, a knowledge which they constantly deepened, they could learn the secrets of beings and of things, foresee their reactions and, to some extent, control them.

Some writers believe that TRIGRAMS were invented before hexagrams. It is obvious that permutating the six lines will provide sixty-four different hexagrams, while only eight permutations of the trigram are possible.

Each of the twelve months is under the influence of several different hexagrams, one of which controls the activities of the month and hence is known as the 'ruling' hexagram.

The symbolism of change is to be found in the work of the seventeenth-century poet, Li Li-feng: 'Gaze first at the hills in the picture and then the picture made by the hills.'

hill The Ancient Egyptians regarded these outcrops of earth as a symbol of what first emerged from Chaos when the air howled in gales across the primordial waters. The gods stood on the first hill and created light (MORR pp. 230–1).

Thus hills were the first manifestation of the creation of the world, standing high enough to be set apart from primeval Chaos, but lacking the majestic size of MOUNTAINS. They mark the beginning of differentiation and emergence from Chaos; their gentle slopes provide them with one aspect of the godhead which is upon a human scale.

In many Irish legends the SID, or Otherworld, is located in mounds (or lakes), hence its meaning in Middle or Modern Irish of 'hill'. This is, however, a recent lexical development due to the obscuring of the original meaning of *sid* (OGAC 14: pp. 329–40). In Celtic fashion, instead of symbolizing the creation of *this* world, hills symbolize the *Other* world.

hind Hinds in the dreams of men symbolize the primitive, undifferentiated, instinctive state of animality. In women's dreams they generally suggest the dreamer's own femininity, still scarcely differentiated – and sometimes only grudgingly accepted – and still in a primal and instinctual state and one not fully revealed, either through moral censure, fear, lack of opportunity, psychic infantilism or an inferiority complex, the animus being too powerful and negative. According to one legend, Siegfried was suckled by a hind (mother). The hind's image is that of the virginal persisting into the maternal and sometimes of the castrating power of female virginity. In Greek mythology, hinds were sacred to Hera (Juno), goddess of love and marriage.

The hind is basically a feminine symbol. It can play the part of nurse–mother in respect of innocent children. Its beauty is displayed in the extraordinary brilliance of its eyes and its gaze is often compared with a girl's. In fairy stories, princesses are sometimes changed into hinds.

The Song of Solomon (2: 7) uses 'hinds' in a spell to preserve lovers from interruption: 'I charge you, O ye daughters of Jerusalem, by the roes, and by the hinds of the field, that ye stir not up, nor awake my love, till he please.'

In Mongol and Turkic symbolism, the hind stands for the Earth in the basic sacred marriage of Heaven and Earth. Mongols believed that Genghis Khan was born of a wild hind mating with a BLUE wolf and even today, at Konya in Anatolia, once the capital of the Seljuk Turks, there is a saying 'that when the hind gives birth, the Earth is lit by a holy light' (ROUF p. 321, quoting Oguz Tansel). All Eastern mythology contains this basic mating of carnivore with herbivore, and a common artistic theme is the predator on its victim's back. Jean-Paul Roux observes that, on the symbolic plane, the key fact is that the predator is not depicted hunting its victim, but mating with it, adding: 'I have no doubts whatsover that this depicts the mythical sexual intercourse of male and female, Earth and Heaven' (ROUF p. 321).

Pindar's 'hind with golden horns' and brazen hoofs was a creature dedicated to Artemis. The goddess had four of them harnessed to her chariot and Herakles (Hercules) hunted the fifth for a whole year as far as the land of the Hyperboreans. Since it was his task to take it alive, he managed to immobilize its front legs by shooting his arrow between bone and tendon without spilling a drop of blood. He then carried the hind back to Mycenae, the ancient city of palaces built like castles, symbol of impregnable safety. 'He pierced the brazen-footed deer', says Virgil (*Aeneid* 6: 802).

The symbolism of the hind with brazen hoofs is studied from the metallic angle in the entry BRONZE: the animal side of the legend may, however, yield a further meaning. The hind is a delicate creature which runs as fast as an arrow and, if one were to emphasize this point, one might say that it was tireless and that its hoofs never wear out. In this sense they might be brazen hoofs. On the other hand, if one considers its shyness and its distant flight to the land of the Hyperboreans, those primeval sages, the hind with the brazen hoofs which Herakles attempted to catch alive after a long chase into the north might symbolize wisdom, so hard to attain. Here the symbols of the sacred metal and fleeing hind come together.

In mystic Celtic tradition, too, hunting the hind symbolizes the pursuit of wisdom which is only to be found under the tree of knowledge, the apple. Now the Hyperboreans lived far away in the north and, in some versions of the legend, the hind was either taken under a tree or sought refuge in the mountains. This would seem ample confirmation that, in this context, it represented wisdom, tirelessly pursued by Herakles. However, there is no definite literary evidence to support what can only be an intelligent hypothesis, admittedly of an inconclusive nature.

hippopotamus Because it so often devoured or trampled down part of their crops, the Ancient Egyptians 'usually regarded [the bull-hippopotamus] as a manifestation of the perverse forces in the world. . . . As the enemy of mankind [it] was considered sacred to the wicked Set' and a sacred body of harpooners was maintained whose duty it was to destroy it. And yet the cow-hippopotamus was venerated and even worshipped as a fertility symbol under the name of Thoueris. 'By tradition, she helped in childbirth the mothers of the gods, of kings and of simple mortals. Herein lies the explanation of the numerous figures, statues, amulets and representations in temples which show Thoueris standing on her two hindfeet leaning on the magic knot' (POSD p. 126).

In the Old Testament (Job 40: 15ff.), the hippopotamus – its name, Behemoth, probably derived from the Egyptian – symbolizes brute strength, which God can master but which man cannot tame: 'Lo now, his strength is in his loins, and his force is in the navel of his belly. He moveth his tail like a cedar; the sinews of his stones are wrapped together. His bones are as strong pieces of brass; his bones are like bars of iron. . . . He lieth under the shady trees, in the covert of the reed, and fens.'

Symbolically interpreted, this description embraces all those human impulses and vices which the individual cannot master, affected by original sin. This enormous lump of flesh needs God's grace if it is to raise itself through spiritualization.

Hiram Freemasons acknowledge as their founder this craftsman of genius who is mentioned in the Old Testament. To some extent he is reminiscent of Hephaistos or Daedalus in Greek mythology. He lived during the reign of King Solomon and played the leading part in decorating the King's palace and the Temple, for which he cast all the metalwork.

'And king Solomon sent and fetched Hiram out of Tyre. He was a widow's son of the tribe of Naphtali, and his father was a man of Tyre, a worker in brass: and he was filled with wisdom, and understanding, and cunning to work all works in brass. And he came to king Solomon, and wrought all his work' (1 Kings 7: 13-14).

Once he had finished his masterpieces the master vanished from history, but legend took him to itself and changed his life and death into an initiation myth. Masonic ritual made it a symbolic drama inspired by the ancient mystery religions, and the centrepiece of initiation into their society (see FREEMASONRY).

The myth, as invented or embroidered in the eighteenth century, runs as follows. Work on the Temple at Jerusalem had ended, but not all Hiram's fellow workers had been initiated into the Master's wonderful secrets. Three of them determined to force them out of him. Standing at different doors of the Temple, each called on him to reveal his secrets. As Hiram fled from door to door, he told each in succession that they would not get what they wanted by threats, but would have to wait until the time was ripe. It was then that they struck him down; one with a blow of his rule to the throat, another with his iron square on the left side of his chest, while the third finished him off with a blow on the forehead from his hammer. They then asked one another what the Master had told them and, when they realized that none of them had gained the secret, they despaired at the pointlessness of their crime. They hid the body and buried it by night near a wood, planting an acacia over the grave (BOUM p. 262, quoting Rayon).

When the symbolism of the myth is applied to the ceremonies of initiation into the grade of Master Mason, the candidate plays the part of Hiram. He has first to die, the three blows in the legend symbolizing a threefold death – of the body (throat), the feelings (left side of chest) and of the mind (forehead). However, like the 'deaths' in all initiation rituals, this is the prelude to rebirth, a rebirth which is physical, psychic and mental, creating a new Hiram who will symbolize those qualities described in the Old Testament and by the acacia bough placed upon his grave. Initiation is a process of individualization. Hiram's secret, the Master's words, are embodied in this law of inner development, in a spiritual transformation and in the quest for personal integrity. Invested with Hiram's qualities, the initiate in his turn becomes the Master. Symbol descends to allegory when we remember that the three murderers represented Ignorance, Hypocrisy or Fanaticism, and Ambition or Envy, in contrast with Hiram's real qualities of Knowledge, Toleration, and Detachment or Generosity.

hive Hives are the BEES' houses and, by metonymy, the bees themselves, collectively, as a tribe. Their symbolic quality is therefore clear. In so far as it is a house, the hive is maternal reassurance and protection: in so far as it is a hard-working collective – and how hard-working: its hum is like that of a workshop or factory – the hive symbolizes the type of organized and directed confederation, subject to strict regulation, which is regarded as soothing and pacifying the individual's basic anxieties. Thus, in some initiation societies and religious communities, patterns of organization call to mind symbolically those through which some heads of state or business chiefs nowadays ensure their personal power in the names of order, justice and security.

hole Holes are a symbol of the threshold of the unknown through which 'one steps into the beyond (Otherworld in relation to the physical world), or into the hidden (Otherworld in relation to the visible world).... Holes allow one line to pass through another (coordinates on the dimensional plane)' (VIRI p. 44). Upon the level of the imagination, holes carry a greater wealth of meaning than the mere void. They are pregnant with all the potentiality of what will fill them or pass through their opening. They are a vigil or a sudden revelation of a presence. Through a hole which Hephaistos with his axe opened in Zeus' skull sprang Athene, goddess of wisdom. Holes may be regarded symbolically as a 'passage through which ideas naturally come to birth' (VIRI p. 95).

There is the same difference between a hole and a void as there is between deprivation and annihilation. This distinction is so true that holes may be seen as a symbol of all potentialities. In this respect they are related to fertility symbols on the biological plane and to those of spiritualization on the psychological.

American Indians regarded the hole both as an image of the female genital organs through which the new-born come into the world and as a GATEWAY through which the dead are enabled to escape from the restrictions of earthly life. The Chinese JADE disc with a hole in the middle, the Pi, is a precise symbol of Heaven in so far as the latter is an Otherworld. The hole thus possesses a double immanental and transcendental meaning: it is the threshold of the internal to the external and of the external world to the Otherworld.

hollow Its symbolism is the opposite to that of the MOUNTAIN, and related to that of the CAVERN, emphasizing its character of depth, and of EMPTINESS or potentiality. It stands for the passive or negative, the other side of being and life. It is the yet-empty reservoir of being. Thus it is made the home of death, the past, the unconscious or of the possible. In more general terms, it is the dark or negative side of all symbols (see hollow TREE) and, it might be said, of all ideas and all beings.

Holy of Holies The inner shrine of a TEMPLE, the most private and the holiest place, where the Ancient Egyptians kept the statues of their gods or, at the Temple in Jerusalem, where the Ark of the Covenant was stored; the Holy of Holies was the House of God. 'The whole world is enclosed within the holy effigy of the Tabernacle', St Jerome wrote (Letter 26 to Fabiola) when, drawing upon ancient tradition, he visualized in the very shape of the tabernacle the symbol of the four elements and the four corners of the world. The prayers which were sent up from around the Holy of Holies should embrace the whole universe in the sense that they came from it in its entirety and return to it in its entirety to seek its blessing. The Jewish philosopher, Philo of Alexandria, in his *Life of Moses* (3: 3–10) thought that if the Tabernacle was an image of the world, it was also an image of the individual and of the human state. The intersection of verticals and horizontals in building this miniature temple, the Holy of Holies, symbolized the division of the individual between sensual drives towards the external world (horizontals) and the call to inward and contemplative concentration (verticals).

Origen, too, called it 'an image of the whole universe', but of a universe conceived as the dialectic of the temporal and the eternal, the human and the divine, the created and the uncreated, the visible and the invisible. The tabernacle is not merely an image, it suggests the conjunction of two worlds or, if preferred, of two different aspects of the same universe in the sense in which one can say that the eternal resides within the temporal, the transcendent within the immanent.

Image and, at the same time, intersection and energy-centre, the 'shrine is a geometric shape calculated to act as a force-field. The dynamic of the holy is, at bottom, to be measured by the golden number. The objective is to trap the power which comes from God and hold it imprisoned within a space intended for humans. Through its very structure the Holy of Holies condenses cosmic energy' (CHOM p. 202).

homa The symbolism of this mythical bird, so famous in Persian literature, is related to that of good fortune and of glory. Its wandering flight takes it to the highest Heavens and it bestows its blessings upon those whom it covers with its wings. In his *Gulistān*, Sa'dī sometimes contrasts the homa with the owl, symbolizing curses and misfortune, while others contrast the nobility and sobriety of the homa with the greed of the raven. Folklore tells how the homa feeds upon fragments of bone so as not to be a charge upon other creatures. The mystical master is compared with the homa for his nobility of soul and for the blessings which he confers. All things deriving from the power of blessing are attributed to this bird.

The legendary *homā* has served as an ornamental motif and its head, in wood or metal, has often been used to decorate furniture (MOKC 1: p. 35).

homecoming See RETURN.

honey (see also BEE) Primeval nourishment, both food and drink, like MILK, with which it is so often associated, honey is first and foremost a rich symbol of wealth, fullness and especially of sweetness. It stands in sharp contrast with the bitterness of gall, and it differs from sugar as those things which Nature offers to mankind differ from those which she keeps hidden. Every Promised Land flows with milk and honey as did all those primeval lands from which mankind was driven. Both Eastern and Western sacred writings associate them and extol them in very similar terms, and often give the symbol a distinctly erotic tone. The land of Canaan may be a land of milk and honey, but it is also the honey of immortal love in the Song of Solomon: 'Thy lips, O my spouse, drop as the honeycomb: honey and milk are under thy tongue' (4: 11), and (5: 1) 'I am come into my garden, my sister, my spouse: I have gathered my myrrh with my spice; I have eaten my honeycomb with my honey; I have drunk my wine with my milk.' Isaiah prophesies (7: 14–15): 'Behold, a virgin shall conceive, and bear a son, and shall call his name Immanuel. Butter and honey shall he eat, that he may know how to refuse the evil, and choose the good.'

In the *Rig-Veda*, too, honey is praised as a fecundating principle, a source of life and of immortality, like milk and SOMA. 'The wave of honey arose out of the ocean; mingling with the [soma] stalk, it became the elixir of immortality' (VEDR p. 126).

Celtic tradition as strongly sings the praises of MEAD as the beverage of immortality, as does an archaic source, the 'Food of the House with two Goblets' which probably antedates the spread of Christianity. This speaks of milk tasting like honey as all that Eithne had as food. Honey is the basic ingredient of mead, the beverage of immortality which flows in rivers in the Otherworld. However, honied sweetness can be dangerously seductive, like the honey dripping from the courtesan's lips (Proverbs), flattery and the fly-trap or booby-trap.

As sole source of nourishment, honey widens its symbolic applications to include skill, knowledge and wisdom, and its sole consumption is confined to exceptional beings both in this world and the Otherworld. Chinese traditions associate honey with the element Earth and with notions of the CENTRE. For this reason the sauces on the dishes served to the emperor had always to be linked to honey (GRAP). Greek tradition maintained that, like the Celtic hero, Pythagoras only ate honey throughout his life.

According to the Pseudo-Dionysius the Areopagite, God's teachings may be compared with honey 'for their purifying and saving virtues' (PSEO p. 357). Honey might well denote religious culture, mystic knowledge, spiritual benefits or revelations to the initiate. Virgil was to call honey 'the heavenly gift of dew', dew being, itself, a symbol of initiation. Honey was also to come to denote the peak of spiritual bliss and the state of Nirvana. As a symbol of all that is sweet, it made the annihilation of pain a reality. The honey of knowledge is the foundation of social and individual happiness. Here again Eastern and Western mystical thought coincides. In the mystical Shi'ite brotherhood of Bektāshī Dervishes, honey denotes *haqq*, transcendental reality, the goal of all spiritual pilgrimage where the individual melts into the godhead. This takes place in *fanā'*, a state of anaesthesia in which even the notion of pain is annihilated. Honey was also a symbol of knowledge for St Clement of Alexandria and of wisdom in Orphic tradition, while Buddhist countries associate it with teaching. 'My teaching is like eating honey: sweet to start with, sweet in the middle and sweet at the end.' So perfect is honey that it was easy to make it a powerful propitiatory offering, the symbol of protection and appeasement. The Athenians used to offer honey-cakes to the Great Serpent, to keep him in his cave. According to the *Hadīths* of al-Bukhārī, the Prophet and Islamic tradition regarded honey as the pre-eminent panacea able to restore sight to the blind, preserve the health and even restore the dead to life. Honey was part of the medicine ceremonies of the North American Indians, playing a major role in these rites and rituals. The Hopi chief from Arizona, Don C. Talayesva, records that during the medicine ceremonies at the time of the feast of the Winter solstice (Soyal), the priest poured libations of flour and honey (TALS pp. 163ff.). His description of the ritual shows that the Hopi endowed this use of honey with the twofold property of purifying and fertilizing, something absolutely concordant with the foregoing. By its association with ritual purification, honey defines its initiatory qualities. In his work on *The Cave of the Nymphs* (quoted in MAGE p. 344), Porphyry states that when candidates were initiated into the Leontica (Mithras in the form of a lion) 'honey, not water was poured over their hands, to wash them.... Furthermore, honey cleanses the tongue from all sin.' Similarly worshippers of Mithras in other shapes were given honey to eat and candidates washed their hands in honey.

The traditions of the Mediterranean peoples, and especially of the Greeks, give full expression to this rich symbolism in its entirety. As food which inspires, it gave the gift of poetry to Pindar as it had given the gift of learning to Pythagoras. Both were initiates in the fullest sense of the word. When Greek religion stated that honey was 'the symbol of death and life, of sluggishness – it was claimed that it caused deep and dreamless sleep – and of clear sight', surely this slyly alludes to the key-words in rites of initiation – darkness and light, death and rebirth. The Eleusinian Mysteries confirm this hypothesis, since honey was given 'to the higher grade of initiate as a sign of new life' (MAGE pp. 13–36). Honey therefore played its part in the initiatory awakening of Spring. It was linked to immortality by its yellow-gold colour and by the eternal cycle of death and rebirth.

In modern psychoanalytic thought honey, 'taken to be the end result of a process of distillation', may become 'the symbol of the Higher Ego, or Self, in so far as the latter is the end-result of internal working upon the self' (TEIR p. 119). Being the product of the transformation of short-lived pollen-powder into the succulent food of immortality, honey symbolizes the transformation effected by initiation, the conversion of the soul and the ultimate integration of personality. This, in fact, reduces to the oneness of a balanced individual a multitude of disparate elements. Similarly, we remain as ignorant of the processes of that biochemical mutation as we do of the very real but hidden workings of mystic grace and spiritual exercises, which take the soul from worldly dissipation (flitting from flower to flower) to mystic concentration (honey). Similarly, the processes whereby the ego becomes integrated on the road to individuation remain unclear, and this is also true of the transformation achieved by initiation.

hood (see also CAUL; HEADDRESS) The hooded cloak – the Latin word *cucullus* being derived from the Celtic – was a regular item of dress in ancient Gaul and there are very many depictions of its wearers, including the mythological figure of the *Genius Cucullatus*. The Irish god, the Dagda, owned a hood with many of the properties of Siegfried's *Tarnkappe* (or helmet of invisibility) in the *Nibelungenlied*. In the tale of the Drunkenness of the Ulates, the Dagda, unseen by all, wore no less than seven hoods one on top of the other; and he covered his head with them in battle, too. Indeed, the tradition of hooded gods, heroes, genii, demons and witches is very widespread.

To Jung hoods symbolized the highest sphere of the celestial world, as did bells, vaults and the skull. Covering the head therefore meant far more than becoming invisible, it meant to vanish and to die. Candidates in rites of initiation often covered their heads with hoods or veils. During the initiation rites of the Nandi in East Africa, the recently-circumcised have to make a very long circuit, and for the journey they are concealed by huge conical hats made of long dried grasses.

Some regard the hood, like the pointed hat, as a phallic symbol.

hook From Marsilio Ficino to Hafiz and Master Eckhart, the hook is often used symbolically, as might be expected, in relation to FISHING. It is the tool with which, Coomaraswami says, 'the Fisher-King catches his human prey.' 'Love', says Master Eckhart, 'is like the angler's hook.' In this respect it is significant that the same symbolism should filter down to such clichés of everyday conversation as 'swallow hook, line and sinker' and 'let off the hook'.

hoopoe The Koran describes this bird as acting as messenger between Solomon and the Queen of Sheba and it plays a prominent legendary part elsewhere. In his *Conference of the Birds*, the poet Farīd al-Dīn 'Attār tells how all the birds in the world set off in quest of a king. The hoopoe was their guide and is portrayed as the 'messenger from the invisible world'; it is described as wearing 'the crown of truth upon its head'. The journeyings of the birds symbolize 'the mystic pilgrimage of the soul in quest of the godhead'. This is why a Persian key to the meaning of dreams describes it as 'a wise and righteous man'. The hoopoe is also reputed to have been 'the only bird able to tell King Solomon where underground springs were'.

In one Persian legend 'the hoopoe was a married woman. She was combing her hair in front of the mirror when her father-in-law entered unannounced. She was so stricken with fear that she turned into a bird and flew away with her comb still in her hair' (hence the bird's Persian name – *shāneser*, comb-in-head). According to another legend, it was 'a good woman married to a worthless husband. One day, discovering her at her prayers, he beat her. She besought God, who changed her into a hoopoe and she flew away. Hoopoes are regarded as birds of good omen.'

In the tale of the western exile of Suhrawardi, the hoopoe symbolizes personal internal inspiration (see also under CRANE).

In addition, the hoopoe possesses many magical properties. If its entrails are removed and dried and worn as a sort of talisman, they preserve against the evil eye and counteract spells. In Tangiers, they are hung up by shopkeepers as a protection against thieves. They are also used to preserve milk and butter against witchcraft. They keep evil spirits away from places where money is buried and they strike down anyone attempting to dig it up. Some tribes believe that a hoopoe's right eye worn between the wearer's own two eyes enables that person to find buried treasure. The bird itself is also believed to be able to do as much and this is why it cries *hut, hut, hut* (there, there, there), prompting its Arabic name, *hadhud.* Hoopoes' blood and hearts are used as medicines, while the former is a substitute for ink in writing spells (WERS 2: pp. 338–9). The hoopoe is a symbol of the sagacity which can not only uncover buried treasure, but guard against ambush.

Hop o' my Thumb See under THUMB.

horn Horns convey a feeling of eminence and loftiness. Their symbolism is that of power, which is, in any case and generally speaking, that possessed by the animals which bear them. This symbolism is linked to Apollo-Karneios

and to Dionysos and was used by Alexander the Great when he adopted
the emblem of Amon, the ram, whom the Egyptian *Book of the Dead* calls
the Lord of the Two Horns. It recurs in the Chinese myth of the terrible
Ch'e Yu, with his horned head, whom Huang Ti could only defeat by blowing on a horn. Huang Ti used his rival's standard, which bore his portrait
and was infused with his strength, to impose his own power. In many countries – and especially in Gaul – warriors used to wear horned helmets. The
power of horns is not, however, restricted to the temporal sphere.

Guénon observes that rams' horns possess a solar quality, while bulls'
horns have a lunar character. The association of bulls with the Moon is a
well-known characteristic of both Sumerian and Hindu culture. A Cambodian inscription describes the Moon as a 'perfect horn' (see CRESCENT) and
emphasizes the 'horned' aspect of Shiva's bull. The *Mahābhārata* talks of
Shiva's 'horn', since Shiva is identified with Nandi, the bull on which he
rides (BHAB, GRAC, GUES).

'The horns of oxen, for instance, which are used to characterize the great
divinities of fecundity, are an emblem of the divine *Magna Mater*' (Menghin
quoted in ELIT p. 164). Horns suggest the prestigious aura of the life force,
the cycle of creation, the inexhaustible well of life and fertility. Hence they
have come to symbolize the majesty and the munificence of kingly power.
Like Dionysos, Alexander the Great was depicted horned to symbolize his
power and genius which established his kinship with the gods and to which
the prosperity of his rule was due.

If horns often derive from a lunar and therefore a female symbolism
(bulls' horns), they may also carry a solar, male symbolic force (rams' horns).
This explains why they are so often seen as a symbol of the powers of
virility, and this other aspect of the symbol naturally applies in the case of
Alexander the Great.

Marie Bonaparte has observed that in Hebrew *queren* means simultaneously 'horn' and 'power' and 'strength', as does *lingam* in Sanskrit and
cornu in Latin. Horns, through their strength, suggest power, while their
natural function evokes the thrust of the male sexual organ (*corno* is Italian
slang for 'penis').

Power comes to be conjoined to aggression. Agni possesses indestructible horns,
sharpened by Brahmā himself, and in the final analysis horns come to mean
aggressive power for good as well as for evil. . . . In the association of horns with
a political or religious leader [Iroquois chieftain, Alexander the Great, Siberian
shaman and so on] we discover a process of annexation of power through the
magical appropriation of symbolic objects. . . . Horns, as trophies, are an exaltation and appropriation of strength. Victorious Roman soldiers decorated their
helmets with little horns.

(DURS pp. 146–7)

Sun and Moon, Fire and Water are seen intertwined in Dogon beliefs,
although they may more often be tinged by a lunar symbolism, in the myth
of a celestial ram bearing a calabash (see GOURD) between its horns. This
is none other than the solar matrix. The ram's horns are testicles, balancing
the calabash which it fertilizes by means of the penis growing out of its
forehead, while it urinates rain and mists which come down to make the

Earth fruitful (GRIE p. 36). This ram moves across the vault of Heaven
ahead of the storms during the rainy season. It is a golden ram, but its
fleece is made of red COPPER, symbolizing the fecundating waters. In another version of the myth the fleece is composed of green leaves, an echo
of the symbolic analogy between the colours GREEN and RED.

According to Fulani legend, a goat's virility may be measured by the
spread of its knotty horns (HAMK p. 17).

Some Siberian shamans' robes were decorated with horns, generally made
of iron and shaped like antlers. These attributes would seem to play the
same part as the wings of eagle-owls which decorated the robes of shamans
from the Altai region and especially those of the Tungus, Samoyed and
Yenisei (HARA p. 345).

In Jewish and Christian tradition, too, horns symbolize strength and have
the meaning of a ray of light or a lightning flash, as in the passage where
Habakkuk (3: 4) describes the glory of God: 'And his brightness was as the
light: and he had horns [lightning] coming out of his hand.' Similarly, when
Moses is described coming down from Mount Sinai (Exodus 34: 29), 'he
wist not that his face shone', the verb 'shone' translating the 'horns' of light
which the Vulgate says came from his head. This is why medieval artists
depicted Moses with horns jutting from his forehead. These two horns bear
the aspect of the crescent Moon. The four horns of the altar of sacrifice in
the Temple denote the four quarters of space, that is the limitless extent of
God's power.

In the Psalms, the horn symbolizes God's strength, which is the most
powerful defence available to those who call upon it: 'The Lord is my
rock . . . my buckler, and the horn of my salvation' (18: 2). But it may also
symbolize the aggressive and vaunting strength of the proud whose arro-
gance the Lord will bring down; 'Lift not up your horn on high: speak not
with a stiff neck' (Psalm 75: 4). On the other hand the Lord imparts strength
to the righteous: 'There will I make the horn of David to bud' (Psalm 132:
17). The word 'horns' is sometimes used to denote the cross-beams of the
Cross.

In Celtic tradition, mythological or heroic sources mention two or three
times a certain Conganchnes, with 'horny skin', who was completely invulnerable except for the soles of his feet (OGAC 10: pp. 375–6). In this
instance horns, by their natural hardness, would symbolize a defensive power
like that of the shield.

Contemporary analysts regard horns as images, too, of divergence, able,
like the pitchfork, to symbolize ambivalence and, in this context, regressive
forces, the Devil being depicted with horns and cloven feet. On the other
hand, they may just as well be able to stand as symbols of receptivity and
initiation, as in the myth of the ram with the golden fleece (VIRI). Jung
discerned a different ambivalence in horns. Their shape and powers of
penetration made them an image of the active male principle, while the lyre
or urn shape of their spread made them as much an image of the passive
female principle. By marrying both principles in the formation of his or her
personality and taking them upon him- or herself, the individual achieves
maturity, balance and inner harmony. Nor is this irrelevant to the Sun–
Moon ambivalence already discussed.

horn of plenty The horn of plenty, or cornucopia, in Classical tradition
was a 'symbol of fruitfulness and happiness. With its mouth upwards, and
not, as in modern art, pointing down, it was the emblem of many deities,
including Bacchus, Ceres, the river-gods, Plenty, Constancy, Fortune, etc.'
(LAVD p. 206). When Jupiter (Zeus) was playing with Amalthea, the goat
who had suckled him, he accidentally broke off her horn. To make amends,
he promised that thereafter the horn would always be filled with whatever
fruit she desired. The horn of plenty symbolizes the unasked profusion of
gifts from the gods.

According to another legend, which does not compromise the properties
of the symbol, the horn of plenty was a horn belonging to the river-god,
Achelous. The greatest river in Greece, he was the son of Ocean and the
sea-goddess, Tethys, the eldest of over 3,000 rivers and father of countless
springs. Like all river-gods, he possessed the power to change himself into
whatever shape he wished. When fighting with Herakles (Hercules) for
possession of the lovely Deianeira, he changed himself into a bull, but when
Herakles broke off one of his horns, he acknowledged defeat. He asked
Herakles to give back his horn and in exchange offered him Amalthea's
horn, which he owned. The horn of plenty was either the one belonging to
Achelous, the river-god, which a nymph picked up and filled with the most
delicious fruit, or else Amalthea's. Depending upon the version chosen,
plenty comes either from the sky or the waters; and yet, surely, it is the sky
which feeds the waters in the shape of rain.

With the passage of time the cornucopia became less a symbol than the
attribute of generosity, of public prosperity, of good fortune, of the hard
work and foresight which are the springs of plenty, of hope, of charity, of
the autumn harvest-season, of righteousness and of hospitality (TERS pp.
116–21).

horse A belief, firmly seated in folk memory throughout the world, associates the horse in the beginning of time with darkness and with the chthonian
world from which it sprang, cantering, like blood pulsating in the veins, out
of the bowels of the Earth or from the depths of the sea. This archetypal
horse was the mysterious child of darkness and carrier both of death and
of life, linked as it was to the destructive yet triumphant powers of Fire and
to the nurturing yet suffocating powers of Water. The multitude of symbolic roles which the horse plays derives from that complexity of meaning
attaching to all major lunar figures, when imagination associates by analogy
Earth, as the mother-figure, with her planet the Moon, water with sexuality,
dreams with divination and plant life with its seasonal renewal.

Analysts, too, have made the horse a symbol of 'unconscious psychosis'
or of the 'non-human psyche' (JUNA p. 312), an archetypal neighbour of
the 'Mother, the world-memory', or even of time, since it is linked to 'the
major natural clocks' (DURS p. 72); or yet again of 'the onrush of desire'
(DIES p. 305). Day, however, follows night and, in the process, the horse
steps out of the darkness from which it came and rises aloft to the very
skies, caparisoned in light. Majestically robed in white, the horse is no
longer a lunar figure from the Underworld, but a sky or solar creature in
the land of kindly gods and heroes – another factor to enlarge the scope of

its symbolic meaning. This white, celestial horse stands for the control, mastery and sublimation of the instincts and, according to the new system of ethics, is 'the noblest conquest of mankind'. There is, however, no such thing as permanent victory, and despite this shining image, the horse of darkness continues its hellish gallop deep down in the individual. The horse thus veers from the benign to the malign, for it is no ordinary creature. Carrying men and women on its back, it is their vehicle, their vessel, and its fate is inextricably bound up in theirs. A special dialectic comes into existence between them, fountain of peace or of confrontation on both the psychic and the mental planes. In the noonday sun, the horse gallops blindly on, while the HORSEMAN, clear-sighted, anticipates its fears and guides it towards its predetermined goal. At night, however, when the horseman himself becomes blind, it is the horse which sees and guides, and it is the horse which takes control, since it alone can with impunity pass through the gates of mystery beyond the reach of reason. Should conflict arise between horse and rider, they may well gallop to madness and death: if they are at one, it will be a triumphal ride. Tradition, ritual, myth, folklore and poetry in their evocation of the horse do no more than give expression to the manifold potential of this subtle interplay.

Creature of darkness and magical power
Tradition and literature from the steppes of central Asia, the land of the shaman and the horseman, have preserved an image of the chthonian horse with mysterious powers which take over at the point where human strength fails, at the gates of death. Habituated to the darkness, clairvoyant, it performs the role of guide and intercessor, in other words, of a conductor of souls. In this respect the Kirghiz epic poem, *Er-Töshtük*, is significant (BORA). Although Töshtük may be the perfect hero, in order to recover his soul, which a wizard has stolen from him, he has in some sense to abdicate his own individuality and trust the paranormal powers of his magic horse, Chal-Kuiruk, which enables him to reach the Underworld and escape all its traps. This Asian Bayard, Chal-Kuiruk, is endowed with human speech and understanding. At the outset of this fantastic ride, it warns its master of the role reversal which will take place: 'Your chest is broad, but your spirit is narrow. You are heedless. You do not see what I see, you do not know what I know.... You are brave but stupid' (BORA pp. 136, 106). Lastly, to add the finishing touch to its powers, it says: 'I can walk through the depths of the seas.'

However, although Chal-Kuiruk is a creature of both worlds, it can only pass from the one to the other at the cost of cruel suffering. Every time the situation demands it, it begs its rider to beat lumps of its flesh 'as big as sheep' from its flanks with his whip, so that its powers may become effective. This is a significant image: each occasion calls the process of initiation into effect.

One has only to read this epic poem to gain a deep understanding of some shamanistic traditions. Thus, throughout most of the Altai region, the dead man's saddle is placed and his horse tethered close to his body to guarantee his last journey (HARA). The Buryat, believing that a sick person had temporarily lost his soul, tethered his horse at his bedside, 'the horse [being] the first to perceive the return of the soul and [showing] it by quivering' (ELIC p. 217). When a shaman died, he was laid on his saddle-cloth, with his saddle as a pillow, his reins, bow and arrows placed in his hands (HARA p. 212).

The Beltir sacrificed the dead man's horse, so that its soul would guide its master's, and it is significant that its flesh was then fed to the DOGS and BIRDS, themselves conductors of souls and familiar with the transcendent upper and lower worlds. Horse sacrifice was so widespread that it is re-garded as one of the key characteristics by which primitive Asian civiliza-tion may be recognized (DELC p. 241). It is in evidence among many Indo-European races and extended in antiquity as far as the Mediterra-nean. In the *Iliad*, Achilles sacrifices four horses at the funeral pyre of Patroclus so that they shall carry his friend to the kingdom of Hades. Through its clairvoyance and knowledge of the other world, the horse played a major part in shamanistic ceremonies. The good spirit of the shamans of the Altai region, which accompanies them on their soothsaying journeys, possesses 'horse's eyes which enable it to see thirty days' journey ahead. It watches over mankind and tells the supreme deity of their doings' (HARA p. 112). Most of the adjuncts of the shaman's trance were related to horses. Thus the skin of the ritual drum, rhythmically beaten to induce trance and bring it to its climax, was more often than not that of horse or stag, and Yakut and other tribes expressly called it 'the shaman's horse' (HARA p. 351). Lastly, shamans often use for their passage into the Otherworld a stick with a carved horse's head, called the 'horse-stick', used, in a way reminiscent of the witch's broomstick, like a live horse (HARA p. 333).

Human metamorphoses into horses: possession and initiation
The key role played by the horse in shamanistic trance rituals naturally leads us to consider the part played by this animal in Dionysiac rites and, more widely, in those of initiation and possession in general. From the outset it becomes all too apparent that in Haitian and African Voodoo and in Ethiopian Zar, just as it had in the ancient mystery religions of Asia Minor, the role reversal between horse and rider, to which we have already briefly referred, is carried to its most extreme conclusion. In all these tra-ditions, man, the possessed, becomes a horse to be ridden by a spirit. In both Haiti and Brazil those possessed by the spirits of Voodoo are ex-pressly termed the 'horses' of their Loa. Similarly in Ethiopia when, in the mass dance of the possessed, 'the *wajada*, the possessed, identifies with his *Zar*, he becomes no more than its horse, lifelessly obedient to the whims of the spirit which rides him' (LEIA p. 337). According to Jeanmaire the same ritual, employing the same terms, was practised in Egypt down to the be-ginning of the present century (JEAD).

The Dionysiac cults of Asia Minor were no exception to what appears to have been a rule. Initiates into their mysteries were said to be 'ridden' by the gods. Horse-like figures abound in the train of Dionysos, supreme master of ecstatic worship. The Sileni and satyrs who accompany the Maenads in the Dionysiac rout are part-horse, part-man, just like the CENTAURS whom the God made drunk, thus causing their battle with Herakles (Hercules) (JEAD, GRID). In legend, the women associated with the Dionysiac orgy,

Jeanmaire observes, 'with remarkable frequency bear names ending in
hippe... or epithets which as strongly give rise to notions of horsiness'
(JEAD p. 285). Hence it is understandable that in Ancient Chinese tradition candidates at the time of their initiation were known as 'young horses'.
Those conducting the initiation, or those who preached new teachings, were
known as 'horse-traders'. To hold a more or less secret initiation ceremony
was to 'unbridle the horses'. If the horse stands for animal elements within
the individual, it owes this above all to those powers of instinct which make
it seem endowed with second sight. Horse and rider are intimately entwined. The horse teaches its rider: in other words, intuition enlightens
reason. The horse imparts secrets: its path is straightforward. Whenever its
rider sets it on the wrong path, it can see the ghosts and shadows there. But
it risks becoming the Devil's accomplice.

In the West, the medieval initiation into knighthood has some similarities
with horse symbolism, since the horse was privileged to bear the knight on
his spiritual quest. In some respects its prototype is the battle between Bellerophon, mounted on PEGASUS, and the Chimera.

Thus, having been regarded as seer and conductor of souls, the horse
becomes the possessed, an initiate into divine mysteries, who abdicates his
own personality so that that of a higher spirit can make itself manifest
through it, a passive role indicated by the twofold meaning of 'to ride' and
'to be ridden'. It needs to be observed, at this point, that not all members
of the Voodoo pantheon, the Loas who ride those whom they possess, are
evil. Among the most important Loas are the White Loas, heavenly sky-
spirits. Thus the horse, a chthonian symbol, reaches the acme of its positive
valence when both the upper and the lower planes are made manifest without distinction through its mediation, that is to say when its significance
becomes cosmic. This links up with the Vedic horse sacrifice, the Asvamedha,
an essentially cosmogonic ritual, as Mircea Eliade emphasizes: 'The horse
is [thus] identified with the Cosmos and the sacrificing of it symbolizes –
that is *reproduces* – the act of creation' (ELIT p. 96).

Some figures in Greek mythology, among them Pegasus, represent not
the fusion of the upper and lower planes, but the passage through sublimation from one to the other. Pegasus carries his thunderbolts to Zeus: he is
a sky-horse, and yet his origins were chthonian since he was either the fruit
of the love of Poseidon for the Gorgon, or born of Earth impregnated by
the Gorgon's blood. Pegasus may therefore be said to stand for the sublimation of instinct and to be no longer the necromancer or the possessed, but
the initiate who has acquired wisdom.

Horses and death
The negative valence of the chthonian symbol makes the horse a manifestation of the power of the Underworld and of death, on the same plane as
the figure with the scythe in Western folklore. In Ireland the hero Conal I
Cernach owned 'Dew Red', a horse with a hound's head, which tore the
sides of its enemies. Cùchulainn's horses, the Macha Grey (called King of
the Horses of Ireland) and Black Hoof had human understanding. The
Macha Grey refused to allow anyone to harness him to the chariot being
made ready for the hero's last battle and wept tears of blood. Later it was

to guide Conal I Cernach, his avenger, to its master's body, while Black Hoof drowned itself in despair.

Horses which either foretell or carry death proliferate from Classical Greece to the Middle Ages and spread throughout European folklore. 'In Greek society, as early as the the the oldest version of the dream-book compiled by Artemidorus, for a sick person to dream of a horse was a sign he or she would die' (JEAD p. 284). The Arcadian Demeter was often depicted as horse-headed and identified with the Erinnyes, those dreadful agents of the justice of Hades. Like Poseidon, she gave birth to another horse, Areion, Herakles' steed. The Harpies, those 'evil spirits of storm, devastation and death' (JEAD), were sometimes depicted as half-woman, half-bird, at others as half-woman, half-mare. One of them was the mother of Achilles' chariot-horses, another of the chargers which Hermes gave to the Dioscuri. Ahriman, the Devil of Zoroastrianism, often appeared in the guise of a horse to kill or carry off his victims.

Most death-horses are black, like Charos, the modern Greek death-god, but some are pale, and these are often confused with the white sky-horse, with a completely opposite significance. Although these pale horses are sometimes called WHITE, this must be understood as being the colour of the night, a cold lunar whiteness comprising emptiness and the absence of colour, while the whiteness of day is solar, warm and comprising the sum of all colours. The pale horse is as white as a shroud or a ghost. Its whiteness is akin to the commonest symbolic application of black – mourning. It is the pale horse of the Apocalypse and the white horse which in English and German folklore is the forerunner of death. Franco-German folklore, too, is full of creatures of ill omen, horses leagued with swirling rivers, such as the *Schimmel Reiter*, which destroys dykes during storms, to the *Blanque Jument* in the Pas-de-Calais, the *Bian Cheval* of Celles-sur-Plaine and *Drac*, the fine white stallion which seized travellers and drowned them in the River Doubs in France (DOND, DONM). In the Middle Ages biers were called 'St Michael's horses' in France and the horse symbolized the tree of death. These last quoted examples serve to show the negative valence of the lunar horse associated with water: its positive valence will be examined later. Lastly it is the disturbing, fixed stare of the war-horse which seems to haunt Albrecht Dürer's imagination.

In terms of semantics, Krappe regards this sinister horse, be it black or white, at the root of the French *cauchemar* or English *nightmare*. The *Mahrt* (German: 'mare') is an evil spirit from the Underworld, as the word indicates (cf. Old Slavonic *mora*, 'witch'; Russian *mora*, 'ghost'; Polish *mora*, Czech *mura*, 'nightmare'; Latin *mors, mortis*, 'death'; Old Irish *marah*, 'death, plague'; Lithuanian *maras*, 'death, pestilence'; Latvian *meris*, 'pestilence'; and the sinister Irish *Mor(r)igain*) (KRAM p. 229). Celtic folklore is haunted by death- or nightmare-horses. The March-Malaen (*malaen = malignus*, Latin) was one of the three scourges of the Isle of Britain; Scottish kelpies are horselike water demons, and Breton folklore is full of tales and stories of diabolical horses which lead travellers astray or dash them into quagmires or morasses. In Breton folklore, black horses are, as often as not, the Devil himself or else one of his imps, or a soul from Hell or Purgatory. On other occasions they may be ridden by some wild huntsman, of which King

Arthur is the most famous, doomed eternally to chase a quarry which he will never catch. It is significant to observe in passing that in the oldest versions of King Arthur's hunt, the king, with a pack of white hounds, should pursue so typically a lunar creature as a HARE.

Dontenville regards this King Arthur as a Celtic homologue of the Germanic Wotan. A related legend, that of the White Lady, should be studied since it reverses the symbol's polarization by giving it a sexual significance. At the same time the steed in this wild ride becomes 'all gleaming white. In such regions as the Jura and the Périgord, the Lady in the White Dress rides through the wind-tossed woods, and the sound may be heard of her horses, hounds and huntsman and the music of her horns. At first they play a warlike march, and then the tune softens into one able to open the glowing gates of pleasure' (DOND p. 35). A glittering white steed and music which starts as tunes of battle and ends as tunes of pleasure – such are the beginnings of the rise of the horse symbol from the realms of the Underworld to those of the sky.

Horse sacrifice
The symbolic links between Earth and Mother, Moon and Water, sexuality and fertility, and plants and the rebirth of the seasons enable us to lay bare other aspects of this symbol. Many writers have explained the process whereby in agrarian societies the Underworld deities became deities of the soil. The horse is no exception to the rule of this symbolic change. Frazer provides countless instances. In Rome horses selected as chargers for the cavalry were dedicated to Mars during the Equiria, horse-races held annually between 27 February and 14 March. This marked the opening of the campaigning season. When it closed seven months later, on 15 October, at the end of the harvest, every year a horse was sacrificed to Mars. Its head was decorated with ears of corn in thanksgiving for the harvest just gathered in, since Mars protected the community as much against disease which might attack their crops as human enemies which might attack their members. The animal's TAIL

was cut off and carried to the king's house with such speed that the blood dripped on the hearth of the house. Further, it appears that the blood of the horse was caught and preserved till the twenty-first of April, when the Vestal virgins mixed it with the blood of unborn calves which had been sacrificed six days before. The mixture was then distributed to shepherds, and used by them for fumigating their flocks.

(FRAG 8: p. 42)

Such a horse sacrifice would constitute 'a sort of royal capitalization on victory', as Dumézil puts it. 'The custom of cutting off the horse's tail', Frazer observes, 'is like the African custom of cutting off the tails of oxen and sacrificing them to obtain a good crop. In both the Roman and the African custom the animal apparently stands for the corn-spirit, and its fructifying power is supposed to reside especially in its tail' (ibid. p. 43). As we have seen, its swiftness associates the horse with time and hence with its continuity, while, being able to pass unharmed through regions of death and cold (Winter), the horse as bearer of the corn-spirit from Autumn to

Spring fills the breach made by Winter and ensures essential renewal. Count-less other traditions confirm this role of corn-spirit. Thus it used to be the custom in France and Germany for the youngest horse in the village to be fêted and petted at harvest time since it was the one which ensured the germination of next year's crops. Until the next seed-time the horse was said to bear the corn-spirit in it (FRAG 7: p. 292).

In Ireland Frazer also records an eye-witness account (FRAG 10: pp. 203–4) of the ceremonies on Midsummer's Eve when, after the country-people had jumped through the bonfires, a clumsy wooden frame about eight feet long appeared on the scene. At one end it had a horse's head and it was covered with a white sheet concealing the bearer. It was greeted by shouts of 'the White Horse!' The hobby leaped over the bonfire and then began to chase the spectators. When the witness asked what the horse meant, he was told: 'All the livestock.' From being the corn-spirit, the horse became a symbol of plenty in general, a development explicable in terms of its dynamism, its driving power and generous strength. Details from other agrarian ceremonies corroborate this interpretation. Thus the Garo in Assam celebrated the conclusion of the harvest by showering with EGGS the figure of a horse, painted white like the Irish midsummer hobby-horse, while dancing round it. The figure was then thrown into a river. Water-spirits are known to control germination and plant-growth. The association of horse and egg strengthens the powers of this rice-spirit. Frazer notes that the head from the figure was kept until the following year, just as in Rome the head of the sacrificial horse was kept nailed to the gates of a fortress.

The kinship between horses and running WATER is brought out most clearly in a custom once practised by fishermen on the Oka, a tributary of the River Volga. On 15 April, the start of Spring and the date on which the ice finally melted, it was their custom to steal a horse and drown it as a sacrifice to the Grandfather of the Waters, who woke from his slumbers on that day. 'Here, Grandfather,' the fishermen would shout, 'take this gift and keep our family [tribe] safe!' (DALP p. 878). Horse sacrifice by drowning in rivers appears to have been practised by other Indo-European races, in-cluding the early Greeks, if one is to believe Achilles' curse on the slayers of Patroclus: 'Not even the fair-flowing river with his silver eddies shall aught avail you, albeit to him, I ween, ye have long time been wont to sacrifice bulls full many, and to cast single-hooved horses while yet they lived, into his eddies. Howbeit even so shall ye perish by an evil fate' (*Iliad* 21: 130–3).

Water-god
Because the horse shares the secret of the waters of fruitfulness it knows their underground meanderings. This explains why from western Europe to the Far East the horse is regarded as having the gift of causing wells to spring from the ground struck by its hoofs. In the Massif Central in France there is a whole series of Bayard-wells or -SPRINGS along the route taken by the Four Sons of Aymon on the back of this famous magic horse. Pegasus himself started the tradition when he called into being the fountain of Hippocrene not far from the wood sacred to the Muses. The Muses gath-ered round it to sing and dance and 'its waters were believed to aid poetic

inspiration' (GRID p. 211). In this context the horse 'awakens' the imagination, just as it 'awakened' nature at the time of seasonal renewal.

Hence it will be appreciated that the horse may equally be regarded as an avatar (embodiment), or assistant, of the rain-gods. In Africa the Ewe believe that the rain-god gallops across the sky on the back of his horse, a shooting star. Initiates into the Kwore society among the Bambara in Mali mount wooden horses. These stand for the winged horses on which the spirits which they invoke fight their battles in the sky against the powers trying to prevent the showers of fecundating RAIN (DIEB). In more general terms, according to Zahan (ZAHV), among the Bambara the horse symbol encompasses notions of swiftness, imagination and immortality and is therefore closely akin to Pegasus. By analogy, the Bambara horse corresponds to the child and the word, which explains why the same plant, the *koro*, which 'is associated with strength and fluency of speech, should be used indiscriminately to strengthen sickly children and to cure barrenness in mares' (ZAHV pp. 161–2).

This example adds to those already mentioned the image of the child who, like the Spring, displays the awakening of the powers of drive and of imagination.

Driving force of the libido

Once past puberty, the young man takes the horse as the symbol, in the fullest sense of the term, of what Paul Diel calls 'the driving force of the libido', with all that this implies in terms of fire, fruitfulness and warm-heartedness. As a symbol of strength, of the creative forces and of youth, and acquiring a sexual as well as a spiritual valence, the horse now shares symbolically in both the chthonian and the celestial planes. This would incline us to evoke the white horse, in its shining, solar aspect, but it is interesting to observe, in passing, that there are two aspects of the BLACK horse as well. In Russian popular poetry what we have hitherto regarded as exclusively a death-horse becomes a symbol of youth and the triumph of the life force. These are the black horses which, in fairy stories, are harnessed to wedding-coaches; they are thus the horses of the libido set free. Taken to their extreme, the words 'horse', 'stallion', 'mare' and 'foal' take on an erotic significance possessing the same double meaning as the verb 'to ride'.

Just as the stallion stands for the powers of fertility, instinct and, through sublimation, of spirit, so the mare embodies the part played by Mother Earth in the original sacred marriage of Heaven and Earth which dominates the beliefs of agrarian societies. We have already mentioned the horse-headed Demeter as a fertility-goddess. It was said that she coupled with a mortal, the handsome Iasion, in the furrows of a freshly ploughed field. This orgiastic performance was not simply mythical. In the twelfth-century coronation ritual of Irish kings as Schröder describes it (KOPP), the king-to-be went through a solemn ritual coupling with a white mare. The mare was promptly sacrificed and its flesh was stewed and served at a ritual banquet in which the king did not take part. However, he had then to bathe in the CAULDRON and in the water in which the meat had been cooked. Analysis of the ritual speaks volumes. In fact, it would seem as if the coupling of man and mare was a repetition of the marriage of Heaven and Earth, the future king acting as the surrogate of the sky-god to impregnate Earth, in the shape of the mare. However, in the last phase of the ritual, the bath in the cooking water, a true return to the womb took place, the cauldron standing for Mother Earth's womb and the cooking-water for the placental waters. In a style characteristic of all initiation rites, the king-to-be was reborn from this bath, having received, as if during the period of a second gestation, the most subtle and secret powers from Mother Earth, whom he had aroused in the shape of a mare. Through this two-phased ordeal he was able to raise himself from the human level to the sacred, part and parcel of the condition of kingship.

The horses of the Sun

Although its origins were in the Underworld, the horse gradually became a creature of the Heavens and the Sun. In the light of the foregoing it is striking to observe the Uralo-Altaic belief that the sacred marriage of Earth and Heaven was accomplished by the coupling of the White Stallion and the Dun Cow, the stallion being a manifestation of the sky-god (ROUF pp. 343–4).

Such, too, was the Indian horse, the *asha*, literally meaning 'that which pierces', its penetration being that of light. The horse-headed Ashvins, related to the daily cycle of light and darkness, were born of mare and stallion – both solar symbols – embodying *dharma* (the law) and knowledge. Mircea Eliade (ELIT) lays emphasis upon the fact that both the Ashvins and the Dioscuri were twins.

As the Tantric emblem of the Bodhisattva Avalokitesvara, the horse symbolizes the power of his grace scattered to the four quarters of the Earth. In the *Bardo Thödol*, Ratnasambhava, the Buddha of the South and a solar symbol, sits on a throne built up of horses. He is also a symbol of wisdom and physical beauty.

In Buddhist, as well as in Hindu texts and in Greek writers under Plato's influence, horses are above all else symbols of the senses harnessed to the chariot of the spirit and controlled by the Self who is the charioteer. In the same way, the teachings of *Bardo* are said to be like 'the bridle which controls the horse's mouth'. There is more than a hint of the symbolism of Pegasus here. This context provides an example, not only of all winged horses, but also of the association of horse and BIRD, of which mythology and tradition offer countless examples, always in a solar or celestial context – for example, in the *Rig-Veda*, where the Sun is either stallion or bird (ELIT p. 144). In a further development of these interlinked analogies, the horse's liveliness often makes it, in the celestial sense of the symbol, a manifestation of the wind. In Arabic folk tales four horses stand for the four winds of Heaven, and in China Vāyu, the wind-god, rides a horse. Boreas, his counterpart in Greek mythology, turned himself into a stallion in order to seduce the mares of Erichthonius. Thus they brought forth 'twelve foals so light-footed that when they galloped across a field of corn, the stalks did not bend under their weight and when they galloped across the sea, they did not leave a ripple on its surface' (GRID pp. 66–7). Boreas was also responsible for begetting horses on one of the Erinnyes and then on one of the Harpies. In these instances, the horses were born of a marriage of the chthonian with the celestial and were instruments of violence. Within the pattern of ascension, this example shows that the horse cannot cut itself completely free from its origins, and it gradually became a warlike symbol and even the creature pre-eminently associated with battle.

As we have seen, the annual horse sacrifice at Rome was to Mars. In fact, the warrior plays a part at both celestial and chthonian levels; death-dealer in battle, he belongs to the Underworld, while his victory or his own death raise him to the skies. Warrior-horses are a constant theme of Celtic heroic literature, often characterized by their chestnut coats, the colour of fire. A Celtic hoard excavated in France at Neuvy-en-Sullias contained the votive statue of a horse with an inscription to Rudiobus (the Red). This is the red horse of the Apocalypse which foretells war and bloodshed.

In Vedic tradition, the sacrificial horse symbolized the cosmos. In the *Rig-Veda*, the chariot of the Sun was drawn by one or seven horses. (In Greek mythology the chariot of the Sun was also horse-drawn, and the horse was one of Apollo's attributes as charioteer of the Sun.) The horse therefore partakes of a twofold solar symbolism with a double valence – a life force when the Sun is shining and a death force when it sets at night. Horses also drew funeral chariots.

The horse majestic
The white horse of the Sun, drawing the Sun-god's chariot, becomes an image of that beauty gained when the spirit (the Charioteer) controls the senses.

The white horse, whose whiteness is dazzling, is the symbol of majesty. Generally it is ridden by him whom the Book of Revelation (19: 11) calls Faithful and True, that is by Christ. St John goes on to describe the heavenly host mounted on white chargers and this is why, in medieval iconography, angels are depicted on horseback.

This whole process of ascension culminates in the figure of the majestic white horse, the steed of heroes, saints and spiritual victors. All great Messianic figures ride such horses. Thus in Hinduism Kalkin, the future avatar (incarnation) of the god Vishnu, will be a white horse; while at his expected second coming, the Prophet Muhammad will also be riding a white horse. Lastly the white horse which the Buddha rode at the Great Departure, riderless, stands for the Buddha himself.

To conclude, it would seem as if the horse were one of those basic archetypes firmly embedded in folk-memory. Its symbolism encompasses both poles of the cosmos, the upper and the lower, and hence it is truly universal. In the chthonian world of the lower pole we have seen how the horse stands as an avatar or friend of the three elements which it comprises, Fire, Earth and Water, and of the Moon which gives it light. At the same time we have seen how the horse is associated with the three elements which comprise the celestial world of the upper pole, Air, Fire and Water – the last two bearing the celestial connotation of their symbolism – and of the Sun which gives it light. On the pediment of the Parthenon, horses draw the chariots both of the Sun and of the Moon. The horse passes as easily from day to night and back again, as from life to death and from the active to the passive role. It therefore links these opposites in continuous manifestation. Essentially the horse is manifestation, life and continuity, overriding the discontinuity of our lives and deaths. Its powers are beyond comprehension, it partakes of the miraculous and it is therefore easy to see why mankind should in both prehistoric and historic times so often have made it holy. Only one creature in the symbolic bestiary of Nature surpasses it in subtlety – the SERPENT. Like the horse, it is at home on every continent, and like it and as an image of time itself, it 'flows' ceaselessly from the heights to the depths and from the depths to the heights, between the Underworld and Heaven. The hidden routes for this constant coming and going of both horse and serpent are the waters – both haunt wells and streams. Thus horses and serpents often play interchangeable roles as the heroes of many a wonder-tale. Or else they are combined to create a weird monster, a cross between horse and snake. This is Long-Ma, the Chinese 'horse-dragon', which brought the Ho-t'u – a plan of the river, also called Ma-t'u, or plan of a horse – to Yu the Great. This is clearly related to the symbolism of the word and draws a fresh parallel with the GARUDA. In countless Chinese legends, from the *Li-sao* of Chu-yuan to the *Si-yu Chi*, horses take the place of dragons. In both cases they take part in the quest for knowledge or for immortality. Nor is it by chance that the ancestors of the secret societies, the pedlars of Taoist knowledge, the apostles of Amidism in Japan, wore the guise of 'horse-dealers', nor that Matso, who spread Zen teaching to China, was called in a pun upon his name, 'the young foal who kicks over the traces and tramples all the peoples of the world'.

The steed of the gods
Strength and swiftness are the qualities which the *I Ching* attributes to the horse. Since the god of the wind and the element of Air, Vāyu, rode on horseback, Granet may well be correct in suggesting that the eight horses of King Mu correspond to the eight winds of Heaven. In any case, in China the horse is a typically *yang* creature. In days gone by sacrifice was offered to the 'First Horse', the name given to a constellation but one suggestive of pastoralist tradition. The frequent presence of horses in Shintō temples in Japan, either alive or in the shape of statues, has never been satisfactorily explained. They would seem to have been the steeds of the *kami*, but in Japan horses are also associated with notions of protection and longevity, as is also the case with the Chinese 'horse-dragon'.

Instead of combining into a single mythic figure, the conjunction of horse and dragon can also split into two component parts. Each takes on an opposing quality and they meet in mortal combat, which becomes a battle of good with evil. Clearly the horse is given a positive value, since it represents the humanized facet of the symbol, while the dragon stands for the beast-in-us, which must be killed, in other words rejected. The myth of St George and the Dragon is an instance of this.

horseman (see also KNIGHT) Equestrian statues or portraits inflate the importance of the conquering hero and are symbols of his triumph and his glory, for just as he has subdued his charger, so he has overcome the forces set against him. They display his ascent into the Paradise of the gods, heroes and the elect, like the famous vision of the Prophet Muhammad on his mare Borak, led by Gabriel and with a retinue of angels to the foot of God's very throne. They may then partake of a spiritual significance, such as the accomplishment of the holy word or the attainment of perfection. Special signs sometimes distinguish the HORSE, its harness or caparison and also the horseman, his dress, distinguishing marks or arms. They lay bare a complete philosophy of which the following is a little-known but strangely rich example.

Most striking among Dogon equestrian carvings are those of Orosongo, horseman of the skies. Marcel Griaule regards this as an illustration of an episode in the myth of the ARK which came down from Heaven with the originals of all living things. Jean Laude quotes this opinion to apply to the figure a less mythical but far deeper interpretation:

The initiate would notice that it contained a group of signs, a jagged line with the surface meaning of vibration. Now if that meaning were explored in depth, the more knowledgeable would find in it a wealth of basics lacking in the outline of the myth itself. They would touch upon a concept of matter, a cosmogony, a wisdom and a structure of social behaviour. The vibration would suggest the spiral descent of the blacksmith [who brought the ark]. At a higher level of initiation it would represent the vibration of matter, light and water. A work of art expresses here in concrete shape a philosophy in the pre-Socratic sense of the word.

The concept of the cosmos as a vibration is so widespread in primitive cultures that no inferences need be drawn in respect of contemporary theoretical physics.

As is the case with all images charged with hidden meanings, any symbolic interpretation of the horseman must take into account every least detail of his depiction. From being an expression of military or spiritual triumph, the image of the horseman came to signify perfect mastery of self and of the powers of nature. Jung, however, maintains that in modern art the opposite is true and that the image of the horseman, instead of expressing tranquillity, now expresses 'tormenting fear' and a measure of despairing panic in the face of forces over which the individual or the consciousness has lost control. The interpretation of symbols must include all these different meanings, provided that they comply with actual experience.

The Four Horsemen of the Apocalypse attest this polyvalence of the symbol. Their description (Revelation 6: 1–8) is inspired by the visions of Ezekiel and of Zachariah and the four horsemen themselves stand for the four terrors of Israel which impend over the Roman Empire – wild beasts (the Parthians), war, famine and pestilence. The rider on the white horse 'went forth conquering and to conquer', but the bow with which he is armed denotes the Parthians, who spread terror among the Romans in the first century AD. Christian tradition also identifies Christ in this victorious horseman, while a mystical interpretation even sees in him the triumph of the word of God, which spreads worldwide in a continuous and irresistibly victorious tide, from the tomb of the risen Christ to the ends of the Earth and the consummation of time. The second horseman rode a red horse and his errand was to 'take peace from the earth, and that they should kill one another'. He carried a sword and represented war. The third appeared upon a black horse holding a pair of scales in his hand and announcing: 'A measure of wheat for a penny, and three measures of barley for a penny: and see thou hurt not the oil and the wine.' He represented famine. The fourth horseman galloped away on a pale horse; he was pestilence, with Hades at his heels, ready to engulf mankind. In oriental literatures these natural calamities have acquired the quality of symbols and represent the worst punishments which threaten the fate of the world on the 'great day of the Lord', should mankind continue to disregard the word of God.

Horus The falcon-headed Ancient Egyptian god, son of Osiris and Isis, was frequently represented by an EYE, the 'Eye of Horus', or by a solar disc borne by a pair of falcon's wings. He symbolized the mercilessly keen eye of justice, from which no action in private or in public life can escape.

He took especial care to see that religious ritual and law were strictly followed. His legendary battle with SET, whom he cut to pieces but who tore out one of his eyes, is an example of the struggle of light and darkness and of the need to be vigilant, to keep one's eyes open, so as to avoid falling into sin or the traps of the enemy. Of course perception of Horus developed in the long course of Egyptian history, and the sky-god became a Pharaonic god battling for the sovereignty of the world. Despite this, he was always seen as being embattled, seeking to preserve the balance against the powers which came against him and to bring about the victory of the forces of light.

host Derives from the Latin word *hostia*, defined by Ernout and Meillet as 'the victim sacrificed to the gods in expiation and to propitiate their anger, in contrast with *victima*, the victim sacrificed in thanksgiving for favours received.' 'Host' would therefore denote all victims sacrificed to a great cause in the hope, like that of the martyr, that it will triumph. For Christians it is Christ, whose sacrifice upon the Cross and in the breaking of bread at the Last Supper are commemorated liturgically in the Eucharist. Christ's dead and resurrected body is represented and symbolized by a small slim disk of unleavened bread, called the Host and given in communion. Its shape and ingredients have inspired preachers to a welter of symbols:

Surely the small size of the host signifies humility, its simplicity perfect obedience, its thinness virtuous temperance, its whiteness purity, the absence of leaven benignity, its baking patience and charity, the inscription which it bears spiritual discretion, its unaltered composition permanence and its circular shape consummate perfection? O bread of life, unleavened bread, hidden abode of the Almighty! Under humble visible accidents lie hidden astounding and sublime realities!

(attributed to St Thomas Aquinas)

hour-glass The hour-glass symbolizes the eternal passage of time, inexorably slipping away until, in the human cycle, it runs out into death. However, it also carries the significance of a potential reversal of time and return to one's beginnings.

The shape of the hour-glass with its two containers displays the analogy between the upper and the lower, and the need to turn the hour-glass upside down to produce a flow from bottom to top. Thus, unless we completely

reverse our attitudes and activities, we shall always be drawn towards the
base. Nor should we forget how restricted is the contact between upper and
lower through the narrow passage which allows a continual flow from one
to the other.

Fullness and emptiness must follow one another in succession. There is,
therefore, a flow from the upper to the lower, from the celestial to the
terrestrial, and then a reverse flow from the terrestrial to the celestial. Such
is the image of alchemical or mystical choice.

Both in Asia and in Arab lands drums are sometimes built like hour-
glasses and hence gain kinship with the CALABASH or FURNACE used by Chinese alchemists and with Mount Kun-Lun, the centre of the world. This is
because the two sand-containers correspond to Heaven and Earth and the
trickle of sand, which flows in the opposite direction when the hour-glass is
inverted, represents the exchanges between the two worlds, the manifestation
in nature of what is celestial and the reintegration of the manifest world
with its divine source. The thin neck between the containers is the 'strait
gate' through which these exchanges are made, the pole of manifestation.
The final running-out of the sand marks the end of a cycle which, Schuon
observes, is in precise conformity with the initially imperceptible movement
of the sand, which gradually accelerates until its final spurt.

Similar symbolism recurs in Shiva's hour-glass drum, the *damaru*. Its two
halves comprise two inverted triangles, *lingam–yoni*, their point of contact
being the BINDU, or seed of manifestation. The *damaru* emits the primordial
sound, or *shabda* (DANA, MALA, SCHT).

house Like cities and temples, houses are at the CENTRE of the world and
are images of the universe. The traditional Chinese house (*ming-t'ang*) was
square. Its entrance faced east and the owner's room faced south, like the
emperor in his palace. The centre-point of the building was determined
according to the rules of GEOMANCY. There was a smoke hole in the roof
and a rain-water tank sunk into the floor. Thus the house was pierced at its
centre by an AXIS joining the three worlds together. The Arab house, too,
was square, enclosing a square courtyard with a GARDEN or FOUNTAIN in its
centre. It was a closed, four-dimensional universe, the central garden an
echo of Paradise and, furthermore, exposed exclusively to celestial influences. The Mongol tent or yurt is circular, the shape associated with no-
madism, since the square on the cardinal points implies fixity in space. The
central tent-post, or simply the column of smoke from the yurt's smoke-
hole, coincides with the World Axis.

Specific types of house – admittedly close relatives of the TEMPLE – express this cosmic symbolism even more clearly. Into this category fall those
'communal houses' built at the intersection of the north–south, east–west
axes of cities in many parts of the world and more especially in Indonesia
and East Asia. The same role is played by the Sioux Sun Dance Lodge,
circular, like the yurt, and with a central pole. It not only suggests the solar
cycle, but also spatial manifestation and, because its twenty-eight supporting poles are linked to the central pole, lunar manifestations as well. The
lodges of Western secret societies in which the cosmic nature of the lodge
is openly affirmed and in which a plumb-line replaces the axis should be

included, as should Chinese lodges. These are square and have four doors
oriented to the cardinal points, each corresponding to the element and
colour associated with its own cardinal point. The centre, corresponding to
the element of Earth, is occupied by the 'City of Willows' or 'House of
Great Peace', lying directly below the Great Bear and representing the
abode of the Immortals. But above all, this is true of the Chinese Temple
of Heaven, which Granet calls the 'Calendar House', but which is pre-
eminently the 'Hall of Light'. The Temple of Heaven may perhaps originally have been circular and surrounded by a moat in the shape of the Pi,
or jade disc. It was thus a reservoir of celestial influences at the centre of
the Chinese world. It next became square, on the pattern of the Earth,
perhaps with five rooms in a cruciform arrangement or perhaps with nine
set out on the pattern of the nine provinces; it was covered by a round
thatched roof to represent the Heavens, supported on eight pillars corresponding to the eight winds of Heaven and the eight trigrams. The Temple
of Heaven comprised four walls oriented towards the four seasons, each
with three doorways so that the twelve doors in all corresponded to the
twelve months and with the twelve signs of the Zodiac, like the gates of the
Heavenly Jerusalem. The emperor's progress from one room to another
determined the divisions of time and ensured that the government of the
empire harmonized with the celestial order.

Although Taoists devised various 'palaces' (corresponding with the subtle centres) in the human body, Buddhism identifies the human body itself
with the house. The Patriach Hui Neng called it an 'inn', thus implying that
it could only be regarded as a temporary refuge. In the Tibetan Wheel of
Life, the body is depicted as a house with six windows corresponding to the
six senses. Canonical writings describe release from the individual state or
from the cosmos by such phrases as breaking 'the roof of the palace' or the
'roof of the house' (see DOME). The opening in the CROWN of the head
through which this *brahmarandhra* or release takes place is significantly
termed the 'smoke-hole' by Tibetans (COOH, COOD, FRAL, GOVM,
GRIL, GUET, HEHS, LIOT, WARH).

In Ancient Egypt the name 'houses of life' was given to a kind of religious seminary attached to shrines. In them, scribes copied liturgical writings and mythological paintings and physicians, surgeons and trepanners
were trained, while the temple attendants went about their duties. In Black
Africa Marcel Griaule has described the Dogon 'great family house [as
representing] the great living body of the Universe in its totality' (CHAS
p. 246).

It would appear that in their concepts of living space, the Ancient Irish
saw the house as symbolizing the status and attitude of mankind to the
sovereign powers of the Otherworld. The palace of the King and Queen of
Connaught, Ailill and Medb, was circular (the circle being a celestial symbol) comprising seven sections, each section containing seven beds or rooms
symmetrically grouped around a central hearth. The dome-shaped roof was
a further adjunct to potential communication with the Heavens. The royal
house was thus both an image of the human cosmos and an earthly reflection of Heaven.

According to Bachelard the house signifies the inner being, and its floors, from cellars to attics, symbolize different states of the soul. The cellars correspond to the unconscious, the attics to spiritual elevation (BACE p. 18).

The house is also a feminine symbol in the sense of being a sanctuary, the mother, protection or the womb (BACV p. 14).

Analysts, especially, recognize differences of meaning in dreams about houses depending upon the rooms seen and the different levels of the psyche with which these correspond. The outside of the house is the human mask or appearance; the roof is the head and the spirit, controlling consciousness; the lower floors denote the level of the instincts and of the unconscious; kitchens may well symbolize the place of alchemical transmutations or psychic transformations, that is, a moment in inner development. Similarly one may move from one room to another on the same floor or go up or down stairs in the house, thereby expressing a stationary or stagnant phase in psychic development or a developing phase, which may be either progressive or regressive, towards spirituality or materialism.

hummingbird The Aztecs believed that the souls of dead warriors came back to Earth in the shapes of hummingbirds or BUTTERFLIES. They also regarded hummingbirds as sources of the Sun's heat (KRIR p. 65).

The Hopi Indians of Arizona, related at least linguistically to the Aztecs, have a myth in which the hummingbird appears as the hero who intercedes with the god of germination and plant growth to save mankind from famine (Leo W. Simmons in TALS pp. 431–2).

The same positive valency determines the view of the Colombian Tukano Indians that the hummingbird, or fly-bird, has sexual intercourse with flowers and stands for glowing virility as the erect male phallus. In Brazil the bird is known as the *passaro beja-flor*, or flower-kisser sparrow.

hundred This number individualizes a part of the whole, which is in itself part of a larger grouping. For example, Persian love poetry will describe a woman who is both lovely and endowed with all the virtues as having 'a hundred hairs'. The Chinese will say that a doctrine has 'a hundred flowers', far more in the sense that it has all the virtues than that it has a hundred different facets. A great military leader will ask for a hundred men when assembling a force sufficient to attain his objective.

A hundred is a part which forms a whole within a whole, a microcosm within the macrocosm, distinguishing and individualizing a person, group or thing within a larger grouping. The entity so individualized will have specific qualities which will give it special efficacy within that larger grouping.

Multiples of a hundred will strengthen this principle of individuation by the characteristics of the multiplier. For example, at the time of the Moon Festival (Coya Raimi: 22 September–22 October) the Inca used to parade 400 warriors on the great square of the Temple of Coricancha, a hundred on each side. Each detachment of a hundred set off in the direction indicated by that particular side, in other words towards one or other of the four cardinal points, to drive sickness away (MEAA). Four symbolized Earth; one hundred symbolized each of the individualized groups whose task it was to march through one of the four predetermined areas.

hunt Naturally enough the symbolism of the hunt has two aspects. There is the slaying of the beast, which is the destruction of ignorance and the tendency to evil, and there is the search for the quarry and its tracking, which bear the sense of spiritual quest. 'The Sufi', wrote Jalālal-Dīn Muhammad Rūmī, 'must follow his quarry like a hunter who sees the tracks of the musk-deer and follows its hoof-prints.' Similarly Master Eckhart speaks of 'the soul ardently hunting its prey, Christ'. There is no difference in this symbolism for North American Indians, to whom hunting was an occupation of the greatest importance. To follow an animal's tracks was to follow the path which led to the Great Spirit.

In Ancient China hunting was in disrepute as being a profane occupation, Lao Tzu holding it to be evil and a cause of woe. However, its only lawful form, the ritual aspect, permitted animals to be taken if they were used for sacrifice or for communal feasts, as well as if they were totem-animals (= *wu*, essence). By eating these totem-animals the monarch increased his kingly qualities, and by catching them and sharing them out gave a display of those qualities. Mastery of divine creatures contributed to the good order of the empire by appropriating and sharing out the symbols – and hence the celestial influences – of which they were the manifestation. It also served to rout the baleful influences of evil spirits (COOH, GRAD, HEHS).

In Ancient Egypt 'hunting was an extension of the creative activity of the gods in so far as it drove back the borders of CHAOS, represented by wild animals, which always subsists on the edge of ordered society' (DAUE p. 640). Hippopotamus-hunting in the Nile Delta, in particular, partook of a magico-religious significance. Set, the god of evil, was incarnate in this clumsy, bulky creature which was 'regarded as a manifestation of the perverse forces in the world'. To harpoon a hippopotamus was to behave like Horus, the god of good, and to destroy these maleficent powers. The Pharaoh often dealt the death blow in person, and in the town of Edfu, sacred to Horus, the persons of the harpooners were sacred, dedicated to the worship of the god (POSD p. 126).

Naturally hunting in Ancient Egypt was a sport, as well, and a test of skill, while remaining a religious act of great social significance.

But it was also magic. All game, whether winged, furred or scaly was supposed to be dedicated to the evil powers. Silent spells were cast by the action of the hunter on foreigners, demons, magicians who could murder departed souls and private and public enemies actual and potential.... Hunting was above all for the king a trial of strength and a continual proof of his youth. By a ritual privilege the king could confront fierce lions.

(POSD p. 133)

In the Roman Empire, lion-hunting was an imperial privilege, too.

In North Africa, as in other parts of the world, hunting is the privilege of the upper classes. 'The Lord alone has the right to hunt' since, as Jean Servier explains, 'hunting is a ritual desacralization of the fields before ploughing. What we have here is the need to drive from arable land the wild animals which are manifestations of the Invisible.' In the West, hunting etiquette calls for a royal fanfare to accompany the death of the ten-pointer stag (SERH pp. 326, 270).

The individual in the sacral state, that is to say when he is temporarily consecrated by going on a pilgrimage and wearing distinctive dress, is forbidden to hunt by the Koran. This ban tests the believer and the genuine fear which he feels for his God. This is shown by the duty imposed upon him of remaining ritually pure, despite his natural love of hunting. It provides a typical test of character (Koran 5: 94–5). Allah's pilgrim must remove the temptation to kill, in order to reach the Ka'ba purged of all desire other than that of honouring his God and submitting to God's laws.

Hunting dances are almost as old as humanity. Those performed by central Asian shamans are described by Jean-Paul Roux (SOUD pp. 308–10). In them the hunter copies the way in which the game moves, so that he 'becomes the quarry which he hunts and only by so becoming is he able to hunt it'; or else by copying the behaviour of another animal persuades his quarry that it is not he, the man, who is hunting it. Two different thoughts seem to have motivated these practices. The first is that the hunter identifies with his quarry through dance and the actual hunting process; the second, close to unconscious ecological thinking, is that although the hunter disturbs animal life, he does not wish to drive the prey from his tribal hunting-grounds. Having to maintain an ecological balance, he preserves them by identifying with their behaviour. In these trains of thought the processes of seduction and appropriation are discernible.

Paul Diel's ethico-biological interpretations turn hunting from a spiritual quest for the divine into the indulgences of a DIONYSOS Zagreos, the Great Hunter, displaying the god's lust for sensual pleasure. Hunting now only symbolizes the pursuit of ephemeral enjoyment and a sort of servitude to an endless repetition of the same actions and the same satisfactions. On the other hand ARTEMIS, the huntress with the silver bow, aims her arrows symbolically at animals, at men who indulge their base instincts and at monsters and giants. The Lady of the Beasts may, therefore, symbolize the internal struggle against instinct, violence, brutality and barbarism. What she hunts is bestiality rather than beasts. She it was who saved Iphigenia from being sacrificed by setting a hind in her place.

hurricane (see also STORM; TEMPEST)   In Amerindian tradition, hurricanes, cyclones, tornados, and whirlwinds are regarded as conspiracies by three of the elements (Air, Fire and Water) against the Earth in a revolt of the elements. Hurricanes are almost Dionysiac orgies of cosmic energy. They symbolize the ending of one period of time and the beginning of another as tireless Earth repairs the damage.

hut (see also TENT)   Huts symbolize the dwellings of nomads or travellers with no permanent city and may aptly be applied to Christians, dwelling in a strange land; since their home is in Heaven, Earth is an alien country and a hut denotes their bodily life on Earth. The reeds and branches from which it is made denote the precariousness of that life. The hut itself is an image of weakness and instability and its cramped confines fit a life of solitude and contemplation.

This is why William of St Thierry in his *Epistola aurea ad fratres de Monte-Dei*, conjures up the hermits of Chartreuse, writing: 'Like the Children of Israel, that is, like passing travellers, you who are spiritual, having no abiding place on earth and seeking the city that is to come, must build for yourselves little huts.'

Huts also play a role in initiations, as the threshold of the Otherworld. They are the equivalent of the MONSTER's jaws or belly, of the dragon, of the funerary urn, or of the man-eating woodcutter's cottage where the ogre lurks ready to eat up Hop o' my Thumb and his seven little brothers. Death and putrefaction are the gates of the Otherworld, but initiates will leave the hut invigorated by a new life and 'possessed of mysterious treasures, symbols of the spiritual riches of initiation. From now on their seven-league boots give them mastery of space, their goose-with-the-golden-eggs mastery of mankind, their secret key mastery of the invisible' (SERH 103–4, 119).

hybrid In African legend there is a wealth of significance in whatever suffers from DEFORMITY or is abnormal. There must be some purpose behind such a disturbance of custom and the natural order. A supernatural force is involved: the monstrous is a mark of holiness.

Certain laws govern the depiction of hybrids. For example such fabulous creatures as CENTAURS, SIRENS or SPHINXES, which are part human and part animal, are depicted sometimes with the human portion uppermost (as in the case of the sphinx), sometimes the animal (as in the case of the falcon-headed god Horus). There is a logic to this. The upper part was considered to be closer to higher things, and there are very good reasons why such a part should be given either animal or human shape. In a serpent-man, for example, the fact that the human feet are given the animal shape of a snake's body, while the head remains human, is a favourable omen. The being, in fact, belongs to a higher plane in its upper portions, that is to say that the upper portion of its body has a higher specific quality than the lower portion, since the one is human and the other completely animal. Thus the snake-man is often regarded as the mystagogue who puts his disciples or pilgrims to the test. Another example is the lion-headed man as a symbol of kingship, in which strength rather than justice predominates, and of bull-headed men, mystagogues in agrarian cults.

Lions and eagles are often associated. The composite creature with eagle's head, wings and claws will then represent the human body and soul. If 'sometimes they are depicted biting one another, the primary notion is not one of fighting, but of two creatures bound together and interpenetrating one another, which can only be achieved by eating one another so that they constantly pass from one to the other. The motif becomes all the more clear when a human figure is associated with these two' (CHAS pp. 265–6). At other times they may symbolize the savage confrontation which takes place within the individual between temptation to evil and aspiration to good.

Hydra This monstrous serpent with seven or nine heads, which grew again as fast as they were cut off, has often been likened to the delta of a mighty river with its countless channels rising and falling with the tide. It represents

the whole catalogue of vices (as much in the shape of those pursued in the heated imagination as of those committed by a sordid greed).... Because its home was a marsh, the hydra has become characterized as the symbol of the more sordid vices. While the monster lives, and so long as human vanity is uncontrolled, its heads, symbolizing the vices themselves, will grow again even if one or two of them are cut off by ephemeral efforts at self-control.

(DIES p. 208)

The Hydra's blood was poisonous and Herakles (Hercules) dipped his arrows in it. This confirms the symbolic interpretation: contact with vice and its consequences are corrupting and corrupted.

hyena The fact that the hyena is both a nocturnal creature and a carrion-eater give it a doubly ambivalent symbolic meaning in Africa.

It is characterized in the first place by the animal's greed, its scenting powers – hence the powers of divination attributed to it – and the strength of jaws able to crack the toughest bones. These factors make the hyena an allegorical figure of knowledge and understanding. However, despite its extraordinary cleverness, it remains a completely terrestrial and mortal creature. Its knowledge and understanding become coarse and heavy-handed simplicity, verging on the ridiculous, and stupidity and even cowardice when contrasted with God's transcendental wisdom and knowledge. It is in this sense that the Bambara regard it as standing opposed to the vulture, even if it complements its symbolism; like the hyena, the vulture is a carrion-eater, but airborne and therefore divine. The hyena stands for an initiatory stage on the path of wisdom which corresponds to the acquisition of real but profane knowledge. It should not attempt to compete with divine knowledge, embodied in a much higher grade of initiate, the LION, a symbol of calm, untroubled wisdom. In the sacred drama staged by the Kore Society, a glance from the 'Lion', a senior grade of initiate, is enough to put the 'Hyena' to flight. In the hierarchy of this secret society, the hyena is allotted the role of 'captive', who in former Bambara social structures had the task of guarding the king and his dwelling. In fact, initiates with the grade of Hyena have the task of guarding the sacred grove in which the society meets.

Hyperborean Greek mythology often mentions the Land of the Hyperboreans: but where was it? Herodotus admitted that he did not know. Undoubtedly it was somewhere in the north, in the far north, beyond the land in which Boreas blew, at the back of the north wind. It may perhaps have been a folk memory, homesickness for the lands from which the Hellenes migrated to Greece in the second millennium BC. Gallet de Santerre believes that 'it would seem as if the Greeks came to regard the Land of the Hyperboreans in much the same way as they regarded Ethiopia or Atlantis, for example, as a sort of distant Paradise, home of the Blessed but geographically ill-defined' (quoted in SECG p. 217). Geographical accuracy is in any case hardly necessary for a knowledge of the Greek imagination. The land was the gilded land of dreams, of ideal childhood and of every Golden Age. It had been Apollo's childhood home, where his mother, Leto, had been born, and periodically he returned to it after a nineteen-year astral cycle. It was there that he hid from Zeus' anger and from there that he shot the miraculous arrow which became the constellation, Sagittarius. Olen, a Hyperborean, was supposed to have founded the oracle of Delphi and, when the invading Galati approached the shrine, they were frightened away by the sight of Hyperborean phantoms. Pythagoras was supposed to have been the reincarnation of a Hyperborean. Hyperboreans became a sort of supermen – or space aliens, as they would be called today – living in a kind of Utopia in wisdom and happiness and a vague aura of magic.

hyssop   In the Old Testament hyssop is constantly associated with purification ceremonies. It was a constituent of lustral water, used for aspersions and mingled with blood for the purification of lepers. Hyssop branches were used to sprinkle the door-posts with the blood of the Passover lamb. Thus hyssop is associated with the original Covenant and with the Second Covenant made by Christ, the Pascal Lamb. What the Synoptic Gospels term the reed offered to Christ on the Cross, is described as hyssop in St John's Gospel.

According to Philo, hyssop was used as a condiment by the most refined gourmets at banquets.

St Bernard of Clairvaux in his forty-fifth sermon on the Song of Solomon wrote: 'Beauty of the soul is humility. I do not say this of myself since the Prophet said before me "Purge me with hyssop and I shall be clean" [Psalm 51: 7], taking this humble herb which cleanses the breast as a symbol of humility. It was with hyssop that, after his heavy sin, the prophet-king cleansed himself and thus regained the snow whiteness of innocence.'

I

ibis (see also HERON; STORK)   Incarnation of the Ancient Egyptian god Thoth, patron of astronomers, scribes, magicians, healers and enchanters. His assimilation with the Greek god Hermes generated the syncretic and esoteric writings attributed to Hermes Trismegistus, the title given to Thoth meaning 'Thrice Great'. With its pointed beak, the ibis might well symbolize the practical application of the intellect, but however practical it might be, its knowledge would not preclude recourse to esoteric wisdom.

As it did to the cock, the Old Testament attributed to the ibis the gift of foreknowledge, for as the cock heralded the dawn, so the ibis heralded the flooding of the Nile. Some would regard the ibis as a lunar bird because its beak curves like the crescent Moon (SOUL p. 39). The shape, however, has inspired a different and far less poetic interpretation. The ibis might well stand for a symbol of health, since its beak is shaped like a clyster (enema syringe) and might be used for the same purpose, Pliny (*Natural History* 8: 27) believing that the bird itself so used it. Hence both Greek and Roman poets, Callimachus and Ovid for example, sometimes use the epithet 'ibis' as a pejorative (TERS p. 221).

Icarus   Son of Daedalus and a slave-girl, his father's inventions caused his death because he disregarded parental warnings when making use of them. Because his father had helped Ariadne and Theseus to kill the Minotaur, they were both imprisoned in the Labyrinth. With the help of Pasiphaë and thanks to the wings which Daedalus had made and fixed to his shoulders with wax, Icarus was enabled to escape from their prison. He flew across the sea but, disregarding his father's prudent warning to take the middle course and not to fly too high, he rose ever closer and closer to the Sun. The wax melted in the heat and Icarus tumbled into the sea and drowned. As an image of the spirit's overweening ambition, Icarus is the symbol of 'deadened intellect and of perverted imagination. He is a mythic embodiment of psychic disorder characterized by self-centred emotional exaltation of the spirit. Icarus stands for the neurotic and his fate. Icarus' senseless exploit has remained proverbial for neurosis taken to extremes, for a form of spiritual sickness, megalomania' (DIES p. 50). Icarus is the symbol of the rash and uncontrolled, the twofold perversion of judgement and courage.

Early Christian writers considered Icarus' downfall as an image of the soul which raises itself aloft on the wings of false love when only the wings of divine love can support its ascent.

icon   By the word 'icon' is meant divine or holy images in general and not specifically the form they take in the Eastern Church.

Icons are unrelated to portrait painting; whatever resemblance there may be is ideal rather than real and depends upon the extent to which the image shares the divine reality which it is intended to express. For, first and foremost, the icon is a representation – within the limitations inherent in the basic impossibility of adequately conveying the divine – of transcendent reality and an aid to meditation. It is intended to fix the spirit upon the image, which itself reflects the spirit, and concentrate it upon the reality which the image symbolizes.

Icons are generally recognized as not having been made by the hand of man, which insulates them from any notion of physical representation. Although the image of Our Lady was attributed to St Luke, the Mandilion originated miraculously; while the image of the Buddha was either projected by him upon canvas or taken up from the shadow which he cast upon the ground. All subsequent icons were reproductions of supernatural prototypes, created under conditions involving strict preparation and according to precise rules.

Of course the image of Christ is distinct from its divine model. The image of the Buddha is no more than an illusory reflection, an artifice (*upāya*). Nevertheless, Christ's icon partakes at the same time of the nature of its model and extends his incarnation, while the Buddha's icon allows a comprehension of the reality beyond shape which it evokes in this illusory fashion. It is the result of the original vow of the Bodhisattva, to remain on Earth until the last being attained deliverance. This twofold aspect explains why the Jōdō sect teaches that, while an image of the Blessed One may be a means of grace and even of salvation, it can be used to light a fire if one is cold. A Zen apologia denies that it is sacrilege to use statues of the saints in this way.

An icon is never an end in itself, but always a means, being, it has been said, a window on Earth open to Heaven, but a window which allows a two-way traffic. The gilded background of Byzantine icons – and the gilding, too, of the Buddha – is, properly speaking, heavenly light, the glow of the transfiguration. Set, as they are in the Greek Church, upon an iconostasis, icons are on the dividing line of the sensory and spiritual worlds. They are a reflection of the spiritual in the sensory and a means whereby the latter can accede to the other.

The icon as an end in itself justifies outbreaks of iconoclasm, and if iconoclasm occurs in the teachings of the Buddha it would appear to have been directed against human images which can only be the focus of idolatry and not against channels of spiritual influences. The non-human image is the gift of the Buddha's grace and is its privileged assistant (BURA, BENA, COOI, OUSI, SCHO, SCHD, SECA).

incense The symbolism of incense derives from the combinations of those of SMOKE, PERFUME and of the imperishable resins from which it is made. The trees which provide them have sometimes been taken as symbols of Christ. It is the duty of incense to carry prayer heavenwards, and in this sense it is a symbol of the priestly office. This is the reason why one of the Three Wise Men brought incense to the Christ-child. Burning incense is universal and everywhere carries the same symbolic property, associating human beings with the godhead, the finite with the infinite and the mortal with the immortal. Hence to rise in a cloud of smoke has more often a positive rather than a negative significance. In this context, there is little difference between the smoke of a funeral pyre, of Maya copal, of Christian incense or of the tobacco of the North American Indians. The significance of the North American Indian CALUMET is only comprehensible in terms of a symbol which, with some trifling exceptions, seems to speak a universal language. Whether it was the pipe of peace or the pipe of war, the calumet ratified covenants or treaties through the presence of the godhead, invited to preside over the celebrations by the cloud of smoke ascending skywards. As countless Ancient Chinese rituals bear witness, smoke – from rushes or reeds – was used in the same way as an agent of purification. Although the smoke of the funeral pyre was supposed to carry the dead person's soul upwards, alchemists had no need of one, claiming that it was possible to see the soul in the shape of a smoky vapour leaving the body in its death agony. Celtic tradition contains the same symbolic notion.

In Hindu ritual, incense (*dhūpa*) is related to the element of Air and is supposed to stand for 'the perception of consciousness' which is 'omnipresent'.

Although the smoke of incense is used as an artificial stimulant in certain Yoga practices, in Buddhist meditation the burning of joss-sticks is used to mark the passage of time (AVAS, DANA, GRIF, GUER).

In Central America the symbolism of incense derives from that of blood, sap, semen and rain. Like clouds, the smoke of incense is an emanation of the divine spirit, 'smoke' and 'cloud' being related words in the languages of Central America. Hence the sending up of clouds of smoke (sympathetic magic) in rain-making rituals. In the *Popol-Vuh*, the culture-heroine, an Underworld deity, extracted sticky, red sap from the copal and gave it to mankind as her own blood (myth of the origin of copal). From that day to this the Maya-Quiché have used copal in all religious rituals to drive off evil spirits. The *Chilam Balam Chumayel* states that 'incense is a heavenly resin, its scent drawn up to the midst of Heaven.' Thus the use of incense derives from fertility-rites linked to the lunar cycle. The relationship between 'copal' and 'Moon' is, furthermore, expressed in their common root *uh* in the Chorti language. As representations of the rain-gods, the hierophants would set alternately upon the holy table slabs of copal and sacred pitchers full of 'virgin water'. Even nowadays, priests still go in procession to tap the sap of the copal and burn incense at midnight on the last day of the dry season, to speed the coming of the first rains (GRID pp. 106–8).

incest Incest symbolizes the tendency of like to marry with like, even to the point of exalting the individual's own essence and discovering and conserving the most deeply embedded ego. It is a kind of 'autism'. In most mythologies it occurs among gods, kings and pharaohs, and in closed societies which attempt to preserve and strengthen their essential supremacy: among the Ancient Egyptians (Isis married her brother, Osiris, and bore four children to her son, Horus), the Inca, Polynesians, Greeks and so on.

In Irish mythology, incest between brother and sister would appear to be the rule for the births of the gods. In the same way the hero Cùchulainn was the son of King Conchobar (surrogate for the god Lug) and his sister Medb, who, before her marriage with Ailill, had had sexual intercourse with both

her brothers. In the tale 'The Courtship of Etain', the Queen of Ireland is
ready to commit adultery with her husband's brother and, in the original
version of the legend, the Dagda does commit adultery with his sister Boann,
his brother Elcmar's wife. It would seem that here we have an explanation
for the polyandry which Caesar reports of the Bretons in *De bello gallico*.
A sole and single goddess balanced the four gods of the Irish pantheon.
While remaining a virgin, she was wife of all four, like the Hindu Pandavas.
Incest, which has nothing whatever to do with the potential immorality of
these mythical Irish figures, may well be an echo of the Adamic age of the
Book of Genesis (OGAC 18: pp. 363–410; CELT p. 15).

Analysts regard the unconscious or repressed temptation towards incest
as constituting 'the Oedipus or Electra complex, as the case may be, which
would represent a normal phase of infantile sexuality in the course of an
individual's development. Neurosis would, however, result solely from
fixation' (PORP p. 214). A distinction should, nonetheless, be drawn between semi-animal incest, which varies between the infantile norm, the
social taboo, sexual perversion and neurosis, and semi-religious incest, rife
with symbols and based upon belief.

The incestuous unions of antiquity were not a result of a love inclination, but
of a special superstition, which is most intimately bound up with . . . mythical
ideas. . . . A Pharaoh of the second dynasty is said to have married his sister, his
daughter and his granddaughter; the Ptolemies were accustomed also to marriage with sisters; Kambyses married his sister; Artaxerxes married his two
daughters; Qobad I (sixth century AD) married his daughter. The satrap
Sysimithres married his mother. These incestuous unions are explained by the
circumstance that in the Zend Avesta the marriage of relatives was directly
commanded; it emphasised the resemblance of rulers to the divinity.

(JUNL p. 257)

There is no certainty that in all cases the teachings of the Avesta were
decisive. Incest would seem to correspond not merely to the situation within
closed societies, but also to closed or restricted psyches which are incapable
of assimilating the 'other'. It evinces deficiency or regression. Although it
may appear normal at one given stage of development, incest is evidence
of a barrier, a bottleneck or a halt in the moral and psychic development
of a society or of an individual.

Although Greek mythology is full of incestuous marriages and primitive
endogamy has left its mark on both society and the psyche, incest inspired
a feeling of religious horror in the Greek tragic poets and in the collective
soul of their audience. Sophocles' *Oedipus Rex* bases its entire dramatic
strength upon this feeling of horror. In Rome, incest was forbidden by law
and those found guilty of it were flung from the Tarpeian Rock.

initiation To initiate is to bring one in. At the same time, it has the meaning
of the Greek word *teleutan,* to die, in some way to put to death, or cause
to die. Death, however, is not regarded as the end, but as an escape, crossing the threshold of a gateway leading to another life. Going out of the one
is followed by going into the other.

The initiate passes through the fiery curtain which separates the sacred
from the profane. By passing from one world to another the initiate

undergoes a transformation, changes the plane of existence and becomes a different being.

The transmutation of metals, in its alchemical, symbolic sense, is another initiation demanding death and the rites of passage. Initiation works a metamorphosis.

The 'death' of the initiate is unrelated to human psychology, but is death to the world in so far as it implies surmounting the profane state. The candidate seems to undergo a process of regression, and his or her rebirth has been compared with a return to the foetal state within the mother's womb. Of course the candidate delves into the darkness, but the darkness concerned is to be compared, not so much with that of the womb, but far more with cosmic darkness.

Mircea Eliade has discussed these rituals (ERAJ 23: pp. 65ff.): they all involve the 'death' of the candidate, with specific differences. In some, for example, he or she may be laid in a grave specially dug for the purpose, covered with branches and dusted with a white powder to a corpse-like whiteness. They are rites of passage symbolizing the birth of a new being.

On the Christian level, suffering is linked to the transition from one state to another, from the old to the new man, with its various ordeals. To appreciate their nature, one has only to go back to the Desert Fathers and to the ordeals which they suffered from diabolical powers. Hence the name 'temptations' applied to these phenomena, the most celebrated, and the most grotesque, being those endured by St Anthony. Christianity identified the powers of evil with the devils tormenting the individual as he passed from a profane state to one of sanctity, not through personal choice but by election.

The 'death' of the initiate prefigures physical death, which itself should be considered as an essential initiation into a new life. However, before this physical death, the individual can create the body glorious by constant repetition of that initiatory death in the sense in which St Paul (1 Corinthians 15: 31) demands it of Christians. In fact, through grace and while living in the profane world to which the Christian does not cease to belong, he or she can enter into eternity. Immortality is not something acquired after death, it is no post-mortem condition, but is shaped in the temporal state and is the result of death by initiation.

ink (see also RED) Wounds inflicted upon the martyrs were compared with WRITING in honour of Christ. Prudentius (*Peristephanon* 3: 136–40) has St Eulalia exclaim: 'See, lord, thy name is being written on me . . . The very scarlet [*purpura*] of the blood that is drawn speaks thy holy name.' It should be observed that in Byzantium, purple ink was kept by the imperial chamberlain, who alone was allowed to use it. This ink had special properties and should be distinguished from the red ink used in medieval writing and illumination. Purple ink is writing in blood, writing which links in indestructible union.

insects In Central America, small flying insects were often regarded as the souls of the dead revisiting Earth. In Guatemala, where the belief endures, they are associated with the stars (THOH).

intoxication (see also CIRCUMAMBULATION; DANCE) Because intoxication is linked to fertility and harvesting the riches of the soil, it derives from lunar phenomena. In fact, in traditional symbolism, the Moon controls the cycle of plant life, pregnancy and growth. Hence fertility-gods and -goddesses are, generally speaking, lunar deities.

Spiritual intoxication is a universal symbol. It is as much at home for esoterics themselves as it is in the language of both Christian and Muslim mystics, for whom it produces the loss of consciousness 'of everything which is foreign to the Truth, even forgetfulness of our own state of forgetfulness'. Spiritual intoxication is more than a mere 'transport' of the mental faculties, since wine is itself a synonym for knowledge. Nor is it entirely a verbal symbol, an analogy. Almost throughout the world recourse is had to physical intoxication as a means of inducing spiritual intoxication, by freeing oneself from the constraints of the external world and from life ruled by consciousness. This is as true of the Greek mysteries as of Taoism where the Sages were famous drinkers, and Lu-ling writes that when drunk one no longer feels heat or cold, the passions disappear and the swarming masses of humanity are no more than 'drops of water floating on the Chi-an or Han rivers'. In the beginning of things, Yu the Great, who used to perform ecstatic dances, indulged in drunkenness.

A Tantric author assures us that 'if you drink and drink afresh and drink again and drink until you collapse, and then, if you get up and start drinking all over again, you break for ever the cycle of rebirth.' This might be an acceptable symbol of spiritual intoxication, but is concerned with something very different, the drinking-bout, in this context the symbol of the breath control exercises and the arousing of *kundalinī* (sexual energy). Falling to the ground is the downward return of energy to the 'root-centre' (*mulādhāra-chakra*), corresponding to Earth. Repetition leads ultimately to deliverance (CORM, ELIY, GRAD, MAST, SCHO).

Drunkenness was the rule at the great Irish feast of Samain when beer and mead flowed in oceans. Most literary sources extol the 'confusion of drunkenness', without intending or even hinting that the phrase should be taken pejoratively. It is quite understandable that it should be a feature of a festival symbolically celebrated outside the human time-scale and during which the Celts believed that they communicated directly with the gods of the Otherworld. This contact was only possible through a sacred intoxication which allowed the individual to escape for a few hours from his normal condition (OGAC 13: pp. 481–506).

Iris In Greek mythology, Iris was the messenger of the gods and especially of Zeus and Hera. She was the female equivalent of Hermes. Like him she was winged, light-footed and swift. She wore winged sandals, carried a caduceus and dresssed in a rainbow-coloured veil which fluttered in the breeze. 'She symbolized the rainbow and, more generally speaking, the links between Heaven and Earth, gods and humans' (GRID p. 238). Because in his *Theogony* Hesiod describes her as the daughter of Thaumas (wonder) and Electra (AMBER) some are inclined to regard her as the symbol of and channel through which flows a divinely derived psychic fluid.

Iris is also the name of a spring flower which in Japan is used as a purifier and preservative. Iris-leaves (*shōbu*) are put in baths to protect the body against disease and evil spirits and upon house roofs as a preservative against evil external influences and fire. They were sometimes planted on thatched roofs with the same objective in mind (OGRJ). On 5 May the Japanese take an 'iris-bath' to obtain these favours in the year to come.

iron (see also BLACKSMITH; EMBRYO; LODESTONE; METAL) Iron commonly symbolizes durability, hardness, obstinacy, harshness and inflexibility, qualities not wholly shared by the metal itself.

Both in Old Testament and Ancient Chinese tradition iron is set in opposition to copper or bronze, as the base opposed to the noble metal, Water to Fire, north to south, black to red, *yin* to *yang*. The Iron Age is the 'hard' age when the cycle finally 'set' into its mould, the Bronze Age was its penultimate stage. The iron or bronze foreheads of mythic heroes and the iron and bronze planks of the symbolic bridge in the legends of the Hong demonstrate the same polarization.

The idea of iron being a base metal is not held consistently and many races have, on the contrary, given it a positive sacred quality, perhaps because meteoritic iron was regarded as having fallen from Heaven, or perhaps because it seemed to corroborate the traditional view of metal as embryonic in the womb of Earth. Nevertheless, the symbolism of iron is ambivalent, as is that of metal-working in general. Iron may be a preservative against evil influences, but it is also their instrument. It is the agent of the active principle which changes inert substances (see CHISEL; KNIFE; PLOUGH), but it is also the diabolical instrument of war and of death. The changes effected to matter by cutting tools do not in themselves possess a positive aspect since iron tools were forbidden in the building of Solomon's Temple (1 Kings 6: 6–7). In India, iron-working is clearly Asuric, that is to say the department of gods of the second rank. The Ancient Egyptians identified iron with the bones of Set, essentially a god of darkness. Iron is, however, what gives the shaman power and makes him effective. It is, in any case, regarded as a fertility symbol with power to protect the harvest. Its ambivalence is always that of the smithy (ELIF, GRIH).

In Mali, the Dogon cosmology also sets the symbolism of iron in opposition to that of copper. Iron is lord of darkness and night, while copper is essentially the symbol of brightness and day (GRIE). Hence iron is an attribute of the evil Demiurge Yurugu, the pale fox, lord of the first word and of divination, who rules darkness, barrenness, drought, disorder, pollution and death (DIED). However, the second Demiurge, Nommo, the benefactor who guides mankind, all-powerful lord of heaven, water, souls and fertility, restricts the disruptive activities of Yurugu. Mankind is not subjected to the duality of these conflicting forces and the blacksmith, created by Nommo, can make iron his servant and from it hoes, the essential tools of the farmer, hunting weapons and weapons of war. The blacksmith made Yurugu his hidden friend, feared by women but from whom men could draw benefit. The pale fox or its surrogate, the jackal, is the creature most employed by the Dogon in their divination and their blacksmiths often have the added function of soothsaying (GRIE, DIED, PAUC).

Among the Watchaga, a Hamitic tribe from Kenya, the women wear iron necklaces and bangles to stimulate pregnancy and cure their children's ill-nesses. The Tiv in northern Nigeria regard iron as a sure means of com-munion between the living and the dead (CLIM).

In his *Works and Days*, Hesiod paints a terrifying picture of the cruelty, perfidy and blood-thirstiness of the fifth race of men, the Iron Age. In his apocalyptic vision they symbolize the rule of materialism and of regression towards brute force and the unconscious.

Coming from the Underworld, iron was a base metal which needed to be kept isolated from life. According to Plato (*Critias* 119e) the citizens of Atlantis hunted with wooden spears and nets, not with iron weapons. Simi-larly, the druids could not use iron implements, but cut the sacred mistletoe with a golden sickle.

Iron symbolizes harsh, 'dark', polluted and hellish strength.

Isis (see also VULTURE)   The most illustrious of all Ancient Egyptian god-desses, Isis is depicted searching for her murdered brother and husband, Osiris, whom she restored to life with her breath (see HALCYON); suckling her son, Horus; or in funeral processions protecting the dead in the shadow of her wings and bringing them back to life. From her faithfulness and devotion, she would appear originally to have been a hearth-goddess, but, according to legend, she 'obtained the secret NAME of the all-powerful god', Ra, and became his equal in power, spreading her influence across the universe. Every living being was a drop of Isis' blood. In fact, Isis was worshipped as the all-powerful universal goddess all round the Mediterra-nean Basin, as devoutly in Greece and Rome as in the Near East: 'I am the mother of the whole of Nature, mistress of the elements, the origin and principle of the ages, the supreme divinity, queen of the shades, the first of the dwellers in the sky, the unrivalled model of all the gods and goddesses. The pinnacles of the sky, the beneficial sea-breezes, the desolate silences of hell, I rule them all according to my will' (quoted by Serge Sauneron in POSD p. 138). All esoteric groups regarded her as the mystagogue who held the secrets of life and death and resurrection. The ANKH was the sym-bol of her boundless power. In all mystery religions of the early centuries of the Christian era, she was the embodiment of the female principle and sole magic source of fertility and transmutation.

island   Islands which can only be reached at the end of a long voyage or flight are pre-eminently symbols of a spiritual CENTRE or, more exactly, of the primordial spiritual centre.

Primeval 'Syria', mentioned by Homer and with the same root as the Sanskrit name for the Sun, *Sūryā*, was an island, the central or polar island of the world. It is to be identified with Hyperborean Tula (the Thule of the Greeks), its name recurring among the Toltec who came originally from the island of Aztlan (or Atlantis). Tula was the 'White Island', its name (*Svetadvīpa*) recurring in myths of Vishnu, current from India to Cambo-dia, where it is given to the temple of Prasat Kōk Pō. The 'White Island' is the abode of the Blessed, as is the Celtic 'Green Island' – from which rises the polar 'White Mountain' – its name recurring in that of Ireland. The primordial Japanese island, Awa, the foam-island, and especially Onogorojima, formed by the crystallization of the salt water dripping from

Izanagi's spear-point, were also 'white islands'. In Muslim tradition, the earthly Paradise is an island, Sri Lanka. Zeus was born on Minos' holy island, Crete, home of the mysteries.

Chinese myth also located island Paradises in the eastern sea and many emperors, victims of charlatanism, tried to reach them with their fleets. However, it was common knowledge that such islands could only be reached by those who were able to fly, namely the Immortals. Imperial fleets are believed to have discovered Taiwan and perhaps Japan. However, Yao had already reached the Isle of the Four Masters, called Chu-che, and identical with Tula (*Chuang Tzu* ch. 1); or had he merely reached the centre of his own self?

That central, lofty island which the Grail epic calls Monsalvat finds its precise equivalent in Khmer architecture. This is the tiny temple of Neak Pean, set in the middle of a square lake. This is perhaps that Lake Anavatapta which cured sickness of body and mind, but it is also that 'ocean of existences', that 'sea of passions' of the yogi. The temple is that 'isle beyond compare', mentioned in the *Suttanipāta*, located 'beyond the fearful tide of existence', polar stability in worldly flux, lastly Nirvana. St Isaac of Nineveh is writing on precisely similar lines when he compares the different sorts of knowledge obtained by a monk through his mysticism with 'so many islands, until at last he comes ashore and makes his way to the City of Truth, whose inhabitants do not trade, but each is rich in his own possession.' This is the Kingdom of the Spirit, the home of great peace, the island of Pong-lai (BHAB, COEA, PHIL, GRIA, GUER, GUES, SILI).

Celts have always depicted the Otherworld and the Beyond of the Irish wonder-voyagers in the shape of islands lying to the west (or north) of the world. The Irish gods, or Tuatha De Danann, 'Children of the Goddess Dana', came with their magic charms from 'four islands to the north of the world', and Ireland, with her central province of Meath (*Mide*, 'middle') was itself a holy island. Nevertheless, it would seem that Britain was the pre-eminent island since it was there, according to Caesar (and as Irish sources confirm), that the druids went to finish their training, to obtain their knowledge of holy things and to strengthen their doctrinal orthodoxy. A number of mythical islands were solely inhabited by women and they reflect the fact that colleges really did exist on islands off the coast of Gaul. On Sena (the Isle of Sein), for example, lived priestesses who foretold the future and claimed to be able to change themselves into whatever creature they wished. Mona (Anglesey), was the great centre of Druidism, destroyed by the Romans during the first-century AD British revolt. Islands were thus miniature worlds, complete and perfect images of the cosmos, because they represented a concentration of sacral qualities. In this way they are notionally linked to temples and shrines. Symbolically, islands are dwellings of the elect, of knowledge and of peace in the midst of the sea of ignorance and disorder of the profane world. They represent a primeval centre, holy by definition, and their essential colour is white. The original name of Britain was 'Albion', the 'White Island' (LERJ pp. 1052–62).

Modern psychoanalysis has laid particular stress upon one of the essential features of islands – they evoke sanctuaries. One of the basic themes of literature, dreams and desires is the quest for the desert island, the unknown island, the island with a wealth of surprises, and this perhaps makes space exploration a facet of this quest. Islands may be sanctuaries where will and consciousness come together to escape the assaults of the unconscious, as rocks provide a refuge from ocean waves.

From the psychoanalytic viewpoint the desire for earthly or eternal happiness is transferred to Fortunate Islands. Thetis was supposed to have carried the body of Achilles to the White Island at the mouth of the Danube, where the hero married Helen and enjoyed a life of eternal happiness with her. Apollo ruled the Isles of the Blessed. They were to become one of the fundamental myths, along with legends of a Golden Age, in Orphism and neo-Pythagoreanism. In his *Works and Days* (170–5), Hesiod describes how the divine race of demi-gods and heroes dwell 'untouched by sorrow in the islands of the blessed along the shore of the deep-swirling Ocean . . . for whom the grain-giving earth bears honey-sweet fruit flourishing thrice a year.'

ivory By its whiteness ivory is a symbol of purity. In addition, its use in King Solomon's throne might associate it with the symbolism of power, in the sense that its hardness makes ivory virtually unbreakable and incorruptible. Homer, who perhaps never saw ivory, contrasts ivory with horn as an expression of lies contrasted with the truth. Such dualism would seem difficult to justify. It is only given expression in an interpolated passage in the *Odyssey*, riddled with puns and of doubtful authenticity. Despite this, it has been frequently quoted and copiously commented upon. It is useless to offer the explanation that horn is transparent like the truth, while ivory is opaque like lies. The passage in question (19: 562–9) is the famous description of the Gate of Dreams: 'For two are the gates of shadowy dreams, and one is fashioned of horn and one of ivory. Those dreams that pass through the gate of sawn ivory deceive men, bringing words that find no fulfilment. But those that come forth through the gate of polished horn bring true issues to pass, when any mortal sees them.'

'Pliny reports that the stone called *chernites* is like ivory and like ivory preserves the body from all decay. Because of this quality, Darius' tomb was built of *chernites*' (PORS p. 58). This belief of the Persians confirms the quality of incorruptibility linked to the symbolism of ivory.

ivy DIONYSOS is generally depicted wreathed in ivy which, as an evergreen, symbolizes the enduring strength of plant life and the persistence of desire. Numerous Tanagra statuettes are decorated with ivy leaves or tendrils. They assured their wearers of the god's protection. Perhaps this need for protection has made the ivy a female symbol.

Dionysos used ivy as he used the vine, to carry away in mystical delirium those women who refused him worship. But once caught up by the divine frenzy they fled, like the daughters of Minyas, to join the Maenads in the mountains (GRID p. 229).

Ivy was also sacred to Attis, loved by Cybele, goddess of Earth and harvest. It stood for the eternal cycle of death and rebirth and the myth of the eternal homecoming.

Ixion Having lured his father-in-law into an ambush and murdered him, Ixion was shunned by gods and mortals. Zeus, however, took pity on him, pardoned him, delivered him from his madness and allowed him to enter Olympus. Here Ixion fell in love with Zeus' wife, Hera, and attempted to seduce her. Zeus saw this and substituted for Hera a cloud shaped like the goddess. Ixion raped the cloud and from this coupling a monster was born which, in turn, fathered the centaurs. As punishment, Zeus bound him with serpents instead of ropes to a winged and flaming wheel. It spun Ixion through the air and landed him in Hell among all those who had outraged the gods. 'In this symbolic image of an imaginary fall are condensed spiritual perversion, pride (taking Zeus' place) and sexual perversion (seducing Hera).' Furthermore, by coupling with a cloud which Ixion took to be a yielding Hera, 'Ixion convinced himself that Hera preferred him, that is to say, his suppressed and guilty impurity was transformed into megalomaniac pride which made him believe he was enjoying perfect sublimity', symbolized by Hera. Deceiving Zeus, he deceived the spirit. 'He believed himself to be higher than the godhead.' All illusions of this sort cast their possessors into Hell. Ixion was thrown down 'from the sublime into the torments of subconscious life . . . . The myth of Ixion describes precisely the true cause of sexual impotence which is, in truth, simply the consequence of an inability to realize spiritual sublimity. This is the deepest significance of the guilty lust of this false hero who, in his pride, attempts the sublime (Hera) although he is powerless really to attain it' (DIES pp. 78–83). The wheel with wings of flame is a solar symbol, but Ixion is not identified with it and he is not, therefore, himself a solar symbol. He is merely tied to the wheel, which means that he has been raised to a solar level, that is the celestial and divine, which is not his own nature. That his bonds should be serpents, means that Ixion has perverted the links which joined him to the celestial symbols. He is to retain the privilege of eternal life, but in an eternity of torment, symbolized by these serpent-ropes. Ixion on his solar wheel is a mock-image of the Sun. His Heaven is a Hell.

J

jackal Becuse of its death-howl, its haunting of graveyards and its feeding on corpses, the jackal is a beast of ill omen, in the same category as the wolf. In Hindu iconography it is the steed of Devī in her sinister aspect.

Some Hindu writers make the jackal the symbol of lust, greed, cruelty and sensuality, in short, of all violent feelings and emotions.

The jackal has been regarded as the symbol of the Ancient Egyptian god Anubis, who was believed to be incarnate in the wild dog and was customarily depicted with a jackal's head. In fact, there were no jackals in Ancient Egypt and what we have are '"roving dogs", animals resembling the wolf, with large pointed ears and long muzzles, lithe bodies and long, bushy tails' (POSD p. 139). They were feared for their fleet-footed aggressiveness and roamed the mountains and graveyards. Anubis was the god whose duty it was to care for the dead, watching over their funeral rites and their voyage to the Otherworld. He was called 'Lord of the Necropolis' and his most famous shrine was at 'Cynopolis, city of dogs' (POSD pp. 11–12). This DOG- or jackal-like conductor of souls symbolizes death and the wanderings of the dead person until he or she reaches the Valley of Immortality. Although there are some superficial similarities, it would be wrong to identify him with CERBERUS of the Greek Underworld.

jade Like GOLD, jade is charged with *yang*, that is with cosmic energy (see YIN AND YANG). As the very symbol of *yang*, it 'is consequently endowed with a whole collection of solar, imperial and indestructible qualities'. Hence the important role which it played in Ancient China:

In the social order it embodied sovereignty and power; in medicine it was a panacea and was taken internally to obtain the regeneration of the body; it was also thought to be the food of the spirits, and the Taoists believed that it guaranteed immortality; hence the importance of jade in alchemy, and the place it has always held in burial beliefs and practices. We read in the writings of the alchemist Ko-Hung: 'If there is gold and jade in the nine apertures of the corpse, it will preserve the body from putrefaction.' And T'ao Hung-King (fifth century) gives us the following details: '... According to the regulations of the Han dynasty, princes and lords were buried in clothes adorned with pearls and with boxes of jade, for the purpose of preserving the body from decay.' Recent archaeological researches have borne out what these texts tell us about funeral jade.

(ELIT p. 438)

If jade, the *yang* principle in material form, was to preserve the body from decomposition, pearl, charged with *yin*, would assure the dead of rebirth.

A distinction is drawn between nephritic jade (silicate of calcium and magnesium) and jadeite (silicate of aluminium and sodium). The word 'jade' derives from the Latin *ilia* ('guts') via the Spanish *ijada* ('side') and the adjective 'nephritic' alludes to the specific use of this mineral in European medicine in cases of kidney disease. There is no such distinction in the Chinese word *yu* and old descriptions relate only to the beauty of the stone. In fact jadeite only supplanted nephritic jade in China during the eighteenth century, when the usurping Manchu Ching dynasty came to power, a fact of undoubted significance given that jade is linked with the exercise of the Mandate of Heaven.

Its beauty makes jade an emblem of perfection; of the five transcendent qualities of benignity, lucidity, resonance, immutability and purity; of most of the moral virtues of charity, prudence, justice, grace, harmony, sincerity and good faith; as well as of Heaven and Earth, of righteousness and, the *Li-Chi* adds, 'of the way of righteousness'. Thus, says Ségalen, to praise jade 'is to praise righteousness itself'. Jade is comfort, warmth and preciousness. It is not simply the sight or feel of jade which inclined a person to righteousness, perhaps it should be described rather by the successive stages of sight and contemplation followed by touch and physical perception. Another factor was resonance. Court officials wore jade ornaments on their girdles. Their resonance was precisely calculated so that, when he rode in his chariot, the sound would maintain the wearer in the paths of loyalty and righteousness. This resonance was in fact an echo of the chord which ruled the harmony of Heaven and Earth. As the *Pi*, the disc with a hole in the middle, jade symbolized Heaven.

It was for this reason that the imperial seal was made of jade and from earliest times transmission of the seal in practical terms was the same as passing on the Mandate of Heaven. Jade therefore symbolized kingship. Furthermore the ideogram *yu* is almost detail for detail similar to the ideogram *wang*, denoting the sovereign in the character of a ruler. In fact *wang* derives from the root *yu* and thus it might be said that 'jade' makes the 'sovereign'. The ideogram comprises three horizontal brush-strokes cut by a vertical stroke and is unanimously regarded as an image of the Supreme Triad – Heaven, Mankind and Earth – united by the World Axis, or Way. The Central Way (*Chung-tao*) is identified with the Royal Way (*wang-tao*) – 'the One uniting the Three, is the King' (Tung Chung-chu).

If, therefore, *wang* is confirmed graphically as the 'Son of Heaven and Earth', the same is true of *yu*. Jade was believed to be formed in the womb of Earth through the agency of lightning, that is of cosmic activity. Cosmic impregnation was also the image of the way in which the 'Embryo of Immortality' was formed in internal alchemy. After all, the jade of Pien Ho which was used to make the talisman of the Chou was revealed by a phoenix. Alchemists also claimed that jade took shape in the womb of Earth in the slow 'ripening' of the embryonic stone. This made them regard it as to be identified with gold. Furthermore, knowing that the jade of these fabulous accounts is always white jade and that white is the colour of alchemical gold, it will be seen that jade and the Philosopher's Stone are identical and that jade is a symbol of immortality. It might be added that there exists another ideogram for *yu*, a combination of *kin* (gold) and *yu* (jade) with the meaning of 'pure gold'.

There was jade in plenty in the abode of the Immortals. As an elixir of longevity it was eaten in powdered form or liquefied or mixed with DEW and drunk from a jade chalice. Some objects placed in the grave and inscribed with 'jade characters' enabled the dead person to be reborn. Jade (or gold) inserted in votive statues endowed them with life. Jade partakes of the character of gold as the essential *yang*, it helps revive the individual and return him or her to a primeval state.

It should also be observed that many critics maintain that the primitive ideogram *yu* comprised three pieces of perforated jade joined by a thread or stalk. If this is so, it is an exact image of the primitive Vedic altar, its three pieces corresponding to the three worlds – Earth, Intermediate World and Heaven – with the stalk representing the World AXIS.

In Central America 'this stone symbolizes the soul, spirit, heart or nucleus of an individual' and is by analogy identified with bone (GIRP p. 57). In Mexico it was customary to place a piece of jade in the dead person's mouth.

According to Krickeberg (KRIR pp. 24–5), in Ancient Mexico, because of its translucency and green colour, 'jade was a symbol of water and the burgeoning of plant life.' The La Venta civilization regarded jade objects as essential items of grave-furniture. During the Classical period in Central America, priests offered the rain- and food-god 'precious water', containing jade chips or dust (KRIR). Jade was a Maya symbol of fructifying RAIN becoming, by extension, the symbol of BLOOD and of the new year.

When known as *Chalchiuatl*, 'precious water', green jade symbolized the blood of human sacrifice spurting out to revive the Sun or offered to the rain-god.

African races traditionally place the same symbolic meaning upon green stones. Thus, in a Dogon myth, a water spirit appeared, rising out of a storm-swollen stream. Round its head a 'rain-green' serpent was wreathed. When the spirit emerged from the waters, in the guise of a woman, the snake changed into a green stone which the woman hung from her neck. Similar stones endowed with sacred properties which link them to fertility are kept in Sudanese shrines (GAND).

For the highly important symbolism of the jade object, see under RING (GIEJ, GRIJ, JAQJ, LAUJ, LIOT, VUOC, SEGS).

jaguar   Central American Indians thought of four jaguars watching over the four tracks leading to the centre of their villages. This custom may have derived from the ancient Mayan belief that four mythic jaguars at the beginning of time guarded the maize-fields.

During the third Maya-Quiché age, corresponding with the cultivation of food-plots and hence with the pre-eminence of Moon-worship, the jaguar represented the Moon–Earth goddess. 'In Mayan and Mexican manuscripts the Earth–Moon goddess is normally depicted with jaguar's claws. It should be observed that the Quiché of Santander-Xecul still call the pot-bellied idols of the archaic period *balam* [jaguar]' (GIRP p. 172).

A stylized pair of jaguar-jaws symbolizes Heaven on monuments from the Classical period of Central America. During the historic era (from about 1000 AD onwards) jaguar and eagle, as decoration on monuments, stand for 'the earthly army whose duty it was to nourish the Sun and the Morning Star with the blood and hearts of human sacrifice' (KRIR p. 52).

The Maya, however, regarded the jaguar as being, above all, a god of the Underworld, the highest incarnation of the internal powers of the Earth. The jaguar was the god of the number NINE, a manifestation of the land 'below'. As lord of that Underworld he sometimes undertook the duties of conductor of souls. At dusk, the Earth is depicted as swallowing the Sun, the latter within the open jaws of a jaguar. Lastly the jaguar became a solar deity corresponding with the Sun's night journey. When the Sun is depicted as a jaguar it is the 'Black SUN' (THOH).

As an Underworld deity, the jaguar carries a CONCH-shell on his back, a symbol of his grandmother, the Moon, and, by extension, of birth (THOH). Again as an Underworld deity, the jaguar is also lord of the mountains, echoes, wild beasts and message-drums. He was called 'Heart of the Mountains'.

In the symbolism of earthly and heavenly powers, the jaguar was the counterpoise to the EAGLE and gave its name to one of the two highest orders of Aztec chivalry, the other being the Eagles (SOUA).

There are countless examples of the association of jaguar with eagle, as representatives of the mighty powers of Earth and Heaven, in Amerindian tradition. The Aztec emperor accepted the homage of his warriors while seated upon a throne set upon a carpet of eagle-plumes and backed by a jaguar-skin. When males are born into the Tupinamba tribe in Brazil, they are given jaguar-claws and eagle-talons (METT).

However, the Tupinamba regard the jaguar as a sky-god, celestial, looking like a sky-blue dog. Its home is high in the sky. It has two heads to eat the Sun and the Moon – this explains eclipses – and at the end of the world it will come down and eat up mankind (METT).

One might ask whether these two symbolic meanings given to the jaguar are not complementary, the powers of the upper and under worlds coming together to accomplish the final destruction of the world.

Alcide d'Arbigny recorded this myth from the Yurucari in Brazil in his *Voyage dans l'Amérique méridionale* (Paris, 1884). A human hero, seeking vengeance for the killing of his own family, hunted the last of the jaguars and forced it to climb a tree. Here it begged the Sun and the Moon for help. The Sun ignored the plea, but the Moon gathered the jaguar up and hid it. Thereafter it lived with the Moon and this is why jaguars are nocturnal creatures.

The same beliefs are to be found among countless South American Indian tribes, in Peru, Bolivia, Ecuador and the Guyanas, especially among the Chané, Uitoto (Colombia), Bakairi (Brazil), Guarani and Tupi (Brazil), Carib, Makusi and Warai of Venezuelan Guyana.

A jaguar with four eyes features in many South American Indian myths. It represents the gift of second sight possessed by the spirits of darkness and the Underworld. In Brazilian myths of the origin of fire, the jaguar is seen as a culture-hero giving mankind not only fire but their first crafts and especially that of extracting cotton fibre. However, the jaguar is not depicted as the discoverer of fire, but rather as its guardian to whom it was entrusted and who was the first to use it. It does not teach fire-making, which emphasizes its chthonian origins. The jaguar is not a Demiurge but perhaps an ancestor.

Janus   Janus, the ambivalent Indo-European deity with two faces, one on each side of the head, was one of the most ancient gods of Rome. Originally the god of gods and benevolent creator, he became the god of change and such transitions as that of development of past to future, of one condition to another, of one vision to another and of one universe to another. He was god of the GATE.

He was the presiding deity of the beginning of anything. The opening month of the year (January, from *janua*, 'gate') was sacred to him, as was the first day of each month. He presided over the start, and the Vestals the completion, of any enterprise. He ruled the birth of gods, the cosmos, mankind and its undertakings.

As warden of gates, which he opened and closed, his attributes were a doorkeeper's keys and staff. His two faces meant that he watched entrances as well as exits and saw into the internal as well as the external world, left and right, above and below, before and after, for and against. He was both vigilance and perhaps an image of an empire which knew no bounds. His shrines were archways, such as gateways or arcades at crossing places. Coins were struck with his head and, on the reverse, a ship.

jar (see also CAULDRON; POT; URN; VASE)   Jars, or amphorae, are commonly used as symbols in India and, above all, as the jar of inexhaustible plenty from which liquid flows as from a spring. Hence jars are attributes of river-deities. Jars also contain the beverage of immortality (*amrita*) and consequently of life itself. Jars act, too, as surrogates for the 'Guardians of Space' at places of sacrifice and are symbols of the 'treasures' guarded by Kuvera. In this context they are the same as COFFERS.

The symbolism of the jar of plenty is as familiar, too, to the Montagnards of Vietnam, where the jar full of rice-beer is most important as the focus of the communal drinking-party.

The Ancient Chinese used jars to hold wine, but for them jars were images of Heaven. To rap on a jar was to copy the thunder – locked underground during the Winter with all the *yang* forces – while a cracked jar let the lightning out, like the storm clouds.

Han dynasty potters and metal-workers produced 'mountain-jars' with conical lids on which were depicted the Isles of the Immortals. The jar was thus simultaneously the sea from which the island rose and a container for the beverage of immortality (GRAC, GROC).

It was in an amphora rather than in a tub that the philosopher, Diogenes, decided to live. In Crete, the bodies of dead children, arranged in the foetal position, were placed in amphorae which, in this instance, would seem to have been symbols of the source of physical and intellectual life, the mother's womb. They provided a sort of return to one's beginnings. In the *Iliad*, amphorae symbolize the sentences pronounced by Zeus which they hold. At the gates of his palace, the god deposited two amphorae, the one containing good, the other evil. Drawing alternately upon one or the other, Zeus showered mankind with good and evil. From this symbol of the overriding indifference of the god to the concerns of mankind, might develop theories either of blind chance or of providence.

jasper This stone was believed to influence women's diseases and was a symbol of childbirth. 'The obstetric virtues of the jasper may be explained by the fact that, when shattered, its womb gave birth to several other stones.' This makes the symbol abundantly clear. From the Babylonians the obstetric role of the jasper passed to the Greco-Roman world and continued down to the Middle Ages. Marbodius, the eleventh-century Bishop of Rouen, states that a jasper 'placed on the belly of a woman in childbirth relieves her pangs' (GOUL p. 201). Similar symbolism accounts for the similar regard in which 'eagle-stones' were held by Classical Antiquity, Pliny observing that they were useful to pregnant women. When shaken, they gave off a strange sound, as though they carried another stone concealed within them. The qualities of these gynaecological and obstetric stones derives directly, either from their share in the lunar principle, or else from their shape, setting them apart and marking them down as coming from some uncommon source. The basis of their magic resides in the fact that they are alive. They must have sexual organs since they are pregnant. All metals and all other stones were believed to be alive and to be sexed. They differed in that their life was more peaceful and their sexuality less marked. They grew in the womb of the earth immeasurably slowly and very few reached maturity. Hence the Indian belief that diamonds are 'ripe', while crystals are 'unripe' stones (ELIT p. 441).

This notion should be compared with alchemical teachings concerning the 'ripening' of metals in transmutation.

In the Book of Revelation (4: 3), St John sees the Ancient of Days seated upon a throne, 'to look upon like a jasper and a sardine stone'. The Pseudo-Dionysius the Areopagite explains that the colour green denotes the full freshness of youth. This symbol is especially fitting for the Ancient of Days or the Creator who enjoys eternal youth.

Jerusalem Psalm 122 makes Jerusalem the symbol of the peace, justice and unity of the twelve tribes of Israel. It then became the symbol of the Messiah's kingdom which the Christian Church opened to all peoples.

In the description given in the Book of Revelation, Jerusalem symbolizes the new order of creation which will replace the existing world at the end of time. It no longer denotes the traditional PARADISE, but something which surpasses all tradition – an absolute newness.

And I saw a new heaven and a new earth: for the first heaven and the first earth were passed away; and there was no more sea. And I John saw the holy city, new Jerusalem, coming down from God out of heaven, prepared as a bride adorned for her husband. And I heard a great voice out of heaven saying, Behold, the tabernacle of God is with men, and he will dwell with them, and they shall be his people, and God himself shall be with them, and be their God. And God shall wipe away all tears from their eyes: and there shall be no more death, neither sorrow, nor crying, neither shall there be any more pain: for the former things are passed away. And he that sat upon the throne said, Behold I make all things new.... I am ALPHA AND OMEGA, the beginning and the end.
(Revelation 21: 1–6)

At this point the square shape of the Heavenly Jerusalem should be emphasized. It distinguishes it from the Earthly Paradise, generally depicted as round. This is because the latter was 'Heaven on Earth' while the New Jerusalem is 'Earth in Heaven'. Circular shapes are related to Heaven and squares to Earth (CHAS p. 76). The transformation of the universe which the New Jerusalem denotes is in no sense a return to an idyllic past, but an unprecedented leap into the future.

jet In the Mediterranean Basin (in Italy and Egypt) and in India jet amulets, like those of coral, were worn as preservatives against the evil eye. In the British Isles, jet was believed to drive off storms and evil spirits and to act as an antidote to poisons, demoniac possession, magically implanted diseases and serpents' bites. Irish women used to burn jet, a highly inflammable bitumen, to ensure the safety of their husbands when they were away from home (BUDA p. 316).

According to Marbodius, Bishop of Rouen, 'suffumigation of jet restores regular menstruation to women ... It is believed to preserve against evil spirits ... It overcomes enchantment and looses spells and is supposed to be a touchstone of virginity' (GOUL p. 208).

At all events, jet, a gleaming black stone, appears as a tutelary symbol protecting from unseen mischiefs.

jewellery In esoteric science, the components of jewellery – its glittering GEMS and METALS, chiefly incorruptible gold – are, in the alchemical sense of the word, the 'ripest' of materials, which make them emanations of primordial energy. Chthonian, because they spring from the womb of Earth, in a different context they suggest the drive of the libido. Jewellery and precious gems, which so many myths and legends link to serpents and DRAGONS, are thus endowed with a secret of immortality which does not come from the gods but from the bowels of the Earth. As a result, the ambitions, passions and worship which they arouse suggest the ambience of Shakespearean drama rather than that of Racinean tragedy. It is as if, in this context, sublimation of desire beats its head against the wall of the human condition.

To make jewellery a symbol of the vanity of human possessions and wishes can only be the result of a debased view of the symbol itself. Jewellery symbolizes hidden knowledge in the precious gems and metals and the shapes they take. From the starting point of the Jungian 'soul' they come to stand for the unseen wealth of the unconscious. Because they are energy and light, they have the tendency to pass from the level of hidden knowledge to that of primeval energy. Many legends claim that precious stones are born from the heads, teeth or spittle of serpents (see EMERALD), as the pearl comes to birth in the oyster. They always wed with opposites: what is precious with what is terrifying. Nonetheless, their legendary birth shows that the glitter of the diamond is a chthonian light and that their infrangibility is an energy from below. In this context, and despite their hardness, jewels evoke a passion and tenderness which has a hint of the protective and the maternal, like Earth and caverns.

However, jewellery is not the precious stone in its natural state, it is the cut and polished gem in its setting, the work of both jeweller and goldsmith, as well as the person who has commissioned or chosen it. Now a union of soul, knowledge and energy takes place and in the end the piece of jewellery comes to symbolize both its wearer and the society which values it. In every age the development of the individual and of society as a whole must be taken into account in interpreting the symbolism of jewellery.

joints Among the Bambara the symbolism of the joints is related to that of knots – they use the same word for both. The joints allow the body to act, move and work. The six Bambara secret societies, initiation into which marks the six stages of the individual's life, are associated with the six principal joints in the human body. These societies ensure the functioning of human society and give the individual the means of self-realization (ZAHB).

Like knots and bonds, the joints may symbolize the process needed to pass from passive to active existence.

The main joints in the body play a basic part in Dogon and Bambara thought. These Mali peoples believe that, at the beginning of time, the human body was flaccid and without joints and that mankind could not work. The mythic ancestors of the present human race were the first people to be endowed with joints. These ancestors were EIGHT in number, eight thereafter becoming the number of creation. Male semen is produced in the joints and when it pumps down to fertilize the egg in the female womb it filters into the foetus's joints to bring them to life. With the coming of humans with jointed limbs came the 'third word', the word in all its fullness, and with it knowledge of those traditional crafts appropriate to these tribes, farming, weaving and metal-working (GRID).

The Bambara also believe that male post-coital fatigue proves that semen is generated in the joints (GRID).

The Likuba and Likuala of the Congo Basin number the important joints in the human body at fourteen, seven – neck, shoulders, elbows and wrists – in the upper part of the body and seven – groin, hips, knees and ankles – in the lower, forming the source of procreation. Their order from top to bottom, from neck to ankles, is the order in which life makes itself manifest in the new-born baby and life may be seen receding from the dying by the progressive paralysis of those fourteen joints, the last to retain its function being the neck (LEBM).

The Carib Indians who once lived in the West Indies believed that the individual was endowed with a number of souls located in the heart, head and those joints where the beating of the pulse was visible.

Joints are one of the symbols of communication and of the path through which life makes itself manifest and along which it passes.

journey Rich in symbolism though journeys may be, this wealth is condensed into the quest for truth, peace or immortality, and into the search for and discovery of a spiritual CENTRE. VOYAGING, crossing RIVERS and looking for ISLANDS are discussed under their appropriate headings. Chinese journeys were expeditions either to the Isles of the Immortals, an Eden in the east which corresponded to the paradisal state, or to Mount Kun-Lun, the centre and World Axis. The islands are Ho-chu (*Li Tzu* ch. 2) and Chuche, visited by Yoa (*Chuang Tzu* ch. 1), both corresponding to the primordial centre, but especially the 'five great islands', Pong-lai (*Li Tzu* ch. 5) to which Ch'in-che Huang-ti and later the Han Emperor Wu sent abortive expeditions. All failed, states the *Pao-p'u Tzu*, because there was no qualified spiritual pilot, or because, as Li Chao Wong taught, Pong-lai can only be reached after a spiritual preparation which enables the seeker to 'rise up to Heaven'. Other journeys include those of Hoan Chen-tai and Princess Miao-chu to the Island of Truth and of Ch'u-yuan to the City of Purity, which was the primordial centre. Huang Ti reached Mount K'ong-tong – a tree and therefore an axial symbol – and may even have attained Mount Kun-Lun itself. Ch'u-yuan's guide, the Immortal Ch'e-song Tzu, reached it easily, as did the Chou Emperor, Mu. However, both Chang-liang and Chang Ch'ien failed, since the centre of the Earth had become inaccessible. In fact, such journeys only reach their objectives within the individual: journeys which are an escape from self always fail.

CHALICES and BOOKS also symbolize this inaccessible centre, and quests for them produce the wealth of adventure in the story of the Grail or in the *Si-yu Chi*. Since these are quests for knowledge, they correspond to the journeys of Aeneas, Odysseus, Dante, Christian Rosenkreuz or Nicholas Flamel, or of the Indian Prince in the *Acts of Thomas*. Without departing from this line of thought, journeys are also the series of ordeals which prepare the candidate for initiation and are to be found in the Ancient Greek Mysteries, in Freemasonry and in Chinese secret societies. Like a spiritual progress, the journey – occurring in Buddhism in the shape of ways, vehicles and 'crossings' – is often expressed in terms of movement along the World Axis. This is true of Dante's journey. The Prophet Muhammad was taken up to Heaven during his *mi'rāj* and Chinese tradition holds that the same was true of Chao Chien-tzu and K'i, sons of Yu the Great. While the quest for the central mountain may be progression towards the axis, its ascent is the equivalent of an ascent into Heaven. The same is often true of crossing BRIDGES.

Advancing towards the centre is often expressed in terms of a quest for the Promised Land as well as by pilgrimage (see PILGRIM). Such was the Exodus from the Land of Egypt, the crossing of the Wilderness and that of the Red Sea, which Origen expressly describes as stages in spiritual development. De Saint-Martin observes that Jethro's Well, beside which Moses halted, was a secondary spiritual centre. Other journeys are Avicenna's (Ibn Sinā's) *Tale of the Bird* and Suhrawardi's *Tale of the Western Exile* and *Letter from the Towers*, where both define their quest as that for their original and not their earthly homeland. *Al sālik*, the Traveller, is a title conferred by some Muslim brotherhoods. 'But who is that traveller?' Shabistari asked. 'Even he who turns his face towards the Prophet . . . Journey within thy self', he added. And it is within the self that the individual attains the Great Peace (*tai-ping*) of the Chinese, Hindu tranquillity, the City of Truth of St Isaac of Nineveh and, lastly, the Grail as well.

The symbolic journey is often undertaken after death, the best-known instances being those recorded in Ancient Egyptian or Tibetan books of the dead. However, the same motif recurs in such very different parts of the world as northern Vietnam (Black Thais) and Central America (Maya). Here again we are clearly concerned with the progress of the soul through states which enlarge those of its manifestation in human form – the super-human goal is still to be achieved.

Literature throughout the world presents many different examples of journeys which, without having the scope of traditional symbol, are intended to have some degree of significance – be it merely satirical or morally instructive – but which are, nevertheless, quests for truth. Instances of these would include Rabelais's *Pantagruel* and Swift's *Gulliver's Travels*, as well as many works of Japanese literature such as the *Utsubo-monogatari* or the *Wasōbyoē*.

An utterly different point of view is presented by 'the longest journey in the world' which, according to the *Digha-nikāya*, is the unbroken chain of cause and effect to which the individual is condemned unless enlightened to the 'Four Noble Truths' of Buddhism (CORT, ELIF, PHIL, GRAD, GRIL, GUED, GUEM, KALL, LECC, KALT, MAEV, MASR, MAST, SAIR, GUEI, GUES, WOUS).

In dreams and legends, journeys under the Earth's surface denote entry into the esoteric realm; those through air and sky, entry into the exoteric realm. A journey up the side of a mountain symbolizes effort; down, relaxation (HAMK 7: p. 16).

Journeys give expression to a deep-seated desire for internal change and a need for a fresh range of experience rather than change of location. According to Jung, they are evidence of a lack of satisfaction, which prompts the search for and discovery of new horizons. Although Jung may suggest that the longing for travel may be the quest for the 'lost' mother, Cirlot rightly observes that it could as easily be escape from the mother. In fact we should remember that this word comprises two aspects – the generous and the possessive.

Journeys to the Underworld denote either a return to one's beginnings, as in the *Aeneid* Book VI, or, in current interpretation, a descent into the unconscious. Both cases perhaps betray a need for self-justification, the Ancient Romans wishing to claim noble descent from dead heroes and moderns trying to find the causes of their behaviour. A journey to the Underworld may more often be regarded as self-defensive or self-justificatory, rather than self-punitive.

Other journeys, such as those of Odysseus, Herakles (Hercules), Menelaus, Sinbad or so many others have been interpreted as quests on the psychic and mystic planes. Throughout literature, journeys symbolize adventure and quest, whether wealth or simply knowledge, the material or the spiritual are at the end of them. But this quest is at bottom no more than a search for and, more often, a flight from one's self. 'True travellers', Baudelaire wrote, 'are those who set out for the sake of setting out.' Never satisfied, their constant dream is of the more or less inaccessible unknown and they never find what they have been trying to escape – themselves.

In this sense journeys become signs and symbols of the deliberate and constant self-blindness and of that avoiding of awkward questions of which Pascal spoke. One is therefore forced to conclude that the only worthwhile journey is the one which the individual undertakes within him- or herself.

Judgement, the   The Judgement, Resurrection or Awakening of the Dead, the twentieth major arcanum of the TAROT, expresses 'inspiration, the redemptive breath' [Wirth] . . . 'a change of position and understanding, matters of law' [R. Bost]... 'return to status quo, the end of an ordeal, amends, forgiveness, compensation for or rectification of error, rehabilitation, cure, setting matters right' [Terestchenko]. Like Justice, it corresponds to the Eighth House of the Horoscope.

Set between the SUN and the WORLD in the Tarot, the Judgement refocuses the mind on death. An angel with a white halo, surrounded by a circle of blue clouds from which dart alternately ten red and ten yellow beams of light, holds in his right hand a trumpet and in his left a sort of pennon, bearing a yellow cross on a white ground. His trumpet appears almost to touch a mountain or mound, also yellow and barren.

At the foot of the card a naked man, seen from behind, appears to be emerging from a green vat or grave, green being the colour of resurrection, in front of which and facing him, their hands clasped in prayer, stand two older figures of a man and a woman, also naked. They may, perhaps, be Jung's Mother and Old Man.

It seems obvious that the trumpet is the Last Trump and that this is the Resurrection of the Dead. But one can delve deeper into this interpretation. The angel's wings and hands are flesh-coloured like those of Temperance. This might be taken to mean that he is made of the stuff of humanity, that he is the brother of mankind and that all individuals may acquire the wings of his spirituality, provided that they preserve moderation and balance in their spiritual ascent. His forearms are red because he is always active, but his hair is the colour of the 'gold of imperishable truth' (WIRT p. 243). These endow him with solar symbolism. He is enclosed within a circle of BLUE clouds, the lunar colour of occult powers and of the truth of the soul. From these clouds dart RED and YELLOW rays of instrumentality and spirituality to show that there can be no action which does not proceed from the powers of the soul, in which intuition and the emotions intermingle. Perhaps it also denotes that human intelligence is confined within these spirals and that there is always a circle which we cannot pass. Human beings stand naked before this angel, herald of the Last Judgement which will sift the wheat from the chaff, rising from the grave, which was their bodies. They are stripped of all worldly attributes except their hair, blue, the colour of the soul and the same colour as the hair of the HANGING MAN, TEMPERANCE and the STAR, three cards with markedly initiatory qualities and which symbolize deaths and rebirths. To be able to be reborn into the true life, one must have heard the call of the golden trumpet through which passes the voice of God. In this case it is the son who has attained the highest grade of initiation without having renounced the lessons of the past, symbolized by his parents. Instead of falling over his shoulders, his hair is shaped like a CROWN and he alone faces the angel.

Thus, as the final stage before the vision of the World, the Judgement symbolizes the victorious summons of the Spirit, the unifying principle which penetrates and sublimates the material.

Juggler, the By an extraordinary paradox, a conjuror and illusionist, who builds an imaginary world with a touch of his hands and a word of his voice, opens the suit of twenty-six major arcana in the TAROT. A YELLOW belt round his waist divides into two halves a garment in which RED and BLUE are precisely balanced. He stands with feet at right angles, his left leg blue stockinged and shod in red, his right leg red and shod in blue. The hand holding his wand emerges from a blue sleeve and points skywards, symbolizing the development required of material things, while the hand which holds a coin emerges from a red sleeve and points downwards, symbolizing the spirit which penetrates matter. All these outward signs emphasize the divided nature of a being who is the product of opposing principles, and the balance and supremacy of the spirit which dominates his duality. The Juggler's hat, yellow with a green brim rimmed with red, is in shape reminiscent of the mathematical sign for infinity (∞). 'The Juggler's head-covering symbolically crowns the range of what he can stand for. The lemniscate with a red rim reminds us of the final triumph of the spirit in Unity' (RIJT p. 212).

The Juggler stands in front of a flesh-coloured table – the colour emphasizing his human nature – of which only three legs are to be seen and which 'might well bear the signs for sulphur, salt and mercury, since they are the three pillars of the phenomenal world' (WIRT p. 117). Lying on the table are such various objects as shekels, cups, swords and wands, corresponding to the four suits of minor arcana and displaying the links which bind the seventy-eight cards of the Tarot.

The Juggler is the dealer who opens the game; but is he really an illusionist playing with us or, under that white hair tipped with golden curls as if its owner was outside time, does there lurk the depth of wisdom of the Magus and knowledge of the secrets of being? 'Generally speaking, he denotes the consultant and may as easily display personal will-power, skill and drive as imposture and lies. Once again, we discover the ambivalence and the bright and dark side of every symbol' (Virel).

His place in the pack, and his very symbolism, invite us to delve beneath the surface. One is the number of the First Cause and, while on the planes of psychology or fortune-telling, the Juggler may denote the 'Consultant', on the spiritual plane he 'manifests the mystery of Unity' (RIJT p. 28).

Simultaneously symbolizing the three worlds – God, in the sign of Infinity, Man and all the variety of the Universe – he is the point of departure and all that it implies, with all the two-edged weapons given to the created being to accomplish his or her destiny.

jujube-tree (sidrat) In Muslim tradition the jujube is a symbol of the extent and limits of space and time. According to the Koran (53: 16), the Prophet Muhammad had a vision 'near the Sirdah [jujube] tree, which marks the boundary . . . when the Sirdah-tree was covered with what covered it.'

This jujube tree has been the object of prolonged discussion by Muslim mystics. It is regarded as marking the frontier beyond which no living creature, not even one closely linked to God, may proceed. Tradition tells that Gabriel here took leave of the Prophet, merely giving him guidance as to how to continue on his way alone. Since jujube trees are sometimes the only living things on the face of the desert, one is perhaps here on the threshold of the desert of the Unknowable.

(CORH)

The mid-Sha'ban festival is linked to the tradition that the jujube tree which grows in Paradise bears as many leaves as there are human beings alive on Earth. On these leaves are said to be written the names of all these individuals, each leaf bearing the name of a person and those of his or her parents. They claim that during the night of 15 Sha'ban, a little after sunset, the tree is shaken and that when a person is fated to die during the coming year, the leaf which bears his or her name falls off. If that person is fated to die very soon, the leaf will be almost completely withered and only a tiny portion will remain green, the size of the green portion depending upon the length of time that person still has to live. A special form of prayer is used at this festival (LANM p. 201).

The jujube may also symbolize a means of defence against attack. Among some Moroccan tribes, when a male child is born, the midwife immediately puts a jujube twig into his hand, so that he may grow up as dangerous as the thorns of that tree. Its thorns are also used against the evil eye and graves are sometimes covered with branches of this thorny shrub.

Traces of this tradition of the jujube as a symbol of defence may be found in Greek legend. Priapus was enamoured of the nymph Lotis and the more she rejected him the harder he pressed his suit. Having narrowly avoided rape she prayed to be turned into a thorny shrub with red flowers, believed to be the jujube.

In Europe, jujube berries were used for chest complaints, but Chinese Taoists regarded them as the food of immortality. The berry upon which the Immortals fed was, it must be admitted, of extraordinary size – as big as a gourd or water-melon. Jujubes were used as food after following a diet of gradual 'abstinence from cereals', being pre-eminently a pure and almost immaterial diet (KALL, LECC, MAST).

jumping The Celts regarded jumping as a warlike skill and one of the ploys of which the hero made use either to escape from or to overwhelm his enemy. It might also be linked to a display of insult or violent anger, and the young Ulster hero, Cùchulainn, often had recourse to the practice. Its symbolism is therefore completely military, drained of any recreational or theatrical quality. A Gallic tribe, the Lingones, bore the name of 'leapers', which suggests that the notions which left their traces in Ireland were shared upon the Continent (OGAC 11: pp. 37–9).

However, in other traditions jumping formed a part of some liturgical ceremonies and then was a symbol of heavenward ascension.

Juno There is no exact equivalent in Greek mythology for this Roman goddess, wife of Jupiter, although Zeus' wife, HERA, is most closely akin to her. Jean Beaujeu explains that her name 'is derived from an Indo-European root which expresses the idea of the life force and which recurs in *juvenis*, the young man at the height of his powers. In Rome, she was both queen and fertility-goddess, presiding over marriage and childbirth . . . while the great festival, the Matronalia, observed on the Kalends of March, was dedicated to Juno' (BEAG p. 232). She was the mother of the war-god and guardian of crops. Other features characterizing this goddess included the fact that the goatskin from which the Luperci (priests of the Lycian Pan) made their whips was called 'Juno's cloak' and that on the first day of each month a sow and a ewe-lamb were sacrificed to her. Originally she was a personification of the lunar cycle. Young, but fully mature, at the height of her powers, commanding, aggressive and fertile, she symbolizes the female principle.

She was above all guardian of married women and children born in wedlock. However, nobody could attend ceremonies honouring her in this role unless 'all knots were untied, since should they have about them any band, girdle, or knot, this could inhibit the safe delivery of the woman for whom sacrifice was being offered' (GRIF p. 241).

Jupiter The Greek equivalent of the Roman king of the gods was ZEUS. The Romans regarded Jupiter as 'the sky-god, the god of light, of the day and of the seasons which he created, as well as of thunder and lightning . . . . [He was] the supreme power, presiding over the councils of the gods, and from him emanated all authority' (GRID p. 244). Jupiter symbolizes externally imposed authority and order. Confident in the justice of his cause and his power to decide, he seeks neither to discuss nor to persuade – he thunders.

In Gaul, the Celtic Jupiter was called Taranis, 'the Thunderer' (from the Irish, Welsh and Breton word *taran(n)*, meaning 'thunder'). Iconographically, his most frequently depicted attribute was the wheel. However, this wheel, contrary to the majority view of modern scholars, is not the symbol of thunder, but the Cosmic Wheel, like the wheel of the Irish druid Mog Ruith, 'the Wizard of the Wheels'. Nonetheless, the principal Irish aspect of the Celtic Jupiter was the Dagda, 'the good god', who possessed the two talismans of kingship, the cauldron of abundance and rebirth, a pre-Christian archetype of the Grail, and a club which slew at one end and restored to life at the other. This is the attribute which corresponds to Jupiter's thunderbolt and Indra's vajra. Other aspects of the Celtic Jupiter include Sucellus ('Hard-hitter') in Gaul and, in Ireland, Manannan (Lord of the Otherworld). The Dagda fathered Brigit (Minerva) and she in turn was mother of all the gods. The Dagda was also the father of Oenghus (Apollo in his youthful aspect) by adultery with his sister, married to their brother, Elcmar (dark, evil), god of night. He was one of the chief warriors in the cosmic Battle of Mag Tuired against the Fomorians. With his brother, Ogma (Elcmar is undoubtedly another name for him), he is one of the two aspects of the all-powerful dualism represented by Mitra–Varuna in India. The Dagda is Mitra, god of friendship, oath-taking and, also, of chicanery. The Celtic notion, however, lays greater stress upon his aspect as 'Lord of Manifestation' than upon his aspect as all-powerful sky-god. He is pre-eminently the druid-god invoked by the priestly caste, while the bards (*filid*) had recourse to Ogma (OGAC 11: pp. 307ff.; 12: pp. 349ff.).

Its size and position give Jupiter a central place among planets in our solar system. Mercury, Venus, Earth, Mars and the asteroids are closer to the Sun; the same number of heavenly bodies, Saturn, Uranus, Neptune, Pluto and their satellites further away. Analogous to this prime site, in astrology Jupiter embodies the principles of balance, authority, order, steady progression, plenty and the preservation of the established structure of society. It is the planet of social legality, wealth, optimism and assurance. The Ancients recorded their gratitude by calling the planet the 'Great Benefactor' of mankind. In the Zodiac, Jupiter rules Sagittarius, the sign of Justice, and Pisces, the sign of philanthropy. Medicine and the law are its favoured professions while it protects the circulation of the blood and the functioning of the liver in human physiology.

Bulkiest of our planets, majestically rotating upon its vertical axis, and with a host of satellites in its retinue, Jupiter provides a pageant for the watcher of the starry vault of Heaven. Like Zeus, Lord of Olympus, Jupiter stands out and easily gained the astrologers' allegiance. Zeus may have been the nurseling of the she-goat, Amalthea, and carry as his attribute her horn of plenty, he may rule and ordain each person's share of the good things of life, but Jupiter embodies the twilight hour when the child sucks its mother's milk and begins to learn how to bring its instincts to maturity. Thus an individual's 'Jupiterian' condition is displayed in the long unbroken train of accumulating attainments, advantages, profits, gifts and graces, all destined to satisfy the consumer appetite, the landowning instinct and material status since it is all a matter of having something or of being somebody. This scenario of the good life, a concomitant of lively appetite, confidence, generosity, optimism, altruism, peace and good fortune, helps to feed the health and ripen the development of individuals born to ever better social conditions under the rule and government of moral principles and in which everyone is able to develop his or her potential and obtain complete mastery of self.

Justice The eighth major arcanum of the TAROT is the first card in the second sequence of seven which relates to the soul and is thus set midway between Spirit (cards 1–7) and Body (cards 15–22) (WIRT p. 158).

On her head, Justice wears the judge's YELLOW cap, on which is depicted a solar emblem, and sits on a throne. This, too, is yellow, as are her coiled necklace, the sword which she carries in her right hand, the left sleeve of her robe, her scales and the ground beneath her. She wears a BLUE coat over a RED dress (like the Female POPE and the HERMIT), but in this instance the three colours – red, blue and yellow – are almost balanced. The occult knowledge possessed by the Female Pope (in blue), is divulged by the Pope in a red cloak and leads to the triumph of GOLD, a solar colour. Sword and scales are traditional attributes of Justice. The scales are like those before Osiris' judgement-seat, of which merely one of Maat's feathers set the trays in balance, and here they are quite still. The straight and merciless sword, like the arm of the scales, will be used to punish the guilty. In this context it should be remembered that sword and scales are also 'symbols of the two ways in which Aristotle maintained Justice could be envisioned. The sword stands for her power to inflict – *Justitia suum cuique tribuit* – and the scales her vocation to restore the balance of society' (RIJT p. 126).

Justice, with the symbolic figure EIGHT, is human conscience in the highest sense of the word. Those who attempt to misuse their powers will feel the weight of her sword and condemnation, while for true adepts, the scales will maintain the balance between the Pope (V) and Necessity (XI), that strict balance being the very law which brings order out of the chaos in the universe and within ourselves.

K

ka One of the most difficult Ancient Egyptian concepts for the Western mind to grasp is that of the *ka*. According to Serge Sauneron,

> the *ka* was, in fact, a manifestation of the *vital energy* both as a creative force and a sustainer of life. Thus the word *ka* could mean both the divine creative power and the forces of continuity which animated Maat, universal order.... In a sense the *ka* was the receptacle of the vital forces from which all life came and through which all life survived.
>
> (POSD p. 142)

The expression 'to pass to one's *ka*' meant 'to die'. This might be interpreted as meaning that this principle led an existence independent from the body with which, notwithstanding, it was created. *Ka*-statuettes were placed in the dead person's tomb and it was to these statuettes that food offerings were brought. Funerary priests were known as 'Servants of the *Ka*'.

André Virel regards this principle as 'an aspect of cosmic power absorbed by the personality', and agrees with Christiane Desroches-Noblecourt in distinguishing between the individual and the collective *ka*, the latter being 'an undifferentiated, universal creative power of continuous interaction'. It tended to become differentiated into the individual *ka* as Ancient Egyptian society developed an 'individualizing and socializing awareness' (VIRI p. 134). The *ka* might symbolize a life force amenable to ever greater personalization as individual and collective awareness developed.

karma (see also SAMSĀRA) A Sanskrit word (from the root *KR*, meaning 'to do'), it denotes the linkage of cause and effect which assures the stability of the universe. With this cosmic meaning is mingled an ethical significance, human actions being inextricably linked with their consequences and these consequences producing situations for which those who committed the acts are responsible, either in this life or in past lives. During the Vedic period, *karma* carried with it a ritual, evidence of that awareness that whatever happens may be regarded as just reward or punishment. All is contained within a span of time far longer than an individual's life. 'Human beings are the heirs of their actions', said the Buddha. 'Awareness is based upon intentions, plans and preoccupations.... From this rises that whole burden of pain.' By its definition, *karma* depends upon awareness. It is a magnificent vision linking human freedom with the universal order in an organized physical and moral system. Cosmic determinism is confined to unenlightened awareness.

katabami See WOOD-SORREL.

Kaydara The Fulani god of gold and knowledge is 'the ray of light cast by the fire which is Gueno [their supreme deity]'. He takes many different shapes when he manifests himself but, for preference, disguises himself as an ugly, little, old beggar-man, the more easily to entrap the unscrupulous and the unwary. Hence legends call his kingdom 'the land of dwarfs', 'land of shadows' or 'land of pygmy genii'. Since pygmies are regarded as the original inhabitants of the country, they often play a supernatural part in African legends.

Being the god of gold, his home, like that of gold, is underground and the journey below the ground in quest of him passes through eleven layers of depth, in other words, eleven ordeals or eleven symbols, until the traveller stands before the supernatural spirit who bestows the sacred metal.

He is depicted with seven heads (seven days of the week), twelve arms (twelve months in the year), thirty feet (thirty days in the month) and sits upon a throne with four legs (the four elements, the four cataclysms which will destroy the human world and the four seasons). This throne revolves continuously, the Fulani having fathomed out the Earth's rotation. Thus Kaydara symbolizes the structure of the world and of time. He revolves on his throne like the Sun which rules time. Knowledge of him is understanding of the cosmic order and also of the causes of disorder, since annihilation of beings, like their birth, comes from other beings. He is called 'the distant and the close-at-hand' since he is inexhaustible and, while one may believe him to be there or not to be there, he is everywhere at all times (HAMK).

Kaydara would seem to be the symbol of the synthesis between the cosmic and the moral and of the light revealed in the ultimate phase of initiation.

key Obviously the symbolism of the key relates to its twofold function of 'unlocking' and 'locking'. It plays the double part of letting in and shutting out, a role underlined by the attribution of the keys of the Kingdom of Heaven to St Peter. The power of the keys is that of binding or loosing and of opening or shutting Heaven, a power effectively granted by Christ to St Peter. (In alchemical terms this power is that of 'coagulation' and 'dissolution'.) This power is emblazoned in the papal coat of arms by the two keys, one of silver and one of gold, which had previously been emblems of the Roman god, Janus. These dual aspects of power, one light and the other dark, correspond to spiritual authority and the duties of kingship, of which the respective aims, according to Dante, are admission to the Heavenly and to the Earthly Paradise or, in Hermetic terms, to the Greater and Lesser Mysteries. Janus' keys also opened the gates of the solstices granting admission to the waxing or waning phases of the cycle of the year or to the respective realms of *ying* and *yang* which come into equilibrium at the equinoxes. Janus was also regarded as a conductor of souls, hence his two faces, one gazing earthwards and the other heavenwards. With his staff in his right hand and his key in his left, he guarded all gates and ruled all roads.

The symbolism of the key unlocking the door of initiation finds expression, too, in the Koran which states that the *Shahada* ('There is no God but God') is the key to Paradise. Esoteric interpretation makes each of the four words of the *Shahada* one of the four teeth of the key which, provided it is whole, will open 'all the gates of the Word of God' and therefore those of Paradise.

In Japan, keys are, generally speaking, a symbol of prosperity because they open the rice-store. But it is patently clear that the rice-store can contain spiritual food and that, in this context, the key with which one gains entry has the same significance as those already discussed (BENA, CORT, GUET, GUES).

Because keys open and shut gates, they are regarded by the Bambara as symbols of power and authority because 'all that is said and all that is done in the individual, in the state and in the world at large, is a gate' (ZAHB p. 82). Chief, God, Sun, all three are keys. God is the key to creation and the world; the Sun, the key of the day which he opens when he rises and closes when he sets. Stools (see THRONE) and the human foot are keys. Keys symbolize chiefs, rulers and mystagogues who possess decision-making powers and responsibility.

On the esoteric level, to hold the key means to have been initiated. It not only shows the power to enter a place, town, or house, but to accede to a spiritual state or abode or to a level of initiation.

In legends and folktales, the keys mentioned are very often three in number and they allow their owners access to three successive enclosures, or SECRET ROOMS, which are as many approaches to the mystery. Be they silver, gold or diamond, they mark separate stages in purification or initiation (LOEF p. 98). In this context, the key symbolizes a mystery to be unravelled, a riddle to be solved or a difficult task to be done; milestones, in short, on the road of enlightenment and revelation.

Khidr In Muslim tradition the Khidr is the guide, mystagogue, lord of the inner life or Green Man (see under GREEN).

khirka (see also CLOAK) The original Arabic meaning of a scrap of torn material came to be applied to the homespun garment of the mystic. Hujwiri, author of the earliest treatise on Sufism, said that it symbolized 'the inner fire [*harka*] which makes the Sufi'.

Originally the *khirka* was woven from blue cloth – blue is the colour of mourning – and became a symbol of the vow of poverty. In Christian tradition, the monastic habit or homespun garment is also a symbol of poverty, of dedication to God, of separation from the world and of membership of a community.

The Sufi only receives the garment after a three-year period of initiation. 'Donnning the *khirka*', Suhrawardi wrote, 'is a tangible sign that a man has entered the path of truth, the symbol of his entry into the mystic path and sign that he has abandoned his own individuality and surrendered himself completely into the hands of the Shaykh [spiritual leader].'

There are two types of *khirka* – the Khirka of Good Will which the candidate has to ask his Shaykh to confer upon him, fully aware of the duties which its assumption entails, and the Khirka of Blessing which the Shaykh himself confers upon those whom he thinks fit to enter the mystic path. The first is naturally much superior to the second and marks out genuine Sufis from those content with mere externals (ENCI 2: p. 1012).

The great Persian poet and mystic Abū Saʿīd (967–1049), in his treatise on the unity of the godhead, studied the significance of donning the *khirka*. First he lists the qualities which should be possessed by the spiritual Master conferring the garment. He must be worthy of imitation, that is to say he must have perfect knowledge, both in theory and in practice, of the three stages of the mystic life – the Law, the Path and the Truth – and no trace of his lower self must be left in him. When such a Shaykh knows a disciple well enough to be certain that he deserves it, he places his hand upon the disciple's head and clothes him with the *khirka*. Through this act he expresses his conviction that the disciple is worthy to be numbered among the Sufi and this declaration has the force of law for them. Thus, when a strange Dervish comes into a monastery or wishes to join a Sufi brotherhood, he is asked 'Which Master taught you?' or 'From whose hands did you receive your *khirka*?'

The Sufis had a custom, when in a state of ecstasy, of ripping up and giving away scraps of a *khirka*, especially when it had been worn by a highly revered Master. 'The purpose behind ripping up and giving away [these scraps] was to bestow the BLESSING believed to be possessed by them. Thus the garments which had belonged to saints acquired miraculous powers, like Elijah's mantle.'

Ibn ʿArabī said that the *khirka* was the symbol of Sufi brotherhood and the sign that they shared the same spiritual culture and practised the same ethos.

There is a widespread custom among mystic Masters that, when they notice something lacking in a disciple, the Shaykh will identify in spirit with the state of perfection which he intends to transmit. When that identification has taken place, he will take the *khirka* which he was wearing at the time when he attained to that spiritual state, strip it off and with it clothe the disciple whose spiritual state he intends to perfect. Thus the Shaykh conveys to the disciple the spiritual state which he has attained within himself.

This interpretation, taken in conjunction with the symbolism of the cloak, identifies the garment with its wearer.

kid See under GOAT.

kidneys In his commentaries upon the symbolic representation of angels, the Pseudo-Dionysius the Areopagite wrote that the kidneys were an emblem of the fructifying power of celestial intelligences.

In the Old Testament expression 'to try the reins [kidneys] and the heart', the kidneys are regarded as the seat of hidden desire, while in this context the heart denotes the most intimate thoughts.

The kidneys often symbolize power, either procreative or the strength to suffer any adversity.

king The Chinese ideogram denoting 'king' (*wang*) comprises three parallel horizontal strokes, for Heaven, Mankind and Earth, linked centrally by a vertical stroke. 'Who better able to act the part of intermediary,' Chuang Chou asked, 'set between them to act as a link and to co-ordinate their activities by sharing in them, who better than the Prince? The one whose nature derives from Heaven is endowed with the qualities which he absorbs from Heaven.' This summarizes the meaning of kings and kingship for the Chinese. The king, fortified by the Mandate of Heaven (*t'ien-ming*), sets his throne in the centre of his realm, and it would seem that this was true originally of the central province of Honan and its capital Lo-yang. Around it, the spatial area expands like a series of squares welded together. The quintessence of royalty is wafted to the four cardinal points, while homage and tribute is paid along these selfsame axes. The king was identified with the central pillar of the Temple of Heaven or with the pole bearing the awning of a chariot. With his feet on the chariot floor and his head brushing this celestial awning, the *wang* became one with the World AXIS, which is both the Royal Way (*wang-tao*) and the Heavenly Way (*t'ien-tao*). Moving through the Temple of Heaven like the Sun through the sky, the sovereign bestowed upon his realm times and seasons, the rhythm and harmony of the Heavens, his regulatory function extending from the cosmic to the social realm.

The role of initiating and regulating cosmic movement may also be applied to the Hindu symbol of the king – *chakravartī* – he who makes the wheel turn, the universal sovereign. He is the motive force of the world, abiding motionless in the void at the hub of the WHEEL. The primeval legislator, Manu, might be cast in a similar role, filled, above all, by the Buddha. The ceremonies performed in the Tantric mandala relative to the sovereignty of the Buddha are rites of kingly consecration. The symbol is given its clearest expression in the shape of that massive structure, the centre of the Bayon at Angkor, a MANDALA, or eight-spoked wheel, at the centre of which stood a statue of the Buddha as king. The duties of the kings of Angkor – like those, furthermore, of the Javanese Kings of the Mountain – were expressly identified with those of the *chakravartī* and this is the meaning behind the initiation undergone by Jayavarman II in 802 on the top of the Phnom Kulōn. Shiva, or the lingam, possess qualities identical to those of other rulers. The Lordship of the Universe is kingship. One of the ancestors of the kings of Angkor was Bālāditya, Prince of the Rising Sun, whose activities were identified with the course of the Sun through the signs of the ZODIAC. Nor should it be forgotten that the emperor of Japan is a direct descendant of the Sun-goddess, Amaterasu-omikami.

The basic duties of these 'centre' rulers was the establishment of justice and peace, that is, the balance and harmony of the world. Thus Manu's Old Testament counterpart, Melchizedek, is the King of Righteousness who rules over Salem, City of Peace. His attributes were the sword and the scales. According to Dante, the duties of an emperor were of the same nature. Guénon, too, has drawn attention to the symbolism of the Three Wise Men, representatives of primordial tradition, whose presents to the Christ-child bear witness to their recognition of his duties as king (gold), priest (frankincense) and prophet (myrrh).

Al-Malik ('King') to the Muslim is one of the Names of God, basically corresponding to the duties of the judge.

By analogy with the central and regulatory qualities of the office of kingship, Shabistarī compares the human microcosm with a kingdom in which the heart is sovereign. If the soul cannot administer justice, 'the spirit decays and the body falls into ruin'. The Chinese *Secret of the Golden Flower* similarly suggests the functioning of the central, imperial power in the 'celestial heart', the point of spiritual concentration (BHAB, COEA, CORT, ELIY, GRAD, GRAP, GRAR, GUED, GUEM, GRIC, GRIF, GUET, GUES, JILH, LECC).

The title of Ancient Egyptian sovereigns, Pharaoh, was taken from a word meaning 'great house', first denoting the palace and then its occupant, who was regarded as of the same nature as the Sun and the godhead. His regalia

identified him with the gods. Like the latter he wore attached to his belt an animal's tail which hung from his waist. He had a false beard which was itself a god and he carried a sceptre with the head of the god Set [originally a god of great valour who was degraded by later tradition to a Typhon or base demon]. His faithful subjects sang hymns to his crowns which were imbued with supernatural life. In the middle of his forehead a uraeus spat flames which consumed rebels.

His power inspired fear, his progeny were countless, his decrees infallible and his judgements instinct with justice and goodness. 'Every change on the throne had a cosmic significance. Although Chaos threatened the order of the universe at the death of a king, the accession of a new pharaoh revivified the original creation and reestablished the equilibrium of nature' (POSD p. 212).

Celtic kings were elected by the nobles from members of the warrior caste, but under the supervision and religious sanction of the druids. A warrior by birth and training, the king was closely akin to the priesthood and his symbolic colour was like that of the druids, WHITE. Kings no longer did battle themselves, but their presence on the field was essential, as a Middle Irish proverb has it: 'Battles are not won unless the King is there.' However, his major role was not warlike – the good king was the one who ensured the prosperity of his subjects. Taxes and tribute were brought to him and these he shared out in gifts and rewards. He was the 'giver', and bad kings were those who levied taxes and gave nothing in return. Under such a ruler, all fruitfulness vanished from soil, trees and animals. Usurpers' reigns were often those which turned out badly and from whom kingship was wrested. The king who was either deposed or had reached the end of his reign, or the usurper, died by violence, drowned in a butt of beer or wine and with his palace burned over his head. Controlled by the druids, kings acted as intermediaries between the priestly caste and their subjects. Dio Chrysostom wrote (Forty-Ninth Discourse) that: 'The Celts appointed those whom they call Druids, these also being devoted to the prophetic art and to wisdom in general. In all these cases the kings were not permitted to do or plan anything without the assistance of these wise men, so that in truth it was they who ruled, while the kings became their servants and the ministers of their will.' One of the taboos set upon the Ulates was not to speak before the king had spoken and upon the king not to speak before the druids had spoken. Thus druids took precedence over kings, but kings spoke before the rest of the people. The royal festival was Lugnasad, the Feast of Lug, the god conceived as the mediator between Earth and Heaven. It was also the harvest festival. Unlike the druid who enjoyed complete freedom of action, Celtic kings were hedged around with a host of taboos and duties which could not be infringed without incurring serious risks. Should he suffer mutilation, the loss, for example of a limb or an eye, or any physical disability, he was disqualified from ruling. King Nuada lost an arm in the first Battle of Mag Tuired and could not regain his throne from the usurper, Bres, until he had been given an artificial arm of silver. However, the king's presence, as giver of gifts and holder of the balance, was essential to maintaining the fabric of society. When kingship began to vanish from Gaul in the first century BC, a state of almost complete anarchy resulted. The Celtic was almost the complete opposite to the Roman system, based upon the supremacy of the temporal power under which the flamen rather than the king was hedged with taboos (OGAC 4: pp. 225ff.; 6: pp. 209–18; 10: pp. 67–80).

A Gaulish cognomen of Mars was *Albiorix*, which should be translated as 'King of the World'. *Albio* means both 'white' and 'world', thus hinting at a religious significance, white possessing a fully sacred character in the Indo-European world. Another epithet based upon office is the name of the tribe which occupied central Gaul, the Bituriges or Kings of the World. However, while *Albio* corresponds to the aspect of kingship as mediation, *bitu* is also a synonym for 'time', 'age' and 'eternity', denoting the timeless aspect of kingship. The Bituriges were thus simultaneously 'Kings of the World' and 'Kings for Ever'. By contrast with both Albiorix and Bituriges, Dubnorix (or Dumnorix) – an important member of the Aeduan nobility, according to Caesar – was 'King of the World' in the temporal sense of the word. Livy mentions a fifth-century BC Gaulish emperor, the ambidextrous King of the Bituriges, Ambigatus. By this ambidexterity should be understood his possession of the two powers, spiritual and temporal, a symbolism which Livy undoubtedly failed to understand. This concept of universal kingship, a concentration of the two powers over the three worlds, is less clearly expressed in Ireland. Nevertheless heroic literature frequently calls King Curoi *Ri in Domuin*, King of the World, a title which the writers of the lives of the Irish saints applied to Christ alone (CELT 1: pp. 173ff.; OGAC 15: pp. 369–72).

In African beliefs, the king symbolizes 'the one who holds all life, human and cosmic, in his hands; the key-stone of society and the universe' (LAUA p. 152).

The king is also conceived as a projection of the higher ego, an ideal to be realized. From that point onwards, he ceases to hold any historic or cosmic significance, but becomes a mere ethical or psychological quality. Upon his image are concentrated all longings for independence and self-governance, of basic understanding and awareness. In this sense the king becomes, along with the hero, saint, father and sage, the archetype of human perfection and energizes every spiritual element to that end. This image, however, may be depraved into that of the tyrant expressing the ill-controlled urge to power.

kingfisher Kingfishers flying in pairs, often to be seen in China, are symbols of faithfulness and happy marriage. The Chinese appreciate their beauty and contrast their nobility and refinement with the coarseness of such 'raucous' birds as kites (BELT).

king's daughter, the (see also WATER)   The king's daughter is a recurrent theme in nearly all traditions. She is given to the hero as a reward for his courage and audacity in tasks which the latter will have had to perform successfully and at the risk of his life. Such are the pairings of Atalanta and Hippomenes, Andromeda and Perseus, Ariadne and Theseus and so on.

The king's daughter is associated with the symbol of water as a primordial element. Thales and Anaximander held that all living things came from water and cosmogonies describe water as being the oldest of the elements. Genesis (1: 2) speaks of the Spirit of God moving upon the face of the waters at the time of the Creation, when God divided the waters which were under the firmament from those which were above it. Sea-deities were endowed with prophetic gifts, being the children of the Old Man of the Sea who had perfect understanding of the workings of fate. So Water, like Fire, was used in ordeals and delivered judgement. Consequently those who drowned in shipwreck and storm were the unrighteous. Water not only fills the office of judge, but acts as purifier and provider as well. In fact, the water-ordeal does not simply punish the wicked, it absolves the innocent, too. In old stories, it is the king's daughter who appeases the ocean's wrath – to which she is sometimes even sacrificed – and saves the shipwrecked mariner. In illustration of this, one need only quote the story of Odysseus who flung himself into the raging sea when Poseidon destroyed his raft. He swum desperately and would have drowned without Ino's help. She gave him her veil, so that he was not overwhelmed by the monstrous waves which tried to suck him under. Coming ashore on Scheria, the isle of the Phaeacians, he was found by the king's daughter, Nausicaa. Sometimes the hero is a child destined to do great deeds and the waters which prophesy and pass judgement will steer the wicker basket or reed box which holds him into the hands of the king's daughter who has come to bathe or wash her linen. Thus Moses passed his ordeal by water and was found by the Pharaoh's daughter. There are, however, similar stories much older than that of Moses, such as that of the Greek twins, Neleus and Peleus, set adrift in a wooden trough and found by their own mother, the king's daughter of Elis (PIEF pp. 193–200).

The king's daughter is the symbol of help from an unexpected quarter, of the virgin-mother whose purity and impartiality helps the individual threatened by the waters. She is the favourable aspect of those waters, the other aspect being that of the waters which swallow up their victims. She is part of those waters above the firmament which, at the Creation, God separated from the waters below the firmament. She is the heavenly waters of salvation, the comforting aspect of the MOTHER.

The king's daughter may also be explained in terms of the almost universal myth of the Old King (LOEF pp. 7–18). The Old King is world-memory, the Collective Unconscious, which has gathered to itself all the archetypes throughout human history. He generally keeps his daughter prisoner. She stands for the individual unconscious which, lacking experience of its own, has failed to emerge from the Collective Unconscious, her father, who burdens her with his past. However, Prince Charming, or the active principle of consciousness, will come to waken her and relieve her of the burden of this inhibition. In return, she will endow him with a fragment of that world-memory and from this foundation the conjoint action of Prince Charming and the king's daughter can expand, symbolizing the coming together of the Collective Unconscious (the Old King), the individual unconscious (the king's daughter) and consciousness (Prince Charming).

king's highway   The king's highway signifies the direct route, the straight road in contast with winding paths. In antiquity the term was often also applied to the ascent of the soul.

When used in the Book of Numbers (21: 22), the term has both historic and symbolic meaning for Bible commentators. The Children of Israel sent an ambassador to Sehon, King of the Amorites to ask leave to cross his lands in order to reach their Promised Land. They undertook not to 'turn into the fields or into the vineyards . . . drink of the waters of the well; but . . . go along the king's highway' until they were clear of his territory.

The king's highway was therefore regarded as a direct road, safe from all danger of going astray and thus causing delays. The king's highway was also interpreted as the road leading to the capital of a kingdom or to the residence of its king. Philo of Alexandria wrote: 'Let us enter the king's highway, we who judge that the things of this world should be cast aside; the king's highway of which no man is lord, but only he who is true king is its lord. . . . Who travels along the king's highway will be unwearied when he meets the king at its end' (DANP p. 195).

Thus when the highway leads to the Heavenly Jerusalem, it denotes Christ himself who, in his own words, announced: 'I am the way, the truth, and the life' (John 14: 6) and returned an ambiguous answer when Pilate asked him if he were a king (John 18: 37).

The term passed via Origen and Cassian to the Middle Ages, and in the twelfth century was applied to the monastic life, in so far as it was a strictly contemplative life regulated by God. In his treatise on the love of God, St Bernard of Clairvaux alludes to the king's highway, the *via regia*, which does not turn aside, avoiding roundabout routes and detours, that is to say all those things which might distract the mind and corrupt the soul. Made one with God, the monk clings to God alone (*De diligendo Deo* 21).

kiss   Symbol of joining together and of mutual adherence, which took on a spiritual significance from earliest times. 'In the *Zohar* we find a mystical explanation of the word "kiss". The source is of course a commentary upon the Song of Solomon (1: 2), but there is another, deriving from the rabbinical notion that some righteous persons, among them Moses, were spared the agony of death, leaving the earthly world in the ecstatic rapture of God's kiss' (VAJA p. 210).

In support of this, Georges Vajda quotes a passage from the *Zohar* referring to the divine kiss:

'Let him kiss me with the kisses of his mouth' – Why should Scripture employ this phrase? In fact kisses mean the joining together of spirit to spirit. This is why the bodily organ which administers the kiss is the mouth, through which breath is inhaled and exhaled. Then again, kisses of love are given with the mouth [thus] inseparably linking spirit with spirit. It is for this reason that he whose soul goes out in a kiss, sticks fast to another spirit, to a spirit from whom he will be separated no more. Their joining together is called a kiss. When they

572   KITE (BIRD)

say 'Let him kiss me with kisses of his mouth', the People of Israel calls for this sticking fast between spirit and spirit which will never be separated.

Both the early Fathers and medieval commentators on the Song of Solomon explained 'kiss' in precisely identical terms. William of St Thierry regarded the kiss as a sign of unity. The Holy Spirit might be considered as proceeding from the kiss of the Father and the Son; the Incarnation was the kiss of the Word and human nature; the union between the soul during its earthly existence and God prefigures the perfect kiss which will take place in eternity. St Bernard of Clairvaux, too, in his commentary on the Song of Solomon, writes at length about the kiss which results in unity of spirit. The soul-spouse alone was worthy of it. The Holy Spirit, St Bernard was to say, was the kiss of Father and Son, mouth to mouth, equal to equal and theirs alone. The kiss given by the Holy Spirit to mankind which copies the kiss of the Triune God, is not and cannot be a kiss, mouth to mouth, but a kiss which replicates and is communicated in the form of another kiss. The 'kiss of the kiss' replicates in the human being God's love, the love of God becoming the love of man for God, similar in objective and mode of loving to the love which God has for himself. St Bernard held that in some peculiar manner the human being was involved in the embrace of Father and Son, the kiss which is the Holy Spirit. Mankind was thus united with God through a kiss and even deified by it.

A kiss was given by adepts in the Mysteries of Ceres as a sign of concord, submission, reverence and love. It bore witness to their spiritual communion. In an identical sense St Paul recommends his readers (Romans 16: 16) to 'Salute one another with an holy kiss. The churches of Christ salute you.' This was the usage of the primitive Church. Pope Innocent I replaced this custom by a metal plate (Pax), which the celebrant kissed and gave to the congregation to kiss with the words *Pax tecum* ('Peace with you'). This plate later came to be known as the *Patena* and was to remain in use. The custom of kissing the relics of saints exposed to the veneration of the faithful still exists.

Formerly the feet and knees of kings, judges and those enjoying a reputation for sanctity were kissed. Statues were kissed to beg their protection.

In the Middle Ages, under feudal law, vassals were compelled to kiss the hand of their Lords. In the old books of ritual which relate to the ordination of priests and the final vows of nuns, the bishop's kiss is mentioned. For reasons of decency, the nun was absolved from the duty of giving the kiss on the mouth and had only to touch the priest's hand with her lips. In feudal society, the kiss raised many problems when a lady gave or received homage. As a symbol of joining together, the kiss, in fact, preserved the polyvalency and ambiguity of the countless different meanings of the term (DAVS).

kite (bird) In Chinese literature, the kite is alluded to as a raucous and chattering bird, the equivalent of the European magpie. However, the reverse is true in Japan where it is regarded as a divine bird. According to the *Nihon-gi*, a golden kite alighted on the bow of the first emperor, Jimmu, to show him the way to victory. Thus, during certain ceremonies, the figure of a kite was always placed beside the emperor and may have been a clan-totem, as was the case in Ancient Egypt (BELT, HERJ, OGRJ).

Kites were among the birds sacred to Apollo and their flight was particularly prolific of omens. Apollo changed himself into a kite when Typhon attacked Olympus. The high-flying kite with its keen eyesight was watched for significant movements by the augurs. It was generally associated with Apollo and symbolized second sight.

kite (artefact) Kites are flown for recreation throughout East Asia, but in Vietnam a kite with whistle attached plays a protective role, driving away evil spirits in times of epidemic. To enhance its curative properties the whistle is loaded with powdered sulphate of arsenic which it sprinkles through the air (HUAV), giving the kite a significance akin to that of the bull-roarer.

knee The Bambara call the knee 'the knob of the head's staff' and locate the seat of political power in it (ZAHB).

They agree in this with very many ancient traditions which make the knee 'the main seat of bodily strength ... symbol of man's authority and power in society' (LANS 6: pp. 1, 26). Hence the meaning of the phrases 'to bend the knee' (perform an act of self-abasement), 'bring to their knees' (impose one's will upon, or even kill someone), 'kneel before someone' (perform an act of allegiance or worship), 'clasp someone's knees' (beg them for protection) and so on. Pliny the Elder noted the religious nature of the knees as symbols of power.

knife The symbolism of all cutting tools in general, that of the active principle which changes passive matter, noted under the entry CHISEL, is fully operative here. The importance given to this symbol varies with the races using the particular tool. The Montagnards of southern Vietnam use knives or machetes for virtually every task and the two words are used to cover all male work indiscriminately.

In Hindu iconography, knives as attributes are confined to the gods who inspire fear and in whose hands knives are to be viewed as the instruments of their cruelty. The same is true of Mexican and Mayan hieroglyphics.

In China knives were primarily emblems of the Moon, in the first place because they were curved and in the second because they were consonant with the 'paring away' of the waning Moon.

In many different parts of the world knives were believed to have the power to ward off evil spirits, a power apparently linked to one of the aspects of the symbolism of IRON (DAMS, ELIF).

The symbolism of knives is often associated with notions of judicial execution, of death, vengeance and of sacrifice, Abraham being armed with a knife when he went to sacrifice Isaac. Knives are the essential sacrificial instruments and were employed in many initiatory rituals, most notably in circumcision. This provides a direct link with the phallic symbolism of knives which Freud so often detected in interpreting his patients' dreams.

Knives with blades of bone, flint or obsidian survived from neolithic times for ritual and sacrificial use among some races long after iron had replaced them for everyday employment.

knight The ideals of knighthood, chivalry, as an element of universal culture and a type of higher humanity have persisted in literature from the Middle Ages to the present day. These ideals may be summed up as utter devotion to beliefs and undertakings to which the whole life is dedicated. They find expression in total rejection of the corruption of the outside world and, above all, of treachery. In practice, however, knights were not always wholly immune to these influences and the violent, brutal, lustful, coarse, quick-tempered medieval knight was no model of perfection. Yet some displayed a high degree of refinement in the context of the morality of their age and were civilizing influences upon it. However, we are less concerned with their history than with what they typify. If the symbol of the knight is completely internalized, that is to say if, as some authorities claim, it is concerned solely with spiritual struggle, it tends to become confused with that of the saint. In this context St Louis of France and St Ignatius Loyola may be instanced. The symbol also loses all specific meaning if it is identified with that of the king. It would be better, therefore, to characterize it as 'skill at arms', horsemanship, of course, but also self-mastery, exercised either in the service of his lord, or in obedience to his lady, or in the performance of public office or in the conduct of war. This skill, which comprised possession precisely of those means necessary to the achievement of the given end, went arm in arm with a sort of mystical surrender to some higher authority, God, king, country, his lady, service itself. The knight was not the master, but the servant who achieved self-realization in promoting some great cause.

The ideal of knighthood might degenerate in the directions of power (the Teutonic Knights), wealth (the Templars) or unreality (Don Quixote), and the knights themselves set themselves up as defenders of their own lands, their own wealth or their own delusions. The acquisition of material goods brought self-alienation.

Knights belonged to the warrior CASTE. Caesar chose the word *eques* (HORSEMAN or knight) to describe a member of the Celtic warrior class by contrast with the druids, the priestly caste and, conjointly with the latter, by contrast with the mass of the people who had no recognized political, social or religious existence. The choice of word symbolizes precisely the nature, duties and very essence of the military portion of Celtic society, its members corresponding to the Hindu Kshatriyas.

The symbol of the knight is therefore enshrined in the notion of fighting and in the tendency to spiritualize the battle. Such spiritualization took place either by choosing some noble cause, or by choosing honourable means, or by admission to an élite order, or by finding some extraordinary leader to whom allegiance might be pledged. The knight's dream betrayed his longing to take part in some great exploit distinguished by a high moral character which made it in some sense holy.

Chivalry gave a particular tone to war, love and death. Love was seen as single combat and war as a love affair, in both of which the knight was prepared to lay down his life. He fought the powers of evil, even when they were embodied in the social structure, should they seem to outrage his inner standards.

St Michael was the patron saint of knighthood, famed for his fight with the Devil, whom he hurled down headlong, and with the powers of evil which he routed. His image, the hero in shining armour, lance in hand, haunted the enraptured minds or generous hearts of those eager to sacrifice themselves to make the world a better place. The ideals of knighthood would seem to be wrapped up in a religious fervour. Huizinga (HUID) emphasizes the way in which medieval chivalry took St Michael as its pattern, orders of knighthood being likened to the orders of angels around God's throne. Being knighted was, in the view of the Spanish writer, the Infante Don Juan Manuel (1282–1348), like such sacraments as baptism or marriage.

Yet the image of the knight was not simply the image of what a man might hope to become. It was also the image of the sort of man one longed to have, in whose brave and loving arms one longed to rest. Old King Mordrayns, in *The Tale of the Sankgreal*, provides an example when he falls into Galahad's arms saying:

Sir Galahad, the servaunte of Jesu Cryste and verry knight, whos commynge I have abyddyn longe, now embrace me and lette me reste on thy breaste, so that I may reste betwene thyne armys! For thou arte a clene virgyne above all knyghtes, as the flour of the lyly in whom virginité is signified. And thou art the rose which ys the floure of all good vertu, and in colour of fyre. For the fyre of the Holy Goste ys takyn so in the that my fleyssh, whych was all dede of oldeness, ys becom agayne yonge.

(MALW p. 731)

The true knight is one who, like Sir Perceval, joins in the quest of the Holy Grail and from whom all the world awaits its celestial nourishment. It is he, who, through all the vicissitudes of life, leads one to the heart of the Spiritual Palace. Himself fed by the sacred host, he becomes the embodiment of that host to others.

knot (see also ANKH)   Knots carry many different meanings, but the chief notion which they convey is that of attachment in a predetermined position or state and of concentration. To untie a knot corresponds to crisis or death, or else solution or liberation. This is an immediate example of the ambivalence of the symbol. Knots are constraints, complications, complexities and entanglements and yet, through their ropes, they are linked to their First Cause. Knots may thus embody the entanglements of Fate. In religious literature and art they symbolize the power to bind and loose. They may also symbolize the marriage of two individuals, a social bond, or even a cosmic bond with primal life.

The Upanishads use the phrase, the heart's knot (*granthi*): and to untie this knot is to attain immortality. The parable of the Untying of the Knots, expounded in the *Surangama-sutra*, is well-known. The Buddha taught that untying the knots of being was the process of liberation, but the knots had been tied in a given order and could only be untied in the reverse order. It was a problem of strict method which Tantrism set itself to solve.

Untying, loosing or slipping through – but not slicing through, as Alexander the Great did the Gordian Knot – may be given different forms of expression. It may literally be unravelling, but it may also be slipping through the loop of the *pāsha*, the noose, without getting trapped in it. The symbol is the same as that of being swallowed by the monster – if the jaws (noose) close, it means death, but by being allowed to slip through one attains liberation in a higher state of being. As in the case of Dürer's *Knoten*, knots may provide a sort of maze. Once the centre is reached, dissolution and release ensue.

Another form of knot is that in the Chinese bamboo stem, their vertical order marking out a gradation of levels of being along the axis joining Earth and Heaven, similar to Tantric *chakra* as well as to the Taoists' nine-knotted bamboo. Unravelling 'knots' (*granthi*) is one of the basic exercises in the practice of Yoga. The Ajnāchakra is located in the area between the eyebrows and is also known as the *Rudragranthi*, Rudra's knot. Granet observes that Chinese knots possess the power of 'trapping reality', in other words of fixing or concentrating states of being or elements. Hence arose the custom, paralleled in pre-Columbian America and among the Maoris, of using knotted cords as the earliest form of recorded language. Aside from this specific use, knotted strings possess the same qualities as bamboos and have, in addition, that of the linkage of their successive knots with their First Cause, as demonstrated in the entries SPIDER and THREAD (AVAS, GOVM, GRAP, SEGI).

The Ancient Egyptians considered the knot to be the emblem of life, the Knot or Girdle of Isis being a symbol of immortality. It was often worn on the head or carried by important figures, or else borne on the girdle. The knot was often tied with the thongs of a sandal, the sandal leaving an active print on the ground. Otherwise it was made with textiles, vegetable fibres, string, etc.

According to Abraham Abulafia (twelfth century), the purpose of life is to break the seal of the soul, or to loosen the different bonds which tie it down. When the knots are unravelled, death, or rather real life, ensues. The same notion recurs in northern Buddhism, for example in the Tibetan *Book of the Loosening of the Knots*.

On a spiritual level, loosing bonds means freeing oneself from earthly attachments in order to live upon a higher plane.

According to the Midrash, commenting on Psalm 92: 12 ('the righteous shall flourish like the palm tree'), the palm tree itself is straight and without knots. The palm tree's heart strains heavenwards, and so it is with Israel's heart (VAJA p. 57).

In practical magic knots and bonds are divided into so many different categories as to acquire a regular morphology. 'We would classify the most important facts under two main headings: (1) the magic "bonds" employed against human adversaries (in war or in sorcery), with the converse operation of "cutting the bonds"; and (2) beneficent knots and bonds, means of defence against wild animals, against diseases, witchcraft, demons and death' (ELII p. 110).

Ethnologists have recorded that in different parts of the world men and women are forbidden to wear 'any knot in their attire at certain critical times – childbirth, marriage or at death' (ELII p. 111).

According to Frazer, to assist childbirth everything should be loose and untied. However, the Kalmuck use a net as a protection against evil spirits during childbirth and, similarly, in New Guinea, widows wear nets to protect them from attack by the souls of their dead husbands (ELII p. 111, fn 54).

In Russia knots played an important part in courtship and marriage rites. The wedding dress was bound by a plaited girdle with knots to keep off the evil eye. There was a peasant belief that if the knot in the village priest's girdle came undone, it presaged a forthcoming birth (DALP p. 146). Married women kept their PLAITS unadorned: unmarried girls tied theirs with a ribbon.

The magical practices of Russian peasants displayed the diametrically opposed properties attributed to knots. In some regions, among them Byelorussia and Carelia, the sorcerer would sate his revenge by 'tying up the corn', leaving a handful of knotted stalks by the roadside. On the other hand, in other regions after the harvest, the peasants would leave a plaited sheaf of corn on the bare earth to ensure the new crop. They called this 'tying a knot in Ilya's beard'.

Sailors from the Baltic would carry about them a piece of ROPE or a handkerchief with three knots in them. They believed that untying the first knot brought fair winds, untying the second, storms and untying the third, calm. In Estonia, they believed that the first knot brought fair winds, the second a good catch and that the third should never be untied since it held storms in check.

In Ancient Greece and Rome charms shaped like plaits (see PIGTAIL), coils of hair, spirals, KNOTWORK, as well as rosettes, crosses, swastikas, axes, discs, and so on, were worn as preservatives.

Knots, however, could have an evil influence and women loosed their hair in Dionysiac processions. In Rome, the flamen of Jupiter was forbidden to wear a knot in clothes or headdress. Knots block psychic traffic.

In Dürer's engraving of Ogmios, the Celtic god, as god of eloquence with chains running from his tongue to the ears of his followers, the flaps of his tunic are knotted. These knots symbolize 'the god's capture' (OGAC 12: pl. 27), a capture by or of the god.

In Islamic tradition knots are regarded as symbols of protection. Arabs tie knots in their beards to ward off the evil eye. 'A pre-Islamic custom retained by the Arabs was for the husband to tie together two bunches of twigs before setting out on a journey. This was known as "marrying the twigs". If the traveller on his return found the twigs in the same state, he would conclude that his wife had remained faithful; if not, he believed himself to have been cuckolded' (DOUM p. 90).

In Morocco twigs in the trees around a shrine are often knotted. The practice is consonant with that of bringing stones and has the same significance – the transfer of ill luck. To get rid of disease, knotted rags or hairs are tied to the trees. In the shrine itself, little bags are left containing earth, hair or nail-clippings. These are the means through which the evil influences work which the depositors want to be rid of. To protect corn from ants, a palm leaf is knotted and left at the exit of the ant's nest (WERS p. 233).

Pilgrims caught in a storm at sea tie knots in their clothes (WERS p. 91). However, the pilgrim should wear no knot in his clothes when in Mecca. To tie a knot is thought to bind the saint being invoked and he is told, for example; 'O Holy One! I shall not let you free until you answer my prayer.'

In Palestine, 'when an Arab is attacked and in danger, he can escape from his enemies by tying a knot in one of the strings of the fringe of his headdress and by uttering the name of Allah' (PIEP p. 214).

In Morocco the groom may not have sexual intercourse with his bride until he has untied the seven knots in her garments (WERS 1: p. 583).

The 113th *sūra* of the Koran alludes to the witches' practice of tying magic knots on which they breathed to fix an individual fate upon them, by recommending that prayer should be offered to God against the evil brought by those who breathe on knots.

Tying and loosing are ambivalent symbols and can be related to those of the GIRDLE.

The explanation of the Gordian Knot remains a matter for dispute. Gordius had been King of Phrygia. The yoke of his chariot was tied with so complicated a knot that nobody could untie it, despite the fact that the oracle had promised that whoever succeeded would become ruler of Asia. Many had tried and failed; Alexander cut through it with his sword. He conquered Asia, but his rule soon ended. This was because cutting the Gordian Knot had been an illusion. It had constantly retied itself, being, in reality, the entanglement of invisible realities. According to Deonna (REGR p. 55), the Gordian Knot had 'neither beginning nor end, being a cosmic knot of a plant substance, linked to a sky-god of thunder, lightning and light. It may also be termed a social, psychological and cultural knot.' Although Alexander's sword may symbolize a stroke of genius cutting the ropes, it is in fact simply an act of violence and the ropes will knit together again. In the event he lost his empire and the knot was retied.

The image of the knot is also associated with the notion of death:

Strings, knots and ropes are associated in Indian mythology with death-gods, such as Yama, and with evil spirits and disease. In Iran the demon Astōvidhātusch tied up the dying person. In Australia, the Aronda believe that evil spirits kill humans by throttling their souls with a rope. In the Danger Islands, the God of Death ties up the bodies of the dead with ropes to carry them to the Land of the Dead. These myths must surely be related to those of the Fates with which we are so familiar.

(VIRI p. 61)

As we know, the Fates, or Moirae, personified the fate of each individual being, weaving and knotting the thread of their existence.

To obtain release from a complex by cutting the Gordian Knot cannot be regarded as a psychological victory; its consequences are as short-lived as Alexander's conquest of Asia. The conqueror's sword-stroke was a false solution, that of violence. Patient unravelling, rather than cutting through, ensures a more settled cure and a longer-lasting victory. (See also EIGHT; SPIRAL.)

knotwork   In works of art or as an ornamental motif knotwork is an aquatic symbol, embodying the shimmer and surge of the waves, or else the vibration of the air. In many cosmogonies, vibration is part and parcel of the act of creation, of energy and of all life.

Knotwork is one of the constant motifs of Celtic art, especially in Irish manuscript illumination. It symbolizes the same ideas expressed by the OUROBOROS, perpetual motion developing and coiling through the intertwining of human and cosmic activities (HENI).

Both Leonardo da Vinci and Albrecht Dürer, as we know, had a predilection for knotwork. 'The German painter', Marcel Brion writes:

> had found an element of intellectual curiosity, plastic beauty and mystery in knotwork and this corresponded with his own anxieties and aspirations.... Both artists made the design of knotwork an integral part of their attempt to recover lost primeval oneness.... Knotwork encapsulates a sort of symbolic shape of da Vinci's entire quest for that lost unity, an image of his thought processes, a portrait of the man himself, an abridgement of his philosophy and a projection of the circumvolutions of that fascinating intelligence.
>
> (BRIV pp. 193, 194, 197)

Da Vinci's knotwork has been compared with a baptistery on an octagonal plan (see OCTAGON) and with its developments in multiples of eight it then embodies 'the place where enlightenment and transfiguration take place, the central point from which human vision encompasses the system of the universe in its totality and in its unity and lays bare its secrets and in which the sublime natural order is revealed to mankind in all its structural harmony' (BRIV p. 210).

Among the illustrations to the entry CROSS, those which change the wooden instrument of torture into a knotwork design deepen its significance until it enfolds within the same unity both the natural world and the world of grace. This knotwork can now be regarded less as an invitation to escape from this unity, than to enter it and share its mysterious energy and to identify the adept's soul in some way, not simply with the soul of the world, but with the very nature of the godhead.

The ropes entwined in recumbent figures-of-eight painted on the walls of Masonic Lodges or embroidered on robes are not simply there for decoration, but symbolize the bonds which unite the members of a social body, their repeated coils proclaiming a lifelong union. The latest discoveries in the electronics and biology of the nervous system might well make knotwork a symbol of the mass of electrical and chemical connections within the human brain, with its millions of neurons and synapses. Knotwork might also symbolize the control panel of a telecommunications network and, going a step further, complex thought itself (nothing may be defined unless as a network of active interrelations), which when systematically applied is capable of upsetting not only traditional logic, but scientific method and understanding of communication as well.

kola See COLA.

L

labarum The labarum was an important symbol in the early Church and took two shapes. The first comprised the Greek capital letters I and X (*Chi*) the initials of *Iesous Christos* (Jesus Christ); the second, known as the Labarum of Constantine, comprised the capitals X and P (*Rho*) the first two letters of *Christos* (see CROSS).

Whenever the first figure is set within a circle, as is often the case, with a horizontal line added, it becomes a six-spoked or eight-spoked WHEEL. The wheel is both a cosmic and a solar symbol and this reminds us that in the liturgy Christ was called *sol invictus*, 'the unconquered Sun'.

The second differs only by the addition of the loop of the capital Rho which, as Guénon has observed, might represent the Sun raised to the top of the World Axis, or again the 'eye of the needle' or the 'strait gate' or even the 'Gate of the Sun' through which may be made that 'release from the Cosmos' which is the fruit of Christ's redemptive power.

laburnum The tree's elegant golden flowers fill the heart with happiness, beauty and grace. In Slav counties it is associated with marriage rites.

labyrinth See MAZE.

ladder All the different aspects of ladder symbolism bring us back to the single problem of the relationship between HEAVEN and Earth.

Ladders are pre-eminently symbols of ascension and realization of potential, related to the symbolism of verticality. However, they display a gradual ascension and a channel of communication, in both directions, between different levels. All realization of potential, Bachelard observes, is conceived as elevation, and all elevation is depicted as a rising curve. Verticality is the line which describes the quality and height of that elevation, horizontality its quantity and extent. Height would be the individual's dimension viewed externally, depth that same dimension viewed from within. In art, ladders are the imaginary stairways of spiritual ascension.

They are also symbols of the intercommunication and the comings and goings between Heaven and Earth. As in Dante's *Paradiso* 21: 28–34:

. . . I saw rear'd up,
In colour like to sun-illumined gold,
A ladder, which my ken pursued in vain,
So lofty was the summit; down whose steps
I saw the splendours in such multitude
Descending, every light in heaven, methought,
Was shed thence.

Ladders may be made of pegs hammered into mountain-sides, or even, according to the Pacific legend, of flights of arrows, each one shot into the tail of the one before, and the first sticking into the vault of Heaven. Ladders may also be made of such airy substances as the RAINBOW or, on the spiritual plane, from the stages of inner perfection.

The notion that in the beginning Heaven and Earth were joined and that this connection was subsequently broken, is almost universal. In Shintō there is a belief that this connection was preserved by Amaterasu, who borrowed 'the Ladder of Heaven'; and this belief is current, too, among the Montagnards of southern Vietnam. In these different contexts the ladder clearly plays the same part as the World TREE. Its symbolism is exactly the same as that of Jacob's Ladder, with its angels descending and ascending; as that of the ladder made from two NĀGA, on which the Buddha came down from Mount Meru; as the *mi'rāj* of the Prophet Muhammad; and as the seven-notched birch trees of Siberian shamans. It should also be observed that the Vietnamese Emperor Minh-Hoang reached the Moon with the help of a ladder.

It is significant that the Siberian birch has SEVEN (or NINE or SIXTEEN) notches, that the Buddha's staircase is of seven colours, that the ladder in the Mithraic Mysteries was made of seven metals and that used in the Kadosch by Masons of the Scottish Rite has seven rungs. To pass from Earth to Heaven requires the passage of seven cosmic stages, corresponding to the seven Planetary Spheres and Dante's Seven Liberal Arts which are also mentioned on the Kadosch ladder. These liberal arts may correspond to more esoteric knowledge, the rungs to grades of initiation, as is patently the case with the Mithraic Mysteries. Passing from Earth to Heaven is accomplished in a series of spiritual states, their order marked by the rungs of the ladder and symbolized as well by the angels on Jacob's Ladder.

If we confine ourselves to the means, we shall find that the notion of the ladder (*klimax* in Greek) recurs among the early Fathers and especially in St John Climacus, who derives his surname from one. The means involved are a strict gradation of spiritual exercises, mounted rung by rung. 'Thus,' wrote St Simeon the New Theologian, 'the individual will succeed in raising himself from Earth and ascending into Heaven.' St Isaac the Syrian adds: 'The ladder of this kingdom is hidden within thee, in thy soul. Cleanse thyself, therefore, from sin and thou shalt find the rungs whereon to mount up.' Buddhist *jhāna* are similarly depicted (COEA, ELIM, PHIL, GUED, GUES, HERJ).

In Mithraic initiation it was the symbol of mystical ascension:

The ceremonial ladder (*climax*) had seven rungs, each made of a different metal. Acording to Celsus (Origen, *Contra Celsum*) the first rung was lead, and corresponded to the 'heaven' of Saturn, the second tin (Venus), the third bronze (Jupiter), the fourth iron (Mercury), the fifth 'the alloy of money' (Mars), the sixth silver (the moon) and the seventh gold (the sun). The eighth rung, Celsus tells us, represents the sphere of the fixed stars. By climbing this ceremonial ladder, the initiate was in fact going through the 'seven heavens' and thus attaining the empyrean.

(ELIT pp. 104–5)

Christ and the Cross are both ladders, as is the human individual, and the same is true of trees and mountains. The monastery itself is a ladder, since it is from within the cloister that the religious can scramble up to Heaven.

Some Cistercian and Carthusian houses bore the name of *Scala Dei* (Ladder of God).

As we have said, ladders are one of the symbols of ascension. They stand as units where the upper and the lower, Heaven and Earth, can meet. They make a bridge in the sense used by Iamblicus (d. 330), when he issued the invitation to rise to the heights as though on a bridge or ladder. The whole of spiritual life is expressed in terms of elevation, which is why St Ambrose was to speak of the 'soul of the baptized person rising to Heaven'.

The Hebrew word *sullām*, translated as *scala* in the Vulgate, recurs throughout the Old Testament. Jacob's Ladder may be the best-known example, but there are other significant uses, as in the three storeys of Noah's Ark (Genesis 6: 16), the six steps of Solomon's throne (1 Kings 10: 19) and the steps in Ezekiel's Temple (Ezekiel 40: 26, 31). Psalms 120–34 are known as Gradual Psalms or 'Songs of Degrees'.

During her martyrdom, St Perpetua saw her ascension as a brazen ladder of extraordinary length mounting from Earth to Heaven, but so narrow that people could only climb it one behind the other. On the rungs were set spikes, hooks and blades to tear the flesh of the unwary and underneath the ladder a huge dragon which tried to catch at the climbers and frighten them away from the ascent. St Perpetua says that as she set her foot on the bottom rung of the ladder she trod down the dragon's head and that as she climbed she caught sight of a vast garden (quoted by Louis Beirnart in ERAJ p. 19). In his commentary on this vision, St Augustine was to say (*Sermons* 280: 1) that the DRAGON's head formed the bottom rung of the ladder. Nobody can begin to climb until he or she has trampled the dragon underfoot.

Early Fathers and medieval mystics constantly use the rungs of the ladder between Earth and Heaven in their symbolic shape. The soul always accomplishes its own ascent step by step. The three stages of beginning, persevering and completing, of body, soul and spirit, or the ways of purgation, enlightenment and union, are so many different degrees which were to become traditional under a variety of titles. In his *Homilies on the Song of Solomon*, Origen describes the seven stages through which the soul must go before it can celebrate its marriage to the Word, thus proving how universal is this use of the number seven.

Each stage corresponds to a book from the Old Testament, starting with Proverbs, continuing with Ecclesiastes and reaching the peak with the Song of Solomon. William of St Thierry, in writing of the seven steps of the soul, was to say that it makes its *anabathmon*, or ascension, up the steps of the heart until it arrives at the life of Heaven.

The Pseudo-Dionysius the Areopagite compares the three paths, purgation, enlightenment and union, with the triads of the Church hierarchy. Jacobus of Sarug (d. 521) alludes to the CROSS standing like a miraculous ladder between Heaven and Earth. '[Christ]', he wrote, 'stood on Earth like a ladder abounding in rungs, stood so that He could raise up all earthly beings. [The Cross] is a broad way. It is like a ladder between heavenly and earthly beings. It is so easy to climb that even the dead will step up it. It has emptied Hell and even mortal men climb up it' (quoted by Carl Martin Edsman in ERAJ p. 19).

According to St John Cassian, the ladder which will reach to Heaven has ten rungs, while St Benedict holds that they are twelve in number and describes them in Chapter 7 of his *Rule*. St John Climacus, in his treatise entitled *The Ladder*, speaks of thirty rungs commemorating the thirty years of Christ's hidden life. Jacob's Ladder provided a basic theme for many writers, including St Gregory the Great and St Isidore of Seville. From this rich and well-proportioned treasury, the writers of the Middle Ages were to construct their varied explanations of the mystic ladder linking Earth with Heaven, which the soul is invited to climb in proportion to its longing, its knowledge and its love.

Such an ascensional symbol is an indication of both hierarchy and motion. The earthly condition is the point of departure; the angelic state the goal of arrival. Between them the different rungs, or temporary halts, not only indicate resting-places but glimpses of the beauty and peace which reassure the climber and encourage him or her to persevere and face the struggles which lie ahead. The more the climber can strip off and cast aside, the easier the climb will become. This is why self-denial is so important. It should be observed that the seven rungs described by the mystics bear some relation to the seven gates of Heaven to be found in Mithraic rites of initiation. Each of these was guarded by an angel and the adept had, each time, to strip himself, so that he could attain to the resurrection of the body.

It should also be made quite clear that, in the vertical plane of ascent (*ascensus*) and descent (*descensus*), the peak is directly over the base. Thus Master Eckhart can write: 'What is most high in unfathomable godhead, corresponds with what is most low in the depths of humility.' There is the same meaning behind Macrobius' statement that 'in nature one thing follows another in continuous succession descending, like the rungs of a ladder, from the highest to the lowest rung. Examined with balance and in depth, it will be seen that all things from Almighty God down to the foulest slime are one and are linked mutually by bonds which can never be broken' (*In somnium Scipionis* 1: 14, 15).

Clearly this aspect of ladder symbolism is true to the Platonic tradition which describes the ascent of the soul from the phenomenal to the intellectual world (DAVS, *passim*).

As a symbol of ascension, a ladder has come to represent the ascent (*mi'rāj*) of Muhammad. When the angel Gabriel snatched the Prophet up to Heaven, as he ascended through the darkness, a magnificent ladder (*mi'rāj*) appeared. It is towards this ladder that the dying direct their gaze and it is used by the spirits of mankind to rise up to Heaven. Sufis consider ascension the symbol of the elevation of the soul as it slips the bonds of Earth and attains mystic knowledge.

The rungs of a ladder also symbolize the years of a human life. 'Algerian peasants at Zakkar in the Sheliff Valley still set headboards of olive wood on their graves, standing diagrammatically for the seven Heavens reached by the earthly ladder' (SERH p. 148).

In Ancient Egyptian tradition, Ra's ladder linked Heaven and Earth. The *Egyptian Book of the Dead* refers to a ladder which allows one to behold the gods. In Ancient Egypt, the notion of the ladder was associated with the myth of the CENTRE of the world. However, all holy places can become centres and thus make contact with Heaven.

'The Egyptians preserved in their funeral texts the expression *asket pet* (*asket* means "step") which shows that the ladder offered to Ra for him to climb from earth to heaven was a real ladder. "The ladder is in place for me to see the gods", says the Book of the Dead. . . . In a great many tombs of the Old and Middle Kingdoms amulets have been found bearing a picture of a ladder (*maqet*) or a staircase' (ELIT pp. 102–3).

The Uralo-Altaic shaman performed his ascent to offer the soul of the sacrificial horse to Bai-Ulgen by means of the seven rungs notched in a birch tree. Each of these rungs also marked his passage through one of the planetary spheres. As in the Mithraic Mysteries, the sixth rung corresponded to the Moon and the seventh to the Sun. Travelling from Asia to America, shamanism is found to preserve the same symbolic framework. As Métraux explains, among the Taulipang Indians in Amazonia 'in order to reach the land of spirits, the shaman drinks an infusion made from a liana whose form suggests a ladder' (quoted in ELIC p. 328).

The Turks have the same ascension symbol. 'In the Uighur poem *Kadatku Bilik*, a hero dreamed that he was climbing a fifty-runged ladder, at the top of which a woman gave him water to drink; thus revived he was able to get to heaven' (ELIT p. 107).

Eliade sums up the lesson to be drawn from all these examples, that all ascension symbols 'signify a transcending of the human and a penetration into higher cosmic levels' (ELIT p. 108).

Ladders, however, may be used by deities to come down to Earth from Heaven. In eastern Timor the Sun-Lord, the supreme deity, comes down once a year into a fig-tree to make his wife, the Earth Mother, pregnant. To help him down, a seven- or ten-runged ladder is set up against the fig-tree. This festival is held at the start of the rainy season.

In many accounts of Amerindians there are references to a ladder which leads up to the RAINBOW, and the rainbow itself is often depicted as a ladder, for example by the Pueblo Indians (LEHC). The rainbow is the road taken by the dead. It is, however, a road which leads down as well as up, and along it the inhabitants of Heaven make contact with those on Earth, as if by means of a ladder.

From the rainbow one is led naturally to consideration of the especial symbolism of the double ladder. This is an extremely ancient image, believed to originate with the Chaldaeans. Sometimes it is drawn within a star or a crowned circle. It is the symbol of justice since ascent and descent are precisely matched, as crime and punishment should be. Similarities have been drawn between the two equal lengths of ladder swivelling upon the bar which joins them at the top, and the scales and the symbol of immanent justice. All crime automatically releases destructive forces upon the guilty party and, in a series of concentric circles, upon his or her sphere of influence. Punishment is subject to a sort of psychic determinism.

Climbing, STAIRWAYS and ladders occupy an important place in psychoanalytic writing. In dreams, in so far as ladders are means of ascent, they engender terror, fear and anxiety or their opposites, happiness, a sense of security and so on. Waking dreams offer all sorts of suggestions of rising and falling and their interpretation is mainly derived from a dialectic of verticality, with the occasional anxious fear that the ladder may over-balance. When associated with the notion of rhythm (see DANCE) the ladder symbol may sometimes hold an erotic explanation, the ascent becoming the swelling of the libido into orgasm.

lake Lakes symbolize the Earth's eye, through which the inhabitants of the Underworld are able to gaze upon humans, animals, plants and so on. Marshes symbolize those eyes which have wept too much (BACV, BACE).

In Egypt a vast lake filled the Wadi Fayum. 'Local theologians in the Late Period regarded it as the manifestation on earth of the Cow of Heaven, a liquid sky in which ... the Sun ... had mysteriously hidden ... the over-flow from the Primordial Ocean ... "Mother of all the gods, giving life to men".' Artificial lakes were dug beside temples. Their banks were the scene of nocturnal mysteries and in their waters the priests performed their ritual ablutions (see WASHING). They symbolized the abiding powers of creation (POSD pp. 84, 249).

The Gauls regarded lakes either as deities or as the abode of gods. Into their waters they cast offerings of gold and silver, as well as trophies of their victories.

Lakes were also regarded as underground palaces made of diamonds, gems or crystal out of which rose nymphs, sirens, fairies or witches, but which also lured humans to their deaths. They could then acquire the ter-rifying significance of paradisal mirages. They symbolize the creations of the overwrought imagination.

lamb Through every stage of development, from nomadic pastoralism to settled agriculture, Mediterranean civilizations regarded the first lamb to be born to the flock, spotless, white and shining, as a manifestation of the power of Spring. It embodied the triumph of renewal, of the victory, always to be won afresh, of life over death. It was this archetypal office which made the lamb the ideal victim of propitiatory sacrifice, the victim to be slain in order to ensure its own salvation. In this, as in so many other rites and customs, the adepts of the Dionysiac Mysteries are antetypes of the supreme revelation to come. Thus, to allow the god to reappear on the shores of Lake Lerna, into which he had dived in search of his mother in the Underworld, 'they would cast into its depths a lamb to appease Pylaochos, the warder of the gates of Hell' (SECG p. 294).

The revelation to the Jews gave this symbol its full meaning. In the first place the lamb symbolized the Children of Israel who belonged to God's flock, led to their feeding-places by their SHEPHERDS (political leaders) (1 Enoch 89: 12ff.). 'Behold, the Lord God will come with strong hand, and ... he shall feed his flock like a shepherd, he shall gather his lambs with his arm, and carry them in his bosom, and shall gently lead those that are with young' (Isaiah 40: 10–11). This was an image to which the Christian evangelists returned (Luke 10: 3, 15: 3ff.; John 21: 15–17).

Most importantly of all, and with undeviating consistency, to this day the lamb has been the sacrificial victim for all occasions for Jews and Christians and Muslims as well. This is especially true of the rites which have suc-ceeded those of vernal renewal, the Jewish Passover, Christian Easter – the death and resurrection of Christ, the Lamb of God – and the Muslim Ramadan sacrifice, the *Kurban*.

A detailed study of these three rituals reveals the continuity of their symbolic meaning down to the smallest detail. Thus, the redemptive blood which Christ shed upon the Cross is not unrelated to the saving blood of the sacrificial lamb with which the Jews daubed their doorposts and lintels to ward off the powers of evil.

When, at the sight of Jesus, St John the Baptist exclaimed: 'Behold the Lamb of God, which taketh away the sins of the world' (John 1: 29), he was referring, in part at least, to this theme of sacrifice. This paschal note is what is so strongly heard in the First Epistle of St Peter (18–19). The Christian is set free, as the Children of Israel once were in Egypt, by the blood of a lamb, Jesus Christ.

Both St John (19: 26) and St Paul (1 Corinthians 5: 7) bear equal witness that the death of Christ perfectly fulfils the sacrifice of the Passover lamb.

Nevertheless, when referring to Jesus as the Lamb, early Christians referred as strongly to another Old Testament prophecy, the mysterious passage in which Isaiah (53: 7 especially) foretells the suffering Messiah symbolized in the metaphor of the lamb led to the slaughter (see Acts 8: 32).

In the Book of Revelation, the Lamb stands on Mount Zion in the centre of the Heavenly Jerusalem. Basing himself upon a description of the Brahma-pura in the *Bhagavad Gītā* (15: 6) almost identical with that of the Heavenly Jerusalem, Guénon suggests a kinship – purely phonetic – between the Lamb (Latin *agnus*) and the Vedic Agni, the god who rode on the back of a ram. The similarity is more than a piece of pure chance since, apart from Agni's sacrificial character, both are seen as the light at the centre of existence, the goal of the quest for supreme Knowledge. This comparison of the Lamb with the Vedic fire-god emphasizes the solar, virile and luminous aspects of the Lamb. This is the Lamb's leonine aspect, which is also displayed in the Book of Revelation which uses the word 'lamb' to denote Christ on twenty-eight occasions. Since, on the one hand, the Greek word used is not precisely the same as that employed in other examples and, on the other, this lamb displays its anger (6: 16ff.), makes war and wins victories (17: 14), it is not unreasonable to detect the influence of star symbolism (Aries, the Ram of the Zodiac). Be that as it may, earlier symbolism is still there, for this is a lamb which is sacrificed (5: 6, 9: 12), the victim and even the Passover victim. This, however, is a return to the risen and glorified Christ and it reveals fresh harmonies: this Lamb has overcome Death (5: 5–6) and the powers of evil (17: 14), it is almighty, divine (5: 7–9) and judge (6: 16).

It was doubtless to avoid all confusion in worship and belief which could arise from the similarity of symbols which led the Council held in Constantinople in 692 to give orders that Christian art should depict Christ upon the Cross in human form and no longer in the shape of a lamb, nor flanked by Sun and Moon.

lameness Rulers of fire and smithies in virtually all mythologies will be lame if they are not ONE-LEGGED. Their infirmity makes them partners in all

the ambiguity – holy left and holy right, divine or diabolical – which underlies odd numbers. Loss of bodily wholeness is most generally regarded as
the price they have had to pay for their supra-human knowledge and for
the power which it confers upon them.

As thieves or robbers, they may, like Prometheus, have awakened the
jealousy of the supreme deity who has branded their flesh, exacting, as it
were, the payment of ransom. This is the fate of culture-heroes in many
mythologies. And yet *Deus impari gaudet* (God delights in the uneven).
This deity is all too human if he becomes jealous of what delights him.

Lameness is a sign of weakness, of the unfinished and of something out
of balance. In myths, legends and folk stories, lame heroes evoke cycles
which begin with the end of one journey as the prelude to a new one.
Lameness suggests sunset or else the Sun at the end of one year and the
beginning of the next.

In his description of a journey to the Underworld, Apuleius explains that
'when the best part of your journey is done, you will meet a lame man with
a bundle of faggots on his back and an ass as lame as he.' The symbol
remains the same whether a god, a king, a prince, a dancer or a donkey-
driver is concerned, and it recurs in 'lame-footed' dances. The lame man
often follows the BLACKSMITH's trade and the smith hammers out swords,
sceptres and shields, symbolizing the Sun's limbs, its rays. Yet his work
cannot bear comparison with that of a god, of a Demiurge or of the Sun.

If the FOOT is a symbol of the soul, then a defect in the foot or in the gait
betrays a weakness in the soul. This, in any case, is what all those mythological or legendary examples of lame men reveal. Achilles may not have
been lame, but he was invulnerable except for his heel, and this was because of his proneness to anger and violence, which are weaknesses of the
soul. From the symbolic point of view, to limp means to have a spiritual
disability.

This disability may not necessarily be on the moral plane, but may indicate an injury on the spiritual. For this reason, the vision of God carries
with it a mortal danger and can leave, as it were, a scar, symbolized by
lameness, in the soul of those who have only enjoyed that vision for a
snatch of time. This was the fate of Jacob after wrestling heroically with the
Lord. He himself explained that his lameness was caused by his vision of
God. 'I have seen God face to face, and my life is preserved. And as he
passed over Penuel the sun rose upon him and he halted upon his thigh'
(Genesis 32: 30–1).

HEPHAISTOS (Vulcan) was a lame and deformed god. Like Jacob after his
wrestling with Jehovah, Hephaistos became lame after a bout with Zeus in
defence of his mother (*Iliad* 1: 590–2). In Olympus he was the smith and
fire-god. His disability was surely a sign that he, too, had seen some secret
of the godhead, some hidden aspect of the supreme deity and in consequence remained forever disabled. Again, what he had seen must surely
have been the secrets of fire and of metals, which may be liquid or solid,
pure or alloyed and may change themselves into either swords or plough-
shares. To pay for stealing this secret from Heaven he had to lose his
bodily wholeness. In many other mythologies we find such blacksmith-
gods as Varuna, Tyr, Odin or Alfödr, gods with knowledge of fire and

metal-founding, wizard-gods who were either lame, one-eyed, one-armed, or otherwise disabled. The loss of bodily wholeness is the price of knowledge and power and a reminder, too, of the punishment which threatens excess. Beware lest you misuse this magic power for the supreme deity is jealous and will brand you with the marks of his power, the sign that you are still his subject.

Lameness symbolizes this brand left upon all those who have come near the power and glory of the supreme deity and demonstrates their powerlessness to rival the almighty (see also DEFORMITY).

lamentation The Book of Lamentations, attributed to the prophet Jeremiah, describes the pitiful state of Jerusalem and Judea, but simultaneously gives vent to complaint and petition. It is a confession of sin and a cry of anger, but, at the same time, an outpouring of hope and a confident appeal.

The Ancient Egyptians had set rituals of lamentation. They seem to have been designed as spells and petitions, appealing to the gods to safeguard the voyage of the sacred boat, to ensure happiness and resurrection and to inflate the dead person's merits through the howling of professional female mourners. The Ancient Greeks, too, had their funeral hymns, threnodies and such lamentations as that of Achilles over Patroclus. Lamentation is part of the funerary ritual of all peoples.

An important part of the funeral ceremonies of the peoples of northern Europe was played by lamentation, and all insular literary sources describe the lengthy ritual of funeral games, lamentation, burial, and the erection of a memorial stone, sometimes accompanied by a mound, on which the name of the dead man was carved in Ogham script. Obviously such rites were confined to kings and chieftains. There does not appear to have been a class of professional mourners, but the task of organizing lamentations seems to have been left to the women. When his brother Ailill was on the verge of death, the King of Ireland, Eochaid Airem, entrusted his wife Etain with the task of arranging his funeral. The symbolism of lamentation is not clear-cut, and it is uncertain as to whether it is solely a matter of displaying sorrow in the face of death. One is more inclined to believe that, in the cultural environment of northern Europe, lamentation was, as in any case in Africa it still is, a spell cast upon, or a warning given to the dead to prevent their return amongst the living.

The poplar, with leaves which shiver in the lightest breeze, is a symbol of lamentation.

Lamia Lamia was a very beautiful woman with whom Zeus fell in love, but Hera, his wife, in a fit of jealousy pursued her and killed all her children. Lamia took refuge in a cave and, jealous of other mothers, hunted, stole and ate their children. She is a symbol of the jealousy of the childless woman.

Lamia was unable to sleep and, taking pity on her ceaseless wakefulness, Zeus granted her the privilege of being able to take out and replace her eyes at will. From then on she was able to enjoy sleep, but only when she was drunk or had removed her eyes – a merciless image of unsleeping jealousy.

Lamia was the name given to unnatural she-monsters who hunted children to drink their blood. The Ancient Greeks also applied the name to creatures of the imagination used to frighten children like bogey-men or vampires.

lamp Lamp symbolism is linked to that of the diffusion of light. The lamp, the Zen patriach Hui Neng taught, 'is the framework of light and light is the manifestation of the lamp.' From this derives the 'oneness' of the one with the other which is like that of 'concentration and Wisdom'. Similarly, Tibetan Buddhists speak of the 'lamp of discipline' which lights the way to Wisdom. Ismaili esoterics also teach that light is the manifestation of the lamp, the lamp being both God and light, the Divine Attributes and the Imam as such.

Hui Neng regarded the uninterrupted transmission of the flame of the lamp as a symbol of the transmission of the Law and there is an important Zen treatise on the transmission of the light of the lamp. In Buddhism, it is, in more general terms, the handing on of life, the cycle of 'rebirths in which there is continuity but not identity'. Release from this cycle, Nirvana, is blowing out the lamp.

Furthermore, the yogi who achieves spiritual concentration is compared by several writers, and especially in the *Bhagavad Gītā*, with a motionless flame sheltered from the draught. Even in the West, the lamp is sometimes taken as a symbol of holiness and the contemplative life.

'Exist, with the Self for lamp', the Buddha taught, in other words, with the Universal Spirit. The same injunction recurs in the Upanishads, and in the same way Mahmūd Shabistarī makes the lamp a symbol of the Divine Spirit (*ar-Rūh*) or the World Soul.

In the West, lamps are frequently used as a sign of the Real Presence of God. They are set on the tops of Buddhist pagodas as 'lighthouses of the Dharma' and Taoists once employed them to summon spirits. In the lodges of Chinese secret societies a red lamp enables 'the true to be distinguished from the false'; it is a reminder of the manifestation of celestial influence, but 'enlightens' the faithful as well. In Hindu iconography, the lamp is the emblem of Ketu, the comet. Ketu also means 'lamp' or 'flame' and the symbolism of Ketu may not be unrelated to the *āratī*, the Hindu rite of hanging lamps in front of images of the gods. Hanging lamps suggests images of rejecting thoughts of the profane world, the lamp itself being, of course, related to the element of FIRE (COOH, CORT, DANA, DAVL, HOUD, MALA, MAST, GRIL, SAIR, SECA).

Berber women say that every time a child is born a lamp is lit:

This lamp is lit near the head of the new-born baby during the first nights he sleeps on Earth. It is the lamp which was carried in front of the young bride and which burned throughout her wedding night, summoning the Invisible to assume bodily shape.

The lamp stands for the human being. Like it, it has a body of clay, a vegetative soul or life-principle, the oil, and a spirit, the flame. To offer a lamp in a shrine is to make an offering of oneself and to place oneself under the protection of the Invisibles and the guardian genii. This is the reason why, in North Africa, lamps are piled in their hundreds in the corners of shrines, in the hollows of rocks and between the roots of sacred trees. . . . In houses in which marriages are celebrated, lamps summon wandering souls so that one of them, lured by the flame, will come down into the bride's womb.

(SERH pp. 71–2)

The Christian custom of offering and burning candles in the sanctuary and before statues of saints symbolizes the FLAME of sacrifice, love and the divine presence.

lance See SPEAR.

language (see also LETTERS; NAME; SOUND; WORD; WRITING) Written and spoken language is infused with symbolic qualities, not only in all that is given expression in image, idea, feeling, resonance, graphics and so on, but also, to a certain extent, in what remains unexpressed. In India, the passage from word to actuality is termed *sphota*, the 'opening' of the bud. Language may be a channel of communication between humans, but by means of prayer and invocation it is the *dhikr* or *japa*, the means of communication between the individual and the godhead. As a symbol of the Word, or *Logos*, it is the instrument of the divine Intelligence, Action and Will in the Creation. The world itself is the consequence of the divine Word. 'In the beginning was the Word' (John 1: 1). 'In the beginning was Brahmā,' say the Vedic writers, 'and with him was *Vāk*, the Word.' In Islam the Word is called *Kalimat Allāh*, 'the Word of God', or 'the Word which Establishes'. Abū Ya'qūb Sejestānī took the four consonants of the word *kalimat* (klmt) to be the fourfold manifestation of primal unity. The *Sepher Ietsirah* states that 'the Word (*Memra*) created all being and all things by its one Name.' *Vāk*, the creative Word, is the bride of Prajāpati, but above all Brahmā's SHAKTI. *Vāk* is also the breath of Shiva-Maheshvara as well as being the cosmic breath, *Vāyu*.

Language is at one and the same time a symbol of God's creative will and of primeval revelation. Brahmā's creative energy, *sarasvatī*, is also Knowledge, Wisdom and the Mother of the Vedas. Hence the enormous importance of the languages in which these secondary revelations have been received and of which they are reflections – of Arabic, for example, the only language in which the Koran may be read, since that language is the very fibre of the book itself. The quest for the 'Lost Word', so often invoked, is that for the Primordial Revelation, for which the symbolism of primeval language is another synonym. In Muslim tradition, the language concerned is 'Syriac', or 'Solar', a patent way of expressing the 'light' drawn into the primeval spiritual centre. It is significant that the language of Paradise was understood by animals. The shaman's acquisition of the language of beasts is, contrariwise, a symbol of the return to the paradisal state. An even clearer expression of this is the fact that so often the language concerned is the language of birds. Now the language of birds is a heavenly or angelic language – symbolically analogous with 'Syriac' – and one which can only be understood by somebody who has risen to certain spiritual levels.

Closely connected with traditional knowledge is the twofold symbolism of 'the gift of tongues' and 'the confusion of tongues'. The latter was a direct consequence of the attempt to build the TOWER OF BABEL and marks the development both of different languages and, at the same time, of different traditions. This is the result of that spiritual befogging which directs the gradual passage from unity to multiplicity, doubtless a normal development and not simply a divine punishment.

Contrariwise, 'the gift of tongues' marks a return to a 'central' state, a synthesis from which modalities of form and expression are seen as necessary adaptations, but of contingent order. The gift of tongues which the Holy Spirit conferred upon the Apostles is the clue to the universal appeal of Christianity. Rosicrucians were said to possess it, as were the twelve sent out by the first Adam, according to Ismaili esoterics who point to the text in the Koran (14: 4): 'We have not sent any Apostle, save with the speech of his own people.' The same gift appears to have been highly regarded by some African pygmies and this might be regarded as a dim memory of a paradisal state.

If the paradisal state implies knowledge of the language of animals, Adam is said to have given them their names (Genesis 2: 19) and hence to have made them subject to him. Now, it is one of the constants of Chinese thought that the order of the universe is controlled by *ming*, correct nomenclature. The *cheng ming*, taught by Confucius, was the essential nature of this correct nomenclature. As the French poet, Milosz, remarks: 'These nouns are neither brothers, nor sons, but the fathers of tangible objects.' In the force of language remain traces of primeval cosmogonic strength.

Another power of language is the one conferred by initiatory MANTRAS or at least the one broadcast by Buddhist teaching. In the *Samyutta Nikāya* (2: 221) Kashyapa is told that he is 'The natural child of the Blessed One, born from his mouth, born and shaped by the *dharma*.' But the *dharma*, in fact, goes straight back to the primeval language spoken by Manu, who made the laws at the beginning of the cycle.

Another very special and often half-understood symbol relating to language is the Tibetan prayer-wheel. It has nothing to do with prayers, but with holy words which its motion scatters abroad like a universal blessing (AVAS, CORT, DANA, ELIY, ELIM, GRAP, GUEV, GUEC, GUEO, GUES, SAIR, SCHC, VACG).

Language is also a symbol of intelligent entities, be they individuals, cities, ethnic groups or nation states. In this context, by language is meant strictly written or spoken language or dialect which is one of the countless forms of language and one of the components of intellectual or social structures. A deep reality resides in the relation between language and the individual. Together they develop and together they preserve all their common experiences. Language is the soul of cultures and societies. Thoughtless harm inflicted upon language affects society as a whole, damaging the roots of its bonding and helping to sever them. Language is, in fact, an intellectual and social structure. It is the main channel of communication between one individual and another and between group and group. It is the most highly refined and subtle means of exchange and interfusion. It transmits a measure of unity to the individual and is a socially cohesive factor. Societies break up when they abandon or weaken their language, and this is why ethnic minorities endeavour to preserve their languages as emblems of their own identity. Mastery of language develops individuation. Knowledge of languages bonds its possessor with the individual or group. To attack a language is to attack an individual; to respect a language is to respect the person who speaks it. Language discharges an energy which proceeds from the whole being and is directed at the whole being. It is steeped in the strength of the symbol and opens the gates to full participation in life.

lantern   Originally lanterns (*toro*) simply filled a decorative function in Japanese temples and shrines. They were symbols of enlightenment and spiritual light. From the Muromachi period (1333–1573) onwards, when the arts of gardening and the tea-ceremony evolved, lanterns had a dominant role in aesthetics and became an indispensable part of the Japanese garden. Merchants offered up lanterns in Buddhist temples to bring success to their ventures, and soldiers to crown their arms with victory.

Western tradition observed the use of funeral lanterns, which burned either beside the corpse or in front of the dead person's house. They symbolized the immortality of the soul in contrast with the corruptible body.

lapis lazuli (see also TURQUOISE)   In Mesopotamia, Sassanid Persia and pre-Columbian America, this stone was a cosmic symbol of the starry night (ELIT pp. 271–2).

larch   Like all conifers, the larch is a symbol of immortality. Hence Siberian tribesfolk cast it as the World TREE, down which the Sun and Moon descended in the shape of gold and silver birds. When associated with the Moon alone, as is the case of the cypress in Europe, the larch sometimes also partook of a funerary character.

lark   Its habit of rising swiftly heavenwards and as rapidly falling to Earth might make the lark a symbol of the evolution and involution of manifestation. Passing successively from Earth to Heaven and from Heaven to Earth, it links together the two poles of existence and acts as an intermediary.

Thus the lark stands for the marriage of Heaven and Earth since it flies high up into the sky and nests at ground level among scraps of dried grass. Its flight into the bright dawn light suggests youthful enthusiasm, ardour and happiness in being alive. By contrast with the nightingale, its song is a song of joy.

The lark in the morning sunshine symbolizes the human drive for happiness. To mystic theologians the lark's song symbolizes pure and happy prayer rising before God's throne.

The Gauls regarded the lark as a sacred bird and throughout the long history of French folklore it has remained a bird of good omen, sometimes even used in charms. 'Whoever carries about his or her person real lark's legs or models of them cannot be harrassed; this charm will overcome the forces of man and nature alike' (CAND p. 17).

laurel   Like all evergreens, laurels symbolize immortality, a factor of which the Romans certainly had not lost sight when they made it the emblem of both intellectual and military glory. In the past, the laurel was also believed to preserve from thunder, a quality deriving from the first of these.

This immortality symbolism was equally familiar to the Chinese. The Moon, one is assured, contains an Immortal and a laurel-bush. At the foot of the laurel (a medicinal plant), the Moon Hare brews the herbs from which it distills the drug of Immortality (SOUL).

As a shrub sacred to Apollo, the laurel symbolized immortality acquired through victory and this is why its leaves were used to crown heroes, geniuses and wise men. An Apollonian tree, it also signified the spiritual conditions of wisdom and valour under which victory was won.

Before the Pythoness delivered her prophecies in Ancient Greece she either chewed or burned laurel leaves which, being sacred to Apollo, conferred the powers of second sight. Those who had gained a favourable reply from the the Pythoness 'returned home wearing a crown of laurel' (LOEC p. 52). Laurel symbolized Apollonian qualities, a sharing in these qualities by touching the plant sacred to the god and, consequently, a special relationship with him which ensured his protection and transmitted a share of his powers. Like milk, laurel displays symbolic association – immortality and hidden knowledge.

In North Africa at seasonal rituals of the Beni Snus, the masked participants carry wands of rose-laurel:

The shrub is deliberately chosen since it grows in damp places and peasants credit it with many purificatory qualities. . . . Once they have been sanctified by dipping in the blood of the sacrificial victim, these branches are tangible signs of the covenant made between humans and the invisible beings; and by this fact become protective charms which drive away all evil influences.

(SERP p. 370)

lead The symbol of heaviness and of impregnable individuality. 'This heavy metal is traditionally an attribute of Saturn, the god who divided and set boundaries. Thus, in order to transmute lead into gold, alchemists attempted, symbolically, to cut themselves free from their limitations as individuals and to embrace collective and universal qualities' (VIRI p. 175).

According to Paracelsus, lead was 'the water of all metals. . . . If alchemists knew what Saturn contained, they would desert all other matter to confine their work solely to this metal' (PERD p. 390). This corresponds to the stage in the 'work' when the matter becomes black, so white lead would be identified with alchemical mercury. It would symbolize matter, in so far as it was interfused with spiritual powers, and the potentiality for transmutation from one body into another, as well as for the general properties of matter into spiritual qualities. Lead symbolizes the humblest level from which spiritual ascension can evolve.

leaf Leaves share the symbolism of PLANTS in general. In the Far East they are one of the symbols of good fortune and prosperity. A bunch or sheaf of leaves denotes a group as a whole in joint action or common purpose.

leaping See JUMPING.

leech A Bengali tradition recounts that the leech, the third Demiurge, was sent after the tortoise and the crab by the all-powerful Sun-god, the consort of the Moon, to recover the Earth from the bed of the Ocean (ELIT). Leeches are among the many geomorphic and cosmomorphic creatures which symbolize the primordial elements which make up the universe.

left See RIGHT AND LEFT.

leg The limb for walking, the leg is a symbol of social bonding. It allows
individuals to approach one another, promotes contact and removes separation and therefore derives its importance from the social order. Hence its
esoteric significance for the Bambara as a marriage-broker, grouping it with
the tongue, nose and sexual organs as a welder and unraveller of society.
For the Bambara, these organs assume a basic importance, they are group-
workers responsible for the cohesion – or dissolution – of the social group.
The foot is an extension of the leg, and they complement one another
symbolically. The latter forges the chains which bind society together and
the former is its ruler and key. By extension, the leg is to the body of
society what the penis is to the human body. It is the instrument of maternal and social relationships as the penis is that of consanguinity. Like the
penis, the leg is a symbol of life. 'To bare one's leg means to display one's
power and virility.' To go through the motions of putting a boot on one's
foot in front of somebody is to cast the most serious aspersions upon the
latter's mother (ZAHB 82, p. 173).

lemures The Latin name for frightening, ghostly apparitions, taken to be
the souls of the dead in general, or of members of one's family in particular,
which came to haunt the living with their own anxieties. Their aid was
sought during the yearly festival of the Lemuria described by Ovid in his
Fasti. Lemures symbolize ancestral shades which haunt dreams and memories like so many reproaches directed by the subconscious to the conscious.

  Bernard Frank records a similar Japanese belief in GENII, like the Lemures.
They are Underworld spirits, ghostly apparitions which haunt and torture
human imagination.

Leo (23 July–22 August) The fifth sign of the ZODIAC fills the height of
summer. The sign is, therefore, characterized by Nature's fruition under the
heat of the Sun, its ruling planet. Placed at the heart of the Zodiac, this sign
expresses lust for life, ambition, pride and exaltation.

  Leo brings us back once more to the element of Fire. However, a change
of principle develops between Aries and Leo so that from brute animal
strength, as spontaneous and instantaneous as a spark or flash of lightning,
conscious strength emerges to become a controlled and operable force, like
a flame giving a full and constant heat and light. We have, in any case, come
from the morning light of Spring to the splendour of Summer's noontide.
The sign is denoted by the royal majesty of the King of Beasts, an emblem
of sovereign power, of strength and nobility, and it is coupled to the Sun.
Both the sign and the Sun symbolize life governed by heat, light, glamour,
power and the glitter of the élite. Thus Leo-types are like triumphant odes
sung to the accompaniment of sounding brass, aflame with the life force.
This zodiacal type corresponds to the high-powered character of the strong-
willed fanatic driven by the obsession to do. The love of action, that emotionally active strength, is controlled and directed towards a goal and
subservient to long-term designs. A strong nature, inherently endowed with
a full-blooded enjoyment of life, finds justification for existence by making
the heavens ring with its achievements. This power can be expressed as

horizontal deployment, as a Herculean type of efficiency, as physical presence, physical activity, the here and now. However, it may also be deployed in vertical tension and provide an Apollonian type of idealism, in which the powers of enlightenment tend to rule unrivalled.

leopard   Ancient Egyptian priests wore leopard skins during funeral ceremonies. The skin symbolized the genius of Set, the god of evil, the enemy and the adversary of gods and men. Wearing leopard-skin meant that Set had been sacrificed, the adversary defeated, and that the wearer carried about him evidence both of that sacrifice and of the magic power it conferred. The sacrifice of which the skin was witness warded off the evil influence of the wicked spirits who haunted the dead. Similar beliefs and practices recur among Asian shamans and in Amerindian civilizations.

The leopard is a symbol of pride, but it is also a hunter. In many respects it is related to Nimrod and, in more general terms, may be regarded as a symbol of the warrior and kingly castes in their aggressive aspects. The leopard symbolizes blood-thirstiness as well as strength and cunning.

In China leopards are among those animals which hibernate and of which the disappearance and reappearance corresponds with the rhythm of nature. The leopard – or a very similar species – is identified with the *p'o-ching*, a mythical beast which is supposed to have eaten its own mother. However, *p'o-ching* also means 'broken mirror', which would seem to associate it with the cyclical waning of the Moon. While the lion is a solar animal, the leopard would seem to be a lunar creature (DEVA, GRAD, GRAP, GUES).

In his apocalyptic vision, Daniel saw 'four great beasts [coming] up from the sea, diverse one from another. . . . [One] like a leopard, which had upon the back of it four wings of a fowl; the beast had also four heads; and dominion was given to it' (7: 3, 6). Critics identify this creature with the Kingdom of the Persians, but without disputing this view and simply passing from a historical to a symbolic explanation, this leopard may be regarded as the monstrous image of an overwhelming disaster striking with unbridled speed. (Four wings represent either the acme of rapidity, or a gale blowing simultaneously from all four quarters, a full-throated tornado; while the four heads stand for the power which overshadows and imposes its authority upon the whole region.) On this level, the leopard symbolizes the ruthless lightning stroke of force.

letters of the alphabet   (see also DA'WAH; LANGUAGE; WRITING)   In Kabbalistic tradition, the letters of the Hebrew alphabet possess creational powers which humans cannot know. 'No one knows its [right] order, for the sections of the Torah are not given in the right arrangement. If they were, everyone who reads it might create a world, raise the dead, and perform miracles. Therefore the order of the Torah was hidden and is known to God alone' (SCHS p. 167).

The book *Bahir*, which is written in the form of a Midrash, or collection of judgements, contains a theory about the vowels and consonants in Hebrew. 'Exclusive of the consonants, the vowels in the Torah may be compared with the living soul within a man's body.' What the book *Bahir* suggests was first enunciated by Judas Halevi. According to Scholem, 'vowels stand for the spiritual in contrast with the corporeal represented by consonants.' Vowels may be regarded as dots and therefore as circles, while consonants are shaped like squares. Hence correlations may be established between 'God–soul–vowel–circle' and 'tribe–body–consonant–square' (SCHO pp. 74–5).

In many alphabets or collections of ideograms, letters or ideograms correspond to the phases of the Moon. This was true of Babylonians, Greeks and Scandinavians (ELIT p. 178).

As in Kabbalistic, so in Islamic tradition a highly refined science of letters is based upon their symbolic qualities. Hurufis, who are adepts in this science, regard a noun as being no less than the essence of the object to which it is applied. Furthermore, all nouns are comprised of the letters used in speech. The whole universe was produced by these letters, but it is in mankind that they make themselves manifest. The letters which God taught to Adam were thirty-two in number, but some of them were lost.

A high proportion of those letters recur in the sacred books of the revealed religions – twenty-two in the Jewish Pentateuch, twenty-four in the Christian Gospels and twenty-eight in the Koran.

These twenty-eight letters also possess numerical properties, as different prophets have observed. They have the potential for different permutations which hold numerous subtle truths.

Thus the first letter, *alif*, takes precedence over the arrangement and combination of the twenty-eight letters. As a number, its value is one. Now unity is an attribute of God, and this is why this letter is the initial letter for the names of Allah and of Adam since it 'doth encompass all things' (Koran 41: 54).

The Hurufi regard God as a power transmitted through a word, that is, a phoneme or a voice. It finds expression in the thirty-two letters of the Arabic-Persian alphabet, twenty-eight of which were used to write the Koran which is the Word of God, and the sound articulated by using these letters is the Essence of God.

The thirty-two letters are manifestations of the Word itself and are the inseparable attributes of its Essence 'as indestructible as Absolute Truth. Like the person of the godhead they are immanent in all things. They are merciful, noble and eternal. Each of them is invisible [hidden] in the Divine Essence.'

Adam's (or the human) face is an exact representation of the face of God, provided one is capable of analysing its lines. Thus, there are SEVEN lines (eyebrows, eyelids and hair) on this face and, if they are multiplied by the four elements, the product is twenty-eight, the number of letters in the Arabic alphabet.

Similarly there are seven signs, or *āyāt*, in the first *sūra* of the Koran. Man, the microcosm, is analogous with the Koran.

So far as the mysterious isolated letters in the Koran are concerned, Professor Massignon describes them as 'abbreviations for the classes of concept spelled out to the Prophet in dreams'. The letters of the alphabet were, in any case, conceived very early in their history 'as the Word of the godhead in material form' (MASH p. 589).

According to the Sufi master, 'Abd ar-Rahmān al-Bistāmi, the letters of the alphabet should be classified like the elements into letters of Air, Fire, Earth and Water.

By taking into account their fundamental and astral nature and their numerical value, letters enable us to attain to esoteric knowledge inaccessible by any other route. In some sense they supplement revelation by making flash before the astonished eyes of the mystic the redemptive enlightenment of the *kashf* [revelation of divine truths] and a perception of events hidden in past, present or future time.

(FAHD p. 228)

Islamic esoteric speculation has been allowed to range freely in this field, from which it has garnered a whole science of divination based upon individual letters and their correspondences (see DA'WAH).

Letters may thus be regarded as symbols of the mystery of individual being, with their basic oneness deriving from the Word, and their countless diversity resulting from their potential for infinite permutation. They are the image of the multiplicity of created life, perhaps the very substance of the beings to which they give their names.

The letters of the ancient Irish or Ogham alphabet were simple notches cut in groups of up to five at right angles or diagonally to or across a line which served as a spine. Examples of up to a sentence or two on wood survive from what were probably longer inscriptions. What we have are, in the main, to be used in magic or divination, incantations which rivet a curse, taboo or obligation upon a named person. Ogham letters possess no curves in them and were simple to cut. They were originally intended to be notched into wood and there is, interestingly enough, an almost perfect homophony between the Celtic words for 'knowledge' and 'wood' – *fid* in Irish; *gwdd* in Welsh; *gwez* or *gouez* in Breton; and *uissu* in Gaulish. They form a 'tree alphabet' since each letter is given the name of a tree. The most ancient Irish alphabet is called the Beth-Luis-Nion Alphabet, from its first three letters – B (Beth) = Birch, L (Luis) = Rowan and N (Nion = Ash). Traditionally, its inventor was named as the god Ogmios, standing for the dark side of the godhead, the primeval sovereign.

However, Ogham was never used as a literary or educational medium – this was exclusively oral – although it is possible that this was due to the development of an archaic system of writing borrowed from the Roman alphabet. Ogham, in any case, symbolized the dark and magic side of Celtic tradition. When Cùchulainn notched Ogham letters on an oak branch, he halted the army of Ireland in its tracks. By carving Ogham letters on a slip of yew, the druid Dallan found the place where Etain was, the Queen of Ireland whom the god Midir had carried off. Dead persons' names were cut in Ogham to tie them to their graves and prevent them troubling the living. The Celts had, nonetheless, an ordinary system of writing – the Gauls used the Greek alphabet – but this could not be used to transmit what was a living tradition. This had to be an oral tradition, for writing killed what it made permanent and unchanging. This is the reason for the absence of Gaulish literary remains, except for inscriptions upon stone or bronze and, of course, on coinage (LERD pp. 122–6).

Letter-forms have stimulated most interesting comparative and historical research. W. F. Albright maintains that the first letter in most ancient alphabets, 'a', or *aleph*, represents a bull's head; the second, 'b', *beth*, a house; 'h', *heth*, a man praying; 'm', *mem*, water; 'n', *nun*, a serpent; 't', *tau*, a cross and so on. Most letters originally depicted an animal, a human gesture or a physical object.

The Kabbalah has built an edifice of cosmogonic and mystical speculation on the shape of letters. *Aleph* suggests the crown of the All-Highest, the right tip pointing upwards denoting wisdom, the left tip pointing downwards corresponding to the mother suckling her baby. Alternatively the upper part denotes the beginning, or wisdom, whose power gives all things their being; the central line, the intellect, the child of wisdom; while the lower part denotes the end of this development in knowledge herself, the daughter of the intellect. *Aleph* thus possesses the beginning and the end of all higher forms of being and this letter symbolizes spirituality. The next letter, *beth*, is the house of wisdom which makes itself manifest in countless ways and fashions. It is God's seal imprinted upon all beings. The house so depicted is open on the left side to the spiritual influences of *aleph*, but closed upon the right so that the seeds of wisdom may ripen in it. 'Through wisdom is an house builded; and by understanding it is established: And by knowledge shall the chambers be filled with all precious and pleasant riches' (Proverbs 24: 2–4).

The sixth letter, *vav*, has been compared to the Pillar of the World, a stream watering plants in a garden, the Tree of Life, a leaping flame, a ray of light, a head and so on (KNOS).

There is an endless fund of such examples of explanations based upon metaphor, homonym and analogy, but not always upon symbolism. However fertile the imagination, it does not always function symbolically.

level With the PLUMBLINE, the level is an important feature of Masonic symbolism. Both are attributes of the two Watchers and, in this respect, their twofold function corresponds to that of the two pillars of Solomon's Temple.

The level comprises a SQUARE, from the upper angle of which hangs a plumbline. If its essential purpose is to determine the horizontal, it is equally able to determine the vertical as well. This enables it to share the symbolism of the CROSS on a cosmic scale. Both are manifestations of the Heavenly Will at the centre of the cosmos and of a harmonious diffusion on the cosmic plane. To pass from the perpendicular to the horizontal is to pass from Entered Apprentice to Fellowcraft Degree which, overall, expresses the reality of this promotion derived from knowledge of the way in which Heaven acts and the acquisition of the influence which it manifests. Oswald Wirth had sound grounds for emphasizing the morphological relationship between the level and the alchemical symbol for sulphur. In fact, the synthesis of the perpendicular with the horizontal is realized by the square alone, an attribute of the Worshipful Master.

Moral or social application of the symbol to notions of equality or of levelling out are clearly inadequate. However, the idea of balanced judgement may usefully be suggested since it is akin to that 'horizontal' diffusion which we have discussed (BOUM, GUET), as well as to the preservation of the same level on a vertical line.

Leviathan In Phoenician tradition, the Ros-Shamra was the symbol of the storm cloud which Baal overpowered to bring fertilizing rain to the Earth.

However, historically and psychologically this symbol acquired infinitely wider dimensions than those of the agrarian myths from which it originated.

The Bible describes Leviathan as a monster which should not be aroused and it is often mentioned in the Psalms and in the Books of Job and Revelation. The name is derived from Phoenician mythology which applied it to 'a monster of primeval chaos . . . there was a common superstitious fear that a powerful curse against the present order might stir him to action. The DRAGON of Revelation 12: 3, who embodies Evil's hostility to God, has certain characteristics in common with this serpent of chaos' (BIBJ on Job 3: 8). This SERPENT when roused was able to swallow, even if temporarily, the Sun itself and witches took advantage of this eclipse to cast their spells. Chapters 40 and 41 of the Book of Job draw a terrifying picture of Leviathan. 'Shall not one be cast down at the sight of him? None is so fierce that dare stir him up: who then is able to stand before me?' (Job 42: 9–10).

He lives for ever in the seas where he lies sluggish until he is aroused. Historically, the reference in Job is to the crocodile, a symbol of Egypt, which had such unhappy memories for the Jews. It also conjures up images of 'the monster which in the beginning the Lord defeated, itself a type of the powers opposed to God.'

The sea monster conjured up in Job 7: 12 comes from Babylonian cosmogony. 'Tiamat (the Sea) co-operated in the birth of the gods and was then conquered and subdued by one of their number. The imagination of the people, or of poets, seized on this story: Yahweh became the conqueror who then set Chaos in order and ever after held the Sea and its monsters in control' (BIBJ).

In this context it is interesting to note that if you accept that the sea is also the symbol of the unconscious, reservoir of shadowy monsters and the forces of instinct which need the power of God to bring to heel, then you have implicitly a theology of grace which is correlative to the power of this Leviathan, a monster capable of swallowing the Sun, itself a symbol of the godhead. These are bound to bring to mind the mysterious and primitive powers of instinct and the unconscious.

In political philosophy, Leviathan symbolizes the state which allots to itself absolute monarchy, rivals God and arrogates to itself absolute power of life and death over all beings whom it brings under its control. A pitiless and uncontrolled monster, arbitrary, cruel and tyrannically totalitarian, seeking to control the personality as well as the person. This absolutist concept of the state derives from Thomas Hobbes, as a logical consequence of a materialist philosophy which claims to protect individuals and groups, but at the cost of their freedom and of passive obedience to the ruler.

levitation See ASCENSION.

liana Thai peoples believe that the liana was the original link between Heaven and Earth, in universal tradition a link that was ruptured. Some regard GOURDS, the fruits of the liana or World Axis, as the source of their tribe.

The twofold nature of the liana and the tree around which it twines is a symbol of love. More precisely, in India the liana is Pārvatī and the tree, Shiva in the shape of the LINGAM. This symbol is somewhat akin to that of the BETEL. The spiral entwining of creepers naturally conjures up, in addition, SPIRAL sybolism in general (DANA, FRAL, ROUN).

Libra (23 September–23 October) When the Sun enters this sign it is at the mid-point of the astronomical year. Its passing from the northern to the southern hemisphere marks the balance between the house which has been built and the forces waiting to pull it down, as well as that between day and night. The sign is depicted by SCALES with a beam and pair of pans. This precise mid-point, upon which everything is balanced, displays the equipoise of external Autumn dusk and internal Spring dawn. It is at this mid-point that one is peculiarly aware of the neutralization of opposing forces, as the equidistant pans of the scales hang in balance – brake and engine, modesty and boldness, artistry and artlessness, fear and rashness, denial and response to the call to live. From it is derived the golden mean, the measured response, half-tones, shades and colours of meaning. Before our eyes opens a world of discrimination of the subtlest character, symbolized by the element of Air. The airy environment of Libra is to that of Gemini what the heart is to the soul. The ego occupies it with someone other than itself, equal in worth, opening an emotional dialogue between the I and the You. The sign which governs parties of pleasure is in any case ruled by Venus, Saturn bringing a measure of detachment and spiritualization to her company. The Venus concerned is the Aphrodite of Autumn roses, the goddess of ideal beauty, of spiritual grace and of sacramental marriage as well as of serenade and stately dance.

library Libraries are our reservoirs of knowledge, treasure-houses open to all. Generally speaking, in dreams libraries allude to intellectual knowledge and book-learning.

Nonetheless, in them one sometimes discovers mysterious books of spells, generally glowing with light, symbolizing knowledge in the full sense of a recorded lifetime of experience.

light In many instances the boundaries between light as a symbol and light as a metaphor remain ill-defined. For example, it might be a matter of dispute as to whether light, 'the ultimate aspect of matter moving at a known speed, and the light of which the mystics speak, have anything in common apart from being ideal goals and boundaries' (VIRI p. 259). On the other hand, we realign with the symbol when we regard light as 'a first aspect of the unformed universe. By setting our course towards it, we set off along a path which seems to take us beyond light, that is to say, beyond all form and even beyond all physical sensation or intellectual emotion' (VIRI pp. 265ff.).

Light is paired with darkness to symbolize the complementary or sequential qualities of an evolution. This law is confirmed by images from Ancient China, among those of so many civilizations. Their meaning is that, just as at all levels of human life,

at every cosmic level a 'dark' period is followed by a 'light', pure, regenerate period. The symbolism of emerging from the 'darkness' can be found in initiation rituals as well as in the mythology of death and the life of plants (buried seed, the 'darkness' from which the 'new plant' (*neophyte*) arises), and in the whole concept of 'historical' cycles. The 'dark age', *Kālī-yuga*, is to be followed, after a complete break-up of the cosmos (*mahāpralaya*), by a new, regenerate era.

Mircea Eliade wisely concludes:

It is in this sense that we can talk of the positive value of periods of shadow, times of large-scale decadence and disintegration; they gain suprahistorical significance, though in fact it is just at such times that 'history' is most fully accomplished, for then the balance of things is precarious, human conditions infinitely varied, new developments are encouraged by the disintegration of the laws and of all the old framework.

(ELIT pp. 183–4)

Phrases such as 'Divine Light' or 'Spiritual Light' reveal the content of a wealth of Far Eastern symbolism. 'Light' is knowledge and the two senses of the word are to be found in the Chinese ideogram *ming* as well. It synthesizes sunlight and moonlight and has the meaning of 'Enlightenment' for Chinese Buddhists. In Islam *En-Nūr*, Light, is basically identical with *Er-Rūh*, Spirit.

According to the Kabbalah, the diffusion of light (*Aor*) from the primordial 'dot' created space. This is the symbolic meaning of the words 'Let there be light' in the Book of Genesis, light which is also enlightenment and order out of chaos, through vibration, according to Guénon, and in this respect the physical theory of light may itself even be regarded as symbolic. According to St John (1: 9), primeval light is identical with the Word. This expresses, in some sense, 'diffusion of spiritual sunlight which is the true heart of the world' (Guénon). St John explains that this diffusion is apprehended by 'every man that cometh into the world', linking with the symbolism of light as knowledge apprehended without 'refraction', that is to say, by direct intuition, without any intervening distortion. This is the essential nature of enlightenment by initiation. This direct knowledge, which is sunlight, stands in contrast with moonlight which, being reflected, stands for rational and discursory knowledge.

Light follows darkness in the order of cosmic manifestation as in that of inward enlightenment. Their succession is as clearly observed by St Paul as it is by the Koran, the *Rig-Veda*, or by Taoist writers, or again by the Buddhist *Anguttara-nikāya*. It is another instance of Amaterasu coming out of the cavern. In more general terms, light and darkness constitute a universal duality expressed most clearly in that of YIN AND YANG. It is in any case a matter of indivisible correlatives, depicted by *yin–yang*, in which *yin* contains traces of *yang* and vice versa. In Zoroastrianism the opposition of light to darkness is that of Ormazd to Ahriman; in the West that of angels and devils; in India that of *deva* and *asura*; in China that of celestial and terrestrial influences. 'The Earth appoints the darkness, and the Heavens the light', Master Eckhart wrote. Once again in China, the conflict of *chin-ming* is to be found in the motto of secret societies. *Chin* (to destroy) and *ming* (to re-create) do not carry the sole meaning of conflict between two dynastic principles, but re-creation of enlightenment through initiation. In Ismaili esotericism, the duality is also that of body and soul, symbols of the principles of light and darkness coexisting in the same individual.

In India and China, as in the Book of Genesis, the first work of Creation was the separation of light and darkness, which were interfused in the beginning. A 'return to the beginning of things' might therefore find expression in the resolution of this duality and the re-creation of primordial unity. 'Follow me', Chuang Tzu wrote (ch. 2), 'beyond the two principles [of light and darkness] into oneness.' The patriarch Hui Neng taught that: 'The common run of mankind regards enlightenment and ignorance [light and darkness] as two different things. Wise men who have achieved the inward reality know that they are of the same nature.'

This is a symbolism which belongs to certain mystical experiences, since the beyond of light and darkness, the essence of the godhead, cannot be apprehended by human reason. This notion is as clearly expressd by some Muslim mystics as it is by St Clement of Alexandria, St Gregory of Nyssa – on Mount Sinai Moses entered the darkness of the godhead – or by the Pseudo-Dionysius the Areopagite.

To increase the intensity of inward light, Taoists employed such different methods as the absorption of sunlight and ingestion of the light of dawn. It is a point of some interest that ultimately they conceived of the immortal body as a body composed of light.

In Celtic tradition light in its various forms is the end or the source of comparisons and flattering metaphors, with which the dictionary is especially well-supplied. Light clearly symbolizes the intermediacy of the sky-gods and Lug is called *grianainech*, 'Sun-Face'. In process of time, in the Christian era, Nuada's sword became the *claidheamh soillse*, 'the Sword of Light' of the Christian faith. All evil influences or ill omens were blamed upon darkness and night. Additionally there was a symbolic equivalence between light and the EYE. Welsh poets called the SUN *llygad y dydd*, 'the eye of the day', while the Irish phrase *li sula*, 'light of the eye', is a well-chosen metaphor drawn from the flash of sunlight. In Gaul there was a god called Mars Loucetius, a later form of Leucetius, 'the shining one', reminiscent of the epithet 'Sun-Face' applied to Lug and occasionally to Ogma. God is light.

Light manifests the forces of fertility released by the sky, just as water is often a manifestation of those same powers released by Earth. In countless central Asian myths, light 'is conjured up either as life-giving heat or as the force which penetrates a woman's womb' (ROUF p. 228). It is a commonplace, Roux adds, that 'throughout the world the most efficacious revelation of the godhead takes the form of light'. Both in Christian and Islamic iconography all revelations of the godhead and all appearances of sacred shapes or emblems are surrounded by haloes of pure, astral light, in which the other-world presence may be recognized.

Roux quotes in support the testimony of a Tibetan monk that 'at the beginning of time, the ancient peoples multiplied by light emanating from the man and entering the woman's womb to make her pregnant.' Similarly, the symbol may be transposed to the spiritual plane, the light of grace making fruitful the heart of the individual whom God summons.

In China, a number of heroes or founders of dynasties were born after 'their mother's bed-chamber had been flooded with miraculous light' (ROUF p. 289). Furthermore, the blue wolves, lions or horses, which figure so largely in the zoos of wonder-animals in Mongolo-Turkic legend, are no more than revelations of celestial light. The same might be said of the spiral of red copper which is twined round the Dogon solar matrix and which cuts the clouds to make the Earth bear fruit. Whether it be water or light, it is celestial semen in the sacred marriage of the elements.

If sunlight is an emanation of celestial power, human hopes and fears do not regard it as an unchanging factor. It may quite easily vanish and with it life might disappear as well. Throughout human history there are records of a host of rituals inspired by solar eclipse and of daily human sacrifices to the Sun, their blood feeding its light. Among some pre-Columbian races, such as the Aztecs or the Chibcha in Colombia, these were on a massive scale. Here Sun-worship led to the growth of what were civilizations of fear, linked to the recurrent phases of the agricultural cycle.

Although the Sun may die each night it is reborn each morning, and humanity links its fate with that of the Sun's light and derives from it hope in the continuity and power of life, for 'there is an essential kinship between mankind and the upper world' (LEER p. 57). Sunlight is human salvation and that is why the Ancient Egyptians sewed an amulet symbolizing the Sun to the wrappings of their mummies.

The ruling dynasties of the Mongols which preceded Genghis Khan sprang from an unmarried princess who explained away the three children to which she gave birth by saying: 'Every night a shining golden man entered through the smoke-hole of her tent, caressed her belly and penetrated her womb with his shining light. . . . He left her by climbing out like a yellow dog along the shining beams of the Sun or Moon. Those who can read the signs will realize that her three sons must have been children of heaven' (ROUF p. 322).

The dove, embodying the Holy Spirit, which in Christian tradition came down to Our Lady, may be regarded as a revelation of the power of light. However, light may also be revealed as the ancestress whom the male impregnates rather than as the revelation of male powers of fertilization. Thus, in a fragment of the *Oghuz-name*:

One day while Oghuz was offering his prayers to Tangri [the sky-god] a blue light descended from heaven. This light was brighter than that of Sun or Moon. Oghuz drew near and perceived that in the midst of this light there was a maiden . . . of extraordinary beauty. . . . He loved her and took her. . . . And she bore three sons. To the first they gave the name of Sun, to the second, Moon, and to the third, Star.

(quoted in ROUF p. 372)

The famous *Emerald Table*, of which the authorship is attributed either to Apollonius of Tyana or to Hermes Trismegistus and which was revered like the Tables of the Law by alchemists and esoterics for hundreds of years, conjures up the creation of the world in these words: 'The first thing to appear was the light of the Word of God. Light bore action, action bore movement and movement bore heat.' Jacob Boehme believed that light derived from fire, but fire 'brings pain, while light is kindly, gentle and fruitful' (*Mysterium Magnum* 5: 1).

This Divine Light, which Jacob Boehme associated with Venus, is the

awakening of desire, or love fulfilled after purification by fire. The light
contains the Revelation, since 'in the light there is a good and merciful
God, and in the power of the Light he calls himself over and above all else
God. And moreover, this is none other than God revealed' (ibid. 2: 10).
Thus, in the mystical sense, the glorification of Light is absolute, since it
becomes in itself the first revelation of the godhead, in which the perceptible quality is so strong that God reveals himself without needing to take
any shape, light providing a manifestation in conflict with darkness. Light
is love, since light derives from fire, just as the desire of love derives from
the will of God (ibid. 2: 18). It should be remembered that in the primitive
Church, baptism was called 'Enlightenment', as the writings of the Pseudo-
Dionysius the Areopagite bear especial witness.

The Old Testament marked itself sharply off from the religions which
surrounded it by declining all theorizing on a Sun-, Moon- or star-God, the
adversary of the powers of darkness. This is why Genesis 2: 3 speaks of day
and light as God's creations and very little of the celestial body which is
their patent cause.

Throughout, light symbolizes life, salvation and happiness granted by
God (Psalms 4: 7; 36: 10; 97: 11; Isaiah 9: 1), who is himself light (Psalm 27:
1; Isaiah 60: 19–20). God's Law is a light unto the paths of individuals
(Psalm 119: 105), as is his Word (Isaiah 2: 3–5). The Messiah, too, brings
light with him (Isaiah 46: 6; Luke 2: 32).

Darkness is correspondingly a symbol of evil, misfortune, punishment,
damnation and death (Job 18: 6, 18; Amos 5: 18). These realities, however,
do not derive from a power alien to God; since he himself created darkness,
he, too, inflicts punishment. Furthermore, God's light pierces and scatters
the darkness (Isaiah 60: 1–2) and he himself calls mankind to the light
(Isaiah 42: 7).

Christian symbolism merely continues along the same lines. Jesus is the
Light of the World (John 8: 12; 9: 5), and those who believe in him should
be so, too, (Matthew 5: 14) by becoming reflections of the light of Christ (2
Corinthians 4: 6) and conducting their lives in accordance with it (Matthew
5: 16). A way of life inspired by love is the sign that the person walks in the
light (1 John 2: 8–11). Nevertheless, in some passages in the New Testament the conflict between light and darkness partakes of a more fundamental nature; it seems to have been influenced by the dualist ideas current in
some late Jewish circles into which Zoroastrian ideas had been introduced.

For example, among the Dead Sea scrolls there is *The Book of the War
between the Children of Light and the Children of Darkness*, which draws a
distinction between the elect, who from all eternity are predestined to belong
to the divine army of light, and others whose true home is the Kingdom of
Darkness. In consequence, the entire history of mankind and of the world
is seen as a pitched battle between two armies led by their supreme commanders, the God of Light and Satan – or Belial, or Mastema – the Prince
of Darkness.

Although it has been carefully Christianized, it must seem that such notions
linger in the background of the opening of St John's Gospel, since he speaks
of light which the darkness cannot and will not accept (John 1: 4–5). Later
Christian voices eagerly took up this theme in *The Manual of the Two*

Ways, upon which the authors of the *Didache* and *The Epistle of Barnabas*
both draw. In it, the individual's moral life is described as two paths along
which he or she walks, guided either by God or by an angel of darkness.

Gnostics enlarged what had been the strictly moral field of this symbolism by speculating upon the conflict between primeval heavenly light and
supernatural powers of darkness. The phenomenal world is a trick played
by the powers of darkness in an attempt to steal the light, which succeeds
only in trapping its reflections in matter. Hence the elect, those in whom a
spark of the divine light dwells, must strive their utmost to repel and annihilate the ascendancy of matter, in order to regain their true nature which
is essentially divine and of the light.

Light, for the Fathers, was a symbol of the Kingdom of Heaven and of
Eternity. According to St Bernard, when the soul is separated from the
body it will be 'plunged into a vast ocean of eternal light and of bright
eternity.' Noon (see MIDDAY) is the pole of this light which, in its symbolic
sense, is 'when time stands still . . . the supreme moment of divine
inspiration . . . the brightness and intensity of meeting God face to face'
(DAVS pp. 52, 160).

The symbolic meaning of light derives from a study of the natural world.
Both Persia and Ancient Egypt, and indeed all mythologies, make light an
attribute of the godhead. 'The Ancient World as a whole bears the same
witness – Plato, the Stoics, the Alexandrians, as well as the Gnostics. St
Augustine was to pass on the Neoplatonist influence in praising the beauty
of light. The Bible had already proclaimed its grandeur when it called the
Word, Light of Lights' (DAVS p. 159). The whole of the first epistle of St
John has as its theme that God is light.

In Islamic tradition, light is pre-eminently the symbol of the godhead.
The Koran (24: 35) states:

God is the light of the Heavens and of the Earth. His light is like a niche in
which is a lamp – the lamp encased in glass – the glass, as it were, a glistening
star. From a blessed tree is it lighted, the olive neither of the East nor of the
West, whose oil would well nigh shine out, even though fire touched it not! It
is light upon light. God guideth whom He will to His light, and God setteth
forth parables to men, for God knoweth all things.

All Muslim mystics have meditated upon this *sūra,* and a Sufi treatise
entitled the *Mirsadulabād* comments upon it as follows:

Man's heart is like a glass lantern set in the recess (*mishkāt*) of his body. That
is to say, it is the most closely concealed consciousness (*sirr*) enlightened by the
light of the spirit (*ruh*). The atmosphere within the recess is irradiated by the
light reflected by the glass. This atmosphere stands for the physical faculties,
while the beams of light which shine through the glass are the five senses. By
degrees, God's light diffuses beauty and purity to the lowest and highest faculties of the human soul and this is what is meant by 'light upon light'.

(MASP p. 530)

The first part of al-Ghazālī's *Niche for Lamps* is devoted to a study of
this essence of light. He states that 'God is the sole light from which all
other lights derive in a way similar to the physical diffusion of light throughout the universe. It might be likened to moonlight, itself reflected sunlight,

which enters a room through the window, is reflected from a mirror hanging on one wall onto another wall, which in its turn reflects the light onto the floor' (WENG pp. 14–15).

Psychologists and psychoanalysts have noticed that 'ascension is linked to images of brightness accompanied by feelings of euphoria, while falling is linked to images of darkness, accompanied by feelings of fear' (PALP p. 96). These observations confirm that light symbolizes the maturing of the personality in harmony with the higher levels of being to which it rises, while darkness, blackness, would symbolize a state of anxiety and depression.

In Ancient Egypt the god Set symbolized the terrifying and evil light from dark places, while the god Anubis symbolized the life-giving, favourable and uplifting light from which the universe arose and which conveys the soul to the Otherworld. Light symbolized the power of giving and of taking away life. Life was dependent upon light, which it received and which determined both its level and its nature.

In the language and rituals of Freemasonry, to receive the light is to be accepted for initiation. Having taken part in certain rituals, the Entered Apprentice takes an oath, wearing a blindfold. When this is eventually removed, he is 'as if dazzled by the sudden brightness, and receives the light. All the lodge members point their swords at him. The light is given by the Worshipful Master with the aid of a flaming SWORD, a well-known symbol of the Word.' Giving the Light is a ritual performed at the opening of a meeting. The Worshipful Master alone is allowed to hold the lighted candle. He gives the light to the two Watchers who each carry a flaming torch and with them he lights the other candles set in front of the pillars. Finally, 'when a Mason of high standing is introduced, the Master of Ceremonies walks in front of him carrying a star which symbolizes the light represented by the visitor' (HUTF pp. 148, 158, 162). The light to which the rituals so often refer is none other than knowledge, which transfigures and which it is the duty of Masons to acquire.

lightning Lightning symbolizes the spark of life and the powers of fertilization. It is fire from Heaven, vastly powerful and terrifyingly swift, which may be either life-giving or death-dealing. The Hebrew word used in the Creation story may be translated either as light or as lightning. Lightning has been compared with seminal ejaculation, symbolizing God's virile action in creation. Australian Aboriginal mythology is more explicit in stating that lightning is a tumescent penis. According to the Atjiraranga-Mitjina myth, studied by Geza Roheim (GEZH 313ff.), lightning and bull-roarer are the erected penis of the son who is to be killed by his father, the thunder. In the same sense Psalm 29: 9 speaks of the voice of the Lord making 'the hinds to calve'. When God speaks it is to the accompaniment of crashes of thunder and flashes of lightning (Exodus 19: 16–18). The Old Testament God is a god of lightning and also of fire, and lightning is his instrument (Job 37: 3ff.).

Jeremiah presents the God who created the world as a god of thunder and lightning (10: 12–13) while Psalm 77: 18–19 also alludes to thunder and lightning. The primitive Elohim was the god of the thunderbolt. God's face flashes like lightning (Daniel 10: 6) and his hands are covered with lightnings (Job 36: 32).

Ancient Babylonian tradition takes up this theme. To the Greeks, too, Zeus was the god of the thunderbolt.

On the spiritual plane, lightning produces inward light since it forces the individual to close his or her eyes, that is, to meditate. Lightning marks the individual deeply in the sense of Job's 'he hath set his mark upon me' (16: 12).

Lightning is a sign of power and strength, the manifestation of an energy which restores equilibrium (Job 37: 14–18).

In African tradition, too, lightning, as well as thunder, is the attribute of the almighty sky-god. According to a Pygmy myth, lightning was the instrument – the divine phallus – of the elemental sacred marriage of Heaven and Earth, an echo of Indo-European mythology in which it was the instrument of Indra. The Pygmies also regard it as the instrument with which the sky-god punishes adultery.

Its association with rain – celestial semen – is almost world-wide. Together they comprise two facets of the same symbol, based upon the twofold nature of Fire and Water, which can be either positive or negative. They may be the agents of fertility, but they can also be divine punishments wiping mankind out by fire or flood.

Eastern thought constantly associates symbolically lightning with fertility, as this Taoist prayer makes evident: 'As that powerful and resistless element the thunderbolt cleaves the cloud to turn it into rain, so open this woman's womb so that she may soon give birth' (HENL quoting Granet).

In Ancient Peru, the fertilizing Sun assumed the aspect of lightning with which it became confused and which, in turn, became embodied in the image of a serpent, frequently with two heads, which was a symbol of rain (TRIR).

As the weapon of Zeus, forged in FIRE (symbol of the intellect) by the Cyclops, lightning is 'the symbol of intuitive and spiritual enlightenment' (DIES p. 118), or of the sudden flash of inspiration. However, while it enlightens and stirs the spirit, lightning strikes down 'the drive of unsatisfied and uncontrolled desire', represented by the Titans. The symbol is ambivalent – it both enlightens and destroys. Dionysos' mother, Semele, was destroyed by lightning, unable to bear the sight of Zeus as a god.

In Vedic tradition, the acolyte invoking Agni touches the water and chants: 'You are the lightning; cleanse me from evil. From the priestly order I go to the Truth.'

In this context the association of Fire and Water is particularly striking. If lightning is truly fertilizing, it also acquires a twofold sense of purification, since the Truth demands purity. Lightning and water are associated in the *Chāndogya Upanishad*, as well, in a description of the fecundating monsoon storms. For lightning is not simply a phenomenon, not simply light or fertilizing rain, but is in truth the symbol of another reality, that of the shining realms of Brahmā. The *Kena Upanishad* makes it plain that the Brahman is that which 'gives fire to the lightning . . . and thus belongs to the ranks of the gods. But this truth can only be known, understood and grasped in overall intuition by him who has expelled evil and who has his roots in the infinite and unassailable world of Heaven.'

Lilith   Lilith was the name given, in Kabbalistic tradition, to the woman created before Eve, at the same time as Adam, and not from his rib but, like him, fashioned directly from earth. She claimed equality with Adam, since both were created from dust. This led to a quarrel and Lilith, having in her anger pronounced the name of God, fled to begin her mission of she-devil. In another tradition Lilith was a first Eve, and Cain and Abel quarrelled over possession of her, since she had been created independently of Adam and was not related to them. Some detect traces of HERMAPHRODITE in the first man and of INCEST in the first man and woman.

Lilith was to become the foe of Eve, promoting adultery and extramarital relationships. Her dwelling was to be set at the bottom of the sea and anathemas were pronounced to confine her there and to prevent her troubling the lives of mortal men and women (SCHS pp. 157ff.).

As a wife supplanted by or deserted for another woman, Lilith was to stand for hatred of family life, of marriage and of children. She was to echo the tragic figure of LAMIA in Greek mythology. Unable to integrate within the structure of human society, with its interpersonal and group relationships, she was cast into the abyss of the ocean depths where she continues to be tortured by perverted desire which prevents her from taking part in normal relationships. Lilith is 'the nocturnal female satyr who tries to seduce Adam and to give birth to the phantom creatures of the wilderness; the vampire-nymph of inquisitiveness, who can take out and replace her eyes at will and who suckles the children of men with the poisoned milk of dreams' (AMAG p. 199). She is to be compared with the Black MOON, with the shadowy world of the unconscious and with dark impulses. Eaten up by jealousy, she devours the new-born.

lily (see also DAY-LILY)   Although lilies are synonymous with whiteness and consequently with purity, innocence and virginity, becoming, for Jacob Boehme and Angelus Silesius, symbols of heavenly purity, they are, nonetheless, liable to quite other interpretation.

A lily was what Apollo's catamite, Hyacinthus, was changed into and in this context the flower evokes unlawful passion, although the flower concerned is the martagon or red lily. Persephone was gathering lilies, or narcissi, when Hades, who had fallen in love with her, carried her down to his Underworld kingdom through a chasm which he had opened in the ground. Lilies might therefore symbolize temptation or the Gates of Hell. In his plant mythology, Angelo de Gubernatis considers that lilies are undoubtedly attributes of Venus and the satyrs, because of their phallic pistils, and that, in consequence, lilies are symbols of procreation. This, the author feels, is why they were chosen by the Kings of France as symbols of the prosperity of their line. Ignoring the phallic aspect, in his novel, *The Cathedral*, Huysmans denounces their spicy-sweet scent as being akin to Levantine and Oriental aphrodisiacs, the very opposite of the odour of chastity. To the poet Mallarmé, lily symbols had lunar, female and even aquatic overtones. The lily thus became the flower of love and of a love which, although intense, might in its ambiguity be unfulfilled and either repressed or sublimated. When sublimated, lilies are flowers of glory.

This notion is not foreign to the equivalency which can be established between the lily and the LOTUS, which springs up from the muddy unformed waters. It then becomes a symbol of the potential of the individual to realize the antitheses of his or her being. Perhaps the words Anchises addressed to Aeneas, prophesying the wonderful destiny of their descendants, should be interpreted in this sense. 'Thou shalt be Marcellus... Give me lilies with full hand, let me scatter purple flowers' (Virgil, *Aeneid* 6: 883–4). The offering of lilies to the shade of the young Marcellus when Aeneas descends to the Underworld amply illustrates the flower's ambiguity. When he sees it growing on the banks of Lethe (6: 709), Aeneas is 'thrilled by the sudden sight' of the mystery of death. On the other hand, these purple flowers offered to Augustus' adopted son help to stir in Aeneas' heart 'love of the glory to come'. The symbol thus possesses the power to exalt or to bring down in death.

The six-petalled heraldic lily again may be identified with the six spokes of the WHEEL of which the rim remains undefined, that is to say, with the six rays of the Sun (GUEC, GUES) – the flower of glory, the well of fruitfulness.

In Biblical tradition, the lily is the symbol of election of the beloved's choice. 'As the lily among the thorns, so is my love among the daughters' (Song of Solomon 2: 2). Such was Israel's privileged position among the nations and Our Lady's among the daughters of Israel. Lilies also symbolize surrender to the will of God, that is, to providence which provides for the needs of the elect. 'Consider the lilies of the field, how they grow: they toil not neither do they spin' (Matthew 6: 28). Thus, placing themselves within the hands of God, lilies are more finely arrayed than even Solomon in all his glory. Lilies thus symbolize the mystical surrender to God's grace.

lily of the valley Origen's second sermon on the Song of Solomon records the second-century mystical interpretation of the valley as signifying the world and the lily denoting Christ. The lily of the valley is directly related to the Tree of Life planted in the Garden of Eden, since it is the lily (Christ) which will restore a pure life, the promise of immortality and salvation.

Limbo Limbo was apparently the fruit of Orphic tradition which Virgil (*Aeneid* 6: 426–9) locates at the entrance to the Underworld, abode of the souls of still-born or prematurely dead babies. 'At once are heard voices and wailing sore – the souls of infants weeping, whom, on the very threshold of the sweet life they shared not, torn from the breast, the black day swept off and plunged in bitter death.' Christianity adopted this idea of Limbo to denote the place into which the souls of unbaptized babies descended and where they suffered the consequences of Original Sin. It was also the place for the souls of adults who had lived their lives in obedience to natural law but who, through lack of the gift of supernatural grace, were deprived of eternal bliss. However, the notion has given rise to considerable controversy among Catholic theologians and is no clearly defined part of the Christian faith. In current terms, Limbo symbolizes the anteroom of Heaven or the preliminaries to a new era of civilization.

lime-tree The lime, with scented flowers which have sedative properties, has always been regarded as a symbol of friendship. Its Greek name is that of the mother of the centaur Chiron, whose powers were always exercised to the benefit of mankind. In his *Metamorphoses*, Ovid tells how Baucis and Philemon were granted the privilege of dying at the same instant for having entertained Zeus and Hermes, disguised as poor mortals. After their deaths, he shows how they were changed into two trees which overhung the shrine to Zeus which they had served. One was an oak – Zeus' tree – and the other a lime, the emblem of loving faithfulness.

line (see also PLUMBLINE) Through its everyday use, the line has come generally to be a symbol first of straight lay-out and then of intellectual and moral rectitude. 'Ritual', the *Li-chi* teaches, 'keeps the State upon its course. . . . The [cabinet-maker's] blackened line [distinguishes between] the straight and the crooked' (ch. 23). As the guide-line towards this rectitude it also symbolizes the prop, method, master and path in any striving towards spiritual realization. Thus in the Taoist *Secret of the Golden Flower*, this kind of methodical element should be used at the start of such an experience, but gradually abandoned as it has performed its task. 'That is the way a mason hangs up his plumbline. As soon as he has hung it up, he guides his work by it without continually bothering himself to look at the plumbline' (35).

lingam The word *lingam* means 'sign', but it should be noted that its root is the same as that of *langalā* (PLOUGH), a root common to the words for 'spade' and 'phallus'. Thus the lingam is very definitely a phallus and the symbol of procreation. Yet it should be stressed that it is totally devoid of erotic overtones. The 'subtle shape', known as the *lingam-sharīra*, is always distinguished from the 'gross shape', the *sthūla-sharīra*. The lingam is the sign of the well-spring of life.

The base of the lingam, which is concealed within its plinth, is square; the central section is octagonal and the upper part cylindrical. These sections correspond respectively to Brahmā, Vishnu and Rudra, as well as to Earth, the intermediate world and Heaven. In its entirety the lingam is the symbol of Shiva as First Cause and as procreator. The lingam is not an attribute of Shiva but *is* Shiva. However, the lingam, by itself, is part of the realm of the unformed, of the non-manifest. It is only its duality with the *yoni*, a representation of the female sexual organ, which allows the lingam to pass from principle to manifestation. The *yoni*, or WOMB, is the altar or basin surrounding the lingam, the receptacle for semen.

Fertilization of the Earth ideally finds expression in natural lingams with their own existence as standing stones on mountain peaks, such as the *lingaparvata* of Funan and Champa. These most forcefully conjure up Jacob's BETHEL or Beith-el, 'the House of God', which the patriarch anointed with oil in the same way as lingams are anointed with water. The symbolic kinship between the egg and the lingam is demonstrated, furthermore, by the fact that the *swāyambhuva-lingam* is none other than the OMPHALOS or navel of the world which contains within itself every potential manifestation. In Japan, stone carvings or pottery models of miniature phalli are buried to ensure fruitful harvests.

The lingam is both a central and an axial symbol. The lingam of light, which Shiva made manifest and of which Brahmā-as-boar sought the base and Vishnu-as-goose sought the tip, corresponds to the World AXIS and this is why Vishnu and Brahmā are regarded as the guardians of the zenith and nadir respectively. In many temples built in the shape of a mandala, some of the best examples being found at Angkor, the central lingam is surrounded by eight minor lingams corresponding to the eight essences (*astamurtī*) of Shiva, to the four cardinal and their intermediary points of the compass and to the eight *graha* round the Sun. This is not the only instance in which Shiva, generally associated with the Moon, plays a solar part.

In Yoga, the lingam is an axial symbol. Standing in the middle of the 'root-centre' (*muladhāra-chakra*) which corresponds to the *yoni*, it is pictured as a light-lingam around which is entwined the *kundalinī*-serpent. This lingam is the power of knowledge, knowledge being born from the union of lingam and *yoni*. In the course of the yogic experience the column of light rises to the crown of the head and passes beyond it. It is identified with Shiva's flaming lingam.

In Indian alchemy, the lingam is composed of mercury. This is because alchemy derived from Shiva and, as mercury corresponds to the Moon, it consequently corresponds to Shiva.

It may also be noted that the lingam symbol seems to subsist in the Cambodian *popil* ceremony of circumambulation during which a tray (*yoni*) surmounted by a lighted candle (lingam) is carried processionally (BHAB, DANA, ELIF, MALA, PORA).

It is very likely that among those who adore the *lingam* of Shiva, a great many see it only as an archetype of the generative organ; but there are others who look to it as a sign, an 'image' of the rhythmic creation and destruction of the universe which expresses itself in forms, and periodically returns to its primal, pre-formal unity, before being reborn.

(ELIT p. 7)

The Chinese equivalent of the Hindu lingam is the Chui, an elongated triangular piece of jade. It is often to be found in the centre of temples, at crossroads and on mountain peaks, a reminder of the mystery of life and of the sacred nature of the act of procreation. It symbolizes sacred marriages.

lion A solar symbol of overpowering brightness, the powerful, sovereign King of the Beasts, the lion is burdened with the virtues and defects which are inherent in its status. Although he may be the embodiment of power, wisdom and justice, overweening pride and self-confidence, on the other hand, may turn him into the symbol of the father, the master and the monarch dazzled by his own power and blinded by his own light to become the tyrant when he believes he is the guardian. He may be as admirable as he is insupportable, and facets of his symbolism waver between these two extremes.

The *Gītā* calls Krishna 'a lion among wild creatures'; the Buddha is 'the Lion of the Shakyas' and Christ 'the Lion of Judah'. Muhammad's son-in-law, Ali, whom the Shi'ites honour, is the Lion of Allah and it was for this reason that the old Iranian flag was blazoned with a crowned lion. The Pseudo-Dionysius the Areopagite explained the reason for some angels being given the faces of lions as being the fact that the lion's shape expressed the authority and irresistible strength of mental holiness and its overriding, fierce and uncontrollable effort to copy God's majesty. It also expressed the secret of the godhead given to angels, who shroud the mystery of God in the majesty of darkness by piously hiding from the vulgar gaze all hint of their traffic with the godhead in the same way as the lion uses its tail to wipe out its spoor when pursued by the hunter. He quotes both the Book of Revelation, in which the first of the four living creatures, 'filled with eyes before and behind', which surround the throne of Heaven is described as a lion, and Ezekiel 1: 4–15, where Jehovah's chariot appears as four creatures, 'their appearance . . . like burning coals of fire', each with four faces, one of which was the face of a lion.

The arms of Ashoka (d. 232 BC), the Buddhist king who reunited India and drove out the Greeks and Persians, comprised three lions seated back to back on a pedestal in the shape of a wheel, with the device: 'Truth Vanquishes'. These are the arms of the modern Indian Republic. Given the strength of Ashoka's faith, these three lions might stand for the Tripitaka, the 'Three Baskets', or canonical collection of the teachings of the Buddha, or the Triratna, 'the Triple Refuge', the Buddha (the Founder or Enlightened One), Dharma (the Law) and Sangha (the Community).

As a symbol of justice, the lion stands surety for physical and spiritual power. Many divinities are depicted riding or seated upon lions, and lions decorated Solomon's throne as well as the thrones of the Kings of France and of medieval bishops. The lion is also the symbol both of Christ as judge and Christ as teacher, and carries his book or scroll. In this context, the lion is the well-known emblem of St Mark. The 'Lion of Judah' a constant Biblical theme from the Book of Genesis (49: 8) onwards, culminates in the person of Christ. It is 'the Lion of the tribe of Juda . . . [who] . . . hath prevailed to open the book, and to loose the seven seals thereof' (Revelation 5: 5). More strictly speaking, in medieval iconography the forequarters of the lion correspond to Christ's divine nature, the hindquarters – often deliberately set in contrast by their weakness – with his human nature.

Lions were also used as the Buddha's throne and that of Kubjīkā, an aspect of Devī.

The lion is divine energy, the power of the *shakti*. The avatar Nara-simha (incarnation of Vishnu as 'Man-Lion'), strength and courage, destroyer of evil and ignorance, takes a lion's shape. As both the sovereignty and power of the *dharma* (Law), the lion corresponds to Vairocana, the absolute and 'central' Buddha, and also to Manjusrī, the bearer of knowledge. The Buddha 'roared with the roarings of a lion [like Brihaspati in the Vedas] when he taught the Law to a community – this was his lion-roar' (*Anguttara-nikāya* 5: 32). This expresses the strength of the Law, its power to shatter and to enlighten and its propagation in space and time.

Hindu iconography also includes a lioness, *shardulā*, a manifestation of the Word, expressing the terrifying aspect of Māyā, the power of manifestation (BURA, COOH, CHAV, DANA, DEVA, DURV, GOVM, GUEM, GUER, EVAB, MALA, MUTC, SECA).

There is little change in the proud role of the lion from Europe to Africa. The Bambara, impressed by its effortless strength, have made the lion a symbol of divine knowledge, and a rank in their traditional social hierarchy only one step below that of priest–sage.

However folk-wisdom, as well as philosophy and mysticism, have been well aware of the defects of this 'effortless strength' once its powers have ceased to be accepted unquestioningly. Thus contemporary women's liberation has come to regard the proud and noble lion as a male phallocrat unable or unwilling to see that his power is strictly relative. This is somewhat reminiscent of St John of the Cross, who noted the lion's 'heedless, angry appetite', a symbol of imperious will and uncontrolled strength. This links it to the 'pot-bellied lion', the symbol of blind greed which Shiva treads down. This blindness takes us straight from the lion as symbol of Christ to the lion as symbol of Anti-Christ, as strongly based in Scripture. Psychoanalysis sometimes makes the lion a symbol of depraved social drive – a tendency to tyrannical domination and to unfeeling imposition of strength and authority. However, the roar and gaping jaws give a totally different twist to lion symbolism: it ceases to be bright and solar and becomes dark and chthonian. In this disturbing image, the lion becomes akin to those Underworld deities, such as the CROCODILE, which in so many mythologies swallow the Sun at dusk and regurgitate it at dawn. This was the case in Ancient Egypt where lions were often depicted in pairs, back to back, each looking to a different horizon, one to the east and one to the west. They thus came to symbolize the two horizons and the Sun's course from one end of the Earth to the other. Watching, as they did, the birth and death of daylight, they came to represent yesterday and tomorrow. 'Since the sun's underworld journey brought him from the jaws of the lion of the West to the jaws of the lion of the East, whence he was reborn in the morning, the lions became of fundamental importance in the rejuvenation of the sun' (POSD p. 150). In more general terms they symbolized that revival of strength ensured by the cycle of day and night, of exertion and rest.

Similarly, although lions in the Far East are merely emblematic animals, they have affinities with the DRAGON and come to be identified with it. Lions play a protective part against malign influences. Lion-dances (*Shishimai*) take place on 1 January and at other festivals in Japan. They are held in front of Shintō shrines, in the streets and even in private houses. Musicians accompany the dancers, who wear lion's-head masks, one of them actually wearing the mask and two or three others covering themselves with a sheet to represent the body. The lion's head is red. This lion is supposed to drive away evil spirits and to bring health and wealth to families, villages and districts.

As we see, the nightmare vision described above ends by being exorcized, the chthonian symbolism reversed and the image of death becomes a pledge of rebirth, that is of life. Similar phenomena are also observable on other cultural planes in which 'the seasonal eating of the bull by the lion has for thousands of years given expression to the fundamental and conflicting dualism of day and night, Summer and Winter' (CHAS p. 53). The lion has come not only to symbolize the return of the Sun and the revival of cosmic and physical energy, but rebirth itself. Some Christian graves were decorated with lions since 'standing on its own, the lion is a symbol of the resurrection' (CHAS p. 278).

liver The liver is commonly linked to outbursts of rage, the gall, from the bitter taste of bile, to animosity and to deliberately spiteful designs.

Whatever the culture, there are few meanings without some similarity with
the foregoing, Islam attributing the passions to the liver and suffering to the
gall.

Taking his hint from Jeremiah (Lamentations 3: 9) and from Deuteronomy 32: 33, St John of the Cross likens gall to memory, to 'death of the
soul' and to 'utter deprivation of God'.

'Dragon's gall' is contrasted with wine as the opposite to the drink of life.
The *Suwen*, the basic treatise on Chinese traditional medicine, states that
the gall has a bitter taste and a green tinge. It states that the liver generates
strength. It is 'the general who elaborates his strategems', while the gall is
'the judge who decides the case and gives his verdict'. While the liver may
generate strength, it also generates anger and valour, the basic soldierly
qualities. In Far Eastern languages, many terms for the liver – and especially for the gall – also bear the sense of 'valour'. The meaning of 'bitterness' is equally common to Europe, as sometimes is that of 'joy'. In Ancient
China it was customary to eat the livers of one's enemies. Not to do so
would have been to cast doubts upon their valour which the eater believed
he assimilated. Hare's gall was used in smelting sword-blades. Chong-ying
cut himself open to replace his own liver with that of his lord, slain in battle.
In Cambodia, Laos and Champa, every year people were secretly waylaid
and their galls removed to make a liquor for the generals to drink and an
unction for the heads of the war-elephants (CADV, CHAT, FRAL, CORT,
PELC, PORA).

lizard   The lizard's symbolism might be regarded as deriving from that of
the SERPENT, of which it is a paler version. However, unlike the serpent, so
far as Mediterranean civilizations are concerned, lizards are old family
friends. The Ancient Egyptians depicted the lizard in their hieroglyphic for
'plentiful'. They provide a decorative motif ceaselessly repeated in the arts
of Black Africa, where the creature is often regarded as a culture-hero, intercessor or messenger of the gods. 'In the beginning,' relates a myth from the
Cameroons,

God sent two messengers to Earth. The CHAMELEON was to tell mankind of the
resurrection of the dead: the lizard was to tell them that death was final. The
first message to be delivered would be the one to take effect. The lizard tricked
the chameleon by telling it to go slowly, ever so slowly, because if it ran it would
shake the world to pieces. It then took the lead and told mankind that there was
no life after death.

                                                                (MVEA p. 61)

The Bantu of the Kasai River believe that the birth of a male child is
foretold by dreaming of lizards, while their neighbours, the Luala and Luba,
make their medicine pouches from the skins of monitor lizards (FOUG).
The lizard's antiquity is stressed in Melanesia, where it is regarded as the
oldest of the four ancestors who established the four classes into which
their society is divided (MALM). Lastly, it is clearly classed as a culture-
hero by the islanders of the Torres Straits, who believe that it was a long-
necked lizard which brought fire to mankind (FRAF).

The way in which lizards lie motionless hour after hour in the sunshine
make them Christian symbols of contemplative ecstasy. For the same reason

St Gregory the Great observed that the lizard might symbolize the soul which humbly seeks enlightenment, by contrast with the bird which has wings to fly up to Heaven.

locust   A devouring swarm of locusts is the very image of a destructive scourge. From Exodus 10: 14 to Revelation 9: 3 they are to be seen in this light, although in the latter instance critics judge them to stand for historic invasions or for hell-born torments. This aspect should most certainly not be overlooked, since exorcisms were long used against locusts.

In the Old Testament, although God himself may have decided to send an invading swarm of locusts, their visitation is regarded as something on the natural plane; in the New Testament (Revelation 9: 1–6) the symbol takes on a different shade of meaning and a swarm of locusts becomes spiritual and moral torment.

From the same point of view, Chuang Tzu regarded an untimely swarm of locusts as a cosmic disorder known to be caused by the microcosm being ever so slightly out of rhythm. In fact, in Ancient China locusts possessed very different qualities, their swarming symbolizing large numbers of descendants and hence the blessing of Heaven. The insect's rhythmical hopping was associated with seasonal fertility rites and with the rules of well-balanced family and social life (GRAD, GRAR).

lodestone (see also IRON)   In about 587 BC, Thales discovered magnetism through a lodestone, a black and gleaming form of magnetite. The lodestone symbolizes all the mysterious and almost irresistible forms taken by magnetic attraction. It was regarded as being related to lime formed from magnetic dust, with which all individuals were charged like a lodestone. The whole universe was saturated by it and through it kept its cohesion and its movement. The lodestone became a symbol of cosmic, emotional and mystical attraction.

In magical practices lodestones were used as love-charms, to attract and to seduce.

The Ancient Egyptians would seem to have regarded

the natural lodestone or magnetized iron as holy substances, since they believed that they derived from Horus. Non-magnetized iron, on the other hand, was abominated as a substance deriving from Set, or Typhon. This explains why it is so seldom that pieces made from iron are to be found among Egyptian antiquities, since their original owners would only have used them with vast repugnance or in deliberate defiance of their religion.

(PIED p. 17)

The lodestone, however, was interfused with Horus' solar virtues and, like the god, took part in regulating the movements of the universe.

Loki   The Scandinavian evil spirit of the destructive element of FIRE, who fathered such dreadful monsters as the serpent of the Midgard and the wolf, Fenrir. At the end of the world Loki will utter a diabolical laugh of triumph.

Several questions are raised by his twofold nature, his friendships with gods as well as with evil spirits, his powers over the forces of evil and his clear similarity of character with Lucifer. He would appear to symbolize the triumph of expediency over conscience, the trickery and lies which deprave the spirit.

Lorelei The German equivalent of the sirens of Greek mythology, they sat on outcrops in the River Rhine and lured boatmen onto the rocks with their songs. These water-nymphs symbolize the fatal enchantment of sensuality, overpowering reason and leading the individual to ruin.

loss To dream of losing things is related to feelings of ownership or of longing for some TREASURE, as well as with the concern to rid oneself of some possession. Hence arises the ambivalence of the symbolism of loss, since it is linked to guilt if a treasure has been lost, to greed if a treasure is to be found and to repulsion if the intent is to reject the object.

Cirlot agrees with Jung in associating feelings of loss with signs of final purification, of journeys or pilgrimages, as well as with the idea of death and resurrection. From the analyst's point of view, the image and sense of loss correspond with the fact that consciousness is confined exclusively to the perception of material things and is completely closed to spiritual realities which, by definition, are invisible and imperceptible.

lots See O-MIKUJI.

lotus This might be called the first of all flowers, generally blossoming on stagnant and murky waters with so sensual and imperious a perfection that it is easy to imagine the lotus as the very first sign of life upon the undifferentiated vastness of the primeval waters. Ancient Egyptian iconography certainly treated the lotus in this way, the flower being the first to appear and from its expanded petals springing the Demiurge and the Sun. The lotus is therefore pre-eminently the archetypal sexual organ or vulva, pledge of the continuity of birth and rebirth. From the Mediterranean to India and China its symbolic importance, manifest in so many different ways both sacred and profane, arises from this basic image. In the land of the Pharaohs, where it was regarded as the holiest of flowers, 'the blue lotus . . . suggested the perfume of divine life. On the walls of the tombs at Thebes, the living and dead of a family are shown solemnly smelling the blue flower in an attitude partly of delight and partly inspired by the magic of rebirth' (POSD pp. 152–3).

In Chinese erotic literature, where a love of metaphor is wedded to an underlying realism, the word 'lotus' is used expressly to denote the vulva and the most flattering name which a courtesan can receive is that of 'Golden Lotus'. Despite this, Hindu and Buddhist spirituality would read a spiritual and moral meaning into the lotus's spotless colour, flowering uncontaminated by the grubby world below. 'I am unsullied by the world, even as the pure and lovely lotus is unsullied by the waters' (*Anguttara-nikāya* 2: 39).

Chu Tun-i, in an apparently bisexual and therefore totalizing context, reverts to this notion of purity, adding to it those of sobriety and righteousness, to make the lotus an emblem of the wise man. Generally speaking, while the notion of purity remains constant, it is supplemented by those of resoluteness (stiff stalk), wealth (abundant growth), many descendants (prolific seeding), married harmony (two flowers on the same stalk) and time past, present and to come (the plant simultaneously bears the three stages of its development – bud, flower and seed).

The major writers of Hinduism make the lotus a symbol of spiritual fulfilment from its rising out of darkness to blossom in full sunlight. If the waters are taken as an image of the undifferentiated primeval state, the lotus will stand for manifestation, which emanates from them and which blooms on their surface like the hatching of the World Egg. Indeed, the tight bud is the precise equivalent of that egg, and the hatching of the egg corresponds to the opening of the bud. Both are the realization of the potential contained in the first seed, as well as the potential of every individual whose heart is also a lotus bud.

Since the traditional flower has EIGHT petals, just as there are eight major points of the compass in space, the lotus is the symbol of cosmic harmony. It is used in this sense when depicted in many mandalas and yantras.

Hindu iconography depicts Vishnu sleeping on the surface of the ocean of the First Cause. From his navel a lotus emerges and within the inner whorl of blossom sits Brahmā, principle of 'expansive' tendencies (*rajas*). One should in any case add that the Ancient Egyptians made the lotus-bud a symbol of the seed of manifestation. However, in Khmer iconography, the Earth is substituted for the lotus as an attribute of Vishnu, standing for the passive aspect of manifestation. For the sake of completeness, it should be stated that Indian iconography distinguishes between the pink lotus, or *padma*, (described above), which is a solar emblem and also a symbol of wealth, and the blue lotus, or *utpala*, an emblem of the Moon and of Shiva.

From the Buddhist point of view, the lotus – upon which Shakyamuni sits enthroned – is the Buddha's nature, untouched by the polluted atmosphere of *samsāra*. *Mani padme*, the Jewel in the Lotus, is the universe as the receptacle of *dharma*, and illusion, or *Māyā*, from which Nirvana emanates. Alternatively, the Buddha in the middle of the eight-petalled lotus sits at the hub of an eight-spoked wheel, of which the *padma* is the equivalent, thus evincing his office as *chakravartī* (king), as might be deduced from the Bayon of Angkor Thom. In other contexts, the centre of the lotus is filled by Mount Meru, the World AXIS. In myths of Vishnu, the stalk of the lotus itself is identified with this axis and, since the latter is generally accepted as being phallic, it would corroborate the bisexuality or the totalizing sexuality of the symbol. In Tantric symbolism, the individual's seven subtle centres through which the spinal column runs, that of the *sushumna*, are depicted as lotuses of 4, 6, 10, 12, 16, 20 and 1000 petals. The lotus with 1000 petals stands for revelation in its wholeness.

Japanese literature reduces the symbol to a more commonplace level by frequently making the lotus, flowering unsullied on the muddy waters, an image of moral standards maintained unsullied and unaffected by a sordid social environment, without the need for retreat into solitude.

Lastly, it would seem that the lotus has a significance in Far Eastern alchemy. In fact several Chinese organizations have assumed the white lotus as their emblem, including an Amidist community founded on Mount Lu in the fourth century and a major Taoist secret society. The latter might well have used the Buddhist symbolism as a cloak, but may also have related their emblem to the symbolism of 'inward' alchemy, its 'Golden Flower' being white (BURA, DURV, GRIF, SOUN).

Love (Eros)   In Orphic cosmogony, the world originated in Night and the Void. Night produced an egg and from this egg Love hatched, while Heaven and Earth were formed from the two halves of the broken shell.

Hesiod believed that 'at the first Chaos came to be, but next wide-bosomed Earth, the ever-sure foundation of all . . . and Eros [Love], fairest among the deathless gods, who unnerves the limbs and overcomes the mind and wise counsels of all gods and all men within them' (*Theogony* 116–22). Undoubtedly Eros had many other lines of descent, being most often regarded as the child of Aphrodite and Hermes. Plato, in his *Symposium*, says that he has a twofold nature depending upon whether he is the child of Aphrodite Pandemos, the goddess of brute lust, or of Aphrodite Urania, the goddess of spiritual love. In the symbolic sense, he may also be born of the marriage of Poros (Expediency) and Penia (Poverty), since love is never satisfied, is always seeking the object of its desires and is full of tricks to achieve its ends. Love is generally depicted as a child or youth, naked and winged, 'because he embodies a longing which has no use for intermediaries and cannot be concealed' (Alexander of Aphrodisias: quoted in TERS p. 15). The fact that Love should be a child undoubtedly symbolizes the eternal youthfulness of all deep-seated love, but also a degree of irresponsibility as well. Love toys with the mortals whom he hunts, sometimes without even seeing them, and whom he blinds or burns, his bow, arrows, quiver, blindfold and other attributes being his symbols in all cultures. The orb which he sometimes holds suggests his universal and sovereign power. However much the poets may prettify him, Love remains foremost among the gods since it is he 'who ensures not only the continuity of the species but the internal cohesion of the Cosmos' (GRID p. 147b).

Love also derives from the overall symbolism of the marriage of opposites. He is the libido, the individual's fundamental driving force, motivating all beings to express themselves in action. He realizes the individual's potential. However, this passage to action is only effected by contact with another individual and following on from physical, sensual or spiritual encounters which are so many confrontations. Love tends to overcome these conflicts, to assimilate different forces and to integrate them into a single structure. In this context it is symbolized by the cross, a synthesis of horizontal and vertical streams, and by the Chinese *yin–yang* binomial. From the cosmic viewpoint, single being first fragments into multiple being and love is the force which empowers the RETURN to oneness, the reintegration of the universe marked by the passing from the unconscious oneness of primeval chaos to the conscious unity of a definitive order. The libido shines out of the conscious state in which it may become a spiritual force for moral and mystic progress. The individual ego develops along the same lines as the universe. love being a search for a centre which will allow the dynamic synthesis of the individual's potential. Two individuals who give and surrender themselves to each other then discover themselves in each other, but raised to a higher level of being, provided that their surrender has been total and not simply confined to one level of their being, more often than not that of the flesh. Love is an ontological well-spring of progress in so far as it is truly union and not confiscation. When depraved, instead of being the long-sought centre of unification, it becomes a principle of division and death. Its depravity comprises the destruction of the quality of the other person in an attempt selfishly to exploit that person instead of joint self-enrichment by mutually and unstintingly giving of oneself, so that each becomes both greater and more individual. Love is the soul of the symbol and is the realization of the symbol since the latter is the welding together of two separated parts of knowledge and being. The major error of Love is taking one part for the whole.

The famous mythical drama of Psyche and Eros is an illustration of the conflict between soul and love. Although the maiden Psyche surpassed all others in beauty, she could not find a husband, since her very loveliness set up a barrier. In their despair, her parents consulted the oracle and were told that they were to dress her in bridal clothes, lead her to a mountain and leave her alone on a cliff-top, where a monster would come to take her for its bride. She was accordingly led in funeral procession and abandoned at the place commanded. Soon a gentle breeze lifted her into the air and carried her to the floor of a deep valley. There stood a magnificent palace in which voices proffered their service to her like so many slaves. That night she felt a presence at her side, but did not know who it was. This was the husband of whom the oracle had spoken. He did not tell her who he was, simply warning her that if she ever saw him she would lose him for ever. Days and nights passed in this way in the palace, but although Psyche was happy, she wanted to see her parents again and was allowed to spend a few days with them. Her jealous sisters awoke her misgivings and, on her return to the palace, by lamplight she found a handsome youth sleeping at her side. Unfortunately Psyche's hand shook and a drop of hot oil fell upon Eros. Thus Love was revealed and fled away. Now Psyche's misfortunes began. Aphrodite made her the victim of her anger, setting ever more difficult tasks to fulfil as punishment. Eros, however, could no more forget Psyche than she him. He obtained permission from Zeus to marry her: Psyche became his wife and was reconciled to Aphrodite.

In this myth Eros symbolizes love and more particularly the longing for physical satisfaction, while Psyche personifies the soul, tempted to experience this love. Her parents stand for reason which provides the requisite framework. The palace is an epitome of images of luxury and physical enjoyment, all the product of dreams. Darkness, agreement not to look at the lover and the feeling of a presence all denote the resignation of spirit and consciousness to overweening longing and imagination, a blind surrender to the unknown. The return to the parents' home is the awakening of the rational faculty: the sisters' questions are those of the unsure and inquisitive spirit. Consciousness still slumbers, these are merely doubts and curiosity aroused once the senses have been sated. On her return to the palace, Psyche wants to see her lover and she snatches up a torch. This is still the smoky and flickering light of a spirit hesitant to break the bargain and obtain the truth. At the sight of this lovely and splendid body the soul intuitively knows that it clothes something monstrous at this dim level of reality. Love flees when he is exposed. Enlightened but tormented, Psyche

wanders through the world hunted down by Aphrodite, doubly jealous, as
a woman of Psyche's beauty and as a mother of the love which the girl has
aroused in her son, Eros. The Soul (psyche) experiences even the abyss of
Hell where Persephone, nevertheless, gives her a flask containing the water
of youth, the principle of renewal after expiation. Psyche falls asleep and is
awakened by an arrow shot by Eros who has also been searching desperately for her everywhere – this represents the survival in her of desire.
However, this time permission to marry is sought from Zeus – this means
that Psyche and Eros will no longer come together simply upon the level of
carnal lust, but in accordance with the spirit. With love thus deified, Psyche
and Aphrodite, two aspects of the soul, desire and consciousness, are
reconciled. Eros no longer appears as a solely physical presence and is no
longer dreaded as a monster: love is integrated into life. 'Psyche weds the
sublime image of physical love: she becomes the bride of Eros: the soul
rediscovers the capacity to unite' (DIES pp. 132–4: slightly modified).

Baudelaire in his study of Richard Wagner demonstrates the striking
similarity of this myth with the legend of Lohengrin. Elsa pays heed to the
witch, Ortrude, just as Psyche listened to her sisters and Eve obeyed the
serpent. Elsa fell 'victim to the diabolical impulse of curiosity and, unwilling
to respect her divine husband's incognito, lost all happiness when unveiling
the mystery.... The eternal Eve had fallen into the eternal trap.'

Lover, the   The sixth major arcanum of the TAROT. The essence of the
Lover's symbolism is the ordeal of choosing which faces all young men
when they reach the crossroads of puberty; hitherto they have followed a
single path, but now it forks away to right and left. This is Pythagoras'
upsilon (Y): which are they to choose? The number six, associated with this
card, stresses its symbolic aspect of sexual initiation since, as St Clement of
Alexandria observed, six is a sexual number and for this reason is called the
marriage number. Choice arouses conflicts yet stimulates a longing to settle
them by uniting the parties concerned.

A youth wearing a tunic striped vertically in BLUE, RED and YELLOW stands
in the centre of the card between two women. On his left a fair-haired
woman, in a blue dress with a blue cape trimmed with red, points her left
hand (see RIGHT AND LEFT) at the young man's chest, while her right is held
palm downwards. On the Lover's right a woman, in a red dress with dark
blue sleeves and with blue hair topped by a sort of yellow headdress or
crown, lays her left hand upon his right shoulder and points to the ground
with her other hand. The first of the women is attractive: the second is long-
nosed, elderly and severe. Above the young man a winged angel, or an
Eros-Cupid, hovers in the middle of a solar disc with blue, yellow and red
beams. He holds a bow and aims a white arrow at the young man.

All writers on the Tarot compare this card with the parable of Herakles
(Hercules), forced to choose between virtue and vice, or with Orphic and
Pythagorean traditions of the path which the soul follows after death when
it comes to a fork and has a choice between the left hand, which in fact
leads down to Hell, and the right hand, which goes to the Fields of the
Blessed. There is only one road to true happiness and we have to be able
to choose it. The arrow, a dynamic symbol of decision and 'vector of the

Sun and of intellectual enlightenment' (VIRI p. 73), which helps to solve the riddles of ambivalence, is there to guide or dictate the Lover's choice. In this instance it aims to insulate him from delusive attractions.

However, this card also symbolizes emotional values and the projection of the twofold image of woman which men create for themselves. Venus Urania or Venus of the Crossroads, angel or demon, inspiring carnal lust or platonic love, woman continually changes shape and man wavers before her because at root he does not know his own nature:

Whether the man conceals a suppressed conflict or whether he wavers when faced by a conflict on terms just revealed, it is up to him first to take stock of the elements which tear him apart. He has then to study them objectively, that is to take up a position which will insulate him from them. Only then can constructive synthesis occur, such being the basic dialectic of all development of the consciousness.

(VIRI p. 77)

And such, we might add, is one of the lessons which the Lover teaches us, that emotional ego which must face and decide all our choices.

lozenge Lozenges are female symbols. They sometimes decorate Amerindian serpent images to which erotic significance is attributed – the lozenge stands for the vulva, the serpent for the phallus – and express a dualist philosophy.

According to Henri Breuil, during the Magdalenian period the lozenge represented the vulva and consequently the womb of life. It acquired the extended meaning of the gate to the Underworld, through which the initiate passed, the entrance to the home of the chthonian powers.

In Guatemala, women stress its function as a symbol of womanhood by wearing lozenge-patterned dresses. The goddesses in the temple of Palenque wear lozenge-patterned robes. In Mexico the lozenge occurs, too, in association with the image of the Moon- and Underworld-goddess Chalchiuhtlicue. 'She who wears a skirt of precious stones' (or of green jade), is the goddess of fresh water, the wife of Tlaloc, the great storm-god (SOUP, SOUA, GRIP). In Central America, Chalchiuhtlicue is often depicted in association with the JAGUAR. The only female figure carved on a stele from Copan wears a skirt patterned with lozenges like the spots on a jaguar's skin. In Mayan art, these spots take the shapes of circles within a lozenge. Tortoiseshell is often depicted as marked with lozenges, the tortoise generally being regarded as the manifestation of a Moon- and Underworld-deity, as, for example among the Chorti (GIRP).

The Bambara use as the conventional sign for a girl's sexual organs a small oval like a lozenge with rounded ends in one of which there is a small dot (ZAHB).

A lozenge shape in coffee-grounds is a sign of success in love (GRIA).

In China it is one of the eight most important emblems and the symbol of victory.

When very elongated – like a pair of isosceles triangles joined at their bases – the lozenge signifies contact and communication between Earth and Heaven, between the upper and the lower worlds and, sometimes, coitus.

lute   See under LYRE.

lynx   Although Celtic legend makes no mention of the lynx, it is curious that in Irish its name is an exact homonym of that of the god Lug – *lug, loga* (genitive). It is therefore possible that because of its keen sight, it may have been regarded as a symbol or image of the god Lug. Harps were strung with lynx-gut and their music considered divine (CHAB pp. 300–1).

In the Middle Ages, it was believed that the lynx 'was able to see through walls' and in Renaissance engravings of the five senses, a lynx stands for that of sight.

lyre   (see also HARP; ZITHER)   The lyre, the invention of HERMES or of Polyhymnia, one of the nine Muses, was, with its marvellous notes, Apollo's and ORPHEUS' instrument and is the symbol of poets. In more general terms it is the symbol and instrument of cosmic harmony. The walls of Thebes arose to the music of Amphion's lyre. In Christian iconography it conjures up active participation in the beatific union. This is the part played by David's harp. The seven strings of the lyre corresponded to the seven planets. Their vibrations harmonize in the same way as do the latter in their cosmic revolutions. When the number of strings was increased to twelve, this was seen as corresponding to the signs of the Zodiac.

This idea of harmony finds its expression, too, in the harps of those who, in the Book of Revelation, have overcome the Beast. The delightful fable of Chen-wen, told by Lao-tzu, is no less significant in this respect. When P'ao-pa struck the strings, he made the birds and fishes dance; but Chen-wen was able to bring to birth the four seasons by touching the individual strings, and the harmony of all four of them, the common chord of the world of the Immortals, by striking the four strings together. The lute or zither is the emblem of Sarasvatī, Brahmā's *shakti*, a personification of the Word and of the creating sound, as well as that of the *kinnara* bird.

On the Tibetan Wheel of Existence, Avalokitesvara is depicted in the world of the *dēvas* with a lute which he uses to awaken the gods from their illusions with the sound of the *dharma*.

'Imitate the zither-player', wrote Callistus II. The zither is the heart, its strings the senses, the player is the intellect and the bow 'remembrance of God' (BURA, BENA, DANA, GOVM, GRAD, HERJ, MALA, PHIL).

The lyre is one of Apollo's attributes and symbolizes the god's powers of divination. As an attribute of the Muses Urania and Erato, the lyre symbolizes poetic and musical inspiration.

Basing himself upon the mythical account of its invention, Jean Servier regards the lyre as 'a symbolic altar joining Heaven and Earth together'. Hermes stole Apollo's cattle, covered a tortoise's shell with the hide of one of them, fixed its horns to one end and strung this sound-box with strings made from its guts. 'Now, to Mediterranean civilizations, the bull stood for the Heavenly Bull. . . . To make the strings vibrate was to make the world vibrate. The cosmic marriage took place, Earth was made fruitful by Heaven; rain fell upon the fields and all female creatures became gravid. All musical instruments would seem to have been so many means of touching the secret harmony of the world' (SERH p. 151).

M

macaw   Because of its long red feathers, the Maya regarded the macaw as a symbol of fire and solar energy. 'The hieroglyphic *kayab*, depicting a macaw's head, denoted the solstice and this the Chorti translated with a blazing Sun' (GIRP p. 163). In the fives-court at Copan, six statues of macaws are drawn up in lines of three facing east and three facing west. They mark the astronomical positions of the six cosmic Suns – the fives-ball standing for the seventh in the middle – and represent the seven-person theogony of the Sun God (GIRP p. 255).

The Bribi Indians, in Colombia, have been recorded as using a red parrot as a psychopomp (conductor of souls) (KRIE p. 359).

All equatorial and tropical American tribes put the macaw's feathers to decorative or ritual use as a solar symbol. Métraux (METT) quotes an observation made by Yves d'Evreux among the Tupinamba which marks a distinction between its symbolic significance and that of the EAGLE's feather. 'Great care must be taken when making the flights for an arrow to avoid placing an eagle's feather next to a macaw's feather, for the latter might be eaten by the former.'

The Bororo Indians believe in a complex cycle of transmigration of souls during which they are temporarily reincarnated as macaws (LEVC).

In Brazil, macaws make their nests on the tops of cliffs or steep rock-faces and to reach them is an achievement. The macaw, a solar symbol, is the avatar (embodiment) of heavenly fire, so hard to gain possession of. In this context it is the opposite of the JAGUAR, associated with chthonian fire. Many Amerindian myths on the origins of fire bear witness to this, since their heroes often need to come to grips with chthonian–celestial duality in the shapes of jaguar and macaw.

Maenads   See BACCHANTES.

magic square   There is a wealth of tradition surrounding magic squares. The square itself, with its rigid boundaries, conjures up a feeling of some secret and occult power. The magic square is a means of entrapping and storing the potential of a power by enclosing it within the symbolic representation of the name or number of the person who rightfully exercises that power.

The invention of the magic square goes back to the birth of science. According to the *Lutfi'l Maqtūl*, 'the science of the magic square is a science which God created in the beginning. He himself instructed Adam in this science' and then it was handed down by his prophets, wise men and saints.

Arabic bibliography records that Thābit ben Kurra (826–890) wrote about magic squares. The Sabeans were the first to establish a relationship between these squares and the planets.

The simplest form of the magic square, or *wafk*, comprises nine compartments in which the first nine numerals are written so that the sum of each vertical or horizontal line of figures is always fifteen:

4	9	2
3	5	7
8	1	6

This arrangement is to be found as early as the tenth century in Jabir ben Hoyān's *Kitab-al-Mawazm*, and a hundred years later al-Ghazālī describes a charm which is still in use today and known as 'the Seal of Ghazālī'. These charms, attributed to Balinas (Apollonius of Tyana) should be written on pieces of brand-new cloth and placed beneath the feet of a woman in labour. They are regarded as helping childbirth. (ENCI: 'Wafk').

There is also a large charm, a square of forty-nine compartments, linked to the different days of the week and through them to the planets.

Planetary seals are made as follows:

Saturn: a magic square of nine compartments on lead;
Jupiter: sixteen compartments on tin;
Mars: twenty-five compartments on iron;
Sun: thirty-six compartments on gold;
Venus: forty-nine compartments on copper;
Mercury: sixty-four compartments on silver alloy;
Moon: eighty-one compartments on silver.

In the West, this conjunction of magic squares with planets and metals runs right through to Cornelius Agrippa's *Occulta Philosophia* (1533) and Cardan's *Practica Arithmetica*. In the Muslim world their popularity began in the thirteenth century and reached a peak in the seventeenth and eighteenth centuries.

Jadwal, meaning plan or diagram, is derived from the magic square. It is a technical term in Arabic magic denoting those often square diagrams divided into compartments in which are written numerals corresponding in value to the letters of the Arabic alphabet and, for example, making up the name of the person seeking a charm. The numerical value of the letters is derived from the *abjad* process (A = 1 etc.). In most cases the *jadwal* is framed by words drawn from the Koran.

All sorts of permutations are feasible. Numerals need not necessarily be written in the compartments, but names or magic words instead. Thus a very common *jadwal* comprises seven times seven compartments in which are written: (1) Solomon's Seal; (2) the seven *sawakit*, or consonants not found in the first *sūra* of the Koran; (3) the seven names of God; (4) the names of the seven Spirits; (5) the names of the seven kings of the Jinn; (6) the names of the seven days of the week; (7) the names of the planets. These charms can be written on paper which is then crushed to pieces, or else the writing is washed off and the water drunk. They are employed in a wide range of circumstances.

Budūh is a magic word made up from elements of the simple magic square divided into three parts by taking the numerical value of the LETTERS OF THE ALPHABET into account. Thus al-Ghazālī describes it as 'an incomprehensible but reliable aid to the solution of the most difficult problems.'

The common people believe that Budūh became a jinn whose help is sought by writing his name either in numerals or in letters (DOUM p. 298).

They believe that Adam invented this spell and that he in turn transmitted it to al-Ghazālī. The *budūh* is used as a charm and as a preservative, and is sometimes associated with such other practices as the ink-mirror (ENCI: 'Budūh').

The four letters of *budūh* may also be arranged in a magic square, the sum of the numbers allotted to each of them being twenty at each line end:

8	6	4	2
4	2	8	6
2	4	6	8
6	8	2	4

'This should be written on a parchment, tied beneath the wing of a white dove and the bird released in front of the home of a girl who has refused an offer of marriage. This will reverse her decision' (DOUM p. 193).

By sympathetic magic, the numerals and letters which comprise the Names of God are believed to be effective. For example, *el-Muccavwir*, 'the Maker', is believed to be a cure for sterility in women (the Maker of Children). Countless examples of these squares are extant.

S	A	T	O	R
A	R	E	P	O
T	E	N	E	T
O	P	E	R	A
R	O	T	A	S

Pliny the Elder (*Natural History* 28: 20) refers to the existence of this magic square, many examples of which have been discovered in what was Gaul, some of the most recent in Hebrew letters. It is composed of five letters so arranged in five lines that the meaning of the words remains unchanged whether they are read horizontally or vertically, from left to right, from top to bottom or vice versa. It is therefore firstly a palindrome, more carefully constructed than many others.

It is possible, even probable, that this magic square was of Celtic origin, since the meaning of the word *arepo* may be found in the Gaulish adverb *arepo*, 'in front' or 'at the end of', related to the Gaulish noun *arepennis*, 'head' or 'piece of ground' (cf. French *arpent*, 'acre', and Irish *airchenn*).

Numerical and esoteric symbolism was not a feature peculiar to the Celtic world and yet the intrusion of a Gaulish word must suggest druidical influences. The current state of research does not allow us to confirm this hypothesis and it is possible that the spell simply refers to the cosmic wheel in general (AIBL (1953) pp. 198–208; ETUC (1955) 321: pp. 27–8).

The sentence in Latin – SATOR AREPO TENET OPERA ROTAS (The sower at his plough (or, in his field) controls the work) – written in a twenty-five-compartment magic square, has been interpreted in thousands of different ways by alchemists and students of the occult. Their explanations combine simultaneously the symbolism of the letters themselves with that of the numeral traditionally assigned to each letter and that of the black or white background on which the letter is written. Some students of tradition derive from a magic square containing 'creative whorls' (ROTAS) 'the cosmogonic marriage of Fire and Water, from which creation itself was born'.

The central vertical and horizontal lines of this square contain the word TENET, forming a cross which may be read in any direction. This Latin word means he, she or it 'holds'. Some students have noticed this and see the significance of the word and its central place in the square as the indication that 'the cross holds up the world.' This would provide the square with coherent meaning. Thanks to this symbolism, this explanation would make the magic square intelligible in some degree, despite the difficulties posed by the translation of the other words.

In all astrological traditions the Earth, matter and the finite are represented by a SQUARE, too, while a CIRCLE stands for Heaven, the universal and the infinite. In astrology the square is embodied in an aspect of 90°, standing for barriers, divergences, difficulties, prohibitions, inhibitions and the need for concerted effort, and in quadruplicates which divide the signs of the Zodiac into three groups according to their position in relation to the cardinal points. The cardinal group contains Aries, Cancer, Libra and Capricorn; the fixed group Taurus, Leo, Scorpio and Aquarius; and the mutable, Gemini, Virgo, Sagittarius and Pisces.

The peculiarity of this division of the Zodiac – one among many others – is that each group brings together signs from different elements and often of conflicting tendencies, those of Fire (Aries, Leo and Sagittarius); of Earth (Taurus, Virgo and Capricorn); of Air (Gemini, Libra and Aquarius); of Water (Cancer, Scorpio and Pisces). Thus the square, which in astrology conveys the notion of conflict, tension, confrontation and basic incompatibility, is associated in the Zodiac with notions of activity and drive (the prime significance of the cardinal quadruplicate); of adaptation and diffusion (the mutable quadruplicate); and of firmness, rootedness and stability (the fixed quadruplicate). The square, therefore, embodies above all the idea of materialization, by contrast with that of spirituality linked to the circle and the sphere.

Nor should it be forgotten that horoscopes, maps of the heavens and the astrologer's working-tool, were until the nineteenth century in Europe and in India are still drawn up in the shape of squares. This is clearly of symbolic significance. The celebrated problem of 'squaring the circle' was to medieval and Renaissance astrologers that of introducing the individual's material body into the spirituality of God and the cosmos. In other words, this mathematical and astrological problem was exactly analogous with the meaning given by mystics and initiates to the alchemists' 'Great Work'. Like alchemy, astrology displays two different facets, its 'material' and mathematical base being the foundation and guide for its workings on the ego. The circular shape for horoscopes – clearly far more handy for practical work and therefore more 'rational' and 'scientific' – was invented by English astrologers in the eighteenth century, and in modified form popularized in France by Paul Choisnard early in the present century. It has, however, clearly lost all its old symbolic context.

magpie Magpies are commonly synonymous with tattlers and thieves, a fact easily explicable in terms of the bird's behaviour. This is also why the magpie-thrush, the *börling-börlang*, symbolizes for the Montagnards of southern Vietnam the ancestor who taught them the art of conducting trials – or at least of holding palavers – while the Sioux are convinced that magpies are omniscient.

In China, magpies know if the wife is unfaithful, since the half-mirror which the husband has given her turns into a magpie and tells the husband if the wife has deceived him during his absence from home. The identification of magpie with mirror is odd, until you remember the attraction shining objects have for the bird. On the other hand, the magpie is also the means to marital fidelity, these birds forming the bridge over the Milky Way for the bridal procession to pass when the celestial Weaver goes to meet the Cowherd. This is the reason why magpies are supposed to have bald heads.

The magpie is a fairy (*chen-nu*) since the daughter of the Fire-king, Yenti, changed herself into a magpie and flew up to Heaven when her nest was burned – a Taoist Immortal's apotheosis. In this context, the magpie played a similar part to that of the CRANE. Furthermore, ashes from magpies' nests were used to wash the eggs of silk-worms, a custom which conjures up hatching symbolism (DAMS, GRAD, GRAR, HEHS, KALL).

Magpies were sacrificed to Bacchus so that, with the help of wine, tongues might be loosened and secrets revealed.

According to the Greek legend, the Pierides, nine Thracian maidens, attempted to rival the nine Muses. Defeated in a singing match, they were changed into magpies. As told by Ovid, the magpies of the legend might be regarded as symbols of envy, presumption, idle gossip and snobbery.

In Western folklore, the symbolism of the magpie is generally dark and appearances of the bird seen as evil omens (MORD p. 184).

Maia The nymph whose dalliance with Zeus was concealed within a cavern and who became the mother of Hermes. In Roman tradition it was perhaps a Maia other than this Arcadian nymph who personified 'the awakening of Nature in the Spring' and who was to become the familiar of Hermes. The Romans celebrated her festival in May and perhaps she gave her name to the month. She would be a fertility-goddess representing the projection of the life-force. Psychoanalysts have, by extension, made her a symbol of the externalization of the Ego. In Vedic thought, the Sanskrit word *Maya* denotes the illusion comprised by the phenomenal world which is merely the product of a magic worked by the gods.

maize In Mexican and related cultures maize is the comprehensive manifestation of the Sun, the world and of mankind. In the *Popol-Vuh*, it took three attempts to create mankind. The first man was made of clay and was destroyed by a flood; the second, of wood, was washed away in a rainstorm; the third, from whom we are descended, was made of maize (ALEC pp. 96–7).

Maize is a symbol of wealth and, when its origins are investigated, of semen.

makara In Hindu iconography the *makara* is a sea-monster, based upon the DOLPHIN, but also related to the CROCODILE. It is pre-eminently a symbol of water. It is Varuna's and Ganga's steed, on this level replacing the NĀGA, which in turn replaces it as Varuna's steed at Angkor. The *Bhagavad Gītā* proclaims its important status in the world of waters: 'The makara is to other fishes what Ganges is to other rivers and Rama to other warriors' (10: 31). In Tantric symbolism the *makara* is the steed of the Mantra Vam, who corresponds with the element of Water. In iconography the Makara's Bow is the symbol of beneficent rain and of the fertilizing waters poured down from Heaven. It is identified with the RAINBOW.

The *makara* (Chu-sin in Tibetan) is depicted upon the *phurbu*, a magic dagger with a triangular blade like some tongue designed to swallow the demons it pierces. In this ritual object of Tantric Buddhist transmutation, the mouth of the water-dragon, the *makara*, like the dagger, spits lightning, flames and smoke to a thousand crashes of thunder (STEI). Similarly at the principal 'gates' of the mandala, 'emanations of glorious light' are vomited from the mouths of the *makaras* to the glory of the Wheel of the Dharma. Stein believed that a link existed between the different meanings borne by the *vajra* ('terrible weapon and phallus') and the *phurbu*'s burning energy-tip, which both ingests and exudes, *bodhicitta* (spirit of enlightenment or semen) being concentrated at the tip of the blade. The *makara* which came out of the unsullied lotus gave birth to four of the five symmetric flames which burn at either end of the *vajra*.

The Indian Zodiac substitutes the *makara* for CAPRICORN and it therefore corresponds to the Winter solstice (which is, in any case, itself related to the element of Water). In so far as it marks the beginning of the ascendant phase of the annual cycle, it is the solar gateway or Gateway of the Gods. The symbolism of the MONSTER's gaping jaws as a gateway is well known: it may either be saviour or DEVOURER. In this context, it may be either dolphin or crocodile, a gate of salvation or a gate of death, depending upon whether the swallowing up is annihilation or a passing beyond the constraints of temporal existence. The *makara*-crocodile on the stupa at Bharut appears to be gobbling up, or liberating, a temple and, especially, a bird, and cannot fail to remind us of the QUAIL gobbled up by the wolf in the Ashvin legend.

Another aspect of its beneficent symbolism is provided by the *makaras* which form Vishnu's earrings: they represent intellectual and intuitive knowledge (AUBJ, BURA, CORF, DANA, GOVM, GUES, MALA).

male and female The meaning of these two words should not be confined exclusively to the biological plane, defining the individual's sexual characteristics, but should also be understood at a higher level and in a wider context. Thus the SOUL is a combination of male (*nefesh*) and female (*chajah*) principles which give the living soul its full meaning.

According to the *Zohar*, the soul's male and female elements derive from the cosmos. The male principle radiates the life force, but this principle of life is subject to death; the female bears life, it animates. In this context Eve, who proceeded from Adam, signifies that the spiritual is beyond the vital element. Adam was pre-existent to Eve and the vital is earlier than the spiritual element. A similar theme is picked up in the myth of Athene springing from the brain of Zeus. In this respect, the *Zohar* uses the example of the candle with its elements of light and darkness signifying male and female.

Distinction between male and female is a sign of separation, like the upper and lower waters and Heaven and Earth. In the earliest accounts of the Creation, the first human was HERMAPHRODITE, since this separation had yet to take place.

On the mystical plane, the spirit is regarded as male and the soul which animates the body as female. This is the well-known duality of animus and anima.

When the words male and female are used at a spiritual level they do not denote sexuality, but giving and receiving. In this esoteric sense the celestial is male and the terrestrial female. The more firmly one sets oneself upon the biological plane and explains male and female in sexual terms, the more confused one becomes.

Westerners are prone most frequently to be scandalized or aroused by the erotic symbolism of Oriental art and particularly of Indian art. Nor is it uncommon to find readers bewildered by the symbolism of the Song of Solomon and disconcerted by the commentaries which it has provoked. One has to base oneself upon a spiritual plane to grasp the meaning of the symbols. Nothing should be taken literally, 'for the letter killeth, but the spirit giveth life' (2 Corinthians 3: 6).

Even if we stand on the plane of sexuality, it is clear that men and women are neither wholly male nor wholly female. Men possess a female element, and women a male one. All male and female symbols display opposite characteristics. Thus trees are female, yet may appear male, like the symbolic tree sprouting from Adam's penis.

Paul Evdokimov has posed clearly, if from the Orthodox viewpoint in which mysticism, ontology and symbolism are united, the problem of male and female. In the Christian context his theories possess universal validity. Having reminded his readers that in Christ there is neither male nor female and that each finds in him his or her own image, and that human fulfilment is wholly integrated in Christ, he writes: 'Historically we are individual men meeting individual women. This is, however, a situation created for us to transcend, not to remain set in it. . . . Thus during our earthly lives each person goes through the erotic phase, burdened with mortal poison and celestial revelation, to discover at last Eros transfigured in the Kingdom of Heaven.' It is impossible to outline more fairly the problem of male and female, 'the two dimensions in the single pleroma of Christ' (EVDF pp. 23, 24). What St Paul had declared concerning Christ, St Gregory of Nyssa was to state concerning mankind (*De hominis opificio* 181d). Thus male and female cease to confront one another, they cease to be opaque, while still preserving their own individual energies.

Male and female are present in the One God. Christ, the perfect image of God, is one in his male and female wholeness. 'In accordance with the hypostatic division, the male relates to the Holy Spirit. The "uni-duality" of Son and Holy Spirit expresses the Father' (EVDF p. 26).

The two words, male and female, are therefore not confined to an expression of sexuality. They symbolize two aspects, complementary or wholly one, of the individual, of mankind and of God.

man Humanity has been bound to see itself as a symbol. In many traditions, including even the most primitive, man is described as a small-scale copy of the universe, a microcosm or synthesis of the world. Man is the centre of the world of symbols. So many writers, from the Wise Men of the Upanishads, to Christian theologians and those who searched out the secrets of alchemy, have drawn analogies and seen correspondences between the elements which make up the human frame and those which make up the universe and between the principles which control human emotions and those which govern the universe. Some saw the bones of man's body as being linked to Earth, his blood to Water, his lungs to Air and his head to Fire, while for others the nervous system was related to Fire, the respiratory to Air, the circulatory to Water and the digestive to Earth. Man is in touch with the three levels of the cosmos, his feet with the terrestrial, his chest with the atmospheric and his head with the celestial. He is a citizen of the three kingdoms, animal, vegetable and mineral, and in spirit he can communicate with the godhead. The number of comparisons which may be made is endless and sometimes owes more to phantasy than to symbolism.

In the *Atharva-Veda* (10: 7) man was originally regarded as the cosmic pillar, a sort of Atlas, with the duty of holding Earth and Heaven together, both being threatened with constant dissolution and disintegration. Man is thus both centre and principle of unity, ultimately identical with Brahman, the supreme principle.

The idea of man being made in God's image is Biblical. 'And God said, Let us make man in our image, after our likeness . . . And the Lord God formed man of the dust of the ground, and breathed into his nostrils the breath of life; and man became a living soul' (Genesis 1: 26; 2: 7). Commentators observe that the idea of likeness weakens that of image by utterly removing any notion of identity. This concept from Genesis became the cornerstone of astrological teaching, welding the relationship between the microcosm – man – and the macrocosm – not simply the universe, but the all-embracing mind of God, the idea and power of the universe. His or her birth is to each individual like the creation of the world, since to that individual coming into being and the birth of the world are one and the same, as are death and the end of the world. When an individual dies it is one and the same that he or she dies to the world or that the world dies with them. The entity, God–Universe–Man, is expressed as a sphere, the traditional image of the world in the centre of which each man stands. His place in the world and the world's place in him are defined by their mutual ties. Man symbolizes a network of cosmic relationships.

The Chinese regard each individual human being as a complex corresponding to given elements. These components are never considered as being wholly spiritual or wholly material. Each person's nature is thus produced by specific ingredients mixed more or less harmoniously. Man's bodily condition is characterized by the proportions of *yin* to *yang* which it contains and it is this balance which is upset by illness.

Chinese physicians had evolved the following correspondence between the cosmos and the human body:

the round head: sky;
the hair: stars and constellations;
the eyes and ears: Sun and Moon;
the breath: wind;
the blood: rain;
the bodily vessels and humours: streams and waters;
apertures and veins: valleys and rivers;
the four bodily seas (stomach, Sea of Water; aorta, of Blood; mediastinum,
    of the Lungs; brain, of Bone Marrow): the four cosmic seas;
the body: the element Earth;
the skeleton: mountains;
the heart: Great Bear;
the seven apertures in the heart: the seven stars in the Great Bear;
the five internal organs: the five elements;
the eight parts of the body: the eight trigrams;
the nine apertures in the body: the nine gates of Heaven;
the four limbs: the four seasons;
the twelve principal joints: the twelve months;
the 360 minor joints: the 360 days of the year.

Chinese medicine recognized five digestive organs and nine apertures in the body – the two eyes, the two nostrils, the two ears and the mouth were seen as being *yang*: the two lower apertures as being *yin*.

All that was required to obtain a more or less accurate diagnosis was to combine the theory of the apertures and of the five internal organs with their correspondences with the five elements, the lower apertures being attributed to the kidneys, the nostrils to the lungs, the eyes to the liver, the mouth to the spleen, the ears to the heart. In his study of Chinese thought, Granet provides a portrait of Confucius drawn in accordance with this theory:

Confucius was descended from the Yin who had been rulers by virtue of water. His family name means 'hollow' and his personal name 'hollow mound' and at the crown of his head he had a slight depression like the hill-top which holds a pool of standing water. Water corresponds to the kidneys and to the colour black. Black is a sign of depth. His spirit was characterized by wisdom and the kidneys are the source of wisdom.

Man is flesh and spirit, but there are beings bearing the names of men who are so spiritually impoverished as to feel at home in a world which has turned away from God and who experience no transcendental longings. The Gnostic, Basilides, asked himself whether such men were men in the true sense of the word and most emphatically denied it (ERAJ (1948) p. 116). In prophetic terms Basilides spoke of a time to come when spiritual men had been replaced by ignorant beings who rejected all that which pertained to the spiritual. Each would be quite happy with the world in which he or she lived and would have no more interest in eternal life. When that time came, a man who spoke of the spiritual life would seem as foolish as a fish trying to crop the mountain pastures with a flock of sheep. Once the world was filled with such ignorance, quest and longing on the spiritual plane would come to an end and the world would be completely denuded of spiritual longing (ibid. 123–4). Thus Basilides demonstrates the end of the man of flesh and spirit, and thus the day will come when man will symbolize the flesh alone. When this happens he will be in danger of losing his immortality.

mana   Mana is not a symbol, but is itself symbolized in charms, stones, leaves, different images, idols, objects hung round the neck or worn on belts, other items of clothing and so on. The word 'mana' is of Melanesian origin, but the meaning which it conveys is the same as that of the Sioux *wakan*, the Iroquois *orenda*, the Huron *oki*, the West Indian *zemi* and the *megbe* of the African Pygmy tribe, the Bambuti. Although the concept of 'mana' is so widespread that some sociologists have gone so far (and too far) as to suggest that all religious phenomena derive from it, it is by no means universal. Wherever it occurs, it denotes a particular relationship with the sacred:

that mysterious but active power which belongs to certain people, and generally to the souls of the dead and all spirits. The tremendous act of creating the cosmos could only be performed by the *mana* of the Divinity; the head of a family also possesses *mana*, the English conquered the Maoris because their *mana* was stronger. . . . But men and things only possess as *mana* because they have received it from higher beings, or, in other words, because and in so far as they have a mystical sharing of life with the sacred. . . . Everything that *is* supremely, possesses *mana*; everything, in fact, that seems to man effective, dynamic, creative or perfect.

(ELIT pp. 19–20)

mandala   Strictly speaking, the word 'mandala' means 'circle', although it is a complex piece of drawing and often framed within squared borders. Like the YANTRA (an emblematic medium), but more powerfully schematic, the mandala is simultaneously an abridgement of spatial manifestation and an image of the world, the depiction and realization of divine powers, as well as a visual aid to spiritual instruction and enlightenment.

The traditional Hindu mandala determines through ritual orientation the central holy area comprising altar and temple. The mandala is the spatial symbol of the presence of the godhead at the centre of all things – *purusha* (Vāstu-Purusha mandala). It is depicted as a square subdivided into smaller squares, the simplest (dedicated to Shiva and to Prithivī) comprising four or nine compartments, the more common sixty-four or eighty-one compartments. The square (or squares) at the centre are the *Brahmāsthana*, the

Place of Brahmā, and contain the *Garbhagriha*, or womb-chamber, the cella of the temple. The outer framework of squares is related to the solar and lunar cycles. If this arrangement is to be found in the ground-plan of temples, such as that at Khajurāho, in India itself, it is also true of places such as Angkor, in particular, to which Hinduism was exported.

The Tantric mandala comes from the same symbolic source. It is painted or drawn as an aid to meditation or marked out on the ground for rites of initiation. Basically it is a square with gateways at the four points of the compass. These gateways are filled with circles, lotuses, images and symbols of the godhead, those on the outer perimeter being provided with guards. Passing through them in succession corresponds to similar stages in spiritual development or grades of initiation, until the centre is attained, the undifferentiated state of Buddha-*chakravartī*. The mandala may also be internalized and formed in the cavern of the heart. Temples like that at Borobudur in Java display precisely what is meant by the internal development of the mandala.

Far Eastern Shingon Buddhism depicts the mandala as a lotus, on whose centre and individual petals there is an image of the Buddha or of a Bodhisattva. An especial feature is the double mandala, again with Vairocana in its centre, comprising that of the non-manifest *vajradhātu*, or Diamond Cycle, and that of the *garbhadhātu*, or Womb Cycle, which although universally manifest bears the fruit of liberation.

Japanese Buddhists of the Shingon sect regard the concentric designs of these mandalas as images of the two complementary and ultimately identical aspects of supreme reality. One is the primeval power of reasoning, inborn in humans, which employs the images and ideas of the illusory world; the other is ultimate knowledge, gained by spiritual exercises, acquired by the Buddha and with him interfusing the intuition in Nirvana. The mandala is an image both of synthesis and of a driving energy source; it both stands for and yet also helps to overcome the conflict of the many and the one, the diffused and the concentrated, the disjoint and the conjoint, the differentiated and the undifferentiated, the external and the internal, the visible illusion and the invisible reality, and space-time and extraspatial timelessness.

Henry Corbin has observed Ismaili circular diagrams strikingly akin in concept and meaning to the mandala (BURA, CORT, COOI, DAVL, ELIY, GRIC, KRAT, MALA, SECA).

In Tibetan tradition, the mandala provides a temporary guide to the imagination during meditation. In its varying combinations of circles and squares it displays the spiritual and material universe as well as the dynamic which links them on the triple cosmic, human and divine planes. 'The ritual use of the mandala is as an adjunct to the divinity of which it is the cosmic symbol. As a visible projection of a divine world at the centre of which sits enthroned the divinity in question, there can be no mistake about its meaning. The Master's voice is able to bring it to life' (TONT p. 12). In one example, five large concentric circles might encompass an eight-petalled lotus in the centre of which there is a structure comprising a number of squares one inside the other, each with four gates opening to the four points of the compass. Within, twelve Buddhas in meditation would surround another square in which a circle is drawn. Once again, in the centre of this circle would be another eight-petalled lotus in the middle of which the deity would be seated. In the blank spaces would be seen symbols of flame, thunderbolt and cloud. Around and outside the large circles, deities and protective or destructive creatures would be depicted against a background of cloud and flame. Through the magic of its symbols, the mandala is both the image and the moving force of spiritual ascension. It derives from the ever-increasing drive to internalize existence by progressively concentrating the manifold upon the one, with the ego reintegrated into the whole and the whole into the ego.

Jung uses the image of the mandala to express

a symbolic representation of the 'nuclear atom' of the human psyche – whose essence we do not know. . . . Similar pictures are used to consolidate the inner being, or to plunge one into deep meditation. The contemplation of a mandala is meant to bring an inner peace, a feeling that life has again found its meaning and order. The mandala also conveys this feeling when it appears spontaneously in the dreams of modern men who are not influenced by any religious tradition of this sort. . . . Roundness (the mandala motif) generally symbolizes a natural wholeness, whereas a quadrangular formation represents the realization of this in consciousness. In the dream the square disk and the round table meet, and thus a conscious realization of the centre is at hand.

The mandala incorporates a twofold efficacy: it preserves psychic order if it already exists and restores it if it has vanished. In the latter case it has a stimulant and creative function (JUNS pp. 213–15).

mandorla See under ALMOND.

mandrake The mandrake is a fertility symbol, it foretells the future and acquires wealth. In magical practices, although the mandrake may be found in both male and female shape, it is always regarded as the male principle. Its medicinal virtues and spiritual efficacy depend upon the extent to which it has a tap-root. It is, however, poisonous and must be carefully prescribed to be beneficial.

The mandrake is supposed to grow from the semen ejaculated by a hanged man (SCHM).

In Ancient Egypt mandrake berries, the size of a nut and white or russet-coloured, were symbols of love, doubtless because of their aphrodisiac qualities.

In Ancient Greece the mandrake was known as the sorceress Circe's plant and inspired a reverential awe. Pliny the Elder, following Theophrastus, observes: 'The diggers avoid facing the wind, first trace round the plant three circles with a sword, and then do their digging while facing the west. . . . The pounded root, with rose oil and wine, cures fluxes and pain in the eyes' (*Natural History* 25: 94).

In folklore and legend the mandrake is associated with the symbolism of fertility and wealth, provided that it is treated with care and reverence. It is one of those plants most fertile in superstitious and magical practices.

manikin In his *De bello gallico*, Julius Caesar describes the Celtic ritual CREMATION of men shut in human figures, or manikins, of willow, which were set on fire.

'Laodamia is also supposed to have fashioned a life-size figure of her dead husband in wax and was accustomed secretly to copulate with it. Her father discovered it and threw this manikin upon a fire: Laodamia cast herself after it and was burned alive' (GRID p. 251).

The manikin is one of the symbols of identification: of an individual's identification with perishable matter, with a group, or with another individual; or of identification with a perverse desire or with guilt. Later ages burned their enemies in effigy. Laodamia died with the object of her desire, an object with which she had identified. This was to take the image for the reality, a spiritual deviation under the impulse of passion which made the soul blind and servile.

Manitu The Algonquin Indians regarded the Manitu as the life force immanent in humans, animals, plants and all natural phenomena. The individual's energies are part of the Manitu which the individual shares. The sum of that energy is the Supreme Being, the Great Manitu who gives life to all creation (KRIE p. 61).

manna The Book of Exodus (16) speaks of manna, the food with which God's providence miraculously fed the Children of Israel during their forty years in the wilderness. From the outset it was the ideal foundation for an elaborate symbolic structure, since its very name was supposed to be derived from the question asked by those who first found this strange substance – 'Man hou? What is it?'

A heavenly food, manna might be 'the corn of Heaven' or 'angels' food' (Psalms 78: 24–5).

This miraculous food could not simply have vanished from the face of the Earth, and rabbinical writings enable us to follow step by step the speculations which led them to conclude that manna was now stored in Heaven and kept for the righteous. When the Messiah appeared it would once again fall down on Earth for this second Moses in a second Exodus. It is to similar beliefs that St John alludes: 'To him that overcometh will I give to eat the hidden manna' (Revelation 2: 17).

From this traditional data both Jewish and Christian writers have added far richer meanings to the symbolism of manna. Philo regarded it as a type of the Logos and as the heavenly food of souls. In St John's Gospel (6: 31–5) the Eucharist becomes the true manna, the Bread of God, coming down from Heaven and giving life, the Bread of Life.

Following St Paul (1 Corinthians 10: 3–16), the early Fathers emphasized one of the harmonics of this basic theme. Just as the Children of Israel had eaten this miraculous food, but had been quite capable of faithlessness immediately afterwards, so Christian neophytes should not think that the bread of the Eucharist would act like some magic charm to prevent them falling into sin (St John Chrysostom, *Baptismal Catachesis* 5: 15ff.).

mantra In Hinduism and Buddhism, the resonant ritual phrase passed by the master to his disciple is believed, when recited, to have the power to set in motion its corresponding spiritual influence. It allows the one who uses it to become part of the vibrations which, according to Hindu cosmology, comprise the universe and to share in the control of their energy. In this case the symbol partakes of the strength of sacramental communion with the cosmos.

maraca   Used by Amerindian shamans as a sacred musical instrument in exactly the same way as their Siberian confrères use DRUMS. The Tupinamba make offerings of food (METT pp. 27ff.), while the Yaruro carve on them stylized representations of the deities they visit in trance states (quoted in ELIC p. 178). Pawnee Indians regarded maracas as symbolizing the breasts of the First Mother (FLEH).

The Tupinamba of Brazil used to take their maracas into the Otherworld 'to tell the ancestors they had arrived' (METT). It is one of the symbols of making contact with the godhead and presences.

market-place   In Ancient China, market-places were not only trading places but the scenes of Spring dances, marriages, rain-making ceremonies and ritual connected with fertility and other celestial influences. In fact, if one wanted to stop the rain, women were forbidden to enter market-places.

As places where *yin* and *yang* met in equal balance, market-places were centres of peace in which blood-feuds could not be pursued (Granet). The rituals of secret societies take the symbolism a stage further when they speak of a 'market-place of the Great Peace' (*t'ai-p'ing*), the goal of a 'voyage' and identical with the 'City of Peace' or the 'Abode of Peace'. It is the image of a spiritual state or a rung upon the ladder of initiation (GRAD, GRAR).

marriage   Marriage is the symbol of the loving coitus of man and woman, which, in a mystical sense, is also that of Christ's union with his Church, of God with his Chosen People and of the soul with God. In Jungian analysis, during the course of the process of individuation or of personality integration, marriage symbolizes the conciliation of the feminine principle of the unconscious with the male principle of the spirit.

Nearly all religious traditions contain instances of sacred marriages. They not only symbolize the potential for union between God and the individual, but also the coition of divine principles which will engender definite essences. One of the most famous of these marriages was between Zeus (Power) and Themis (Justice or Eternal Order), from which were born Irene (Peace), Eunomia (Order) and Dike (Law).

Ancient Egypt had its 'wives of Amon' who were generally the daughters of Pharaohs, consecrated as worshippers of the god and vowing their virginity in this sacred marriage. 'Married only to the god, the Divine Wife offered his cult a mildly erotic element, charming the god with her beauty and the music of her sistrums; sitting on his knee, she would put her arms around his neck' (POSD p. 11). Although no link can be established, one cannot avoid comparing the rites of the Worshippers of Amon, a fertility-god, with those of the Vestal Virgins, priestesses of Hestia (Vesta), goddess of hearth and home. In Rome, Vesta was to become the Earth Goddess and the Mother Goddess whose worship laid exaggerated stress upon sexual purity.

Thus marriage, instituted for the transmission of life, seemed surrounded by the halo of a cult which promoted and even demanded virginity. It symbolizes the divine origins of life, of which human coitus is merely an ephemeral receptacle, instrument or channel. Marriage derives from the rites of making life holy.

Mars (see also ARES) The prime significance of Mars in astrology is that of energy, aspiration, enthusiasm, striving and aggression. Since these qualities are used more frequently for evil than for good ends, in the Middle Ages the planet was called 'the star of evil'. Mars governs both life and death. Its chief house, that is to say sign of the Zodiac which best suits it, is ARIES which rules in Spring when nature is reborn, while its second is SCORPIO which rules in Autumn when nature dies. Mars symbolizes the fiery force of desire, forcefulness, violence and the male sexual organs.

The planet glows with a red and fiery light, like some face suffused with passion and murderous rage. All ancient languages gave it a name meaning 'fiery' and mythology completed the process by calling it after the god of war. It would appear that its symbolism is all too easily acquired and yet, when a rigid statistician had the bright idea of finding the position Mars occupied in the horoscopes of 3142 European commanders, he found that the chances that they were born either when the planet was in its ascendant or descendant were a million to one. Similar statistics emerged in a study of a group of 2315 medical graduates and of 1485 leading athletes. Astrologers, however, had not expected such results to show that the armed forces, medicine and sport are under the sign of Mars. The particular indicator of the tendencies associated with this planet is the hostility exhibited in paroxysms of infantile rage occurring during teething and in the earliest attempts at muscular co-ordination and walking. These are the opening shots in the battle for life, fought tooth and claw in a dangerous world of falls and collisions, cuts and scratches and bumps, whinings and disobedience. It continues through all the competition, rivalry and enmities aroused by the need to earn a living, clutch at status and defend interests won, giving one's all to satisfy longings and urges at whatever risk.

marsh (see also LAKE) While Europeans may read into the marsh the sense of sloth and idleness, Asia does not regard absence of movement as something negative. The Chinese HEXAGRAM *t'ui*, which duplicates the sign for still water, carries the meaning of concord, fulfilment and wealth.

In Sumerian mythology, the marsh is passive, female, undifferentiated matter.

In China marshes were places for fishing and hunting, but the hunting was ritual. This was because the powers of Heaven were manifested in marshes and because they, too, were spiritual centres. This is why after the Great Yu had regulated space, he fashioned the marsh of Hia and there built a royal watchtower, the ancestor of the Temple of Heaven (see HOUSE) and centre of the Chinese empire. In the Celtic world, marshes must have carried a very similar significance, if the location of Glastonbury is anything to go by. In Ancient Greece marshes played parts similar to MAZES.

A very different approach is to be observed in the *Samyutta-nikāya*, in which the Buddha takes the marsh as an image of sensual pleasures which are obstacles along the Eightfold Path (GRAD, LIOC, SOUN).

A Fulani tale depicts the path beside the marsh as a phase in initiation.

Hammadi's lament develops the theme still further: 'O you marsh of deception! Woe to the thirsty who rush to your pools! Our throats are dry, our misfortunes have reached their peak, we die in torment!' The deadliest of poisonous snakes writhe round marsh-pools and deny access.

The 'bright' side of the symbol of the marshy pool which denies the stranger access, bears the meaning of a united family, a well-defended country or a secure village, the still water being the image of a peacefulness which nothing can disturb. The 'dark' side of the marshy pool protected by poisonous snakes symbolizes selfishness and the greed which refuses to share the good things of life with neighbours, even if they are dying of poverty (HAMK 12, p. 61). This aspect may also bear a meaning, in line with the symbolism of treasures guarded by monsters, of the difficulties to be overcome before the cool of the oasis or the pool can be attained.

Analysts make pools and marshes a symbol of the unconscious and the Mother, a place where matter germinates in secret.

mask In the East the symbolism of the mask depends upon the use to which it is put, the main types being theatrical, carnival and funeral, the latter a special feature of Ancient Egypt.

Theatrical masks – also used in ritual dances – are one form of manifestation of the universal ego. The wearer's personality is generally left unchanged, which means that the universal ego is immutable and unaffected by its contingent manifestations. And yet, in a different light, the very same performance may aim at modification through the actor's identification in the part which he plays with the particular divine manifestation represented, since the mask – and especially the fantastic or animal mask – is the face of the godhead and more particularly the face of the Sun, radiating spiritual light. Thus, when we are told that the *t'ao-t'i* masks (see DEVOURER) have grown gradually more human, we should not regard this as a sign of growing civilization, but rather of growing forgetfulness of the power of the symbol.

Masks also sometimes externalize demonic tendencies, as is the case in the Balinese theatre where these two aspects (of the actor's own personality and the universal power of the mask) meet face to face. However, much more striking instances are provided by carnival masks which, without exception, depict the lower, satanic aspect with a view to repudiating it. Masks act as liberators and this is also true of those used in the Ancient Chinese No Festival, corresponding to the New Year. They worked as a catharsis. Instead of hiding, the mask revealed those lower tendencies which had to be driven out. Masks, however, are dangerous things to use or handle and are surrounded with ritual and ceremony. This is true not only of Africa, but also of Cambodia, where the masks used in the *trot* dance are paid particular respect. Were this not so, the wearers would be endangered.

The funeral mask is the unchanging archetype in which the dead person was judged to return. Burkhardt also observes that it was intended to preserve within the mummy the 'bone-breath', a 'subtle' lower human modality. To preserve it, however, had its dangers, especially if the person concerned had attained a certain level of spiritual elevation. Although the two forms were different, a mask designed to pin down the wandering soul (*huen*) was employed as predecessor of the funeral tablet (see TABLE(T)). Granet suggests the eyes of the mask were pierced, just as the tablet was pricked, to show that the dead person had been born into the Otherworld (BEDM, BURM, GRAD, GUEI, GUES, GROC, PORA, SOUD).

In the dualistic concepts of the Iroquois, their False Face dances all originate from Flint, the evil one of their TWIN culture-heroes, who rules over darkness. There are two guilds of dancers belonging to their confederacy of secret societies. Their task is basically medicinal, preventing and curing both physical and psychic illness. In their ritual, the men are masked as dwarfs, monsters and other abortive pieces of the evil brother's creation. In the Spring and Autumn, the turning-points in the solar cycle, they drive disease from their villages.

According to Krickeberg (KRIE pp. 130–1), these masked dances originate from hunting rituals. They probably became healing dances because animals sent disease to avenge themselves upon their hunters. This is somewhat akin to the fact that among the Pueblo Indians, animal-gods are chiefs of Medicine Lodges (MULR p. 284). The Pueblo Indians celebrate the Coco Katchina – ancestors and the dead in general – with masked dances (ibid.). The festivals of these animal-gods are only held during the Winter, with the most important ceremonies occurring at the solstice, thus sharing a common symbolism with the Iroquois rituals. They are not only masters of herbal medicine and the rites of curing, but also of sorcery and black magic.

In Africa 'masks are an established feature of fertility-, funeral- and initiation-ceremonies. From the earliest times they belong to that stage in social development at which people become settled tillers of the soil. In his book, *Les arts de l'Afrique noire*, Jean Laude has written one of the most striking chapters on masks, 'sculpture in motion' and the main data for this entry is taken from this source (LAUA pp. 196, 201–3, 250–1).

Masked processional dances at the end of the seasonal agricultural tasks of ploughing, sowing and harvesting conjure up the series of events from the beginning of the world, the regulation of the universe and the ordering of society. They do more than simply recall them, they repeat them in order 'to manifest the here-and-now and in some sense to reinvigorate the present by relating it to that past and legendary age when God with the help of the spirits brought it into being.' As an example, the masked Kurumba dancers 'imitate the actions of the culture-hero, Yirigue, and his children when they came down from Heaven bearing masks.' Dogon dancers wear Kanoga masks – significantly the word means 'Hand of God' – and imitate 'with a circular motion of their heads and the upper portions of their bodies the motion made by God when he created the world and set the bounds of space.'

At regular intervals the masks breathe fresh life into the myths which claim to explain the origins of the customs of daily life. In symbols, morality is shown as the replica of cosmogenesis. The masks perform a social duty, masked ceremonies being

cosmogonies enacted to reinvigorate time and space. By their means an attempt is made to restore humanity and the forces entrusted to mankind to the pristine state which all things lose when subject to time. However, they are also truly cathartic displays, during which human beings take stock of their place in the universe and see life and death depicted in a collective drama which gives them a meaning.

Masks assume a slightly different significance in initiation ceremonies. The masked mystagogue incarnates the spirit which teaches mankind. Masked dances infuse the youth with the realization 'that he is dying to his former state to be born into adulthood.'

The masks sometimes partake of a magic power which protects their wearers against sorcerers and those who would harm them. Contrariwise, members of secret societies use them to impose their will through fear.

Masks are also instruments of possession: 'they are designed to trap the life force which escapes from a human being or an animal at the instant of death. The mask transforms the dancer's body, he preserves his own individuality but uses the mask like some living and moving adjunct to incarnate another being, spirit or mythical or fabulous animal which is temporarily called into being' and its powers tapped.

Masks also act as an agency controlling the movement of spiritual energies scattered throughout the world and all the more dangerous for being unseen. They trap them to stop their wandering.

If the life force set free at the moment of death were allowed to wander, it would disturb the living and upset the universal order. When it is trapped and brought under control in a mask, it can, so to say, be capitalized and then redistributed to the benefit of society as a whole. However, the mask also protects the dancer, who needs to be defended during the ritual from the power of the instrument in his hands.

Masks are designed to subjugate and control the invisible world. These forces move about in so many different shapes as to explain the varied combinations of carved human and animal figures unendingly and sometimes monstrously intertwined.

But masks can bring their wearers into danger. When trying to trap the vital force of another by luring it into the snares of his mask, the wearer may in his turn become 'possessed' by the other. The roles of mask and wearer become interchanged and the life force concentrated within the mask may possess the person who had placed himself under the mask's protection. Protector becomes controller. Accordingly, wearers of a mask, or even people who wish simply to touch it, must from the outset make themselves worthy to make contact with the mask and make preparations beforehand against any adverse reactions from it. This is why they must, over a longer or shorter period of time, abstain from certain foods and from sexual intercourse, purify themselves with baths and ablutions and offer sacrifice and prayer.

It is all rather like the preparations for a mystical experience and ethnologists have, in any case, already compared the use of masks with the practical methods of access to the mystical life. Carl Einstein defined the mask as 'motionless ecstasy' and with more moderation Jean Laude suggests that it might be 'the means dedicated to the attainment of ecstasy at the moment when it contains within it the god or spirit.' Although the examples given by M. U. Beier are not conclusive, he states that some Yoruba masks might display the expression of a living individual in ec-static communion with the Bazimu. The facial expression, the swollen features – and especially the eyes – the rounded prominence of the limbs as if puffed out by the force springing up within them, all make one think of them as expres-sions of receptive concentration such as may be seen on the faces of the faithful in adoration, either about to take God into the soul or immediately after the mystic marriage with God has been consummated.

In this context, it should be remembered that different definitions of mys-ticism depend upon the levels of the different theologies of the religious life.

The trapped force is neither to be identified with the mask, which is a mere representation of the being for which it stands, nor with the wearer, who simply handles it without appropriating it to himself. The mask is the intermediary between the two forces and indifferent to whoever will emerge the victor in the dangerous struggle between the prisoner and his captor. In each case, the relationship between these two terms varies and each tribe gives them a different explanation. Although the coded language of the masks is broadcast throughout Africa, its deciphering is not always, every-where, or in every detail precisely the same.

Celtic languages have no word for 'mask', but borrowed it from the Latin. Archaeology, however, has discovered a limited number of Celtic masks and plenty of depictions of them, while Irish mythological descriptions lead one to conclude that some persons or messengers from the Otherworld wore masks. From the disappearance of any Celtic word after the introduc-tion of Christianity, it would be legitimate to infer the existence of tradi-tional data no longer available to us (REVC 15: pp. 245ff.; 19: pp. 335–6; POKE p. 845; OGAC pp. 116–21; R. Lantier, 'Masques celtiques en métal', in *Monuments et mémoires Piot* 37: pp. 148ff.; CELT 12: pp. 103–13 + plate 47).

Both in Ancient Greek tradition and in Minoan and Mycenean civiliza-tion masks were commonly employed in sacred ritual, ceremony and dance, at funerals, as offerings, as disguise and in the theatre. As in the Japanese theatre, these stage masks were stereotyped and generally emphasized the common characteristics of the person they represented – king, old man, woman, slave and so on. These masks occur throughout the range of plays and characters. When an actor put on a mask, externally or by magical appropriation, he became one with the character he played. His mask was a symbol of identification. The mask symbol has been borrowed for dra-matic purposes in stories, plays and films in which a person becomes so identified with the character or mask as to be unable to rid him- or herself of it. Incapable of tearing off the mask, that person becomes the character it represents. It is easy to imagine the powers of identification possessed by masks and one can also see why analysts are bent on stripping away an individual's masks, to make that person face the fullness of reality.

When shaped like gods or spirits and worn on the clothes or hung on temple walls, masks were 'the very image, all the more expressive as they were only faces, of the supernatural powers invoked by worshippers' (DEVD p. 284).

But this, perhaps, brings us back to the Chinese and Hindu myths of the

lion, the dragon or the ogre which besought the god who had created them
to supply them with victims to eat and which were given this answer: 'Feed
upon yourselves.' They then realized that they were no more than masks,
appearances, longings, insatiable greed, but void of all substance.

mat See CARPET.

maze The most famous maze was the Labyrinth, the Cretan palace in
which Minos stabled the MINOTAUR and from which Theseus was enabled to
escape only because of the thread which Ariadne had given him. All mazes
share its common characteristic of complexity and difficulty of ingress and
egress.

Basically a maze comprises a criss-cross pattern of paths, some of which prove
to be dead-ends, through which a way must be found to lead to the middle of
this strange spider's web. However, it is inaccurate to compare a maze with a
spider's web. The latter is regular and symmetrical, while the very essence of
the maze is to crowd into the smallest possible space the most complicated
system of paths and thus delay for as long as possible the traveller's arrival at
the centre which is his goal.

(BRIV p. 179)

   This artificial network exists in a natural state in the passageways leading
to a number of prehistoric cave-sites; Virgil assures us that it was drawn
upon the door to the Sibyl's cavern at Cumae; it was carved upon the stone
floors of cathedrals; it was danced in many lands from Greece to China, and
it was known to the Ancient Egyptians. The fact is – and its association with
CAVERNS bears this out – that mazes should both allow access to their centres by a sort of initiatory journey and bar it to those who are not qualified
to enter. In this sense the maze is akin to the MANDALA, which in any case
sometimes bears a labyrinthine appearance. Thus we are concerned with
the representation of initiatory tests by choosing, as preliminaries to a journey to the hidden centre.
   The mazes carved into the floors of cathedrals were at one and the same
time the monograms of their builders and substitutes for pilgrimage to the
Holy Land. This is why either the architect himself or the Temple at Jerusalem is sometimes depicted in the middle, either as the chosen one who
has reached the centre of the world or the symbol of that centre. The
faithful who were unable to take part in the actual pilgrimage could journey
in imagination through the maze until they reached the Holy Places. This
was the stationary pilgrimage (BRIV p. 202). At Chartres the pathway
through the maze was over 200 yards long and the journey was made upon
the knees.
   Mazes were used as defences at the gates of fortified towns (see CASTLE);
they are also to be found in ancient clay models of Greek houses and, in
both cases, we have a town or house protected as if it were the centre of
the world. Such defences are to ward off not merely human enemies, but
evil influences as well. The identical part played by screens set in the middle
of temple naves in areas under Chinese influence should also be observed,
since here evil influences were believed always to make themselves felt
along straight lines.

Theseus' dance, known as the Crane Dance, is clearly related to his journey through the Cretan labyrinth; similarly, labyrinthine bird dances, such as the Yu Dance, existed in China and their role belonged equally to the supernatural order (BENA, CHRC, GUES, JACG, KALT).

As the symbol of a defensive system, the maze proclaims the presence of something precious or holy. It may serve the military purpose of defending an area of land, a village, a town, a tomb or a treasure-house, to which it allows admission only to those who know the plans or have been initiated. It has the religious purpose of protection against the assaults of evil, this evil being not only satanic, but also intrusive, from persons prepared to violate the secrets, the holiness and the intimacy of a relationship with the godhead. The centre protected by the maze is the preserve of the initiate, the person who has passed the tests of initiation (the windings of the maze) and has shown him- or herself worthy to be granted a revelation of the mystery. Once that person reaches the centre, he or she is, as it were, made holy, entering the arcane and bound by the secret.

The labyrinth rituals upon which initiation ceremonies are based ... are intended for just this – to teach the neophyte, during his sojurn on earth, how to enter the domains of death [which is the gate to a new life] without getting lost. . . . In a sense, the trials of Theseus in the labyrinth of Crete were of equal significance with the expedition to get the golden apples from the garden of the Hesperides, or to get the golden fleece of Colchis. Each of these trials is basically a victorious entry into a place hard of access, and well defended, where there is to be found a more or less obvious symbol of power, sacredness and immortality.

(ELIT p. 381)

The Cretan Labyrinth might also have a solar significance because of the double axe, of which it might have been the palace and which is carved on so many Minoan remains. The bull shut in the labyrinth is solar, too. In this context, it may symbolize the royal power which Minos exercised over his people. 'While the stepped spires of the ziggurat borrow the three-dimensional spatial projection of a helical maze, the very name, Labyrinth, Palace of the Axe, reminds us that in Knossos the mythical stall of the Minotaur was pre-eminently the shrine of the double axe (emblem of kingship), that is, of Zeus–Minos' archaic thunderbolt' (AMAG p. 150).

In the Kabbalistic tradition taken up by the alchemists, mazes filled a magical function which was one of the secrets attributed to Solomon. This is why the mazes in cathedrals, 'those series of concentric circles broken at given points on the circumference to provide a strange and tangled pathway', came to be called 'Solomon's Maze'. Alchemists saw them as images 'of the whole task involved in the Work, with its major difficulties; an image of the path they needed to follow to reach the centre, arena for the two warring natures; image of the path which the artist must follow to find release' (FULC p. 63). This explanation would run parallel with that provided by one of the teachings of ascetic mysticism – focusing upon oneself, along the thousands of paths of feeling, emotion and ideas; overcoming all that stands in the way of unalloyed intuition, and then returning to the light without becoming lost in the byways. To enter and to emerge from the maze might be the symbol of death and resurrection.

The maze also takes one to the centre of one's self, 'to some hidden, inner shrine, occupied by the most mysterious portion' of the human personality. This conjures up the *mens*, the temple of the Holy Spirit in the soul in a state of grace; or again, the depths of the unconscious. Both can only be reached by consciousness after making many detours or by intense concentration, when that ultimate intuition is attained and everything becomes plain through some kind of enlightenment. Here in this crypt the lost oneness of being, scattered in a multiplicity of desires, is rediscovered.

To reach the centre of the maze, like a stage in the process of initiation, is to be made a member of the invisible lodge which the maze-makers always shroud in mystery or, better still, have always left to be filled by the finder's own intuition and personal affinities. When Marcel Brion writes about Leonardo da Vinci's maze, he conjures up 'that brotherhood of men of all ages and all lands, filling the magic circle which Leonardo left blank, for it was never his intention to describe in detailed terms the shrine in the middle of his maze' (BRIV p. 196).

The maze combines the motifs of SPIRAL and PLAIT and might express

the patent intention of representing infinity under both the guises in which it appears in human imaginations. The first is the spiral, or the infinity of non-fulfilment, since, in theory at least, it can be conceived of as never coming to an end; the other is the infinity of the eternal homecoming embodied in the plait. The harder the journey, the more and the tougher obstacles in his path, the more the initiate will be transformed and acquire a new self in the course of his voyage of initiation.

(BRIV pp. 199–200)

The transformation of the self which occurs in the middle of the maze and which will be manifested in broad daylight at the end of the return journey, through darkness to light, will mark 'the victory of the spiritual over the materialistic and, at the same time, that of the eternal over the ephemeral, of reason over instinct and of knowledge over blind violence' (BRIV p. 202).

mead   Mead was the Celtic beverage of immortality, drunk by the gods in the Otherworld – when the monks came to write these legends down they often substituted wine – and also at the ritual feasts during the great festival of Samain. At Celtic feasts mead and beer were drunk together and mead brought swift and complete intoxication. Mead lingers as a drink in Celtic areas, especially in Brittany (OGAC 13: pp. 481ff.).

In contrast with BEER, which was the drink of the warrior caste, mead, in the Celtic world, was the drink of the gods. The drinking of mead at the festival of Samain was due to the fact, confirmed by all literary sources, that the priestly caste joined in the feasting. The deposed High King died, drowned in a cask of mead – or less frequently of wine – while his palace was burned down (OGAC 7: pp. 33–5; 13: pp. 481–506).

In Africa, mead has remained a divine drink. The Bambara regard it as the drink of their wise men, since it stands for knowledge in its highest form. This is because it is made of WATER and HONEY, fermented and flavoured with pepper. Water is the vital fluid which makes fertile and unites, permitting intercommunication; honey is the symbol of truth and therefore of coolness, light and sweetness. The Bambara say that truth is like honey, because, like a honeycomb, it has 'neither top nor bottom' and is 'the sweetest thing in the world' (ZAHB p. 166). Pepper gives strength and stimulus to the virtues of these two ingredients and lastly FERMENTATION activates and sublimates the virtues of the whole. Mead only becomes intoxicating once it is fermented (see AMBROSIA).

medicine   The Plains Indians regard the attainment of corporeal and spiritual wisdom to be the essential business of life, and the power of 'medicine' as being the basic force governing its acquisition. To gain this power fills a great deal of the Indian's active life.

> The reason for this term [medicine] is that men of great attainments in this medicine were often professional healers . . . But the meaning of 'medicine' extends far beyond the practices of Indian doctor or healer . . . There are also numerous secret societies, also called 'medicine societies' . . . These societies form a structure within the tribal structure . . . and each performs a special function in the total tribal economy: of surgeons, of rain-priests, of clowns, of guardians of seed-corn or devotees of cult-objects. Each of these societies will possess its own 'medicine bundle', which is to the group what the individual's 'medicine bag' is to him – guardian of his life and fate – and with each such bundle there is a body of transmitted learning, in part practical instruction, in part song and ritual, which in sum embodies its wisdom.
>
> (ALEC pp. 185–6)

With the Canadian Athabasca Indians, 'medicine' is the art of acquiring a guardian or animal spirit. At the age of five the child is taken out of the camp and undergoes an ordeal by fasting to produce dreams. He becomes so hungry that he reaches a hallucinatory state of semi-consciousness. The first image which he sees in sleep becomes his guardian spirit and never leaves him. For the rest of his life he will wear a piece of the bodily shape taken by this spirit, which may be an animal, or also a natural phenomenon such as wind or water, or a spirit of the dead. In the latter instances he will wear a symbol cut into a piece of birch-bark. This spirit or medicine-animal may be invoked by song or drum-beat and becomes vital to the hunter – without it he dies. 'A hierarchy of ever more powerful and numerous spirits builds up to the summit of the social and religious pyramid on which the Shaman stands.'

The shamans' cures never fail and their role is essential to the survival of nomadic hunters. 'Their uncanny medicines are the ramparts behind which constantly threatened lives find shelter' (MULR pp. 224–8).

The ancient Greeks believed that the centaur Chiron taught medicine to Asclepios (Aesculapius). His ability to cure diseases and even to restore the dead to life was due to one thing alone – the Gorgon's blood given to him by Athene. The blood which flowed in the left side of the Gorgon was deadly poison, that from the right brought healing. Asclepios proved a skilful practitioner and the numbers of those brought back to life increased. Zeus struck him down with a thunderbolt and changed him into a constellation, Serpens (see CADUCEUS). Similarly Adam was driven from Paradise for having eaten of the fruit of knowledge and for trying to make himself God's equal by acquiring the source of life. The symbol of Asclepios, the physician destroyed by thunder, emphasizes the sacred character of life, which belongs to God alone. The myth will remind us of the sense of proportion which humans need to display in their quest for knowledge. The mortal who is lord of life is the mortal who has usurped the functions of God. It illustrates a phase in the eternal search for the truth in which mortals are in danger of mistaking for the truth what is really pride in making themselves God's equal. The Mackenzie Indians used to say there are no gods, only medicine. And the fear of genetic engineering pervades us today.

Medusa See GORGONS.

Melusine In romances of chivalry she was the legendary woman of extraordinary beauty who sometimes changed into a SERPENT. She was the GENIUS of the Lusignan family who would appear on one of the towers of their castle wailing mournfully every time a member of the family was about to die. A fifteenth-century romance popularized the legend of a FAIRY of wondrous beauty who promised Raimondin to make him the chief man of the kingdom if he would agree to marry her and never to look at her on a Saturday. The marriage was celebrated and brought Raimondin wealth and children, but Raimondin was eaten up by jealousy. Suspecting his wife of betraying him, he watched through a hole bored in the wall as Melusine withdrew to her room one Saturday. When she took her bath he saw that she had become half woman and half serpent, like the SIRENS who were half woman and half fish. Raimondin was overwhelmed with grief while Melusine, her secret revealed, flew off, proclaiming her distress from the top of the castle keep in frightful screams. Re-echoing the myth of Eros and Psyche (see LOVE), this legend symbolizes the destruction of love through lack of trust, or else through refusal to respect the beloved's right to privacy. It may also be interpreted as the disintegration of the individual who seeks openness at all costs and in consequence destroys the beloved and his or her own happiness. In the process of individuation, that person is unable to accept the limitations of the unconscious and the hidden, nor yet his or her own shadow, his or her own animality and their share in the dark and unknowable.

menhir Among the roles played by the menhir would seem to have been that of tomb-guardian, and it would generally be sited over or beside the burial place. 'Stone was a protection against animals and robbers, and, above all, against "death" for, as stone was incorruptible, the soul of the dead man must continue to exist as itself (the phallic symbolism that these prehistoric burial stones later came to have made this meaning still clearer, for the phallus symbolized existence, power, continuance)' (ELIT p. 217). The menhir is a male symbol of protection and watchfulness.

Caesar regarded menhirs as images of Mercury, just as in the Greco-Roman world squared stone COLUMNS were images of Hermes. In Celtic tradition, such cenotaphs or grave-stones were raised in honour of important druids and sited on the borders of the lands of the living looking out over the Happy Fields where the dead dwelt. This lithophany, or manifestation of STONE, conjured up the permanence of a force and a sort of vitality untouched by decay. In this context the stone is akin to the Tree of Life and the World Axis.

Among the less civilized tribes of central India, huge rocks were rolled onto or at fixed distances from the graves of their dead. These megaliths were 'intended to "fasten down" the dead man's soul and provide a temporary dwelling for it near the living so as (while enabling it to influence the fertility of their fields by the powers its spiritual nature gave it) to prevent it roaming about or becoming dangerous' (ELIT pp. 217–18) (see BETHEL). The significance of the menhir is thus related to the symbolism of the tomb-watcher and the guardian of life.

André Varagnac, on the basis of decorative patterns which he has been able to identify with reasonable accuracy, distinguishes between male and female menhir-statues. His researches have led him to discover in these menhirs traces of fire and fertility symbols (VARG p. 25). This is a recurrence of the bipolarity of the life–death symbol.

Mephistopheles 'He who hates the light'. The evil spirit of medieval literature who aided Dr Faustus, once the latter had bartered his soul to the Prince of Darkness. Embittered and sarcastic, his irony hides 'the pain and despair of the being of a higher nature which is separated from the God for which it was created, and is now totally imprisoned in Hell' (DICP p. 418). This evil spirit is recognizable 'by his cold-blooded malignity, his bitter laugh, which mocks at sorrow, and his ferocious pleasure at the sight of pain. He is the one whose mockery undermines the virtuous, who debases the talented by his scorn and tarnishes the brightness of glory with his lies. . . . Next to Satan he is the power of Hell most to be feared' (COLD p. 454).

Goethe transformed the figure of the medieval Mephistopheles into a metaphysical symbol. To prevent mankind from slumbering in deceitful and slothful peace, God gave Mephistopheles the freedom to act in the world as 'creative and fruitful anxiety'. He thus has his place in progressive evolution as an essential factor, albeit negative, in the destiny of the universe. 'I am a part of those forces,' he tells Faust, 'which ceaselessly plot evil and eternally create good.'

However, his limited intelligence is unable to grasp the vision of this harmonious evolution. Mephistopheles believes he is leading mankind to damnation when at the end of the toils in which he has entangled them, they find salvation. It is a case of the biter bitten.

The analyst may see in Mephistopheles the perverted tendency of the spirit to arouse the powers of the unconscious solely to obtain strength and satisfaction from them, instead of integrating them into a harmonious pattern of human behaviour. He is the sorcerer's apprentice who trifles with the unconscious and only raises it to the light in order the better to dazzle the consciousness. But when he arouses the consciousness, this will have to cast aside the harness of the false master and shape its own development along lines appropriate to it. The deceiver will become the deceived.

Mephistopheles also symbolizes the challenge of life, with all the ambiguities which this implies. As Jung points out, Faust had failed to 'live' a substantial proportion of his youth. Consequently he remained an incomplete personality, absorbed in the empty and unrealizable quest of metaphysical goals. He was unable to face the challenge of life and it was precisely this aspect of his unconscious which Mephistopheles was to arouse and lay bare. Such a challenge is one of the essentials in preparing the hero for the battles of life (JUNH).

Mercury (for the God, see HERMES) Mercury is a universal alchemical symbol and in most cases that of the passive, moist principle, *yin*. In alchemical terms, 'solution', bringing back to mercury again, is regression to an undifferentiated state. Just as a woman submits to the male, so mercury is subservient to SULPHUR. Mercury, the Chinese 'liquid silver' (*chui-yin*), corresponded to the dragon, the bodily fluids blood and semen, the kidneys and the element Water. Western alchemists set mercury in opposition to sulphur, but the Chinese brought them together as CINNABAR. The rotation of mercury and cinnabar obtained by successive calcinations is that of *yin* and *yang*, of death and rebirth. Some Western alchemical traditions maintain that mercury is female and sulphur male semen and that metals are born of their subterranean coitus.

In India, on the other hand, mercury was regarded as a concentration of solar energy underground, Shiva's semen to which mercurial lingams were dedicated. Mercury has the power of separating gold. It is a food of immortality, but also a symbol of deliverance. Alchemical mercury is a symbol of soma, which Tantrism uses to govern secretion and circulation. It may well be the means by which this deliverance is effected through strengthening the body. 'Mercury Knowledge' is in any case a term for a science of inward regeneration which we know by the name of Yoga. Mercury was believed to be able to obtain pure gold, as Yoga immortality (DANA, ELIY, ELIF, GUET, MAST).

In astrological analysis Mercury comes immediately after the two great lights the Sun, planet of life, and the Moon, planet of birth, in other words of the manifestations of life in our ephemeral world. If the Sun is the Heavenly Father and the Moon the Universal Mother, then Mercury is their child, the Intercessor. His two houses, that is to say the two signs of the Zodiac with natures most in harmony with that of this planet, are Virgo, which follows the solar sign, Leo, and Gemini, which comes before the lunar sign, Cancer.

Being the nearest neighbour to the Sun, Mercury is the swiftest planet, ceaselessly spinning. Mercury, the busy mythological god with wings at his heels, was the messenger of Olympus (see HERMES). This is as much as to say that Mercury is basically a principle of liaison, communication, movement and adaptation.

If one goes on to observe that the CADUCEUS is Mercury's attribute, one will readily appreciate the twofold nature of this symbol, in which the opposing yet complementary principles of light and dark, high and low, left and right, male and female meet head on. This internal ebb and flow comprises the first stage in intellectual development – distinguishing differences to avoid confusing one thing with another and standing outside oneself. Such interplay helps strengthen the rational by reducing reliance on instinct and repressing purely sensory responses. On these foundations, the structure is built of the socialization of the individual through acceptance of custom and submission to the laws of logic, the intercommunication of ideas clothed in words and of physical objects by a regulated system of exchange. In every individual the Mercurian process assists the ego to divert us from the attractions of a subjectivity which keeps us in darkness. The process pushes us to the point where the world around us comes together in a network and wealth of contacts. Mercury is the best channel for adapting to life in the face of the twin pressures of internal drives and external stimuli.

messenger In nearly all Celtic literary sources, the messenger of the gods was a woman who would appear to the chosen person during the night of the Festival of Samain (1, November). She was wonderfully beautiful, inspired love in the man she had chosen and, when she left him, even for a short time, he wasted away. Sometimes she brought a branch of apple-blossom. Her uncanny song was a narcotic. Sometimes, again, she brought an APPLE, the fruit of immortality and a never-ending source of food. Very often she would appear in the shape of a SWAN, singing a magic song. The Christian scribes who wrote down the legend turned it into a love story, like that of Zeus and Leda, but with the roles reversed. Cùchulainn was the only one to refuse these gifts and he was punished by a year's wasting-sickness (OGAC 18: pp. 136ff.; CHAB p. 541).

In Greek mythology both Hermes and Iris are messengers of the gods. In place of the fruit of immortality, Iris carried to the gods the waters of the River Styx which she gathered in a golden ewer.

metal (see also ALLOY; BLACKSMITH; BRONZE; COPPER; EMBRYO; GOLD; LEAD; MERCURY; SILVER) The word 'metal' is derived from the Greek *metallon* (mine) and René Alleau relates it to the root *me*, or *mes*, the oldest word for the Moon (ALLA pp. 62–3).

There are two distinct sides to the symbolism of metals. Metal-workers, such as blacksmiths, were on the one hand often partly excluded from society since their trade appeared to have links with the Underworld and was on this account judged dangerous. On the other, they often played the opposite part of a major role in society, their trades underpinning initiatory cults such as those of the CABEIRI in Ancient Greece and of Chinese and African secret societies. The first aspect is likely to have been the more important, since the most significant factors were the underground source of the ore and kinship of the forge with the fires of the Underworld. The beneficent aspect is based upon purification and transmutation, as well as the cosmic function of the person affecting the transmutation. Smelting pure metal from rough ore, said Jacob Boehme, 'was releasing the spirit from its accidents so that it became visible'.

Metals provide suitable subjects for effecting transformations, of which the objective in ALCHEMY was to extract the sulphur. The fusion of metals may be compared with death; the sulphur extracted being its essential quality, the nucleus or spirit of the metal.

In China the smelting process was likened to the acquisition of immortality and is the source of the alchemical symbolism; the Chinese ideogram *chin* – a stylization of metal fragments in the soil – carries the selfsame meaning of both 'metal' and 'gold'. Nevertheless, gold is pure *yang*, while the element Metal is of the essence of *yin* and corresponds to the west, to Autumn and to the colour white. 'Melt down the universe and refashion it', is a phrase used in the ritual of a secret society. This is the alchemists' *solve et coagula*, the rotational influences of Heaven and Earth, of the *yang* aspect and the *yin* aspect. The creation of alloys is on a par with marriage, since metals are substances endowed with life and sexuality. They have blood, which Nicolas Flamel describes as the mineral spirit which resides in metals. Metals are married by smelting and this is why success relies upon the sacrifice of the smith and his wife in the crucible (*yang* and *yin*) or at least of such surrogates as their hair or nail-clippings.

The impure aspect of metals, sign of their cyclical solidification, may be found in the Jewish prohibition of metal in their altars and of metal tools in the construction of Solomon's Temple. This ban was directed especially against iron since, as the doctrine of *yuga* (the ages of gold, silver, bronze and iron) shows, the symbols of metal are set in descending hierarchical order of 'solidification', the gradual hardening of the four ages of the world (ELIF, GRAD, GUER, GUES).

In fact there is a system of correspondence between metals and stars or planets which runs in ascending order to provide the following hierarchy of metals:

lead	=	Saturn
tin	=	Jupiter
iron	=	Mars
copper	=	Venus
mercury	=	Mercury
silver	=	Moon
gold	=	Sun

This cosmic hierarchy is to be found among the myths of many peoples and ages, such as in Hesiod, for example. The Golden Age and its people are wholly marvellous, while the Iron Age and its people are wholly brutalized and despotic. A hierarchy of metals also recurs within the social hierarchy, gold, silver or iron plate being allocated by class, while in the Middle Ages, gold spurs were for knights and silver for squires. This distinction was less a matter of cost than of the notion of hierarchy based upon the symbolism of metals. Such symbolism, however, recognized alloys, such as bronze.

Metals are the planetary elements of the Underworld and planets the metals of the Heavens, the symbolism of each running parallel with the other. Metals symbolized cosmic energy in condensed and solid form, with different influences and attributes.

As symbols of energy, Jungian symbolism has identified them with the libido. Their chthonian character relates them to sexual desires and, if the latter are sublimated, it is as if base metal had been transmuted into pure gold. In this context, the analogy is not only with astrology, but also with alchemy. The issue is release from an enslavement to carnal appetite which plays the same role as harmful planetary or metallic influences. The path of individuation may be compared with that of transmutation. Sublimation or spiritualization, like the alchemists' Great Work, proceeds through fire and destruction to reintegration on a higher level. Alternatively, and following another line of reasoning, it is less a matter of liberation from planetary or metallic influences than integrating them into a completely balanced lifestyle.

To lay aside all metal is a very ancient initiatory and symbolic ceremony and is undoubtedly related to the 'impure' aspect of metals. It has been likened to 'the myth of the Babylonian goddess, Ishtar, who was forced during her descent into the Underworld, successively to cast aside all her jewels and garments as she passed through seven successive outworks to appear stark naked before her sister, the terrifying ruler of the kingdom of the dead.' Something similar is to be found in Masonic initiatory rituals, in which the candidate is asked to remove from his person all metal objects such as rings, small change, watches, chains and so on, to show his indifference to all material goods and conventions and his willingness to regain his original state of innocence (HUTF p. 147).

metamorphosis All mythologies are filled with stories of metamorphoses, of gods changing either themselves or other beings into human or animal shapes or, more often, into birds, trees, flowers, fountains, rivers, rocks, mountains or statues. From Greek mythology alone Grimal quotes over a hundred examples.

In all Welsh and Irish literary sources there are accounts of a sorcerer, either a druid or a bard, or else a sibyl changing, for some reason or other, a hero or heroine into some creature such as a pig, bird or fish. Often, too, gods or goddesses effect such transformations and, in addition, there are druids who agreed for sacrificial purposes to change themselves into cattle. In Gaul, the priestesses of Sena claimed to be able to change themselves into whatever animal they wished. Such temporary metamorphoses should, however, be clearly distinguished from METEMPSYCHOSIS which, in the strict sense of the word, is transmigration, an utter and complete passing from one state to another (LERD pp. 126–34; OGAC 15: pp. 256–8).

These metamorphoses may be to higher or to lower states depending upon whether they represent a reward or a punishment, or upon the ends for which they are designed. Zeus did not intend it as a punishment when he appeared before Leda in the shape of a swan.

Such metamorphoses betray a definite belief in the basic oneness of being, outward appearance having a passing or illusory quality. Changes of shape do not seem to have affected the inner personality, persons generally retaining their original names and psychic make-up. From the analyst's viewpoint, one might conclude that metamorphoses rise from the depths of the unconscious and are shaped by the creative imagination as expressions of desire, guilt, inhibition or idealism. Metamorphosis is an identification symbol in a personality in process of individuation who has yet to take on fully the role of his or her ego and realize the full range of his or her potential (see SOUL).

metempsychosis In different shapes and under different names a belief in the transmigration of souls is to be found in many different cultural environments, such as the Indian, Greek and north European. Judaism, Christianity and Islam reject it, since they espouse a linear rather than a cyclical notion of time.

This is not the place to discuss these beliefs, but whatever their moral, anthropological, cosmological or theological premises and whatever theoretical or pragmatic arguments are their base, they all have a symbolic bearing. On the one hand, they manifest the yearning to grow into the light of the One and on the other a feeling of responsibility for past actions. The twin forces, the weight of those actions and aspirations towards purity, set in motion a cycle of rebirths until perfection is gained, opening the doors of eternity and freeing from the wheel of life. Metempsychosis may be seen as a symbol of ethical and biological continuity. Once an individual is brought into being, he or she can escape neither from life nor from the consequences of his or her actions. Life is no longer a gamble: belief in metempsychosis does away with chance.

In their abridgement or short descriptions of the religious beliefs of the Celts, ancient writers often confused the immortality of the soul with metempsychosis. In fact, immortality of the soul was the privilege of those who went into the Otherworld, while metempsychosis was actually restricted to a few divine beings who changed their nature and state for soundly based reasons. In the Welsh tale of Ceridwen's CAULDRON, Gwion, having gained knowledge of all things from the broth he was cooking, changes himself successively into hare, fish, bird and grain of corn. To pursue him, Ceridwen changes herself into greyhound, otter, hawk and black hen. She pecks the grain of corn, becomes pregnant and gives birth to the famous bard, Taliesin. In this instance, transmigration relates to three conditions, the hare standing for Earth (corporeality), the fish for Water (the 'subtle' state) and the bird for Air (formlessness). The grain of corn symbolizes reabsorption into the First Cause. In Ireland, the bard Amorgen was successively bull, vulture, drop of dew, flower, wild boar and salmon. The case of the goddess Etain is even more complicated, since it affects a multitude of states of being. It may be stated that, in the Celtic world, metempsychosis only affected those individuals predestined and set apart for a particular mission or possessing the manifold aspects of truth and knowledge (CELT p. 15).

In some instances it is hard to separate metempsychosis from METAMORPHOSIS, the latter affecting only the outward appearance and not the inner essence, and not requiring death as its channel, while the former is part of the much weightier cycle of death and rebirth. Despite what Herodotus wrote and despite the charms and spells of the *Book of the Dead*, Serge Sauneron raises doubts as to whether the Ancient Egyptians really believed in the transmigration of souls. 'But such transmigrations were, on each occasion, only temporary and the soul did not pass through a vast cycle of reincarnation. It remained tied to the embalmed body in the tomb and could only be absent for brief periods' (POSD p. 289).

The *Tibetan Book of the Dead* reveals what happens during the forty-nine symbolic days of ordeal, between the individual's drawing his last breath and choosing a new womb. During this time the disembodied being, led by the conscious principle, is reduced to the product of his or her actions in earlier lives. The individual is, in fact, free and responsible for his or her fate, choosing the place of transmigration according to the *karma* accumulated during those existences.

The *Book of the Dead*, or *Bardo Thodol*, is mainly concerned with the nature of the human spirit and of its projections, pleasant or frightening, equable or wrathful. To the dead, these projections are infinitely more powerful, since the conscious principle is adrift and bewildered when it sees its bodily moorings snap. The *Vajrayāna*, the 'Diamond Vehicle' of Tibetan Tantric Buddhism, teaches its disciples how first to recognize and then to master this world of self-hallucinatory projections, so as to overcome fear and realize the true nature of the diamond spirit. The word *bardo*, meaning 'between the two', is applied both to the passage from death to rebirth as well as to any pause between two thoughts.

One Buddhist concept distinguishes six paths. Three of them are patently bad – rebirth in Hell, rebirth as a ghost subject to the tortures of hunger and thirst, and rebirth as an animal – the fourth, rebirth as a Titan, is equally wretched, while the other two are in contrast relatively good – rebirth as a god or as a mortal. 'Both these conditions are, however, temporary and cease once the effects of the actions which had ordained this rebirth are exhausted' (MYTF p. 155). To become fully enlightened, the individual has two choices: either to merge into Nirvana, or, if he or she possesses a Bodhisattva ideal, although freed from the Wheel of Life to return freely to Earth to help his or her fellows free themselves from the world of suffering.

meteorite　See SHOOTING STAR.

mica　In Ancient China, mica was a highly prized food of immortality, perhaps because of its immutability and its golden glitter. It needed to be made palatable by means of 'liquid jade'. Another explanation is that its name (*yun-mu*) means 'Sea of Clouds' and that its eater was enabled to fly and to ride the clouds like the Immortals.

In Hindu alchemy, mica (*abhra*) was the complement to mercury, uniting with it like Gauri's ovum to Shiva's semen. From such a marriage came the fruits of immortality (ELIY, KALL).

midday (midnight)　Like the solstices in the annual cycle, so midday and midnight are not simply points of the greatest concentrations of *yang* and *yin*, but also starting points for ascending movement of opposing principles, since the ascendant portion of the day runs from midnight to midday, its descendant from midday to midnight. This is why, in China, the most favourable time for conception is at midnight at the Winter solstice, while in the West, Christ was born in the middle of the night at that same Winter solstice. The *I-Ching* teaches that the prince who possesses greatness and plenty is 'like the Sun at noon' (his body casts no shadow, his voice throws back no echo), but also 'after it has reached midday, the Sun starts to sink; the Moon wanes after it has reached the full.' In the north, *The Secret of the Golden Flower* observes, at midnight at the Winter solstice the *yin* is at rest and the *yang* set in motion. It is the middle line (*yang*) of the trigram *K'an* (north) turning back to the trigram *Ken* (complete *yang*).

This is close to esoteric Tantrism, which draws a correspondence between midnight and the condition of absolute repose in a state of beatitude. This, Guénon observes, is because the spiritual Sun is at its zenith at midnight, in converse analogy with the material Sun. Initiation into the ancient mysteries was linked to the 'midnight' Sun.

There is a wealth of similar concepts in Ismaili esotericism. Noon, when there are no shadows, is the Seal of Prophecy, the zenith of spiritual light. Midnight is the entanglement, confusion and befogging of conformity to the letter and the point from which the ascent to solar revelation begins. Thus in the writings of someone like Shabistarī such apparent paradoxes occur as 'shining night' or 'dark noon', these being the points of disjunction in the two cyclical half-courses of the spirit (CORT, ELIY, GRAP, GRIF, GUES).

In Biblical tradition, noon symbolizes light in all its fullness. Origen explains the importance of this symbol in Holy Scripture in his first and third sermons on the Song of Solomon, when he observes that Lot was unable to face the full light of noon, while Abraham was able to do so. To see God face to face is to see him in the midday light.

Midday marks a sort of sacralized moment, a pause in cyclic motion before the fragile balance is broken and the Sun totters into a decline. It conjures up the Sun halted in its course – the only moment when there is no shadow – an image of eternity.

midnight See MIDDAY above.

milk According to the *Rāmāyana*, *amrita*, the nectar of life, was produced by the churning of the Sea of Milk. This was the first food and the first drink, in which all other beverages resided in a state of potentiality, and hence milk was naturally the symbol of plenty and fertility, and also of knowledge. The meaning of the word was extended in an esoteric sense and, as a channel of initiation, milk was lastly a symbol of immortality. No sacred writings have celebrated milk to the extent of those of India. The morning hymn, the *agnihotra*, sung every day since the Vedas began, tells how 'Indra and Agni with joyful song give life to this milk so that it confers immortality to the righteous man who makes sacrifice.'

There is a similar note in Orphic hymns in which milk is not only the drink, but the place, of immortality. Similarly Herakles (Hercules) imbibed the milk of immortality at Hera's breast, while the Pharaoh was suckled by a goddess and by this means attained to a new and wholly divine life, from which he drew the strength to fulfil his mission as an earthly ruler. Again, milk was poured on the 365 altar tables around the tomb of Osiris, one table for each day of the year, and this sprinkling helped the god's rebirth each morning.

The Celts, too, regarded milk as the nectar of immortality when a drunken stupor was not required. Furthermore, milk possessed medicinal virtues. A Pictish druid, Drostan, advised the King of Ireland to heal his soldiers, wounded by the Bretons' poisoned arrows, by collecting the milk from 140 white cows and pouring it into a hole in the middle of a field. Those who bathed in it would be healed (LERD pp. 66–7).

The Pseudo-Dionysius the Areopagite compared God's teachings with milk, because the strength instilled in them furthers spiritual growth.

Suckling by a divine mother is a mark of adoption and hence of absolute knowledge. Herakles was suckled by Hera and St Bernard by Our Lady, making him the adoptive brother of Christ. The Philosopher's Stone is sometimes called the Virgin's Milk, milk in this context being a food of immortality.

There are many instances of Muslim commentators giving milk this sense of the initiatory. For example, in a *hadīth* recorded by Ibn Omar, Muhammad is supposed to have said that 'to dream of milk is to dream of learning or knowledge' (BOKT 4: p. 458).

In the language of Tantrism, 'milk' is *bodhicitta* meaning both 'thought' and 'semen', rising to the *manipūra-chakra*, or umbilical centre.

Lastly, it should be added that milk, like all symbolic vehicles of Life and Knowledge as absolutes, is a lunar symbol, predominantly female and linked to the springtime renewal of nature. This is the essential quality of libations of milk and of such milk-white sacrificial victims as the cow which the Yakut sprinkled with milk at the Spring festival in May and which somehow signified the transfer to the fields of the powers inherent in the symbol (HARA pp. 161, 177).

Milky Way All tribes of North American Indians regard the Milky Way as the pathway which souls follow to the Otherworld. At the end of it lies the land of the dead (ALEC p. 200).

In Maya-Quiché mythology (*Popol-Vuh*) the Milky Way is described as a great white serpent (FGRP p. 151).

The Aztecs believed that the Serpent of the Milky Way was eaten each day by an eagle standing for Uitzilopochtli, the god of the midday Sun, associated with the south and the colour blue. This god was one of the FOUR sons of the divine pair who ruled the creation – 'the Lord and Lady of Duality' (SOUM).

The Zuni Indians of New Mexico have a secret society called after the Milky Way. It bears the emblem of the goddess of butterflies, flowers and the Spring, who is also the Sun's jester and acts as intercessor between him and mankind. At festivals, members of this society put on shows of un-bridled obscenity. The Milky Way is called the roof-tree of Heaven.

In Peruvian Inca mythology, the Milky Way was the great river flowing through Heaven, from which the thunder-god drew the water which he sent down as rain (LEHC). However, their descendants the Quechua Indians regard the Milky Way as a heavenly road as well as a river.

Baiame, the supreme deity of the Aborigines of south-western Australia, lives in the sky, seated on a crystal throne beside which flows a broad stream – the Milky Way (ELIT).

In the Turkic and Tatar languages the Milky way is known as 'the birds' road' or 'the road of the wild geese', as it is by the Finns in the Volga region. To Estonians and Lapps it is the birds' road as well. The Buryat and many Yakut regard the Milky Way as a seam across the sky. The Samoyed of Turukhansk call it the sky's spine. It is not just European folklore which says it was formed from milk spilled in the sky, as the legend of Hera confirms. She grew angry with the infant Herakles (Hercules), tore her nipple from his lips and the milk which spurted out formed the Milky Way. Similar legends are to be found among such Altaic tribes as the Buryat. In

China, too, the Milky Way is a river, the Celestial Stream, as it is for the northern Siberian tribes and for Koreans and Japanese as well. Tatars from the Caucasus and Ottoman Turks call it the straw-thief's road, according to a legend which Uno Harva (HARA p. 144) believes originated in Persia. Some Yakut believe that the Milky Way is the track left by the snow-shoes of a hunter-god pursuing a six-legged stag. This stag would be the Great Bear and the god's house the Pleiades. The Tungus believe the hunter is a bear and the Milky Way becomes 'the track of the bear's snow-shoes'. Muslim Tatars hold it to be 'the pilgrim road to Mecca' (HARA).

For the Celts, the Milky Way was the chain belonging to the Irish god, Lug, patron of the arts and lord of peace and war (MYTF p. 25).

The Finns believed that:

it was the branches and trunk of an enormous tree felled across the sky. This was an oak which grew so tall that it shut out the light of the Sun, the Moon and the stars. The clouds stopped moving across the sky because they were caught in its monstrous branches. Then a tiny little creature emerged from the sea or from underground and struck the tree with a gold or copper hatchet. The tree came down, darkening a part of the sky but setting the Sun, the Moon, the stars and the clouds free.

(MYTF p. 110)

Sallustius, a fourth-century Neoplatonist philosopher who refused the Emperor Julian's offer to make him his heir, provided a semi-symbolic, semi-scientific explanation. He regarded the Milky Way as the upper limit of mutable matter.

In all traditions the Milky Way is regarded as a roadway, built by the gods, linking their world with the Earth. It has also been compared with serpents, rivers, footprints, spurts of milk, seams and trees. Souls and birds use it for travelling between the two worlds. It symbolizes the road taken by pilgrims, explorers and mystics from one place to another on Earth, from one plane to another in the cosmos and from one level to another in the psyche. It also marks the boundaries between the busy world and the stillness of eternity.

millet This basic cereal crop is needed not only to sustain human life, but, the Chinese believed, to ensure the survival of the ancestors through ritual offering. They even regarded it as the very symbol of the fertility of the soil and of the natural order. Millet was synonymous with reaping and harvesting. Rulers of the Chou dynasty were above all others lords of millet, their celestial ancestor being Prince Millet. He was the giver of rain, hence of heavenly blessings, which the sovereign, as his surrogate, shared with his people.

Libations with a base of black millet seeped right down to the Underworld to call up the *p'o* soul (*yin*) so that it could be united with the *huen* soul (*yang*) to rise up to Heaven in quest of the smoke of sacrifice. This was a repetition of the birth of the ancestor (GRAR). Millet provided a channel of communication between the two worlds, celestial and subterranean.

mimosa In Masonic symbolism the mimosa is sometimes confused with the ACACIA, but Jules Boucher makes the distinction quite clear. 'In flower symbolism, the mimosa is the emblem of security, or in a wider sense, of certainty.' This certainty is that death is a change and not the total destruction of being. 'When the Initiate emerges from the grave or the coffin, what was once a caterpillar or worm crawling in darkness on the ground comes out of its chrysalis and flies upwards a bright-winged butterfly towards the Sun and the light. The mimosa heralds this Sun and light with its golden yellow flowers, the symbol of might and power' (BOUM p. 271).

minaret See TOWER; ZIGGURAT.

Minotaur (see also AURA) This was the monster with a man's body and a bull's head which King Minos imprisoned in the Labyrinth, or palace of the double axe (see MAZE), which had been built for it. At regular intervals, either annually or every three years, it was fed with seven youths and seven maidens paid as tribute by Athens to Crete. Theseus, the king's son, offered himself as one of their number, managed to kill the monster and, thanks to the ball of twine which Ariadne gave him, to escape from the Labyrinth. This monster symbolizes a psychic state of perverted domination by Minos. However, the monster was Pasiphae's child, which means that Pasiphae is also at the root of Minos' perversion. She symbolizes sexual guilt, unnatural lusts, undue dominance and sins repressed and hidden in the Labyrinth of the unconscious. The willing sacrifices made to the monster are so many lies and evasions to lull the conscience. They accumulate as fresh sins. Ariadne's ball of twine stands for the spiritual assistance needed to overcome the monster. In its totality the myth of the Minotaur symbolizes the 'spiritual struggle against repression' (DIES p. 189). However, this struggle cannot be won without the weapons of light since, according to the legend, it was Ariadne's luminous crown, lighting the gloomy passageways of the palace, and not simply her ball of twine, which enabled Theseus to emerge from the depths of the Labyrinth after killing the Minotaur with his bare hands.

mirror The Latin word for mirror (*speculum*) has given us the verb 'to speculate'; and originally speculation was scanning the sky and the related movement of the stars by means of a mirror. The Latin for star (*sidus*) has also given us the word 'consideration' which, etymologically, means to scan the stars as a whole. Both abstract nouns which now describe highly intellectual activities are rooted in the study of the stars reflected in mirrors. It follows, then, that mirrors, as reflecting surfaces, should be the basis of a wealth of symbolism relating to knowledge.

What is reflected in the mirror if not truth, sincerity and what the heart and conscience hold? An inscription on a Chinese mirror in the museum in Ho Chi Minh City (Saigon) reads: 'Like the Sun, like the Moon, like water and like gold, be clean and bright and reflect what is in your heart.' Mirrors are used in this role in Western folk stories of initiation and in the rituals of Chinese secret societies.

Although its deepest meaning may be different, in Japanese tradition mirrors are related to the revelation of the truth as well as to purity. The same line of thought is behind the use of a 'mirror of the *karma*' by Yama, the Indo-Buddhist Lord of the Kingdom of the Dead, when he sits in judgement. Magic mirrors, instruments to reveal the word of God, may be debased by use in divination, but in different forms of shamanism – rock-CRYSTAL being the material – and among African Pygmies, they may be employed to astonishing effect. The 'truth' revealed by the mirror may obviously be of a higher order and this conjures up the magic mirror of the Ch'in, which Nichiren compares with the Buddhist 'Mirror of the Dharma', which shows the causes of past actions. The mirror may be the instrument of enlightenment. In fact the mirror is the symbol of wisdom and knowledge, a dusty mirror being the symbol of the spirit darkened by ignorance. The Tibetan Buddhists' 'Wisdom of the Great Mirror' teaches the ultimate secret, namely that the world of shapes reflected in it is only an aspect of *shunyata*, the void.

These reflections of the celestial Intellect or Word of Heaven have made the mirror seem as if it were the symbol of the manifestation of the creative mind. It is also the symbol of the divine intellect reflecting manifestation and creating it as such in its own image. This revelation of identity and difference was the cause of the fall of Lucifer. In less specialized terms it is the outcome of the most intense spiritual experience, as St Paul (2 Corinthians 3: 18) and many Christian and Muslim spiritual writers bear witness. 'The human heart [is] the mirror which reflects God' is, for example, how Angelus Silesius expresses it, while for Buddhists the mirror of the heart reflects the Buddha's nature and for Taoists Heaven and Earth.

The heavenly intelligence reflected in a mirror is identified symbolically with the Sun and this is why the mirror is so often a solar symbol. It is, however, also a lunar symbol in the sense that the Moon, mirror-like, reflects the light of the Sun. The best-known solar mirror occurs in the Japanese myth of Amaterasu, in which the mirror draws the divine light out of the cavern and reflects it upon the world. In Siberian symbolism, two great heavenly mirrors reflect the universe and, in his turn, the shaman traps this reflection in his mirror. This reflection of cosmic perfection also finds expression in the Mirror of Devī and, in a secondary state, in that of the Sarasundarī who are her messengers. In Vedic tradition, the mirror is the solar mirage of manifestations, symbolizing the succession of the shapes of transitory and ever-changing beings.

Although the reflection of light or reality does not change its nature, it nevertheless carries with it some illusory aspect ('catching the Moon in the water') or falsity with respect to the First Cause. Hindu writers speak of 'identity in difference'. 'As the light is reflected in the water but does not penetrate it, so is Shiva.' Thus 'speculation' is indirect, 'lunar' knowledge. In any case the mirror presents a negative image of reality. 'What is above is as what is below', says the alchemical *Emerald Table*, but with an opposite meaning. Manifestation is a negative image of the First Cause, displayed in the two inverted triangles of the star-shaped hexagon. The symbol of the ray of light reflected upon the surface of the waters is the cosmogonic sign of manifestation, it is active *purusha* on passive *prakrti*, vertical Heaven on horizontal Earth. Nevertheless, passivity, which reflects things while remaining unaffected by them, is in China the symbol of the non-activity of the wise man.

Again, as a female and lunar symbol, in China the mirror was the queen's emblem. The mirror 'takes fire from the Sun'. It is, in any case, the sign of harmony and of happy marriage, a broken mirror being that of separation. (In the end, the broken half of the mirror takes the shape of a magpie and reports the wife's infidelities to the husband.) The creature called the *p'o-ching*, or 'Broken Mirror', was related to the phases of the Moon. The marriage of the king and queen was celebrated at full Moon when the mirror was made whole once more.

The use which the Taoists made of the magic mirror was somewhat specialized. By revealing the nature of evil influences, it drove them away and afforded protection against them. Hence the survival of the custom of setting an octagonal mirror inscribed with the eight trigrams above the entry to a house. Octagonal mirrors – undoubtedly signs of harmony and perfection in the case of Amaterasu – in China are intermediaries between the round mirror (Heaven) and the square mirror (Earth). Humans do not see their reflections only in polished bronze or still waters, as this passage from the T'ang Chronicles, quoted by Segalen, shows: 'Men use bronze as a mirror. Men use the past as a mirror. Men use their fellow-men as mirrors.' In Japan the mirror, or *kagami*, is a symbol of the perfect purity of the soul, of an unsullied spirit and of a reflection of self upon consciousness. It is also a symbol of the Sun-goddess (Amaterasu-Omi-Kami). Sacred mirrors are to be found in many Shintō shrines, like crucifixes in Catholic churches. A mirror is also one of the principal imperial attributes and the Sacred Mirror is housed in a special building in the Imperial Palace.

The use of mirrors is one of the oldest forms of divination and Varro says that it originated in Persia. According to legend, Pythagoras had a magic mirror which he, like the Thessalian witches, would turn towards the Moon before reading the future in it. Its use is the opposite to necromancy, conjuring the spirits of the dead, since it calls up individuals who may be still unborn or who are engaged in activities still to be performed (GRIA p. 334).

By virtue of the analogies between mirrors and water, fragments of mirror are often used, as for example by the Bambara, in rain-making ceremonies (DIEB).

Both mirrors and water surfaces are used to interrogate the spirits in divination and their replies to the questions asked are written by reflection upon them. Congolese fortune-tellers employ this process, sprinkling a mirror – or the surface of a bowl of water – with chalk dust. The white powder is an emanation of the spirits and the pattern in which it falls reveals their answer (FOUC). In central Asia, shamans practised divination by mirrors, by pointing them at the Sun or Moon, the latter being also regarded as mirrors on which is reflected all that occurs on Earth (HARA p. 130). Furthermore, shamanistic robes were often decorated with mirrors which 'reflect the activities of men or else protect the shaman [during his spirit flight] against the arrows of evil spirits. After such shamanistic experiences the sorcerer sometimes has to make the same number of scratches on these shields as arrows which have hit them' (HARA p. 348).

Both Plato and Plotinus sketch the notion of the soul regarded as a mirror and this theme was developed by St Athanasius and St Gregory of Nyssa, in particular. According to Plotinus the image of a being is ready to receive the influence of its model as in a mirror. According to his line of reasoning, the individual, like a mirror, reflects beauty or ugliness. The first essential is that the mirror itself should be clean and polished to receive the clearest reflection. This is why, according to St Gregory of Nyssa, 'as a well-made mirror reflects upon its polished surface the image of whatever is set in front of it, so the soul, cleansed from all earthly corruption, receives in its purity the image of incorruptible beauty.' This is no longer mere reflection, but participation, in which the soul becomes a part of that beauty to the degree to which it lays itself open to it. (Jean Daniélou in ERAJ (1954): p. 395; Régis Bernard, *L'image de Dieu* (1954): p. 75).

The mirror's task is not simply to reflect an image. When the soul becomes a perfect mirror, it becomes part of that image and, through becoming part, undergoes transformation. There therefore exists a relationship between the object contemplated and the mirror which contemplates it. In the end the soul becomes part of that beauty to which it exposes itself.

In its very different aspects, the mirror has become an especial theme for Muslim philosophers and mystics inspired by Neoplatonism. The mirror is even called the symbol of symbolism itself (MICS).

The numinous aspect of the mirror, that is, the terror which self-knowledge inspires, is characterized by the Sufi legend of the PEACOCK. The mirror is Psyche's (DURS) and analysts have stressed the dark side of the soul.

Al-Ghazālī exerted a deep influence on Sufism by using the Neoplatonist notion of the two sides of the soul, 'its lower side directed at the body, its upper at the mind'.

Attār said that 'in its dullness the body is like the back of a mirror; the soul is its polished face' (RITS p. 187). When discussing the two sides of the mirror, Rūmī explained that God created this world which is dull and dark so that his light might be made manifest.

By virtue of the theory of the microcosm as an image of the macrocosm, the individual and the universe play their respective parts as two mirrors. Similarly, individual essences are reflected in the Divine Being, according to Ibn 'Arabī, and the Divine Being is reflected in individual essences.

The magic mirror which enables its user to see past, present and future is, in any case, a classic theme of Muslim literature. The CHALICE of Jamshid, the legendary king of Persia, was really a mirror. In its turn it symbolized the initiate's HEART.

If the heart is symbolized by a mirror – which used to be made of metal – then rust symbolizes sin, and polishing the mirror purification.

In Iran, Afghanistan and Pakistan, they still use the Mirror of Our Lady Mary (*Ayin-i Bībī Maryam*) when betrothed couples first meet. It is hung on the far wall of the room in which the meeting takes place, the couple entering from opposite doors and being expected to look at their mirror images, instead of straight at one another. In so doing they will meet as if they were in Paradise, seeing their faces corrected and not inverted as in this world. The mirror's image-correcting facility becomes a symbol in this context of things seen in their essential reality.

Sufis regard the whole universe as comprising a group of mirrors in which the Infinite Being gazes at itself in its manifold shapes or else which reflect in different degrees the radiation of the One Being. The primary significance of the mirrors is that they symbolize the self-determining potentiality of the Being. They also convey the cosmological meaning of material receptacles in respect of pure action (BURS).

Lastly, a different meaning makes the mirror a symbol of reciprocal awareness. A famous *hadith* declares that 'the faithful is the mirror of the faithful.' The more the face of the mirror of the soul is polished by self-denial, the better it is able to reflect faithfully its surroundings and even the thoughts of others. Sufi literature contains a wealth of instances of men made pure who were capable of this sort of 'reflection'.

mist Symbol of the indeterminate, of a phase in development when shapes have yet to be defined or when old shapes are vanishing and have yet to be replaced by definite new shapes.

Mist is also a symbol of the mixture of Air, Water and Fire which existed prior to the creation of solid matter, like the original TOHU-BOHU as it was before the six days' Creation and before all things were given their shape.

Japanese painters often depict horizontal or vertical mists (*kasumi*). They denote a break in the thread of a story, a transition in time-scale or a passing into a world of fantasy or wonder.

Some Irish literary sources associate fog or mist with the music of the Otherworld (*sid*) or with the Otherworld itself. *The Voyage of Bran* speaks of a 'lovely mist' which conjures up or symbolizes indistinction, the period of transition between two states of being. Similarly, when Senchan Torpeist sends his son Muirgen to raise the soul of King Fergus to teach him the tale of the cattle-raid of Cooley, which no poet then knew in its entirety,

Muirgen stood on the rock and sang as if addressing Fergus himself. . . . A thick mist encompassed him and for three days and three nights he lost sight of his companions. Then Fergus came to him, finely clad, in a green cloak, hooded tunic embroidered in red, with a golden-hilted sword and bronze shoes and his hair was brown. And he taught him the whole of the cattle raid of Cooley, as it had happened, from beginning to end.

(OGAC 9: p. 305; WINI 5: p. 1111; LERD p. 101)

Thus mists are regarded as preludes to important revelations, prologues to manifestations. 'And the Lord said unto Moses, Lo, I come unto thee in a thick CLOUD, that the people may hear when I speak with thee, and believe thee for ever' (Exodus 19: 9).

mistletoe Modern Breton is the exception to the rule that throughout the Celtic world mistletoe bears names which characterize its symbolism. In the celebrated passage in which he describes how it was gathered, Pliny states that the Gauls called mistletoe by a name meaning 'all-heal'. This is precisely the meaning of *uileiceadh* and of *olilach*, and it should be seen a symbol of immortality, strength and physical regeneration. In the Norse myth, Balder was killed with a mistletoe spear and this may symbolize the passing from one form of life to another higher, semi-divine state. In the Breton dialect of Vannes, among the many words used instead of mistletoe, there is the curious name of *deur derhue*, 'oak-water'. It cannot, however, be established that this has any ancient linguistic or symbolic quality. Oak bears mistletoe very infrequently, and this undoubtedly explains in part the use to which Gaulish druids put it. It was very rare to find mistletoe growing thus, and when it was found it was gathered at a solemn religious ceremony

on the sixth day of the moon (which for [the Gauls] constitutes the beginning of the months and years and, after every thirty years, of a new generation) because it is then rising in strength and not one half of its full size. Hailing the moon in a native word that means 'healing all things', they prepare a ritual sacrifice and banquet beneath a tree and bring up two white bulls, whose horns are bound for the first time on this occasion. A priest arrayed in white vestments climbs the tree and with a golden sickle cuts down the mistletoe, which is caught in a white cloak. Then finally they kill the victims, praying to God to render his gift propitious to those on whom he has bestowed it. They believe that mistletoe given in drink will impart fertility to any animal, and that it is an antidote for all poisons.

(Pliny, *Natural History* 25: 250–51)

The ritual which Pliny describes is probably related to the festival at the beginning of November which marked the start of the Celtic year and this fits well with the mistletoe's symbolism of immortality and regeneration. While the plant symbolism of the druids themselves influenced their choice of mistletoe growing on oaks, it is unlikely that mistletoe also symbolizes wisdom, since the tree is itself the symbol both of strength and wisdom (wood = learning). The priestly caste, however, possessed healing powers. It might be added that the fact that mistletoe is propagated by birds consolidated its immortality symbolism (see GOLDEN BOUGH) (LERD pp. 60–2).

Mithras The saviour god of the mystery religions, dispensing the life force, patron of soldiers and known as the Unconquered Sun (*Sol invictus*), identified with the god of endless time, he was at the beginning of the living universe which he ruled. He was depicted either as a hero cutting the throat of a BULL, the first living creature from whose blood plants and animals were to come to birth, or as a lion-headed man with a serpent coiled round his body, representing the cycle of time and of the Sun. He was born from a rock on 25 December, a day on which the Sun's rebirth (*Natalis Solis*) was celebrated after the Winter solstice. His worship competed strongly with early Christianity. It came to Rome from Persia, and passed to Gaul and the whole Mediterranean area with the legions and the soothsayers in their train at the close of the Republican era and in the early years of the Empire. Its initiates enjoyed the cult of the *taurobolum*, the bloody sacrifice of a bull, in order to share the powers attributed to the god and to the bull and of which they were symbols.

The devotee who wished to participate went down into a trench especially dug for that purpose and covered over with a board pierced with holes. A bull had its throat cut with a sacred spear immediately above and its blood splashed down through the holes and over the devotee's entire body. Whoever underwent this sprinkling with blood was *renatus in aeternum*, reborn to eternal life. The energy and vitality of the bull, commonly held with the lion to be the strongest of all animals, would regenerate the body, and perhaps the soul, of the participant.

(BEAG p. 254)

Mithraic worship symbolized physical and spiritual rebirth through the energy possessed by blood, by the Sun and, ultimately, by the godhead and provides an excellent example of symbols superimposed along the same axis. It resulted in glorifying, not simply the energy and vitality of the soldier, but of whoever might be called upon to fight against all the powers of evil, so that spiritual purity, truth, self-sacrifice and the brotherhood of all living beings might triumph.

mole If ever there was a chthonian animal, it is the mole which symbolizes all the powers of Earth. Its Greek name links it to lizards and to owls, which share its blindness and beneficence. Asclepios, the god of healing, was originally a mole-god, as was Rudra, the Indian archer-god of healing. Moles, with their system of underground tunnels, may even have provided the model for the ancient maze at Epidaurus, sacred to Asclepios and conceived both 'as the tomb and as the underground dwelling of the god' (SECH p. 237).

Moles were regarded as symbols of the person who unfolded the mysteries of Earth and of death which, once acquired, preserved the initiate from sickness or brought a cure. From the physical plane, that of the agrarian cult-animal, the symbol permitted transition to the spiritual plane, that of the master who guides the soul through the gloomy underground maze and heals it of its passions and anxieties.

Moloch To present one's children to Moloch (Melek) was to burn them in sacrifice to the Canaanite god. Moses, as the Lord's mouthpiece, forbade the Children of Israel to practise such rites: 'Thou shalt not let any of thy seed pass through the fire to Molech, neither shalt thou profane the name of thy God' (Leviticus 18: 21). 'He ... that giveth any of his seed to Molech, ... shall surely be put to death; the people of the land shall stone him with stones.... Then I ... will cut him off and all that go a whoring after [Moloch]' (ibid. 20: 2, 6). However, the Children of Israel and even Solomon and other kings, often relapsed into this form of idolatry. Children were either burned alive upon the altar or within the hollow body of bronze statues dedicated to the god, while their cries were drowned by the shouting and drum-beating of his priests.

In Semitic languages *Melek* means 'king' and became the name of a deity worshipped by the people of Moab, Canaan, Tyre and Carthage and often confused with BAAL. This cruel cult has often been compared with the myth of the Minotaur (who periodically devoured his allocation of young people), with that of Cronos (who ate his own children) and with the sacrifices offered to the Inca gods. Moloch should, undoubtedly, be regarded as an ancient image of the jealous, vengeful and pitiless tyrant who demands that his subjects obey him to the death and who levies their goods and even their children, doomed to death in battle or on the altar. His defenceless subjects yield complete submission to the direst threats of this all-powerful king.

In modern times, Moloch has become the symbol of the tyrannical power of the all-devouring State.

money See COINS.

monkey The monkey is a commonplace for agility, comicality and a capacity for imitation. A disconcerting aspect of its nature is what Schuon calls its 'random consciousness'. Li-tzu classifies it as a stupid and ill-tempered animal. The monkey's agility, however, finds immediate application in the Tibetan Wheel of Life, on which it symbolizes consciousness, but in the pejorative sense of the word, since this is the consciousness of the phenomenal world which hops from one thing to the next like a monkey hopping from branch to branch. Buddhist methods of meditation compare control of the heart's wanderings with training a monkey.

It is, nevertheless, true that the Tibetans' ancestor was a monkey, whom they have made a Bodhisattva, while the *Si-yu-chi* states that he was the child of Earth and Heaven born when the primeval egg split apart. This monkey accompanied Huan-chang when he journeyed in quest of Buddhist holy books, and not simply as a light-hearted companion, but as a Taoist magician of enormous skill. It is also true that in India there is a royal monkey, Hanumān, in the *Rāmāyana*. Once again one should take note of several abiding characteristics which are carried over into myth – Hanumān's quick-witted diplomacy and the unbridled powers of imagination and agility, as well, once again, as the fickle-mindedness of the Monkey King, Suen Hingcho. An explanation of the foregoing may be found in the traditional relationship between monkeys and the wind, which is, in any case, the reason why in Cambodia hunting monkeys is believed to be a means of making rain. In India, barren women strip off their clothes and clasp the statue of Hanumān in order to cure their sterility.

In the end the Monkey King became a Buddha. In Far Eastern art monkeys are often depicted in attitudes denoting wisdom and detachment from worldly things, perhaps by way of satirizing human pretensions to wisdom, as in Mori Sosen's touching picture. The three famous monkeys of the Jingoro, in the temple at Nikko, one shutting its eyes, the other its ears and the third its mouth, are yet another display of wisdom and hence of good fortune. Furthermore, in Ancient Egypt the dog-faced baboon was the incarnation of the god Thoth (GOVM, GRIF, GUES, PORA, SCHP, WOUS).

In Ancient Egyptian symbolism the role allotted to the monkey was in broad outline the one which it would play in Central America. Taking the shape of a great white dog-faced baboon, the god Thoth – who also took the form of an ibis – was patron of the wise and the men of letters. He was the scribe of the gods, writing down the words of the creator, the god Ptah, as well as the verdicts passed by Anubis when he judged the souls of the dead. He was thus simultaneously an artist, a patron of flowers, gardens and feasting, a mighty magician able to read the most mysterious hieroglyphics and, of course, a conductor of souls. He ruled the hours and the days and was lord of time. Notwithstanding, as the god Baba, he was the dominant '"male among baboons", quarrelsome, libidinous ... and a dribbler.' The Ancient Egyptians were keenly aware of the aggressiveness of baboons and 'in hieroglyphic writing the sign written after the verb "to be angry", showed a baboon, his teeth bared, standing on all fours, his tail arched in rage' (POSD p. 173). Baboons howl at daybreak and were supposed to stand on the edge of the world and help the sun to rise each morning with their prayers. In the Egyptian city of Babylon the hot-blooded baboon was the image of the Sun itself and this simian Apollo wielded bow and arrows.

During the journey which the Ancient Egyptians believed that the soul made from death to reincarnation, Champollion describes how, in the area in space between the Earth and the Moon where the soul dwelt, the god Pooh (the Moon), in human form, is always depicted as being 'accompanied by a dog-faced baboon crouching towards the Moon-rise' (quoted in MAGE p. 141).

The monkey symbolism of the Aztecs and Maya was to some degree Apollonian. Those born under the sign of the monkey – monkeys were patrons of one of the calendar days – were adepts in the arts, singers, orators, writers and sculptors, or at least hardworking and gifted craftsmen, blacksmiths, potters and so on. Sahagun explains that the Aztecs believed them to be 'equable, cheerful and universally beloved'. Maya pictography shows the association of monkeys with the Sun: the Sun, called 'Prince of the Flowers' and patron of singing and music, often being depicted in the shape of a monkey. 'Monkey' was used as a title of honour and meant a sensible or hard-working man. 'Monkey' also bore a sexual connotation, as the symbol of a hot and even promiscuous nature (THOH). However, in several codices the monkey is depicted as the twin of the death-god and midnight, standing for the night sky and symbolizing all that is offered in sacrifice at dawn for the Sun's return.

In the Chinese Zodiac the monkey rules the sign of Sagittarius.

In Japan it is customary to avoid using the word 'monkey' during a wedding ceremony in case it should make the bride run away. On the other hand, monkeys are supposed to drive off evil spirits and it is for this reason that children are often given monkey-dolls. These are also given to pregnant women to ease childbirth.

The association of monkey and blacksmith observed among the Aztecs is also found among the Fali of the northern Cameroons, the black monkey being the avatar (incarnation) of the Blacksmith who stole Fire (LEBF).

Indian scholars are agreed that, in India, monkeys are a symbol of the soul (PORS p. 199).

In a Bororo Indian myth collected by Colbacchini and Albisetti and quoted by Lévi-Strauss (LEVC pp. 126–7), the monkey, who was 'formerly like a man', is seen as a culture-hero who discovers the art of fire-making by friction. The fact that he tricks the JAGUAR, deceives him, is swallowed by him and then vomited up again, is significant. In this context the jaguar stands for the powers of the Underworld, his jaws are the mouth of Hell and the monkey's journey is typically Orphic, making him an initiate at the time of his discovery and mastery of fire. This myth then, concentrates the essential elements of monkey symbolism – the mischievous sorcerer concealing his powers, and chiefly his intelligence, under the mask of buffoonery.

Many other Amerindian myths stress the dangers for humans who laugh at the tricks and jokes of their brother-in-law the monkey, a Dionysiac and Priapic character who conceals his knowledge and lures humans into debauchery and drunkenness to display his control over them (LEVC p. 121). And the temptations of this world are but a foretaste of the same ones which will await the soul after death, when humans will meet that great initiate and tempter, the monkey. While the Ancient Egyptians believed that in the Otherworld their souls would have to escape the nets cast for them by monkeys (POSD), 'the same theme is to be found in the cosmology of the Bolivian Guarayu; along the road leading to the Great Forefather, the dead have to undergo various ordeals, which include tickling by a sharp-nailed marimondo monkey' (LEVC p. 122).

The monkey-highwayman, the cheerful rogue whose jokes disarm ill humour, is illustrated by the Greek myth of the Cercopes (who gave their name to a genus of African long-tailed monkeys, the Cercopithecus). The Cercopes

were tall and burly brigands who robbed travellers and put them to death. One day they attacked Herakles [Hercules] as he lay asleep. Awaking, he soon subdued them and, in his rage, trussed them up and slung them over his shoulder like goats being taken to market. However, their jokes restored him to such good humour that he agreed to set them free. Their life of robbery and theft so angered Zeus that he changed them into monkeys.

(GRID p. 86)

Or, in other words, they showed themselves to be monkeys.

These Cercopes of Greek mythology are closely related to the Trickster, the mythological hero of the North American Winebago Indians, whom Paul Radin regards as the Hero in his most primitive form.

The Trickster cycle corresponds to the earliest and least developed period of life. Trickster is a figure whose physical appetites dominate his behavior; he has the mentality of an infant. Lacking any purpose beyond the gratification of his primary needs, he is cruel, cynical and unfeeling.... This figure, which at the outset assumes the form of an animal, passes from one mischievous exploit to another. But, as he does so, a change comes over him. At the end of his rogue's progress he is beginning to take on the physical likeness of a grown man.

(JUNS p. 112)

Henderson rightly compares this hero, who acts entirely upon instinct, with the monkey of the Chinese classical theatre. However, it must be remembered that just as elsewhere, so in China, this aspect of the monkey corresponds only very superficially with the animal's complex symbolism. Like many others, the Chinese monkey is both sage and initiate, concealing his true nature under this mask of buffoonery. This trickster, this cheeky mountebank, although related to Thoth and Hermes, is surely also the JUGGLER, the first major arcanum of the Tarot, who initiates the quest for knowledge which the pack symbolizes, a quest of which the goal is the 'Secret of the Universe'.

The Indians often depict Trickster as a coyote and we have already seen the symbolic relationship between monkeys and the DOG tribe.

Later, Henderson shows how, in Navaho mythology, Trickster 'invented the necessary contingency of death, and in the myth of emergence he helped lead the people through the hollow reed whereby they escaped from one world to another above it where they were safe from the threat of flood' (JUNS p. 126). This is truly the recurrent image of the mystagogue standing, like Hermes, at the CROSSROADS of the visible and the invisible.

In Christian iconography, the monkey often provides an image of humanity degraded by sin (CHAS p. 267), and especially by lust and malice.

Perhaps these contradictory yet homogeneous traditions might be brought together by explaining the monkey as the symbol of the actions of the unconscious. Unregulated manifestations of the unconscious occur either in the dangerous shape of the release of the uncontrolled and therefore degrading forces of the instinct, or else in the unexpected and beneficial shape of the sudden flash of light or happy inspiration which makes clear what course of action to follow. The unconscious has these twin aspects, it can be as maleficent as an evil sorcerer, or as kindly as a good fairy, but each is as irrational as the other (CIRD p. 202).

Such an explanation might receive strong and unusual confirmation in the Tibetan story of the monkey, Mani bka'bum, and his wife, the She-Devil of the Rocks, whom the monkey had married solely upon the advice of the gods and moved by pity when intimidated by the cunning She-Devil. From their marriage six half-human beings were born. Gradually their hair fell off, their tails grew shorter and they became humans. Thus mankind came into being in Tibet through the kindness of a monkey and a She-Devil of the Rocks who fell in love with him. These first parents gave their children the ten virtues of mankind and drew down upon them from the gods corn, gold and precious stones.

The appearance of monkeys in dreams is seen by psychoanalysts as being primarily an image of obscenity and lust, of a disturbed state, of impudent self-satisfaction. A sense of irritation is also perceptible arising from the resemblance between men and monkeys, furry forefathers, caricatures of the ego, brutish, greedy and lustful. Dream-monkeys are despicable images of all that human beings should avoid in themselves. However, as Ernest Aeppli so rightly remarks:

Those who see monkeys in their natural state regard them in a totally different light and look upon them as particularly lively and agile creatures living a life of freedom. They admire their astonishing gifts and think that the gods have shown them especial favour. They even see them as incarnations of gods and spirits. The great epic poem of Hindu mythology, the *Rāmāyana*, makes a monkey God's saviour during the famous crossing of the bridge. Some tribespeople go so far as to say that the orang-utan does not speak because it is too wise to do so! Dreams of monkeys are primeval calls towards development of the personality along lines which are at one and the same time varied yet strictly bound up with nature.

(AEPR p. 263)

monster Monsters symbolize the guardian of a treasure, immortality for example. In other words, they symbolize the sum of difficulties to be overcome and of obstacles to be surmounted if in the end this material, corporeal or spiritual treasure is to be won. The monster is there to stimulate effort, mastery of fear and a display of heroism, and in this guise is to be found in numerous rites of initiation in which the candidate has to prove his capabilities and his worthiness. To acquire the higher good one covets, dragons, thorn-bushes, serpents and all sorts of monsters, including one's self, have to be vanquished. Monsters mount guard at the gates of royal palaces, temples and tombs. In many cases the monster is no more than an image of one aspect of the ego, the ego which must be overcome in order to develop a higher ego. In antiquity this struggle was often depicted as a battle between an eagle and a serpent.

In so far as monsters are guardians of treasure, they are also signs that this is holy ground. The presence of a monster might be axiomatic for the presence of treasure. There are few holy places which have not set at their approaches some monster such as a dragon, boa, naga, tiger, or gryphon. Gryphons watch over the Tree of Life; the Golden Apples of the Hesperides were guarded by a dragon, as was the Golden Fleece at Colchis; Dionysos' goblet was protected by serpents and all the treasures of pearls and diamonds under land or sea were guarded by monsters. All paths to wealth, glory, knowledge, salvation and immortality are similarly protected and they may not be gained except through some act of heroism. Once the monster, be it within or outside ourselves, is killed, the way to the treasure is open.

Monsters are also related to rites of passage, they swallow the old individual so that the new individual may be born. The world which such monsters guard and of which they are the gateway, is not the external world of fabulous treasure, but the internal world of the spirit, which can only be entered after an inner transformation. This is why every civilization provides examples of man-eating monsters, conductors of souls, as symbols of the need for rebirth. What is generally regarded as the 'monstrous' aspect of revolutions, for example, takes on a quite different meaning in the light of this explanation. It means that revolutions aim to go so far as radically to transform mankind and to fit humanity for life in a new world. 'Let the old man die and the new man live' summarizes the symbolism of the monster.

Sometimes, however, to be swallowed by the monster is terminal. Such is the descent into Hell of the damned, torn and swallowed by the frightful jaws of devils or wild beasts.

In Biblical tradition, monsters symbolize irrational forces and possess the characteristic of the increate, chaotic, dark and abyssal. Monsters are therefore regarded as disordered and unrestrained and conjure up the period preceding orderly creation. Ezekiel (1: 4) speaks of their four aspects; they are manifest in storms as thick cloud and shafts of fire; they seem to signify the four winds and the four points of the compass (Ezekiel 1: 17). They are the storm, with its black clouds, thunder and lightning. Monsters are frequently associated with water as well as with wind. This water comes from the Underworld, and the underground realm is also the monsters' domain. The same is true of mankind. Humans are born of wind (spirit) and water and hence every individual carries within him- or herself his or her own monster with whom he or she must constantly do battle. Wherever monsters go, they spread terror, and individuals must confront them ceaselessly.

Monsters are also resurrection symbols, since monsters swallow individuals in order to set their rebirth in motion. Each individual must go through his or her own chaos before his or her personality can be restructured; he or she must go through the darkness before stepping out into the light. One has to surmount the incomprehensible within oneself; something which is terrifying because it is incomprehensible and appears to be uncontrolled. And yet what is uncontrolled does have its own set of rules. Jonah is an illustration of this thesis. He was swallowed into the belly of a sea-monster (see WHALE; LEVIATHAN) and when he emerged he was a changed being.

Diel sees monsters as symbolizing a psychic function, that of the over-active and misguided imagination, an unhealthy distortion or diseased func-tioning of the life force. While monsters may stand for external threats, they also reveal internal dangers, since they are like the ugly shape of aberrant desires. They are images of the definitive anxiety which causes them, since anxiety is a definitive, convulsive state composed of two utterly opposed attitudes, unbridled desire and timid inhibition. Monsters gener-ally arise from the Underworld, from dark cracks and gloomy caverns, all so many images of the subconscious (DIES p. 32).

Moon, the (planet) Lunar symbolism is to be seen as correlative with that of the SUN. Its two most basic characteristics spring on the one hand from the fact that the Moon has no light of its own and simply reflects the light of the Sun, and on the other that as it goes through its regular phases the Moon changes shape. This is why it symbolizes dependence and, invariably, the female principle, as well as periodical change and renewal. On both counts the Moon is a symbol of change and of growth (see CRESCENT).

The Moon is a symbol of life-rhythms:

a body which waxes, wanes and disappears, a body whose existence is subject to the universal law of becoming, of birth and death. The moon, like man, has a career involving tragedy, ... but this 'death' ... is never final .... This per-petual return to its beginnings, and this ever-recurring cycle make the moon *the* heavenly body above all others concerned with the rhythms of life.... It gov-erns all those spheres of nature that fall under the law of recurring cycles: water, rain, plant life, fertility.

(ELIT p. 154)

The Moon also symbolizes passing time, living time, which it measures by its successive and regular phases.

The moon becomes the universal measuring gauge ... the same symbolism has linked together the moon, the sea waters, rain, the fertility of women and of animals, plant life, man's destiny after death and the ceremonies of initiation. The mental syntheses made possible by the realization of the moon's rhythms connect and unify very varied realities; their structural symmetries and the analogies in their workings could never have been seen had not 'primitive' man intuitively perceived the moon's law of periodic change, as he did very early on.

(ELIT p. 155)

The Moon was also the first thing to die since, every lunar month, for three days and nights it vanishes as if it has died. Similarly the dead were believed to acquire a new form of existence. To humans the Moon became the symbol of this passage from life to death and from death to life and was even regarded by some peoples as the place where this transition took place, in parallel with a location below the ground. This is why so many lunar deities are at the same time chthonian death-deities like Men, Perse-phone and, probably, Hermes. Some, however, believed that the journey to the Moon or even life for ever on it was confined to such privileged classes as rulers, heroes, initiates or sorcerers (ELIT p. 171; see also chapter 4, 'The Moon and its mystique', ibid. pp. 154–87).

The Moon is a symbol of knowledge acquired coldly, logically and in graduated stages. While the Moon, as the star of night, may conjure up metaphorical visions of beauty shining against the vast black background of Heaven, this light is merely a reflection of the light of the Sun and hence the Moon is the symbol of knowledge acquired through reflection, that is, theoretical, conceptual and rational knowledge (see MIRROR). In this respect Moon and OWL are linked symbolically together. This is also the reason why the Moon is *yin*, being passive and receptive, relative to the Sun's *yang*. The Moon is Water relative to the Sun's Fire, cold relative to heat, and symbolically north and Winter in opposition to south and Summer.

The Moon produces water and Hui-nan Tzu claimed that water-creatures waxed and waned with it. As the passive source of water, the Moon is both well and symbol of fertility, identified with the primeval waters from which came manifestation. The Moon holds the seeds of cyclical rebirth and is the CHALICE which contains the beverage of immortality, and for this reason it was called soma, as was the drink. Similarly Ibn al-Farid made the Moon the chalice of the *yin* of knowledge and the Chinese saw on the Moon the HARE pounding the ingredients for the elixir of life. They believed that dew, with similar properties, rained down from the Moon.

In Hinduism the 'way of the ancestors' (*pitri-yāna*) leads to the 'sphere of the Moon'. This is not a place where they are freed from their mortal state, but they set in motion cyclical renewal. It is where finished shapes dissolve and from which undeveloped shapes emanate. This is not unrelated to Shiva's role of Transformer, his emblem being a crescent Moon. The Moon, in any case, rules the weekly and monthly cycle. This cyclic movement of waxing and waning can be related to the lunar symbolism of Janus. The Moon is simultaneously the gates of Heaven and Hell, Diana and Hecate, Heaven in this context being no more than the roof of the cosmic building. Release from the cosmos can only be effected through the solar gateway. Diana is therefore the good and Hecate the evil aspect of the Moon (DANA, GRAD, GUEV, GUED, GUES, SOUL).

One of the three major Chinese annual festivals is the mid-Autumn festival of the Moon-goddess Heng-ugo, which takes place during the full Moon of the Autumnal equinox on the fifteenth day of the eighth month. Offerings are made of fruit and sugar-cakes, made and sold especially for the occasion, and bunches of crimson amaranth. Men are excluded from the ceremonies. This is clearly a harvest festival and, once again, the Moon is a fertility symbol. The Moon is water and the essence of *yin*: like the Sun it is the home of an animal, either a toad or a hare (MYTF pp. 126–7).

Altaic peoples greeted the new Moon and prayed for 'good luck and happiness' (ibid.). Estonians, Finns and Yakut celebrated weddings at the new Moon, they, too, regarding it as a fertility symbol.

The Moon was sometimes taken as an unlucky sign, the Samoyed regarding it as Num's (the Heaven's) 'bad' eye, the Sun being his 'good' eye.

For example, the Maya god, Itzamna ('House of Raindrops' = Heaven), son of the Supreme Being, was identified with the Sun-god Kinich Ahau ('Lord Sun-face'). 'This is why the Moon-goddess, Ixchel, was his companion and also his evil, hostile aspect, depicted exactly as he, although wearing a head-band of serpents, the attribute of goddesses' (KRIR p. 98).

Since the Moon ruled the cycle of renewal on the cosmic plane as well as on the plane of Earth, together with plant, animal and human life, the Aztec lunar deities included the gods of intoxication. This was because, on the one hand, the drunkard exemplifies the cycle of renewal since when he wakes from drunken sleep he has forgotten all that has gone before; and, on the other, because feasting and drunkenness always go together and exemplify fertility since they are held at harvest-time. This is a further example of the harvest-rites to be found in all agrarian societies. The Aztecs called the deities of drunkenness 'the four hundred rabbits', which serves to underline the importance of the rabbit among animals associated with the Moon (see under HARE).

The Aztecs also believed the Moon to be the daughter of the rain-god, Tlaloc, associated with fire as well. In most Mexican codices, the Moon is depicted as 'a sort of crescent-shaped receptacle full of water over which sits the silhouette of a rabbit' (SOUM).

The Maya made the Moon a symbol of idleness and sexual laxity (THOH), as well as being the patroness of weaving, and in this context having a spider as an attribute.

Means (MEAA) holds that the Moon had four symbolic meanings for the Inca. Originally it was regarded as a goddess unconnected with the Sun; next as the women's god, the Sun being the men's; then as the Sun's wife, their children being the stars; lastly, at the final phase of their religio-philosophical thinking, as the incestuous bride of the Sun, her brother, both deities being children of the all-powerful sky-god, Viracocha. In addition to the primary task of ruling the skies and being the root from which the imperial Inca line sprang, the Moon ruled the winds and the waves, queens and princesses, and was patroness of childbirth.

Deification of the two great lamps of Heaven did not always result in the Moon becoming the Sun's bride. The Gé Indians of central and northeastern Brazil, for example, regard the planet as a male deity quite unrelated to the Sun (ZERA).

Similarly throughout the southern Semitic world (Arabia, the Sahara and Ethiopia) the Moon is male and the Sun female. This is because night is cool and restful and the best time for these nomads to travel with their herds and camel-caravans. The Moon is also regarded as male by many settled races (SOUL p. 154). It guides in the darkness.

In Jewish tradition, the Moon symbolizes the Children of Israel. Just as the face of the Moon changes, so the wandering Children of Israel constantly changed their route. Adam was the first man to follow a nomadic life (Genesis 3: 24); Cain was to be a wanderer (ibid. 4: 14); while God commanded Abraham to leave his father's house and country (ibid. 13: 1). His descendants were to suffer the same fate – the Diaspora, Wandering Jew and so on. Because the Moon hides and then shows its face, the Kabbalists compare it with the KING'S DAUGHTER.

When Tamar was pregnant with twins and upon the point of giving birth to them (Genesis 38: 28–30), one of the babies thrust out a hand and the midwife tied a red thread to it saying that it would be the first-born.

However, the baby's hand was withdrawn and his brother was born first. He was named Pharez and his brother, Zarah. Now the word for 'palm-tree' is *tamar* and the palm is bisexual. This is why, the Bahir says, Tamar's children were compared with the Sun and the Moon, the latter appearing only to withdraw and give the Sun precedence (SCHK pp. 107, 186).

The Moon – *qamar* in Arabic – is often mentioned in the Koran. Like the Sun, it is one of the signs of Allah's power (41: 37). Allah created the Moon (10: 15) and the Moon pays him homage (22: 18). Allah has subjected it to mankind (14: 37), especially in measuring time by means of its phases (10: 5; 36: 39) and periods (2: 185). The lunar cycle enables the date to be calculated (55: 4; 6: 96). But on the Day of Judgement the Moon will be darkened and the Sun and Moon shall be together (75: 8–9) (RODL).

Islam has two calendars, a solar calendar for the needs of agriculture and a lunar calendar for religious observance, the Moon ruling all canonical activities.

The Koran itself employs Moon symbolism, the phases of the Moon and the crescent Moon being used to suggest death and resurrection, while to Maulavī (1207–73) 'the Prophet reflects God as the Moon reflects the Sun. The mystic, too, who has seen God's glory is like the Moon which pilgrims use to guide them through the darkness.'

In Irish customary forms of oath the Moon (*esca*), like the Earth and the elements, was called as witness (see BLOOD-BROTHERHOOD). Although we know of a lunar–solar example from Coligny, Celtic calendars were originally lunar: 'The moon . . . for [the Gauls] constitutes the beginning of the months and years and, after every thirty years, of a new generation' (Pliny, *Natural History* 16: 249). (OGAC 13: pp. 521ff.)

The imaginations of different races has turned the pattern of the craters on the Moon into a lunar zoo. In Guatemala and Mexico they are seen as a rabbit and sometimes as a dog, while in Peru they form a jaguar or a fox.

However, and once more in Peru, some traditions follow European folklore and make out the features of a human face. According to an Inca tradition, the pattern of craters is dust which the jealous Sun threw into the Moon's face to darken it because it shone more brightly than his (MEAA, LEHC).

The Yakut see this pattern as 'a girl carrying two buckets from a yoke across her shoulders' while the Buryat complete the picture by adding an osier-bed. Similar configurations were common in Europe and recur among such northwestern American Indian tribes as the Tlingit and Haida (HARA pp. 133–4).

The Altaic Tatars can see an old cannibal in the Moon – the gods put him there to spare mankind from him – while other tribes see a hare. In central Asia, and especially among the Goldi, Ghilyak and Buryat, dogs, wolves and bears either live in the moon or are involved in myths explaining its phases.

The Moon, its disc apparently the same size as that of the Sun, plays a major role in astrology. It symbolizes the passive but fertile principle, night, moistness, the subconscious, imagination, parapsychology, dreams, receptivity, woman and all that is shifting, ephemeral and by analogy with its astronomic role as a reflector of the Sun's light, subject to outside influence.

The Moon's passage through the Zodiac takes twenty-eight days and some historians believe that the Lunar Zodiac of twenty-eight houses (now obsolete in Western astrology) is considerably older than the Solar Zodiac of twelve houses – something which would explain the importance of the Moon in all religions and traditions.

Buddhists believe that the Buddha meditated for twenty-eight days under a fig-tree, that is, a lunar month or complete cycle of our sublunary world, before he attained Nirvana and acquired perfect knowledge of the mysteries of the universe. Brahmans teach that there are twenty-eight angelical or paradisal states above the human condition, that is, that the Moon exerts its influence as strongly upon the 'subtle' and superhuman planes as it does upon the material universe. The Jews link the Lunar Zodiac with the hands of the universal man, Adam Kadmon, twenty-eight being the number of the word *cHaLaL* = life, and the palms of both hands. The right hand, the hand of blessing, is comparable with the waxing Moon, the left, the hand of cursing, with the fourteen days of the waning Moon.

The Moon is the well-spring of countless myths, legends and cults, providing such goddesses as Isis, Ishtar, Artemis, Diana or Hecate with its image, and is a cosmic symbol throughout every age, from time immemorial to the present, and common to every culture.

In myth, legend, folklore, folktale and poetry the Moon is the symbol of the female deity and the fruitful forces of life incarnate in the deities of plant and animal fertility and mingled in the worship of the Great MOTHER goddess. Astrological symbolism carries this endless and universal stream still further by linking the Moon with the infusion into the individual of the influence of the Mother as food, warmth, love and an emotional world.

The Moon is also the symbol of dreams and the Unconscious as properties of darkness. The Dogon master of divination, the pale fox Yurugu, the only creature to know 'the first word spoken by God', which only comes to mortals in their dreams, symbolizes the Moon (ZAHD).

Dreams and the unconscious form part of the world of darkness. Thus the symbolism of both Moon and the unconscious associates with darkness the elements of Water and Earth, in opposition to the symbolism of the Sun and consciousness which associates light with the elements of Air and Fire and the properties of heat and dryness.

Paul Diel would interpret the Moon and darkness as symbolizing the unhealthy imaginings which stem from the subconscious, in the meaning of 'overheated and repressive imagination' given to it by this writer (DIES p. 36). In many different cultures this symbolism has been applied to a whole line of heroes or deities who are lunar, nocturnal, unfulfilled and malignant.

The Black Moon is an imaginary point in the Heavens and of considerable importance in astrology. It is depicted schematically as a scythe with a line through it or as two crescent Moons set point to point with a dot in the centre of the circle which they form – the unicorn's eye, a metaphysical location if ever there was one.

The Black Moon is associated with Adam's first wife, LILITH, whose sexual organs were in her head. Basically it is linked to notions of the intangible, the inaccessible, and to the overwhelming presence of absence (and the converse), as well as of a hyperlucidity which agonizes by the very intensity of its strength. The Black Moon is something more than a hidden centre of repulsion, embodying as it does a mind-boggling loneliness and a void so absolute that it is none other than the fullness of density.

This immaterial power is also the black hole haloed by black flames which annihilates whatever it lights upon. It can, nevertheless, transfigure the astrological house in which it occurs as a birth sign, on the basis of sublimation or complete self-surrender. On other occasions, when it is the receptacle of evil influxes, disintegration is to be expected.

Hadès associates the Black Moon with that dark and heavy element, *tamas*. It then might symbolize the energy which must be mastered, the darkness which must be scattered and the *karma* which must be cleansed. It is always linked to utterly opposed phenomena, veering wildly between the extremes of repulsion and fascination. Whoever is marked by the Black Moon would rather renounce the world, even at the cost of his or her own destruction and that of others, than fail in their frantic quest for the Absolute. However, should that person be capable of transmuting its poisonous properties into healing ones, the Black Moon will give access to the 'strait gate' which opens upon such release and such light. Jean Carteret, who has devoted his studies to lights which shed darkness, emphasizes the similarities between the Black Moon and the UNICORN which either destroys or divinely fecundates, depending upon whether the individual is cleansed of passion. The Black Moon denotes a dangerous path, but one which may provide a short cut to the luminous centre of Being and Oneness.

The Black Moon is the unlucky aspect of the Moon. It is a symbol of annihilation, of dark and maleficent passions, of hostile energies to be overcome, of KARMA, of the absolute void and of the black hole with its terrifying powers of attraction and absorption.

Moon, the (Tarot) According to different commentators, this eighteenth major arcanum of the Tarot expresses: 'the sullying of the spiritual by the material' (Enel); 'neurasthenia, depression, loneliness and disease' (Muchery); 'bigotry, treachery, false security, deceptive appearances, misdirection, theft by servants or close associates, worthless promises' (Tereschenko); 'either work, the laborious acquisition of truth and learning by painful experience, or illusions, deceptions, traps, cheating and delusion' (Wirth). This tarot complements the meaning of the LOVER and, like that card, in astrology corresponds to the Sixth House. It should be added that the early eighteenth-century French tarot, mentioned by Gérard van Rijnbeck, does not depict the two barking dogs of the current version but a cow, a stork and a lamb, which can be parallelled by the traditional attribution of domesticated animals to the Sixth House.

Nevertheless this card needs to be examined in closer detail. It has three distinct levels. In the uppermost, on the full BLUE face of the Moon a human face is outlined in crescent and from it radiate twenty-nine beams – seven blue, seven WHITE and fifteen smaller RED beams. Between Heaven and Earth there are eight blue, six red and five YELLOW droplets which look as though they were being sucked up by the Moon.

On the uneven foreground only two tiny plants, each with three leaves, grow, while in the background, to right and left, rise two crenellated towers with the corners cut off, one of which seems to be open to the sky, the other roofed. In the middle distance there are two flesh-coloured dogs (or else a dog and a wolf), face to face, jaws open, apparently howling, while the one on the left may even have caught one of the blue droplets in its mouth.

Lastly, on the third and lowest level of the card we have a rear view of a huge blue crayfish moving across the middle of a blue pool of water shot with black.

The three clear and separate levels are those of the stars, Earth and waters. The Moon which dominates the picture only provides reflected light, but draws to itself all that emanates from this world, whether it bears the colours of the spirit and of blood, of the soul and its hidden power or the triumphant gold of material things. The two DOGS, like Cerberus, are both guardians and conductors of souls. They bay at the Moon and remind us that throughout Greek mythology they were the creatures sacred to Artemis, the huntress and Moon-goddess, and to Hecate, as powerful in Heaven as she was in Hell as the two towers would suggest, marking as they do the boundaries between these two opposing worlds. Because of its ability to move backwards as well as forwards like the Moon, the crayfish itself has often been associated with it. However, the Moon has always been regarded as a liar and we should not rely upon what would appear to belong to the cosmic order since this card bears a deeper meaning and one on the psychic level. 'The Moon, as Plutarch remarked, is where good men go after they die. There they lead a life which may not be godlike, but is yet free from care until they die for a second time. All men must die twice' (RIJT p. 252). Thus the Moon is the abode of individuals between the time when they leave their bodies and the second death which is the prologue to their rebirth.

Thus souls in the shape of droplets, the different colours of which correspond perhaps to the three degrees of spiritualization, rise up towards the Moon and, if the dogs try to frighten them, it is only to stop them crossing forbidden bounds into which the imagination might make them stray. The world of reflection and externals is not the real world. The crayfish is the only creature in the blue waters bathed by moonlight to remind us that the astrological sign of Cancer is traditionally the home of the Moon and propitious to inward study and examination of conscience. Like the Ancient Egyptian scarab, it consumes all that is ephemeral and takes part in moral regeneration.

The Moon lights us along the path of mystic enlightenment to which the seventeenth arcanum (the Star) has led us. It is still endangered by magic and imagination until the SUN (nineteenth arcanum) opens up the KING'S HIGHWAY of enlightenment and objectivity.

morning In the Bible, the word denotes the time of God's blessings and of human justice. It symbolizes the time when light is fresh, of beginnings when all is still uncorrupted, pure and uncompromised. Morning is a symbol of both purity and of promise, it is the time of Edenic existence. It is also the symbol of trust in oneself and in others and in life itself.

mortar The sexual significance of PESTLE and mortar is easy to understand. By extension the Bambara make the mortar a symbol of education (ZAHB).

Like the CAULDRON, the mortar plays a major part in European and Asian mythology. In Russia, the old ogress, Baba-Yaga, personifying Winter storms, travels in a mortar. 'The mortar is her coach, the pestle her whip and with her broom she sweeps away the track of her passing' (AFAN 1: p. 157).

The Vedas glorify mortars and soma – the liquor of life and semen of the gods – in poetry in which the sexual symbolism is made holy until it is given a cosmic dimension. The womb, instrumental in passing on life, is associated in this context with the drum, while the phallic pestle is compared with a stallion.

mosquito Perseveringly pursuing his victim and sucking his blood has made the mosquito a symbol of aggressiveness.

An expert in Greek mythology has suggested that the famous Theban Sphinx, which Sophocles described as 'the virgin with the hooked claws and riddling song', who asked her riddle of everyone who passed her and ate them when they failed to answer it, was really none other than the malaria mosquito. The monster died when OEDIPUS solved the riddle by draining the marshes.

This explanation casts some light upon the Oedipus complex. When the King of Thebes was unable to deal with the Sphinx and became resigned to her malign presence, he identified himself in some sense with the monster. A ruler becomes responsible for evils which he cannot cure. Laios became the mosquito, malaria, and to overcome the latter, the king had to be deposed. Hence his killing and, since he was Oedipus' father, the killing of the father who stood in the son's way.

On the other hand, MARSHES are symbols of the unconscious. Their stagnant waters, on which mosquitoes breed, are not removed until the drainage channels are opened; and these channels from the unconscious are such routes of self-expression as dreams, speech, poetry, painting and music. The father is the marsh which breeds fever and, by a strange reversal of the symbol, Oedipus in this context may stand for the analyst, since it is he who helps to open the channels of communication and drain the father away. The two roles, however, are united when an internal riddle needs to be solved. Oedipus is his own analyst, as every analyst must become at a certain stage in his analysis. At that point the cure has been effected and the dissociated parts of the personality are brought together. The channels are open, the mosquitoes dead and the monster has vanished. No one can ever save you except yourself.

moth The night BUTTERFLY which shrivels the leaves on which it settles, the moth is the constant symbol of the soul seeking the godhead and consumed by a mystical love, attracted like the insect fluttering round the candle until it burns its wings. The theme is a thread which runs through Persian mystical poetry and the moth becomes the symbol of humanity in the chilly darkness, yearning for wings to take flight towards the heights of divine love.

On the other hand, the notion of the moth burning its wings in the candle – shared by more than one culture – causes it to be regarded, like the butterfly, as a symbol of faithless frivolity. 'Men rush to their doom like moths flying to their death in the candle-flame', says the *Bhagavad Gītā*.

mother The symbolism of the mother is related to that of EARTH and the SEA, in the sense that all three are WOMBS and wells of life. Earth and sea are themselves symbols of the mother's body.

All the great Mother Goddesses were fertility-goddesses – Gaia, Rhea, Hera and Demeter among the Greeks; Isis among the Ancient Egyptians and in Hellenistic cults; Ishtar among the Assyrians and Babylonians; Astarte among the Phoenicians, and Kālī among Hindus.

The same ambivalence existing in sea and Earth symbolism recurs in the symbol of the Mother. Life and death are interdependent. To be born is to emerge from the mother's womb; to die is to return to Earth. Mothers are anchors of shelter, warmth, love and nourishment. On the other hand they may run the risk of suppressing their children by limiting their horizons and of stifling them by exercising the office of nurse-maid and governess to excess. She who gave life devours what should procreate; the giver entraps and castrates.

Christianity mystically transposes the Mother into the Church, conceived as a community from which Christians can draw nourishment in the life of grace, but from which they may also suffer intolerable spiritual despotism, such is the human capacity to corrupt.

On the other hand, the Divine Mother symbolizes the most perfect sublimation of instinct and the most profound harmony of love. In Christian tradition, Our Lady is the Mother of God, conceiving Jesus through the Holy Spirit. In the dogma of the Catholic Church, she expresses a historical reality and not a symbol. The event is no less significant on two counts, namely, that virginity does not inhibit a very real maternity and that God can impregnate one of his creatures independently of the laws of nature. This dogma emphasizes with equal force that Christ is directly rooted in the human nature of his Mother and in the divine nature of his Father and nothing can better express the Word made Flesh than the unity of the person in two natures. The early Fathers enjoyed exploring the verbal consequences of this paradoxical event. Our Lady was her son's daughter in so far as he is God, her creator: she was also the mother of her God, in so far as he was a man incarnate through her. If we consider her son's divine nature, clearly she never conceived him, yet if we consider the person of Christ as an individual, she is really his mother since it was she who gave him his human nature. Hence her name, Theotokos, Mother of God, so fiercely debated in the councils of the primitive Church and expressive of motherhood in its perfection.

This manifestation of divine motherhood has nothing in common with the Divine Mother of Hindu theology, and this difference stresses the divisions between a history-based theology, founded upon what is regarded as an event which took place, and a symbolic theology, based upon what is regarded as a symbol. For the one, the historical fact that the Mother of God exists expresses the spiritual reality of the Incarnation; for the other the absolute symbol of the Divine Mother translates the spiritual reality of the female principle. Notions can be absolute symbols and, in India, the notion of the Divine Mother is 'a synthesis of . . . mythology, theology, philosophy and metaphysics. These four angles of vision are represented by symbols, such, for example, as that of Kālī.' Now in Indian iconography,

Kālī is depicted as a hideously ugly woman, blood dripping from her long pendulous tongue, dancing upon a corpse. How then can she symbolize the Divine Mother? Swami Siddheswarānanda explains that in this symbol of Terror 'we do not worship either violence or destruction, but in a vision of a single modality we comprehend the three impulses which together form creation, stabilization and destruction.' These are three aspects of a single experience of life. The Divine Mother is thus the life force made manifest, and this force is 'the Spiritual Principle displayed in a female shape'. Other aspects may be seen in symbols other than Kālī – DURGĀ, Lakshmi, Sarasvatī, GANESHA, for example. All assume a cosmocentric attitude of mind tending to include within its range of vision macrocosm and microcosm, atom and globe. The Divine Mother is like a continuum which unites and underpins the universe, *prakrti* and *māyā*, the oneness of all that is manifest from simple outward shape to pure illusion. She is consciousness of manifestation, of Shiva's self manifest in countless outward shapes, of those waves of energizing power which are beings and of matter raining down in fleeting lightning-flashes. She is the consciousness of the wholeness made manifest and liturgies invoke her in such terms as: 'Divine Mother I worship you under the shape of creative energy, I fall before you!' (*Vedanta* 4–5 (1967): pp. 5–26).

Brigit was the mother of the three primeval Celtic gods, Brian, Iuchar and Iucharba, who fought and killed Lug's father, Cian, their own father's brother. Brigit was invoked by poets, learned men and smiths. However, she was also daughter of the Dagda, just as Minerva-Pallas was the daughter of Jupiter-Zeus and the Dagda was Lug's brother . . . but it is pointless as well as impossible to draw up a coherent and rational family-tree. Unimpaired, Brigit symbolizes what Goethe called the Eternal FEMININE, without the need to make her a mother-goddess with the ethnographic accent upon fertility. 'Mother' may also be found in the Gaulish river-name, *Matrona* (Marne), and in the name of the Welsh deity *Modron.* 'There would seem to be an active symbolic relationship between the Eternal Mother and water (salt or fresh) which stands for the full range of potential retained by a certain state of being' (GUEI p. 306 n. 4). In Ireland, the primeval mother-goddess is called Dana (= 'art'). She was the mother of the gods (*Tuatha Dé Danann*, 'People of the Goddess Dana') and corresponds to Elatha (= learning). She was also known as Ana and as was the case with the Roman goddess Diana and St Anne, the mother of Our Lady, we may see her as (dé) Ana, 'the goddess Ana'. At the functional level of the craftsman, the Celtic Minerva, another of her aspects, counterbalances Gobniu, the blacksmith. However, in her primary role of mother and virgin she stands simultaneously for universal potentiality and divine bliss. At the same time she may be identified with the universal father who, without begetting children, is the Almighty Father (CELT p. 15).

It would seem that in Celtic religious concepts, women played an important role either as messengers from the Otherworld or as sole possessors of the right of kingship and as war-goddesses. There was, however, one sole and unique female deity with varied aspects, in contrast with separate and distinct male deities. This female deity counterbalanced the 'Almighty Father' (*Ollathir*) and since, although he was the father of mankind, he lacked virility, she was both virgin (see VIRGINITY) and mother of the gods (OGAC 18: p. 136).

In the structure of the Gaulish pantheon described by Caesar and reconstructed by comparison with the Irish, a single goddess corresponded to the four major gods identified with Mercury, Apollo, Mars and Jupiter. This was Minerva, the Irish Brigit who survives in the Gallic place-name, Brigantia. This is reminiscent of the Hindu Pandavas, the five brothers who shared a single wife, and simultaneously explains the series of incestuous unions in Irish mythology. In Ireland, Brigit was the mother.

In contemporary psychoanalysis, the mother symbol acquires an archetypal quality. The mother is 'the first form in which the individual experiences the anima', that is, the unconscious. The latter is to be seen under two aspects, the one creative, the other destructive. It is destructive in so far as it is 'the well-spring of all instinct ... the totality of all archetypes ... the residuum of all human experience since the remotest beginnings, and the site of supra-individual experience'. However it needs consciousness to actualize itself, since it exists only by interdependence with the conscious, the distinguishing feature of humans by contrast with animals, the latter being said to have instincts but not an unconscious. It is precisely within this relationship that the forces of the unconscious may become established and breed. By reason of the relative superiority which it derives from its impersonal nature and the properties from which it originates 'it may turn against the conscious, which derives from it, and destroy the latter. Its role then becomes that of the mother who consumes her offspring, oblivious of the individual and totally absorbed in the blind cycle of creation.'

On the child's side may be discovered a distorted image of the mother and an involutionary attitude in the shape of a 'mother-fixation'. In this instance the mother 'continues to exert an unconscious spell which threatens to paralyse development of the ego.... The subject's mother dons the maternal archetype, symbol of the unconscious, that is, of the non-self. This non-self is regarded as being hostile, because of the fear which the mother inspires and the unconscious domination which she exercises.'

In dreams the mother is sometimes symbolized by a BEAR. In those circumstances, the animal stands for 'all those instincts which the dreamer has concentrated and projected upon his mother ... the bear being the personification of his infantile fixation upon the maternal image. The bear remains the predominantly instinctual creature for as long as the dreamer's instincts remain undeveloped, primal and entirely governed by the infantile longing to be cuddled and kissed.' At other times the animal may be a WOLF, 'the big, bad wolf', which may allude to the maternal image. A 'frightening, fierce, and hungry predator', it confronts the dreamer with 'the contradictory nature of the instincts, since his longing to be cuddled and protected by his mother clashes with what is exactly opposite, the uncontrollable rage and consuming fire of the instincts' (ADLJ pp. 53, 54, 111, 206).

motley Motley is the primitive symbol of the countless beauties of the natural world, its shapes and colours. Parti-coloured clothes, gardens, carpets, frescoes and pottery all conjure up this inexhaustible wealth of living things and offer an implicit plea for good fortune; they pledge their identification with the protean and constantly regenerated world of nature.

Fertility-gods and goddesses, kings in many countries and priests vested for their offices were often dressed in parti-coloured cloaks or tunics.

mountain Mountain symbolism takes many forms deriving from height and CENTRE. In so far as mountains are tall, lofty, rising abruptly to meet the Heavens, they form part of the symbolism of transcendence and, in so far as they are so often numinous places where the gods have revealed their presence, they share in the symbolism of manifestation. Mountains are places where HEAVEN and Earth meet, where the gods have their home and human ascension its boundary. Viewed from above, the vertical point of their peaks make them the centres of the world: seen from below, they stand against the horizon like World Axes, their slopes like a LADDER to be climbed.

Thus, in all lands and among all peoples, most cities have their holy mountain. This twofold symbolism, of height and of centre, recurs in spiritual writing. St John of the Cross describes the stages of the spiritual life as though it were an ascent and St Teresa of Avila in her *Interior Castle*, as if it were climbing Mount Carmel.

Mountains also give expression to notions of stability, changelessness and, sometimes, even of purity. The Sumerians believed them to be undifferentiated masses of primal matter, the World Egg, which, according to the *Chu-wen*, brought forth 'ten thousand beings'. In more general terms, mountains are both the centre and the axis of the world, pictorially represented as right-angle triangles. They are the homes of the gods and their ascent is represented as an exaltation heavenwards and as a means of entering into a relationship with the godhead, like a return to the First Cause. Chinese emperors sacrificed on mountain peaks; Moses received the Ten Commandments on the top of Mount Sinai; Shiva-Maheshvara 'ceaselessly descended' upon the peak of Ba-Phnom, the site of a capital of the former kingdom of Funan; Taoist Immortals ascended into Heaven from mountain tops and it was there that messages for Heaven were placed. The best known axial mountains are Meru, in India, Kun-Lun in China (*see also below*) and Li-tzu's Mount Li-ku-ye; and there are many more: Fuji-yama, for which ritual purification is an essential preliminary to any ceremonial ascent; Greek Olympus; Persian Alborj; Samaritan Garizim; Masonic Moriah; Elbrus and Tabor (the latter derives its name, significantly, from the root for 'navel'); the Ka'ba at Mecca; Montsalvat in the Grail legend; the Muslims' Kāf; the Celts' white mountain; Potala in Tibet and so on. In every case we are concerned with mountains central or 'polar' in any given tradition. Montsalvat and Li-ku-ye stand on islands which have become inaccessible while Kāf can be reached neither by land nor by sea. Implicit in this is a removal from the primeval state like the transfer of the spiritual centre from the peak of the mountain, on which it may be seen, to the CAVERN lying beneath it. Dante places the Earthly Paradise on the peak of Mount Purgatory. Taoists stress the difficulties, the dangers even, of climbing a mountain without training oneself through spiritual exercises. Mountains are sometimes inhabited by fearful beings who bar all approaches to the summit. Clearly the ascent is of a spiritual nature, moving upwards towards knowledge. 'The ascent of this mountain', Richard of St Victor wrote, 'belongs to self-knowledge and what happens at the top of the mountain leads to the knowledge of God.' 'The Sinai of one's being' is a symbol common to Suhrawardi of Aleppo and to Ismaili esoterics. In Sufic terms, Mount Kāf is man's *haqīqāt*, his deepest truth, his very nature as the Buddhists would say. Similarly for the Chinese, Mount Kun-Lun corresponds to the head, and its peak touches the point at which the release from the cosmos may be effected.

Once again the cosmic symbolism of mountains as centres needs to be stressed. In India, in addition to Mount Meru, there were such other axial mountains as Kailāsa, the abode of Shiva, and Mandara, which was used as a plunger in the famous Sea of Milk episode. Apart from Kun-Lun – which was also a pagoda to nine storeys corresponding to the nine degrees of heavenly ascension – the Chinese had the four world-pillars, one of which was P'u-Chou which gave access to the Underworld, and the four mountains at the cardinal points, T'ai-shan, to the east, being the best known. 'If the heavens were in danger of falling,' wrote Chairman Mao, 'this mountain would hold them up.' To the Taoist Celestial Masters, Mount Kun-Lun symbolized the abode of immortality, rather on the lines of the Western Earthly Paradise. Its fame derives from the fact that Chang Tao Lin, the Heavenly Master, went there for the two swords which, it seems, drove evil spirits away. It was from this mountain, too, that having drunk the beverage of immortality discovered by one of his ancestors, he rose up to Heaven on the five-coloured dragon.

In Taoist mythology it was upon this mountain, called 'the Mountain in the Middle of the World' and around which the Sun and Moon revolved, that the Immortals went to live. On the peak of the mountain they located the Gardens of the Queen of the West, in which grew the peach-tree with the fruit which conferred immortality.

Guénon believes that, from the etymology of her name, Cybele was a mountain-goddess and this is undoubtedly true of Pārvatī. She was the symbol of ether and also of strength. Furthermore, she was Shiva's *shakti*, while he was Girisha, 'lord of the Mountain'. His role is best displayed in Cambodia, where his lingams are set up either on natural mountain peaks, such as Lingaparvata, Mahendraparvala or Phnom Bakheng, or on the tops of mountainlike step-temples such as Bakong, Ko-Ker or Baphuon. Such temple-mountains are the centres of kingdoms, as Meru is the centre of the world. They are the axes of the universe, as were Maya or Babylonian temples. In such centres, the king was the surrogate of the Lord of the Universe, Shiva-Devarāja, being the *chakravartī* or Universal Monarch. The Kings of Java and Funan were Kings of the Mountain for, as the Javanese saying goes, 'where the king is, there is the mountain'. Echoes of this artificial central mountain are to be discerned in Celtic rock-piles, their tumuli and cairns; in the man-made hills in Chinese capital cities; perhaps, as Durand claims, in Vietnamese citadels and watch-towers; and certainly in the sand-mountains and sand-pagodas created at New Year in Laos and Cambodia. They are to be seen with equal clarity in Buddhist stupas, of which the most grandiose is at Borobudur in Java.

Because mountains are ways leading to Heaven, they were the refuges of

Taoists who, as Demiéville observes, 'entered the mountain' when they left the world behind, as a means of identifying themselves with the Heavenly Way (*T'ien Tao*). Taoist Immortals are called *sien*, literally, 'mountain-men'.

In Chinese classical painting mountains are contrasted with water as *yang* with *yin*, the changeless with the ephemeral, the former being most often depicted as a ROCK, the latter as a WATERFALL (BENA, BHAB, COEA, COOH, CORT, DANA, DAUM, DEMM, ELIF, GRAD, GRAP, GRAR, GRIC, GUEV, GUED, GUEM, GUEC, GUES, HUAV, KALL, KRAA, LIOT, MAST, PORA, SCHP, SECA, SOUN, SOUP, THIK).

The Old Testament contains echoes of the mythological symbolism of the primordial or cosmic mountain. Like fortresses, the high mountains are symbols of safety (Psalm 30: 7).

Mount Garizim is called, in passing, 'the middle of the land' (Judges 9: 37), while such phrases as 'the everlasting hills' occur in Genesis 49: 26. Hills and mountains are associated with Jehovah (Psalm 36: 7; Psalm 48; Isaiah 14: 12ff.), while Ezekiel 28: 11–19 would imply speculative thought which equated to some extent the Mountain of the Lord with the Mountain of Paradise. Such a concept cannot be found in Genesis, but surfaces in late Jewish writings (Jubilees 4: 26; 1 Enoch 28: 1ff.; 8: 3). These are signs of how popular and attractive the theme of the holy mountain was.

This is transmuted into eschatological terms in two passages from the prophets Isaiah (2: 2) and Micah (4: 1): 'But in the last days it shall come to pass, that the mountain of the house of the Lord shall be established in the top of the mountains.'

At the cost of some modification, the symbol may be found at the very heart of the Jewish religion. Heir to the primeval holy mountain, the mountain now often symbolizes the presence or proximity of God, such as his revelation upon Mount Sinai and the sacrifice of Isaac (Genesis 22: 2) upon a mountain later identified as the Temple Mount. Elijah was granted the miraculous shower of rain (1 Kings 18: 42) after praying on the top of Mount Carmel and God revealed himself to him on Mount Horeb (1 Kings 19: 9ff.). Jewish apocalyptic writings merely added to the number of these visions of revelations of the godhead on mountain tops.

Nor should the Sermon on the Mount (Matthew 5: 1ff.) be forgotten; no doubt it corresponds in the New Covenant to the Ten Commandments of the Old, handed down from Mount Sinai. It should also be observed that Christ's Transfiguration took place upon 'an high mountain' (Mark 9: 2) and his Ascension on the Mount of Olives (Luke 24: 50; Acts 1: 12).

Furthermore, mountains were widely regarded as symbolizing human pride and pomp, which could not, however, escape God's almighty power. Pagan worship was often celebrated upon high places (Judges 5: 5; Jeremiah 51: 25) and this is why Judaism and after it the early Church expected the mountains to be levelled and to vanish. This was because, when God brought his chosen people back from exile, 'every mountain and hill shall be made low' (Isaiah 40: 4) and the end of the world would make the mountains disappear (1 Enoch 1: 6; Ascension of Isaiah 4: 18; Revelation 16: 20).

There are two aspects to the symbol: God reveals himself upon the mountain tops, but the mountain tops upon which men stand only to worship man and idols and not the true God, are no more than signs of pride and omens of disaster (see TOWER; TOWER OF BABEL; ZIGGURAT).

The links in this chain of sacred symbolism – God–mountain–city–palace–refuge–temple–centre of the Earth – shine out in all their clarity in these verses of Psalm 48:

Great is the Lord, and greatly to be praised in the city of our God, in the mountain of his holiness. Beautiful for situation, the joy of the whole earth, is mount Zion, on the sides of the north, the city of the great King. God is known in her palaces for a refuge. . . . We have thought of thy lovingkindness, O God, in the midst of thy temple. According to thy name, O God, so is thy praise to the ends of the earth.

As we have seen, Biblical tradition invested many mountains with the quality of holiness and in consequence they came to symbolize the revelation of the sacred. Such were Sinai or Horeb, Tabor, Garizim, Carmel, Golgotha and the mountains of Christ's temptation, of the Beatitudes, the Transfiguration, the Crucifixion (Calvary) and the Ascension; and the so-called Gradual Psalms (120–34) rise step by step to these heights. In the early Church mountains symbolized the centres of initiation into the monastic life founded by the Desert Fathers.

The Acropolis of Athens stands with its temples upon the top of a holy mountain, access being through the Propylaea for the pilgrims to the ritual and hymns of the festival of the Panathenaea. When temples were built on flatlands, a central man-made mountain was provided, such as, for example, the Mount Meru in the temple of Angkor Thom.

In Africa and America, among all peoples and in all lands, mountains have been marked out as the abode of the gods who signal their reactions to human behaviour by mists, clouds and lightnings.

To summarize Biblical traditions and those of which Christian art gives so many examples, Champeaux and Sterckx stress three main principles of mountain symbolism: (1) mountains link Earth and Heaven; (2) holy mountains stand in the centre of the universe of which they are the image; (3) temples are identified with these mountains (CHAS pp. 164–99).

In Muslim cosmology, the mountain which dominates the terrestrial world is called Kāf. Early Arab thinkers generally regarded the Earth as a flat disc and Mount Kāf as being separated from the terrestrial disc by a region which could not be crossed. In the words of the Prophet, this was a region of darkness which it would take four months to traverse.

Some describe Mount Kāf as being made of emerald and its reflection as tingeing the vault of Heaven, which the West would call blue, with green.

Another version claims that only the rock upon which Mount Kāf stands is composed of a sort of emerald. This rock is also called 'the post' because God created it to support the world. In fact, some maintain, the Earth could not remain steady of itself and needs a support of this kind. If Mount Kāf did not exist, the Earth would be in a state of continuous quaking and life of any sort would be impossible.

Once again we have a recurrence of the symbolism of centre and navel of the world (see OMPHALOS). Mount Kāf was often viewed in the same light as the mother-mountain of all the mountains in the world. 'The latter were

joined to it by a complex of underground roots and veins and when God
wished to destroy any country he had only to command one of these roots
to move and an earthquake would follow' (ENCI 11: 'kāf').

Inaccessible to human beings and standing on the edge of the world,
Mount Kāf represented the boundary between the visible and the invisible
world. Nobody knew what lay behind it and only God knew what creatures
lived upon it.

However, the most important thing about Mount Kāf was that it was the
home of the fabulous bird, the SIMURG, which had existed from the beginning of the world. This wonderful bird then retired to Mount Kāf, where it
lived in happy and cloistered solitude, a wise counsellor consulted by kings
and heroes. Kāf owes the name which the poets have given it of 'Mountain
of Wisdom' and, symbolically, 'Mountain of Happiness', to the bird which
made its home there.

Mount Kāf is often mentioned in the *Thousand and One Nights* and other
Arabic stories.

Mystical writers have made it a more esoteric symbol. In his *Rose Garden
of Mystery* Shabistarī asked what Mount Kāf and the simug were. Lāhijī
provides the answer in his commentary that 'Mount Kāf, like the cosmic
mountain, is internalized in a psycho-cosmic mountain. The simug signifies
unique and absolute Selfhood. Mount Kāf on which it dwells is the eternal
human reality; which is the revelation in perfect form of divine *haqīqāt*,
since the Divine Being (*haqq*) is revealed in it, with all its names and
attributes' (CORT pp. 123–4).

Africans often regard mountains in the shape, and playing the parts, of
fabulous beings and of places haunted by gods, spirits and hidden powers
which one should not risk disturbing. The sound and song of the mountains
are replete with mystery, not to be understood by the uninitiated. The
mountains themselves are a hidden world full of secrets, holy places which
are not to be entered without a guide (mystagogue) under pain of mortal
danger. They symbolize the longing for initiation as well as its perils (HAMK
p. 24).

The Celtic world provides scarcely any evidence of the general symbolism of mountains except for the mythical Welsh place name Gwynvryn
('White Mount'), from the tale of Branwen the daughter of Llyr in the
Mabinogion, where it is the central place where Bran's head was buried. So
long as it was left undisturbed, the head would perform the task of keeping
the isle of Britain safe from all invasion or disaster. Since white was a
priestly colour, Gwynvryn can only stand for a primeval centre and this
detail in the Welsh tale must come from a much earlier source. Holy mountains are places of solitude and meditation, by contast with the lowlands
where mankind lives (LOTM p. 45; GUER).

A mountain peak rising to the sky as depicted by Leonardo da Vinci, say,
or by some Chinese artists, is not just a beautiful decorative motif, but
symbolizes the abode of solar deities, the higher properties of the soul, the
supraconscious functioning of the life force, the opposition of the warring
principles of Earth and Water, which comprises the world, and the destiny
of mankind to move ever upwards. As the focal point of an area, mountain
peaks symbolize the bounds of human development and the psychic function

of the supraconscious which is, in fact, to lead mankind to the peak of its development (DIES p. 37).

mourning See LAMENTATION.

mouse See under RAT.

mouth As the channel through which pass breath, speech and food, the mouth is the symbol of creative force and, in particular, of the insufflation of the soul. As the organ of speech and of breathing, it also symbolizes an elevated state of consciousness and the power to control through use of reason. However, as with all symbols, there is another side to this positive aspect. A power able to build, animate, legislate and elevate is also capable of destroying, killing, disorganizing and debasing – the mouth undermines its castles of words as fast as it erects them. It is the intercessor between the situation of the individual and the higher or the lower world into which it can lead that person. Iconographically it is depicted throughout the world either as the jaws of a monster or as the lips of an angel and can as easily be the Gates of Hell as the Doors of Paradise.

The Ancient Egyptians practised the post-mortuary ritual known as 'the opening of the mouth'. This rite was intended to fit all the dead person's bodily organs for their new life. Anubis presided over the ceremony, which took place on the day of the burial over a carefully prepared body. The specially trained priest touched the dead person's face twice with a small adze and once with a chisel or pincers. He then opened the mouth with a hook shaped like a bull's leg and a golden implement in the shape of a human finger. The ceremony ensured the dead person the ability to speak the truth, thus satisfying the gods who would be his or her judges, and to receive a new life. A solar disc placed upon the mouth showed that the dead person now shared the life of the Sun-god, Ra. From now onwards he or she was summoned to eat the food of Heaven (ERMR p. 308; PIED pp. 334, 401). The Egyptian *Book of the Dead* contains such prayers as: 'Give me back my mouth, so that I may speak.'

There were secret societies with a religious rite of initiation in which the candidate was first gagged in the presence of their officers, their high priests not removing the gags until the candidate had successfully passed the initial tests. This ceremonial closing of the mouth symbolized the need rigorously to observe the rules of secrecy, never to speak without the society's permission and to pass on only what the mouths of its Masters had taught.

Carvings from southern Gaul depict faces without a mouth. When the Irish bard Morann, son of the usurper Cairpre, was born, his father ordered him to be thrown into the sea since he had no mouth. Lack of a mouth must surely be related to eloquence, poetry or the expression of thought. Since blind men were endowed with second sight, men without mouths were orators and poets employing other than a common tongue.

The 'mouth of darkness' is a chthonian or infernal symbol, a gaping entrance to the Underworld, swallowing the Sun each dusk to vomit it up again at dawn. It is the transition from light to darkness, life to death, and hence both entrance and exit of ritual initiation, traditionally regarded as a form of ingestion in which the initiate is sometimes said to have been swallowed by a monster when he remains hidden in his retreat.

Hieroglyphics, temple statues and buildings all bear witness to the importance which this symbol has held for so many peoples in those fortunate places where religious knowledge and astronomical observation had yet to become separate branches of science. Whether set at the foot of Central American step-pyramids or Asian stupas, the mouths of wolf, lion, crocodile, jaguar, python, *nāga* or dragon all had the same meaning. In mouth symbolism the monster Quetzalcoatl is the brother of LEVIATHAN or Jonah's WHALE. The subtle interplay of the colours green and red, regarded here as what symbolizes and what is symbolized, was often associated with the mouths of monsters, green on the outside and red as hell-fire within.

Because of the associations in so many cultures of Fire with the mouth – the tongues of fire at Pentecost, dragons spitting fire, the lyre of Apollo, the Sun-god and so on – Jung saw a link and a deep relationship between the mouth and fire. The two chief characteristics of the human race are the use of speech and of fire. Both derive from psychic energy or MANA. The symbolism of the mouth derives from the same sources as that of fire and displays the same twofold characteristics as Agni, the Indian god of manifestation, creator and destroyer. The mouth is also shaped in the curve of the primeval egg, the palate corresponding with the upper world and the lower jaw with the Underworld. The mouth is thus the point of departure or of convergence of two directions and symbolizes the source of opposites, contrarieties and ambiguities.

mud   The symbol of fertile primeval matter from which, according to Biblical tradition, mankind, in particular, sprang. As a mixture of Earth and Water, it joins the receptive womb-principle (EARTH) with the energizing principle of change and transformation (WATER). If one takes Earth as one's point of departure, then mud will symbolize the beginning of development, Earth moving, fermenting and becoming plastic.

On the other hand, taking Water, pure and unsullied, as one's point of departure, then mud will be seen as the beginning of retrogression and degradation. Hence it will become identified in moral symbolism with lees, silt, the lower levels of existence – water which has become filthy and contaminated.

All levels of cosmic and moral symbolism range between Earth brought to life by Water and Water polluted by Earth.

mulberry-tree   In Ancient China the mulberry was the tree of the east. It was the abode of the Mother of Suns and the tree up which the rising Sun climbed. When Huang Ti left the hollow mulberry-tree (*ch'ong-san*) to climb the throne, he clearly followed the ascendant path of the Sun. This same path was accompanied by the rhythmical beating of a drum of mulberry-wood or of paulownia. A forest of mulberry-trees (*san-lin*) was planted at the eastern gate of the capital and the same word is used for a dance which would appear to have been related to the vernal equinox.

However, Yen-ti's daughter, transformed into a magpie, used a mulberry-tree to rise to Heaven.

Bows of mulberry-wood, as well as bows of peach-wood, were used to shoot arrows to destroy evil influences at the four points of the compass.

Consequently, it is somewhat surprising to find that the appearance of miraculous mulberry-trees in conjunction with some dynastic event was regarded as ill-omened. This is doubtless because the Sun's ascendant presages drought, which is patent evidence of Heaven's curse (GRAD, KALL).

In legends its red flowers, which gleam at night, have been compared with the stars. Ovid relates that its fruit was originally white, but became red after the suicide of the two lovers, Pyramus and Thisbe, who used to meet in the shade of a mulberry-tree beside a spring.

mushroom Mushrooms, and in China especially the agaric or tinder agaric, are symbols of longevity, the reason, perhaps, being that they last a very long time when they are dried. A mushroom was one of the attributes of the god of longevity. The Immortals ate them, together with cinnamon, gold and jade. Mushrooms, Wang Ch'ong wrote, gave them bodily lightness.

Agaric (*lin-che*), furthermore, was believed to flourish only when the empire enjoyed peace and good rule. To see it growing was a sign that Heaven's mandate was being put to proper use.

Additionally some ancient writers considered it to be a love philtre.

On a different plane, Taoist cosmology made the mushroom an image of primeval Heaven because of the domed shape of its cap.

Chuang Tzu (ch. 2), furthermore, regards the mass of mushrooms growing from the same moist patch as an image of the ephemeral modalities of being, fleeting outward appearances of one and the same essence (DURV, KALL, ROUN).

The Dogon symbolically associate mushrooms with the coating of the stomach and with musical instruments. Drum-skins are rubbed with ashes of mushrooms to 'make them speak' (DIED).

The Oroch, a Siberian Tungus tribe, believed that the souls of the dead were reincarnated in the shape of mushrooms on the Moon and dropped down to Earth again in the same form (ELIF).

Some Bantu tribes in the central Congo also make mushrooms symbols of the soul. The Lulua use the terms 'kraal mushrooms' and 'bush mushrooms' for the worlds of the living and the dead (FOUC). A wise man added: 'A kraal mushroom and a bush mushroom are the same mushrooms.' All these beliefs share one point in common: they make mushrooms symbols of life regenerated by fermentation and organic decomposition, that is, by death.

music (see also SOUND) The Ancient Greeks generally attributed the invention of music to Apollo, Cadmus, Orpheus and Amphion; the Ancient Egyptians to Thoth or Osiris; Hindus to Brahmā; the Jews to Jubal and so on. Musical historians praise Pythagoras, who invented a monochord to determine mathematically the musical scale. Equal praise is given to Pindar's master Lassus who wrote the first musical treatise *c.* 540 BC. Two thousand years before these masters lived, the Chinese had carried a musical form to a point of real perfection. In fact a generally accepted chronology sets the Emperor Huang Ti's reign at about 2697 BC. Under this emperor, one of his ministers, Lin-Len, formed an octave of twelve semitones, which he called twelve *lu*. These twelve *lu* were divided up into *yang lu* and *yin lu*, and corresponded to the twelve months of the year and the twelve states of the soul, each *yang lu* being followed by a *yin lu*, and each *lu* being fraught with symbolic meaning.

Pythagoreans also regarded music as a harmony of numbers with the cosmos, the latter itself being reducible to sound-numbers. This was to endow numbers with the mind and feelings of animate beings. Their school is responsible for the concept of a 'music of the spheres'. Music with its different harmonics, tones, tempi and instruments is a means of identifying with the life of the cosmos in all its fullness. In every civilization, the high points of social or personal life have been punctuated by events in which music has played the part of a mediator which widens contact until it borders upon the divine. Plato categorized the types of music appropriate to the activities of the citizen.

Traditional Celtic music was played on the HARP rather than on wind instruments such as the bagpipes which were kept for battle or amusement. All competent harpists were able to play in three modes, bringing sleep, laughter or tears respectively. They echo, without corresponding precisely to, the three modes of ancient Greek music, the Lydian sad and mournful, the Dorian manly and warlike and the Phrygian exultant and Bacchic. The mode which brought sleep was linked to the Otherworld, it was the music of the gods which brought enchanted sleep, as well as that of the SID and of its messengers who came either in the shape of mortal women or of swans. When the children of Lir were changed into swans, they sang god-like songs which charmed all the people of Ireland who heard them (OGAC 18: pp. 26–9; CHAB pp. 545–7).

Christian tradition retained much of the Pythagoreans' music symbolism, handed down via St Augustine and Boethius. According to Carcopino: 'Ternary rhythm was called perfection while binary was always regarded as being flawed. The symbolism of the number seven was echoed on the musical plane, the musical number, Athene's number' alight with her wisdom. Boethius distinguished three symbolical types of music: the music of the universe 'which corresponded with the harmony of the stars and derives from their movement, from the passing seasons and from the combination of the elements . . . [the tune] is shriller the faster they move and lower the slower. . . . The cosmos is a magnificent concerto.' The second type is the music of humanity: 'It controls the individual and each individual hears it within him- or herself. It implies a harmony between body and soul . . . a harmony between the faculties of the soul . . . and the elements which constitute the body.' Lastly there is instrumental music which governs the playing of musical instruments. If, as Varro would have it, music is 'the art of modulation', to the degree in which it controls the order of the cosmos, of humanity and of the instruments themselves, it becomes the art of attaining perfection (DAVS pp. 249–51).

mutilation (see also BLINDNESS; DEFORMITY; ONE-ARMED; ONE-EYED; ONE-LEGGED)　Mutilation is most generally regarded as a disqualification; thus Celtic tradition relates that King Nuada ceased to be able to reign after losing an arm in battle with the earlier inhabitants of Ireland. The god Midir was threatened with the loss of his kingdom because he was accidentally blinded in one eye.

However, this purely social consequence of mutilation does not really reveal the symbolic meaning of the word. In order to understand this, it should be remembered that much of civilization is based upon even numbers – human beings walk on two legs, work with two hands and absorb visual reality through two eyes. In opposition to the divine or human order is the hidden transcendental order of darkness, based primarily upon 'one' and standing on a point like a dancer or an inverted pyramid. The deformed, limbless and handicapped have this in common, that they are marginalized by human or 'daylight' society, since their 'evenness' is affected, and must perforce now belong to the other order, that of darkness, be it celestial or infernal, divine or satanic.

The Latin proverb remarked *Numero deus impari gaudet* (God delights in odd numbers), but the odd man out can carry the meaning of somebody who has offended the social code, either criminally or heroically. Both criminal and hero derive from the sacred and are differentiated only by the direction their lines of development take – right-hand or left-hand. Queen Medb blinded each of the children of Calatin – probably another name for the goddesses of war – in one eye to turn them into sorcerers to bring down Cùchulainn, her chief enemy. The Celtic donor – the essential property of kings – has no arms; the second-sighted are blind; and the genius of eloquence is a stammerer or a mute (CELT 7: *passim*; OGAC 13: pp. 331–42).

In Ancient Egypt, to secure magical protection, the hieroglyphics on temple walls for creatures inspiring fear, such as lions, crocodiles, snakes and scorpions, were defective and depictions of the animals themselves were cut in half, limbless, or disfigured in such a way as to be reduced to powerlessness (POSD p. 157).

myth In Paul Diel's ethico-psychological interpretation (DIES p. 40), the most significant figures of Greek mythology each stand for a function of the psyche; and their interrelationships display human psychic life divided between the opposing drives to sublimation or perversion.

The spirit is called Zeus; harmony of desires, Apollo; intuitive inspiration, Pallas Athene; repression, Hades and so on. The developmental drive – the essential desire – is represented by the hero, and the confrontational situation of the human psyche by battles with the monsters of perversion. All aspects of psychic life, be they sublimated or aberrant, may thus be susceptible to representational formulation and their explanations verified symbolically with the help of the symbolism of the victory or defeat of any given hero in combat with any given monster of determinate or determinable meaning.

This key to interpretation has enabled the writer to restore an understanding of myth by making it a dramatization of the inner life. Other interpreters, from the fourth-century BC Euhemerus onwards, have regarded myths as the past life and history of peoples, with their heroes and their exploits being in some sense restaged symbolically on the level of gods and their adventures. Myth, therefore, becomes a dramatization of social life, poeticized history. Other commentators, especially philosophers, 'regard them as a collection of very ancient symbols, originally intended to enfold philosophic dogma and ethical ideas, of which the meaning has been lost . . . poeticized philosophy' (LAVD p. 684). For Plato they were a means of translating what derived from opinion and not from scientific certainty. Whatever the system of interpretation, they help to enlighten one dimension of human reality and show the symbol-making side of the imagination at work. They do not claim to transmit scientific truth, but to give expression to the truth of some perceptions. The interpretations employed in the present work have no other aim than to demonstrate that, beneath the dramatic diversity of myths and the analogy of their structures, what it is important to discover is their symbolic quality, which reveals the depth of their meaning.

N

nadir See ZENITH.

nāga (see also CROCODILE; MOUTH; PYTHON; SERPENT) The finest and most numerous examples of this seven-headed serpent are depicted on the temple at Angkor Thom in Cambodia. To the Khmer, the *nāga* was 'the symbol of the RAINBOW, regarded as the magic bridge giving entry to the abode of the gods.' In this, the most famous temple in south-east Asia,

> the gods at the south gate hold one end of the *nāga* which writhes symbolically round the Meru [the Indian holy mountain, which the temple itself is supposed to represent] while its other end is grasped by the demons at the north gate. Taking it in turns to tug, they can rotate the central mount and churn the sea to obtain ambrosia. From time immemorial the Khmer kings were compared with Vishnu churning the Sea of Milk to obtain *amrita,* that is, plenty.
> (GROA pp. 155–6)

The rubbing motions of the serpent wrapped round the sacred mount stimulate secretions of prosperity. Khmer beliefs laid great symbolic stress upon the churning of the Sea of Milk, whence came the APSARA and the phenomenal world.

Furthermore, like the python, the *nāga* is a symbol of the MOUTH which swallows either the human individual or the Sun itself at one end of the horizon to vomit them up at the other, and is therefore an initiatory symbol of death and rebirth. The significant facts in the traditions quoted above are the north–south axis and the *nāga*'s SEVEN heads, the latter being the symbol of fulfilment and especially of human fulfilment. The *nāga* is often depicted in India at the foot of the majestic stairways of stupas, re-echoing the gaping crocodile-mouths found at the foot of stairways on Central American pyramids.

nakedness Although in the West the naked body is often regarded as a sign of sensuality and physical depravity, one should remember, in the first place, that this point of view is not shared universally and, furthermore, that in Christian tradition this concept is the consequence of Original Sin and of the Fall of Adam and Eve. It relates to the fall from one level to another – from that of the First Cause to that of manifestation – and to an externalization of perspective. Something very like this is to be found in the Shintō myth in which, after their descent into Hell, Izanagi and Izanami were humiliated when they realized their condition. Although after the veiling of the body in the Middle Ages the Renaissance rediscovered the nude aesthetic, it was from a purely naturalistic point of view and one completely devoid of symbolic properties. Nor was it the point of view of Classical antiquity if one calls to mind the unveiling of Mystica in the House of the Mysteries at Pompeii with its wealth of symbols. In fact the symbolism of nakedness evolved in two directions – that of physical, moral, intellectual and spiritual purity, and that of provocative, empty sensuality, stimulating the senses and the flesh at the expense of the spirit.

From the traditional viewpoint, bodily nakedness is in some sense a return to the primeval state and to a 'central' perspective. This is true of Shintō priests who purify their naked bodies in the cold, unsullied winter air; of Hindu ascetics 'clad in the void' and of the Jewish priests who entered the Holy of Holies naked to show their self-abnegation before the mystery of the godhead. Nakedness is the destruction of what separates humans from the natural world around them so that in consequence natural energy may pass unscreened from the one to the other. This was the reason for the ritual nakedness, that may have been purely legendary, of the Celtic warrior in battle. It was certainly true of some temple dancers and even of some sorcerers who, in some circumstances, bared themselves to Underworld forces.

The uncovering of the Buddhist Dākini is like the European concept of the naked truth in the context of pure knowledge. Abū Ya'qūb Sejestānī applies a similar meaning to Christ on the Cross – the uncovering of the esoteric. Kālī's nakedness is the power of time, the spoil from the destruction of the Universe, and also displays the fact that she is outside the conventional dress of *Māyā*. In Tantrism, the ritual nakedness of the *yoginī* is the very symbol of *prakrti*, the cosmic substance, at the sight of which the spirit (or being) is still and untroubled (AVAS, BURA, DANA, ELIY, HERS, PALT, SAIR, VARG).

In Biblical tradition, nakedness may be taken primarily as a symbol of a condition in which all is manifest and nothing hidden – that of Adam and Eve in the Garden of Eden. It will be observed that the first two humans only saw the need for clothes after the Fall, thus showing, amongst other things, that the relationship between God and those he had created in his image had lost its original and unsullied simplicity.

Very naturally nakedness denoted poverty and spiritual weakness as well. Thus mankind will stand naked before God's judgement (Ecclesiastes 5: 15); while Ezekiel (16: 4ff.) chronicles the history of Israel by comparing it to a girl who was naked until the Lord chose her and clothed her.

Its symbolism is sometimes patently pejorative – nakedness is shame. Thus, through the prophet Nahum (3: 5), the Lord threatens to expose Israel and show her nakedness to the Gentiles, thus revealing the shame of the chosen, but idolatrous, people. It will be observed how far this is from the highly favourable view of nakedness formed by Hellenism, for whose athletes and artists the nude was an ideal.

In so far as ritual nakedness is concerned, there may well be an instance of this in the account of David dancing naked before the Ark of the Covenant (2 Samuel 6: 16, 20–2). His wife, Michal, felt he had shamed himself, but David replied that shame was nothing compared with his religious duties towards his God.

There is a clean division between Canonical and Gnostic writers, the latter viewing nakedness as an ideal to be achieved. This is the nakedness of the soul which casts aside the body, its clothing and its prison, to regain its primeval state and to ascend once more to its divine beginnings.

This would lead us to study the symbolism of DRESS, which will considerably clarify that of nakedness.

Female nudity has an awesome power. The Irish epic, *The Cattle Raid of Cooley*, tells how, when Cùchulainn returned from his first bloodthirsty foray on the borders of Ulster, he was in such a state of fighting-madness that he was unable to distinguish friend from foe. He turned the left side (the sinister side; see RIGHT AND LEFT) of his chariot towards Emain Macha, the capital of Ulster. Thereupon, King Conchobar ordered fifty women led by the queen to go out naked to meet him. The youthful hero lowered his eyes so as not to look at them and this provided the opportunity to seize him and duck him in three vats of icy water. The first was shattered, the water in the second evaporated in steam and only in the third was the water left at a bearable temperature. Another incident occurs in *The Madness of the Ulates*, when Richis, to avenge the death of her son, exposed herself in front of Cùchulainn. When the latter looked away, a warrior was supposed to strike him down, but Cùchulainn's charioteer, Loeg, inflicted a mortal wound on Richis, breaking her spine with a sling-shot. Male nudity is related to battle-madness. *The Cattle Raid of Cooley* tells of warriors who, in the heat of battle, melted the snow for thirty yards around them. This heat generated by Gaulish warriors explains why Classical writers reported that they fought naked. But such authors mistook myth for historical truth. There is overwhelming archeological evidence that the Gauls used body-armour (OGAC 18: pp. 368–72).

name (see also DA'WAH; LANGUAGE; LETTERS; SOUND; WORD; WRITING) Both the symbolism and the employment of the Name of God are constants in all theistic religions and in those Buddhist sects which approach them.

The importance the Children of Israel attached to the employment of the Name is well known. Three Names were said to express the very essence of the godhead, the chief one being the Tetragrammaton (JHVH or YHVH), which only the High Priest was allowed to pronounce. Other Names (Adonai, Shaddai and so on) denoted attributes or properties of the godhead. This same notion of properties or attributes applied to the ninety-nine names of God in Islam, upon which (Er-Rahmān, Er-Rahīm, El-Malik and so on) al-Ghazālī, among others, has left his commentary. It also applies, but without Scriptural foundation, to the Pseudo-Dionysius the Areopagite's Divine Names (Good, Beautiful, Life, Wisdom, Power and so on). In all these cases we are clearly dealing with aids to meditation and to spiritual exercises.

However, the best-known employment of the Divine Name – and this is often mentioned in the Psalms – is as an invocation, by means of which the invoker in some mysterious way becomes identified with the godhead itself. There is, as it were, a 'real presence' in the Name invoked. Invocation of the name calls up the being and this is why St Bernard can call it food, light and medicine. Hesychasm practises invocation restricted simply to the Name of God, sometimes combined with rhythmical breathing derived from the practice of Nicephorus the Hermit, while St John Climacus wrote: 'Let Jesus be in your minds as you draw breath.' The Arabic word *dhikr* (referring to a form of liturgical ritual) brings together both invocation and mental activity, since it conveys both meanings, and its relationship with Hesychasmic

practices is marked. ('Say "Allah" and leave the universe and all it contains.') It is also related to the Hindu *jāpa* employed by some swamis, the
basic spiritual exercise comprising the repetition of the Name of Rām. Other
names, such as Vishnu and Krishna, are employed in this invocation since,
Shri Rāmakrishna used to say, 'God and his Name are identical.' Amidism
claims that one has only to invoke the Name of the Buddha to bring about
a rebirth in the 'Pure Land' of Amida, hence the fervent recitation of the
Nembutsu in Japanese temples.

It should also be observed that some aspects of the invocation of the
Name derive from the symbolism of sound and language. In fact, in Indian
teaching, the Name (*namā*) is no different from the sound (*shabda*). The
name of something is 'the sound produced by the activity of the mobile
forces which comprise it' (Avalon). Furthermore, to pronounce a name is
in some sense effectually to 'create' or 'present' it. Name (*namā*) and form
(*rūpa*), being essence and substance of the individual manifestation,
determine its nature. Hence it is simple to deduce that naming a person or
thing is the same as taking control of them. For this reason the Ancient
Chinese attached enormous importance to correct designations since the
universal order derived from them. The School of Names (*Ming-kia*) carried these consequences to their extremes. Genesis 2: 19 also states that
Adam was entrusted with the task of naming all living creatures. This was
to grant him power over them and this power remains one of the characteristics of the paradisal state (AVAS, GRAP, PHIL, SCHC, SCHU,
WARK).

The Ancient Egyptians believed that 'the personal name was much more
than a means of identification. It was an essential part of the person. The
Egyptians believed in the creative and compelling power of the word. The
name was a living thing.' All characteristics of the symbol recur in names.
(1) They are 'full of significance'; (2) when writing or speaking the name of
a person, that person 'is given life and survival', which corresponds to the
dynamics of the symbol; (3) knowledge of the name 'gives power' over that
person, which corresponds to the magical aspect, the mysterious bond of
the symbol. Knowledge of the name is part of the ritual of conciliation,
casting spells, destroying, taking possession of and so on, and the phrase
'his name will no more be among the living' was the most extreme form of
the death-sentence (POSD p. 181).

Belief in the power of the name was not something exclusively Chinese,
Egyptian or Jewish, it is part of primitive thought-processes. To know a
name and to utter it correctly is to be able to exercise power over a person
or thing. In this respect Jewish thought and Biblical tradition were in strict
agreement. The divine Tetragrammaton was charged with energy and this
is why it was used in incantation. Were the name to be shouted aloud the
whole universe would be struck dumb, and this is why learned Jews tried
to keep its pronunciation secret. To reveal it would have been to allow
blasphemers and sorcerers to put it to evil use.

The Divine Name denotes the very identity of God. Juda ben Samuel
Halevi (d. 1141) compares the meanings of the name Elohim with the
Tetragrammaton. The meaning of the latter derives from no process of
reasoning, but from an aspiration and prophetic insight. Thus the individual

who seeks to apprehend the name separates himself from the elect of his kind and rises to the angelic plane. Through it he becomes a different person (VAJA pp. 107, 211).

In Muslim tradition the Great Name, *al-ismu'l-a'zam,* is the symbol of the hidden essence of God. A prophetic *hadīth* states: 'God has ninety-nine names, or one less than a hundred. He who learns them all will enter Paradise.'

In the Koran (7: 179), it is said: 'Most excellent titles [names] hath God: by these call ye on Him, and stand aloof from those who pervert his titles.'

The 'Great Name' is the unknown name to make up the 100. Knowledge of the Great Name of God

enables the knower to work miracles and it was thanks to this knowledge that Solomon bent demons to his will. It is the only one unknown of the 40,000 names borne by God. To discover it, one should burn a Koran, and it will be the only word left. Or else one should count the words in the Koran in reverse order, coupling the last with the first until one last word is left in the middle, and that will be the Great Name. If it is uttered in invocation, all one's wishes will be fulfilled.

(PELG p. 104)

It is said that Muhammad said that the name was to be found in the second, third or twentieth *sura*s, in which God is designated by the titles Living (*al-Haiy*), Self-sufficient (*al-Qaiyum*) or Him (*Hu*) (HUGD p. 220).

Because of the belief that it forces God to answer a prayer, the Great Name is endowed with magical properties. The enduring aim of sorcerers is therefore to discover it. Amulets and charms often bear the names of God.

This notion of an all-powerful name of the godhead, known only to a few initiates, is in all likelihood a Muslim borrowing from Judaism.

For a mystic such as El Būni, the Great Name was that of Man himself.

In the Celtic world name was closely joined to function. Names of individuals, of tribes, of towns or of places were always chosen by a druid with reference to peculiarities or remarkable events. Cùchulainn was originally called Setanta. He was given his new name by the druid Cathbad because, when he had killed a hound belonging to the blacksmith, Culann, he had proposed so fair an indemnity that all present, including both king and druid, had been astonished by it. Both in Gaul and in Ireland, a significant number of personal names are known which derive from the names of gods. From a very early period Celtic tradition, therefore, assigned a real identity between a person's name and his or her religious or social duties, or between name and appearance or behaviour.

narcissus Although open to dispute, the derivation of this word from Greek *narkē* (numbness) would help to explain the connection of this flower with the cults of the Underworld and with the initiation ceremonies associated with the worship of Demeter at Eleusis. Narcissi were planted on graves. They symbolize the numbness of death, but of a death which is perhaps no more than a sleep.

Wreaths of narcissi were offered to the Furies, who were believed to paralyse the guilty. The plant flowers in the Spring in damp places. This relates it to the symbolism of water and the seasonal cycle, and in consequence to fertility. This is the meaning of its ambivalence – death, sleep, rebirth.

In Asia, narcissi are symbols of good fortune and are given as New Year gifts.

In the Bible, narcissi, like lilies, characterize Spring and the end of the world (Song of Solomon 2: 1).

The flower also serves as a reminder, but at a lower level of symbolism, of that version of the myth of Narcissus in which he drowned in the pool in which he was complacently admiring his own beauty. This is why the moralists see him as the emblem of vanity, selfishness, self-love and self-satisfaction.

Persephone was drugged with the scent of narcissi when Hades, enraptured by love of her beauty, seized the girl and carried her off to the Underworld.

Because of its straight stalk, Arab poets see the narcissus as a symbol of the righteous man, the faithful servant and the pious man who tries to devote himself to God's service. The Greek myth is foreign to a view which deploys in so many poems all the metaphors evoked by the flower's graceful appearance and powerful scent.

navel See OMPHALOS.

Necessity

The eleventh card in the TAROT symbolizes will-power directed towards the realization of moral values. The will can be pointed in different directions. In the JUGGLER, it is concentrated to acquire internal balance; in the victorious Charioteer [see CHARIOT] it spreads out a dominant force projected into the astral plane; in the HERMIT it seeks the heights of mystical ecstasy. . . . In this eleventh card it is applied to moral cleansing, the foundation and support of all mystical, occult or magical practice. The Tarot, Necessity, is the symbol of moral purity and of the perfect innocence which in this state itself possesses the strength to give battle.

(RIJT p. 240)

A fair-haired young woman demonstrates the way to resolve the ambivalence of the WHEEL OF FORTUNE and shows us how to take control of any situation. Round her head she wears a blue and white ribbon embroidered with yellow, reminding us of the Juggler. With both flesh-coloured hands she holds open the jaws of a yellow lion, seen in profile. A long fold of her red cloak falls across her blue dress with white sleeves and lace. One of a pair with JUSTICE, she wears its opposite colours and matches those of the EMPEROR and the POPE, the red of power and activity overshadowing the blue of inward illumination. However, power in this context is no physical force, since the young woman seems to hold the lion's jaws open with her finger-tips. She conjures up no picture of Samson, David or Herakles (Hercules) since she exercises 'a feminine strength far more impossible to resist in its softness and subtlety than any outburst of rage or explosion of brute force' (WIRT p. 176). It would serve no useful purpose to kill the lion; what is required is to use its energy and strength since 'the initiate scorns nothing inferior and regards even the basest instincts as holy, since they provide the necessary spur to all action. . . . What is lowly should not be destroyed, but ennobled by transmutation, just as one attempts to raise lead to the dignity of gold' (WIRT p. 176). The symbolism is obvious at the psychological level, at which our will-power must control and use the forces of the unconscious to develop our personality.

'Necessity, or the Lion tamed by a Virgin, stands for moral strength, the confidence which masters any test, freedom of action, self-possession' (Tereschenko) . . . 'bringing the passions under control, success' (Wirth). In astrology it corresponds to the Eleventh House.

The contrast between the lion, an image of brute force, and the virgin, an image of spiritual strength, is transformed into a victory of spirit over flesh, and signifies not destruction but sublimation of the instincts.

Remembering that the figure eleven is of prime importance in initiation, both because it is the sum of three and eight (corresponding here to the Empress and to Justice) and because, using the Theosophical method of reduction, it equals two, it is hardly surprising to find the Female Pope (II) (see under POPE) under Necessity. Similarly, knowing that in order to find the origin and derivative of the card one has to take the third card immediately preceding and the third card immediately following it, we find that Necessity derives from Justice (VIII) and leads to Temperance (XIV), underlining the connection between these three cardinal virtues (Necessity standing for Moral Purpose). However, Necessity is the only card in the Tarot which has not got a complementary card, that is, one of which the number when added to its own produces the sum of twenty-two. This, surely, is a sign that in our struggle for self-control we are always on our own and we must redouble our efforts to be able to keep to our purpose.

neck The Likuba and Likuala of the Congo Basin regard the neck as the location of the principal JOINT in the human body through which procreative energy circulates. This joint is the first through which the new-born baby shows signs of life and it is the last through which the dying person does the same, as procreative energy retreats joint by joint (LEBM).

The Guarani Apapocuva Indians of Brazil locate the individual's animal soul in the neck. This governs individual temperament, gentleness coming from a butterfly's soul, cruelty from a jaguar's (METB).

The neck symbolizes the communication of soul with body.

Persian-Arabic love poems describe the neck in these five ways – as a camphor tree (from its scent and slender trunk), a candle, an ivory comb, a branch of blossom and a silver ingot, as in the verse: 'Whoever lays his hand upon my Turkish beauty's neck is seized with the yearning to possess this silver ingot' (HUAH p. 75).

These three examples, taken from three totally distinct cultures, show the neck to be among the select portions of the human anatomy, whether it be a sign of life, of the soul or of beauty.

necklace The symbolism of the necklace also includes that of chains of office and the collars of civil and military orders of chivalry as well as the collars put round the necks of prisoners, slaves and domestic animals. In general terms the necklace or collar symbolizes a bond between the wearer and whoever has given it to or forced it upon him or her. In this context it becomes an obligation or link, sometimes with erotic overtones.

In the cosmic and psychic sense, it symbolizes the reduction of the manifold to the one, a drive towards regulating and setting in order a more or less chaotic state of diversity. Conversely, to unstring a necklace is the same as destroying the established order and scattering what had been gathered together.

There was but one necklace in Celtic mythology and this was the necklace of the mythical judge, Morann, which had this property, that it would tighten around its owner's neck if ever he delivered a wrong verdict and grow loose when his verdict was just (OGAC 14: p. 338). In the traditional Chinese novel *Hsi-yu chi* (*Monkey*), when the Monkey King became a priest in the service of the gods, he wore a golden headband endowed with precisely the same properties.

nectar See AMBROSIA.

Neptune (for the god, see POSEIDON) In this article we treat only two interpretations of the astrological symbolism of this planet. In astrology Neptune embodies the principle of passive receptivity displayed equally in inspiration, intuition, mediumistic powers and paranormal faculties as in unworldliness, madness, aberration and irrational fears.

It is for this reason that his House is in the psychic sign of Pisces, which some have christened the Hospital of the Zodiac. This planet rules the subconscious and brings on mental illness, depression and neurosis. On the social plane, it has a marked influence upon Anarchism and its opposite number, Communism, upon irrational or surrealist movements and also upon the police. Under its influence, too, are gases, mainly the toxic ones, narcotics and radiation (including radiology, broadcasting and television). When first sighted by Le Verrier on 23 September 1846, Neptune was in the sign of Aquarius, which traditionally rules Russia; and the Soviet Union is supposed to have been particularly affected by its influence. The Soviet denial of present comfort for some future state of bliss, its sharp contrasts, propaganda, policies, foolhardy social and scientific experiments, its atheistic or religious mysticism, all were deeply tinged by Neptunian influence.

Throughout the wide gamut of all his different guises, whether like Titea he stands for primordial slime, First Matter, primeval waters or the dust of cosmic infinity and ultimate fusion, Neptune is the archetype of universal integration or dissolution. It may comprise lack of differentiation from the group, or attachment to some superior order, identification, contemplation, communion. This may devolve at one extreme into the twilight state of the comatose or the schizophrenic, afflicted with total confusion, unrestrained attachment and the incomprehensible blackness of ego and non-ego mingled together, and, at the other, into the saint's ecstasy or the yogi's *samādhi*, through the intermediate stages of clairvoyance, a sort of probing of the cosmic unconscious, prelogical thinking and surrealism. The Neptunian process is the expansion of awareness beyond the self, response to the soul-music of group, race or class; participation in the community, attachment to the rhythm of time, alignment with an infinity of cosmic subjectivity, becoming one with the universe so that all streams flow through one's own veins, all fires burn in one's own body, the hearts of all mankind beat in one's own and the star which twinkles within one revolves with all the galaxies.

net In Ancient Rome a class of gladiator, the *retiarius*, was armed with a net which he used to immobilize his opponent by entangling him in the meshes, thus placing him at his mercy. In psychology, this fearful weapon has become the symbol of those complexes which entangle the subject's internal and external life and the meshes of which it is so difficult to loosen and unravel.

In the Old Testament, too, nets are an expression of anguish: 'The sorrows [or snares] of death compassed me and the pains [or nets] of hell gat hold upon me: I found trouble and sorrow. Then I called upon the name of the Lord' (Psalm 116: 3–4).

In the Gospels, however, nets symbolize divine instrumentality which, after the Last Judgement, moves to gather up mankind to bring the just into the Kingdom of Heaven. This 'is like unto a net, that was cast into the sea, and gathered of every kind. Which, when it was full, they drew to shore, and sat down, and gathered the good into vessels, but cast the bad away. So shall it be at the end of the world' (Matthew 13: 47–9).

In oriental tradition, the gods, too, are provided with nets to catch men in their meshes, either to draw them to them or to bend them to their will. In these images analysts perceive symbols of trawling in the unconscious, anamnesis aimed to bring to the brink of the conscious, like fish from the depths of the sea, the most deeply repressed memories. The sky is sometimes compared with a net, the stars being the knots of its invisible meshes. This would mean that it is impossible to escape from this universe and from the laws which govern it.

In Persian tradition, the opposite takes place, and it is the mystic, especially, who arms himself with a net in an attempt to capture God. In some original writings and especially in the *Dawar-i-Dāmyārī*, the tradition of the Followers of the Truth, an Iranian Shi'ite sect, has richly embroidered upon this theme in a multitude of symbols unique in Iranian religious thought and Muslim tradition by their extent and originality.

Although nets as such were common features of Iranian folklore, of the heroic tales of the *ayyār* (roughly equivalent to the European romances of chivalry in the feudal era) as well as among urban story-tellers, a net becomes the spiritual weapon of Pir-Binyāmin, a manifestation of the Angel Gabriel and of Jesus Christ.

The *dam*, a weapon translated as 'net' or various associated forms such as the lasso, fishing-line, snare and so on, symbolizes a supernatural power with which Binyāmin is endowed. Following a covenant in eternity between God and his angels, this net was loaned to Binyāmin as the receptacle of divine forces, thus assigning him the role of divine huntsman.

The net also symbolizes all human capacity and potentiality in the person of Binyāmin, created by God before the world itself came into being, and representing primeval man dedicated to the sublimation of his being.

Given that the godhead is symbolized by a 'Royal Eagle', the 'net' is fated to trap this Eagle, that is to say to claim fulfilment of the divine promise which God embodies.

Although Binyāmin may be the particular owner of the net, the latter in itself alone symbolizes mankind's passionate search for the godhead. This quest, or mystical hunt, conjures up the image of a life-and-death struggle waged by mankind in the person of its intercessor, Binyāmin, and of the exertions without which the godhead would escape like the Royal Eagle flying away from the clumsy hunter. Whoever possesses the net – that is the individual who takes up this dangerous and difficult quest – is, like Binyāmin, alert to cast his net at the right moment. Nets may also be compared with the web in which spiders lurk for prey.

In all these symbolic images, when nets are regarded as holy things they are used as a means of entrapping a spiritual power (MOKC).

Nibelungen The heroes of Scandinavian and later of German mythology, these DWARFS were lords of the riches hidden underground and underwater, but thirsted for more gold and power, eager to be the masters of mankind and of the elements. Their lives enjoyed precarious and derisory happiness, since they dreamed always of establishing their empire by force and fraud, its structure doomed to speedy destruction. It was if they were obsessed with the need to humiliate, taunt, insult or domineer over all those bigger, stronger or richer than they. They symbolize the megalomania of petty minds with inflated ideas of their own capabilities and unbounded human ambition. They are like the forces of the unconscious which provoke an insatiable greed which finally leads to death. They also symbolize human ambitions doomed, like the universe itself, to inevitable annihilation.

After Siegfried's victory, the Burgundians were to despoil the Nibelungen of their wealth and take their name. And the saga was to begin all over again, since by taking their name the Burgundians took with it their ambitions and their doom as well.

niche The niche is a universal architectural symbol which very plainly conjures up a 'CAVERN, with the sky for its roof and the Earth for its floor', as the Chinese would say, its upper portion domed and its base horizontal. Niches are, above all else, where the divine presence is lodged, the 'abode of the gods' in Hindu phraseology. This is also their function in Christian basilicas, where the apse is shaped like a niche as, indeed, it is in most later churches. Porches of medieval cathedrals, too, were niches, defining another aspect of cavern symbolism, that of gateway or passage. The *mihrāb* in a Muslim mosque is a perfect example of the niche, since it, too, is the place where the godhead, symbolized by a lamp, is present. 'His light is like a niche in which a lamp is set', says the Koran. However, the primary role of the niche – both symbolic and actual – is to re-echo the words uttered in front of it. It is the Word of God which is thus reflected and revealed to the world, perfectly defining the essential aspect of the Divine Presence (BURA, KRAA).

In so far as the top of the niche follows the lines of the bowl of an upturned chalice, its symbolism may be likened to that of the HALO, as Champeaux and Sterckx have likened that of the archway. 'The lines of an archway are none other than the perfect outline of the person wearing a halo. They apply with special force to the saint who has attained to the assumption of the flesh by the spirit, and who has actualized the mystery of divine in-dwelling symbolized by the stone-built church' (CHAS p. 270).

night The Greeks regarded Night (Nyx) as the daughter of Chaos and mother of the Sky (Ouranos) and the Earth (Gaia). Night also gave birth to death, dreams, sleep, vexation, friendship and deceit. The gods often lengthened nights by halting Sun and Moon, so as the better to achieve their ends. Night moves across the sky, veiled in darkness on a chariot drawn by four BLACK horses and followed by a retinue of maidens, Fates and Furies. The sacrifice to this Underworld goddess was a black ewe-lamb.

The Maya used the same hieroglyphic to mean night, the Underworld and death (THOH).

In the Celtic conception of time, as the year began with Winter, so night began each day. In Ireland the period of 'a night and a day' legally defined twenty-four hours, and, symbolically, eternity. The Welsh for 'week' is *wythnos* (eight nights) and the concept survives in 'fortnight' in English, although 'sennight' (week) is obsolete. The period of the 'three nights of Samain' in Irish calendars is found word for word in the Gaulish calendar from Coligny. Caesar states that the Gauls reckoned time by nights (OGAC 9: pp. 337ff.; 18: pp. 136ff.).

Night symbolizes the period of gestation, germination or conspiracy which will burst out into life in broad daylight. It is endowed with every potentiality of being, but to go into the night is to return to a state of indeterminacy and intermingle with nightmares, monsters and 'black thoughts'. Night is the image of the unconscious and, in the darkness of sleep, the unconscious is set free. Like all symbols, night displays a twofold aspect – that of the shadowy world of the brooding future, and that of the prelude to daylight when the light of life will shine forth.

In mystical theology, Night symbolizes the disappearance of all knowledge which may be defined, analysed or expressed and, further still, the state of being deprived of all proof and psychological support. With such other terms as 'obscurity', Night applies to the wiping clean of the intellect, 'emptiness' or 'nakedness' applies to that of the memory and 'dryness' or 'aridity' to that of all longings, sensual emotions and even the highest aspirations.

nightingale Nightingales are universally esteemed for their perfect songs. According to Plato, the nightingale was the emblem of the ancient Thracian bard, Thamyris.

The bird is especially respected in Japan, where its song is regarded as repeating the title of the Lotus Sutra, the *Hokkekyo*, so cherished by the Tendai sect (OGRJ).

In *Romeo and Juliet* (III: v) the nightingale is contrasted with the lark: as the songster of love in the enclosing darkness with the songster of dawn and parting. If the two lovers listen to the nightingale they will remain together but in danger of death; if they trust the lark they will save their lives, but will have to part.

By the beauty of its song, which enthralls the listening darkness, the nightingale is the magician who makes his hearers oblivious of the dangers of the day.

All poets make the nightingale the songster of love, but the bird most strikingly displays by the feelings which it arouses the close link between love and death (cf. Keats's 'Ode to a Nightingale').

nightjar The Montagnards of southern Vietnam call the nightjar 'the black-smith-bird' and compare its call with the blow of hammer on anvil. The bird is in fact the patron of smiths and forges the AXES of the thunder. By dreaming of the nightjar one can master the art of ironworking (DANA, KEMR).

nimbus See HALO.

nine In Homer, nine possesses ritual properties. Demeter wandered through the world for nine days in search of her daughter Persephone; Leto suffered the pains of childbirth for nine days and nights and the Nine Muses were the fruits of nine nights of Zeus' love-making. Nine would seem to be the mean for gestation and successful search and to symbolize the successful outcome of exertion and the fulfilment of creation.

The Pseudo-Dionysius the Areopagite classifies angels in nine choirs, or three triads – perfection of perfection, order in order and unity in unity.

Each world – Heaven, Earth and Hell – is symbolized by the ternary figure of a triangle. Nine is the totality of the three worlds.

Nine is the number of the celestial spheres and, in counterpoise, of the circles of Hell. This is why there are nine joints on the Taoist bamboo and nine (or seven) notches on the Siberian axial birch-tree. This is also why there were nine steps up to the Chinese imperial throne and nine gates shutting it off from the external world, since the microcosm was an image of Heaven. In contrast with the Nine Heavens were the Nine Springs, the abode of the dead. Buddhists also believe in nine Heavens, but the *Huai Nan Tzu* says that the Chinese Heaven comprises nine plains and 9999 corners. Under the Han Dynasty, the number nine was the foundation of most Taoist ceremony. Nine is the number of fulfilment: nine is the number of *yang*. This is why Yu's cauldrons were nine in number and why alchemical cinnabar had to be transmuted nine times before it could be drunk.

Nine was also the Chinese spatial standard, being the square of *lo-chu*, the number of regions from which the nine shepherds brought the metal from which the nine cauldrons were cast. In times past, China numbered eighteen provinces – twice nine – but according to Ssu Ma Ch'ien she occupied one eighty-first of the world. In the myth of Huang Ti, Ch'eyu is not one, but either seventy-two or eighty-one, expressing the totality of a guild, and it is no accident that the *Tao Te Ching* should comprise eighty-one, or nine times nine, chapters.

If Dante, like all others, regards nine as the number of Heaven, it is also Beatrice's number and she herself is a symbol of love (GRAP, GUED).

For Muslim esoterics, to walk down nine steps without falling means that their nine senses have been tamed. Nine is also the number which corresponds with the apertures in the human body and symbolizes for the esoteric the channels of communication with the world.

Among the Aztecs, the Texcoco king, Nezahualcoyotl, built a temple with nine storeys to match the nine Heavens or the nine stages through

which the soul must go to reach eternal rest. It was dedicated to 'the Unknown God, creator of all things, who is close to us', the god through whom
we live and move (MYTF p. 187). In Central American mythology, the
number nine symbolizes the nine Heavens over which the Sun climbs. On
the other hand, nine is also the number sacred to the Moon-goddess. In
Maya hieroglyphics, Bolon Tiku, Goddess Nine, is the goddess of the full
Moon (GIRP p. 309).

The Aztecs regarded nine as being the number specifically symbolic of
things earthly and nocturnal. Hell comprises nine plains and the Aztec
pantheon included nine gods of darkness ruled by the god of Hell, his name
coming fifth in their list, that is, in the middle of the eight others. In most
other American Indian cosmogonies there are also nine Underworlds. The
Maya belief was the opposite to this, nine being considered a lucky number,
especially useful in magic and medicine (THOH). The serpent was the god
of the ninth day and also ruled the thirteenth. However, Aztec commoners
believed that nine was a number to be feared because of its connections
with the deities of night, Hell and death.

The number nine played a leading part both in the mythology and in the
shamanistic practices of Mongolo-Turkic tribes. Belief in the nine layers of
Heaven was often coupled with that in the nine sons or servants of God,
corresponding, according to Goncharov, to the nine stars worshipped by
the Mongols. The Chuvash, on the Volga, set their gods in groups of nine,
following rites of sacrifice often including nine priests offering sacrifice,
nine victims, nine chalices and so on. Pagan Cheremis offered the Sky-God
nine loaves of bread and nine goblets of mead and the Yakut, too, set nine
goblets of mead on their sacrificial altars. 'By way of comparison, we would
mention that, according to Masmoudi, in Syria the Sabeans had nine colleges
of priests corresponding to the nine celestial circles' (HARA pp. 117–18).

According to René Allendy (ALLN pp. 256ff.) the number nine was seen
as 'the complete number in the last analysis'. It is the symbol of the manifold returning to the one and, by extension, that of cosmic solidarity and
redemption. 'Every number, no matter what it may be, as Avicenna said,
is none other than the number nine or its multiple, with one exception,
since the figures for numbers comprise nine different shapes and values
together with nought.' The Ancient Egyptians called nine 'the Mountain of
the Sun':

Their Grand Ennead derived from the development in the three worlds, divine,
natural and intellectual, of the archetypal trinity of Osiris, Isis and Horus, standing
for Essence, Substance and Life. The Alexandrian Platonists also perceived a
triple division within this primeval trinity of deities to form nine principles.
Christian architects eagerly sought to give expression to the number nine, the
sanctuary of the church at Paray-le-Monial in France, for example, being lit by
nine windows.

Nine universal principles are also to be found in the teachings of the
oldest school of Indian philosophy, the Vaisheshika. Orphic initiation would
similarly seem to have accepted three triads of principles, 'the first comprising Night, Sky and Time; the second, Air, Light and the Stars; and the third,
Sun, Moon and Nature, these nine principles making up the nine symbolic

aspects of the Universe. Parmenides stated that the number nine related to absolutes.' The nine Muses stood for the sum of human knowledge as represented by the sciences and the arts. Liturgically a novena stands for 'something fulfilled, a complete time-span'. Zoroastrianism, too, had its novenas; they recur in the Zend Avesta where many rituals of purification comprise the triple repetition of a triad of ceremony. Thus the shrouds of the dead should be washed nine times, three times with urine, three times with earth and three times with water. Such three times threefold repetition recurs in many rituals of magic and sorcery.

Since THREE is the number of innovation, its square stands for universality. It is significant that, in so many folktales drawn from all over the world, the supernumerary, infinity, is expressed by such repetitions of the number nine as the 999,999 Fravashis who, the Ancient Iranians believed, watched over the semen of Zoroaster, from which all prophets were to spring. The OUROBOROS, the serpent which bites its own tail and the image of the return of the manifold to the one and hence of primeval and of final Oneness, is related graphically to the way the number nine is denoted in many alphabets such as the Tibetan, Persian, Egyptian hieratic, Armenian and so on. The mystical meaning of nine relates it, too, to what the Sufis term *haqq*, the final stage of the Way, bliss leading to *fanā*, the annihilation of the individual in the rediscovery of the whole, or, as Allendy has it, 'the loss of personality in universal love'. Indian tradition defines more clearly the redemptive meaning of the symbol nine through the nine successive incarnations of Vishnu who, each time, offered his life for the salvation of mankind. Similarly, according to the Gospels, Jesus was crucified at the third hour; his death agonies began at the sixth hour (dusk), and he died at the ninth hour. Claude de Saint-Martin considered that in nine 'the physical body and all its properties were annihilated'. Allendy concludes that Freemasons have made it 'the eternal number of immortality, nine masters discovering the grave and body of Hiram.' In Masonic symbolism

the written shape of the number nine stands for a downward and therefore material germination, while by contrast the figure six represents an upward, and therefore spiritual germination. Both numbers form the start of a spiral. On the human level, nine is, in fact, the number of months needed for the foetus to attain birth size, although completely formed by the seventh month. (It may also be observed that six was the number for the fulfilment of Creation which culminated in the creation of man on the sixth day.)

(BOUM p. 227)

The number nine often recurs in the world picture painted by Hesiod's *Theogony*. Nine days and nights is the space of time between Heaven and Earth and Earth and Hell (720–5). Similarly Gods were punished for their perjury by being banished for 'nine full years' from Olympus where they kept council and feasted (60–1).

Nine being the last of a series of figures heralds both an end and a fresh beginning, that is to say, a removal to a new plane. This notion of rebirth and germination in association with that of death is, as we have shown, recurrent in the concepts of symbolic properties of the number held in several different cultures. As the last of the numbers in the manifested universe, it starts the phase of transmutations. It gives expression to the end of a cycle, the completion of a journey, the tying of a knot.

It is in this sense that we may explain both the title and the arrangement of the writings of Plotinus, such as they were handed down by his disciples and by Porphyry in particular, under Pythagorean influence. The *Enneads* (groups of nine) comprise fifty-four short tracts, somewhat arbitrarily arranged, but equalling the product of six times nine – two numbers, each of which is a multiple of three and both of which emphasize the symbolism of three. Porphyry was delighted 'to find that this was the product of the perfect number, six, multiplied by nine.' This numerological arrangement helps to symbolize the master's teaching as a complete, cosmic, human and theological vision from the beginning of time to the end of the world. The universal knot is tied when the emanation of the One returns. By their title alone, the *Enneads* comprise the global manifesto of a school of philosophy and a vision of the world.

Nirvana   A Sanskrit word (privative *nir* + radical *va*, 'to breathe'), its literal meaning denoting extinction by loss of breath in the sense of achieving ultimate peace. This is not a return to nothingness, but rather the extinction of the Ego within the Self, whether the latter be the Brahman of Hinduism or the Buddha. The word is in no sense negative, except in relation to the cycles of rebirth, but has a very positive meaning.

In this respect it is in sharp contrast with SAMSARA. A Tantrist writer describes the two conditions corresponding to them:

Samsāra, said the bearer of the VAJRA, is the spirit darkened and afflicted by countless figments of the mind, flickering like the lightning in the storm and indelibly stained by attachment to the world and other passions. Nirvana is best and brightest and free from all figments of the mind and cleansed from all stain of attachment to the world and other passions. . . . Its essence is almighty. Nothing is beyond it. . . . Nothing other than it exists for those who yearn for release and long for the disappearance of endless pain and the attainment of the bliss of enlightenment . . .

(SILB p. 307)

The Tree of EMPTINESS leads to Nirvana, which is sometimes described, or rather suggested, by the Sutras as 'the intuitive vision of the world as it really is. . . . As a result of inverting the cluster of sensory phenomena and the awareness which identifies them, that mystical Knowledge of the inner life is achieved which is the property of the Tathāgata or disciple who has attained to the state of a Buddha.' Nirvana is symbolized in the image of the Moon shining out after the wind has blown the clouds away.

north (see also CARDINAL POINTS)   According to the book *Bahir*, north is the abode of evil; and Satan, the principle of temptation and of evil, comes from the north. In the Old Testament we read: 'Out of the north an evil shall break forth upon all the inhabitants of the land' (Jeremiah 1: 14). Destruction was to come from the north (ibid. 46: 20). The north wind was regarded as a destroying wind.

Its destructive powers were of the symbolic order. Jeremiah saw 'a seething pot; and the face thereof [was] toward the north' (ibid. 1: 13). The pot symbolizes the source of a revelation, but that revelation is not of Yahweh.

Jeremiah's god pronounces sentence upon the kingdoms of the north whence come unrighteousness and idolatry.

By contrast the Greeks looked to the Hyperboreans for wisdom. However, the prophet's north is not the north of Greek mythology and the two revelations and the two wisdoms are, in any case, very different things.

nose Like the eyes, the nose is a symbol of clairvoyance, perspicacity and discernment, but intuitive rather than rational.

In Black Africa many of the powders used to establish contact with the spirits, souls and invisible forces are prepared from dogs' noses or pigs' snouts (FOUC).

Similarly the Sudanese use for the same purpose the snouts of hyenas, in the light of the creature's unrivalled sense of smell.

The Bambara regard the nose, together with the legs, sexual organs and tongue, as one of a band of four 'workers'. As the organ of smell which separates the pleasant from the unpleasant, it directs desires and speech, points the legs in the right line of march and complements the activities of the three other workers responsible for the efficient or inefficient functioning of the group as a whole (ZAHB).

Yakut, Tungus and many hunter-tribes in Siberia and the Altai region set aside the snouts of fox and sable, since 'this is where the creature's soul is hidden' (HARA p. 292). Chukchi kept the snouts of wild animals, believing that they guarded their homes. Gilyak cut off seals' snouts, and similar customs are to be found in other Finno-Ugrian tribes. In the nineteenth century the Lapps used to skin the bear's snout and 'the man who had cut off the bear's head, wrapped his own face in the skin.' In Finland a similar custom related to hares. The meaning of these customs is explained in a Finnish song which speaks of taking the bear's snout to acquire its sense of smell. Hunter-tribes observe similar customs in connection with the eyes of their game, the Sagay removing the bear's eyes so that he will no longer be able to see a man.

In Japan the proud and boastful are supposed to have long noses and are called *tengu*. *Tengu* are evil spirits depicted as mountain demons with long noses or greedy beaks.

numbers (see also ZERO; ONE; TWO; THREE; FOUR; FIVE; SIX; SEVEN; EIGHT; NINE; TEN; ELEVEN; TWELVE; THIRTEEN; SEVENTEEN; TWENTY; TWENTY-ONE; TWENTY-FOUR; THIRTY-SIX; FORTY; HUNDRED; THOUSAND; TEN THOUSAND) One should perhaps emphasize here more than anywhere that philosophical or mathematical notions regarding numbers have no place in this work, which attempts to deal purely with symbols and not to act as a substitute for general or specialized dictionaries.

From earliest times numbers, seemingly used simply for counting, have been the favourite foundation for elaborate symbolization. They not only express quantity, but ideas and powers as well. Since the traditional mind does not admit of the operation of pure chance, the numbers of things or actions themselves possess great importance, and sometimes simply by themselves allow a true understanding of existence or causality to be attained. Each number possesses its own individuality and in this context we have listed above those which we have described for their own particular properties.

Numerology is one of the oldest sciences of symbols. Plato called it 'the highest level of knowledge' and the essence of cosmic and inward harmony, while Pythagoras and Boethius regarded it as one, at least, of the instruments of the latter. Traces of it are to be found in China in the *I Ching*; the *Li Tzu* (ch. 8) recounts the tale of the 'Master of Numbers', while the historian P'an Ku derives the science from the families of Hi and Ho of the Ming-t'ang in the days of the Emperor Yao. Others attribute its discovery to Huang Ti himself, representative of primeval tradition.

The Chinese, especially, regarded numerology as the key to the harmony of the microcosm and macrocosm and of their empire with the laws of Heaven. Pythagoreans were perfectly familiar with the notion of cosmic rhythms in relation to numerology, as it was associated in one way or another with MUSIC and architecture – hence the use in the latter of the celebrated Golden Number, which had been recognized as providing the key to proportion in living creatures. However, these are merely practical applications of higher principles, since Boethius assures us that ultimate knowledge is conveyed in numbers and Nicholas of Cusa that numbers are the best way to approach Divine Truth. 'Numbers rule all things', Iamblichus quotes Pythagoras as saying.

'Numbers', said de Saint-Martin, 'are the outer shell of beings.' They not only govern their physical harmony and the laws of space, time and life, but also relations with the First Cause. It is not, however, a matter of simple 'arithmetical expressions', but of 'principles co-eternal with Truth'. They are ideal, and they are properties, not quantities. Geometry did not apply to the measurement of space, but to the harmony of forms; astronomy did not simply study distance, weight or weather, but the rhythms of the universe. Created beings are themselves numbers, since they derive from the One and First Cause. They return to this First Cause as numbers return to unity. 'God', Angelus Silesius wrote, 'is in all things as unity is in all numbers.' (BURA, BENA, GRAP, SAIR).

Numbers need to be handled with care since they conceal a hidden power. In Fulani tradition, numbers are the bait which attracts the mysterious. They are produced by word and sign and yet their essence is more mysterious than their components. Thus one never mentions 'the numbers of one's children, cattle or wives, any more than one's age, if one knows it.' On the other hand, the individual is perfectly ready to enumerate things which do not affect him or her directly, being lessons, motifs or symbols to be explained. The reason for this derives from animism. Like names, when numbers are uttered they release forces which start to flow like some underground stream, alive but unseen. Uttering a name or number which is yours, gives a hold over you, the proof being 'that if a stranger utters your name when he is calling somebody else with the same name, it upsets you. It is this current which has affected you since he has touched no part of your body.' The spoken word has always influenced human beings, but while the power of words may be great, the power of numbers is even greater. Words may explain the sign, but numbers are its hidden root, since they are the product of sign and sound and therefore both more powerful and more mysterious (HAMK p. 56).

Aztec thought also clothed numbers with cosmic significance. Each of them was associated with a particular god, colour and point of the compass, as well as with a group of good or evil influences.

Generally speaking, multiples of any given number have the same basic symbolic significance as the number itself. However, they can either stress and accentuate this significance, or else give it a special accentuation which must be sought out in each instance.

Some believe that each number tends to generate the number immediately above it, one generating two, two generating three and so on, because each of them is driven to step outside its own bounds. Others, however, hold that this is because they need an opponent or a partner. Numbers are thus endowed with the motives of living beings.

nut-tree (see also HAZEL; WALNUT) All insular Celtic writers regarded the lexicographically confused nut-tree, service-tree and hazel (*coll*) as trees with a magical character. As such, they were often used by druids and bards as aids to incantation, the most noteworthy being cutting *ogham*, or magic writing, on their wood. In this context, the nut-tree was the associate of yew and birch, and the nut itself often enough the fruit of knowledge. One of the mythical kings of Ireland was called MacGuill, 'Son of the Hazel-tree'.

The nut-tree is also a symbol of perseverance in the development of mystical experience, since it keeps one waiting for its fruits.

nymphs These deities of streams, springs and fountains – Nereids, Naiads, Oceanides – were sisters of Thetis. They gave birth to heroes and brought them up. They also lived in caverns and watery places, and hence share a terrifying, chthonian aspect, all birth being related to death and vice versa. In the development of the personality they represent an expression of the female aspect of the unconscious. Deities of birth, and especially of those born to heroic deeds, their worship was not untinged with fear. They stole children away and troubled the spirits of those to whom they revealed themselves.

The middle of the day was the moment when the nymphs manifested themselves. Whoever saw them became seized with a nympholeptic mania .... That is why it was advisable, at midday, not to go near fountains or springs, or the shadow of certain trees. Later superstition had it that a prophetic madness would seize anyone who saw a form emerging from the water ... the ambivalent feeling of fear and attraction ... the 'fascination' of the nymphs [which] brings madness, the destruction of personality.

(ELIT p. 205)

They symbolize the lure of heroic madness which manifests itself in warlike or erotic feats of all descriptions.

O

o The letter 'o' is one of the most widely used alchemical symbols, as shown in the accompanying table, based upon that given by Dom A.-J. Pernéty in his *Dictionnaire mytho-hermétique* of 1787. Note particularly the way the symbols for 'night' and 'day', and 'purification' and 'sublimation' are inverted.

ȣ	Alkaline salt	☿	Mercury
o	Alum	☿ precipitate	Mercury precipitate
♁	Antimony	☿ sublimate	Mercury sublimate
o–o	Arsenic	℞℞	Night
8	Arsenic	⊕	Nitre
‡	Black sulphur	✚	Oil
♁	Cinnabar	∘°	Oil
⊖	Common salt	‡	Powder
♀	Copper, Venus	℞℞	Purify
♀	Copper calcinate	☿	Quicksilver or Mercury
♂	Crocus of iron	♂	Red arsenic
♉	Day	♋	Red arsenic
8	Digest	o–	Salammoniac
℞	Double salt	⊶	Spirit
⊙	Feu de roue	♋	Sublimate
o⊣	Glass	⊕	Verdigris
⊙	Gold or sun	⊕	Vitriol
♂	Iron, steel or Mars	⊖	Vitriol
♋	Lodestone	✧	Wax
♂	Mars	⊶	Yellow arsenic

oak In many traditions the oak was a sacred tree to which the privileges of the supreme sky-god were attributed, doubtless because it attracts lightning and is symbolic of kingship. Oaks were dedicated to Zeus at Dodona, to Capitoline Jove in Rome, to Ramow in Prussia and to Perun among the Slavs. Herakles' (Hercules') club was made of oak. It is an especial indicator of strength, power, longevity and height in both the spiritual and the material senses of the words.

In all ages and among all peoples the oak has been synonymous with strength, the overwhelming impression made by the fully grown tree. Furthermore, in Latin the same word, *robur*, is used for both 'oak' and 'strength' and it may as easily symbolize moral as physical strength.

Among both Greeks and Celts the oak was the prime representative of the World AXIS or Tree, and the same is true of the Yakut in Siberia.

It should further be observed that both at Sichem and at Hebron Abraham received the divine revelation in an oak grove. Here again, therefore, the tree played its axial role as a channel of communication between Heaven and Earth (GUEM). In Homer, Odysseus on his return went twice to Dodona 'to hear the will of Zeus from the high-crested oak of the god' (*Odyssey* 14: 327; 19: 296). The Golden Fleece, guarded by a dragon, hung from an oak-tree, the latter having the properties of a temple.

Pliny the Elder drew a comparison between the Greek word for oak (*drus*) and the word 'druid'; in consequence druids were called 'oak-men', an etymological relationship which has often managed to slip into works of modern scholarship. However, all Celtic languages have a different word for 'oak', including the Gaulish *dervo*. Nonetheless, this is a valid symbolic relationship in the sense that the druids' priestly quality entitled them to both wisdom and strength and the oak symbolizes both these properties (OGAC 12: pp. 48–50; 18: pp. 111–14). The oak was worshipped by the Celts, for whom its trunk, knotty branches, thick foliage and the symbolism it possessed, made it the emblem of hospitality and the equivalent of a temple.

oath See BLOOD-BROTHERHOOD.

obsidian A very hard, dark green, volcanic rock, most commonly found in desert regions or their vicinity. When polished, it is extraordinarily beautiful and it was much used by Ancient Egyptian sculptors. In pre-Hellenic times, obsidian chips were used as scrapers, knives and spear-heads. Towards the end of the Bronze Age, this metal replaced obsidian. The STONE's symbolism is closely related to that of flint.

The blades of sacrificial knives were originally made of flint – or obsidian – and the stone has preserved its 'white' magical property among Central American Indians. It preserves against 'black' magic and drives evil spirits away.

The Ancient Mexicans regarded flint as being associated with cold, darkness, the kingdom of the dead and the north. 'Flint' years were ruled by this symbolism and brought with them drought and famine. Mayan hieroglyphs substitute a hand for the flint. In Mexico the deified flint was the son of the goddess of the primeval man and woman, who presided over all creation (SOUM, THOH).

The association of contrasting functions in the same symbol is illustrated by the Aztec practice of healing cuts by covering them with a salve containing powdered obsidian (SOUA p. 196). Having the power to cut open human flesh, obsidian also had the power of knitting it together again.

ocean See SEA.

octagon Baptismal fonts are often supported by EIGHT pillars rising from an octagonal base. The octagon symbolizes resurrection, while the HEXAGON stands for death in the Christian symbolism which St Ambrose inherited from Classical antiquity. An octagon conjures up 'the eternal life which the neophyte acquires when dipped in the baptismal font' (BRIL p. 208). The hexagonal shape which is sometimes adopted stresses another aspect of baptism, the burial in its grave of the sinful creature as a prelude to its rebirth into a state of grace.

octopus   This shapeless, tentacled creature stands significantly for the monsters who regularly symbolize the spirits of the Underworld and even Hell itself.

The octopus was a decorative motif in northern Europe from the Greek world to that of the Celts, which might help to account for its Hyperborean origins. The octopus corresponds to the zodiacal sign of Cancer and is opposed to the dolphin. This identification is not unrelated to the creature's 'infernal' aspect, the Summer solstice being the gate of the Underworld (GUES, SCHC).

Odin   See WOTAN.

Oedipus   The legendary hero of Greek tragedy has provided a mainstay of modern psychoanalysis – the Oedipus complex.

His father, Laios, was warned that if he had a son that son would kill him. Accordingly, at birth he had Oedipus' ankles pierced and bound to a strap, hence the name 'swell-foot' (Oedipus). The servant who should have left him exposed to die gave him to strangers – some legends say they were kings, others shepherds – who reared the child. As a man, he was travelling to Delphi when he met Laios in a narrow gorge and, because he would not give way, killed him, not knowing that he was his father. Thus, in his ignorance, he fulfilled the oracle. On the road to Thebes he met the SPHINX, a monster laying the country waste. Having killed it, he was made king and given Laios' widow and his own mother, Jocasta, in marriage. Through the cryptic oracles delivered by the soothsayer, Tiresias, Oedipus learned that he had killed his father and married his mother. Jocasta committed suicide and Oedipus tore out his own eyes.

We all know what the Freudians have made of this situation by applying it in general terms to make it typical of relations between parents and children. The dual tendency, with countless variations, of erotic fixation which the child has for the parent of the opposite sex, and the aggressive hostility felt for the parent of the same sex, has to be overcome if the individual is to achieve maturity.

Paul Diel's explanation, based upon careful examination of all of its details, has, however, brought fresh life to the legend. 'The cutting of the baby Oedipus' tendons symbolizes a lessening of the resources of his soul, a handicap to the psyche, which was to be characteristic of the hero throughout his life.' In fact, the FOOT in many traditions

serves as an image of the soul, its condition and its fate. Thus, in myth, the way in which a person walks is compared with the behaviour of that person's psyche ... (the vulnerability of Achilles' heel symbolized the vulnerability of his soul, his proneness to anger, the cause of his doom), while in the quest of the Golden Fleece, Jason's unshod foot made him lame. ... Now the person with a lame psyche is the neurotic. Oedipus is the symbol of the individual wavering between the neurotic and the commonplace. He overcompensates for his inferiority (his wounded soul) by actively seeking a domineering superiority. But his outward success was to become the reason for his inner defeat.

The legend contains another symbol – the narrow gorge in which Laios was killed. Now, 'like all other cavities (dragon's cave, Hell and so on), a sunken road is a symbol of the subconscious.' The road down which Oedipius met his father therefore, was rooted in the subconscious, and it is in the subconscious that its meaning must be sought. It stands for 'the murderous conflict which tears the soul of the handicapped. The ambivalence between wounded vanity and vanity triumphant.' Although Oedipus may have defeated his father he did not escape from his own vanity.

If the part played by his mother, Jocasta, is explained symbolically, it may be said that to marry one's mother is 'to become synonymous with over-attachment to earthly things'. Oedipus exaggerates his physical cravings, becomes their prisoner and his life becomes commonplace. When at last the revelation burst upon him that he has killed his father and married his mother, he does not accept responsibility for it, he rejects it and tears out his eyes.

In this gesture he displays his paroxysmal despair, but at the same time it is a symbol of his ultimate refusal to see. He is blinded by looking inside himself. Guilt is repressed instead of being sublimated and panic-stricken remorse is not allowed to become redemptive penitence. The blindness of self-love is total, inner light is put out and the spirit is dead.

At this point his daughter, ANTIGONE, comes on the scene, takes him by the hand and leads him to the shrine of the Eumenides at Colonos, where Oedipus dies. This last scene signifies that he has at last found peace in a proper understanding of his sin and in knowledge and acceptance of himself and of his fate. 'Symbol of the human soul and of its conflicts, of the neurotic overwhelmed yet able to recover from his neuroses, Oedipus is brought down by his weaknesses, but draws strength from the very fall to rise up once more and, in the end, to stand forth as the conquering hero' (DIES pp. 149–70). Oedipus epitomizes 'the complete span of the neurotic's psyche and of his neuroses, of the neurotic creature of impulse who only achieves self-mastery in the acceptance of death.'

office Office symbolizes order in life and society and directed movement. In the sociological system devised by Dumézil, Indo-European society is divided into three classes which, between them, include all potential activities of body or mind. Proof of the existence of this tripartite division comes from a comparison of the data provided by the Hindu system (which hardened into the CASTE system) and with Indo-European systems in general (Roman, Germanic, Celtic and so on). The first class is priestly (Brahmans), the second warrior (Kshatriyas) and the third mercantile or artisanal (Vaishyas), and there is an echo of this under the French monarchy in the divisions of Clergy, Nobility and Third Estate (the English Lords Spiritual, Lords Temporal and Commons). Celtic society was based upon a very archaic tradition and reserved the highest prestige for the first two offices, those of priest and warrior. Within the priestly class were numbered all druids, poets, seers, healers, historians and judges, while the warrior class comprised all those of noble birth and free men who owned cattle. The third office seems to have been filled only by craftsmen, smiths and wood- and textile-workers who, in Gaul at least, were both wealthy and active. No place was to be found for those who tilled the soil, nor is there any sign that a mercantile middle class existed like the Vaishyas in India. The common folk linked to the land did not count: they had no official place, like Untouchables and outcasts in India.

As defined in Ireland, non-gods were tillers of the soil and gods were all those with either an intellectual or a manual skill. This is the concept of society belonging to nomadic warriors and herdsmen, ruled by an all-powerful priesthood. However, there would seem to have been local variations. In India, for example, the office of the healer-gods, or Ashvins, belonged to the third category. In Ireland, women were free to enter the first or second class and similarly in Gaul there were instances of female druids and seers. In Ireland, too, free women owed military service. At the top of the hierarchy, the god Lug, master of many crafts, transcended the three offices. In the epic, *The Battle of Mag Tuired*, he explains that when he came to Tara he was at one and the same time druid, warrior and craftsman, the master of all intellectual and manual skills. Any connection, however, with tilling the soil is the result either of a later and generally Christian and hagiographic interpolation or of failure to understand something handed down by tradition. The god–druid, or the Dagda, was therefore never a tiller of the soil except by subsequently being relegated from God to King of the Tuatha Dé Danann and by the latter taking refuge underground when the Irish arrived and retaining the magical power of providing dearth or plenty of corn and milk. By methodical and sensible correlation of this system of offices, basic traditional data can often be identified or more conveniently classified. Iconographic symbols are related to these different offices (DUMI; OGAC 12: pp. 349–82).

A Celtic king would receive tribute, but would then make sure that it was fairly apportioned among all his subjects. His office was to apportion and distribute. As the intermediary between the priestly class, which closely scrutinized his activities, and the warrior class from which he was sprung, the king was also a pledge of continuing social cohesion. In this context, it was his office to ensure that productive tasks were properly performed by those responsible for them. In this sense Celtic kings were generally responsible for the fruitfulness and fertility of soil, animals and women. However, they did not assume personal responsibility for that fertility, but oversaw it, and the Celtic world does not appear to have had any symbolism specific to that office. The king's role of apportioning and distributing covered every field of human activity, since he was also both judge and warrior. He was present on the battlefield, but took no part in the fighting, his presence being indispensable for victory (OGAC 4: p. 245; 10: p. 307).

ogre The ogres of folktale are reminiscent of Giants, Titans or CRONOS. They symbolize blind and greedy force. Ogres need their daily ration of fresh meat and a Hop o' my Thumb (see THUMB) easily tricks them into eating their own daughters.

Perhaps ogres are an image of self-begetting, self-destroying time; or exaggerated caricatures of the father anxious to preserve his dictatorial power indefinitely, unable to bear the thought of sharing it or giving it up, and readier to see his children die rather than grow up and one day take his role from him. While ogres may perhaps be distorted and aberrant father-figures, used to frighten children, they are also images of the state, of taxation, tyranny and war.

The ogre symbol is therefore connected with that of the MONSTER which swallows and regurgitates its victims in a metamorphosis from which they emerge transfigured. In the context of Cronos and monsters, the image of the ogre may be classified with the traditional myth of time and death:

All that is derived from physical birth serves momentarily to sustain the Immortal Spirit, but is doomed to annihilation. Only through the co-operation of Time was Earth enabled to give birth to the visible shapes of the universe on the six planes of physical life, but it is Time's task to undo this work. Time is half the fate of forms, unless the Immortal Spirit snatches up one of his creations to make it immortal. It was thus that Cybele managed to save some of her children whom she made gods.

(LOEF pp. 165–6)

oil   The use of oil in ritual and in sacrifice is characteristic of the peoples of the Mediterranean Basin and of the Near (or Middle) East, or, to be more precise, of all social groups in which the OLIVE-TREE, because it provides both food and light, is especially highly regarded. Directly deriving from this twofold use, oil is at once a symbol of purity and light as well as of prosperity.

In North Africa and once, it would seem, in the traditions of all Mediterranean peoples, women poured oil over altars of undressed stone and men oiled their PLOUGH-shares before cutting the first furrow. 'In both cases, it is a matter of an offering to the invisible power' (SERP p. 120). In such an offering oil, the colour of the sun and the symbol of lubricating and fertilizing power, simultaneously proffers a prayer for fertility and injects its symbolism into the open furrow. The oiled share penetrating the earth may also, perhaps, signify the gentleness, infused with an almost holy reverence, of this communication with Earth. This is the predominant emotion surrounding this fertility rite, a symbol of human coitus.

Embodying the notion of a family of cultures in material form, oil became the very sign of divine blessing and a symbol of joy and of brotherhood (Deuteronomy 33: 24; Psalms 48: 8; 133: 1–2).

Nevertheless, there was a far deeper symbolism behind ritual anointing. The kings of Israel were anointed and the oil then endowed them with God-given authority, power and glory, the Lord being in any case regarded as the real power behind the anointing. This is why the oil of the anointing was regarded as a symbol of the Spirit of God (1 Samuel 16: 13; Isaiah 11: 2; the latter, it should be remembered, in the context of the king who is to come). Because the person anointed has, as it were, been raised to the sphere of the godhead, no mortal should touch him (1 Samuel 24: 7–11; 26: 9).

At this point it is well to remember that when transcribed, the Hebrew word for 'anointed' has given us our word 'Messiah' and that its translation into Greek is 'Christos'. Jesus was therefore regarded as the king who was to come without a priori setting aside all reference to his priestly and prophetic ministry. However, as he patently was never anointed physically, the path towards spiritualization is clearly marked, the Holy Spirit, which the oil symbolized, being conferred fully upon Jesus like an unction (Luke 4: 18). Since the primitive Church at once related baptism to the gift of the Spirit (Acts 2: 38; 9: 17ff.), a rite of baptism was soon instituted in which anointing with oil was employed (Hippolytus, *Apostolic Tradition* 2: Tertullian, *Treatise on Baptism* 7).

Oil, which is thus present at the beginning of life as it is in Extreme Unction at its end, comes to play an extraordinary sacral role in the Christian world and is perhaps best summarized by the comments of the Pseudo-Dionysius the Areopagite:

After the salutation the Hierarch pours oil upon the defunct. But remember, that in course from the Birth from God, before the most Divine Baptism, the oil of Chrism, as a first participation of the holy symbol, is given to the neophyte, after the entire removal of the former clothing. And now, at the conclusion of all that is done, the oil is poured upon the defunct. The first anointing with the oil summons the initiated to the holy contests; but the pouring of oil now shows the defunct to have struggled through those same contests, and to have been made perfect.

(PSEN 95)

On the other hand, the natural consistency of oil made Shintō mythology regard it as the image of the primeval undifferentiated state, the primordial waters being of oil.

It is not surprising, therefore, that alchemy should have given oil so important a symbolic role. It is present at the beginning and end of life, but Claude de Saint-Martin regards it as a symbol of the intermediary bond, since it is an element in the alchemists' Great Work in which bread and wine are mercury and sulphur. Oil, he stresses, 'is composed of four elemental substances which give it an active relation to the four cardinal points.' Its nature is such that it immobilizes and stops external influences, another aspect of its cleansing and protective role.

old age Where old age is regarded as a sign of wisdom and righteousness – priests were originally old men, in the sense of wise men who gave guidance – and where, as in China, old age has always been respected, this is because it is the image of longevity, of experience and wisdom acquired over the years, itself no more than a flawed image of immortality. Tradition would have it that Lao Tzu was born with white hair and the face of an old man, hence a name meaning 'Old Master'. Under the Han dynasty, Taoism recognized as the supreme deity Huang Lao Kun, or 'Old Yellow Lord', a completely symbolical phrase which Maspéro has rightly compared with the Ancient of Days in the Book of Revelation and, one might also add, with the Druses' Old Man of the Mountains. Again in the Book of Revelation, the Word is depicted as being white-haired; yet another emblem of eternity. However, escape from the bounds of time can find expression in the past as well as in the future and to be an old man is to have existed before time began and to continue to exist after the universe has passed away. Thus the Buddha gives himself the title of elder brother of the universe. Sometimes, and especially in the Cambodian context of Angkor, Shiva was worshipped under the name of Vriddheshvara, 'Old Lord'. The Chinese secret society, Ch'ien-ti hui, is sometimes called 'the True Ancestor Society', as for example by the Vietnamese Emperor, Gia Long, in the edict in which he banned it. The 'Ancestor' is Heaven, at least for the 'True Man', the son of Heaven and Earth (BHAB, ELIM, GRAD, GUET, MAST).

olive-tree This tree possesses a wealth of symbolism – peace, fruitfulness, purification, strength, victory and reward.

In Ancient Greece the tree was sacred to ATHENE and the first olive, which sprang from her quarrel with Poseidon, was preserved as a treasure behind the Erechtheum. It would seem that graftings from this tree still flourish today on the Acropolis. The olive shares the symbolic properties attributed to Athene, to whom it was sacred.

Olives used to flourish on the plains of Eleusis. They were protected and anybody harming them was brought before the courts. They are almost deified in the 'Homeric' hymn to Demeter, which associates them with the Eleusinian Mysteries.

All European and Eastern countries endow them with the same significance and in Rome they were sacred to Jupiter and Minerva. According to a Chinese legend, olive-wood was an antidote to some poison and venom, giving the tree the properties of a preservative. In Japan it symbolizes friendship, as well as success in study and in civil or military enterprises. It is the tree of victory.

In Jewish and Christian tradition, the olive is a symbol of peace and it was an olive-branch which the dove brought back to Noah when the Flood was over. An old legend tells that Christ's cross was made of olive- and cedar-wood. In medieval terms, it was, furthermore, a symbol of gold and of love. 'Were I to behold olive-wood gilded at your door, I would at once call you a temple of God', Angelus Silesius wrote, fired by a description of Solomon's Temple.

For Islam, the olive is the central tree, the World AXIS, a symbol of Universal Man and of the Prophet. The 'Blessed Tree' is associated with light, since its OIL is used as lamp fuel. It would appear that, to Ismaili esoterics, 'the olive-tree on the top of Mount Sinai' stands for the Imam and is at one and the same time Axis, Universal Man and source of enlightenment.

Each leaf of the olive, in its character as a sacred tree, is said to bear one of the names of God written on it, while the *baraka* of its oil is so strong that it swells the quantity of oil by its very self and becomes dangerous. In some tribes, men drink olive oil to increase their powers of procreation.

(WESR p. 107)

A beautiful passage in the Koran (24: 35) compares the light of God with 'a niche in which is a lamp – the lamp encased in glass – the glass, as it were, a glistening star. From a blessed tree it is lighted, the olive neither of the

East nor of the West, whose oil would well nigh shine out, even though fire touched it not.'

Another explanation of the olive-tree symbol identifies the 'blessed tree' with Abraham and with his hospitality, and holds that it will endure until the Day of the Resurrection (HAYI pp. 285, 294). The tree of Abraham mentioned in the *hadīth* which follows that passage, was also an olive. The olive symbolizes the Paradise of the chosen.

om (see also AUM)   The symbol most highly charged with Hindu tradition is the monosyllable, Om. It is the primeval and inaudible SOUND, the creational sound from which manifestation evolves, and is hence the image of the Word. It is imperishable and inexhaustible (*akshara*), the very essence of the Vedas and hence of Indian traditional knowledge. It is the symbol of Ganesha and corresponds to the SWASTIKA, emblem of the cyclical evolution of manifestation expanding from its immovable primeval centre.

The sound 'Om' may be broken down into three elements – A, U and M (AUM) – controlling an inexhaustible list of threefold divisions: the three Vedas (Rig, Yajur and Sama); the three states of being (wakefulness, *jāgaritsa-sthāna*, corresponding to Vaishvanara; dream, *svapna-sthāna*, corresponding to Taijasa; deep sleep, *sushupta-sthāna*, corresponding to Prajnā); three periods of time (dawn, noonday and dusk); three worlds (Bhū, Earth; Svar, Heaven; Bhuvas, atmosphere) and hence the three states of manifestation (gross, shapeless and subtle); three elements (Agni, Fire; Aditya, Sun; Vāyu, Wind); three modalities or *guna* (*rajas*, expansive; *sattva*, cohesive or ascendant; *tamas*, destructive or descendant); three gods (Brahmā, Vishnu and Shiva); three powers (action, knowledge and will) . . . There is, furthermore, a fourth aspect to the monosyllable: its sound as a whole is indeterminate when analysed independently of the three elements which comprise it. It corresponds to the undifferentiated state of Oneness and therefore to a spiritual actualization of the highest importance, the mantra of mantras. The Upanishads tell us that it is the bow, the self being the arrow and Brahmā the target. In addition Guénon has noted the correspondence between the monosyllable and the three elements of Vishnu's CONCH, the shell which holds the seed from which will spring the cycle to come.

It is important to observe that in the Middle Ages there was a Christian equivalent which was commonly used as a symbol of the Word. This was the siglum ☐ which latterly was quite wrongly compared with the words 'Ave Maria'. In fact this siglum, pronounced in Latin with a sound similar to the Sanskrit *Aum*, meant 'ALPHA AND OMEGA, the beginning and the end' (Revelation 21: 6) and hence the evolution and involution of the cycle of manifestation. This symbol gains added significance by its frequent association with the swastika in medieval iconography (BHAB, COOH, DAMS, DAVL, ELIY, GOVM, GUEV, GUEM, SILI, VALA).

o-mikuji   At a very small charge, the visitor to a Japanese Shintō shrine may gain the right to rattle a cylindrical box full of wands. When he or she manages to shake one out, a number may be read on it. The person is then given a printed slip with a corresponding number, upon which there are prophecies or instructions. If these are, unfortunately, unlucky, the slip of paper is stuck on a branch of one of the trees growing in the temple enclosure. This is why foreign visitors are amazed to see trees near Shintō temples completely covered with slips of paper. The slip symbolizes chance, on which human fate depends. The word *Kuji* means drawing lots. However, fate may be affected by invisible forces and, when these forces are seen to be hostile, the slip of paper in the holy tree tries to immobilize or exorcize them.

omphalos (see also LINGAM)   The omphalos or navel-stone is a worldwide symbol of the CENTRE of the world. In many traditions, the creation of the universe originates in a navel, from which manifestation radiates to the four points of the compass. Thus in India, the *Rig-Veda* speaks of the navel of the Uncreated upon which rested the seed of the worlds, and it was from Vishnu's navel stretched out upon the primeval ocean that the LOTUS of universal manifestation sprang.

The navel, however, is not simply the indicator of the centre of physical manifestation, it is also the spiritual centre of the world. This is true of the BETHEL erected by Jacob in the shape of a column, as well as of the omphalos at Delphi, centre of the worship of Apollo. 'This god,' as Plato wrote, 'as the traditional religious interpreter, has his shrine at the world's centre and navel, to guide mankind.' It is also true of a number of menhirs, the Celtic equivalent of the omphalos; of the island of Ogygia, which Homer calls the navel of the world, as of the Easter Islands which bear the same title; and of the stone on which the Ark of the Covenant rested in the Temple at Jerusalem and the omphalos which is still exhibited near the Holy Sepulchre. (Ogier d'Angelure wrote in the Middle Ages that 'many say that Our Saviour said that it was the navel of the world.') The *nabhī*, or navel, is the 'motionless hub of the wheel', the tree, in Hindu terminology, under which the Buddha sat when he attained enlightenment at Bodhgaya. Upon the world's navel the Vedic sacrificial fire was symbolically lit, but all altars and hearths are, by extension, similar centres. The Vedic altar was the 'navel of the immortal', the central point from which the dimensions of the human state were drawn in space and time, the point of return to the beginning of things, the mark of the World Axis. In some African carved doors, panels, stauettes and so on a central disc is sometimes to be seen, in all likelihood standing for the navel of the world. In African carved figures, the navel is often given great prominence, becoming a jutting or hanging cord (LAUA pp. 307–9).

In both Yoga and Hesychasm, the navel is also the centre of the human microcosm. Spiritual concentration centres upon the navel, an image of the return to the centre of things. In fact, in Yoga the navel is made to correspond to the *manipūra-chakra* (or *nabhī-padma*), the centre of transformational energy and of the element of Fire. This is the meaning of 'omphaloscopy', a term so frequently misunderstood (AVAS, BENA, CHOC, COOH, ELIY, ELIM, GOVM, GUEM, GUES, SILI).

In the Celtic world navel symbolism is primarily represented by the title 'Nabelcus' borne by the Gaulish Mars and confirmed by a number of inscriptions from south-eastern Gaul. The word is related to the Gaulish *naf*, 'chief' or 'lord', and on an Indo-European level provides a correspondence with the Greek *omphalos*, 'central point' or 'centre', the Irish *imbliu* only meaning 'navel' in the strictly physical sense of the word. Thus Mars Nabelcus was a 'master', 'lord' or yet again 'god' of a central point. The Celts, too, had holy centres, Caesar mentioning a 'consecrated place' in the Carnutian forest at which the druids met to choose their leader. Such places were regarded as the centre of the country and even in Gaul there are some tens of examples of the place-name Mediolanum, 'centre of perfection' or, as modern etymologists prefer, 'central plain'. In Ireland all religious life was concentrated upon the central province of Midh, the modern Meath (CELT 1: pp. 137–41; OGAC 15: pp. 372–6).

In symbolic art, the omphalos is generally depicted as a white standing STONE with an ovoid tip, frequently wreathed by one or more serpents. According to Pindar, the omphalos at Delphi was more than the centre of the world or even the centre of the created universe, it symbolized the channel of communication between the three worlds, of mortals living on Earth, of the dead dwelling in the Underworld and of the gods. The omphalos at Delphi was believed to stand upon the spot where Apollo killed the serpent Pytho and also upon the crevasse through which the waters of Deucalion's flood had drained away. It symbolized the life force which controls the blind and misshapen powers of Chaos, or as we might say today, a rationally structured way of life. Such a rational structure is, however, gained by internal self-control and by a victory over self, and not through external aids.

The cosmic omphalos has been contrasted with the cosmic EGG as the male with the female principles of the universe. The world was born from their sacred marriage in the same way as the child is born from sexual intercourse. The serpent wrapped round the omphalos symbolizes this synthesis or sexual congress as it does when wrapped round the lingam.

Just as there is a 'navel of the world', so the Pole Star, round which the firmament appears to rotate, is frequently called the 'navel of the Heavens' or their hub or hinge. This is especially the case among many northern European and Asian peoples such as Finns, Samoyed, Koryak, Chukchi, Estonians and Lapps. Scandinavian folk poetry calls it the 'navel of the world' (HARA p. 32).

onager The onager, often loosely and inaccurately termed the wild ass, symbolizes the wild man, temperamentally hard to tame. The Old Testament has some dozen references to the onager to which the Angel of the Lord compared Ishmael (Genesis 16: 12) because of his adventurous and nomadic life.

Mysticism also uses the symbol of the onager. Thus the twelfth-century Guiges II the Carthusian compares himself with the solitary onager reluctantly accepting God's yoke.

one One is the symbol of *homo erectus*. Human beings are the only species to walk upright and there are anthropologists who see in this their distinguishing characteristic, a characteristic more profound even than their powers of reasoning.

One may be found in the images of the standing stone, the erect phallus and the upright staff. It stands for human activity associated with the work of creation.

One is also the immanent First Cause from which, nevertheless, all manifestation originates and to which, once its fleeting essence is exhausted, it returns. It is the active principle: the creator. One is the symbolic place of being, the beginning and end of all things, the cosmic and ontological centre.

As well as being the symbol of Being, it is also the symbol of Revelation, the intercessor which raises mankind through knowledge to a higher plane of being. One is the mystic centre, too, from which the Spirit radiates like the Sun.

There is justification for the distinction which Guénon draws between one and Oneness. The latter is an expression of absolute being, incalculable, transcendent, the One God, while the former allows reproduction in its own likeness and reduction of the many to the one within a pattern of departure and return in which both external and internal pluralism have parts to play.

Aside from its general and universal characteristics as a foundation and point of departure, the figure one displays certain more specific developments, especially in Iranian literature and folklore.

First and foremost one (*yak*) stands for the One God. The figure is written in the same shape as the letter *alif* ('a') in the Arabic-Persian alphabet. In the *abjad* alphabet (A B J D) this letter also has the properties of one (see DA'WAH).

The heroes of the legends and literature of chivalry proudly affirm their adherence to an Islamic culture which flourishes and spreads throughout the East and of which the battle-cry is 'There is no other God than the One God.' The hero sets himself up as defender of the faith in which he has been nurtured and, to defend his own Muslim community, wars upon the believers of other faiths, especially Christians, Jews, Zoroastrians and Hindus. It is a struggle in which the figure one in some sense stands for what is at stake.

When a Muslim paladin enters the court of an infidel king or emir he announces defiantly: 'I greet those within this court who know that in the eighteen thousand universes there is One God.'

In legend and folktale, the One God is often symbolized by the figure one.

Jung classifies separately a whole series of what he calls 'unifying' symbols. These are the symbols which tend to reconcile opposites and to achieve a synthesis of contradictions, such as, for example, squaring the circle, mandalas, the Star of David, hexagrams, wheels, the Zodiac and so on.

The unifying symbol would be charged with extremely powerful psychic energy. Jacques de la Rocheterie has observed its occurrence in dreams only when the process of individuation is well advanced. The subject is then able to draw on all the energy of the unifying symbol in order to achieve within him- or herself harmony between consciousness and the unconscious, a dynamic balance of resolved contradictions and the cohabitation of irrational and rational, intellect and imagination, real and ideal and concrete and abstract. Totality is unified within the subject whose personality develops fully.

one-armed (see also DEFORMITY; MUTILATION) . Hands separated day from night and hold the office of creation. To lose an arm or a hand sets the victim outside time. When Sleeping Beauty pricked her finger on a spindle, she slumbered for a hundred years. This isolation is, however, only relative and temporary. It takes the individual into a different order of things, the 'odd' or sacred, be it the left-hand world of black magic or the right-hand world of white magic – like the ONE-LEGGED, ONE-EYED and all those creatures afflicted with deformity, which destroys an element of evenness or physical symmetry. This explains why the one-armed man is the archetypal beggar. The one hand he holds out possesses power from the fact that it is his only hand, like the hand of justice. Mutilation endows with properties of its own.

The one-armed are not irrevocably outside time. As the seed in the furrow is in some sense outside time but will emerge in the Spring thanks to the sunshine, so the one-armed may be reinstated in time through fresh use of hand or arm. The one-armed symbolize those summoned to live on a different plane of being.

In Norse mythology the sovereign god of justice was Tyr the One-armed. He agreed to lose an arm to save the other gods. By consenting to this sacrifice, he ensured the truth of his promise, his limb being the corporeal pledge of his bond. By this very action he acquired supreme power in matters of law. He who offers a pledge becomes responsible, and he who is responsible is in command. The one-armed symbolize this law.

one-eyed (see also CYCLOPS; DEFORMITY; MUTILATION; ONE-EYED; ONE-LEGGED)   A Roman hero, Horatius Cocles, was one-eyed, but the glare of that remaining eye was enough to halt the enemy in their tracks and stop them crossing the Pons Sublicius, the bridge which led into Rome. The Norse god, Odin, too, had lost an eye, only to gain the power of seeing the Invisible. He was the god of magic and the force of his spells could paralyse or scatter his enemies in battle.

The one-eyed person's remaining eye is a symbol of second sight and of the magic powers which a glance possesses, just as the physically handicapped or the limbless seem by the very weakness or loss of one limb to have acquired exceptional properties for the limb which remains sound. It is as if its strength were not reduced nor doubled, but increased tenfold, or rather as if they themselves were removed to a different plane. In the dialectic of symbolism, it is as if the loss of an organ or a limb were compensated by an increase in the powers of the remaining limb or organ.

In the *Eddas*, Allfodr goes to Mina, the spring from which 'all knowledge and wisdom flows. He asked leave to drink from the spring, but was not allowed to do so until he had given one of his eyes as a pledge.' He thus sacrificed in part his powers of one sort of vision in return for what would give him sublimated vision, access to divine knowledge.

The French painter Gustave Courbet wrote in the opposite sense: 'I see too clearly, I should pluck out an eye.' In both cases it is relinquishment of diurnal vision to acquire the visionary's nocturnal vision.

one-legged (see also DEFORMITY; MUTILATION; ONE-ARMED; ONE-EYED) Aztecs and Maya in Mexico and Guatemala (SOUM, THOH) and Incas in South America (LEHC) believed that the thunder-god, lord of the rains and therefore of the Earth's fertility, was one-legged. The same belief is found among the Samoyed in Asia (they also believe that storm-spirits have only one foot, one hand and one eye) and the Wiradyuri in southern Australia (HENL).

Father de Avila (AVIH) records a strange ancient Peruvian myth, according to which the thunder-god, son of the almighty sky-god, suffered LAMENESS, like Hephaistos-Vulcan, after battling with the chthonian fire-god.

Legba, great god of the Voodoo pantheon and intercessor between mankind and the supernatural, is depicted in Haiti as a lame old man leaning on a crutch. He is derisively called 'broken-foot', but his manifestations are terrifyingly brutal and those of whom he takes possession are thrown senseless to the ground where they remain 'as if struck by a thunderbolt' (METV). In Benin, the Fon god Arui, who brought fire to mankind, is depicted as a tiny little man with one arm and one leg and a single eye in the middle of his forehead (VERO).

Nommo and Faro, the Dogon and Bambara water-gods, lords of the thunderbolt and the rains which make the Earth fruitful, are both one-legged. These gods, however, who provide the archetypes of all water-spirits, are sometimes also depicted with fishlike attributes. The Dogon and Bambara say that the upper portions of their bodies are human but the lower part is, according to the Bambara, of red copper (a water symbol) or, according to the Dogon, in the shape of a fish or a serpent (GRIH, DIEB). This would explain why all these deities are one-legged, originating in the myth of the siren, a creature half-human, half-fish.

In the cave paintings of South African Bushmen depicting the Sorcerer in conjunction with the ox, avatars (incarnations) of rain-gods, the former is one-legged. In Ancient China, the sight of a one-legged bird foretold rain and hopping dances were used in rain-making (HENL).

The southern Nigerian Ekoi culture-hero who stole heavenly fire from the Supreme Deity was doomed to lameness when the latter discovered the theft. 'For this reason myths call him the Boy-on-Sticks and, in their stilt-dances, there is a character who acts the part of the mythical fire-bringer' (TEGH p. 90).

The fire-god Hephaistos (Vulcan), son of Hera and Ouranos (Uranus) and husband of Aphrodite, was lame (GRID).

In Greek mythology, those pre-eminently chthonian deities, the Cylopses, who sublimated chthonian fire by giving Zeus thunder, lightning and the thunderbolt, had only one eye, set in the middle of their foreheads. They were three in number. One may well wonder whether these one-eyed, lame or one-legged deities, all connected with the secrets of fire and metal-working, were not essentially gods of the order of odd numbers, the most secret, most awesome and most transcendent of all orders since, in the human scale of values, the word 'order' is always associated with even numbers. Odd numbers – one leg, one eye, three Cyclopses, three Gorgons – would be an order symbolizing an awesome power, as it were divine might taken over and channelled to selfish ends. The human world, which is temporal, is governed by the number two, and not by the number one, the number of the timeless, the increate, the forbidden world of God.

Depending on whether it is explained as being beneficent or maleficent, this power may take the form of a Supreme Deity, like Kierkegaard's

Jehovah, or Lord of Hell. In both cases, the one-legged awakens in the depths of our beings fear of Fate.

onion This alliaceous plant enjoys so high a reputation that a religious sect was devoted to its cultivation. Its bulbous shape, strong smell and layers of skin one on top of the other provide subjects for symbolic interpretation. Rāmakrishna compares the laminated structure and lack of a central core with the structure of the ego. Spiritual experiences strip it away layer by layer until there is voidness and then there is no barrier to the Universal Spirit and union with Brahmā. On a magical level, the Ancient Egyptians protected themselves against certain diseases with onion stalks, while Plutarch says that the Romans forbade the plant because they believed that it waxed while the Moon waned and its smell weakened the life force. Aphrodisiac properties have also been attributed to it, as much because of what it suggests to the imagination as because of its chemical composition.

onyx The stone is generally regarded as bringing discord and is also supposed to produce nightmares and to be fatal to pregnant women, in whom it causes still-births. However, in India and Persia it was endowed with beneficent powers, especially those of preserving against the evil eye and easing childbirth (BUDA p. 320).

orange (colour) Lying mid-way between yellow and red, orange is the most actinic colour. Lying between celestial gold and chthonian red, the primary symbolism of the colour is that of the point of balance between the spirit and the libido. However, this balance tends to be upset in one direction or the other, so that orange may become the revelation of divine love or the emblem of lust. Both the saffron robe worn by Buddhist monks and the orange velvet cross of the Knights of the Holy Ghost are instances of the first.

Portal regards the orange veil, the *flammeum* worn by Roman brides, as an emblem of the permanence of marriage – a significance corresponding on the profane level to the Oriflamme on the sacred. Virgil describes Helen of Troy as wearing a saffron veil, while the Muses, regarded by some commentators as daughters of Heaven and Earth and of recognized importance in the worship of Apollo, were also robed in saffron. The orange-coloured precious stone, the jacinth, was considered as a symbol of fidelity (BUDA p. 129). It was an emblem of one of the Twelve Tribes of Israel on the High Priest's breastplate, and in Britain the Crown Jewels contain a jacinth symbolizing 'regal temperance and sobriety' (MARA p. 277). Exposure to fire does not affect the jewel's colour, which Portal sees as an expression of faithful constancy conquering and extinguishing the flames of passion.

However, it is an extremely difficult task to maintain the balance between the spirit and the libido, and hence orange has become a colour which symbolizes lust and infidelity. According to traditions going back to the worship of the Earth Mother, this balance was sought in the ritual ORGY, regarded as bringing with it initiatory sublimation and revelation. Dionysos was said to be dressed in orange.

orange (fruit)   Like all fruit containing a mass of seeds or pips, oranges are a fertility symbol. Young married couples in Vietnam used to be given presents of oranges.

Probably for the same reason, in Ancient China a formal offer of marriage was accompanied by a gift of oranges to the girl concerned (DURV, KALL).

orb (see also CALABASH; EGG; SPHERE)   Among the objects conjuring up the power of kings, emperors, popes and gods, an orb held in one of their hands stands for the domain or empire over which their sovereign authority extends and the totalitarian nature of that authority. The spherical shape of the orb, in fact, may partake of a twofold significance – the geographical totality of the universe and the juridical totality of absolute power. The latter meaning alone is valid when the orb denotes the limited area over which the individual exercises power. The power itself is limitless and this is what the orb signifies.

orchid   In Ancient China orchids were associated with Spring festivals in which they were used to drive off evil influences, most specifically that of barrenness. As its name implies, the wild orchid is a symbol of fertilization (it derives from the Greek *orkhis*, 'testicle'). In China again, orchids furthermore stimulated procreation and were pledges of fatherhood. However, the deaths of children were regarded as falling under the orchid's influence and resulted from cutting the flowers. A flower with a double aspect, which takes back what it gives; nonetheless, its beauty is a symbol of purity and of spiritual perfection (BELT, GRAD, MASR).

orgy   Orgiastic festivals, such as Bacchanalia or even ordinary drunken revels, are, on the one hand, symptoms of regressive behaviour, of a return to Chaos, with drunken debauchery, singing, licentious display, outlandish costume, carnival monstrosities and complete abdication of authority by the reason. On the other hand, they may be a sort of recharging of the personality, diving deep into the elemental powers of life after the wear and tear of everyday living and the social pressures of urban society. Thus orgies are observed to have been the main feature of festivals connected with seedtime, harvest and the vintage. They symbolize a violent yearning for change but, although driven by the yearning to escape from the everyday, they fall into something far worse, the life of brute instinct. Only mystical orgies or mystical intoxication with Vedic soma, the Sufi's dance, ascetic self-denial or saintly ecstasy – whatever the differences among them – in principle set the course away from the commonplace along a path which leads to the sublimation of desire and the renewal of being.

Orgies may be regarded as an image of the life of the gods, free and unfettered by laws; they take their participants out of themselves and even raise them to the level of gods, but they are a waste of energy which apes the force of creation. When the show is over they seep away with a bitter aftertaste left by the brevity, uncertainty and cramping and illusory nature of the experience. They end in debasement and in destruction rather than creation. The experience may, however, be able to inspire a fresh drive and a new mustering of energy towards a higher goal, so that one surpasses one's own self on the way to higher things. Such an inversion of values implies a deep feeling of humility. In that case, instead of aping God, the image implores his aid. The vain attempt to identify oneself, even for a moment, with him changes into a humble admission of one's difference.

oriole In China the oriole is a symbol of marriage. In the art of the common people orioles are often depicted with peach-blossom as symbols of Spring. Through a roughly similar sound of the words, the oriole is sometimes made the symbol of gladness, like the chrysanthemum.

The 'yellow birds' which perched on the doorway of the Immortal Chi Tzu T'ui were undoubtedly orioles and here again may well have been bound up with the proclamation of Spring (DURV, GRAD).

Orpheus A mythical character; although described in different ways by poets and further confused in so many legends, Orpheus emerges in every case as the pre-eminent musician. With LYRE or ZITHER he calmed the elements unleashed in storm and tempest and charmed plants, animals, humans and gods. Through the magic of his music he succeeded in persuading the gods of the Underworld to set free his wife Eurydice who had died from snake-bite when fleeing the advances of Aristaeus. But one condition was laid down – Orpheus was not to look at her until she had returned to the light of day. Half-way there, in a fit of anxiety, he looked back and Eurydice vanished for ever. Orpheus would not be consoled and met his death when he was torn to pieces by the Thracian women whose love he had scorned. He is supposed to have inspired the Eleusinian Mysteries. Some early Christian writers regarded Orpheus as the victor over the brute powers of nature (Dionysos), like Jesus who had conquered Satan. He has given rise to a wealth of esoteric writings.

Each feature of his legend reveals Orpheus as the seducer at all levels of the cosmos and of the psyche – Heaven, Earth, the ocean and the Underworld; the subconscious, the conscious and the superconscious; he dissolves anger and resistance; he enchants. However, in the end he failed to bring his beloved back from the Underworld and his own remains were scattered in pieces and thrown into a river. He may, perhaps, be the symbol of the embattled individual who can suppress but not destroy evil, and who dies because he or she is incapable of overcoming his or her own deficiencies. On a higher plane, Orpheus would stand for the pursuit of an ideal to which lip-service is paid but no real sacrifices are made. Such a transcendent ideal is only ever attained by those who root out and effectively abdicate their own self-centredness and exorbitance of desire. Orpheus might symbolize lack of soul-force. He never managed to resolve the contradiction between his yearning for both the sublime and the commonplace and died because he had not the courage to choose between them (DIES pp. 569, 136–43).

Jean Servier compares the ban laid upon Orpheus and Eurydice in the Underworld with certain taboos surrounding the ploughing season in the eastern Mediterranean.

While the first furrow is being cut, the ploughman must remain silent, as weaver-women must remain silent when making the warp and men must remain silent when digging a grave. He is not allowed to look behind him or to retrace his steps, just as members of a funeral procession are not allowed to look back.

Invisible powers are there who could be insulted by an inadvertent word or
annoyed at being seen by a sideways look or a glance over the shoulder.

(SERP p. 148)

Orpheus is the man who broke the taboo and dared to gaze at the Invisible.

Osiris In Ancient Egypt Osiris began as an agrarian god, symbolizing the
inexhaustible power of plant life, and then was identified with the Sun in its
nocturnal aspect and symbolized the continuance of birth and rebirth.

Osiris is the universal life force whether active in Heaven or on Earth. In the
visible shape of a god he goes down into the realm of the dead to enable them
to be reborn and eventually to rise again in the glory of Osiris, since all the
righteous dead are like grains of life in the depths of the cosmos exactly as
grains of wheat in the bosom of the Earth.

(CHAM p. 17)

He was to become the god of agriculture. Having been shut in a chest or
COFFER by his jealous brother Set and other enemies, and set adrift on the
Nile, he became the object of a quest, like that of the medieval Holy Grail.
His mutilated and dismembered body was restored to life when the two
goddesses, Isis and Nephthys, often depicted with great wings, breathed
upon it. Osiris symbolizes the drama of human life, doomed to death but
at intervals victorious over it. As god of death and resurrection, he holds an
important place in mystery religions. In Ancient Egyptian iconography he
is generally depicted as god and king with the three royal attributes of
sceptre, flail and the staff of longevity, in the shape of a solar ray.
     According to the Ancient Egyptian legend, after death Osiris' body floated
on the Nile and became dismembered. Isis gathered all the pieces together,
except for one, the penis, which a fish had swallowed. In explanations of the
myth this detail is generally ignored and yet it contains something of prime
importance. The invention of farming in the Nile valley was attributed to
Osiris by at least one Ancient Egyptian religious text. Plant germination is
linked to disintegration, just as annihilation is a prelude to new life. 'If the
grain die not . . .' The fish which swallowed the penis may be regarded as
the mystagogue who initiates into a new life. Hence one may perceive that
a corpse is like the penis after castration or, having lost its seminal fluid,
like a parched seed. Funeral libations will therefore enable it to regain
its vital fluids in the Otherworld, just as when the seed in the ground is
watered it is reborn in the shape of a plant. Death is seen as the ultimate
castration of life, but also as the state which makes another life possible.
     The myth of Osiris displays the three phases of individuation postulated
by the analyst André Virel:

1 Osiris in the chest is an image of the integration of the ego. 'The chest
   sets the bounds of individuality and stands for the separational and
   pattern-forming aspect of individuation.'
2 The mutilation of Osiris is an image of dissociation and disintegration.
3 Osiris restored and endowed with an immortal soul is 'reintegration in
   a higher form, possessing spiritual significance'. It corresponds to the
   final phase of integration, characteristic of individuals or groups which
   have reached the peak of their development (VIRI pp. 148, 181, 228).

ostrich In Ancient Egypt the ostrich feather was a symbol of justice, right-eousness and truth. In antiquity this meaning was seen to be derived from the fact that all ostrich feathers were the same length, but this point is scarcely relevant. The goddess Maat wore an ostrich feather on her head, and she was the goddess of justice and truth who sat in judgement at the weighing of souls, the feather itself being used as a just weight on the scales of judgement. Like the goddess of which it was the emblem, the ostrich feather signified universal order based upon justice.

The ostrich feathers from which the fans of pharaohs and their court dignitaries were made symbolized the basic duty of their office – the admin-istration of justice.

In the traditions of the Dogon, a West African farming people whose whole system of symbols is lunar and aquatic, the ostrich sometimes takes the place of wavy lines or chevrons symbolizing water-courses. In this con-text the ostrich's body is depicted as a series of concentric circles and chev-rons. According to Griaule, the bird's characteristic zigzag run, like the twisting course of a stream, accounts for this interpretation (GRID).

Otherworld See BEYOND.

otter The otter, which rises to the surface of the water and then dives below it, possesses lunar symbolism and from this derive the properties for which it is used in initiation. Otter-skin is used in initiation societies both among North American Indians and among Black Africans, especially the Bantu of Cameroon and Gabon.

The Ozila, the female initiates with magical powers of conferring fertility, who dance especially at birth and marriage ceremonies, hold a horn in one hand and wear otter-skin girdles.

The shamans of the North American Ojibwa Indians keep their magic shells in an otter-skin bag. The messenger of the Great Spirit, who acts as intercessor between him and mankind, is supposed to have seen the wretched state of human weakness and disease and to have revealed the most sub-lime secrets to the otter and interfused its body with *Migis* (symbols of the Midé or members of the Midewiwin Medicine Lodge) so that the creature became immortal and could, by initiating humans, make them holy (ELIT, ELII). All members of the Midewiwin carry otter-skin medicine bags (ALEC p. 213). These are the bags which are aimed at the candidate at initiation ceremonies as if they were fire-arms and 'kill' him. They are then laid on his body until he is restored to life. After song and feasting the shamans present the new initiate with his own otter-skin bag. The otter is therefore an initiating spirit which kills and restores to life.

In Europe evidence of the role of conductor of souls being assigned to the otter comes from a Romanian folk-song which speaks of the otter, with its intimate knowledge of rivers, guiding the soul across fords unharmed to the cool spring from which it can find refreshment.

In the Celtic world the symbolism of the otter (Irish *doborchu*; Welsh *dyfrgi*; Breton *dourgy*; literally 'water-hound') complements that of the DOG. Cùchulainn began his succession of exploits by killing a hound and he ended it, a few moments before his own death, by killing an otter with a sling-shot (CELT 7: p. 20; CHAB p. 317).

Ouranos (Uranus)   The sky-god in Hesiod's *Theogony*, he is the symbol of boundless, undifferentiated creative abundance, which smothers what it begets through its very proliferation. It characterizes the initial phase of any activity with its alternations of elation and depression, the ebb and flow, life and death of the project. Thus Ouranos comes to symbolize the cycle of evolution. The BULL is the emblem of this sky-god of Indo-Mediterranean religion who is one of many fertility symbols.

But with Ouranos, this fecundity is dangerous. As Mazon notes in his commentary on Hesiod's *Theogony*, the mutilation of Ouranos puts an end to his hateful and unproductive fecundity, and introduces into the world through the appearance of Aphrodite (born of the foam bloodied by Ouranos' genital organs) an order, a fixedness of species which was to prevent all disordered and dangerous procreation in the future.

(ELIT p. 77)

On the basis of Greek mythology, André Virel perfectly characterizes the three essential phases of creative development. Ouranos (for whom there is no Roman equivalent) stands as the first phase – chaotic and undifferentiated effervescence, which he calls *cosmogenesis*. In the second phase of *schizogenesis* Cronos (Saturn) steps in to cut and slice. With his scythe he cuts off his father's sexual organs and brings his ceaseless seminal ejaculations to an end. He represents a stationary period of time. He is the controller who 'brings the entire creation of the universe to a halt . . . with life at a standstill, ever the same and without progressive evolution.' The rule of Zeus (Jupiter) is characterized by fresh advances, no longer anarchic and disorderly, but organized and controlled, and this Virel calls *autogenesis*. After the discontinuity of the previous phase, during which the pause and the imposition of strict limits had allowed the first series of classifications to be made, progressive development began afresh. This was the moment at which 'individuals became clearly self-aware and simultaneously aware of the connections of causality, of the definition of beings and of objects perceived in their similarities and differences. . . . The mythological history of the gods [then] began to become the history of mankind.' Mythology is thus presented as a 'psychology projected upon the external world', not merely as a psychology of the individual, as Freud understood it, but also as a collective psychology as Jung conceived it (VIRI pp. 84–6).

ouroboros (see also SERPENT)   A serpent biting its own tail symbolizes a closed cycle of development. At the same time this symbol enshrines ideas of motion, continuity, self-fertilization and, consequently, of the eternal homecoming. The image's circular shape gives rise to another explanation – the marriage of the chthonian world, represented by the serpent, and the celestial world, represented by the circle. Confirmation of this interpretation might be found in some examples in which the ouroboros is part black and part white. It would thus bear the meaning of the marriage of opposing principles, Heaven and Earth, night and day, the Chinese *yang*, and *yin*, and of all the properties possessed by these opposing elements (see also DRAGON).

Another interpretation may see in the ouroboros the contrast between two different planes of being. The serpent biting its tail falls into the shape of a circle, a break with its linear development which would seem to mark as big a change as emergence upon a higher level of existence, a level of celestial or spiritualized existence, symbolized by the circle. The serpent thus transcends the plane of brute life to move forward in the direction of the most basic living impulses. This explanation, however, depends upon the symbolism of the circle, the image of celestial perfection. An opposite image may be conjured up by the serpent biting its tail, ceaselessly revolving around itself enclosed within its own cycle, and that is the image of the SAMSĀRA, the WHEEL of Life. As one condemned never to escape its own cycle and raise itself to a higher plane, the ouroboros symbolizes eternal return, the endless cycle of rebirth and a continual repetition which betrays the dominance of a basic death-wish.

owl The owl is the bird sacred to Athene, goddess of wisdom, and shares the goddess's attribute. A nocturnal bird, related to the Moon and unable to bear sunlight, it is in this respect in sharp contrast with the eagle, which gazes directly at the Sun. Guénon observes that in this particular may be seen the relationship of the owl with Athene–Minerva, symbol of rational knowledge – perception of reflected (lunar) light (see MIRROR) – by contrast with intuitive knowledge – direct perception of (solar) light. This is also perhaps the reason for the owl being the traditional attribute of seers, symbolizing their gift of second sight, exercised by their interpretation of omens. 'Athene's bird, the owl, symbolizes reflection which rules the darkness' (MAGE p. 108).

In Greek mythology the owl is represented by Ascalaphos, son of Acheron and the nymph of darkness. It was the owl which saw Persephone swallow the food of the Underworld (a pomegranate seed) and denounced her, thus removing whatever hope she had of escaping forever to the light of day (GRID). It was also the interpreter of Atropos, one of the Parcae (Fates), who cut the thread of fate herself. In Ancient Egypt the owl was the image of cold, darkness and death.

In Hindu iconography, the owl is sometimes an attribute of Vārāhi, the mother, although no precise significance can be attached to it (GRAD, GRAC, MALA).

In Ancient China the owl played an important part, being a terrifying creature which was supposed to have devoured its own mother. It symbolized *yang,* and even a superabundance of *yang.* Its manifestation occurred at the Summer solstice and it was identified with the drum and with thunder. It was also related to smelting. It was the emblem of Huang Ti, the Yellow Emperor and first blacksmith. As a symbol of superabundant *yang,* the owl was believed to cause drought. Children born at the solstice (the Day of the Owl) were believed to inherit natural violence and might even become parricides. Owl stew, given on that day to the nobleman's vassals, may perhaps have been ritual ordeal, purification or communion, or perhaps a combination of all three. Whatever the case, owls were always considered savage unlucky creatures.

The owl is also one of the most ancient symbols of China, going back to times known as the mythical period. Some writers maintain that it is confused with the Dragon-Torch, the emblem of the second dynasty, the Yin.

It was the emblem of the thunderbolt and was depicted on royal standards. The bird was sacred to the solstices and to metal-workers and in ancient times presided over the days on which smiths made swords and magic mirrors.

The Plains Indians believed that the owl had dominion over the night, hence owl feathers were used in some rituals (FLEH, ALEC p. 118).

In the medicine lodge during the initiation rites of the Midewiwin society among the Algonquin Indians, was perched the figure of 'the owl-being, that guides into the Land of the Setting Sun, the land of the dead' (ALEC p. 212). In this context the owl played the part of conductor of souls (ALEC p. 258).

The owl may equally be regarded as a messenger of death and consequently of ill omen. The Maya-Quiché say: 'When the owl hoots, the Indian dies.' Chorti sorcerers, the powers of evil incarnate, are able to turn themselves into owls (GIRP p. 79).

To the Aztecs, the owl was the creature which symbolized the god of Hell, as did the spider. In many of the codices, the owl is depicted as the 'wardress of the dark house of Earth'. Through its association with chthonian forces, it was also an avatar (embodiment) of darkness, rain and storm. This symbolism associated it with both death and the lunar–terrestrial powers of the unconscious which govern the waters, plants and growth in general.

The grave furniture of the pre-Inca Peruvian Chimu civilization often includes depictions of a sacrificial knife with a half-moon blade and a handle in the shape of a god who is half human and half night-bird, or owl. The symbol is clearly linked to the idea of death or of sacrifice and the deity wears a necklace of pearls or sea shells, his chest is painted red and he is flanked by a couple of dogs, recognized conductors of souls. This owl often holds a sacrificial knife in one hand and in the other an urn to catch the victim's blood (GRID).

In the apocryphal Welsh tale of that name, the owl was one of the 'Ancient Things of the World', replete with wisdom and practical experience. One ought therefore to classify it among primeval creatures, although it does not seem to have been part of Celtic religious symbolism. Under Christian influence, it was regarded askance, so that the benign symbolism of the owl was probably pre-Christian. In the tale of Math the son of Mathonwy, Llew's faithless wife, Blodeuwedd, is changed into an owl to punish her adultery with a neighbouring lord (MABG p. 79; CHAB pp. 461–70).

ox In contrast with the BULL, the ox is a symbol of kindliness, tranquillity and peaceful strength, or, as Devoucoux has written of the ox in Ezekiel's vision and in the Book of Revelation, 'of the power of work and of sacrifice'. However, this particular ox may, in fact, be a bull. There are certain differences between the two in terms of their symbolism and its explanations. The ox-heads of the Emperor Shen Nung, inventor of agriculture, and that of Che-yu may as easily be identified as bulls' heads, the same ideogram, *nu*, serving for both animals. The bull Apis, at Memphis, a hypostasis of Ptah and of Osiris, may as easily have been an ox, the same word denoting all cattle. In this respect its lunar character is not the determining factor.

Throughout East Asia the ox, and more especially the buffalo, are venerated as mankind's most valuable helpers. They were the steeds of the sages and notably of Lao Tzu in his journey to the western borders. In fact there is something about these animals, a gentleness and aloofness, which suggests contemplation. Statues of oxen are common features of Shintō temples, but in Ancient China, a clay figure of an ox represented the cold and was thrown out of the house in the Spring to encourage the renewal of nature. It was a typically *yin* emblem.

The buffalo is a more lumbering, rough, peasant creature. In Hindu iconography it is the steed and emblem of the death-god, Yama, and in Tibet, too, the death-spirit has a buffalo-head. Nevertheless the Gelugpa – one of the Yellow Hat sects – give a buffalo-head to the Bodhisattva Manjushrī, who destroyed death. The classic representation of the *asura*, Mahesha, is as a buffalo. He was defeated and beheaded by Candī, an aspect of Umā or Durgā. It may well be that, as buffaloes are fond of marsh-land, this one was related to water and defeated either by the Sun or by drought and, in fact, a buffalo is sometimes sacrificed in India at the end of the monsoon. However the *asura* is sometimes depicted in human form, gradually freeing himself from the shape of the decapitated beast, and this has a significance of a spiritual order.

The Montagnards in Vietnam, whose most fundamental religious act is to sacrifice a buffalo, treat the creature as the equal of a human. The ritual execution of the buffalo makes it an intercessor for the community with the higher spirits (DAMS, DANA, DEVA, EVAB, FRAL, GRAR, HERV, MALA, OGRJ, PORA).

The Ancient Greeks regarded oxen as sacred animals and often offered them in sacrifice, a hecatomb meaning the sacrifice of one hundred oxen. The ox was sacred to certain gods and, when Hermes robbed Apollo of his oxen, he was only able to obtain pardon for his sacrilegious theft by giving Apollo the lyre which he had invented by stretching the hide and tendons of an ox over the shell of a tortoise. The Sun had his herd of spotless, white oxen with golden horns. Odysseus' hungry crew slaughtered them for food on the island of Trinacria in contravention of their captain's orders. They all perished; Odysseus alone was saved because he had not shared the food.

Sacred oxen were reared by the clan of the Buzyges; the animals' task was to commemorate the invention of the plough by Triptolemos during the holy rites of ploughing celebrated in the Eleusinian Mysteries. Throughout North Africa, too, oxen are sacred animals offered in sacrifice and connected with the rituals of ploughing and making the soil fruitful (GRID, SERP).

Doubtless because of its sacred character and its connection with most religious rites either as victim or as the one who offers sacrifice, as for example when it ploughed a furrow in the earth, the ox was also the symbol of the priest. For example, and although the interpretation is open to argument, the oxen of the three-headed giant, Geryon, might well be 'members of a primitive priestly college at Delphi and Geryon their high priest. He might well have been conquered and killed by Herakles (Hercules) and a new order of worship instituted at Delphi' (LANS 2: p. 163).

The Pseudo-Dionysius the Areopagite summarizes the mystic symbolism of the ox thus: 'The image of the ox denotes the strong and the mature, turning up the spiritual furrows for the reception of the heavenly and productive powers. The Horns [symbolize] the guarding and the indomitable . . .' (PSEH p. 48).

There was a Gaulish divinity, the familiar spirit of Borvo, or Apollo Borvo, the protector of thermal springs, called Damona, a name containing the root *dam*, the Celtic word for cattle in general. However, within the Celtic world the ox was never endowed with anything but the normal Christian symbolism. Nonetheless, Welsh legends are evidence of the existence of primeval oxen. The two principal beasts belonged to Hu Gadarn, a mythical character who first came to the Isle of Britain with the tribe of the Cymry (Welsh). Before these two oxen came, the only creatures in Britain were bears, wolves, beavers and horned cattle. The *Book of Invasions* mentions other mythic oxen without any specific detail. Oxen thus played a part similar to that of the culture-hero (CHAB pp. 127–8; MYFA p. 400; OGAC 14: pp. 606–9).

oyster   In Ancient China ashes of oyster or mussel shells were often used as a drying agent, especially in graves. Apart from the effectiveness of these ashes in purely material terms, there was an attempt to obtain magical benefits from the bivalve SHELL, which because of its shape symbolized the female principle.

Oysters are also creatures which conceal pearls within their shells. In this respect they symbolize true humility, the source of all spiritual perfection and, consequently, wise men and holy persons as well. They only open their shells to the sunlight, and pile up inner wealth which they carefully cover up so that it may not be profaned. The oyster is inextricably linked to the symbolism of the PEARL.

P

Pactolus King Midas had been initiated into the Dionysiac Mysteries. One day he recognized the prisoner whom his guards brought before him as the god's companion Silenus, who had lost his way. Midas at once freed him and brought him back to Dionysos. As a reward, the god promised to grant any wish, and Midas asked that whatever he touched might be turned to gold. This nearly killed the king, since every time he put food or drink to his lips it turned to solid gold. He besought the god to take back the privilege. Dionysos agreed, provided that he purified himself at the source of the River Pactolus. The king dipped himself in the water and the gift left him, but for ever after the river became a river of gold, or at any rate one in which nuggets were to be found. Homer (*Iliad* 2: 460) tells how this river, with its golden sands, became the place where swans gathered. In the light of their symbolism, it would seem as if in this context gold is poetic inspiration, the divine afflatus received by those who approached the sacred spring.

In the well-known legend, Midas was punished by Apollo by being given ass's EARS. Paul Diel compares this with the legend of Pactolus and provides a fresh explanation. 'His misfortune symbolizes the punishment of all those who long solely for wealth. They suffer impoverishment of the life force and place themselves at risk of gradually losing the power of enjoying what they take for good fortune. They are threatened by starvation. Physical death by inanition symbolizes the death of the soul through lack of spiritual nourishment' (DIES p. 129).

palace Palaces provide an extra touch of magnificence, wealth and hidden secrets to the general symbolism of the HOUSE. The sovereign dwells in the palace, wealth accumulates there and it is a place where secrets are guarded. It symbolizes power, good fortune and knowledge, all the things beyond the scope of ordinary mortals.

Its very structure is subservient to the rules of orientation, making it part of a cosmic order. Palaces may therefore be seen both as the products and the sources of physical, individual and social harmony. In this respect palaces are CENTRES of the universe for the countries in which they are built, for the monarchs who live in them and for the people who look to them. The buildings themselves always comprise some portion in which the vertical dominates, thus making the centre the AXIS as well. They conjoin the three levels of subterranean, terrestrial and celestial; the three classes of society and their three offices. They might symbolize in psychoanalytic terms the three levels of the psyche – the unconscious (secrecy), the conscious (power and knowledge) and the superconscious (wealth or the ideal).

In alchemical terms, the mysterious Hermetic palace 'stands for alchemical or live gold, despised by the ignorant and hidden under rags which conceal it from sight, although it may be very valuable indeed to the person who knows its true properties' (FULC p. 129).

palm Palms and branches of foliage are regarded universally as symbols of victory, ascension, regeneration and immortality. This is true of the Golden Bough in the *Aeneid* and that used in the Eleusinian Mysteries; of the Chinese willow and the Japanese *sakaki*; of the Masonic acacia and the druidical mistletoe; of the willow branches in *The Shepherd* of Hermas and of the box-sprigs which the French place on graves on Palm Sunday.

The palms of Palm Sunday prefigure Christ's resurrection after the tragedy of Calvary, and the palms borne by the Christian martyrs carry the same meaning. Similarly, the French box-sprig signifies sure belief in the immortality of the soul and in the resurrection of the dead (GUED, ROMM). Jung makes it a symbol of the soul.

Pan Pan, the shepherds' god, had half human, half animal shape; bearded, horned and hairy, lively, agile, swift and crafty, he expressed animal cunning. He preyed sexually upon nymphs and boys indifferently, but his appetite was insatiable and he also indulged in solitary masturbation. The gods gave him the name of Pan, meaning 'All Things', not only because all things are to some extent like him in their greed, but also because he is a universal tendency incarnate. He was the god of All Things, doubtless indicative of the procreative current charging All Things, All Gods or All Life (GRID p. 342).

He gave his name to the word 'panic', the terror which fills all nature and all beings when the feeling that this god is there disturbs the spirit and bewilders the senses.

Later, when he had lost his original uncontrollable sexuality, he came to personify the grand totality of a state of being. Neoplatonist and Christian philosophers made Pan the synthesis of paganism. Plutarch records the legend of sailors on the high seas hearing mysterious voices proclaiming 'great Pan is dead!' No doubt the voices mourning among the waves foretold the death of the pagan gods, epitomized in Pan, and the birth of a new age and one which made the Greco-Roman world shiver with fear.

The phrase 'great Pan is dead' is sometimes used to mean the end of an era. Proudhon, for example, applied it to a society which has sunk to its nadir. The death of Pan symbolizes institutional collapse, a strange development for a symbol which passed from that of unbridled sexuality to that of a social order whose disappearance through the failure of its will to live can cause such deep despair.

Pandora Zeus commanded all the gods to hasten to the birth of Pandora, the first woman, saying:

'I will give men . . . an evil thing in which they may all be glad of heart while they embrace their own destruction.' So said the father of men and gods, and laughed aloud. And he bade the famous Hephaestus make haste and mix earth with water and put in it the voice and strength of human kind, and fashion a

sweet, lovely maiden-shape, like to the immortal goddesses in face; and Athene
to teach her needlework and the weaving of the varied web; and golden
Aphrodite to shed grace upon her head and cruel longing and cares that weary
the limbs. And he charged Hermes the guide, the Slayer of Argus, to put in her
a shameless mind and a deceitful nature. So he ordered. And they obeyed the
lord Zeus the son of Cronos. . . . Also the Guide, the Slayer of Argus, contrived
within her lies and crafty words and a deceitful nature at the will of thundering
Zeus, and the Herald of the gods put speech in her. And he called this woman
Pandora, because all they who dwelt on Olympus gave each a gift, a plague to
men who eat bread.

(Hesiod, *Works and Days* 58–82).

Pandora symbolizes the origin of the evils which afflict mankind. According to this myth, they came through the woman who had been created at
Zeus' command to punish the disobedience of Prometheus, who had stolen
fire from Heaven to give to mankind. In the legend of Pandora, in spite of
the gods, mankind enjoyed the benefits of fire and, despite itself, humanity
suffered the damage caused by womankind. The woman was the price of
fire. Only the symbols retained by the legend are worth our concern. It
shows the ambivalence of FIRE, which gives enormous power to mankind
but may, however, result as easily in misfortune as good fortune, depending
upon whether human ends are righteous or sinful. And it is often woman
who directs the flames towards misfortune. The fire thus symbolizes love,
for which all humans long, at whatever cost in suffering. Man who stole fire
from the gods was to undergo in consequence burning by the fire of his
desires. Pandora symbolizes the fire of lust which brings misfortune upon
mankind.

Papal Bull See BULLA.

paper Currently the symbolism of paper is linked either to the writing on
it or to its fragile texture.

In Shintō worship, an important symbolic part is played by strips of folded
paper known as *gohei*. This is the Japanese pronunciation of the Chinese
ideogram and *mitegura* is the strictly Japanese word denoting the ritual and
perhaps magical folding of the paper. There are a score of different ways
of folding it and each has a different meaning, being at one and the same
time an offering and a sign of the 'real presence' of the *kami* in the temple.
Gohei are used in spiritual exercises. Mountains of these strips of folded
paper are to be seen outside temples, reminding us of the candles lit at
Christian shrines.

Folded pieces of paper very similar to the *gohei* symbolize the four *mitama*,
the four traditional aspects of the soul and of the timeless part of the
individual.

Mention should also be made of the *harai-gushi*, an instrument of ritual
purification comprising a staff round which strips of white paper have been
wound. The *tamagudhi*, which is an offering but which probably symbolizes
a link between the soul and the *kami*, is a *sakadi*-branch bearing strips of
folded paper. The notion of purity and, it would seem, of 'subtlety' is constant throughout (HERJ).

Paper, the image-bearer, is a fragile substitute for reality – a paper tiger.

papyrus Papyrus is a transliteration of the Greek word *papyros* (which gives us 'paper'), itself derived from an Ancient Egyptian word meaning 'royal'. The papyrus was the equivalent of the BOOK. In the days when its tufted growth thickly covered the marshes of the Nile Delta, 'the papyrus became the vigorous symbol of the world in gestation; in the form of the bulbous column it served as a support in temples, the scene of the daily rebirth of the universe. Verdant and perennial, the sign for "joy" and "youth" (= "green" in hieroglyphics), it was the magical sceptre of goddesses; it was used in splendid bouquets, symbols of triumph which were offered to the gods and to the dead' (POSD p. 206).

In hieroglyphics the papyrus roll signified knowledge. Unrolling it and rolling it up again corresponded with evolutionary and involutionary drives, with the twofold aspect of knowledge, exoteric and esoteric, with the alternation of the secret and the revealed and the immanent and the manifest. In psychological terms this exhibits tension and relaxation, elation and depression.

Paradise Works of art and both waking dreams and those in natural or drug-induced sleep are full of visions inspired by what might be termed '"the nostalgia for Paradise". I mean by this,' Mircea Eliade explains, 'the desire to be always, effortlessly, at the heart of the world, of reality, of the sacred, and, briefly, to transcend, by natural means, the human condition and to regain a divine state of affairs: what a Christian would call the state of man before the Fall' (ELIT p. 383). Or, as some latter-day magician might remark, his eye upon the future rather than upon the past, 'a super-human state'.

Such indeed was Adam's condition in the Earthly Paradise, in a state of supernatural grace. One thing alone was missing – the right to touch the Tree of the Knowledge of Good and Evil, growing in the midst of the Garden. The breach of this commandment brought with it the Fall of man. The Book of Genesis describes this Paradise in these words:

And the Lord God planted a garden eastward in Eden; and there he put the man whom he had formed. And out of the ground made the Lord God to grow every tree that is pleasant to the sight, and good for food; the tree of life was also in the midst of the garden, and the tree of knowledge of good and evil. And a river went out of Eden to water the garden; and from thence it was parted, and became into four heads. And the name of the first is Pison: that is it which encompasseth the whole land of Havilah, where there is gold; And the gold of that land is good: and there is bdellium and onyx stone. And the name of the second river is Gihon: the same it is that compasseth the whole land of Ethiopia. And the name of the third river is Hiddekel: that is it which goeth towards the east of Assyria. And the fourth river is Euphrates. And the Lord God took the man, and put him into the garden of Eden, to dress it and to keep it. And the Lord God commanded the man, saying, Of every tree of the garden thou mayest freely eat: But of the tree of the knowledge of good and evil, thou shalt not eat of it: for in the day thou eatest thereof thou shalt surely die.

(Genesis 2: 8–17)

Paradise is the Sanskrit *paradēsha*, the all-highest place, the Chaldean *Pardes*. With its central spring and four rivers flowing to the four points of the compass, it is the first spiritual CENTRE, the birthplace of tradition. It is also, universally, the abode of immortality. It is the immovable centre, the heart of the world and the point at which Heaven and Earth enter into communion. Hence it is to be identified with the central or polar mountain, the Hindu Meru or the Muslim Kāf. Uttarakura, the earliest Hindu paradise, was a land to the north, the Hyperborean centre. Muslim esoterics also mention Adam's CAVERN and its symbolism is linked to that of the MOUNTAIN. That the Earthly Paradise is inaccessible is due to the breach of communion between Earth and Heaven, caused by the Fall. Yearning after this Paradise Lost is universal and is manifested, as several theologians have observed, by praying towards the east. On the other hand, Amida's Paradise and that of Mount Kun-Lun lie in the west, as did that of the Ancient Greeks, who also shared a belief that it was in the north. This may lead us to presume that all peoples intuitively believe in one primeval centre, not confined, naturally, to any one particular locality, since this disturbing unanimity is focused upon a condition rather than upon a place.

Paradise is most frequently depicted as a GARDEN luxuriating in plants growing of their own accord and as a direct result of the action of Heaven. The part played by the SPRING or central well from which life and knowledge derive, has been mentioned already. Animals wander freely, their language understood by human beings, who are accepted as their masters. This is a typical feature of the paradisal state springing from Adam's task of giving animals their names. Theologians maintain that this displays the triumph of the intellect over the senses and instincts, as well as knowledge of the specific natures of living creatures. In China, the same notion is to be found in the Isles (see ISLAND) of the Immortals or the Paradise of Kun-Lun inhabited by tame animals. The circular garden, the P'i Yong round the Forbidden City, was filled with animals, and Buddhist paradises are filled with birds, angelic symbols.

As we have said, the emphasis is less upon place than upon condition, and the return to the paradisal state is, in fact, to attain a condition of centrality from which may be made the spiritual ascent along the axis between Earth and Heaven. Furthermore, the Heavens are themselves often many in number and set in hierarchical order, to symbolize the successive attainment of ever higher states of being. The 'centre of the world' corresponds with Brahmaloka, which is in the centre of each being, a state of potential immortality. Similarly Abū Ya'qūb states that just as the Garden of Eden is filled with trees, plants and running waters, so the inward garden of clear perception is filled with the knowledge of higher things and with those gifts imparted by Intellect and Soul (CORT, ELIY, ELIM, GROC, GUEV, GUED, GUEM, GUER, GUES, LIOT, SCHC, GRIB).

Muslim tradition provides an ever more ample and detailed description. Eight gates open onto Paradise and there are one hundred steps in the stairways leading to each storey, the highest being that of the seventh Heaven. A famous *hadīth* states that the key to these gates has three pins – proclamation of the Oneness of God (*tauhīd*), obedience to God, and abstinence from all evil-doing.

Paradise is also described as possessing eternal daylight and eternal spring. One day in Paradise is the same as a thousand days on Earth. Four rivers flow from mountains of musk between banks of pearl and ruby. There are

four mountains – Uhud, Sinai, Lebanon and Hasid. It would take a galloping horse a hundred years to emerge from the shadow cast by the banana
tree growing in Paradise and a single leaf of the JUJUBE-tree growing on its
borders would cover the entire body of the Faithful.

Wonderful music, angels, the elect, hills, trees and birds all combine to
create the univeral song of paradisal bliss.

The sweetest music of all is the voice of God welcoming the Elect. Every
Friday the Almighty invites them to visit him. Men follow the Prophet,
women his daughter Fatima, mounting from one Heaven to the next, passing the Heavenly Ka'ba, surrounded by angels at prayer; and they approach
the Guarded Tablet on which the QUILL inscribes the Decrees of God. The
Veil of Light is raised and God appears to his guests like the full Moon.

The Mu'tazilites explain the anthropomorphic attributes of God metaphorically, but take the sensual pleasures of Paradise at their face value.

The early Ash'ari stressed the incomparable and indescribable bliss of
Paradise as in no way to be set beside earthly pleasures.

Philosophers, and especially Avicenna, taught that the wise man should
regard Resurrection and Paradise as symbols and allegories.

Sufis elaborated a higher spiritual meaning revealed by the *kashf* (unveiling). Ibn al-'Arabī regarded Paradise as an abode of life, the raised beds
standing for degrees of perfection, brocaded bed-covers for the soul's lower
face, Houris for heavenly souls and so on.

In the High Middle Ages, Irish monks assimilated the traditional Celtic
sid into the Christian Heaven. However, because their intimate knowledge
of Celtic tradition enabled them to identify certain elements in it with traditional Biblical chronology, they also identified Ireland with a promised
land and with an image of the Earthly Paradise – rich soil, pleasant climate
and an absence of serpents or other noxious creatures (LEBI 1, *passim*).

parasol   The parasol is a symbol of Heaven and, in consequence, the Asia-
wide emblem of kingship; hence the White Parasol of Laos. In the first
place it is the regalia of the *chakravartī*-king, the universal monarch seated
at the hub of the wheel. The ribs of a parasol radiate from its axis like the
spokes from the hub of a wheel. The monarch is identified with this cosmic
AXIS represented by the staff of the parasol. AWNINGS themselves are Heaven
and very clearly related to dome symbolism. In Laos, so legend assures us,
a parasol was set upon a 'sand-mountain' as an image of the World Axis,
Mount Meru. Thai funeral ceremonies include the setting of a parasol on
the top of a short column fitted with cross-pieces for the soul's ascent into
Heaven, while the staff, or *danda*, of the Hindu parasol is itself divided into
a number of sections. The Ancient Chinese royal chariot had a round awning
representing Heaven, while the pole which held it up represented the World
Axis and the square body of the chariot the Earth. The Emperor was iden-
tified with the pole since Heaven covers and Earth underpins. The parasol,
Vishnu's emblem, is simultaneously an emblem of kingship and a symbol of
Heaven.

In aniconic depictions of the Buddha, the meaning is the same – the
parasol stands for Heaven; the throne, for the intermediate world; and his
footprints, for the Earth. The parasol is, however, the emblem of the

chakravartī, the Buddha himself. The stepped series of parasols on the tops of STUPAS and pagodas are celestial levels. It should be observed that they are placed above the dome, on the portion of the axis which emerges from it, that is to say, that they stand for extra-cosmic levels and superhuman states. In Tibetan symbolism they correspond to the element Air, but above them there is a 'tongue of flame', the element Ether.

In Tantrism, the *chakra* (wheels) set at intervals along the spinal column (microcosmic axis) are overtly identified with parasols. However, the very crown of the Brahmarandhra, with a hole in the centre, is a parasol. It is the flowery awning, the Chinese imperial insignium which Taoist symbolism, for its part, identified with the eyebrows, sheltering the Sun and Moon. Guénon notes the twofold aspect under which the parasol should be considered. Seen from below it shades against the sunlight: seen from above, its ribs (*salākā*) are the very rays of sunlight which embrace the whole world (BENA, JILH, MALA, MASR, PORA).

As a solar symbol, it is, as it were, the halo of the person which it shades, who is related to the Sun by his rank and authority. Among the retinue of servants surrounding a king, one held a parasol over his head, and this was often decorated with richly coloured feathers. In Chinese tradition, the parasol was an emblem of elegance and the display of wealth. The parasol attracts attention, not to the Sun above it, but to the Sun below it, that is to the individual concerned. It tends towards interiorization.

If one considers its everyday use alone, it is patently a symbol of protection.

partridge Although the Chinese, like Europeans, regard the cry of the partridge as discordant, they sometimes treat it as a love-call. Partridges used to be regarded as preservatives against poison.

In Indian iconography, the partridge is a type of the beauty of the eyes (BELT, MALA).

In Iran, the partridge's strut is compared with the walk of an elegant and high-born lady (SOUS p. 185).

In Kabyle folk poetry and tradition, the partridge is 'the symbol of womanly grace and beauty' (SERP p. 155). Eating its flesh is the equivalent of swallowing a love-potion.

Christian tradition makes the bird a symbol of temptation and of damnation, an incarnation of the Devil. Ancient Greek legend also made it a bird of somewhat evil cast. When Daedalus became jealous of one of his nephews and threw him off the top of the Acropolis, Athene took pity on him and saved him by turning him into a partridge as he fell. However, the bird was a delighted spectator 'at the funeral of Daedalus' son, Icarus, who had fallen to his death' (GRID p. 358).

As may be seen, partridge symbolism is rather ambivalent.

pasque-flower See SNOWDROP.

paulownia In Ancient China, the paulownia was a 'cardinal' tree, the Paulownia Gate being the North Gate. It is true that in this instance the tree concerned was the hollow paulownia (*K'ong-tong*). Wood from the paulownia was used to make musical instruments, and especially soundboxes on which the Sun's course could be followed in rhythm. It was also used to make war-drums. The ideogram for paulownia (*t'ong*) has the same sound as the ideogram *t'ong*, meaning drum-beat.

As regards the location of the Paulownia Palace in which T'ang the Victorious was buried, and to which T'ai-kia was exiled, this may very well have been in the north, if one bears in mind that this quarter was the abode of the dead. The process of regeneration follows the Winter solstice and, in the north, paulownia is a substitute for that well-known emblem of immortality, the ACACIA (GRAD).

peace Nations at peace and societies at peace are both symbols of peace at heart and are both its consequence. The Heavenly Peace of the Chinese (*Taiping*) was indeed displayed in the social harmony and undisturbed government of the empire. Yu the Great regulated the world by pacifying Earth and Waters. The Han dynasty *Taiping-Chao* was a Taoist organization, while Hung Hsiu-chuan, who led the Taiping Rebellion in the nineteenth century, proclaimed himself the Son of God. The Chinese secret societies' 'City of Willows' is also known as the House of Heavenly Peace (*Taiping chuang*). This is the image of the spiritual centre and even of the Still Centre lying above the Great Bear. Hence peace is the peace to be found in a 'centred' paradisal state, free from all earthly cares. It is perhaps that Salem ('peace') of which Melchizedech was king, Jerusalem meaning 'Vision of Peace'. The voyage described in the Ancient Egyptian *Book of the Dead* is to a 'City of Peace', just like that described in the legends of Chinese secret societies. 'Heavenly Peace' is literally the Arabic *sakīnah*, corresponding to the Hebrew *shekinah*, the Real Presence of God. It is also the *Pax Profunda* of the Rosicrucians and the Heavenly Sanctuary of the medieval guilds, the 'peace in emptiness' of which Li Tzu speaks and the Hindu philosopher Shankara's 'Tranquillity', and the Beatific Vision of Christian mystics.

The Peace of Christ, so cherished by the Greek Fathers, was a state of spiritual contemplation. The Hindu *shānti* is the quest for inner peace. 'Pacification' is the extinction of worldly cares and the fires of passion, as well as sacrificial death. The Buddhist *shāntipada* or state of peace is identical with the bliss of the *samādhi*. Buddhist scriptures state that the Buddha attained 'repose', since for them Heavenly Peace is NIRVANA (CORT, CORM, GRAD, GRAP, GRAR, GUEV, GUEC, GUET, SCHP, SILI).

peach Because it blossoms early, the peach-tree in flower is a symbol of Spring. The same line of thought – rebirth and fertility – makes it also a Chinese emblem of marriage. The *Momo* or festivals held in honour of peach-blossom in Japan seem to reinforce this with the twofold notion of purity and faithfulness – peach-blossom symbolizing virginity.

Its fruit, on the other hand, is connected with the myth of Izanagi who used it as a protection against thunder. It plays the part of a preservative against evil influences and has properties used in exorcism, as is clearly shown in Chinese practices, a peach-wood staff being employed for the purpose. This is perhaps because Yi the Archer was killed by such a staff, which was a royal weapon. At New Year, little figures carved from peach-wood were set over doorways to drive off evil influences.

Often both the tree and its fruit are symbols of immortality. The peach-tree belonging to the Siwang Mu, the Royal Mother of the West, every three thousand years bore fruit which conferred immortality. The Immortals fed upon peach- and plum-blossom or, like Koyeu, upon the peaches which grew on Mount Sui. Sap from peach trees, the *Pao-p'u zu* relates, makes the body luminous. Folk art assures us that the peach brings 'a thousand Springs'.

In their legends, Chinese secret societies symbolically take up the historical theme of the 'Peach-orchard Oath'. Some versions indeed turn it into a 'Garden of Immortality', a sort of Paradise of regeneration, identifying the peach-tree with the Tree of Life in the Earthly Paradise, in this context the goal of the journey undertaken by the initiate.

It may be added that the sight of peach-blossom brought enlightenment to the monk, Lin-yun, that is to say that it spontaneously caused his return to the centre and to a paradisal state (COUS, DURV, GRAD, HERS, KALL, LECC, RENB).

According to a mythological treatise on geography written in the third century BC, the *Book of Seas and Mountains*, there was once a gigantic peach-tree with a trunk 3000 *lis* in diameter (about a mile), and among its branches was the Ghosts' Gateway. Watchmen at the gate were charged with the task of arresting malignant ghosts and feeding them to the tigers, since tigers only eat persons of ill repute. The famous Emperor Huang Ti had the notion of simply hanging figures of the watchmen carved from peach-wood beside the gates instead of the watchmen themselves. Peach-wood was also used to make the the Ki-Pi, the brushes used in divination. They were a sort of red lacquered fork which wrote the ideograms which provided the oracular message.

peacock Although we readily make the peacock an image of vanity, the bird sacred to Zeus' (Jupiter's) wife Hera (Juno) is first and foremost a solar symbol, stemming from the way in which it spreads its tail in the shape of a wheel.

It was the emblem of the Burmese monarchy, descended from the Sun. The Burmese Peacock Dance and the use of the peacock in the Cambodian *trot* dance relate to droughts caused by the Sun. Sacrificing a peacock, like the sacrifice of a stag, is a prayer for rain and for the heavenly gift of fertility. Kumāra (Skanda), whose steed is the peacock – there is a very famous depiction of this at Angkor Wat – is identified with solar energy. Skanda's peacock certainly destroys serpents – that is, attachments to the physical and temporal – but the identification of serpents with the element Water confirms the kinship of the peacock with the Sun and the element Fire, the antithesis of Water. In any case, according to the *Bardo-Thodol*, the peacock is also the Buddha Amitābha's throne, to which the colour red and the element Fire correspond.

In this context it is also supposed to be the symbol of beauty and the power of transmutation, since the loveliness of its plumage is believed to derive from the natural transmutation of the poisons which it swallows when it destroys serpents. Undoubtedly in this context we are, above all, concerned with immortality symbolism. This is the Indian explanation, and, furthermore, Skanda himself transforms poisons into a beverage of immortality.

In Buddhist *Jataka*, the peacock is a shape under which the Bodhisattva teaches renunciation of worldly attachments. In the Chinese world, the peacock is used to express wishes for peace and prosperity. It is also called 'the Pimp', both because it is used as a decoy and because one glance from the bird is supposed to make a woman pregnant.

Men of the southern Vietnamese Maa tribe wear peacock feathers in their hair. This doubtless serves to identify them with the race of birds, but is perhaps also not unrelated with sun-ray symbolism. In Vietnam, peacocks are emblems of peace and prosperity (BENA, BELT, DAMS, DANA, DURV, EVAB, GOVM, KRAA, MALA, PORA).

In Christian tradition, too, the peacock symbolizes the solar wheel and hence is a sign of immortality. Its tail evokes the starry sky.

It will be observed that Western iconography sometimes depicts peacocks drinking from the eucharistic chalice. In the Middle East they are shown on either side of the Tree of Life, symbols of the incorruptibility of the soul and the twofold nature of the human psyche.

Peacocks are sometimes used as steeds, but to some extent they control their riders. Known as the creatures with a hundred eyes, they became signs of eternal bliss and of the Beatific Vision of the soul, face to face with God. They are to be found in Romanesque sculpture and in funerary symbolism (CUMS).

To Muslims, the peacock is a cosmic symbol and when it spreads its tail it represents either the whole universe, or the full Moon, or the Sun at its zenith.

A Sufi legend, probably of Persian origin, tells that God created the Spirit in the form of a peacock and showed it in the mirror of the Divine Essence its own image. The peacock was seized with reverential awe and let fall drops of sweat, and from these all other beings were created. The peacock's outspread tail imitates the cosmic deployment of the Spirit.

                                                                    (BURD p. 85)

In esoteric tradition, the peacock is a symbol of wholeness, in that it combines all colours when it spreads out its tail in a fan. It exhibits the intrinsic identity and the short-lived nature of all manifestation, since its forms appear and vanish as swiftly as the peacock displays and furls its tail.

The Yezidi, originating in Kurdistan and notable for the similarities between them and Sufi Dervishes and Buddhists, make much of the power known as Malik Taus, the Anga-peacock, in which opposites are reconciled.

pear In China pear-blossom was sometimes used as a symbol of mourning, because it is white, but more especially as a symbol of the fleeting nature of life itself, because it is so short-lived and so very easily scattered.

In dreams the fruit is 'a typically erotic symbol, fraught with sensuality. This is probably due to its sweet taste, juiciness and also to its shape which has a suggestion of the feminine about it' (AEPR p. 283).

pearl The consistency of meanings applied to this lunar symbol, linked to water and woman, is as remarkable as their universality, as the varied writings of Mircea Eliade and other ethnologists go to show.

Born of Water or the Moon and found in a shell, the pearl stands for the *yin* principle and is the essential symbol of 'a femininity wholly creative.... The sexual symbolism of shells communicates to them all the forces involved in it; and finally the similarity between the pearl and the foetus endows it with generative and obstetrical properties.... All the magic, medicinal, gynaecological and funereal properties of pearls spring from this triple symbolism of water, moon and woman' (ELIT p. 439). As a typical example, pearls are a panacea of Indian traditional medicine, being specifics against bleeding, jaundice, madness, poisoning and eye and lung diseases. In Europe they were used to treat melancholy, epilepsy and madness.

In the East, it is their fructifying, aphrodisiacal and talismanic properties which predominate. If pearls were arranged in a grave they 'regenerated the dead by placing them within a cosmic rhythm which is supremely cyclic, involving (in the pattern of the moon's phases) birth, life, death, rebirth' (ELIT p. 440).

Modern Hindu healers use powdered pearls for their tonic and aphrodisiacal properties.

The Ancient Greeks regarded pearls as symbols of love and marriage.

In some parts of India, a dead person's mouth was stuffed with pearls and there was a similar custom in Borneo. Meanwhile, Streeter describes the Florida Indians as decorating the tombs of their kings with pearls just as the Egyptians had done in the time of Cleopatra. He states that de Soto's Spanish troops found wooden coffins in one of their great temples, in which the embalmed bodies of the dead had been placed and beside them small baskets filled with pearls. Similar customs have been recorded in Mexico and in Virginia.

The use of artificial pearls falls under the same symbolic heading. Madeleine Colani has described how, in funeral sacrifices and ceremonies in Laos 'the dead were provided with pearls for their heavenly existence. They were stuffed into the body's natural apertures. Even today the dead are buried with belts, caps and clothes decorated with pearls.'

Chinese traditional medicine employed the 'virgin' pearl, that is one which had not been drilled, as a panacea for diseases of the eyes, and Arabic medicine acknowledged the same properties in it.

Gnostic Christianity both enriched and made pearl symbolism more complex, while developing it along its original lines.

St Ephrem used this ancient myth as an illustration both of the Immaculate Conception and of Christ's spiritual birth in baptism by fire. Origen was another to identify Christ with the pearl and he was followed by many writers.

In the famous Gnostic 'gospel', the *Acts of Thomas*, search for the pearl symbolizes the spiritual drama of Man's fall and redemption. It finally came to mean the mystery of the transcendent made amenable to sense-perception, the manifestation of God in the Cosmos (ELIT).

The pearl may also be seen in the role of mystical CENTRE. It symbolizes the sublimation of instinct, spiritualization of matter, transfiguration of the elements, the gleaming goal of evolution. The pearl is like Plato's spherical man, the image of the ideal perfection of human beginnings and ends. Muslims depict the faithful in Paradise as being enclosed within a pearl with a Houri for company. Pearls are the attributes of angelic perfection, of a perfection which is nevertheless acquired by transmutation and not freely given.

Pearls are rare, pure and precious. They are pure because they are regarded as being flawless and white, and this is unaffected by their being dredged from the muddy depths or taken from a clumsy shell. Their value makes them stand for the Kingdom of Heaven (Matthew 13: 45–6). Diadochus of Photike taught that, by the 'pearl of great price' which the merchant bought by selling 'all that he had', is meant the light of the intellect within the heart, the beatific vision. Here is a hint of the pearl being 'hidden' in its shell, like truth and knowledge, which require effort for their attainment. Shabistarī saw pearls as 'the heart's knowledge: when the Gnostic has found the pearl, his life's task has been accomplished.' The Eastern prince in the *Acts of Thomas* goes in quest of the pearl in the same way as Perceval seeks the Grail. Once this 'pearl of great price' has been acquired, it should not be 'cast before swine' (Matthew 7: 6): knowledge should not be broadcast heedlessly to those unworthy of it. Symbols are pearls of speech concealed within the shell of words.

According to legend, pearls are born from a lightning flash or from a drop of dew falling into the shell; they are, at all stages of being, imprints of celestial action and embryos of physical or spiritual birth, like the BINDU in the conch or the Aphrodite-pearl in its shell. Persian myth associates pearls with primeval manifestation, the pearl in its shell being like the genie in the darkness. In many parts of the world a more down-to-earth view is taken of the oyster which holds the pearl – it is compared with the female sexual organs.

Pearls are naturally associated with the element Water – dragons keep guard over them at the bottom of the sea – but they are also linked to the Moon. The *Atharva-Veda* calls them 'daughters of soma' which, as well as being the beverage of immortality, is also the Moon. In Ancient China, pearls, along with aquatic creatures, were observed to 'change' with the phases of the Moon. Carbuncles, those 'shining pearls', borrowed their light from the Moon. They were preservatives against fire. They were, however, both Fire and Water, images of the spirit coming to birth in matter.

The Vedic pearl, 'that daughter of soma', prolonged life. In China, too, it was a symbol of immortality. A shroud decorated with pearls or pearls inserted in the natural apertures of the corpse prevented it from decaying. The same belief was current with regard to jade and gold. It should be observed that pearls came to birth in the same way as JADE, possessed the same properties and served the same uses.

A symbol of similar order was provided by pearls strung on a thread, becoming a rosary or *sūtrātmā*, the linked series of worlds penetrated and linked by the Universal Spirit, *ātman*. Thus pearl NECKLACES symbolize the cosmic unity of the manifold, the integration of the scattered elements of a being in the oneness of personality and the establishment of a spiritual relationship between two or several individuals. The broken necklace is, however, the image of the disintegration of personality, universal upheaval and the destruction of oneness.

In Iran, pearls have particularly rich symbolic qualities, as much from the sociological viewpoint as from the history of religion.

The twelfth-century Persian poet Sa'dī repeats in his *Būstān* the legend of the growth of the pearl from a drop of rain falling into the shell, which rises to the surface of the sea and opens to receive it. This drop of water, celestial semen, becomes the pearl. This legend has its origins in Persian folklore and is a commonplace of literature. Futhermore, a *hadīth* may be quoted in which the Prophet states: 'God has servants who are like the rain. When it falls on dry land it gives birth to corn: when it falls on sea, it gives birth to pearls.'

In Persian literature and folklore, the unflawed pearl is regarded as a symbol of virginity, as it is in the writings of the Ahl-i Haqq sect and in more general terms among the Kurds. The phrase 'to pierce the pearl of virginity' is used to mean the consummation of a marriage.

On another level, the belief of the Ahl-i Haqq that the mothers of the avatars of God were all virgins and that their chief name was Ramz-bār ('Secret of the Ocean') relates to this symbol. According to their cosmogony 'in the beginning no creature existed except the all-highest, sole, living and venerable Truth. Its dwelling-place was in a pearl and its essence was hidden. The pearl was in a shell and the shell was in the sea and the waves of the sea covered them both.'

In his poem the *Iskandar-Nāma*, Nizāmī likens the birth of Alexander the Great to the growth of a royal pearl in a shell fertilized by the Spring rain.

Ancestral lineage is sometimes compared with a string of matched pearls, and the same image is also used for versification. In Persian literature, a subtle thought is called a 'pearl', as much from its beauty as from the fact that it is a product of its author's creative genius. For example, the phrase 'a subtle thought finer than the rarest pearl' may be used. 'To scatter shining pearls from lips of coral' is to speak brilliantly. 'Threading pearls' is versification.

In a mystic sense, pearls are also taken as symbols of enlightenment and spiritual birth, as may be seen especially in the famous 'Hymn of the Pearl' in the *Acts of Thomas*. Mystics constantly seek to attain their ideal or their goal, the 'pearl of the ideal'. This quest for the pearl stands for the search for the Sublime Essence hidden in the Self. The archetypal image of the pearl evokes something which is pure, hidden, buried in the depths and difficult to reach. The word 'pearl' may denote the Koran, knowledge or child. 'If a person dreams that he has pierced a pearl, it means that he has expounded the Koran well. Dreams of selling pearls mean that thanks to the dreamer, knowledge has been spread abroad.' Hafiz speaks of 'the pearl which the shell of time and space cannot contain' and Hariri praises 'the pearl of the Mystic Way preserved within the shell of divine Law'.

In the East, and especially in Persia, the pearl generally speaking is endowed with a nobility which derives from its sacrality. This is why it decorates the crowns of kings. Traces of this same characteristic are to be found in pearl jewellery, especially ear-rings decorated with rare and precious pearls which cast a shadow of this holy nobility upon their wearers.

In oriental dream symbolism, pearls preserve these special characteristics and are generally interpreted as children or else as wives and concubines. In addition they may be regarded as symbols of knowledge and wealth.

pedestal See THRONE.

Pegasus Pegasus, the winged horse, is often associated in Greek legend with water. Poseidon fathered the creature on one of the Gorgons and its name is similar to *pege*, 'spring'. Pegasus was born at the Ocean springs, Bellerophon found it drinking from the Pirenean spring and Pegasus made water spring from the mountain-side by striking it with his hooves. The horse was also linked to storms, 'bearer of thunder and the thunderbolt for wise Zeus'. Any symbolic explanation of Pegasus must take account of WINGS and SPRINGS, while fertility and elevation provide an axis for understanding the myth. Pegasus is the cloud carrying the fructifying rain.

Traditionally HORSES stand for the driving force of desire. When the human partakes of the horse's body, he or she is reduced to that mythical monster the centaur, identified with animal instincts. The winged horse, on the other hand, stands for 'creative imagination and its real powers of elevation' and for 'sublime and spiritual values', able to raise humans above 'the perils of aberration'. In fact, it was by using Pegasus as his steed that Bellerophon was able to overcome the CHIMERA. Pegasus may thus be regarded as 'the symbol of sublimated imagination ... objective imagination which raises the individual to sublime levels' (DIES pp. 86–7).

This explanation brings together the two meanings of springs and wings – spiritual creativity.

In more general terms, Pegasus has become the symbol of poetic inspiration.

pelican The mistaken belief that the pelican fed its young with its own flesh and blood made the bird in the past a symbol of parental love. This is the reason why, in Christian iconography, it is a symbol of Christ. There is, however, a deeper reason: as a water-fowl, the pelican is a symbol of the moist humour which ancient physical science believed disappeared under the growing heat of the Sun, only to re-appear in Winter. The pelican was thus taken for an image of Christ's death and resurrection, as also that of Lazarus. Its standing as a Christ symbol was also based upon the wound in its heart from which flowed water and blood, life-giving draughts. 'Dead Christian, awake!' Angelus Silesius wrote. 'Behold, our Pelican waters you with his blood and the waters of his heart. If you accept them fittingly ... you will at once be alive and well' (DEVA).

pen The symbolism of pen (*qalam*) and book – or quill and tablet – plays an extremely important part in Islamic tradition. The Sufis teach that the Supreme Pen is Universal Intelligence. The Guarded Tablet, on which this pen writes the fate of the world, corresponds to *materia prima*, the increate or non-manifested which, under the impulse of the Intelligence or Essence, produced all that creation contains (BURA p. 17).

In his *Chronicles*, Tabari wrote that God created the *qalam* a thousand years before he created anything else. He also wrote that the *qalam* was created from light.

The first thing which God created was the Hidden or Guarded Tablet. On it he wrote all that would be until the Day of Resurrection. God is the only being who knows what is written on it. It is made from white pearl and its length is the distance which separates Earth from Heaven and its breadth the distance between East and West. It is bound to the Throne and ever ready to strike the forehead of Isrāfil, the angel closest to the Throne. Whenever God wishes to bring into being something in his creation, the Tablet strikes Isrāfil on the forehead. He looks in it and reads the will of God. Allah, it is said, blots out or confirms whatever he wishes and in him is the archetype of the Written Word. God glances at this Tablet three hundred and sixty times a day. Whenever He looks at it, He gives life or brings death, He raises or abases. He confers honour or inflicts humiliation, He creates what He will and determines what seems good to Him.

Allah created the Quill or Pen from a precious substance so as to write upon the Tablet. The Pen has one end split so that light flows from it like ink from our quills. God said: 'Write!' 'What shall I write?' asked the Pen. 'Fate!' it was told. It began to write on the Tablet everything that was to happen until the Day of the Resurrection. The Tablet was filled: the Pen dried up, and the fate of all was fixed for good or ill (SOUN). The quill is regarded as the symbol of predestination.

pentacle Treatises on magic call a pentacle a magic seal impressed on virgin parchment made from goat-skin, or engraved upon such precious metals as gold and silver. Triangles, squares and six- or five-pointed stars are drawn inside the circles on the seal and within these geometric patterns are written Hebrew letters, Kabbalistic signs and Latin words. These seals are believed to bear a relationship to those invisible realities of whose powers they obtain a share. They can be used to cause earthquakes, inspire love, bring death and launch spells of all sorts. They both symbolize, entrap and deploy occult powers.

pentagram Pentagrams take either pentagonal or star shape. Their symbolism is manifold, but is always based upon that of the number FIVE, which expresses the conjunction of inequalities. The five points of the pentagram come together in fruitful marriage of three (the male principle) with two (the female principle). In this context, the pentagram symbolizes hermaphrodism. Pentagrams were used as recognition signs between members of the same group or society, as for example the followers of Pythagoras in Classical antiquity. The pentagram united them: it was one of the keys to Higher Knowledge and opened the door to what was secret.

The pentagram also bears the meaning of marriage, good fortune and fulfilment. The Ancients regarded it as a symbol of the idea of perfection. Paracelsus judged the pentagram to be one of the most powerful signs.

In Europe the pentagram of Pythagoras became that of Hermes Trismegistus and was regarded, not simply as a symbol of knowledge, but as a means of casting spells and of obtaining power (GHYN 2: p. 77). Sorcerers used representations of the pentagram to exercise their powers and there were pentagrams specific to love, ill luck and so on.

In its stellar, rather than pentagonal shape, Masonic tradition calls the pentagram the Blazing Star. With some reservations Boucher quotes Ragon's interpretation of the Blazing Star as being 'the image in Ancient Egypt of the son of Isis and the Sun, begetter of the seasons and emblem of motion, of that Horus, symbol of primeval matter, inexhaustible well-spring of life, spark of holy fire and universal seed of all beings. To Masons, it is the emblem of the Genius which raises the soul to great deeds.' Boucher reminds us that 'the pentagram was the favourite symbol of the followers of Pythagoras. . . . they inscribed it upon their missives as a form of greeting like the Latin *vale*, or "Good health". The pentagram was also called *ugeia*, Hygeia being the goddess of health, and the five letters making up her name in Greek were set at each of its points' (BOUM).

The pentagram gives expression to a force which is the synthesis of complementary powers.

peony   In China, the peony is a symbol of wealth and honours because of the way in which the flower grows and its RED colour. The Chinese name, *mutan*, includes *tan*, the word meaning CINNABAR, the medicine of immortality (DURV).

The phrase, 'to blush like a peony', has led to the swift corruption of the flower into a pejorative symbol of shame.

Its former use as a medicinal plant gave rise to numerous superstitions connected with it, recorded by Theophrastus and current until modern times.

perch   In the Far East this fish is a symbol of sexual appetite and in China is regarded as an aphrodisiac. The meaning of such circumlocutions as 'to be hungry for perch' or 'to be greedy for perch' are self-explanatory (BELT).

perfume   The Roman Missal speaks of the 'savour of sweetness' (*odor suavitatis*) and this is one of the elements of a sacrificial offering designed to make it acceptable to God. Aromatic perfumes played a particularly important part in Jewish ritual. Similarly, perfumes were widely employed in Ancient Greek and Roman religious ceremonies. They were poured over statues of the gods, corpses were embalmed in them, scent-bottles were placed in graves and even the grave-stone itself was rubbed with perfume. In Ancient Egypt, essential oils for perfumes were extracted and blended in the temples and the goddesses were regarded as surpassing all other women in the perfumes they used. The intangible but very real scent of a perfume relates it symbolically to the presence of a spirit and to the nature of the soul. The way in which a perfume lingers long after the person wearing it has departed, evokes notions of the enduring strength of remembrance. Perfumes thus symbolize the memory and it is perhaps in this sense that they were used in funeral ceremonies.

Perfumes are, however, expressions of the virtues, as Origen remarks in connection with the 'very sweet scent of cedar'. In Yoga they are also the manifestation of a degree of spiritual perfection, for the scent which the individual gives off may well relate to his ability to transmute seminal energy. Were he a *urdhvaretas*, he would give off the scent of lotus.

Perfume plays an important part in purification, the more so because it is often an exhalation of such incorruptible substances as resin (see INCENSE). It stands for perception of consciousness.

The Gandharvas are called 'Perfumes', but rather than give off sweet-scented emanations, these celestial beings take their nourishment from them. They are akin in part to soma and in part to breath or the life force. To

Tibetan Buddhists their 'cities' are typical of phantasmagoria, mirage or unsubstantial building (AVAS, DANA, EVAB, SAIR).

Perfumes are also symbols of light, and Hindu ritual associates them with the element Air.

In their experiments with mental imagery, Doctors Fretigny and Virel have proved the powers which perfumes exercise in psychology. They encourage the appearance of significant images and scenes. In their turn, these images arouse and redirect emotions and desires and can also be related to a distant past. Essence of heliotrope, especially, induces images of flowers, gardens and scented articles, and stimulates the senses. Essence of vanilla conjures up food images and emotions associated with the oral stage. Phenomena of symbolization through sensory environment have been little studied to date.

Persephone   Daughter of Zeus and Demeter, the fertility-goddess who, in Plato's words, 'provides food like a mother'; or, according to another tradition, of Zeus and Styx, nymph of the Underworld river. Her symbolism brings these two legends together, since Persephone lived for three parts of the year on Earth and for one season in the Underworld. She thus symbolizes seasonal change. For the three Winter months of the year she returns to the company of Hades, god of the Underworld, the uncle who ravished her and became her husband. She is his prisoner, too, since he persuaded her to eat a POMEGRANATE-seed, thus breaking the fast which must be observed in the Underworld and condemning her to it for ever.

When dwelling on Earth she is supposed to have fallen in love with Adonis, whom she forced to follow her to the Underworld. It would, however, be an exaggeration to make her goddess of the Underworld to the exclusion of all else. Rather she would seem to symbolize the paradox that, if the grain die not, the harvest shall not arise.

The Ancient Romans identified her with Proserpina and she was also called Cora, 'the Maiden'. She played an important part in mystery religions and especially in the rites of initiation at Eleusis, where she might well symbolize the candidate for initiation who suffered death to be reborn and went through Hell to attain Heaven.

Perseus   The myth of Perseus illustrates the complexity of the father–son and son–father relationship present in all men. Perseus had no human father. He was directly descended from Zeus (metamorphosed into a shower of gold) and Danae. Danae's father, Acrisius, however, had been told by an oracle that he would be killed by his grandson and, in his fear, set Danae adrift on the sea in a wooden chest with her baby. They reached an island, where Perseus grew up and became famous for his great deeds. It is pointless in this context to explain the myth in elaborate detail, it suffices to observe that, as Paul Diel explains, it symbolizes the simultaneous existence in each individual of two images of the father – the first of an overbearing and hostile person, the second of a man of sublime and generous nature, the first being no more than a perverted image of the second. The negative aspect might be regarded as that of 'the old Adam', responsible for Original Sin and for all the ills and weaknesses and painful duties which are consequent upon it and, on top of all this, swollen with self-conceit. The

positive aspect is that of the father as symbol of the spirit which enlightens,
and of the strength which creates, shares and comforts. Which of these two
fathers was he to kill? That is to say, which was he to choose? The myth
is as it were a symbol of choice.

Perseus was, however, also the conqueror of Medusa, Queen of the
GORGONS, thanks to PEGASUS, the winged horse which had enabled
Bellerophon to overcome the Chimera. If Medusa stands for an exaggerated image of guilt, cutting off her head is decisively to master exaggerated,
paralysing and morbid feelings of guilt and to gain the strength to see
oneself undistorted by belittlement or self-aggrandisement. This is clear-
sightedness without the distorting mirror reflecting the morbid world of sin.
In this repect also, Perseus symbolizes a choice between standing as if
turned to stone before the image of sin distorted by the seductions of self-
conceit, or cutting off the head of that image by overcoming self-conceit
through the exercise of a balanced judgement and with the sharp SWORD of
the truth (DIES pp. 90–105).

As a reward for overcoming self-conceit and the monsters of his own
creation, Perseus at Zeus' command became one of the heavenly constellations. He symbolizes the realization of an ideal at the cost of hard struggle
and courageous and careful choice.

persimmon The famous persimmons by the Chinese painter Mu-k'i are
not so much a formal symbol as an attempt to express the inexpressible –
the subtle mark of enlightenment.

In the Far East, the persimmon is denoted by the ideogram *che* pronounced in the same way as the ideogram for 'business'. Hence persimmons
are used to send good wishes for success in business (DURV).

pestle The pestle occurs in different guises in Hindu iconography and
bears correspondingly different meanings. When held by Balarāma, it is
associated with the ploughshare and is the implement which rules the soil;
in the hands of Samskarsana, it is a death symbol; in those of Ghantākarma
it has a selective function, since pestles separate the grain of rice from the
husk. Ghantākarma is believed to drive off disease: he is the 'destroyer of
death'.

The rising and falling of the pestle in use follows the line of the World
Axis. Devoucoux compares this aspect with the vertical shaft of the Cross,
in the sense that they unite 'things heavenly with things earthly'.

Pestles are also endowed with phallic symbolism, something not unrelated to the shape and meaning of the LINGAM, as some Cambodian legends,
for example, graphically express (DEVA, MALA, PORA).

In Burma there is the tale of the pestle which, for a woman's lifetime, had
crushed spices and become so impregnated with their aroma that it could
bring the dead to life, restore their youth to the aged and make the young
immortal. The Moon stole it to preserve eternal youth, but a dog chased
her and made her drop the pestle (eclipse) and this is why the Moon grows
old and has to die each month.

The Vedas often use the sexual allegory of pestle and MORTAR.

petrifaction See under STONE.

phallus A symbol of the powers of procreation, the well-spring and channel of semen as representative of the active principle. Many symbols, such as the foot, the thumb, standing stones, columns, trees and so on, carry a phallic meaning, but their depiction is neither necessarily esoteric (see LINGAM; OMPHALOS) nor erotic. It merely conveys the sense of the powers of procreation which are worshipped in that particular shape by many religions.

Phallic symbolism plays, as it does in all ancient traditions, an important role in Kabbalistic thought. *Jessod*, the ninth *sefirah* (see SEFIROTH), relates to the powers of procreation as the foundation of all living things. In the *Sefer Bahir*, the phallus is compared with the righteous man, the latter being a column which is at one and the same time the foundation and the point of balance between Heaven and Earth. Because of the close links binding the microcosm and the macrocosm, the deeds which the righteous man accomplishes on Earth are the counterpart of cosmic energy. The presence or absence of the righteous upon the earthly plane strengthens or weakens the bonds of Heaven and Earth. Similarly the phallus hardens or softens in the presence or absence of energy. 'The righteous is an everlasting foundation' (Proverbs 10: 25): the phallus is the foundation of life, as the column is the foundation of the universe. Throughout the Middle Ages Galen's belief that semen originated in the brain and descended through the spinal marrow was the prevailing opinion. This is why the phallus symbolized the Orient, the dawn, the mystic East, the abode and origin of life, of heat and of light. It was known as man's seventh limb. It was the centre from which branched legs, arms, the spinal column along which semen flowed and the head which generated the semen. It was opposed by the eighth (female) limb to which it transmitted semen like a river flowing into the sea. According to the *Sefer Yerira*, the phallus not only performed the duties of procreation but, on the structural level of mankind and of the world order, that of maintaining equilibrium. Hence the notion of the relationship of the seventh limb, the balancing factor in human structure and dynamism, with the seventh day of the Creation and with the righteous man whose role is to sustain and balance the world. In different guises the phallus has stood for the life force and been worshipped as the source of life (SCHC pp. 165–9).

pheasant Both the cock and hen pheasant play important parts in Far Eastern mythology. Its call and display make the cock a symbol of cosmic harmony, a prefiguration of the coming of Yu the Great, regulator of the world. The call of the hen to the cock is related to thunder. *Ch'en*, thunder, Spring, cosmic disturbance and conception, also describes the beating of a pheasant's wings. It is a sign of the awakening of the *yang*. With the round of the seasons' rhythm the pheasant transforms itself into the serpent and vice versa, the pheasant being *yang* and the serpent *yin*, since this is the rhythm of universal alternation. This, too, is doubtless the reason for the roofs of pagodas being curved like flying pheasants' wings.

The call of the hen pheasant is also used in Shintō mythology. The bird was the emissary of Amaterasu-omikami to the *kami* (divinity) who regulated the world, Ame-wakahiko. The latter had abandoned himself to earthly pleasures and cut his links with Heaven. The sinful *kami* and his companions regarded the hen pheasant's call as an ill omen. For all that, the call was still a summons and, as it were, a shaft of primeval sunlight, a symbol of colour, light and order.

On the other hand Chuang Tzu makes the marsh pheasant a symbol of a careworn, toilsome existence, but one unhampered nonetheless (BELT, GRAD, HERJ). Throughout, the bird was regarded as a manifestation of solar power.

phoenix (see also HERON)   From the accounts given by Herodotus and Plutarch, the phoenix would seem to have been a mythical bird of matchless splendour and extraordinary longevity which came from Ethiopia and, having been cremated upon a funeral pyre, had the power to be reborn from its own ashes. When the time of its death drew near, it built a nest of aromatic twigs in which it burned from the heat of its own body. This clearly displays the aspects of its symbolism – the cycle of regeneration, resurrection and immortality. This is why, throughout the Middle Ages, the phoenix was made the symbol of Christ's resurrection and sometimes that of his divine nature, as the PELICAN was of his human nature.

In Ancient Egypt the phoenix was a symbol of the solar cycle and was associated with the town of Heliopolis. There is always the possibility that this 'City of the Sun' was not originally Egyptian, but belonged to that primeval 'Land of the Sun', Homer's 'Syria'. Arabs believed that the only place upon which the phoenix could settle was Mount Kāf, the pole and centre of the world. Be that as it may, the Ancient Egyptian phoenix, or *bennu*, was associated with the daily cycle of the Sun and with the annual flooding of the Nile, hence its relationship with regeneration and life.

Since, in Ancient Egypt, the bird concerned was the purple heron, this suggests the alchemists' 'red art'. Taoists called the phoenix the 'cinnabar bird' (*tan-niao*), cinnabar being red sulphur of mercury. Furthermore, the phoenix corresponds, emblematically, to south, Summer, Fire and the colour red. Similarly, its symbolism is akin to the Sun, life and immortality. It was the emblem of Nu-Kua, who invented the *cheng*, a musical instrument which copied the shape and imitated the supernatural song of the phoenix.

In China, the male bird was a symbol of happiness and the female an emblem of the empress, in contrast with the Imperial Dragon. Male and female phoenixes were together emblems of happy marriage. Yet again, not only did Suo Che's and Lon Yu's phoenixes display married bliss, but guided married couples to the Paradise of the Immortals. It was a phoenix which guided Pien-ho to the Ch'u dynasty jade, jade being a symbol of immortality, and it was the *Fong-hoang*, a manifestation of pure *yang*, which made its appearance during prosperous reigns.

Al-Jili made the phoenix the symbol of what exists only in name, meaning 'what exists beyond the grasp of the intellect or of thought'. Thus, since the idea of the phoenix can only be apprehended through the name which it bears, so God cannot be apprehended except through his Names and Virtues (CORA, DEVA, DURV, GUES, JILH, KALL, SOUN).

This splendid and fabulous bird rose at dawn from the waters of the Nile like the Sun, and legend states that it burnt itself to ashes and went out like the Sun in the darkness of the night, only to be reborn from those ashes. The phoenix conjures up an image of creative and destructive fire, from which the world began and in which it will end. The bird is a surrogate Shiva or Orpheus.

It was a symbol of the resurrection which awaited dead people after their souls had been weighed, provided that they correctly followed the ritual of sacrifice and the judges of the dead had accepted as truthful their denial of sin. The dead person became a phoenix. The phoenix often bore a star to display its celestial nature and the nature of life in the Otherworld. 'Phoenix' is Greek for the bird called the 'bennu'. It is depicted at the prow of many of the sacred BOATS which launched 'into the vast gulf of light . . . a symbol of the universal soul of Osiris, endlessly self-creating so long as time and eternity shall last' (CHAM p. 78).

Phurbu See under MAKARA.

pig The pig is almost worldwide the symbol of gluttony and greed, gobbling up whatever is set before it. In many myths insatiability is attributed to it.

In the broadest terms, the pig is the symbol of those obscurantist tendencies to ignorance, gluttony, lust and selfishness, since, as St Clement of Alexandria points out, quoting Heraclitus in his *Stromata*, 'the pig delights in filth and dung.' This is the spiritual basis for the ban on eating pig-meat, and especially in Islam. St Clement goes on to observe that those who eat such meats are generally those who live for the lusts of the flesh. Pigs are depicted in the middle of Tibetan Wheels of Life and bear the same significance, especially that of ignorance. In this context the Gospel parable of 'casting pearls before swine' should not be forgotten, an image of spiritual truths thoughtlessly revealed to those who are neither worthy to receive them nor able to understand them.

In Greek legend, the witch Circe turned into swine the men who pressed their suit upon her. On other occasions, she would touch the guests at her table with her magic wand and turn them into such unclean beasts as pigs, dogs and so on, 'each in accordance with their underlying character and their nature' (GRID p. 94).

The pig is the ancestral animal which founded one of the four classes into which Melanesian society is divided (MALM).

The Kirghiz regard pigs not only as symbols of depravity and uncleanness, but of wickedness as well (BORA p. 293, n. 318).

There is, however, one notable exception to this general rule. Because of its sleek looks, which they keenly appreciate, the Sino-Vietnamese make the pig a symbol of plenty, which the sow and her litter reinforce with the ideal large families (DURV, GOUM, PALL, SCHC). Despite the taboos laid upon pigs and swineherds, the Ancient Egyptians depicted on their amulets Nut, 'the sky-goddess and eternal mother of the stars' as a sow suckling her litter.

pigeon (see also DOVE) In Victorian slang the pigeon was the 'sucker', although in more poetic terms it is also a symbol of love. Its shy habits explain both these attributions. A pair of pigeons make more explicit the love symbol, which is common to such other birds as ducks, kingfishers and phoenixes. In the pigeon's case, there is the added factor of the male brooding the eggs.

In Ancient China the basic pattern of the seasons, the alternation of YIN AND YANG, was expressed by the transformation of pigeon to hawk and of hawk back to pigeon. The former became a symbol of Spring, reappearing after the vernal equinox (GRAR).

In northern Algeria pigeons flutter round the tomb of the Muslim saint who protects the Kabyle village; however, 'elsewhere they are regarded as birds of ill omen since their cooing is the groans of souls in torment' (SERP p. 49).

pigtail Like beards, HAIR plaited into pigtails is proof of and a channel for virility and the life force. In addition to this symbol, pigtails stand for a probable link between this world and the Beyond, the home of the dead; and for the intimate entwining of relationships, the mingling of currents and influences and the interdependence of individuals upon one another. Gaulish grave-stones from various places in France depict individuals with a single large pigtail hanging down one side of the face, while on some small copper coins there is a squatting figure holding a pigtail in each hand. In Ireland – and among the Germans, too – a shaven head was a mark of inferior social status or of humiliation. The young hero Cùchulainn 'had fifty plaits of golden hair from one ear to the other, like the dazzling golden rays shining from the face of the Sun' (OGAC 10: pp. 201–2; 11: p. 335).

The pigtail was a symbol of the Maya Sun-god and used by his earthly representatives (GIRP p. 83).

pilgrim A religious symbol corresponding to the earthly situation of the individual who goes through a time of trial so as to reach, at the moment of death, a Promised Land or Paradise Lost. The word denotes the person who feels a stranger to his or her environment, through which they pass in search of their ideal city. The symbol not only expresses the ephemeral nature of the human condition, but inner detachment from the present and an attachment to distant and higher ends. It may also be observed that with the pilgrim symbol are associated ideas of cleansing and expiation, as well as those of paying homage to the Person – be that Christ, Muhammad, Osiris or the Buddha – who has made holy the place of pilgrimage. By journeying thither the pilgrim identifies himself with and assimilates himself to that Person. In addition, the pilgrim makes his journey not in comfort but in poverty, a further connection with notions of detachment and purification. The pilgrim's STAFF symbolizes both the endurance test and self-denial. All these conditions are preparation for the enlightenment and divine revelations which will be the reward at journey's end. Pilgrimage is related to rites of initiation: it identifies the pilgrim with the chosen master.

pillar See under COLUMN.

pine Throughout most of the Far East, the pine is a symbol of immortality, due to its evergreen foliage and the incorruptible nature of its resin.

Taoist Immortals fed upon pine kernels, needles and resin, doing away with the need for any other nourishment and making their bodies light and able to take flight. If pine-resin was allowed to drip down the tree-trunk and seep into the soil, after a thousand years it would produce a sort of miraculous mushroom, the *fu-lin*, which itself furnished immortality. Flowers from the pines in the Pure Jade Heaven 'gave a golden complexion to whoever ate them' (MAST).

Symbolism of the same character led, in Japan, to the choice of pine and *hinoki* (CYPRESS) as building material for Shintō temples and the wood used in cult-implements. The notion also occurs in Chinese secret societies: both pine and cypress stand at the gates of the City of Willows or the Circle of Heaven and Earth, both abodes of the Immortals. Confucius, too, relates that beside altars to the Earth 'the Hia planted pines and the Yin, cypress.'

In Japanese art, the pine is regarded as a symbol of the life force; in everyday life as an omen of good fortune; in literature, as the result of a pun, of delay. Two pine trees are reminders of the legend of Takasago and symbolize love and faithfulness in marriage.

Western iconography sometimes depicts two cocks fighting over a pine-cone, which inevitably conjures up the picture of the two dragons fighting over a pearl. It is the symbol of the truth made manifest (DEVA, KALL, MAST, OGRJ, SCHL, STEJ, DUSC).

In China, the pine is often associated with other symbols of longevity such as the mushroom and the crane, or the bamboo and the plum. The Chinese, regarding long life as the highest bliss, perhaps imagine that by bringing these symbols together they can correspondingly augment their power. For unless they are assured of having the time to enjoy them, they have little real regard for wealth, honours, love or children.

In Japan, the pine (*matsu*) is also the symbol of irresistible strength tempered by a lifetime of daily struggle. It is also the symbol of those who have held to their opinions unaffected by the criticisms of those around them, because the tree emerges unscathed from the assaults of storm and tempest. During the week-long New Year festivities, the Japanese set on either side of the entrance to their homes two pines, carefully chosen of the same height. This is from the Shintō tradition that *kami* (divinities) dwell in the branches of trees and, as the pine is an evergreen, they prefer it to all others. Pines are therefore placed at the entrance of the house to attract the *kami* and their blessings.

DIONYSOS often holds a pine-cone in his hand like a sceptre. Like the IVY, it is an expression of the perpetuity of plant-life, with the additional nuance of a sort of lordship over nature, regarded as an elemental and intoxicating force, on the part of the god. It stands for the elevation of the life force and the glorification of fertility. The Orphics consecrated a mystery-cult to Dionysos in which the god died, was eaten by the Titans and was then restored to life again, a symbol of the perennial return of plants and of life in general. Dionysos was also seen at Delphi for three months when he ruled the shrine, vanishing for the rest of the year. Historians regard this as an agrarian religious myth. The pine was also sacred to the fertility-goddess, CYBELE. It was supposed to have been a nymph changed into a tree to escape the amorous attentions of Pan. The pine-cone symbolizes the immortality of plant and animal life.

What Franz Cumont calls 'that great mystical drama', the cult of Cybele at Rome, with its echoes of the mysteries of Isis, in fact gave the pine a place of honour:

A pine-tree was cut down and carried to the Palatine Temple by a guild bearing the name of *dendrophori* (tree-carriers). The tree was bandaged like a corpse and wreathed with violets to represent the dead body of the goddess's lover, Attis. Originally the latter had been no more than a vegetation-spirit, and thus the vastly ancient cult of Phrygian peasants subsisted beside the palace of the emperors in the honours paid to this tree of Mars. The next day was one of sorrow, during which the faithful fasted and mourned beside their god's body . . . The mystic eve of longed-for resurrection . . . From wails of despair they passed to delirious rejoicing. . . . With the rebirth of Nature, Attis awoke from his long death-sleep and the delight in his return to life was given full rein in unrestrained rejoicing, licentious masquerades and lavish banquets.

The pine symbolized the body of the god who died and was restored to life again: the image, in the worship of Cybele, of the cycle of the alternating SEASONS (BEAG p. 253).

pipe Pan, personification of the pastoral life, who from his half-human, half-animal origins became god of woods and caverns, is supposed to have invented the pipe, and with it to have delighted gods, men and beasts. The pipe also conjures up the legend of Hyagnis and, on a more homely level, that of the Pied Piper.

The Chinese legend of Suo Che and Lon Yu also invokes the supernatural properties of the sound of the pipe (*cheng*). The latter summoned gentle breezes, painted clouds and, above all, phoenixes which guided the pair to the Paradise of the Immortals. In the same way the Pied Piper's tune opened a cavern in the mountain-side into which he led the children. Both stories represent reintegration into a paradisal state. The sound of the pipe is heavenly MUSIC, the voice of angels. It should also be observed, as is so often the case in Chinese legend, that the pair were carried into a state of bliss by BIRDS, playing the same symbolic role as that of angels.

Another Taoist musical instrument was the Pipe of Iron which 'cut the roots of the clouds' and 'split rocks' which might well seem to relate it to thunderbolts and rain (KALL, LALM) and make it a fertility symbol.

The REED pipe (*ney*) played by Dervishes during their ritual sessions (*dhikr*), and especially used by the Mevlevi Order (Whirling Dervishes) as an accompaniment to the chants sung to their dances, is a symbol of the soul separated from its Divine Source and yearning to return to it. This is why it mourns. Thus Jalāl-al-Dīn Rūmī, founder of the Mevlevi Order, addresses God: 'We are the pipe, the music comes from You' (*Mathnavi* 1: 599). Sufis say that the pipe and the man of God are one and the same thing.

Rūmī tells the story of how the Prophet confided secrets to his son-in-law, Ali, forbidding him to tell anyone else. For forty days Ali succeeded in keeping his promise, but then, overcome, he went into the desert and, thrusting his head down a well, began to repeat these hidden truths. They provoked him to a state of ecstasy in which some of his spittle fell into the water. A little later a reed grew from the well. It was cut by a shepherd who bored holes in it and played it as a pipe. The tunes he played became famous and ecstatic crowds came to listen to his playing. Even camels formed circles round him to listen (see ORPHEUS). The news reached the Prophet, who summoned the shepherd and asked him to play. All those who listened fell into an ecstasy. 'These tunes', the Prophet then said, 'are commentaries upon the mysteries which I imparted secretly to Ali. However, if one of the pure loses his purity, he cannot hear the secrets contained in the tune played upon the pipe nor enjoy them, since the complete Faith is pleasure and passion' (*Mathnavi* 4: 2232; 6: 2014; HUAB 2: p. 8).

pipe of peace   See CALUMET.

piranha   Horror stories and the fears of some explorers have lifted these little carnivorous Amazonian fish to the level of a nightmare castration or ingestion myth. They have come to symbolize the very misery engendered by a tormented imagination. Some tribes identify them with river spirits or death in the shallows while ethnologists discern in this fear of piranhas a resurgence in a different shape of that old fear of the *vagina dentata* (see VULVA). It is in this sense that Bateson observed that the crocodile's jaws used as a gateway to the enclosure where initiation rites were performed was called, in Iatmul, *shurvi iamba*, literally 'the Gate of the Clitoris'. The analyst would see in the piranha myth the imaginary transposition of a potential danger into an actual danger or else the transference to an animal of the unconscious terrors engendered by so terrifying a region as Amazonia or its Indian population. 'The aggressive piranha is, unconsciously, burdened with the hostility of the jungle and the unyielding nature of the Indians' (MCPM p. 11).

Pisces (19 February–20 March)   Twelfth and last sign of the ZODIAC, Pisces falls immediately before the vernal equinox. In terms of the psyche it symbolizes that inner, shadowy world in which we talk either with God or the Devil. In horoscopic terms this translates as a highly impressionable and receptive nature lacking firmness. Its traditional ruling planet was Jupiter, to which Neptune was added after its discovery.

The astrological period of the triad of watery signs may be compared with the Winter floods and the waves which wash away and cleanse, as well as with the anonymous and moving mass of the oceans into which all things are plunged. Here the Moist holds undisputed sway as the principle which diffuses, dilutes, enfolds and welds individual parts into one whole, the latter being as wide as the vastness flowing around us, even as the infinity of the cosmic ocean. The sign is depicted traditionally as a pair of fish back to back joined at their mouths by a sort of umbilical cord. Under their influence we become part of that great universal tide and belong to the community of all peoples on Earth, like a drop of water in the ocean. We are placed, too, in an undifferentiated world, one without distinguishing marks, drowned and confounded in the obliteration of individuality to the benefit of the limitless, going from zero to infinity. The underlying fabric of the Piscean type is woven from an extremely pliable psyche. In their inner world, knots are untied, cohesive forces baffled and shapes blurred. There reigns an impressionistic atmosphere, conducive to the amorphous, the relaxed, emotional dilation and inflation by means of which the individual can escape from self to become interfused with the awareness of qualities surpassing the self, but enveloping it and making it part of a far wider structure.

pitchfork Akin to the CROSSROADS, it is the symbol of ambivalence itself. 'The outcurving prongs [display] the tendency of individualities sprung from a common origin to become differentiated. On the other hand, the very way in which the two prongs of the pitchfork remain linked to their single common origin, make the pitchfork the symbol of an undifferentiated state' (VIRI p. 38). In this respect it is the opposite of the ARROW; 'the latter is a male symbol, while the other is female. They are respectively movement as opposed to passivity, penetration as opposed to openness, orientation as opposed to laterality, differentiation as opposed to lack of differentiation, oneness as opposed to ambivalence' (VIRI p. 194). However, the significance of the pitchfork may be completely reversed when it is used as an objective implement, attempting by its very ambivalence to stab, hold and retain within its two prongs as if they were some creature's jaws. The pitchfork then becomes the Devil's emblem, 'the arrow of darkness, an image of the power of magic, of the dynamism of affectivity and the strength of the unconscious' (VIRI p. 202).

Pitchforks were also used as instruments of torture upon slaves, their faces pressed into the ground by prongs on either side of their necks, as though caught in some monster's jaws. The pitchfork was the instrument which returned them to the undifferentiated state of death.

plain Plains are symbols of space and of the boundless Earth, but always in the horizontal as opposed to the vertical sense. When transposed to Heaven, the word denotes the boundless immensity in which the sky-gods dwell and to which psychopomps (conductors of souls) lead souls at death. Mithras was often called 'Lord of the Plains'.

In the Celtic world-view the plain was a specific designation of the Otherworld – *Mag Meld*, 'Plain of Joy'. The word was, however, often transferred or applied to that other Earthly Paradise, Ireland itself, one of its names being *Mag Fal* 'Plain of Fal', *Fal* being itself a metaphor for kingship. One personification of the 'plain' was the goddess Macha (*magnosia-Macha*), who gave her name to the former capital of Ulster, Emain Macha. She thus symbolizes the kingship of the warrior. Plains seem to have been the ideal places for mortals to inhabit, mountains, by contrast, being the preserve of the gods. One of the tasks imposed upon a deity in exchange for services rendered or in fulfilment of some oath sometimes took the form of reclaiming one or several plains. This, for example, was the task imposed upon the god Midir by King Eochaid Airem, who had defeated him in a game of chess, a task which the god performed with ill grace. When the same task was imposed upon the goddess Tailtiu, she performed it successfully, but died of exhaustion. The plain was named in her memory and because that was where the shamrock first grew, the plant became the emblem of Ireland. Meldi, the Gaulish name for the modern French city of Meaux, may have been called 'pleasant' in the context of religious notions comparable with the Irish Mag Meld (OGAC 17: pp. 393–410; J. B. Arthurs, 'Macha and Armagh', in *Bulletin of the Ulster Place-name Society* 1: pp. 25–9).

The Plain of Joy was also the Land of Youth, an Elysium where centuries passed in minutes, where the inhabitants never grew old and where the fields were covered in flowers which never died. Similar fields of Paradise, replete with every delight, were the Elysian Fields of Greco-Roman mythology and with them corresponded the Fields of Ialu of the Ancient Egyptians. The latter were also known as the Fields of REEDS, of Food, or of Offerings, and to them went the dead who had passed the test of weighing the soul. There they spent a godlike life of pleasure contemplating the Cosmic Egg, or the Sun-god Ra in his egg preserving 'the primeval vibration which was at the origin of that of light and of the word' (CHAS p. 49). An antithesis of Hell, fields are a symbol of Paradise to which the righteous attain after death.

plait As opposed to the SPIRAL, which he regards as 'open and optimistic', Marcel Brion considers the plait to be a 'closed and pessimistic' motif:

The motif of the plait is far more complicated and harder to define. The motif is as widespread as that of the spiral, but it has a very different meaning. This is due, in the first place, to the fact that it is a 'closed' motif and hence a pessimistic one, unless, that is, we regard it in the reassuring light of the theory of the Eternal Homecoming, so rich in hope, and of which the plait forms the simplest formulation and the clearest image. Were one to conceive a spiral as long and as entwined as the mind could imagine, it would necessarily end at some point, while the most rudimentary plait is a prison without hope of escape.
(BRIL p. 198)

The plait may thus be regarded as a symbol of involution.

planet (see also SEVEN; STAR; and specific symbolism under headings for individual planets) From the very earliest times, planetary symbolism derived from supposed parallels between the celestial and the terrestrial or human order, whereby a special relationship existed between the movement of the stars and human fate. The thinking upon which this belief was based premissed a twofold operation: in the first place that the relationship between the planets was of the same nature as that subsisting between human beings or within each individual, and in the second that the phenomena observed in the movement of the planets impinged directly upon human behaviour. Each planet exerted some influence upon life on Earth and each was endowed with some power over its human inhabitants. To the seven planets corresponded seven Heavens, seven days of the week, seven bearings in space, seven states or operations of the spirit, seven moral and theological virtues, seven gifts of the Holy Spirit, seven metals, seven stages in the Great Work and so on. Planetary symbolism is virtually inexhaustible and is the sign of a belief in the symbiosis of Heaven and Earth animated by the ceaseless interaction of the three levels of the cosmos.

A characteristic of the Kabbalah is its search for correspondences between all parts of the universe and every human tradition. It correlated the spheres (called planets in the original sense of the term), the angels, their cosmic functions, spatial bearings and the operations of the spirit (see table). Christian tradition has not followed this angelic and functional astrology (see ANGEL).

Planets: The Kabbalistic system of correspondences

Planet	Angel	Cosmic function	Spatial bearing	Operation of the spirit
Sun	Michael	give light to the world	zenith	will
Moon	Gabriel	strengthen hopes and send dreams	nadir	imagination
Mercury	Raphael	civilize	centre	motional and intuition
Venus	Amael	love	west	love and fellowship
Mars	Samael	destroy	south	action and destruction
Jupiter	Zachariel	organize	east	judgement and command
Saturn	Oriphiel	watch over	north	patience and perseverance

planetary ages   In astrology each planet symbolizes a specific period of life
– the Moon, early childhood; Mercury, childhood; Venus, adolescence; Mars,
the prime of life; Jupiter, maturity (or old age, according to Junctinus of
Florence); and Saturn senility. We know that statues of Apollo, symbol of
the Sun, are always beardless, as are those of Mercury, while Jupiter is
depicted as a fully mature and Saturn as an old man. Historically, this
theory of planetary ages goes back to the Greeks, but it varies greatly
depending upon the authority in question. The fourth-century Sicilian astrologer Firmicus Maternus (2: 29) is one, but it appears from these scattered and fragmentary sources as if there were some confusion between the
theories of those who believed that each planet ruled in succession a phase
of human life of determined length and the theories relating to planetary
cycles. For example, the twelve months of Jupiter seem to have some connection with the twelve years it takes the planet to pass through all the signs
of the Zodiac, while Venus's eight months reflect her shorter eight-year
sidereal period and so on. In any case most writers are in agreement in
regarding the first 4 (or 7) years of a human life as being ruled by the
Moon; the years 5 to 14 (or 7 to 15), by Mercury; 14 (or 15) to 22 (or 23
or 24, according to Junctinus of Florence) by Venus; 22 (23 or 24) to 34,
37 or 41 by the Sun; 34 (or 37 or 41) to 45 (or 52 or even 56) by Mars; 45
(52 or 56) to 56 (or 68) by Jupiter; and the last 28 or 30 years by Saturn.
Modern astrologers apparently ignore the symbolism of these planetary
ages, although in their writings Mercury is interpreted as a child, Venus as
a girl, Jupiter as a grown man and Saturn as an old man.

plant (see also HERB; VEGETATION)   Plants symbolize solar energy concentrated and made manifest.

Plants suck up the strength of terrestrial fire and draw in solar energy.
They amass this power, from which they derive their healing or poisonous
properties and which is the basis of their use in magic.

In relation to the male principle of life, plants signify growth, in the words of Psalm 144: 12: 'That our sons may be as plants grown up in their youth.'

Plants bear their own seed. Some, the hyssop, for example, are used as purifiers.

Just as the solar spectrum breaks down into different colours, so plants symbolize the manifestation of energy in its different forms. As manifestations of life they are as inseparable from Water as they are from the Sun.

It is easy to understand why the two symbols, plants and water, should be linked. Waters bear seeds, all seeds. Plants – roots, shrubs, lotus blossom – display the manifestation of the cosmos and the appearance of form. What the LOTUS symbol (or root) expresses, rising from the waters (or from an aquatic emblem), is the cosmic process itself. In this context the waters stand for the non-manifest; the seeds for latency; the floral symbol, manifestation or cosmic creation (COOH). Plants, the first stage in life, above all symbolize perpetual birth, the ceaseless flow of life-giving energy.

In Vedic tradition, those plants with medicinal properties were themselves the gift of Heaven and the roots of life; prayers were offered to them as though they were deities.

plantain   In Ancient China the plantain was regarded as a fertility symbol, no doubt because of its many seeds. Picking plantain was believed to encourage pregnancy.

In Indian traditional terms, 'plantain flesh' expresses something extremely delicate. It is compared, in particular, with the *kundalinī* slumbering in the 'root-centre' (GRAD).

Pleiades   The principal star (third magnitude) of this small constellation is Alcyone (Peace) which many astronomers, both ancient and modern, have regarded as the central sun in our galaxy. It is interesting to observe that the Babylonians called it Temennu (Foundation Stone); Arabs, Al Wasat (the Centre); and Hindus, Amba (the Mother). As for the Pleiades themselves, the constellation was called Kimtu (the Family) by the Assyrians and Kimah by Arabs and Jews, meaning 'the Pile' for the former and 'The Seal' for the latter, while the Greeks symbolized it as seven maidens or as Aphrodite's seven doves. According to the Hindus, the Pleiades are the seven nurses of the war-god, Kārttikeya, identified with Mars, which explains the Martian character which astrologers attribute to this constellation. It is interesting to observe that, like the Ancient Greeks, Australian Aborigines regard the stars as sacred maidens singing at a corroboree; North American Indians as sacred female dancers; and Lapps as maidens.

The most likely reason for the astrological importance of the Pleiades would seem to be that this star cluster marked the beginning of Spring in the distant past of the third millennium BC. The name of the first house, or division, of the Chinese lunar Zodiac is that of the Pleiades, Mao. Both in Polynesia and in Peru the new year began when this constellation reappeared for the first time over the horizon. In both these areas, as in Ancient Greece, it is still regarded as the patron of farmers.

The Pleiades played a starring role in the Inca religio-cosmogonic system. Their link with agriculture deified them and their appearance in June, coinciding with the New Year, was honoured by human sacrifice in which the victims willingly hurled themselves over precipices. They were regarded as protectors of harvests, presiding over the ripening of fruit and guarding the maize from drought. Father Francisco de Avila observed of the Ancient Peruvians that the Yunca carefully watched for the appearance of these stars. 'If they were unusually large, they concluded that it would be a year of plenty: if small, it was a sign of dearth' (AVIH).

The Turkic peoples of central Asia regarded the Pleiades as the heralds of winter and there was a similar belief in Europe and among the Lapps. Yakut and many other Altaic peoples said that in the middle of the constellation there was a hole, piercing the vault of Heaven, and that the cold came through this hole (HARA p. 129).

An eastern Sudanese tribe, the Manjia, believe that the constellation is the home of pretty women after death and, by a further twist in their mythology, they believe the stars themselves to be maidens desired by the culture-hero, Seto (bird-eating spider), represented by the constellation Orion (TEGH pp. 110–11).

By extension, the word Pleiad has come to mean any group of seven wise, handsome or famous people.

plough Throughout the world, ploughing was considered as a sacred activity and, specifically, as an activity which made the Earth fruitful. Sociologists call the festival which accompanied the cutting of the first furrow in Ancient China and in India (the Buddha's first miracle occurred at this festival), a festival still celebrated in Thailand and Cambodia, a 'desacralization' of the soil. It might, perhaps, be more accurately termed a 'deflowering' since it is above all the transcendent Male, the intercessor between Heaven and Earth, who takes possession of and fertilizes virgin soil. On the one hand, it is noteworthy that before the ceremony, the emperor of China used to pray for rain, celestial semen; that the first furrow was perhaps cut by married couples, sometimes to the accompaniment of coitus. Both spades and ploughshares possess phallic symbolism (see below), while the furrow corresponds with woman. Thus Rāma's bride Sītā ('Furrow') was allegedly born from the furrow cut by the phallic plough of Vishnu's avatar (i.e. Vishnu's incarnation as Rāma). However, this symbolism should not, as we shall show, be restricted to its literal expression. Earth receives celestial influences so that the harvest of this celestial penetration of Earth is, in Taoist parlance, 'the Embryo of the Immortal'.

A more immediate symbolism of ploughing is to be found in the Buddhist Pali scriptures, and this is that of spiritual exertion and self-denial. 'And this is how the ploughing is done and from it will come the harvest which shall never die (*suttanipāta*).' Clearly the end result, despite this, is virtually the same and very little different from that conjured up by St Paul, when he compares God with the ploughman, or labourer. 'For we are labourers together with God: ye are God's husbandry' (1 Corinthians 3: 9). (BURA, DANA, ELIM, GRAD, GRAP)

Ploughing does not feature in Celtic mythology, typical of the absence of any agricultural activity among the gods of northern Europe. Such activities being regarded as servile, they were simply ignored. Those elements of the neo-Celtic vocabulary relating to farming techniques – including the word for plough – are of Latin origin. The farmer Amaethon, whose help was essential in the vast task of ploughing in the tale of Culhwch and Olwen, has the secondary title of *ambactos*, 'servant'. It was only after the battle of Mag Tuired that the captured Fomorian king, Bres, to save his life taught the Irish how and when to plough, sow and harvest (REVC 12: pp. 104–6; MABG p. 115).

Ploughing symbols appeared only at a later stage when warrior societies became agricultural and peasant societies, and are also related to the transition from nomadic to settled society.

Like most cutting implements, spades and ploughs symbolize the action of the male principle upon passive, and therefore female, matter. The ploughshare symbolizes the penis which penetrates the soil which is analogous to the female sexual organ. Ploughing the soil stands for coitus, the marriage of Earth and Heaven, and childbirth is, as it were, the harvest. This identification of the plough with the organ of procreation, Mircea Eliade observes, is illustrated by the linguistic kinship between the words *lāngala* (plough) and *lingam*, both deriving from a root-word denoting both spade and phallus. The same derivation occurs in different southern Asian languages.

In India, the plough is essentially the attribute of Bala-Rāma ('Rāma the Strong'), Vishnu's avatar and Krishna's brother, a symbol of kingly virtues but, undoubtedly, of lordship of the land in particular. When the plough is an attribute of the *nāga* (Bala-Rāma is also the *nāga* Ananta), its relationship with lordship of the land is even more clear (BURA, MALA).

When Isaiah speaks of the conversion of the nations, he writes (2: 4): 'And they shall beat their swords into ploughshares, and their spears into pruninghooks; nation shall not lift up sword against nation, neither shall they learn war any more.' This passage from Isaiah was often taken up and interpreted by the early Fathers and Irenaeus, in particular, uses this verse as an example of the pacific nature of Christians in his tract *Adversus Haereses* (4: 34). He explains the meaning of the text in the clearest fashion, writing:

For Our Lord himself is he who made the ploughshare and brought the pruninghook, for by this is denoted the first sowing of mankind, which had its representation in Adam, and the gathering of the harvest by the Word at the Last Day. And because of this, he who brought together the beginning and the end is the Lord of both, has made manifest at the end the plough, of wood and iron, and has thus cleared his land. The abiding Word, effectively made one with the Flesh and stabilized in this fashion, has cleared the untilled soil.

In Jewish and Christian tradition the plough was a symbol of creation and of the Cross. The wood and the iron of which the plough is made symbolize the unity of Christ's two natures.

The plough and the stylus also symbolize the labours of the writer. Isidore of Seville compares the stylus with the plough and alludes to the Ancients ploughing their lines of writing like a ploughman drawing out his furrows. Blank pages are compared with fields untouched by the ploughshare. Medieval writers often use this symbolic meaning.

plum-tree   Far Eastern painters frequently use plum-trees as their subjects, since the tree is primarily a symbol of Spring. It is sometimes a symbol of Winter, as well, since it blossoms at the end of that season and marks renewal and the season of youth which is on the verge of manifestation. It is also a symbol of purity, since the blossom appears before the leaf. A Sung dynasty monk, Chung Jen, devoted an entire book to the plum-tree in blossom, making it a symbol of the universe.

It is true that there is a relationship between plum-blossom and immortality, that the Immortals feed upon it and that it was in fact the badge of Lao Tzu, since he was born under a plum-tree and announced that he would make it his patronymic.

In Japan the plum is one of the trees of good omen (DURV, GROC, KALL).

The North American Pawnee Indians regard the wild plum as a fertility symbol, since it is so prolific (FLEH).

In dreams, its fruit sometimes has an erotic significance, evidence of a craving for sexual satisfaction.

plumbline   The plumbline is an important element in Freemasonry. It is depicted hanging from the keystone of an arch and touching the ground. This is a clear representation of the Cosmic AXIS and the direction taken by celestial activity. Furthermore, in some instances it is shown joining the Great Bear, or its surrogate the letter 'G', to the centre of a swastika drawn upon the ground, that is to say joining the celestial to the terrestrial POLE.

A more immediate meaning is that linking it to proportion in building or, and this amounts to the same thing, righteousness in spiritual endeavour. However, the goal of such endeavour is still identification with the Middle Way or with the World Axis (BOUM, GUET, GUES).

In some works of art, the plumbline symbolizes Justice tempered by Mercy, Architecture, or Geometry (TERS p. 181). It is the living rule of all building, both material and spiritual, which, as Le Corbusier remarked, should be used in the vertical plane with Heaven. It is the pliant symbol of the vertical.

Pluto   Astrologically, this planet rules the powers which control the vast changes which took place in the evolution of the geology of the Earth and the zoology of species, as well as those taking place in the heart of matter, in the world of nuclear physics, in the conquest of space, in lasers and in transplant surgery. Pluto is the symbol of radical restructuring upon fresh foundations, rejecting harmful or unnecessary elements. Its effects often seem as sudden and as unexpected as those engineered by Uranus and Neptune but, unlike those two planets, Pluto's influence stands out clearly as being beneficent and inspired by deep feelings of justice even though the results may seem immoral or abnormal when judged by purely human standards. Antibiotics, computers and, in general terms, all ultramodern technology, including television, come under Pluto's sway. Astrologers, however, have still to reach agreement upon the House which it rules and have successively suggested Aries (trumpeted by Caslant), Cancer (Muir, in England), Pisces (Wemyss, a view shared by Vouga and his successors),

Scorpio (Brunhübner) and Sagittarius (Volguine). Over the last twenty years, this last-named attribution has been gaining ground. When first sighted in January 1930, Pluto was in the sign of Cancer, which traditionally rules China. We are at present watching the birth of a typically Plutonian civilization in what has become the third great world-power, its outlines emerging since about 1971. Current events are comparable with what took place in the USA during the first quarter of the nineteenth century and in what was the Soviet Union during the first decade of the Russian Revolution.

In analytic astrology, Pluto is the Prince of Darkness, symbol of the depths of our own inner darkness which is linked to the primordial night of the soul, that is, to the most ancient stratum of the psyche. When Jung states that civilized mankind still trails its saurian tail behind it, he provides the definitive chthonian image of the individual's mother-country over which this planet rules. It is the range of the affective tendencies of the sado-anal stage and its powers of evil – all that is black, ugly, dirty and bad, rebellion, sadism, anguish, absurdity, annihilation and death. Similarly we are within this same compass when Jung summons us to encounter our own dragon and to develop our awareness of the invisible, to assure ourselves that we are the owners of buried treasure, to clear the way to this hidden wealth, to uncover the most deeply buried secrets for spiritual fulfilment or to actualize the metaphysical. Alignment of the ego upon the most profound truths of being provides the power, or at least the hidden strength of purpose, which has the last word in human affairs. Conversely, if we reject these most basic of all requirements of living, inner eruptions destroy our balance and Pluto, by means of disasters which cut the ground from under our feet, opens the gulf into which we shall promptly fall and be swallowed – our final damnation.

point See CARDINAL POINTS; DOT.

pole By definition a pole is a fixed point round which the world rotates. It is the symbol of stability in the midst of flux. It is the unchanging CENTRE (*Chung Yung*), the hub of the Cosmic Wheel. The World Tree or AXIS joins the terrestrial to the celestial pole, the centre of the universe in the Northern Polar Constellation. It is for this reason that the pole is often represented by a mountain like the Muslim Mount Kāf. And this is also why primeval tradition is often regarded as being Hyperborean.

The pole is depicted in the centre of the swastika, the image of rotational movement on a fixed point. In some Masonic lodges, a plumbline (World Axis) is hung from a representation of the Great Bear (or the letter 'G' standing for it), as the celestial pole, and touches the centre of a swastika drawn on the floor, as the terrestrial pole.

In China, the polar star or constellation was called 'the Celestial Roof-ridge' or 'Supreme Roof-ridge' (*T'ai-ki*) and was the dwelling of the Supreme Being (*T'ai-yi*). Directly below, the emperor, at the terrestrial pole, regulated the rhythms of Earth, just as the Pole Star regulated the rhythms of the stars. This is because once primeval 'polar' tradition had become differentiated, the symbolic pole was located in each and every spiritual centre. The Islamic pole rises directly over the Ka'ba at Mecca; the Chinese, over the Temple of Heaven; the Judeo-Christian, over Jerusalem.

This is the meaning of the orb surmounted by a (polar) cross, at least as used by Dante in the *Divine Comedy*. The entrance to Hell lies immediately below Jerusalem: at the opposite pole is the mount of Purgatory and the entrance to Heaven. Such axial duality relates to the Suffering Christ and the Christ in Glory. This is the meaning of the Carthusian motto – *Stat crux, dum volvitur orbis*, the Cross stands firm (like a pole), while the world revolves around it.

In Islam *al-Qutb* (the Pole) by analogy denotes the centre and peak of a spiritual hierarchy. Moses is designated *Qutb*, as is the Imam of the Ismailis, and as such bears upon his shoulders the balance and stability of the world. He is located 'in the north', on 'the peak of Sinai'. Sheikhs and Masters of Sufi Orders are often given the title of honour of 'Pole' (CORT, ELIM, GUED, GUEM, GUEC, GUET, GUES).

pomegranate Broadly speaking, the symbolism of the pomegranate is related to that of all fruit (such as citron, gourd or orange) which contains large numbers of pips or seeds. Primarily they are fertility symbols and symbols of innumerable descendants. In Ancient Greece, the pomegranate was an attribute of Hera and Aphrodite, while in Rome the headdress of married women was fashioned from pomegranate twigs. In Asia the image of a pomegranate split open conveys good wishes when it does not specifically denote the vulva. The caption beneath a piece of Vietnamese folk art would serve to confirm this; it reads: 'The pomegranate opens and allows a hundred children to emerge' (DURV). Similarly, in Gabon, the fruit symbolizes maternal fruitfulness. In India, women used to drink pomegranate juice to combat barrenness.

Christian mysticism transposed this fertility symbolism to the spiritual plane. Thus St John of the Cross made pomegranate-seeds the symbol of divine perfection in all its varied effects, adding the roundness of the fruit as expressing the eternity of God and its sweet juice as the bliss of the soul which knows and loves. Lastly, in this 'the pomegranate stands for God's highest mystery, His deepest judgements and his most sublime greatness' (DURV). The early Fathers also sought to make the pomegranate a symbol of the Church herself. 'Just as beneath a single skin the pomegranate contains innumerable seeds, so the Church joins in one faith many different peoples' (TERS p. 204).

In Ancient Greece, pomegranate-seed was to have a significance in relation to sin. Persephone was to confess to her mother that, in spite of herself, she had been tempted and that in the words of the 'Homeric' hymn to Demeter 'he secretly put in my mouth sweet food, a pomegranate seed, and forced me to taste against my will.' The pomegranate-seed which doomed her to the Underworld is a symbol of sugared poison. Thus, because Persephone had eaten it, she had to spend one third of the year 'in darkness and gloom' and the other two-thirds with 'the deathless gods'. In the context of the myth, the pomegranate-seed might mean that Persephone yielded to temptation and thus deserved her punishment of having to spend one third of her life in the Underworld. On the other hand, by eating the pomegranate-seed she had broken the law of fasting which ruled the Underworld. Whoever ate anything could not return to the land of the living. It was only by the especial favour of Zeus that she was able to divide her life between the two realms.

Although the hierophants, the priests of Demeter at Eleusis, 'were crowned with pomegranate-branches during the Great Mysteries', the pomegranate itself, the sacred fruit which had doomed Persephone, was strictly forbidden to initiates because, 'as a fertility symbol, it contains the power of drawing souls down into the flesh' (SERP pp. 119, 144). The pomegranate-seed which Demeter's daughter had swallowed consecrated her to the Underworld and, by an apparent reversal of the symbol, doomed her to barrenness. The enduring law of the Underworld was stronger than the fleeting pleasure of tasting the pomegranate.

It would, however, be simpler to say that this red and burning seed conjures up, better than anything else, the spark of chthonian fire which Persephone stole for the benefit of mankind, since her return to the Earth's surface signified vernal renewal and thus, indirectly, fertility. From this viewpoint, Persephone is to be numbered among those countless culture-heroes who, throughout the world, stole fire to ensure the permanence of life and of the universe itself.

In Persian love-poetry, the pomegranate evokes the breast, Firdausī, for example, writing: 'Her cheeks are like pomegranate flowers, her lips like their juice and her breasts swell like a pair of pomegranates' (quoted in HUAS p. 77). A common Turkish riddle likens the betrothed to 'a rose unsmelled or a pomegranate unpeeled'.

Pope, the The Pope, the fifth major arcanum in the TAROT, is separated from the Female Pope (II: see below) by the Empress (III) and by the Emperor (IV). The Female Pope and the Empress, female powers, wear BLUE robes on RED. Like the Emperor, the Pope wears red on blue, his blue robe being enveloped by a red cape trimmed with YELLOW. Its sleeves are white, since his arms remain unsullied. His left hand is gloved in yellow and marked with a cross and holds the staff of a papal cross with three crossbars. These symbolize 'creative power over the three worlds of the divine, the spiritual and the material' (PAPT). 'This ternary begets a septenary formed by the globular tips of the staff and cross-bars. Now seven is the number both of harmony and of the second causes which govern the universe, these causes corresponding to planetary influences and the seven notes of the gamut' (WIRT p. 142). The Pope is seated between two blue columns, reminiscent of Solomon's Temple. His right hand blesses two persons with tonsures, one on each side of the foot of the card. One, dressed in red with a yellow stole, has his left hand raised, while the other, in a yellow cloak with a red hood and a blue hat, has his right hand pointing down in a precisely reversed gesture. The latter is the humble and passive recipient of traditional and dogmatic teaching from on high, the former its active disseminator. Thus, following on from the Emperor who simply announces his strength and activity, the Pope is the one who passes on his knowledge. He no longer needs the book lying open in the lap of the Female Pope. As a symbol of the man of knowledge, he transmits that knowledge to others, and as the fifth arcanum of the Tarot, he bears the number of Man, regarded as the intercessor between God and the Universe.

From his elevated position, he commands his disciples: 'Go and teach all nations of the Earth.' 'The Belgian Tarot often replaces the Pope, or Master of Secrets, with Bacchus. He stands for the cause which sets mankind upon his predestined forward path' (Enel)... 'duty, morality and conscience' (Wirth)... 'moral strength and responsibility conferred upon mankind' (Rolt-Wheeler). In astrology the Pope corresponds to the Fifth House.

The Pope is the last of the first group of arcana in the Tarot, the group setting the subject (the JUGGLER) face to face with the object, the manifold aspects of knowledge symbolized by the four powers invested with either religious or secular duties. After them man has to make his first choice and this will fall to the LOVER.

Pope, the Female The second major arcanum of the Tarot; by contrast with the standing figure of the Juggler, she sits, a motionless and mysterious woman. Beneath a blue cloak with yellow collar and clasps, she conceals a long red dress over which two yellow ribbons cross. This symbolizes latent spiritual powers. She wears the triple Papal tiara, the last of its three crowns slightly impinging upon the frame of the card (see WORLD). Over her shoulders falls a white veil and her head is framed by flesh-coloured drapery, as are her hands, the visible portion of the sleeve of her dress and the book which she holds open before her. The white veil is reminiscent of Isis and of the inscription which Plutarch tells us was carved upon her statue at Sais: 'I am all that has been, all that is and all that is to come and no mortal has yet succeeded in lifting my veil.' Sometimes known as 'the Gate of the Hidden Shrine' (RIJT p. 229), the Female Pope possesses the Book of Books, the Book of the Last Judgement which contains all things and from which the world will be judged. She is also compared with Juno, standing for wisdom and wealth, stability and self-control; a sluggishness which may be either needful or harmful. In astrology the Female Pope corresponds to the Second House.

The tale of a Female Pope in the Middle Ages is irrelevant. What this Tarot symbolizes is Woman, priestess or goddess herself, who possesses all the secrets of the universe and is reluctant to reveal them. She is the latent manifestation of the Mother-goddess. Behind the veil of appearance, she hides her strength (red) beneath a cloak of blue (like the EMPRESS, JUSTICE and the HERMIT); she is the waiting figure, 'moral law... priesthood... knowledge as opposed to power' (WIRT p. 125); 'inner contradiction of duality, eternal antithesis of Being and Essence' (RIJT p. 228).

poplar In Ancient Greece the poplar was sacred to Herakles (Hercules). According to legend, when he went down into the Underworld, he crowned his head with a wreath of poplar. The sides of the leaves which were against his head remained pale, those exposed became smoky dark. Hence the difference between the colours of the two sides of the leaf and upon this is based the tree's symbolism – the twofold natures of all beings.

Phaeton's sisters, the Heliades, who had allowed their brother to drive the chariot of the Sun without permission, were changed into poplars. One of the Hesperides, too, was changed into a poplar for losing the apples from the sacred garden. The wood of the white poplar was the only one permitted in sacrifices to Zeus. Hades changed Leuce into a poplar and planted her at the gates of the Underworld so that the mortal woman whom he loved should always be near him.

The tree seems as strongly linked to the Underworld, to pain and to sacrifice as to grief. A funereal tree, it symbolizes the regressive powers of Nature, memories rather than hopes and time past rather than rebirth in the time to come.

poppy   In Eleusinian symbolism, 'the poppy offered to Demeter symbolized the Earth, but also stood for the power of sleep and forgetfulness which possesses humans after death and before rebirth' (MAGE p. 136). In fact, Earth is the place on which these transmutations occur – birth, death and oblivion, resurrection. It is understandable that the poppy should be an attribute of Demeter and identified with her symbolically.

In Russia a girl is said to be 'as pretty as a poppy', while to 'remain a poppy' is to remain an old maid.

porcupine   In divination, the Ekoi of southern Nigeria prefer this animal to all others. It is closely linked to the spirit-realm and often plays the part of culture-hero. In particular, the porcupine taught women how to grow TOMATOES (TEGH pp. 90–1). It will be remembered that the Bambara believe that tomatoes contain a fragment of life-producing power, which makes the tomato akin to the POMEGRANATE. It was a porcupine, too, which organized the first sacrifice to the spirits. On the other side of Africa, the Kikuyu regard the porcupine as the discoverer of fire (myth recorded by FRAF).

Poseidon (Neptune)   God of seas, oceans, rivers, springs and lakes, dominion over the WATERS is his, as the Underworld belongs to Hades, the Heavens to Zeus and Earth to all three brothers. His attribute is the trident or three-pronged harpoon, analogous with Zeus' thunderbolt; it may originally have stood for foaming waves and flashing lightning, for Poseidon was a terrifying god 'of stormy rather than of calm seas' (SECG p. 103). The ficklest of the gods, he enjoyed love affairs with countless goddesses and mortal women, but his offspring were always monsters or rogues. Pausanias states that 'only the initiate knows the name' of the daughter he fathered on Demeter. The secret remains hidden.

Poseidon is just as much a chthonian force, god of earthquakes, their shocks, the Ancients believed, being produced by storms at the sea on which the land-masses rested. Homer remarks that he confounds land and sea together and Humbert was also able to state that Poseidon 'must originally have symbolized that active force which stirs the receptive and passive Earth, whether in the form of vital fluid or of seismic shock' (quoted in SECG p. 104). Furthermore, he was to be depicted in the guise of those animals, such as bulls, horses or dolphins, which embody the fertility principle. The mane of the one, the bellowing of the other and the way the third swims with swift and undulating movement might provide, at a purely metaphorical level, an explanation of this through their similarity with the surge and thunder of the waves. Symbolical interpretation goes wider and deeper, beyond outward appearance, to an apprehension of the fertility principle, confirmed in each of the animals mentioned, and manifested with all the greater intensity in Poseidon as the concentration of the generative force of all the animals represented. It was to Poseidon that Plato (*Critias* 113e) was to attribute the power in the fable of Atlantis 'of making two fountains spring from the soil, one hot and the other cold, and to make the Earth bear nutritious plants in abundance.'

Poseidon, god of sea and earthquake, comes to be the symbol of the lower rather than the upper primeval waters in which life began, but in a stormy, monstrous and undifferentiated state. Dry land starts to emerge from the maelstrom of the seas, but it must still be developed and harmonized. Poseidon expresses the creational powers of the Underworld and is an embodiment of the elemental and still indeterminate forces of a Nature in quest of solid and enduring shape.

From the ethical point of view, Paul Diel was to condemn severely the type of behaviour symbolized by Poseidon. The god would undermine every attempt at spiritualization and would legitimize a type of aberration. He 'is the ruling spirit which legitimizes the perverted satisfaction of desire, the mundane and vicious' (DIES p. 123).

pot (see also JAR; URN; VASE)   This everyday object is open to other symbolic meanings than those of dullness and stupidity. Buddhist teachers (*Suttanipāta* 721) compare the half-filled pot with the fool, since 'fullness' alone corresponds to wisdom and a state of repose. The vessels shaped by the potter are the elements of our *karma*, fashioned daily by what we do and how we behave – in other words, *samsāra*. Under BETEL we have referred to the evil monk of the legend whose belly was likened to the pot in which betel-chewers ceaselessly stir the corrosive lime with their spatulas. Lime-pots are in any case regarded by the Vietnamese as household gods who ward off marauding thieves.

These are, however, specific cases. A more general attribution is that current in India, where the pot is a water and especially a female symbol. In some cults of Dravidian origin, the goddess herself is represented by a pot. In classical iconography a cosmetics jar (*ānjanī*) is a typical attribute of Devī. The Pot Dance was an extremely ancient fertility rite which displayed the utensil's sexual symbolism, the water within it being the very stuff of the manifestation which proceeded from celestial fertilization (ELIY, GOVM, LEBC).

In Africa, too, the immediate symbolic identification of the pot is, in fact, with the womb. Such, for example, is the meaning to be attached to the Dogon image of the Sun as a pot surrounded by a spiral of red copper. The pot stands for the female half of this bisexual symbol, the SPIRAL being the male seed which makes it fertile.

The Bambara, by extension, make the pot a symbol of knowledge. When the newly-circumcised go into an initiatory retreat, they learn that they must strive to obtain the master's pot, that is, try to match their master in knowledge (ZAHB).

In fact, the Bambara regard knowledge as the peak of felicity, the physical pleasure of sexual intercourse being a substitute for it. To some extent their concept is akin to Sufi mystical thought, since they, too, regard all knowledge as being in God, and therefore consider that the highest form of knowledge comprises identification with Him who is the source of bliss.

The Fali give the first wife the title of the large pot in which they brew millet beer; the second, that of the jar in which water is stored; the third, that of the common cooking-pot; and the fourth, that of the long-necked pot used to fetch water (LEBF).

poverty Poverty is broadly speaking the symbol of that stripping away of spiritual inessentials which is part of the quest of the ascetic. It is the Evangelist's 'Blessed are the poor in spirit' (Matthew 5: 3). For Master Eckhart it meant 'stripping off self, to put on the eternity of God' (see DRESS), the one being a precondition of the other. 'And every one that hath forsaken houses, or brethren, or sisters ... for my name's sake, shall receive an hundredfold, and shall inherit everlasting life' (Matthew 19: 29). 'Perfect Poverty' is a classic medieval expression for spiritual development through baring to the essentials. Poverty is like childhood, being a return to simplicity and a detachment from the phenomenal world, childhood being a return to one's beginnings. The same notion exists in Islam, in which spiritual poverty is known as *faqr*, the 'poor' contemplative being the *faqīr*. It is separation from the manifold, and exclusive dependence upon the First Cause. The *Chuang Tzu* itself (ch. 4) distinguishes between 'the heart's fasting' (*sin-chi*) and material poverty which is merely 'self-denial as a prelude to sacrifice' (ECKT, GUEC, SCHP). All these writers stress the positive aspects of poverty. Casting aside material objects is merely the accidence; the triumphant joy of possessing God and God alone is the substance, as St Francis of Assisi bears witness.

prayer-wheel In Tibetan tradition, and recurrent in other different religious and cultural environments, the *hkhorlo* or prayer-wheel is believed to possess 'an energizing spell. By setting it in motion contact is established between the person at prayer, the microcosm, and the gods who rule the universe, the macrocosm. Such contact is both essential and beneficent ... Sorcerers insert a fragment of a human skull between the handle and the body of the wheel.' Inside the wheel there may be the spell from the 'Jewel in the Lotus' (see BELL), a passage from a holy book or a complete paper scroll (TONT p. 4). Undoubtedly use of the prayer-wheel is linked to a belief in the power of the word, either in general terms, or at least to some specific words. The wheel is the container or vehicle for a sacred force enveloped in the sound of the word, which may be set in motion to an individual's advantage.

prince(ss) Princes symbolize the promise of supreme authority, of primacy among equals in any particular realm – literature, painting, science or poetry. Prince Charming awoke the Sleeping Beauty; young men's dreams are haunted by the far-off princess. On the other hand, princes give expression to kingly qualities at the youthful stage when those qualities have neither been fully acquired nor exercised. The idea of youth and glitter is linked to that of the prince. He cuts a larger figure as a hero than as a sage. He is associated more with heroic deeds than with the maintenance of law and order. Princes and princesses are idealizations of men and women in terms of beauty, love and heroism. In legends, princes are often the victims of witches who transform them into monsters or wild beasts, and they can only regain their princely shape as a result of heroic love. For example, in 'Beauty and the Beast', the prince symbolizes the transformation of the baser self into the higher self through the power of love. Princely virtues are the reward of total love, that is of absolute self-sacrifice.

The symbol has its dark side, too. Lucifer is the Prince of Darkness. The bearer of light now only sheds darkness around him. This is the corruption of the best into the worst. The princedom of evil, night and death, is the extreme condition of a lack of good, light and life. It is an inversion of the symbol.

Procrustes In Greek mythology he was the brigand who seized travellers, placing the tall upon a short bed and cutting off the portion of their legs which protruded from the end, and the short upon a long bed, stretching them until they fittted its length. He thus forced whoever came into his clutches into the mould of his own desires and provides a perfect symbol of 'reduction to the commonplace and shrinking the soul to fit the conventional' (DIES p. 128). It is the perversion of idealism into conventionality and a symbol of the tyranny exercised by those who only tolerate the activities and opinions of others when they satisfy their own standards. Procrustes is a symbol of totalitarianism, whether exercised by individual, party or state.

Prometheus The myth of Prometheus finds its place in the history of expanding creation, marking the attainment of awareness and the appearance of mankind. Prometheus was supposed to have robbed Zeus, symbol of the spirit, of the seeds of FIRE, another symbol of Zeus and of the spirit, either by snatching them from the Sun's wheel, or by taking them from Hephaistos' smithy, to carry them down to Earth. Zeus was then believed to have punished him by chaining him to a rock and by setting on him an eagle which ate his liver. He is a symbol of the torments of a repressed and unexpiated guilt complex. 'And ready-witted Prometheus he bound with inextricable bonds, cruel chains, and drove a shaft through his middle, and set on him a long-winged eagle, which used to eat his immortal liver; but by night the liver grew as much again everyway as the long-winged bird devoured in the whole day' (Hesiod, *Theogony* 521–4). Herakles (Hercules), however, freed him from his torments by breaking his chains and killing the eagle with his arrow. When the centaur Chiron longed for death to put an end to his sufferings, he bequeathed his immortality to Prometheus who was thus able to take his place among the gods. While Hesiod attributes to Prometheus trickery, perfidy and 'evil-thinking' against the gods, Aeschylus praises him because

even flashing fire, source of all arts, he hath purloined and bestowed upon mortal ceatures ... fire that hath proved to mortals a teacher in every art and a means to mighty ends. . . . Aye [said Prometheus] I caused mortals no longer to foresee their doom [of death] . . . I caused blind hope to dwell within their breasts. . . . And besides it was I that gave them fire. . . . Aye, and therefrom they shall learn many arts. (*Prometheus Bound* 7, 110, 250ff.)

The meaning of Prometheus' name – Forethought – makes clear the meaning of the myth. As a descendant of the Titans, the spirit of revolt was innate within him; however, he symbolizes not a revolt of the senses, but that of the spirit, the spirit which, if it cannot make itself the equal of the divine intellect, at least tries to steal a few sparks of its light. This is not a quest of the spirit for its own sake, along the path of gradual self-spiritualization, but the use of the spirit for purposes of self-gratification. 'The stolen fire symbolizes the intellect reduced to being the mere means of satisfying a host of cravings and of which the exaltation runs counter to the developmental direction of life. The rebellious intellect chooses the material in preference to the spiritual. By unleashing material cravings, liberation becomes imprisonment in matter' (DIES pp. 237, 243, 250). Prometheus' final deification was to follow his freeing by Herakles, that is to say, after his chains were broken and the eagle killed. But it was also to be conditional upon the death of the CENTAUR, that is to say, by the sublimation of desire. The latter was to be a victory of the spirit at the end of a fresh phase of creative development in the direction of the being and no longer towards power.

Gaston Bachelard regards the Prometheus myth as illustrating the fact that 'there is in man a veritable *will to intellectuality*', but a life of the intellect on a par with that of the gods, and not 'under the absolute dependence of the principle of utility'.

We propose, then, to place together under the name of *Promethean complex* all those tendencies which impel us *to know* as much as our fathers, more than our fathers, as much as our teachers, more than our teachers. Now it is by handling the object, it is by perfecting our objective knowledge, that we can best hope to prove decisively that we have attained the intellectual level which we have so admired in our parents and in our teachers. The acquiring of supremacy through drive of more powerful instincts naturally will appeal to a much greater number of individuals, but minds of a rarer stamp also must be examined by the psychologist. If pure intellectuality is exceptional, it is nonetheless very characteristic of a specifically human evolution. The Prometheus complex is the Oedipus complex of the life of the intellect.

(BACF p. 12)

prostitution Sacred prostitution, the symbol of divine marriage, generally took place within the enclosures of temples and shrines built to ensure the fertility of crops, animals and so on. The custom is recorded during antiquity in many traditions, and continues today within some African tribes.

It was not merely a fertility rite. It symbolized union with the godhead and, in some instances, the oneness of the living in the wholeness of being, or else the receiving of a share of the energy of the god or goddess represented by the prostitute.

Proteus A sea-god of the second rank, his special duty according to the *Odyssey* was to act as seal-herd. He conjures up a picture of the waves of the sea which, during storms, are able to suggest the fleeting images of horses, sheep, pigs, boars, lions and other animals, since Proteus was 'endowed with the power of changing himself into any shape he wished. He could not only become an animal, but an element like Fire or Water.

He made especial use of this power when he wanted to escape his question-
ers. For he possessed the gift of prophecy, but refused to enlighten those
mortals who questioned him' (GRID p. 398).

He may thus be made a symbol of the unconscious, manifesting itself in
thousands of different shapes, never replying plainly and only expressing
itself in riddles.

psychostasis See under SCALES.

pumpkin See GOURD.

puppet These little figures in painted wood, ivory or cloth, manipulated
by an invisible puppeteer either with his fingers or on the end of strings,
symbolize individuals lacking in sense of purpose who give way to any
external pressure, light-weight, frivolous and both unprincipled and want-
ing in character.

However, their symbolism goes far deeper. In his allegory of the cave,
Plato compares life on Earth with a shadow theatre, its inhabitants mere
puppets compared with the pure and changeless ideas of the upper world,
of which they are the feeble images.

The Ancient Egyptians, the Greeks and the Chinese were all familiar
with these articulated dolls and displayed them in religious processions.
Like STATUETTES, they possessed sacred properties in relation to the deity or
important person they depicted, but these were almost those of the buffoon
since they provided a ridiculous travesty, throwing into sharp relief upon
their stage the follies of mankind. Travelling puppet-shows flourished
throughout the Hellenistic world. The Church forbade their use in medieval
mystery plays.

In Europe and in Asia (and especially in Japan) type-characters have
been created which have, as it were, become the archetypes of human
behaviour and emotions. In Kyoto puppetry has reached the pitch of being
able to give expression to the subtlest as well as to the most violent feelings.
This traditional and almost standardized form of drama produces cathartic
effects upon its audience, which spends hours watching it. Before their eyes
unfold cosmic, national, family and individual dramas, into which they project
all the force of their unconscious. Puppets effect both abreaction and integration by causing the emotions to flow along the channel of communal
legend and tradition.

The puppet itself becomes charged with all these forces and, in the end,
comes to possess vast magical power. In its battered old age it passes from
the theatre to the junk-shop but is still regarded as preserving its secret
properties, and poetry endows it with the respect due to a miraculous symbol of mankind. Puppets are able to express what dare not be said openly,
they are the heroes and heroines of secret longing and hidden thought, the
quiet confession made to others of oneself and of oneself to one's self.

Puppets also carry a mystic meaning. The *Mahābhārata* has the words:
'Human behaviour is controlled from the outside like that of a wooden doll
on the end of a string.' And in the Upanishads there is: 'Do you know the
thread by which is attached this world and the other and all the beings in
them, and the hidden Master who controls them from within?' When the

craving for the One is satisfied, the human will be absorbed in Plato's golden thread which governs us, puppets that we are. Plato said that, by virtue of all that is best in it, mankind is the plaything of God, while Jacob Boehme wrote: 'You will achieve nothing until you abdicate your own will, that is, what you call "I" or "myself".' Ananda Coomaraswamy conjures up the ecstatic rapture of the puppet 'acting without action' in the sense taught by the *Bhagavad Gītā* and the Taoist doctrine of *wi wu wi*. Freedom is not to be gained by uncoordinated movement, but by becoming aware that in joining in 'the dance of phenomena' we may identify with the puppet-master who controls us. In the Hindu *Kāthā Sarit Sāqara*, the king who peopled his city with puppets provides a perfect example of puppet symbolism. The city is the body, its parts linked to their master, the self, at the heart of the Golden City. Heinrich von Kleist in his *Über das Marionettentheater*, and Novalis intuitively accepted the superiority 'of this created thing over the run of mankind' (COOE).

purification Every religion has its rites of purification and the list of taboos and rituals is endless. Whatever displeases God, be they deeds, foods or animals, is unclean and this uncleanness may be physical or may take the form of disobedience to the law. This must be cleansed. In Ancient Greece, the notion of moral purity, of purity of conscience, of the soul becoming sullied and of repentance only made its appearance with the cult of Delphic Apollo. Ritual washing was rigidly enforced at certain times or before entry to certain places, and took the form of washing the hands, rinsing out the mouth, bathing and so on. Purification was one of the duties of the lower orders of the Ancient Egyptian priesthood, whose task it was daily to open and close the temples. The ritual took place at dawn at the lake-side. *Agnihotra*, in the Vedas, was the rite of purification by fire, since both fire and water have cleansing as well as propitiatory properties. Purification from murder, however, could only be obtained by blood. The guilty party had to be sprinkled with the blood of a sacrificial victim.

Purification is linked to water, fire and blood, while uncleanness derives from Earth. Purification symbolizes the restoration of original purity, a consciousness of being sullied by sin and worldly intercourse, and an aspiration towards what may in some respects be a heavenly life and a return to the springs of being.

putrefaction (see also EXCREMENT) The reduction of matter to dust or its rotting away symbolizes the death of its old nature and its rebirth in another mode of being, able to bear fresh fruit.

The alchemists regarded putrefaction as

the chiefest chemical operation ... the death of the body and the separation of the matter of which it is composed which provokes their corruption and disposes them to generation. Putrefaction is caused by the continuous internal warmth of the body and not to any manual application of heat. One must therefore take care not to increase the external heat beyond a modest degree, in case the matter is reduced to dry, red ashes, instead of black, and all is destroyed.

(PERD pp. 418–19)

The matter should be allowed to putrefy in a slow and controlled way, one might say, rather than disappear in a flash.

The Christian liturgy of ASH Wednesday symbolizes the return to the dust from which we were created, but only to prepare the soul for its eternal bliss.

Putrefaction, generally speaking and in accordance with the etymology of the word, means to rot away. However, the symbolism is the same – death and rebirth into another life. This new life, the sequel to putrefaction, is generally conceived as being in a higher or sublimated form, or else it denotes the transformation of a purely material existence into an ideal and patterned existence.

An example of this type of putrefaction symbol is provided by the legend of the 'dragoness', Pytho, slain by Apollo, recounted in the 'Homeric' hymn to Pythian Apollo (358–74):

Then she, rent with bitter pangs, lay drawing great gasps for breath and rolling about that place. An awful noise swelled up unspeakable as she writhed continually this way and that amid the wood: and so she left her life, breathing it forth in blood. Then Phoebus Apollo boasted over her: 'Now rot there upon the soil that feeds man! You at least shall live no more to be a fell bane to men who eat the fruit of the all-nourishing earth, and who will bring hither perfect hecatombs. Against cruel death neither Typhoeus shall avail you nor ill-famed Chimera, but here shall the Earth and shining Hyperion make you rot.'

Thus said Phoebus, exulting over her: and darkness covered her eyes. And the holy strength of Helios made her rot away there; wherefor the place is now called Pytho, and men call the lord Apollo by another name, Pythian; because on that spot the power of piercing Helios made the monster rot away.

Now, it should be remembered that Pytho, being a monster, was born of Earth and that she uttered oracles. She was a chthonian creature. Apollo, himself sky-born, by killing her and substituting his own for her oracles, confirmed the triumph of Heaven over Earth. The monster's putrefaction was one of the conditions of Apollo's victory as well as being the result of the action of the Sun, Apollo's ARROW being the symbol of the Sun's rays. From now on oracles were to come from the sky of Delphi, not from the bowels of the Earth.

pyramid The pyramids, the most famous tombs of the kings and queens of Ancient Egypt, fall into different categories. There is the regular, square-based pyramid, like that of Cheops; the step-pyramid, like that of Jeser; or the pyramid with a rhomboidal base, like that of Snefru. All were constructed in accordance with religious beliefs and magical practices for which professional Egyptologists have far more sober explanations than those of the army of longwinded amateurs. Although one should approach with caution 'pyramidology', in so far as it relates the scientific knowledge of the Pharaohs with that of modern scholars, it is perfectly in order to study ancient beliefs and to draw from them the reasons for the existence of these gigantic buildings. The pyramid shares in the symbolism of the mound which covered the bodies of the dead: it is a stone mound, its perfection and colossal size exploiting to the very full the magical assurances expected of the humblest funeral ceremony. 'It is not difficult to imagine that the mound, although purely practical in origin, was thought to resemble the hill which emerged from the primeval waters when the earth came into being and thus represented existence. Death could be magically countered by the presence of this potent symbol' (POSD p. 233).

A second explanation may be added which does not contradict the first and is especially valid in the case of kings. Heliopolitan belief maintained that when the king's earthly life came to an end he returned to the Sun-god and perhaps became identified with him. This is why pyramids are symbols of ascension as much in their external shape – step-pyramids being reminiscent of LADDERS or STAIRWAYS – as in their internal passageways, which often slope steeply. The lines of the pyramid and the slope of the internal passages might well represent 'the sun's rays shining down to earth through a gap in the clouds' (POSD p. 233). All these arrangements symbolize the power of the dead king to ascend into Heaven and to descend again at will. Albert Champdor regarded 'these massive pieces of architecture [as being] designed to strike the people dumb and to protect the tiny mortuary chamber which was, as it were, its ridiculous soul and in which the ritual of the rebirth of Osiris was performed before the mummified remains of the Pharaoh in the depths of inviolable mystery' (CHAM p. 10).

According to Sertillanges, the inverted pyramid is the image of spiritual development. The more spiritualized the individual becomes and the higher he or she rises, the wider and broader grows his or her life. Similarly, and at group level, the greater is the society of individuals in whose lives he or she shares.

Both at individual and group levels the pyramid conveys the twofold meaning of integration and convergence. 'The plainest and most perfect image of synthesis', it may, in this context, be compared with a tree, but an inverted tree with the foot of the trunk uppermost.

Scattered communities coming together as cities integrated into an organized State with convergent cities, such is the meaning of the pyramids built at a period during which groups in Ancient Egypt tended to coordinate their efforts to construct a national synthesis. . . . This tendency towards social synthesis finds initial expression in the physical projection of the symbol of that synthesis, construction of the pyramid, an image of upward convergence. Building the pyramids gave expression to a synthesis of which the builders were largely unaware. However, by the projection in physical shape of the results of their internal synthesis, the builders emphasized their tendency towards national synthesis. From then on, the pyramid which they had erected provided the Ancient Egyptians with a motivating image, strengthening in each the tendency towards awareness of themselves as individuals and as members of society.

(VIRI pp. 154, 246)

In addition to its role in upward convergence and awareness of synthesis, the pyramid was also the meeting-place between two worlds. The one was the world of magic linked to funeral rites designed to preserve life indefinitely or to ensure the passing to an existence beyond time; the other, the logical world of geometry and architecture. 'It was inevitable that mystery-mongers should gaze in wonder at this meeting, seeing it sometimes as the divine elucidation of geometry and at others as magic justified by mathematics' (VIRI p. 155).

The geometrical proportions of the Great Pyramid at Giza have opened the doors to other explanations that take us back to the symbolism of the alchemists. It is well known that this pyramid's 'square base has a perimeter equal to the length of the circumference of a circle with a radius equal to its height, which is the same as saying that the relationship between the square base and the circle is expressed in terms of elevation.' Nothing is easier, then, than to picture a circle, its radius equal to the height of the pyramid, pivoting upon its tip, either vertically in the shape of a WHEEL or horizontally in the shape of a DISC, or obliquely on a different plane. One might as easily picture a sphere with a circumference equal to the perimeter of the base and its axis that of the pyramid itself. Alchemists would have regarded this as a solution to the problem of squaring the circle. A second comparison, however, may be made since the pyramid's 'four triangular faces meeting at the peak would correspond to the alchemical synthesis of the four elements moving upwards until in the end they created a circle, corresponding to ether, of which the alchemical symbol was the circle ... The dialectic of SQUARE and CIRCLE symbolize the dialectic of Heaven and Earth, material and spiritual' (VIRI p. 243).

Matila Ghyka concludes, after studying the geometrical proportions of the Great Pyramid, that

> it is probable that whoever designed the Great Pyramid was unaware of all the geometric properties which we can observe with hindsight. These properties are not, however, due to chance, but in some way flow organically from the master-plan consciously embodied in the meridian triangle. This is because a clearly organized geometric concept always provides a good master-plan. This one has the originality of incorporating in the crystalline and abstract rigidity of the pyramid a dynamic pulsation which itself may be regarded as the mathematical symbol of living growth.
>
> (GHYP p. 27)

Perhaps 'living growth' best expresses the all-embracing symbolism of the pyramid. It was intended to ensure the apotheosis of the Pharaoh in an assimilation of the dead with the Sun-god, the uppermost and eternal limit of growth.

A similar notion has been attributed to Hermes Trismegistus, the tip of the pyramid symbolizing: 'The Word as Demiurge, the first-born Power, but proceeding from the Father and ruling all created things, totally perfect and fruitful.' Thus at the upper limit of the pyramid, the initiate would await marriage with the Word, just as, in a chamber in the stone, the dead Pharaoh awaited assimilation with the immortal god.

Pytho (see also CROCODILE; MOUTH; NĀGA; PUTREFACTION) Apollo, according to the 'Homeric' hymn to Pythian Apollo (300–5), 'with his strong bow the lord, the son of Zeus, killed the bloated, great she-dragon, a fierce monster wont to do great mischief to men upon earth, to men themselves and to their thin-shanked sheep; for she was a very bloody plague.' This Underworld deity and serpent was to be given the name of Pytho on the very spot at Delphi where the cult of Pythian Apollo was celebrated. Like the CHIMERA, this serpent was one of the monsters most frequently depicted on archaic monuments. As a pre-eminent representation of the chthonian,

Pytho was equipped with the initiatory mouth which gapes to swallow the setting Sun and spit it out again at day-break. Apollo's victory over the serpent is that of reason over instinct, of consciousness over the unconscious. This symbolic struggle of action with emotion, of thought, the diurnal aspect, with the nocturnal aspect, inspiration, has only begun to be settled in the West with the resolution of the quarrel between the Ancients and the Moderns, which, from the Romantics to Freud, at last and after two thousand years of fear gave corporate rights to the unconscious.

Pythoness   See SIBYL.

Q

quail In figurative language quails are symbols of heat or, more basically, of love-heat. It will be observed that in China the quail was the bird of the south and of Fire, being the Red Bird, the symbol of Summer. In Chinese astronomy it gave its name to the central star of the Summer Palace.

Notwithstanding, quail symbolism is linked especially to the behaviour of a migratory bird and to its underlying cyclical nature. What is more, this was of a rather strange character, since it led in China to the phoenix being substituted for the quail. Like the swallow, in Ancient China the quail returned with the fine weather and was believed to change itself into a fieldmouse or FROG during the Winter. Springtime jousting imitated the mating habits of quail (and partridge and wild goose). This seasonal rhythm, this coming and going of migratory birds, was an image of the alternations of *yin* and *yang*, birds (celestials) changing into animals which lived either underground or in the water.

The Vedic myth of the deliverance of the quail by the horse-headed twin gods, the Ashvins, is well known. It would appear to possess a significance of the same order, even if it forms part of a cycle of different scope. Current interpretations link the Ashvins to Heaven and Earth, to day and night. The quail (*vartikā*) which they freed from the jaws of the wolf must therefore be the dawn, the sunlight previously swallowed and shut in the CAVERN. It will be remembered that the Chinese dawn-clouds have five colours 'like the quail's egg' and also that the quail always flies by night. Christinger observes that *vartikā* means 'she who returns' and derives from the same root as *ortyx*, the Greek name for the bird. Ortygia, 'Quail Island', was the birthplace of Artemis (Moon) and Apollo (Sun), whose alternation bears some relation to that of the Ashvins. It goes without saying that this light, set free from the clutch of darkness – or from the Underworld – is not simply that of the rising Sun but also that of the spiritual Sun or, more accurately, the enlightenment which comes from intellectual effort or initiation (CHAT, CHRC, GRAR).

Nor should it be forgotten that, along with manna, quails provided the miraculous food on which the Children of Israel were nourished in the Wilderness.

quarantine See under FORTY.

quartz (see also CRYSTAL; STONE) Quartz symbolizes the celestial element in initiation. In the initiation rites conducted by Australian medicine-men, the 'holy, powerful water' is regarded as liquid quartz (ERAJ 26: p. 195).

quaternary number (see also FOUR) In this context, these words (see SQUARE) are taken to mean the arithmetical progression of the first four digits – 1, 2, 3, 4. Their sum is the DECADE, a symbol of perfection and the key of the universe. The quaternary is the sacred number in this the human world. It is placed equidistant from impenetrable oneness (4 – 1 = 3) and from the septenary (7 – 4 = 3), which expresses its marriage with the divine triad, that is with the one regarded under its three relationships with creation – power, intelligence and love.

The equidistance of the quaternary from one and seven provides an adequate definition of human vocation. Issuing from the One, the individual is marked out as the creature of the creator, but is called upon to RETURN to the creator and to unite with him so as to manifest his power, intelligence and love. Thus the individual follows the same path in reverse, the Three, for the first time in the direction of differentiation and in the second in the direction of reintegration. The quaternary number is a good example of a situation, but of a developing situation, mankind being set on this Earth in a dynamic which concerns the whole universe.

quill See under PEN.

R

rabbit See under HARE.

rags and tatters Are the symbol of anxiety and lesions of the psyche as well as of that material poverty which, in folktales, is sometimes adopted as a disguise by princes, princesses and wizards. It denotes simultaneously poverty and anxiety or cloaks inner riches under an appearance of wretchedness, thus displaying the superiority of the inner over the outer self.

rain Rain is regarded universally as the symbol of the celestial influences which the Earth receives. It is self-evidently a fecundating agent of the soil, which gains its fertility from rain, and countless agrarian rites were devised in dance form, in offerings to the Sun, in Cambodian 'sand-mountains' or by using the smithy to summon a storm to send down rain. However, this fecundation had wider application than to the soil alone. Indra, the god of the thunderbolt, brought rain to the fields, but also made animals and women fertile. What comes down to Earth from Heaven is spiritual fertility, light and spiritual influences as well.

The *I Ching* teaches that from rain came the *k'ien* principle, the active celestial principle to which all manifestations owe their existence. In his *Risālat*, Ibn al-Walid equates cosmologically celestial rain, the 'Upper waters', with semen; and Isaiah 45: 8 reads: 'Let the skies pour down righteousness; let the earth open, and let them bring forth salvation' In the *Tao Te Ching* (ch. 39), the ideogram *lin*, used to denote celestial influences, comprises the ideogram *wu*, denoting magical incantations, together with three open mouths drinking in the rain of Heaven. This, of course, gives expression to the rites mentioned earlier, but their effects are felt in the realm of the intellect. Islamic esoterics say that 'with every drop of rain God sends his angel.' Apart from the special meaning which they give the phrase, its literal symbolism is obvious, as is also the comparison with the Hindu teaching that 'subtle' beings come down to Earth from the Moon, dissolved in drops of rain. This lunar rain also possesses the usual fertility symbolism and that of bringing back to life. If rain is grace, it is also wisdom. The Master Hui Neng taught that: 'The Highest Wisdom, immanent in each individual's nature, may be likened to the rain.'

If rain symbolism is usually very close to dew symbolism, it will be observed that in China they are sometimes opposed to one another, since the nature of rain is *yin* and that of dew *yang*. And yet both originate in the Moon. However, the fact that they work together is a sign of world harmony (CORT, DANA, ELIM, GUET, GUES, HOUD, LIOT, PORA).

The Greek legend of Danaë reveals how Heaven-sent rain makes the Earth fertile. To avoid all danger of her conceiving a child, Danaë's father imprisoned her in an underground room walled in bronze. Here she received a visit from Zeus, who had taken the shape of a shower of gold which seeped through a crack in the ceiling and made her pregnant. Here are closely linked the sexual symbolism of rain, regarded as semen, and the agricultural symbolism of plant growth, which needs rain before it can take place. The myth also contains reminders of the pairings of light and darkness, Heaven and Hell and gold and bronze, conjuring up those marriages of opposites from which spring all manifestation and fecundity.

In Amerindian tradition rain is 'the storm god's "sowing"' (ELIT p. 93). Rain was the sperm which made fruitful the sacred marriage of Heaven and Earth. All agrarian civilizations attribute the same symbolic properties to it.

In the Maya-Quiché languages water, rain and plants are equated and expressed by the same word (GIRP p. 92).

While rain may be regarded as sperm or seed, it was also seen as blood, whence the beginnings of human sacrifice, fertility-rites characteristic of agrarian civilizations.

Itzamna, the Maya god of agriculture, is the self-proclaimed 'substance of the skies, the dew from the clouds' (GIRP p. 93).

In Maya-Quiché languages the word *quic* has the simultaneous meaning of 'blood', 'resin' and 'sap', as well as any human or animal liquid excretion which is assimilated to rain (GIRP p. 107).

The Aztec rain-god, Tlaloc, was also the god of the THUNDERBOLT and of LIGHTNING, 'fire-rain'. Lightning, like rain, was recognized as having the same property of celestial semen. Tlalocan – Tlaloc's Heaven – was the abode of those who had died by drowning or by lightning, the god himself being depicted with rings round mouth and eyes made of the bodies of two serpents. These serpents stand for both lightning and water (SOUM).

The Peruvian Inca believed that rain was cast down from Heaven by the thunder-god, Illapa, who drew the water from the Milky Way, the great celestial river (LEHC).

The association of Moon and Water and Spring rains and purification is clearly shown in the ceremonies with which the Inca celebrated Coya Raimi, the festival of the Moon (22 September–22 October). This month marked the end of the dry season, and strangers, sick persons and dogs were driven out of the city of Cuzco before the ceremonies to call down the Spring rains began (MEAA).

In India, a fertile woman is called 'the rain', that is, a spring, of all prosperity (BOUA).

Daughter of the clouds and the storm, rain brings together the symbols of Fire (lightning) and Water and also conveys that twofold sense of spiritual and physical fecundation. The part played by the rain is perfectly expressed in the *Chāndogya Upanishad*. As it falls from the sky, rain also expresses the twofold blessing of the gods, in both spiritual and material terms.

rainbow Rainbows are both intermediaries and pathways between Heaven and Earth. They are the bridges used by gods and heroes when they travel between this Earth and the Otherworld. Evidence from Pygmies and Polynesians, Indonesians, Melanesians and Japanese, to give examples from non-European societies, shows that this function is virtually worldwide.

In Norse legend, the bridge Byfrost was a rainbow, as was the Japanese 'floating bridge of Heaven' and the seven-coloured staircase down which the Buddha returns from Heaven. The same notion recurs from Iran to Central Africa, and from North America to China. In Tibet, the rainbow is not a bridge in itself, but the souls of monarchs rising up to Heaven. There is something akin to the notion of the pontiff or pontifex here (see under BRIDGE). It is a place of passage. There is an etymological and symbolic link between the rainbow and the sky. The Breton word *kanevedenn* assumes an Old Celtic prototype, *kambonemos*, 'curve of the sky'. Rainbow symbolism would thus be linked to that of the sky and of bridges (OGAC 12: p. 186).

The ribbons used by Buryat shamans are called rainbows; 'in general they symbolize the shaman's journey to the sky' (ELIC p. 135). Central African Pygmies believe that God uses the rainbow to show what he wishes to communicate with them.

Rainbows are an example of the transfer of the attributes of the sky-god to the Sun-god. 'The rainbow, regarded in many places as a manifestation of the sky-god, is associated with the sun and the Fuegians believe it to be the Sun's brother' (ELIT; SCHP p. 79).

The Dogon believe that the rainbow which allows the heavenly ram, which fertilizes the Sun and whose urine is the rain, to come down to Earth. The chameleon wears the colours of the rainbow and is related to it. Again, according to Dogon belief, there are four colours in the rainbow, black, red, yellow and green, and these are the hoof-prints of the Heavenly Ram, when he gallops (GRIE).

In Ancient Greece, the rainbow was Iris, swift-footed messenger of the gods. It was also, in more generalized fashion, a symbol of the relationship between Heaven and Earth and gods and mortals – a form of divine speech.

In China, the conjunction of the five colours attributed to the rainbow is that of *yin* and *yang* and is a sign of universal harmony and of its fecundity. While Shiva's bow is said to resemble the rainbow, Indra's is directly attributed to it and, in Cambodia, the rainbow is still called 'Indra's Bow' (*einthna*). Now, Indra scatters rain and thunder over the Earth and these are symbols of celestial activity.

The seven, rather than five colours of the rainbow provide Muslim esoterics with an image of the properties of the godhead reflected in the universe, since the rainbow 'is the reversed image of the Sun upon the broken curtain of the rain' (Jīlī). In India and Mesopotamia, these seven colours were assimilated to the seven Heavens. According to Tibetan Buddhists, clouds and rainbows symbolize *Sambogha-kāya* ('bliss-body') and when they dissolve in rain they symbolize *Nirmāana-kāya* ('Buddha-nature').

The marriage of opposites is also the reuniting of divided halves or resolution. Thus, Guénon suggests, the rainbow which appeared above Noah's Ark reunited the 'Lower Waters' with the 'Upper Waters', the two halves of the World EGG, as a sign of the restoration of the cosmic order and the birth of a fresh cycle. More explicitly, the Old Testament makes the rainbow the covenant in material form. 'And God said, This is the token of the covenant which I make between me and you, and every living creature that is with you, for perpetual generations; I do set my bow in the clouds, and it shall be for a token of a covenant between me and earth' (Genesis 9: 12–13).

De Champeaux carries the same image into the New Testament, linking Peter's barque with Noah's Ark.

Within this shell is contained the Mystery of the Church which, by its vocation, is co-extensive with the Universe symbolized by the SQUARE. In Noah's case God prefiguratively drew the square of the New Cosmos within the rainbow circle of divine loving-kindness. He sketched the plans of the New JERUSALEM. This covenant was already an assumption, an accomplished fact, since God is faithful. In both Byzantine and Western religious art, Christ in Glory is often depicted enthroned in the midst of a rainbow.

(CHAS p. 108)

The association of rain and rainbows means that in many traditions the rainbow conjures up images of the mythic serpent. In East Asia, this is the NĀGA, offspring of the Underworld. This symbolism recurs in Africa and also, perhaps, in Ancient Greece, for the rainbow embossed upon Agamemnon's breast-plate took the form, Guénon observes, of three serpents, related to the cosmic currents which flow between Heaven and Earth. The newel-posts of the Buddha's rainbow-staircase are formed by a pair of *nāga*. At Angkor Thom, Prah Khan and Bantai Chmar, the same symbolism is to be found in the causeways with *nāga* balustrades. That these are images of the rainbow is confirmed by the presence of Indra at the end of the causeway at Angkor Thom. It should be added that, at Angkor, the same idea is expressed in the gateways – Gates of Heaven, of course – of which the lintels carry carvings either of Indra or of the MAKARA vomiting two serpents. Generally speaking, a *makara*-arch symbolizes a rainbow and celestial rain. There is a Chinese legend of the Immortal who was changed into a rainbow coiled like a serpent, and it should be noted that there are at least five ideograms denoting rainbows, all of which contain the root, *ho-i*, that of the serpent.

It must be added that, while rainbows are generally heralds of good things to come and are linked to the cycle of rebirth – it was for this reason that a rainbow was seen when Fu-hi was born – they may also serve as prologues to disturbance to the harmony of the universe and even take some terrifying meaning. This is the other sinister, or nocturnal, aspect of the same complex symbol. 'When the state is in danger of destruction,' Huai Nan Tzu wrote, 'the aspect of the heavens changes and . . . a rainbow appears.' The Montagnards of southern Vietnam regard the relations between Heaven and Earth established by the mediation of the rainbow to wear an ill-omened aspect concerned with death and sickness. The rainbow *Borlang-Kang* springs from something sinister and to point at it can cause leprosy. Pygmies call it 'the perilous sky-serpent' and see it as a solar arch formed by a pair of serpents welded together. The Semang Negrito believes that the rainbow is a python-snake. From time to time 'he slithers into the sky to take a bath. Then he gleams brightly. When he tips the water out of his bath it falls to the Earth as Sun-rain, a water most perilous to humans.'

The Andaman Negrito regards the rainbow as malevolent. It is the forest-spirit's drum and its appearance heralds death and disease (SCHP pp. 157, 167). On the other hand the Chibcha in Colombia regarded it as a goddess who protected pregnant women (TRIR p. 130).

The Inca believed that rainbows were the feather-crown of the god of thunder and rain, Illapa. He was regarded as being both cruel and inexorable and for this reason the Ancient Peruvians did not dare look at a rainbow and covered their mouths with their hands when one appeared (LEHC). The Pueblo Indians call by the name of rainbow the ladder leading down to their underground temples, which hence gives access to the realm of the chthonian powers.

The Inca also believed the rainbow to be unlucky since it was a sky-serpent. 'When it was no more than a little worm it was nourished by mortals, but it ate so greedily that it grew to enormous size. The mortals were forced to kill it because it demanded human hearts for food. Birds dipped their feathers in its blood and their plumage became dyed with the bright colours of the rainbow' (LEHC).

In central Asia there was a lingering belief 'that rainbows suck up or drink the waters of lakes and rivers. The Yakut go so far as to believe that they may even suck men up from the ground.' In the Caucasus, children were warned not to let the rainbow carry them up into the clouds (HARA p. 152).

ram The ram, by its fire, masculinity, strength and instinctive reactions symbolizes the procreative forces which arouse mankind and the world at large at the springtime of life, as well as the Spring of the year, and ensure that the cycle of life continues on its way again. This is why the ram combines warmth and generosity with an obstinacy verging upon blindness. Such at least is what astrologers understand by the Ram, ARIES, the sign which enters the Sun every year on 21 March, the day of the vernal equinox. To them it stands for the cosmic image of a force which is animal or rather animating, for fire which both creates and destroys, for a power which is both blind and rebellious, profuse and disorderly, generous and sublime and which radiates outward from a central point in every direction. This fiery force is assimilated to the outpouring of primeval life, to that very first surge of being, and to all those elements of pure animal drive, uncontrollably shattering everything in its lightning path, carried away in the fire-breathing frenzy which such a primal process possesses. Alchemical tradition held that one was in the presence of a Word of which the echoes were in RED and GOLD and in affinity with Mars and the Sun. A contentious Word, to match a passionate, ebullient and tumultuous nature. Astrology identifies individual human characteristics with each sign of the Zodiac, but explains that, to resemble the type denoted by the sign, one does not simply have to be born in that Zodiacal month or under that particular sign. Now the typical Arietan belongs to what the modern science of character calls the 'Choleric' (emotional–active–of limited vision), with blazing vitality, eager to live life to the full, tumultuously, intensely giving full play to strong emotion, uncontrolled feelings, to danger and daring and all the ups and downs of an over-active existence.

Evidence for such characteristics is to be found throughout the world in many symbol-creating myths, customs and images. Thus the Ancient Egyptian air- and fertility-god, Amun, later to be given fresh life as Jupiter-Amon, was depicted as ram-headed, just like Hermes Kriophoros, the ram-bearer, renowned in a temple in Boeotia for having saved a city from the plague by carrying a ram on his shoulders around its walls. In a similar pastoral cult, the Dorians worshipped Apollo Karneiros, the ram-god, as renowned in Sparta for driving off wild beasts, protecting flocks and teaching the shepherds their craft. Undoubtedly such Mediterranean ceremonies and beliefs lie behind Christ the Good Shepherd and the countless Christian depictions of shepherds carrying a LAMB or a ram on their shoulders. The ram thus became 'a variant on the Lamb of God, which offered itself as a victim for the salvation of sinners' and the symbol not only of Christ, but of 'the faithful who, after him and in him, accepted death as a means of redeeming others' (CHAS p. 278); this within the sublimation of the symbolism of fire, blood and fertility which renews life.

Among the countless other examples one might take that of the potter-god, Khnum, who, the Ancient Egyptians believed, had fashioned all created things, as the archetypal ram-god, the procreative ram. Countless mummified rams have been excavated. 'In them resided, from earliest times, the forces which ensured the powers of reproduction of the living. Their horns, forming part of several magical crowns worn by kings and gods, were the very symbol of the terror which radiated from the supernatural' (POSD p. 262).

The same belief survived to Ptolemaic times and Jean Yoyote records: 'a priest from Mendes set up his statue in the temple of the Ram, fertility-god and lord of the city, trusting in the prayers of the pilgrims on his behalf: "You who come down the river to visit the great sacred rams, pray to God for this statue of me!"' (SOUP p. 20)

From Gaul to Black Africa, from India to China there was the same joyful worship of that symbolic chain which linked creative fire to fertility and even, by the mediation of the principle of life itself, to immortality.

Thus in the Vedas, rams are related to Agni, lord of fire, and especially to sacrificial fire. In Tantric Yoga, the allegory of the ram is the *manipūra-chakra*, which corresponds to the element Fire. Lastly, according to the *Bāskala-mantra Upanishad*, the sage Indra changed himself into a ram to teach the doctrine of 'the oneness of the Supreme Principle'.

A ram, too, was the steed of the Hindu god Kuvera, warden of the north and guardian of treasure. This is somewhat suggestive of the Golden Fleece, but although the quests for the Golden Fleece are primarily quests for a spiritual treasure, that is to say, for wisdom, they are perhaps also kingship-ordeals as well. In Ancient China, rams played the role of unicorns in trials by ordeals. At the same period and at the same cultural level, a ram was also sometimes the steed of an immortal (Ko Yu) and even the shape into which the Immortal was transformed (GRAD, KALL, MALA, RENB). Remember, too, that in Black Africa, amongst other evidence, Marcel Griaule has recorded the painting upon the wall of a shrine of the Celestial Ram, an agrarian deity, standing over an ear of maize and with its tail ending in a serpent's head, symbolizing superabundant fertility.

Returning to Europe, we find that large numbers of Gallic stone or terracotta rams-head andirons have been found, which seem not unconnected with the creature's fire symbolism and fecundity within the family (CHAB). Second only to its fleece as a receptacle of symbolic properties is the creature's HORN, a source of countless customs, traditions and images deriving from the original symbolism and of which undoubtedly the most highly-charged is the HORN OF PLENTY. Modern analysis and psychology recognize its importance, which has been visualized and summarized as follows by Virel. The ram is not only

the inseminator of the flock but, in the shape of the battering-ram, was also the weapon which enabled besiegers to smash their way through the walls and gates of cities and hence to shatter the protective shell of societies. The spiral shape of the horns gives an additional notion of development and emphasizes the initiatory and introductory properties suggested by the points of all animal horns. The ram provided an excellent example of initiation. It was endowed with reason and the Word. It symbolized physical strength and the sacred power of sublimation. It flew and its fleece was golden.

(VIRI p. 174)

Its penetrative power is, however, always ambivalent – it fecundates and yet it wounds and kills.

rat Were the rat not regarded as a frightening and even an infernal creature it might have shared the metamorphosis into a love symbol of its fellow-rodent, the rabbit, which shares its hungry nocturnal habits and its prolixity. It is, therefore, a chthonian animal, which played an important part in pre-Hellenic Mediterranean civilizations and was often associated with SERPENTS and MOLES.

As Freud demonstrates in his classic analysis of the 'Rat Man', the creature is regarded as unclean, rummages in the bowels of the Earth, has distinctly phallic and anal connotations and is associated with notions of wealth and money. For this last reason it is often regarded as the image of avarice and greed and of sinister and shady activities. (The *I Ching* is at one with European tradition on this point.) Positive analysis would emphasize the creature's fecundity and in Japan, for example, it is the companion of Daikoku, the god of wealth. The same interpretation is current in China and Siberia. This would explain why, in Freudian analysis, rats become the avatars of children, both being signs of wealth and plenty. Rats are, however, insatiable pilferers and are thus regarded as thieves.

In India, Ganesha's steed is the mouse, *mūshaka*. As such, it is associated with ideas of theft and the misappropriation of riches. The 'thief' is the *ātman* within the heart. Under the veil of illusion it alone benefits from the specious pleasures of the individual and even from the good which self-denial brings (DANA, HERA, OGRJ).

In the *Iliad*, Apollo is invoked under his name of Smintheos, derived from a word meaning 'mouse'. The ambivalence of the title given him corresponds with the two aspects of the symbol. The mouse which spreads pestilence is the symbol of Apollo who destroys by plague – and in a passage in the *Iliad* the old man Chryses calls on the god to avenge an insult – while, as a harvest-god, Apollo protects the grain from the ravages of mice. In this symbolism it may be seen that the destructive role played by rats and mice is grounds for applying that role in two different ways – actively employing it as vengeance and suppressing it as benefaction. Hence arises the twofold aspect of the god called Smintheos.

This primitive, agrarian tradition of Apollo as a mouse-god who sends disease and cures it, should be compared with the Indian tradition of a rat-god, supposedly the son of Rudra, with the power to inflict and cure disease. Apollo Smintheos and Ganesha embody 'the beneficent and healing powers of the soil' (SECG pp. 216, 236).

raven Recent comparative studies of the customs and beliefs of a wide range of peoples would seem to show that the purely negative aspect of the symbolism of the raven is very late and an accretion almost entirely localized to Europe. In fact, here its appearance in dreams is considered of ill omen and allied to fear of misfortune. It is also the great black bird of the Romantics, hovering over battlefields to feast on the bodies of the slain. Such an image, it is worth repeating, is recent and highly localized, although it recurs in India, where the *Mahābhārata* compares ravens with messengers of death, and perhaps in Laos as well, where water soiled by ravens cannot be used in ritual aspersion. Despite this, nearly everywhere, in both East and West, the symbolism of the raven is founded upon its positive aspects.

Thus in both China and Japan it is a symbol of filial gratitude, the Han considering the fact that it feeds its parents as auguring the reinstatement of the social order. In Japan, too, it is taken as the expression of family affection.

In Japan it is regarded at the same time as a messenger of the gods, while the Chou regarded it as a bird of good omen, the herald of their victories and the mark of their virtues. The bird in question was, it is true, a red raven, bearing the colour of the sun, for in China ravens were solar birds. The symbol of the ten ravens which flew from the mulberry-tree in the East to fetch light into the world, would seem to have passed into Shintōism. However, Yi the Archer shot nine with his arrows, otherwise the universe would have caught fire.

Han dynasty stone carvings show a three-legged raven in the centre of the Sun. It would seem to be the principle giving life to the Sun and perhaps stands for *yang* (odd-numbered) (MYTF p. 126). Like the tripod, the raven's three feet, which became the emblem of the Chinese emperors, corresponded to the solar symbolism of dawn, noon and dusk.

In the Book of Genesis the bird is a symbol of clear-sightedness, since it was sent out to see if the lowlands had emerged from the waters of the Flood. 'And it came to pass, at the end of forty days, that Noah opened the window of the ark which he had made: And he sent forth a raven, which went forth to and fro, until the waters were dried up from off the earth' (8: 6–7).

In Ancient Greece, too, the raven was a solar bird sacred to Apollo. Although Plutarch says that eagles determined the siting of the omphalos at Delphi, Strabo states that this task was performed by ravens. At least both birds have this in common, that they acted as messengers of the gods and performed prophetic roles. Ravens were also attributes of Mithras, and these were believed to be endowed with the power of casting evil spells.

Ravens are common features of Celtic legend, in which they play prophetic roles. The Pseudo-Plutarch who undoubtedly based himself upon Gaulish tradition, translated Lugdunum (the Celtic name for Lyons) as

'Ravens' Hill' rather than the accepted 'Lug's Hill', since a flight of ravens had shown the city's founders where to build.

In Ireland, the war-goddess took the name of 'Bobd' or carrion-crow and often appeared in this shape. The crow is the nocturnal aspect of the raven and in Ancient Greece was sacred to Athene while, as we have seen, the raven was Apollo's bird.

In any case, ravens play a fundamental part in the Welsh tale, 'The Dream of Rhonabwy': when Arthur's men slaughtered Owein's ravens, the surviving birds reacted violently and in their turn hacked the soldiers to pieces. Ravens still occupy a respectable place in folklore (LERD p. 58). The birds were sacred to the Gauls and in German mythology were the companions of Wotan (Odin).

In Scandinavian mythology, two ravens perched on Odin's throne, Hugin (Mind) and Munnin (Memory), and a pair of wolves crouched beside the god. The two ravens stand for the creative and the two wolves for the destructive principle (MYTF p. 148).

'Among the Tlingit Indians (North-West Pacific), the central divine figure is the Crow, primeval hero and demiurge, who made the world (or, more precisely, set it in order, and spread civilization and culture through it), created and liberated the sun, and so on' (ELIT p. 53). The Crow endowed it with the dynamic and regulatory element.

'In North America the Supreme being of the sky generally tends to become amalgamated with the mythological personification of the thunder and the wind, represented as a large bird (the crow, etc.); he beats his wings and the wind rises, his tongue is the lightning' (ibid.).

In the Mandan Spring Festival, the 'First Man', herald of renewal who commemorated the 'retreat of the waters', had his naked body painted white, wore only a cape made from the pelts of four white wolves and had two tufts of ravens' feathers stuck in his hair (LEVC).

The messenger of the Mayan god of thunder and the thunderbolt was a raven (*Popol-Vuh*).

From Black Africa comes evidence of the raven's role of guide and guardian spirit. The Likuba and Likuala in the Congo Basin regard the raven as 'a bird which warns men of the dangers threatening them' (LEBM).

Ravens may also be regarded as symbols of solitude, or rather of the deliberate self-isolation of the individual who has determined to live upon a higher level. They may also be seen as emblems of hope with their constant cry, according to Suetonius, of *Cras! Cras!* ('Tomorrow! Tomorrow!') (TERS p. 111).

Thus most beliefs surrounding the raven depict the bird as a solar hero and often as a Demiurge or messenger of the gods. The bird is in any case a guide, and even guides souls on their last journey since, as a conductor of souls, his keen sight pierces the darkness and he is not led astray. It would seem as if this positive aspect is linked to the beliefs of nomadic hunters and fisherfolk and that the raven only became negative when mankind settled and agricultural communities developed.

Alchemists have always associated the stage of PUTREFACTION, when matter becomes black, with the raven. They call this stage 'the Raven's Head': it is leprous and must be bleached by 'bathing seven times in the waters of

Jordan'. These are the imbibitions, sublimations, cohobations or digestion of matter, all practised under the lordship of fire alone. This is why the black bird is so often depicted on the pages of ancient treatises of Hermetic lore (PERD).

ray   At all cultural levels in works of art rays are drawn from the SUN, from HALOES or from other forms. These rays symbolize an emanation of light radiating from a centre, sun, saint, hero, genius or other individual. They express a fecundating influence, whether of the spiritual or material order. An individual emitting rays belongs to the element Fire, and is related to the Sun. The recipient of the rays determines whether they instil warmth, stimulus or fertility, or else burn, dry up or sterilize.

razor's edge   An image which symbolizes the difficulties of rising to a higher condition.

The most usual symbol to express the break through the planes and the pene-tration into the 'other world' – the transcendent world, whether that of the living or the dead – is . . . the razor's edge or the 'strait' gate of Matthew 7: 14. It is hard to pass over the sharpened blade of the razor . . . the narrow and perilous bridge . . . or find the door in the wall where none can be seen, or go up to Heaven by a passage that half-opens only for an instant, or pass between two millstones in constant motion, between two rocks that may clash together at any moment, or between the jaws of a monster.

All these images, presenting an apparently insoluble problem, 'express the necessity of *transcending the "pairs of opposites"*, of abolishing the polarity that besets the human condition, in order to reach the ultimate reality' (ELII pp. 83–4) by setting oneself along the axis of a different polarity.

Rebis   The Rebis (from *res bina*, 'twofold matter') is a symbol of the HER-MAPHRODITE. Alchemists call the first decoction of mineral spirit mixed with its own body the Rebis because

it is made of two substances, namely of male and of female, that is of the dissolvant and of the dissoluble body, although at bottom it is the same sub-stance and the same matter. . . . Philosophers have also given this name to matter in the work which has reached the 'white' stage, because then it has become a mercury enlivened with its own sulphur and these two separate substances derived from the same source are really one homogeneous whole.

(PERD pp. 426–7)

As a result they assimilate this to the hermaphrodite, the matter being sufficient in itself 'to bring into the world a royal child more perfect than its parents'.

The illustration of the Rebis taken from Basil Valentine's *Theatrum Chemicum* (Strasbourg: 1613) depicts an oval frame suggestive of the alche-mists' 'Philosophers' Egg' and also of the Cosmic Egg, of which the splitting into two halves corresponds to manifestation by the polarization of prime-val Oneness. The seed within this egg is nothing less than a hermaphrodite figure, of which the female half is crowned by the Moon and holds a Mason's SQUARE in her hand, while the male half, crowned by the Sun, holds a COMPASS. Unlike the near example of Fu Hi and Nu Kua, there is

REBIS: Hermaphrodite Mercury (Basil Valentine, *Theatrum Chemicum*, Strasbourg, 1613)

no exchange of attributes in sacred marriage. The *Emerald Table* describes the Rebis as being engendered by the Sun and Moon and resembling the essentially united, externally polarized properties 'of Heaven and Earth'. The dragon on which the hermaphrodite stands and which provides a further link with the Chinese symbol, is its strength of manifestation.

red   Red, the colour of FIRE and of BLOOD and regarded universally as the basic symbol of the life-principle, with its dazzling strength and power, nevertheless possesses their same symbolic ambivalence; speaking visually, this doubtless depends upon whether the red is bright or dark. Bright, dazzling, centrifugal red is diurnal, male, tonic, stimulating activity and, like the Sun, casting its glow upon all things, with vast and irresistible strength (KANS). Dark red is its complete opposite. It is nocturnal, female, secret and, ultimately, centripetal and stands, not for manifestation, but for the mystery of life. The first is the red of flags, ensigns, posters and publicity material. It carries along, heartens and stimulates. The second warns, holds back and awakens vigilance and ultimately anxiety. It is the red of traffic-lights, the red light barring entry to film or broadcasting studios, as well as being the red lamp which used to mark the entry to French licensed broth-els. This last might appear contradictory since, instead of forbidding access, it invited it. This is not, however, the case, considering that the invitation was to transgress the most powerful taboo of the period, the taboo on sexual drive, libido and the sexual instincts.

This nocturnal, centripetal red is the colour of the fire which burns within the individual and the Earth, that of the womb and of the alchemists' athanor in which, through the making of the Red Stone, the generation or regenera-tion of the individual or of the 'work' takes place through dissolution and ripening. Western, Chinese and Muslim alchemists all used the meaning of red in precisely the same way, and the Arabs' 'red sulphur', denoting 'Uni-versal Man', springs directly from the making of the Red Stone, maturing in the athanor. The same is true of the Chinese 'red rice'; this, too, is the fire – or blood – of the athanor, allied to cinnabar, in which it is alchemically transmuted to symbolize immortality.

Below the green of the Earth's surface and the blackness of the soil, lies this redness, pre-eminently holy and secret, the mystery of life hidden on the dark floor of the primeval ocean depths. Dark red is the colour of the soul, of the libido and of the heart. It is the colour of knowledge and of esoteric lore forbidden to the uninitiated, which the wise man conceals beneath his cloak. In the Tarot, the HERMIT, the FEMALE POPE and the EMPRESS are dressed in red beneath a blue cape or cloak and all three, in different degrees, stand for hidden knowledge.

As we have seen, dark red is related to the womb. It might only lawfully be seen in the course of an initiatory 'death' when it was endowed with sacramental properties. In the mysteries of Cybele, candidates went down into a trench and their bodies were washed by the blood of the bull or ram ritually sacrificed upon a grid placed over them (MAGE), while a serpent sucked the blood from the victim's wound.

In Fiji, in a similar ritual, novices were shown

a row of dead or seemingly dead and murdered men, their bodies cut open and covered with blood, their entrails protruding.... Suddenly [the High Priest] blurted out a piercing yell, at which the counterfeit dead men started to their feet and ran down to the river to cleanse themselves from the blood and guts of pigs with which they were beslobbered.

(FRAG 11: p. 245)

The 'wine-dark sea' of the Ancient Greeks and the 'Red Sea' derive from the same symbolism, standing for the womb in which life and death are transmuted the one into the other.

While dark and centripetal red is initiatory, it is also a funereal colour. 'According to Artemidorus, the colour purple is connected with death' (PORS pp. 136–7).

For such, in fact, is the deep ambivalence of blood-red – when hidden, it is what conditions life: when exposed, it means death. This is the basis of the taboos relating to menstruating women. Menstrual blood is impure because it inverts its polarity when it passes from the darkness of the womb to the light of day and passes from the sacred right-hand to the sacred left-hand. Such women are untouchable and, in many societies, they have to go into retreat to be cleansed before they can be restored to their place in the society from which they have been temporarily excluded. For a long time this same taboo was extended to men who, even in a just cause, had shed another's blood. The medieval French executioner, dressed in red, was, like the BLACKSMITH, an untouchable; both had handled the very essence of the mystery of life embodied in the centripetal red of blood or of molten metal.

Malinowski records a myth of the Melanesian Trobriand Islanders which illustrates how ancient and widespread are such beliefs. At the beginning of time, a man learned the secrets of magic from a crab. It was red because it was charged with magic and, after gaining its secrets, the man killed it. This is why nowadays crabs are black. They have been deprived of their magic. All the same, they are still slow to die because they were once lords of life and death.

Bright, diurnal, solar, centrifugal red is, on the other hand, a spur to action. It is the image of ardour and beauty, of all that is impulsive and generous, of youth and health and wealth and love, free and victorious, this last explaining how, in many customs, including that of the red lamp mentioned above, both aspects of the symbol are present. It is the red dye, generally diluted in vegetable oils which enhance its strength and vitality, with which women and girls in Black Africa paint their faces and bodies after the taboo following their first menstruation has been lifted, on the eve of their marriage or after the birth of their first child. Among North American Indians, young people of both sexes painted themselves with red – again diluted with oil – since they believed that this aroused their strength and quickened their desire. Red acquired healing properties and became an indispensable heal-all. This too is the meaning behind the countless traditions, from Russia, China and Japan, which associated red with all folk-festivals and especially with those celebrating Spring, marriage and birth. Frequently 'red' was used as a metaphor for 'handsome' or 'lovely' when applied to a boy or girl and this is still true of Irish Gaelic.

Although it might embody the ardour and enthusiasm of youth, in Irish tradition red was above all the colour of the warrior, and there were two very common adjectives in Gaelic, *derg* and *ruadh*, to describe it. There are hundreds, if not thousands, of examples of this, and the druid–god, the Dagda, is called *Ruadh Rofhessa*, 'the Great Red Sage'. In literature, and especially in the tale of the destruction of the hall of Da Derga, there are examples of red druids, a reference to their warlike skill and to their two-fold office of priest and warrior. In Gaul there was a cult of Mars Rudiobus or Rudianus (red) (WINI *passim*; OGAC 12: pp. 452–8).

Thus it would seem that, with this warlike symbolism, red will always be the spoils of the war – or of the dialectic – between Heaven and Earth, the fire of the Sun and the fires of Hell. It is the colour of Dionysos, the liberator and orgiast. Alchemists, whose chthonian interpretation of the colour has already been noted, also said that the Philosopher's Stone 'bore the sign of the Sun'. Red is also called the Absolute; 'it is pure because it consists of concentrated rays of sunlight' (YGEA p. 113). When solar symbolism bore it off and Mars supplanted Vulcan in Venus' arms, the warrior became the conqueror and the conqueror the emperor. A richer red, slightly tinged with violet, became the emblem of power and was soon reserved for exclusive imperial use. This was purple, and that variety of red 'in Rome was the colour of generals, nobles and patricians. Consequently it became the imperial colour. Byzantine emperors were dressed entirely in red. . . . In the beginning of heraldry there were laws forbidding the use of gules (the colour red) in coats of arms' (PORS pp. 130–1). Justinian's laws condemned to death those who bought or sold purple cloth. This was the same as saying that it had become the very symbol of supreme power. 'Red and white are the two colours sacred to Jehovah as God of love and wisdom' (PORS p. 125 n. 3), which would seem to confuse wisdom with conquest and justice with force. The Tarot provides the true answer. NECESSITY, the eleventh major arcanum, depicts a man forcing open the jaws of a lion with his bare hands. He is dressed in blue with a red cape, while the eighth arcanum, JUSTICE, like the Empress, wears a blue cloak over her red robe.

When externalized, red is dangerous as the uncontrolled lust for power, leading to self-absorption, hatred, 'blind passion and hell-born love' (PORS p. 131). Mephistopheles wears the red cloak of the Princes of Hell while cardinals wear that of Princes of the Church, and Isaiah (1: 18) puts these words into Jehovah's mouth: 'Come now, and let us reason together, saith the Lord: Though your sins be as scarlet, they shall be as white as snow; though they be red like crimson, they shall be as wool.'

There is no single nation which – each in its own way – has not given expression to the ambivalence from which the colour red derives its powers of fascination. Intimately connected within it are the two most profound human impulses – doing and suffering, freedom and tyranny – as so many red flags fluttering in the winds of the twentieth century go to show!

In heraldry red is called 'gules' an Old French word suggesting *gueule*, MOUTH, with all the symbolic ambivalence of the latter, basically that of undifferentiated libido which haunts childhood dreams, children throughout the world being attracted by the colour red. According to La Colombières (PORS p. 135), 'Gules, the heraldic colour red, stands for the spiritual virtues of love of God and of one's neighbour; for the worldly virtues of courage and self-sacrifice; for the vices of cruelty, murder and slaughter; and for the Choleric humour in persons.' For their part, the wise men of the Bambara say that the colour red 'reminds one of heat, fire, blood, corpses, flies, annoyance, hardship, Kings, the untouchable and the inaccessible' (ZAHB p. 19).

Generally speaking, in the Far East, too, red conjures up notions of heat, intensity, activity and passion. It is the colour of the *rajas*, the colour of the full Moon.

Throughout the Far East red is the colour of fire, the south and sometimes of drought. (It should be noted that red, the colour of fire, is used to ward off fire especially in rites connected with house-building.) It is also the colour of blood, of life, of beauty and wealth and of marriage (symbolized by the red threads of Fate, tied in Heaven). As the colour of life, it is also the colour of immortality, obtained by means of red cinnabar (red sulphur of mercury) or by the red rice of the City of Willows. Here, as we have seen, Chinese symbolism converges with both Western and Islamic alchemy.

In Japan, red (*aka*) is worn almost exclusively by women. It is a symbol of true-heartedness and good luck. Some Shintō sects teach that red denotes harmony and expansiveness. Japanese conscripts used to wear red belts when they joined their regiments, as a symbol of their loyalty to the emperor. Rice coloured red may be sent as a token of good wishes for birthdays, success in examinations and so on.

reed Broadly speaking reeds are taken as symbols of what is fragile as well as what is flexible. The latter is Aesop's reed (as opposed to his oak), the former, perhaps, Pascal's 'thinking reed'.

In the Far East, the symbolism of the plant takes two distinct forms. In Shintō mythology the reed which sprouted from the primeval waters stands for manifestation and equates with the LOTUS. Mythical Japan was a 'reed-bed'.

On the other hand reeds are also believed to be endowed with cleansing and protective powers. When Izanagi returned from the realms of the dead he cleansed himself with reeds, and Yi-yin was cleansed in reed-smoke before he became a minister. The genii who guard GATEWAYS use reed-ropes to control evil spirits. Some Shintō rites of purification involve crossing a circle of reeds (*chi-no-wa*). Entrance to the lodges of some Chinese secret societies is under an arch of reeds, beside which the wardens stand. White reed mats are used ritually.

In India the reed (*vetasa*) is sometimes regarded as an image of the World Axis and a comparison with the axial reed which emerged from Japanese primeval waters is unavoidable (GRAD, HERS, HERJ).

In the legend of King Midas, a reed grew from the hole in which the barber had buried his secret, 'King Midas has ass's ears'. Paul Diel regards that reed as standing for one of the symbols of reduction to the mundane which is the consequence of inordinate desire. In the context of the legend, 'the reed represents the depraved soul which bends to every pressure and bows to every change of fashion' (DIES p. 132).

The reed plucked from the Earth becomes the *ney*, the sacred PIPE of the Mevlevi, or Whirling Dervishes. This is the basic instrument used in their religious music and, in the words of Jalāl-al-Dīn Rūmī, the Order's founder, 'sings the pains of separation'. In this context, the reed pipe symbolizes the mystic who has been torn away from God and by his wailing and his songs displays his aspiration to find him once more in eternal life.

This symbol of the soul expressing its burning longing in song and tears recurs in the folklore and superstitions of some eastern European and Asian peoples. Ukrainians, Byelorussians and even Lithuanians say that 'the reed which grows from the grave of a drowned man will name his murderer if it is made into a pipe.' The reed is a voice.

The years in the Aztec calendar were set under four signs, one of which was that of the reed. The green reed was associated with the east, the land of rebirth. The Ancient Mexicans regarded it as a symbol of fertility, plenty and wealth (SOUP).

reef As a symbol, reefs are the very opposite of ISLANDS. The latter are the sought-after places of refuge; the former objects of fear. Reefs have been compared with sea-MONSTERS. In such tales of voyages as the *Odyssey*, they become a veritable obsession. They are implacable foes along the path of fate, obstacles to success. They are all the more to be feared since the voyager encounters them when he is already in such impossible situations as storm, fog or darkness. Reefs are there to apply the final stroke of misfortune.

From the psychological point of view reefs symbolize turning to stone, that is the hardening of consciousness into an attitude of hostility and of stagnation on the path of spiritual progress. Cirlot regards them as examples of the major myth of regression.

reincarnation See METEMPSYCHOSIS.

reindeer The reindeer occupies the same symbolic place among the peoples of the far north, who use it for food and transport, as does the HORSE among equestrian races. The cultures of these northern peoples reflect a lunar symbolism and the reindeer, like the rest of the stag family, is part of the general structure of Moon symbolism. The role of the reindeer is nocturnal and funerary and that of conductor of souls: 'Wherever the reindeer has been domesticated and used as a riding-animal, as among the various Tungus tribes, it accompanies the dead person into the other world' (HARA p. 225). In this respect, its symbolic role is akin to that played by the DEER on the prairies of North America and on the steppes of central Asia (see also STAG).

resin Because it is incorruptible, because it is flammable and because it is generally produced by evergreen trees, such as conifers, resin is a symbol of purity and immortality. The trees from which it comes have sometimes been taken as symbols of Christ. In China, resin, and especially those resins produced by CYPRESS and tamarisk, were sometimes used as medicines of immortality and, in the case of cypress, to acquire weightlessness. It should not be forgotten that resin is among the ingredients of INCENSE (GUEM, KALL), as was Mayan copal.

respiration The most varied traditions have all fastened upon the binary rhythm of respiration, exhalation and inhalation, symbolizing the expansion and contraction of the universe, what the Indians call *kalpa* and *pralaya*. These are centripetal and centrifugal movements from a centre which, in human beings, is the heart. This is why Taoists allow that respiration is controlled by the heart. The two phases of respiration are 'the opening and the closing of the Gates of Heaven', *yang* and *yin* respectively. Respiration is to become assimilated into the power of air and, if air is a symbol of the spirit, of BREATH, then respiration is to become assimilated into a spiritual power.

While the practice of rhythmical breathing adopted by Yoga and similar Chinese exercises – the 'counting of breaths' features in Buddhist *T'ien-tai* and in Muslim *dhikr*, too – is designed to produce the best environment for meditation, *The Secret of the Golden Flower*, nonetheless, mentions a 'subtle respiration' which is inaudible to the senses, being the internal rhythm of life, of which physical breathing is a clumsy approximation. The same of course may be said of 'foetal breathing' (*T'ai-si*). Holding, swallowing and allowing one's breath to circulate internally clearly has little physiological reality; what is meant is imitation and integration of the respiration, the life-rhythm, within the closed circuit of the foetus and the return to a primal state with the aim of acquiring immortality (ELIY, GRIF, GUES, MAST, MASN).

A close symbolic parallel is provided by the Persian poet, Sa'dī, in his *Gulistān*: 'Each respiration holds two blessings. Life is inhaled, and stale, foul air exhaled. Therefore thank God twice every breath you take.'

rest The 'rest' which God took after the work of Creation was unrelated to a condition of stasis. 'Rest' does not mean inactivity and calling a halt to a process of development. God's rest is to be seen as a 'creative pause', initiating a fresh aspect. This rest was devoted to blessing and making holy, that is to say, to a fresh infusion of energy into creation, raising it to a fresh level which might well be that of awareness. God's rest after the work of creation symbolizes the fulfilment of time itself. The seventh day was related to the first as perfection was achieved and the cycle began. The same meaning is to be found in the image shared by so many different traditions, the OUROBOROS or serpent biting its tail. Beginning and end are joined together and cosmic energy circulates through the whole. St John's words 'I am ALPHA AND OMEGA' (Revelation 21: 6) illustrate this concept of circularity of which the foregoing is an example.

Rest is the reward of labour, or rather it is its limit. Whoever walks 'where there is the good way . . . shall find rest for [the] soul' (Jeremiah 6: 16): human bliss. The Old Testament meaning is continued by the New (Matthew 11: 29). Here, rest is understood in the sense of 'security' and may therefore be seen as a conditon of harmony and oneness.

In Rabbinical tradition, it was not the case of a creator exhausted by his huge task taking his rest. God's activity in the world appears to have ceased, in the sense that having set creation on its way he has handed to mankind the responsibility for its progress and for bringing it, by direct action and by prayer, to a state of perfection. This is a transfer of power which raises mankind to the rank of joint-creator. However, the universe will only obey mankind to the extent that mankind itself respects the order of creation.

resurrection This is the clearest symbol of divine manifestation, since all traditions hold that the secret of life can belong to God alone. Apollo's son, Asclepios (Aesculapius) the god of healing, was taught the art of curing disease by the centaur Chiron. When he had progressed so far that he was able to restore the dead to life, Zeus, King of the Gods, struck him down with his thunderbolt. Such knowledge was forbidden.

There is a curious Lydian legend which, in one aspect, re-echoes the scene in the Garden of Eden by introducing a serpent which possessed the secret of life and was therefore able to raise the dead. One day a serpent bit Moria's brother, Tylos, on the face and he died instantly. Moria summoned a giant, Damasen, who crushed the serpent. The serpent's mate slithered swiftly to a neighbouring wood and returned with a herb which she laid on her mate's nostrils. He immediately came to life and the pair escaped. Moria, who had seen all this, used the herb to bring her brother back to life. In the present context, the legend is of interest because it shows that the secret of life is not in human hands. Only the serpent knew of the herb which restored to life, and thus it was that, in the Garden of Eden, it was a serpent, entwined around the tree of Life, which tempted Eve with the offer of some secret knowledge and led to our first parents being punished by loss of immortality.

Mystery religions, and especially the Eleusinian Mysteries, as well as the Ancient Egyptians' funeral ceremonies, are all evidence of the lively human hope of resurrection. The rites of initiation into the major mysteries were symbols of the resurrection which the initiates expected, but they set the principle of that resurrection beyond human control. Resurrection, as myth, idea or fact, is a symbol of transcendence and of the absolute power over life which belongs to God alone.

return All cosmic symbolism, all spiritual progress and the symbols which it shares, the MAZE, MANDALA, LADDER or ALCHEMY, denote a return to the

centre or to the Garden of Eden, a reintegration of manifestation with its
First Cause.

Since the DOT, according to Angelus Silesius, 'contains the CIRCLE' within
itself, the circle has completed its return to the dot. When 'primeval man'
or 'true man' (*chen-jen*) has achieved a return to the paradisal state, he will
have returned 'from the circumference to the centre'. Now the centre of the
world and the centre of the Garden of Eden were and are that specific point
of contact between Heaven and Earth, the point from which the individual
can rise to superhuman states. But before looking at specific applications
of this symbolism, let us observe another aspect of it – time-cycles. One
of these is the return of light and the vanishing of darkness linked to the
myths of Isis and Osiris, of Artemis and Apollo, of the Hindu Ashvins and
of Amaterasu. Another is the return of Summer and the passing of Winter,
linked to the symbolism of Janus and the gates of the solstices, to the
trigams *k'ien* and *k'uen* and to the alternation of *yang* and *yin*. Yet another
is the return of the QUAIL, released 'from the jaws of the wolf' and, in a
different sense, the return from the Underworld. It is also, as Shabistarī
said, a return to 'the dawn of the Resurrection' after the gradual dimming
of the Faith, as well as being the light of the Second Coming and the
apotheosis of the Heavenly Jerusalem.

An involuted spiral expresses this return to the centre. The Chinese ideogram conveying this notion, *hoei*, was originally spiral in shape. 'The return
[*fan*] is the movement of the Tao' (ch. 4). Departure and expansion, the
Tao Te Ching also teaches, 'imply return' (ch. 25); and again, 'to return to
the root is to find rest' (ch. 16). It also employs, but in a more technical
sense, the term *huan-yuan* (to cause something to return to its beginnings).

'Yoga', wrote Arthur Avalon, 'is a flowing back to the well-spring', the
opposite of the process of manifestation, reintegration into the centre of
being. This is expressed in such phrases as 'to go against the stream' (*ujāna
sādhana*), 'regressive' motion (*ultā*), 'swallowing breath', 'return-flow of
semen' or 'the internal marriage of Sun and Moon'. This return to an
undifferentiated state, to the foetus, the womb or the beginning of time,
finds expression, too, in the Buddhist awareness of earlier existences. In
psychoanalysis, recall is also a return to the well-spring.

Taoist techniques – as well as those described in *The Secret of the Golden
Flower* – ally Yoga with alchemy. The 'backward' or 'regressive' motion of
breath or semen, *ch'i* or *hsin*, are practised in both. 'True strength returns
drop by drop to its spring.' They come together like fire and water, *yang*
and *yin*, to engender the 'Embryo of Immortality', corresponding to the
state existing prior to the separation of *min* and *hsin*, Heaven and Earth.
The 'Embryo' itself escapes bodily restrictions to make its return to the
First Cause.

The 'return to the womb', that is to the primeval undifferentiated state
or 'moistness', is what Western alchemists called PUTREFACTION, when the
matter of the Work became black: the darkness and death which were the
prelude to the return of the light and rebirth.

A very similar symbolism was present among Muslim esoterics who sometimes expressly identified it with alchemy. The word *ta'wil*, denoting the
interpretation of symbols, itself carries the meaning of 'coming back' or

'returning to the well-spring', that is to say, of passing from the appearance to the reality, from the accidence to the substance. The spiritual path is a 'regressive' path, leading from the manifold to the One and from the circumference to the centre. 'The end is the return', Shabistarī wrote, since, according to the Koran itself, Creation, made by God, returns to him (AVAS, CHRC, CORT, ELIY, ELIF, ELIM, GRIF, GUED, GUET, LIOT).

The dynamics of Neoplatonist philosophy are conceived on the plan of emanation from the One and return to the One. This is the same metaphysical model upon which the mighty *Summa Theologica* of the Middle Ages, and especially that of St Thomas Aquinas, are based. His set out from a study of God and of creation to pass to a study of morality which is a return to God through Christ. The symbol of return is that of the final phase of the cycle.

Allowing for differences of content, the whole of Hermetic thought rests, too, upon such a model of cosmic unity. In traditional iconography this is expressed by the OUROBOROS; this 'image of the One – the Whole – its circular shape, a symbol of the world, also alludes to the cloistral principle or to Hermetic secrecy. It expresses additionally eternity, conceived in terms of an eternal homecoming, without beginning or end' (VANA p. 18).

Only a linear concept of time, its duration limited for each individual who would then suffer complete annihilation, could predicate death as a journey without return, from which no one ever came back and which led to nothing. This is to confine the centre of the cosmos and of life uniquely to this Earth and uniquely to a specific individual who vanishes. This is the reverse of those concepts which accept transcendence and for which death is only one of the GATES through which life passes.

ribbon   Ribbon symbolism is related to that of KNOTS and CHAINS, but its significance is more generally positive even when the ribbon is tied. When a ribbon is tied in a bow it may be given the appearance of a FLOWER: it is a sign of blossoming rather than of arrested development. Furthermore, ribbons may be fashioned into diadems, necklaces or crowns, or be used as sashes or garters, or may ornament dress, tie up gifts, and so on. The circular pattern which they then make evokes, like the circle, notions of a share in immortality, perfection, generous or even heroic deeds. The lady presented ribbons to her knight and ribbons were thrown to the victor in the joust. A medal ribbon is a reward for valour or a distinguished career, it denotes success, victory and fulfilment. Although ribbon symbols are pointed in the direction of the display of triumph, they do not escape all potential danger. The ribbon which marks a person out may also isolate him or her in self-esteem and compromise his or her spiritual development. Ribbons have been used to strangle people and this may be understood in the sense of moral or psychological suffocation. The colour of the ribbon may alter or 'colour' interpretations of specific cases.

rice   Just as bread or corn is the basic food of Europeans, so in Asia is rice, and it conveys the same symbolic and ritual meaning.

Rice originates with the gods. Not only did it take its place in the primeval GOURD on the same footing as the human species, but, like manna in the Wilderness, it grew spontaneously and filled granaries. This is an article of faith in Asian legend. The toil involved in rice-growing was a consequence of the destruction of the intercourse between Heaven and Earth. Rice was brought to Japan by Amaterasu's grandson, Prince Ninigi, and was the focus of a ceremony involving the community as a whole, during which the emperor 'tasted' the cereal in company with the Sun-goddess.

Rice is both the staff of life and the food of immortality and as such 'red' rice is the content of the Chinese secret societies' bushel-baskets. It comes, the ritual manuals state, solely from 'the power of the Lord Min', that is to say from 'light'. Like bread, it is also a symbol of spiritual food. Rice changes alchemically into cinnabar, red sulphur of mercury. This may be compared with Muslim esoterics' 'red sulphur' and the 'making of the Red Stone' in Western alchemy.

Rice is wealth, abundance and primeval innocence. It should be observed that even in the West it is a symbol of good luck and of fertility, since handfuls of rice are thrown at weddings (GRIL, GUET, HERS, HERJ, MAST, ROUN).

rift A broken column, a sinking ship, a ruined temple or house, a tree blasted by lightning, and so on, can no longer be interpreted solely in terms of what they meant when they were complete and perfect columns, ships, temples, houses or trees. Such is the general significance of breaking, rift or ruin in the case of these images. Hence all rift symbolizes, in whatever displays it, the duality of all being. Whatever lives or has been made, may be killed or destroyed and, furthermore, it bears the seeds of its own destruction. 'In the midst of life we are in death.' In Hindu tradition, Vishnu and Shiva, gods of destruction and reconstruction, are no more than two names for one and the same reality. Rift, although it lays most of its emphasis upon the negative phase, signifies the alternation of integration and disintegration. The negative aspect is, however, the condition for rebirth and renewal. On the internal psychological plane, as in the physical world, to rise above or to heal a rift is to reach a fresh level of being. Gloomy pleasure in rifts, on the other hand, sets the person along the road of regression and involution.

right and left In the Old Testament, to look to one's right hand is to look towards the side upon which one's protector stands (Psalm 142: 4). This is to be the place of the elect at the Last Judgement, the damned going to the left. The left is the direction of Hell, the right that of Heaven.

Some Rabbinical commentators explain that Adam, the first man, was hermaphrodite, his right side being male and his left female (see REBIS). When God created 'male or female' he split him down the middle (ELIT p. 423).

This tradition affected medieval Christian thought, which held that the left side was the female side and the right, the male. Being female, the left, in accordance with deep-seated prejudice, was nocturnal and satanic as well, while the right was diurnal and divine. Thus the sign of the cross was made with the left hand at Black Masses and the Devil marked the children consecrated to him 'on the left eyelid with one of his horns' (GRIA).

A print in Father Gucci's *Compendium Maleficorum* (Milan, 1626) shows

Satan setting his mark upon his new followers with his claw over the left eyelid, thus blinding them to the light divine and making them able only to see by his light.

To the Ancient Greeks, the right was the side 'of the arm which shakes the spear' (Aeschylus, *Agamemnon* 115). Good omens appeared on the right hand, which symbolized strength, skill and success. The Latin word for 'left', *sinister*, still strikes an ominous note in many modern European languages.

The Celts shared the same views as Classical antiquity with respect to the properties of right and left, that is, that the right was lucky and of good omen, while the left was fatal and of evil omen. Classical writers sometimes contradict one another. Posidonius states that the Gauls worshipped their gods by turning to the right, Pliny that they turned to the left. However, the sole valid distinction between right and left, apart from the cardinal points east and west, is the transit of the Sun. Whatever follows its path is 'right', whatever goes in the opposite direction is 'left'. When the Celts took their bearings, the observer stood facing the rising Sun, which meant that the south lay on his right hand and the north on his left. The north is, therefore, the 'low' in which the Sun sets and from which it begins its daily ascent: the south is the 'high' where the Sun ends its climb and starts to set. The eccentricity of the Irish lay in the way in which they melded or assimilated north with left, and consequently right with south, through their taboo upon uttering the word 'left' (*clé*; Welsh, *cledd*; Breton, *kleiz*), which was replaced by a number of euphemisms, the chief one being *tuath*, 'north'. This was in fact the name of the tribe which took the meaning of 'north' because the pagan Irish gods (*Tuatha Dé Danann*, 'People' or 'Tribes of the Goddess Dana') originated, according to ancient tradition, in the north and after Ireland became Christian the latter was looked upon with suspicion (OGAC 18: pp. 311–22; see also EAST AND WEST).

In South America, in the Inca temple of Coricancha at Cuzco, the statue of the all-powerful god, Huiracocha Pachacamar, was flanked on the right by the Sun-god and on the left by the Moon-goddess.

In Africa, the Bambara regard four, the number of woman, as synonymous with 'left' and three, the number of man, with 'right'. The right hand is the symbol of order, righteousness, work and faithfulness, while the left symbolizes disorder and doubt, expressing 'the differences in human awareness' (DIEB).

The Dogon have the funeral custom of laying the corpses of men on their right sides and women on their left (GRIE).

On the other hand, in the Far East, it is the left which would seem to be the propitious side. This would stem from a precedence of the nocturnal over the diurnal and of the hidden reality over the apparent, consistent with Chinese thought and art. For example, in Yunnan, Dto Mba Shi Lo, who established shamanism among the Moso, was born 'from his mother's left side, like all heroes and saints' (ELIC p. 445).

The contrast between right and left in China in no sense contains the seeds of confrontation, since in this, as in other instances, the governing forces are those of *yin* and *yang* and these do not conflict. Just as the Chinese do not set religion against magic, or the clean against the unclean, the sacred against the profane, so the right hand, more generally devoted to earthly activities and to profane works, is not for that reason set up as a rival to the left.

The left is the honourable side since it stands for Heaven and is therefore *yang*, taking precedence on occasion over the right which is Earth and *yin*. Since the right is *yin*, it belongs to women, Autumn, harvesting and food.

In *The Way and its Power*, Lao-tzu wrote: 'The left is the place of honour in good times and the right in bad. In battle the subordinate stands on the left and the commander on the right, in so doing equating war with burial rites.'

The belief that it is unlucky to extend a house towards the west (right and *yin*) probably arose from the fear of bringing a new wife into the household since, in ancient times, the women's quarters lay on this side.

Basing themselves upon the principle that the right was *yin*, and therefore female, while the left was *yang*, and therefore male, doctors placed strong reliance upon the position of the foetus when predicting its sex during pregnancy. Another factor was whether the year of its conception was *yang* or *yin*!

The same principles were applied when it came to vaccinating boys and girls. The insufflation for smallpox was made in the girl's right nostril and in the boy's left. The same rule applied to aphrodisiacs when administered to men or women.

Since all that is noble was left, Chinese men hid their right hands under their left when offering greetings, while women did the opposite. However, during the time of mourning, which was *yin*, men did the opposite, hiding their left hands under their right.

During the archaic period, prisoners had their left hands cut off and their left eyes put out.

Generally speaking, in China the left hand was used for giving and the right for taking.

In human relationships, right and left governed protocol and precedence. The host received his guests standing and facing south, to benefit from the *yang*-principle, his guests facing north (less honourable and *yin*).

Similarly, in Japanese tradition the left is the side of wisdom, loyalty and instinct. It is linked to the Sun (*hi*) which is the male element. The Sun-goddess, Amaterasu, was born from Izanagi's left eye, the Moon from his right. The right is associated with the Moon, with water and with the female element.

Reasons have been sought for these different interpretations of right and left. In ritual circumambulation in India, for example, motion from left to right is propitious, while that from right to left is regarded as unlucky and performed only at funerals. In black magic, the left takes precedence, too: the first step is taken with the left foot, the left side is the side nearest the fire and so on. Boucher offers Goblet d'Alviella as his authority for the explanation that 'righthandwise rotation carries lucky and lefthandwise rotation unlucky associations, because the first is Sunwise and the second in the opposite direction.' Furthermore, in Brahmanical funeral ceremonies a first lefthandwise circumambulation would set a course towards the ancestral realms of the dead, while a second circumambulation, righthandwise, would indicate a return to this world (BOUM p. 113). It needs to be emphasized

that the righthandwise motion of the Sun is only apparent in the northern
hemisphere if one faces the Sun east and south. In the southern hemisphere, of course, the motion would appear to be lefthandwise. Any symbolic comparisons made from such observations must be both tenuous and
fanciful or reversed for the southern hemisphere. Furthermore, because of
the rotation of the Earth, the starry firmament moves from right to left.
Stellar or polar motion is, therefore, apparently always the opposite to that
of the Sun.

In Western Christian tradition, right has the connotation of the active
and left of the passive. Again, the right came to denote the future and the
left the past over which mortals had no control. Lastly, the right possessed
beneficent and the left maleficent properties.

In his commentary on the Song of Solomon (8: 3), 'His left hand should
be under my head, and his right hand should embrace me', William of St
Thierry explains that the right hand represents knowledge acquired by reason
exercised in works while the left, propitious to rest, denotes wisdom and the
contemplative life, expressed in peace and silence.

The conclusions to be drawn from all these examples are that, overall, in
Western tradition right and left contrast with one another in exactly the
same way as male and female, active and passive, day and night, extroversion and introversion and so on, while Far Eastern tradition reverses these
symbolic analogies point by point by labelling left *yang* and right *yin*. It
should nevertheless be observed that in both cases the male principle, or
yang, is given precedence over the female, or *yin*, with this one exception
that, in the West, the left or female side is seen as governing life itself, since
left is the side of the heart.

In politics, the right is taken to symbolize order, stability, authority, hierarchical structures, tradition and a degree of complacency, while the left
stands for dissatisfaction with the social order, demand for one's rights,
dynamism, the quest for greater justice and progress, liberation, innovation
and risk-taking. In fact, such generalizations are over-dependent upon day-
to-day political reality and merely correspond with the myths and fantasies
which motivate the minds of the electorate.

righteous persons   Their symbolic meaning is denoted by the verse (Proverbs 10: 25): 'The righteous is an everlasting foundation.'

The righteous set everything in its place, regulating all things with moderation and, in so doing, respond to their regulating and creative role.

The righteous fulfil in themselves the duties of the scales with both pans
in perfect balance and on the same level. The righteous are, therefore,
beyond conflict and confrontation, actualizing oneness within themselves
and thereby becoming already part of eternity, which is one and whole and
unaffected by the disjunctive effects of the temporal. This is why the righteous occupy such an important place in the Bible, thinking and acting with
serious and orderly moderation.

While the righteous symbolize human perfection by their resemblance to
a Demiurge which creates order – they bring order first to their inward
nature and then to their environment – they also fill the role of what is truly
a cosmic force. Thus they are often compared with COLUMNS, links between

what is above with what is below (see SCHO p. 165). Hence the saying in the Talmud 'Were there only one righteous man upon the face of the Earth, he would sustain the world.' Gnostic thinkers exalted the role of the righteous into that of hypostasis: they became 'columns of splendour'.

ring To demonstrate that rings serve essentially to display links and bonding, one need only cite two among countless examples – wedding rings and pastoral rings like the Fisherman's Ring used as a papal seal and broken on the death of the pope who wore it. Rings may thus be regarded as signs of a covenant, vow, community or common fate.

The ambivalence of the symbol arises from the fact that rings simultaneously bind and isolate, something not unrelated to the dialectic relationship of master and slave. The image of the falconer ringing a hawk, which thereafter will hunt for him alone, may be compared with that of the bishop, surrogate for the godhead, placing the wedding ring upon the finger of the novice, who thereafter becomes the mystic Bride of Christ and servant of the Lord, with this difference only, that the nun, unlike the bird, submits of her own free will. This is what gives rings their sacramental properties, since they are manifestations of a promise. In this context, it should be observed that tradition requires bride and groom to exchange rings during the wedding ceremonies. This shows that the relationship described above is established between them, but with twofold force and in twin directions, a dialectic of double subtlety in that each of those involved becomes simultaneously master and slave of the other.

The interpretation of ring symbolism may be compared at all levels with that of GIRDLE symbolism and especially upon the spiritual plane, since it derives from the old Roman custom of forbidding the priests of Jupiter, the flamens, to wear rings unless they were broken and had no stone set in them (Aulus Gellius 10: 15). The reason for this taboo was that 'any sort of bond completely encircling any part of the celebrant's body would lock up his supernatural powers and prevent them operating in the outside world' (BEAG).

That no stone was set in the flamen's ring brings us to a fresh symbolic aspect of rings. When they bear a seal which is a symbol of power, they cease to be symbols of submissiveness but become those of spiritual or physical dominion. Such was the ring to which, legend says, Solomon owed his wisdom. The Fisherman's Ring, on the other hand, superimposes these two properties since it is simultaneously the symbol of temporal power and of spiritual submissiveness.

There have been several famous rings, with different symbolic meaning, especially among the Ancient Greeks. As a condition of his liberation by Herakles (Hercules), Prometheus had an iron ring on his finger in which was set a chip of rock as a reminder of the chains which had bound him to the rock in the Caucasus and, above all, as a sign of his submission to Zeus. Here again the symbolism is twofold, since his submission to Zeus conjures up what caused the hero's greatness and his punishment, the one inseparable from the other. The bezel of this ring may not hold a seal, but it at least contains a signature.

In China, the ring was the symbol of the endless cycle of unbroken continuity, the closed circle, by contrast with the spiral. It corresponded to the trigram *li*, which is that of the Sun and of Fire. On the other hand, the ring into which pommels of swords were shaped would appear to have been associated with the Moon.

The greatest emphasis should, however, be placed upon the jade ring (*pi*) which possesses a symbolism of the highest importance. The *pi* is a thin, flat disk, the diameter of the hole in the middle either equalling or more frequently being half of the thickness of the ring. In the entry on JADE, the royal components of the symbolism of this mineral have been described. *Pi* were royal jades and, significantly, the ideogram for *pi* was a combination of *pi* (prince) and *yu* (jade). Because the *pi* is round, it was a symbol of Heaven by contrast with the square *ts'ong*, a symbol of Earth. Ritual offerings of *pi* to Heaven and *ts'ong* to Earth were made at the solstices.

The hole in the middle of the ring is the receptacle for, or the channel of, celestial influence. It lies directly below the GREAT BEAR or the POLE Star like the emperor in the Temple of Heaven. It is therefore an emblem of the emperor as 'Son of Heaven'. Furthermore, the Temple of Heaven was surrounded by a circular moat called the Pi-yong, since it was in the shape of a *pi*. It is important in this context to observe that the Celts also employed very fine jade rings and that one of them was found in Brittany associated with an AXE, its point marking the centre of the ring. Now axes are associated with thunderbolts, themselves a manifestation of celestial activity. The hole in the middle of a ring is the Monad, as well as being the void in the hub on which the WHEEL turns. It symbolizes and helps to actualize the void in the centre of the individual into which the celestial influx should pour down.

Some *pi* are extant, notched in such a way, it has been shown, to provide so accurate a map of the circumpolar heavens as to calculate the direction of the pole and the date of the solstices. This is because observing the heavenly bodies is an appropriate way of paying due honour to Heaven, to conform to the harmony which it teaches and to receive its beneficent influence.

Coomaraswamy has observed that the *pi* corresponds to the perforated brick on the top of a Vedic altar, which stood for Heaven, the two lower bricks corresponding to the *ts'ong*.

Jade rings are sometimes decorated and this might represent an alteration to the primitive symbol which called for austerity and restraint. When decorated with a pair of dragons, the ring signifies the changing *yin* and *yang* around the changeless essence in the centre. In rings decorated with the eight trigrams, the central void is very clearly *yin–yang* (or *T'ai-chi*) the undifferentiated state of primordial Oneness. Instead of alteration, this may well be the display or explanation of a symbol no longer understood directly and intuitively (BELT, GRAD, GUES, SOOL, VARG).

In Christian tradition, rings symbolize faithful affection freely given. They are linked to time and the cosmos. Pythagoras' dictum, 'Do not carry God's image on your ring', shows that God must not be associated with time. There are two further interpretations of the saying. The biblical is that one should not take the name of the Lord in vain; the pagan, that it is wisest to make sure one's life is free and untrammelled.

The early Christians copied the Gentiles in the wearing of rings and St Clement of Alexandria advised his contemporaries that the bezel should bear the image of a dove, a fish or an anchor.

Knights were permitted to wear gold rings.

On the esoteric plane, rings are possessed of magical powers, being miniature versions of the girdle which guards places which hold treasure or secrets. To obtain a ring is, in some respects, the same as opening a door or entering a castle, a cave or Paradise itself. To set a ring on one's own finger or to place it on somebody else's, is to take a gift for oneself or to accept it from someone else, as a treasure kept for one's own exclusive use or mutually shared.

In Irish poetry, legend and song, rings serve as a means of recognition, symbols of a force or bond which cannot be broken, even if the ring itself is lost or left forgotten at the roadside. In the second Battle of Moytura, a woman of the Tuatha Dé Danann, Delbaeth's daughter Eri (Eri is a variant of *Eriu*, 'Ireland', and *Delbaeth* means 'shape') had a brief love-affair with an unknown man who arrived in a miraculous boat. When they parted, he told her that his name was Elada ('Knowledge'), son of Delbaeth – they were therefore brother and sister – and gave her a ring which would enable him to recognize their child. In another legend, Cùchulainn treated Aoife, a female warrior whom he had conquered and seduced, in exactly the same way with respect to the child whom she would bear him (OGAC 17: p. 399; 9: pp. 115ff.).

Legend attributes Solomon's wisdom to a ring. Arabs tell the story of the day when he sealed with his ring the demons whom he had assembled for his work of divination and they became his slaves. One day he lost his ring in the Jordan and did not regain his wisdom until a fisherman found it and brought it to him. Esoteric writers have suggested that perhaps it might have been stolen by a jealous jinnee to use its power, until God forced him to throw the ring into the water so that it could be found and returned to Solomon (GRIA p. 89).

This ring may thus be regarded as a symbol of Solomon's knowledge and the power which he possessed over others. It is like the seal of fire, the gift of Heaven, which was the badge of his spiritual and physical dominion. It is reminiscent of other magic rings.

Mention has already been made of Prometheus' ring, and among other rings famed in Greek legend is the one which belonged to Polycrates. This king enjoyed such a steady run of good fortune that he became convinced that his privileged position could not last. He therefore decided to sacrifice of his own accord something precious and to which he was particularly attached. So, from the top of a tower, he cast into the sea his ring in which a splendid EMERALD was set. However, it was swallowed by a fish, the fish was caught and taken to Polycrates. The latter had attempted to confine his fate within the magic circle of the ring, but the sea had rejected his offering. Oroetes, the Persian governor of Sardis, lured him from Samos and crucified him. The ring thus symbolized the fate from which no human can escape, as well as manifesting the indissolubility of a bond. Polycrates tried to offer it as compensation, but the gods accept only what they themselves have decided to take and their decrees are not to be altered by some showy material offering. The only sacrifice is the inner sacrifice, the acceptance of one's fate, and this is what Polycrates' ring would seem to mean.

The story which Plato tells of Gyges' chance finding of a ring is as rich in symbolic meaning. When he put the ring on his finger, Gyges accidentally discovered that it possessed the power of making him invisible . . . and this was the beginning of his good fortune. Is the meaning of this ring so very different from that of Polycrates? Since it was found upon a dead man and in such unusual circumstances as an earthquake which exposed it in a brazen horse, the ring could only be the gift of the forces of the Underworld and was to pass to those who dwelt on this Earth extraordinary powers. However, its magic only operated when Gyges 'rotated the bezel of his ring in front of him and in the palm of his other hand'. Here again, true strength lies within us and the invisibility conferred by the ring is a withdrawal from the external world to acquire or to repossess those essential teachings which come from the world within. Gyges' ring might therefore symbolize the high point of inner life and perhaps mysticism itself. The symbol's bipolarity resides within us. The ring's powers may result as easily, should its magic be perverted, in the successful commission of crime and the establishment of tyrannical rule as in mystical attainments. And this is what happened in the story of Gyges.

The Ring of the NIBELUNGEN was the pledge of their power. WOTAN snatched it from them with a thrust of his spear. In this context, the ring symbolizes the bond which can be created between man and nature through the exercise of the will. When the human being wears the ring it is a sign of man's dominion over nature, but it enslaves man to the destructive passions of lust and greed which are the painful consequences of the exercise of that power. Man, thinking that he rules, feels himself manacled and ruled by that golden ring which binds him to every sort of craving. It is an image of the drive for power. Wotan, however, as a god, was unwilling for what he had created to steal from him his power over creation, and returned the ring to mankind. Later, SIEGFRIED and the god's daughter, BRUNHILD, were to cast the ring back into the Rhine as a sign that, in order to destroy evil in the world and because of their awareness of the power of love, they themselves rejected power. The symbolism of the ring of the Nibelungen may be graduated to different political and social, moral and metaphysical, and even mystical levels.

river (see also CONFLUENCE) The symbolism of rivers and running WATER is simultaneously that of 'universal potentiality' and that of 'the fluidity of forms' (Schuon), of fertility, death and renewal. The stream is that of life and death. It may be regarded as flowing down into the sea; as a current against which one swims; or as something to be crossed from one bank to another. Flowing into the sea is the gathering of the waters, the return to an undifferentiated state, attaining Nirvana. Swimming against the stream is clearly returning to the divine source, the First Cause. Crossing the river is overcoming an obstacle separating two realms or conditions, the phenomenal world and the unconditioned state, the world of the senses and the state of non-attachment. The Zen patriarch Hui Neng taught that the far bank was *pāramitā*, that is, the state which is beyond being and non-being, a state, furthermore, which is symbolized not simply by the far bank but by the smoothly flowing stream as well.

The celestial stream of Jewish tradition is the river of grace and heavenly influences. However, this heavenly stream flows vertically down along the World AXIS, and then from the centre flows horizontally out to the FOUR points of the compass until it reaches the rim of the world, and these four streams are the four rivers of the Garden of Eden.

The celestial stream is the Gangā (Ganges), in India the cleansing river which flows from Shiva's tresses. It is a symbol of the Upper Waters but, additionally, in so far as it cleanses all things, it is an instrument of liberation. In Hindu iconography the Gangā and Yamunā (Jumna) are attributes of Varuna as Lord of the Waters. The Gangā's stream really is an axial stream since it is said to flow along a triple bed traversing Heaven, Earth and the Underworld.

In Ancient China, the symbolism of crossing a river possessed considerable importance. This was undertaken by young couples at the vernal equinox and was a true passage from one year and from one season to another, from *yin* to *yang*. Additionally, it was a ritual cleansing as a prelude to the fecundation which would be consequent upon the restoration of the power of *yang*, as well as a prayer for RAIN, itself the fecundation of the soil by celestial activity. At the equinox, the legendary Weaver crossed the celestial river (the Milky Way) for her marriage to the Ox-herd. This seasonal ceremony had its prototype in the landscape of Heaven (BHAB, DANA, GUEC, GRAR, HOUD, SCHP).

The Ancient Greeks made rivers the objects of worship and elevated them to the rank of demigods, such as the sons of Oceanus and the fathers of the Nymphs. Sacrifice to them took the form of drowning live bulls and HORSES in their waters, and they could not be crossed without first undergoing ritual purification and offering prayers. Like all the forces of fecundation, their actions were arbitrary and they could both irrigate and flood or wash away the fields, carry or sink the boats on their waters. They inspired both adoration and fear.

Hesiod laid down the rule never to cross rivers with their ever-flowing streams until the traveller had said a prayer as he gazed upon their shining waves and bathed his hands in their clear and pleasant waters. Whoever crossed a river without first cleansing his hands from the evil with which they were sullied, would attract the anger of the gods who would send down the direst punishment.
(LAVD p. 430)

The rivers of the Underworld mark the punishments reserved for the damned – Acheron (pain), Phlegethon (burning), Cocytus (mourning), Styx (terror) and Lethe (oblivion).

One of the chief rivers of Ireland, the Boyne (Boann), was regarded in a passage from the 'History of Place-names' (*Dindshenchas*) as an aspect of the great cosmic river from which all comes and to which all returns. It is to be seen in other lands under such other names as Severn (England), Jordan (Palestine), Tiber (Italy) and so on (CELT 15: pp. 328ff.).

As they flow down from the mountains, wind through valleys and are lost in lakes and seas, rivers symbolize human existence and its winding passage through desire, emotion and intent. In this respect Heraclitus' theory is significant. In Fragment 12 of Diels's standard edition we read: 'Those who enter the same rivers receive the current which has come from other streams and washed other people, and souls exhale moist substances.' Plato was to put it more concisely: 'You cannot step twice into the same stream' (*Cratylus* 402a).

Patri observes of the Heraclitan symbolism of fire and water (*Revue de Métaphysique et de Morale* 2–3: p. 131) that the the plural 'rivers' does not denote plurality of streams. Every bather has his own river. In the symbolic sense of the term, to enter a river is for the soul to enter the body. 'River' takes on the meaning of 'body'. The dry soul is drawn in by fire, the moist soul is enfolded in the body. The body leads a precarious existence, it seeps away like water, and each soul possesses an individual body, its temporary habitation, its river.

robe See DRESS.

roc The bird described in *The Thousand and One Nights* was well known to medieval European literature since Crusaders had returned with legends in which this fabulous creature was described in the greatest detail. Marco Polo, too, mentions it in his account of his travels. He relates that natives of the island of Magastar had described the roc as a bird 'with a wing-span of over thirty paces and with wing-feathers each twelve paces in length'. It was so huge and strong that it could seize an elephant and carry it high up into the air quite unaided, to let the elephant fall and shatter on the ground. The vulturine bird would then swoop down to tear and eat the carcass, returning to finish its meal at its leisure.

In the Kurdish legend of Prince Ibrāhīm and Princess Nūshāfarīn, the roc is described as a white bird sixty feet tall and dwelling beside the sea of Muhīt (Mediterranean) and performing the same feats as the SIMURG.

The author of the *Nuzhat-ul-qulūb* also mentions the roc among the birds and animals to be found beside the China Sea.

All the symbols relating to the simurg may be equally applied to the roc, although its legendary aspect often takes precedence over its symbolic significance.

The roc may also symbolize a powerful king or an emir famed for his valour.

rock (see also SYMPLEGADES) There are different aspects of rock symbolism, but the most obvious is that of unchanging motionlessness. In Chinese landscape painting rocks are contrasted with WATERFALLS in the sense of *yang* contrasted with *yin*, the active but non-acting principle with the passive but impermanent principle.

This changelessness may be that of the supreme First Cause, as is the case when the Psalmist applies the term 'Rock of Israel' to none other than Jehovah himself. The same is true of the Song of Moses (Deuteronomy 32: 4): 'He is the Rock, his work is perfect: for all his ways are judgement: a God of truth and without iniquity, just and right is he.'

A similar identification may be made in the case of the rock in the Wilderness from which Moses struck water, as a spring of life and a manifestation of primeval potentiality. In the Old Testament, the rock is the symbol of Jehovah's strength, of the firmness of his Covenant and of his faithfulness. The Psalmist in his distress (Psalms 18: 3; 19: 15) calls upon God as his rock. Moses may also be regarded as the man of the rock from which he made fresh water spring by striking it with his STAFF. This rock is a prefiguration of Christ who is positively identified by St Paul as that 'spiritual Rock' from which flow the waters of life (1 Corinthians 10: 4).

In Hindu tradition, Shiva's *svāyambhuvalinga*, the natural lingams formed by bare rocks on mountain peaks, possess this same property of the active principle, the source of cosmic manifestation. In Japanse mythology, rocks symbolize firmness (see FUDO).

Ismaili esoterics believe rocks to be underground condensations of the mass which fell with the rebellious Angels since rocks are thick, hard and compacted (see REEF).

One very special case should be mentioned, that of the two famous rocks in the Bay of Ise linked by a rope. The rising Sun is to be seen between them, symbol of the birth of life (BURA. BHAB. CORT. OGRJ).

Sisyphus' rock or boulder, which always rolls to the bottom of the hill and has to be pushed up again, characterizes the insatiable nature of desire and the ceaseless nature of the struggle against its despotism. Sated, pushed away or sublimated, it is constantly reborn and returns in some fresh shape. Its own bulk makes it roll backwards and become a burden. Human laws prescribe a ceaseless attempt to shoulder this burden of one's desires and raise them to a higher level.

Sisyphus' rock is 'the symbol of the crushing burden of Earth [earthly longings]' (DIES p. 183).

rod See STAFF; WAND.

rope Broadly speaking, like TREES, LADDERS and SPIDER's webs, ropes are one of the ascension symbols, since they provide the means, as well as standing for the desire, to ascend (ELIT p. 103). When knotted they symbolize CHAINS or bonds of all sorts and possess hidden or magical properties.

Varuna is generally depicted holding a rope, a symbol of his power to bind and loose.

In Ancient Egyptian hieroglyphics a knotted rope denotes a person's name or a separate and individual being. It is the symbol of a stream of life reflected upon itself and, as such, constituting a person.

The Greeks had a legend of a cordwainer, Ocnos, 'a symbolic character depicted as plaiting a rope in the Underworld which a she-ASS ate as fast as he plaited it. This was generally interpreted as being a symbol of a hard-working man (Ocnos) who had married an extravagant wife' (GRID p. 322a). As in other instances, the rope symbolizes the punishment of Nemesis and it is possible to suggest that Ocnos' eternal plaiting of the rope eternally eaten by his wife, the she-ass, symbolizes the eternal punishment inflicted upon evil marriage-partners. Fortune is also often shown holding a rope, since she can bring life to an end by cutting the thread of existence at whim.

African witch-doctors use ropes as instruments for their magic and they are believed to become serpents, staves, fountains of milk and so on.

Central American civilizations regarded the rope as a divine symbol and, in Mayan and Mexican art, ropes hanging from the sky symbolize divine semen falling from Heaven to fecundate the Earth. This symbolism is echoed in the name of the month which ushers in the rainy season. In the Ancient Mexican calendar it was called Toxcatl, meaning 'rope' or 'lasso' (GIRP p. 99). Local fabrics continue the tradition of Mayan manuscripts by symbolizing rain as ropes. In Mayan architecture these ropes became slender columns.

The Chorti bury their dead with a rope to be used to fight off the wild animals to be encountered on the way to the Underworld.

In Shintō, the sacred rope is called the *shimenawa*, meaning 'rice-straw rope', from *shime*, 'tightly-plaited', and *nawa*, 'rope'. This is, however, an abbreviation of the original name *shirikumenawa*, which meant 'a straw rope plaited in such a way that the roots of the straw may be seen at either end'. It is set in holy places to keep out evil spirits and evil influences and to stop accident, injury or misfortune affecting the place as well. It is a protective symbol which the Japanese set on *torri*, in Shintō temples, on new buildings, on the rings where traditional Japanese sumo-wrestling matches take place and, during the week of New Year, at the doors of all houses. Since they are holy, the old *shimenawa* are burnt.

Northern wizards used to tie the winds which they controlled into a rope. A woodcut in Olaus Magnus' *Historia de gentibus septentrionalibus* (Rome, 1555) shows two sailors bargaining with a wizard standing upon a lonely rock in the sea, over his price for 'the rope with three knots which he holds in his hand and which contains the winds which he has tied up. By unpicking the first knot they would release a gentle west-southwesterly; by unpicking the second, a stiff northerly; but if they were to unpick the third then a most dreadful storm would follow' (GRIA p. 105).

In the Koran, too, ropes are symbols of ascent, reminiscent of the rope the shaman or the oriental juggler throws into the air and uses to climb skywards.

'Yet how paltry it is to try to throw ropes into the air!' The Prophet's remarks about ropes contain a heavily ironic challenge. Heavenly ropes can only come from Heaven and, try as man may, he can never make them rise up from Earth. In other words, grace alone makes ascent into Heaven possible.

rosary The rosary is those rows of pearls on a thread, mentioned in the *Bhagavad Gītā* (7: 7), their string being *ātman* on which all things are threaded, that is, all worlds and states of manifestation. *Atman*, the universal spirit, links these worlds together and is also the breath which gives them life. In this context, Guénon emphasizes that, in principle, the prayer spoken to each rosary bead should be linked to the rhythm of respiration.

In Hindu iconography, the rosary is an attribute of several deities, but especial of Brahmā and of the goddess Sarasvatī, herself the alphabet, potent creator of language. Her rosary (*aksha-māla*) comprises fifty beads (*aksha*) which correspond to the fifty letters of the Sanskrit alphabet from *a* to *kasha*. As ever in the case of the 'Wreath of Letters', the Hindu rosary is linked to its creator (*shabda*) and to the sense of hearing.

However, in India again and especially in the Buddhist world, the rosary has 108 beads (12×9), which is a cyclical number and therefore normally used to express the development of manifestation. Ninety-nine, the number of beads in the Muslim rosary, is also cyclical and linked to the Names of God. The hundredth bead is 'latent' and expresses the return of the manifold to the One, of manifestation to the First Cause. Similar observations might be made of the Christian rosary, which comprises sixty beads ($10 \times 5 + 5 + 1 + 3 + 1$) even though their arrangement seems to have been the result of quite diffferent concerns.

In all traditions, repeated prayer has its own particular qualities, independent of whatever symbolism is possessed by the object used as a mnemonic aid (GUES, MALA).

As in India, the Tibetan Buddhist rosary comprises 108 beads and its decades are sometimes separated by silver rings. The materials of which they are made and their colours vary with their user. 'Yellow beads are for Buddhas; beads of white shells for Bodhisattvas; coral beads for the man who converted Tibet; for the terrifying Yamāntaka, Lord of Death, the cranial bones of different hermits; for the deities of Yoga, the bark of a shrub called *tulosi* . . . and for ordinary mortals, ordinary wood' (TONT p. 5). To the extent to which prayers, all much the same, are recited over each bead of the rosary, its symbolism may be compared with that of the PRAYER-WHEEL. In Africa rosaries made from human teeth are known.

rose In beauty, shape and scent, the rose is outstanding and hence has become the most commonly used floral symbol in the West. Broadly speaking the rose corresponds status-wise to the LOTUS in Asia, both being very close to the WHEEL in symbolic terms. The commonest aspect of this floral symbolism is that of manifestation, rising from the primeval waters to blossom above them. This aspect is, in any case, familiar in India where *triparasundari*, the Cosmic Rose, is used as a point of comparison with the Divine Mother's beauty. It denotes the attainment of perfection, unsullied fulfilment. As we shall see, roses symbolize the chalice of life, the soul, the heart and love. They may be contemplated in the same way as a MANDALA and regarded as mystic CENTRES.

In Christian iconography, the rose may be either the chalice into which Christ's blood flowed, or the transfiguration of those drops of blood or, again, the symbol of Christ's wounds. A Rosicrucian symbol depicts five roses, one at the centre and one on each of the four arms of the Cross. This conjures images of the Grail or else of the 'Heavenly Rose' of the Redemption. In the Rosicrucian context, it should be observed that its emblem sets a rose in the very centre of the Cross, that is, where the Sacred Heart, Christ's heart, is located. This symbol is the same as the *Rosa Candida* in Dante's *Divine Comedy*; and that in turn conjures Our Lady's title, 'Mystic Rose', in litanies of the Blessed Virgin; and that of the medieval poem the *Roman de la Rose*. Angelus Silesius takes the rose for an image of the soul, as well as of Christ who leaves his mark upon it. The Golden Rose, which the Pope used once to bless on the fourth Sunday in Lent, was a symbol of his 'spiritual power and teaching' (DEVA), but doubtless a symbol of resurrection and of immortality as well.

Gothic rose-windows and the seaman's compass-rose mark the way in which the symbolism of the rose is transformed into that of the wheel.

Finally, a special case should be observed, that of Sa'dī of Shiraz, for whom, as a Muslim mystic, the rose-garden is a garden of contemplation. 'I shall pluck roses from the garden, but I am drunk with the scent of the rose-bush.' Christian mystics would certainly not reject such language as a commentary upon the Rose of Sharon in the Song of Solomon.

Because of their relationship with blood, roses seem often to have been regarded as symbols of mystical rebirth: 'On battlefields where a number of heroes have been slain, roses or eglantines will grow; . . . roses and anemones [grew up] from [the blood] of Adonis when [the young god was] dying' (ELIT p. 302). 'Human life', Mircea Eliade writes, 'must be completely lived out if it is to exhaust all its potentialities of creation and expression; if it is interrupted suddenly, by violent death, it will tend to extend itself in some other form: plant, fruit, flower' (ibid. pp. 301–2).

Abd al-Qadir Jīlānī compares scars with roses and attributes a mystic meaning to them.

According to Portal, roses and the colour pink became the symbol of rebirth because of the semantic kinship between the Latin words *rosa* (rose) and *ros*, meaning 'DEW' or 'RAIN'. 'The flower and its colour were primary symbols of rebirth and of initiation into the Mysteries. . . . In the *Golden Ass*, Apuleius regained his human shape by eating a garland of roses given to him by the high priest of Isis.' The rose-bush, he adds, 'is an image of the born-again, just as dew is a symbol of rebirth' (PORS pp. 218, 220). This interpretation receives confirmation from the frequent juxtaposition in Scripture of GREEN with roses. Thus Ecclesiasticus 24: 14 has: 'I was exalted . . . as a rose-plant in Jericho, as a fair olive tree in a pleasant field.' The olive was sacred to Athene, who was born on Rhodes, the Island of Roses – and this would suggest the secrets of initiation – and rose-bushes were sacred to Aphrodite as well as to the grey-eyed goddess. The Ancient Greeks knew the rose as a white flower, but when Aphrodite's lover Adonis was mortally wounded, the goddess, running to his help, pricked herself on a rose-thorn and her blood tinged the flowers sacred to her.

It was because they were a regeneration symbol that, in Classical antiquity, the custom was established of placing roses upon graves. 'The Ancients called this ceremony the *Rosalia*. Every year during the month of May they offered dishes of roses to the spirits of the dead' (PORS p. 222). Hecate, goddess of the Underworld, was sometimes depicted wearing on her head a garland of five-leafed roses. FIVE, which follows the number of fulfilment, four, is the acknowledged mark of the beginning of a fresh cycle.

According to Bede, in the seventh century the Holy Sepulchre was painted in a mixture of WHITE and RED. These two elements of the colour rose-pink, with all their traditional symbolic properties, recur at all levels, in the sacred and the profane, in the distinctions drawn between offering white or red roses, as well as in the distinctions drawn between ideas of passion and of purity and those of transcendent love and divine wisdom. The *Palais de l'Honneur* states that 'over the coats-of-arms of nuns is set a garland comprising white rose branches with leaves, flowers and thorns, denoting the chastity which the bearers have preserved amid all life's thorns and mortifications.'

Roses became a symbol of love and, more strongly still, of the offerings made by a love which was pure:

Roses took the place of Egyptian lotus or Greek narcissus as the flowers of love. These were not the frivolous flowers of which Catullus wrote . . . but Celtic roses, proud with life and, though equipped with thorns, fraught with a gentle symbolism. This is the symbolism of the *Roman de la Rose*, in which Guillaume de Lorris and Jean de Meung created the mysterious garden of love and chivalry, of the Mystic Rose of the litanies of Our Lady, of the Golden Roses which the Popes sent to princesses worthy of them and, lastly, of that vast symbolic rose which Beatrice showed her faithful lover when he reached the last circle of Paradise, a flower simultaneously rose and rose-window.

(GHYN 2: p. 41)

Dante was to compare heavenly love with the centre of the rose. 'Into the yellow of the rose/Perennial, which, in bright expansiveness,/Lays forth its gradual blooming, redolent/Of praises to the never-wintering sun . . . Beatrice led me' (*Paradiso* 30: 124–7).

Whether white or red, roses were the favourite flowers of alchemists, who often entitled their treatises *The Rosary of the Philosophers*. White roses, 'like lilies, were linked to the white stone, the objective of the first stage of the Work, while the red rose was associated with the red stone, the objective of the second stage. Most of these roses have seven petals, each petal relating either to a metal or to an operation in the Work' (VANA p. 27). A blue rose was to become the symbol of the impossible.

ruby (see also ALMANDINE) According to Portal, in Classical antiquity rubies were regarded as emblems of good fortune. 'It was an evil omen if they changed colour, but they would regain their blood-red tint as soon as trouble had passed. They banished sorrow, restrained lust, resisted poison, were preservatives against plague and warded off evil thoughts' (PORS p. 128).

As a blood-stone, the ruby was used homeopathically in the preparation of medicines to staunch bleeding. For the same reason, Russian popular tradition maintains that it is good for the heart, brain, memory and vitality and that it clears the blood (MARA). However, if we are to believe good Bishop Marbodius, it is the solitary and glowing eye which dragons and wyverns carry in the middle of their foreheads. It is then known as a carbuncle. They 'surpass all other fiery stones, casting rays like blazing coals, so that the darkness is quite unable to dim their light' (GOUL p. 210).

rudder Like the tiller it is a symbol of responsibility and, on those terms, means foresight and overriding authority. It may be found on medals, memorial columns and in coats-of-arms.

rukh See ROC.

rule Because rules are used to draw straight lines they are a symbol of righteousness: however, their significance goes far beyond this. As 'measuring staves' (*mānadanda*) they are an attribute of the heavenly architect, Vishvakarma, and they recur as the 'golden reed' in the Book of Revelation and as a nilometer (for measuring the height of the Nile) in the hands of the Ancient Egyptian god Ptah. The Memphis theologians regarded Ptah as 'the creator of the world by means of his heart (= thought) and his tongue

(= creation by utterance). . . . One ancient tradition attributed to him the invention of crafts, and artisans came under his protection. . . . The Greeks identified Ptah with HEPHAISTOS' (POSD p. 226).

Above all, the rule is an instrument used in building and hence universal manifestation. It is employed as such in Masonic symbolism, particularly in passing to the Fellowcraft Degree. Rules allow plans of buildings to be drawn and ensure that they have been correctly executed. Their twenty-four gradations correspond to that most obvious manifestation of celestial activity, the daily course of the Sun. 'The rule symbolizes making perfect. Without it, labour would be at random, the arts would be defective, the sciences would exhibit a series of uncohesive systems, logic would be unsettled and capricious, law-giving arbitrary and oppressive, music would be discordant, philosophy would be reduced to metaphysical darkness and the sciences would lose their clarity' (Ragon in BOUM p. 20).

In religious orders, the Rule – be it that of St Augustine, St Benedict, St Dominic, St Theresa of Avila, or any other founder or foundress – is also the instrument used to build the spiritual self and shape spirituality. National constitutions play the same role by giving states their structure. In the deepest sense of the word, rules are symbols of proportion within the individual, of his ideals and of their realization. As St Augustine said, all things have been made to a rule which gives each weight, shape and proportion.

S

S The shape of the letter 'S', whether horizontal or vertical, was often used as a decorative motif in ancient and primitive art and many examples survive from India, Greece, Rome and elsewhere. Like the SPIRAL, it would appear to symbolize movement in the direction of oneness, whether seen as horizontal or vertical, between Heaven and Earth, the male and female principles, the mountain and the valley, the waves of the sea, gusts of wind, waterspouts and whirlwinds. A number of commentators also regard it as the symbol of the twofold process of development, opening to higher influences and bowing to the lower. It can also be seen as the sacrificial smoke curling up. But however it is viewed, 'S' is the symbol of a unifying movement which brings together different beings, elements, planes and even foci.

sabbath The sabbath symbolizes REST after labour. The seventh day imposed the cessation of activity upon the Jews, it was a day dedicated to God. In the account of the Creation (Genesis 2: 2–3), God is said to have finished the work which he had done and to have rested on the seventh day. As a day of rest, the sabbath reproduces the seventh day of Creation. This period of rest carries with it a degree of sanctification, hence the words of Exodus 20: 8: 'Remember the sabbath day to keep it holy.' The sabbath thus denotes a time devoted to God and does not relate simply to human beings, but to animals as well. Thus oxen and asses should not be put to work. The law prescribing a sabbath day's rest held an important place in the Old Testament and, although its position was to alter with the ages, Judaism still enacts thirty-nine prohibitions on certain activities.

In the New Testament and among the early Fathers and medieval mystics the sabbath still stood for God's resting and the day was dedicated to him, but its significance partook of a spiritual as well as of a material character. The true sabbath of the righteous becomes that of the religious and demands a fresh dimension beyond merely earthly labour. When creation is restored, it will be set at the disposal of the righteous and they will enjoy a true sabbath day's rest. The seventh day, fundamentally a specifically Jewish idea, came to mean eternal life (DANT pp. 350–1).

The Sabbath of Sabbaths, which the Children of Israel termed the Great Jubilee and which took place every fifty years (Leviticus 25: 8), signifies eternal rest and bliss.

The twelfth-century Cistercian monk, Aelred of Rievaulx, pointed out in his *Speculum caritatis* that the six days of the Creation each had its own morning and evening, showing thereby its beginning and its end. The seventh day had neither morning nor evening, it stood outside Creation and belonged to the divine order alone. 'The day on which God rested was not within time, it was eternal'; it was God's sabbath since it involved God alone. This is why the soul's true sabbath is God and it is attained by chastity. Before beatitude the individual has a foretaste of the Sabbath of Sabbaths. Aelred separately distinguishes three sabbaths, each interconnected as the soul rises ever higher. Each sabbath is a stepping-stone on this upward ascent, but the Sabbath of Sabbaths alone brings with it the vision of God. Peter of Celle (d. 1183) regarded monastic life and heavenly life as neighbours; passage from one to the other was like passing from one sabbath to the next. Contemplative life might be compared with a cessation from toil and with the seventh day on which God rested from his Creation.

Eternal sabbath signifies sabbath without limit. In a poem attributed to a twelfth-century monk from Hirsan, the sabbath is compared with Easter and with Summer. Neither old age nor disease, nor even death, can hold any sway over such a sabbath. Rest consists above all in the knowledge and love of God (LECM p. 62).

Sabbath denotes a sacred as opposed to a profane period of time. Rest is made holy by meditation upon creation. Henri Baruch makes the important point that the Hebrew word for 'rest' is the verb *chabot*, 'to rest', which has the literal meaning of going on strike. This rest is also *hinnafèch*, meaning to regain one's soul. While the individual who observes the sabbath may meditate upon creation, he or she will also call to mind the flight from Egypt, since 'only free men and women rest.' It is not simply a matter of putting all work aside, but of expelling from the spirit all inward anguish and oppression, to attain a rest which sets free the soul.

The coming of the sabbath is a reason for joy. According to the liturgy of the School of Safed (fifteenth century) a man should make ready for the sabbath like a groom for his bride. It is a day of rejoicing (BARH p. 9).

But the sabbath did not always have this religious connotation. The curses which the prophets Isaiah and Hosea called down upon those who celebrated the new Moon and other sabbaths and festivals of the lunar cycle 'seem to show that the remnants of an ancient tradition from their days of wandering had survived, which prescribed feasts and rejoicing on the sabbath in accordance with a Moon-cult' (SOUL p. 143), and that these had no connection with the Lord's day. The sabbath (from *shabater*, 'to cease') would seem originally to have been a feast of the full Moon, the point at which the Moon ceases to grow. It was then extended to each of the four phases of the Moon, coinciding with the festival of the seventh day. Witches' sabbaths are connected with this ancient tradition rather than with the Old Testament account in Genesis. According to legend, they would set off astride broomsticks to meet in a clearing to hold their tumultuous and fearful orgies. This is the nocturnal aspect of the symbol of the seventh day: when God rests the Devil gets busy.

sacrifice Is the act of making some object or being holy, that is separate from the person offering sacrifice, whether the latter be his or her property or even his or her own life. The sacrifice is set apart, too, from the rest of the world which remains profane, separated from itself and given to God as a token of dependence, obedience, repentance or love. What is offered to God in this way becomes God's property absolutely – this is why it was so often broken or burnt – or untouchable, and as God's property it is something which produces fear and awe.

Sacrifice is a symbol of 'the renunciation of the ties of Earth through love of the spirit' or of the godhead. All traditions contain symbols of son or daughter being sacrificed, Abraham's intended sacrifice of Isaac being, perhaps, the best known. But the meaning of sacrifice may become corrupted, as was the case of Agamemnon and Iphigenia, when obedience to an oracle concealed other motives and in particular the empty ambition of gaining revenge. 'The only valid sacrifice is to cleanse the soul of all vain thoughts, and one of the most enduring symbols of this purification is that innocent creature, the ram' (DIES p. 69). Sacrifice is linked to the notion of interchange on the level of spiritual or creative energy. The more valuable the material object, the more potent will be the spiritual energy given in return, whether the object of the sacrifice be purification or propitiation. The symbol is seen fully formed in the notion of sacrifice. Because a material asset symbolizes a spiritual asset, to offer the former attracts the gift of the latter as a reward or, one might well say, in fair and strict compensation. The properties of sacrifice, which will be corrupted by magic, reside in this relationship between the material and the spiritual and in this conviction that positive action results from the impingement or mediation of material and spiritual powers.

In the Old Testament, the act or motion of sacrifice symbolizes human recognition of God's supremacy. In Jewish thought, sacrifice had a very special meaning. Life should always be preferred to death. Sacrifice of one's own life, or martyrdom, is only valid in so far as in sacrificing one's mortal life one bears witness to a higher life in the Oneness of God. Human sacrifices were strictly forbidden and animal sacrifices took their place. In matters of self-denial, physical needs were never to be sacrificed at the risk of repression. Sacrifice never involved impairment of one's nature since there is a unity between body and soul, both coming together to offer one another mutual assistance in their respective spheres. Such a marriage was all the closer and more intimate because, according to Jewish thinking, blood provided the soul with physical support.

Self-sacrifice should only be considered after balanced study since self-sacrifice arising from a pride disguised as humility would be mistaken and a misdirection of true love into mere masochism. Nevertheless, God demanded sacrifice and his demands had to be obeyed. In this repect, the case of Abraham and Isaac was typical. There was no denying the agony inflicted by any agreement to sacrifice something and it was felt to its full in Abraham's grief. It was even stronger in the case of Sara, whose inability to accept the idea of the death of her son, Isaac, caused so great a shock to her system that it killed her (BARH).

In Celtic tradition the old word for 'sacrifice' is known only from comparison with the neo-Celtic *idpart* (Middle Irish), *aberth* (Welsh) and *aberzh* (Breton). Etymologically this was *ateberta*, an oblation, and there is therefore no firm evidence of it being a blood-sacrifice, despite the legends purveyed in the lives of the saints, and these should be treated with caution. It may well be that Caesar's accounts of human figures stuffed with men and then set on fire, as well as that of the Berne scholia of sacrifice by fire, drowning and hanging, are based upon a misunderstanding of mythological data. If there were human sacrifices, despite what Classical authors say they must have been very rare and restricted to certain carefully determined ceremonies. In these circumstances, one cannot escape the general properties and symbolism of surrogacy, which are those of sacrifice. At the end of their reigns some Irish kings were sacrificially slain by having their palaces burned about them while they were either stabbed or drowned in a butt of wine or of beer. That is to say, they were sacrificed by the two chief elements controlled by the druids, Fire and Water, the sacrificial draught and the funeral pyre. Their fate was perhaps ritual purification before natural death. When Ireland became Christianized, the druids whose presence was essential to the sacrifice, either as officiants or as static organizers of the religious ceremony, vanished as such, but may well have survived as bards (*file*) and it was through them that Ancient Irish literature was handed down to us (OGAC 12: pp. 197–200, 450).

Sacrifice, for the Ancient Greeks, was a symbol of expiation, purification, appeasement and propitiatory entreaty. Light coloured victims were offered to the deities of Heaven and dark coloured to those of the Underworld. The blood which flowed from the victim's throat had to splash the ALTAR.

In sacrifices to the dead and to the gods of the Underworld, the whole victim belonged to those on whose behalf it was being offered; while in other sacrifices, the flesh was shared among those present, once the entrails and the gods' portion had been removed. 'Once the offering had been made, the person who had offered the sacrifice took care not to look behind him when he left the scene' (LAVD p. 844). In fact, he could not act as surrogate either for the person providing the victim or for the victim itself and was no more than the instrument of sacrifice. The victim was the surrogate for the person who offered it up for sacrifice, and it was the latter who expected benefits to flow from the sacrifice.

The walls of Egyptian temples depict their pharaohs slaughtering their foes and this has led historians to believe that human sacrifice existed in Ancient Egypt. This does not, however, seem to have been the case, at least during the historic period. These bloodthirsty scenes simply symbolize the victory which all kings are supposed to gain over their foes. Naturally, the Pharaoh entreats the gods to help him, but this does not imply the necessity of human sacrifice. Nevertheless, these symbolic depictions of victory were charged with magical powers since they were bound to actualize what they depicted. Reality is only a thought made manifest, the exteriorization of an internal word.

Indeed sacrifice primarily celebrates an internal triumph and the Jungian school was to interpret the famous scene of Mithras sacrificing the bull, as they did other sacrifices and especially certain Dionysiac rites, 'as a symbol of the victory of man's spiritual nature over his animality – of which the bull is a common symbol' (JUNS p. 147).

saffron According to Gilbert of Hoyland (d. 1172) saffron, with its bright golden colour, is related to wisdom. It is the colour of the robes of Buddhist monks.

Sagittarius (22 November–20 December) The ninth sign of the ZODIAC, occurring just before the Winter solstice at a time when country people have a pause in working the land and can devote their energies to hunting. It is a symbol of movement, of nomadic instincts, of independence and of quick reaction. The sign is ruled by Jupiter.

We have now reached the last of the three 'fiery' signs. If the strength of Fire was visceral in Aries and in Leo was accompanied by a will dedicated to self-glorification, in Sagittarius the force is that of spiritual enlightenment and infusion and an internal flood tide on which ego and instinct transcend their limitations and approach the superhuman. This sign stands as the image of sublimation. The four horse's hooves are planted firmly on the ground while the human part of the centaur faces the Heavens, draws his BOW and points his ARROW at the stars, providing the portrait of something bursting with life and oriented towards its widest fulfilment. The ruler of this sign is, of course, Jupiter, the principle of cohesion and unification, welding into one broad, global synthesis things heavenly and things earthly, flesh and spirit, unconscious and superconscious. A Sagittarian structure is thus related to that of epic poetry, symphonic music, cathedral architecture and the path taken by the pantheistic urge towards integration into the life of the universe. In the typical Sagittarian individual may be seen basically an ego which grows wider or deeper, seeking its own limitations and attempting to overcome them, driven by a species of instinct for the large-scale and grandiose. Hence Sagittarians aspire to heights or space sought in a sort of rapture, which may be the drive to an ideal participation or assimilation in collective life, or else simply rebellion against overweening power, or merely an inflation of the ego which becomes perverted into intoxication with their own importance.

sakaki In Shintō the holiest of all trees is the *sakaki*. This is because the mirror which brought Amaterasu out of her cavern was hung upon a *sakaki* planted for that purpose in front of her refuge. Thus the Sun-bearing *sakaki* acquires an 'axial' character.

Sakaki branches are used bunched as offerings, or in ritual purification. On the one hand the leafy branch is, broadly speaking, associated with primeval innocence, and on the other, because the tree is evergreen, the *sakaki* is seen as a symbol of regeneration and immortality (HERS, OGRJ).

salamander In Classical antiquity, this amphibian, a close relative of the newt, was believed to be able to live in FIRE without being burned up. It was identified with fire, of which it was the living manifestation.

On the other hand, it was believed to be able to put out fire through its extraordinary coldness, and the Ancient Egyptians used the salamander as their hieroglyphic for a man who had died of cold. The French king, François I, took a salamander surrounded by flames as his badge with the device *J'y vis et je l'éteins* ('I live among them and I put them out').

In medieval iconography, the salamander stands for the righteous person who never relinquishes peace of soul or trust in God in the midst of tribulation.

Alchemists regard the salamander as 'the symbol of the Red Stone . . . and call their incombustible sulphur by its name. The salamander, which feeds on fire, and the phoenix, which is reborn from its own ashes, are the two most common symbols of this sulphur' (TERS).

saliva   Saliva is both a creation and a destruction symbol. Christ restored sight to the blind man with his spittle (John 9: 6), while Job (17: 6) complains of the enemies who spit in his face.

Saliva may be seen as a liquid bodily secretion possessing magic or supernatural powers with twin effects, bringing together or sundering, healing or inflicting disease, soothing or insulting.

The Bambara hold that 'to spit is to give one's word, to take one's oath' (DIEB), thus expressing the belief that when saliva is an adjunct to speech it enhances the properties of the word. Countless myths from Africa, the East and from the Americas accord saliva the powers of semen and countless heroes owe their birth to a god's or a hero's spittle.

salmon   In the Celtic world virtually all fish symbolism was concentrated upon the salmon, which was once a common and abundant food-source among North European peoples. Other fishes – with the exception of the WHALE for which they used a word borrowed from the Germanic – were practically speaking non-existent and in literature, unless the word 'fish' is qualified, it is nearly always synonymous with 'salmon'. The salmon is of the same essential nature as the BOAR, in that both are creatures of sacred wisdom. Wells of knowledge recur in Irish literature overhung by hazel- or rowan-bushes and in them live the salmon of knowledge who feed on the scarlet berries or the nuts dropping into the water. Whoever eats the flesh of these fish acquires second-sight and knowledge of all things. This is what happened to Finn as a boy. He was the pupil of a bard or *file* and was busy one day grilling a salmon for his master. As he turned the fish on a spit he burned his finger and sucked it. He instantly became omniscient and was given a prophetic tooth. Thereafter he had only to put his thumb on his wisdom tooth and chew it to become gifted with second-sight. Salmon, again, was the food of Eithne, the allegorical figure of Ireland, after her conversion to Christianity. With the boar and the WREN, the salmon was a particularly druidic creature and one of the symbols of wisdom and spiritual nourishment. It recurs as a primordial creature in the Arthurian tale of Culhwch and Olwen and in the apocryphal account of the Sages of the World in Wales, and in the adventures of Tuan mac Cairill. The body of the salmon is the last stage in his metempsychosis, and after he has lived for a hundred years in this shape, Tuan is caught and taken to the Queen of Ireland. She eats the fish and becomes pregnant by it.

salt   The different aspects of the symbolism of salt arise from the fact that it is produced by the evaporation of sea-water, being, as de Saint-Martin says, 'fire, born of water, both its quintessence and its opposite'. It was with the help of the salt which he had drawn from the primeval waters which he 'churned' with his spear that Izanagi called into being Onogorojima, the first central island. By a reverse process, a grain of salt dropped into and melted in water is a Tantric symbol of the reintegration of the ego into the Universal Self. Salt is both a preservative of food and a corrosive of materials and, as a symbol, is applicable 'to the laws of both physical and moral and spiritual transformation' (Devoucoux). Christ's apostles are like 'the salt of the earth' (Matthew 5: 13), being possessed naturally of its strength and flavour, but also of its powers of preservation against corruption. This is undoubtedly the very quality to which may be attributed its use as a cleansing agent in Shintō. When Izanagi returned from the Kingdom of the Dead, he was purified in salt sea-water. The cleansing and protective properties of salt are used in everyday Japanese life as well as in Shintō, and gathering salt is hedged around with important ceremonies. Salt set in small heaps at the entrance to houses, on the rims of wells, at the corners of the wrestling ring or scattered on the ground after funerals has the power to cleanse objects and places which may accidentally have become defiled.

Salt is a basic seasoning and physiologically essential to food. The Catholic baptismal liturgy alluded to the salt used on food and similarly made the salt of wisdom a symbol of the seasoning of spiritual nourishment. In this context, the penitential character sometimes attributed to salt is at best secondary, at worst mistaken. Following this train of thought, salt was an important ritual element to the Children of Israel, all sacrificial victims needing to be dedicated with salt. Eating salt as a communal action sometimes partook of the qualities of communion and a bond of brotherhood. Salt was shared in just the same way as bread.

By combining, and hence neutralizing, two complementary substances, in addition to being their end product, salt is shaped in cubic crystals. This is the root of its Hermetic symbolism. Salt is the product and the balance of the properties of which it is composed. The notion of 'mediation' expressed in the crystals is linked to that of 'crystallization', solidification and stability (AVAS, DEVA, GUET, HERS, SAIR).

Salt also symbolizes incorruptibility. This is why 'the covenant of salt' (2 Chronicles 13: 5) denotes a covenant which God cannot break. Leviticus 2: 13 refers to the salt with which all sacrificial offerings were to be seasoned. As 'the salt of the covenant', it was an essential ritual provision. The Children of Israel regarded communal eating of bread and salt as the sign of a friendship which could not be broken. The same significance recurs in Philo of Alexandria's description of the food eaten on the Sabbath by the Therapeutae, a pre-Christian Jewish monastic community in Egypt. This comprised bread, salt of hyssop and fresh water. The shew-bread was seasoned with salt and, because of its ritual nature, salt was later adopted by Christians in fasting, baptism and so on (JAUA pp. 47ff.).

Salt may, however, have a quite contrary symbolic meaning and be the very opposite of fertility. In this context, land sprinkled with salt denotes an arid and rock-hard soil. The Romans sprinkled salt over the sites of cities which they had razed to the ground to make permanently barren the soil. Mystics sometimes compare the soul to soil sprinkled with salt, or by contrast to soil made fertile by the dew of grace. William of St Thierry, inspired by Psalm 107: 34, speaks of 'removing the salting brought by the former condemnation'. The soil is barren, William was to add, quoting Jeremiah 17: 6, because it was a salt land. All that has been salted is bitter: salt water is therefore a water of bitterness by contrast with the fresh water which fecundates.

We have already observed that in Japan salt (*shio*) is regarded as a powerful cleaning agent, especially in the form of sea-water. The oldest Japanese Shintō scripture, the *Kojiki*, provides a mythological explanation for this. The great *kami*, Izanaki-no-Mikoto, became defiled when he attempted to see his wife once more in the Kingdom of the Dead. He therefore went and cleansed himself in Tachibana, an inlet in the island of Kyushu. His name and that of his wife mean 'those who engage in mutual seduction'. Some Japanese scatter salt daily on the thresholds of their homes as well as throughout the house once a hated visitor has left it. Sumo wrestlers sprinkle it over the ring before a bout as a sign of purification and in order that the bout shall be fought according to the rules.

Salt was a symbol of friendship and hospitality to the Ancient Greeks, as it was to the Children of Israel and is to Muslims, because it is shared; and a symbol of a binding promise, because it is indestructible. Homer bears witness to its divine nature and its use in sacrifice.

samsāra In Hindu art, this term, meaning literally 'wandering' and deriving from the Sanskrit to denote the cycle of births and deaths and the current of coming into being, is symbolized by a six-, eight- or twelve-spoked WHEEL radiating from a hub, each spoke standing for a particular aspect of life or of the Law. This is 'the stormy sea in which the ignorant happily flounder', a world of disorder, pain and anxiety. The hub stands for the centre, to which the individual awareness should look if it is to find peace. It is the path of wisdom without which none can escape the wheel of existence through an endless succession of reincarnations. Conduct in previous lives thrusts the living into a flow of being which has neither beginning nor end, until they are at last delivered by NIRVANA. The pleasures deriving from *samsāra*, like knowledge of phenomenal or intellectual structures, have no existence of their own.

In Buddhism, a more subtle concept identifies *samsāra* with Nirvana in that both terms denote a subordinate state, but the one is in the shape of an awareness disturbed by sensual cravings and in the aspect of worldly defilement, while the latter conjures the spirit of purity and awareness of the absolute. When the Buddha had achieved this inner level of mysticism, whereby awareness mastered the turmoil of the phenomenal, 'he escaped from being and non-being, which is neither gain nor loss' and duality was entirely obliterated (SILB pp. 258–60).

sanctuary (see also HOLY OF HOLIES; TEMPLE) Sanctuary means a place of secrets. This is certainly the meaning attached to the word by Philo of Alexandria when he speaks of entering the sanctuary as denoting uncovering divine mysteries. This is the name applied to a place which is set apart, taboo, and enshrining some basic treasure.

Celtic sanctuaries were essentially woodland. Caesar described the Gaulish druids as having their holy place in the Carnutian Forest and most written evidence also points to forests (see WOOD). Etymologically *nemeton*, the word for 'sanctuary' common to all Celtic languages, denotes 'a circular space in a wood', which the Romans often translated by the Latin word *lucus* (grove). During the Christian era in Ireland, *nemeth* was the word used for a sacred enclosure, while in eleventh-century Brittany *nemet* meant 'forest'. According to Strabo the supreme council of the Galati met in a *drunemeton* (sanctuary or holy place) in Asia Minor. Etymologically the noun for sanctuary is related to that meaning Heaven (*nemos*). TREES deeply rooted in the Earth and with their branches reaching to the skies were the natural intermediaries between gods and mortals (OGAC 12: pp. 185–97).

sand The symbolism of sand derives from its innumerable grains. The Buddha taught that past ages 'were more in number than the grains of sand from the source to the mouth of the Ganges (*Samyutta-nikāya* 2: 178). A similar idea occurs in Joshua 11: 4: 'And they went out and all their hosts with them, much people, even as the sand that is upon the sea shore in multitude.' The ritual heaping of 'sand-mountains' in Cambodia – clear surrogates for the 'central mountain' – is also linked to the symbol of the multitude, the grains of sand being the numbers of sins for which forgiveness is sought or years of life asked to be enjoyed.

The handfuls of sand ritually scattered in some Shintō ceremonies stand for rain, which is yet another form of a symbol of plenty. In special circumstances, Islam uses sand instead of water for ritual ablution (HERS, PORA, SCHC). It is a cleansing agent since it flows like water and burns like fire.

Shifting and penetrable, sand adopts the shapes of the bodies resting in it and in this respect is a womb symbol. The enjoyment received from walking or lying upon sand or from burying oneself in it – so clearly marked on resort beaches – is unconsciously akin to what the analysts term *regressus ad uterum*. It is effectively a quest for rest, safety and regeneration.

sandal (see also FOOT; SHOE; SLIPPER) Sandals are, as Segalen would phrase it, 'what comes between the surface of the Earth and the live weight of the body', hence the importance of the symbolic act of removing the sandals, a Masonic rite, reminiscent of Moses' action on Mount Sinai when his bare feet made contact with the holy ground. Among the Children of Israel it was once the custom to remove one's sandal and give it to the other party as a token of the binding nature of an agreement (Ruth 4: 7).

To the ancient Taoists, sandals were substitutes for the bodies of the Immortals such as Huang Ti, whose sandals were his sole visible sign, as well as being their means of locomotion through the air. 'Men soled with air', their sandals were winged and may even have been birds. It is easy to imagine Immortal cobblers producing such sandals since they were instruments of Immortality and even symbols of the Elixir of Life.

A symbol of mystic elevation, as well as of swift flight, is provided by the winged sandals of Hermes and Perseus, sometimes depicted with the wings growing from their heels.

sap (see also SOMA) Sap is the plant's nourishment, its vital juice, its very being, and the Sanskrit word *rasa* means both sap and being. From this derives the pure plant symbolism of the Ancient Greeks' ambrosia and nectar, the Zoroastrians' *haoma* and the Hindus' soma. 'I pervade the Earth,' Krishna says in the *Bhagavad Gītā*, 'and my strength sustains all beings. I am soma, juice of juices, which feeds every plant.' It should, nevertheless, be clearly realized that soma is to be taken as a symbol and not as the beverage of immortality itself since the latter can be produced only by spiritual action, a real transubstantiation of plant juices which can only take place in the domain of the god. Soma is identified with the Moon, which is the chalice in which it is offered. To extract soma from the plant itself features a ritual which symbolizes the stripping away of the fleshly covering, liberation and the ejaculation of the self from out of its shell. It is also said that at some time in the past soma was lost and replaced by different substitutes, including wine, itself a plant 'essence'. This must in some way connect with the myth of Dionysos. Yoga identifies soma, as an elixir of life and immortality, with the seminal fluid which has to be raised and inter-fused throughout the body like sap throughout a plant. Even in the West the symbolism of sap was applied to the attainment of spiritual perfection and immortality, Ramon Llull claiming that the Philosopher's Stone brought plants to life. This regeneration of plant life is associated with Spring and here is a recurrence of the favourite notion of Chinese tradition, the sea-sonal cycle, the universal rhythm with its alternation of *yin* and *yang* which is seen in the growth of plants and the circulation of their sap and which should be observed when the vital bodily fluids, breath and semen, are set in motion. This is the way in which the microcosm may conform to the harmony of the macrocosm and become part of it.

Ibn al-Walid's 'divine sap' was the 'column of light', supernatural energy derived from the supreme First Cause, and also gnosis, the food of the intellect, which allows direct access to life divine (COOH, CORT, DANA, ELIY, ELIF, GRAP, GUEM, GUES).

sapphire (see also BLUE) As the supremely celestial jewel, the sapphire absorbs all the symbolism of blue. According to a medieval treatise on precious stones, 'meditation upon this stone carries the soul to heavenly contemplation' (MARA). Again, as in Ancient Greece, so in the Middle Ages there was a belief that sapphires cured eye-diseases and set prisoners free. Alchemists related it to the element Air. The eleventh-century Bishop Marbodius described it in these words: 'Sapphires possess a beauty like that of the heavenly throne; they denote the hearts of the simple, of those moved by a sure hope and of those whose lives shine with their good deeds and virtuousness' (GOUL p. 214). Similarly, Conrad of Haimbord regarded the sapphire as the jewel of hope (ibid. p. 218). Since divine justice was seated in it, such varied powers were attributed to the sapphire as 'to stave off poverty, to protect against the anger of the great, against treason and against miscarriage of justice, to increase valour, joy and vitality, to drive away ill humour and to strengthen the muscles'. In India and Arabia, sapphires are valued as preservatives against the plague, a burning disease linked to chthonian fire (BUDA). The baroque statuette of St George in the Treasury at Munich depicts the saint dressed in sapphires set in gold, defeating an emerald dragon. Christianity took the sapphire as a symbol both of purity and of the enlightening power of the Kingdom of God.

Like all blue stones, in the East, the sapphire is regarded as a powerful charm against the evil eye.

sarcophagus A symbol of the Earth as the receptacle of the life force and the place where it undergoes its metamorphosis, the sarcophagus may be compared with the alchemists' Philosopher's Egg, the Kabbalists' URN and with the mother symbol, in so far as the latter is the nurse and the centre of rest.

Coffin texts are one of the richest sources of our knowledge of Ancient Egypt. The sarcophagus was regarded simultaneously as the sanctuary of life beyond the grave, as a safeguard against the visible and invisible foes surrounding the dead person and as the scene of the transformations which would open the doors to eternal life. It was the dead person's house which he could leave through the door painted on the side and from which he could see out through the eyes painted on the coffin-lid.

In Ancient Greece sarcophagi tended to develop into TEMPLES, with a greater or lesser wealth of architectural adornment, the most famous being the mausolea of Hellenistic Asia Minor. The dead person's life and his ascent into Heaven were depicted in carving.

Satan (see also DEMON; DEVIL)   Among devils and demons, Satan by antonomasia denotes the Adversary, an adversary as proud as he is evil. 'Now there was a day when the sons of God came to present themselves before the Lord, and Satan came also among them. And the Lord said unto Satan, Whence comest thou? Then Satan answered the Lord, and said, From going to and fro in the earth, and from walking up and down in it' (Job 1: 6–7).

The translators of the *Jerusalem Bible* observe that the word 'Satan', the Adversary, is apparently borrowed from legal phraseology (Psalm 109: 6–7). The word came more and more to denote 'an evil being ... and eventually a proper name ... [that] of the power of evil ... synonymous with the dragon, the devil, the serpent ... alternative names or personifications of the evil spirit.... Satan, like the serpent of Genesis 3, tempts man to sin.'

The word reached African tradition via Islam, but in this context he is no anti-god, for nothing can exist which is against Guéno. He is an evil spirit who works through hints and promptings to evil (HAMK p. 37).

In Hermetic tradition,

Satan is another name for SATURN in the guise of the principle of the Spirit taking material shape. The Spirit turns in upon itself, sinking into matter, and from this rises the myth of the fall of Lucifer, the bearer of light.... The myth of Satan epitomizes the problem of what may be termed evil.... Its existence, relative to human ignorance, is no more than a distortion of primal light which, although buried in matter, shrouded in darkness and reflected in the turmoil of human awareness, perpetually struggles to break free. Through the suffering which it causes, this distortion may nevertheless become the means through which a true scale of values gains recognition and the starting-point for the transformation of awareness which, from then on, becomes able to reflect without distortion primeval Light.

(SENZ p. 315, n. 417)

The Cathars regarded Satan as the Demiurge who created the world. Satan was visible and spoke through his prophets since the God of Goodness was invisible to human eyes. There are undoubtedly links between the ideas of Jewish ascetics of the twelfth century and the teachings of the Cathars and between the latter and the Book of Bahir in repect of Satan's cosmic role, and between the demonology of the Cathars and that of the Kabbalists in respect of Satan's wives. LILITH, especially, was held traditionally to be the wife of Satan. Despite the inevitable contacts between Provençal Jewish scholars and the Cathars, the former were all too well aware of the gap which separated them from the Cathars' demonology and their belief that the world was so evil that it could only be Satan's creation (SCHK pp. 250ff.).

satire The Ancient Egyptians used satire to mock the behaviour of those who followed different trades and professions, from those of scribe or government official to those of baker, cobbler, blacksmith and so on. This satire was a source of inspiration to the writers of the Old Testament. In Ecclesiasticus 38: 24ff. there is a prominent example of their tendency to show that while manual work is essential to the social fabric, it monopolizes the spirit in worldly concerns, so that wisdom is the fruit of leisure alone. Such satire was motivated by moral and social concern and by an extremely aristocratic and priestly concept of wisdom.

In the Celtic world satire embodied a very different power. It was a verse incantation rather than a poem in the true sense of the word, which the Irish bard or druid uttered against whoever had refused his requests. (Generally speaking this was some king.) The semi-automatic effect of satire, even when unprovoked, all literary sources confirm, was for three boils to appear on the victim's face. The latter was then forced either to die of shame or to abdicate, since the physical deformity disqualified him from office. However, even without the physical blemish, the Fomorian king Bres' fortunes took a sudden turn for the worse when the bard Cairpre, whom he had entertained meanly, composed a satire against him. Luaine, the wife or concubine of Conchobar, King of Ulster, died of shame because the druid Aithirne and his sons uttered the all-powerful spell (*glam dicinn*) which raised three pimples – Shame, Guilt and Ugliness – on her face, she having refused them her favours. The word for the specialist in incantation, *cainte*, is related to that for 'song' and 'complaint' (in the legal sense), but the latter was one of the weapons of the entire priestly caste and symbolized their fighting power as magicians (OGAC 16: pp. 441–6; 17: pp. 143–4).

Saturn Contrary to the somewhat superficial views of some commentators, it was only at a comparatively late period that the Romans identified their god, Saturn, with the Greek god, CRONOS. Saturn's association with King Janus, who appears to have welcomed him to Rome, left behind memories of a golden age and, in this context, he symbolizes the culture-hero and especially the one who teaches the arts of agriculture. At his festival, the Saturnalia, the social order was reversed and slaves ruled their masters, the latter serving their slaves at table. This may perhaps have been a faint echo of the fact that Saturn had dethroned his father Uranus (OURANOS), before being dethroned in his turn by his son Zeus or Jupiter. Similarly, such ceremonies might be interpreted in the psychoanalytic sense of the Oedipus complex, the overthrow of the god, father or master. For the brief period of the Saturnalia the people imposed upon their leaders the fate which the latter had imposed upon their fathers, and the fate which Saturn had held in store for his own father.

The Sumerians and Babylonians regarded the planet Saturn as that of righteousness and justice (DHOB p. 94) and here we find echoes of the significance it must originally have had in Rome. Saturn was apparently

connected with the Sun's office of fecundation, of government and of continuity, one ruler succeeding another as season succeeds season.

In Hermeticism, while mere chemists regarded Saturn as lead, to philosophers Saturn was the colour black, the colour of matter after solution and
putrefaction, or else of common copper, first of metals, or of Ramon Llull's
azoic vitriol, which separates metals (PERD). All these are images of the
office of divider, which is both an end and a beginning, the halting of one
cycle and the beginning of a fresh one, the stress being laid more strongly
upon the break in or slowing of development.

In astrology, Saturn embodies the principle of concentration, contraction,
fixation, condensation and inertia. In short it is a power which tends to
crystallize and to set the existing order of things in a rigid frame, and thus
to be opposed to all change. That extraordinary powers of working evil are
attributed to the planet is only just, since it symbolizes obstacles of all sorts,
barriers, dearth, misfortune, impotence and paralysis. Its good influence
provides a depth of penetration which is the fruit of profound reflection and
constant striving, and corresponds with loyalty, constancy, knowledge, self-
denial, chastity and piety. Its two Houses – Capricorn and Aquarius – are
opposed to those of the stars and therefore to the light and joy of being.
Physically, Saturn rules the skeletal frame.

Saturn is the astrologers' 'wizard' planet with the baleful fleeting light
which, from earliest times, has conjured up the disappointments and trials
of life and which has been depicted allegorically as a skeleton sharpening
a scythe. At the base of the biological and psychological functions which
Saturn symbolizes is to be found the phenomenon of renunciation, the
succession of trials of separation which mark out the life-cycle of every
individual, from the severing of the new-born baby's umbilical cord to the
loss of natural faculties in old age, via all the different surrenders, self-
denials and sacrifices which life itself imposes. Throughout this process,
Saturn is thus given the task of setting us free from the internal prison of
our animal nature and our worldly ties and striking off the fetters of living
instinctively and by our passions. In this sense Saturn provides a strong
restraining influence which benefits the spirit and is the motive force of
intellectual, moral and spiritual life. A Saturnine complex is a reaction
displayed in a refusal to give up whatever one has become attached to in
the course of one's life, a fixation which crystallizes in childhood, from
weaning and from the different situations producing affective frustration
which lead to the stimulation of greed in the varied shapes of bulimia, lust,
jealousy, avarice, ambition and pedantry, linking with the cannibalistic aspect of the myth of Cronos devouring his own offspring. The reverse of this
Janus-face displays, therefore, exaggerated renunciation in the varied forms
of self-effacement, impoverishment of the ego, insensitivity, coldness and
detachment verging, in extreme cases, upon pessimism, melancholy and
renunciation of life itself.

scales Scales are the acknowledged symbol of justice, moderation, prudence and balance because their purpose corresponds precisely with the
weighing of actions or activities. When associated with the sword, scales
still symbolize Justice, but in double harness with Truth. On the social level,

they are the emblems of administrative and military duties, those of kingly power and one characteristic, in India, of the Kshatriya caste. This is also why scales, in this instance associated with the potter's wheel, were one of the mandarin's attributes in China. When depicted in the lodges of Chinese secret societies, scales stood for Justice and Righteousness.

'In the City of Willows all is fairly weighed' takes on a special significance if we remember that the City of Willows corresponds to the changeless Centre.

It is simply a matter of extending the foregoing meanings to divine justice to make scales the symbol of the Last Judgement. In Ancient Egypt, Osiris weighed the souls of the dead; in Christian iconography, St Michael, the Archangel of the day of Judgement, holds a pair of scales; the scales of the Last Judgement are also alluded to in the Koran; in Tibet, the pans of the scales used to weigh the individual's good and bad deeds are loaded with white and black pebbles respectively. In Persia, the angel Rashnu stood beside Mithras and weighed souls at the Bridge of Fate, while a Greek vase depicts Hermes weighing the souls of Achilles and Patroclus.

In Ancient Greece, Themis, the goddess who ruled the world in accordance with a universal law, represents the scales with their concomitant notions not only of justice, but of moderation, order and balance as well. According to Hesiod, the goddess was the daughter of Ouranos (Uranus: Heaven) and Gaia (Earth) and therefore of matter and of spirit, of the visible and of the invisible. In Homer she is viewed as a symbol of Fate, as the battle between Achilles and Hector shows:

When for the fourth time they were come to the springs, lo then the Father [Zeus] lifted on high his golden scales, and set therein two Fates of grievous death, one for Achilles, and one for horse-taming Hector; then he grasped the balance by the midst and raised it; and down sank the day of doom of Hector, and departed unto Hades; and Phoebus Apollo left him.

(*Iliad* 22: 208–13)

Since the notion of fate bears with it that of the individual's life-span, it is easy to understand why the scales were as much the emblem of Saturn or Cronus. The latter, as both judge and executioner, measured out human life and also held the scales, whether they balanced or not, between years and seasons, days and nights. It should be noted that the zodiacal sign of the scales, LIBRA, brings in the Autumnal equinox (the Spring equinox being brought in by Aries, the Ram) when day and night are of equal length and thus balance. It is also noticeable that the movements of the scale-pans, like those of the Sun in its annual cycle, correspond to the relative 'weight' of *yin* and *yang*, of darkness and light, something running without any major difference from Ancient Greece to Ancient China. When the pans are in balance (at the equinoxes), the pointer on the scales, or the sword which is identical with it, becomes the symbol of the changeless Centre. The polar axis which stands for it points to the Great Bear which, in Ancient China, was called the Jade Scales.

Sometimes, however, the two pans of the celestial scales were represented by the Great and Little Bear. Ritual texts of Chinese secret societies add that the scales in the City of Willows 'are magnificent and shine like stars and constellations' of which they are effectively the reflection at the foot of the Cosmic Axis. Furthermore the Sanskrit word for scales, *tūla*, is the same as that for the 'Holy Land', located in the north, that is at the Pole (see THULE).

Scales, yet again, are the balance of natural forces and of what Devoucoux terms of 'all things made to be made one', of which earlier symbols were rocking-stones.

Bringing matter and time and the visible and the invisible into balance, it is hardly surprising that both hermeticism and alchemy should be familiar with what was termed 'knowledge' or 'mastery of the scales', since this 'knowledge' was that of the correspondences between the material and the spiritual universe, between Heaven and Earth. Muslim esotericism transposed these scales (*mizān*) to the planes of language and writing, the 'scales of letters', striking the same balance between letters and language as that between what the former denoted and their essential nature. To bring the beam of such scales to the horizontal was undoubtedly to have attained to supreme wisdom (CORT, CORJ, DEVA, EVAB, GUEM, SOUJ).

Psychostasis, or the weighing of souls, is a famous subject of Ancient Egyptian theology and art, symbolizing God's judgement of the individual after death and all the formidable apparatus of justice. The scene is generally set as follows: the scales stand in the centre with the symbol of the dead person's conscience, the heart, enclosed in an urn, in one pan. In the other is the goddess Maat's OSTRICH-feather, the symbol of justice. The IBIS-headed god, Thoth, stands on the right ready to record the judgement, while on the left stands the JACKAL-headed god, Anubis, holding the dead person's hand and leading him towards the scales. In his other hand the god holds an ANKH, the symbol of the eternal life which the dead person hopes to obtain. Anubis casts a keen eye upon the beam of the scales while the dead person makes a confession. This is really a negative confession in the sense that the sins listed are those which have not been committed. At the God's feet the CROCODILE Devourer, with gaping jaws and a group of hippopotami behind it, waits for Thoth to give his verdict. If the feather is heavier, the dead person is saved, but if it is his conscience, then he is doomed. The scene sometimes takes place in the presence of the great gods, Ra, Osiris and Isis, assisted by forty-two assessors armed with knives, the latter being the canonical number of sins. Psychostasis means that no human action is insignificant in God's sight. It symbolizes judgement, but, at a deeper level, responsibility as well.

Scales are often depicted on Christian graves, Judeo-Christian thought on this subject being the same as that of pagan antiquity. Several Old Testament writers compare notions of good and evil with those of scales. Thus Job 31: 6: 'Let me be weighed in an even balance, that God may know my integrity.'

Good means what has struck a balance between the internal and the external. In Jewish thought devils were always regarded as being powerless against what had achieved this balance.

Knowledge is an exact and strict science. It weighs in the balance. This meaning comes out in Ecclesiasticus (16: 24–5): 'My son, hearken unto me, and learn knowledge. . . . I will shew forth doctrine in weight, and declare his knowledge exactly.'

Strict control is as strong an element of scholarship as it is in the weighing of souls or of metals.

The balance, which scales symbolize, is an indicator of a return to oneness, that is to say, to latency, since everything which is manifested is subject to dualism and to contrarieties. The balance achieved when the two pans of the scale hang level signifies the attainment of something beyond the confrontations which are part of time and space and matter. If we start from the centre of the scales and the fixity of their pointer we can see these confrontations as complementary aspects. The Kabbalah says that before the Creation, 'the Ancient of Days held the scales.' In his commentary on this passage, Enel said 'that before the manifestation of the act which set Creation in motion, the Latent had envisaged the duplication which was to give birth to all successive separations right down to those of the cell.' The scales, with its two pans, stands for this duplication.

scapegoat The first Old Testament mention of the scapegoat occurs in Leviticus. The High Priest was to receive two goats as a sin offering from the Children of Israel. Lots were to be drawn and one of them was to be sacrificed, the other set free, but it was a freedom burdened by the sins of the people. The latter was brought out of the Tabernacle, laden with the sins of the people, and taken either into the Wilderness and there abandoned or, according to other authorities, thrown over the edge of a cliff. 'And Aaron shall bring the goat upon which the Lord's lot fell, and offer him for a sin offering; But the goat on which the lot fell to be [Azazel's], shall be presented alive before the Lord, to make an atonement with him, and let him go for a scapegoat into the wilderness' (Leviticus 16: 9–10).

The despatch of the goat to Azazel exhibits archaic characteristics foreign to the Law of Moses. Azazel is the name of the demon which dwells in the Wilderness, the accursed land which God did not make fertile and to which Jehovah's enemies were exiled. The animal sent to Azazel is not sacrificed to him. The goat driven into the Wilderness, the demon's abode, simply stands for the demoniac share of the people, the burden of their sins, and this the goat carries into the place of punishment, the Wilderness. Meanwhile another goat is actually sacrificed to Jehovah in ritual atonement.

A goat was sacrificed to Jehovah for 'the sins of the people' and sprinkling with its blood was regarded as cleansing. On the other hand, the scapegoat bearing the people's sins suffered the ordeal of banishment, separation and rejection, symbolizing the condemnation and rejection of sin and its permanent removal. The same underlying motives recur in the rite of purification following healing from leprosy. The beneficiary offered two birds; one of them was immediately sacrificed, while the other was sprinkled with its blood and promptly released (Leviticus 14: 4–7). The scapegoat carried evil away and it was no longer a burden upon a sinful people. Individuals are termed 'scapegoats' in so far as they are charged with the crimes of others without being able to appeal to justice, offer anything in their defence or be lawfully condemned. The tradition of the scapegoat is almost worldwide; it occurs on all continents and extends to Japan. It stands for the deep-seated human tendency to project one's own guilt upon someone else, thus appeasing one's own conscience which always requires some victim to bear responsibility and punishment.

scarab The scarab is best known as an Egyptian symbol; as such it symbolized both the Sun's cycle and, at the same time, resurrection. It was the image of the self-renewing Sun, the god who returns, and in Ancient Egyptian painting scarabs are depicted carrying huge solar balls. As the Sun returns from the shades of night, so the scarab was believed to be reborn from its own corruption; or else it rolled a fiery ball in which it had deposited its own seed. Since it symbolized the daily and nightly cycle of the Sun, it was also often called Khepri, god of the rising Sun. The Egyptian hieroglyphic of the scarab with legs outstretched corresponds to the verb *kheper*, meaning something like 'to come into existence by assuming a given form'. Scarabs were also worn 'as cheap protective AMULETS, for the insect had concealed in himself the power of eternal renewal of life.' Scarabs were given the spreading wings of hawks, like those on Tutankhamen's coffin, and used as talismans, being invoked in the words of a spell in *The Book of the Righteous* as 'the god who is in my body, my creator who maintains my limbs'.

In depictions of psychostasis (see under SCALES) the dead person's heart bore witness to his morality and judged his conscience. The accused had, therefore, to conciliate this portion of himself since it could determine his salvation or his damnation. Thus, on the deceased's heart, was placed an amulet shaped like a scarab to prevent it bearing witness against the dead person. 'The heart was the conscience; it dictated a person's actions and rebuked him; it was an independent being of a superior essence dwelling in the body. Written on a coffin in the Vienna Museum are the words: "A man's heart is his own god"' (POSD pp. 61, 259–60).

A further source of symbolism is the habit of the scarab, or dung beetle, of rolling its ball, an image of the World Egg from which all life and regular manifestation arose. The scarab was thus regarded as being self-generated, and the same explanation was given in China. 'The scarab rolls its ball,' we read in *The Secret of the Golden Flower*, 'and in that ball life is engendered, the fruit of its undivided effort of concentration.' If an embryo could be generated in the dung-ball, why, they concluded, could not concentration of the spirit give birth to the Embryo of Immortality in the 'celestial heart'?

Taoist commentators cite the activities of the dung-beetle as an example of the skill of what is to all appearances skill-less, and of the perfection of what seems imperfect, of which Lao Tzu spoke (ch. 45), and which are the criteria of Wisdom (GRIF, SOUN, WIET).

A little-known passage in *The Book of Chilam Balam*, recounting Mayan religious tradition, depicts the scarab as the filth of the Earth, in both material and moral terms, which, despite this, is called to become divine. 'Two scarabs then appeared, evil creatures who had sowed the seed of sin within us, the filth of the Earth ... Wait, speak and you will become the gods of this Earth.' It is not beyond the bounds of probability that the authors of this satire, descended from the natives who had fought against the Christianity preached by their conquerors, depicted these foreign priests in the shape of invading dung-beetles.

sceptre Sceptres are an extension of the arm and signs of power and authority. To break one's sceptre is to abdicate.

Above all sceptres symbolize supreme authority, being

small-scale models of the ruler's staff. Being a pure vertical enables the sceptre to symbolize the individual as an individual, and then the superiority of that individual in the office of ruler and, finally, the power received from on high. The sceptre of Western monarchs is a small-scale version of the COLUMN of the world with which other civilizations identify their priests and kings.

(CHAS p. 377)

A majestic figure of Zeus was carved on the pediment of his temple at Olympia and, in the middle of this temple, stood the richly decorated throne on which sat his statue of gold and ivory. Phidias had shown him as master of the universe, holding in his left hand a sceptre tipped by an EAGLE. In Greek tradition, sceptres symbolized the right to deliver judgement rather than the soldier's authority as such. In Rome, the sceptre was to become part of the panoply of the consuls.

The Egyptian goddesses' magic sceptres were symbols of joy, of joy in being able to accomplish whatever they wished. The tip of the Pharaoh's sceptre was carved in the likeness of the face of the god Set, whom Plutarch made the incarnation of evil, to be compared with Typhon and Baal.

Certainly, the Red God was never the personification of friendliness. The Typhonian animal was traditionally associated with the representations of storms and ideas of violence. In the ancient myths he was certainly the murderer of Osiris and the formidable rival of the young Horus whose eye he tore out .... [But it was he, too, who] stabbed the horrible Apopis with his lance. [Later] he was not the personification of dryness, but the patron of the produce of oases.

(POSD p. 259)

At the tip of the Pharaoh's sceptre he doubtless preserved this dual symbolism of prince of fertility, as well as of a prince who was merciless in his wrath and who punished his personal enemies as severely as those of his people. Power was in his hand and he could launch it like a thunderbolt.

schekina God's dwelling-place on Earth which, in Talmudic and Jewish Rabbinical literature, stands for God himself in his actions carried out on Earth and especially in Israel. Where the Old Testament alludes to the 'face' of God, Rabbinical literature uses the term *schekina*.

In the Kabbalah the meaning of *schekina* is different and it is used of the female element in God. The third *sefirah* displays the power of the Demiurge as that of a higher form of mother or *schekina*. From her seven powers emanated, of which the first six stand for the chief limbs of the original higher form of man. They were regarded as the phallic substructure which stood symbolically for justice (*Zaddik*). God and the first man retained their procreative powers within well-defined limits. God animates all living beings with this life force which is, in any case, confined within his own Law. *Schekina* is also identified with the Children of Israel and with the soul (SCHK pp. 123–4).

scissors Scissors were an attribute of Atropos, the Fate with the task of cutting the thread of life. They are a symbol of the possibility of sudden death and of the fact that life depends upon the gods.

Scorpio (23 October–21 November) The eighth sign of the ZODIAC, mid-way through the three-monthly period of Autumn when gales blow the yellowing leaves away and animals and trees prepare for a fresh existence. Scorpio has Mars for its ruler and is a symbol simultaneously of resistance, of fermentation and of death, of dynamism, endurance and struggle.

Scorpio conjures up a picture of the natural world at Hallowe'en, with fallen leaves and hoar-frost, of the return to the chaos of unformed matter, while below the soil makes ready to spring to life once more. It is the 'watery' quarter between the spring-waters of Cancer and the waters drawn from the ocean of Pisces, that is the deep, standing waters of silent stagnation. Scorpio, the black scorpion which flees the light and lives concealed, is equipped with a poisoned sting. Together they comprise a world of gloomy properties which rightly conjure visions of the torments and tragedies of life, including the absurd, annihilation and death itself. Hence the sign has for its ruler Mars as well as Pluto, that mysterious and pitiless power of shadows, Hell and internal darkness. This takes us to the core of the Freudian sado-anal complex, but the psychotic properties of the anus combine with those of the sexual organs. A dialectic of destruction and creation, of death and resurrection, of damnation and salvation takes shape since Scorpio is the love-song on the battlefield and the war-cry on the fields of love. Against such a red and black background, the individual becomes rooted in the convolutions of his inhibitions and is only really an individual when torn by the brutal fits of the inner demon which thirsts, not for well-being, but for fuller being, even if this involves the bitter anguish of living torn between divine vocation and diabolic temptation. This volcanic nature makes the Scorpio-type a bird which can only confidently stretch its wings in the midst of gales, its temperament being storm and its environment tragedy.

scorpion Many Africans use a euphemism for the scorpion since, like the hyena, the insect is evil and to use its true name would be to release its powers against oneself.

According to a Malian legend, the scorpion said:

I am neither an elemental spirit nor a demon. I am a creature which brings death to whoever touches me. I have two horns and a tail which I brandish. My horns are called savagery and hate and the dagger in my tail is called the avenging stabber. I give birth only once. Pregnancy, a sign of increase among all other creatures, is for me the signal of forthcoming death.

(HAMK p. 10)

With its tail ending in a poison-sac feeding a sting which is permanently unsheathed and ready to strike death into anyone who touches it, the scorpion's nocturnal aspect is the embodiment of aggression and of a malevolence which always lurks ready to kill. In its diurnal aspect it symbolizes a mother's self-denial and self-sacrifice, since legend affirms that her young come to birth by digging through and eating their way out of her belly (HAMK p. 60).

The scorpion was a Mayan god of hunting and was used in their hiero-glyphics as a symbol of repentance and also of surgical blood-letting (THOH). The Dogon, too, associate it with surgical operations, the removal of the clitoris in fact. The poison-sac and sting symbolize the organ, the poison being the blood and liquid released by the operation (GRIE). In this context, the scorpion stands for a woman's second (male) soul, but else-where the scorpion, having eight legs, is the guardian of twins, with eight limbs in all. 'Nobody can touch them without risking being stung' (GRIE). These two symbolic meanings given to the scorpion are not contradictory, but complementary, for, as Griaule explains, 'the birth of twins is an occa-sion of considerable importance. It repeats the occasion when the first woman gave birth and her clitoris was changed into a scorpion.' (In those days circumcision was not practised until after a woman had given birth.)

In Ancient Egypt, this dangerous insect's shape was used for one of the oldest hieroglyphics and its name was borne by one of the pre-dynastic kings, 'King Scorpion'. Some of the Pharoah's SCEPTRES were tipped by scorpions with the head of Isis. Divine honours were paid to the insect in the shape of the goddess Selket, 'a fundamentally benevolent person in as much as she gave power over her earthly manifestations to the "Charmers of Selket", an ancient body of sorcerer-healers' (POSD p. 254). In this context the scorpion possesses all the symbolic ambivalence of the SERPENT.

In Ancient Greek tradition, the scorpion avenged Artemis (the Roman Diana), the eternally youthful virgin huntress, archetypal man-hater. Of-fended when Orion offered violence to her, the goddess had a scorpion sting him in the heel. For his services, the scorpion was turned into a con-stellation. Orion was also sent up to Heaven and became a constellation, too. This resulted in the saying that 'Orion is constantly running away from the Scorpion' (GRID). The scorpion in this context was regarded as the instrument of divine vengeance.

scythe   A symbol of death in so far as the scythe, like death, brings all things down to the same level. It was, however, only early in the fifteenth century that the scythe first started to be seen, when held by a SKELETON, as standing for the pitiless equalizer. In both Old and New Testaments it is the sickle which will be used to cut down the tares, not the scythe. It is, how-ever, depicted as an instrument of punishment, and therefore one which chooses its victims, rather than the general instrument of death which strikes indiscriminately. Saturn, the old, lame god of time, is generally the one to handle sickle or scythe as the blind instrument which cuts down all living things. The change from SICKLE to scythe reflects the development of farm implements. Nevertheless it should be observed that the thirteenth major arcanum of the Tarot, Death, depicts a scythe which cuts down not life but worldly illusions. This agrees perfectly with the symbolic meaning of the number THIRTEEN – the beginning, not the end of a cycle – and gives the implement positive properties showing it, in this context, to be the instru-ment which opens the door to the realm of true and invisible reality, the *haqq* of the Sufi.

sea   Because of their apparently limitless extent, seas and oceans are im-ages of the primal undifferentiated state of primeval formlessness. Such was the ocean upon which Vishnu slumbered. It was *arnava*, the dark and shapeless sea, the LOWER WATERS over which the Spirit of God broods and from which arises the primeval burgeoning of EGG, LOTUS, REED or ISLAND. The boar (*Varāha-avatāra*) brought the Earth up to its surface; Izanami stirred it with his spear and by coagulation formed the first island; the *deva* and the *asura* 'churned' it and from it distilled *amrita*, the draught of immortality.

Seas are also symbols of the Upper Waters, of Divine Being, of Nirvana and of Tao. This is expressed in the writings of the Pseudo-Dionysius the Areopagite, of Tauler, Angelus Silesius ('the uncreated sea of the One God'), Master Eckhart ('the unfathomable sea of the nature of God') and even in those of Dante and of Sufism. The Upanishads elaborate on this theme as does Buddhism – the dew-drop dissolves in the sparkling sea – and in Taoism the *Tao Te Ching* (ch. 32) speaks of the Tao being to the world what the sea is to rivers. 'All waters flow into it without filling it: all waters flow from it without draining it. This is why I go to the sea' (Chuang Tzu ch. 12). It is, furthermore, the 'Ocean of Joy' to the Béguines, Ibn Mashish's 'Ocean of Divine Solitude' and al-Jīlī's 'Ocean of the Glory of God'. In Tantrism, the ocean is the Universal Spirit, *Paramātmā*, into which is mingled the drop of the water of life, *jīva*, or *jīvātmā*, the individual soul. In Mahāyāna the ocean is Dharma-kāya, the Enlightened Body of the Buddha which mingles with *bodhi*, primeval intellect. Its calm surface symbolizes both emptiness (*shunyāta*) and Enlightenment. According to Shabistarī, the ocean is the heart; its shores, gnosis; its shells, language, and the pearls which they contain, the 'knowledge of the heart', the hidden meaning of language.

But when the sea is stormy, to reach the further shore entails a dangerous crossing of its treacherous stretch of water. It is Shankarāchārya's 'sea of passions'; the ocean of the world of the soul crossed in stages in St Isaac of Nineveh's allegory; the 'ocean of existences' represented by the lake of the temple of Neak-Pean at Angkor; and the sea of the realm of the senses in the *Samyutta-Nikāya* (4: 157): 'Whoever crosses the sea with its sharks and demons, its terrifying waves which are so hard to surmount, may be said to have gone to the ends of the Earth and have departed to the beyond.' (AVAS, COEA, GRAR, DANA, CORM, CORT, GOVM, HOUD, JILH, SILI)

In Ancient Egyptian mythology, the coming into being of Earth and life was conceived in terms of emergence from the ocean, just as mudbanks emerged from the falling floodwaters of the Nile. Thus creation, including even that of the gods themselves, arose from the primeval waters. The first god was called 'the earth which emerged' (POSD p. 67).

The Ancient Greeks and Romans offered HORSES and bulls, themselves symbols of fertility, in sacrifice to the sea.

But monsters rise from its depths, and so the sea is an image of the unconscious which has currents of its own which may be either lethal or regenerative.

The sea played a highly important part in Celtic traditional concepts. The gods – Tuatha Dé Danann, People of the Goddess Dana – reached Ireland by sea and it was by sea that the Otherworld was reached. One of the most notable mythological themes relative to water symbolism is that of the child

who is cast adrift. When Morann, son of the usurper, Cairpre, was born, he
was a dumb monster who was cast into the sea. The waters broke the mask
which covered his face; he was saved by servants and became a famous
judge during the reign of his father's lawful successor. Dylan eil Ton ('Dylan,
Son of the Waves'), son of the Welsh goddess Arianrhod ('Silver Wheel')
entered the sea as soon as he was born and swam like a fish. Merlin, the
enchanter, was *Mori-genos*, 'born from the sea', and Pelagius (Morien) was
Mori-dunon, 'fortress of the sea'. One of the epithets of the Gaulish Apollo
was *Moritasgus*, 'he who comes [?] from over the sea'. The sea partakes of
the divine property of giving and taking life (OGAC 2: pp. 1–5).

Manannan, the Dagda's brother and lord of the Otherworld in the Irish
pantheon, was called Mac Lir, 'son of the sea'. Sea symbolism is linked with
that of water in the context of the origin of all life. However, neither Manannan nor the Welsh god, Manawyddan, who corresponds to him, was a sea-
god in the sense sometimes attached to them by modern researchers. He is
in fact linked to the primeval state through the sea symbolism which reinforces his mythological office.

The Old Testament was certainly to some extent familiar with the Eastern symbolism of the primeval waters, sea or ABYSS, of which even the gods
stood in awe. 'In Babylonian cosmogonies Tiamat (the Sea) co-operated in
the birth of the gods and was then conquered and subdued by one of their
number. The imagination of the people, or of poets, seized upon this story:
Yahweh became the conqueror who then set Chaos in order and ever after
held the sea and its monsters in control' (BIBJ, Job 7: 12). This is why, in
the Old Testament, the sea is so often a symbol of God's enmity. Ezekiel
prophesied against Tyre foretelling that the Lord would 'bring up the deep
upon thee [Tyre], and great waters shall cover thee' (26: 19). In the New
Testament, St John rhapsodizes on the new world in which there will be no
more sea (Revelation 21: 1).

This is also the reason motivating the old Jewish writers to state plainly
that the sea is part of God's creation (Genesis 1: 10); that it should submit
to his commands (Jeremiah 31: 35); that he could dry it up to allow the
Children of Israel to pass through the midst of it (Exodus 14: 15ff.); and that
he could raise or calm storms upon it (Jonah 1: 4). The sea thus became the
symbol of creation assuming the place of, or being taken for, its creator.

The Christian mystics were others who took the sea as a symbol of the
human heart as the seat of the passions. In the dedication to his *Moralia
super Job*, St Gregory the Great describes his entry into the monastic life
as 'an escape from the shipwreck of life'. According to the twelfth-century
Aelred of Rievaulx, a sea lay between God and ourselves. This denoted the
present age. Some drowned in it, others crossed it. A boat was needed to
cross the sea: the married state was a leaky skiff, but the life of the Cistercian
was like a stout ship.

In sum, the sea is a symbol of the dynamism of life. Everything comes
from the sea and everything returns to it. It is a place of birth, transformation and rebirth. With its tides, the sea symbolizes a transitory condition
between shapeless potentiality and formal reality, an ambivalent situation
of uncertainty, doubt and indecision which can end well or ill. Hence the
sea is an image simultaneously of death and of life.

seal (animal) When regarded as a slippery, smooth-furred creature which shuns humans and slips through their fingers, the seal is the symbol of a virginity inspired not by higher motives, but by fear of self-surrender and by lack of love. Thus, in Greek legends, nymphs pursued by gods changed themselves into seals. The sea-god, Poseidon, had flocks of seals of which he made the minor deity, Proteus, the shepherd, the latter having the power to change himself into whatever shape he wished. Today, seal symbolism may be described with greater clarity. Seals symbolize the unconscious or at least that portion of it which derives from repression, carefully controlled by Proteus, but, like its shepherd, capable of taking any form it chooses.

Legends also tell of female seals stripping off their skins on the sea-shore and walking the sands in the shapes of lovely women.

seal (artefact) (See also TATTOO; for Solomon's Seal see STAR OF DAVID) In ancient Eastern civilizations, the seal was an item of major importance. It was used in many spheres and upon numerous occasions.

Kings put their seals upon documents setting out their decrees. Seals are thus marks of power and of authority. A seal has the force of a signature. Seals authenticate public or private contracts. They reserve such documents as wills for future publication, hence to seal means to lock away, to lay aside and preserve. Seals thus become symbols of secrecy.

Seals mark people or things as the unquestionable property of those whose stamp they bear and under whose protection they stand by the same right. Seals are symbols of lawful ownership.

These different uses are the theme so richly developed in symbolic variations.

Thus St Paul regarded the church in Corinth as the legitimation of his apostolate 'for the seal of mine apostleship are ye in the Lord' (1 Corinthians 9: 2). The Father marked the Son with his seal, indicating thereby that he had chosen him and sent him in his name to bestow eternal life (John 6: 22).

God seals his instructions (Job 33: 16); he sets a seal upon the stars forbidding them thereby to show themselves (Job 6: 7). He commands Daniel to seal his visions, in other wrds, to keep them secret (Daniel 12: 4; see also Revelation 22: 10). On the other hand St John (Revelation 22: 10) was not to seal the revelations made to him since they were of immediate effect.

Rabbinical writers regarded the seal as the symbol of circumcision, initiating the individual into God's people. St Paul takes this a step further by explaining that true spiritual circumcision is a seal of membership of the righteous (Romans 4: 11) and that the Holy Spirit may be termed a seal in so far as it is a pledge of salvation (2 Corinthians 1: 22). Hence it is a short step from this to acknowledgement that the divine seal possesses semi-magical properties, a step often taken at different and widely separated periods of time, as witness the seal-charms bearing the Tetragrammaton (God's name in Hebrew). That these properties were undoubtedly those of preservatives against evil is apparent from Mandean and Gnostic writings.

God marks individuals with his seal (Ezekiel 9: 4; Revelation 7: 3ff.) showing thereby that they belong to him and are under his protection. In this context, the author of Revelation would seem in all probability to have in mind the letter X (that is to say *chi*, the initial letter of Christ's name in

Greek). Even in this context, the word 'seal' begins to return to a realist meaning without, however, losing any of the symbolic load it has gathered on the way.

In fact, while Christianity subsequently continued to use the word 'seal' in the sense or senses indicated above, it began to use it as well with a new and technical meaning. Hermas states that the seal is water, and by water should be understood the water of baptism. Irenaeus, Tertullian and Clement of Alexandria all understood this sense of the word, so that in the end 'seal' was made the technical term for baptism. Was it not this which marked the individual as belonging to God, who justified and protected that person? It is quite possible that, very early on, the ceremony of baptism itself incorporated that clear rite of deposition to be found at the end of the second century in the *Apostolic Tradition* of Hippolytus. (See, for example, baptismal rituals and liturgies.)

The Gnostics were to speculate about the symbol and to see in the seal the mysterious means whereby the soul was safeguarded during its journey through the lower worlds to the light on high.

To close this line of thought, mention should be made of an interesting development of the seal symbol by Philo of Alexandria, who regarded the seal as the idea, the model, which stamps the world of the senses. The primeval seal was, therefore, the ideal world, the Word of God (*On the Creation of the World* 25). Plato's influence is all too evident.

Lastly, there is a passage in Revelation which speaks of a book with seven seals (Revelation 5ff.), of which the interpretation raises difficult questions. To determine the symbolism of the image, one has first to decide on what the book represents – is it the Book of Fate, God's testament, or the Old Testament, hitherto misinterpreted? Whatever the document may be, it should be noted that it can only be opened by a person invested with absolute divine authority – the Lamb, Christ himself.

The betrothed in the Song of Solomon says of his beloved: 'Set me as a seal upon thine heart, as a seal upon thine arm: for love is strong as death.' The commentators in the *Jerusalem Bible* remark: 'The seal, attesting the wishes of its owner, here symbolizes the wishes of Yahweh, i.e. the Law' and Jehovah is a jealous god. The passage could be interpreted in a more inward-looking way if the seal were taken as being the symbol of ownership. The lover does not force his law of faithfulness, he invites the bride to imprint upon her heart and arms, in letters of fire which nothing can put out, the sign of their mutual love which surrenders them into a relationship as decisive as death. This is no longer obedience but willing self-surrender.

seasons The seasons have been depicted in different ways in the arts – Spring by a lamb, a kid, a bush or a wreath of flowers; Summer by a dragon spitting fire, by a sheaf of corn or a sickle; Autumn by a hare, vine-leaves or a Horn of Plenty brimming with fruit; Winter by a salamander, a wild duck or a blazing hearth. Spring is sacred to HERMES, the messenger of the gods; Summer to the Sun-god, APOLLO; Autumn to DIONYSOS, the god of wine; Winter to HEPHAISTOS, god of metal-work and the arts which depend on fire. The alternation of the seasons, like the phases of the Moon, punctuate the rhythm of life and the stages in the cycle of development – birth, growth, maturity and decline. This is a cycle applicable to human beings as well as to their societies and civilizations. It also illustrates the myth of the eternal homecoming. It symbolizes cyclic alternation and perpetual rebirth.

sea-urchin Fossil sea-urchins, according to Pliny (*Natural History* 29: 52–4), enjoyed great popularity in Gaul. He terms them *ova anguinum* (serpents' eggs) and discounts the druidical belief that they were engendered from the spittle of masses of serpents coupling together in the Summer; and from direct personal experience he disproves the belief that they were sovereign charms to conciliate the powerful and to win court cases.

Archeologists excavating burial mounds have discovered fossil sea-urchins within cists where there is no human burial and this practice finds its parallels in Iran (OGAC 17: pp. 218, 224; 6: p. 228).

The basic symbol of the sea-urchin is the World Egg, but there are close links with the general symbolism of EGGS, SERPENTS, STONES and TREES. Because of the shape of the sand-dollar there are further developments in cavern and heart symbolism and again in Rosicrucianism and the symbolic meaning of Easter-eggs (CHAB pp. 943–54; LERD p. 62).

The primal egg, the symbol of concentrated life, in Cathar doctrine stood for Christ's dual nature, the union of divine and human powers.

In its symbolic history the fossil sea-urchin has followed the most perfect ascending curve from serpent's egg, through World Egg to manifestation of the Word. Unlike regression, it symbolizes evolution destined to reach its peak.

seaweed Edible seaweed, which forms an important part of Japanese diet, is gathered according to Shintō ritual, not so much because the weed is produced by the SEA as because it is regarded as possessing protective properties, safeguarding sailors and easing childbirth (HERS). Coming from the depths of the sea, that reservoir of life, seaweed symbolizes boundless life which nothing can destroy, elemental life, primeval food.

secrecy A secret is one of the privileges of power and a sign that one shares in that power. It is also linked to the notion of TREASURE and it has its guardians. Further, it is a source of anxiety because of the inner burden it imposes both upon those who carry it and those who fear it.

Prometheus was released from the claws of the vulture which devoured his liver, without Herakles (Hercules) having to risk the anger of the almighty god, by revealing to Zeus a secret entrusted to him by Themis. The fate of the gods hung upon this secret and this was Prometheus' weapon. He only used it after he had made Zeus suffer as severely as he and after he had gained release from his chains. From the psychoanalytic viewpoint one might say that revealing a secret relieves the soul from anxiety. The god who benefits thereby, Zeus, is the spirit, free from anxiety, who can now rule untrammelled. The subject who benefits thereby is the whole being who guarded the secret and who now finds freedom from its bonds and is therefore able to follow his or her spiritual drive. It is healthy to unburden oneself; however, anyone able to keep his or her secrets, unfalteringly and unconstrained, gains a matchless strength of domination which gives him or her a keen sense of superiority.

To alchemists,

the secret of secrets [was] the art of making the Philosopher's Stone. If, like Egyptian priests, philosophers kept the secret to themselves, it was because of its very excellence. One of the excuses made by philosophers for not divulging a secret so useful to those with knowledge of it, was that all the world would wish to try it and would abandon the arts and crafts so essential to life. Society itself would be troubled and overturned.

(PERD p. 455)

Another reason advanced by esoterics was that persons unprepared properly to accept such a secret would not only fail to understand it, but would also either misuse or mock it. One should not cast pearls before swine.

secret room   All rites of initiation may be seen as an ordeal consisting of passing through a secret room. It may be a cellar, vault, locked room, hole dug in the ground or forest clearing. Whatever it may be, it is somewhere far from prying eyes where the candidate is sprinkled either with lustral water or with the blood of a sacrificial victim. Often he spends the night there and is regarded as having been given a revelation of the godhead either in sleep or during his vigil. The Salt Papyrus of Ancient Egyptian magic describes a secret room in which the 'signs of breath' are given and the dead resurrected and prepared for their new lives. In the *Golden Ass* (11: 23) Apuleius describes one of these rooms. During his initiation into the mysteries of Isis, 'I approached near unto hell, even to the gates of Proserpine', he makes Lucius say, '. . . I saw likewise the gods celestial and the gods infernal.' This secret room symbolizes the place where the old man dies and the new man is born. It may, perhaps, be compared with the Christian baptistery. All initiation, be it the most straightforward, shares elements of secrecy and withdrawal, based upon some sort of death, and elements of self-surrender.

In his study of the symbolism of fairy-stories, Loeffler-Delachaux (LOEC pp. 98–100) distinguishes three secret rooms which correspond to the three degrees of initiation and which each possesses its locks and keys of silver, gold and diamond. These are the successive places of initiation in which the candidate is first cleansed (silver key), then instructed so as to gain mastery over the powers of nature (gold key) and finally enlightened by supreme knowledge and the acquisition of power (diamond key). These three rooms correspond to progress towards something holy, going ever more deeply inwards. They are like the spiritual pilgrimage from the enclosure without, to the temple within, until the holy of holies is reached where the godhead resides, something not dissimilar to the Sufi doctrine of the four GATES.

seed   The seed which dies and sprouts is the symbol of the variability of plant life. It is often alluded to in 'Homeric' hymns. The symbolism, however, rises above the cycle of plant reproduction to acquire the meaning of the alternation of life and death, of life in the realms below ground and of life in the realms of light, of the latent and of the manifest. 'Except a corn of wheat . . . die'. Rites of initiation, and especially the Eleusinian Mysteries, had as their goal deliverance from this alternation and permanence in the world of light.

seesaw See under SWING.

sefirot These basic elements of Kabbalistic tradition generate so complex a symbolism that only its outlines may be given here.

Sefirah (the singular) has the sense of numeration and, as we have shown NUMBERS establish the relationship between the First Cause and manifestation. This is the role of *sefirot*, emanations, properties or attributes of God, through which his down-poured activity is made manifest and through the mediation of which it can return in the opposite direction to the First Cause, to comprehend the incomprehensible Essence, *Ayn Soph*.

The *sefirot* are ten in number grouped in three triads – Crown (*Kether*), Wisdom (*Hocmā*) and Intellect (*Binā*); Grace (*Hesed*), Strength (*Geburā*) and Beauty (*Tiphereth*); Victory (*Netzā*), Glory (*Hod*) and Foundation (*Yesod*) – and lastly the Kingdom (*Malchut*).

In a different pattern they may be set as three columns: on the right, Wisdom, Grace and Victory; on the left, Intellect, Strength and Glory; and, in the centre, Crown, Beauty and Foundation standing over the Kingdom. The right-hand column, the active or male column, is the column of mercy; the left-hand, passive or female column, is the column of austerity; while the central column is the balancing axis, the Heavenly Way. One cannot fail to be reminded of Tantrism's three *nadī* in this context.

The Crown stands over the head of ADAM Kadmon, the Kingdom lies beneath his feet, Intellect and Wisdom on either side of his head; Grace and Strength are his arms, Victory and Glory his legs; Beauty corresponds to his heart and Foundation to his sexual organs or, as Tantrism would say, to the *chakra manipūra* and *anāhata*, to Earth and Fire.

There are, in addition, complicated systems of correspondences between the *sefirot* and the names of God (BOUM, WARK).

semen Galen believed that semen originated in the brain and this theory was widespread throughout the Middle Ages. We read in the Bahir that the spinal marrow stretches from the brain to the phallus and through it semen flows. Semen symbolizes the powers of life, and human life can derive only from what characterizes man, his brain, the seat of his own faculties.

Seraphim (see also FIRE) The name of these heavenly beings means 'burning' (*saraf*) like that of the serpent or winged dragon mentioned in Numbers 21: 6: 'And the Lord sent fiery serpents among the people, and they bit the people; and much people of Israel died.' Isaiah is, however, the first to give this title to angels:

Above it stood the seraphims: each one had six wings: with twain he covered his face [for fear of Jehovah], and with twain he covered his feet [euphemism for sexual organs], and with twain he did fly. And one cried unto another, and said, Holy, holy, holy, is the Lord of hosts: the whole earth is full of his glory ... Then flew one of the seraphims unto me, having a live coal in his hand, which he had taken with the tongs from off the altar: And he laid it upon my mouth, and said, Lo, this hath touched thy lips; and thine iniquity is taken away, and thy sin is purged.

(6: 2–3, 6–7)

These two passages show the symbolic properties of 'burning'. In Numbers, the earlier of the two, it describes the serpent sent as a punishment by the Lord, while in Isaiah, the later text, it is the angel of the Lord who cleanses by fire. The same linguistic root is the basis of the twofold development – the semantic development of the symbol of burning and the spiritual development of religious awareness. Originally the goal of burning was death; later it was purification.

The Pseudo-Dionysius the Areopagite exactly apprehends this significance of seraphim:

Those that know Hebrew affirm that the holy designation of the Seraphim denotes that they are fiery or burning ... their ever moving around things Divine, and constancy, and warmth, and keenness, and the seething of that persistent, indomitable, and inflexible perpetual motion, and that vigorous transformation of the subordinate, by precept and example, as giving new life and rekindling them to the same heat; and purifying through fire and burnt-offering, and the light-like and light-shedding characteristic which can never be concealed or consumed, and remains always the same, which destroys and dispels every kind of obscure darkness.

(PSEH p. 27)

Such are the properties of seraphim deriving from their very name.

This astounding synthesis incorporates all the properties of fire – heat, cleansing, self-identification, light and enlightenment, the power to scatter darkness. The seraphim symbolize all these powers on the highest level of spiritual awareness.

serpent Serpents are as different from all animal species as the human race, but at the opposite end of the scale. If mankind may be regarded as standing at the end of a long evolutionary struggle we must set this cold-blooded, armless, hairless, featherless creature at its very beginning. In this sense mankind and serpents are opposites, complementary and rivals the one to the other. In this sense too, there is something of the serpent in all human beings, and strangely enough in that portion of them over which they have the least control. An analyst has remarked that 'the serpent is a vertebrate creature embodying the lower psyche, hidden psychosis and what is unusual, incomprehensible and mysterious.' There is nothing so simple or so commonplace as a serpent, and yet by virtue of this very simplicity nothing which shocks the spirit more.

At the well-springs of life: the serpent as soul and libido
Travellers in the southern Cameroons have observed that in their hunting language the Pygmies depict serpents as a line on the ground and doubtless similar cave-drawings have exactly the same meaning. They may be said to take the serpent back to its original manifestation. It may only be a line, but it is a living line, what André Virel calls 'an abstraction in flesh and blood'. Lines have neither beginning nor end and, once they come alive, they become capable of depicting whatever you like or of changing into any shape. All that can be seen of the line is what is immediately made manifest in space and time, and yet one is aware that, at either end, it is produced into invisible infinity.

The same is true of the serpent. When made visible on Earth, the serpent in the instant of its manifestation is the sacred made manifest. Above and beyond this, there is a feeling that it is a continuation of the infinite materialization which is none other than primordial formlessness, the storehouse of latency which underlies the manifest world. The serpent which we see is the manifestation of the holiness of nature, a holiness which is material and in no sense spiritual. It makes its appearance in the sunlit world like a ghost which one can touch, but which slips through one's fingers. So, the serpent evades time which can be clocked, space which can be measured and logic which can be rationalized, to escape to the lower reaches from which it came and in which it can be imagined timeless, changeless and motionless in the fullness of its life. Swift as lightning, the serpent streaks from the dark mouth of some crevice or cranny to vomit life or death, before returning again to invisibility. Or else the serpent discards its male appearance to become female, coiling up, entwining around, squeezing, throttling, swallowing, digesting and sleeping. The she-serpent is the invisible serpent-principle which dwells in the lower levels of consciousness and the deeper strata of the Earth. It is secret and equivocal, its decisions are unpredictable and as swift as its transformations. Ever ambivalent, it toys with its own sexuality; it is both male and female, twins within the same body, like so many of the culture-heroes who are always depicted initially as cosmic serpents. The serpent does not therefore depict an archetype but an archetypal complex, linked to the freezing, clammy subterranean darkness of the beginning of things. 'All possible snakes together form one single primordial manifoldness, an inseverable primordial Something which yet is ever coiling and uncoiling, which is ever melting away and re-emerging' (KEYM p. 222). Yet what is this 'primordial Something' if it is not latent life or, as Keyserling puts it, 'the lowest layer of life'? It is the well-spring, potentiality, from which all manifestation derives. 'Nethermost Life', he continues, 'must needs be reflected in daylight consciousness in the form of a snake, as indeed the Chaldeans had but one word for Serpent and Life' (KEYM p. 21). René Guénon makes the same observation: 'Serpent symbolism is, in fact, linked to the notion of life itself. In Arabic the word for "serpent" is *el-hayyah*, and that for "life", *el-hayat*' (GUES p. 159), adding, and this is of prime importance, that El-Hay, one of the principal names of God, 'should not be translated as "the Living", but as "the Life-giving", the one who bestows life or who is the principle of life itself.'

The serpent which we see should, therefore, be regarded simply as a fleeting incarnation of a Great Invisible Serpent, causal and a-temporal, lord of the life-principle and of the powers of Nature. The serpent is an 'Old God', the first god to be found at the start of all cosmogenesis, before religions of the spirit dethroned him. He created life and sustained it. On a human level he is the dual symbol of soul and libido. 'The serpent is one of the most important archetypes of the human soul', wrote Bachelard (BACR p. 212). In Tantrism, the serpent is the *kundalinī*, coiled round the base of the spinal column, on the sleep-state *chakra*, 'its mouth closes the urethral meatus' (DURS p. 343). When the serpent awakes, hisses and stiffens, ascent through the successive *chakra* takes place. This is the rising tide of the libido, the fresh manifestation of life.

The cosmic serpent

From the macrocosmic viewpoint, the *kundalinī*'s equivalent is the serpent Ananta which wraps its coils round the base of the World Axis. Ananta is associated with Vishnu and Shiva and symbolizes cyclical expansion and contraction, but, as guardian of the nadir (see ZENITH), he carries the world upon himself and ensures its stability. When building a house in India, as with all houses which should stand at the CENTRE of the world, a pile is sunk into the head of the subterranean NĀGA, once geomancy has established where it lies. Those who carry the world are sometimes ELEPHANTS, BULLS, TORTOISES, CROCODILES and so on, but they are only surrogates for, or different animal shapes of, the serpent in its original role. Thus the Sanskrit word *nāga* means both 'serpent' and 'elephant' (KRAM p. 193) and this may be compared with the equivalence of serpent and tapir in the Maya-Quiché world-picture (GIRP pp. 267ff.). These 'animals of power' are very often depicted by their heads at the end of a serpent's body, or they may themselves be supported by a serpent. In every instance, they stand for the terrestrial aspect, that is the strength and aggression of the manifestation of the great god of darkness who, throughout the world, is a serpent.

There are two ways of sustaining something. It may either be carried, or enfolded by creating an unbroken circle round it to prevent its falling apart. This second role is filled, once again, by the serpent biting its tail, the OUROBOROS. In this context, the circumference complements the centre so as to suggest Nicolas of Cusa's notion of God himself. The ouroboros is also the symbol of cyclical manifestation and return, sexual auto-intercourse, perpetual self-fertilization (as the tail penetrating the mouth would indicate), continuous transformation of death into life, since its fangs inject their poison into its own body; or, in Bachelard's words, it is 'the material dialectic of life and death, death springing from life and life from death'. While it conjures up the image of the CIRCLE, it is predominantly the circle's dynamism, that is, the first WHEEL, apparently motionless because it revolves on its own axis, but with perpetual motion since it is continuously self-renewed. Universal life-giver, the ouroboros provides the motive power, not only of life, but of time, creating both within itself. It is often depicted in the shape of a twisted chain, its links the hours. Setting the stars in motion, it is also the first representation and mother of the Zodiac. An old symbol of an Old God of Nature dethroned by the spirit, the ouroboros remained a powerful cosmographic and geographic deity and, as such, was carved round the edges of the earliest representations of the world, like what is undoubtedly the earliest Black African *imago mundi*, the Benin Disc (FROC pp. 147–8). Its sinuosities frame all things, bringing together opposites, the primeval oceans on which floats the SQUARE shape of the Earth.

Terrifying in its anger, it becomes the Jewish LEVIATHAN or the Norse Midgardorm which, the Edda tell us, 'was older than the gods themselves', causing the tides when he drank and storms when he belched. Returning to the cosmogenetic level, the serpent is Ocean itself, its nine whorls encircling the Earth and its tenth, so Hesiod states in his *Theogony*, running beneath it to form the Styx. In the final analysis this emanation of formless primeval matter, from which all things spring and to which all things return to be renewed, may be likened to an object thrown from one hand and caught by the other. Underworld and ocean, primordial waters and the depths of the Earth, simply compose that *materia prima*, primeval matter, from which the serpent is made. The serpent was the first water-spirit, and is the spirit of the waters below, on and above the Earth's surface. Krappe (KRAM p. 205) stresses the fact that countless rivers in Greece and Asia Minor bore the names of *Ophis* (Snake) or *Draco* (Dragon), and then there were 'Father' Rhine and 'Mother' Volga and the river-god, *Deus Sequana*, the Seine. Very often the attributes of the animal-shape adopted explain the heavenly or earthly functions of the river-deity. Virgil's 'horned' Tiber may be explained as a depiction of the serpent which has taken to itself the strength of the bull, typified by its horns. Similarly, the Acheloos, the greatest river of Ancient Greece, successively took the shapes of serpent and bull to combat Herakles (Hercules). As the deity of clouds and fecundating rain, serpents sometimes take to themselves the powers of the RAM – hence the horned serpents so common in Celtic and, particularly, in Gaulish iconography – or of birds. These are the Far Eastern winged DRAGONS and their Central American counterparts, the Plumed Serpents.

We are familiar with the basic importance attaching to symbolic images in these two great agrarian civilizations and the particular attention which they paid to meteorological phenomena. In the Far East, celestial dragons were the founding fathers of many dynasties and the Chinese emperors carried one embroidered on their banners to denote the divine origins of their empire. In American Indian mythology from Mexico to Peru, Alexander stresses (ALEC pp. 94ff.), the myth of the Serpent-Bird coincides with the oldest religious rituals connected with the cultivation of maize:

the myth-being is associated with moisture and with the waters of the world-regions . . . yet always in his greater forms, with the sky. He is not only the 'Green-Feather Snake' and the 'Cloud Snake', bearded with rain, but he is also the 'Son of the Serpent' and again the 'House of Dews' and . . . 'Lord of the Dawn'. . . . The Plumed Serpent is first of all the rain cloud, and in a special right the high-terraced, silver-shining cumulus cloud of midsummer (whence he is also called the 'White God') from whose black belly falls the reek of rain. . . . In New Mexico [he is represented as] a serpent body whose dorsal burden is the cumulus cloud and whose tongue is the jagged levin. The Chinese Dragon, it will be recalled, swims in just such billowing cumulus.

(ALEC pp. 94–5)

The 'Old God' and mythic ancestor

When the serpent became the mythic ancestor and culture-hero – most familiar in the shape of the Toltecs' Quetzalcoatl which the Aztecs also adopted – the serpent became flesh and sacrificed itself for the human race. Indian iconography explains the meaning of this sacrifice. Thus the Dresden Codex depicts

a bird of prey striking its talons into the serpent's body so that the blood from which civilized mankind is to be created will flow. The god [the serpent] in this context turns the celestial powers of his own attribute, the Sun-bird, against himself to make fertile mankind's land, for this god is the cloud and his blood is the rain which will enable the maize to grow and mankind to live from the maize.

(GIRP p. 269)

One could elaborate upon this sacrifice, which is not only that of the cloud, but the death of desire as well, in the fulfilment of its loving mission. On a more clearly cosmogonic level – and one which in Sufism becomes the foundations of a mysticism – it is the splitting of primordial Oneness, the two in one, into its two components to create the human order. Jacques Soustelle regarded Quetzalcoatl's sacrifice as a variation upon the classic theme of initiation, death followed by rebirth. Quetzalcoatl became the Sun and died in the west to be reborn in the east. Within himself he was two-in-one and dialectic and became the guardian of twins.

The same symbolic complex recurs in Black Africa. The mythic ancestor and culture-hero of the Dogon is the water-god Nommo. He is depicted with a snake's body instead of human lower limbs. He brought mankind the most valuable cultural gifts – metal-working and corn – and is also 'two and one'; he too sacrificed himself for the good of the new human race. Many other examples might be quoted from African tradition and especially that of Dan or Da, the great god from Benin and the Slave Coast, who is the serpent and the fetish rainbow (MAUG). In Haitian Voodoo, he became Damballah-Weddo and is the lord of springs and rivers, for both movement and water are in his nature. The thunder-stone is sacred to him and he forbids his servants, that is those who become possessed by him, to invoke any deity who works both good and evil, except twins who are his neighbours. He is also lightning and, above all, god of strength and fertility (METV). Now, Dan is still the 'Old God of Nature' in present-day Benin, the ouroboros of the Benin Disk described above, hermaphrodite and himself twin (MERF). This would explain the worship of the sacred pythons kept in the temples of Abomey and girls are dedicated to them, being ritually betrothed to these gods at the time of crop-sowing. The Yoruba regard Dan, whom they call Oshumare, as the rainbow, linking the upper and the lower levels of the world and only to be seen after rain. Frazer (FRAG 5: p. 67) cites Bozman for evidence that the Guinea coastal tribes 'invoke the snake in excessively wet, dry, or barren seasons'.

All these examples, taken from cultures which have developed independently of our own, explain how the serpent's connections with the weather, of which there are survivals in European folklore, have originated. 'There is a widely held belief', Krappe writes (KRAM p. 18), 'that rainbows are a serpent drinking from the sea. This notion occurs not only in France, but among the Nevada Indians in North America and the Boro in South America, in Southern Africa and in India . . .' All these attestations are no more than so many applications in their specific areas of the myth of the Great Primeval Serpent, an expression of formless primal matter. It is the beginning and the end of every manifestation and this explains its prime eschatological significance through which we return to the highly complex development of the serpent symbol in European civilization. But first we should remember that the Batak in Malaysia believe that a cosmic serpent lives in the Underworld and that it will destroy the world (ELIC p. 286). The Huichol cosmic serpent has two heads, which comprise two pairs of monstrous jaws gaping at east and west. From the one he vomits the rising Sun and with the other he swallows the setting Sun. And now we come to the oldest creator-god in the Mediterranean world, the serpent Atum, father of the nine deities of Heliopolis. He was the one who spat out the whole of creation at the beginning of time, after he had emerged by his own efforts from the primeval waters. As he was alone, written sources are divided as to the origins of his 'spittle' and some state that it came not from his mouth but from his penis, Atum in fact masturbating rather than spitting. Thus the first pair of gods sprang into existence, 'Chu and Phenis, who brought into the world Geb and Nut, respectively air and moisture, Earth and Heaven' (DAUE). Then Atum rose up before his creation and, according to the *Book of the Dead*, addressed it in these words: 'I am he who remains . . . The Earth shall return to formless chaos, and then I shall transform myself into a serpent which no man knows and no god sees!' (MORR pp. 222–3). No mythology has depicted the Great Primeval Serpent so baldly. Atum has no need to swallow the Sun. He has nothing to do with the Underworld, the chthonian realm in which our life dies and is reborn every day. He is serpent only before and after the totality of the space–time continuum in a region to which neither gods nor mortals have access, and is truly the first of the Old Gods, the *deus otiosus* of Nature in his pitiless transcendence.

Nevertheless, the realms below the Earth, which the Sun must traverse every night to ensure his own rebirth, were set wholly under the sign of the serpent in Ancient Egypt as elsewhere. Although Atum may have had no part to play within the drama, it is, nevertheless, he who illuminated it externally. Stripped of his serpent-shape, each evening he became god of the setting Sun, pointing in the west the way to the depths below. He then plunged underground on a boat on which he took his place surrounded by all his heavenly retainers.

The notion of the belly of the Earth in which this alchemical regeneration occurs being under the predominant influence of the serpent is described in minutest detail in the *Book of the Dead*. The route taken by the Sun is divided into twelve halls corresponding to the twelve hours of darkness. The Sun-boat first crosses sandy shoals inhabited by serpents and soon changes into a serpent itself. At the seventh hour a fresh snake-form appears, Apophis, the monstrous embodiment of the lord of the Underworld and a prefiguration of the Old Testament Satan. 'His coils entwine a mound 450 cubits long . . . his voice attracts the gods who will wound him.' This incident marks the climax of the drama. At the eleventh hour, the Sun-boat's tow-rope becomes a serpent. Lastly, during the twelfth in the chamber of the dawn, the Sun-boat is dragged through a serpent 1300 cubits long and when it comes out of the mouth, the rising Sun is to be seen in the shape of a scarab on the bosom of Mother Earth. The Sun is reborn to begin afresh its ascent of the heavens (ERMR pp. 271–2). To sum up, the Sun has to change into a serpent in order to do battle with other serpents – one in particular – before being swallowed and expelled through the Earth's serpent-like gut. One might elaborate at great length on this evolution of a swallower–swallowed complex, beside which Jonah's fate seems quite straightforward. The serpent may be regarded, worldwide, as the great regenerator and initiator, lord of the Earth's womb and, like that womb, simultaneously the enemy – in the dialectic sense of the word – of the Sun, hence of light and therefore of mankind's spiritual side.

In order more effectively to develop the contradictory facets of the original symbolic entity, the Egyptian sacred book divides them into a similar number of serpents, but the overriding importance of the role given to Apophis demonstrates that of all the potentials combined within the original, the one that was to take precedence, namely that of the serpent as a hostile force, was about to emerge. This runs in parallel with the positive qualities attributed to the spirit and the negative ones attributed to the inexplicable, dangerous powers of Nature, from which the notion of intrinsic Evil, Evil which was no longer physical but moral, was gradually to take shape. Apophis falls short of this, but the path is clear and it will soon become the king's highway. The significance of Apophis remains doubtful. On the one hand, at the seventh hour, he of his own accord draws to his body the gods who are going to wound him. He therefore plays a positive part and, at the last resort, one counter to his own selfish interests in effectuating the rebirth of the Sun. On the other hand, the priests of Heliopolis regarded him as the Enemy when, during their ritual conjurations, they trod his image underfoot on the floors of their temples to help Ra, prince of light, triumph over this first 'prince of darkness. This was done at dawn, noon and dusk, as well as at certain set times of the year, during storms, in heavy rain or at an eclipse of the Sun' (JAMM p. 180). Maspéro explains that this eclipse 'meant that Ra had been worsted in his struggle against Apophis.'

Giver of life and inspiration: the serpent as healer and seer

The foregoing should be regarded less as an attempt to assert the hegemony of the spirit over the forces of nature, than as an attempt to balance these two basic forces of existence by preventing the one, which is subject to no control, from trying to overmaster the other. The same concern may be traced in the myth of Zeus' struggle with TYPHON, Apophis in another shape. Typhon, the son of Gaia (Earth) or of Hera, was not, in fact, a serpent, but a hundred-headed dragon clothed in vipers 'from the waist downwards and more vast than the mountains' (GRID). He was, therefore, an excellent embodiment of the uncontrolled forces of Nature, rising in rebellion against the spirit, and it is significant that to crush this rebel Zeus had only the help of his daughter, Athene, Reason. All the other Olympians fled in panic to the safety of Egypt – that mythical Egypt which was to become the symbol of brute creation – where they changed themselves into animals. Typhon's infernal nature is betrayed by the creatures which he begot – the Delphic Hydra, the Chimera and the hounds Orthos and Cerberus. Cerberus (see DOG) was not, however, maleficent in himself. The dog played a dialectically positive part in the Greek Underworld, in which the ceaseless cycle of regeneration was effected.

Like Ancient Egyptian thought, Greek thought only disapproved of the serpent to the extent that it attempted to reduce the cosmos to its original chaos. On the other hand, to the degree that it remained the essential other side of the spirit, the life-giving force which inspired the sap to rise from the roots to the crown of the tree, it approved and even glorified it. Thus all the great goddesses of nature, those Mother-goddesses which Christianity refashioned as Mary, Mother of God made Flesh, had serpents as attributes.

However, the Mother of Christ, the second Eve, was to crush the serpent's head instead of listening to it. First in this line was Isis, wearing the royal cobra on her forehead, the pure gold URAEUS, the symbol of divine sovereignty, knowledge, life and youth. She was followed by Cybele and Demeter and that Cretan serpent-goddess who was chthonian as well. It is also significant that during the reign of the Pharaoh Amenophis II, the uraeus was also depicted as carrying the solar disc (DAUE, PIED, ERMR, GRID). However celestial her origins, Athene herself had a serpent as one of her attributes, and what plainer symbol of the marriage of reason with the powers of Nature than the myth of Laocoon, in which the serpents which emerged from the sea to punish the priest guilty of sacrilege should subsequently coil round the feet of Athene's statue?

The inspirational role of the serpent may be seen in all its clarity in the myths and rituals surrounding the worship of the two great gods of poetry, music, healing and above all of divination, Apollo and Dionysos. Apollo, the most solar of gods and Olympian of the Olympians, started his career, if one may use the term, by freeing the Delphic oracle from that other larger-than-life symbol of the powers of Nature, the serpent Pytho. This is not, however, to deny Nature soul and intellect, as Aristotle was to emphasize, but rather to free that soul and that deep and inspiring intellect which together must fecundate the spirit and thus ensure the order which the spirit strives to establish. In this sense APOLLO is very far from being DIONYSOS' antagonist, as all modern writers agree (GUTG, MAGE). Dionysos is simply set at the opposite pole and knows that the two poles must complement one another if they are to achieve that harmony which is their supreme goal. Thus, however Dionysiac trance and ecstasy may be, they are not excluded from the Apollonian world, the Pytheness, who only prophesied when in a state of trance, being an example of this.

In this respect, the story of Cassandra, with whom Apollo was to fall in love, is highly significant. Cassandra had a twin brother, Helenus, and after the feasts celebrating their birth, their parents left them forgotten in the temple of Apollo. 'The next morning, when they came to fetch them, they found them sleeping with two serpents licking their sensory organs in order to cleanse them. The parents screamed in fear and the reptiles slithered away into the sacred laurel grove. Subsequently both children revealed a gift of prophecy imparted to them when the serpents had cleansed them' (GRID p. 80). This cleansing seems akin to the Pythagorean *catharsis*, in which there is general agreement that there are Apollonian influences. 'Generally speaking,' Grimal adds, 'Cassandra was reputed to be an inspired prophetess. The God possessed her and she uttered his oracles in a delirium. Helenus, on the other hand, used to foretell the future from the flight of birds and external signs.' This is incontrovertible evidence in a belief that the two facets of divination, both Apollonian and Dionysiac, derived from the serpent.

Another significant myth is that of Iamos, Apollo's son by a mortal woman. He was brought up by serpents and fed upon honey before becoming a priest and ancestor of a long line of priests (GRID). Melampus, who was both seer and healer, had his ears cleansed by serpents, with the result that he was able to understand the language of birds. His name means 'Black

Foot' since according to tradition when he was born his mother placed him in the shade but carelessly left his feet exposed to the Sun (GRID p. 282). In this context, the serpent's field of knowledge extends its power over the realms both of light and darkness, reconciling soul and spirit, the two areas of awareness, sacred left and sacred right.

However, in the Greek world, Dionysos most fully embodies the sacred left and he is basically associated with the image of the serpent. Guthrie explains how the worship of Dionysos reached its peak in Greece at precisely the same time as Greek literature achieved perfection and that the greatest of Dionysos' gifts was the feeling of complete freedom (GUTG pp. 145ff.). Thus the Great Liberator appeared upon the scene at exactly the moment in history when the *Logos* in its perfected written form took its triumphant place in the Greek city-state. Mass ecstasy, trance and possession – the serpent within the individual rising in revolt – may be regarded from now on as Nature's revenge upon the Law, daughter of reason alone, with its oppressive tendencies. To sum up, this was a return to harmony through excess and to balance through fleeting madness – a therapy provided by the serpent. Of course trances, ecstasies and possession had existed long before the appearance of Dionysos. They came into being with the worship of Nature and of the great goddesses of the Underworld, all of whom, as we have said, had serpents among their attributes. However, at that particular moment in history when Athens was sketching the lines of modern thought and society, they were given a burst of fervour so powerful that its effects were to endure in a world in which society's grip upon the individual was to close ever more tightly. It is this obstinate determination of the individual to be free from the tyranny of reason which was to spawn Gnostic sects, Sufi orders and, in the Christian world, the whole range of heresies which did battle with the Roman Catholic Church. Each of these movements in its own way fought the arraignment of the serpent: '"no being," proclaimed the third-century Gnostic sect, the Peratae, "either in heaven or on earth, was formed without the Serpent"' (DORL p. 51). The Ophites – whose name alone was a profession of their faith – added: 'We venerate the Serpent . . . because God made it the cause of Gnosis for mankind. . . . Our bowels, thanks to which we nourish ourselves and live, do they not reproduce the form of the serpent?' (DORL p. 44). The analogy they drew, which echoes that between the serpent and the labyrinth (see MAZE), amazingly foreshadows modern discoveries in the fundamentals of the psyche. Simultaneously they enlighten us as to the origin of divination by the examination of entrails. Some animist societies, still uncrushed by the modern world, continue to keep alive and active this current of parallel thought which elsewhere has been repressed by force of circumstances into a barren esotericism. The cults of Zar in Ethiopia and of Voodoo in Benin and Haiti (see HORSE) may be taken as examples.

However, the story of Dionysos holds the seeds of all this and makes it perfectly clear in images. Cretan, Phrygian and, lastly, Orphic traditions provide a variant of the legend of his birth under the names of Zagreos or Sabazios, not from Zeus' coitus with Semele, but with Persephone, that is to say from the marriage of soul and spirit, of Heaven and Earth. To accomplish his purposes, tradition says that Zeus turned himself into a

serpent. That is to say, that however deified the spirit might be, it acknowledged the priority of the primeval uncreated state from which it had itself
sprung and into which it had to return in order to be reborn and bear fruit.
Yet Dionysos was also himself fundamentally the initiate who had to sacrifice
himself in order to be born again and effect his purpose. Thus he was torn
to pieces by the Titans, to be restored to life at the express command of
Zeus, the Spirit. Only then were the Bacchantes and retinue of those whom
the god possessed able, like Athene, to handle serpents. The sense of the
fable is plain and shows that serpents in themselves are neither good nor
bad, but possess both potentialities ... 'for the serpent-being', Jacob Boehme
was to write, 'has great power. . . . This is well understood by sage students
of Nature, namely, that within the serpent dwells an excellent art and that
there is even virtue in its being.' The serpent is not the healer, but the
healing, and this should be understood by the CADUCEUS with its staff, designed to be handled. The spirit is the healer who has first to try the healing upon himself in order to learn how to use it to the benefit of society
at large. Otherwise he will kill instead of cure, by bringing discord and
character-disorder instead of harmonizing the relationship between instinct
and reason. Hence the importance of Spiritual Guides, the heads of guilds
of initiates. They were, in some sense, soul-healers, analysts born out of
time, or rather, shepherds of souls. If they had not killed and brought to life
the serpent within them, they were only able to perform a crude and harmful form of analysis. And this is precisely what was to afflict the Dionysiac
guilds, driven underground by the modern world. When this modern world
brags of the Ancients, it would seem to have forgotten their lesson of the
Golden Mean which emanates from all their myths dealing with the serpent. Implicit in any notion of balance, the Golden Mean in some respects
seems close to 'the wisdom of serpents' of which Christ spoke.

This is the inspiration behind such major works of esotericism as the
Tarot, in which the Golden Mean is represented by the fourteenth arcanum
– Temperance, set between Death and the Devil – bearing a plain meaning.
An angel dressed half in red and half in blue – half in Earth and half in
Heaven – pours first into a red vase and then into a blue one a colourless
and serpentine liquid. These two vases symbolize the two poles of being
and what joins them together and is the means of their endlessly repeated
interchange is the water-god, the serpent. The historian of the Tarot, Van
Rijnberk, states that this card is the symbol of alchemy and adds that it
expresses clearly the belief in reincarnation and the transmigration of souls
(RIJT p. 249). 'One has only to recall that in classical Greek *metagiosmos*,
the act of pouring something from one vase to another, was regarded as the
synonym of metempsychosis.' This confirms our theory that the fluid depicted on the fourteenth arcanum represents the serpent, since Greco-Latin
tradition repeatedly depicts reincarnation in the shape of a serpent. This was
the old Athenian belief regarding the sacred serpent on the Acropolis which
was supposed to protect the city. It stood for the soul of the serpent-man,
Erechtheus, regarded as a former king of Athens and often identified with
Poseidon. In a variant legend, he was a culture-hero who brought corn from
Egypt (GRID; FRAG 4: pp. 84–6). Similarly the Thebans believed that, on
their death, their kings and queens were changed into serpents (FRAG

ibid.). Throughout Greece, folk-custom dictated that libations of milk were poured on graves for the souls of the dead, reincarnated as serpents. When Plotinus died, a serpent was said to have emerged from his mouth with his dying breath. Finally, in Rome, the symbol of the *genius*, or guardian-spirit, was a serpent. Many more instances might be quoted from the past and from more recent examples taken from the animist cultures of New Guinea, Borneo, Madagascar, Bantu Africa and elsewhere.

Such similarities show that these cultures differ only from our own in openly acknowledging symbolic beliefs which, through the pressure of history, our own has buried without altogether losing sight of them. One must therefore look to the current of what is termed alternative philosophy or thought to disinter the serpent's archetypal function. Despite centuries of concentrated official indoctrination, designed to diminish the serpent's manifold potentialities, he will still be seen to be the lord of the dialectic of life, the mythic ancestor, culture-hero, the master of womankind, Don Juan, and hence the father of all those heroes and prophets who emerge, like Dionysos, at some given moment in history to regenerate the human race. Thus the mother of the Emperor Augustus was said to have been visited in a dream by a serpent in the temple of Apollo, and the same legend explained the miraculous births of Scipio Africanus and Alexander the Great. Small wonder then that the legend should have found its way into apocryphal lives of Christ himself. Aelian in his *De natura animalium*, reports that in the days of King Herod a Jewish maiden was visited by a serpent and, according to Frazer (FRAG 5: p. 81), there is every reason to believe that this is a reference to Our Lady. In any case, we all know the affinities which join serpent and dove in sexual symbolism, but what are we to make of the custom which Frazer records among the Nandi of East Africa? There 'if a snake goes on to the woman's bed, it may not be killed, as it is believed that it personifies the spirit of a deceased ancestor or relation, and that it has been sent to intimate to the woman that her next child will be born safely' (FRAG 5: p. 85).

That the tradition of the serpent as 'the master of women' because he is lord of fertility is worldwide has been made abundantly clear by Eliade (ELIT pp. 165ff.), Krappe and by ethnologists specializing in the study of particular continents. Baumann (BAUA), for example, stresses that in Africa this is characteristic of matriarchal societies. Thus, in Angola, the Chokwe place a serpent carved from wood under the nuptial bed to ensure that the bride conceives. In the Volta region, 'when a Senufo woman conceives she is taken into a hut decorated with depictions of serpents, while the Nuruma and Gugoro say that a woman will become pregnant if serpents enter her hut' (BAUA p. 423).

In India, women anxious to bear children will adopt a cobra. The Tupi-Guarani of Brazil beat the thighs of barren women with serpents to make them fertile. Elsewhere, serpents keep the spirits of children, which they allocate to the human race as and when the need arises. In central Australia, two ancestral serpents ceaselessly travel the Earth and each time they stop they leave *mai-aurli*, spirits of children. In Togo, a giant spirit which lives in a lake takes children from the hands of the Supreme Deity and brings them to the town.

We have mentioned the serpent's sexual ambivalence and, in this aspect of its symbolism, this is shown by the fact that it may simultaneously be womb and phallus. There is a mass of iconographical evidence for this both from Stone Age Asia and from Amerindian cultures in which the reptile's body (phallic overall) is decorated with a pattern of LOZENGES, the vulva symbol. Eliade (ELIC p. 340) records a Negrito myth which is a clear expression of this womb symbolism. On the way to Tapern's palace a huge serpent lives under the carpets which it weaves for Tapern. In its belly there are thirty beautiful women, headdresses, combs and so on. A Chinoi called the Weapon Shaman lives on its back, as the keeper of this treasure. Any Chinoi who wishes to enter the serpent's belly must first undergo two ordeals of the magic door type and which therefore possess an initiatory character. If he succeeds he may choose his bride.

As lord both of womankind and of fertility, the serpent was also often regarded as being responsible for menstruation, which he caused through his bites. Krappe supports the antiquity of this belief by showing its existence in pre-Zoroastrian legends of Ahriman. This same belief recurs among Rabbinical writers who attribute menstruation to Eve's coitus with the serpent, as Salomon Reinach shows, and the belief is still alive among the Papuans of New Guinea. All these instances show the affinity between the serpent and the shadow, the latter, too, being regarded as a fecundating soul. Lastly the serpent is a Don Juan, as the analyst Rank shows in his essay on the Don in which the shadow is considered as the serpent's double. 'In Central India there is widespread fear of being made pregnant by shadows. Pregnant women avoid men's shadows for fear that the child they carry will look like the man in question. . . . Thus the shadow is the symbol of male procreative power which not only stands for procreation in general, but also for rebirth in one's descendants' (RANJ p. 98).

Such beliefs have left their traces in European folklore. In his *Tradizioni popolari abruzzeri* (quoted in ELIT), Finamore records the belief in the Abruzzi still current that serpents copulate with women. In some regions of France, Germany, Portugal and elsewhere women are frightened that serpents will creep into their mouths while they are asleep – especially during menstruation – and make them pregnant.

The serpent arraigned
Although, as a general rule, Christianity has retained only the negative and accursed aspects of the serpent, Christian scriptures for their part bear witness to the symbol's dual aspect. Thus, in the Book of Numbers, when the serpents sent by God caused the deaths of many of the Children of Israel, his Chosen People were restored to life by the serpent itself, following the instruction the Almighty gave Moses:

And the Lord sent fiery serpents among the people, and they bit the people; and much people of Israel died. Therefore the people came to Moses, and said, We have sinned, for we have spoken against the Lord, and against thee; pray unto the Lord, that he take away the serpents from us. And Moses prayed for the people. And the Lord said unto Moses, make thee a fiery serpent, and set it upon a pole: and it shall come to pass, that every one that is bitten, when he looketh upon it, shall live. And Moses made a serpent of brass, and put it upon a pole: and it came to pass that if a serpent had bitten any man, when he beheld the serpent of brass, he lived.

(Numbers 21: 6–9)

Although Christian theology made this incident a prefiguration of the Crucifixion, when Christ regenerated the world from the Cross, the serpent more often in the medieval mind was Eve's serpent, doomed to crawl upon his belly, and the cosmic dragon of the Book of Revelation. There St John does not controvert its antiquity, but announces its defeat. 'And the great dragon was cast out, that old serpent, called the Devil, and Satan, which deceiveth the whole world, he was cast into the earth, and his angels were cast out with him' (Revelation 12: 9). From now on, the seducer becomes the creature of repulsion. None can dispute the existence of his knowledge and powers, but their origin can be called in question. They were regarded as the fruits of theft and, in the eyes of the spirit, became unlawful. The serpent's knowledge became damnable knowledge and the serpent within us was to give birth to vices which brought us death instead of life. Our vices, wrote the fifth-century Christian Spanish poet, Prudentius, are our children, but when we give them life, they give us death, as its young give death to the viper which bears them:

She does not bear her young by an organ of sex, nor does her womb swell from intercourse, but when she burns with the excitement of the female's heat the lewd beast opens her mouth wide in thirst for a mate that is doomed. He puts his three-tongued head into his spouse's jaws, eagerly entering her alluring mouth and inserting his baneful seed by oral union. The bride, smitten with the strong pleasure, takes her lover's head between her teeth and breaks his neck with a bite in the midst of their fond compact, drinking in the injected slaver while her dear one dies. With these allurements the sire is destroyed; but the young shut up within her kill their dam. For when the seed develops and the tiny bodies begin to creep about in their warm hiding-place and to shake the womb with their waving and lashing ... For because there is no passage to give them birth, the belly is tortured and gnawed by the young as they struggle into light, till a way is opened through the torn sides ... and the young creep about licking the corpse that bore them, a family of orphans at their very birth. ... just so does our soul conceive.

(*The Origin of Sin*, 584–96, 600–2, 605–6, 608)

Long before the word was invented, the age, as may be seen, was baroque and the baroque spirit was to flourish for centuries in this 'reversal of the wonderful' which made demonology its chosen field. The serpent crawls amid the poisoned flowers of a landscape of the damned and is the asp coiled on Cleopatra's breast or lurking in a ROSE-bush. The serpent, too, is every cosmic dragon which peoples our mythologies, flapping its wings and vomiting fire and smoke from its hiding-place in the darkness. Here it jealously protects its treasures – including the most precious of all, immortality – no longer allowing humans access to them, but keeping them from them, since however satanic the serpent may be, he remains immortal. Krappe (KRAM pp. 288ff.) draws comparisons which explain how the serpent gained this immortality and sheds light upon the rivalry between mankind and the serpent upon which the Christian world has raised its own mythology:

In the Babylonian epic of Gilgamesh, [the serpent] steals from the hero the Herb of Immortality which the gods have given him. In New Britain a good spirit willed that serpents should die and that humans should change their skins and live for ever. Unfortunately an evil spirit discovered a way to reverse the arrangement and this is why serpents shed their skins and regain their youth while humans are doomed to die.... In the archetype of the Old Testament account, it would seem as if the serpent made Adam [or rather Eve] believe that the tree of death was really the tree of life. He, naturally enough, ate the fruit of the tree of life.

The serpent, with every sin laid to his charge, is proud, selfish and greedy. The 'good being' of the serpent, to use Jacob Boehme's words, has vanished and all that is left is what Boehme terms 'that false being who loves to take material shape in pride ... the one who allows the poor to suffer starvation while he sets his heart upon temporal wealth and amasses possessions, he is no Christian but the child of the serpent.' Lord of the life force, the serpent no longer symbolizes fertility, but lust. 'Having been the most evil of all creatures,' Boehme continues, 'and having ravished Eve's virginity, he sowed the seeds of bestiality and all unnatural lust within mankind.'

The sole vestiges of the serpent's 'good being' survived in his chthonian task of executing divine justice in a way somewhat reminiscent of the myth of Laocoon. This is how Dante displays him in the *Inferno*. At the beginning of Canto 25, having seen a thief, guilty in addition of sacrilege, stifled by a serpent, the poet exclaims:

At once I liked the snakes; for one came sneaking
About his throat, and wreathed itself around
As though to say: 'I will not have thee speaking';
Another wrapped his arms, and once more bound
All fast in front, knotting their coils till he
Could give no jog, they were so tightly wound.

Later, in the same Canto, Dante describes the extraordinary fusion which takes place between a serpent and one of the damned in a marriage of which the wild grandeur displays all the ambivalence of the serpent in its sexual connotation. 'Till like hot wax they stuck; and, melting in, / Their tints began to mingle and to run, / And neither seemed to be what it had been.'

What Durand terms the 'sum total' would seem to be the meaning given to the serpent-dragon in the notion of the hero evolved in the Middle Ages and surviving to the present day. The dragon is the obstacle which must be overcome to reach the level of the sacred, it is the 'beast within' which all good Christians must strive to slay like St George or St Michael. The pagan myth of SIEGFRIED is turned round to point in the same direction. By his dedication, the 'new hero' becomes the superman through whom a so-called Christian civilization falls into precisely those excesses which Christianity is meant to control. The consequences are all too plain, and not the least serious is a sketchy morality of Good and Evil. It is outrageously oversimplified and traumatic because it ruptures the unity of the human personality by repressing into the unconscious the deepest aspirations and inspirations of being. In the last resort the vital principle is itself affected,

producing that sickness in our civilization of which Keyserling so perti-
nently explains the cause, writing that 'Original life . . . must indeed appear
evil to day-time consciousness which has grown self-assured' (KEYM p.
24). This extremist self-assurance, as we now know, under the pretext of
enlightenment leads only to deeper obfuscation.

Revaluation of the serpent symbol
To deny primeval life and the serpent which embodies it, is to deny all the
nocturnal properties of which it partakes and which are the spirit's clay. It
was not until the nineteenth century that a warning note was sounded by
the Romantic Movement. Once again poets and painters were the movers,
and for this reason the greatest of them were branded as 'damned' by the
society which they had undertaken to set free. 'Let what you have seen in
darkness emerge into the light of day' wrote the German painter Friedrich,
while the French 'realist' Courbet replied: 'I see too clearly; I should put
out an eye.' The breach was opened, and through it in the twentieth century
poured a revolution in thinking in which a leading role was played by the
Surrealist Movement. In 1924, in the first Surrealist manifesto, André Breton
wrote: 'I believe that those two apparently so contradictory states of dream
and reality will soon be resolved into a sort of absolute reality, or superreality
if one may use the word.' Meanwhile Freudian psychoanalysis had invented
the clinical method of reintegrating human personality by rooting out guilt
complexes which had become pathogenic. Nor should one be astonished
that Freud, the father of psychoanalysis, should have been arraigned, since
this merely reopens the case against the serpent.

At this particular point in time, Western thought also yielded to the
impulse to examine, from motives other than an interest in the outlandish,
those so-called primitive cultures which still survived on our planet, mainly
in Africa, America and Oceania, wherever animism was still practised. While
the serpent arouses only feelings of repulsion in the modern Westerner,
those areas had preserved him as a complete archetype, keeping alive and
acknowledging his positive properties. The ordinary African or Indian is
not necessarily afraid of snakes, even if modern and recently imposed structures tend to conceal the serpent's traditional role from him or her. For
example, in Benin the old god, Dan, whose story we have sketched, takes
everything in his stride and sees where his writ runs in each fresh development. As lord of energy and motion he has become the patron of TRAINS,
steamers, motor transport and AIRCRAFT.

As a basic archetype, linked to the well-springs of life and the imagination, the serpent, it becomes apparent, has retained worldwide his seemingly utterly contradictory symbolic powers. If the strongest of them were
censured (or indeed censored) at a particular point in human history, they
are now beginning to emerge from incarceration to restore harmony and
freedom to mankind. Their channel is poetry, painting and medicine, which
have always had the serpent as an attribute. The physical sciences, through
their revolutionary discoveries, are added to their number, at least that is
what Einstein's famous theory would lead one to believe.

Thus, in spite of all the upheavals of our present century, Athene, goddess
of all true knowledge, still goes on clutching to her bosom the serpent
which gave birth to Dionysos, Satan and the emperors of China.

sesame Although the plant does not originate in China, sesame is the traditional Chinese tonic. Its seeds are regarded as enabling one to abstain from cereals and to achieve longevity. When Lao Tzu and Yin Hi set out for the western regions – Kun-Lun, the centre of the world – they ate sesame for their food (KALL, MAST).

The word sesame is inseparable from the magic spell 'Open, sesame!' uttered by Ali Baba to open the doors of the mysterious CAVERN in which the Forty Thieves had hidden their plunder. It is impossible to determine the origin of the phrase as a practical command, but it remains as a symbol undoubtedly linked to fertility, since when the seed-pod opens it provides all the wealth of the Earth. From the psychological point of view, 'Open, sesame!' is not without significance in the context of those closed doors which are individuals isolated from one another. Some small magic password is required, to open not only hearts, but also the secret pathways of the unconscious. 'Open, sesame!' is an appeal to the riches hidden in the cavern, whether that cavern be the seed-pod which gives food and fecundates, or whether it be a CHEST stuffed with material wealth, the sanctuary of spiritual revelation or the maze of the unconscious.

Set The Egyptian god whom Plutarch compared with TYPHON and the Palestinian BAAL, was identified with the principle of evil and often depicted as a black pig gobbling up the Moon in which the soul of his brother, the kindly OSIRIS, had taken refuge. He was the Devil of Ancient Egyptian mythology, worshipped by some, execrated by others, but feared by all. A perverted power and a character in the cosmic and moral struggle between good and evil, he symbolizes primeval power misdirected to evil ends.

seven Seven corresponds to the seven days of the week, the seven planets, seven rungs of perfection, seven spheres or celestial stairs, the seven petals of the rose, the seven heads of the *nāga* of Angkor, the seven branches of the shaman's cosmic and sacrificial tree and so on.

Some groups of seven symbolize other groups of seven: thus the rose with its seven petals conjures up the Seven Heavens and the seven orders of angels, both perfect groupings. Seven denotes the fullness of the planetary and angelic orders, the fullness of the heavenly mansions, the fullness of the moral order and the fullness of energies and principles in the spiritual order. Seven was an Ancient Egyptian symbol of eternal life. It symbolizes the dynamic perfection of a complete cycle. Each phase of the Moon lasts for seven days and the four phases of the Moon (7×4) complete the cycle. In this context, Philo of Alexandria observed that the sum of the first seven digits ($1 + 2 + 3 + 4 + 5 + 6 + 7$) equals the same figure – 28. Seven conveys the meaning of a fresh start after a cycle has been completed and of positive regeneration.

Seven characterized the worship of Apollo and ceremonies in his honour were held on the seventh day of the month. In China, too, popular festivals were celebrated on the seventh day. Seven recurs in countless Ancient Greek traditions and legends – the seven Hesperides, the seven gates of Thebes, Niobe's seven sons and seven daughters, the seven strings of the lyre, the seven spheres and so on. There are seven emblems of the Buddha. The CIRCUMAMBULATION of Mecca is completed in seven circuits. If the centre is included, it is also to be seen in the hexagram (see STAR OF DAVID). A week consists of six working days and one day of rest, representing the centre; the heavens contain (according to the old computation) six planets with the Sun as their centre; the hexagram has six sides, six angles or six star-arms, its centre acting as the seventh; the six directions of space have a mid-point or centre which gives the number seven. Seven symbolizes the fullness both of space and of time.

As the sum of the numbers FOUR (symbolizing Earth, with its four points of the compass) and THREE (symbolizing Heaven), seven symbolizes the fullness of the universe in motion.

A group of seven comprises the fullness of moral life if the three theological virtues of Faith, Hope and Charity are added to the four cardinal virtues of Prudence, Temperance, Justice and Fortitude.

The seven colours of the rainbow and the seven notes of the diatonic scale display seven as the governor of vibration, that vibration which many primitive traditions hold to be the very essence of matter. Hippocrates is credited with stating that through its hidden properties the number seven maintained all things in being, bestowed life and motion and that its influence extended to heavenly beings.

As we observed at the beginning, seven is the number of the completed cycle and of its renewal. Having created the world in SIX days, God rested on the seventh day and made it holy. The SABBATH is, therefore, not really a day of rest standing outside Creation, but its crowning achievement. This is what the week, the length of a phase of the Moon, conjures up.

Islam is equally familiar with the concept of seven adding perfection to a group of six, and this is especially true of the Ismailis who hold that every solid body possesses seven sides – its six facets and its fullness, corresponding to the Sabbath. 'All things in this world are seven, because all things possess their own individuality and six facets.' The gifts of the intellect are seven – six, plus *ghaybat*, suprasensory knowledge. There are seven Imams to each period – six, plus the Qā'im, the Imam of the Resurrection. Furthermore each of these series corresponds to the others. The Religion of the Letter is to evolve over a six-day cycle, each day being a thousand years, and they will be followed by a seventh, the Sabbath of Religion in Truth, the day of the Sun and of enlightenment and of the manifestation of the Hidden Imam.

A Hindu tradition attributes six rays to the sun, six corresponding to the six quarters of space and the seventh to the centre. The rainbow apparently has six colours, not seven, the seventh being white, the synthesis of the other six. Similarly, the seven sides of Mount Meru each face one of the seven continents (*dvīpa*) corresponding to the seven quarters of Hindu space (six, plus the centre). Clement of Alexandria wrote that from God 'the Heart of the Universe, emanate six divisions and phases of time.' This was the secret of the number seven: a return to the centre, to the First Cause, seven, deriving from the group of six, perfects the whole.

Seven is clearly a worldwide symbol of wholeness, but of a wholeness which is not static, a dynamic wholeness. As such it is the key to the Book of Revelation, with its seven churches, seven stars, seven Spirits of God, seven seals, seven trumpets, seven thunders, seven heads, seven plagues, seven cups, seven kings. Seven is the number of the Buddhist Heavens. Avicenna also describes 'Seven Archangels, Princes of the Seven Heavens', who correspond to Enoch's Seven Watchers and to the Veda's seven Rishi. The latter live in the seven stars of the Great Bear, which the Chinese relate to the seven apertures in the body and the seven openings in the heart. The red lamp of the Chinese secret societies has seven arms like the Jewish seven-branched candlestick.

Some Muslim writers relate the seven esoteric meanings of the Koran to the seven subtle centres of the human body, and this reminds us that Yoga also acknowledges seven subtle centres – the six CHAKRA, plus the *sahasrāra-padma*. Abū Ya'qūb claimed that Spiritual Shapes were made manifest by the Seven Supreme Letters which are the Seven Intellects and the Seven Cherubim.

The Heavens are seven in number and so, according to Dante, are the planetary spheres, and these the Cathars made to correspond to the seven Liberal Arts. We have noted (see LADDER) that the Seven Heavens should also be identified with the seven notches in the Siberian axial tree, with the seven colours of the Buddha's staircase, the seven metals of the ladder in Mithraic mysteries and the seven rungs of the ladder of the Kadosh in Scottish Freemasonry, since seven is the number of the ascending order of spiritual levels which allow the individual to pass from Earth to Heaven.

At birth, the Buddha had measured the universe by taking seven steps to each of the four points of the compass. Four of the essential stages in his liberation correspond to the pauses, each of seven days, which he made under four different trees.

Ssu Ma Ch'ien wrote that the *yang* numbers achieved their perfection in seven. Seven different sets of indicators are considered in divination by yarrow-stems, in sets of seven each, which employs forty-nine in all. Forty-nine is also the number of Bardo, the intermediate state in Tibetan belief of the soul after death. This state lasts for forty-nine days and, originally at least, was split into seven periods each of seven days. In Japan, the souls of the dead are believed to dwell on the roofs of their homes for forty-nine days, a belief carrying the same meaning (CORT, EVAB, GRAP, GUED, GUEM, GUES, HERA, SAIR).

The number seven is frequently used in the Old Testament. There is the seven-branched candlestick; the seven spirits resting on Jesse's rod; the seven Heavens in which the orders of angels dwell; and the seven years which Solomon spent building the Temple (1 Kings 6: 38). Not only the seventh day, but the seventh year, was a time of rest, and every seven years slaves were set at liberty and debts wiped clean. Seven is used seventy-seven times in the Old Testament. Through the changes which it ushers in, the number seven itself possesses powers and is a magic number. When Jericho was captured, seven priests with seven trumpets were ordered to walk seven times round the city walls on the seventh day. Elisha sneezed seven times and the child was restored to life (2 Kings 4: 35). Naaman the leper bathed seven times in the Jordan and was cleansed (2 Kings 5: 14). 'The just man falleth seven times, and riseth up again' (Proverbs 24: 16). Seven unblemished creatures of each species were saved from the Flood. Pharaoh dreamed of seven fat and seven lean kine.

Seven is not, however, exempt from care since it indicates the passing from the known to the unknown: one cycle has ended, but what will its successor be?

By Sumerian times seven (with some of its multiples) had become a sacred number and it was certainly the darling child of Biblical numerology. Since it corresponded to the number of the planets, it always characterized perfection (the Gnostics' *pleroma*) if not the godhead itself. The week comprises seven days in memory of the length of Creation (Genesis 2: 2ff.). If the Passover feast of unleavened bread lasted seven days (Exodus 12: 15, 19), this was undoubtedly because the Exodus itself was regarded as a new creation and one which brought salvation.

Zechariah (3: 9) speaks of the seven eyes of God. Then there are the groups of seven in the Book of Revelation. The seven lamps which are the seven spirits of God signify the spirit of God in its fullness (4: 5); the seven letters to the seven churches signify the Church as a whole; and there are the seven trumpets, cups and so on. All these herald the final accomplishment of God's will in the world.

This is why seven is also the devil's number, since Satan, 'the ape of God', always strives to imitate God – hence the Beast with Seven Heads (Revelation 13: 1). However, the visionary of Patmos more usually kept half seven, three and a half, for the powers of evil, thereby showing that the designs of the Evil One were doomed to failure (Revelation 12: 6). For example, the dragon was only able to threaten the Woman, that is God's people, for 1260 days, or three-and-a-half years, and there is a reference (12: 14) to 'a time, times, and half a time'.

Seven is the key to St John's Gospel – seven weeks, seven miracles, seven references to Christ as 'I am.' Seven recurs forty times in the Book of Revelation in groups of seven: seals, trumpets, cups, visions and so on. The book is composed in series of seven. The number also denotes the fullness of a period of time, such as Creation in Genesis; the ending of a period of time, an era or a phase; the plenitude of the graces given to the Church by the Holy Spirit.

There have been many symbolical explanations of the mystical meaning of the seventh day. This was the day on which God rested from the task of Creation and signifies, as it were, the recruitment of the divine strength in the contemplation of the finished work. The seventh day's rest marks a compact between God and humanity.

Seven symbolizes the end of the world and the fullness of time. According to St Augustine it measures the length of history and the period of humanity's earthly pilgrimage. If God ordained a day for rest, St Augustine was to remark, it is because he wished to separate himself from his creation and to be independent of it, so as to repose in it. On the other hand, the number seven, indicative of rest and cessation of toil, invites humanity to turn to God to repose in him alone (*De Genese* 4: 16). St Augustine was also to speak of the miraculous draught of fishes as standing for the end of the world: Christ had seven disciples with him and by this means set in motion the end of time.

Lastly, six denotes a part only, since work comprises the part and only rest signifies the whole, since it denotes perfection. We suffer in the degree in which we know only in part without the fullness of encountering God. What is in part will vanish and seven will crown six (*City of God* 11: 31).

On the evidence of the Talmud, the Jews also regarded the number seven as a symbol of human wholeness, simultaneously male and female. This is because it is the sum of four and three; Adam during the hours of his first day received the soul which gave him full being at the fourth hour and at the seventh hour was given his companion, that is he was duplicated in Adam and Eve.

In Islam, too, seven is a lucky number and the symbol of perfection. There are seven Heavens, seven Earths, seven seas, seven divisions of Hell and seven gates; seven verses in the *Fatiha* (the first *sura* in the Koran); the seven letters not used in the Arabic alphabet which 'fell under the table'; the seven words which comprise the Muslim profession of faith, the Shahāda; and so on.

During the pilgrimage to Mecca, the faithful should make seven circuits of the Ka'ba and travel seven times between Mount Cafā and Mount Marnia.

The Companions in the Cave (*Ashab al-Kahf*: Koran 17) were seven in number (Seven Sleepers). Charms are written using their names to which is added that of the dog which guarded them for 300 years (LANN 1: p. 314).

The seven gates of Paradise open to the mother of seven daughters. When a pregnant woman is in a critical condition seven verses of the *sura* are read over her. In Iran, at the moment of birth, a lighted lamp is placed upon a napkin and the napkin is decorated with seven different kinds of fruit and with seven different aromatic spices. Children are generally given their names on the seventh day. Sometimes a girl will go to the riverside on her wedding eve, fill and empty her water-jar seven times and then throw seven handfuls of corn into the stream (MASP pp. 35ff.). This is a magic fertility symbol.

In Morocco barren women wrap their girdles seven times round the trunks of certain trees and then tie them with one of the seven cords attached (WERS 1: p. 77). In Syria girls without suitors exorcize the evil influences which prevent them from finding husbands by bathing in the sea and allowing seven waves to pass over their heads. If a naked sword is displayed before a seven-day-old baby it will become valiant. Seven elements are essential to a woman's adornment.

To ensure that a dead person is pardoned for his or her sins, seven lines should be drawn on the grave. After burial one should step seven paces backwards and seven paces forwards again. There is a common belief that the souls of the dead remain for seven days close to their graves.

To beg the favours of a saint, his tomb should be visited on seven days, or four times a day for seven days. Travellers who are forced to spend the night in an uninhabited place should first walk seven times round the spot.

There are countless instances of this belief that seven is a sacred number and that its influence, while generally beneficent, may sometimes be evil. A proverb states that 'seven is hard.'

Nizāmī's famous work, *The Seven Princesses*, blends colour symbolism with astrology. There are seven palaces, each the colour of one of the seven planets, and in each dwells a princess from one of the seven different parts of the world.

Muslim mystics affirm that the Koran conveys seven meanings, and sometimes seventy meanings are claimed. A *hadīth* states that the Koran possesses both exoteric and esoteric meaning, and that the esoteric meaning itself has an esoteric meaning, and so on, through seven esoteric meanings in all.

Mystical physiology, so characteristic of Persian Sufism, is also based upon the number seven. Writers such as Semnāni distinguish seven different organs or subtle sheathings 'each of which typifies a prophet in the human microcosm.... The first marks the subtle corporeal organ and denotes, as it were, the Adam of your being.... The sixth is the Jesus of your being.... The seventh is the Muhammad of your being' (CORL pp. 238ff.).

These subtle sheathings are associated with different colours – matt black for Adam; blue for Noah; red for Abraham; white for Moses; yellow for David; glossy black for Jesus; green for Muhammad (ibid. p. 242).

In his famous poem, *The Conference of Birds*, Farīd al-Dīn 'Attār symbolizes the seven stages along the mystic way as seven valleys. The first is that of the quest (*talab*); the second is that of love (*eshq*); the third, of knowledge (*ma'rifa*); the fourth, of independence (*istignā*); the fifth, of unity (*tauhīd*); the sixth, of wonder (*hayrat*); and the seventh, of spiritual poverty (*faqr*) and of mystical extinction (*fanā'*).

The Plains Indians regard seven as being the number of the cosmic coordinates of mankind, through adding the four cardinal points (the immanent plane) and the World Axis running through the centre of this plane which is the 'here and now' (mankind) and ending in the upper and lower. Seven = 4 (points of the compass) + 2 (vertical axis) + 1 (centre), this 1 being the result of the incidence of 4 and 2. The transcendental opposition of the upper and the lower is resolved by their incidence upon the immanent plane in oneness, which is the place of mankind (ALEC pp. 47–8).

The same symbol recurs among the Pueblo Indians, but upon the social plane. The holy town of Zuni, 'the centre of the world', is divided into seven sections corresponding to the seven quarters of the world. It comprises the joining together of seven former villages, standing for the same division of the cosmos. The social division is based upon the same plan, clans being attached in groups of three to each of these sevenfold divisions, with the exception of the parrot-clan, the principal clan in the tribe which occupies on its own the centre or 'here and now' (MULR pp. 277–8). Cosmic colours were allocated according to the same 'cosmic palette'.

The great sky-god of the Maya-Quiché, who becomes the thirteen-god with the twelve stars (rain-gods), also becomes the seven-god with the six cosmic Suns. He thus forms the group of agrarian gods. The ideogram of the seven-god depicts the Great Bear.

The Mame, descended from the Maya, fashion their hearths from six stones (three large and three small) which comprise the number seven when the cooking-pot is placed upon them. Seven is an attribute of the corn-god and is also that of fire in its different forms – thunderbolts, the fire of the gods; subterranean fire, that warms the great Earth-Mother; the hearth, the fire of mankind (GIRP p. 81).

The corn-god is the seven-god because the number seven is associated with the astronomical phenomenon of the transit of the Sun through the zenith which determines the start of the rainy season (*Popol-Vuh*). Since this god is the archetype of the Perfect Human, he imposes his numerical symbol upon the human family, the latter in fact comprising ideally six children. They comprise the body of the number, seven, the head being composed of the Sun–Moon symbiosis of the parents, recalling the divine Twins who initiated the creation (GIRP p. 237).

The Maya placed the seventh day, falling in the middle of their thirteen-day week, under the sign of the jaguar, giving expression to the inner forces of the Earth. It was a lucky day (THOH).

The seven-goddess, called 'seven serpents' or 'seven ears of corn' and set in the middle of the series one to thirteen, symbolized the human heart and the maize-cob. Days numbered seven were lucky (SOUM, THOH).

In the Temple of Coricancha at Cuzco, where the entire Inca pantheon was represented, a wall close to the Cosmic Tree bore a design depicting seven eyes and called 'the eyes of all things'. Lehman-Nitsche regards this as relating simultaneously to the Pleiades and, undoubtedly, to the eyes of Viracocha, the supreme sky-god. He notes that the prophet Zechariah (4: 10) speaks of seven as 'the eyes of the Lord, which run to and fro through the whole earth'.

The Dogon regard the number seven as the symbol of the marriage of opposites, of the resolution of duality and, hence, as a symbol of oneness and accordingly of perfection. However, this marriage of opposites, which in very precise terms is the marriage of the two sexes, is as much a symbol of fecundation. Because of this, the Word being analogous with semen and the ear with the vagina, the Dogon regard the number seven as the emblem of the Lord of the Word, a rain-god, and hence god of storms and of BLACKSMITHS (GRIE, GRIL).

The Bambara, too, consider seven as the number of perfection since it is the sum of four (female) and three (male). The supreme deity, Faro, god of water and the Word, dwells in the seventh Heaven with the fecundating waters which he bestows in the form of rain. It is in the seventh Heaven, too, that the Sun sinks each evening at the end of his transit. Like Heaven, Earth is divided into seven levels and the waters of Earth, too, are seven in number, as are its metals. Seven is the number both of mankind and of the universal First Cause.

As the sum of four and three, it is the sign of human wholeness (combining the spiritual principles of the two sexes), of the universe in its totality, of creation fulfilled and of natural growth. Seven is also the expression of the Perfect Word and thereby of primal oneness.

Altaic Tatars, when boasting of the shrines in their native land, give them a common appellation – 'my country with its Seven Gates and my waters' (HARA p. 177).

Jean-Paul Roux emphasizes how Mongol and Turkic tribes regard seven as 'a holy cosmic number' (ROUF p. 98).

Since seven is the number of human perfection – that is, of the perfect actualization of the individual – it is easy to understand why it should be the number of the HERMAPHRODITE, as in Africa it is the number of the mystic Twins, since it is patently obvious that hermaphrodite and twins are one and the same. The combinations of TAROT cards giving the number seven are also significant. The pairing of Emperor and Empress (four and three) gives Father and Mother, perfection in the manifested, the inner and outward forms assumed by temporal power, the harmonious sum of the four elements and three principles of esoteric knowledge. On the other hand the spiritual pairing of Pope and Female Pope also produces seven, but as the sum of five and two. It is hardly surprising that the seventh arcanum itself, the expression of both these pairings, should be the CHARIOT, the sign of fulfilment.

In folk stories and legends the number would seem to express the seven states of matter, the seven degrees of awareness and the seven stages of evolution:

1 awareness of the physical body; cravings satisfied simply and brutishly;
2 awareness of the emotions; impulses become more complex through feeling and imagination;
3 awareness of intellect; the individual classifies, arranges and reasons;
4 awareness of intuition; relationship with the unconscious becomes apparent;
5 awareness of spirituality; detachment from worldly things;
6 awareness of will; thought is transmitted into action;
7 awareness of life; directing action towards eternal life and salvation.

Madame Loeffler-Delachaux regards Hop o' my THUMB and each of his brothers as symbols of each of these states of awareness (LOEF pp. 197–8).

seventeen This number, together with seventy-two, the first being the sum of nine and eight when added, the second of their product when multiplied together, have vast symbolic importance.

In Islamic tradition, seventeen is the number of the liturgical gestures (*rak'a*) employed in the five daily prayers and it is also the number of words used in the call to prayer. In Muslim folklore, the symbolic number seventeen constantly recurs, especially in legends, 'more particularly the seventeen pieces of advice whispered into the king's ear during his coronation and the seventeen components of the standard' (M. Mokri, *Les secrets de Hamza*).

In Shi'ism, above all, and through its influence in the religious epic poetry of the Anatolian Turks,

a quasi-magical importance attaches to the number seventeen. . . . Shi'ite mystics from a very early period held the number seventeen in veneration, a veneration stemming from far earlier Pythagorean speculations based upon the Greek alphabet. . . . Seventeen was the number of those who were to be brought to life again, each of these individuals being bound to be given one of the letters of the alphabet from which the supreme name of God was composed.

This is not unrelated to the Star, the seventeenth arcanum of the Tarot, which is a symbol of change and rebirth and what Dr Allendy explains as 'deliverance from Karma' (ALLN p. 364). Furthermore, according to the Sufi alchemist Gābir ibn Hayyān, the shape (*sura*) of all things in the world is seventeen. Seventeen stands for the very foundation of the theory of balance and should be regarded as the law of equilibrium in all things.

'The number seventeen is especially important in the tradition of trade-guilds which recognize seventeen initiates or companions of Ali, seventeen patrons of the founders of the Muslim guilds begun by Selmān-i Fārsī, and seventeen major guilds' (MELN pp. 455ff.).

The Ancient Greeks regarded seventeen as standing for the number of consonants in the alphabet, successively broken down into nine (the number of mute consonants) and eight (the number of semi-vowels or semi-consonants). These numbers are also closely related to their theory of music and to the harmony of the spheres.

As we have observed at the outset, seventeen and seventy-two are first the sum and second the product of eight and nine. Furthermore the sums of the digits comprising these two numbers give eight for seventeen (1 + 7) and nine for seventy-two (7 + 2). Nine and eight constantly recur in Ancient Greek numerological speculations, whether it be on the planes of grammar, of music (the ratio nine to eight is represented by the median chords of the lyre), of prosody or of cosmology.

The Ancient Romans seem to have regarded the number seventeen as unlucky since an anagram of the letters of which it is composed (XVII) gives the word VIXI, I have lived.

seventy (see also NUMBERS; SEVEN) All derivatives or multiples of seven carry with them the idea of wholeness. Turkish tradition notes that seventy-two is a co-partner with seventy (as it is in the case of THIRTY-SIX). Seventy is ten times seven – a superlative equal to twofold perfection – and seventy-two may be divided by nine numbers – 2, 3, 6, 8, 9, 12, 18, 24 and 36. It is also eight times nine and, above all, one fifth of 360, that is to say one fifth of the Zodiac. Seventy-seven and seven times seven are self-explanatory as well as 700, 7000, 70,000 and 700,000. In short, this is an incidence of all the perfect numbers.

In a famous *hadīth*, the Prophet declared: 'After me, my community (*umma*) will divide into seventy-three sects of which seventy-two shall perish and one shall be saved' (MASM p. 137).

In an allusion to the seventy-two diseases, another *hadīth* has the Prophet say to Ali: 'Start and finish your meals with salt, since this is a remedy against the seventy-two diseases.'

The Shi'ites are just as partial to the number seventy-two. The Imam Hosayn died of thirst with seventy-two companions. There are seventy-two witnesses in the *taziye*, the dramatic equivalent of the medieval mystery-plays. The Persian psaltery (*sentūr*) has seventy-two strings (three per note).

According to Philippe de Commines (*Mémoires* 2: p. 4), when Philip the Good, Duke of Burgundy, forced the citizens of Ghent to accept the Treaty of Gavre (24 July 1453), he took away the right of their guilds to carry banners. The latter were seventy-two in number. It is interesting to compare this conventional number of guilds with that of the sects, two notional orders which often intersect in history (DENJ pp. 395ff.).

The Bible contains a wealth of examples of the number seven and its derivatives being used to denote to the highest degree the wholeness of actuality and even of potentiality. St Augustine's ten times seven corresponds to a complete development, a cycle of development wholly fulfilled.

The gift of a fool shall do thee no good . . . for he looketh to receive many things for one.

(Ecclesiasticus 20: 14)

And the light of the sun shall be sevenfold, as the light of seven days, in the day that the Lord bindeth up the breach of his people, and healeth the stroke of their wound.

(Isaiah 30: 26)

In this context the prophet is describing the prosperity that is to come. It will be incomparably greater than anything in the past, since its source, the light of the Sun, will have been infinitely increased sevenfold.

Then came Peter to him, and said, Lord, how oft shall my brother sin against me, and I forgive him? till seven times? Jesus saith unto him, I say not unto thee, Until seven times: but, Until seventy times seven.

(Matthew 18: 21–2)

In the Bible the number seventy always denotes universality. Genesis 10 lists seventy tribes of the Earth, scattered after the sacrilegious building of the Tower of Babel, a sin for which mankind as a whole was punished.

seventy-two See under SEVENTEEN; SEVENTY; THIRTY-SIX.

shadow On the one hand, shadow is the opposite to light, and on the other, the very image of fleeting, unreal and mutable things.

Shadow is the *yin* aspect opposed to the *yang* aspect (see YIN AND YANG). It may well be – and etymology would seem to bear this out – that the basic dualism of Chinese philosophical definition was originally represented by the shady side of a valley opposed to its sunny side. The study of shadows seems to have been one of the fundamentals of ancient geomancy and hence of orientation. The lack of a shadow, a characteristic the Chinese record in the case of a number of individuals, may be explained in three different ways. It was due to the fact that purification had made their bodies translucent, or that they had escaped the limitations of bodily existence; both these conditions were the case of the Immortals; or it was due to the 'central' position of the body itself, immediately below the Sun at its zenith, and that was, roughly speaking, the position of the emperor. Beneath the *Kien* tree, the World Axis up and down which monarchs ascend and descend, there is neither shadow nor echo. This central position, the position of the solstices and of the noonday, is also that of the Ismaili mystic at the moment when the soul casts no shadow, when the Devil Iblīs casts no shadow – the moment of inward peace.

Li Tzu regarded the shadow, without independent existence or movement, as a symbol of all unpremeditated actions. Buddhists go further, seeing all phenomena as shadows – 'dreams, bubbles, shadows' – as do Taoists, judging the reality of Heaven and Earth as shadows. Nevertheless, magical practices relating to human shadows or the Indonesian shadow-theatre might, perhaps, provide a different viewpoint, shadows being regarded, in these instances, as charged with the individual's complete subtle being (CORT, GRAD, GRAP, KALL, MAST).

Many African tribes regard shadows as the second nature of people and things and as being linked, generally speaking, to death. The Semang Negritos believe that in the kingdom of the dead you lead a shadowy life, feeding on the shadow of things.

The Indians of northern Canada believe that at death shadow and soul, separated entities, both leave the body. While the soul journeys to the kingdom of the wolf, in the west, the shadow lingers by the grave. It is the shadow which maintains relations with the living, and hence it is to the shadow that grave-offerings are made. The soul is able to return and by uniting with the shadow become a fresh being. People who are born a second time in this way sometimes dream of their previous existence.

In many South American Indian languages, the same word is used for shadow, soul and picture (METB).

The Yakut regarded the shadow as one of the three human souls. Shadows were respected and children not allowed to play with them (HARA p. 182). Tungus avoid treading upon another person's shadow.

Tradition states that the person who has sold his or her SOUL to the Devil loses his or her shadow. The meaning of this is that being without a shadow, the person no longer exists as a spiritual being or as a soul. The Devil ceases to create the shadow of that person because it no longer exists.

Muslim mystics regard every manifestation of divine reality – and such is creation in the eyes of the believer – as 'the shadow of God, black light, darkness at noon. Shape determines the limits of all beings, which are no more than the shadows cast by a light from on high which hides all as it reveals all. The loveliest human beauty, the mystic Rūzbahān wrote, is no more than shadow. Jungian analysis (JUNS pp. 168–76) classes as 'shadow' all that which the subject refuses to recognize or admit and which dominates him or her, despite this, directly or indirectly, through traits of character which he or she feels lowering, or in impulses which he or she regards as incompatible with him- or herself. This shadow is projected in dreams in the shape of persons who are simply reflections of the unconscious self. The shadow is also displayed in impulsive and unpremeditated words or actions which suddenly reveal an aspect of the psyche. The shadow also makes the subject more sensitive to certain individual or collective influences which arouse and reveal in him or her hidden tendencies. These are not necessarily harmful, but they run the risk of becoming so the longer they remain repressed in the shadow of the unconscious. There is everything to gain by allowing them into the light of consciousness. However, the subject often dreads their appearance for fear of having to bear their burden, to master them or to make them beneficial and of having to face up to his or her complexes. 'I feel two beings within me . . .' The coexistence of opposites is hard to bear, but rich in potential.

Shakti In Indian art the *shakti*, personified as the goddess Shakti, stands for the female element in all being and symbolizes cosmic energy, with which she is identified. The Shakti is generally depicted tightly clasped to Shiva who stands for latency and the Father, while the Shakti is manifestation and the Divine Mother. Shiva in his wisdom becomes the Shakti, but she must be reabsorbed into him in order to return to primeval Oneness. Shiva and the Shakti are but one in the Absolute, being the two aspects, male and female, of Oneness. In folk-art and imagination, the Shakti were merely powers, and depicted as goddesses and wives of the gods.

shala The shala or sal-tree was a royal tree with magnificent trunk and foliage and it was a synonym for temporal power or even the power of the Brahman. It was regarded by Buddhists as a sacred tree because under its shade the Buddha's birth and his final release from the cycle of rebirths took place. The Chinese sometimes regard the Buddhist shala as a Moon-tree, which makes it akin to symbols of immortality (see CINNAMON; LAUREL).

shamrock In Christian art, triple-leafed shapes and trilobate arches, which remind the viewer of the shamrock-leaf, symbolize the Trinity.

sheaf The sheaf is a symbol of harvest, plenty and prosperity. There were rituals in honour of the first and last sheaves to fall to the scythe since they were infused with 'the weight of sacred power . . . The force of the whole of vegetation dwells in that sheaf, just as it is concentrated in the few ears that are not cut down' (ELIT p. 337). That force was, however, itself ambivalent and could become harmful if a few grains or the entire sheaf were not cast on a neighbour's land or offered up in propitiation to bring assurance of food, heavenly blessing, protection against all ills, good fortune and, some-times, the gift of prophecy.

In so far as it is tied together, or is a gathering of stalks, or a bundle or a group of similar objects, the sheaf symbolizes the reduction of the many to the one, the integration of disparate elements into a whole, the strength which is the consequence of unity and social concord. In the opposite sense, the sheaf, like the KNOT, can mean something which inhibits the free development of the individual.

Like the sheaf, bunches of flowers, cascading fountains or fireworks symbolize the joyous profusion of life, the way in which it leaps up in thousands of flashing sparks or germs of life, the prodigal nature of its fleeting gifts and a sort of perpetual offering.

Throughout North Africa 'harvesting the last corner of a field and cutting the last sheaf partake of the nature of ritual slaughter, to ensure that the souls which have made the soil fertile make their departure.' Jean Servier describes these agrarian ceremonies and in particular the sacrificial slaughter of the sheaf. The last sheaf, which is kept until the following year, is never burned, 'since one should never use fire to bring to an end the moist fecundity of the folk from the Underworld' (SERP pp. 226, 230ff.).

sheep (see also SHEPHERD) The symbolism of the sheep differs little from that of the LAMB, the latter closely linked to values given to the symbol by Christianity. The Welsh tale of Peredur in *The Mabinogion* describes two flocks of sheep, one white and the other black, with a river running between them. Every time a white sheep bleated, a black sheep crossed the river and turned white, and every time a black sheep bleated, a white sheep crossed the river and turned black. Beside the river – in all probability symbolizing the boundary between this world and the Beyond – grew a tall tree, one half of which was in flames from the root to the top and the other in full leaf. The white sheep which turned black symbolized souls descending from Heaven to Earth, while the black sheep which turned white symbolized the opposite – souls ascending from Earth to Heaven. Such symbolism may, however, antedate Christianity and be an adaptation of the belief which Caesar describes in his *De bello gallico* that the gods required a life in return for a life. This was one of the basic principles of the transmigration of souls.

On the other hand, in the Irish tale of the siege of Druin Damghaire sheep are symbols of diabolical maleficence. The evil druids of Cormac, King of Ireland, in his war against the refusal of the province of Munster to pay an unjust tribute, employed three maleficent black sheep with fleeces that curled into iron spikes. They easily overcame a number of warriors (CHAB pp. 176–9; REVC pp. 43, 22; MABG p. 203; MEDI pp. 10, 35).

shell (see also CONCH; COWRIE)   Shells conjure up the waters in which they are formed and share the fertility symbolism which belongs to WATER. In shape and depth they are reminiscent of the female sexual organs, while the fact that they sometimes contain pearls may perhaps have inspired the legend of the birth of Aphrodite, rising from a shell. This would corroborate the dual aspect of the symbol – erotic and fecundating. Countless paintings of the birth of Venus, like those by Botticelli or Titian, illustrate this association of fertility linked to sexual pleasure. From there it is easy to pass to notions of prosperity and good luck, and this is what the Chinese did, seldom failing to picture their emperors in association with a shell.

Following this same symbolic line, we find the Aztecs calling their Moon-god Teccaciztecatl, Shell-man, and depicting him as a womb, standing for birth and procreation.

However, links between Earth and Moon go to the former's very essence, that is to say to the Earth's entrails and to those chthonian powers often depicted in the shape of an aged lunar-Earth goddess. This is true of the Maya, to whom shells symbolized the Underworld and the kingdom of the dead. When a shell-shape is added to the solar hieroglyphic, it means the Black Sun, that is the Sun going about his nocturnal duties of visiting the Underworlds (THOH). In the West Indies, shells are placed on graves in cemeteries and lighted candles are placed in them on special occasions.

Shells are thus linked to the idea of death, in the sense that the prosperity which they symbolize for individuals or for generations of individuals stems from the death of the earlier occupant of the shell, the death of the preceding generation. In the Stone Age, the sea-shells used as funeral ornaments 'welded the dead person to the cosmological principle – Moon, Water, Woman – gave that person new life by inclusion within the cosmic and presupposed birth, death and rebirth on the pattern of the phases of the Moon' (Breuil in SERH pp. 37–8).

Malinowski discovered in the islands of the Western Pacific a strange trade (*Kula*) in shells worked into armlets (*mwali*) or strung as necklaces (*sulava*). This trade was subsidiary to other bartering and was more like a religious ritual than a commercial transaction. *Kula* means 'circle' and 'the same word is applied to the journey made by the souls of the dead who, according to tradition, set off for the Island of Tuma, to the northwest of Boyuna; home . . . of the *mwali*. *Mwali* are broad arm-bands made from the upper portions of a large conical shell' and are regarded as male. They travel in a westerly direction and symbolize the human quest whose goal is death. *Sulava* are long necklaces of red shells, regarded as female, and travel from west to east. They stand for the impurities of the flesh and for menstrual blood, incarnation, the descent of the soul into matter and fertility deriving from the dead. These sea-charms stimulate trade and engagements of all sorts between individuals.

(SERH pp. 285–91)

The foregoing explains why, in dreams, shells are an expression of the libido. The vagina which they portray is the entrance to the cavern or to the treasure-chamber, since all shells may possibly contain pearls. To dream of shells is therefore to be summoned to make a journey which is always charged with positive properties (AEPR).

Sheol In the Old Testament all those who rejected Jehovah went down alive into Sheol (translated as 'the pit' or 'the grave').

And it came to pass, as he had made an end of speaking all these words, that the ground clave asunder that was under them: And the earth opened her mouth, and swallowed them up, and their houses, and all the men that appertained unto Korah, and all their goods. They, and all that appertained to them, went down alive into the pit, and the earth closed upon them: and they perished from among the congregation. And all Israel that were round about them fled at the cry of them: for they said, Lest the earth swallow us up also. And there came out a fire from the Lord, and consumed the two hundred and fifty men that offered incense.

(Numbers 16: 31–5)

The Psalmist beseeches God: 'Return, O Lord, deliver my soul: oh save me for thy mercies' sake. For in death there is no remembrance of thee: in the grave who shall give thee thanks?' (Psalm 6: 5–6). And Job describes Sheol as 'A land of darkness, as darkness itself; and of the shadow of death, without any order, and where light is as darkness' (Job 10: 22); 'As the cloud is consumed and vanisheth away: so he that goeth down to the grave shall come up no more' (ibid. 7: 9).

The word is of unknown origin. It inspired fear, but conveyed no very clearly defined idea. It meant the diminished life of silence, utterly separated from God, which the dead spent, damned for their earthly deeds. Their abode was in the depths of the Earth, to which the dead descended to pass a gloomy afterlife. Their sufferings were described as being without reprieve and as the deprivation of all those things which conjure up symbolically the light of the Sun.

shepherd In the nomadic society of herdsmen, the image of the shepherd is impregnated with religious symbolism.

God is the Shepherd of Israel (Psalm 23: 1; Isaiah 40: 11; Jeremiah 31: 10). He leads his flock, watches over it and guards it. However, since God delegates part of his authority to temporal or spiritual leaders, the latter may also be termed shepherds of the people. The Judges were the shepherds of God's people (2 Samuel 7: 7). David was a shepherd boy whom God chose to be the leader of his people (2 Samuel 7: 8; 24: 17). In this respect the Children of Israel merely followed the religious customs of their neighbours in Egypt and Mesopotamia. Nevertheless, an important difference may be seen in that, in the Old Testament, the title of shepherd is only granted to leaders, and especially to kings, in a secondary manner. They are the shepherds chosen by God, but the flock itself belongs to God and God is the true shepherd.

This is why, even during the reign of Ahab, a prophet could denounce the king's apostasy in these words: 'I saw all Israel scattered upon the hills, as sheep that have not a shepherd' (1 Kings 22: 17). This was because the king was not the born shepherd by divine right. Jeremiah (23: 1–6) and Ezekiel (34) both charged the Shepherds of Israel with failure to perform their duties and went on to proclaim faithful shepherds or even God's direct intervention as he took charge of a flock which hirelings had neglected.

Latterly Judaism developed this symbolism in three directions:

1 human leaders are no longer considered other than mere instruments of the true shepherds, who are the good or evil angels of the people (1 Enoch 89);
2 the symbolism of the shepherd and his flock is no longer restricted to the relationship between God and Israel; God is the shepherd of mankind (Sirach 18: 13);
3 lastly, expectation of a new shepherd, after God's heart, culminates in the Messianism of the *Psalms of Solomon*; the Messiah 'leads the Lord's flock in faith and righteousness' (17: 45).

These last two aspects point directly to the Christian symbolism of the shepherd. Jesus said 'I am the good shepherd' (John 10: 11ff.); no hireling, but the one to whom the flock belongs and who is ready to die for it. He added (ibid. 10: 16) that, in his vision, the notion of the flock was not restricted to one seeming category of religion or of race.

The Book of Revelation also emphasizes this point, but by promoting another aspect of the symbol. Christ will lead all the nations of the Earth to the pasture, but with a rod of iron. He will be both shepherd and judge (Revelation 2: 27; 12: 5; 19: 15).

The picture of Christ as the Good Shepherd which so often recurs in such early Christian writings as *The Shepherd* of Hermas, culminates in a process already shown in the Old Testament whereby spiritual leaders are termed shepherds or pastors, whose ministry is constantly related to that of their Lord, 'that great shepherd of the sheep' (Hebrews 13: 20), 'the chief Shepherd' (1 Peter 5: 4).

This gospel symbolism is of a spiritual leader guiding the body of his disciples along the path of truth and salvation. According to the *Samyutta Nikāya* the Buddha employed very similar notions. 'The monk's pasture, his birthright' is the domain of spiritual realization, from which he should not stray for fear of running into serious danger. The danger resides, 'among the four stages of watchfulness, in the forbidden pasture', the domain of the senses. In this context, the basic emphasis is upon the fact that here the 'shepherd' is not personalized, but is identified with *dharma*, destiny, the chain of cause and effect.

The symbolism of the shepherd also contains the sense of a wisdom which is both intuitive and the fruit of experience. The shepherd symbolizes watchfulness. His duties entail the constant exercise of vigilance. He is awake and watching. Hence he is compared with the Sun, which sees all things, and with the king. Furthermore, since, as we have stated, the shepherd symbolizes the nomad, he is rootless and stands for the soul which is not a native of this Earth but always a stranger and pilgrim. In so far as his flock is concerned, the shepherd acts as a guardian and to this is linked knowledge, since he knows what pasture suits the animals in his charge. He observes the Heavens, the Sun, the Moon and the stars and can predict the weather. He distinguishes sounds and hears the noise of approaching wolves, as well as the bleating of lost sheep.

Through the different duties which he performs, he is regarded as a wise man whose activities are the result of contemplation and inner vision.

On a more basic level he represents the herdsman as opposed to the farmer, that is nomadic society associated with space as opposed to settled society imprisoned within time or, to take it to the uttermost extreme, as Being as opposed to Having. If we substitute the second for the first, it is CAIN's murder of Abel, a phase of 'fixation' or cyclic 'coagulation'.

Chinese mythology provides a parallel. Ch'e Yu was worshipped by herdsmen. He fought on horseback and this associated him with the nomadic tribespeople of Manchuria, renowned as horse-breeders. He had horns on his head and was, in addition, a wind-god. Now Ch'e Yu was defeated by Huang Ti, the inventor of agriculture, ritual, metal-working and alchemy. This would appear to have been the victory of a settled society of farmers and metal-workers over a society of nomadic herdsmen, of the *yin* aspect of one civilization over its *yang* aspect. Furthermore, since the metal needed to forge the NINE dynastic cauldrons was brought to Yu the Great from the nine regions by nine shepherds, this can be seen to have been a phenomenon of fixation and of ingathering from Chinese space to its centre and, therefore, of organization and lasting settlement (GRAD, GUET).

In Assyro-Babylonian civilization, the shepherd symbol took on cosmic significance. The Moon-god Tammuz was given the title of shepherd, the stars being his flock. He was a vegetation-god who died and came to life again. According to Krappe (in CIRD p. 280), like Adonis and Aphrodite and Osiris and Isis, Tammuz was joined in passionate love with Ishtar. Their relationship followed the pattern of the phases of the Moon in a series of disappearances and returns. During the 'dark' phase, the shepherd acted as a conductor of souls down to Earth. Cosmic powers stood for his flocks and he was revealed as the lord of all things.

shield Although it may sometimes be death-dealing, the shield is the symbol of the passive, defensive and protective WEAPON. To the strength given by the leather or metal of which it is made, the shield magically adds the strength of whatever is depicted upon it. In many cases the shield is, in fact, a representation of the universe, as if the warrior carrying it confronted his opponent with the cosmos and as if the blows which the latter struck went far beyond his opponent and sank into the reality depicted. The shield of Achilles is a case in point:

[Hephaistos] on it wrought many curious devices with cunning skill. Therein he wrought the earth, therein the heavens, therein the sea, and the unwearied sun, and the moon at the full, and therein all the constellations wherewith heaven is crowned. . . . Therein fashioned he also two cities of mortal men exceeding fair. In the one there were marriages and feastings . . . But around the other city lay two hosts of warriors in gleaming armour. And twofold plans found favour with them, either to lay waste the town or to divide in portions twain all the substance that the lovely city contained therein.

Hephaistos also depicted upon the shield 'soft fallow-land, rich tilth and wide ... a king's demesne-land ... a vineyard heavily laden with clusters ... a herd of straight-horned kine ... a great pasture of white-fleeced sheep ... and the great might of the river Oceanus, around the uttermost rim of the strongly-wrought shield' (*Iliad* 18: 483ff.). Upon this shield were concentrated all that makes life worth living, all the beauty the universe contains, all symbols of strength, wealth and happiness brought together This astounding display also symbolizes what is at stake in battle – all that is lost in death and all that is won in victory. The shield was broad enough to cover all the warrior's body and ultimately to be used as a stretcher to carry him dead or wounded from the field.

Instead of attractive scenes, shields sometimes depicted a face so terrifying as to paralyse an enemy. This was a psychological weapon. Perseus had conquered the frightful Gorgon, Medusa, without looking at her. He had polished his shield until it was like a mirror and, when Medusa saw her own face, she was petrified with horror and the hero cut off her head. Athene placed upon her shield the decapitated head which turned to stone those who looked upon it and used it against those who dared attack her.

St Paul's description of 'the whole armour of God' (Ephesians 6: 13–17), which the Christian uses in the spiritual battle for salvation, includes 'the shield of Faith' against which all the blows of the Evil One will shatter. To be more precise, he says that Faith will be 'able to quench all the fiery darts of the wicked'. Extinguishing the flames is to allow the sense of the symbol to give a wholly spiritual meaning to the part played by the Shield of Faith, which should be used against the temptations of heresy, pride and the flesh.

The Irish tale of the cattle-raid of Fraech is evidence that warriors' shields depicted in relief, or engraved, figures of imaginary or fabulous animals which acted as badges. This was the birth of heraldry, since each Irish hero would seem to have used a different pattern or emblem. By its very nature, the shield possesses all the qualities for warding off evil. Celtic words for 'shield' (Irish: *sciath*; Welsh, *yscwyd*; Breton, *skoed*) are related to the Latin word *scutum*, 'shield'. In medieval Irish literature 'shield' acquired a range of metonymic or metaphoric meanings such as 'warrior', 'protection', 'legal warranty' and so on. Shields are first and foremost passive weapons, submissive like the warrior caste to the priestly caste and not, in the first instance, weapons of aggression (Celtic languages have no native word for 'breastplate': the Irish word *luirech* is derived from the Latin *lorica*: but they were used by the Celts). There are plenty of protohistoric examples of notched round shields depicted on gravestones from southern France and Spain (of which they are a most important decorative element), alongside the usual military equipment of chariot, bow, spear and so on (OGAC 11: pp. 76–7; 14: pp. 521–46; WINI 5: pp. 667–79; ROYD under letter S cols 91–2).

In Renaissance art, the shield is the attribute of Virtue, Strength, Victory, Vigilance and Chastity. In Mantegna's painting 'Wisdom defeating the Vices' (in the Louvre, Paris) Minerva carries a translucent shield on her arm (TERS pp. 50–1).

ship (see also BOAT)   Ships conjure up ideas of strength and safety in the dangers of a voyage and the symbolism is as applicable to space-flight as to sea-travel. The ship is like a star which orbits about its pole, the Earth, but under human control. It is a picture of life in which the individual must choose a goal and steer a course.

In Egypt, and subsequently in Rome, there was a ship-festival in honour of Isis which took place in March at the start of Spring. A freshly-built ship, inscribed with holy words and purified by blazing TORCHES, with white sails set and laden with perfumes and baskets of flowers, was launched into the sea and left for the winds to take it. It was intended to ensure fair winds and calm seas for the rest of the year. Isis' ship was a symbol of sacrifice to the gods to ensure the safety and protection of all other ships and stood for human society, passengers aboard the same ship of state or fate.

The old Scandinavian legend of the ghost-ship, on which Wagner based his *Flying Dutchman*, symbolizes the quest for fidelity in love and the ship-wreck of that ideal, exposed as nothing more than a phantom. In desperation the Dutchman wanders the seas, hoping to meet the woman who will be eternally faithful. Senta, for her part, emotionally absorbed by the same ideal, swears that she will be faithful to the Dutchman until death. However, in so doing she betrays her fiancé, Birk, and suffers the same damnation as the Dutchman whom she has tried to save. The Dutchman puts to sea, but his vessel founders, while Senta leaps from the rocks and is drowned. However, the pair are seen rising from the now-calmed waters, transfigured and redeemed by their sacrifice. Salvation is no impossibly idealistic dream, but exists in the courageous acceptance of reality. The ghost-ship symbolizes those dreams inspired by the highest ideals, but which are impossibly idealistic and cannot be realized.

shirt (see also TUNIC)   According to Celtic tradition, the Dagda was told by the people of 'the great world in the east that no disease can affect the skin covered by a shirt': shirts are therefore symbols of protection.

To be shirtless is a sign, not only of the deepest material deprivation, but also of utter moral loneliness and social abandonment, unprotected materially, by any group or even by any love. To give the shirt off one's back, on the other hand, is a gesture of unbounded generosity. In so far as a shirt is a person's second skin, it is to give oneself and share one's very being.

The material from which the shirt is made subtly influences the sense of the symbol, since it is directly in contact with the wearer. Whether it be the coarse hemp of the peasant or ascetic, the fine linen of the fashionable or the silk of the rich, or the richly embroidered ceremonial garment, it is emblematic of the individual. The proverb 'the happy man has no shirt' means that he claims nothing, since he does not rely for his happiness upon material goods, however scanty. Free as air, he does not burden himself with any personal attachment or piece of clothing.

shoes (see also FOOT; SANDAL; SLIPPER)   Jean Servier observes that 'to walk shod is to take possession of the ground' (SERP p. 123) and the sociologist supports this statement with examples taken from Greece, the Ancient East and North Africa as well.

He reminds us of the Old Testament passage: 'Now this was the manner in former times in Israel concerning redeeming and concerning changing, for to confirm all things; a man plucked off his shoe [or sandal], and gave it to his neighbour: and this was a testimony in Israel' (Ruth 4: 7). In fact, in the *Jerusalem Bible* the commentators observe: 'Here the gesture merely validates a contract of exchange. To put one's foot on a field, or to throw a sandal on to it, is to take possession of it. . . . The sandal thus becomes the symbol of the right of ownership. By taking it off and handing it to the purchaser the owner transfers the right to him.'

Jean Servier also observes that 'HERMES, protector of boundaries and of travellers crossing those boundaries, was a god who was shod, since he was the lawful possessor of the land on which he stood.' Similarly, Servier adds, 'in Islam, a visitor must take off his shoes when he crosses the threshold of his host's house, showing thereby that he has no thought of claiming or attempting to obtain possession of it. The ground on which mosques or shrines stand does not belong to human beings, and they must therefore remove their shoes before they tread upon it' (SERP pp. 124ff.).

In Western tradition, shoes have a funerary significance – a dying person is about to take his leave. The shoes at the bedside show that that person is no longer well enough to walk: they are a sign of death.

This, however, is not their only meaning. If they symbolize travel, it is not towards the other world alone, but in every direction. They are the symbols of the traveller. This is perhaps the subconscious reason for the comparatively recent custom in some places of setting shoes by the fireside to receive presents from Father Christmas on Christmas Eve. They might show that their owners are also travellers and need something to help them on their way. Without shoes their journey is broken and they wait for Heaven to provide them with the means to continue on the next stage of their journey.

An old Russian custom ordained that, at the wedding-feast, the bride's napkin should be folded in the shape of a swan and the groom's in the shape of a slipper as a symbol of his authority. At church, the bride would try to be the first to step on the pink satin carpet on which the Orthodox religious ceremony was held, so that she would hold the upper hand over her husband. On the wedding night, she had to pull off her husband's boots, one of which held money and the other a whip. Samoyed custom prescribed that the suitor should make good his promise by sewing a pair of fur boots for his intended bride (AFAN). Russian peasants were not allowed to go barefoot on the day on which their livestock was put out to pasture for the first time in case they caused a plague of snakes and wolves.

To remove one's shoes is the first step towards intimacy.

In Classical antiquity shoes were the mark of a free man: slaves went barefoot.

Shoes are a sign that the individual is his or her own master, self-sufficient and responsible for his or her actions.

Shoes partake of the FOOT's threefold symbolism: 'Freudians regard them as phallic, Diel as a symbol of the soul and, in our opinion, they are as much a point of contact between the body and the Earth' (CIRD p. 106), perhaps as a symbol of the principle of reality ('he has his feet on the ground').

shooting-star Regarded as a divine or celestial manifestation or as a message from Heaven, since it looks like a spark of heavenly fire or a seed from the godhead coming down to Earth. Primitive belief held that the stars were, in fact, gods and that the fragments which they cast off were, as it were, seed. Shooting-stars performed a mission similar to that of angels by communicating between Heaven and Earth. Shooting-stars are symbols of a higher form of life which communicates with man or reminds him of his vocation.

shoulder The shoulders signify power and the strength to bring into being. In the fragments of the Gnostic writings of Theodotus we read: 'The cross is the emblem of the boundaries of the Divine Being. This is why Jesus, by this mark, having borne seed on his shoulders injected it into the Divine Being. For Jesus is called the shoulders of the seed.' St Irenaeus was to write: 'Power is upon his shoulders.'

The Pseudo-Dionysius the Areopagite also said: 'The shoulders . . . denote the power of making, and striving, and accomplishing' (PSEH p. 46).

The Bambara locate the seat of strength and even of violence in the shoulders (ZAHB).

shout In ancient Irish law, a shout had the properties of a legal protest, but to achieve this it had to satisfy conditions of time and place generally defined with great precision. From the point of view of religion or tradition, the shout possessed properties which caused harm or paralysis. For example, all the Ulates who had heard the goddess Macha's shout were at least once in their lives stricken with weakness and had no more strength than a woman in childbirth. This was the punishment inflicted for King Conchobar's having forced Macha to run against his horses. Macha, who was pregnant, won the race but, as she passed the goal, she gave birth to twins and died. The tradition of the baneful shout lingers on in the Arthurian cycle where Culhwch threatens to give a shout of protest if he is not admitted to Arthur's court. It also survives in Breton folklore in the *hoper noz* (night-crier), *c'hwitellour noz* (night-whistler) or, in the region of Vannes, *bugul-noz* (night-child or -shepherd), whose shout leads travellers astray. This mythic gift may be compared with the shout of Reuben, Jacob's eldest son, which killed whoever heard it with terror, or with the braying of the three-legged ass in the Bundeshesh (REVC 7: pp. 225, 230).

All traditions have their baneful and paralysing shout. There is the well-known Indian war-whoop, and Greeks and Trojans shouted *Halala* as they rushed to battle. Pindar calls the war-goddess Halala.

The Romans uttered their *clamor* as they launched their attack. Tacitus mentions the *barditus*, or *barritus*, the Germans' war-cry which they shouted with their shields in front of their mouths so as to act as amplifiers. Later, the Romans borrowed these barbarian war-cries for their own forces. They uttered them by gradually increasing the sound from a barely audible hum to an enormous bellow.

(LAVD p. 308b)

In the Koran, the Shout is personified and identified with disaster, being the punishment which suddenly overwhelms the impious and the unjust (7: 78). The shout is compared with a whirlwind sent by God. 'And a violent tempest overtook the wicked, and they were found in the morning prostrate in their dwellings, as though they had never abode in them' (11: 70).

War-cries symbolize the punitive wrath of the gods, as cries of pain symbolize the protests of humanity and shouts of joy, life bubbling over. According to magical theory, to shout is, in some sense, to create and, by shouting out the vengeful wrath of the Almighty, is to summon up his powers against the enemy. Imitating the sounds of thunder, whirlwind and earthquake is to rouse the storm and set it upon the enemy. The human shout is a means of trapping the heavenly shout. Some Japanese practices confer upon those who attain the highest grade of initiate the power to kill with a shout.

In Ancient Greece, shouts of celebration resounded from the procession which solemnly carried the *hiera* (holy mysteries) along the Sacred Way from Athens to Eleusis. A god, Iacchos, personified this shout. 'Enthusiastic shouts of *Iacchos, o Iacchos* were uttered in honour of the young god. The personification of a shout . . . he had become the Eleusinian avatar of Dionysos. . . . Aristophanes calls him the inventor of the festal song, Demeter's companion and guide . . . and Strabo goes on to call him Demeter's daimon and founder of the Mysteries' (SECG p. 150). When associated with Dionysos and Demeter, the shout expresses fecundity, love and life and symbolizes all the joy of living. The first sign that air has entered the lungs of a new-born baby is when it utters a cry. One cry kills, another confirms the existence of life. As a weapon which attracts and repels, the shout brings salvation or annihilation.

sibyl (Pythoness) This was the name given to legendary prophetesses, the most famous being the Trojan, Cassandra, with whom Apollo became enamoured. He granted her the gift of prophecy but, because she rejected him, he caused all that she foretold to be disbelieved. Other famous sibyls in Classical antiquity were those of Delphi, Erythrea and Cumae.

The sibyl who prophesied in Apollo's name, seated upon the tripod at Delphi, was known as the Pythoness through the connection with the serpent Pytho. The Pythoness had to be a virgin, or at least, once chosen had to preserve complete chastity and solitude as 'Bride of the God'.

The sibyl symbolizes the human being who is raised to a transnatural level which enables him or her to communicate with the godhead and to act as a channel of communication with it, just as the person who is possessed and prophesies is the voice of the oracle and the instrument of revelation. Sibyls were even regarded as emanations of divine wisdom, as old as the world, and repositories of primeval revelation. On these terms they might symbolize revelation itself. Thus there have been frequent comparisons between the number of the twelve sibyls and that of the twelve apostles, and they have been subjects of Church painting and sculpture.

sickle Because of its shape, the sickle is often compared with the crescent Moon and it has been the attribute of many agrarian deities such as Saturn and Silvanus. Curved weapons generally relate to lunar symbolism and to fertility. They are a mark of female nature.

The sickle may thus symbolize the harvest-cycle, self-renewing, and death and the hope of rebirth.

There is the well-known ritual use by the Celts of a golden sickle to harvest the MISTLETOE, the symbol of immortality. In addition, in Celtic art, the cock's tail-feathers are stylized in a sickle shape. Since the cock is a solar bird, we see a complete reversal of the symbol from lunar to solar. However, in this case the cresent, too, is reversed, and points earthwards. This position on the cock, some scholars believe, is a hermaphroditic sign.

The Hindu *shastra*, with which the *asura* were armed, has a sickle shape but does not seem to be assimilated to it.

In Japan, the sickle was used as a 'support' for the real presence of the *kami* (divinities) in some temples. The sickle remained sacred and was set on house-roofs as a preservative against thunder (HERJ, MALA, VARG).

The sickle is also the attribute of Death and of Time, which destroys all things (see also SCYTHE). It was the implement which Cronos used to castrate his father, Ouranos (Uranus), to prevent untimely creation. In this context the sickle is the symbol of decisive resolve, of determined differentiation on the path of individual or collective evolution. It is the sign 'of temporal progress and of evolutionary necessity itself', the sprouting of the primeval seed (DIES p. 113).

The bipolarity of the symbol is patent. It signifies both death and harvest. Yet the harvest can be gathered only by cutting the stalk which, like some umbilical cord, links the grain to the earth which feeds it. Harvesting is condemning the grain to death either in the form of food or of seed-corn. 'If the grain of wheat die not . . .' This is why the sickle is the attribute both of Saturn and of Ceres.

sid (see also PARADISE)   In Old Irish, the word *sid* is used for 'peace' and the 'Otherworld' which is, by definition, outside time and space and human fate. By extension, the word is also used to describe the gods or divine creatures from the Otherworld. Mythical geography located the *sid* in the west or north of the world (Celtic sense of direction was often confused on this point), beyond the seas. A new extension to the meaning of the word was given by Christian monks when they copied the legends and applied the word *sid* to the real or mythical hills, burial-mounds and sometimes even lakes under which the pre-Christian gods had gone to dwell. The arrival of the Gaels (or sons of Mil) had the effect of dividing the world into two parts: the Earth's surface belonged to the Irish and the Underworld to the gods or Tuatha Dé Danann, or Children of the Goddess Dana. All writers describe the *sid* as a place of wonder, its houses built of bronze, tiled with gold and silver and decorated with precious stones. There were trees bearing fruits, APPLES and nuts, which imparted knowledge and eternal health. Warriors engaged in endless feasting at which the flesh of magic pigs was eaten and the traditional beverages of immortality and intoxication flowed in rivers of milk, beer and mead. It was an enchanted place where there was no sin, death, dispute or sickness of any sort. Its inhabitants remained eternally young and healthy. In any case the majority of them were women of an otherworldly beauty. These characteristics provide the basis for the different names commonly used in literature for the Otherworld – *Tir na nog*, Land of Youth; *Tir nam-Beo*, Land of the Living; *Tir nam-Ban*, Land of Women; *Mag Meld*, Land of Pleasure; *Tir Tairngire*, Land of Promise.

However the *sid*, or Otherworld, was generally invisible and hidden from the sight of mortals who were unable to perceive or enter it except in exceptional circumstances. The Irish monks confused the gods' Otherworld with mortals' Beyond, of which they no longer understood the meaning and which they lumped together as an assimilation with the Old Testament and Christian Paradise (OGAC 14: pp. 329–40; 18: pp. 13–150).

Siegfried Mythical incarnation of the raw and violent young hero, avid to do great deeds and to enjoy his pleasures. Intoxicated with the carelessness of youth, he scorns the lessons of the past and the hardships of the future, believing only in the ordeal of battle, in which he feels himself invincible and invulnerable, and intent upon satisfying all his desires until the fatal day of the death he knows has been fixed by a fate which he accepts from the outset. He is the Germanic symbol of the 'iron-age soul' and the incarnation of self-destructive violence. His character became subtly altered in the interpretation given to it by Wagner's *Ring* cycle. He embodies 'the universal religious theme of the imaginary hero drawn by earthly reality, of the god seduced by humanity' and, at a deeper level, 'the world of elemental energy, primeval innocence and joy, a power still the prisoner of the old pagan cosmogony which the new Christian world tries (in vain) to convert'. Later he would come to stand for the superman which the modern secular world summons to replace the gods. He would know no other law than the pitiless law of nature. He then embodied a Nietzschean dream. Another interpretation makes Siegfried the man of the future destined to free the world from selfishness by making the Will submit to Conscience through his defeat of the DRAGON and marriage with BRUNHILD. This development of the myth shows the influence of Christianity upon pagan legend; sometimes they fight, sometimes they make love. And a new meaning is instilled into the symbol, betraying the existence of opposites within the complexity of the human psyche, when Siegfried with all his violence becomes a Christ-figure. (See also NIBELUNGEN.)

sieve Symbol of the separation of good from evil, of the righteous from the wicked, of the critical spirit, of pitiless choice and of impartial and loveless judgement, the sieve symbolizes the application of a mechanical principle to the weighing of moral actions and spiritual creations. Christ attributes this way of judging, as if by sifting with a sieve, to none other than Satan. 'Simon, Simon, behold, Satan hath desired to have you, that he may sift you as wheat: But I have prayed for thee, that thy faith fail not' (Luke 22: 31–2). The sieve proves the firmness and quality of dust-free grain.

It is also the ordeal of persecution or of punishment and in this sense becomes an instrument of divine justice. Isaiah describes God's anger as acting 'to sift the nations with the sieve of vanity: and there shall be a bridle in the jaws of the people' (30: 28). Sifting is a threat with which Jehovah threatens sinners. 'For, lo, I will command, and I will sift the house of Israel among all nations, like as corn is sifted in a sieve, yet shall not the least grain fall upon the earth' (Amos 9: 9). In this context, the sieve is pictured as retaining good deeds, down to the smallest kindness; all righteousness, no matter how slight, is to be taken into account.

In fact, there are two ways of looking at the manner in which a sieve is operated. Either the sieve retains the grain (the righteous) and gets rid of the chaff and dirt (sinners), or else it retains the pebbles (sinners) and lets the fine sand (the righteous) through – in which case 'grain' in the passage quoted should be translated as 'pebble'. In the first instance the prophet uses sifting in a pejorative sense. What falls from the sieve is unworthy and valueless since, when sifting wheat, what passes through the sieve is rubbish, the stuff of cheats and fraudsters. What the sieve rejects is doomed to death and punishment (Amos 8: 6).

The Ancient Egyptians often depicted scribes with their attributes of ink and reed-pen to write with and winnowing-basket, or sieve, with which to weigh up. The scribe counted and wrote down the number of bushels of sifted grain. In this context, the sieve in the scribe's lap symbolizes apprehension of real values, since he will not record tares as wheat, evil deeds for good or lies for the words of the gods. The sieve might be said to symbolize a sense of values.

Sieves were also regarded as instruments of divination and investigation. When the name of the guilty party was uttered, the sieve, held in a pair of tongs and hanging from the index fingers of two assistants, would begin to turn. This is an example of the divinatory properties invested in things which rotate, since giration always conveys something mysterious and often malign (GRIA p. 329).

silence Silence and dumbness (whether deliberate or involuntary) convey very different meanings. Silence prefaces the opening of a revelation while dumbness is a state which precludes it, either through refusal to receive or to transmit it, or as a punishment for having drowned the revelation in a hubbub of activity or emotion. Silence opens the doors, dumbness closes them. Tradition holds that there was silence before the Creation and that there will be silence at the end of the world. Great events are clothed in silence but hidden under dumbness. The former endows things with greatness and majesty, the latter devalues and degrades them. The one is a sign of development, the other of regression. Monastic rules stated that silence was a major ceremony. God comes to the soul in which silence reigns but strikes dumb the person who spends his or her time in idle gossip, and will not enter the soul which shuts itself off and remains obstinately dumb.

silver In the scale of correspondences between metals and planets, silver relates to the Moon and belongs to a symbolic scheme, or chain, linking Moon to Water to female principle. Traditionally gold, the active, male, solar, diurnal and fiery principle, is opposed to silver, the passive, female, lunar, watery and cold principle. The colour of silver is WHITE; that of gold, yellow. The Latin word for silver, *argentum*, derives from a Sanskrit word meaning 'white' and 'shining'. Small wonder then that this metal should be associated with the dignity of kingship. When the Irish King Nuada lost his arm in the first battle of Moytura and through the loss of a limb became disqualified from kingship, the god of healing, Dian Cécht, made him an artificial arm of silver which allowed him to return to the throne. This is reminiscent of the mythical king of Tartessos, Argantonios, who, according to Herodotus, lived for one hundred and twenty years (CELT 9: pp. 329ff.).

According to Ancient Egyptian myths, their gods' bones were made of silver and their flesh of gold (POSD p. 263).

Since it is white and shining, silver is also the symbol of purity in all its forms. 'It is pure light such as passes unsullied through transparent crystal, clear water, the reflection of a mirror or the flashing of a diamond. It is like clear conscience, pure intent, open-heartedness, fair dealing. It summons faithfulness to follow in its footsteps' (GEVH).

In Christian symbolism it stands for Divine Wisdom, just as gold conjures up God's love for mankind (PORS p. 57).

The Bambara regard silver as a symbol of cleansing streams. God, uniting in himself the two cleansing elements, Fire and Water, is simultaneously gold and silver (ZAHB).

In Russian folklore, too, silver is a symbol of purity and of purification. The heroes of countless folktales realize that they are threatened with death when their silver snuff-boxes, forks or other everyday items start to tarnish (AFAN). The silver ermine which guards spinning-women, sometimes makes them the present of an especially slender and strong silver thread. The Kirghiz cured epilepsy by making the patient watch the healer slowly forge a silver cone. It apparently had a hypnotic effect, the patient relaxed, grew sleepy and calmed down.

On the moral plane, however, silver also symbolizes the object of all desires and the harm which they cause, such as the progressive decay of conscience. This is its negative aspect, the perversion of its qualities.

simples See HERBS.

simpleton (see also CLOWN; FOOL) Some aspect of their behaviour often makes those who are inspired, such as poets or initiates, appear to be simpletons, since they overleap the bounds of convention. For those who only know the rules of common sense, nothing seems more foolish than wisdom.

A Fulani legend states that there are three kinds of simpleton. The first is the person who had everything and suddenly lost it all; the second, who had nothing and as suddenly acquired everything; and the third, the mental defective. A fourth sort might be added: the person who sacrifices everything to gain wisdom, the initiate being a prime example.

(HAMK p. 33)

The last named might be none other than the Fool in the Tarot. The simpleton is beyond the bounds of reason and social convention. According to the Gospel, the wisdom of men is folly in the eyes of God and the wisdom of God folly in the eyes of men. 'Transcendence' is concealed by this word 'folly'.

simurg Persian literature and mysticism has endowed the simurg with a wealth of symbolism. It is the name given to a species of mythical bird known as the *saéna* in the Avesta. The *saéna*'s characteristics are reminiscent of those of the EAGLE.

In the *Shāh-Nāme*, the simurg's nest is located on the peak of Mount Elbrus, which corresponds to Hara-barazaiti in the Avesta (Yasnā 10: 10), but in Muslim Persian literature the simurg dwells on the fabulous Mount

Kāf, with jinns and peris. Sa'dī, proclaiming God's praises, says that even the simurg on Mount Kāf shares in his munificence.

The simurg speaks a human language and acts as messenger and confidant. He carries heroes vast distances and gives them a few of his feathers. When they burn one of them, they can summon the simurg from afar. This is a favourite motif, and is found not only in relation to the simurg, but to other fabulous birds such as the HOMA and the ROC.

The simurg's feather was believed to be able to heal wounds and the bird itself was regarded as a wise physician (hakīm). This is a favourite theme in Firdausī's Shāh-Nāme. When the simurg leaves the hero Zāl whom he has brought up, he gives him some of his feathers, telling Zāl that whenever he has need of him he has only to burn one and the simurg will appear. Zāl puts these feathers to many uses. He strokes the wound in the side of his wife Rūdāba with a feather and it heals; he does the same for his son Rostam.

Under Islam, the simurg symbolized not only the mystic master and manifestation of the godhead, but also the hidden Self. Farīd al-Dīn Attār, in his Conference of the Birds, treats the simurg as a symbol of the quest for Self. He plays upon the bird's name and the thirty birds (sī morgh) who set out in quest of a transcendental goal, only to find at the end of it that the simurg is none other than their own selves, the sī morgh (thirty birds).

siren The sirens were sea monsters with the heads and breasts of women and the bodies of birds, or, according to later legends originating in northern Europe, with the bodies of fish. Their sweet songs and lovely faces seduced passing sailors, whom they lured into the sea where they devoured them. Odysseus was forced to tie himself to the mast to prevent himself yielding to their summons. They were as evil and as much to be feared as HARPIES or Furies (see ERINNYES).

They have been held to portray the dangers of navigating the seas and then even to portray death itself. Under Ancient Egyptian influence, which depicted the souls of the dead as human-headed birds, sirens have been regarded as souls of the dead who have failed to achieve their destiny and been changed into hungry VAMPIRES. However, despite the fact that they were regarded as evil spirits or Underworld deities, some sarcophagi depict them as deities of the Beyond, charming the Blessed by their harmonious songs in the Fortunate Isles (GRID p. 425). Nevertheless, sirens remained traditionally imagined as symbols of fatal attraction.

If life is compared with a journey, the sirens represent the traps set by passion and desire. Since they rise from the indeterminate elements of Air (birds) or Water (fish) they have been made creatures of the unconscious, dreams which bewitch or terrify and in which are displayed the dark and primitive impulses of the human psyche. They symbolize the self-destructive power of desire, to which the depraved imagination offers only a senseless dream instead of objective reality and viable action. Like Odysseus, one must lash oneself to the mainmast, the spirit's vital axis, if one is to escape the delusions of passion.

six (see also NUMBERS; STAR OF DAVID) Allendy regards sixes as basically indicating 'the indefinitely counterpoised confrontation of creature and creator' (ALLN p. 150). This confrontation is not conflictual, and may only indicate a simple difference, but may nevertheless be the source of all the ambivalences in the number six since, in fact, it embraces the network of actions embodied in two groups of three. It may have as strong a tendency towards evil as towards good, towards rebellion against God as towards union with him. Six is the number of mutual giving and hating, that of mystic destiny. It is perfection in the form of power, pictorially expressed by the symbolism of six equilateral triangles within a circle. Each side of each triangle equals the radius of the circle and six is almost exactly the ratio of the circumference to the radius (2π). However, this potential perfection may come to grief, and this danger makes six the number of the trial between good and evil.

In the Book of Revelation the number six has a clearly pejorative meaning, and would seem to be the number of sin. It is also the number of Nero, the sixth Roman emperor. In this instance, the balance would seem to have inclined towards evil.

Similarly, the false prophet, Anti-Christ, would have 'the mark, or the name of the beast, or the number of his name. . . . Let him that hath understanding count the number of the beast: for it is the number of a man; and his number is Six hundred threescore and six' (Revelation 13: 17–18). The number is the sum of the numerical values possessed by the alphabet (see DA'WAH) and denotes Caesar-Nero (in the Hebrew alphabet) or Caesar-God (in the Greek). It is legitimate to universalize the designation since history has progressed since the death of the historic Nero and, although fresh Neros have arisen, to regard the Number of the Beast as symbolizing the deification of power or the state.

From an analysis of fairy stories, six would seem to be 'the corporeal individual without the saving element, that final part of the self which allows communion with the godhead. Additionally, the number six was dedicated by Classical antiquity to Venus-Aphrodite, goddess of physical love' (LOEF 199). This is a further example of unrealized potential.

Six is also the number of the Old Testament Hexameron – the number of the days of Creation and the number which is intermediate between the First Cause and manifestation.

The world was created in six days and, as St Clement of Alexandria observes, created in the six orientations of space, that is the four points of the compass, the nadir and the zenith. Jewish tradition holds that it went on for six thousand years. Just as St Clement makes cosmic development correspond both in space and in time, so Abū Ya'qūb Sejestānī makes the perfect number, the six days of Creation, correspond to the six cosmic energies, the six facets of a solid body and, esoterically, with the prophets (*notaqā*) of the six ages. Luc Benoist has observed that in Hindu and in Chinese art, as well as in Classical Vitruvian architecture, there are six rules which reflect God's creation. De Saint-Martin writes that the shew-bread of the Children of Israel, set out six by six, provides us with a picture of 'the two sixfold laws, fountains of all things temporal and intellectual'.

Nevertheless, in China six was above all else the number of Heaven, although this was solely from the point of view of manifestation. It might be said to be the hexagram *K'ien*, 'the chariot drawn by six dragons' of the

I Ching. The celestial influences are six in number. More generally speaking, the HEXAGRAM itself displays the characteristics of the number six (= 2 × 3), two interlocking triangles.

The number six is expressed either in the hexagon, or, better still, in the six-pointed star formed by a pair of inverted triangles. This, in Hindu terms, represents the lingam penetrating the *yoni*, the counterpoise of Fire and Water, symbol of *rajas*, the expansionist tendency of manifestation. In the West, the star became the emblem of Israel, the Seal of Solomon or the Star of David. It was still an expression of the marriage of opposites, of a principle and of its reversed image mirrored in the waters. The regular triangle may thus be regarded as an expression of Christ's divine nature, the inverted triangle of his human nature and the star as a whole as the union of the two natures.

The six-pointed star is also the macrocosm or universal man, and the five-pointed star the microcosm or the ordinary individual (BENA, CORT, DANA, GRAP, GUEC, GUET).

To the Chorti, descendants of the Maya, six is a female number in terms of the six synodic returns of the Moon, while seven is male (GIRP p. 280). Six derives from the Moon's cyclical symbolism and seven from the Sun's light symbolism. The former marks the completion of a transit, cycle or phase of evolution; the latter its perfection, or rather the enjoyment of its perfection. Hence, one may deduce that to pass from six to SEVEN is to move from manifestation to awareness of manifestation, seven being the individual human being, an enlightened person, as it is the number of full spatial orientation, if one adds the centre at which the lines joining the six points intersect.

The Maya allotted the sixth day to their rain- and storm-god. Six was an unlucky number, and the day was also associated with death. On it, divination into the causes of sickness was undertaken, its augural creature being the OWL, sight of which was supposed to foretell death (THOH).

On the other hand, like all even numbers as expressions of the twinship of all fulfilled creation, the Bambara consider six to be a lucky number. It is the sign of male twins (3 + 3) (DIEB).

sixteen (see also FOUR; SWASTIKA; TOWER)   As the square of four, this number is indicative of the attainment of physical power. As such, it possesses a dangerous moral significance through exaggerated pride and unbridled lust for power. Jacob Boehme uses this number to denote the ABYSS, in contradistinction to Nirvana.

If, on the other hand, sixteen is regarded as twice EIGHT, it becomes 'the multiplication of cycles of change and rebirth for the individual' (ALLN p. 364), or else the duplication of the eighth *sefirah* of the Kabbalah – 'Hod, glory, splendour' (FRCH p. 158), a situation just as uncomfortable.

sixty-four   The square of EIGHT clearly expresses perfect, actualized wholeness. Although it is fulfilment, plenitude and bliss, it is also the lists of a tournament expressed in the sixty-four squares of the chessboard. This symbol recurs if transposed from space to time. Allendy (ALLN) emphasizes a strange relationship between Eastern and Western tradition. The Buddha's mother was born into 'a family endowed with sixty-four sorts of virtue'.

Confucius belonged to 'the sixty-fourth generation from the founder of his line Hoang Ti', just as, according to St Luke, Jesus was 'sixty-fourth in line of descent from Adam'. Sixty-four mules drew the hearse when Alexander the Great was buried and, in China, sixty-four persons bore the corpses of their dead emperors. Sixty-four is the number of earthly fulfilment.

skeleton The skeleton is the personification of Death and sometimes of the Devil. In alchemy, it is the symbol of blackness, PUTREFACTION and solution, colours and operations which preface transmutation. The skeleton does not stand for death as an end in itself, something static, but, if one may use the phrase, for a dynamic death which is the herald and the channel of a new form of life. With its ironic smile and pensive attitude, the skeleton symbolizes the knowledge of the person who has crossed the threshold of the unknown and, by dying, acquired the secrets of the Beyond. In dreams, skeletons foreshadow an imminent event which will transform the dreamer's life, by shattering a state to which the dreamer is accustomed and of which he or she dreads the disappearance, without yet knowing what is to succeed it.

In Classical antiquity, if we are to believe Apuleius, impressions or statuettes of skeletons were commonly used in magical practices. These skeletons were regarded as images of Mercury (HERMES), the god who was the conductor of souls and enjoyed the privilege of being able to go down to and return from the Underworld. This use may be seen as an attempt symbolically to identify the god with death, so that the practitioner might share the same privilege of escaping from the Underworld as did the god; or, in an opposite sense, of dooming a given individual to death and leading him or her to the Underworld.

In Petronius' *Satyricon*, a jointed skeleton made of silver circulates at Trimalchio's banquet to symbolize death in general and the brevity of human life, rather than a particular god or an individual death. The sight of the skeleton, while the feasters were in their cups, was designed to spur them to an ever keener enjoyment of these fleeting moments of pleasure. In Classical antiquity, skeletons at the feast were as common as the *danse macabre* in medieval art.

skink Like Arabs and Egyptians, the Bambara regard this type of lizard as a creature of good omen and do not eat its flesh, although other lizards are considered delicacies. They still use it for some kinds of medicine and, if a sick person sees a skink, it is a sign foretelling that person's cure. 'The Markos call the skink "the women's SERPENT" since it is quite harmless and it is regarded both as kindly and as holy. According to a Fulani folktale, when the skink grows old it turns itself into a double-headed serpent' (HAMK 12). It stands for the serpent's diurnal and beneficent aspect.

skull As the seat of thought, and hence of overall control, the skull is the chief of the four 'centres' in which the Bambara epitomize their macrocosmic depiction of the human individual, the other three centres being located at the base of the sternum, in the navel and in the sexual organs. The secret initiatory society, the Kore, set four earthenware jars on their altars. These jars are filled with heavenly water collected from the first and last of the annual rains and stand for these four points. The central jar, standing for the skull, contains four thunder-stones, celestial fire in material shape, expressions of God's spirit and intellect and the human brain, his microcosmic avatar in the shape of the Cosmic Egg and, like it, the womb of knowledge (ZAHB).

In many Asian and European legends the human skull is regarded on a par with the vault of Heaven. Thus in the Icelandic *Grimnismal*, the skull of the giant Ymir becomes the vault of Heaven after his death and similarly, in the *Rig-Veda*, the vault of Heaven was fashioned from the skull of the first man (HARA pp. 81–2). Gilbert Durand (DURS pp. 143ff.) in fact establishes a parallel between the valorization of verticality on the level of the social macrocosm (archetypes of monarchy) and of the natural macrocosm (sacralization of mountains and of sky) and the human macrocosm. This also offers an excellent explanation for skull-worship in all its countless shapes, from ancestral skulls to skulls taken as trophies, as well as for the cosmogenetic analogies already mentioned. From the same law of analogy between the human microcosm and the natural macrocosm derive the likening of the eyes to the stars and the brain to the clouds in the sky (see also COLUMN).

Skull-worship is not restricted to human skulls. Among hunter-tribes, animal trophies play an important ritual part. This is simultaneously linked to confirmation of human superiority, demonstrated by the presence in the village of the skull of a big-game animal, and to a concern for the preservation of life. Since the skull is, in fact, the apex of the skeleton and the latter comprises the imperishable matter of the body, it is therefore a soul, and in this way the village acquires the animal's vital energy.

Livy records that when, in 216 BC, the Cisalpine Gauls ambushed and destroyed the army of the Roman ex-consul Postumius, they carried off this magistrate's head with the rest of the spoils with great pomp. 'They adorned his skull with gold according to their custom. And it served them as a sacred vessel from which to pour libations at festivals and at the same time as a drinking cup for the priests and keepers of the temple' (Livy 23: 24). The symbolism of the skull is related to that of the HEAD, regarded as the spoils of war, and that of the CHALICE. In this context one should mention the skulls found in a number of Celtic shrines in southern Gaul (OGAC 11: p. 4; 10: pp. 139ff.; BENR).

The location of the head, the dome-shape of the skull and its role as a spiritual centre have often led to its being compared with the Heaven of the human body. It was regarded as

the seat of the life-force of both body and spirit.... By cutting off a corpse's head and preserving the skull as a possession ... primitive man attained several goals. First he possessed the closest and most personal memory of the dead person, and then he acquired that person's life force and its use to the benefit of those coming after. The more skulls he could accumulate, the broader the extent of this spiritual underpinning.

Hence the mounds of skulls unearthed from time to time by archeologists (GORH). Hence, too, the employment of skulls, reservoirs of life at its highest level, in the alchemists' work of transmutation.

In Freemasonry, the skull symbolizes the cycle of initiation through the death of the body as the prelude to rebirth at a higher level of life and in a state in which the spirit rules. As a symbol of physical death, the skull is similar to the alchemical process of putrefaction, as the grave is to the athanor – the new man rises from the crucible in which the old man was annihilated, in order to become transformed. The skull is often depicted with cross bones, a St Andrew's cross, symbol of nature quartered under the overwhelming influence of the spirit, and hence a symbol of spiritual perfection.

sky See HEAVEN.

sling The Peruvian Inca armed their rain- and thunder-god, Illapa, with a sling. Thunder was caused by the noise it made when the god whirled it and the sling was therefore symbolically equivalent to the BULL-ROARER, which plays a basic role as the voice of the great sky-god.

In Greco-Roman tradition the sling was a weapon and no more. It did not even become a motif of the plastic arts, like the bow, or lend itself to any symbolic interpretation.

It was, however, the weapon which enabled the shepherd-boy, David, to lay the giant Goliath low. Slings symbolize the strength of the weak and resistance to established power structures.

slipper The first version of the Cinderella story goes back to the third-century AD Roman orator and writer, Aelian, and shows how slippers have always tended to be identified with their owners. He tells how an eagle stole the slipper belonging to the courtesan, Rhodopis, while she was bathing and carried it to Pharaoh. The latter was so struck by the slenderness of the sole that he instituted a search for the owner. Needless to say, when she was found he married her. Similarly, the slipper which Cinderella dropped when she fled the prince's palace on the stroke of midnight, was the means by which she was identified.

The surprise was complete when Cinderella drew from her pocket in sign of recognition, irrefutable proof of identity, the other little slipper and put it on. Once he had found her again, the prince, who had gone into a decline from the moment she had left him, despite her rags and poverty married her for her beauty alone. Some critics have taken the symbol of identification for a sexual symbol, or at least as a symbol of sexual appetite sharpened by sight of the FOOT. Those who regard the foot as a phallic symbol, all too naturally see the slipper as a symbol of the vagina and between the two a problem of adaptation which may cause severe stress.

In northern China the words for 'slipper' and 'mutual agreement' are pronounced in the same way. Thus a pair of slippers symbolizes domestic harmony and they are given as wedding presents.

smoke (see also INCENSE) Smoke depicts the relationship between Heaven and Earth. It may rise as prayer or homage to God in incense or the smoke of sacrifice, or, as in Ancient Chinese rituals, it may call down from Heaven in smoke from burning fat or artemisia the *huen*-soul to be reunited with the *p'o*-soul so that life may be restored. Also in China, and in Tibet, smoke raises the soul to the Beyond, and thus Taoist self-immolation by fire was a form of release. A column of smoke, from whatever source, may be identified with the World AXIS and this is clearly displayed in the column rising from the hearth in the centre of a Mongol yurt and escaping through the hole in the roof. It is, as has been noted in reference to CAVERNS and DOMES, a release from the cosmos.

In Ancient China, smoke from burning reeds and canes played the same part in ritual cleansing as water and fire (GRAD, GRAR, KALL).

There are many references to the extraordinary gifts of the druid Fingen, an Ulster healer, who had only to see the smoke from a house to know how many of its inhabitants were sick and the diseases from which they suffered. It is not certain whether this detail is due to the Irish love of exaggeration or if there is something symbolic behind it. If the latter is true, the symbolism would be related to the paranormal powers of the druid and it would be proper to regard the smoke as merely developing Fingen's powers of diagnosis – he was credited with being able to name the person who had inflicted a wound simply by looking at it. The smoke might be regarded in some sense as the breath of the house and in more general terms as an individual's breath (WINI 5: p. 795).

Materials used in the principal smoke-ceremonies, rites of purification among North American Indians, include incense, resins (including copal), tobacco and cedar-wood. Columns of smoke rising into the air symbolize the joining together of Earth and Heaven and the spiritualization of mankind.

Alchemists believe that the sort of steam which seems to rise like smoke from a person in death-throes, symbolizes or really is the soul leaving the body. This belief is fairly widespread throughout the world.

snail Universally regarded as lunar symbols, snails are signs of the regular cycle of rebirth; as the Moon waxes and wanes, so snails expose and retract their horns; they are signs of death and rebirth, motifs of the eternal homecoming.

The snail, with its spiral shell, linked to the phases of the Moon, and the tumescence of its horns, also stands for fertility. 'Thus the snail becomes the scene of a lunar theophany, as in the ancient religion of Mexico in which the moon god, Tecciztecatl, is shown enclosed in a snail's shell' (ELIT p. 157).

Like all molluscs, the snail displays sexual symbolism in the analogy between its substance, motion and excretions with those of the vulva.

It also symbolizes the enduring within the changeable. 'The helical shape of the land- or sea-snail's shell provides an universal glyph of the eternity of being within the fluctuations of change' (DIED).

For the Aztecs, snails were symbols of conception, pregnancy and birth (ELIT p. 186). In Benin they are regarded as reservoirs of semen (MAUG).

In Egyptian hieroglyphics, the snail stood for the SPIRAL. Like that geometric shape, present throughout the natural world, it might well have symbolized the evolution of life.

In North Africa, snail's shells are made into necklaces.

Snails have shells of the pattern of ram's horns. . . . In addition they partake of moisture and only come out, as the peasants say, after rain. They are linked to the agricultural cycle and have become the symbol of the fertility bestowed by the dead, a necklace of their shells being the almost essential adornment of the ancestor who returns to mortal earth to make it fertile, bearing with him all the symbols of the face of Heaven and of the beneficent rain-storms.

(SERP p. 371)

snake See SERPENT.

sneezing The simple act of sneezing, 'stimulated by devils tickling a person's nose', may drive the soul from the body. The Lapps believed that a violent sneeze could cause death and from this belief stems the custom, dating back to Classical antiquity, of well-wishing the sneezer (HARA).

In some African tribes, sneezing when speaking to somebody means that God approves of what has been said. A sudden sneeze during a period of silence is taken as a good omen and is the occasion for an exchange of good wishes and even of presents (HAMK).

Sneezing symbolizes a manifestation of the sacred to reward or punish, through its suddenness marking a break in the time continuum.

snowdrop In the West, this tiny, strongly-scented white flower which blossoms at the end of Winter and heralds the Spring has become a symbol of consolation and hope.

To the Plains Indians its North American equivalent, the pasque flower, is a symbol of courage, endurance and faithfulness to death (ALEC pp. 194–5).

Snow White See under ALCHEMY.

solstice The symbolism of the solstices should attract our attention since it does not coincide with the character of the seasons in which they occur. In fact, it is the Winter solstice which inaugurates the ascendant phase of the annual cycle, while the Summer solstice inaugurates its descendant phase. Hence arises the Greco-Roman symbolism of the gates of the solstices represented by the two faces of JANUS and, later, by the two feasts of St John, in Summer and Winter. It is easy to observe that it is the Winter gateway from which the 'light' phase of the cycle emerges and its 'dark' phase from the Summer gate. It has been observed in this context that Christ's birth falls at the Winter solstice and that of St John the Baptist at the Summer solstice, hence the remarkable passage in the New Testament in which the Baptist says: 'He [Christ] must increase, but I must decrease' (John 3: 30).

In Chinese symbolism, the Summer solstice corresponds to the trigram *li*, Fire, the Sun, the head; and the Winter solstice with the trigram *k'an*, Water, the abyss, the feet. Despite this, the descendant phase of the *yang* principle originates from the former, the *yin* from its ascendant phase. In internal alchemy, the stream of energy flows upwards from *k'an* to *li* and downwards from *li* to *k'an*. It was also said that the *yang* line of the trigram *k'an* tended to deviate towards the trigram *k'ien*, which is pure *yang* or active perfection, whereas the *yin* of *li* tended towards *k'uen*, which is passive perfection. In the first instance, it was a matter of an ascendant movement and in the second of a descendant one. There is a pre-existent tendency towards light in *k'an*, and towards darkness in *li*. Furthermore, although the Winter solstice may correspond to the kingdom of the dead, it is a token of their rebirth. It is associated with gestation and birth and is a favourable period for conception.

Apparently in Hindu tradition the Winter solstice inaugurates the 'way of the Gods' (*devayāna*) and the Summer solstice the *pitriyāna* or 'way of the ancestors'. Naturally enough these correspond to the gates of gods and mortals in Pythagorean symbolism (GRAP, GRIF, GUES, MAST).

The solstices also play their part in Christian iconography. The Summer solstice (around 21 June) marks the apogee of the Sun's transit when it is at its zenith and stands at its highest in the sky. This was the day chosen to celebrate the festival of the Sun. To the degree to which Christ is compared with the Sun, he is depicted as the Summer solstice. From this, the entire symbolism of Christ as lord of time originated in Romanesque art (CHAS pp. 407ff.).

soma (see also SAP)   Soma was the sap of the plant of that name which in India was transformed into a goddess to whom hymns were sung and sacrifice made. It was the sap or HONEY of immortality carried by an eagle to mortals (*sandharva*), offered to the gods and drunk by mortals so that they could communicate with the godhead. Soma is the symbol of sacramental intoxication.

song   Song is the symbol of the word which links the creator's power to what it has created, in so far as the latter recognizes its dependence as a creature and gives it expression in joy and worship or prayer. It is the creature's breath responding to its creator.

In the Celtic world, the poet-seer, the *file*, when acting in his official capacity, employed song as a formal mode of expression. In Gaulish, we know that religious songs were called *cantalon*, a word related to the Irish word for 'incantation' and to the Breton for 'reading', *cetal*, and in the realm of the Italic languages with the words for 'song' – *canere* in Latin means 'to sing'. A mythical Irish poet was called Amorgen, 'the Birth of Song' (OGAC 12: pp. 448–9). The Children of Lir were changed into swans by their stepmother and they lulled the Tuatha Dé Danann to sleep by singing, without harp accompaniment, in the 'drowsy mode'. By comparison with instrumental music – and this shows how ancient the tradition is – song was primeval. Music, even sacred music, was no more than a craft. Harpists were freemen with the right to own cattle (*bo aire*) but not members of the priestly class like the poets (*filid*) (OGAC 18: pp. 326–9).

sorcerer   See under WITCH.

soul   The word 'soul' conjures up an invisible power which either has separate existence as part of a living individual or is simply the phenomenon of life. It may be either material or immaterial, mortal or immortal; it is a governing, active principle; except for fleeting appearances, it is invisible and displays itself only in its activities. Through its mysterious power it suggests supernatural strength, a spirit or an energy-centre. Openly to acknowledge the existence of the soul is to invite contradiction on philosophical or scientific grounds, and its existence is either rejected or, even when accepted, accepted as a concept on slightly different terms. These two attitudes will mark out basic differences in anthropology, ethics and religion. And yet, be it as something which conjures up an invisible power or something which stimulates knowledge, which either accepts or rejects it, the soul has at least a twofold claim to symbolic properties as much by the words and gestures which express it as the images which depict it. The soul underpins a whole series of symbols.

The chief of these symbols is *breath*, and all its derivatives. The etymology of the Latin word *animus* is in itself related to 'breath' and 'AIR' as principles of life. *Animus* is the intellectual principle and the seat of desire and the passions, and corresponds to the Greek *anemos* and the Sanskrit *anitī*, meaning 'breath'. Its properties are intellectual and emotional and its range, male, while the *anima* is the principle of inhaling and exhaling air and its range is female.

There are as many different ways of depicting the soul as there are beliefs in its nature, and yet some notion of these beliefs, however abbreviated it may be, is essential to an understanding of the symbols. For example, the Ancient Egyptians regarded the sacred ibis as representing the principle of immortality (*akh*), its nature celestial, shining and powerful and apparently common to gods and mortals. The human-headed bird corresponds to the individual's own spirit (*ba*), after that person's death able to haunt the scenes of his or her life. 'The *ba* is thus the spiritual principle which could appear independently of its physical support and act on its own account, as the representative, as it were, of its owner . . . the itinerant soul of a living being, capable of physical action.' In addition to these two principles, the human being comprised a number of elements, including shadow and NAME, of which the latter 'formed his very essence' (POSD pp. 266–7).

Canadian Indian hunters, the Naskapi, believed that the soul was a shadow, a spark or tiny flame which comes out of the mouth (MULR p. 233). The Delaware Indians believed that it resided in the heart and it was called an image or reflection, a visual phenomenon lacking corporeal substance (ibid. pp. 243–4).

South American Indians often have only one word meaning soul, shadow and image, or else soul and heart (Carib) or soul and pulse (Witoto).

The individual often has several souls (two, three, five and upwards) with different functions, all consisting of more or less subtle matter. Generally only one soul goes up to Heaven after death, the others remaining with the body or else, since they were of animal origin, being reincarnated in animal shape. These Indians, generally speaking, believe that sleep, as well as fits and trances, is caused by a temporary loss of soul (METB).

In the province of Kasai, the Bantu of the Congo Basin also believe that the soul leaves the body during sleep and that the dreams which it brings back from its travels have been told to it by the souls of the dead with whom it has spoken (FOUC). The soul also leaves the body in fits, trances or under hypnosis, but ranges even further and may chance to reach the very land of spirits, bringing back evidence of this on awaking.

According to Dr Fourques, the Baluba and Lulua believe that three 'subtle vehicles' are associated with the human personality. The coarsest vehicle is the *mujanji*, identical with the ghost. It governs the animal functions and is analogous with the etheric body in occultism. The *mukishi* is the double, the vehicle for feelings and the lower levels of intellect, analogous with the astral body in occultism. Lastly there is the *m'vidi*, the vehicle of intuition and higher levels of intellect. Reincarnation can only take place if all three subtle vehicles are brought together. Humans alone possess these three principles, animals, with the exception of the DOG, only having a *mujanji* (ghost). The latter also has a *mukishi* (double) and this explains its ritual importance. The *mujanji* governs corporeal existence; the *mukishi* escapes from the body during sleep and converses with the *mukishi* of the dead (dreams); while the *m'vidi* warns individuals of hidden dangers 'or those of which the signs of their coming are too slight for apprehension' (FOUC).

Folk-belief in North Africa is that two souls inhabit the human body – the *nefs*, or vegetative soul, and the *rruh*, the breath or subtle soul. The vegetative soul corresponds to the passions and emotional behaviour; it is carried by the blood and resides in the liver. Breath, or the subtle soul, corresponds to the will and travels through the bones: it resides in the heart.

(SERP p. 23)

The marriage of these two souls is symbolized by the pairing of rock and tree:

The one represents the female principle, the other the male. . . . The tree gives the *nefs*, or vegetative soul shade and moisture, but it is predominantly the especial support of the *rruh*, the subtle soul which comes to perch on its branches like a bird. The *nefs* is there in the rock or stone while waters springing from rocks are simply symbols of fertility welling up from the Underworld.

(SERP p. 28)

The soul may leave the body in the shape of a bee or butterfly, but most frequently manifests itself in the shape of a bird.

Siberian peoples believed that animals as well as humans had one or several souls which were often assimilated to the shadows of the creatures to which they gave life. The Yukagir of northern Siberia maintained that a hunter could not take game unless one of his dead relations had taken the creature's shadow beforehand (HARA p. 184).

The soul and the 'little souls' play a constant and mysterious part in the lives of Eskimo and in their funeral ceremonies. Yakut, Chuvach and others believe that the soul comes out of a sleeper's mouth to travel. It usually takes material shape as an insect or BUTTERFLY. In some central European legends it takes the form of a mouse.

Like so many other 'primitive' peoples, and especially the Indonesians, the North Asian peoples believe that man can have as many as three or even seven souls. At death one of them remains in the grave, another descends to the realm of shades, and a third ascends to the sky. . . . The first soul resides in the bones, the second – which probably resides in the blood – can leave the body and move about in the form of a wasp or a bee; the third, which resembles the man in every particular, is a kind of ghost. At death the first soul remains in the skeleton, the second is eaten by spirits, and the third appears to humans in the form of a ghost.

(ELIC pp. 215–16, 216 n. 4)

Harva cites Baratov (HARA p. 264) for the Buryat belief that the individual has three souls: one goes to Hell, the other remains on Earth in the shape of a mischievious spirit (*bokholdoi*), while the third is reborn in another person.

Most Turkic and Mongol peoples believed in the existence of a soul outside its owner's body and generally taking the shape of an animal, insect, bird or fish (HARA). The hero of the Kirghiz epic of Er Töshtük had an iron file for a soul because of his prodigious strength and valour. Humans could be killed by magic if the creature or object in which their soul was incarnate were destroyed.

The Volga Tatars' *ubyr* was a very special type of soul and not all individuals necessarily possessed one. After its owner's death the *ubyr* survived and escaped by night 'through a little hole near the corpse's mouth to suck the blood of sleeping people' (HARA p. 199). It may thus be compared with the VAMPIRE-myth. To destroy the *ubyr*, the corpse was dug up and pinned to the ground by a stake driven through its chest. A living person's *ubyr* was just as baneful and often left its owner's body to perpetrate all sorts of evil deeds. It might be encountered in the shapes of a pig, a cat, a ball of fire or a dog. 'The *ubyr* loses it powers when whoever sees it splits a wooden dung-fork or any forked piece of wood' (HARA p. 198).

Elephants, tigers, leopards, rhinoceroses, sharks and a number of other animals, especially those regarded as chthonian, have sometimes been believed to be reincarnations of dead kings or chiefs. Frazer provides many examples of this belief from Asia (Semang and Malaysia) and Black Africa (Dahomey (now Benin) and Nigeria) (FRAG 1: pp. 84ff.).

The Chinese believed the soul to be made from two principles –

kuei and *shen*. *Kuei* was the heavier of the two, weighing down the desires of its owner. It haunted the grave and the places which its owner had frequented. . . . *Shen* was the genius, the spark of divine fire present in the human body. . . . In the fourth century BC, the dualism of this folk belief became linked to the grand dualism of an official cosmogony based upon the oppositions of the two principles, female, earthly *yin* and heavenly, male *yang*.

(SERH p. 76)

The Celtic world affords no exact equivalent to the legend of Cupid (Eros) and Psyche (see LOVE). However, dictionary definitions of the word 'soul' in modern Celtic languages give us, in Irish Gaelic *ainim*, and *ene* and *anaon* in Breton for 'the souls of the dead'. This shows that, in Classical antiquity, the Celts, too, recognized both in language and in religious and metaphysical thought the distinction between *animus* and *anima*, the soul as respectively spirit and breath, although this distinction was lost from the fourth century AD onwards in liturgical language, in which *animus* was replaced by *spiritus*. The panceltic word for 'soul', *anamon*, also relates etymologically precisely to the word for 'harmony' (*anavon*) and to the name of the primeval goddess, Ana (or Dana). It thus symbolizes the fullness of the individual's potential as a spiritual being.

Irish and Gaulish druids taught the immortality of the soul as one of their basic doctrines. After their death, the deceased went to the Beyond where they continued in a way of life similar to the one which they had enjoyed on Earth. A survival of this concept of the Beyond lingers in the Breton *anaon*, who return to their old homes along familiar roads on All Souls'

Day, the day after All Saints and corresponding to the Irish festival of Samain. In antiquity, writers often confused this doctrine of the soul with that of metempsychosis. They are, however, quite separate – the gods being by definition immortal have no need of immortality of the soul, and mortals only fleetingly and in extraordinary circumstances visit the Otherworld (OGAC 18: pp. 136ff.), which is quite different from the Beyond.

Death is surrendering one's soul: bringing to life or animating is giving a soul. Jewish thought provided the soul with two drives, one to higher things (heavenly) and one to lower things (earthly). It also conceived of a male principle (*nefesh*) and a female principle (*chajah*), both called upon to transform themselves in order to be able to become a single spiritual principle, *ruah*, spirit or breath. The latter is linked visually to the divine and cosmic image of the cloud or of MIST. The vital or terrestrial element denotes externality: the celestial or spiritual element, internality.

The motif of the soul's heavenly journey is depicted in the shape of the Sun's daily transit from dawn to dusk. In so far as its substance is light, the soul (soul-spirit) is generally depicted in the shape of a flame or of a BIRD.

In the Homeric Age, the Greeks, Jean Defradas writes,

> used the word *psyche* for 'soul' in precisely the same sense of the Latin *anima*, as 'breath'. *Eidolon*, shade, is, strictly speaking, an image. Lastly, for 'spirit' they used a word with a physical meaning, *phrenes*, the diaphragm, the seat of thought and feeling inseparable from a physical framework.

Under the influence of their philosophers, the Greeks next distinguished different parts, principles, powers or faculties in the human soul. To the Pythagoreans, *psyche* corresponded to the life force; *aisthesis* (perception) to sense-perception; *noös* to the intellectual faculties, the solely human principle. Then there are the well-known parallels which Plato draws (*Republic* 4) between the parts of the soul and the classes and duties of society. In the *noös*, Aristotle distinguished active and passive intelligence, which later thinkers were to identify with the Logos and with God. The concept of *pneuma* only came later in writers of a theological cast, for whom it was a soul called to live in the company of the gods, purely spiritual 'breath', Heaven-bent. Although rooted in Plato's thought and developed six centuries later by Plotinus, 'pneumatology' only came really into its own in the early centuries of Christianity and blossomed into Gnosticism.

Pneuma, translated by the Latin word *spiritus*, as Jean Beaujeu observes, was regarded simultaneously in Rome as 'the principle of generation for all living beings and, in its purely intellectual and spiritual aspect, as the principle of human thought. The fire which was embodied in *pneuma* came from pure ethereal fire and not from any earthly flame, and its origins established a real kinship between the soul and Heaven.'

The concept of *pneuma* as a mixture of air and vital heat, the latter closely related to and often identified with pure ethereal FIRE, which is the soul of the universe, seems to have as its starting point one of Aristotle's early treatises, from which it passed on to the Stoics. The likening of the cosmos to a living being, would, however, appear to have originated with the Pythagoreans and to have passed, via Plato, to the Stoics as well. Similarly, the idea that the body paralyses and stupefies the soul, making it simultaneously the slave of darkness and the passions and in some sense imprisoning it, was promulgated by a long line of thinkers, philosophers and religious teachers from Plato onwards.

Without claiming to teach a complete and coherent system of anthropology, St Paul distinguishes within the individual spirit (*pneuma*), soul (*psyche*) and body (*soma*). If Thessalonians 5: 23 is compared with 1 Corinthians 15: 44, it will be seen that it is the soul-*psyche* which vitalizes the human body while the spirit-*pneuma* is that part of the individual which is exposed to a higher level of life and to the direct influence of the Holy Spirit. It is the latter which is to benefit from salvation and from immortality and the latter which Grace makes holy. However, its influence should be radiated by the psyche throughout the body and consequently throughout the individual as a whole, that is the body which lives and moves in this world and will be resurrected in the life to come.

Scholastic tradition, and Thomist thought in particular, was to distinguish three levels in the human soul. There was the vegetative soul which controlled the elementary functions of eating, reproduction and physical movement; the sensitive soul which regulated the sense-organs; and the rational soul upon which depended the higher functions of knowledge (*intellectus*) and love (*appetitus*). In the present context we may ignore later divisions into powers, faculties and so on of the soul.

It is possession of a rational soul which distinguishes human beings from other creatures and gives them the title to be created in 'the image and likeness of God'. The needle-point of the soul is the *mens*, its highest level designed as a receptacle of Grace, to become God's temple and directly to enjoy the Beatific Vision.

Christian tradition developed the mystical meaning of the soul. The spiritual levels attained by mystics owed nothing to physiology, their souls being vitalized by the Holy Spirit.

The soul displays different facets or levels of action and energy. Mystics followed in the footsteps of St Paul by distinguishing the vital from the spiritual principle, the properties of the *psyche* from those of the *pneuma*, the spiritual individual alone being moved by the Holy Spirit. When he speaks of God's word, St Paul compares it with 'a two-edged sword, piercing even to the dividing asunder of soul and spirit' (Hebrews 4: 12), claiming that spiritual transformation is needed 'to put on the new man' (Ephesians 4: 24).

The early Greek Fathers of the Church were to take up the categories suggested by Plotinus under which human beings may be classed as governed by senses, reason or intellect, in other words three levels of humanity. William of St Thierry held that these three categories were to be found in monasteries. Stability can never be constant, hence there are continual fluctuations between the last two categories of rational and spiritual. Each category has a corresponding quality of love proportionate to the degree of its union with God.

In terms of psychoanalysis, Jung shows that the soul is a concept which may be explained in many different ways and goes on to say that it

refers to a psychological content that must possess a certain measure of auto-
nomy within the limits of consciousness. . . . The soul does not coincide with the
totality of the psychic functions. We define the soul on the one hand as the
relation to the unconscious, and on the other as a personification of unconscious
contents. . . . It is evident from the ethnological and historical material that the
soul is a content that belongs partly to the subject and partly to the world of
spirits, i.e., the unconscious. Hence the soul always has an earthly as well as a
ghostly quality.

(JUNT pp. 247, 250)

It is earthly because it is set in touch with the natural maternal image, the
Earth; celestial, because the unconscious constantly and ardently yearns for
the light of awareness. It is in this way that the *anima* acts as a mediator
between the ego and the self, the latter comprising the nub of the psyche.

According to Jung, there are four stages in the development of the *anima*.
The first, symbolized by EVE, represents purely instinctual and biological
relations. The second is higher but retains sexual elements. The third is
represented by the Virgin Mary in whom love utterly attains the spiritual
level. The fourth Jung denotes as typified by Sapientia, wisdom (JUNS pp.
184–5). The meaning of these four stages would seem to be that the earthly
Eve, conceived as the female element, progresses towards a spiritualized
state. If we concede that all earthly things possess their heavenly counterparts, then the Virgin Mary may be considered the earthly aspect of wisdom
(Sophia), which is itself heavenly.

Let us take yet another definition given by Jung: 'the *anima* is the female
archetype which plays an especially important part in the male unconscious.'

If the *anima* is the female indicator in the male unconscious, then, according to Jung, the *animus* is the male indicator in the female unconscious,
or, again, the *anima* is the female component of the male psyche and the
animus is the male component of the female psyche (JUNM pp. 183, 437).
The activity of the soul, that female archetype, varies at different periods
of history. (See FEMININE, THE ETERNAL.)

Traditionally, in black magic a person may sell his or her soul to the
Devil in return for the heart's desire. The legend of Faust's bargain with
Mephistopheles recurs in different shapes, but a German legend adds that
once a person has sold his or her soul to the Devil, he or she loses his or
her SHADOW (TERS p. 26). This may perhaps be an echo of belief in two
souls and of the Ancient Egyptian belief in doubles, but is more likely to
symbolize the fact that the party to such a bargain has destroyed his or her
own existence. The shadow would thus become the symbol of the lost soul
in physical terms, since the soul now belongs to the world of darkness and
can no longer show itself in the light of day. Lack of shadow is a sign of lack
of light and substance.

It would need volumes to elucidate even one of the many and varied
concepts of the soul or souls which are embodied in the works of art,
legends and traditional depictions which are so many symbols of the invisible realities which are active in human beings. Such symbols would remain
a closed book without reference to the beliefs about the soul held by the
peoples who have conceived them.

All this article has done is briefly to sketch some of these beliefs as a

SOW 899

warning to those seeking an explanation of symbols, to use every discretion and caution when speaking of soul symbols. First it is a matter of determining whether it is the *animus* or the *anima*, and the celebrated arguments about them only scratch the surface of the incoherent mass of human intuitions on the vital principle. This principle does more than merely bring together a scrap of matter and a breath of the spirit, but unites them in the same object.

sound (see also AUM; LANGUAGE; OM)   A dictionary defines sound as 'a transmitted disturbance perceived or perceptible by ear: esp[ecially] a tone produced by regular vibrations', and it is from this aspect that sound has been made a basic symbol in India. Sound lies at the beginnings of the cosmos. If speech or the Word (*vāk*) brought the universe into being, it was by the effect of the regular vibrations of primeval sound (*nāda*). *Nāda* is the manifestation of sound (*shabda*) or of the property of sonority, which corresponds to the element Ether (*ākāsha*). Indian literature states that whatever may be perceived as sound is SHAKTI, or divine power. What lacks sound is the First Cause itself. It goes on to define sound as latent (*parā*), subtle (*pashyantī*) or articulated (*vaikharī*). Sound is perceived before shape, hearing is anterior to sight. From the sound (*shabda*) is born the BINDU, or seed of manifestation. Similarly a person's birth is sometimes called a 'sound'.

Knowledge is regarded not simply as something seen, but as something heard as well ('auditive light', says *The Secret of the Golden Flower*, in which Tantric influence is clear). MANTRAS display the echoes of that primordial vibration, and of these the monosyllable *om* is the most prestigious since it reproduces the very process of manifestation. The first mantras, or mental incantations, are attributed to the primeval lawgiver, Manu, and are charged with all the *shakti*'s power, a power which is even exercised upon the physical plane. However, their prime faculty is their ability to allow the heart (*anāhata*) to hear those 'inaudible' sounds which correspond, in other words, to the vision of Brahmā obtained by the 'eye of the heart'. There are many Hindu techniques for hearing internal sound, which is compared with the ringing of bells, the blowing of conches and so on, and there is even a Yoga of sound (*shabda-yoga*). Such auditory practices are linked to the Muslim *dhikr* (AVAS, DANA, ELIY, GRIF, GUEI, VACG).

sow   If the pig is generally regarded as the uncleanest of animals, the sow has received opposite attention, being deified as a symbol of fecundity and plenty, rivalling the cow in this respect. Thus the Ancient Egyptians depicted the great goddess, Nut – embodied in the vault of Heaven and forming the female half of the elemental sacred marriage of Heaven and Earth – sometimes as a cow and sometimes as a sow reclining in the sky and suckling her piglets, embodied in the stars (POSD). As a Moon-goddess, the sow is the mother of all the stars, which she swallows and regurgitates turn and turn about, as they are diurnal or nocturnal, to let them journey across the sky. Thus she swallows the stars at dawn to regurgitate them at dusk, while she adopts the opposite course in relation to her child, the Sun. Sows were the favourite victims in sacrifices to Demeter, the mother-goddess of the Earth. Sows symbolize the female principle reduced to its basic reproductive role.

space (see also CARDINAL POINTS)   Space, inseparable from time, is simultaneously the place where all is potential – and in this sense it symbolizes primeval chaos – and the place where all is actualized – and in this sense it symbolizes the cosmos or ordered universe. It constantly bubbles with dissipative energy, resulting in fresh and quite unpredictable orders. Space is like a vast area which cannot be measured, of which the centre cannot be determined and which is expanding in all directions. Space symbolizes the infinity in which the universe moves and is itself symbolized by a three-dimensional cross of six arms, as well as by the sphere, but a dyanmic sphere of limitless expansion. Space therefore embraces the entire universe, actual and potential.

In the sense of the positioning of an object or an event, space symbolizes a collection of co-ordinates or bearings which form a dynamic system of relationships to one given point, body or centre, radiating in any number of directions. These are reduced in practical terms to three axes, each of two directions – east–west, north–south, zenith–nadir; or else left–right, forewards–backwards, up–down. To this one adds time (before–during–after) and speed (faster–equal–slower). Thus, in general terms, space symbolizes the internal or external environment in which all living things, persons or groups move.

Internal space is used in reference to all human potential which may progressively be deployed, the agglomeration of conscious, unconscious and unforeseeable.

Whether you regard astrology as a science or not, it, too, rests upon the meaning of the mysterious spatial connections between planets, stars and galaxies. Nor can astronomy itself, however detached, fail to engender amazement tinged with awe when facing a space which defies measurement and has no limit to its extent. The cosmonauts who walked upon the Moon's surface openly admitted to semi-religious feelings and realized that mankind and Earth itself are not to be measured in relation to the vastness of space.

sparrowhawk   Because the male is smaller and clumsier than the female, the sparrowhawk symbolizes the marriage in which the wife is the dominant partner.

In Ancient China, this bird, metamorphosed from the ring-dove, was an emblem of Autumn, the season both of hunting and of life in retirement.

In addition it was a sparrowhawk, according to the *Cho-Ching*, which, in association with a tortoise, taught Kun how to build dykes and stop inundation during the flood.

In Ancient Egypt the sparrowhawk was the bird of Horus, and hence a solar emblem. Like the eagle, it symbolized the Sun's powers. Greeks and Romans also saw the Sun's image in the sparrowhawk (GRAR, MASR).

spear   The spear is universally regarded as an axial, phallic, fiery or solar (*yang*) symbol.

In Japanese Shintō mythology, Izanagi and Izanami thrust a spear decorated with jewels (the solsticial AXIS) into the sea and, when they withdrew it, the salt which dripped from it formed the first island, Onogoro-jima. Next they set up the Celestial Pillar, in other words the World Axis. Some writers, however, very naturally identify this pillar with the spear. Like the axis, the spear is also a Sun-ray, symbolizing heavenly activity, the action of Being upon undifferentiated Matter, which was precisely the case of the spear decorated with jewels.

In Grail-legends, the drops of blood which flowed from the upright spear and were collected in the chalice, express the same idea. This spear was the one which the centurion Longinus thrust into Christ's side. It was alleged to have the power of healing the wounds which it had inflicted, a power shared by Achilles' spear.

In Celtic tradition, Lug's spear was brought by the Tuatha Dé Danaan from the ISLANDS to the north of the world. Basically it was a fire-spear which never missed its mark and which inflicted wounds which always proved mortal. It produced many offspring in epic in the hands of such heroes as Cùchulainn and his brother Conall of the Victories. Sometimes such spears killed bystanders or even those who wielded them. Celtchar the Cunning was killed in this way, by a drop of blood which ran down the shaft.

Its symbolism complements that of the Dagda's CAULDRON, for the cauldron of magic blood (that of cat, druid and hound) was needed to damp the spear which, without it, would cast sparks and of its own accord kill princes and the sons of kings. Here the sexual symbolism is explicit, and the fact that the spears held by Irish heroes are often compared with CANDLESTICKS or pillars only serves to corroborate this.

Almost exactly the same symbolism is to be found in Black Africa where a bundle of spears, as the agglomeration of power, denotes the king.

A custom in the Greco-Roman world, in which, as we know, the spear was one of the attributes of Athene (Minerva), shows how much all elements affecting the libido may be both honoured and restrained or controlled. Officers or ordinary soldiers who had performed some outstanding deed of bravery were rewarded with a spear. This spear was, however, usually blunt, not simply because it was awarded as an honour, but because it conferred no position of authority in either civil or military affairs. For the strength which the spear expresses, and this is evidence of it, had to be that of public authority overriding that of the private individual. This is why the spear held a symbolic place in all things deriving from the law, protecting contracts, and the legal process as a whole (LAVD p. 573).

sphere The sphere is, as it were, a CUBE of the CIRCLE, and shares its symbolism. It adds a third dimension to the meanings of the circle, throwing them into relief and corresponding better to actual experience. 'The wholeness of Heaven and Earth is wonderfully expressed in terms of the pairing of cube and sphere. In architecture we see this in the shape of the quadrilateral surmounted by the sphere. The latter is generally reduced to a hemisphere, as in the semi-domes of an apse' (CHAS p. 32). Examples are provided in Byzantine churches, mosques and in such specimens of Renaissance architecture as St Peter's at Rome.

In Christian iconography, there occurs the figure with the vault overhead and the square stool at his feet. This is the symbol of God coming down to Earth from his heavenly throne. The passing from sphere, circle or arch to rectangular shapes also symbolizes the incarnation (CHAS p. 79). The same

Person partaking of the two natures, human and divine, provides the link, bridge or marriage between Heaven and Earth. The reverse process, the passing from the square to the circular, symbolizes the return of the created to the uncreated, of Earth to Heaven: the wholeness of fulfilment or the perfection of the completed cycle.

In Greek tradition, and with Parmenides and Orphic literature in particular, two concentric spheres stand for the terrestrial world and the other world, death providing the passage from one to the other. 'I have left the circle in which one is burdened by the weight of terrible grief and I have entered, quick-footed, the longed-for circle. I have entered the womb of the Mistress who rules the underworld' (Orphic Fragment 32c).

In his *Timaeus* (31b), Plato presents the cosmological picture of the universe as a sphere:

And he [the Creator] bestowed on it the shape which was befitting and akin. Now for that Living Creature which is designed to embrace within itself all living creatures the fitting shape will be that which comprises within itself all the shapes there are; wherefore he wrought it into a round, in the shape of a sphere, equidistant in all directions from the centre to the extremities, which of all shapes is the most perfect and the most self-similar, since He deemed that the similar is infinitely fairer than the dissimilar.

In fact the primal HERMAPHRODITE was frequently pictured as a sphere. It is a well-known characteristic that 'the sphere symbolized perfection and totality from the time of the most ancient cultures' (ELIT p. 423).

Being 'the pre-eminent figure of symmetry', the sphere is a symbol of ambivalence. Primitively, Australian tribesfolk believed, like Plato, that 'the primeval hermaphrodite (the image of ambivalence) was spherical (symmetrical). This same association of the beginning of things with bisexuality and with the sphere recurs in Plato's *Symposium*' (VIRI p. 99).

According to the prophets, three spheres emanated from God to fill the three Heavens. 'The first, the sphere of love, was red; the second, the sphere of wisdom, was blue; and the third, the sphere of creation, was green' (PORS pp. 181–2).

Muslim cosmogony has constant recourse to this idea of the sphere. Ibn Abbas records a tradition which describes the creation of water as that of a white pearl the shape and size of Heaven and Earth. The Seven Heavens were pictured as round tents one on top of the other.

This is how al-Fārābī (d. 950) describes the process of creation in his theory of emanations:

After the emanation of the Higher Sphere, emanation continued by the simultaneous creation of an Intellect and a Sphere. Thus from the second Intellect there came a third and the Sphere of the Fixed Stars; from the Third Intellect a fourth, and the Sphere of Saturn; from the Fourth Intellect, a fifth and the Sphere of Jupiter; from the Fifth Intellect, a sixth and the Sphere of Mars; from the Sixth Intellect, a seventh and the Sphere of the Sun; from the Seventh Intellect, an eighth and the Sphere of Venus; from the Eighth Intellect, a ninth and the Sphere of Mercury; from the Ninth Intellect, a tenth and the Sphere of the Moon.

(FAHN p. 237)

The essence of this theory recurs in Avicenna. According to other theories of emanation, like those promulgated by the Brotherhood of Purity, the universe was composed of spheres, from the Sphere of the Primum Mobile to the one lying in the centre of the Earth. The notions of spheres and orbital motion always predominated and was an expression of perfection. If any being was conceived as perfect, it would be pictured symbolically as a sphere. It actualized an equal distance from its centre to any point on the surface of the sphere.

Sphinx In Ancient Egypt Sphinxes comprised massive stone structures in the shape of a crouching LION with a human face emerging from the mane and wearing an enigmatic expression. The most famous of these stands on the edge of the desert, below the PYRAMID of Chefren among the pyramids and tombs at Giza.

The Sphinx still watches over these gigantic cemeteries, its red-painted face staring at the sole point on the horizon from which the Sun will rise. It is the warden of these forbidden thresholds and royal mummies. It listens to the song of the planets; it watches on the brink of eternity over all that has been and all that is to come; it gazes at distant Niles flowing across the Heavens and the Sunboats floating on their waters.

(CHAM p. 10)

In fact, these divine lions bore the heads of Pharaohs and, according to Jean Yoyotte, stood for 'a royal power, merciless towards rebels but protecting the good. By virtue of its bearded face it represented either the king or the sun-god and it possessed the same attributes as the lions. Being a feline it was irresistible in battle' (POSD p. 267). Instead of the look of anguish which Romantic poets invented, their expression and their attitude expressed the serenity of complete assurance.

In Greece, Sphinxes were winged lionesses with cruel and enigmatic faces, a type of fearsome monster which may be seen as a symbol of womanhood perverted.

In the Greek legend, a Sphinx ravaged the land of Thebes. It was a monster, half woman, half lioness, which 'asked riddles of those who passed it, and ate them if they failed to give the right answer' (GRID p. 324). It would symbolize 'debauchery and overriding depravity' and, like 'the plague devastating a country ... the destructive consequences of the reign of a depraved monarch' (DIES p. 152). The Sphinx may have wings, but cannot fly and is doomed to be swallowed up by the abyss. Instead of expressing the certainty, however mysterious, of the Egyptian Sphinx, the Greek Sphinx, according to Paul Diel, expresses only the destructive emptiness of absolute power.

In the course of its evolution in the imagination, the Sphinx has come to symbolize, too, something from which there is no escape. The very word 'Sphinx' conjures up the idea of riddles, the Oedipan Sphinx, a riddle which overpowers and constricts. In fact, the Sphinx stands on the brink of a fate which is both necessity and mystery.

spider The spider is regarded in the first place as a lunar manifestation, devoted to spinning and weaving. While the thread is reminiscent of that of the Fates, as the Koran emphasizes, what is woven is of extreme fragility. 'But verily, frailest of all houses surely is the house of the spider' (Koran 29: 40).

This fragility evokes the fragility of a reality which is no more than illusory and deceptive appearance. Whether the spider wove the fabric of the world, or the veil of illusion which conceals the Supreme Reality, was a question which the most ancient of the Vedas asked in India in the second millennium BC with the myth of Māyā, the SHAKTI or companion of Varuna. This myth received differing interpretations. In Buddhist philosophy, *māyā* was to suggest an illusory reality, because it was empty of being, that is to say devoid of all metaphysical substratum. Brahmanism, on the other hand, regarded it as reality, existence being 'real' since it is a manifestation of Being. Māyā's veil, like the spider's web, expresses the beauty of creation and Māyā was an important goddess.

The dialectic from which the spider's symbolic ambivalence derives, a fundamental question for Buddhism and Hinduism, is also the dialectic of existence versus being, which may be detected at the very beginnings of Mediterranean culture, if the structure of the myth of Arachne is examined closely.

Athene was the goddess of the Higher Logic, since she sprang fully armed from the head of her father, Zeus. She was the mistress of weaving, but Arachne, a young Lydian girl, a mere mortal, was so gifted in that art that she dared to challenge the goddess. Each sat at their looms facing one another. Athene wove portraits of the twelve Olympians in all their majesty and at the four corners of the fabric depicted the punishments inflicted on mortals who dared to defy them. In reply to this transcendental picture of a higher reality to which mortals cannot attain, Arachne depicted the loves of gods for mortal women. Athene, enraged, struck Arachne with her shuttle. The girl then tried to hang herself. Athene saved her life but changed her into a spider, endlessly swinging at the end of its thread. There is something decidedly Sartrean about a girl challenging a goddess, since it sets this world over the other and even makes Olympus itself subject to human passions. The spider with its contemptible web also symbolizes the failure of the individual who tries to rival God, the punishment of ambition to ape the creator.

Spider symbolism as a whole forms part of the Indo-European cultural heritage and, subject to many different interpretations, occurs scattered at countless cultural levels separately or in isolation. Thus the spider makes its easy appearance in the role of cosmic creator, higher deity or Demiurge. This occurs among many peoples.

In West Africa, Anansi the spider prepared the material from which the first humans were made and created the Sun, the Moon and the stars. Then Nyame, the sky-god, breathed life into mankind. The spider continued to play the part of go-between between gods and mortals and, as a culture-hero, brought mankind corn and the hoe (MYTF p. 242).

In myths from the Gilbert Islands (Micronesia), Nareau, the Lord Spider, is depicted as the first of all beings and the creator-god (MYTF p. 225).

The Ashanti have turned the spider into a primeval god; mankind, they say, was created by a great spider. A legend from Mali describes the spider as the counsellor of the supreme deity, a culture-hero who 'disguised himself as a bird, flew away and, without his master's knowledge, created Sun, Moon and stars. . . . Then he created day and night and brought down the dew' (TEGH p. 56).

Since the spider wove the fabric of reality, it rules fate, and this explains its worldwide role as seer. For example, the Bamun in the Cameroons believe that the bird-eating spider has been given

the heavenly privilege of foretelling the future. . . . Under another of its names, Ngaame, it vies with the royal serpent for first place in the Bamun artists' bestiary. . . . Its significance is all-embracing and complex. Since it is linked to human destiny and the drama of life on Earth, divination with the Ngaame has produced an art of deciphering the signs. . . . This involves placing at the opening of the bird-eating spider's hole emblems which the insect will disturb when it emerges with the darkness and will transform into a message. These, the seer will sift to find cures for illness, protection against enemies and enjoyment of life.

(MVEA p. 59)

Divination through spiders is still practised in the former Inca Empire in Peru. The seer takes the lid off a jar in which the fortune-telling spider is kept. If any one of its legs is straight, this is an evil omen (ROWI).

Lastly, spiders are sometimes symbols of the soul or are among those creatures which conduct souls. The peoples of Siberia and the Altai in central Asia, particularly, regarded the spider as a soul freed from the body. Although the Muisca in Colombia may not believe the spider to be a soul, yet on its boat of spider's web it carries souls across the rivers on their way to the Underworld. To the Aztecs, the spider was a symbol of the god of the Underworld. The Montagnards of southern Vietnam regard the spider as a shape taken by the soul when it leaves the body during sleep and, hence, to kill a spider is to risk killing the sleeper.

All these properties – Demiurge, seer, conductor of souls and hence intermediary between the two worlds of the human and the divine reality – have turned the spider into a symbol, too, of a higher grade of initiation. The Bambara, for example, call spiders a class of initiates who have attained 'internalization, the creative power which the individual draws from meditation and intuition' (ZAHV p. 116).

On the other hand, this internalization, suggested by the spider lurking in the middle of its web, provides the analyst with 'an excellent symbol of introversion and Narcissism, the individual swallowed by his or her own centre' (Beaudoin).

But this embracing and centripetal image should not cause us to forget that other image of the intercessor provided by the image of the spider bouncing like a yoyo at the end of a thread which it seems ceaselesly to be trying to climb. A latent sexual content is detectible (see SWING), fully confirmed by studies made in Sardinia and Apulia of 'tarantulism' and its social setting (EMTR pp. 230ff.). On the mystical plane, the thread is reminiscent of the umbilical cord or of the golden chain joining creator and created by which the latter attempts to climb to the former, a motif evoked by Plato and which the Pseudo-Dionysius the Areopagite echoes.

This is yet another example of unison in Indo-European thought, since

906   SPIKENARD

the Upanishads turn the spider, spinning its long thread, into a symbol of deliverance. The yogi's thread is the monosyllable AUM, thanks to which he can raise himself until he finds release. The spider's thread is the means and support of spiritual self-realization.

spikenard   Athough this plant is often mentioned by oriental writers, it was unknown in the West. From it, one of the most valuable PERFUMES was extracted, a scent which evoked the qualities of kingship. 'While the king sitteth at his table, my spikenard sendeth forth the smell thereof. A bundle of myrrh is my wellbeloved unto me; he shall lie all night betwixt my breasts' (Song of Solomon 1: 12–13).

It is a component of the Paradise in which love blossoms. When the wellbeloved describes his rapture, he compares his spouse with a spring or a GARDEN (ibid. 4: 12), 'spikenard and saffron: . . . with all the chief spices. A fountain of gardens, a well of living waters, and streams from Lebanon.' (ibid.: 14–15).

It was also with spikenard that Mary Magdalene anointed Christ's feet, taking 'a pound of spikenard, very costly' (John 12: 3).

In their commentaries upon the Song of Solomon, the Church Fathers made spikenard a symbol of humility, reducing somewhat the perfume's regal and luxurious character. However, the conflict is resolved when the symbol is explained. Spikenard is a tiny grassy plant which grows in mountainous areas. When its roots are crushed they give the most wonderful perfume. Thus it is with humility, which produces the highest fruits of holiness. Medieval writers often mention this plant, taking their information from Pliny's *Natural History*.

spindle (see also DISTAFF; THREAD; WEAVING)   Plato's 'spindle of fate' symbolizes the fate which rules the heart of the universe.

The spindle turns at a regular rate and makes the whole of the cosmos turn with it. It is the sign of a sort of robotic movement within the planetary system, the law of the eternal homecoming. On these grounds it may be compared with Moon symbolism. The Moirae, daughters of Necessity (fate) sing with the sirens as they make the spindles turn. Lachesis (past), Clotho (present) and Atropos (future) rule the life of each individual with a thread which one spins, the other unwinds and the third cuts.

This symbolism displays the inevitability of fate. Pitilessly the Parcae (the Roman name for the Moirae) wind and unwind time and life. The twofold aspect of life is made plain. The necessity of movement from birth to death reveals the contingency of being. Necessity of death resides in the non-necessity of life.

The spindle, instrument and attribute of the Fates, comes to symbolize death.

spiral   The spiral, a frequent natural formation in both the vegetable and animal kingdoms, in the shape of vines and convolvuli or snail- and sea-shells, conjures the development of strength or condition.

Its shape is to be encountered in all cultures, heavy with symbolic meaning. 'It is an "open" and optimistic motif. Nothing is simpler than setting out from one end of the spiral and reaching the other' (BRIL p. 198).

It displays the appearance of motion rotating outwards from a fixed point of origination, continuously expanding and lengthening into infinity. It is typical of those unending lines which constantly link the two ends of the future.... [The spiral is and symbolizes] emanation, extension, evolution, cyclical but progressive continuity and rotational creation.

(CHAS p. 25)

The spiral is linked to the cosmic symbolism of the MOON, to the erotic symbolism of the vulva, to the watery symbolism of the SHELL and to such fertility symbols as helix or HORN. In short, it stands for the repetitive rhythm of life, the cyclical nature of evolution and the permanence of being beneath the flux of movement.

In fact, this applies to the helical spiral, but its symbolism differs slightly from that of the flat spiral. The latter is more closely related to that of the MAZE, evolution from the centre, or involution returning to it. The double spiral symbolizes simultaneously the two directions of this movement, birth and death, *kalpa* and *pralaya*, or the 'death' and the rebirth as a changed person which occurs in initiation. It marks the action in a reverse direction of the same power around the two poles and in the two halves of the World Egg. The double spiral is the outline of the line dividing YIN AND YANG, separating the black and white halves when their symbol is depicted. The alternating rhythm of the movement can hardly be better expressed, not even by the ancient ideogram *chen*, which depicts with a double spiral the alternate expansion and contraction of *yin* and *yang*.

The double spiral is also the double wreathing of the serpents round the CADUCEUS, the double helix around the Brahman's staff and the twofold movement of the *nādī* around the central *sushumna* artery – the polarity and balance of the two opposing cosmic currents. The same symbol may thus be expressed in the spiral's alternating rotation, now in one direction, now in the opposite, as in the Hindu myth of the Churning of the Sea of Milk when the serpent Vashūki was hauled turn and turn about by *deva* and *asura*. The same is true of the bow-driven fire-stick which some have attempted to compare with the Celtic double spiral and with Jupiter's office as Lord of Fire. In Asia, drills are still used which employ very similar principles. What should be noticed in this context is that fire is produced in much the same way as *amrita*. It is the result of alternation and equilibrium between two streams of energy flowing in opposite directions. The double spiral is also related to some depictions of the DRAGON.

On the other hand dragons are coiled in helical spirals around the columns of some temples, as is the serpent of the *kundalinī* around the *svayambhuva-lingam* at the base of the spinal column. This is, however, an embryonic and undeveloped spiral. *Yin* and *yang* may be regarded as sketches on the horizontal plane of the evolutionary helix. The latter continues into infinity and symbolizes the evolution and continuity of states of being – as well as degrees of initiation, as is the case in the symbolic use of the spiral staircase (AVAS, BENA, EPEM, GUED, GUEC, GUET, GUES, LIOT, MATM, VARG, WIEC).

The spiral is a lunar and aquatic fertility symbol. It is engraved upon paleolithic statuettes of goddesses and is the equivalent of all centres of life and fecundity (ELIT): a centre of life because it marks movement in a certain unity of order, or, conversely, the permanence of being beneath its flux.

It is to be found in every culture.

The spiral is an abiding leitmotif. . . . The symbolism of the spiral sea-shell is reinforced by mathematical speculation which turns it into the sign of equilibrium in a state of disequilibrium and of the stability of being in the womb of change. Spirals, and especially logarithmic spirals, have the remarkable property of growth in a way which retains ultimate shape, the overall shape of the figure remaining unaltered, and thus of having permanence of shape despite asymmetrical growth.

(GHYN)

On the first day of their major Winter solstice festival, which is also their New Year, the Zuni (Pueblo) Indians light a New Year fire on the altar and then chant 'spiral' songs and dance 'spiral' dances (MULR p. 292). Their custom may well provide the key to the origin of all giratory dances, the most celebrated of which is that of the Mevlevi or Whirling Dervishes in Turkey, since as Gilbert Durand remarks (DURS p. 338), the spiral 'ensures the permanence of being in the flux of change'. In Mayan cosmology the Winter solstice was symbolically zero in time and its own symbol was the spiral. This was the critical point in time when the restarting of the annual cycle had to be ensured or else the end of the world would follow. It is common knowledge that terror of this threat drove the Aztecs to practise human sacrifice upon a maniacal scale in order to provide the Sun with the strength and the blood to start out again on his journey.

The S-shaped, counter-rotating, double spiral is a symbol of thunder and of the phases of the Moon, storms often being associated with the changes of the Moon. It expresses graphically the symbolism of fecundity associated with the network of storm, thunder and lightning and in this context may stand for the BULL-ROARER (HENL).

Many of the peoples of Black Africa regard the spiral or helix as the symbol of the dynamic of life, the movement of souls in the created and expanding universe. In this respect, the Dogon and Bambara solar hieroglyphic is most revealing. It comprises a pot (the primeval womb) around which are three (the masculine symbol) spiral coils of red copper. The latter symbolizes the primordial Word, the first utterance of the god Amma, in other words, the spirit and seed of godhead. The Bambara depict Faro, Lord of the Word, as a spiral at the centre of the four points of the compass. He takes material shape in the wicker-work hat with eight whorls which was once worn only by kings. With the spiral which he made his own when the world was set in order, 'Faro travels every four hundred years to inspect the borders before returning to the centre from which he watches over and rules the universe' (DIED). Similarly, in procreation, the man's seminal fluid and his word enter the woman through her sexual organs and through her ear, regarded as another sexual organ, and coil in a spiral round the womb to make the seed of life fertile (GRIE pp. 38, 51, 62; DIEB pp. 40, 43; GRIG, ZAHD).

Further south, a similar symbolism governs the use of the spiral in the cosmogonic thinking of the Lulua and Luba, Bantu tribes from Kasai in

Zaire. Souls, spirits and genii move in helical or spiral lines within the four planes of the universe. Among their hieroglyphics, a large spiral, flanked by two smaller ones, depicts the Supreme Deity creating Sun and Moon. A single spiral stands for the coiled and parti-coloured serpent which is an image of the creator and of the cyclical current of life. It also stands for Heaven and for the soul's cyclical wanderings, in succession incarnate, disincarnate and reincarnate. A spiral with its coils streaked at regular intervals signifies 'the course of human life, alternating between good and evil'. On this analogy, the shell of the giant land-snail, which is also helical and streaked, 'is an ingredient of those medicines which may be used for good or ill' (FOUA p. 66).

The powerful Voodoo god, Dan, a symbol of continuity, is generally depicted in Benin in the shape of a serpent biting its tail. It is, incidentally, assimilated to the rainbow and is regarded as a doubly bisexual being since it is its own twin, the two in one, 'coiled in a spiral round the world which they preserve from disintegration'. In this context the spiral clearly partakes of its basic significance of primeval motion, the 'creational vibration' of the Dogon, which is the basis of all created things. Paul Mercier uses this striking phrase to describe it: 'doing nothing of itself, but without it, nothing can be done' (MERF).

Pictorially the Lulua depict Earth, Moon and Sun as a series of spirals or concentric circles, only distinguished from one another by their size or numbers. The Earth is the smallest and the Sun the largest, with respectively two spirals or concentric circles for the Earth, three for the Moon and four for the Sun (FOUA).

With its dual meaning of contraction and expansion, the symbolism of the spiral is linked to that of the WHEEL and is found as often or even more frequently in Celtic carvings or as a decorative motif in metalwork, pottery, coinage and so on. Modern scholarship has attempted to make it the equivalent of the Latin *fulmen* and a Celtic symbol for the thunderbolt, but this explanation is inadequate since the spiral is in fact a cosmic symbol. It was a motif which the Celts often carved on dolmens and megalithic monuments (OGAC 11: pp. 307ff.).

The Germanic peoples set a horse's eye, ringed by a spiral, on the Sun's chariot to symbolize the source of light.

The spiral also symbolizes the soul's journey, after death, along ways unknown to it, but leading by preordained byways to the central home of eternal being. 'I believe that in all the primitive civilizations in which it occurs, from the North Cape to the Cape of Good Hope, and in many civilizations in America, in Asia and even in Polynesia as well, that the spiral stands for the journey which after death, a person's soul makes to its ultimate destination' (BRIL).

spittle See SALIVA.

spleen In China, the spleen was regarded as being a reservoir of terrestrial, or *yin*, energy. It corresponded to sweetness of taste and to the colour yellow, which is habitually that of the centre. Despite this, the system of correspondences was somewhat complicated. Essential energy was located in the spleen at the Spring equinox, while the *Hong-fang* makes the spleen correspond to the element Wood, and to the Spring – hence to the colour green (CHAT, CORT, GRAP).

In the West, too, there were contradictions. According to one view, the spleen was the seat of melancholy and irritability and to another – shared by the Arabs – it was linked to cheerfulness, laughter being caused by a dilation of the spleen. Both were based upon physiological theories rejected by modern medicine.

In both East and West the spleen was the symbol of changeability, like the volatile humours.

spring Throughout the world, springs are held to be holy because they are the source of fresh or pure water. They are channels of the primary manifestation, on the level of human reality, of basic cosmic matter without which fecundation and growth of all living things could not be assured. The fresh water which they diffuse, like RAIN, is divine blood and heavenly seed. Springs are symbols of motherhood. For this reason they were often protected by taboos and the Maya-Quiché of Central America are still forbidden to fish in springs or to lop the trees which overshadow them. Spring-water is lustral water, 'part and parcel of purity' (DURS).

The symbolism of the spring of living waters is best expressed by the spring welling up in the middle of the GARDEN, at the foot of the Tree of Life, in the centre of the Earthly PARADISE, and then dividing into four rivers and flowing to the four points of the compass. This spring was variously termed the Fountain of Life, the Fountain of Immortality or of Youth, or else the Fountain of Knowledge. The tradition persists that the Fountain of Youth springs from the foot of a tree. Because its waters are ever changing, the FOUNTAIN symbolizes constant rejuvenation rather than immortality. Such divine or sacrificial beverages as ambrosia, soma or mead were all 'Fountains of Youth'. Whoever drank from them broke through the limitations of the temporal state to acquire longevity through youthfulness perpetually renewed, a state which the alchemists achieved with their Elixir of Life.

Eastern tradition speaks of a polar, or Hyperborean, Fountain of Life and it was in quest of this that Alexander the Great set out. But his impatience prevented him from reaching it and he died at the age of thirty-three.

This Spring of Life is sometimes compared with the water and blood which flowed from Christ's side and which Joseph of Arimathea is supposed to have caught in the Grail. Alexander's quest, mentioned above, is akin to a quest for the Grail.

In Arab countries especially, the buildings round a square courtyard with a fountain in the middle are the very image of the Earthly Paradise (CORM, GUEC, GUES).

In Irish accounts of the Battle of Mag Tuired, mention is made of a healing spring into which wounded members of the Tuatha Dé Danann were thrown so that they would rise from its waters the next morning healed and ready for battle. Around this spring grew large numbers of healing or medicinal plants, because this was where Dian Cécht, the god of healing, had set one specimen of every plant which grew in Ireland. The symbolism of this spring or fountain is that of regeneration and purification.

In southern Gaul the fountain of Glanum ('pure'), now St-Rémy-de-Provence, was placed under the patronage of Valetudo ('Health') and its name is reminiscent of the Irish Fountain of Health (*Slante*) of the Tuatha Dé Danann. Many Irish princes and warriors regularly took a morning bathe in a spring and when King Eochaid surprised and approached his future bride Etain, she was loosing her hair before bathing in a spring. Boann went to the fountain of Segais to cleanse herself after the birth of Oenghus (Apollo in his youthful aspect) and the water surged out as a river (the Boyne) and carried her down to the sea and drowned her. The cult of springs and fountains is very much alive in present-day Celtic areas, especially in Brittany where they are generally believed to have curative properties for the widest range of illnesses, from fevers to skin diseases, frequently through the intercession of St Anne and more often still of Our Lady. However, such cults existed long before in Gaul and several deities of hot springs are known, including Apollo Borvo ('Boiling'), hence the name of the modern Bourbon-les-Bains and so on. The best known of these Celtic springs was the Fontaine de Barenton in the Forest of Brocéliande (modern Paimpont in Brittany) and springs and fountains are often mentioned in the Arthurian Cycle, especially in the Welsh tale of Owen and Lunet (see also SIMPLES; BUSHEL) (OGAC 11: pp. 279ff.; 12: pp. 59ff.; KERA).

In Scandinavian legend, Mimir's Well contained the waters of knowledge. This 'water was so precious that in order to be allowed to drink it, the god Odin was forced to pay with the loss of an eye. At this cost he drank the waters of knowledge, prophecy and poetry' (MYTF p. 44).

The leaves of gold found in the graves of Orphic initiates in southern Italy provide such a wealth of material for symbolic elucidation, especially by the psychoanalyst, as is wellnigh inexhaustible. Fragment 32a describes a spring of fresh water which leads those who drink of it to the realm of heroes. But great care must be taken not to mistake another for it:

In the House of Hades, on your left hand, you will see a spring. Close to it grows a white cypress. Be careful not even to approach this spring. You will find another with fresh water flowing from the Marshes of memory. Wardens stand beside it. Say to them: 'I am the child of Earth and the starry Heavens as you yourselves know well. I am parched with thirst and dying. Give me the fresh water which flows from the Marshes of memory at once.' And then they will give you water to drink from the divine spring and you will go to reign among the heroes.

In traditional cultures springs are well known as symbols of the beginning of life and, in more general terms, of all beginnings, of genius, power, grace and all good fortune. If the spring itself flows from the 'Marshes of Memory', what more powerful evocation can it provide of the unconscious? This is because Memory was worshipped as the repository of all learning. The spring mentioned above is, in fact, the spring of knowledge, mother of that knowledge which leads to perfection and which derives from memory. As Defredas comments in his French translation of the Orphic fragment:

As wife of Zeus, Memory became the mother of the Muses. According to then-current ideas, the dead, drinking the waters of Lethe or forgetfulness, lost all memory of their past lives. One can readily see, therefore, why memory should play a pre-eminent part in a religious system in which initiation received during the lifetime and comprising, in part, the possession of spells which allowed their owners to follow the right road in the Otherworld, had to be kept safe in order to reach the state of bliss.

The first spring, therefore, mentioned in the Orphic fragment and which had to be avoided, was that of Lethe which would lull into the sleep of death. The other spring is the spring of Memory, which assures the wakefulness of immortality. If one is a 'child of Earth and the starry Heavens', it is from the second spring that one must drink.

This is the same symbolism of the archetypal spring which Jung translates as an image of the soul, in so far as it is the origin of the inner life and of spiritual energy.

square (see also MAGIC SQUARE) The square is one of the geometric figures most frequently and universally employed in symbolic language. With the CENTRE, CIRCLE and CROSS, it is one of the four basic symbols, according to de Champeaux (CHAS p. 28).

It is the symbol of Earth as opposed to Heaven, but as well, and upon another level, it is the symbol of the created universe as opposed to the uncreated and to the creator. It is the antithesis of the transcendent.

The square is a positively static shape, its four corners firmly moored. It symbolizes the halt or pause. Implicit in the square is the notion of stagnation and solidification, even of becoming permanently set in perfection, as in the case of the Heavenly Jerusalem. While smooth motion is circular and rounded, stoppage and stability are associated with angular shapes and harsh, jerky lines.

(CHAS pp. 30–1)

Many areas set apart for religious or other special reasons – altars, temples, cities, military camps – adopt a quadrangular form. Often this takes the shape of a square within a circle, like camps or temples on hill-tops, or like the city of Rome within a circle of hills.

The illustration opposite (CHAS p. 269) depicts 'the clear image of the individual who is spiritualized without becoming disincarnate'. The central cube, with its squares, chequer-boards, mason's squares and dots, suggests the physical world of the creation, limited and bounded by time and space. The oval shape of the head, the arch of the eye-sockets, the almond eyes and the crescent of the lips symbolize concentration and the spiritual. The conjunction of the two displays the relationship between Heaven and Earth, between the transcendent and the immanent, a relationship which culminates in a marriage within the individual. It depicts what Champeaux describes in more general terms as 'a dynamic image of a dialectic between the transcendent and the heavenly, to which humans naturally aspire, and the earthly which is their present location' (CHAS p. 131).

Plato regarded the square – and the circle – as being 'absolutely beautiful in itself'. Abū Ya'qūb said that FOUR, the number of the square, was 'the most perfect of numbers' since it was the number of the Intellect and of the letters making up God's name (*Allh*). The symbolism of square and number four come together. From the Tetragrammaton, the Israelites composed the unutterable Name of God (JHVH or YHVH). The Pythagoreans used the TETRAKTYS (as four squared, or sixteen) as the basis of their teaching.

Composite symbol of male figure and square in enamelled bronze (Bergen University History Museum)

In some sense, therefore, the number four is that of Divine Perfection, although more generally speaking it is the number of the complete evolution of manifestation, symbol of the established universe.

Manifestation evolves from a fixed centre to the four points of the compass along the arms of an imaginary CROSS. A cross within a square expresses the dynamic of the number four, while the materialization of the manifestation is expressed by the square alone. This is true of settled societies; nomadic peoples inhabit circular camps and round tents.

The ages of the world, human life and the phases of the Moon are all attuned to the number four, while the four phases of cyclical motion expressed in a circle divided along its horizontal and vertical diameters is truly squaring the circle. When projected on the basis of its four cardinal points, the Earth is a square. It is divided into its four regions inhabited by its four castes by the four arms or faces of the godhead – Shiva's or Vishnu's or Ganesha's four arms; the four faces of Tumburu at Angkor, but more plainly in the multiple Lokeshvara in the temple of Bayon there. Tantric or architectural MANDALAS, being images of the cosmos, are squares with their gates at the four points of the compass. The square is the basic figure for space, as the circle, and especially the SPIRAL, are for time.

Similarly in China, space is square, each point of the compass being dominated by a cardinal mountain.

The notion that the Earth was square goes back to very ancient times in China and has become part of the language. Space was measured by the four *yang* directions, but that word also means 'square'. This is why the Earth-god is represented by a square mound, and why the capital city and the imperial palace were both square. Space comprises a series of squares set one within the other [relative to the centre of the world] or set side by side [around secondary centres].

(MYTF p. 124)

At the centre the emperor received good influences from the four points of the compass and drove away harmful ones. Square space was divided into square provinces in accordance with Yu the Great's 'Magic Square' and also, according to the *Chou Li*, into square fields. The city, as the centre of space, was square with gates at the four points of the compass. If the world were to be properly regulated, vassals would be received at these four gates and they would gather in a square formation. Houses and altars were square. The Temple of Heaven (see HOUSE) was square with four times three gates corresponding, like the gates of the Heavenly Jerusalem, to the twelve months of the year. The lodges of secret societies were square with four doors corresponding to the four elements. The ancient Chinese universe – and this must also have been the ideal arrangement of a lodge – comprised a series of squares one within the other, an arrangement which cannot but remind us of the triple enclosure, a Celtic and Christian symbol of the three grades of initiation or of the three worlds over which the Cross stretched its redemptive power.

Of course, this same cosmic symbolism of the square aligned upon the four points of the compass recurs in Korea and Vietnam, but it is especially prevalent in Cambodia, not only in the ground-plans of temples or of the capital Angkor, but also in the subdivision of the kingdom, once comprising four provinces at the four points of the compass.

Even more than the square, the CUBE is a symbol of solidification, stability and the stoppage of the cycle of evolution, since within its three dimensions it sets and determines space. In Masonic symbolism the Perfect Ashlar possesses this notion of fulfilment. Nor is the notion of basis, foundation or stability foreign to the symbolism of the Ka'ba at Mecca, it being a stone cube. The Muslim *qubbah* is the earthly square supporting the heavenly dome, often with the aid of four pillars.

The next entry (SQUARE (MASON'S)) mentions the Christian symbol, the gammadion, which is more or less a square enclosing a cross, and hence synthesizes the two aspects of the number four. The cross depicts Christ surrounded by the four Evangelists or else by the creatures which serve as their emblems.

If Heaven is generally round and Earth square, one may sometimes alter one's viewpoint and reverse the symbolic correspondences. In Hindu temple-building, while the square may be fixation and crystallization of the heavenly cycles, it may also signify quite the opposite – the changeless First Cause by contrast with the circular motion of manifestation. However, one always returns to the original notion in respect of the building of Vedic altars, which were cosmic cubes. Granet has also observed that the 'celestial tree-trunks' of the Chinese cycles were ten in number and arranged in a square, while their 'earthly branches' were twelve in number and set in a circle, reminiscent of the exchange of attributes between Fu-hi and Nu-kua described under COMPASS (BURA, BENA, BHAB, CORT, DANA, CHAE, GRAD, GRAP, GRAR, GRIR, GUEM, GUEC, GUER, GUET, GUES, KRAT, NGUC, SAIR, SCHU, SECA, SOUN).

In Platonic theory four is compared with the material shape of the idea and three with the idea itself. The former is an expression of phenomenon, the latter of essence: the one of matter, the other of spirit. While the number three is related to the symbolism of the vertical, the number four belongs to that of the horizontal. One joins the three worlds and the other divides them, if each is considered at its respective level.

According to Plutarch (*Isis* 106), the Pythagoreans stated that the square concentrated the powers of Rhea, Aphrodite, Demeter, Hestia and Hera. In his commentary on this passage Mario Meunier explains that: 'The square signified that Rhea, the mother of the gods, the source of time, made herself manifest through changes in the four elements represented by Aphrodite (Water, source of life), Hestia (Fire), Demeter (Earth) and Hera (Air).' The square symbolized the synthesis of the elements.

Because the four sides of the square are of equal length, in Christian tradition too it symbolized the cosmos and the pillars standing at each of its four corners symbolized the elements.

The fifteenth-century Denis the Carthusian was to state that square bodies are not destined to rotate like spherical bodies. Furthermore the square displayed a stable character. The quadrangle was employed as the plan of many public squares, such as the Agora in Ancient Athens. Square plans were adopted for town-building in the Middle Ages and the chapel of the Grail was square.

The thirteenth-century architect, Villard de Honnecourt, who made a collection of stylized drawings, preserved the plan of a twelfth-century Cistercian church drawn 'on the square' (*ad quadratum*). This has points of comparison with the proportions of the microcosm, or human being, according to St Hildegard. The Hildegardian man, with feet together and arms outstretched, is eight equal units of measurement in length and eight in breadth, these units of length and breadth being expressed as squares. The ground-plan of such a church *ad quadratum* may be contained within a rectangle, its length comprising three squares of the same size. The ground-plan of the Cistercian church comprises twelve equal units of measurement in length and eight in breadth, in other words, a ratio of 12:8 or 3:2.

Square churches are common in England and include Christ Church Cathedral (Oxford), the parish church at Ramsey (Essex) and St Cross (Winchester). It would seem clear that not all English square churches were built under Cistercian influence, though all English Cistercian churches are square. In Germany, the majority of churches with square apses derive from the Cistercian abbey church of Morimond. In France, square churches are Cistercian. Their apses are rectangular and flanked by four, six or eight square side-chapels. Their ambulatories are rectangular.

The apses of all early Cistercian churches are rectangular, but in churches built towards the end of the twelfth and during the thirteenth centuries apses become polygonal. A vast body of spirituality is symbolically contained in these square shapes of stability, a stability which is the basis of the inner life.

The medieval author of a guide for pilgrims to the shrine of St James at Compostella compares a church with the human body. The nave is the trunk and legs, and the transepts the arms. The proportions of the human body provided the basis for drawing the ground-plan.

The square man with feet together and arms outstretched denotes the four points of the compass. This brings us back to the significance of the cross and the four directions implicit in it. Medieval writers enjoyed drawing comparisons and they related the square man to the four Evangelists, the four rivers of Paradise and, since Christ took on a human nature, he too was regarded as the epitome of the square man. Thierry of Chartres went so far as to say that oneness was the very foundation of the square since it was four times repeated. Symmetry and proportion are vital ingredients of architectural composition. The inspiration for Romanesque churches was the Temple which, according to tradition, displayed the temple of the human body in its proportions. Its ground-plan could be contained within a square. However, Romanesque churches were not exclusively built *ad quadratum* on the lines of Villard de Honnecourt's design of a Cistercian church. Sometimes they were round, and this takes us to a different symbol. We pass from space and time to the eternity of Heaven. The church is no longer the point of departure for spiritual development, but symbolizes its ultimate goal.

Square shape is not unique: it is temporal, while eternity is represented by the circle. The latter progresses through possessing the property of the year, to being the measure of time and eternity and, finally, signifying infinity. Circle and square symbolize two fundamental aspects of God – oneness and manifestation. The circle expresses the heavenly and the square the earthly, not by contrast with the heavenly, but simply as being created. There is both separation and conjunction in the relationship between square and circle. The circle, therefore, will be to the square what Heaven is to Earth or eternity to time, but the square is confined within the circle, that is, Earth depends upon Heaven. The quadrangular is no more than the perfection of the sphere upon an earthly plane (DAVS pp. 185–90).

The square and the number four occupy an equally important place in Islamic tradition. 'If Islam is compared with a building, then profession of faith (*shahada*) is the roof, its four pillars being worship (*salāt*), almsgiving (*zakāt*), fasting (*saum*) and pilgrimage (*hajj*)' (SOUP pp. 101, 132).

This idea of monolithic unity is symbolized by the Ka'ba. Originally the word meant both 'something square' (*trabba'a*) and 'something round' (*istadāra*). It is significant that the Ka'ba's shape lends itself to this dual meaning, being partly cubic and partly semi-circular. 'The supreme symbol of Islam, the *Ka'bah*, is a square block; it expresses the number four which is the number of stability. The Arab house is square' (SCHU p. 129n.). So, too, are the domed tombs (*qubba*) of Muslim saints. The square tomb stands either for Earth or for the body and its four elements, and the dome for Heaven or the spirit.

One of the basic rituals involved in pilgrimage is the procession which 'circles' the 'square' House of God (*Beit ul'lah*).

Thus at two levels, ritual and architectural, we may detect the conjunction of square and circle implicit from the very first in the etymology. The Ka'ba has four sides and four lines running from the centre to its four corners (*arkan*). It is oriented upon the four points of the compass and each of its four corners has a separate name. The white marble, semi-circular wall which marks a space around it is called *hatīm* or *hijr*. In the distant past there could have been wells into which offerings were thrown.

Additionally, and long before the advent of Islam, Mecca was called *Umm al-Qurā*, Mother of Cities (Koran 6: 92; 42: 5). Folk literature also calls it the Navel of the World, like the OMPHALOS at Delphi.

If we study Plutarch's account of the foundation of Rome, we find that Romulus was taught the ritual by the Etruscans, as if initiated into a mystery. The first thing to be done was the digging of a circular ditch into which offerings were thrown, and this was given the name *mundus*, a word also meaning 'world', or 'cosmos'. Although the shape of the city was circular, Classical antiquity referred to Rome as *urbs quadrata* (square city) and Plutarch himself calls it *Roma quadrata*. He regarded Rome as being simultaneously a circle and a square. Some critics, however, maintain that *quadrata* means 'quadripartite', that is to say that the circular city was divided into four parts by two main streets which crossed at the *mundus*. Others hold that the contradiction should only be seen in terms of a symbol, and that this is the visual representation of the insoluble mathematical problem of squaring the circle.

The *mundus* was regarded as the centre which linked the city to the spirit-world just as the umbilical cord joins the baby to its mother.

Ibn-al'Arabī observes that the Ka'ba is the earthly equivalent of the THRONE of God round which the angels circle (Koran 29: 75). The human HEART, he says, is the house of God, nobler and of more moment than the Ka'ba itself.

Ordinary human hearts are square, for they are open to four sorts of inspiration – divine, angelic, human or diabolical. The hearts of prophets are triangular, since they are immune to the suggestions of the Devil. Similarly, although the Ka'ba would seem to have four sides, it really only has three if the semi-circular side is taken into account.

In addition it should be observed that in ancient times in the East, the Babylonians used the square to denote a sum total. It expressed the notion of gathering within defined bounds and corresponded to field boundaries. It does not occur so early as the circle, and may possibly be derived from it. 'In any case, circle and square express a sum total, but the square ... employed in accounts where it was sometimes even duplicated to denote the total of totals ... serves also to express all notions of limitation ... it is a repository' (RUTE p. 233).

The association of circle and square always calls to mind the pairing of Heaven and Earth (see SPHERE; CUBE). Jung regarded threefold and fourfold as the basic archetype of fulfilment. Muslim art is a perfect illustration of this symbol.

square (mason's)   The entry COMPASSES covers the conjoint symbolism of these two instruments of measurement. This entry will only touch lightly upon them with the view of clarifying specific points.

The square is used to draw right-angles and to measure the Earth. In Ancient China, the Earth was seen as square and its subdivisions were squares too (see SQUARE). This is why the two arms of the mason's square are equal. Originally the ideogram *fang* (square) was shaped as two squares facing one another to form a rectangle, or else as a right-facing swastika formed from four squares and therefore marking the boundaries of the four regions. The square was an imperial emblem since the emperor was Lord of the Earth and, like Yu the Great, its governor. Traditional comment on the ideogram *kong* (mason's square) shows that the instrument 'shapes all things; it shapes the right-angle, which shapes the square which itself shapes the circle' (WIEC). Other sources confirm the construction of CIRCLES within squares. This is why Granet claims that the instrument is the emblem of the sorcerer, who is *yin–yang*. Furthermore, a circle drawn inside a square is a symbol of the primordial hermaphrodite.

The Greek capital letter gamma is shaped like a square, hence the ancient figures known as *gammadia*. These comprised either four squares meeting at their angles and thus outlining within them a cross, or else four squares forming a rectangle, its centre marked by a cross. In both cases the central cross is the symbol of Christ and the four squares that of the four Evangelists or of the four beasts of the Book of Revelation. Guénon further observes that the first shape of the *gammadion* corresponds to the internal lines of the *lochu*, the magic square revealed to Yu the Great, and could thus be a recurrence of the notion of the measurement of terrestrial space (GRAP, GUEC, GUES, WIEC).

The square symbolizes space because it can be employed in both horizontal and vertical planes. However, since it is used to draw rectangular shapes or right-angles, the square also symbolizes righteousness and respect for rules and regulations. In Freemasonry 'hanging from the girdle of the Venerable Master, it signifies that the head of any lodge can only have one resolve, to follow the statues of the Order and one course of action, that of the good.' Other writers make it a symbol of the equilibrium resulting from the marriage of active and passive, especially when the square is a T-square. On the other hand, the asymmetric L-square displays activity and dynamism. The square straightens and governs matter. In astrology, a 90° angle is regarded as maleficent. Some writers condemn the square as a broken cross, the banner of the Lord of Hell. By contrast with the compasses, and in so far as the latter draws curves and is active, the square is linked to matter and in that sense is passive and submissive (BOUM pp. 1–4).

squid   See CUTTLE-FISH.

staff (see also WAND)   In symbolism, the staff appears in different roles, but basically as: a weapon, and especially a magic weapon; the support for the pilgrim on his travels and the shepherd in his wanderings; and the World Axis.

In Hindu iconography it bears all these meanings. It is a weapon in the hands of several gods, but especially of Yama, warden of the south and of the kingdom of the dead where his *danda* is used to punish and to keep in subjection. On the other hand, the *danda* becomes a pilgrim's staff in the hands of Vishnu's avatar (incarnation) as Vāmana the Dwarf, and we might call it the World Axis in those of the Brahman. Ninurta's staves strike the Earth and are related to thunderbolts.

The bishop's crozier is another form of shepherd's crook, Segalen emphasizing that 'its stately processional use is a splendid and antiquated revival of the progresses through their pastures of shepherd-kings in ancient days.' The shepherd's crook and the staff of office support the wayfarer and are badges of authority. The Buddhist monk's *khakkhara* supports his steps, is the weapon of peaceful resistance and signals a presence. It has become the symbol of monasticism and the weapon of exorcism, driving off evil influences, freeing souls from Hell, taming dragons and making the waters spring from the ground – pilgrim's staff and magic wand.

In Ancient China staves, and especially PEACH-wood staves, played an important part, being used at the New Year to drive away evil influences. Yi the Archer was killed by a peach-wood rod. The staff, and especially the red staff, was used to punish the guilty. In the hierarchy of a Chinese secret society, the 'red staves' still survive as ministers of justice. BAMBOO staves with seven or nine KNOTS (the numbers of Heaven) were widely used in Taoist ritual. The knots might be said to correspond to degrees of initiation. Be that as it may, these staves are reminiscent of the Hindu *brahma-danda*, its seven knots standing for the seven *chakra*, wheels, or lotuses of Yoga physiology which mark the steps in spiritual realization.

The Taoist Heavenly Masters are often depicted holding red staves. Theirs is a knotty staff, for it must show the seven or nine knots which symbolize the seven or nine doors through which the initiate must pass to acquire knowledge. Once he has gained this knowledge, he will be able to ascend into Heaven, rising by as many steps, seated on the staff held in a crane's beak. There are echoes of the Tao's journey in the legends of medieval witches riding to their Sabbaths astride a BROOMSTICK, although there is a vast difference in the sign which affects this very symbol. Generally speaking, the shaman's, pilgrim's, Master's or magician's staff is 'a symbol of the invisible steed on which he travels through planes and worlds of being.' In legends of witchcraft, the staff became 'the wand with which the good fairy changed the pumpkin into a coach and the wicked queen into a toad' (SERH p. 139).

Staves are also related to axial symbolism in much the same way as the SPEAR. Around the World AXIS (*brahma-danda*) two spiral lines coil in opposite directions, reminiscent of the coiling of the two Tantric *nādī* around the spinal column (*sushumna*) or of the two serpents coiled round another staff, from which Hermes fashioned the CADUCEUS. In this way, the development of the contraflow of two currents of cosmic energy is expressed. Mention should also be made of Moses' rod (Exodus 7: 8–12), which changed itself from rod to serpent and from serpent to rod. Some critics see this as a demonstration of the supremacy of the God of Israel, others as a symbol of the soul transfigured by God's spirit. Other writers again have regarded this alternation of rod and serpent as a symbol of alchemical alternation – *solve et coagula* (BURS). Other associations of rod (or staff) and serpent include the staves of Aesculapios and Hygeia, emblems of healing which embody the currents of the caduceus, the currents of bodily and spiritual life. They, in turn, remind us of Moses' other rod which became the brazen serpent, a prefiguration of the redemptive power of the Cross (BURN, ELIF, FAVS, GRAD, GUET, MALA, MAST, SEGS, SOYS).

From support, defence and guide, the staff became the sceptre: a symbol of kingship, power and authority as much in the spiritual and intellectual spheres as in the social hierarchy. The Field Marshal's baton, the Lord Chamberlain's staff and the rods of the Gentlemen Ushers stem from the sceptre, as their authority stems from the Crown.

The symbolism of the staff is also related to that of FIRE and, consequently, to those of fertility and regeneration. Like the spear and the PESTLE, the staff has been compared with the phallus, Rajput miniatures being especially explicit on this point. According to Greek legend, fire spurted from the staff. Besides what Prometheus brought down from Heaven, fire was invented by Hermes rubbing two rods, one of hard, the other of soft wood, against one another. This earthly fire had a chthonian character which differed from the nature of the heavenly fire which PROMETHEUS stole from the gods. The latter would never have become earthly unless, in the words of Aeschylus, it had descended from Olympus, the abode of the immortal gods, to the Earth, the abode of mortal men.

Fire, whether born of a spark, of lightning or of a thunderbolt, is fecundating. It brings rain and makes the springs overflow. When the Children of Israel rebelled against Moses because they were tormented by thirst in the Wilderness, he struck the rock with his rod and water gushed out (Exodus 17: 1–6). The priest of the goddess Demeter struck the earth with his staff in 'a ritual designed to promote fertility or to rouse the powers of the Underworld' (SECG p. 136). One night, the ghost of Agamemnon appeared to Clytemnestra in a dream, going over to the sceptre which his murderer, Aegisthus, had stolen from him. He took it up and stuck it into the ground as if it had been a staff and immediately Clytemnestra saw it sprout branches and leaves like a tree (Sophocles, *Electra* 13–15). The staff which came alive and put out shoots foretold the speedy return of Agamemnon's son and avenger. It symbolized human vitality, regeneration and resurrection (LANS 2: p. 59).

stag (see also DEER; GAZELLE; HIND) Because of the spread of its antlers, which regularly drop and grow again, the stag is often compared with the TREE of Life and symbolizes fecundity and the rhythms of growth and rebirth. These properties are to be found as commonly in the decorations of Christian baptisteries as, for example, in Muslim, shamanistic, Mayan or Pueblo Indian tradition. It is 'one of the symbols of continual creation and renewal' (ELII p. 164, n. 8).

In their dances and their cosmogonies, North American Indians demonstrate this link between stag and Tree of Life:

The close association of the deer-kind with the pine tree [in the Pueblo Deer dance around a pine tree set up in the dancing plaza] may in part be mere forest imagery ... but it is not improbable that far more deeply lies that symbolism which associates deer not only with the east and dawn but also with the beginnings of life at the creation of the world. In more than one American Indian cosmogony it is the elk or buck that bays into existence created life, and sometimes in Indian art the tree is shown springing from the pronged horns of the animal – as in the European lore of the vision of St Hubert.

(ALEC p. 37)

The Hopi Indians cut their sacred image of the Sun-god from deerskin (TALS). In the sixteenth century the Florida Indians, at their Spring Sunfestival, used to erect a pole 'at the summit of which was mounted the skin of a deer, taken from an animal ceremonially captured, stuffed into lifeform with plants, and adorned with suspended fruit or vegetation. This image was oriented to the rising sun, and around it was held the dance, with prayers for a fruitful season' (ALEC p. 138). Krickeberg records a similar custom at the Timucua Spring-festival (KRIE p. 129).

The stag is also the herald of daylight and guide to the light of the Sun, as in this Pawnee hymn to the light of dawn: 'We call to the Children; we bid them awake. ... We tell the Children that all the animals are awake. They come forth from their places where they have been sleeping. The deer leads them. She comes from her cover, bringing her young into the light of day. Our hearts are glad' (ALEC p. 113).

In other traditions, this property acquires a cosmic and spiritual breadth and the stag is regarded as an intercessor between Earth and Heaven and as the symbol of the rising Sun in its transit to the zenith. One day a cross would appear between its antlers and the stag would become the image of Christ, the symbol of the mystical gift of the gospel of salvation. As the messenger of the godhead, it then became a link in that chain of symbols which are so often seen together – the Tree of Life, HORNS and the CROSS.

The stag is also a symbol of swiftness as well as of timidity. In Classical antiquity it was sacred to the virgin huntress Artemis (Diana) and its iconography depicted her chariot as being drawn by stags which she drove with golden reins. The animals doubtless owed this privilege to their agility. Their sacred nature finds its echo, in almost the same fashion, in the Buddhist *Jataka* stories. The golden stag is none other than a Bodhisattva who saves mankind from despair by calming their passions. The gazelles of Benares (symbols of the first sermon) are also stags. 'The strength of the wild stag' (Wang Chou) is the power of the master's instruction and selfdenial, which radiates with the speed of a race-horse and does not fail to arouse a degree of fear because it is so difficult to achieve.

The golden stag recurs in Cambodian legends, but there the creature's solar character is regarded in a maleficent light. As is so often the case, a solar animal is linked to drought. To obtain rain, the 'stag' must be killed, and this is the object of the *trot* dance so popular in Cambodia and especially in the Angkor region. In other areas, the appearance in a village of a stag heralds fire and forces the villagers' departure. Ancient China fostered the same notion of the stag as the baneful bringer of drought. It is interesting to observe how Origen makes the stag 'the enemy and destroyer of serpents', that is to say, the symbol of Christ expressly as the enemy of evil. Now the serpent is the creature of earth and water and it is confronted by the animal of sky and fire. Like the EAGLE which devours serpents, the stag is an exceptionally favourable sign, but it is bipolar since it destroys by fire, drought stifling all things which live in water.

St John of the Cross attributes to stags and hinds 'two different consequences of their lustful appetites' – boldness to the former and timidity to the latter, a consequence of what he assumes are the creatures' reactions to their sexuality.

In Japan, on the other hand, at Nara the countless stags and hinds which wander freely conjure up by their complete absence of fear the vision of a return to primeval purity. The hind has a peculiarity in that she sets her hind-hooves in the prints of the fore-hooves. This might symbolize the fashion in which one should follow the Path of the Ancestors. It approaches the symbolism of the HUNT.

Stags also have associations of lesser importance, such as the Chinese attribution of aphrodisiac properties to stags' antlers. In so far, however, as the medicine was regarded as strengthening the *yang*, it is still of some importance since it brings us close to techniques for obtaining immortality. Stags are also mentioned as symbols of longevity, but more particularly as those of prosperity, based upon the usual folk-pun, since *lu* means both 'stag' and 'salary'. When depicted in this role, the stag is generally accompanied by the pine-tree (longevity) and the bat (good luck) (BELT, DURV, GRAD, HERS, KALL, PORA, VARG).

A clear sign of the importance of the stag in Celtic symbolism is its comparatively frequent appearance in legend and iconography. There was a Gaulish god called Cernunnos, 'he whose head is crowned like the stag's'. He is depicted on the silver Gundestrip Cauldron, seated in a Buddha-like posture, holding a torque in one hand and a serpent in the other and surrounded by animals of all descriptions including, most notably, a stag and a serpent. Perhaps the antlers which crown the god's head should be regarded as a radiation of heavenly light (see HORN).

Another notable monument is that from Rheims, on which Cernunnos is depicted as the god of plenty. And other monuments, too, are known. Despite this, it would seem that the god really should be regarded as the Lord of the Beasts. In Ireland the son of Finn, the great hero of the Ossian cycle, was named Oisin (fawn), while St Patrick changes himself and his companions into stags (or deer) to escape the trap laid by the pagan King Loegaire. He succeeded in so doing thanks to a magical practice called *feth fiada*, normally used to confer invisibility. In the Celtic world the symbolism of the stag is widespread and undoubtedly goes back to the dawn of time. Lacking an overall study, one must provisionally confine the symbolism to its relation to longevity and plenty. The Celts used stag-horn to carve many of their charms and, in burials in Switzerland, the Alemanni interred stags alongside horses and humans. Comparisons have been drawn with the stag-masks found in fifth- and sixth-century BC horse-sacrifices in the Altai. The Breton St Edern is depicted riding a stag (CHAB pp. 240–57; ZEIP 24: pp. 10ff., 155ff.; OGAC 5: pp. 324–9; 8: pp. 3ff.; 9: pp. 5ff.).

Like reindeer and hinds, stags seem to have played the part of conductors of souls in some European traditions, especially Celtic. Morholt of Ireland, Yseult's uncle, slain in single combat by Tristan, was shown lying wrapped in deerskin (BEDT p. 20).

In Holy Scripture, the stag is often associated with the gazelle. In his third sermon on the Song of Solomon, Origen observes that the gazelle is keen-sighted and that the stag slays serpents, using its breath to drive them from their lairs. Origen compares Christ in his *theoria* with the gazelle and, in his *praxis*, with the stag.

In Ancient Hebrew the word for 'stag' was *'ayyāl*, derived from *'ayīl*, 'ram'. Stags were often regarded as a sort of giant RAM or wild GOAT, hence the variety of Latin translations in the Vulgate.

The stag symbolizes speed and leaping. When thirsty or when seeking a mate, his wild and raucous bellowing seems irresistible. Hence Christ summoning the soul and the soul-bride seeking her beloved are compared with the stag. The stag is as powerful a symbol of the Divine Bridegroom, swift and tireless in his quest for souls, his brides, as the soul itself, seeking the divine spring at which to slake its thirst.

In some works of art the stag becomes the symbol of the melancholy humour, no doubt because of its liking for solitude.

Sometimes one sees a stag depicted which has been wounded by an arrow and holds a herb in its mouth which it expects to heal it. The device *malum immedicabile* conveys the sense of an incurable wound. The wound concerned is clearly caused by love and derives from Ovid (*Metamorphoses* 1: 523), who puts the words 'Alas, no herb can cure my love' into Apollo's mouth when Daphne has escaped him.

(TERS pp. 67, 416)

Writers and artists have turned the stag into a symbol of prudence, because it sniffs the wind to catch a hostile scent and because it instinctively knows which plants have healing properties. It is also the symbol of sexual ardour and is depicted in the backgounds to Aphrodite and Adonis, and to Susannah and the Elders and so on. It is a symbol of hearing because it pricks up its ears and cannot be approached undetected; of lyric poetry because it is beside the Muse, Erato, with whom a stag fell in love; and of music, which it will even sit to listen to and because its antlers are lyre-shaped (TERS pp. 65–8).

A winged stag may signify swiftness to act. However, if the image is interpreted from the aspect of WING symbolism, the entire stag symbol is raised to the level of spirituality – the prudence is that of the saint, the ardour is to unite oneself with God, the keen hearing is attention to God's word and the promptings of his spirit and awareness of God's presence.

The stag is often associated with the unicorn, and is then the symbol of alchemical mercury. A plate illustrating Lambsprinck's masterpiece, the fourteenth-century Philosopher's Stone (LAMP), depicts these two creatures face to face in the undergrowth. The poem which accompanies this third figure reveals that the stag symbolizes mercury (the male aspect) and the spirit, while the unicorn symbolizes sulphur (the female aspect) and the soul, while the forest is salt and the body.

stairway The stairway is the symbol of the acquisition of learning and of the ascent to knowledge and transfiguration. If it rises skywards, the knowledge is that of the divine world; if it leads underground, it is to knowledge of the occult and of the depths of the unconscious. A white stairway sometimes stands for higher knowledge, a black for black magic. Like the LADDER, it symbolizes the quest for exoteric knowledge when it goes up, and for esoteric when it goes down (HAMK p. 6).

The Ancient Egyptians were familiar with this symbol of ascent as early as the PYRAMIDS. These are similar to stairways, as is especially clear in the case of step-pyramids. Works of art depict the souls of the dead climbing a stairway of seven or nine treads to reach the throne of Osiris and undergo the weighing of their hearts. Boats are depicted with a seven- or nine-tread stairway amidships, instead of mast and sails, 'symbolizing the last, decisive ascent of the soul to the stars where it mingles and becomes one with the light of Ra'. Such are the 'Boats of the Stairway to Heaven, symbols of the ascent of the soul' (CHAS pp. 139, 171).

This classic symbol of ascent can denote not only the ever higher pursuit of knowledge, but a concerted elevation of the whole being. It partakes of the symbolism of the World AXIS, of verticality and of the SPIRAL. When it is a spiral staircase, it focuses attention upon, as it were, the newel-post of this axial evolution, which may be God, a principle, love, art, consciousness, or the personality of the individual who leans his or her entire weight upon this newel as they climb the steps splaying out from it. Like all symbols in this category, the stairway possesses a negative aspect of descent, falling, returning to Earth and even to the Underworld. This is because the stairway links the three cosmic worlds and is as apt for regress as for ascent and epitomizes the whole gamut of the vertical.

standard See BANNER.

star (see also BEAR; POLE)   The best-remembered property of the star is its luminosity and the fact that it is a source of light. The stars painted on the ceilings of temples or churches explain their heavenly significance. This celestial character turns them into symbols of the spirit and especially of the warfare between spiritual forces, or light, and material forces, or darkness. Stars shine through the darkness and are guiding-lights in the night of the unconscious.

The Blazing Star in FREEMASONRY derives from the Pythagoreans' pentagram, although it is sometimes mistakenly call the Seal of Solomon, this term being in practice more often confined to the six-pointed STAR OF DAVID. The five-pointed Blazing Star is the symbol of the central manifestation of light, of the mystic centre and of the focus of an expanding universe. Set between square and compasses, Heaven and Earth, it stands for the regenerated individual blazing like light itself in the darkness of the profane world. Like the number FIVE, it is a symbol of perfection. On the tracing board of the Fellowcraft Mason, the Blazing Star bears the letter 'G' in its centre (see G). This is the same as *iod*, the Divine Principle in the initiate's heart (BOUM, GUET).

If, in addition, the five-pointed star is a symbol of the human microcosm, the six-pointed Star of David, the emblem of Judaism, with its inverted and interlaced triangles, may be said to symbolize the bonds of flesh and spirit, of the active and passive principles, the rhythm of their dynamic and the laws of evolution and involution. The seven-pointed star partakes of the symbolism of the number SEVEN. Bringing together square and triangle, it is a figure of the cosmic lyre, the music of the spheres, of universal harmony, of the seven colours of the rainbow, of the seven planetary zones, of the individual in his or her wholeness and so on.

In the Old Testament and in Judaism, stars obey and proclaim the will of God (Isaiah 40: 26; Psalm 19: 2). They do not belong, therefore, wholly to inanimate creation and an angel watches over each of them (Enoch 72: 3). From this it was a short step, and one quickly taken, for stars to be regarded as symbols of angels and the Book of Revelation (6: 13) speaks of the stars which fell from Heaven as though speaking of the fallen angels.

When Daniel describes the lot of mankind at the resurrection he can use only the symbol of the stars to characterize the eternal life of the righteous – ascent to the condition of the stars of Heaven.

On the other hand, there can be little doubt that when St John refers to the seven stars which Christ holds in his hand (Revelation 1: 16–20; 2: 1; 3: 1), he is speaking of the seven planets.

Finally, it should be observed that the prophecy in Numbers 24: 17 of 'a star out of Jacob' influenced Messianic symbolism and that the star was often regarded as the image or even as a name of the expected Messiah. This would explain why the coins struck by Simon Bar Kokhba ('Son of the Star'), politico-religious leader of the second Jewish Revolt (132–5 AD), bear a star.

There was a Gaulish goddess called 'Star', as the presence of the name *Sirona* in a Gallo-Roman inscription bears witness. The name of another Welsh goddess, Arianrhod, means 'silver wheel', a term which Joseph Loth states was applied to the constellation Corona Borealis. Given the tendencies apparent in the Celtic pantheon, it is legitimate to infer that these names of goddesses denoted one of the aspects of the primeval Great Goddess, but no detailed interpretation is possible. The current state of scholarship allows us only to state that astral symbolism was known to the Celts (LOTM 1: p. 191).

The Yakut believed that stars were the windows of the universe. They were opened and closed to allow the different spheres of Heaven (generally nine in number, but sometimes held to be seven, twelve or fifteen) to be ventilated. Uno Holmberg observes that this mythico-religious notion was current throughout the northern hemisphere. It is yet another expression of the widespread symbolism of access to Heaven through a 'strait gate'. The gap between the two cosmic levels only opens for an instant to the minute dimensions of a star, and then the hero, initiate or shaman must seize the fleeting moment to reach the Beyond (ELIC p. 260).

In Aztec myths, the stars were called *mimixcoatl* ('cloud-serpents') because Mixcoatl, god of the Pole Star, coexisted in them. They had preexisted him when the Sun had used them for food (KRIK p. 62).

In Mayan hieroglyphics, stars are often depicted as eyes with rays of light shooting out of them (THOH). In Guatemala, the folk-belief still persists that they are the souls of the dead. Insects emanate from them and come down to visit the Earth. According to Father Cobo the same belief existed in Peru – the stars were the souls of the righteous – but the Inca Garcilaso, for his part, tells us that the stars were regarded as the Moon's ladies-in-waiting and her retinue (GARC). Yet undoubtedly it is Father Cobo who, in his *Historia del Nuevo Mundo*, provides us with the most interesting explanation for the Incan cosmic symbolism of the stars. He tells us that not only all humans, but all animals and birds were represented in the Heavens by stars or constellations which, the Indians believed, were as it were a Second Cause, set there by the creator to 'ensure the preservation and increase of living things'. Father Acosta was of the same opinion, writing, in his *Historia natural y moral de las Indias*, that 'they believe that in the heavens there is a DOUBLE of every animal and bird on earth, which is responsible for their birth and increase.'

This belief may be compared with that of the Bambara who hold that water, the mirror of creation and the substance from which the Seventh Heaven is made, contains duplicates or specimens of all created species, so that the great Demiurge, who regulates the world and also resides in the Seventh Heaven, can govern his creation (DIEB).

According to the Finnish epic, the *Kalevala*, the stars were made from fragments of the shell of the World Egg.

The Morning Star possesses an especial significance. Because of its reddish colour and because it heralds the perpetual rebirth of daylight (the principle of the eternal homecoming), it is the symbol of the principle of life itself. This is the aspect in which it is honoured by the Plains Indians (ALEC p. 42).

The Cora Indians, from the south-west of the USA, near the Mexican border, make the Morning Star one of an all-powerful trinity with Sun and Moon. A culture-hero, the star slew the Serpent, Lord of the Waters and the Night Sky, to give its body to feed the Eagle, God of the Day Sky and of Fire (KRIE p. 103).

According to the chronicler, Sahagun, the Mexicans dreaded the planet Venus, the so-called Morning Star, and closed their doors and windows at daybreak to escape its dangerous starlight (THOH). The star unleashed disease and, because of this, is often depicted with bow and arrows and sometimes, even, wearing a mask in the shape of a skull (SOUP). The Maya regarded the star as the Sun's elder brother and depicted it as a coarse and obese man with a tangled beard. As patron of the forest animals, hunters offered it copal incense and prayers at daybreak.

In Arabic and Persian elegiac verse the serene and unwrinkled forehead of the beloved is compared with Venus rising in the pale light of dawn (HUAS p. 21, quoting Farrukhī).

In symbolism worldwide, the Pole Star plays a commanding role as 'the absolute centre around which the whole firmament revolves for ever' (CHAS p. 17). The whole Heaven turns about this fixed point which simultaneously evokes the motionless First Mover and the centre of the universe. The positions of the stars themselves are fixed by their relationship with the Pole, as is that of sailors, nomads, travellers and all those who wander across the emptiness of land, sea or air. In many parts of Europe and Asia the Pole Star is called pivot, hub, navel, life-centre, Gate of Heaven, umbilical North Star. The star is also connected with the mystery of birth. In China the princely, noble and wise are compared with the Pole Star 'the fixed star round which all other stars turn in cosmic homage' (*Lun-yu* 2: 1). Shakespeare compares human constancy with the 'Northern star' (*Julius Caesar* 3: v). In short the celestial pole symbolizes 'the centre to which all things relate, the First Cause from which all things emanate, the force which sets all things in motion and the leader around whom the stars turn like courtiers round their king.' In some primitive religions, the Pole Star is the abode of the Divine Being to whom they attribute 'the preservation and government of the universe. The Pole Star is supremely the throne of God. From its height he surveys all things, rules all things, intervening to reward or punish and making the laws and swaying the fate of the heavenly world of which the Earth is a mere copy' (CHAS pp. 17–18).

In Turko-Tatar tradition, 'the Pole Star shines in the middle of the sky and is the Tent-pole of the Heavens.' The Samoyed call it the 'Nail of Heaven', or 'Nail-Star' and the same is true of Lapps, Finns and Estonians. The Turkic peoples of the Altai regard the Pole Star as if it were a pillar – the Golden Pillar of the Mongols, Kalmuk and Buryat; the Iron Pillar of the Kirghiz, Baskirs and Siberian Tatars; and the Pillar of the Sun of the Telyut. The Buryat picture the stars as a herd of horses tethered to the Pole Star.

Von Fulda called the Saxons' 'Irminsül' *Universalis Columna, quasi sustinens omnia* ('the Column of the Universe, bearing, as it were, all things'). The Scandinavian Lapps inherited this belief from the ancient Germans and called the Pole Star 'Pillar of Heaven' or 'Pillar of the World'. Irminsül may have been compared with the COLUMNS of Jupiter. Similar ideas still survive in southeast Europe, in, for example, the Romanians' 'Column of Heaven' (ELIC p. 261).

The Chukchee hold that the 'hole in the sky' is the Pole Star, that three worlds are connected by similar 'holes', and that it is through them that the shaman and the mythical heroes communicate with the sky. And among the Altaians – as among the Chukchee – the road to the sky runs through the Pole Star. . . . In his mystical journey the Yakut shaman, too, climbs a mountain with seven storeys. Its summit is in the Pole Star, in the 'Navel of the Sky'. The Buryat say that the Pole Star is fastened to its summit.

(ELIC pp. 262–3, 266)

In Indian mythology Mount Meru rises up in the centre of the world; above it the Pole Star sends forth its light. The Uralo-Altaic peoples also have a central mountain, Sumbur, Sumur or Sumeru, above which hangs the Pole Star.

(ELIT p. 100)

'According to the tradition of Islam, the highest spot on earth is the Ka'aba for "the Pole Star proves . . . that it lies against the centre of heaven"' (ibid.). The star is also a manifestation of God when faith grows dim, to guard it against all the obstacles which lie on the path of the creature towards its creator. The Pole Star not only shines in the physical sky, but in the human heart, clouded by the passions and, as it were, plunged into sensual darkness.

Uno Harva quotes Anokin (HARA p. 39) for the belief that the Pole Star is not the last but the fifth of the seven or nine obstacles which the shaman has to overcome during his ascent to the Heaven of the Supreme Deity.

Another shamanistic tradition, which Harva quotes from Baratov, is that 'all the worlds are interconnected through openings located close to the Pole Star.' Alexander records a similar belief among the Blackfoot Indians.

Shamanistic esoteric lore taught that the Pole Star was the pivot round which the firmament turned, its position being regarded as fixed. It was in the vicinity of this star that the vault of Heaven reached its highest point.

Most Asiatic traditions from Asia Minor, India and central Asia place the Pole Star, the Navel of the Universe, over the peak of the World Mountain to show where the almighty sky-god lived. This is the reason why the inhabitants of those areas often set altars at the northern end of their temples, Ruysbroek writing in the thirteenth century that they all prayed towards the north (see CARDINAL POINTS) (HARA). But prior to this, the Old Testament (Isaiah 14: 13) has: 'I will sit also upon the mount of the congregation in the sides of the north.'

The Pole Star being the centre and pivot of the universe was invoked in Vedic marriage ceremonies by the bridal couple. In the miniature universe of the home, the groom played the part of the Pole Star.

Four fixed stars of the first magnitude are generally termed Royal Stars by astrologers and are of especial importance to them. They served as markers for the Babylonian calendar. They comprise: Aldebaran, alpha of the constellation Taurus, Guardian of the East; Regulus, in the constellation Leo, Guardian of the North; Antares, alpha of the constellation Scorpius, Guardian of the West; and Fomalhaut, alpha of the constellation Piscis Austrinvs, Guardian of the South. This is not the only list: different writers list different stars and thus Regulus is sometimes replaced by Rigel, beta of the constellation Orion (its Indian name is *Raja*, 'king' or 'lord', which emphasizes its status as a Royal Star); while Antares (a star of ill omen which the inhabitants of Mesopotamia called 'The Travellers' Gravedigger') is replaced by the kindly Spica, Virgo's Ear of Corn. Sirius, however, although the brightest star in the sky, never occurs in any list of Royal Stars. Several symbolic images are associated with each of these stars. Generally Aldebaran is represented by an eye; Regulus by a heart or a crown; Antares, since its name derives from Ares-Mars, by a dagger or a scimitar; and Spica by a female sphinx, or by an ear of corn.

Most historians regarded the Star of Bethlehem as a concession made by the infant Church to the then all-powerful astrological thought and it was but one of the similar and extraordinary cosmic phenomena which ushered in the births of nearly all the Sons of God, including the Buddha. Thus, for example, according to later legend, the birth of Agni (who, like Jesus, was laid by Maya, his Virgin-Mother, and by his earthly father, Twāstri the carpenter, between the mystic cow and the ass which carried the soma) was proclaimed by the appearance of a star called SaVaNaGRaHa.

It would be a mistake to think that the date of Christ's birth can be established either by astronomy or by astrology. All astronomical research into the Star of Bethlehem has been fruitless. Many theories have been advanced. It was the appearance of a comet, the fourfold conjunction of the planets, a new star and so on, but all such explanations are clearly forced and inadequate. The phenomenon was probably symbolical and psychological rather than physical. At the time of the presumed date of Christ's birth, astronomical observation was so widespread that had some extraordinary phenomenon occurred it would have been noted and recorded by Roman or oriental writers. Lack of written sources makes it impossible to establish precisely when these first attempts to make Jesus a subject for astrology first took place.

In the TAROT, following on from the Devil, 'centre of darkness' and the Tower, 'an explosion of frustration', comes the seventeenth major arcanun, the Star, 'a centre of light' (VIRI p. 81). In astrology it corresponds to the Fifth House.

The card depicts a naked girl, with blue hair curling over her shoulders, kneeling on her left knee and holding a red vase in each hand from which she pours the blue contents into a sort of lake, which is blue, too. From the yellow, undulating ground spring a plant with three leaves and two green bushes, standing out against the sky. On the larger of the two, on the left, perches a black bird, symbol of the immortal soul. In the sky there are six stars, set one above the other in groups of three, of different sizes and colours. (Two are yellow with seven points, and two red and two blue with eight points.) They are symmetrically arranged around a seventh star at the top of the card. This is much the largest and would seem to comprise two eight-pointed stars, one red, the other yellow, set one on top of the other, and representing, according to some critics, human and divine nature (MARD p. 314). Immediately above the head of the girl – doubtless personifying either Eve or mankind in general – there shines an eight-pointed yellow star. This arrangement of seven stars grouped round a larger star reminds us not only of the Pleiades, but also of the eighth arcanum, Justice, as 'the intellect which co-ordinates natural action and reaction' (WIRT p. 222). This is the first occasion on which stars feature in the Tarot and the next two cards will be Moon and Sun. Hitherto mankind has been enclosed in its own universe, but now it mingles with the life of the cosmos and is 'open to those celestial influences [arcana 18–21] which will lead it to mystical enlightenment' (WIRT p. 224). The naked girl is in a state of perfect receptivity since she retains nothing which she has been given. The waters which flow from her vases, coiling like those of Temperance, are BLUE like her hair and will meet, without actually mingling, with other waters, blue too, or will irrigate a parched earth. This surely is to make the material elements Earth and Water partake of a celestial character. As intercommunication between different worlds, as the soul linking the spirit to matter or as 'a passage to guided development . . . the seventeeth arcanum depicts the symbolism of creation, birth and transformation. The image of water pouring from a vase reminds us that, in dreams and myths, birth is associated with images of water or expressed through them. . . . The Star is the world in process of formation, the original centre of the universe (VIRI p. 81).'

The Star is closely linked to the Heavens on which it depends, and also conjures up the mysteries of sleep and darkness. The individual must conform and harmonize with the strong rhythm of the cosmos, to shine in personal brightness.

This arcanum, with its vegetation and its waters, its two vases from which the waters pour, and its seven- and eight-pointed stars, symbolizes a creation which is not yet complete and perfect. It demonstrates the movement which shapes the universe and the individual self, a return to the springs of light and water, to the centres of celestial and terrestrial energy. It symbolizes inspiration materialized, or the communication of artistic aims hitherto impossible to express.

Star of David Also known as the Seal of Solomon, this SIX-pointed star is formed by the intersection of two equilateral triangles and is truly an epitome of Hermetic thought. In the first place it contains the four elements. The regular triangle stands for Fire and the inverted triangle for Water. The 'Fire' triangle cut by the base of the 'Water' triangle stands for Air, while the 'Water' triangle cut by the base of the 'Fire' triangle stands for Earth. The hexagram in its entirety comprises the four elements which make up the universe.

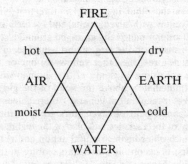

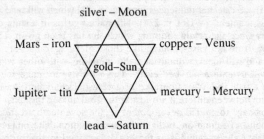

Taking the four lateral points of the star and conveniently allocating to them the four basic 'humours', it will be seen (as in the diagram above) that they display the correspondences between the four elements and pairs of humours.

Fire combines hot and dry; Water, moist and cold; Earth, cold and dry; Air, moist and hot. Their permutations and combinations produce the different sorts of living things. The Star of David may thus be seen as the marriage of opposites and an expression of the oneness of the cosmos at the same time as its complexity.

Again, in Hermetic tradition the Star of David also encompasses the SEVEN basic metals, that is the totality of metal, as well as the seven planets which epitomize the totality of the Heavens. The centre (see figure) is

occupied by gold (Sun); the upper point by silver (Moon) and the lower by
lead (Saturn). On the right, the upper point is copper (Venus); the lower,
mercury (Mercury), while on the left the upper point is iron (Mars) and the
lower tin (Jupiter).

Many more examples might be given of the interplay of correspondences
between elements, humours, metals and planets with their varied range
of symbols based upon this hexagram. The entire theory and practice of
ALCHEMY lay in obtaining the transmutation of the imperfect, lying on the
margins, into a single state of perfection which lay at the centre and was
symbolized by gold and by the Sun. The reduction of the manifold to the
one, of the imperfect to the perfect, of which sages and philosophers
dreamed, is epitomized by the Star of David.

Some critics have unhesitatingly passed from the material to the spiritual
plane and regard the Great Work of alchemy as a form of asceticism and
mysticism aimed at bringing the individual, fragmented by so many different drives, back to a union with the divine principle. Others regard the
superimposed triangles as the union of male and female principles.

statuette African statuettes are not intended to provide portraits of ancestors or of any particular individual but, according to Jean Laude, are supposed to 'hold the ancestor's life force and to ensure the welfare of his
descendants'. They are often associated with the remains of the dead person or emerge from baskets or bags containing bones. When families split
up, a fresh statuette is carved and carried away by the members of the
family who are leaving so that they can preserve the link to the group-
ancestor. When it leaves the sculptor's hands, the carved figure is uncharged
with its powers. 'It is only after appropriate rituals that it becomes consecrated and steeped in religious strength. Deconsecrated carvings may be
sold, given or thrown away. They are powerless. Africans never confuse the
image with what it is the image of.'

The Ba-Kongo carved *mintardi* (guardians) first in wood and later in
stone and these statuettes are regarded as embodying the spirit of a dead
chief and showing his continuing presence watching over the fate of his
family and his people. They are symbols of the protection the ancestors
extend to their descendants.

The Dogon sometimes consider statuettes as if they were prayers to obtain
fecundating rain (protection) or, when the limbs are carved in high relief,
as plastic representations of the myth which explains 'how the human body
was given joints to allow it to work' (cosmogony). This context gives the
symbol its ethical and cosmic meaning. 'A statuette does not have just one
definite meaning which would allow its pose and gesture to be related to a
definite event in a fixed and rigid myth. It has several different meanings
and knowledge of them is, apparently, a progressive acquisition linked to
the stages of an initiation which lasts until death.'

As an aid to knowledge acquired by initiation, the symbol is sometimes
also imbued with a magic power. Some peoples have established a correlation between such a power and the pose of the statuette. Some of these
carvings, in which the length of the limbs is exaggerated or in which they
are violently stretched or contorted, are regarded as aiding growth and

increasing physical strength. The symbol in this context becomes an effective instrument, like the sacraments in Christian theology. The statuette is however conceived in more materialistic terms 'as the repository of the strength of an ancestor or a spirit' (see MASK) (LAUA pp. 138, 140, 153, 181, 185, 280, 286).

Dogus, idols from the prehistoric Jōmon period in Japan, are little abstract statuettes which archeologists believe were symbols of fertility and of belief in supernatural forces, imbued with magic powers.

In the Minoan Age and throughout the Mediterranean world, statuettes of the gods in human or animal shape were made from terracotta, bronze, wood or stone. They had religious significance and were deposited in graves or dedicated to the gods in shrines and in private homes, where they must have exercised a protective influence upon the dead, upon the community or upon the family. They were tutelary symbols.

stilts Stilts allow their user to identify with wading birds and especially with the CRANE, which was regarded in Ancient China as a symbol of immortality. 'Those who can get up on stilts,' the *P'ao Pu Tzu* suggests, 'can travel the wide world in any direction they please unhindered by mountains and rivers.' In imagination they are able to fly and hence to attain the Isles of the Immortals, a power which Huang Ti is supposed to have acquired. In Ancient China, Kaltenmark observes, the Crane Dance was probably a stilt-dance and would therefore be related directly to BIRD symbolism and through it to immortality (KALL).

stone (see also BETHEL; DIAMOND; EMERALD; JADE; JEWELLERY; MENHIR; PEARL) Stones hold a prominent place in tradition and there are close links between the soul and stone. According to the legend of Prometheus, begetter of the human race, stones retain a human redolence. Stones and humans display the twofold movement of rising and falling. Humans are born of God and return to God. Raw stone comes down from Heaven and when transmuted rises to the sky. TEMPLES should be built of raw stone, not of dressed stone, for 'if thou lift up thy tool upon [the stone] thou hast polluted it' (Exodus 20: 25; cf. Deuteronomy 27: 5; 1 Kings 6: 7). In fact, dressed stone is the work of human hands and desacralizes God's work, symbolizing human activity substituted for creative energy. The raw stone was also the symbol of freedom, dressed stone of slavery and darkness.

Raw stone was also regarded as HERMAPHRODITE, this property comprising the perfection of the primeval state. Once dressed, its principles were separated. It might be shaped either as a cone or a cube. A conical stone stood for the male element, a cubic stone for the female. When the cone was set on a square base it reunited the male and female principles. Celtic dolmens and menhirs are good examples of this and the same is true of church-towers. When worship took place on or before stones, the stone itself was not the object of worship, but the deity which had taken up residence in the stone. Today, the Mass of the Roman Rite continues to be celebrated on a stone set in a cavity in the altar and containing relics of the saints.

Stones are not lifeless masses. Living stones fell from Heaven and they remain alive after their fall.

As an element in building, stone is linked to the establishment of sedentary societies and to a type of cyclic 'crystallization'. Stone also plays an important part in the relationship between Heaven and Earth, both in the shape of 'stones which fell from heaven' and in the shape of stones, either standing or heaped, in the form of bethels, megaliths or cairns. Different peoples from as far afield as Australia, Indonesia and North America have regarded pieces of QUARTZ as being splinters of the sky or of the heavenly throne and their shamans have used them in divination. Stones which fell from Heaven are in any case frequently 'talking' stones, the channels of oracles and messages. Such stones are very frequently meteorites, like the Black Stone of Cybele and its Greek equivalents, the Palladium of Troy, the *Ancile* or shield which fell from Heaven and upon which the prosperity of Rome depended, the Black Stone enshrined in the Ka'ba at Mecca and the stone the Dalai Lama was given by the 'King of the World'. Thunderstones fall into a different category since they are symbols of thunder itself, and therefore of heavenly activity and not of its presence or of its effects. (Into this category fall Parashurāma's stone axe and Thor's stone hammer.) Another example might be the stone which fell from Lucifer's forehead and from which, according to Wolfram von Eschenbach, the Grail was carved. The frequency with which stones fell from Heaven was often regarded – and this is especially true of Ancient China – as being due to the fact that the sky was itself the roof of a cave. The reverse of this proposition is the reason why the stalactites hanging from the roofs of caves were regarded as the rock's marrow and used as an ingredient in the medicines of immortality so highly regarded by Taoists.

Whether or not the Black Stone of Cybele, the conical image of a mountain, was an OMPHALOS, to act as navel-stones was the especial function of standing-stones, the best-known of which was Jacob's Beth-el, the House of God. This, undoubtedly, is the significance of some Celtic standing-stones, while stones heaped into cairns are evocations of the central mountain. The Omphalos at Delphi, the altar at Delos, the stone which bore the Ark of the Covenant at Jerusalem and even the altar stones in Christian churches are all symbols of the presence of God or, at the least, aids to spiritual influence. Such is true of the Stone of Destiny in Westminster Abbey on which Irish, Scottish, English and British kings have been seated at their coronation. The same meaning recurs in Vietnam, where standing-stones are always the abode of guardian spirits and a screen against evil influences, which avoid them.

Stones are also symbols of the Earth-Mother and this was one of the aspects of Cybele's symbolism. In a number of traditions, precious stones are 'born' from rocks, having 'ripened' within them, the rock itself being a living thing which transmits life. In Vietnam, stone is said to bleed when struck by the pick. In Ancient Greece, after the Flood, human beings were born from the stones scattered by Deucalion. Semitic tradition contains accounts of humans born from stone and in some Christian legends Christ is so born. Undoubtedly this should be compared with the Gospel account (Matthew 4: 3) of the stones turned into bread. Bethel (the House of God) becomes Bethlehem (the House of Bread) and the bread of the Eucharist takes the place of the stone as seat of the Real Presence. In China, Yu the

Great was born from a stone, as was his son, K'i, the northern face of the rock splitting apart. It is undoubtedly no accident that in alchemical symbolism the Philosopher's Stone is the instrument of regeneration.

Raw stone is ambivalent, passive matter. As we have seen, if subjected to the slightest human action it becomes polluted. On the other hand, if subjected to heavenly and spiritual action, so that it ultimately becomes dressed stone, it is ennobled. It is the transition from the soul in darkness to the soul enlightened by divine knowledge when it is God, not man, who accomplishes the transition from raw to dressed stone. Did not Master Eckhart teach that 'stone' was synonymous with 'knowledge'? For the Israelites, the symbolism was different. The transition from raw to dressed stone for the altars in Solomon's Temple was a sign of the Chosen People becoming a settled society and, as we have observed above, of 'cyclic stabilization' or crystallization, of involution rather than evolution. In Masonic symbolism, the Perfect Ashlar also expresses the notion of stability, balance and fulfilment and corresponds to alchemist's salt.

In the same context, the pyramid on a cube base is a symbol of the Philosopher's Stone, the spiritual principle founded upon 'salt' and Earth. Building, stone upon stone, clearly conjures up a spiritual edifice, and this notion is developed at length in *The Shepherd* of Hermas, but has two Gospel-passages as its source. The first is the one which makes Peter (Cephas) the foundation stone, the rock upon which Christ will build his church (Matthew 16: 18). The second is the one in which Matthew (21: 42) and Luke (20: 17) quote from Psalm 118: 'the stone which the builders rejected is become the head of the corner.' This notion of corner-stone recurs in Freemasonry and is unintelligible without the correction which modern commentators have supplied to the translation, since 'corner-stone' is really the key-stone of the arch. This is the stone which completes and crowns the work and the symbol of Christ who came down from Heaven to fulfil the Law and the Prophets.

The notion of the fulfilment of the Great Work applies exactly to the Philosopher's Stone which, furthermore, is sometimes regarded as a symbol of Christ. It is 'the bread of the Lord', Angelus Silesius wrote. 'We seek the gold-stone [*Goldstein*] and ignore the corner-stone [*Eckstein*] which can make us healthy, wealthy and wise for evermore.' (Remember, too, that *Eckstein* may also mean 'diamond'.) The stone which is the Elixir of Life and which, according to Ramon Llull, regenerates plants, is the symbol of the regeneration of the soul by divine grace. 'Can one make gold with stones?' the commentator on *The Secret of the Golden Flower* asks ironically. The *P'ao Pu Tzu* assures us that all one will obtain is lime. And yet the great guru Nāgārjuna declared that transmutation was possible by virtue of a sufficiency of spiritual energy. If gold is immortality and stones are human beings, the operations of spiritual alchemy are well calculated to this end. 'The corner-stone which I desire,' wrote Angelus Silesius, 'is my tincture of gold and the stone of all the sages' (BENA, BHAB, CADV, ELIF, GRIF, GUED, GUEM, GUET, GUES, KALL).

In his study of the beliefs of Altaic peoples, Jean-Paul Roux contrasts the symbolic meaning of the stone with that of the TREE. True to their nature, stones, 'from the days when our remotest ancestors set them up or carved their messages upon them, are eternal and the symbol of static life, while the tree, subject to the cycle of life and death, but which possesses the ineffable gift of perpetual regeneration, is the symbol of dynamic life' (ROUF p. 52).

This stone-principle is represented in standing-stones which sometimes embody the souls of ancestors, especially in Black Africa, but which on the other hand have a known association with the phallus, thus explaining their association with orgiastic rites in some places, particularly Brittany. The Manchu custom of setting up great tree-trunks or stone columns epitomizes this distinction between the two archetypal aspects of Life, the static and the dynamic, attributed by Roux to stones and trees. From the sociological point of view, peoples' hesitation and alternating transition between 'perishable' and 'hard' civilizations – hardness of course being that of stone in the first place – might therefore be regarded as being the result of choice between these two aspects or complementary properties of Life.

People thought the so-called 'thunder' stones – which are for the most part nothing more than prehistoric flints – were the very arrowpoints of the lightning, and they were venerated and piously preserved as such. Everything that fell from above partook of the holiness of the sky; that is why meteorites, absolutely saturated with it, were venerated.

(ELIT p. 54)

Such stones, especially in Africa, were associated with the cults of sky-gods and were sometimes objects of worship. Thunder-stones, generally meteorites, were regarded as fertility instruments since they fell from the sky like rain. Furthermore

the baetyl [bethel] ... marks the place of god's descent; it is the most ancient and far-cast of all human implements, the universal symbol of the liberation of human-nature from brute-nature, and so of the conception of divinity.... 'Thunderstones' primarily are themselves charged potencies, magical, fetishistic. Later the arrowheads and axes and other stones which are viewed as 'bolts' from on high are taken to be the missiles thrown down by a Thunderer or Fulminator. Then man-made emblems of these bolts – the Minoan double-axe, the pronged image of the lightning, the Roman *bidens*, the Hindu *tribula*, the Greek *triaina*, weapon of 'earth-shaking' Poseidon, and the *keraunos* of Zeus which seems to combine the lightning's fork with the double striking power of the two-blade axe – all these became symbols of the awesome Power, and later were pictured attributes of the God to whom the power is ascribed.

(ALEC pp. 53–4)

The Mexican Chorti retained the polished stone axe as the symbol of the THUNDERBOLT (GIRP p. 27) and the same is true of the Bambara. The latter believe that thunder-stones both preserve against and attract thunderbolts. When hung from the roofs of huts, they drive away but, when placed in a shelter in the bush, they draw down thunder (DIEB). In their symbolism of the human microcosm, thunder-stones are associated with the skull and hence with the brain, the realm of thought (ZAHB pp. 216ff.).

P. Alexandre has recorded a tradition among the Fang in Gabon of setting a stone axe or a thunder-stone between the legs of a woman in labour to ease childbirth. In central Asia, Yakut 'women after childbirth drink water in which chips of this sort of stone have been placed to ease disposal of the afterbirth. The same remedy is employed to clear blockage of the intestines or urinary tract' (HARA p. 151).

Rain-stones are personifications of ancestors turned to stone (LEEC p. 183), or rather symbols of the ancestors' abode or of the strength of the stone to retain them indefinitely in one place. The stones, so to speak, bind the ancestors' souls, appease and preserve them to fertilize the soil and to draw down the rain (hence, rain-stones). They are culture-objects and come to stand not only for ancestors, but for tutelary gods and heroes as well. Stones and rocks give spiritual powers material shape and hence they become objects of worship. Young husbands call upon them to beget children and women rub themselves against them to become pregnant, perhaps by the ancestors (love-stones). Traders anoint them with oil to ensure their prosperity, but they are feared as guardians of the dead and prayers are offered to them to protect family or group.

Rain-stones are generally meteorites and they, too, are regarded as emblems of fertility. During droughts, offerings are made to them, as well as in the Spring, to ensure good harvests.

A close analysis of innumerable 'rain stones' has always brought to light the existence of a 'theory' to explain their power of governing the clouds; it is something to do either with their shape, which has some 'sympathy' with the clouds or with lightning, or with their celestial origin (they must have fallen from heaven), or with their belonging to 'ancestors'; or perhaps they were found in water, or their shapes recall snakes, frogs, fishes or some other water emblem. The power of these stones never originates in themselves; they share in a principle, or embody a symbol. . . . These stones are the *signs* of a spiritual reality beyond themselves, or the instruments of a sacred power of which they are merely containers.

(ELIT pp. 226–7)

According to the chronicler Sahagun (SOUC p. 228), rain-stones, which the ancient Mexicans called 'rain-gold', were supposed to preserve against thunder and to cure fevers. Most Buryat villages used to have their own 'sky-stone' kept in a casket fixed to a pillar (celestial column) erected in the centre of the village. In the Spring the stones were ritually sprinkled and sacrifice was offered to them to bring rain and to assure Summer fertility. Agapitov detected traces of phallic worship in this custom (HARA p. 110).

In Mongolia, it was thought that concealed in the mountains or in the head of a stag, serpent or water-fowl, or in the belly of an ox, there was a stone which brought wind, rain, snow and frost (HARA p. 159). Similar beliefs were current among such other peoples as the Yakut and Altaic Tatars. During the height of summer such stones were hung on their horses' manes to protect them against drought. To bring rain, they were soaked in a vase of cold water. The same belief existed in Persia, which explains why the Tatar word for this stone is of Persian origin.

The Black Stone from Pessinus (now Bala-Hisar, Turkey) was the concrete expression of Cybele, the Great Mother Goddess worshipped by the people of Phrygia. At the beginning of 204 BC the stone was transported to Rome and erected with great pomp on the Palatine Hill. This Black Stone symbolized the enthronement of an Eastern deity in Rome, the first mystic conquest of a wave which was to engulf and sweep away the city's most ancient traditions. The stone stood for and exercised all the invisible but irresistible strength of a real presence.

To the Omaha Plains Indians 'a black stone represented the thunder, just as a translucent pebble was the symbol of the water's potency' (ALEC p. 53).

Standing-stones, whether Indian LINGAMS or Breton MENHIRS, are universal symbols. With similar rites women in India and Brittany approached them to cure their barrenness. This meaning attached to the stone is close to that belonging to vast sacred trees, they too being phallic. In both cases, the fertility-rites attaching to them employ thunder-stone (neolithic AXE) and SERPENT in the same chain of lunar symbolism. The most favourable day on which to visit these stones, bearing offerings of milk, butter and so on, was a Monday (the Moon's day) or Friday (Venus' day).

Boulnois writes that in Brittany women used to rub their bellies with the stone-dust from a dolmen or menhir, as well as with the moisture which had collected on its rough surface (BOUA p. 12). The dolmen was regarded as the abode of the ancestors who made it fertile. He adds that 'the majority of Dravidians regard stones as having the same power as trees and water to tie down spirits', good or evil. Hence they are used therapeutically by being placed upon the heads of sick people to drive out of their bodies the spirits of fever. Hence, also, the custom (ibid. p. 13) of casting a stone onto the path behind one, on returning from a funeral service, to prevent the spirit of the dead person from trying to return.

There are stones with holes through them through which coins, hands, arms, heads or even whole bodies are thrust, since they are regarded as preservatives against spells and also as possessing the powers of fertilization and fecundation. Some ethnologists share the view of John Marshall that passing through a hole in a rock or stone implies belief in regeneration through the cosmic female principle. In the Ancient East and in Australia, this type of stone, when associated with initiation-ordeals, is a vaginal symbol.

Stones shaped like a millstone with a hole in the middle are related to solar symbolism and to a cycle of liberation through death and rebirth in the womb.

There is a Fulani belief that a flat stone stands for the two types of knowledge – exoteric (light side) and esoteric (dark side). It thus symbolizes the knowledge which is the gate to the way which links the two realms of the living and the dead (HAMK p. 5).

There were also stones reputed to give utterance. The Stone of Sovereignty or *Lia Fail* (incorrectly termed the Stone of Destiny) in Ireland was one of the talismans of the Tuatha Dé Danann. It uttered a cry when touched by a prince to whom kingship rightly belonged. Because it remained dumb when he set his foot upon it, the hero Cùchulainn broke it in pieces. It was symbolically located at Tara, the capital of the High King (OGAC 16: pp. 432–3, 436–40).

Other stones were the essential tools of divination, acting as intermediaries between the god and the seer. The sibyl carried a stone with her and sat upon it when making her prophecies. When Apollo was building the walls of Megara, he rested his lyre upon a stone. Thereafter, if a pebble was thrown against this stone it uttered a most musical note.

Symbolic properties also attach to heaps of stones. From the mountain passes of the Andes to Siberia there is a custom for travellers to add their stone to a heap which in course of time grows to the size of the Pyramids. Jean-Paul Roux regards this custom as an example of the 'collective soul'.

Any accumulation of small objects endowed with souls strengthens their individual potential and in the end creates a new and extremely powerful soul. The soul of an ordinary pebble is feeble enough but, when added to the souls of countless other pebbles, the collective soul of the heap becomes a mighty numinous force. This power is created by heaping up stones in selected places and, here again, the sacred and collective soul of the *obo* is inseparable from the sacred soul of the ground upon which it has been heaped.

(ROUF p. 89)

In Islamic tradition, during the *hajj*, or pilgrimage to Mecca, one should go to Mina to cast stones at 'the Devil's landmark' (*Jimār*). The custom of throwing stones upon a tomb is widespread. Stoning was considered a means of combating the harmful contagion of sin and death. This magic ritual became Islamicized. Stones were taken to the tombs of saints as symbolic offerings. There was a custom of throwing a stone on a heap of stones to drive off ghosts, the soul of a dead person or jinn. Sick people, and especially women, seeking a cure at tombs of the saints, would rub the diseased parts of their bodies with stones. These stones should not be touched afterwards since the disease had been transferred to them and might perhaps be passed on by contamination. These heaps of stones might bear different meanings. Sometimes they were no more than signposts to roads, wells or tombs, while at others they might act as memorials of particular events. They would be raised at the scene of a murder or at a place where somebody had died in a way deserving of pity and these were known as *menzeh*. The latter were also erected over graves in cemeteries. Sometimes oaths would be taken over heaps of stones. At places from which tombs are visible, particularly upon high ground and especially in mountain passes, little pyramids of stones are to be found. Travellers add another stone or two in honour of the saint in the tomb or to ensure a safe journey. Some heaps of stones themselves stand symbolically for tombs of saints.

Some sociologists see this as a sacrifice or offering to gods, spirits or the souls of the dead, while for others, among them Doutte, 'the stone added to the heap is a symbol of the believer's union with the spirit or god of the cairn or sacred pile.' Frazer observes that the transference of disease into a stone or into a human or an animal by means of a stone is a magical practice to be found worldwide in primitive societies.

To rid oneself of dreams of the dead, you whisper your dreams to a hole in the ground and then cover it with a stone.

Curses were often embodied in stones. Seven stones were cast at the person to be cursed or else cursing-stones were piled in a heap and the heap then scattered with the prayer that the things which made happy the person on whom the curse was to fall should be scattered in the same way (WERS 2: p. 460).

Precious stones are the symbol of the transmutation of the opaque into the translucent and, in a spiritual sense, of darkness into light and imperfection into perfection. Thus the Heavenly JERUSALEM is completely encrusted in precious stones.

And the building of the wall of it was of JASPER: and the city was pure gold, like unto clear glass. And the foundations of the wall of the city were garnished with all manner of precious stones. The first foundation was jasper; the second, SAPPHIRE; the third, a chalcedony; the fourth an EMERALD; The fifth, sardonyx; the sixth, sardius; the seventh, chrysoly; the eighth, beryl; the ninth, a topaz; the tenth, a chrysoprasus; the eleventh, a jacinth; the twelfth, an AMETHYST. And the twelve gates were twelve PEARLS.

(Revelation 21: 18–21)

This means that in this new universe all states and levels of existence will have undergone a radical transformation in the direction of a perfection unequalled in this world and characterized by spirituality and luminosity.

According to Léonard's *Speculum lapidum* (Paris, 1610), emeralds restrain lust and fortify the memory; RUBIES maintain good health, are preservatives against poison and reconcile enemies; and sapphires make their wearers peaceable, pious and kindly while, according to Cardano, they are a preservative against the bites of snakes and scorpions. According to St Hildegard a DIAMOND in the mouth prevents lying and aids fasting; the topaz neutralizes poisoned liquors; while the pearl is sovereign against diseases of the head (GRIA).

In astrology, precious stones correspond to metals and planets as follows: CRYSTAL – silver and the Moon; lode-stone – Mercury (metal and planet); amethyst and pearl – copper and Venus; sapphire and diamond – gold and the Sun; emerald and jasper – iron and Mars; carnelian and emerald – tin and Jupiter; TURQUOISE and all black stones – lead and Saturn.

In Islam, precious stones were used for countless magical practices, acting as charms or counter-charms to ensure the efficacy of a spell or deliverance from one. CORAL, carnelian, mother-of-pearl and AMBER were regarded as preservatives against the evil eye. When seen in dreams, according to a Persian treatise, precious stone possessed the following symbolism. Carnelian and ruby were signs of rejoicing and prosperity, as was coral. Agate was a sign of fame and fortune; turquoise of victory and long life, while emeralds and topaz denoted the valiant, faithful and pious individual as well as lawfully-gotten wealth.

One could go on listing the permutations in these correspondences, few authors agreeing between themselves. However, the essence of their symbolism is elsewhere.

Because of its changeless nature, in Biblical tradition the stone symbolizes wisdom. It is often associated with water. Thus when entering and when leaving the Wilderness, Moses caused the waters to spring up by striking a rock (Exodus 17: 6). In this context water symbolizes wisdom. Stones are also related to notions of honey and oil (Deuteronomy 32: 13; Psalm 80: 17; Genesis 28: 18). Stones may also be compared with bread. St Matthew tells of Christ being led into the Wilderness, where the Devil tempts him to turn the stones into bread.

The word 'Bethel', which occurs in Jacob's dream, means 'House of God' in Hebrew. As we have noted above, the meaning of Bethlehem ('House of Bread') is closely linked to it. In his commentary upon the Song of Solomon (2: 17), William of St Thierry observed that Bethel meant the House of God, that is to say a house of vigilance and wakefulness. Those who live in such a house are God's children, visited by the Holy Spirit. This house is called the house of wakefulness because those who live in it await the coming of the Bridegroom.

In the Temple, stone was holy not simply because it had been sanctified by the rites of dedication, but because it corresponded to its purpose and responded to its status as stone. St Hildegard of Bingen described the apparently incompatible properties of stone, three in number, as moisture, palpability and fiery strength. The property of moisture prevents its dissolution, thanks to its palpable nature it may be handled, while the fire within its bowels makes it hot and allows it to make its hardness harder still. Hugh of St Victor also studied the three properties of stone and in a sermon preached at a dedication service said that stones stand for the faithful, squared and strong in the stability of the Faith and the virtue of faithfulness.

When they had concluded a treaty, the Ancient Romans would sacrifice a pig to Jupiter by striking it over the head with a flint as a pledge of their oath and of their good faith, Jupiter being the god of oaths (*deus fidus*). If they should break their oaths, the god would strike them down as they had struck the pig down, with all the more violence as Jupiter was the more mighty and powerful (Livy 5: 24).

In this context the flint is clearly a symbol of the thunderbolt, the instrument of divine vengeance. In human hands the flint strikes the pig down, just as the thunderbolt in the hands of god will strike down the perjurer.

In Islam, the stone of stones is the Black Stone in the Ka'ba, at Mecca. It is called *yamīn Allāh*, God's right hand. The faithful take an oath of fidelity by laying their hands upon the stone or even by kissing it. On the Resurrection Day, the stone will bear witness in favour of the faithful who have made their pilgrimage to it (see BLACK).

Petrifaction
MEDUSA's eyes were so glaring that they turned to stone whoever gazed into them. To kill her, PERSEUS used a highly polished shield like a mirror. Medusa saw her own image and was petrified. Perseus escaped petrifaction and cut off her head. Athene then placed Medusa's head on her own shield and at the sight of it her enemies were halted in their tracks and turned to stone. In the Old Testament, Lot's wife was turned into a pillar of salt because she stopped and looked back to see the burning pitch and sulphur falling upon Sodom and Gomorrah (Genesis 19: 26).

The opposite to petrifaction occurred after the Flood when, on Zeus's orders, Deucalion and Pyrrha cast stones over their shoulders and they were changed into human beings. Those which Deucalion threw gave birth to men: those which Pyrrha threw, to women.

The two myths are correlative and reveal a pause and a fresh start in biological and spiritual development. The noösphere and the biosphere regress into the lithosphere, but forward movement can begin again.

What is especially noteworthy is that petrifaction is caused by or through the eyes: those who gazed at Medusa and she who looked back at Sodom and Gomorrah were turned to stone or into a pillar of salt. Similarly, it was because Corydon had watched Artemis bathing; because Lyco and Orpheus had spied upon the loves of Dionysos and their sister, Carya, that they were turned to stone.

Petrifaction symbolizes punishment inflicted for the ill-timed stare. Its consequences are an attachment which persists after the fault itself – the stare which lingers, perhaps from exaggerated feelings of guilt; the paralysing stare, perhaps from pride or greed; and the possessive stare. Petrifaction symbolizes the punishment of human enormity.

stork Although Leviticus 11: 18–19 categorizes the stork among unclean beasts (see TABOO), it is generally regarded as a bird of good omen. It is a symbol of filial piety, since it is claimed that storks feed their parents in their old age. In some countries storks are supposed to bring babies, and this may not be unrelated to the habits of a migratory bird which returns with the reawakening of Nature. However, from the same viewpoint and for the same reason, the stork is endowed with the power of causing pregnancy simply by its glance. In China the same is said of the heron.

In the Far East and especially in Japan the stork is commonly confused with the CRANE and regarded as a symbol of immortality.

It is at all events the most common symbol of longevity and the bird is supposed to reach a fabulously great age. Once it reaches six hundred, it is said to cease to eat, supporting life solely by drink, and after it reaches the age of two thousand to turn completely black. With the hare and the raven, it was the Taoist alchemists' favourite creature (BELT, CORM, GUEM).

storm (see also HURRICANE) The storm is the symbol of a theophany, the manifestation of the awesome and almighty power of God. While it may herald a revelation, it can also be a manifestation of divine anger and sometimes of punishment.

In the Old Testament, Jehovah addresses mankind and challenges it to match his deeds: 'Hast thou entered into the springs of the sea? or hast thou walked in the search of the depth? Have the gates of death been opened unto thee? or hast thou seen the doors of the shadow of death?' (Job 38: 16–17). He teaches mankind a lesson in humility at the same time as he confirms his matchless power. The image of the storm is at the centre of this demonstration.

Conjuring up an image of God's glory and power, the storm can also lay low the enemies of God's people and assure their peace, as in Psalm 29: 'The voice of the Lord is upon the waters: the God of glory thundereth . . . The voice of the Lord divideth the flames of fire. The voice of the Lord shaketh the wilderness . . . The Lord will give strength unto his people: the Lord will bless his people with peace.'

Creative activity is also unleashed in storm. In a cosmic upheaval beyond the power of words, life itself was born. The mighty beginnings and the mighty ends of historical epochs – revolutions, new regimes and even the end of the world itself and the New Jerusalem – are seen in terms of storm. The gods who created and set the universe in order were storm-gods – the

Assyro-Babylonian Bel, the Ancient Greek Zeus (Jupiter), the Germanic Donar, the Norse Thor and the Hindu Agni and Indra. Storms are also heralds of fecundating rain and in this respect beneficent symbols.

Storms were the favourite theme of European Romanticism as symbols of the human aspiration towards a life which, although itself tormented and stormy and swept by gales of passion, was raised above the commonplace. Love of storms indicates a need to live at a pitch of intensity and to escape the commonplace. At bottom it is, perhaps, a longing to suffer the violent action of God.

stranger The word 'stranger' symbolizes a human condition, for when Adam and Eve were driven from Paradise, they left their home country and became strangers and migrants.

Philo of Alexandria observes that Adam was driven from Paradise, that is to say that he was condemned to exile. Every child of Adam is therefore a passing guest, a stranger in whatever land he or she may be, even in their own country. This theme was taken up by the Church Fathers, and especially St Augustine, and further developed by medieval writers into the PILGRIM as a type of humanity. Since one's true home is Heaven, if one is exiled from it one becomes a stranger throughout one's earthly life.

In other traditions, the stranger is perceived as a potential rival and, although benefiting from the laws of hospitality, he may as easily be a dangerous incarnation of the Devil as a messenger from God. He needs to be honoured in the latter capacity and conciliated in the first. The stranger also signifies that part of the self which is still wandering unassimilated from the path of personal identification.

In all societies, the stranger is the person whose love lies elsewhere. Even if they cannot be precisely defined, the stranger's centres of interest are not those of the majority. The stranger typifies the artist's alienation from modern society.

strawberry The Ojibwa Indians of southwestern Ontario believed that when a person died, the soul remained conscious and journeyed to the land of the dead

until it reached a huge strawberry. Strawberries provide summer food for the Indians and symbolize the season of fine weather. If the dead person's soul tastes the fruit it will forget the land of the living and it will be unable thereafter to return to it. If the soul refuses to taste the fruit it retains the ability to return to Earth.

(SERH p. 90)

This belief may be compared with the one recorded in the 'Homeric' Hymn to Demeter and applying to the pomegranate seed which Persephone swallowed and was consequently doomed to remain in the Underworld. The dead must no longer eat the food of the living: earthly food is forbidden to the inhabitants of the Underworld.

stumbler Unlike the ACROBAT, who symbolizes freedom from the laws of everyday life, of gravity as well as of society, the stumbler is a symbol with religious significance. Falling head over heels, the person who stumbles 'loses an upright stance and all which symbolizes upward striving towards the heavenly and spiritual. That person no longer climbs the World Axis towards the heavenly Pole and God, but dives head-first into an animal sub-world and the darkness of the nether regions.' The stumbler has set his sights upon unworthy objects. In the moral combat with sin and self the stumbler is guilty of his or her own failure and the fall is the mark of this defeat.

stupa In India the Emperor Ashoka (third century BC) and in China the Emperor Wen (seventh century AD) erected countless stupas at the road-side and at crossroads as massive and graceful reliquaries symbolizing the loyalty of the State to the Buddha and inciting their subjects to a similar loyalty to the State. The symbolism of the stupa, however, surpasses its politico-religious use.

The stupa is the prime and most characteristic monument of Buddhist India. Originally it was a mound covering the relics of the Buddha and is consequently the aniconic image of the Buddha himself and more exactly of his *parinibbana* (final release from the cycle of rebirth).

However, the stupa is also a cosmic symbol. Its hemispherical shape rep-resents the World Egg (*anda*) while it also stands for the womb (*garbha*) with the relics representing the seed of life (*bīju*). Most commonly the stupa rests on a square pedestal or else is carefully aligned on the cardinal points. Here is a recurrence of the symbolism of the DOME (see also SPHERE) in which Earth supports and Heaven covers. The World Axis is always represented in a stupa and rises above its summit. It is release from the cosmos, the spiritual drive beyond the contingent constraints of manifesta-tion. This cosmic symbolism is made clearer still by ritual CIRCUMAMBULATION round the monument. There are some similarities between the stupa and the Buddha's body, its floors, like the parts of the body, signifying an as-cending order in levels of existence or celestial planes, release taking place through the crown of the head. In Tibet, these different levels are in any case identified with square, triangle, chalice and flame, corresponding from base to summit to the five elements – Earth, Water, Fire, Air and Ether – as well as to the five chief CHAKRA in Tantrism.

The PARASOLS, set one above the other along the shaft emerging from the hemispherical summit, represent a heavenly hierarchy which is extracosmic and superhuman (BURA, GOVM, SECA).

substitutes The image may alter, but humanity remains the same, or at least the image changes more quickly than the human. Only within the last two or three generations have such images as TRAINS, AIRCRAFT and AUTOMOBILES acquired in the imagination those powerful properties once possessed by horses, serpents and chariots to give expression to our psychic lives. They comprise typical symbolic substitutes. They can be reduced to archetypes in the collective unconscious, replacing images from the latter when these are so closely tied to phenomena at a particular stage of civil-ization that they are bound to become less important or to disappear as that civilization advances. The symbol remains, but its verbal, visual, audible and emotional settings live and die or remain dormant. Without claiming to be comprehensive, a list can be made of symbols being formed and becom-ing substitutes for long-standing images. However, in this field just as there can never be exact equivalence between synonyms, so there can never be a perfect equivalence between symbols, nor definitive agreement upon their interpretation. According to Jung and other psychoanalysts, these are some of the symbols currently undergoing substitution: train, car or aircraft for *dragon*; motor, rail or air crash for *fighting dragons*; lift for *ascension* and *spiritualization*; machine-gun beside an opening for *Cerberus*; hypodermic syringe for *sacrificial knife*; leaking fuel tank for *bleeding wound*; priest, teacher or cab-driver for *wise old man*; road-map, department store for *maze*; aircraft for *Zeus' eagle*; market-woman at the vegetable stall for *Earth Mother*; headlights piercing the darkness for the *awakening and call of the anima*; sexual liberation for the *return of Dionysos*; industrial energy for *Promethean fire*; mass media, public relations for *Hermes*.

This substitution-phenomenon merits attention, especially since it indicates the future of symbols, a future which can affect group representation as well as individual images and which cannot be interpreted on the basis of predetermined patterns.

sulphur   In alchemy, sulphur is the active principle and the one which acts upon inert mercury and either impregnates it or kills it. Sulphur corresponds to Fire as mercury to Water. It is the male principle of generation which acts upon mercury to produce metals under the ground. It is a manifestation of the will of Heaven – the fire and brimstone (sulphur) which rained down on Sodom corresponds in a strange way with this notion – as well as being a manifestation of the activity of the Spirit. In Muslim esotericism, 'red sulphur' denotes the Universal Man (also represented by the PHOENIX) who is therefore the product of the alchemist's process of the Red Stone.

The action of sulphur upon mercury 'kills' it and as it transmutes it produces cinnabar, the medicine of immortality. The constant coupling of sulphur with Fire sometimes connects it, too, with the symbolism of the Underworld (ELIF, GUET). Job 18: 15 regards sulphur (brimstone) as a symbol of sterility, as it were a disinfectant. It is scattered 'upon the habitation' of the king of terrors. This is the destructive, infernal aspect of the symbol, its positive sense inverted to the opposite meaning.

Other esoteric traditions, connected with the former, regard sulphur as the symbol of fiery breath and a designation for mineral semen. Hence it is as strongly linked to the active principle. It conveys light and colour (ALLA p. 245).

Red sulphur (*kibrīt ahmar*, in Arabic) 'of which the very existence partakes of legend, is allegedly found in the West, near the sea, and is excessively rare. Hence it is used as a term to describe the peerless individual' (ENCI).

Jildāki compares the transmutation of the soul through ascetic practices with red sulphur (MASH p. 931).

In the alchemical symbolism of Muslim mystics, the soul which is imprisoned in harsh wastes must first be 'liquefied' and then 'congealed', these operations being followed by 'fusion' and 'crystallization'. The powers of the soul are compared with the natural forces of heat, cold, moisture and dryness. In the soul, the corresponding forces are connected to two complementary principles, similar to the alchemist's sulphur and mercury. In Sufism, mercury denotes the plasticity of the psyche and sulphur the action of the spirit. Ibn 'Arabī used the word 'sulphur' to denote the Divine Act (*al-Amr*) and 'mercury' for Nature as a whole (BURD p. 109).

It is common knolwedge that the Philosopher's Stone was red.

The alchemists regarded sulphur as being to the body what the Sun was to the universe (MONA p. 60). When given the infernal sense of their symbolism, gold, light and the colour yellow 'denote selfish pride which seeks only in itself for wisdom and which becomes its own god, principle and goal' (PORS p. 84). In Christian tradition, it is this fatal side of the symbolism of the Sun and of the colour yellow for which 'diabolical' brimstone (sulphur) stands in both Old and New Testaments alike. Sodom was destroyed by fire and brimstone and the punishment which the Book of Job (18) holds out to the wicked uses the same image. 'The light shall be dark in his tabernacle . . . brimstone shall be scattered upon his habitation. . . . He shall be driven from light into darkness.' The smoky yellow flame of burning sulphur stands in the Bible for the anti-light which flows from Lucifer's pride – light turned into darkness. 'Take heed therefore', says St Luke (11: 35), 'that the light that is within thee be not darkness.' Sulphur is a symbol of guilt and punishment because 'paganism used it to cleanse the guilty' (PORS p. 86).

Sun, the   The symbolism of the Sun, as multivalent as the reality of the Sun, itself provides a wealth of contradictions. When the Sun was not a god, for many peoples it was a manifestation of the godhead (celestial epiphany). It could also be conceived as the Supreme Deity's son or the rainbow's brother. Semang Pygmies, Fuegians and Bushmen regard it as the Supreme Deity's eye, Australian Aborigines as the Creator's son, kindly disposed to mankind. The Samoyed considered Sun and Moon as the two eyes of Num (the Heavens), the Sun being the good and the Moon the evil eye. The Sun may also be regarded as what makes fertile, yet at the same time as what burns up and kills.

The immortal Sun rises each morning and

descends nightly to the kingdom of the dead; it can, therefore, take men with it and, by setting, put them to death; but it can also, on the other hand, guide souls through the lower regions and bring them back next day with its light. That is its twofold function – as psychopomp to 'murder' and as hierophant to initiate. It explains the belief . . . that merely to glance at the setting sun may induce death. . . . The Upanishads say that the Sun engenders and devours its offspring. In his *Republic* (508 BC), Plato makes it 'the image of the good as expressed in visible things; to the Orphics it was the intellect of the world'.

(ELIT pp. 136, 151, and see chapter 3)

The Sun is the source of light, heat and life and its rays represent the celestial or spiritual influences which the Earth receives. Guénon observes that these rays are sometimes presented iconographically as alternations of straight and wavy lines. In this context it is an attempt to symbolize both the light and heat or, from another viewpoint, the light and the rain, which are alike the *yin* and *yang* aspects of the Sun's lifegiving radiation.

In addition to giving life to things, the Sun's rays make them manifest, not simply by making them perceptible, but because the rays represent extension of the primeval dot and in so far as they measure space. The Sun's rays – to which Shiva's tresses are assimilated – were traditionally seven in number, corresponding to the six dimensions of space and to the extra-cosmic dimension, represented by the centre itself. This relationship between the Sun's rays and cosmic geometry is expressed in Pythagorean symbolism. It is also Blake's Ancient of Days, the Sun-god measuring Heaven and Earth with his compasses. Hindu writers attribute the beginnings of all things which exist to the Sun, the First Cause and end of all that is manifested, the one which nourishes (*savitri*).

It is true that under a different aspect the Sun is also the principle of drought – the opposite to the fecundating principle of rain – and the destroyer. Thus the Chinese believed that excessive heat from the Sun had to be destroyed by shooting arrows at it and sometimes – as for example in Cambodia – rain-making rituals involved the sacrifice of a solar animal. Cyclical creation and destruction make the Sun a symbol of Māyā, mother of the differentiated universe and of cosmic Illusion. In another way, the cycle of the Sun symbolizes the alternation of life, death and rebirth, both in its daily manifestation (a universal symbol but one of especial richness in Vedic writings) as well as in its annual manifestation (see SOLSTICE). The Sun is thus regarded as a symbol of resurrection and immortality. The Chinese Immortals fed upon the essence of the Sun as well as upon SUNFLOWER seeds, of which the relationship with the Sun is patent. The Sun is an aspect of the Tree of the World as well as of the Tree of Life, the former in any case being identified with the Sun's ray.

The Sun is the centre of the Heavens, just as the heart is the centre of the body; but in this context it is a spiritual Sun which Vedic symbolism depicted as stationary at its ZENITH and which was also termed the Heart or Eye of the World. It was the abode of Purusha or of Brahmā; it is ātman, the universal spirit. The Sun's ray which binds *purusha* to the individual corresponds to the subtle coronal artery of Yoga. It is reminiscent of the symbolism of THREAD and cannot fail to conjure up that of the spider's web. As the heart of the world, the Sun is sometimes depicted in the centre of the WHEEL of the Zodiac and is manifested in a similar way by the twelve Aditya. Although the universal symbol of the solar CHARIOT is generally related to the Sun's diurnal transit, the chariot-wheel – and Sūrya's chariot had only one wheel – is itself pre-eminently a symbol of the radiant Sun.

If the light radiated by the Sun is intellectual knowledge, the Sun itself is the cosmic intellect, just as in the individual being the heart is the seat of the faculty of knowing. The name Heliopolis, Citadel or City of the Sun, was often given to the primal spiritual centre. It is the seat of the cyclical lawgiver Manu, Homer's Syria (*Sūrya*, 'Sun'), lying beyond the island of Ortygia, an island 'where are the turning-places of the sun' (*Odyssey* 15: 404). The pre-eminent Sun-god and god of initiation, Apollo, came from the Hyperborean world and his arrow was like a ray of sunlight. Similarly, the Sun is Vishnu's emblem, as well as that of the Buddha (some Chinese writers called him 'Golden Man' and 'Sun-Buddha') and of Christ, too. His rays are the twelve Apostles and he was called *Sol Justitiae* (Sun of Justice) and *Sol Invictus* (Invincible Sun). Hesychius of Batos wrote that 'we look upon Jesus as the Sun shining Justice down', that is to say, as the spiritual Sun or heart of the world. Philotheus of Sinai calls him 'the Sun of Truth', reminiscent of the Transfiguration on Mount Tabor when Christ's face shone like the Sun. The LABARUM, Christ's monogram, is reminiscent of the solar wheel. To this one might add that the Jewish High Priest wore a golden disc on his chest, a symbol of the divine Sun.

Similarly, the Sun is a universal symbol of the monarch as the heart of an empire. Although the mother of the Han Emperor Wu may have given birth to him after dreaming that the Sun had entered her womb, this was not merely a symbol of fecundation, it was above all an imperial symbol.

The Rising Sun is not simply the Japanese national emblem, but the country's name (*Nihon*). The ancestor of the dynasties which ruled from Angkor was named Bālāditya ('Rising Sun') and his activities are deliberately assimilated – as were those of the Chinese emperor in the Temple of Heaven – to a revolution of the Zodiac. Circumambulation always follows the Sun, wherever temples look to the East from which its daily transit begins.

The solar principle is represented by large numbers of animals, birds and plants (CHRYSANTHEMUM, LOTUS, SUNFLOWER; EAGLE, STAG, LION, to mention a very few) and by a metal, GOLD, which alchemists designated the Sun among metals.

The MOON is always *yin* relative to the Sun's *yang*, since the latter's light shines directly while the Moon's is only a reflection of the Sun's. The latter is the active principle, the other, the passive. Symbolically, this has a very wide application, the Sun representing immediate, intuitive knowledge, the Moon rational and speculative knowledge acquired by reflection. Consequently Sun and Moon correspond, respectively, to spirit and soul (*spiritus* and *anima*) as well as to their respective seats, the heart and brain. They are essence and substance, form and matter. In the alchemical *Emerald Table* we read, 'his father is the Sun, his mother the Moon'. According to Shabistarī the Sun corresponds to the Prophet and the Moon to the wāli, or the Imām, since the second receives light from the first.

This active–passive, male–female duality – which is also that of FIRE and water – is not a fixed rule. In Japan and among the Montagnards of southern Vietnam, too, the Sun is feminine and the Moon is masculine – as, one is bound to observe, is the rule in German. This is because the female principle is regarded as the active principle, in so far as it is fecund, and among the Radhe, it was the Sun-goddess who impregnated, brooded and gave birth. This is also why, although the right eyes of such primeval heroes as Vaishvanara, Shiva, P'an-ku and Lao-kun are the Sun and their left the Moon, in the case of Izanagi the process is reversed. This correspondence between the eyes leads to another: the left eye corresponds to the future and the right to the past; thus the Sun corresponds to the powers of intellect and the Moon to those of memory.

The solar and the lunar eyes correspond to the two lateral *nādi* in Yoga – *īdā* (lunar) and *pingāla* (solar). Furthermore, the journey which the liberated being undertakes on reaching the central *nādi* may either be directed towards the Sphere of the Sun, that is, along the Path of the Gods, or *devayāna,* or towards the Sphere of the Moon (along the Path of the An-cestors, or *pitri-yāna*): in the first instance, to escape from the cosmos and, in the second, to re-enter the cycle of rebirth. In Tantrism *īdā* and *pingāla* as Moon and Sun correspond to SHAKTI and Shiva, but Shiva's lunar nature sometimes reverses the roles. Yoga is the marriage of Sun (*ha*) and Moon (*tha*), hence Hatha-yoga, represented by the breathings *prāna* and *apāna*, or else by breath and semen, which are fire and water. The same duality is expressed in Chinese alchemico-Tantric symbolism by the trigrams *li* and *k'an*, which the *I Ching* effectively makes to correspond to Sun and Moon.

The duality of Sun and Moon is also that of Vishnu and Shiva and of the *sattva* and *tamas* tendencies. There is an echo of this in the solar and lunar dynasties of India, Cambodia and Champa. The marriage of Sun and Moon is Harihara, part-Vishnu and part-Shiva, a favourite symbol in pre-Angkorian art. In Chinese it is also light (*ming*), its character composed of a synthesis of those denoting Sun and Moon (BURA, BENA, AVAS, DAMS, DANA, ELIY, ELIF, PHIL, GRIC, GRIF, GUEV, GUEM, GUER, GUET, GUES, KALL, KALT, KEMR, LECC, PORA, SAIR, SILI, CORT).

In Central American tradition solar symbolism contrasts with lunar in another aspect. 'Sunset is not recognized as a "death" (unlike the moon's three days in hiding) but as a descent into the lower regions, into the kingdom of the dead. Unlike the moon, the sun has the privilege of passing through hell without undergoing the condition of death' (ELIT p. 136). Hence the genuinely solar properties of the eagle among shamanistic attributes.

The opposition of Sun and Moon generally overlays male–female dualism. Thus Soustelle explains that 'according to ancient tradition, at Teotihuacan men were sacrificed to the Sun and women to the Moon' (SOUM).

The Ancient Mexicans believed that we live under a fifth Sun. The four earlier Suns were those successively of the tiger, of wind, of rain (or fire) and of water. The first was that of Tezcatlipoca, linked to cold, to darkness and to the north; the second, of Quetzalcoatl in his original shape, linked to witchcraft and the west; the third, of the rain-god Tlaloc, linked to the south; the fourth, of the water-goddess Calchiuhtlicue, linked to the east.

Our Sun, the fifth, was placed beneath the sign of one of the fire-gods, Xiuhtecuhtli, sometimes depicted as a butterfly. All these ages, which they called Suns, ended in cataclysms when the four tigers devoured mankind, the four winds blew them away and the four rains and the four waters drowned them. The present age will be brought to an end by four earth-quakes, and that will be the finish of the fifth Sun.

The great god of the midday Sun in the Aztec pantheon, Huitzilopochtli, was depicted as an eagle holding a starry serpent in its beak.

What most strikingly epitomize the basic symbolic dualism founded upon the pairing of Sun and Moon are the attributes of exogamic division among the Omaha Indians. This was given physical expression in the way in which, in their encampments, their tents were separated into two semi-circles. The first presided over all religious activities associated with the Sun, the day, the north, the higher, the male principle and the right side, the second over the duties of politics and society, associated with the Moon, the night, the lower, the female principle and the left side (LEVS).

The whole Dogon system of cosmogony is dominated by lunar symbolism and for them the Sun is not male but female. It is described as a white-hot earthenware POT with a spiral of red COPPER making eight turns round it. It is thus the prototype of the fertilized womb. The earthenware pot represents the female womb holding the life-principle, the red copper coiled round it is male semen which coils round the womb to make it fertile, but this semen is also light, water and the Word. Lastly the number of copper coils – eight – is that of completed creation, of speech and of perfection (GRIE, GRIS). The prototype of the womb was fashioned by the Supreme Deity, Amma, with damp clay, before he set Sun and Moon in the sky.

The Fali in Cameroon depict Sun and Moon as two pieces of earthenware, one a flat plate, the other a hollow pot. Their prototypes, reinforced with iron and lined with copper, were stolen from Heaven by the first woman potter, wife of the first blacksmith, before this primeval pair came down to Earth (FROA).

In Fulani tradition, the Sun is no less than the Supreme Deity's, Gueno's, eye. 'When he had finished the work of creation, Gueno took the Sun out of his eye-socket, so that he became the one-eyed king, for his one eye is enough for him to see all that goes on on Earth while his other gives it heat and light' (HAMK p. 2).

Central Asian peoples, and especially the inhabitants of the Amur Basin, believed that in the beginning there were three or four Suns, their burning heat and blinding light making the Earth uninhabitable. A god or hero saved mankind, according to most of the myths, by slaying the first two or three Suns with his arrows. According to some of these myths, these original Suns actually set the Earth alight and coal was produced by this fire. Similar legends occur in China (ten Suns), India (seven Suns) and Sumatra (eight Suns).

In most nomadic pastoral societies the Sun is female (Mother Sun) and the Moon male (Father Moon): this is true of most of the Mongol and Turkic peoples of central Asia (HARA pp. 130–2).

In Celtic, as in all ancient Indo-European languages, the noun, Sun, is feminine. In myth it was personified by Lug ('Light') who was called *grianainech*, 'Sun-face'. The same epithet is applied, either by analogy or extension, to the war-god, Ogma, who by definition possessed or ruled the dark side of the world. The Sun was, however, regarded above all as one of the basic elements in the universe. It was the most important among those (Moon, water, air and so on) called upon to witness a formal oath.

Many Irish writers of lives of the saints have described or castigated ancient Gaelic Sun-worship, but their reference is to somewhat simplistic and stereotyped concepts in pre-Christian tradition. A glossary (ARCL 3: p. 477, no. 1569) mentions 'high knowledge of the Sun' (*imbus gréine*). All Irish and Welsh writers using the Sun in metaphor or comparison employ it to characterize not only light and brightness, but all things beautiful, pleasant and splendid. Welsh writers often use the metaphor, 'eye of the day', for Sun and the Irish word for eye (*sul*), which is the equivalent of the Brythonic word for Sun, emphasizes the solar symbolism of the eye (OGAC 4; ANEI 5: p. 63; STOG p. 25; PLUV 1: p. cxxxvi).

In astrology, the Sun is the symbol of life, heat, day, light, authority, the male sex and all things radiant. If astrologers seem to have lowered it to the level of a mere PLANET, to be compared with a Mars or a Jupiter, this is chiefly because its influence is, so to speak, divided into two quite separate fields, one of direct influence through its position in the Heavens and the other indirect, being that of the ZODIAC. In fact all influence exerted by the signs of the Zodiac is essentially solar, being, in actual fact, the influence of the Sun reflected or polarized by the Earth's orbit.

In its role of cosmic symbol, the Sun ranks as a true astral religion, its worship dominating the great civilizations of antiquity with their gigantic figures of gods and heroes – Atum, Osiris, Baal, Mithras, Helios, Apollo and so on – embodying the powers of creation and the sources of light and life represented by the Sun. Peoples with astral mythologies regard the Sun as a father-symbol, something reflected in children's drawings and in dreams. In the same way, the Sun has always been the astrologers' symbol of the male principle of generation and of the principle of authority of which the father is the individual's earliest embodiment. This is also true of that area of the psyche created by paternal influence in the form of training, education, awareness, discipline and morality. Thus, in a horoscope the Sun stands for Durkheim's social constraint and Freud's 'censorship' and is the source of social drives, civilization, ethics and all major aspects of existence. Its range of properties stretches from the negative super-ego which crushes the individual with taboos, principles, rules or prejudices, to the positive, idealized ego, a higher image of self to which the individual attempts to lift him- or herself. The day-star therefore locates the individual within a life which may be strictly regulated or highly sublimated; it represents the outlook offered by his personality through psychic syntheses, at the highest level, of the greatest demands, the loftiest aspirations and the strongest forms of individuation, or else in the total failure of pride or power-madness. It stands for the individual achieving the goals of marriage and parenthood, in worldly success which is an extension of his or her personal qualities, and in the very fact that he has achieved success by embodying the powers and authority inherent in the ultimate solarization of guide, leader, hero and ruler.

Paul Diel interprets the Sun as giver of light and the Heavens which it illuminates as symbolizing the intellect and the superconsciousness. As he would say, the intellect corresponds to consciousness and the spirit to superconsciousness. Thus the Sun and its rays, which were once symbols of fecundation, have become symbols of enlightenment (DIES pp. 36–7). This is the key which enables psychoanalysis to unlock the meaning of all myths which show Sun-gods or solar heroes in action.

The Black Sun is the Sun in its nightly transit, when it leaves this world to shed its light upon another. The Aztecs depicted the Black Sun carried on the back of the god of the Underworld. It is the antithesis of the midday Sun, as the maleficent and destroying absolute of death.

The Mayas depicted the Black Sun as a JAGUAR.

Alchemists saw the Black Sun as unworked, primal matter, still to be set on the path of development. To the psychoanalyst, the Black Sun stands for the unconscious, again in its most elemental form.

Traditionally the Black Sun presages the unleashing of destructive forces upon the universe, society or the individual. It heralds disaster, suffering and death, the inverted image of the noonday Sun, hence the universal sense of ill omen attaching to eclipses.

In the TAROT, the Sun, source of light, follows the Moon, a reflection of that light. It is the nineteenth major arcanum and one of the most enigmatic. It expresses 'the happiness of the individual who feels at one with Nature' (Enel); 'true marriage, happiness, the united family' (Tereschenko); 'concord, clarity of judgement and of expression, literary or artistic talents, happy marriage, brotherly love or fulfilment, pretence, histrionics, window-dressing and fallacious appearance' (Wirth). In astrology it corresponds to the Seventh House.

Reading these differing interpretations makes one wonder whether the Tarot Sun means too many things to be expressed in any single card. We should, however, try to examine it more closely. The dominant colour of the card is golden YELLOW, the pre-eminent solar colour, which symbolizes simultaneously intellectual perfection, the wealth of metal and of harvest and the alchemists' Great Work as well. The Sun's disc is personified by a full face from which radiate seventy-five rays. Fifty-nine of these are just black lines, eight are formed by elongated triangles with straight sides (four yellow, two green and two red), alternating with eight others with wavy sides (three red, two white and three blue) which thus emphasize 'the two-fold action of the Sun's rays, bringing both heat and light' (WIRT p. 236).

It should be observed that it is only the RED rays, bearing the colour of the all-powerful spirit, which share this twofold activity. Thirteen droplets, point uppermost, arranged in a symmetrical pattern (five blue, three white, three yellow and two red), fall from the Sun towards the ground. The Sun generously scatters its fecundating energies while the Moon draws to itself the emanations of the Earth and we are reminded here of the shower of gold in which Zeus fell to seduce Danae in a similar symbolic sense.

On the bare earth stand a pair of twins, flesh-coloured, bare-headed, wearing necklaces and holding hands. They are reminiscent of the two persons held fast to the Devil's pedestal in the fifteenth arcanum, but whereas the latter wore nothing except their devilish headdresses, the solar twins are clothed in blue loin-cloths, as if they had already become aware of their differences in the light. Attempts have been made to show that one is 'the spirit, the solar, positive and male element' and that the other is 'the soul, the lunar, negative and female element of the human being' (RIJT p. 256), or else that they are the two opposing yet complementary principles, the active and the passive.

Be that as it may, as twins they are charged with especial powers and 'related to the Sun, which separates beings and things, and doubles them by giving each a shadow . . . they are the very image of similarity, brotherhood and synthesis' (VIRI p. 66). Like Adam and Eve and the hero-twins who are the mythic ancestors of so many peoples, they are an expression of that primeval parthenogenesis and hermaphroditism which marks the start of humanity venturing out in the light of the Sun.

They stand with their backs to a wall built from four courses of stonework as yellow as the ground itself but with red coping running at the twins' waist level. 'The elect, for whom the children of the Sun stand, can only come together in brotherly love within the shelter of a stone wall' says

Oswald Wirth (WIRT p. 235), while Dr Carton regards 'the stone wall as standing for the Philosopher's Stone . . . a hieroglyphic of Truth, the Absolute and the Infinite' (MARD p. 316).

The red coping brands this wall with the mark of the spirit. It stops at waist-level as if mankind, previously cast from a far taller Tower, had at last taken stock in the sunlight, of itself and of its potentiality. For, in the end, illusions vanish and the Sun reveals reality and the truth about ourselves and our world. Through its enlightenment, both physical and spiritual, we can face JUDGEMENT, the twentieth arcanum. The Sun sharpens our awareness of our limitations; it is the light of knowledge and the spring of energy.

sunflower The common name of the heliotrope is sufficiently strong an indication of its solar character, the result both of the sun-ray pattern of its petals and of the way in which the flower follows the Sun's daily transit.

In China, the sunflower was a food of immortality and was most notably used as such by Kui-fu. Its changing colours relate it to the points of the compass and might have characterized the flower as heliotropic (KALL).

sunshade See PARASOL.

swallow Although one swallow may not make a Summer, these birds are messengers of Spring and the Chinese used once to time the precise dates of the equinoxes to their arrival and departure. Fertility rites marked the arrival of the swallows at the vernal equinox, and undoubtedly this relates to several legends recounting the miraculous pregnancies of girls who ate swallows' eggs. (They include the stories of Hien Ti and of the ancestress of the Chang family from whom Confucius was descended, so that he might justly be called the swallow's son.) As another sign of Spring, cakes shaped like swallows used to be nailed above the door, although in this instance swallows would seem to have been confused with another Spring migrant, possibly the oriole.

In addition to the yin–yang seasonal rhythm of its migration, it was also believed to undergo a metamorphosis. The swallow, Li Tzu reports, takes refuge in the waters (yin or Winter), where it becomes a shell, returning to its bird-shape when the Sun rises into the ascendant (yang or Summer).

Similarly, Isis changed into a swallow at night, circling Osiris's coffin with cries of lamentation until the return of the Sun, a symbol of the eternal homecoming and a herald of resurrection (GRAD, GRAP, GRAR, KALL, LIOT, WIEG).

In the realm of Celtic myth, the name of Fand stands for the swallow. She was the wife of the sea-god Manannan and she fell in love with Cùchulainn and wafted him into the Otherworld. He spent a month with her and then abandoned her. He was taken back by his wife Emer and a sorrowful Fand returned to the husband who had set out in search of her. Another mythic person whose name is related to that of the swallow was Fandle, one of the three sons of Nechtan Scene, killed by Cùchulainn during his first expedition to the borders of Ulster. Fandle was so light-footed that he could fight on water (OGAC 11: pp. 325ff.; ETUC pp. 506–13). Here again the swallow was regarded as being linked to the symbolism of fertility, alternation and renewal.

The Bambara of Mali regard the swallow as the assistant – a manifestation – of the Demiurge Faro, lord of the waters and of the word and the highest expression of purity, in contrast with the Earth, unclean in the beginning. The swallow owes this important function to the fact that it never alights upon the ground and is therefore free of defilement. It is the swallow which collects the blood of the victims sacrificed to Faro and carries it into the heights of Heaven, from which it falls in the shape of fecundating rain. The bird thus plays the part of a vehicle in the cyclical mechanism of fertilizing the Earth, as it does of women, by carrying the juice of the wild tomato into Heaven (DIEB).

In Islam the swallow is the symbol of the renunciation of good fellowship. It is called the Bird of Paradise. The Persians believed 'that the twittering of swallows separated neighbours and friends, signifying loneliness, separation and migration', doubtless from the migratory habits of the bird itself (FAHN p. 447).

swan From Ancient Greece to Siberia, via Asia Minor, as well as among Slav and Germanic peoples, a great mass of myth, tradition and poetry has gathered in praise of the swan, the spotless bird whose whiteness (see WHITE), strength and grace have made it a living manifestation of LIGHT itself.

There are, nevertheless, two whitenesses and two lights, the solar, male light of day and the lunar female light of night. The meaning of its symbolism depends upon which of these two the swan embodies. If it remains undivided and, as is sometimes the case, tries to bear the synthesis of both, the swan becomes hermaphroditic and even more highly charged with mystery and holiness. Lastly, just as there is a Black SUN and a Black Horse, so there is a Black Swan, not desacralized, but charged with occult and inverted symbolism.

There is a Buryat tale of the hunter who, one day, surprised three shining maidens bathing in a lonely lake. They were none other than swans which had removed their feathered cloaks to enter the water. The man stole one of the dresses and hid it, so that after their bathe only two of the swanmaidens were able to resume their wings and fly away. The hunter took the third for his wife. She bore him eleven sons and six daughters, but when she found her cloak again, she addressed him before flying away in these words: 'You are an earthly being and will remain earth-bound, but this is not my home, I came from the skies and to the skies I must return. In the Spring, every year, when you see us flying overhead towards the North and every Autumn when you see us flying overhead towards the South, you must celebrate our passing with special rites' (HARA p. 319).

Most of the Altaic peoples have similar stories, with variations, wild GEESE often taking the place of swans. In all these tales, the bird of light, with its spotless, shining loveliness, is the heavenly virgin who will be made pregnant either by Earth or by Water – the hunter of the lake – to give birth to the human race. However, as Roux (ROUF p. 351) so rightly observes, heavenly light in this context ceases to be male and fecundating to become female and fecundated. These myths remind us of the Ancient Egyptian representation of the sacred marriage of Heaven and Earth – Nut, the skygoddess, made pregnant by Geb, the Earth-god – in this instance the light being the soft and milky moonlight of a mythic virgin. This meaning of the swan-symbol seems to have been predominant among all Slav peoples as well as among Scandinavians, Persians and the Turks of Asia Minor. The image – or perhaps one should say the belief – was sometimes pushed almost beyond its limits. Thus in the Yenisei Basin there was a deep-rooted belief that swans menstruated like women (ROUF p. 353). However, the swan has many avatars (embodiments), depending upon the people concerned. We have already mentioned the wild goose, but the GULL played the same role for the Chukchi and the DOVE and PIGEON for the Russians (ROUF ibid.).

As a more general rule, the swan is the embodiment of male, solar, fecundating light. Even in Siberia, although that belief was not widely current, it left its traces. Thus Uno Harva observed that Buryat women made a curtsy and addressed a prayer to the first swan they saw in the Spring (HARA p. 321). It was, however, in the pure light of Ancient Greece that the beauty of the male swan, inseparable companion of Apollo, received its largest measure of praise. In myths, this bird of Heaven through its migrations is the link which joins the peoples of the Mediterranean to the mysterious Hyperboreans. It is common knowledge that Apollo, the god of poetry and prophecy, was born on Delos on a seventh day. On that day sacred swans flew seven times round the island and then Zeus presented the young god with a chariot drawn by white horses, as well as his lyre. His team carried him 'first to their home on the shores of the ocean beyond the home of the North Wind, where the Hyperboreans lived under a sky which was always clear' (GRID p. 41). This causes Victor Magnien to write (MAGE p. 135) that the swan symbolizes 'the powers of poetry and of the poet himself'. The swan might well be the image of the divinely inspired poet, of the sacred priesthood, of the white-robed druid, of the Norse skald and so on. At first sight the myth of Leda would seem to bear the same interpretation of the symbol of the swan as male and diurnal. However, closer examination reveals that if Zeus changed himself into a swan to come to Leda, this was, as the Greek myth explains, only after she 'had turned herself into a goose to escape him' (GRID p. 257). Now, as we have seen, the goose is an avatar of the swan in its female and lunar acceptation, so that the loves of swan-Zeus and goose-Leda stand for the bipolarization of the symbol. This leads one to presume that the Greeks intentionally brought together these two meanings, the diurnal and the nocturnal, to make the swan a hermaphrodite symbol in which Leda and her divine lover are really only one.

This same notion underlies Gaston Bachelard's analysis of a scene in Goethe's *Faust Part II* (7300–6) in which maidens are seen bathing in clear waters and are approached by swans. Bachelard synthesizes this image of the swan with that of Desire, demanding the interfusion of Sun and Moon, the two luminaries through which the universe manifests its polarity. The swan's song may then be interpreted as the passionate outpouring of the lover before a fatal term is set to this exaltation which truly becomes a *Liebestod* (BACE pp. 50ff., 152). The swan which dies singing and sings dying thereby becomes the symbol of the primary desire which is sexual desire.

One example of the inversion of the symbol provided by the image of the Black Swan can be mentioned. In Andersen's story *The Travelling Companion*, drawn from the depths of Scandinavian folklore, a bewitched and bloodthirsty maiden is seen in the shape of a black swan. When the swan is dipped three times into cleansing water, it turns white and the princess, freed from the spell, is able at last to love her young husband.

In the Far East, too, the swan is the symbol of gracefulness, nobility and valour. This is why, Li Tzu reports, the Mongols made the Chou Emperor, Mu, drink swan's blood It is also the symbol of music and of song, while the wild goose, from its well-known wariness, is the symbol of prudence, which the *I Ching* employs to indicate the stages in cautious advance, such an advance naturally being capable of being interpreted in spiritual terms.

It is hard to separate the two birds in Hindu iconography; Brahmā's 'swan' (Hamsa) used as his steed has the appearance of a wild goose. As de Mallmann says, the etymological kinship between *hamsa* and *anser* (Latin for 'goose') 'hits one between the eyes'. The Hamsa which was Varuna's steed was a water-fowl; Brahmā's steed was the symbol of the elevation of the unformed towards the Heaven of knowledge. There is much the same meaning in those Cambodian writings which identify Shiva with the Kalahamsa 'which haunts the yogis' lake of the heart' and with the *hamsa* 'which dwells in the BINDU', *hamsa* meaning both *anser* and *ātman* or self, the Universal Spirit. When an attribute of Vishnu, it becomes a symbol of Nārāyana, one of the titles of the Creator-God, and the soul in the universe personified.

Swan symbolism opens still further perspectives in so far as a swan either laid or brooded the World EGG. This was the role of the 'Nile goose' in Ancient Egypt; and again, that of the *hamsa* which incubated the *Brahmanda* on the primeval waters in Indian tradition; and, lastly, there was the egg produced by Leda and Zeus, from which emerged the Dioscuri, each capped by half the egg and figures of its differentiation. Nor is it irrelevant to add that until comparatively recently there was the widespread belief that babies were born of earth and water and brought by the swans (BHAB, DANA, ELIM, GUET, MALA, SOUN).

In Celtic literature, most of the inhabitants of the Otherworld who, for one reason or another, wish to enter the terrestrial world, take a swan's shape and generally travel in pairs linked by a gold or silver chain. Many Celtic works of art depict a pair of swans, one on either side of the Sunboat, which they steer on its voyage across the celestial ocean. Since they came from and returned to the north, they symbolized higher or angelic states of being in the course of liberation and return to the Almighty Principle. Continental as well as insular Celts often confused the swan with the crane, which explains why Caesar states that there was a taboo upon the Bretons eating it (OGAC 18: pp. 143–7; CHAB pp. 537–52).

The swan is also a part of alchemical symbolism. 'Alchemists have always regarded it as an emblem of mercury, being of the same colour and as mobile. Its volatility, too, is displayed by its wings. It is an expression of the marriage of opposites [Fire and Water] in which its archetypal property of hermaphroditism may be discerned.'

swastika (see also SIXTEEN; TOWER; WHEEL)   One of the oldest symbols in existence is the swastika, and it is one of the most widely spread, from furthest East Asia to Central America, via Mongolia, India and northern Europe. It was well-known to Celts and Etruscans and to Ancient Greece, so that the so-called Greek-key pattern derives from it. Some writers have tried to take it back to Atlantis, which shows its great antiquity.

However complex its symbolism may be, the bare outline of the swastika displays a rotary movement around a fixed CENTRE, which may either be the ego or the POLE. It is therefore a cyclical symbol of activity, manifestation and perpetual regeneration and it is in this last sense that it is often an accompaniment to images of such saviours of the human race as Christ, from the medieval catacombs in the West to the Nestorians of the steppes of central Asia. 'Romanesque depictions of Christ were conceived in terms of the spiral or swastika which harmonized the stance and dictated lines of limbs and drapery. This provided the means for the reintroduction of the ancient symbol, the whirlpool of creation around which are arranged the hierarchies of created things emanating from it' (CHAS p. 25). Another saviour is the Buddha, since he displays the Wheel of the Law (*dharmachakra*) revolving around its still centre, often represented by Agni.

Number symbolism helps to understand better the sense of the power of aggregation conveyed by this symbol. The swastika consists of a CROSS quadrupled, because each of the four arms extending from the centre has a further extension pointing in the direction in which it rotates. Its numerical value is therefore FOUR times four, or sixteen, and is the evolving power of reality or of the universe. As a development of the created universe, it is associated with those major creating or redeeming personages mentioned above: as a development of a human reality, it may well express the furthest development of secular power, which would explain why the swastika was an attribute of Charlemagne and of Hitler. Here again we must pause to take into account the direction in which the swastika rotates. If this is in the path of the Sun, cosmic and linked to the transcendent, then it is Charlemagne's; if it is in the opposite direction, widdershins, attempting to set what is infinite and holy within the finite and the profane, then it is Hitler's swastika. Guénon explains these two opposite directions as 'the world's rotation seen from one or other of the poles' the poles in question being human and celestial, rather than the poles of the terrestrial globe.

In every case this symbolism is one of aggregation, recurring in China, where the swastika is the sign for the number ten thousand, which is the totality of beings and manifestations. It is also the earliest shape of the ideogram *fang* denoting the four quarters of space. It might well be related, too, to the numbers of the *Lo-chu*, which in any case conjure up cyclical and gyratory motion.

When taken in its spiritual sense, the swastika purely and simply replaces the wheel in Hindu iconography, for example as the emblem of the *nāgi*. It is, however, also the emblem of Ganesha, god of knowledge, and sometimes a manifestation of the Supreme Principle. Freemasons fall into a category of strictly observing cosmographical symbolism when they regard the centre of the swastika as the Pole Star and the four gammas which it comprises as the four cardinal positions of the Great Bear around it, which

might help to elucidate Guénon's remark quoted above. There are subsidiary forms of the swastika, such as the one with curved arms employed
in the Basque country and evoking with especial clarity the shape of the
double spiral (see DODECAHEDRON). Another form has each arm ending in
a KEY, a clear expression of key symbolism, the vertical axis corresponding
to priestly office and the solstices and the horizontal to kingly office and the
equinoxes (CHAE, CHOO, DANA, GRAP, GUEM, GUEC, GUET,
GUES, VARG).

sweating 'The steam bath is one of the elementary techniques for increasing "mystical heat," sweating sometimes having pre-eminent creative value;
in a number of mythological traditions man was created by God after a
period of violent sweating' (ELIC p. 334 n. 147). Steam baths in the northern regions of both Europe and Asia, as well as among the Plains Indians,
possess a similar significance.

Mastery over fire, insensibility to heat and, hence, 'mystical heat' which
makes extreme cold as bearable as furnace heat, is a magico-mystic property, which along with qualities as prestigious – ascension, magic flight and
so on – palpably translates the fact that the shaman has risen above the
human state and already shares that of the spirits (ELIC p. 335).

In ancient Central American civilizations, the steam bath bore a sacrificial meaning, the Indian offering his sweat to the Sun-god (GIRP p. 190).
His action carried with it properties both of purification and of propitiation
and has been taken up with renewed enthusiasm by contemporary Plains
Indians to defend and celebrate their cultural identity.

swing The *Brahmana* call the swing, 'the boat which sails to Heaven'
based upon a symbolism of movement which is self-explanatory, but which
Mircea Eliade believes cannot fail to suggest a shamanistic context.

Throughout southeast Asia the swing is associated with rites of fertility
and fecundation, doubtless due to the alternation of its movement, which
Chinese terminology might identify with that of YIN AND YANG.

In the Hindu ceremonies at the solstices, the *mahāvrata*, the priest offering sacrifice, stood on a swing, evoking the three breathings, *prāna*, *vyāana*
and *apāna*, which might well have been related to the disciplines of respiration practised in Yoga. This, however, is a particular application of a
wider cosmic symbolism. The motion of the swing was identified with that
of the Sun which the *Rig-Veda* itself calls 'the golden swing'. The rhythm
of the swing is the same as that of time, the daily cycle and the cycle of the
seasons at the same time as it is that of breathing. In the case of the
mahāvrata, the play of the swing suggested the beginning of the rising of
the *yang* and was generally performed in the Spring, but it was also a
symbol of love and employed in marriage rituals. This is because another
and perfectly explicit symbolism is suggested by the reciprocal motion of
the swing in a doorway.

If at the same time we observe that this doorway is a *torana* – the Sun-
gate, the entrance to and exit from the world – the rhythm is the universal
rhythm of life and death, expansion and contraction, evolution and involution. It is only natural, therefore, that the poet Kabir should compare this

rhythm with that of the SAMSĀRA: 'All beings and all worlds hang from this swing and its motion never ceases.'

In some parts of India use of swings was confined to ritual and they were reserved for communication between Earth and Heaven, and more especially for the manifestation of the Word of God.

This swinging motion, furthermore, was linked to rain-making rituals since its upward arc might foretell the height of the rice-heaps and the seat of the swing might be decorated with a *makara*, thus suggesting rule of the waters or the rainbow. The objective was always, through harmonizing with the natural cycles and by the upward arc of the swing, to call down on the world celestial harmony and blessing.

Implications of the same order most probably resided in the ancient Chinese ordeal of the seesaw, aimed, Granet tells us, to 'weigh abilities' and doubtless virtues as well (AUBJ, GRAC).

Pausanias describes a picture, *The Descent to the Underworld*, in which, among other characters from Greek mythology, he noticed Ariadne's sister, Phaedra, whose body 'swung in the air from ropes which she held in either hand'. This image of Phaedra on a swing has been viewed as the emblem of her suicide – this is disputed – and as 'the survival of a pre-Hellenic ritual, since Minoan figurines have been found designed to go on swings. The significance of the ritual of the swing is difficult to determine. Charles Picard suggests that it represents the drive towards the divine, and yet, in religions in which trees were worshipped as fertility symbols, a goddess swinging from a tree might also be significant' (Defredas in BEAG p. 295). To represent Phaedra in this way might link her with Chinese fertility symbolism and this is confirmed by Pierre Lavedan. Phaedra on the swing 'is the agrarian swing-ritual. Perhaps she was originally regarded as an Aegean goddess connected with soil-fertility' (LAVD p. 751).

On the other hand, the swing ritual celebrated at Athens was an expiatory rite for the murder of Icarios. Having disseminated the planting of vines throughout Greece, Icarios apparently gave some shepherds wine which Dionysos had presented to him. The shepherds became drunk, thought that Icarios had poisoned them and killed him. His daughter then hanged herself from the tree at the foot of which she had found his body. Dionysos struck the Athenian maidens mad and they followed her example. The oracle announced that this crisis-state was the God's vengeance for the murder of Icarios and his daughter's despair. The god felt insulted by mortals who had scorned his gift of wine. A religious ceremony was founded during which maidens swung from trees. Later, dummies took their place, then discs with faces painted upon them and models of human faces or of those of Dionysos himself. The custom was known in Rome (GRID pp. 145, 146). Phaedra's suicide may be discerned in the symbolism of death, but this would only be a prelude to her rebirth, in accordance with agrarian beliefs based upon the recurrent cycles of plant life.

Swing rituals combine two symbols. The swing raises the wind which makes the soil fertile by bringing rain, and it also brings together woman with TREE, which is itself a symbol of life. In Nepal, Estonia, India and Spain, swing rituals were 'prayers for the breezes needed for winnowing and a prayer for the fecundating power of breath' (SERP p. 312).

sword In the first place the sword is the symbol of the warrior caste, its virtues – valour – and its office – power. Power possesses a dual aspect. It is destructive, but what it destroys may well be injustice, crime and ignorance and it thereby becomes positive. As a constructive element, the sword establishes and maintains peace and justice. All these symbols apply literally to the sword as an emblem of kingship, like the sacred swords of the Japanese, Khmers and Shans, the latter still guarded by a society within the Jarai clan. When associated with the SCALES it is related especially to Justice, since it separates good from evil and strikes down the guilty.

The sword is the warrior's symbol, but it is also the symbol of 'holy war'. (This is not, as some would claim in Indian iconography, Aryan conquest except in so far as it relates to spiritual conquest.) Holy war is above all else an inner struggle, and this may also be the significance of the sword brought by Christ (Matthew 10: 34: 'I am come not to send peace, but a sword'). And it is also – in both its creative and destructive aspects – a symbol of the Word and of speech. While he preaches, the Muslim *khītab* holds a wooden sword in his hand and the Book of Revelation describes a two-edged sword in the mouth of the Word. The two edges relate to its dual powers, but may also convey the meaning of sexual dualism. The edges are either male and female, as an Arab writer explains, or else swords are ritually forged by a married couple or by a pair of smiths, in a series of operations which, as in Chinese legend, comprise a marriage.

Swords are also LIGHT and LIGHTNING. Their blades glitter and, as the Crusaders used to say, are fragments of the 'Cross of Light'. The sacred Japanese sword originated in lightning, while the Vedic sacrificial sword was Indra's thunderbolt, which would identify it with the VAJRA. Hence swords are FIRE and the angels who drove Adam and Eve out of Paradise carried flaming swords. In alchemical terms, 'the Philosopher's Sword' is the fire in the furnace. In the world of the evil spirits (*asura*) the Bodhisattva carries a flaming sword and this is the symbol of the struggle for the attainment of knowledge and liberation from desire. The sword slices through the darkness of ignorance or the knot of entanglements (Govinda). Similarly Vishnu's sword, which was a flaming sword, was the symbol of pure knowledge and of the destruction of ignorance. Its sheath was darkness and non-knowing and this, no doubt, is linked to the fact that the sacred sword of the Shans can only be drawn from its sheath by someone who is not a member of its guild of guardians at the risk of gravest danger. Purely symbolically such danger would be expressed as blinding or burning, the sword's brightness and fire being unbearable to those unqualified to handle it.

While swords may be lightning and fire, they are also Sun-rays. In the Book of Revelation the mouth from which the sword comes is in a face which shines like the Sun, the latter, in fact, being the source of all light. In China, the trigram *li*, corresponding to the Sun, also corresponds to lightning and the sword.

The reverse is also true. Swords are also related to WATER and DRAGONS. The tempering of the blade is the marriage of Fire and Water; the sword, being Fire, is drawn to the Water. The Japanese sacred sword was taken from a dragon's tail; the Shan sword was found on the bed of the Mekong River. In China, swords leaped of their own accord into the water where they changed into glittering dragons, while swords stuck into the ground caused springs to break. It is common knowledge that lightning is linked to rain-making.

Swords are also polar and axial symbols and thus the sword is identified with the upright of a pair of scales. In China, the sword was the symbol of imperial power and the weapon of the centre. The Scythians depicted the World Axis and celestial activation as a sword stuck into a mountain peak. The sword stuck into the ground, with a spring flowing from it, is not unrelated to the creative activities of Heaven (CHOO, COOE, HERS).

Swords are both thrusting and cutting weapons and, in the latter role, they are weapons of decision, instruments of active truth. From Paul Diel's ethico-biological perspective they are 'the symbol of the clarity and strength of the Spirit which dares to cut to the heart of the problem – self-centred blindness with its false, contradictory and ambivalent value-judgements' (DIES p. 98).

The sword sometimes appears to be the sole means of solving a problem and reaching a goal. But it may prove a deceptive weapon, for this is the nocturnal aspect of the symbol. The knot which has been cut but not unravelled may be tied again. King Gordias' chariot was tethered with so complicated a knot that none could untie it, although the oracle had promised the empire of Asia to whomever succeeded. With one stroke of his sword Alexander the Great sliced through the knot. He became lord of part of Asia, but lost it almost at once. Cutting through is not unravelling and is an example of short-lived surface solutions. Eagerness to achieve quick results overpowers wisdom, which looks to permanent solutions.

In Biblical tradition, the sword is one of the three scourges – war, famine and pestilence. This trilogy occupies an important place in Jeremiah (21: 7; 24: 10) and in Ezekiel (5: 12–17; 6: 11–12; 12: 16; etc.), where the sword symbolizes invasion by hostile armies.

According to Philo of Alexandria (*De Cherubim* 25–7) the sword denotes the Word and the Sun. As a symbol of solar strength it also possesses phallic significance. However, phallic symbols are not necessarily sexual, and it denotes the powers of generation.

When God drove Adam and Eve from the Garden of Eden he posted cherubim to the east, with swords which whirled like flames, to bar the way to the Tree of Life (Genesis 3: 24). The land of bliss became a forbidden land. The whirling swords threw off lightnings like those from a thunderbolt and drove the profane from the sacred spot. The flame from the sword drew a boundary like a wall of fire.

According to Philo, however, the two cherubim stand for the motion of the universe, the ceaseless movement of the whole of Heaven, or again for the two hemispheres. He provides an alternative explanation, in that the cherubim symbolize the two highest attributes of God – goodness and power. Their swords relate to the Sun which in one cosmic day makes a complete circuit of the universe. The swords also relate to reason, which simultaneously brings together the two attributes of goodness and power, since it is through reason that God is simultaneously all-good and all-powerful (*De Cherubim* 21–7).

In the Celtic world, the sword of Nuada, King of the Tuatha Dé Danann, was one of the four talismans which they had brought with them from the four mysterious islands in the north of the world from which they had come to Ireland. Whoever brandished the sword was invincible. Christian Ireland turned it into 'the Sword of Light', symbolizing the Catholic faith (OGAC 12: p. 353; CELT pp. 441–2).

In Christian tradition, swords are noble weapons in the hands of knights and Christian champions and are often mentioned in the *chansons de geste*. Roland, Olivier, Turpin, Charlemagne, Ganelon and the Emir Baligant own swords which are almost persons, each with its own name, among them Joyeuse, Durandal, Hauteclaire, Corte, Bantraine, Musaguine and so on. These names show how swords were personalized. The sword was associated with notions of light and clarity and the blade was described as glittering.

The sword sometimes denotes speech and eloquence, since tongues, like swords, are two-edged.

sycamore The sycamore, or Pharaoh's fig, was sacred in Egypt and grew as plentifully in the gardens along the banks of the Nile as in the Fields of Ialu. Souls, in the shape of birds, would perch on its branches and its shady foliage symbolized the security and protection enjoyed by the souls in the Otherworld.

In the New Testament, Zacchaeus climbed into a sycamore when the crowd prevented him from seeing Christ pass by. St Gregory the Great called it *ficus fatua* (*Moralia* 27: 29) and to climb into a sycamore means spiritually to partake of a measure of madness in abandoning all interest in earthly things and in all that is created. What Zacchaeus did might, therefore, symbolize the folly of being detached and a certain degree of contempt for public opinion verging upon anti-conformism. If the tree is a sign of vanity (*fatua*), to climb it is to trust in vain things.

symmetry The symbol of unity through the synthesis of opposites, symmetry gives expression to the reduction of the manifold to the one which is the underlying meaning of the act of creation. After a stage of expansion, the universe finds its meaning in a return to the oneness of thought – manifestation of the manifold ends by bringing into prominence the one, the one which is the beginning and the end of all things. Natural like artificial symmetry bears witness to the oneness of conception. Symmetry, however, may sometimes betray artificiality and lack of creative spirit and show a degree of conceptualization in what has to be created or done. Consequently it denotes a rationalization which constrains and may perhaps stifle the spontaneous strengths of pure intuition and imagination. Unity so obtained is a surface unity only. Instead of a synthesis of opposites it is merely duplication, a MIRROR-image. On the other hand, dissymmetry may answer a deep logic, but one hidden from over-regimented minds.

Symplegades (see also ROCK; TUNNEL) The Blue or Clashing Rocks formed an impassable barrier in the Bosporus between the Mediterranean and the Black Sea. Their movements were unpredictable and when they crashed together they would crush any ship which had dared to venture between their threatening masses. Phineus accordingly advised the Argonauts to release a dove between these moving cliffs. The bird managed to get through but, as the rocks closed behind it, they caught its tail-feathers. The Argonauts waited until the rocks parted again and went through at full speed, but the stern of their ship was damaged. Once a ship had succeeded in passing through them, the Symplegades remained parted and fixed for ever. However, severe stress is bred from enterprises which pose a deadly threat and of which the outcome is risky in the extreme. Rocks, shoals and tunnels fall into the category of the fear-inducing, as do storms and thunder. The image of moving rocks, frequent in dreams, betrays fear of failure, confrontation or difficulty, and is an expression of stress. Yet, as the legend of the Argonauts shows, this stress may be overcome by careful appreciation of the problem, by reaching its solution and by accepting the anticipated risk. Thoughtful consciousness can, in this context, overcome unconscious terror.

The Symplegades symbolize difficulties which may be overcome by courage and intelligence. Like the tunnel and so many others it is a paradoxical symbol, showing both the problem and the way in which it may be solved from within, thus displaying the symbolic dialectic so often conjured up by Mircea Eliade, the coincidence of opposites.

T

tabernacle See HOLY OF HOLIES.

table(t) The current meaning of table evokes the idea of the communal meal. Into this category would fall the Round Table of the Knights of the Grail which, prior to its reception of the Grail itself, was the image of the spiritual centre. Of course it was also reminiscent of the twelve apostles round the table at the Last Supper, as well, in shape, as of the Zodiac with its twelve signs, and in India, with the twelve Aditya, which are the twelve stations of the Sun (GUES, JILH).

If the Round Table is compared with the Chinese JADE disc, or *pi*, it may be regarded as an image of Heaven.

In Jewish tradition, 'the Lord said unto Moses, Come up unto me in the mount, and be there: and I will give thee tables of stone, and a law, and commandments which I have written; that thou mayest teach them' (Exodus 24: 12). The moral law has truly come down from Heaven and Jehovah himself has written it upon stone in the shape of the Tables of the Law. They provided the centre which united the Chosen People, the table around which the Twelve Tribes of Israel entered into communion. There were other Tables of the Law, those of Hammurabi, Ashoka, the Ancient Greeks and Romans among them, which played the same role as principal structure, cohesion and life in societies and among individuals. The Tables of the Law were to lead the Chosen People to the New Covenant at the Holy Table of the Eucharistic feast.

In Islam, God writes down the fate of mankind with his PEN upon the Guarded Tablet. Esoterically this is a symbol of universal matter upon which the Pen acts as the activating First Cause. God's tablet is like a MIRROR which existed before life began and upon which the whole course of existence may be read from all eternity. God alone knows what is written upon this holy tablet.

Ibn 'Abbās has given his name to a tradition which describes the Guarded Tablet in these terms:

Its length is the distance which separates Earth from Heaven and its breadth the distance between East and West. It is bound to the Throne and nearly touches the forehead of Isrāfil, the angel closest to the Throne. Whenever God wishes to bring into being something in His creation, the Tablet strikes Isrāfil's forehead. He looks in it and reads the will of God. . . . God glances at this tablet three hundred and sixty times a day. Whenever He looks at it, He gives life or brings death, He raises or abases, He brings honour or humiliation, He creates what He will and determines what seems good to Him.

(SOUN p. 244)

During the Middle Ages, there appeared *The Emerald Table*, a work attributed to Hermes Trismegistus, the 'Thrice-great Hermes', although its real author remains unknown. It held the teachings of Hermeticism, attributed to the god himself. Impenetrably obscure, they were to inspire the alchemists' commentaries, epitomizing their science, a science which was revealed only to the initiate. Its distillation may be epitomized as a belief that

what is below is like what is above and what is above is like what is below; through these things are performed the miracles of one thing only. And since all things are and originate from the One, through the One, all things are created by transmutation from this one thing. . . . Thou shalt separate earth from fire, the subtle from the coarse, gently and with great labour. It rises from Earth and comes down from Heaven and receives the strength of the things above and the things below. By this means thou shalt acquire the glory of the world and all darkness shall flee from thee.

This programme and these methods culminated in the alchemists' Great Work, which was not simply the transmutation of lead into gold, but of matter into spirit or, better still, making the universe divine. It was the germ of the idea, as stated elsewhere, of a development of the lithosphere into the biosphere and of the latter into the noösphere. This table was called EMERALD since this is the most precious of all stones and is 'the Flower of Heaven'. In this context the table symbolizes the revelation of a secret, but in a form understood only by the initiate.

In a completely different context, the use of funerary tablets in the Far East was one of the fundamental elements of ancestor-worship. The family shrine held the tablets of the four previous generations, while older tablets were either buried under the temple floor or stored in chests. The tablet was intended to 'anchor' the dead person's soul, since the souls of the unburied and unworshipped dead became maleficent wanderers. Granet records a proverb to the effect that 'the soul-breath (*huen*) of the dead wanders and this is why we make masks to anchor it.' This leads one to wonder whether the tablet replaced the MASK, the incision in the tablet in some way becoming the equivalent of the eye-holes in the mask which corresponded to the rebirth of the dead person beyond the grave. This is mere hypothesis, but is nonetheless attractive (GRAD, HUAV).

In the Greco-Roman world, as a result of Eastern influence, tablets were also employed to cast spells. The enemy's name, together with an appropriate curse, was inscribed upon a tablet and the latter was consecrated to the gods of the Underworld. Such tablets were generally made of lead and nailed to a tomb. The nail was supposed to pierce the enemy and the grave to close over him for ever.

The Orphic Tablets, gold leaves inscribed with liturgies of initiation and prayers to the gods, were discovered in south Italian cemeteries and relate to funeral rites. They comprise instructions to the dead on their mysterious journey through the Underworld as well as prayers to the gods of Hades. In this context the tablet is to be seen as a symbol of intercession.

taboo (see also ABSTINENCE; DEFORMITY; ONE-ARMED; ONE-EYED; ONE-LEGGED) This word of Polynesian origin symbolizes what is forbidden and untouchable.

Leviticus 11 provides a long list of clean and unclean beasts. The description of unclean derives from the primitive custom of the taboo, which displayed human submission to the divine. Although the principle of the taboo remained the same, the objects to which it applied varied from people to people.

The commentary in the *Jerusalem Bible* shows that in the Old Testament:

Behind all these regulations lie religious taboos of great antiquity. That is 'clean' which is considered worthy to approach God, 'unclean' whatever makes a person unfit for ritual worship or whatever is in fact excluded from it. The clean animals are those that can be offered to God (Genesis 7: 2), the unclean animals those which the pagans offered to their gods or which, since they were unpleasing to man, were thought displeasing to God. . . . Other regulations deal with birth (ch. 12), sexual life (ch. 15), death (21: 1, 11) . . . all these are the mysterious province of God, the master of life. A symptom of decay like leprosy (13: 1ff.), also induces impurity. Because the idea of 'cleanness' is related to worship, it is associated with the idea of sanctity. The prophets, however, will go further and insist on the cleansing of the heart . . . thus preparing the way for the teachings of Jesus . . . who releases his followers from ordinances of which only the formalities have been preserved. . . . The ancient legislation, however, establishes an ideal of moral purity, safeguarded by positive observances.

Taboos might be said to symbolize moral consciousness and be the equivalent of the psychoanalysts' censorship. The taboo evolves with the development of consciousness and changes from an act of obedience to an external order into a rational action inspired by spontaneous adherence to a law. Censorship is no longer imposed by social constraint, habit or fear nor by a submissive spirit of ritual. It is replaced by moral law of which the principles reside in the individual conscience. This cannot, however, be translated in terms of a morality individual to each. Primitive taboos gave birth to moral conscience and direct and inspire it, but it only becomes operative at the level of reason, freedom and self-denial.

Aulus Gellius (*Noctes atticae* 10: 15) lists a number of taboos binding the flamen, or priest, of Jupiter and which derived from the Romans' heritage, as similar taboos affecting Brahmans show. These taboos were designed to preserve the sacred nature of the priesthood and its mission. The purpose of some is to preserve within the priest the supernatural powers with which he was invested, while others aimed, on the contrary, to allow those powers to be exercised externally. This is why the flamens were only allowed to wear RINGS which had been broken.

In Ancient Egypt there were very many taboos constraining avoidance of or indulgence in certain classes of creature, action or gesture. They were linked to local myth and legend. Their special symbolic meaning varied with the nature of their object but the general meaning of the taboo, here as elsewhere, would seem to have derived from a symbolism either of identification with (indulgence in) or of differentiation from (avoidance of) the object. To pay honour to the cow was to assimilate with all for which the animal stood as source of life; on the other hand to avoid an unclean creature was to dissociate oneself from all the uncleanness for which it stood.

The *geasa* or taboos imposed by the druids above all depended upon the circumstances of a person's birth or baptism. Throughout his life Cùchulainn respected a taboo against hounds and the two signs by which he recognized that his death was approaching were when he ate hound's flesh and killed a 'water-hound' or otter. King Conchobar's son was forbidden to listen to the harp of Craiphtine, the harpist of the druid-god the Dagda; to hunt the birds of Mag Da Cheo; to travel with an oak yoke to his chariot; to cross the Shannon dry-shod; and lastly to stop at Da Coca's inn. He died after breaking all these taboos. Those imposed upon King Conaire were stricter still. He was never permitted on his return home to offer the right side of his chariot to the sight of Tara or the left to Bregia; he was forbidden to hunt Cerna's game, nor was he allowed to spend a night in a house in which after sunset the fire was open to and visible from the outside; when he went to the home of 'a man clad in red' he was forbidden to have three 'red men' walk in front of him; no theft was permitted in his kingdom; after sunset he was not allowed to receive the visits of lone men or lone women and he was forbidden to intervene in disputes among his servants. *Geasa* should be classified among the means employed by the druids to confine the warrior-caste to a rule of life which conformed with the religious symbolism which they respected. Dumnorix, brother of the druid Diviciacus, invoked religious reasons which prevented him accompanying Caesar to Britain. But the proconsul suspected him of treachery and had him murdered. Taboos may also be encountered in Arthurian literature (LERD pp. 54–6).

'Taboo ... is the fact of things, or places, or persons being cut off or "forbidden", because contact with them is dangerous' (ELIT p. 15). Taboos may be temporary or permanent; their powers may simultaneously attract and repel, their ambivalence deriving from the unaccustomed. By their separation and isolation from the rest of things, taboos acquire an additional and mysterious quality, as if beneath their outward appearance someone or something else lurked.

Frazer considers the existence of taboos in all human societies as

a system of animism in the act of passing into religion. The rules themselves bear the clearest traces of having originated in a doctrine of souls, and of being determined by the supposed likes and dislikes, sympathies and antipathies of the various classes of spirits towards each other. But above and behind the souls of men and animals has grown up the overshadowing conception of a powerful goddess who rules them all, so that the taboos come more and more to be viewed as a means of propitiating her rather than as merely adapted to suit the tastes of the souls themselves. Thus the standard of conduct is shifted from a natural to a supernatural basis.

(FRAG 3: p. 213)

However imaginary the dangers incurred by breaking a taboo, they are nonetheless dreaded and may even lead to death. The

imagination acts upon man as really as does gravitation, and may kill him as certainly as a dose of prussic acid. To seclude these persons from the rest of the world so that the dreaded spiritual danger shall neither reach them, not spread from them, is the object of the taboos which they have to observe. These taboos act, so to say, as electric insulators to preserve the spiritual force with which these persons are charged from suffering or inflicting harm by contact with the outer world.

(FRAG 3: p. 224)

Taboos make holy, like odd numbers, and this causes many physical infirmities or deformities to set a taboo upon the person suffering from them.

tabor Originating in the East, the tabor produces light, dancing notes, very different from the heavy, deep, mysterious beats of the DRUM. In Greek antiquity, Cybele, 'Mother of Gods and Men', was 'well-pleased with the sound of rattles and of timbrels [tabors], with the voice of flutes' ('Homeric' Hymn to Cybele). The tabor was generally used to accompany the dance, to which it beat the rhythm and symbolized carefree joy. Bacchantes in Dionysiac orgies are often depicted shaking tabors. It nevertheless takes on cosmic dimensions, recalling evolution and the music of the stars which enraptures gods and goddesses.

The sacred tabor used in Dionysiac rites probably produced a deeper note, more like the one employed by Dervishes of the Rufai and Kadiri rites to beat time to their *dhikr*. It is then similar to the East Asian shaman's tabor and, like it, partakes of drum symbolism in general, manifestation of the power of the sky-gods.

tail The Latin word *penis* means both 'tail' and male sexual organ and in many Asian and North American myths the tail plays a phallic role. It is akin to the complex symbolism embraced by the serpent.

The Turco-Mongol standard, the Tug, was made from one or several animal-tails, most frequently from horse-tails, but sometimes from those of ox or yak, and derived its symbolic properties from the fact that 'in this part of the animal's body all its strength resides' (ROUF p. 403). This notion of warlike strength or of virility likens a horse's tail set on the top of a shaft to the *penis erectus*. The Huns appear to have used this emblem and it was certainly employed by the pre-Slav Bulgars. During the reign of Tsar Boris, the Pope enjoined their catechumens to replace it with the cross. As Roux stresses, 'in this period it was felt that symbols were powerful and that the sign with which the standard was decorated should play the same part, as an object of faith, as that played by the Cross' – hence the replacement of the one by the other. This substitution of one emblem for another ought to be the mark of real inner conversion.

tamarind-tree In Thailand, Laos, Sri Lanka and India the tamarind-tree had an important role to play. Since it was regarded as the home of malefi-cent influences, its scent and shade were dangerous. Staves of tamarind-wood and swords with sheaths made from it were considered effective 'even against those who had made themselves invulnerable' since the wood had inherited the dangerous powers of the spirits which had lived in it (FRAL).

tamarisk Because the tamarisk has some of the appearance of the pine and because it is a hardy tree, in China it was a symbol of immortality. Chi-sung Tzu, 'the Master of the Rain', means 'red pine', or tamarisk. It was also called Chu-ti ('virtue of trees'), this 'virtue' or power doubtless deriving from its resin used as a longevity drug.

One might also observe that in the land of Canaan the tamarisk seems to have filled the role of 'central' tree since, before calling upon the Lord at Beersheba, Abraham planted a tamarisk (Genesis 21: 33).

In Japan, the countryside in which the tamarisk grows is reminiscent of the landscapes of the South China school of painters. Formerly the sages would say that it prophesied rain and called the tree the divine rain-maker. It is still called Sole-Three-Spring Tree, because it blossoms up to three times a year.

It conjures sweet solitude, vast empty spaces and the great plains of China, in which whole civilizations have been swallowed unnoticed by the indifference of eternity.

Tantalus In the inward struggle against empty self-inflation, the Tantalus-myth provides a strand which symbolizes the rise and fall of the individual. Tantalus was invited to banquet with the gods and was tempted to make himself their equal. When he returned the invitation, it was to feast on the good things which the gods themselves had given him. When he served up the flesh of his own children, he was cast down to Hell. His punishment fitted his crime. The water, fruit and freedom for which he longed were there before his eyes and yet he could never grasp them. 'The water which seeps away and the fruit which disappears are plainly a symbol of the powers of the imagination weakened into a state of hallucination' (DIES pp. 58–71).

His failure of judgement is that of persons who follow an undeviating course of self-infatuation. To be the equal of the gods, he tried to give them ambrosia, nectar and his own son as if they were his to give instead of being the gifts of the gods in the first place. The gods restored the son, Pelops, to life, but gave the father over to torment. Paul Diel offers a different explanation for the punishment inflicted upon Tantalus after his disastrous banquet. 'He offered the gods flesh, physical desires (man's offspring), instead of a soul made clean (God's offspring)' (DIES p. 66).

Thus the symbol displays three different aspects – a loss of the sense of reality; attributing to oneself such benefits as life, which belong to the gods alone; and offering the gods material objects instead of spiritual riches. The same mistaken relationship between mankind and the gods lies at the root of this symbol. The mortal who tries to ape god by becoming god's equal, will be punished by a keen sense of impotence. But, in simpler terms, Tantalus is also the symbol of the ceaseless craving which cannot be suppressed but remains always unsatisfied because it is in human nature never to find satisfaction. The closer the individual approaches the longed-for object the swifter it vanishes away and the greedy quest goes endlessly on.

Tao This is not the place to discuss Tao as the philosophical foundations of a clearly defined doctrine such as Taoism. Tao is not only a definite philosophical doctrine, but is also the basis of a number of philosophies, their systems differing, just as in Western philosophy notions of essence and being have given rise to several different systems.

In China Tao existed long before the Chinese laid claim to it.

In Chinese, the word *tao* means 'the way' or 'the path'. Like all things Chinese, any explanation of the meaning takes us back to *yin* and *yang*. It is, however, in no sense the sum of the two since *yin* and *yang* either alternate or coexist in a state of opposition. Any summary is an oversimplification, but Tao might be said to govern their alternation. This would explain the basic law at the root of all actual or symbolic mutation, which would allow Tao to be regarded as a principle of order ruling mental activity and the cosmos alike and without distinction. With considerable reservation it may be compared with the Stoic notion of reason, the Logos immanent in the universe as a whole and in each individual in his or her specific fate. In terms of modern physics it might also symbolize a new order born of disorder and the emergence of 'dissipative structures'.

tapir This was the Mayan symbolic equivalent of the SERPENT.

Tarot The Tarot is undoubtedly the most ancient pack of cards and sets a world of symbols working. Nor can there be any doubt that it served over the centuries as a secret channel through which occult teaching was handed down. Where it originated is hard or impossible to say, and the widest variety of theories have been advanced from the eighteenth century onwards, when Court de Gébelin became obsessed with explaining it. Whether deriving ultimately from China, India or Egypt, and whether or not it was the invention of Thoth–Hermes Trismegistus, of the Gypsies, the alchemists or the Kabbalists, or even of 'the wisest of the wise', the Tarot does, in fact, display an iconography which is clearly medieval and mixed with Christian symbols.

Colours and numbers
The Marseilles Tarot – upon which all detailed descriptions in this Dictionary are based – is the Tarot in its most traditional form of a pack of seventy-eight cards, the fifty-six minor arcana and the twenty-two major arcana. The first point to observe is that TWENTY-TWO is the number of letters in the Hebrew alphabet and that, according to the Kabbalah, they represent the universe. In the Tarot, this number comprises twenty-one numbered cards, plus the Fool. TWENTY-ONE, as THREE times SEVEN, is the number of human perfection (and it should be remembered that the twenty-first major arcanum is the World). The Fool, the extra card, as an African sage would say, is speech which gives this perfection its soul. What should be remembered particularly about the fifty-six minor arcana is that they form four groups, one might call them columns, each of fourteen cards which correspond to the four suits of the conventional pack, deriving as it does from the Tarot. It should, however, be stressed most importantly that seventy-eight, the total number of cards in the Tarot, is also the sum and hence, in the language of the occultists who devised the Tarot, 'the hidden meaning of the first twelve numbers'. This Book, outwardly no more than a pack of cards, therefore holds the added substance of the number which provides the framework of all thought and of the universe itself.

All these cards are brightly coloured and, before we study their individual meanings, we shall briefly recapitulate the symbolism of the dominant colours of the Tarot – pink ochre (flesh), blue, red and yellow. Pink ochre always denotes what is human or related to humanity (faces, bodies and buildings); the nocturnal, passive and lunar colour BLUE is the colour of secrecy, emotion, the anima and, above all, of female properties; RED is the male colour of inner strength, potential energy, manifestation of the animus, blood and the spirit; lastly, YELLOW, despite its ambivalence, is simultaneously the colour of Earth and of the Sun, of the richness of honey and harvest and of mental enlightenment in all the purity of incorruptible gold.

(For a detailed application of this symbolism see the separate entries for each of the major arcana.)

Minor arcana

The minor arcana are divided into four suits – Rods, Cups, Swords and Shekels – each of fourteen cards comprising King, Queen, Knight, Jack and ten other cards numbered from ace to ten. (The Knight has disappeared from the conventional pack and Rods have become Diamonds; Cups, Hearts; Swords, Spades; and Shekels, Clubs.) These four suits symbolize the four elements or four basic components of life.

The Rod is 'the Fire of activity, the essential point of departure' for all development (DELT 1: p. 18); but it is also 'the magic wand, the sceptre of male domination, the Father' (WIRT p. 42).

The Cup is 'celestial fecundating Water, the life of the psyche linking created beings to the godhead' (DELT 1: p. 18); but it is also the 'seer's chalice, female receptivity, the Mother' (WIRT p. 43).

The Sword is 'Air, the spirit which penetrates and gives matter form by creating that agglomeration which will become the human being' (DELT 1: p. 19); it is also 'the magician's sword, the weapon shaped like a cross and thus recalling the fecund marriage of the male and female principles; additionally the sword symbolizes a penetrative action like that of the Word or that of the Son' (WIRT p. 44). It is also interesting to see how Jung confirms this – 'the word "spade" derives from the Italian *spada*, which means "sword" or "spear". Such weapons often symbolize the penetrating, "cutting" function of the intellect' (JUNS p. 297).

Lastly, the Shekel is Earth – 'the descent below ground which is the start of every initiation (hence the importance of the cavern) and which gives the individual the support of the world in which he or she is set' (DELT 1: p. 19) – or else 'the five-sided disk, the sign of the supportive power of the will, which concentrates spiritual activity, the synthesis which returns the threefold to oneness, Trinity or Tri-Unity' (WIRT p. 43).

A detailed study might be made of the symbolism of these fifty-six cards, but this would deflect us from our purpose. It should simply be observed that they are closely linked to the major arcana and we shall find them in the first of these, the Juggler, who grasps a Rod to ensure his control over the Earth (Shekel) and over himself, while on the table stand the Cup and the Sword (miniaturized as a dagger) which symbolize the two paths, through heart or through spirit, which the individual must take in quest of initiation.

The major arcana: paths to initiation

The major arcana are paths to initiation, their stopping-places interpreted in countless different ways. They have been represented as the 'quintessence of occultism' and as lofty stages set far above the anonymous masses. They are described in detail in this dictionary under their respective names:

I: the Juggler – II: the Female Pope – III: the Empress – IV: the Emperor – V: the Pope – VI: the Lovers – VII: the Chariot – VIII: Justice – IX: the Hermit – X: the Wheel of Fortune – XI: Necessity – XII: the Hanging Man

– XIII: nameless arcanum (Death) – XIV: Temperance – XV: the Devil –
XVI: the Tower – XVII: the Star – XVIII: the Moon – XIX: the Sun – XX:
Judgement – XXI: the World – unnumbered: the Fool.

Groups of three and groups of seven
Omitting the Fool, which is unnumbered, there are twenty-one arcana which
may be divided either into seven groups of three or into three groups of
seven. Within each group of three 'the lowest number is active and the
highest number is as emphatically passive, while the middle number is intermediary, active in relation to the highest, passive to the lowest. The
lowest corresponds to the spirit, the middle to the soul and the highest to
the flesh' (WIRT p. 68). The seven groups of three comprise: the Juggler
(I), the Female Pope (II) and the Empress (III); the Emperor (IV), the
Pope (V) and the Lovers (VI); the Chariot (VII), Justice (VIII) and the
Hermit (IX); and so on. The same separate aspects of spirit, soul and flesh
are to be found in the three groups of seven: from Juggler (I) to Chariot
(VII) the properties of the spirit; from Justice (VIII) to Temperance (XIV),
those of the soul; and from the Devil (XV) to the World (XXI), those of
the flesh.

The same card may thus be interpreted as spirit and soul, or as soul and
flesh, according to its place in the chosen grouping and according to the
level of analysis. For example, the Empress is flesh in the first group of
three and spirit in the first group of seven. Relationships alter within the
different groups. All keys of interpretation open up different aspects of the
same card and none possesses fixed and absolute meaning. It is a perpetually mobile system of relationships demanding the greatest subtlety of
interpretation.

Even within each group of seven 'the first three arcana oppose the second
three and it is only the seventh which makes a unity of the whole' (WIRT
p. 77), thus validating the synthesizing significance of the Chariot (VII),
Temperance (XIV) and the World (XXI) – the predominance of the will in
the world of the spirit (VII), of balance in that of the soul (XIV) and
ceaseless movement in the world of the flesh (XXI).

Relationship with the Zodiac and the planets
This grouping in threes may be compared with the concept in astrology
whereby the wheel of the ZODIAC in its three successive positions – birth
(or start of evolution), zenith and fall (or involution) – stands for the four
elements. The signs of Fire, Earth, Air and Water begin with Aries, Taurus,
Gemini and Cancer, reach their zenith in Leo, Virgo, Libra and Scorpio
and decline and fall in Sagittarius, Capricorn, Aquarius and Pisces. When
the Tarot is divided into groups of three, the cards on which the symbols of the Zodiac are clearly marked have a corresponding status. The
Archer (Sagittarius) in the Lovers (VI) is in decline, the Scales (Libra) of
Justice (VIII) and the Lion (Leo) of Strength (XI) are both at their zenith,
while the Twins (Gemini) of the Sun (XIX) are at the beginning of their
development.

However, the further one proceeds with the reconstruction of an astrological Tarot, the more sharply divided the authorities become. There are
as many different correspondences between the arcana and the planets and

the Zodiac as there are specialists in the study of the Tarot. Imagination has free rein in this field. For example, Oswald Wirth equates the Juggler with Mercury, while Fomalhaut regards it as the Sun, Terestchenko as Neptune and so on. Without claiming to have made a complete list, one can often discover at least a dozen different and often contradictory astrological correspondences for some cards. Faced by a chaotic mass of hypotheses, Volguine has suggested (*L'Utilisation du Tarot en astrologie judiciaire*, Paris, 1933) that the major arcana should be made to correspond to the astrological Houses, rather than to the planets and signs, since each division stands for a well-defined area. Thus the Juggler and Death are linked to the First House; the Female Pope and Temperance to the Second House and so on. The arcana of the Tarot may also be taken in pairs. In their pairing each displays a more or less obvious similarity of opposites, the link between the cards and the astrological Houses providing the rationale for this pairing.

Kabbalistic interpretation
Kabbalists who have studied the Tarot have been struck by several points. There are the same number of major arcana as there are letters in the Hebrew alphabet and this number is 'precisely the same as the twenty-two paths of wisdom, the channels between the ten SEFIROT, which link together these sublime metaphysical principles of the Jewish Kabbala' (RIJT p. 198). Mystic attributes of God, the *sefirot* themselves evolved 'in the shape of groups of three, in each of which trinities two opposites are linked by an intermediate' (MARD p. 154). Moreover, they agree with the symbolic meaning of the cards – the Crown of the *sefirot* matches the Juggler, First Cause from which all things proceed; the Female Pope matches Wisdom; the Empress, the Understanding; the Emperor, Magnificence and Mercy; the Pope, Fortitude or Judgement; the Lovers, Beauty; the Chariot, Victory; Justice, Splendour; the Hermit, the Foundation; and the Wheel of Fortune, 'representing the whirlpool of involution', the Kingdom (WIRT pp. 71–3). As there are correspondences between all the cards, this has provided the foundations for building a complete Kabbalistic symbolism for the Tarot since 'in the chain of being, everything is magically contained in everything' (SCHS p. 122).

Anthropocentrism in the Tarot
Provided that one or two symbolic traces can be found to link the Tarot to such or such a teaching, alchemy, magic or even Freemasonry has been used to provide the key to its interpretation, and to these passing reference is made in the articles devoted to each of the major arcana. However, the Tarot remains predominantly anthropocentric and the figures which it comprises have psychological and cosmic meaning. They relate to humanity, the world around it and the individuals making it up, and even when human beings are not depicted, as in the Wheel of Fortune (X) and the Moon (XVIII), the animals depicted are caricatures of humans.

If the symbolism of the Tarot is now to be studied from this angle, the cards must be arranged either in a circle in which the Fool is placed between the Juggler and the World, or in two rows, the first from I to XI and the second in the opposite direction from XII to the Fool. It will be clearly seen that the vertical axis of the Tarot links arcana VI and XVII, the

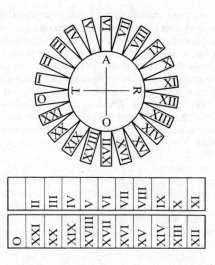

II	III	IV	V	VI	VII	VIII	IX	X	XI

O	XXI	XX	XIX	XVIII	XVII	XVI	XV	XIV	XIII	XII

Lovers and the Star, the one being the emotions and the other hope, as if these two properties were those around which all the rest revolved.

Pathway to the attainment of wisdom
The individual stands alone facing the world and seeking the path of wisdom by acquiring a dual mastery – that of the external world and that of the universe within. Such mastery is the product of a gradual initiation which itself makes a distinction between two paths, two methods or two main phases, predominantly active or passive, solar or lunar:

The first is based upon the principle of developing individual initiative and upon reason and will-power. It suits the wise person who always retains full self-control and relies only upon the resources of his or her own personality, without recourse to the aid of outside influences. The other is completely different and takes a course entirely opposite to the first. Far from developing what is in the self and *giving* in proportion to the expansion of the innermost energies, the mystic sets his or her sights upon *receiving* to the uttermost extent of an especially developed receptivity.

(WIRT p. 49)

Thus the rational and the mystical, like male and female, contrast and complement one another. Necessity (XI) and the Hanging Man (XII) are merely two aspects of the same symbol – the external strength of Necessity and the completely internalized strength of the Hanging Man. In the same sense, too, the Juggler (I) in his quest for initiation encounters the Female Pope (II) who holds all the secrets of the universe, but to read her book requires the intellect of the Empress (III) and of the Emperor (IV). Initiation takes effect with the Pope (V) and the individual succeeds in raising him- or herself through the series of ordeals presented by the other cards, the first being the strain imposed by the Lovers (VI), lying at the centre of the first row of cards, since nothing can be achieved without emotional drive. Having made this choice, with all that it entails, the driver of the Chariot (VII) is in danger of overstepping his powers and becoming proud of his own strength, but Justice (VIII) is a reminder of the fundamental law of balance. Strong in his ideals, he sets out as the Hermit (IX) into the world, but the more the Hermit seeks the truth, the more he passes judgement and sets in motion the Wheel of Fortune (X) which allots to each his due according to inward state and longing for personal development. Necessity (XI) alone can halt the Wheel of Fortune. At the end of this first pathway the initiate has discovered the object of his or her quest – Necessity wears the same headdress as the Juggler, the ribbon wreathed in the symbol of infinity.

The mystical phase

With the Hanging Man (XII) at the beginning of the second row, the initiate enters an inverted world in which physical means have become ineffective. This is the passive, mystic pathway. The anonymous thirteenth arcanum, a red card, the colour of blood and of fire which destroys and burns away illusion, shows us that Death is far from being the end, but rather a beginning. However, we must not force the pace of the new life held out to us – the demands of Temperance (XIV) are the same as those of Justice (VIII) and it is only when one is aware of one's own limitations and has acquired an inner balance that one can face the Devil (XV). He is the symbol of the deadliest of temptations, those which hold out occult powers matching the manifest powers of God, but which weave as many strands linking us to the Lord of Hell. Unfortunately, whatever mankind builds is doomed to fall like the shattered Tower (XVI). Henceforth all that remains for the individual is the Star (XVII) of Venus, the dual star of hope and of love, the centre of the second row of cards and the foundation of the vertical axis of the Tarot. Just as the Moon is the stars' companion in the physical sky, so in the symbolic universe of the Tarot, the Moon (XVIII) follows the Star. She bears the properties of the past, the wealth of the unconscious, the imaginary realm from which dreams recharge their strength. Without the joint strength of Star and Moon, we should be unable to face the Sun's (XIX) bright light and heat. This is the arcanum of total enlightenment and under it the individual is for the first time no longer alone. Henceforth he or she will be judged in his or her fullness, as a person and by his or her deeds. In the sight of the angel of Judgement (XX), the child will symbolize the witness. The individual has now reached the acme of initiation and the World (XXI) is there only as the synthesis of what has been gained. The individual 'has succeeded in transmuting the phenomenal world into a psychic property, that is to say, in alchemical terms, that setting out from the *materia prima* of the Juggler he has finished with pure gold' (DELT 11: p. 488).

Thus, while the first path of initiation ended with Necessity (XI), 'prerogative of the Juggler who has realized his plans' (WIRT p. 53), the second path, the path of the mystic, sets out from the Hanging Man (XII) and takes us to the Fool 'whose passivity here partakes of the sublime' (WIRT p. 55). This is the individual who, having gained all that the world can offer, realizes that this possession is worthless and consequently returns to the unknown and unknowable which both precedes and follows our lives. Faced by this twofold barrier, all that we can do is to continue our search after having at last admitted in our minds and accepted in our physical pains that there is a natural difference between ourselves and God. The only possible relationship with him resides in hope, self-surrender and love. This is the ultimate lesson of the Tarot if conceived as a path of initiation.

Archetypes in the Tarot
The two paths which we have marked out are, however, open to other interpretations. Jung distinguishes the two aspects of the individual's struggle against others and against him- or herself. There is the solar path of extraversion and action, of practical and theoretical reflection upon rational motivation. And then there is the lunar path of introversion, of meditation and intuition in which motivations are all-embracingly dictated by the senses and the imagination. The Tarot also appears to contain a number of basic archetypes – the mother (the Female Pope, the Empress, Judgement); the horse (Chariot); the old man (Emperor, Pope, Hermit, Judgement); the wheel (Wheel of Fortune); Death; the Devil; the house or tower (Tower, Moon); the bird (Star, World); the virgin, the Spring; the star (Star); the Moon; the Sun: the twins (Devil, Sun); the wing (Lover, Temperance, Devil, Judgement, World); the flame (Tower) . . .

Whatever validity these different points of view may possess, we should never forget that the Tarot never submits to any one attempt to systematize it and it always retains something which escapes our grasp. Its fortune-telling aspect is just as evasive. We shall make no attempt to cover these other aspects in this article since their permutations are as endless as their explanations. Although they may be based upon the symbols which we have attempted to clarify, they demand training of the imagination gained only from long practice and a strong measure of scepticism.

tattooing (see also BLUE; SEAL (ARTEFACT)) In Ancient China, tattooing appears to have possessed some importance. Its symbolism is hinted at by the original meaning of the ideogram *wen*, which denoted simple written characters as well as Confucian political wisdom. *Wen* means 'lines which cross one another [which could relate it to weaving], veins, wrinkles and drawings'. In some pictures of a tattooed man we are faced by a permanent prayer to and identification with the heavenly powers, at the same time as a basic means of communication with them. Such is the most generalized meaning of tattooing bestowed in consequence of a rite of initiation which allows this communication to take place. At the same time, this initiation is a rite of admission into a social group and the tattoo is the permanent mark of that initiation, the badge of the tribe.

All in all tattooing belongs among symbols of identification and is interfused with all their magic and mystic potency. Identification always carries a double meaning: it tends to invest the individual concerned with the properties and strength of the creature or thing to which that person is assimilated and, at the same time, to immunize the latter against its potential power to cause harm. This is why tattoos depict dangerous creatures such as serpents or scorpions, or animals which are symbols of fertility, such as bulls, or of power, such as lions, and so on. Identification also carries the sense of surrender or even of consecration to whatever the tattoo symbolically depicts. It then becomes a badge of fealty.

Taurus (21 April–20 May) The second sign of the Zodiac is located between the vernal equinox and the Summer solstice and is the symbol of a vast capacity for hard work and of all the natural instincts, especially those of preservation, sensuality and an exaggerated propensity for pleasure. In astrological terms, this sign is ruled by Venus, in other words this quarter of the sky stands in close and perfect harmony with the planet concerned. Associated with the sign of Taurus is the symbolism of *materia prima*, the primeval substance which may be identified with the element Earth and the Earth Mother. While Aries, the hypervirile ram, leaping forwards and upwards with its massive horns and thick-boned skull, is the dynamic, embodying the element of primeval fire, Taurus, the bull, may be seen as the static of a life-bearing mass. This would be characterized by a powerful, deep-bosomed creature, big-bellied and wide-spreading, in which the predominant spirit would be one of weight, heaviness and thickness, slow-moving, stable, solid, concentrated and fixed. This hyperfemale sign accumulates properties which are clearly terrestrial and harmonize with lush green patures. In the music of the spheres Taurus' score reads like a Dionysiac anthem in praise of Venus, Venus Genetrix, a mass of pulsating flesh and rich red blood throbbing with the emanations of the spirit of Earth, an anthem exalting the Earth Mother in all her lunar fullness. Taurus bestows an animal nature, temperamentally linked to the instincts and especially acute in sensory perceptions in a world of smell, taste, touch, seeing and hearing. To live in it is to surrender to a craving for the fruits of the Earth and the enchantments of alcohol. In Taureans, the lust for life is rooted in a warm-hearted temperament and strong, keen-edged vitality. Its acquisitive drives may be satisfied by a life of pleasure and sexual abandon as easily as in that of the workaholic.

tea An aesthetic, however perfect, is not the sole source of the wonderful Japanese tea ceremony, although economy of setting, gesture and means might make it seem an inimitable cult of the beautiful. However, the Taoists say that the first tea ceremony was Yin-hi's offering of a cup to Lao Tzu when the latter presented him with the *Tao Te Ching*. The disciples of Zen add that the first tea-pot sprang from the Bodhidharma's eye-lids. He cut them off and cast them aside to prevent drowsiness during meditation and this is why monks use tea for the same purpose of keeping themselves awake.

Although the ceremony itself bears all the marks of communal ritual and probably was just this – it is claimed that it was instituted to civilize behaviour, control the passions, appease warlike hatred and bring peace – its main characteristic is its austerity, the economy of action aimed at depersonalizing the participants. As in all the arts of Zen, the goal at which it aims is the elimination of the ego from the action, which is achieved through its own nature or in emptiness. Lastly, tea is the symbol of the Being in which the Self participates. That participation is not in the void of sleep, but in the intense and active wakefulness of silent meditation (OGRJ, OKAT).

tear The teardrop evaporates and dies after bearing witness to the grief or pleading of which it is a symbol. Tears have often been compared with PEARLS or drops of AMBER into which the tears of the daughters of Meleager and the Heliads, the daughters of the Sun, were changed. The tears of the child-victims of their rain-making sacrifices were regarded by the Aztecs as symbols of the rain-water they were intended to promote.

teeth (see also DECAPITATION) The Bambara draw a correspondence between teeth and eyes, both being similarly associated with concepts of intellect and the universe.

The Bambara separate the teeth into three groups – incisors, canines and molars – with different symbolic functions. 'The incisors stand for fame and renown. They appear in the foreground when the lips are parted in laughter and hence are also a sign of happiness and are regarded as giving speech a cheerful and youthful attraction.' The canines are a sign of hard work as well as of relentlessness and of hatred. The molars, 'symbols of protection', are a sign of endurance and perseverance and 'those with strong molars are regarded as sticking obstinately to their opinions' (ZAHB p. 22).

Toothlessness is the sign of the loss of youth and of the loss of the strength both to attack and to defend oneself: it is a symbol of frustration, castration and bankruptcy. It is the loss of the life force, since healthy, well-furnished jaws are evidence of manly strength and self-confidence.

In Vedic tradition, the teeth are endowed with much the same significance, and especially the canines, of which the aggressive strength needs to be controlled.

In Ireland, literary sources show the wisdom tooth being used in a spell known as the *teinm laegda*, or poetic enlightenment. The second-sighted bard or hero placed his thumb on his wisdom tooth, bit it, sang a verse and offered sacrifice to the gods.

Persian love-poetry is like that of Europe in comparing the teeth with pearls or with the fixed stars, as well as with hail-stones (HUAS p. 61).

Teeth are the instruments whereby their owner takes possession of something and even assimilates it. They are millstones which grind to provide a food for the desires.

Teeth symbolize the power of chewing and the aggressiveness which originates from the promptings of physical desire. Dragon's teeth represent the aggressiveness of a perverted lust for domination which grinds to destruction. Iron men sprang up when the dragon's teeth were sown. These were men whose souls were so hardened by their belief in their predestination to power that they fought to the death among themselves to sate their ambitions.

(DIES p. 176)

The ambitious have long teeth. This means of assimilation is, however, a symbol of perfection, since what is eaten tends to be heavenly food. 'The teeth denote the dividing of the perfect nourishment given to us. For each individual Being divides and multiplies by a provident faculty the unified conception given to it by the more Divine Order, in proportion necessary for the instruction of the inferior' (PSEH p. 46).

Temperance   Temperance means moderation, proportion and the mastery of desire. VIOLET is the colour of moderation, a colour combination of red and blue, the dominant colours of the Tarot card. Violet is also the marriage of the active and the passive, symbolizing the invisible, hidden mystery of creation.

The fourteenth major arcanum of the Tarot, originating in NECESSITY (XI) and complementing JUSTICE (VIII), brings us face to face with the fourth cardinal virtue. It is interpreted in many different ways. 'Temperance, or the Two Urns, or the Solar Genius, is an expression of involution' (Enel); 'of retribution' (Jolivet-Castelot); 'of restraint and pause' (Poinsot); 'of the opportune or inopportune event' (Bost); 'of action and effort, of using one's opportunities, management, loss of lawsuits, hostility of traditional powers' (Holt-Wheeler); 'of serenity and an easy-going nature, pliancy able to suit the action to the occasion, or indifference, lack of personality, a tendency to drift with the stream and to follow prejudice and fashion' (Wirth). In astrology, it corresponds to the Second House since this arcanum in some sense complements the Female Pope.

The card should, however, be closely studied. It depicts a woman with BLUE hair in a long skirt, part blue, part RED, who holds a blue urn in her left hand from which she pours a colourless liquid into a red urn held at a lower level in her right hand. 'One might be tempted to regard this attitude as an allusion to the processes of distillation, purification and the development of matter' (RIJT p. 214) . . . 'since this card is generally held to be a symbol of alchemy. Dead and putrefied matter, as the thirteenth arcanum reminds us, is subjected to ablution which turns it from black to grey and finally from grey to white, marking the successful conclusion of the first stage of the Great Work' (WIRT p. 196). This is the penetration of matter by the spirit, symbol of all spiritual transfusions. On the physical plane, the winged genius actualizes and embodies the works of Justice, but creates nothing by its own means, Temperance being content to decant the undulating liquid from one receptacle to the other without losing a drop of what remains the same throughout. Only the urn changes shape and colour. As the article on the SERPENT observes, may this not be the symbol 'of the dogma of reincarnation or the transmigration of souls? One has only to recall that in Ancient Greece, the act of pouring liquid from one urn into another was taken as the synonym of metempsychosis' (RIJT p. 249). Thus the winged figure of Temperance, standing between Death (XIII) and the Devil (XV), reminds us of the great law of the perpetual circulation of life-fluids on the cosmic plane and, on the psychological plane, of the need for that difficult internal balance which must be preserved between the two poles of our being, Heaven and Earth, represented by the halves of blue and red. If the liquid pouring from one urn to the other undulates in defiance of the laws of physics, this is because the serpent has cropped up again, as symbol of the perpetual passage from one world to the other.

tempest   See STORM.

temple   Temples reflect the world of the godhead built in the image which mortals create of the divine – the ebullience of life in Hindu temples, the moderation of the temples on the Acropolis, the wisdom and love in Christian churches and the marriage of Heaven and Earth in Muslim mosques. They are, in some sense, earthly copies of heavenly archetypes, at the same time as being cosmic images. Cosmology and theology are thus as deeply rooted in the human spirit as they are in the work which human hands dedicated to the gods. The universe itself has been conceived as a temple and mystics have made the human soul the temple of the Holy Ghost.

The very word 'temple' is linked to watching the movement of the stars. '*Templum* originally meant that quarter of the sky which the Roman augur marked out with his staff and in which he watched either natural phenomena or the flight of birds. It then came to mean the place or sacred building from which this watching of the sky was practised' (CHAS p. 455). Similarly, the Greek word *temenos*, deriving from the same Indo-European root, *tem* (to cut, mark out or share), 'meant the place set aside for the gods, the sacred enclosure around the shrine and a spot which could not be touched.'

Temples are God's earthly dwelling, the place of the Real Presence. All temples, too, lie directly below the Heavenly Palace and hence at the CENTRE of the world. The temples at Jerusalem, Delphi, Angkor, Borobudur, in Central America and so on are centres of the world from which space originates and which in turn epitomize space. Hence the importance of orientation which is, throughout the world, one of the main elements in temple-building.

Temples are built to divine plans. The design of the Temple at Jerusalem was revealed to David, while, until comparatively recently, Cambodians claimed Indra himself and Vishvakarma as architects of Angkor Wat. The Chaolin monastery of the Chinese secret societies was built by a celestial genius, Ta Tzun Chen, as the Heavenly Jerusalem was constructed by the Angel with the Golden Reed. Temples are crystallizations of celestial activity, as is shown in Hindu building rites and methods. The quadrangular ground plan, the 'squaring-up' of the temple, is obtained by means of a circle radiating from the pin of a dial which casts the shadow which determines the four points of the compass – setting the bounds of space and time. An Ancient Egyptian inscription proclaimed that this temple was like Heaven in every part.

Hindu or Buddhist temples have the horizontal structure of the MANDALA, which is that of the cosmos. Christian and Muslim domes have the hierarchical structure of the three worlds. From India to Angkor and to Java replicas have been erected of Mount Meru, which is both the AXIS and the centre of the world. In the Far East, the Buddhist temple reflects the celestial bliss of the Paradise of Amida. Architectural peculiarities are sometimes needed in order to accept the influence of Heaven. This poured into the Chinese Temple of Heaven through a hole in the roof which was round, like Heaven itself. T'ang the Victorious caused a drought by setting over the altar of Earth a roof which prevented the influence of Heaven from passing through.

While epitomizing the macrocosm, temples are also images of the microcosm, being simultaneously both the world itself and the human individual. The body is 'the temple of the Holy Ghost' (1 Corinthians 6: 9). The opposite is also true – the temple is the body of the Divine Person, with Christ's body outstretched upon the cruciform ground plan of the church, the altar his heart.

The individual's approach to the temple is always a symbol of the spiritual made actual – the Christian by sharing in the Redemption as he or she approaches the altar, the Hindu returning to the centre of being and to the entrance to a hierarchy of higher levels of existence through CIRCUMAMBULA-TION. Since it is the place to which the godhead descends and where it is active, the temple is the way along which the individual can rise to the level of the godhead (BURA, BENA, ALMT, GRAD, KRAT, SECA; see also TOWER; ZIGGURAT).

The Temple which King Solomon built for the Lord is a model of symbolic GEOMETRY. It measured sixty cubits in length, twenty in breadth and thirty in height. The porch standing in front of the Temple was ten cubits deep and twenty broad in relation to the breadth of the Temple itself (1 Kings 6: 3). The Sanctuary was designed as the resting-place of the Ark of the Covenant and its internal dimensions formed a cube twenty cubits long, twenty broad and twenty high (1 Kings 6: 20). The two cherubim, carved from wild olive-wood, which stood in the Sanctuary were ten cubits high and each of their wings measured five cubits and they stood wing to wing (1 Kings 6: 23). Thus the internal dimensions of the HOLY OF HOLIES displays a perfect CUBE, with the altar of acacia-wood apparently a square five cubits long and five broad (Exodus 27: 1). Square and double square dimensions, so popular in the Old Testament, recur in many Romanesque churches, while Solomon's Temple is often cited as a model in manuscripts concerning the medieval guilds. Its cosmic symbolism is obvious. Josephus and Philo are in agreement in demonstrating that the Temple stands for the cosmos and that every object within it had its appointed place. Philo went on to state that the Altar of Incense stood for thanksgiving which proclaimed the perfect goodness of God in his heaven. The seven-branched CANDLESTICK stood for the seven planets, while the Table of Shewbread represented thanksgiving for the operation of the earthly order, the twelve shewbreads themselves symbolizing the twelve months of the year. The Ark of the Covenant was placed below the wings of the cherubim: it symbolized the comprehensible. The Temple's foundation-stone possessed cosmic properties and was to be identified with the BETHEL stone on which Jacob's head rested when he dreamed that the Heavens opened (Genesis 35: 9). This stone was the centre of the world, the point at which Heaven entered into communion with Earth. In his vision (ch. 40–2), Ezekiel gives us the measurements of the new Temple.

Solomon's was not the only temple to possess cosmic symbolism. As Schwaller von Lubicz confirms, all true temples possess this quality. The Ancient Egyptian temple-tradition was handed down, via the temple which Solomon built to the Lord, to the Romanesque church-builders. St Peter Damian was to say that churches offer a figure of the world. Churches built of stone present an image of the vast City of God of which St Augustine wrote, and which comprises all Christian people, just as the building comprises a mass of individual stones.

(DAVR pp. 183–4)

Celtic proto-historic archeology from time to time unearths the remains of wooden cult-buildings as, for example, the one at Libenice in Bohemia, but it was not until the Roman occupation of Gaul and Britain that what may properly be called temples made their appearance. The Celts, in fact, used wood as their main building material and only constructed in stone under their conquerors' influence. Some of these temples were of considerable size and built to ground plans which varied from the rectangular to the square and, very occasionally, the circular. Their symbolism in each instance is that of the geometric figure to which they were built, the square being Earth and the circle Heaven. However, a very large number of small temples, or *fana*, were to be found in remote or isolated places in Gaul. These most certainly carried on the tradition and the symbolism of the *nemeton*, or SANCTUARY, or the forest-clearing which was the real temple of pre-Christian Celtic worship (GREA *passim*; see also CROSSROADS).

Drawing upon HIRAM and Solomon's Temple, Freemasons have built up an elaborate symbolism on this topic. The temple 'may be regarded as a symbolic image of mankind and the World – to acquire knowledge of the heavenly Temple one has to rebuild within oneself and to defend this temple through the life of the spirit.' The temple's very orientation, with its entry to the West and the chair of the Worshipful Master at the east, as in a cathedral, is itself a symbol:

The Temple symbolizes the way which runs from West to East, that is towards the LIGHT. It is a holy and symbolic place. When asked its measurements, a Mason must always reply that its length runs from west to east, its breadth from north to south and its height from the nadir to the zenith. Since the Temple is an image of the cosmos, it cannot be measured. The ceiling of the Temple is patterned like the starry skies, standing for the night sky displaying its multitudes of stars. At the east end, behind the Worshipful Master's chair, is to be seen the Divine Light, the TRIANGLE with an eye in its centre.

(HUFT pp. 42, 158)

ten   Ten was the number of the Pythagorean TETRAKTYS, the sum of the first four digits $(1 + 2 + 3 + 4)$. It possesses a sense of totality, of fulfilment and that of a return to oneness after the evolution of the cycle of the first nine digits. The Pythagoreans regarded ten as the holiest of numbers. It was the symbol of universal creation, upon which they took their oaths, as 'the Tetraktys from which eternal Nature springs and in which it is rooted' (MONA p. 26). If all springs from ten and all returns to it, it is therefore also an image of totality in motion.

It will be noted that ten provides a binary formula similar to TWO in computers, thus confirming its significance as the source of the multiple and manifest as well as its part in finding the sum of things. Furthermore, it is precisely as a multiple or double that it was known in China, ten being, above all, the double of FIVE, emphasizing the duality of being. Five was already a number which found the sum of things and ten displayed the internal duality of all the elements making up five. For example, in the *Hong-hui* there are 5×2 Ancestors, to which the 5×2 lodges correspond – the whole being represented in the *teu* by 5×2 Banners. The ten 'celestial shoots' which were used to measure time are the equivalents, pair by pair, of the five Chinese ELEMENTS. Thus, while it symbolized a group, ten also carried with it the concept of its basic duality, the principle of motion.

In these circumstances, it is hardly surprising that ten should be an expression of death as well as of life, since their alternation, or rather their co-existence, is linked to this duality. Thus the Maya regarded the tenth day as unlucky, since it belonged to the death-god (THOH). Nor should it be forgotten that it followed the ninth day, the day of disease.

Quite the opposite is true of the Bambara – according to their calculations ten is the luckiest number since it is the sum of the first four digits, marking the four stages of creation, and is the sum of six and four, both lucky numbers possessing fundamental significance. Ten is an emblem of fertility, an attribute and one of the names of the water-god, Faro (DIEB). All this is quite understandable within the logic of symbols although it might be quite incompatible with purely conceptual logic.

Ten, as the number which sums up all things, finds its place in the Ten Commandments, symbolizing the fulfilment of the Law in a decalogue which is a single commandment.

tent The tent is the abode of the desert nomad. When the Lord dwelt with the Children of Israel, a tent was set aside for him, which was to become the prototype of the TEMPLE, the tabernacle of the sanctuary. Tents also possess cosmic significance as images of the vault of Heaven. Tents symbolize the presence of Heaven upon Earth and of the protecting Father. 'The Turko-Tatars, like a number of other peoples, imagine the sky as a tent; the Milky Way is the "seam"; the stars, the "holes" for light' (ELIC p. 260).

The Labrador hunters had a custom of particular significance. A band of birch-bark was used to tie the tops of four or eight ten-foot poles stuck in a rough circle in the ground and forming a lean-to into which their shaman crawled to summon the spirits. Outside, his congregation accompanied the shaman's chanting by beating drums. Soon the lean-to would begin to sway as the spirits came, the shaman passing on their messages by shouting out (MULR p. 256). This custom may be compared with that of the 'music rooms' of the men's societies among the Bamileke in Cameroon and with the daily excursions of the sacred musicians during the New Year ceremonies of the Piaroa Indians.

The symbolism remains constant – tents are places to which the godhead is summoned to make itself manifest.

The cosmic tent of the shamans and central Asian nomads, its top touching the Pole Star, gave rise to the mandala as well as to the architectural symbolism of the Buddhist STUPA and *chörten*. Amongst other things, these correspond to the stacking up of the five elements and the hidden meeting points of the subtle channels of the human body.

In the practices of Vajrayāna, it would seem that the tent came from the unsullied Void, to which it will return, as dazzling as it is insubstantial. It announces the complete lack of its own essence in the intrinsic nature of all beings and all things.

Henri Corbin stresses the similarity between the esoteric structure of Ancient Iran and the cosmic tent of which the Imam is the POLE. The angel of the cosmic north, a secretion of his own light, Sraosha watched from the summit of the cosmos, spreading like a tent over the central pillar (see COLUMN) linked to the Pole. This underlines the relationship between what we know of Zoroastrianism and the concepts of the Pole in Taoism. For the latter, the region of the Pole Star was the abode of an angel corresponding to the angel in the Avesta.

In India, the fate of the word 'tent' is noteworthy. *Mandapa*, which originally meant no more than a rough shelter, came to be an element indissolubly linked to the Hindu temple.

Alchemy did not fail to adopt the tent. The adept knelt before it in prayer, with arms outstretched, and in adoration, while the Great Work reached its fulfilment. This stresses the mystical aspects of the Great Work. Through the self-denial imposed by his quest for the Philosopher's Stone, the adept attained to a spiritual universe comparable with that of the religious mystic who transforms his being through the practices of prayer and contemplation. It was a matter of a state of ultimate ecstasy, mystic ecstasy being regarded as the final stage of transmutation.

Well pegged to the ground, tents are miracles of balance between the flow of cosmic energy and the currents of Earth-forces. They are perfect examples of the formula 'Nirvana = *samsāra*'. Their empty space and the office they fill as the nomad's companion rightly designate them as one of the symbols of EMPTINESS. Tents are closely connected with Jehovah's appearances in the Wilderness. 'Who coverest [himself] with light as with a garment: who stretchest out the the heavens like a [tent]' (Psalm 104: 2); 'Also can any understand the spreadings of the clouds, or the noise of his tabernacle [tent]' (Job 36: 29).

The Ark of the Covenant inside the tabernacle (tent), which is the meeting-place with the godhead, was not, Louis Bouhier believes, a coffer but a 'throne which was deliberately kept empty'. In so far as the mystery of the God's presence (*shekinah*) is concerned, the word itself is derived from *schakan*, meaning 'to live as it were in a tent'.

The legend of Tristan and Isolde also makes use of a tent. Under the rich awning raised over the deck of the ship which carried the betrothed of King Mark of Cornwall, the lovers met and drank the love-philtre instead of the death-draught.

ten thousand This number symbolizes fulfilment, fertility and plenty. St Irenaeus (*Adversus Haereses* 5: 33, 3), when describing the time of the Messiah, alludes to the teaching of Christ that then vines will each bear ten thousand branches, each branch will bear ten thousand shoots, each shoot will bear ten thousand bunches of grapes, each bunch will bear ten thousand grapes and each grape provide twenty-five measures of wine. Every grain of corn sown will give ten thousand grains.

Such fertility was to be the feature of Christ's kingdom before the end of time and symbolizes a renewal of the Earth. During this period, the righteous will be given transfigured bodies, while continuing to live on this earthly plane. The number, ten thousand, is the sum of the renewal of the Earth and of its human inhabitants, as if it were a fresh creation (DANT p. 382).

In China, the phrase 'ten thousand beings', or rather 'ten thousand', denoted totality and was the symbol of something so large that no name could be given to it. The number was meant to stand for the totality of beings, essences and things upon Earth.

When the Chinese so enthusiastically wished somebody in power 'ten thousand years', they were not hoping that he would live that length of time but, since the phrase embraced all that exists, they recognized, perhaps unconsciously, that he stood for the marriage of Heaven and Earth and the perfect harmony proceeding from *yin* and *yang*. This was because he had pursued the task of all powerful men and sought to develop his genius to the full in acting for the good of his subjects.

Lao Tzu said that 'ten thousand beings are carried on the back of the *Yin* and enfolded by the *Yang*.' It can be seen that when the Chinese shouted ten thousand years for this or that leader, they were not wishing him anything special, but merely recognizing that he had done his best for the existing order of things and that all they wished, in fact, was the continuance of that order.

Ancient Greek historians related that the Persian king's guards comprised ten thousand men, called the Immortals. One thousand of them carried lances with golden pommels and nine thousand with silver. The number symbolized the almost countless bodies of Persian soldiery, and the title of Immortals, their reputation for invincibility.

termite and termitary Although their lives are, generally speaking, similar to those of their cousins, the ANTS, there are various symbolic elements in them peculiar to termites. In the first place, the object of their existence is regarded in a different light and is seen as the symbol of slow and secret destruction – which it is in fact, from the point of view of the down-to-earth individual.

In India, earth from a termitary is regarded as playing a protective role, doubtless because the insects' underground activities mean that they are in touch with the evil influences issuing from the Earth.

The Montagnards of southern Vietnam believe that from time to time the higher ranking spirit, Ndu, makes his home in a termitary which gives protection to and assurance of good harvests. The termitary is therefore a pledge of wealth. In India, the relationship between the termitary and the *materia prima* is confirmed by its known relationship with *nāga* and this is perhaps the reason, too, why in Cambodia rain is obtained by plunging a staff into a termitary (DAMS, GRIE, PORA).

Termitaries possess an extremely complicated and important esoteric and symbolic meaning in the religious and cosmogonic thinking of the Bambara and Dogon. In their creation-myths they stand primarily for the Earth's clitoris which became erected against the sky and rendered sterile the first marriage of Heaven and Earth. The CLITORIS is male polarity in the female and must for this reason be cut out. The termitary is also the symbol of oneness and, in some sense, the opponent of creation, which is completely controlled by the principle of duality or of twinship. This accepted meaning of the termitary as a solitary and mysterious power results in the occasional higher initiate of Bambara societies, who has attained the highest level of spiritual perfection possible to man, being called one of those 'from behind the termitary' (ZAHB p. 135).

ternary See THREE.

tetraktys This is the sum of the first four digits, equalling TEN $(1 + 2 + 3 + 4 = 10)$ (see QUATERNARY NUMBER). According to Pythagorean teaching, it contained the knowledge of all things when set out in the shape of a triangle with ten dots disposed pyramidally at four levels:

Fire – the creative spirit

O

Air   O O   Matter

Water   O O O   Marriage of spirit and matter

Earth   O O O O   Created forms

At the top a single dot symbolizes the Monad, or the godhead, principle of all things, latent being; below, the source of all manifestation is depicted by Two, symbolizing the first manifestation, duplication by pair or dyad, male and female, Adam and Eve, phallus and egg, light and darkness, Heaven and Earth, *yin* and *yang*, and so on, in other words the inward dualism of all beings; the three dots correspond to the three levels of the world – infernal, terrestrial and celestial – and with the three levels of human life – physical, psychic and spiritual – while the base of the pyramid, with its four dots, symbolizes Earth, the manifold nature of the physical universe, the four elements, the four cardinal points, the four seasons, and so on. The whole comprises a decade, or the totality of the created and uncreated universe.

The tetraktys possessed a sacred character and Pythagoras' followers used to take their oaths on it. Pythagoras himself identified it with the oracle at Delphi. It was the perfect number which provided knowledge of oneself and of the worlds of gods as well as mortals. In terms of music, the tetraktys denoted perfect harmony, the principle of all things. It was therefore invoked as a god, the god of harmony who presided at the birth of all beings (BOUM p. 45; GHYP pp. 15–16).

tetramorph   Tetramorphs include the four figures in the visions of Ezekiel (1: 5–14) and St John (Revelation 4: 6–8) of the man, the bull, the lion and the eagle. Revelation calls them 'the four beasts' and they symbolize the universality of the presence of God, the four pillars of God's throne, the four Evangelists, Christ's message and also Heaven, the realm of the elect, the holy place and all transcendence.

According to St Jerome, the man stands for Christ's Incarnation; the bull (a sacrificial animal), for his Passion; the lion, for his Resurrection; and the eagle, for his Ascension. In the Christian iconography of the Evangelists, when taking into account the characteristics peculiar to each Gospel and especially to their opening chapters, the man in the tetramorph corresponds to St Matthew; the lion, to St Mark; the bull (or ox), to St Luke; and the eagle, to St John.

There are many other tetramorphs in different traditions, in which they would appear to correspond to the four points of the compass and to the way in which the universe is ordered on the pattern of kingdoms, often divided into four peripheral and one central province. They are sometimes, too, expressions of the four elements, occult teaching identifying the eagle with Air and intellectual activity; the lion with Fire, strength and movement; the bull with Earth, labour and sacrifice; and the man with spiritual intuition.

Dr Paul Carton adapted the four 'beasts' in the tetramorph to the Classical doctrine of the four 'humours', each beast corresponding to one of these humours:

The Bull's sides stand for physical matter, bodily nourishment, phlegm, the inertia of Water, the virtue of command with its opposite vice of sensuality, in short, the phlegmatic humour.

The Eagle's wings stand for the life force, breath, blood, the mobility of Air, emotions exploding into passion, in short, the sanguine humour.

The Man's head stands for incorporeal spirit as the seat of thought, earthly knowledge, the Earth, in short, the melancholic humour.

The Lion's claws and limbs stand for consuming Fire, active strength and unifying energy which activates more or less intensely what has been determined by instinct or by will, in short, the choleric humour.

According to him, the Ancients in their wisdom had drawn from the riddle of the Sphinx four basic rules for the conduct of human life – knowledge, with the human brain; will, with the lion's strength; daring (or lifting oneself) with the bold strength of the eagle's wings; silence, with the powerful concentrated bulk of the bull.

(BOUM pp. 47–8)

Generally speaking, like the CROSS, the tetramorph symbolizes a systematic relationship between different fundamental and primal elements, which stems from the centre.

André Leroi-Gourhan stresses how extraordinarily ancient this theme is. It may be truly termed archetypal, since it is as old as the cave-paintings in France, Spain and central Europe and runs through history from the Sumerians to the present day and from Peru to Europe (LERR pp. 184ff.).

theatre   Remembering the distinction which Antonin Artaud drew between 'the Eastern theatre with its metaphysical tendencies' and 'the Western theatre with its psychological tendencies', we see that this is, in fact, a distinction drawn between a theatre which, as is recognized in India, remains conscious of its sacred origin and of its peculiar function as a symbol, and a 'profane' theatre. The *shastra* teach us that theatre-art is the fifth Veda, the Nātyaveda created by Brahmā as a means of universal edification, since the first four could not be understood by those of lowly birth. This provides an epitome of symbols, through which such people may apprehend the path of virtue. It is a representation of the endless strife between the *deva* and the *asura*.

However, the bare liturgical bones to be found on most of the stages of Asia may also be discerned, in part at least, in Classical Greek drama. It evolved more exuberantly and lavishly in the medieval mystery plays and in the Spanish *autos* down to Calderon. Furthermore, it is impossible to overlook the relationship between such plays and those of the other 'mysteries' of Ancient Greece, as well as with the legends of initiation in both Eastern and Western secret societies. Physically the Athenian theatre is a religious monument deriving its sacred character from temples, while the performances staged in it derive from ceremonies performed in honour of the gods.

Medieval mysteries depicted three worlds – Heaven, Earth and Hell, angels, men and devils – symbolizing three states of being and what Guénon calls 'their fundamental simultaneity'. In more general terms, the theatre stands for the world, what the audience sees as the 'manifested'. 'What it arouses,' Artaud adds, 'is the manifested.' And because this is what it represents, the theatre can make apparent its illusory and ephemeral nature. In the parts which he plays, the actor is also the Being made manifest in a series of modalities which, in order to be real, assume a wavering and changeable appearance. Calderon called one of his *autos The World's Great Stage*, and this, in fact, is just what it is (ARNT, ARTT, DANA, GUET, JACT).

On the other hand, the individual stands upon this great stage of the world, just as he or she becomes part of the world of the theatre when becoming a member of the audience. As such, he or she, in fact, is projected into the actor, identifying with the characters played and the feelings expressed, or is at the very least drawn into the dialogue and movement. However, simply giving expression to emotions and unravelling situations, frees the audience from what had remained locked within it, producing the well-known phenomenon of catharsis. The spectator is cleansed and purged of what he or she was incapable of casting off by their own efforts and thus the theatre helps to dissolve complexes. Its effectiveness is increased in proportion to the spectator's playing an actor's part and involving him- or herself in an imaginary situation. Moreno fully understood this phenomenon and employed it by making psychodrama a therapeutic technique, even trying to extend it to such collective psychoses as race riots. The value of the technique, like catharsis itself, resides in the symbolic transference of a situation which the subject has actually experienced, but which remains unexpressed and frequently in the unconscious, to the level of an imaginary situation in which restraint no longer has the same reason for operating. Spontaneity is given free rein and consequently what is in the unconscious is gradually exposed and the complex resolved. When symbols play a fully inductive role, a kind of liberation (catharsis) occurs and a modicum emerges from the depths of the unconscious to the light of retrieval. In Greek, catharsis also carried the meaning of pruning or cutting the dead wood from trees, as well as of assuaging the soul by the real or imagined satisfaction of a moral need and the ceremonies of purification to which candidates for initiation submitted. Theatre symbolism operates at all these levels.

theogony The battles of gods, heroes and giants in various mythologies and especially in Hesiod's poems derive from distant memories transmuted into MYTH, in the archetypes of the collective unconscious, or in the dramatic structure of human passions. There have been many attempts to explain them. One such, by Paul Diel (DIES), suggests that the three generations of the Greek gods Ouranos, Cronos and Zeus correspond to the three levels of the development of consciousness – the unconscious, consciousness and superconsciousness. André Virel (VIRI), on the other hand, regards these three generations as symbols of individual and group development – a first phase of chaotic and irrational proliferation, with a wealth of ambivalences; an abrupt halt to growth; and a resumption of progress under the banner of organization. To sum up, theogony symbolizes an explosion of the life force followed by a sharp separation of ambivalences and then a marriage of opposites, setting the past in order and by-passing it to provide the spring of continuous progress. With such keys and others as well – and these are certainly not those of which Classical authors were in any sense aware – it is possible to provide a perfectly coherent symbolic explanation of what superficial readers would regard as merely the riotous excesses of an over-exuberant imagination.

thigh The bodily function of the thigh is to provide both support and movement. It therefore denotes strength, and the Kabbalah stresses its firmness, like that of the COLUMN.

In the Greek legend, Dionysos underwent a second period of gestation in the thigh of his father, Zeus. This deserves thorough symbolic analysis since the thigh obviously has both sexual and uterine significance. According to the classic pattern of initiation ritual, the legend indicates that the person who was to become Master of the most celebrated of the Ancient Greek Mysteries was given his initiatory training – or second gestation – within the thigh of an all-powerful god who might, in this context, be regarded as the primordial hermaphrodite. In this case 'thigh' might be a euphemism for the womb. It would then immediately be linked to the symbolism of the CAVERN, or rather to that of the hollow tree. This is, however, no contradiction with the thigh being regarded, externally, like the column, that is, as a symbol both of elevation and of strength.

thirteen From Classical antiquity, the number thirteen has been regarded as unlucky. During a procession, Philip of Macedon set his own statue among those of the twelve great Olympian gods and was assassinated shortly afterwards in the theatre.

Thirteen persons, Christ and his apostles, celebrated the Last Supper. The Kabbalah lists thirteen spirits of evil. The thirteenth chapter of the Book of Revelation is that describing Anti-Christ and the Beast.

And yet, in Classical antiquity, the thirteenth member of a group was regarded as the most powerful and the most exalted. Such is true of Zeus among the twelve Olympians, among whom he sits or whom he leads, making a thirteenth who, according to Plato and to Ovid, is distinguished by his higher standing from the rest. Odysseus was the thirteenth member of his crew and escaped being eaten by the Cyclops.

In Allendy's system of numerological symbolism, 'this number stands for a principle of activity, three operating within the unity of the complete decade which contains it' and which consequently restricts its range. Thirteen would correspond to an organized and dynamic system, but one which was predetermined and particular rather than universal. Schwaller, too, interprets it as 'a generative force for good or ill'. Through its static (the group of ten) and its dynamic (the group of three) limitations, thirteen displays development doomed to death, the culmination of a power, since the latter is itself restricted, 'regularly thwarted effort'. Generally speaking, thirteen, as an eccentric, marginal and erratic element, is separated from the normal order and rhythm of the universe.

From the cosmic point of view, thirteen's undertakings are generally bad, since the activities of the creature can only be blind and inadequate for they do not harmonize with the laws of the universe. They may serve for individual development, but they disturb the government of the macrocosm and trouble its rest. They are a unity shaking the balance of the different interconnections in the universe (12 + 1).

(ALLN p. 359)

In Ancient Mexican astronomy, calendars and theology, thirteen was a basic sacred number. In the *Popol-Vuh*, there are 'thirteen gods' and 'the thirteen-god'; there are twelve stars and the Sun at its zenith; while the twelve rain-gods are personifications of the thirteenth who is also the first, or great sky-god.

The Aztecs considered thirteen to be the number of time itself, the figure which stood for the completion of a temporal series. It was associated with the figure fifty-two, the Aztec age (13 × 4), the 'bond of the years' during the course of each of the Aztec 'Suns'. The first and fourth of these Suns each lasted for 676 years and were the most perfect since they comprised these two numbers only – 13 × 52 = 676.

An Aztec week, too, lasted thirteen days.

The thirteenth major arcanum in the Tarot, Death, does not mean an end, but a fresh start after the completion of a cycle – 13 = 12 + 1 – and to this, generally speaking, the number would correspond. It does, however, carry with it the pejorative hint of being less a completely fresh birth than starting the same thing all over again. It would, for example, stand for Sisyphus' unceasing efforts to roll the rock to the top of the hill or the cask which the Danaids could never fill to the brim.

thirty-six (with its derivatives) Thirty-six is the NUMBER of cosmic solidarity, where the elements meet and from which cycles evolve. Its derivatives display the relationships within the triad of Heaven, Earth and Mankind.

Thirty-six is the sum of the sides of a square each of nine units; it is the approximate value of a circle with a diameter of twelve units; while 360 is the number of degrees in a circle and days in a lunar year. It is the Chinese Grand Total and the Hindu Holy Year (the movement in the precession of the equinoxes is one degree in seventy-two years; that of the polar cycle one degree in sixty years; their cycles coincide evey 360 years (6 × 60 = 72 × 5) – J. Lionnet). Most cosmic cycles are multiples of 360. Thirty-six is the sum of the first four even numbers and the first four odd numbers (20 + 16), which won it the title of 'the great quaternary' from the disciples of Pythagoras; it is also the sum of the cubes of the first three digits.

Seventy-two is the number of the length of time Lao Tzu was borne in the womb, the length of time the seasons last (according to Chuang Tzu), the number of Confucius' disciples, that of the Taoist Immortals and of the companions of Huang Ti's apotheosis.

Thirty-six is the number of Heaven, seventy-two of Earth and 108 of mankind. Thirty-six, seventy-two and 108 bear the same interrelationship as one, two and three. An isosceles triangle with an angle of 108° at the apex provides the proportions of the Golden Number and, in fact, displays a particularly harmonious appearance. In different ways, thirty-six, seventy-two and 108 were the favourite numbers among secret societies. Among other symbols, the beads in the Buddhist and Shivite rosary are 108 in number, as are the columns in the temple of Urga and the towers of the

Phnom Bakheng at Angkor. It is the most important symbolic number in both Buddhism and Tantrism.

The Chinese believed that in the microcosm of the human body there were 360 bones, joints and points for acupuncture.

If 72 and 108 are both doubled seven times, the totals produced are 4608 and 6912. These numbers are the values of the 192 even lines of the hexagrams multiplied together (192 × 24) and that of the odd lines similarly multiplied (192 × 36), 24 and 36 themselves being the product of 12 multiplied by 2 (the sign for even) and 3 (the sign for odd). 4608 + 6912 = 11,520 and this, according to the *I Ching*, is the number of the 'ten thousand beings'. 6912 is the value of *k'ien* (Heaven); 4608, that of *k'uen* (Earth). The three numbers are in the ratio of 2, 3 and 5 and correspond to the 'conjunctive' character of 5 = 2 + 3, the marriage of Heaven and Earth in the nature proper to each; 6912 (Heaven) = 4608 (Earth) = 11,520 (Mankind), another way of expressing the Great Triad.

According to Maspéro, 72 and 108 divided by 2 (that is, 36 and 54) gave the astronomical co-ordinates of Lo-Yang, the former Chinese imperial capital, which was yet another meeting-place of Heaven and Earth, the one where the Son of Heaven and Earth held sway.

thistle Thistles are generally regarded at first sight as harsh and unattractive plants and as fit food for asses. Like all prickly plants, they are a symbol of the protective belt defending the heart against external harm and attacks. The device of Scotland is *Nemo me impune lacessit* (None touches me unharmed) and its emblem the thistle. In this respect the plant has become the emblem of austerity, of some degree of misanthropy and of the vengeful spirit.

Nonetheless, it is probable that the 'radiant' aspect of the flower itself would be capable of endowing it with completely different properties linked to the radiation of sunlight.

The Ancient Chinese herbalists regarded the thistle as 'fortifying' the body and conferring longevity, doubtless because when dried the plant seems to last for ever (KALL).

thorn Thorns conjure up visions of barriers, difficulties, external defences and, in consequence, of an unpleasant and unwelcoming exterior. Thorns are a plant's natural defences and this cannot fail to remind us of the role played by an animal's horns. On the other hand, as Guénon has observed, Christ's crown of thorns, woven, it is said, from acacia, is not unrelated to a solar crown, the symbolism of the thorns being reversed so that they are identified with the Sun's rays radiating from the Redeemer's body. In fact iconographically, Christ crowned with thorns is sometimes depicted casting rays of light.

Others interpret the Crown of Thorns which Christ wore during his Passion as celebrating the marriage of Heaven with the virgin Earth and being the wedding ring of the Word – the Son of Man – and the Earth, virgin and still to be made fertile.

In China, arrows, flying thorns, were the weapons used to drive out evil spirits and were the instruments employed to exorcise 'central' space (GRAD, GUES).

In both Jewish and Christian tradition, thorns conjure empty untilled soil and hence it was denoted as 'a land of thorns and thistles'. Since thorns stood for unploughed virgin soil, the crown of thorns – for which a wreath of orange blossom was substituted at her wedding – symbolized a woman's virginity as it did the virginity of the soil.

The Mexicans symbolically linked cactus thorns with flint sacrificial knives. The south, the land of Fire, of the midday Sun (Uitzilopochtli) and human sacrifice – the blood-offering to the Sun – was called the 'thorny side' in the Nahuatl language, doubtless because their priests used cactus thorns as instruments of self-mortification, slashing their legs to offer their blood to the gods.

thousand The number one thousand bears the paradisiacal sense of immortality in a state of bliss.

Each day of the Tree of Life was a thousand years and the lives of the righteous last for a thousand years, too. 'A thousand years in thy sight,' says Psalm 90: 4, 'are but as yesterday when it is past.' Adam should have lived for a thousand years and it was because of his sin that he died sooner. According to Asiatic tradition, the life span in Paradise, judged by the teachings of millenarianism, lasts for a thousand years (DANT p. 391).

Millenarianism, however, is more generally applied to the rule of the Messiah in relation to the Second Coming, Christ's return and his earthly reign with the righteous after their resurrection and before the end of the world. The length of his reign should be a thousand years. The Catholic Church condemned this literal interpretation of the number as heresy and teaches that a thousand should be understood in its symbolic sense of a distant, hidden and indefinite date.

An identical teaching is to be found in St Justin when he alludes to the resurrection of the body. This should last for a thousand years in a rebuilt and enlarged Jerusalem (*Dialogi* 80). St Augustine and other Fathers of the Church regarded this number as being 'the sum total of generations' and 'the fulfilment of life'.

In this context, one should remember the doctrine of the seven periods of one thousand years, as presented in the *Epistle of Barnabas*, and its relationship with Judeo-Christian Gnosticism in Egypt. The cosmic week comprised seven periods each of one thousand years, but this division of the world into seven ages did not derive from traditional Jewish sources but from Hellenized Jewish tradition (DANT pp. 396–7).

thread (see also WEAVING) The symbolism of the thread is basically that of the agent which 'links all states of being to one another and to their First Cause' (Guénon). This symbolism finds its best expression in the Upanishads, where the thread (*sūtra*) is said, in fact, to link 'this world to the other world and to all beings'. The thread is both *ātman* (Self) and *prāna* (Breath). Because it is linked to a main central point, often depicted as the Sun, the thread must 'in all things be followed back to its source'. This cannot fail to remind us of Ariadne's thread which was the active ingredient of Theseus' return to the light of day. One is also reminded of the strings or threads which link puppets to the central will of the person who manipulates them, as in the Japanese puppet-theatre.

On the cosmic plane, distinction should be drawn between the threads of
the warp and the threads of the woof. The warp is the link between worlds
and states of being, while the prescribed and temporal development of each
of them is represented by the woof. Shiva's hair denotes the weaving as a
whole. The Fates, or the thread of time or of fate, symbolize the unwinding
of the single woof thread (see also SPINDLE).

Returning to the concept of 'breath', we should also observe that in
Taoist fashion it is often associated with the backward and forward motion
of the shuttle across the loom – life-state, death-state, evolution and involution of manifestation. Unpicking at night what has been woven during the
day – as in the myth of Penelope – is employed by the *Rig-Veda* to symbolize, once again, the rhythm of life, the endless alternation of inhalation
and exhalation like that of light and darkness.

In the Japanese myth of the Sun-goddess, Susano-wo-no-Mikoto destroyed
what Amaterasu had woven. Different initiation rites for women, especially
in China, included ritual weaving while locked into a room, at night, during
the Winter, since the woman's participation in the act of cosmic weaving
made it dangerous and needed to be undertaken in secret. On the other
hand, daytime labours, in the Summer, were men's work. The heavenly
marriage of the woman Weaver and the Oxherd, is the equinox, balance
and the marriage of *yin* and *yang*.

We have already seen that 'thread' is one of the meanings of the word
sūtra, denoting the Buddhist scriptures. It should be added that the word
tantra is also derived from the notion of 'thread' or 'weaving'. The Chinese
ideogram *ching*, combining *mi* (thick thread) and *ching* (underground
stream), denotes both the warp and basic texts, while *wei* denotes both the
woof and the commentaries upon those books. Warp and woof are what in
India are designated as *shruti* and *smriti*, products of the intuitive faculties
and those of reason. In the case of *tantra*, the weaving may be the interdependence of things and of cause and effect, and yet the tantric 'thread' is
still that of traditional continuity, Ariadne's thread in the labyrinth of the
spiritual quest, the link to the First Cause of all things.

Threading a needle is, furthermore, the symbol of passing through the
gateway of the Sun and escaping from the cosmos. It is also, the meaning
remaining identical, the symbol of the arrow piercing the centre of the
target. In this context, the thread may be regarded as the link between the
different cosmic levels (infernal, terrestrial and celestial) or those of psychology (unconscious, conscious and superconscious) and so on.

To revert to the simplest level and the notion of the thread of fate, it
should be observed that in the Far East marriage is symbolized by a celestial spirit twisting two red silk threads between his fingers – the threads of
fate of bride and groom becoming a single thread. In other southeast Asian
countries the wrists of the bridal couple are linked by the same thread of
white cotton, the thread of their mutual fate (DURV, ELIM, GOVM,
GUEC, GUES, SILI).

All around the Mediterranean Basin, and especially in North Africa,
weaving is to women what ploughing is to men – participating in the work
of creation. 'Through myth and tradition, weaving has an equal place with
ploughing, but is itself a sort of ploughing, an act of creation producing,

patterned in the wool, symbols of fertility and depictions of ploughed fields. In his *Nymphs' Cave* Porphyry wrote: "What better symbol for the souls descending into birth than the weaver's loom?"' (SERP pp. 132–6).

three (see also AUM; TRIAD; TRIANGLE; TRIPLE) Three is regarded universally as a fundamental number, expressive of an intellectual and spiritual order in God, the cosmos or mankind, and either synthesizes the three-in-one of all living beings or else results from the conjunction of one and two produced, in this case, 'from the marriage of Heaven and Earth. The Tao produced one; one produced two; two produced three' (*Tao Te Ching* 42). However, it is more generally accepted that three, being the first odd number, is the number of Heaven, while two is the number of Earth, since one pre-existed their polarization. The Chinese called three a perfect number (*ch'eng*) as an expression of wholeness and fulfilment – nothing can be added to it. It is the culmination of manifestation, since Man, the son of Heaven and Earth, completes the Great Triad. Three is also the perfection of divine unity to Christians, God being One in three Persons. Buddhism finds its fulfilment in the Triple Jewel, or *triratna* (Buddha, Dharma, Sangha) and this was appropriated for their own uses by the Taoists as the Tao, the Books and the Community. Time is threefold (*trikāla*) – past, present and future – and the universe is threefold (*tribhuvana*) – Earth, atmosphere and sky (*bhu, bhuvas, swar*). Again, in Hinduism, manifestation of the godhead is threefold (*trimūrti*) as Brahmā, Vishnu and Shiva, the creator, preserver and destroyer, corresponding to the three *gunas*, or modalities – *rajas, sattva* and *tamas*, the expansive, the ascendant or centripetal and the descendant or centrifugal. In the Cambodian variety of Shiva worship, Shiva is at the centre, facing east; Brahmā on the right, facing south; and Vishnu on the left, facing north. Another notable group of three is the holy monosyllable *om*, comprising the three letters AUM, matching the three states of manifestation. There were Three Wise Men and Guénon remarks that they symbolize the three offices of the King of the World incarnate in the new-born Christ – King, Priest and Prophet. There are three theological virtues, Faith, Hope and Charity, and in alchemy, too, there were three elements employed in the Great Work, sulphur, mercury and salt.

In China, the three brothers, the Hi and the Ho, were lords of the Sun and the Moon and in Classical mythology, too, three brothers were lords of the universe – Zeus, Lord of Heaven and Earth; Poseidon, Lord of the Sea; and Hades, Lord of the Underworld. According to Granet, Chinese 'urban and military organization' was based upon the three, the square and a combination of both (see TRIGRAM), while for Allendy, too, the group of three is the number of 'organization, activity and creation' (ALLN p. 39).

The group of three is expressed graphically in such different symbols as the TRIDENT, the *trinacria* (a fish with a single head and three bodies) and, of course, in its simplest form, by the triangle. The Chinese ideogram *tsi*, which was originally expressed as a triangle, possesses the notion of marriage and harmony. The equilateral triangle, or one with either the Hebrew Tetragrammaton or the Eye of God in the middle, is a symbol of the Christian Trinity as well as being a symbol of the Chinese Great Triad.

In Persian tradition, the figure three seems generally to have been endowed with a magico-religious character. The figure was notably present in ancient Persian religion with its threefold motto: 'Good thoughts, good words and good deeds'. These three *bûkht* were also known as the 'Three Saviours'. Evil thoughts, evil words and evil deeds were attributed to the Spirit of Evil.

There is abundant reference, both in those parts of the Avesta which deal with ceremonial matters and those which discuss matters of morality, to the figure three, which always symbolizes the moral triad of Zoroastrianism. It also contains fairly lengthy descriptions (*Vendidad* 8: 35–72; 9: 1–36) of the ritual purification which the man who had been polluted by a corpse (*nasu*) should undergo. Three series each of three holes had to be dug in the ground and filled with bullock's urine (*gōmez*) or water. The person had always to begin by washing the hands three times and then the priest would sprinkle the different parts of the body to drive out the evil spirits.

There was an ancient magico-religious ceremony of casting lots by shooting three arrows or reeds.

The figure three is also connected with *azlām*, the rite of casting lots with arrows, the third of which always denotes the chosen person or place, the treasure and so on. This was a long-established, pre-Islamic custom among the Arabs and one undoubtedly extremely ancient, being based upon folk tradition over a very wide area. With variations, it occurs as far afield as among the nomads of the steppes, as well as in Iran and among the Arabian Bedouin.

In legends, it is only after a king has called three times for a volunteer to undertake a dangerous mission that the warrior himself comes forward, thus demonstrating how far he surpasses all others in valour. Similarly, a hero about to set out to combat a demon will tell his friends that he will give three shouts, the first when he sees the demon; the second when he gives him battle; and the third when he has overcome the demon. He will also ask his companions to wait three days when he sets out to give the demon battle, or to enter an enchanted palace alone or even go to some amorous assignation. There was implicit belief that his character as a hero would preserve his life for the first three days.

The three successive acts which occur in so many tales of wonder ensured that the enterprise would succeed, and at the same time formed one indissoluble whole.

To make a dream come true and bring good luck, the dreamer must keep it a secret for the next three days. Failure to heed this warning – bordering upon the psychological – risks causing painful consequences. Here again the figure three sets the bounds between the lucky and the unlucky.

In the tradition of the Ahl-i-Haqq, or Followers of the Truth, in Iran, the figure three is endowed with a sacred character and it recurs frequently either in their accounts of cosmogony or in their descriptions of ritual actions.

In the womb of the primeval pearl, before God created the world he brought into being from his own essence three angels or rather three entities called *se-jasad* (the Three Persons) – Pir-Benyāmin (Gabriel), Pir-Dāwūd (Michael) and Pir-Mūsi (Raphael); and it was only later that he created Azrael, the Angel of Death, and Ramzbār, the female angel, Mother of God, standing respectively for his wrath and his mercy. Subsequently he created two other angels to bring the number of divine entities to seven.

In a number of traditional tales, the sect connects the number three with historical or quasi-historical events and believes that it affected their outcome. Ceremonies which are an earthly and symbolic reflection of these events also employ the ternary. Each year, three days' fast commemorates the three-day battle and final victory of the Sultan Sihāk, a fourteenth-century manifestation of the godhead, and of his companions. In another manifestation of the godhead, Khan Atash waved his hand three times and the enemy armies were routed, while the sacrifice of three sheep, which appeared from nowhere, was a substitute for the sacrifice of three believers.

In the sphere of ethics the number three also possesses an especial importance. The three things which destroy an individual's faith are lies, impudence and sarcasm. The things which drag an individual down to Hell are also three in number, slander, hard-heartedness and hatred. On the other hand there are three things which lead the individual to the faith: modesty, courtesy and fear of the Day of Judgement.

Several of the visionary writings of the Ahl-i-Haqq contain instances of the number three being linked to something magic or psychic, such as the vision in which the Khan Atash gained recognition as a manifestation of the godhead by changing his appearance three times in front of his disciples.

Even symbolic objects occur in groups of three, such as the carpet, pot and napkin, objects endowed with magic properties since they belonged to one of these incarnations of the godhead.

The Dogon and Bambara regard three as the number symbolizing the male principle and depict it in a hieroglyphic showing the penis and two testicles. As well as being the symbol of maleness it is also that of motion, in opposition to FOUR, the symbol of femaleness and the elements. Dieterlen describes the Bambara as believing that the original universe was three, but it was not actually made manifest, that is, did not impinge upon the awareness, until it was four. As a result, she adds, the Bambara regard maleness (three) 'as what sets things in motion, ensuring their fecundity, while the latter only comes to fruition and full knowledge through femaleness.'

It is for this reason that, whereas in most cases the triangle, and especially the inverted triangle, has female significance, to the Dogon it is the symbol of the power of the male to fecundate. In the hieroglyphic meaning 'let Hogon see!' it appears inverted. Hogon is the name of the high priest who, covered in pollen, pierces with his needle the end of the egg standing for the maternal womb (GRIS).

To the Fulani, too, the number three is laden with hidden meaning. There are three classes of herdsmen – goatherds, shepherds and oxherds – but, above all, three 'is the fruit of the incest of the Him and His own flesh, since the Monad, incapable of hermaphroditism, couples with itself in order to reproduce.'

Three is also manifestation, disclosing and revealing the first two numbers, just as the child reveals the presence of father and mother, and the tree-trunk standing man-high reveals the presence of leaves and branches in the air above and of roots in the ground below.

Lastly, three equates with rivalry (two) overcome, and gives expression to a mysterious efficacity, synthesis, reunion, marriage or resolution (HAMK).

The Kabbalah has provided a rich field for numerology and seems to have placed groups of three in an especially privileged position.

All things of necessity proceed in threes which simply make up one. Any action, in itself single, may in fact be separated into:

1 the active principle or cause of the action – its *subject*;
2 the subject's action – its *verb*;
3 the effect or result of this action – its *object*.

These three terms are inseparable and mutually interdependent and from them comes the threefold oneness we find in all things.

(WIRT p. 67)

For example, creation implies a creator, the act of creating and the thing created.

Generally speaking, in terms of the triad, the first is pre-eminently *active*, the second *intermediate*, being active in relation to what follows it but passive in relation to what has preceded it, while the third is strictly *passive*. The first corresponds to spirit, the second to soul and the third to flesh.

(ibid. p. 68)

The first *sefirah* in the Kabbalistic numerical system, the SEFIROT, are themselves split into groups of three. The first 'is of the intellectual order and corresponds to pure thought or spirit'; it includes the Father-principle, the creative Word-Thought and the Virgin-Mother who conceives and apprehends. The second group of three is 'of the moral order and is related to emotion and the exercise of will-power, in other words, the soul', bringing together merciful grace, austere judgement and palpable beauty. The third group of three is 'of the dynamic order, related to creative activity and hence to the body', comprehending the principles which guide progress, proper regulation of its execution and the energy capable of actualizing a concept (WIRT pp. 70–2).

Psychoanalysts share Freud's view of the number three as a sexual symbol. In most religions, at least at some phase or point in their development, the godhead itself is conceived as a triad in which may be discerned the roles of Father, Mother and Child. Even such highly spiritualized faiths as Catholicism contain the dogma of the Trinity which introduces into the most absolute monotheism a mysterious principle of living relationships. In order to nip in the bud any tendency towards polytheism, Islam severely bans any form of words which might weaken belief in the oneness of Allah.

The triads of Ancient Egyptian gods and goddesses were no more than arrangements of minor importance dictated by convenience, or social or theological ends. 'It might even be asked whether the idea of a triad is not a modern creation, an attempt to see in a few instances of divinities being grouped together in "families", an ancient rule generally applied' (POSD p. 290).

Three also denotes the levels of human life, material, rational and spiritual or divine, as well as the three stages of mystical development, purgative, illuminative and unitive.

This number is also an expression of the social order in its fullness and particularly the threefold structure of Indo-European society. According to Georges Dumézil, if all social structures are analysed, it will be found that this threefold division only evolved into an all-embracing world-view and value structure among particular peoples. Although its origins are unknown, this threefold division of duties or orders is perfectly clear. It is given expression in various triads which easily embrace religion, warfare and work; kingship, martial strength and fecundity; the priesthood, power and productivity; priests, warriors and producers (Brahmā, Vishnu and Shiva); Brahmans, Kshatriyas (warriors) and Vaishyas (farmers and merchants), Shudras or slaves being as it were outcasts; Jupiter, Mars and Quirinus; the senatorial, equestrian and plebeian orders. Interaction takes place between the socio-political and the mythological organizations, each structure being reflected in the other, but they do not always develop at the same pace. Myth changes more slowly than reality, although sometimes it may anticipate it.

Zoologists have noted many triads within the human body. It would seem as if every important function of an organism possesses this basic structure. Such observations illustrate the fundamental meaning of the triad as the living wholeness of types of relationship within a complex single structure. It is a mark simultaneously of a being's unique identity and of its internal multiplicity, of its relative stability and of the mobility of its components, of its immanent independence and of its dependence. The triad is as useful a channel of dialectic in the logical exercise of thought as of movement in physics and of living matter in biology. The basic rationale of this universal phenomenon of threes must no doubt be sought in a metaphysic of composite and contingent being and in a global view of the manifold oneness of all that exists in nature and which may be summarized as the three stages of being – appearance, development and destruction (or transformation); or birth, growth and death; or again, in astrological tradition, increase, culmination and decrease.

threshold The esoteric significance of the threshold relates to its position in the passage from the external (profane) to the internal (sacred) state.

It symbolizes both separation and the potential of friendship, marriage or reconciliation. This potential can be actualized if the individual who comes is greeted at the threshold and invited in. It will be lost if the visitor is left at the threshold with nobody to welcome him or her. This is the reason why at the threshold of the house or temple should be set those emblems, in the shape of carvings, decorations or paintings, which show the significance of the place to be entered and of the welcome which will be given. To stand at the threshold is to indicate one's readiness to obey the rules by which the place is governed. But this readiness is still indeterminate, incomplete and requires acceptance, so that to drive somebody from the threshold is to deny membership to and to reject that person. To stand at the threshold is also to place oneself under the protection of the master of the house, be he God, grandee or peasant. Crossing the threshold requires a degree of bodily purgation and purity of mind and soul, symbolized, for example, by the removal of one's shoes before entering a mosque or a Japanese house.

The threshold is the borderline of the holy and participates in the transcendence of the centre (see GATEWAY).

The thresholds of temples, shrines and tombs are, in many traditions, untouchable. Care must be taken to step across them without touching them with one's foot. One may prostrate oneself before them and kiss them. In central Asian and Siberian cultures this custom was extended to the threshold of the family home or tent and it is also to be found in the ritual attaching to Voodoo shrines in Haiti (METV). In Asia Minor Shi'ite Sufi say: 'Muhammad is the room and Ali the threshold.'

In Mali, the Bambara regard the threshold as one of the sacred places in the hut and associate it with ancestor-worship. They summon their ancestors by striking the threshold with a stick carved to depict them. Sacrifices are offered annually to them at family altars placed beside the centre-post of the hut and at its threshold (DIEB).

throne The universal duties of throne and pedestal are to support the glory or display of greatness either of gods or of mortals. In the Book of Revelation (4: 2ff.), the 'throne that was set in heaven', surrounded by the four symbolic beasts, was thus a manifestation of God's glory at the end of the world. It symbolizes the final balance of the cosmos, a balance, Burckhardt writes, 'achieved by the complete integration of all natural opposites.'

In China, a throne set upon a pedestal signified the separation of the celestial from the terrestrial world and the supremacy of the former over the latter.

Hindu thrones were of various natures. The *padmāsana*, the lotus seat or pedestal, expresses cosmic harmony. It was the throne of Vishnu – and even that of the Buddha – but it could also, in Tantric terms, be the 'lotus of the heart'. Shiva's throne, the *simhāsana*, like that in the Book of Revelation, was borne by four animals corresponding to the four ages of the world and the four colours. They were called Dharma, Jnāna, Vairāgya and Aishvarya. This throne supports aspiration towards supreme knowledge through mastery of cosmic energy. In fact, *simhā* means 'lion' and, as is amply supported by iconography, the throne was more widely known as the 'Lion Throne'.

In some Christian as well as Islamic writing, God's throne is said to be supported by eight angels corresponding to the eight points of the compass and the subordination of the whole universe to God.

Buddhism locates the Buddha's diamond throne at the foot of the Bodhi-tree, that is to say, in the centre of the world. In aniconic art (i.e. not using figures of humans or animals to portray gods and so on) the throne stands for the Buddha – set between parasol (Heaven) and the Buddha's footprint, it corresponds to the intermediate world.

Sometimes, as in the case of rulers, the throne either confers office or postulates its exercise. In the case of the *simhāsana* of Mysore it conferred temporary deification. Nor should the infallibility of the Pope be forgotten, when he speaks *ex cathedra*.

The throne (*el arsh*) of Islamic esotericism underpins manifestation, itself without form, and even the transcendence of the First Cause, giving expression to the relationship between the First Cause and its manifestation. On the other hand, the pedestal or footstool (*el kursī*) is primal differentiation, the first 'creation' (AUBT, BURA, GUES, JILH, MALA, SCHC).

'Lord of the Throne' is one of the names most frequently applied to Allah by the Koran. He is also known as 'Lord of the Heavens and the Vast Throne' and 'Master of the Throne'. Tradition has it that 'the Throne possesses seventy thousand tongues and that each tongue praises Allah in several different languages'. The Throne is identified with Divine Knowledge.

The Throne encompasses all things. It symbolizes the culminating state of universal manifestation, bringing balance and harmony in its fullness. Upon it stands the glorious manifestation of God in his Mercy and Bliss. God's throne is 'upon the waters' (Koran 11: 9) that is to say it stands supreme over all cosmic potentiality or the ocean of primordial matter. This is reminiscent of the Hindu and Buddhist symbol of the LOTUS which blossoms on the surface of the water and is simultaneously an image of the universe and the seat of the godhead made manifest. Basically, the Throne is to be identified with the Universal Spirit.

'From the Sufi viewpoint, each single thing, seen in its primeval nature, is God's Throne. In particular, it is the mystic's heart which is identified with the Throne, just as in Hindu and Buddhist symbolism, the lotus is identified with the heart' (RITS p. 625).

Thrones are also regarded as epitomes of the universe and are often decorated with an ornamentation which conjures up the elements of the cosmos. Sometimes they rest upon four figures or columns which call to mind the four points of the compass. To sit upon the throne without due right is to usurp almighty power, and becomes the crime of *lèse-majesté* or even of *lèse-divinité*. Thrones symbolize the Divine Right of Kings. They are also symbols of the persons exercising that power, as in a judgement from the throne, and bear witness to the permanance of authority and of its divine origin.

King Solomon's throne has been described and commented upon as if it were one of the wonders of the world. Even the Old Testament account contains a wealth of symbols:

> Moreover the king made a great throne of ivory, and overlaid it with the best gold. The throne had six steps, and the top of the throne was round behind: and there were stays on either side on the place of the seat, and two lions stood beside the stays. And twelve lions stood there on the one side and on the other upon the six steps: there was not the like made in any kingdom.
>
> (1 Kings 10: 18–20)

Commentators have, however, burdened this throne under a weight of marvels. The jinnee Ifrit is supposed to have stolen the throne for Solomon from Balkis, Queen of Sheba, conveying it in the twinkling of an eye through space to the Mount of Jerusalem, together with all her books of magic. Thanks to these, Solomon was able to bring under his sway mortals, jinn and the elements themselves. Above the two lions there were supposed to be two eagles. The lions stretched their paws when Solomon mounted his throne and the eagles spread their wings when he sat down upon it. The pillars of the throne were of precious stones and over and above it hung a crown of rubies and emeralds. The Talmudists added that 'when Solomon mounted his throne heralds on each of the steps proclaimed to him the duties incumbent upon him as sovereign, and that when he sat down a dove flew from the throne, opened the Ark of the Covenant, and took out the Torah and gave it to him so that he might study it; and the twelve golden lions sent forth terrifying roars' (GRIA p. 97).

We shall, however, remain true to the Old Testament version. Although this was written centuries after the death of Solomon and is unencumbered by marvels and legends, we should still observe the symbolic properties of the details which it describes. Again, although it would need a small treatise to describe them fully, we need to gather together the significance of IVORY and GOLD; of such animals as LIONS; and of the numbers SIX, TWO and TWELVE. Summarizing and simplifying some of their characteristics, we find that ivory is the mark of incorruptibility and of invincibility; gold of supremacy and wisdom; and lions of power. The two lions represent the king's power over Israel and Judah which only became separate kingdoms after his death, while the twelve lions stand for the twelve tribes of Israel. The six steps up to the throne separate Solomon from the rest of mankind, marking the king's elevation to the highest level of supremacy and wisdom, only slightly below that of the godhead. They correspond to Solomon's own number, that of the so-called Seal of Solomon, or six-pointed STAR OF DAVID. No more glorious nor flamboyant combination of symbols may be imagined than Solomon's throne.

'Thrones' is the name given to the first order of angels by the Pseudo-Dionysius the Areopagite:

Every appellation of the celestial minds denotes the Godlike characteristic of each. . . . The appellation of the most exalted and pre-eminent Thrones denotes their manifest exaltation above every grovelling inferiority, and their celestial tendency towards higher things; and their unswerving separation from all remoteness; and their invariable and firmly-fixed settlement around the veritable Highest, with the whole force of their powers; and their capacity for receiving the approaches of the Godhead, through the absence of all passions and earthly tendency, and their bearing God; and the ardent expansion of themselves for the divine reception.

(PSEH pp. 27–8)

thuja In Ancient China, this was the tree of Spring and the sunrise and had therefore to be planted on the Earth-altar lying to the east. In addition, like all conifers (see PINE) it was a symbol of immortality and its resin and seeds were eaten by the Immortals (GRAR, KALL).

Thule In Classical antiquity, this island marked the northern limits of the known world – although its precise location was indeterminate – and the epithet *ultima* was always applied to it. The Greek geographer Pytheas is alleged to have discovered Thule lying six days' sail to the north of Britain, and modern scholars have identified it with Unst, most northerly of the Shetland Islands. Its symbolism is comparable with that of the land of the Hyperboreans so often conjured up by the Greeks. In fact, in poetry and legend Thule, with its endless days at the Summer solstice and endless nights at the Winter solstice, became a land of fable. Because the Roman philosopher, Seneca, had already envisaged voyages of discovery to fresh lands beyond these limits, it symbolizes the temporary boundaries of the world. In more general terms Thule might symbolize consciousness, desire and limitation, not only in terms of space, but in those of time and of love as well, in short longing for and awareness of the furthest bounds of what is by its own nature restricted.

thumb A phallic symbol, the thumb signifies creative strength since it is the thumb which provides the other fingers and the hand itself with the power to grasp.

Hop o' my Thumb 'was originally a phallic symbol, and however small the fairy stories make him out to be, he was nonetheless always endowed with the highest attributes' (TEIR p. 53). These fairy stories belong to the tradition 'of families with seven children one of whom is endowed with paranormal powers and bears the name of saviour, or black or white wizard. [These legends] are pastiches of the great five thousand-year-old Asian myth of Krishna'. Although Hop o' my Thumb may stand for the saviour-principle in society, he also symbolizes the driving-principle in human personality which is spread among different elements, just as society comprises a number of different individuals. He stands for total, second-sighted, energetic and active consciousness in the personality guiding life and behaviour on a safe course (LOEF pp. 157–9).

thunder In Old Testament tradition, thunder is the voice of the Lord. It also heralds manifestation of the godhead. Before ratifying the Covenant with the Children of Israel and giving them the Ten Commandments, Jehovah made Heaven and Earth reverberate with a loud noise:

And it came to pass on the third day in the morning, that there were thunders and lightnings, and a thick cloud upon the mount, and the voice of the trumpet exceeding loud; so that all the people that was in the camp trembled. And Moses brought forth the people out of the camp to meet with God; and they stood at the nether part of the mount. And mount Sinai was altogether on a smoke, because the Lord descended upon it in fire: and the smoke thereof ascended as the smoke of a furnace, and the whole mount quaked greatly. And when the voice of the trumpet sounded long, and waxed louder and louder, Moses spake, and God answered him by a voice. And the Lord came down upon mount Sinai, on top of the mount: and the Lord called Moses up to the top of the mount; and Moses went up.

(Exodus 19: 16–20)

Thunder displayed God's power and especially his justice and his anger. It stood for the divine threat of annihilation (Job 36: 29–33) or else heralded revelation.

In Greek tradition, thunder was originally associated with rumblings in the bowels of the Earth, doubtless a memory of the upheavals of creation. But it passed from the Earth into the hands of the sky-god Zeus, when the latter had dethroned and castrated his father Cronos, 'the wily', and freed his brothers. 'And they remembered to be grateful to him for his kindness, and gave him thunder and the glowing thunderbolt and lightning: for before that, huge Earth had hidden these. In them [Zeus] trusts and rules over mortals and immortals' (Hesiod, *Theogony* 503–6). Thunder symbolizes supreme rule which had passed from Earth to Heaven.

The Celtic thunder-god Taranis was the equivalent of the Roman Jupiter, to whom he was assimilated in the Gallo-Roman epoch. The word for thunder is to be found in neo-Celtic languages, but the name of this god is peculiar to Gaul. In the Celtic world THUNDERBOLTS bear the same significance as the Latin *fulgur*, but it would seem as if thunder itself symbolized above all an aberration in the cosmic order, displayed in the wrath of the elements. The Celts had the rooted fear that the sky would fall upon their heads and the Irish called upon sky, Earth and sea as chief witnesses of their oaths. Thus there was a notion of direct human responsibility for the unleashing of thunder and thunderbolts, considered a method of punishment inflicted on the guilty by the all-powerful god. There is no other explanation than this for the panic which struck the Celts when they were caught in a violent storm shortly after they had plundered the shrine of Apollo at Delphi (OGAC 10: pp. 30ff.).

According to Mircea Eliade, thunder is the fundamental attribute of sky-gods, often assimilated to the supreme deity or else to his son. In the *Popol-Vuh*, thunder is the spoken word of God, as opposed to thunderbolts and LIGHTNING which are his Word written in the sky (GIRP p. 26).

Thunder-gods, lords of RAIN and hence of vegetation, derive from the symbolic lunar cycle. In many cosmologies they are related to the Moon-deity. In Australia, the thunder- and storm-god is often depicted sailing in a boat shaped like the crescent Moon (HENL). Thunder is also often depicted as a ONE-LEGGED man, and this is particularly true of the higher civilizations in the Americas – Maya, Aztec and Incan – as well as of the Samoyed and Australian Aborigines. BULL-ROARER and DRUM imitate the sound of thunder and for this reason women are forbidden to see them (HENL, SOUM, THOH, LEHC).

Tlaloc, the Aztec god of storm, thunder and lightning, had his abode in the east, the land of springtime renewal. Together with Huitzilopochtli, the Midday Sun, he was one of the two Great Gods to whom most sacrifices were offered. At the coming of the Spaniards, their altars stood side by side at the top of the great pyramid in Mexico. In Peru, Illapa possessed the same attributes and enjoyed similar honours from the Inca, being especially prominent as lord of the seasons (ROWI). In the great temple of Coricancha at Cuzco he took precedence immediately after the great sky-god, Viracocha, and the Sun and Moon, Demiurges, father and mother of the Inca. He was depicted as a constellation, probably the Great Bear, in the shape of a man holding a club in his left hand and a sling in his right. This sling was the thunder which he released to make the rain fall, the latter being drawn from the Milky Way, the great river in the sky. All along the Caribbean littoral and in the islands, the Great Bear was regarded as the storm-god.

In many myths from Australia and the Americas, thunder and lightning are linked to the mythical Great Mother and to the original Twin Heroes.

In the mythology of the Siberian far north, as well as in continental America at the same latitude, there are mythical birds which cause thunder by beating their wings. Samoyed depict theirs in the shape of a wild duck or 'iron bird'; the Yurak as a wild goose; the Altaic Telyut as an eagle; the

Ostyak from Tremjugan as a black bird rather like a grouse. On the other hand, Mongols, Soyot and some of the eastern Tungus tribes, such as the Goldi, shared the Chinese belief that thunder was caused by a sky-dragon, while to the Turgut it was the work of the Devil in the shape of a flying camel. The thunder-bird was the shamans' ally and guided them in their flights into the upper Heavens. We have mentioned the Telyut thunder-eagle, and when Christianity was introduced into central Asia, it became an avatar (manifestation) of St Elijah, living in the Twelfth Heaven. Sky-gods were 'old' gods and when the lord of thunder took human shape, he was no exception to the rule current among the peoples of central Asia. The traditions of the Buryat and Ostyak from Demyanka, therefore, depicted him as an old man, generally winged and covered in feathers. This old man once lived upon Earth – undoubtedly he was a former shaman – but discovered a way up into the sky one day and remained there for ever after. According to a Buryat legend, he became one of the 'old grey sky-god's' helpers and his task was to execute justice. At the same time as he makes the thunder roll, he casts lightning at thieves.

The lords of thunder had many a BLACKSMITH in their service – seventy-seven, the Buryat believed – to make their arrows. A subtle difference originated among the Buryat: thunder felled trees with its arrows, but 'killed living creatures with its fire' (HARA p. 150). The duty of executioner attributed to thunder occurs throughout many Asian peoples of widely differing cultures and origins, such as the Yakut – strongly influenced by Russian culture – and the Goldi of far eastern Siberia. All these peoples believed that wicked spirits were split in two by the spirit of thunder (HARA pp. 147ff.).

thunderbolt (see also THUNDER; VAJRA) In heraldry the conventional representation of the thunderbolt, the attribute of Jupiter, is a sheaf of barbed lances or arrows, but it may sometimes be depicted as a dart, trident or similar implement. Virgil (*Aeneid* 8: 424–32) describes the Cyclops forging a thunderbolt for Jupiter from iron. 'Three rays of twisted hail had they added to it, three of watery cloud, three of ruddy flame and the winged southern wind', all the shapes and the fullness of the moral or physical storm which the thunderbolt symbolizes.

Thunderbolts display the almighty power of the greatest of the gods. Generally speaking, they symbolize the dual powers of creation and destruction possessed in Hinduism by Shiva and Vishnu and in the Vedic religion by Indra, in whom, like Zeus and Jupiter, both properties were united.

From the remotest past, thunderbolts were regarded as the implements and weapons of the gods, especially when wielded by Zeus or Indra. 'Thunder is a weapon of the sky gods in all mythologies, and any spot he has struck with lightning becomes sacred . . . and any man he has struck with lightning is consecrate' (ELIT pp. 53–4). This is a species of theophany (divine manifestation) which placed a taboo upon whatever it touched. Furthermore, Neolithic 'thunder-stones' (see STONE), Parashu-Rāma's stone AXE and Thor's HAMMER are all symbols of the thunderbolt which strikes and cleaves the Earth. The BLACKSMITH-gods of the Tugen of Kuang-si, of

Tibet, and of the African Dogon are involved in the same symbolism. However, the axe or hammer of these gods does not only destroy, but creates and fecundates. Thunderbolts procreate and destroy at one and the same time; they are both life and death. This is the significance of the two-bladed axe and of the two tips of the Hindu thunderbolt, the *vajra*. Generally speaking, thunderbolts are symbols of celestial activity and of the transforming influence of Heaven upon Earth. They are, in addition, associated with RAIN, which stands for the patently beneficial aspects of this activity.

The *I Ching* associates thunder with fear and with the moderation and balance which it creates. The aspect of destructive fear is also that of Rudra carrying the thunderbolt and also, if you will, of Skandha, the personification of war, with the thunderbolt as an attribute. 'Thunder', Chuang Tzu said, 'is created by the discordancy of *yin* and *yang*.' The reverberations of this discord call down thunderbolts spontaneously in the microcosm, as they did in the case of Wu-Yi, who had shot his arrows against Heaven. Secret societies condoned some sins in the same way. Furthermore, the fact that a storm prevented Ts'in Che Huang-ti from completing the *fong* sacrifice on Mount Tai Shan was supposed to be formal evidence of his virtue. In the trigrams in the *I Ching*, *chen*, which corresponds to thunder, is the upheaval of the world and of nature – it is the sign of Spring. Both classical Hindu and Tantric writers display a point of view of a very similar order when they identify the *vajra* with the phallus as the source of creative energy.

As an instrument of the godhead, the *vajra* corresponds to the Word and to the intellect. In both India and Tibet (where it is called *dordje*), it is Method as opposed to Wisdom or Knowledge (represented by the BELL). 'The thunderbolt was an attribute of the Vedic god Indra which was adopted by several Tibetan deities. As the symbol of the male principle and of the Method (in contrast with the bell), the thunderbolt is restricted to priests and magicians as a weapon against demons and vices' (TONT p. 2). It was the symbol of the infinite, righteous and beneficent power of the godhead. Indra was the god who wielded the thunderbolt. 'Indra the Generous seized his thunderbolt to hurl it as a weapon; he killed the first-born of dragons. Indra . . . you . . . overcame by your own magic the magic of the magicians [and] at that very moment you brought forth the sun, the sky, and dawn' (VEDR p. 149).

The dragon's fatal error was its belief that it was God's equal. In this context the dragon stands for the drought which Indra removed by setting the water free with his thunderbolt, the latter symbolizing the fertility-principle which was the origin of his kingship of the world. The dragon is the fire which shrivels, the thunderbolt the fire which fecundates.

Vajra not only means 'thunderbolt', but also 'diamond', lightning often originating in legend from diamonds or, as in the case in Cambodia, from a gem. Thus, in Tantric Buddhism, the *vajra* is sometimes the image of the Diamond World, or knowledge, as opposed to the Womb World, or outward appearance, represented by the bell.

It should also be observed that thunderbolts in the shape of double tridents are not peculiar to India and similar forms have been found in the

Greco-Roman world and in the Near East. They clearly convey the meaning of the twofold power of creation and destruction (CHAE, DAVL, ELIY, GRAD, GRIE, GUET, MALA, PORA, SECA).

Within the Celtic world, thunderbolts were doubly represented in Gaul, in the very name of the god Taranis ('Thunder') and in the hammer of Sucellus, 'the hard hitter', a name given to the sky-god by function of his office. The Irish counterpart to this hammer was the CLUB belonging to the Dagda, the 'good god', first and foremost a druid-god, who used one end of it to kill and the other to restore mortals to life. The club needed eight ordinary mortals to carry it and left a furrow which could be used to mark the frontier between two provinces (OGAC 10: pp. 30ff.). It symbolized that same power of the godhead to create and to destroy.

In Amerindian tradition, according to the *Popol-Vuh*, thunderbolts and lightning comprise the written word of God, in contrast with thunder, his spoken word (GIRP p. 26).

Lehmann-Nitsche (LEHC) has recorded an Amuesha myth in which the thunderbolt was father of the Sun (regarded as female) and of the Moon (regarded as male). In this myth, characteristic of the way in which lunar symbols are linked, Earth was still only peopled by jaguars and lizards. A female lizard, a virgin, was walking with her brother when she saw some beautiful flowers which she picked and clutched to her breast. All at once the sky grew dark, a storm burst and a thunderbolt fell. When sunlight returned, a rainbow appeared decorated with those very flowers, and the she-lizard found that she was pregnant.

In Peru, the customs surrounding the bezoar (a hard mass of material in the stomach) provided equally strong evidence of the procreative powers of thunderbolts. For the same reason the concretions of sand where a thunderbolt struck were regarded as love-charms (LEHC). Thunderbolts were also linked to divination, and Inca seers claimed to have their gift through having been thunderstruck (TRIR).

In Africa the Bambara believe that thunderbolts are the whips of Faro, the water-god and Demiurge who governs the world (DIEB). By interchange, whips symbolize lightning and thunderbolts. However, Zahan states that the Bambara believe that thunderbolts are particular manifestations of the spirit of God, and even that spirit in physical shape – hence the association of thunder-stones with the skull. To the Dagara of Ghana and Upper Volta, thunderbolts are symbols 'of the male penetrating the female' (GIRD).

Altaic peoples extended to animals the taboo upon persons struck by thunderbolts and the flesh of such an animal was never eaten. The Buryat exposed the bodies of animals struck by lightning upon platforms in the forest in the same way as human bodies. Both belonged from then on to the thunder-god, who would come to hunt their souls when nobody was there (HARA). Generally speaking, in central Asia, thunderbolts made holy whatever they struck and the Buryat would fence such places off to prevent their livestock feeding there. In the Yenisei Basin there was the belief that forest fires caused by lightning should not be put out. However, libations of milk were poured to both thunder and lightning and there was a belief that only milk could put out a fire started by Heaven. Similar customs were to be found from the Caucasus to Mongolia and, underlying them all, was the notion of making a libation of milk to appease the gods.

Those struck by lightning went up to Heaven, while the rest of the dead went down to the Underworld. Such beliefs were common to many Altaic peoples, while eighteenth-century sources add that the Ostyac believed that this privilege of eternal life in the Heavens was extended to all those who had met a violent death (HARA p. 252).

While the thunderbolt symbolizes the abrupt and harsh intervention of Heaven, in this respect its symbolism differs from that of the star and the axe. 'If thunderbolts are violent discharges of energy, then stars are the accumulation of that energy. The star has the properties of concentrated lightning.' Thunderbolts may be compared with axes and thunder-stones, 'but the hand-axe is symbolically a concentrated thunderbolt'. Thunderbolts may be regarded as 'non-concentrated' explosive energy, while, on the other hand, axes stand for 'structured energy . . . instruments of preconceived creation in the alchemical world in which they were traditionally associated with the axe-blow from which Pallas Athene sprang to birth and with the shower of gold' (VIRI pp. 8, 106). Thunderbolts are creation springing up from nothing into a still chaotic state, or which annihilates itself in apocalyptic flames.

thyrsus The long staff, spear or javelin, tipped with a pine-cone and wreathed around with ivy and vine-leaves or clusters of grapes, was the attribute of Dionysos and the Bacchantes. The prose-poem which Baudelaire dedicated to Franz Liszt makes its symbolism crystal-clear. In the first place it is 'the sacerdotal emblem grasped by the priests and priestesses worshipping the god whose mouthpiece they are'. And then it is as though the tendrils, fruit and flowers are all dancing around some hieratic maypole. Lastly the thyrsus, 'Maestro, stands for our twofold nature . . . The staff is your will, standing straight, firm and unshakeable, while the flowers are your fancies tripping round your will, the female element cutting its fantastic capers around the male. What anatomist would be so hatefully bold as to divide and separate the straight line from the curlicues, intention from expression, disciplined will-power from convoluted creative spirit, unity of aim from variety of means, genius welding all together in an all-powerful and indivisible whole?' It may not be an exaggeration to say that the thyrsus is the symbol of the manifold nature of the inner being, of the individual aware of the Bacchic elements deeply buried within him or her.

tiara Attis, Mithras, Ceres and Cybele all wore the tiara, a headdress incorporating three crowns set one above the other and culminating in a pointed cap, which displayed their empire over the three levels of the cosmos – celestial, terrestrial and infernal. When, from time to time, these gods and goddesses made their progresses through the realms of life and death it was as sovereigns.

Wearing the tiara was the privilege of the Great Kings of Persia, the closed triple crown symbolizing the number of their kingdoms and their absolute power.

There have been different explanations of the pope's tiara. The uppermost crown, closed by a cap surmounted by a cross, might well symbolize the pope's supremacy over all archbishops, whose mitres are 'open'. When, in the later Middle Ages, the papacy adopted the tiara, it symbolized the threefold kingship of the head of the Church – spiritual kingship over souls, temporal kingship over the States of the Church and pre-eminent kingship over all earthly rulers.

At papal coronations, when the cardinal sets the tiara upon the pope's head, he tells him that he has received the triple crown because he is not only Father, but Prince, King and Ruler upon Earth, and Vicar of Christ – the three titles which the tiara symbolizes.

It is doubtful whether the three crowns set one above the other may really be taken to correspond to the attributes of the Three Persons of the Trinity – the Power of the Father at the summit; the Wisdom of the Son in the middle; and the Love of the Holy Spirit at the foot. This has not, however, prevented some writers from regarding the tiara as a symbol of the Trinity. Others see in it the symbols of the three theological virtues of Faith, Hope and Charity, which should be present to a heroic degree in the pope who theoretically dwells in a state of sanctity.

tiger Generally speaking, the tiger conjures up notions of strength and savagery, signs simply of the negative. As a hunting-creature, it is, in this respect, a symbol of the warrior caste. In Chinese geomancy and alchemy the tiger was set in opposition to the DRAGON; in the first instance it was a maleficent symbol, but in the second the tiger stood for an active principle, energy, in contrast with the 'moist', passive principle, lead as opposed to mercury, breath to semen.

The 'Five Tigers', symbols of protective strength, were the guardians of the four cardinal points and of the centre. There are several instances in Chinese history and legend of this name (*Wu ho* – Five Tigers) being given to groups of valiant warriors who defended the empire. Tigers are, especially, animals of the north and of the Winter solstice, when they devour evil influences. That tigers are sometimes the steeds of the Immortals is because they themselves are endowed with longevity. In Buddhism, their strength is also a symbol of the power of faith and of the spirit struggling to make its way through the Forest of Sin, itself depicted as a BAMBOO-forest.

In Hindu iconography, Shiva's trophy is a tiger-skin. Natural energy, which does not bind Shiva and which he controls, is represented by the Shakti, who rides a tiger (CHOC, DANA, GRAD, GUES, KALL, LECC, OGRJ).

Tigers are monsters of darkness and the new Moon but are also figures in the higher world, 'the world of life and growing light'. They are often depicted as 'letting humanity, represented by a child, escape [their] jaws (the child being the ancestor of the tribe, likened to the new moon, the "Light that returns")' (HENL quoted in ELIT p. 183).

Malaysian healers have the power to change themselves into tigers, and it should not be forgotten that throughout southeast Asia the mythic Tiger-Ancestor is regarded as an initiatory master. It is he who takes neophytes into the jungle to initiate them, in fact to 'kill' and 'revive' them (ELIC p. 339).

In Siberia the Gilyak believed that 'because of its habits and way of life, the tiger is really a human being who only takes on the appearance of a tiger temporarily' (ROUF p. 303).

The appearance in dreams of tigers causes an agonized awakening. It revives the terrors aroused by approaching the beast in the jungle or seeing it in zoos or circuses. It terrifies and fascinates by its beauty, savagery and swift movement. According to Aeppli, in dreams

it stands for a whole family of urges which have become completely out of our control and are ever ready to take us off our guard and harrow us with their assaults. The powerful feline nature of the tiger embodies a group of instinctive impulses as unavoidable as they are dangerous. It is naturally more cunning and less short-sighted than the bull and just as untamed and even more savage than the wild dog. These instincts display their most aggressive aspects because they have become utterly inhuman by being repressed within the jungle. Despite this, the tiger fascinates through size and strength, although it may lack the lion's dignity. The tiger is a treacherous, unforgiving tyrant. To see a tiger stalking through one's dreams means that one is dangerously open to the animality of one's instinctual impulses.

(AEPR p. 265)

The tiger symbolizes the drowning of consciousness in the unleashing of a flood of elemental desires. Nevertheless, if, as sometimes depicted, the tiger is fighting creatures belonging to a lower order, such as serpents, it stands for the higher consciousness; but if it is fighting an eagle or a lion, then it stands for the instincts attempting to slake their rage against the prohibitions imposed by that higher order. As always, the meaning of the symbol varies with the creatures depicted in conflict.

tile In the Masons' language, to tile or cover the Temple is to protect it from 'rain-damage' caused by the intrusion of the uninitiated and of external influences. Thus one of the Outer Guards is the Tyler who only admits the candidate after he has answered questions suited to his grade. Unless it is 'tiled' or covered, the Temple will let in the rain and hence, in French Masonry, the words 'It's raining' mean that there are uninitiated intruders in the Lodge meeting (BOUM).

Tiles symbolize the protection of a secret, and in their nocturnal aspect utter indifference to spiritual influences and the powers of self-development, a regression into what has been acquired and fixed. Thereupon the secret becomes corrupted and void of meaning.

time Time is often symbolized by the WHEEL, by the twelve signs of the ZODIAC, describing the circle of life as they move round, and, generally speaking, by any circular shape. The centre of such circles is then regarded as the motionless aspect of existence, the pivot which makes the motion of existence possible, the one contrasting with the other like time with eternity. This explains St Augustine's definition of time as the shifting image of motionless eternity. All motion takes circular shape once it becomes part of the evolutionary curve between a beginning and an end, and lays itself open to measurement which is none other than that of a time-scale. In an unconscious attempt to drive out the anguish of the brevity of existence, contemporary watchmakers have found no better way than to give their clocks and watches square faces rather than round, thus symbolizing the human illusion of an escape from the pitiless wheel and of controlling the world by imposing their scale of values upon it. Squares symbolize space, the Earth and matter. This symbolic passing from the temporal to the spatial does not, however, succeed in suppressing all rotary movement, but it conceals the ephemeral nature of existence, since it displays no more than an instant in space.

Christian architecture and sculpture, especially in such examples of Romanesque art as the tympanum of Autun Cathedral, often depicted Christ as the Lord of Time, the Chronocrator who was coupled with the Cosmocrator, the Lord of the Universe and of its harmonies (CHAS pp. 393–407). Art has been conceived as a struggle against death, as also has mysticism. Both symbolize the struggle for eternal life. To Baudelaire, time was 'the watchful deadly foe, the enemy who gnaws at our hearts'.

In speech, as in the tangible, time symbolizes the bounds of duration and provides the sharpest distinction between this world and the world of the Beyond, which is that of the eternal. By definition, human time is finite and divine time infinite, or rather it is a negation of time, timelessness. One is limited, the other perpetual. There is no common ground for comparison between them. This natural difference, which the mind cannot normally conceive, was marked in Ireland by a symbolic discontinuity or break in human time patterns every time a mortal entered the *sid* (Otherworld) or came into contact with its inhabitants. Such mortals believed that they had been away for a few days or months at most when, in fact, they had been gone for several centuries. The consequence was that once they returned to Ireland and set foot on Earth, they suddenly became as old as if they had passed an earthly existence and promptly dropped dead. On the other hand, heroes might have spent several days in the *sid* and only have been gone for a few hours. The Irish overcame this dilemma by confining contact between mortals and the *sid* to the beginning of the Celtic year, the feast of Samain on 1 November. This feast linked together two years, closing one and opening the next, while in reality belonging to neither. It was symbolically outside time (OGAC 18: pp. 135–50). Generally speaking, feasts, ritual orgies and ecstasies are, as it were, escapes from time, but such escapes can only be realized through intensity of inner life and not by indefinitely prolonging the duration of time. To escape from time is to escape utterly from the cosmic order, to enter another order and another universe. Time is indissolubly linked to space.

Titan The Titans, according to Paul Diel, symbolize 'the brute strength of Earth and hence earthly longings in rebellion against the spirit (Zeus)' (DIES p. 102). Together with the Cyclopes, Giants and Ouranids (three giants, each with a hundred hands and fifty heads) they stand for the upheavals of nature at the beginning of time, 'elemental manifestations, . . . the savage untamed strength of Nature in her birth-pangs. They represent the first stage of evolutionary gestation, the eruptions which prepared the Earth to become the place where human life could burgeon' (DIES p. 112).

The sons of Ouranos (Uranus: Heaven) and Gaia (Earth), the Titans tried to seize supreme power after Cronos had castrated their father. However, they were defeated by Zeus, the son of Cronos, who had shackled his father and who, with the help of Apollo, Poseidon, Athene, Hera and all the deities of sky, sea and Underworld, established the third heavenly dynasty.

The brutal, rebellious and ambitious Titans, 'opponents of the spirit of consciousness (represented by Zeus), do not symbolize exclusively the savage powers of Nature. In their struggle against the spirit they stand for the untamed powers of the soul in conflict with the harmonizing tendencies of spiritualization' (DIES p. 117). The battle of the Titans with the Olympians under Zeus' command 'symbolizes the evolutionary attempt to fashion conscious being out of brute nature' (DIES p. 119). Zeus stands for the impulse of the spirit to break free from abject slavery to matter and the senses.

Furthermore, in their struggle against the spirit, the Titans not only symbolize the forces of nature but also 'the tendency towards dominance – tyranny. This tendency is all the more to be feared since it is sometimes hidden under an obsessive ambition to make the world a better place' (DIES p. 144). This is an attitude commonly to be found in the higher reaches of the civil service and the technocracy, which are subject to what some psychologists call a form of moral ague, ague which, it must be admitted, infects a Kafkaesque bureaucracy.

Titans (*asura*) share with mortals and mortal gods (*deva*) the upper part of the Tibetan Wheel of Life, animals, greedy spirits (*preta*) and the spirits of Hell occupying the lower half. The Titans are engaged in a ceaseless war with the gods so as to tear from their grasp the fruits of the tree 'which satisfies all desire'. This is their *karma* born of jealousy and a boundless ambition which dooms them to be swallowed up in endless warfare. A green Chenrezi (see BODHISATTVA) alone can draw them to higher spheres. The six states of being in the Wheel of Life apply not only to future rebirths, but to the stages of everyday life. The Titans stand for styles of living and states of consciousness.

toad The fear inspired by this creature of the twilight makes it generally regarded in the West as a symbol of ugliness and clumsiness. However, if one delves beneath the surface, one discovers that the toad carries all the significance deriving from that great symbolic chain which links water with darkness, darkness with the Moon and the Moon with *yin*. Thus the Chinese regarded the toad as the Moon-goddess and believed that they could see a toad on the Moon. This was the wife of Yi the Good Archer who stole from him the draught of immortality which the Queen Mother of the West had given him, and then fled until she reached the Moon where she was changed into a toad. And there she remained as its goddess. On the other hand, during eclipses, it was a toad which was believed to be eating the Moon. Chinese tradition seems to waver between the toad as an aspect of *yin* or of *yang*. The former is, however, the stronger, explicable in terms of the creature's preference for dark and moist hiding-places. Furthermore, toads are often confused with frogs and, provided that it has been dried, an old toad could be just as effectively employed as a rain-maker. In addition, toads served as protection against armed attacks and turned the weapon against its user.

Toads were highly respected by the Vietnamese, who also knew them as heralds of rain and said that the toad was 'the sky-god's uncle and tells him when to pour out the beneficent water. Whoever strikes a toad will be struck by Heaven's lightning.' In addition, toads are symbols of success and, if they are scarlet, of strength as well – they were used in medicine as a child's tonic – and of valour and wealth. The caption under a piece of Vietnamese folk-art reads: 'The clever child should carry a scarlet toad.' 'Scarlet toad' is synonymous with 'rich man', deriving either from the creature's lucky colour or perhaps from its rarity.

The Maya-Quiché Indians share the Far Eastern belief in the toad as a rain-god. In Mayan lands they still say that the prayers of toads are better than ours in obtaining rain (GIRP p. 151). In Aztec iconography the toad stood for Earth (KRIR p. 41).

In the myths about the origins of fire told by such South American Indian tribes as the Tupinamba and Chiriguano, the toad became the Man's accomplice and helped him steal fire from its original owner, the Vulture (METT).

African traditions relating to the toad are various. The Bambara believe that toads change into mice during the dry season (ZAHB). On the other hand, there are definite links between human beings and toads since the human foetus, it is believed, at a certain stage in its development turns into a toad if it is female and into a grey lizard if male. Linked to water, Earth, woman and moisture, the toad is believed to be able to cure burns and is said to be invulnerable to snake-bite. It appears able to cause torpidity in the snake which has swallowed it and has 'an affinity with the female sexual organs which, during intercourse, effect the post-ejaculatory detumescence of the penis' (ZAHB p. 58). Deriving from this same symbolism, the Bambara

compare the toad with the Earth which the Sun – that other serpent – cannot harm by biting it. Lastly, as with all those symbols associated with the network of Earth, water and Moon, the toad is an esoteric expression of the concept of death and rebirth, and hence its name is used to denote a class within their initiatory society. In this context the musical instrument which stands for the toad is the drum played by rubbing with the hand, and its sexual symbolism is patent.

(ZAHB)

The Bamun tribes call the toad 'Tito'.

It is the synthesis of the horizontal and the vertical. Its silhouette suggests the seated figure or one carrying a burden. It plays a highly important part in their creation-legends.... On the shores of Lake Chad it is to the toad that the women owe the famous fashion of artificially enlarged lips, a fashion derived from the mystic ties between the creature's life and the life of these tribespeople.

(MVEA p. 61)

However, the Bambuti Pygmies regard the toad as a malignant spirit responsible by his perhaps deliberate clumsiness for introducing death into the world (SCHP p. 76).

According to a Fulani tradition, toad's oil seeps into stone (see under STONE, the flat stone which is a symbol of twofold knowledge). When the neophyte asks the mystagogue how to pass from ignorance to knowledge, the latter replies: 'Change yourself into toad's oil.' That is to say that humans can penetrate to the depths of a subject without altering its externals through the subtle fluidity of their spirit (HAMK p. 6).

In France the toad would appear to have been a royal and solar symbol as predecessor of the fleur-de-lis, featuring as such upon Clovis' standard. Guénon, however, suggests that there may have been some confusion here with the frog, the symbol of resurrection. Toads are more often regarded as being the reverse of frogs, of which they are the dark, lunar and infernal aspects, being supposed to intercept star-light and swallow it. The toad's unblinking stare would then be the sign of insensitivity or indifference to light (DURV, GRAD, GUES, NGUC, SOUL).

Like any manifestation of the deity of the Moon, the toad was also an attribute of the dead. 'In Ancient Egypt, like the frog, the toad was associated with the dead, and mummified toads have been found in tombs. . . . In the Middle Ages, toads, as well as snakes, were the natural attributes of the skeleton' (TERS p. 135).

In Ancient Greece a famous courtesan, Phryne, bore the name of toad (*phryne*) and plunged stark naked into the sea to play the role of Venus Anadyomene, having taken part with other courtesans 'in the licentious rejoicings, nominally in Aphrodite's honour, which took place at the end of the festival of Poseidon' (SECG p. 379). She was hailed as the prophetess and priestess of Aphrodite. The toad would seem to have symbolized sexual abandon in her person.

In European traditions of sorcery and magic, toads have a well-defined part to play. 'The toad is one of the shapes assumed by a demon when he sits upon a witch's left shoulder. Thanks to two tiny horns borne on his forehead, a toad was recognizable as a demon, and witches took infinite care of him. They baptized their toads, dressed them in black velvet, put little bells on their paws, and made them dance' (GRIA p. 136). The stone which is said to be found in a toad's head was a precious charm to obtain earthly felicity (GRIA p. 345).

tobacco The Tupinamba Indians of Brazil attributed various properties to tobacco, especially that of clarifying the brain and keeping its users 'fresh and cheerful'. The sorcerer would puff tobacco smoke over the warriors with the words: 'Receive the spirit of strength to overcome your enemies' (METT). It was also said that tobacco smoke puffed over a sick person 'strengthened the magic powers of his breath'. Similar fumigations were always used in initiation ceremonies by Amazonian Indians (GHEO). In the same cultural area, tobacco juice was squirted into the eyes of the would-be shaman to give him the gift of second sight (METB).

toe To the Bambara, the small toe, like the little finger, symbolizes the complete individual and is often decorated by a silver ring, a symbol of the word which dwells within the whole human body, from head to feet.

They also read sexual significance into the gap between the big toe and its neighbour, since they believe that it is the location of one of the nerve-centres of the human body governing the 'strings' or muscles of the sexual organs and anus. It therefore 'mirrors the movement, sexual reproduction and evacuation of the human body' (ZAHB). Zahan gives many practical instances which stress this relationship. Thus, a woman with a very wide gap here is said to have powerful sexual appetites and a liking for their indulgence. On the other hand, it is customary to bind a cotton thread round the big toes of a married couple on their wedding-night. This is to help the groom take the bride's virginity and the bride to bear the pain of defloration.

The myths of the Congo Pygmies, the Bambuti, express the belief that heroes refuse to be born through the vulva, but prefer to come into the world through the big toe on their mothers' right feet. The Pahuinbeti of southern Cameroon have the same belief. The big toe symbolizes an extraordinary birth.

tohu-bohu *Tohu wa bohu* means disorder and void. It relates to primal chaos before the creation of the world. Apart from their use to describe the primal state which preceded the order of creation, we find these words *tohu* and *bohu* used by both Isaiah and Jeremiah, the latter in connection with the destruction of the world: 'I beheld the earth, and, lo, it was without form and void; and the heavens, and they had no light' (Jeremiah 4: 23). Isaiah alludes to destruction. It is a reversion to formlessness and chaos.

Originally tohu-bohu symbolized a completely anarchic situation, forerunner of the manifestation of form and, finally, the dissolution of all form. It is the last stage of regression on the road from individuation into a state of dementia.

tomato Within the system of symbols employed by the Bambara, tomato-juice is assimilated to blood. This vegetable 'is the bearer of the foetus, since its seeds are seven in number and seven is the number of twinship, the primordial principle of being'. This is why, when the great Demiurge, Faro Lord of the Waters and the Word, was setting the world in order, he made women fertile with tomatoes and in return women continue from time to time to make offerings of this vegetable to the god. His messenger, the SWALLOW, collects the juice of these tomatoes, just as he collects the blood of the sacrificial victims, and carries both fecundating blood and juice up into the Heavens, from which they descend to Earth in the shape of rain. The fecundating properties of tomatoes are equally stressed in a number of ritual practices in everyday life, such as the habit Bambara couples have of eating tomatoes before indulging in sexual intercourse (ELIF).

tomb Whether it has the modest proportions of a grave-mound or rises to the skies like a pyramid, tombs remind us of the symbolism of MOUNTAINS. Every tomb is a humble replica of those holy mountains which are the reservoirs of life. They proclaim that life in all its changing shapes is eternal. In this context one can see why, in the words of a Greek (quoted in POSD p. 286), 'an Egyptian took more trouble preparing his eternal resting place than arranging his home.' Similarly, in Greek tradition in the Mycenean Age, tombs stood for the homes of the dead, as necessary to them as their own houses had been during their lifetimes. Later, in the Hellenistic world, the bodies of the dead were generally cremated. In other traditions, especially those current in Africa, tombs were used to localize physically the souls of the dead which might otherwise wander abroad and disturb the peace of the living.

Funerary statues may, as in Ancient Egyptian art, be copies of the dead person. They are the mainstay of the dead person's ghost, but they need not necessarily reproduce his or her physical features. Often the symbolic figure of a sphinx or siren was substituted for the human figure. Sometimes the figure of a lion or a bull was erected as the funerary statue.

(LAVD p. 960)

Jung related the tomb to the female archetype, like everything which embraces or enfolds. It is a place of safety, birth, growth and comfort. The tomb is the place in which the body either changes into spirit or prepares for its rebirth. Yet it is also the abyss into which the being is swallowed up in ineluctable and transitory darkness. The MOTHER and her symbols are both loving and fearful.

Dreaming of tombs betrays a graveyard within – repressed desires, lost loves, failed ambitions, memories of happier times and so on. They seem dead but, in psychological terms, are not completely dead, they lead a twilit life in the tomb of the unconscious. The person who dreams of the dead, of tombs and graveyards

is really looking for a world which still contains some secret life for that person. That person makes his or her way there when life closes in with real existential conflicts from which there is no apparent issue. The person concerned then seeks for an answer on the tombs of those who have carried much of this life into the depths and darkness of the Earth. . . . That person will thus have had recourse to a great and serious symbol – for the dead are powerful, they are legion – so as to regain strength from something which appears lifeless but which is vast and miraculous – for death is life as well.

(AEPR p. 252)

tongue The tongue is regarded as a flame, being as agile and of the same shape. It destroys and cleanses. As the organ of speech it can create or annihilate, and its power is boundless. It has also been compared with the beam of a scales – it weighs and gives judgement. Depending upon the words which it utters, the tongue is wholesome or perverse (Proverbs 15: 4), speaketh proud things (Psalm 12: 3), is lying (Psalms 54: 3; 109: 2; Proverbs 6: 17). The power of the tongue is so absolute that death and life are in it (Proverbs 18: 21). When the Old Testament mentions tongues without qualifying them, it is always in a pejorative sense of evil-speaking.

God's tongue is compared with a devouring fire (Isaiah 30: 27), a symbol of his power and justice. Tongues of fire (Acts 2: 3) symbolize the Holy Spirit, regarded as the power of enlightenment. The 'gift of tongues' allowed its beneficiaries, after receiving the Holy Spirit, to express themselves in the most diverse languages and with irresistible force.

The Haggadah mentions 'the evil tongue' (*lachone hara*) as one of the four scourges, along with murder, shamelessness and idolatry, which cause worldly corruption.

Calumny, the evil tongue, was regarded as so weighty a matter that, in Jewish tradition, twenty-three judges were required to try a slanderer. The case was treated as if it were a matter of life or death. The slanderer (*motsi chem rā*, 'he who has uttered an evil word') was in some degree a criminal (BARH).

A digression in the Irish tale, *The Madness of Cùchulainn*, makes human tongues the equivalent of heads, since it tells how the heroes of Ulster, when boasting of their heroic deeds, would produce the tongues of the enemies whom they had killed in single combat. In a number of Breton folktales, the hero keeps the tongues of the many-headed hydra or dragon which he has killed. He uses them to make good his claim and to confound the villain or traitor who has unfairly gained possession of the heads (see BRAIN; HEAD) (OGAC 10: pp. 285ff.).

The Bambara believe that the body as a whole depends for its prosperity upon four organs, the legs, nose, sexual organs and the tongue – hence the high importance of the last-named. As the organ of speech, it is regarded as the creator of the Word, possessed of a power of fecundation analogous with that of rain, blood, semen and the spittle which is the instrument of the Word. All human intercourse depends upon the tongue, which can either provoke strife and argument or else good fortune and both spiritual and material wealth. In isolation, the tongue is held to be able only to speak the truth. It has 'only one colour' and its specific social duty is to 'give its colour' to society. They also say that liars have 'striped' tongues (ZAHB p. 197).

When the Bambara speak of a person being able 'to hold his tongue' they mean that he has reached the age of manhood and self-control. This is why, in some rites of initiation, candidates try not to utter a sound as they beat themselves with whips which they call 'tongues'. The extraordinary properties which the Bambara attribute to this organ arise, no doubt, from the fact that over and above speech, knowledge, the supreme good, is implicated. 'Knowledge, they say, is the wealth of the tongue' (ZAHB p. 196). On the other hand, the tongue is the organ of taste and therefore of discernment. It divides the good from the bad and parts the one from the other. Combined through another of its aspects with the symbolic structure of the whip, this explains why the Bambara assimilate the tongue to the knife and razor as well.

tonsure The symbolism of the tonsure, the rite of admission to the secular clerical state, derives from that of HAIR, as does that of shaving the scalp among male religious orders and leaving only a narrow ring of hair around the crown of the head. It was a sign of the renunciation of sensual love and of worldly desires and good things, of penitential self-sacrifice and, above all, of laying oneself open to heavenly influences. Shaving the head to leave only a crown of hair recalled the Crown of Thorns worn by the crucified Messiah. In the hierarchy of holy orders, the tonsure was the first of minor orders, the whole hierarchy, in fact, being based upon the spiritual choices which we have mentioned and which were symbolized by the deliberate removal of a circular patch of hair. In medieval iconography, St Peter is sometimes distinguished from the other apostles around him by his tonsure, the symbol being reserved for him to express his primacy in the apostolic order.

Ritual and votive tonsures are to be found in the Far East. Here, too, they symbolize the renunciation of earthly pleasures and obedience. This is why it is also to be found in some warrior castes.

torch This symbol should be compared with those of BIRDS, LIGHT and Iris, the RAINBOW. Demeter, Persephone's mother, went in search of her daughter carrying blazing torches and, when she met Hecate, the latter held a torch. One of the chief priests at Eleusis was called the Daducos, or Torch-bearer.

Herakles (Hercules) succeeded in overcoming the HYDRA with the help of burning arrows and he seared its flesh with blazing torches to prevent its heads growing again.

From these examples it would seem as if the torch was a symbol of cleansing by fire and of enlightenment. Its light illuminated the passage of the Underworld and the paths of initiation.

torii These are gateless GATEWAYS which always mark the entrance to Shintō temples and shrines. They comprise two uprights supporting two cross-beams. The Japanese regard them as perches for the birds and as a thank-offering to those of them which helped the *kami* (deities) when they were trying to make the Sun-goddess, Amaterasu, leave the cave to which she had taken the Sun and thus deprived the world of its light. Their symbolism is related to that of the door. They open the way to light, that of the Sun and that of the divine spirit.

tortoise (see also CROCODILE; DOME; DRAGON) Whether male or female, mortal or cosmic, the symbolism of the tortoise (and the turtle – see below) extends across the whole range of the imagination.

The tortoise is a figure of the universe and comprises a whole cosmography in itself with its shell, the upper half curved like the Heavens – a characteristic relating it to the dome – and the lower flat like the Earth. This was the light in which it was regarded among the Chinese and Japanese in the Far East, as well as among the tribes inhabiting the great bend of the river Niger in Central Africa, of which Dogon and Bambara are best documented.

However, its bulk, its obstinate strength and the notion of power conjured by its four stumpy legs, set like the pillars of a temple upon the ground, have made the tortoise into a bearer of the cosmos and a relation of the other powerful chthonian creatures which bore the world upon their backs, the great crocodile or caiman in Central American cosmogonies, the WHALE or great fish, the dragon and even the mammoth, regarded by most Siberian tribes as an underwater deity.

The Chinese classics stress the part which the tortoise plays in stabilizing the cosmos. Nu Kua cut off its four legs to establish the four poles of creation, while every pillar in an imperial tomb has its base carved in the shape of a tortoise. In some legends, it was a tortoise which supported the celestial pillar thrown down by Kung Kung, Lord of the Titans. Li Tzu tells us that the Isles of the Immortals only came to rest when the tortoises took charge of them and set them on their backs. In India, tortoises support the throne of the godhead. Their chief representative is Kūrma, one of the avatars (incarnations) of Vishnu. He acted as the foundation of Mount Mandara and held it steady when the *deva* and *asura* began to churn the Sea of Milk to obtain *amrita*. Kūrma is still supposed to underpin India. The Brāhmanas associate it with creation itself. As in China, tortoises are associated with the primordial waters – a tortoise supported the *nāga* Ananta like the waters of the new-born Earth.

Its task of supporting the universe and of being the pledge of its stability relates the tortoise to the greatest gods. In Tibet, as in India, the tortoise which carries the cosmos on its back is the incarnation either of a Bodhisattva or Vishnu who, in this shape, is depicted with a GREEN face, a mark either of regeneration or of generation, as he emerges from the primordial waters bearing the Earth upon his back (PORS, HARA). The association of primeval waters with regeneration derives from a nocturnal and lunar symbolism, the tortoise in China symbolizing both north and Winter, which are associated with the phases of the Moon. The Mayan Moon-god was depicted with a tortoise-shell as a breastplate (KRIR p. 96). The well-known longevity of both tortoises and turtles is so well known as to lead them to be associated with notions of immortality. This runs in parallel with the fertility of the primordial waters, ruled by the Moon, so that many Demiurges, culture-heroes and mythic ancestors borrow their shape on the basis of their duties as bearers of the cosmos. Countless traditions worldwide bring these symbolic characteristics together. Thus the Dravidian Munda from Bangladesh regard the tortoise as the Demiurge entrusted by the Sun, all-powerful god and husband of the Moon, with the task of rescuing the Earth from the bottom of the sea (ELIT p. 130). According to the Iroquois, when the Grandmother of mankind fell from the sky there was no Earth. The Turtle rescued the Grandmother on his back and the Musk-rat covered it with mud from the bottom of the sea. Thus the first island gradually took shape on the Turtle's back and this grew into the whole Earth. According to Krickeberg, this myth is of Algonquin origin (KRIE p. 129). The same myth sees the reappearance of the Great Turtle on two occasions to assure the evolution of the human race. Thus it passes from cosmos-carrier to culture-hero and mythic ancestor. On the first occasion the Great Turtle appeared in the guise of a young man 'with fringes on his arms and legs' who by magic made pregnant the daughter of the celestial Grandmother. She gave birth to the warring Twin Heroes who created good and evil. On the second occasion, when the good Twin Hero fell into a lake, he came to the hut of his father, the Great Turtle. The latter gave him a bow and two ears of maize, a ripe ear to sow and a green ear to cook – the Iroquois were a hunting tribe which became farmers (MULR pp. 260–2).

Similar beliefs are to be found among other North American Indian tribes, such as the Sioux and the Huron, as well as among the many Mongol, Turkic or Altaic peoples of central Asia, such as the Buryat and the Dorbot. In Mongol myth, a golden tortoise supports the mountain in the centre of the universe, while the Kalmuk 'believe that when the heat of the Sun has dried and burned up all things, the tortoise which bears the world on its back will also begin to feel the effects of the heat and in its agony will turn over and thus bring about the end of the world' (ROUF p. 82).

As the tortoise evolved in mythic thought in this way, between the heights of Heaven and the depths of Hell, it was only natural that it should have become linked to stars and constellations and, in Yucatec, Orion's Shield is known as the Tortoise (THOH). Snug between the domed and flat surfaces of its shell, the tortoise also became the mediator between Heaven and

Earth. For this reason the tortoise was adjudged to possess the powers of
knowledge and prophecy. In Ancient China we know of archaic fortune-
telling techniques based upon the study of the cracks produced on the flat
portion of a tortoise-shell by the application of heated iron bars. Such
practices may be related to the purposes behind the use of the tortoise-
stool, or stool of judgement, upon which the Tikar judges in Cameroon
used to seat suspects to prevent them from lying under interrogation.

It must be due to its virtues as the omniscient and beneficent ancestor
that the tortoise is so often the companion and family-friend of human
beings. All Dogon families own a tortoise and when the head of the household is away, it is the tortoise which is given the first mouthfuls of food and
water each day. The Japanese pay it the same respect as they do the CRANE
and the pine tree, with which both creatures are associated, attributing tens
of thousands of years of life to it.

The association of crane and tortoise brings to mind the woodcut in the
famous Renaissance book, Colonna's *Hypnerotomachia Poliphili*, depicting
a woman holding a tortoise in one hand and a pair of spreading wings
in the other. The symbolism, patently hermetic, of this ancient allegory
contrasts – or compares – the chthonian and celestial properties represented respectively by the tortoise and the wings. If one follows the famous
eighteenth-century French hermeticist, Dom Pernety, one might be tempted
to regard the wings as an attribute of Mercury and the tortoise as the raw
material for the zither which Mercury was to fashion from a tortoise-shell.
The transformation of the tortoise into a zither would epitomize the art of
alchemy and this is why Dom Pernety regarded the tortoise as 'the symbol
of the raw material of the Art'. The tortoise belongs to Saturn's line, like
lead, the '*materia prima* of the Work'. This links up with the thinking of
Chinese alchemists, who regarded the tortoise as 'the starting point of
development', in line with the myths mentioned above. Instead of marking,
through its chthonian nature, involution or regression, the tortoise is on the
contrary the beginning of the spiritualization of matter, its goal symbolized
by the wings. This may perhaps be why Pliny the Elder regarded the flesh
of the tortoise as 'a salutory antidote to poison' and attributed to it the
properties of 'a preservative against witchcraft'. At this point the symbol
becomes ambivalent, since all antidotes carry in them a poisonous characteristic and this is substantially the meaning of the following passage from
the 'Homeric' Hymn to Hermes (30–8) in which the god addresses the
tortoise:

An omen of great luck for me ... Hail comrade! ... A tortoise living in the
mountains? But I will take and carry you within: you shall help me and I will
do you no disgrace, though first of all you must profit me. It is better to be at
home: harm may come out of doors. Living you shall be a spell against mischievous witchcraft; but if you die, then you shall make sweetest music.

Hermetic philosophers regarded this address to the tortoise as an epitome
of the alchemical Work. The tortoise 'was a deadly poison before it was
prepared and a sovereign antidote afterwards, says Morian. With it Mercury gained such infinite wealth as the Philosopher's Stone obtains' (PERD
pp. 499–500).

Upon a more anthropocentric plane, the tortoise, as we stated at the beginning of this entry, possesses simultaneously both male and female symbolism. It would seem as though this aspect of the symbol, so strongly emphasized in Chinese tradition and Amerindian myth, derives from noticing that the way the creature's head emerges from the shell is not dissimilar from penile erection and this is the source of a number of Chinese metaphorical expressions. The same line of thought regards the retraction of the head into the shell as penile detumescence. This in turn leads to notions of evasiveness, surrender and even of cowardice which, taken to its extreme, would liken the tortoise withdrawing into its shell to the ostrich burying its head in the sand. The final debasement of the symbol lies in the Chinese use of the word tortoise to describe both cuckold husbands and pimps who pretend to ignore the intercourse of which they are the beneficiaries (VANG pp. 285–8). For their part, Amazonian Indians regard the tortoise as a depiction of a vagina which is sometimes, in myths from the Vaupes region, that of the Sun's wife. It is startling to observe that, in this same cultural area, a tortoise-shell sealed with wax at one end is used as a musical insrument employed in some of their initiation ceremonies, an echo of the tortoise-shell which Hermes changed into a zither.

Lastly, we should observe that the tortoise's withdrawal into its shell is, in the traditions of Hinduism, an image of the highest spiritual significance, being a symbol of involution and return to the primeval state and therefore of a basic spiritual attitude.

totem A person's totem is generally revealed to him in a vision during the course of the second stage (adolescence) of his rites of passage. The totem is an animal or plant chosen as guardian and guide, an ancestor as it were, with which bonds of kinship are established with all which this entails in terms of rights and duties.

The word *totem* is an Algonquin term, properly applied to the personal guardian or tutelary which belongs to the individual man, and often represented by picture or emblem in his medicine, or fetish, parcel, or painted upon his clothing or accoutrements. It is in no sense hereditary or genealogical, nor has it anything to do with the social organization of tribe or clan. . . . It has no relation to the social phenomenon of 'totemism,' as commonly discussed.

                                              (ALEC p. 241, n. 7)

Although the theory is strongly disputed nowadays, totemism was, in fact, regarded as the primitive form of all religion and morality. From the totem derived taboos and bans which would have been the earliest bonds of and pattern for organized society.

Setting such controversies aside, totems may be regarded as symbols of a bond of kinship or of adoption to or by a group or superhuman power.

There is a close relation or even identification between the initiate and his totem, his 'bush-soul'. Jungians explain how, through initiation rites,

the boy enters into possession of his 'animal soul' and at the same time sacrifices his own 'animal being' by circumcision. This dual process admits him to the totem clan and establishes his relationship to his totem animal. Above all, he becomes a man, and (in a still wider sense) a human being.

East Coast Africans described the uncircumcised as 'animals'. They had neither received an animal soul nor sacrificed their 'animality'. In other words, since neither the human nor the animal aspect of an uncircumcised boy's soul had become conscious, his animal aspect was regarded as dominant.

(JUNS p. 237)

tower (see also HOUSE; ZIGGURAT)   Building a tower immediately conjures up the erection of the TOWER OF BABEL, that Gate of Heaven which was intended artificially to restore the broken primordial AXIS and by its means climb up to the abode of the gods.

Its symbolism is worldwide. The Tower of Babel was a Babylonian ziggurat; in Khmer and Cham buildings, *prasat* are substitutes for Mount Meru, the decreasing size of the storeys in the tower on their summits suggesting approximations of mountain peaks. The Tower of Babel was supposed to have gone down deep below the ground and this is also true of Meru and, at least symbolically, of the towers which stand for it. They always contain an underground cell with rubble-work below or else with a deep well in the centre. In this way they join together the three worlds of Heaven, Earth and Underworld.

In China, Wen Wang erected the Tower of Beneficent Influences (*ling-tai*), nominally as a celestial observatory but, as its name shows, above all as a receptor of heavenly influences. In addition it was in the middle of a sort of Earthly Paradise in which animals ran free. Nor is there any need to emphasize its 'axial' role. Chu Sin also built his own Tower of Babel and it was upon its summit – or upon that of some similar building – that the celestial WATER-SKIN was set, at which Chu Sin shot his arrows and from which he obtained the shower of blood (COEA, GRAD, GRAC).

In Christian tradition, drawing its inspiration from fortification and feudal buildings, stiff with towers, belfries and keeps, the tower became the symbol of watchfulness and ascension. The tower symbol, which we find in Litanies of Our Lady ('Tower of David', 'Tower of Ivory'), becomes very clearly defined if we remember that 'Our Lady' and the 'Church' are associated terms. In the Middle Ages towers could be used as observation posts to watch for potential enemies, but they also had the meaning of LADDERS, reflected in their staircases, as intermediaries between Heaven and Earth. Each rung of the ladder and each storey of the tower marked a stage in ascent towards the Heaven which the Tower of Babel had attempted to reach until God had confounded human language. With its foundations on a centre (the world-centre) the tower is an ascensional path which, like the steeple, transforms generative solar energy (DAVR pp. 228–9) and broadcasts it earthwards. It was a tower of bronze which was Danae's prison and in which she was made pregnant by Zeus' shower of gold. The alchemists' ATHANOR borrowed the shape of a tower to show that the transmutations which their work sought to achieve were always in an upward direction – from lead to gold and from the dross of the flesh to the purity of the spirit.

According to Aelred of Rievaulx, the Cistercian Order was like a fortified city encircled by walls and towers to protect it from the assaults of the foe. Poverty was its wall and silence the tower which raised the soul to God.

The sixteenth major arcanum of the TAROT depicts a flesh-coloured tower, its pinnacle struck by a thunderbolt and tottering towards the left, while two persons, arms outstretched, are being hurled headlong earthwards on either side of the building. In all, thirty-seven almost spherical bodies, thirteen red, thirteen white and eleven blue, stud the sky around the majestically plumed thunderbolt, its little tongues of scarlet flame emphasizing its glory.

At first sight this card would seem to display divine – indeed heavenly – punishment striking a building which is none other, given its colour, than the human frame itself – except for one very significant point, that the bulk of the tower remains undamaged and it is only what was intended to complete the whole, the human crown with its four golden battlements, which is cast down. This reminds us of Napoleon's famous action at his coronation in 1804 when he snatched the imperial crown from the hands of the Pope and set it on his own head. Acting like another Prometheus on that 2 December brought down upon him the anger of the gods assuaged at Waterloo. It may perhaps have been this picture which made André Virel declare that the Tower was 'to some extent complementary with the Emperor'. The symbolism of their respective numbers would seem to corroborate this statement for, if the Emperor is FOUR, above all the number of Earth, SIXTEEN, four squared, is an expression of absolute power, of complete and dynamic fulfilment, as demonstrated by the swastika. This cross with crooked arms multiplies four by four and is famous for its association with dynamos of power from Charlemagne to Hitler, beneficent if it turns with the Sun, maleficent if against it.

However, as we have seen in the case of the swastika, the number sixteen is in no sense static, but dynamic. It stands not only for the abyss which Jacob Boehme contrasts with Nirvana, but for cyclical renewal, patent in the way in which the shape of the swastika suggests rotation. Although nothing is specified, this may not be a definite casting down from top to bottom of the tower but a coming and going, and the two builders may in any case come to no harm from the disaster which has hurled them earthwards. That is to say that they might well, and indeed will, resume their work, for a topless tower is as unfinished as an unsuccessful existence is unfulfilled. The symbol of the Tower becomes a positive one and, to quote Chaboche, expresses 'an unexpected change of fortune' or a 'crisis of redemption' (FRCH p. 224), or again, as Virel suggests, 'a true attainment of consciousness'. The thunderbolt falling upon the top of the tower echoes Vulcan's axe-stroke upon the head of Jupiter, without which Minerva, the embodiment of Reason, would never have been born. The Tower symbolizes the stroke of fate, its harshness attuned to the ambitions of those whom it strikes, but which alone can unlock doors to the one pathway set before them by the gods, a path which is no longer material but spiritual.

If this warning shot is neither understood nor obeyed in the fullness of its meaning, then the workers upon the human building will be doomed to try for ever to complete what cannot be completed, perpetually hurled into the abyss, and as often climbing from it to continue their efforts. The Tower thus reminds us of the myth of Sisyphus.

Tower of Babel The TOWER of Babel symbolizes confusion, the word Babel itself deriving from the root *Bll*, meaning 'to confound'. Human presumption tried to rise to inordinate heights, but could not surpass its own nature.

This lack of balance produced confusion on both earthly and divine levels. Humans no longer understood one another and no longer spoke the same language, that is to say that there was no longer the slightest consensus between them, each individual proclaiming him- or herself absolute and alone.

The Old Testament account comes at the end of the chapters which describe the beginnings of mankind and before the more circumstantial, less mythological and more chronological accounts of the Patriarchs. It provides a sort of full stop to this first phase of human history, which was characterized by the gradual growth of great empires and vast cities. It is peculiar that a social phenomenon and a social disaster should mark the end of this period (Genesis 11: 1–9).

This tradition of a sacred structure raised to Heaven, doubtless originally the product of a desire to approach the power of the godhead and to channel it towards Earth, became depraved into its opposite. The Old Testament reveals that the Tower of Babel was the work of human pride, an attempt by mankind to raise itself to the level of the godhead. On the collective plane, it was a city built in opposition to God and for this reason Jehovah scattered its builders.

The confusion of tongues might be said to be the punishment of group despotism which, through its very oppression of mankind, causes mankind to split into hostile factions.

Without in the least denying divine intervention in this catastrophe, it is legitimate to hold that the manifestation of the Lord God does not exclude a symbolic explanation in which Jehovah, too, would in this context be a manifestation of immanent Justice and an expression of human conscience in revolt against the tyranny of an organization with totalitarian tendencies. A soulless, loveless society is doomed to dispersal. Unity will only return with fresh spiritual principles and renewed love. 'It was the punishment of a collective sin,' de Vaux observes, 'which, like that of our first parents, was once again a sin of exorbitance. The balance would only be regained in Christ the Redeemer with the miracle of the tongues at Pentecost (Acts 2: 5–12) and with the gathering of the nations in Heaven (Revelation 7: 9–19, 14–17).' In fact this apocalyptic vision of a new society, ruled by the Lamb, is the antithesis of the Tower of Babel with its dispersal of mankind, as the confusion of tongues is the opposite to the gift of tongues at Pentecost.

town See CITY.

Tracing Board See under FREEMASONRY.

train Trains have come to occupy an important place in the drawings and dreams of children and adults, as in life in general, and are as characteristic of this civilization as was the horse and carriage of byegone ages. Trains have invaded the imagination and bulk large in the world of symbols.

Students and analysts of dreams would categorize the train, as successor to serpents and monsters, as an evolutionary symbol. The interpretations which follow are therefore based upon real-life practice and experiment and preserve their form of clinical notes, additionally corroborated by other observers.

The rail network automatically conjures up a vivid picture of Intercity and local trains, expresses, goods trains and stopping trains, passenger coaches and goods wagons. Its timetables are written on tablets of stone and the traveller must conform to them. It operates with clockwork precision, needing the most careful regulation. It offers the public a service by a rigidly time-tabled organization which can only function faultlessly if it preserves its rigid order and system of priorities in which feelings have no place. Because public transport is more important than private transport, when any other system crosses a railway line traffic along it must come to a halt as soon as a train is signalled. Lastly, the rail network provides safe carriage for goods and passengers, linking together all regions within any one country, and even several continents as well, and providing a channel for all types of trade and intercommunication.

In dreams, the rail network is a forceful image of the impersonal cosmic principle, imposing its unchanging law and pattern upon such separate and fragmentary portions of the psyche as the ego and its complexes. Communal interests take precedence over individual interests. The network also stands for the forces of bonding and co-ordination working at the heart of the psyche. It suggests universal life imposed with all its inalterable force.

Trains seen in dreams are images of social life as a member of a group and of the fate which governs us. They conjure up the means of our personal development which, whether they take us in the right or the wrong direction, are so hard to acquire or which we fail altogether to obtain. They are signs of our psychic development and indications that we have become self-aware and are moving towards a new life.

To dream of reaching the station late, of missing our train or of catching it only at the last minute are all dreams which are indicative of our having let slip an opportunity . . . or of our having failed to do so. But our self-awareness has been aroused and it is our task to understand its significance. The dream-picture is generally accompanied by feelings of helplessness, insecurity and inferiority. The ego feels powerless to find the right path.

Physical, psychic and spiritual development is held back because our complexes, unconscious fixations, psychological routines, our persona or mask, our intellectual dogmatism, our disinclination from force of habit to make any effort, our blindness and so on all interfere with our inner development. Or else we suffer from failure- or frustration-complexes which prevent us from realizing our personality. Lack of self-possession and self-confidence makes us give way to nervous agitation or even nervous hurry.

The departure platform is a symbol of the unconscious, the place at which our development begins, the starting point of fresh material, psychic and spiritual ventures. There is a wide choice of destination, but we have to choose the one most suited to us. On the other hand, it may quite simply be the centre of heavy traffic in all directions, an evocation of the self.

We seldom dream of the arrival platform. It shows that the secret workings of inner development have brought us one stage further in our destiny.

We dream only occasionally of station-masters and guards. They may be seen as figures of the impersonal ego and of its transcendent function of self-realization. However, the station-master stands for the 'head' which governs the active, creative and impersonal forces which rule our fate, while the guard is the adviser, guide and, sometimes, judge and executioner.

The engine conjures, as the case may be, the conscious ego which carries along the psyche in its entirety, for good or ill, or else its reverse, the impersonal ego which takes us in the direction in which we have to go. In both instances a dynamic energy is harnessed to the available psychic resources. A massive engine rushing towards the dreamer may be a modern dream-picture of the dragon. It would appear to be about to swallow us up, but we are the ones who use its strength to attain our own ends.

Rail-tickets are signs that we have to give in order to receive. The exchange symbolized by money (our energy) is what allows us to acquire and does not allow us to receive without giving, unlike the person who remains in an infantile state. Development is impossible without sacrifice, and without self-sacrifice.

Travelling without a ticket or in a higher class than that to which our ticket entitles us are signs of self-deception, deliberate or involuntary, about our gifts, qualities, position, importance and so on ... and there is always the risk that we shall have to pay more than if we had bought the proper ticket in the first place.

Dreaming that we are in a lower class than that to which our ticket entitles us betrays a tendency in the dreamer to underestimate his or her gifts, qualities, position, importance and so on.

Uncomfortable, dusty, grimy or antiquated trains are signs of a super-differentiation of the conscious ego and disappointment in discovering that this superdifferentiation impoverishes the dynamism of development; or else cruelly real dream-pictures of a degree of impoverishment in the dreamer's material, psychic or spiritual life, despite illusions to the contrary.

Trains, coaches or compartments noticeable for their power, luxury or comfort are signs that the potential derived from the hidden work of development is being efficiently realized, but that the conscious ego is still unaware of it. Or else these are dream-pictures of material, psychic or spiritual potential ignored by a self-deprecating conscious ego lacking self-confidence and underestimating its own resources.

Derailment: indication of neurosis which derails the process of development, or a complex which is hard to unravel or dubious to resolve.

Rail-crash: comparable with a battle of Dragons and Giants; indicative of a serious situation of internal conflict.

Difficulties in boarding a crowded train show the dreamer's difficulties in becoming part of social living because he or she is too individualistic. This is a condition which may be due to egocentricity, infantilism, isolation or excessive introversion. If the train is packed with children, then the dreamer is infantile, but not child enough in the sense of possessing a soul which is simple, unambiguous and sincere.

The threat or actuality of being run down by a train expresses an extreme anxiety-state, either because the conscious ego feels drowned and as it were annihilated by the unconscious libido – the dreamer risking loss of psychic self-control and being in danger of self-destruction – or else because the dreamer feels crushed by the material and social life which he or she is forced to lead to scrape an existence.

Trains running over a person or thing are signs of intense repression of some undiscovered element. The dreamer's material and social life crushes some psychological element within, and this will vary with the individual.

Luggage is regarded by the dreamer, rightly or wrongly, as holding all the things which he or she cannot do without. Psychologically, therefore, it stands for our own well-being, potential and external signs of wealth, as well as the whole body of things which seem vital to us, such as strength, capability, instinct, skills, habits and things to which we are attached or which we preserve, and so on. Just as when we travel with our luggage, so we believe that we possess all those elements essential to physical, psychic and spiritual life – the equivalent of our intellectual equipment.

To forget or to lose our luggage, like the dream-picture of missing a train, is generally accompanied by feelings of helplessness, insecurity and inferiority. The ego feels powerless to co-ordinate its efforts. This dream stresses our conscious or unconscious oversights in dealing either with our objective or subjective life and is the sign of natural or acquired dysfunction. Lack of self-possession causes nervous anxiety and loss of control, or mental confusion, loss of memory. Sometimes this dream-picture reveals a failure-complex, placing us in unpleasant or even inextricable situations, or a frustration-complex. These two complexes hinder realization of our individuality.

Bulky luggage: we often burden ourselves, physically and psychologically, with the bulky luggage of illusion, self-imposed obligation, intellectual knowledge, projections, unconscious fixations, longing to make a show, a mentality which settles ever more deeply into its prejudices, anxiety, revolt, sentimentality, cravings and so on. Much needs to be left behind, checked and set in order before we can continue our normal development and be able to 'catch the train' with what we need, unburdened by the bulk of false values.

Anxiety through lack of luggage: have we got all that we really need to bring to a successful conclusion something undertaken in conscious life or to cope with the beginnings of self-awareness? What illusions have made us set out without having made provision for what we shall need? This anxiety arises from our uncertainty as to whether our resources are adequate to the task in hand.

Getting rid of our luggage: when we have achieved a certain measure of development, our dream-luggage, that is our attachment to those aids which we believed indispensable, become burdens, that is, dead and useless weight. We therefore rid ourselves of them with a profound feeling of freedom, either by detaching ourselves from them or by inner self-denial. From then on spiritual, internal or personal values predominate. From now on it becomes necessary for us to rid ourselves of whatever has become tarnished and outworn, be it attachments, opinions, feelings, cares, preoccupations or commitments. In this context, it is a matter of eliminating useless constraints.

trapezium   Schneider has likened the trapezium to a bull's head in full face and hence it should evoke notions of sacrifice. It might equally be regarded as a truncated triangle and would then give the impression of incompleteness, irregularity or failure. This might arise from the fact that the figure is un-fulfilled or has been diverted or stopped in the course of its development, or else has been mutilated. All these observations may be transposed, symbolically, from the material to the psychological plane and be epitomized as a measure of constraint in an individual's dynamism. The trapezium is a summons to motion.

treasure Buried treasure – as the *Hadīth* has it: 'I was a buried treasure: I longed to be known' – is the symbol of the Divine Essence in latency. It is also that of esoteric knowledge.

The Hindu goddess Kuvera guards treasures and is mistress of the Earth's riches, metals being traditionally related to buried treasure. However, her eight treasures, like those of the *chakravartī*, are in fact the eight chief emblems of the gods, symbols both of their powers and of universal manifestation. Because she rides upon a ram, Kuvera has been compared with the Argonauts' Golden Fleece, another buried treasure. Generally speaking, these treasures are symbols of knowledge and immortality, the spiritual storehouses which can only be reached after a perilous quest. Lastly, they are guarded by DRAGONS or by MONSTERS which are images of those dangerous psychic entities to which one is in danger of falling victim unless one has the necessary qualifications or has taken the proper precautions (CORT, GUER, MALA).

The treasure generally lies deep in some CAVERN or buried underground. Its position symbolizes the difficulties inherent in its quest, but above all the fact that human effort is essential. The treasure is not freely given by Heaven and is only to be found at the end of a long series of ordeals. This bears witness to the fact that the buried treasure is spiritual and moral and that these ordeals, battles with monsters, with the elements and with robbers along the road belong, like the obstacles themselves, to the moral and spiritual order. The buried treasure is a symbol of the inner life and the monsters which guard it none other than aspects of ourselves.

tree Merely the bibliography of trees, one of the richest and most widespread symbolic motifs, would of itself fill a volume. Mircea Eliade (ELIT pp. 266–7) identifies seven different lines of interpretation. These he does not claim to be exhaustive, but they all stem from the notion of the living cosmos in a state of perpetual regeneration.

In spite of outward appearance and hurried conclusions even sacred trees are not everywhere cult-objects. They may be the representations of an entity larger than they and which may itself become an object of worship.

As symbols of life constantly developing and ever rising to the Heavens, trees conjure up the full range of vertical symbolism; Leonardo da Vinci's tree is an example. On the other hand, they serve to symbolize the cyclical character of cosmic development in death and regeneration. Deciduous trees are especially suggestive of this cycle since they shed their leaves and cover themselves with fresh foliage each year.

Trees also connect the three levels of the cosmos – the Underworld through their roots burrowing deep into the soil; the Earth's surface with their trunk and lower branches; the Heavens with their upper branches and top, reaching up to the light. Reptiles crawl among their roots; birds roost in their branches; and they relate the Under to the Upper World. They bring all the elements together: Water circulates in their sap; Earth becomes part of their body through their roots; Air feeds their leaves; and Fire is produced by rubbing their sticks together.

The article which follows deals only with the symbolism of trees in general: at its conclusion there is a list of those trees for which there are separate entries.

Because its roots delve into the soil and its branches stretch up to the skies, the trees is universally regarded as a symbol of the relationships established between Heaven and Earth. In this sense trees possess the character of CENTRES, to the degree that the World Tree is synonymous with the World AXIS. As axial figures, trees are therefore the upward path along which proceed those who pass from the visible to the invisible. This, then, is the tree, as suggestive of Jacob's Ladder as of the shaman's post in a Siberian yurt, of the centre-pole in a Voodoo shrine ('Spirit-path': METV p. 66), or of that in a Sioux medicine-lodge round which the Sun-dance takes place. In Judeo-Christian tradition it is the central pillar which holds up temple or house and it is also the spinal COLUMN which supports the human body, the temple of the soul.

The Cosmic Tree is often depicted as an especially majestic species. This was the way in which Celts looked upon the oak, Germans the lime, Scandinavians the ash, Eastern Islam the olive and the peoples of Siberia the larch and birch. All are trees remarkable for their size, their longevity or, as in the case of the birch, for their gleaming whiteness. Pegs set in the trunk of the birch-tree marked out the stages of the shaman's ascension. Gods, spirits and souls took advantage of the World Tree as a path between Heaven and Earth. In China, this was true of the Kien Mu, a tree growing in the centre of the world, as the fact that it neither emitted an echo nor cast a shadow bears out. It had nine roots and nine branches through which it reached out to the nine springs where the dead dwelt and to the nine Heavens.

Up and down it went the emperors, who not only mediated between Heaven and Earth but were surrogates for the Sun. Sun and Moon came down the Siberian larch as well, in the shape of birds. Furthermore, on opposite sides of the Kien-tree grew the Fu-tree to the east and the Jo-tree to the west, where the Sun rose and set. The Jo-tree also bore ten Suns in the shape of ten ravens.

To Shi'ite Muslims of the Ismaili rite, the tree 'nourished by earth and water and overtopping the seventh Heaven' symbolizes *haqīqāt*, the state of bliss in which the mystic surmounts the dualism of appearance and reaches Supreme reality, primordial Unity, in which being coincides with God.

Some traditions hold to a plurality of World Trees. Thus the Goldi set one in Heaven, one on Earth and a third in the Kingdom of the Dead (HARA p. 56).

On the opposite side of the world to the land of the Goldi, in the cosmology of the Pueblo Indians, the great pine-tree in the Underworld shares the ascension symbolism of the transmigration of souls by providing the ladder up which the Ancestors were able to climb until they reached the light of our Sun (ALEC pp. 36–7). However, this central tree, which overshadows the whole range of thought, from the cosmos to mankind, with its bulk and strength, is also of necessity the Tree of Life. This is true whether its leaves, like those of the laurel, are evergreen and symbols of immortality, or whether they are deciduous so that their seasonal regeneration is an expression of the cycle of dying and rebirth and hence of the dynamism of life. 'If the tree is charged with sacred forces,' Mircea Eliade observes, 'it is because it is vertical, it grows, it loses its leaves and regains them and is thus regenerated (it "dies" and "rises" again) times without number' (ELIT pp. 268-9).

The sap in the Tree of Life is the dew of Heaven, and its jealously guarded fruits convey a crumb of immortality. This was true of the Tree of Life in the Garden of Eden (its fruits were twelve in number, the sign of the cycle of rebirth and of the Heavenly Jerusalem), of the golden apples in the Garden of the Hesperides, of the peaches from the Si-wang Mu, and of the sap of the Persian *haoma*, excluding all mention of the resin of various conifers. The Japanese *himorogi*, brought to Middle Earth, would seem in all likelihood to have been a Tree of Life. The Tree of Life is a common Persian ornamental motif, standing between a pair of animals facing one another. In Java it is depicted, together with the central mountain, upon the *kayon* (screen) of the shadow-theatre.

The Bodhi-tree under which the Buddha obtained enlightenment is yet another World Tree and Tree of Life, and in early Buddhist iconography it stands for the Buddha himself. An inscription at Angkor states that its roots are Brahmā, its trunk Shiva and its branches Vishnu. This is a classic description of the World Axis. The Cosmic Tree, employed to obtain the beverage of immortality in the churning of the Sea of Milk, is depicted at Angkor with Vishnu at its foot, upon its trunk and at its top. In other contexts, however, Shiva is a central tree and Brahmā and Vishnu its side branches.

The association of the Tree of Life with the manifestation of the godhead is re-echoed in Christian tradition, since there is an analogy, or even a renewal of the symbol, between the tree in the Old Covenant, the Tree of Life in Genesis, and the Tree of the Cross, or Tree of the New Covenant, which renewed mankind. De Lubac regards the Cross, standing on a mountain in the centre of the world, as wholly renewing the ancient symbol of the Cosmic or World Tree. In any case, Christian iconography provides constant examples of the leafy cross, or Tree Cross, where the gap between the upper branches reveals the symbolism of the fork and its graphic representation the letter Y, or Oneness and Duality. At the extreme limit, by metonomy Christ himself becomes the World Tree, the World Axis, the ladder, a comparison which Origen makes explicit.

Both in East and West the Tree of Life was often inverted. According to the Vedas, this inversion derived from a definite concept of the role played by sunshine and sunlight in the growth of living things. They drew life from above and tried to instil life below. Hence the inversion in which the roots were depicted as playing the part of branches and the branches of roots. Life came from Heaven and was instilled into Earth. There is nothing anti-scientific about this concept, but in the East the upper atmosphere is sacralized and photogenesis explained as the power of heavenly beings. The Hindu symbolism of the inverted tree is expressed with particular clarity in the *Bhagavad Gītā* (15: 1) and also bears the meaning of the roots as the principle of manifestation and the branches as the effloration of that manifestation. Guénon postulates a further meaning. The tree rises above the plane of meditation which marks the lower limits of the inverted cosmic realm. It crosses the bounds of the manifest to enter those of meditation and supply the latter with inspiration.

The same notion is to be found in Jewish esotericism where the *Zohar* speaks of the Tree of Life as stretching from the upper to the lower regions and all of it lit by the Sun. In Islam, the Tree of Bliss is rooted in the highest Heaven and its branches stretch above and below the world.

In Icelandic and Finnish folklore the same tradition is firmly present. The Lapps annually sacrificed an ox in honour of their vegetation-god and at the same time a tree was set up close to the altar with its branches in the ground and its roots in the air.

Schmidt records that the medicine-men of some Australian Aboriginal tribes had a magic tree which they planted upside-down. Having soaked the roots in human blood they would then burn it.

In the Upanishads, the universe is an inverted tree, rooted in the Heavens and with branches which enfold the whole Earth. According to Eliade, this image might have a solar significance.

Cf. *Rig Veda*: 'The branches grow towards what is low, the roots are on high, that its rays may descend upon us!' The *Katha Upanishad* describes it like this: 'This eternal Ashvattha, whose roots rise on high, and whose branches grow low, is the pure [*shukram*], is the Brahman, is what we call the Non-Death. All the worlds rest in it!'

The *ashvattha* tree, Mircea Eliade observes, 'here represents the clearest possible manifestation of Brahman in the Cosmos, represents, in other words, creation as a descending movement' (ELIT p. 273).

Gilbert Durand, therefore, concludes: 'This unusual inverted tree, which shocks our sense of ascendent verticality, is a strong sign of the co-existence within the archetype of the tree of cyclical reciprocity' (DURS p. 371). This notion of reciprocity leads to that of the marriage of the continuous and the discontinuous and of oneness and dualism, of the symbolic shading of the Tree of Life into the Tree of Knowledge, that 'tree of the knowledge of good and evil', which is nonetheless an entity separate from the other. In the Garden of Eden it was to be the instrument of Adam's fall, just as the Tree of Life was to be the means of his redemption in Christ's crucifixion. The distinction which the Old Testament draws strengthens still further the notion of reciprocity and, if André Virel is right, should induce 'the parallelism and distinction between two creative developments, biological [represented by the Tree of Life] on the one hand and psychological and historical on the other' (VIRI p. 175).

In fact, it is patently the notion of biological development which has made the Tree of Life a fertility symbol upon which, in the course of time, an edifice of propitiatory magic has been erected of which plenty of evidence survives to this day. Thus, in some nomadic Iranian tribes young women tattoo their bodies with trees, the roots sprouting from their sexual organs and the leaves opening on their breasts. A very ancient custom is the reason for finding isolated trees in the countryside, often growing beside a SPRING, with their lower branches covered with red handkerchiefs which barren women, from the Mediterranean to India, have tied to them as fertility charms.

The Dravidian custom of mystic marriage between humans and trees was aimed to enhance the woman's child-bearing capacities. 'The girl betrothed to a Hindu Goala was obliged to marry a mango-tree before wedding her lawful husband' (BOUA p. 277). There is evidence of similar traditions in the Punjab and the Himalayas. 'The Gujerati Kudva Kunbis in Bombay will first marry a girl to a mango or some other fruit-tree if there are any problems with the marriage, because,' as Campbell wrote in *The Bombay Gazette*, 'evil spirits fear trees and especially fruit-trees.' In this context the analogy of the fruit-tree with the woman plays a complementary part with the analogy of the sappy-tree with male procreative powers. This explains why the Kurmi first marry the groom 'to a mango-tree on his wedding-day. He clasps the tree-trunk to which he is then tied. After a decent interval he is set free but bracelets of leaves from the tree are fastened round his wrists.' Marriage to trees associated with human marriage recurs in North America among the Sioux and among the Bushmen and Hottentots of southern Africa.

The Yakut told how,

at the Earth's navel, grew an eight-branched tree, covered with blossom. . . . From the treetop poured a foaming, yellow liquor of the gods. When passers-by drank of it their weariness fell away and their hunger vanished. . . . When the first man, at his coming into the world, sought to know why he was there, he went to this gigantic tree with a top that overtops the Heavens. . . . Then in the trunk of that wonderful tree . . . he saw a hole in which he could make out the upper parts of a woman who told him that he had come into the world to be the father of the human race.

(ROUF p. 374)

Altaic peoples also said 'that before they come down to Earth, human souls dwell in Heaven or perch on the celestial tops of the Cosmic Tree in the shape of little birds' (ROUF p. 376).

Marco Polo related that 'the first king of the Uighurs was born from a certain mushroom fed by tree-sap' (quoted in ROUF p. 361). Similar beliefs are to be found in China. All these legends occur in two versions only. In one, and this would appear to be the older, the tree is impregnated by sunlight, and in the other two trees couple.

Dravidian customs also married one tree to another as a substitute for human weddings. Thus, in south India, in the case of childless marriages, the couple would make their way to some holy river or lake on the morning of an astrologically favourable day. There they would plant cuttings from a sacred tree side by side, one male, the other female, and would wreath the stiff straight twig of the male tree with the pliant twig of the female tree. The married couple of trees was then fenced off to ensure that it would flourish and through its own fertility ensure that of the human couple who had planted it (BOUA pp. 8–9). However, at this stage the trees were merely regarded as being betrothed. An interval of ten years was needed before the barren wife returned, on her own this time, to the woodland couple and set between the roots of the trees, their branches still entwined, a stone which had been long washed in the waters of a holy river or lake and on which was carved a pair of intertwined serpents. Only then would the mystic marriage of the sacred trees take place and the woman become a mother. The association of the symbols of WATER, STONE, SERPENT and tree in this fertility-rite is especially significant.

Anthropomorphic interpretations of the tree also occur among the Altaic and Turko-Mongol peoples of Siberia. Thus, 'a man may change himself into a tree, the Tungus believe, and then resume his original shape' (ROUF p. 246).

The tree as the source of life, Eliade explains (ELIT p. 302), 'presupposes that the source of life is concentrated in that plant; and therefore that the human modality exists in a state of potentiality, in seed form.' He quotes Spencer and Gillen for the belief of the northern Australian Aboriginal Warramunga tribe 'that "the spirits of children", the size of a grain of sand, exist in certain trees, whence they sometimes come and enter the wombs of their mothers through the navels' (ELIT ibid.). This is very reminiscent of the widely held belief that 'the principle of fire, like that of life, is hidden in certain trees from which it can be extracted by rubbing their twigs together' (GRAF).

All the beliefs which we have been describing show that, sexually, tree symbolism is ambivalent. The Tree of Life may originally have been regarded as an image of the primordial HERMAPHRODITE, but on the level of the phenomenal world the trunk rising to the skies, a symbol of pre-eminently solar strength and power, is really the phallus, the archetypal image of the Father. On the other hand, the hollow tree, as well as the tree covered with thick and interwoven foliage in which birds nest and which bears an annual crop of fruit, conjures up the archetypal lunar image of the fruitful Mother. It was from a hollow oak that the waters of the Fountain of Youth poured (CANA p. 80), while the alchemists' ATHANOR, too, the womb in which the philosophers' gold gestates, was often compared with a tree. This is the meaning in Hieronymus Bosch's painting of the Temptation of St Anthony of the tree which 'he imagines as a termagant tearing from her bark-covered belly a baby wrapped in swaddling-bands' (VANA p. 217). Sometimes one tree may be regarded as male and another as female. 'The Chuvach use lime to cut the grave-posts of their female dead and oak for their males' (ROUF p. 360).

Yet again these two polarities may be brought together, leading Jung to interpret the symbol hermaphroditically.

The myth of Cybele and Attis provided the analyst with an excellent field in which to give his thinking full play. In the first place, he regarded the mother of the gods, Cybele, symbol of maternal libido, as being hermaphroditic just like the tree. She was, however, a hermaphrodite burning with love for her son and since the young god's desires were directed towards a nymph, the jealous Cybele sent him mad.

Driven mad by the insanity-breeding mother enamoured of him, he emasculates himself, and that under a pine tree. (The pine tree plays an important role in his service. Every year a pine tree was wreathed about and upon it an image of Attis was hung, and then it was cut down, which represents the castration.) . . . Cybele now took this pine tree, bore it into her cavern and there wept over it . . . The chthonic mother takes her son with her into the cavern – namely the womb – according to another version. Attis was transformed into the pine tree. The tree here has an essentially phallic meaning; on the contrary, the attaching of the image of Attis to the tree refers to the maternal meaning. 'To be attached to the mother'.

(JUNL p. 260)

In imperial Rome on 22 March a cut pine-tree, a memorial, symbol or image of Attis, was solemnly carried to the Palatine Hill in the festival known as 'Arbor intrat'.

Another myth has been interpreted in the same sense, although the details of the original legends may have been somewhat cavalierly handled. It relates to the same tree, the pine. The hero, Pentheus, was the son of Echion, the serpent, and himself possessed a snake-like nature. In his curiosity to watch the orgies of the Maenads, he climbed up a tree, 'but he was observed by his mother; the Maenads cut down the tree, and Pentheus, taken for an animal, was torn by them in frenzy, his own mother being the first to rush upon him. In this myth the phallic meaning of the tree (cutting down, castration) and its maternal significance (mounting and the sacrificial death of the son) is present' (JUNL pp. 260–1).

This ambivalence of the tree symbol, simultaneously phallus and womb, is even more clearly shown by the double tree, 'symbolizing the individuation process in which the inner opposites unite' (JUNS p. 187).

In tribal legends, the wealth of both 'tree-fathers' and 'tree-mothers' produced the 'tree-ancestor' which ends in modern times, all mythical elements stripped away, as the 'family-tree'. In the course of its journey from deep-seated myth to modern allegory, mention should be made of the Old Testament myth of the Jesse-tree (Isaiah 11: 1–2), source of much artistic inspiration and mystical exegesis. 'And there shall come forth a rod out of the stem of Jesse, and a Branch shall grow out of his roots: And the spirit of the Lord shall rest upon him, the spirit of wisdom and understanding, the spirit of counsel and might, the spirit of knowledge and of fear of the Lord.' The Jesse-tree epitomizes the successive generations, whose story is told in the Bible, which culminates in Our Lady and Jesus Christ. It was highly popular among glass-painters and miniaturists in the thirteenth century, and especially with Cistercians, because of their special devotion to Our Lady. The tree is generally depicted sprouting from Jesse's navel, mouth or side. Its trunk sometimes has branches on which Christ's forefathers, the Kings of Judah, are to be seen.

The Tree of Life as a symbol of the growth of family, city or peoples, or better still of the increasing power of a monarch, can abruptly invert its polarity and become a Tree of Death. A commonplace of this is provided by the dreams which troubled Nebuchadnezzar and which the Prophet Daniel interpreted. 'I saw a dream', said the king,

which made me afraid. . . . I saw . . . a tree in the midst of the earth, and the height thereof was great. The tree grew and was strong, and the height thereof reached unto heaven, and the sight thereof to the end of all the earth: The

leaves thereof were fair, and the fruit thereof much, and in it was meat for all . . . and, behold, a watcher and an holy one came down from heaven; He cried aloud, and said thus, Hew down the tree, and cut off his branches, and shake off his leaves, and scatter his fruit. . . . Then Daniel . . . answered . . . the dream be to them that hate thee, and the interpretation thereof to thine enemies. The tree that thou sawest, which grew, and was strong, whose height reached unto the heaven . . . is thou, O king, that art grown and become strong. . . . [But] they shall drive thee from among men.
(Daniel 4: 5, 10–12, 13–14, 19–20, 22, 25)

Ezekiel compares Assyria with a cedar of Lebanon when prophesying its doom (ch. 31). Tall trees like these cedars are sometimes taken as figures of the enemies of Jehovah and his Chosen People. 'The voice of the Lord breaketh the cedars; yea the Lord breaketh the cedars of Lebanon' (Psalm 29: 5). Isaiah (14: 15) meanwhile denounced tyrants who tried, like the cypress and the cedar, 'to ascend above the heights of the clouds', but who were cut down. This is the negative aspect of these mighty trees, which also stand for the boundless ambition of earthly greatness which perpetually seeks to extend its power and which is brought to nothing.

The Kabbalah also mentions a Tree of Death. It provided the leaves with which Adam covered his nakedness and the *Zohar* regards it as a symbol of the black arts which were one of the consequences of the Fall. It is linked to the existence of the psychic body deprived of the 'body of light' (SCHK p. 193).

But, yet again, it is the Cross, the instrument both of torture and of redemption, which brings together in a single image these two extremes of meaning conveyed by that most significant of all things, the Tree – through death to life; *per crucem ad lucem*, through the Cross to the light.

(See also: ACACIA; ALMOND; APPLE; ARBUTUS; ASH-TREE; BANANA; BIRCH; BOX-WOOD; CATALPA; CEDAR; CHERRY; CHESTNUT; CYPRESS; DATE; DOGWOOD; EBONY; FIG; HAZEL; JUJUBE; LABURNUM; LARCH; LAUREL; LIME; MULBERRY; NUT; OAK; OLIVE; PALM; PEACH; PEAR; PINE; PLUM; POPLAR; SAKAKI; SHALA; SYCAMORE; TAMARIND; TAMARISK; THUJA; WALNUT; WILLOW; YEW)

triad (see also THREE) The Christian dogma of the Trinity – One God existing in Three Persons, separate in their different relationships, but not in their being or essence, and to which the operation of certain specifics is attributed, power to the Father, intelligence to the Son (Word) and love to the Holy Spirit – is conveyed in a number of symbols. These include the equilateral triangle; the three-leafed clover; a combination of throne (power), book (intelligence) and dove (love); a cross with the Father at the top, the Son in the middle and the Holy Spirit at the foot; three intersecting circles, signifying their mutual infinity; a group of three angels of the same size, recalling Abraham's vision under the oak at Mambre.

In all religious traditions and in nearly all systems of philosophy triads, or groups of three, occur corresponding to the hypostasis of primordial forces or with the faces of the Supreme Deity. Although it is not always easy to determine the lines of demarcation between persons of such triads, it would seem safe to say that none is conceived upon so rigid and well-defined a pattern as the Christian Trinity, where the dogma of separate persons and single essence removes the logical contradiction without dispelling any of its mystery.

As an example of such triads we would instance one of the least-known. In his *Nueva coronica y buen gobierno*, Guzman Poma de Ayala states that in ancient times the Peruvians acknowledged the existence of a Supreme Deity (Illapa, 'thunderbolt') in three persons – the father (giver of justice) and an older and a younger son. The latter was lord of the fecundating rains and therefore the power which nourished mankind.

The trinity of thunderbolt, thunder and lightning may also be regarded as a manifestation of the storm-god at the birth of Amerindian agricultural society (GIRP p. 42).

Generally speaking such triads symbolize the chief manifestations of the power of the godhead, or else, when conceived on a more internalized and philosophic basis, as in the *Enneads* of Plotinus, the inner life of the Monad whose actions are imagined by analogy with the spiritual activities of the human soul.

triangle The symbolism of the triangle is part and parcel of that of the number THREE and can only be separated from it in terms of its relationship with other geometrical figures.

According to Boethius, who adopted the Platonists' geometrical theories studied by Latin writers, the primary plane surface is the triangle, the second the square and the third the pentagon. If lines are drawn from its centre to its angles, any figure may be divided into several triangles. The triangle is the foundation upon which the pyramid is built.

Equilateral triangles symbolize the godhead, harmony and proportion. Since all procreation proceeds from division, humans correspond to an equilateral triangle split into two, that is, with a right-angled triangle. Plato, in the *Timaeus*, considers that the latter also stands for the Earth. The transformation of the equilateral into the right-angled triangle involves loss of harmony.

The ancient Mayan hieroglyphic for the Sun-ray was a triangle, similar to the 'tiny nail' formed by the burgeoning maize-shoot when it breaks the surface of the soil four days after planting (GIRP p. 198).

Its connections with the Sun and with maize made the triangle doubly a fertility symbol.

In India, Greece and Rome, triangles were often used as decorative motifs in friezes. Their significance would seem always to have remained the same. Point uppermost, triangles stand for fire and the male sexual organs; point downwards, for water and the female sexual organs. The STAR OF DAVID, comprising two inverted triangles, has the especial meaning of knowledge. In Jewish tradition, the equilateral triangle symbolizes God, whose name may not be uttered.

Apart from its well-known importance to the Pythagoreans, in alchemy the triangle is the symbol of Fire; it is also a symbol of the heart. In this context the relationship between the regular and the inverted triangle should always be borne in mind, since the one reflects the other, they being the respective symbols of Christ's divine and human natures as well as being those of the mountain and the cavern. In India, the inverted triangle is a symbol of the *yoni*, or womb, while the two triangles stand for *purusha* and *prakrti*, Shiva and the SHAKTI, LINGAM and *yoni*, Fire and Water, and the tendencies to *sattva* and *tamas*. When harmonized in the shape of the six-pointed Star of David, they stand for *rajas*, or expansion on the plane of manifestation. When brought together, nadir to apex in the shape of Shiva's *damaru*, they become the BINDU, or 'seed' of manifestation (BHAB, DANA, ELIF, GRAD, GRAP, GUED, GUEM, GUEC, GUET, GUES, MUTT, SAIR).

The importance which Freemasons attach to the triangle is well-known. Their 'shining delta' relates to the shape of the Greek capital letter Δ rather than to the mouths of the Nile. The 'sublime triangle' is one which has an angle of 36° at the apex and two of 72° at the base (for the symbolism of these numbers see under THIRTY-SIX). Each type of triangle is regarded as corresponding to one of the elements – the equilateral to Earth; the right-angled to Water; the scalene to Air; and the isosceles to Fire. Linked to triangles are countless theories about regular polyhedrons derived from equilateral triangles; as also are the theories about the countless TRIADS (see also THREE) in religious history; about such moral triptychs as 'right thinking, right speaking and right doing', 'wisdom, strength and beauty' and so on; about the time phases of past, present and future, birth, maturity and death; and about the three basic principles in alchemy, salt, sulphur and mercury; and so on. Such lists swiftly lead from symbolic to conventional signs.

The meaning of the Masonic triangle was Duration, as the base line, and Light and Darkness as the sides leading to the apex, together forming the cosmic triad. So far as the Shining Delta was concerned, traditionally this was an isosceles triangle with a base longer than the other two sides, like the pediment of a temple, with an angle of 108° at the apex and two each of 36° at the base, such a triangle corresponding to the Golden Number. Furthermore, such a triangle left ample room for the inclusion of the pentagon and Blazing Star (BOUM pp. 86–94).

Trickster See under MONKEY.

trident A symbol of sea-deities, whose palaces lie at the bottom of the ocean depths, the trident was originally a depiction of the teeth of sea-monsters and resembled the foaming crests of the storm-tossed waves. It was also one of the earliest fishing implements. It was the weapon, too, of a class of Roman gladiator known as the *retiarius*, who fought with net and trident.

The trident is the emblem of the sea-god Poseidon (Neptune) and a mark of his command of the waters, which he can raise or still. From the same viewpoint, it is also, with the net, the symbol of Christ as 'Fisher of Men'. Furthermore, when its prongs are of an equal length, it is a symbol of the Trinity and may even serve as a secret representation of the Cross.

In Christian tradition, the trident is placed 'in Satan's hands as an instrument of punishment with which he thrusts into the flames (symbol of torment) the souls of the damned. However,' Paul Diel adds, 'it is as much a guilt symbol, its three prongs standing for the three compulsions (sexuality, nourishment and spirituality) which frame all desires, and these may too easily grow exorbitant. It also stands for the risk of deviance, that basic weakness which places the individual at the mercy of the source of temptation and of punishment' (DIES p. 147).

The trident is a solar emblem, its prongs standing for the Sun's rays, and a symbol of the thunderbolt (its prongs are lightning flashes). Tridents strike their prey and in this respect may be likened to some depictions of the VAJRA, which is both thunderbolt and trident.

Above all, in India the *trishūla*, or trident, is the emblem of Shiva the transformer and destroyer. Its three prongs may represent either *trikāla*, threefold time, past, present and future; or the hierarchy of the three levels of manifestation; or else the three 'properties' (*guna*). The *trikāla* is indicated by raising three of the fingers of the right hand in a gesture known as the *trishūlahasta*.

In Buddhism, the trident is taken as a symbol of the *triratna,* or triple jewel. It may also be regarded as the triple current of energy in Tantrism – the *sushumna* in the centre and the *idā* and *pingalā* on either side. Furthermore these currents are directed towards a central point and suggest the *nadī* coiled round the central axis (COOI, CHAE, GROI, GUES, KRAA, MALA, MUTT).

trigram The principles of the Chinese symbolism of the trigram were supposed to have been reveal to Fu Hi (twenty-fourth century BC) by a water-dragon. They are based upon the combination of two determinants, a solid line corresponding to the *yang* and a broken line corresponding to the *yin*. The whole contingent development of manifestation, from primordial Oneness, may therefore be expressed first in four 'digrams' and then in eight trigrams. These epitomize all the potential combinations of triple, and hence 'perfect', groupings of YIN AND YANG, since, as Chuang Tzu stated, '*yin* and *yang* join forces in perfect harmony.' In these groups of three, the three lines set one above the other correspond to Heaven, Mankind and Earth, hence the divinatory practices derived from the *I Ching*. When paired together to form HEXAGRAMS, the eight trigrams (*pakua*) comprise sixty-four hexagrams, alternately celestial and terrestrial.

The trigrams are arranged in a circle around the *yin-yang*, giving expression to every aspect of manifestation. The *I Ching* is the book of the (rotational) changes of the trigrams. The original shape of the ideogram *I* was apparently that of the chameleon. Trigrams are thus placed in correspondence to the eight winds (the eight points of the compass) and the eight (or rather nine) elements, since Earth is at the centre. They correspond to the eight pillars in the Temple of Heaven, to the eight spokes of the wheel and, by analogy, to the eight paths of the Buddhist Way. There are two traditional arrangements called Fu Ti or Anterior Heaven (*Sien-t'ien*) and Wen Wang or Posterior Heaven (*Hu-t'ien*). Both arrangements seem to have been employed indifferently, the first being related to Hot'u and the other to Yu the Great's Lo-chu. This is the development of the plain cross into the swastika and of primordial stillness into motion. Nor should it be forgotten that although their use in fortune-telling was secondary, and to some extent decadent (but seems to have been comprehended in the ideogram *kua*), it was attributed to Wen Wang himself. Tzu T'uen-i stated that the *I Ching* 'contained the secrets of Heaven and Earth, of ghosts and spirits'. This implies that, with the help of yarrow stalks, they are a potential source of the secrets of fate and also and above all of primordial manifestation. It should be added that because trigrams correspond to the currents of cosmic energy, they have always been used as protective charms and, indeed, are still so used to this day, as may be seen by their presence above the doors of Chinese and Vietnamese houses.

To summarize the systems of correspondences of the eight trigrams:

Ch'ien: active perfection; corresponds to Heaven, the south and Summer, to creative energy, the male sex and the Sun;

K'un: passive perfection; corresponds to Earth, the north, receptivity, the female sex and the Moon;

Chen: the arousing; corresponds to thunder, the northeast and the birth of Spring;

Sun: the gentle; corresponds to the wind, the southwest and the close of Summer;

K'an: the abyss; corresponds to Water, the west and to Autumn;

Li: corresponds to Fire, the east and to Spring;

Ken: stillness; corresponds to the mountain, the northwest and the onset of Winter;

Tui: mist; corresponds to lakes, the southeast and the beginning of Summer.

This description follows Fu-hi's arrangement. In Wen-Wang's, *Li* and *K'an*, Fire and Water, are south and north, Sun and Moon, Summer and Winter, red and black; *Chen* and *Tui*, arousal and standing water, are east and west, Spring and Autumn, wood and metal, green and white. The two arrangements are governed by different but not contradictory systems.

In alchemical symbolism *Li* and *K'an* stand for the release of the celestial and terrestrial principles of *Ch'ien* and *Kun*. They are the two complementary elements of the Great Work. *Li* and *K'an* are lead and mercury, 'breath' (*hsi*) and being (*hsing*). *Kun* and *K'an* are located in that holy region in which the *hsing* (semen) arises, *Ch'ien* is located in the *ājnā-chakra*, between the eyes, from which the gleaming *hsi* comes down. The marriage of *hsi* and *hsing* in the inner furnace, entailing both that of *Li* amd *K'an* and of *Ch'ien* and *Kun*, recreates primordial Oneness, which existed before Heaven was made separate from Earth. This is how immortality is obtained. According to the *I Ching*, such marriages, producers of hexagrams, stand either for fulfilment, or for the fecundating penetration by Heaven of Earth which generates peace, living beings and the embryo of immortality (CHOC, GRAD, GRAP, GRIF, GUET, GRIT, KALT, MAST, MATM, SOOL, WILG, YUAC).

triple (see also THREE; TRIAD)   Animals, humans, heroes or gods depicted as having linked triple bodies may stand for various triads corresponding either to attributes – the three levels of the cosmos; creation, preservation and destruction (Brahmā, Vishnu and Shiva) – or to such properties as strength, holiness and knowledge, vitality, intelligence and soul and so on (CIRD p. 333).

The components of all triads may be separately represented, but this triple-bodied depiction also indicates that below the manifold the One remains, and this is no less important than the multiform manifestation in the symbol.

One explanation for the existence in Gaul during the Roman period of many triple figures, their symbolism being related in general terms to that of the triad, is that this was the consequence of tripling their powers or multiplying their aura of majesty. The commonest religious figure of this type is triple-headed. The suggested explanation cannot, however, be the only one, for there can be no very good reason why the symbolism of a religious figure would need to be intensified. Nonetheless, both in Ireland and in Gaul, the Celtic pantheon contains sufficient members – three primal deities, three primeval druids, three war-goddesses, three Queens of Ireland and so on – either with triple bodies or in groups of three, for whom some unifying explanation is essential. It is far more useful, then, to imagine three states of the same being – sleeping, dreaming and waking – or passage through the three worlds of Celtic cosmology – Heaven, Air and Earth – if not passage through time. In that case, tripling would stand for the totality of time past, present and future. Triple-headed figures occur sporadically in Romanesque art, but Pope Urban VIII's decision in 1628 that they should no longer be permitted as symbols of the Trinity has meant that much of the evidence for their existence wil have disappeared (DURA).

Under the entry HEAD, other examples of many-headed beings are given. In this article we should like to add to the triple-headed figures that of the Slav god Triglav, always depicted with three heads. This has been explained as paying homage to his universal lordship of Heaven, Earth and Underworld.

tripod   By virtue of the number THREE, the tripod is an image of fire and Heaven. This is not, however, in its motionless and transcendent oneness, but dynamic and holding communication. The shape of the chalice or circlet which generally tops a tripod confirms this interpretation.

Sacred tripods were connected with the pronouncement of oracles, making manifest the will of the gods. The Delphic Oracle commanded Coroebos to take a tripod from the shrine, to carry it and to walk away until the tripod fell from his shoulders. On that spot, which the gods had chosen, he was to build his city, and that was how Megara was founded.

Hephaistos was the master-maker of sacred tripods and some which he made were so unusual as to be able to make their own way into the homes of the gods and return. This is a symbol of how the secrets of the gods may be penetrated and shared by mankind.

In everyday life, these three-footed kettles or containers were used to heat water and to mix the wine to be served at banquets. There were also more or less elaborately decorated tripods of honour awarded to the victors at athletic or musical competitions, and these the latter either kept in their own homes or dedicated to the gods. However, the most famous tripod of all was the Delphic tripod, source of prophecy and inspiration.

Seated at this tripod, the Pythoness pronounced her oracles and, since the temple was dedicated to Apollo, the tripod became one of the signs of the god's presence. And it was this tripod which Herakles (Hercules) snatched up when, the Pythoness having refused to answer his questions, he tried to set up an oracle depending upon himself alone and far from Delphi. But Apollo stepped between his angry brother and his priestess and when Zeus himself intervened, Herakles abandoned his plans and restored the tripod. The tripod may thus be regarded as 'a symbol of inspiration, the foundation of harmony . . . [and] the badge of [Apollonian] wisdom' (DIES pp. 204–5).

trowel The symbolism of the trowel, the builders' implement which was an emblem of the medieval guilds, is based upon the triangular or trapezoidal shape of the blade – the 'mark' of the guilds incorporating a trowel surmounted by a cross is a symbol of the Trinity – while the side-view suggests the zigzag flash of lightning. In medieval iconography, the Creator is depicted holding a trowel, which is thus the symbol of the powers of creation and hence of the Demiurge and of the Word. It may also be regarded as the equivalent of the *vajra* or thunderbolt (GUEO, ROMM).

It is also one of the attributes of the Freemason, who is presented with a trowel

at the fifth initiation ceremony into the grade of Fellowcraft Mason. It then acquires this significance. The implement is used to lay the mortar which by cementing together the stones of the building makes it one. The trowel joins, fuses and unites. Hence it is essentially the badge of those feelings of enlightened benevolence, universal brotherhood and wide tolerance which mark out the true Mason.

(quoted by BOUM p. 22)

truffle Truffles, underground fungi, ancient legends attributing their mysterious origins to the effects of thunderbolts or strikes by lightning, are hard to find and have a scent and flavour all their own. These properties and the fact that they were thought to be created by divinely wielded thunderbolts made them symbols of hidden revelation. Truffles grew only round the roots of the sacred oak-tree and from this sprang the notion that they were god-given like rain and revelation. Their scent and flavour were similarly god-given and owed nothing to human cultivation.

trumpet A musical instrument used to mark the most important periods of the day (reveille and lights out), to sound the charge or to proclaim a solemn ceremony, or to usher in so great a cosmic happening as the Last Judgement. The walls of Jericho were brought down by silent CIRCUMAMBULA-TION interspersed by trumpet-blasts (Joshua 6: 1–4). Roman armies knew of and put into practice the terrifying alternation of deep silence and the shrill braying of trumpets.

Angels are often depicted blowing trumpets and the Athene Salpinx (trumpet-player) from Argos clearly carried the instrument which joins Heaven and Earth together in common rejoicing. The start of a battle, too, partakes of a sacred nature, hence the use both in religious ceremony and warlike action of this metallic instrument.

The Greeks used trumpets to mark the step in great processions. . . . They had the power of incantation. In the Dionysiac festival at Lerna it was believed that the god was summoned from the marshes by blowing softly upon the trumpets concealed among the thyrses. Plutarch compares this ritual with the Jewish Feast of Tabernacles when sacred trumpets, too, were concealed by the branches of trees.

In Rome, too, trumpets were essential features of religious ceremonies, and twice a year the sacred trumpets were the objects of solemn lustration. Trumpets were sounded during sacrifices, public games and funerals (as well as at triumphal processions).

(LAVD p. 980)

The trumpet symbolizes an important conjunction of elements and events, marked by celestial manifestation (air, breath and sound).

tunic (see also SHIRT)   'The body is the soul's tunic. The Ancients believed that the sky, too, was a *peplos* (tunic) and a cloak of the heavenly gods' (Porphyry, *The Cavern of the Nymphs* 14).

The Cathars, whose teachings were based upon Manichean beliefs, held that the fallen angels were clad in tunics, which were bodies (MAGE p. 146).

By a tradition based upon reverse principles, of all articles of dress the tunic is the one which in its symbolism is closest to the soul. It displays a relationship with the spirit. All the stains and tears in a tunic conjure up the soul's scars and wounds.

The Tunic of Nessus is a symbol of revenge. Herakles (Hercules) mortally wounded with his arrows the centaur who had tried to rape his wife Deianira. Before he died, Nessus entrusted the young woman with the secret that, if she wished to retain her husband's love, she should make him wear a tunic soaked in a certain liquid – and this liquid was a mixture of the centaur's blood and his semen. When Herakles put the tunic on it stuck to his body and burned it just as the tenacious feelings of jealousy burn the soul. When Herakles tried to take off the tunic, he tore out great lumps of his own flesh and, mad with pain, threw himself upon a pyre, while Deianira committed suicide. The earthly doom of the hero of the Twelve Labours, tormented by the poisoned tunic, symbolizes the leprosy with which his soul was tainted. The centaur's blood, which Herakles had spilled in his rage and with which his tunic was soaked, symbolizes the hero's violence; the Centaur's semen, the lust which made him unfaithful and jealous. The two vices which stuck to his skin were also the centaur's revenge, and the blood- and sperm-soaked tunic was the instrument of his vengeance. However, cleansed by the fires of the funeral pyre, Herakles gained admission to the ranks of the gods after his glorious Labours and cruel sufferings.

tunnel (see also SYMPLEGADES)   This enclosed and dark channel of communication, leading through obscurity from one area of light to another, is found on Earth, in the Underworld and in the world above, as well as being the passageway which occurs in all rites of initiation. Dreams so often offer the ghostly vision of endless gloomy tunnels, symbols of anguish, anxious expectation, fear of hardship and impatience to satisfy a desire.

The Epic of Gilgamesh describes a gloomy tunnel plunging into a mountain with twin peaks. The king, whose heart is anguished by his fear of death, plunges into it in quest of immortality among his ancestors and the gods and intent on questioning his dead father on life and death. For twice nine hours he proceeds before he comes out of this deep darkness. Suddenly he feels the north wind blowing in his face. He goes on and emerges into the dawn. He proceeds again for twice twelve hours, the light shines and he himself becomes shining bright. Like the Sun, he has passed through the long tunnel in twelve long stages. Then he walks into a garden and sees trees covered with precious stones. 'The cornelian bears fruit, a bunch of grapes hangs down, glittering to the sight. There the lapis-lazuli sprouts leaves and carries fruit as cheering to behold.' In this context, the tunnel may be regarded as the passageway in an initiation, as an approach to light, the way to life (with the tree and fruit), access to a new life.

The belief in highroads underground along which the Sun, initiates and the dead travelled to reach the light of a fresh day is very widespread in most traditions, especially in Egypt, Mesopotamia and pre-Columbian America. Tunnels under holy mountains, temples and ziggurats lead thither. A Hittite legend thus describes the hunter Kessi's visit to the Kingdom of the Dead. He stood at the entrance of a long and narrow tunnel down which he slowly proceeded until he reached the Gates of the Dawn. He realized that he had left the world of the living behind and tried to turn back. 'Kessi,' said the Sun-god, 'those who have beheld the mysteries of death must never return to the land of the living. Nonetheless, I am going to give both you and your wife entry into a land of light and give you a place for ever among the stars.' There is no return down the tunnel of death, an image of the irreversible and not simply of an ordeal of darkness, but also of a fresh birth, if it is true that birth is opening one's eyes to a new day. Hieronymus Bosch painted the ascent of souls guided by their guardian angels towards a deep cylindrical tunnel which leads from darkness up to light. A soul, in the shape of a woman veiled in white, is conveyed by angels and, as it were, sucked up by the light shining at the end of the tunnel. This is the path of ascension from the darkness of death to the light of Paradise.

The tunnel is the symbol of all those dark, anguished and painful transitions which can be the start of a fresh life. Hence the extension of the symbol to the mother's womb and vagina, the initiatory passageway for the new-born baby.

turban The turban is a symbol of dignity and power on three different planes: national for the Arab; religious for the Muslim; and professional for members of the civil professions in contrast with soldiers. A *hadīth* states the turban is honour for the believer and strength for the Arab. The Prophet Muhammad was above all others the possessor of the turban and for this reason Turkish turban-makers chose him for their patron.

Another often-quoted *hadīth* recalls that turbans are the Arabs' crowns. Legends tell how Adam was supposed to have worn a turban, which the angel Gabriel wound round his head when he had been driven from Paradise to remind him of the honour which he had lost – hitherto he had worn a crown. Alexander the Great wore a crown to hide his two horns. The same train of thought lies behind the story of the seventh-century Tibetan king, Srong-btsan sgam-po. He 'was supposed to have been born with a lump on the top of his head in the place from which sprouted the rope of light, thanks to which the early Tibetan kings ascended into Heaven. This lump shone so brightly that he wore a turban to hide it' (SOUN p. 435).

The turban is the badge which distinguishes the believer from the infidel and marks the division between faith and its opposite. On the Day of Judgement each man will be given light in proportion to the number of twists his turban makes round his head. Thus to take the turban becomes a symbol of conversion to Islam. The turban is something worn to the glory of God, and God and his angels bless those who wear their turban on Fridays.

White is the most usual colour for turbans. The Prophet is supposed to have liked it and the angels who came to his aid at the Battle of Badr are supposed to have worn white turbans, the colour of Paradise. Angels are also believed to wear yellow turbans because the angel Gabriel had a turban made of light. The Prophet would have liked to have worn a blue turban, but forbade it because this was the colour worn by unbelievers.

So far as red is concerned, the angels at Uhud and Hunain wore red turbans and the angel Gabriel is said to have appeared once to the Prophet's wife Ayesha in a red turban.

Green is the colour of Paradise and allegedly Muhammad's favourite colour, although, according to tradition, he never wore a green turban. Nonetheless, wearing one is the badge of his descendants. Today it is considered the rule that only the descendants of Ali should wear a green turban.

Furthermore, the turban is a symbol of investiture. There are no crowns nor coronations in Islam. The Caliphs invested their viziers with turbans and they also formed part of the robes of honour granted to viziers and emirs. The higher the rank, especially from the religious point of view, the larger the turban.

Lastly, the turban is the badge of the civil professions and to wear the turban is synonymous with being in the service of the state.

Shapes differ from country to country. A special symbolism attaches to the different parts of the turban, and thus Sufis wear it with the point to the left, because this is the side of the heart, while it was the privilege of the Hafsid sultans to wear it with the point hanging over the right ear (ENCI).

turkey For North American Indians the turkey provides the dual symbol of male virility and female fecundity. When the turkey-cock swells its wattles it is reminiscent of the male erection, while the hen is one of the most prolific fowls (FLEH).

turnip Taoists made turnip-seed one of the foods of immortality. Their countless multitude ensures the continuity of the vegetable.

turquoise In ancient Central American civilizations the turquoise was always related to fire or to the Sun. Thus when the warrior-god, the Sun, woke he would drive the Moon and stars from the sky armed with the 'turquoise serpent', identified with fire and the Sun's rays. The Aztec fire-god was called Xiuhtecuhtli, meaning Lord, or Prince, of the Turquoise. As the supreme solar deity, he stood for the Sun at its zenith (KRIR).

The cult-room of the Pueblo Indian High-priest of the Rains (Lord of the Northern Rains), so closely guarded a secret that it is practically never revealed to a European, contains an altar comprising 'two small crystal and turquoise columns and a heart-shaped stone, the heart of the world' (KRIR).

turtle See under TORTOISE.

twelve (see also NUMBERS; TWENTY-ONE) Twelve is the number by which space and time are divided, being the product of the FOUR points of the compass multiplied by the THREE levels of the universe. The vault of Heaven is divided into twelve sections, the twelve signs of the ZODIAC, to which reference has been made from the remotest past. In China, the twelve months of the year were determined by the stance of the emperor at the twelve gates of the Temple of Heaven. Among the Assyrians, Jews and other peoples, twelve split the year into twelve months and, among the Chinese and the peoples of central Asia, into their principal periods of time, twelve-year cycles. Multiplying twelve by five provided a sixty-year cycle, at the end of which both solar and lunar cycles coincide. Twelve symbolizes the universe in its cyclical revolution in space and time.

It also symbolizes the inner complexity of the universe. The group of twelve characteristic of the months of the year and the signs of the Zodiac may also stand for the multiplication of the four elements of Earth, Water, Fire and Air by the three alchemical principles of sulphur, salt and mercury; or else the three states of each element at the successive stages of their evolution, culmination and involution; or even, if we are to believe Allendy, 'each of the four elements regarded in its different cosmic manifestations and from a threefold viewpoint which might, for example, be that of the three Hindu *gunas* – activity, inertia and harmony' (ALLN p. 328).

This number is especially rich in Christian symbolism:

By multiplying the four of the world of space with the three of the sacred period of time measuring creation and recreation, we obtain twelve, which is the number of universal fulfilment which is that of the Heavenly Jerusalem with its twelve gates, of the twelve apostles and twelve foundations and so on, as well as being that of the liturgical cycle of the year with its twelve months and their cosmic expression as the twelve signs of the Zodiac. In a more mystic sense, three relates to the Trinity and four to the creation, but the symbolism of twelve remains the same – a fulfilment of the earthly and created absorbed into the divine and uncreated.

(CHAS p. 243)

It is easy to understand the importance of this number. To Biblical writers twelve was the number of the elect, that of God's Chosen People and of the Church, since Jacob (Israel) had twelve sons who became the ancestors of and gave their names to the twelve tribes of the Israelites (Genesis 35: 23ff.). The Tree of Life bore twelve fruits and there were twelve jewels on the High Priest's breastplate. Thus, when Jesus chose twelve apostles, he openly announced his claim to choose, in God's name, another People (Matthew 10: 1ff,). The Heavenly Jerusalem has twelve gates on which are written the names of the twelve tribes of Israel and its walls have twelve foundations in the names of the twelve apostles (Revelation 21: 12, 14). The Woman clothed with the Sun (Revelation: 12: 1) wore upon her head a crown with twelve stars. At the end of time, the number of the faithful will be 144,000, 12,000 from each of the twelve tribes of Israel (Revelation 7: 4–8; 14: 1).

Similarly this City to come, 'in fine gold', rests upon twelve foundations, each bearing the name of an apostle, and forms a cube with sides 12,000 furlongs long and with walls of jasper 144 cubits high. This symbolic number, 12,000, is the product of one thousand (the symbol of a multitude) multiplied by the number of Israel itself (twelve), and it is that of the old and new Chosen People. As for the number of the faithful, 144,000 is twelve squared multiplied by one thousand, and symbolized the multitude of those who believe in Christ, the figure twelve standing for the Church, the Church triumphant after its successive phases of Church militant and persecuted Church.

The Dogon and Bambara in Mali regard the opposing principles four (female) and three (male), which are the foundation of all things, as being able to be brought together in two different ways, one static and the other dynamic, depending upon the properties of the numbers seven and twelve. If seven, four added to three, is the symbol of mankind and of the universe, twelve, the product of their multiplication, is the symbol of human destiny and of the continuous evolution of the universe (DIEB).

The sound wave which, to African thinking, dominated the genesis of things by forming the Cosmic Egg, before the separation of Heaven from Earth and the birth of the Great Demiurges who directed the work of creation, first 'visited', that is defined, the four points of the compass and at each of them whirled three times round in a spiral. Thus, in the beginning, the complex of space and time was defined by the marriage of four and three: their product, twelve, being the number of activity and not a static principle like the number seven. Thus, Dieterlen explains, the Cosmic Egg took shape, moulded by the spiral movement of the sound wave.

In the Celtic world, the key numbers were three, nine and twenty-seven, and the symbolism of twelve is nothing out of the common run. There were twelve knights at King Arthur's Round Table.

Twelve may be defined as the number of fulfilment and of the completed cycle. Thus in the Tarot, the twelfth major arcanum (the Hanging Man) marks the end of an involutionary cycle, the next card (XIII) being Death, which should be understood in the sense of rebirth.

twenty   The number twenty stood for the Sun-god in his archetypal office of Perfect Man for the Ancient Mayans and, in Quiché numeration, twenty is still called 'man', the twenty fingers and toes comprising a unit. The same custom recurs in other Indian cultures, notably among the Venezuelan Caribs. The Mayan religious calendar comprised eighteen months (lunar number) each of twenty days (solar number) (GIRP pp. 215–16).

Again in the Mayan civilization, in consequence of the sacralization of the number twenty, standing for a man as well as for Primal Oneness which was the divine agrarian and solar archetype of Man, the number four hundred (twenty squared) also became holy. Girard records that, during the colonial period, the unit of land measurement, representing the strip of cultivated maize needed to keep one person alive, was twenty feet squared, or four hundred square feet, and the length of the year corresponded to this at four hundred days. Lastly, when at the final stage of their career, which also marks the establishment of an agrarian civilization among the Maya, the Hero Twins went up to Heaven, they took with them four hundred young men and maidens who became stars near those which formed the Pleiades. Four hundred is the number which the Maya used as a symbol of the innumerable and the ineffable (GIRP pp. 248–50).

This concept of four hundred as a boundary-number oddly coincides with something observed by Allendy. The Hebrew letter for this number is *tau*, which corresponds to the last major arcanum of the Tarot – the World (ALLN p. 403). The Hebrew alphabet ends on the numerical symbol which in this context, too, has a boundary-property.

The Hopi Indians of Arizona, whose language derives from the great Uto-Aztec linguistic family, conduct the ritual naming of a child twenty days after its birth. The accompanying ritual cleansing and lustrations which then take place will have been performed in like manner beforehand on the first, fifth, tenth and fifteenth days. The child, in this tradition, does not become an individual until it has completed four times the five-day cycle, which expresses cosmologically the four points of the compass and the centre where manifestation occurs (TALS pp. 31–2).

twenty-one Twenty-one is a symbol of maturity and in the Old Testament it is, above all, the number of perfection (SEVEN multiplied by THREE) and that of the twenty-one attributes of wisdom (Wisdom 7: 22–3). It symbolizes divine wisdom 'the brightness of the everlasting light, the unspotted mirror . . . [which] passeth and goeth through all things' (ibid. 26, 24). In fact it is best to read the whole of chapter 7 of the Wisdom of Solomon, one of the high points of all sacred literature, if one is to appreciate fully its richness. The symbolic TAROT pack is overt evidence of the properties of completeness contained in this number, which is that of the last numbered major arcanum, the World, denoting fulfilment, plenitude and the attainment of a goal.

Dr Allendy deduces a series of antithetic symbols from the fact that 21 is the digits of 12 transposed:

In the figure twelve (12) the principle of differentiation (2) is to be seen in cosmic oneness (1), regulating it in its various aspects and their normal relationships, while in twenty-one (21) we see individuality (1) resulting from cosmic differentiation (2), that is to say precisely the reverse. In twelve, dualism regulates oneness, in twenty-one oneness takes shape within duality.

Another conflict arises from the fact that one of these numbers is odd and the other even: 'Twelve is even. This is a balanced situation which is the outcome of the harmonious arrangement of perpetual cycles (3×4). Twenty-one is odd. This is the dynamic effort of individuality evolving in the battle of opposites and taking the ever fresh path of developmental cycles (3×7).' In consequence of these two differences, twenty-one symbolizes the individual centred upon an objective and no longer upon itself or upon parental figures, as in infantile states. 'This is the autonomous individual set between pure spirit and negative matter. It is also that individual's free movement between good and evil which makes up the universe. It is therefore the number of responsibility and, curiously enough, the twenty-first birthday is the date at which most peoples consider individuals reach their majority' (ALLN pp. 366–7).

twenty-two This number, perhaps, symbolizes the manifestation of being in all its diversity and during its allotted span, that is, in both space and time. In fact, it is the sum total of the twenty-two letters which, according to the Kabbalah, give expression to the universe. There are the three fundamental letters, the equivalents of alpha, omega and the letter M, which are archetypal figures; the seven double letters which correspond to the intermediate world of the understanding; twelve simple letters corresponding to the world of the senses. Of course this teaching relates to the letters of the Hebrew alphabet, but has its analogies in the Ancient Egyptian hieratic alphabet as well as in Phoenician, Ethiopic and other languages (ALLN p. 371).

However the interpretation of twenty-two as the 'symbol of all natural forms and of created history as a whole' (ibid.) may well go back to the ancient Zoroastrians. Their Avesta was written in books each of twenty-two chapters and their collection of prayers contains twenty-two. The Revelation attributed to St John comprises twenty-two chapters, too, while there are twenty-two major arcana in the Tarot.

In Fulani tradition, 220 means a very long time and this number may well have a secret significance in matters of sacrifice and initiation (HAMK p. 45).

Twenty-two plays a highly important part in the symbolic thought of the Dogon and Bambara. The Bambara believe that all mystic knowledge is contained within the symbolism of the first twenty-two numbers; and for them the number twenty-two stands for the whole span of time between the start of the process of creation until the completion of the universal order. It is the fulfilment of the creator's task, the boundary of speech, the figure of the universe (DIEB).

twenty-four The Old Testament (1 Chronicles 24 and 25) describes the separation of both priests and singers into twenty-four divisions and in Revelation (4: 4) there are 'round about the throne [of God] . . . four and twenty seats; and upon the seats . . . four and twenty elders sitting, clothed in white raiment; and they had on their heads crowns of gold.' In his commentary upon Revelation, Féret remarks that these elders 'denote the passage of time, less astronomical time than the span of human history. . . . They are clad in white and crowned with gold because they have taken part in the great battle of truth in history and now share in its victory.' The *Jerusalem Bible* commentators note that: 'The elders have a priestly function: they praise and worship God . . . and offer him the prayers of the faithful . . . the thrones indicate that the elders are "judges" in the New Israel which is the redeemed world: the crowns are the sign that they share God's royal power.' This number twenty-four would appear to denote the twofold harmony of Heaven and Earth (12×2), the twofold and holy fulfilment of the pilgrimage in time and of eternal life. We have shown how TWELVE was the holy number of the Chosen People (Twelve Tribes of Israel; Christ's Twelve Apostles) and it is possible to conceive that by doubling the number of persons (twenty-four) their priestly and royal role is doubled, one in relation to mankind, the other in relation to God. This is multiplying, or rather intensifying, the sacred character of the officiants.

Dr Allendy comes to the same conclusion, though by a different route, that twenty-four symbolizes a harmonious balance:

Here the cyclical mechanism of Nature (4) is linked to cosmic differentiation (20) in the harmonious balance of creation (2 + 4 = 6). This number expresses the relationship between permanent cycles and the laws of karma (24 = 4 × 6); it is the wheel of rebirth (with twenty-four spokes). . . . Outside the circle of the Zodiac, the Chaldaeans distinguished twenty-four stars, twelve to the North and twelve to the South, which they named the Judges of the Universe.

Lastly Allendy quotes Warrain, remarking that, in this number, 'individuality which is both fully aware and in control of all its energies, combines with the Cosmos to develop its complete harmony' (ALLN p. 373).

Twenty-four is a number which often occurs in both Western and Eastern fairy tales. 'In this context it stands for the sum of human strength and the complete gathering of original matter. It divides into the five elements, five senses, five active organs and the five objects recognized by those active organs, to which are added Mind, Intellect, Individuality and primordial Prakrti (precosmic primal matter)' (LOEF p. 196).

twilight   This symbol is closely linked to the west, the direction in which the Sun sinks, vanishes and dies. It expresses the end of one cycle and, consequently, readiness for the start of a new one. In myth, all those epic deeds which usher in a cosmic, social or moral revolution take place during a journey to the west – Perseus on his way to kill the Gorgon, Herakles (Hercules) killing the dragon in the Garden of the Hesperides, Apollo setting out for the land of the Hyperboreans and so on.

Twilight is an image in space-time – the moment when time stands still. Space and time are about to invert into another world and another night, but the death of the one heralds the birth of another, fresh space and new time, successors to the old. The westward journey is a journey into the future, but a journey through transforming darkness. Beyond the night will be the hoped-for dawn.

Twilight symbolizes the nostalgic beauty of regression and of the past in which it wraps itself. It is the picture of momentary melancholy and longing for that past.

twins (see also GEMINI)   All cultures and mythologies display a special interest in the phenomenon of twin births. In whatever shape they may be conceived, as completely identical, or as one dark and the other bright, or one tending heavenwards the other earthwards, or one black the other white, or one red the other blue, or one with a bull's and the other with a scorpion's head, they are expressions simultaneously of interference from the Beyond and of the twofold nature of all beings and the dualism of their physical and spiritual, diurnal and nocturnal tendencies. This dualism is light and darkness, the heavenly and earthly aspects of the cosmos and of the individual. When they symbolize in this way the individual's internal contradictions and the struggle which needs to be waged to overcome them, they acquire the character of sacrifice, the need for self-denial, destruction or submission, the surrender of one part of the self so that the other may come through victorious. Naturally it will be the task of the spiritual powers of progressive development to ensure the defeat of involutional and regressive tendencies. Sometimes, however, it happens that the twins are completely identical, the doubles or copies the one of the other, and in these circumstances they are expressions, no less, of the oneness of a perfectly balanced dualism. They symbolize the inner harmony gained by reducing the manifold to the one. Once dualism is overcome, duality is now no more than apparent, a mirror-image, caused by manifestation.

Twins also symbolize the ambivalent state of the mythic universe. Primitive peoples always regarded them 'as being charged with particularly strong power which might either be both harmful and protective, or else simply harmful or simply protective. . . . Twins were both feared and worshipped, but always endowed with extreme properties. The Bantu put them to death, while in West Africa they were worshipped as sorcerers' (VIRI p. 65). In all traditions, twins, whether gods or heroes, either helped one another or quarrelled among themselves, emphasizing the ambivalence of their position and symbolizing the position of every individual divided within him- or herself. André Virel regards twin-shaped images, like symmetrical images in general, as

the inner tension of a permanent situation. . . . The fear of the primitive at the sight of something twinned, is the fear of the outer eye at the sight of its own ambivalence, the fear of objectively encountering similarities and differences, the fear of acquiring individuating self-awareness . . . the fear of that individuation, the fear of breaking away from collective lack of differentiation.

Basically twins symbolize 'an unresolved contradiction' (VIRI p. 67).

This primitive fear of twins still survives. When a pregnant woman expected twins, she went to the medicine-man for him to make them into one. The medicine-man

took some corn-meal outside the door and sprinkled it to the sun. Then he spun some black and white wool, twisted the threads into a string, and tied it around my mother's wrist. It was a powerful way to unite babies. We twins began likewise to twist ourselves into one child. . . . They could see that I was an oversize baby, that my hair curled itself into two little whorls instead of one at the back of my head, and that in front of my body I was a boy but at the back there was the sure trace of a girl – the imprint of a little vulva that slowly disappeared. They have told me time after time that I was twice lucky – lucky to be born twins and lucky to just miss becoming a girl.

(TALS pp. 25, 27)

'The belief . . . that the birth of twins presupposes the union of a mortal with a god, and particularly with a sky god, is extremely widespread' (ELIT p. 98). According to Eliade all twin heroes – the Ashvins, the Dioscuri, Castor and Pollux, for example – in Indo-European mythology are benefactors, healing mortals, protecting them from harm, rescuing seamen and so on. One of the most celebrated services performed by the Vedic twins was to rejuvenate an old man and make him 'a husband for young women' (DUMH p. 34n.).

In Mexico and among the Pueblo Indians, it was the Hero Twins, the gods of dawn and dusk, who, in cosmogonic tales, cleared the way for the human race when the latter first made its appearance on Earth. They are 'the monster-slayers and the transformers of old, imperfect things into new. In general they are the deliverers and leaders of mankind' (ALEC p. 86).

Many cosmogonic folktales have as their protagonists twin culture-heroes cast in opposing roles. One is good and the other wicked, the latter constantly attempting to bring to nought the creational and civilizing activities of his twin. In other stories he copies him, but so clumsily that where the former has created useful creatures the latter creates harmful ones. The Iroquois are particularly notable for this Manichean mythology (MULR pp. 261ff.) and the same is true of such South American tribes as the Piaroas on the Orinoco River.

This dualism among mythic twins relates to the Sun on its ascendant (evolutionary) and descendant (involutionary) paths. Iroquois dances, for example, may be split into two categories, those of the 'good twin' (the rising Sun), associated with the colour white, such as the Great Feather Dance, and those associated with the 'wicked twin' (setting Sun), associated with the colour black, such as their war-dances. There is the same division in their annual cycle into Winter and Summer festivals. The Summer festivals are the responsibility of the women and beg for fertility for the crops, the Winter festivals of the men and offer thanks for the gifts received in harvest. Each of these halves lasts for six months and is hinged upon the New Year festival, celebrated in February, and that of the Green Maize in October. Thus there is the same dualism to be found in both the daily and the annual cycles (MULR pp. 260ff.).

This dualist mythology and cosmogony is not unrelated to the ancient Mayan concept of the Monad itself being bifurcate, like the tongue of the maize-god.

The dualist way of thought of the ancient Iroquois has not disappeared with the arrival of modernity. 'In fact the transformation of the world by civilization has been integrated into their system' (MULR p. 272). Within the Iroquois Reserve the 'Good Twin' rules. This is where the Iroquois have their homes and their fields and their protection. Outside is the domain of the 'Wicked Twin', his myrmidons, the Whites, living in a desert of factories, apartment blocks and concrete roadways.

The dualist mythologies of twins would seem to originate in the natural dualism of regions where there is a very sharp difference between the two seasons.

During one of the most famous wanderings in Irish mythology, Macha, the eponymous goddess of the capital of Ulster (Emain Macha, 'Macha's twins'), having raced against King Conchobar's horses, gave birth to twins. Their names have not come down to us, but we should not be far wrong if we regarded them as Dioscuri and as prototypes of such Dioscuric pairs as Cùchulainn and Conall Cernach in Ireland. These pairs were linked by kinship and upbringing. Cùchulainn and Conall Cernach were cousins and foster-brothers. Both were sons of sisters. Conall Cernach was the son of King Conchobar's sister, Findchoem, and the bard Amorgen. Cùchulainn was King Conchobar's son by his sister Dechtire. The pair, however, were ill-matched, Cùchulainn being far superior to Conall Cernach both in ability and in fame. One is forced to compare them with the Gaulish Dioscuric pair, Bellovesus and Segovesus, the nephews of Ambigatus, king of the Biturgi, by his sister, according to Livy's account (*Historiae* 5: 34). Segovesus (the Victorious) led a migration of which no trace remains towards the Hyrcanean Forest. Bellovesus (the Warrior) led his men into northern Italy and founded the city of Mediolanum (modern Milan), meaning 'Centre of Perfection' in its sacred sense, or 'Middle of the Plain' in its profane. The symbolism of the Celtic Dioscuri is that of warfare and individual heroism. However, Cùchulainn was also the son of the god Lug and from that aspect stands for the rash and childish aspects of heroic deeds. By some inconsequential trick of the time scale, which only matters at a mundane level, although Conall Cernach was Cùchulainn's foster-brother (*comalta*), he was already grown up and able to keep watch on the borders of Ulster when the latter, at the age of seven, made the first of his bloodthirsty raids into a neighbouring province. The brotherhood of these Celtic Dioscuri is more a matter of principle than of actuality, and physical kinship was lacking. The Celtic aspect was purely warlike (in India the Dioscuri belonged to the 'third' class). Diodorus Siculus (4: 56, 4) quotes the *Timaeus* for the statement that the Celts of the Atlantic seaboard worship Dioscuri who had come from the sea. The Gaulish Dioscuri, Momoros and Atepomaros (Mighty Horseman), had a further prophetic aspect. They played an important part in the foundation of Lugdunum (modern Lyons), fixing its site, according to the Pseudo-Plutarch, by following the flight of ravens (CELT 1: pp. 15–19, 187; CHAD).

two This number is the symbol of confrontation, conflict and recoil and denotes either balance achieved, or hidden threat. It is the figure which epitomizes all ambivalence and split personality. It is the first to separate and it separates most radically – creator and creature, black and white, male and female, matter and spirit and so on – and is the source of all other divisions. In antiquity, it was the attribute of the Mother, denoting the female principle, while among its most terrifying ambivalences is that it may be the seed either of creative evolution or of fatal involution.

The number two symbolizes dualism, the basis of all dialectic, endeavour, struggle, movement and progress. However, division is as powerful a principle of multiplication as synthesis and multiplication is itself bipolar, increasing or diminishing according to the sign (+ or –) which governs the number.

Two, therefore, gives expression to a hostility which from being hidden becomes manifest; rivalry and mutual feelings, either of love or of hate; opposition which may be sterile and negative, as well as complementary and productive.

In any symbol the twofold image, whether of two lions, two eagles, or two of anything else, may either enhance, by multiplying them, the symbolic properties of the image, or by splitting them may do precisely the opposite and demonstrate the inner divisions which weaken it.

All African symbolism rests upon a fundamental dualism regarded as being the cosmic rule above all else. There is good and evil, life and death in human beings; the same Gueno (god) is the source of both good and ill;

everything has a positive (diurnal) as well as a negative (nocturnal) aspect. It should also be observed that the left and right, the high and low, the better and the worse are rivals within each individual and in the relations of that individual with other individuals, that the points of the compass point in opposite directions, that day is opposed to night and male to female ... (HAMK p. 25).

In the numerology of the Bambara in Mali, the figure of primal duality and twinship is a symbol of marriage, love or friendship (DIEB).

In the Celtic world, a certain number of mythical figures are to be found in pairs, either opposing or complementing one another. The study and interpretation of Celtic mythology is still at too early a stage to name any large number of these pairs with any degree of certainty, but the basic pairing or duality in Celtic regions is that of warrior and druid, often conjoined and concentrated into a single divine entity. One stands for strength and the other for traditional wisdom. All mythological series or structures observe this dualist principle, which easily integrates with a series of numerical symbols covering the whole field of comparative religion (OGAC 12: pp. 209–34, 349–82).

For Chinese dualism see under YIN AND YANG.

In Allendy's numerological system, two is the number of 'relative differentiation' and of 'antagonistic or attractional reciprocity' (ALLN p. 19). Since all progress depends upon encountering some degree of resistance, if only the negation of what one aims to overcome, two is the motivator of differentiated development or progress. It is the one in so far as it is the other. Similarly, if the personality develops from its own internal opposition, two is the motivator along the path of individuation. All traditions contain countless examples of binary symbols or of pairs (see TWINS): they are the source of all thought, every manifestation and all motion.

In Iranian culture we find the figure two associated with the following topics:

- day and night, expressed as two aspects of the ceaseless revolution of time and the movement of the Heavens;
- the sublunary world and the world of the Beyond, symbolized by two houses or palaces (*do-sarā*);
- life on earth, represented by a house of dust with two doors, one to enter and one to leave by (that is, to die);
- the brevity of life, compared with a two-day sojurn (*do-rūza-maqām*) in this world;
- the differences and divergent views of mankind at each different age have been translated as a climate in which two different atmospheres reign (*do-havāī*).

Folk poetry, in its descriptions of female beauty, associates some parts of the body and face as pairs (two eyes, two lips, two legs, two breasts and so on) with images (narcissi, cornelians, ivory columns, sweet Omani oranges) which recur in all folktales.

While pouring wine, the hero out of respect or love will kneel on both knees to offer in both hands the chalice to the princess or the lady whom he loves.

The hero will recite two *rakat* of Muslim prayers to exorcise evil spirits or to break the spell laid upon some castle.

To paint a truly horrific portrait of a demon, great emphasis is placed upon his pair of horns.

The chief Persian forms of words employing the figure two are very many in number and all tend to show that the qualities of the person or object to which they are applied are doubled, or in some way squared, or increased tenfold or made infinite. In Persian symbolism, two multiplies to infinity the object to which it is applied, whatever that may be. For example, a messenger with two horses would imply great swiftness, a tent with two rooms, the height of luxury, and so on.

Typhon This monster of Greek mythology was the child of Hera's rage and brought up by the serpent Pytho. Typhon was half human and half animal, winged and having a hundred dragons' heads instead of fingers. He was swathed with vipers from waist to ankles, his eyes spat fire and he was so huge that his outstretched arms could embrace the remotest east and west. Typhon put all the gods to flight except Zeus and Athene, who resisted his assaults. After a battle upon a cosmic scale, Zeus crushed him with his thunderbolt under Mount Etna, but Typhon continues to spit fire from the volcano. There are many versions of this myth (GRID p. 466) standing for the eruptions of animality, of brute stupidity and of the powers of the mundane, as one 'final attempt to oppose the spirit. Typhon is the most redoubtable of all those monsters which are foes of the spirit. He symbolizes the potential of the conscious being to be reduced to banality and the most determined opposition to spiritual development, a regression towards the immediate satisfaction of desire, so characteristic of animality' (DIES p. 119).

It was because Zeus had begotten ATHENE without the assistance of his wife that she, in her anger, decided to produce by her own unaided efforts a monster to rival Athene. The opposition of Typhon, the monster born of Earth's jealousy and vengefulness, with Athene, springing from the brain of Zeus, the sky-god, confirms the explanation which we have given. The violent powers of aberrant instinct, symbolized by Typhon, are unleashed against the ideal of wisdom, symbolized by Athene. It is the rejection of sublimation and surrender to earthly drives.

Or again, it could be the image of the Earth-goddess, with her volcanic eruptions and lava-flows burning like angry vipers, setting herself up in rivalry with the sky-god with his thunderbolt and lightnings.

U

umbilical cord The Bambara call the child's umbilical cord 'the liana from the gourd', regarding it as the root through which the human being is nourished by the Earth Mother during the period of gestation. Hence, until it drops off – which, according to their beliefs should occur on the seventh day, seven being the number of the whole person – the birth is not fully accomplished. It is not until the eighth day, therefore, that the mother is visited and congratulated and it is not until the eighth day – eight being the number of speech – that the ceremony of naming the child takes place. This symbolic notion of the properties of the umbilical cord is the basis of its use as 'medicine' to ensure fertility. The cord itself is preserved in a bag which the child wears round its neck and which acts as a charm. A fragment of the cord soaked in water and mixed with the first hairs cut from the child's head provides a medicine given to it when it falls ill or, if mixed with seeds before planting, ensures that they will germinate.

The Hopi Indians regard the umbilical cord as the house of the child's soul, as Don C. Talayesva explained in his famous autobiography.

When my navel cord dried and dropped off, it was tied to an arrow and stuck beside a beam overhead in the room. This was to make me a good hunter and to provide a 'house' for my infant spirit in case I died, for my soul could then stay by the arrow in the ceiling and quickly slip back into my mother's womb for an early rebirth.

(TALS p. 30)

umbrella Unlike the PARASOL and the AWNING, their symbolism deriving from the Sun in its brightness, the umbrella, as its name implies (*umbra* is 'shade' in Latin), stands on the side of darkness, withdrawal and protectiveness. It would seem incorrect to regard it as having phallic significance, unless all species of protection is an attribute of the Father. It would also be going too far to interpret its symbolism as that of the inverted chalice, meaning the downpouring of the gifts of Heaven. Symbolically, it is more inclined to reveal a timid refusal of the principles of fecundation, either in physical or in spiritual shape. To shelter under an umbrella is to run away from reality and responsibility. Under a sunshade one stands upright; one hunches under an umbrella. The protection one receives from the latter is expressed in loss of dignity, independence and life potential.

unction See under ANOINTING.

Undines In Germanic and Norse mythology Undines are related to the NYMPHS of Classical myth. Female water spirits, they are generally depicted as maleficent, offering to guide travellers through murk, marsh and forest, only to lead them astray and drown them. Poets, novelists and playwrights have sought inspiration in the Germanic legends of the Undines with their grey-green hair which they combed coquettishly at the water's surface. They were all beautiful and mischievous, and sometimes cruel. They enjoyed attracting fishermen or passing knights, whom they would carry off to the bottom of their lakes and into their crystal palaces where days passed like minutes. Scandinavian legend was darker and more passionate, since the handsome young man carried off by the Undines would never see the light of day again and would die of exhaustion in their arms. They, too, symbolize love- and water-charms linked to death and, from the moral and psychoanalytic point of view, the perils of unconditional surrender to seduction.

unicorn In the Middle Ages the unicorn was a symbol of power, basically expressed by its HORN, as well as of magnificence and purity.

These properties recur in Ancient China where the unicorn was the badge of kingship and symbolized kingly qualities. When these were displayed the unicorn would appear, as it did during the reign of Chuen. Above all it was a creature of good omen. Nonetheless, the unicorn was an adjunct to royal law enforcement, striking down the guilty with its horn. It also did battle with the Sun and with eclipses, swallowing them.

The Unicorn Dance is one of rejoicing, highly popular in the Far East at the Mid-Autumn Festival. However, in it the unicorn seems only to be a variant on the DRAGON in its role of Lord of the Rains. The battle with the Sun, responsible for disastrous droughts, might explain this approximation (GRAD). Like the dragon, the unicorn might be born of the constantly changing patterns of the clouds, the faithful harbingers of fecundating rain.

With its single horn set in the middle of its forehead, the unicorn also symbolizes a spiritual arrow, a sun-ray, the sword of God, divine revelation or the godhead penetrating its creation. In Christian iconography, it stands for the Virgin who has conceived by the Holy Spirit. The single horn may also symbolize a stage upon the way of differentiation, from biological procreation (sexuality) to psychic evolution (a sexual oneness) and to sexual sublimation. This single horn has also been compared with 'a frontal penis' or 'phallus of the psyche' (VIRI p. 202), the symbol of spiritual fecundity. Yet, at the same time, the unicorn is the symbol of physical virginity. Alchemists regarded it as an image of the hermaphrodite, but this would seem to be a misunderstanding – instead of possessing a twofold sexuality the unicorn transcends sexuality itself. In the Middle Ages the unicorn became the symbol of the Word of God made flesh within the womb of the Virgin Mary.

In his *Le mythe de la dame à la licorne* (Paris, 1963), Bertrand d'Astorg gives the symbol fresh life by connecting it with medieval concepts of courtly love, regarding the unicorn as a type of those famous women who decided not to consummate the love which they inspired and which they shared. Unicorns being endowed with the mysterious power of detecting impurity, even the tiniest flaw within a diamond, such persons, in the words of Yves Berger, 'abstain from love through fidelity to love, and to preserve themselves from love's inevitable decay.' The poetry of renunciation confronts the poetry of possession, the survival of maidenhood with the manifestation of womanhood. The myth of the unicorn is that of the fascination which purity continues to exercise over the most corrupted hearts.

Simon perfectly summarizes the properties of the symbol when he writes:

Nonetheless, because of the symbol of its horn which separates pure from contaminated water, detects poisons and can only be safely handled by a virgin, the emblem of active purity, or because when hunted and uncaptured it can only be taken through being tricked by a maiden who puts it to sleep with the scent of virgin's milk, the unicorn always conjures up the notion of a miraculous sublimation of carnality and of the supernatural strength which emanates from what is pure.

Many painted or carved works of art depict two unicorns confronting one another in what would seem to be a cruel struggle. One might see this as an image of the violent inner conflict between the two qualities which the unicorn symbolizes – preservation of virginity (the single horn raised to the skies) and fertility (the phallic significance of the horn). The image of the pair of unicorns in confrontation might well be an expression of the longing, contradictory at a merely physical level, for childbirth without loss of virginity. The conflict is not overcome, nor the unicorn fecundated and appeased, except upon the level of a spiritual relationship.

In the sixth and final piece of the famous series of tapestries in the Musée de Cluny, entitled 'La dame à la licorne', a young woman is depicted as having removed her jewellery and being about to enter a tent, symbol of Emptiness and of the presence of God. The device above the tent reads, *A mon seul desir*, meaning that the created being's only longing is to commingle with that of the will which governs her. In so far as we are, during our lives, the playthings of the gods, our role only becomes free and active when we identify ourselves with the puppet-master who has made us and controls us. This is the point at which the self is dissolved into the Greater Self, within the cosmic tent beneath the Pole Star. The lady is Sophia–Shakti–Shekinah, that is, 'She who is within the tent'. By her grace and wisdom, as much as by her purity, she tames the warring creatures of the Great Work, the lion which symbolizes sulphur and the unicorn which symbolizes mercury. The lady is often assimilated to the Philosopher's Salt. She is very close to Hevajra's coadjutor, whose name means 'she who is selfless'. The unicorn's up-pointing horn, which symbolizes spiritual fecundation and which traps the tide of universal energy, is congruent with the axial symbolism of the tent, elongated to a point by the pair of lances; with the headdresses of the lady and her attendant, topped with plumes; and with the trees which celebrate the mystic marriage of East and West, oak and holly being matched by orange and palm. The coat of arms on the tent – gules, three crescents argent on a bend azur – suggest that these tapestries may have been commissioned by the unfortunate son of Mehemet II, the Conqueror of Constantinople, during his imprisonment in France, since his dream was to marry the Cross to the Crescent. The oval island upon which the scene takes place is sculpted like a lotus, symbol of spiritual efforation, while the little monkey seated in front of the lady denotes the alchemist, 'Nature's ape', watching his mistress, who may be assimilated to the *materia prima*.

The alchemical writings of Lombardi, Lambsprinck, Mylius and others are often illustrated with plates of the unicorn. This fabulous beast, originating in the East and associated with the 'third eye', with attainment of Nirvana and with a return to the centre and to the Monad, was ideally fated to denote for the Western hermeticist the path to Philosopher's gold – the inner transmutation effected when the primordial hermaphrodite is recreated. In China, the unicorn was called *Chi lin*, meaning *yin* and *yang* (CARL).

uraeus The image of the angry she-cobra with hood erect personified the burning eye of Ra and symbolized the fiery nature of the crowns when seen on Pharaoh's brow or on the heads of Sun-gods. It was also identified with the Lady Serpent (POSD p. 293). According to Champdor (CHAM p. 46) the uraeus might symbolize 'the vital fluid, the breath of life, the warmth of Isis'. The fiery serpent which crowned the temple-tops or the heads of the Pharaohs concentrated within itself the life-giving and fecundating properties of the Sun, properties just as capable of dealing death by drought and fire – the twofold aspect of kingship.

Uranus (for the god, see OURANOS.)   This planet was discovered by William Herschel on 13 March 1781 and in astrology stands for the cosmic power which causes sudden, abrupt and unexpected upheavals, interference, fresh creations and progress. Its especial domain is electricity, flight and the cinema. In the view of astrology, the breath of fresh air which for the last two centuries has been blowing upon mankind comes mainly from this planet. Astrologers regard it as the true creator of the modern world, based, on the social plane, upon the principles of the French Revolution and, in the industrial sphere, upon industrialization and mechanization. Its House is Aquarius, which it shares with Saturn. When Uranus was first sighted it was in Gemini, the sign of the Zodiac which rules the USA. For good or ill, American civilization is today the most perfect illustration of the influence of Uranus. Immense dynamism, sexual equality, youthful, pioneering attitudes of mind and democratic principles co-exist with a presidential régime, the greatest industrial structure on Earth, racism, brutality and organized crime; everything, including Hollywood and the electric chair, bears the distinctive mark of Uranus. The planet rules the muscles of the human body and the illnesses caused by its influence are muscular, spasms, cramps and heart attacks.

The Uranian process began with something like a sudden burst of anger on the part of Chaos – primordial fire, as it were, catching light. The god of the oceans was confronted by the sky-god, whose initial aim was to break free from an undifferentiated state in the watery seas and then to rise and launch himself towards the heights, in an effort to individuate himself to the very full. Uranus is patron of whatever raises mankind from the ground and lifts him skywards to his mythological domain in the upward surge of effort to attain to the absolute. This would include such mundane things as skyscrapers and go via aircraft and space-satellites to interplanetary rockets. The Uranian encompasses the men of Prometheus' breed, true thieves of the celestial fire, instinctively motivated to deeds of daring. There is always a record to be broken, further or faster to go than anyone else before. Intoxicated by the thirst for unlimited power, the Uranian is the progressive individual on the track of a new age and prone to suffer the fate of the sorcerer's apprentice. At the heart of this process emerges the archetype of hyper-individuation, which provides the specification for a superpersonalized and original human being, generally in the throes of egomania, with the most explosive of unities for a goal and bent upon the absolute.

urn (see also JAR; POT; VASE)   The funerary urn enclosed the dead person's ashes whereas the sarcophagus held the unburned body. Funerary urns, round or square, in metal, marble, pottery or glass, convey the symbolism of the dwelling or HOUSE.

In the arts, the urn was the vessel from which the waters flowed and it symbolized the fecundating powers of streams (see RIVER). Generally speaking, urns relate to the female principle, strengthening the security of the home with the dynamism of fertility. In Chinese Buddhism, the urn is one of the eight figures of luck.

V

vagina   See VULVA.

vajra (see also THUNDERBOLT)   The Tibetan for this Sanskrit word is *dorje* and it denotes a ritual instrument of Tantric Buddhism. It comprises a central point (BINDU), the seed of the spirit and the axis and heart of the universe, and a symmetrical arrangement of lotus flowers from which flash two groups of five flames expressing the arrangement of the five Dhyany-Buddhas, fated to come together like flames in the transcendent nature of the primordial Adi-Buddha, whose spirit is adamantine, dazzling and boundless EMPTINESS. The lotus itself is an expression of the nature of the individual, born in mire but traversing birth and rebirth unsullied to blossom in Nirvana. The *vajra*, which may be translated as 'diamond', 'sceptre', 'thunderbolt' or 'Philosopher's Stone', displays two identical halves, like a pair of mandalas set symmetrically on either side of the central seed, as an expression of the identity of SAMSARA with NIRVANA. It symbolizes the universal love of the Bodhisattva as well as the 'subtle means' whereby release may be attained. The *vajra* (male polarity) is inseparable from the *drilbu*, a bell surmounted by a demi-*vajra*. The *drilbu* (female polarity) symbolizes wisdom, knowledge and emptiness. Its short-lived notes remind us of the inescapable ephemerality of all beings and things. The marriage of *vajra* and *drilbu*, like that of *upaya* and *prajna*, (the male operative power and enlightening knowledge) enables phenomena to become one with the numinous, like the oneness of all dualities, as well as awareness of enlightenment and the true nature of the spirit, as indestructible as the diamond itself. The *vajra* has given its name to the Vajrayāna, the Diamond Vehicle of Tibetan Buddhism, a short cut which enables the ideal of the Bodhisattva to be attained in a single life-time.

The double, or cruciform, *vajra* symbolizes the perfect enlightenment of the Buddha's nature, by means of knowledge (vertical) and love (horizontal), illuminating the entire being and enfolding all created beings. The double *vajra*, standing on a lotus in the middle of the mandala, engenders all that exists in the heart of this representation of the universe, that is to say, in the very heart of the person meditating, and the whole cosmos is reflected in this spirit as if in a flawless mirror. The cruciform *vajra* often occurs in Tibetan iconography as a reminder that, according to Tantric Buddhism, enlightenment consists in knowing one's own heart for what it is.

Valhalla   'Hall of the Slain', 'Porch of the Dead', 'Heroes' Paradise' in Norse mythology, where the abode of those who have died and the land of the living are as alike as the play of mirrors reflecting scenes of exuberant violence, the difference being that one was visible and the other invisible.

The VALKYRIES passed from the one to the other, escorting heroes killed in battle to the Paradise of which they had dreamed. Valhalla was conceived upon the pattern of a battlefield upon which the hero asserted himself in a superabundance of warlike or amorous energy. It was the dream of the fighting-man – battle after battle, after which the dead came back to life to share in the feasting. It was a symbol of that energy, identical with itself, which passes from one world to the next; symbol of a Paradise identical in the other world to the life of which the warrior dreams in this world.

Valkyries These nymphs from WOTAN's palace have often been compared with the AMAZONS. As messengers of the gods and war-leaders, they led heroes to their death and, having brought them to Paradise, poured their beer and mead. They incited the heroes to battle by the love which their beauty instilled into their hearts and by the bravery they displayed at the forefront of the battle on horses charging as swiftly as the clouds or the storm-wracked waves. They symbolize simultaneously the intoxication of enthusiasm and the sweetness of its reward, death and life, and the warrior's heroism and his repose. Although less fierce and cruel than the Amazons, they were just as ambivalent. They stood for the risks inherent in love conceived as a struggle, with its alternations of triumph and disaster and life and death.

valley While in Sufism valleys are the equivalent of spiritual ways or means of passage, as in Attār's *Seven Valleys*, they were above all familiar symbols to Taoists. In the first place, valleys are empty and open to receive celestial influences from above (*Tao*: 15). Valleys are hollows and channels into which the waters streaming down their sides must of necessity flow. To become a point of convergence, the 'Valley of the Empire', the ruler and sage must adopt a lower level in humility and non-action (*Tao*: 28, 66). The 'Spirit of the Valley' (*kuchen*, ibid. 6) provides an inexhaustible subject for interpretation. Wieger regards it as the spirit in the Celestial Valley, 'an expansive, transcendent power in middle space', the world between Heaven and Earth. It may also be the primordial vibration in the cavern of the heart, where emptiness makes its home. It is also the descent of the spirit into the 'lower fields of CINNABAR' in which the Embryo of Immortality (Yang Chang) is conceived through the process of internal alchemy. On the other hand, esoteric recipes for longevity regard it as the life-giving spirit which must be derived from the 'deep valley' of the female partner (*liesien chuang*). Whatever the precise explanation, each interpretation embraces the same notion of receptacle, hollow and void. The 'Deep Valley' is also the pass which Yin Hi guarded and through which Lao Tzu went to reach the primordial spiritual centre.

In Ancient China, it was believed that at the eastern and western extremities of the Earth there were valleys from which the Sun rose and into which it set at either end of its visible transit.

Valleys are the symbolic complements of MOUNTAINS, just as the *yin* is the complement of the *yang*. Richard of St Victor remarks that the Ark of the Covenant was revealed to Moses first upon a mountain-top and then in a valley, where the extraordinary revelation given on the peak became a familar part of normality. The heights of contemplation give place to the descent of the divine presence (GRAD, GRIF, KALL, LIOT, WIET).

The Valley of the Kings, to the northwest of Thebes, with its cliffs, screes and wadis, may be taken as 'symbolising the Egyptian conception of universal harmony, which vibrates but does not move' (POSD p. 292). The valley with its closely guarded tombs stood for the royal road to immortality.

Jehovah's road runs through a valley, too. 'The voice of him that crieth in the wilderness, Prepare ye the way of the Lord . . . Every valley shall be exalted . . . and the glory of the Lord shall be revealed' (Isaiah 40: 3–6).

Valleys are and symbolize the places for fecundating change, where Earth and the waters of Heaven come together to provide rich harvests and where the human soul and God's grace unite to produce mystic revelation and ecstasy.

However, he or she who 'glories in the valleys', forgetting that their wealth is due to God, should beware (Jeremiah 49: 4). Such a casual attitude is like the soil saying it no longer needs watering. All valley symbolism concentrates upon this fecundating marriage of opposing forces in the synthesis of opposites at the heart of the integrated personality.

vampire   The belief in the dead person who leaves the grave to suck the blood of the living is widespread throughout Russia, Poland, central Europe, Greece and Arabia. The Slavs 'run an alder-stake through the bodies of those whose souls return as vampires' (MYTF p. 94).

Traditionally the vampire's victims become vampires themselves, being simultaneously drained of their own blood and polluted.

Ghosts prey upon the fears of the living, vampires kill them by taking their blood, their survival being dependent upon their victims. Explanations in this context should be based upon the dialectic of persecutor and victim and of the eater and the eaten. The vampire symbolizes the lust for life, which bursts into fresh life every time one thinks that it has been sated and which, unless mastered, leaves one exhausted in a vain attempt to give it satisfaction. In concrete terms, this consuming passion is transferred to 'the other person', although it is simply a self-destructive phenomenon. The individual tortures himself and gnaws his own vitals and, since he fails to acknowledge that he is responsible for his own setbacks, he imagines that it is all 'the other person's' fault. On the other hand, when in full commmand of his faculties and acknowledging his responsibilities he accepts his own mortality, the vampire vanishes. Vampires exist until problems of adapting to oneself and to one's social environment have been solved. Until then one is, psychologically, gnawed and eaten away and one becomes a torment to oneself and to others. The vampire symbolizes the turning of psychic forces against oneself.

vase (see also JAR; POT; URN)   In the Kabbalah, the vase has the meaning of TREASURE. To gain possession of a vase is to obtain a treasue, while to break a vase is to destroy, through ignorance, the treasure for which it stands.

Identical symbolism occurs in Mandaean literature and in the *Pistis Sophia.* In the Bahir, the six days of Creation are termed 'six fine vases'. The Shekinah is compared with a 'beautiful vase'.

In medieval literature such vases as the GRAIL are the repositories of treasure.

The alchemical or hermetic vase always means the place where miracles occur. It is the mother's womb in which new birth takes shape, hence the belief that the vase holds the secret of transmutation.

Vases contain, in different shapes, the elixir of life and are repositories of life itself. A golden vase may stand for the treasure of spiritual life, the symbol of a secret power.

When the top of a vase is open it indicates a receptivity to heavenly influences.

vault As symbols of the sky, the vaulted ceilings of churches, tombs, great mosques, baptisteries, tomb-chambers and DOMES are often decorated with a star-pattern or painted with the heavenly imagery of angels, stars, birds, Sun-chariots and so on. These decorations combine with the rest of the building to stand for all the celestial elements within the cosmos as a whole.

Vaults often rest upon square foundations. This combination of curved lines at the apex and straight lines at the base symbolizes the marriage of Heaven and Earth.

vegetation Symbol of the underlying oneness of life itself, with countless texts and images in every civilization showing the transition from vegetable to animal, to human, to divine – and the reverse process. Trees grow from men's stomachs, women conceive through grains of corn, angels grow out of trees, girls are changed into laurels and so on. There is a constant circulatory movement between the higher and lower levels of life. Folk stories have dramatized the permutations between plants, animals and humans and on these an ethic has been grafted. However, the cosmo-biological symbol appears to have preceded its explanation in moral and psychological terms.

Vegetation is also a symbol of the cyclical character of all being – birth, growth, death and transfiguration. Festivals centred upon the plant kingdom, their ceremonies varying according to culture and culminating at the Summer solstice, honour those cosmic forces. They make themselves manifest in these annual cycles, themselves the images of narrower or broader cycles which comprise the vast canvas upon which is painted the evolution of the created universe. In Ancient Greece, nearly all the goddesses, Hera, Demeter, Aphrodite and Artemis, protected crops, as did such gods as Ares (Mars), the god of war, and Dionysos, the god of love.

Vegetation naturally enough symbolizes evolution and the potentiality realized from the seed or germ, as well as from undifferentiated matter represented by the soil. This realization takes place in what Guénon terms 'the sphere of vital assimilation'. From this derives the symbolism of the primordial GARDEN. It is the symbolism of the lotus blossoming upon the surface of the waters, and of the tree which in the Gospels (Matthew 13: 31–2) sprang from the grain of mustard-seed and on the branches of which perched birds, which are symbols of higher spiritual states. In China, little distinction was drawn between human gestation and plant germination, the fertility of the corn being inseparable from that of the woman. Crops were also linked to the notion of cyclical revolution and the same ideogram, *men*, was used both for 'year' and 'harvest'. It is the fount of all biological development.

Plants grow from the Earth and so, according to Genesis, does mankind. The Koran agrees: 'God made you to grow from the earth like a plant.' Islamic esotericism identifies vegetation and the growth of gnosis (*haqīqāt*). The seed becomes 'a Tree, nourished by Earth and Water, with branches which overtop the Seventh Heaven' (Lāhījī).

Born of Earth, the plant has an underground root (*mūla*) which delves deep into the *materia prima* and this is why Hindu tradition gives it a sub-human 'asuric' nature. Now the *asura* were supposed to have pre-existed the *deva* and Guénon observes that in Genesis the plants were created before 'the lights in the firmament of the heavens' (Genesis 1: 11–14). This is because the plants in the Garden of Eden stand for the development of seeds deriving from the preceding cycle and also because the root precedes the stalk. In fact, the root aspect contrasts with the fruit aspect, the latter's nature being solar and celestial, as is that of the branch aspect, a symbol, when it remains green, of resurrection and of immortality. The part of the plant exposed to the air is the TREE of Life, from which is drawn the SAP, which is the beverage of immortality (CORT, ELIY, GRAR, GUEV, GUED, GUEC, GUER, GUES).

vehicle The Jungian school regards vehicles, whether ancient or modern, as images of the ego when considered symbolically. They reflect different aspects of the inner life in relation to the problems of its development. In dreams and the emotions which they arouse, they are to be interpreted in respect to the position and progress of the ego along the path of individuation. (See also AIRCRAFT; BICYCLE; TRAIN)

veil In Arabic, *hijab*, or veil, conveys the meaning of the separation of one thing from another and hence, depending upon whether one puts on or removes the veil, it has the meaning of hidden or revealed knowledge. Thus in Christian monastic tradition, 'taking the veil' means not simply separating oneself from the world, but also of separating the world from that intimate relationship which arises from a life with God. The Koran (7: 44) speaks of the veil which divides the damned from the chosen. Women should be addressed from behind a veil. The Unbelievers tell the Prophet that 'between us and thee there is a veil' (Koran 41: 4). God only speaks to mankind through revelation or from behind a veil (ibid. 42), as was Moses' case.

In the Temple at Jerusalem one veil shut off the Holy of Holies and another the Holy Place. Matthew (27: 51) states that at the moment of Christ's death 'the veil of the temple was rent in twain from the top to the bottom.' This rending shows the abruptness of revelation effected by un-veiling and bears a sense of initiation. Christ's revelation was unveiling in relation to the Old Law – 'there is nothing covered, that shall not be re-vealed' (Matthew 10: 26). Similarly in Islam: 'We have taken off thy veil from thee, and thy sight is becoming sharp this day' (Koran 50: 21). Re-moval of Isis' veil, or succession of veils, clearly stands for revelation of the light. In his *Lehrlinge zu Saïs*, Novalis says that to lift the veil is to become immortal. And also: 'A man succeeded in lifting the veil of the goddess of Saïs. But what did he see? He saw that wonder of wonders – himself.'

Al-Hallāj said: 'What is a veil? It is a curtain set between the seeker and the object of his search, between the betrothed and the object of his desire, between the marksman and his target. It is to be hoped that veils exist only for creatures and not for the Creator. God does not wear a veil, only his creatures do' (MASH pp. 699–700).

The Sufis say that a person 'is veiled (*majdhūb*) when his awareness is controlled by passions, either of the mind or the senses, so that he cannot perceive the divine Light in his heart' (BURD p. 147).

Mystics use the term *hijāb,* meaning all that which veils the object of quest, to signify the impressions left upon the heart by the outward appearances which comprise the visible world and which prevent the penetration of the Truth. 'The *nafs* [animal soul] is the centre of the veiling.... Substances, accidence, elements, bodies, shapes and properties are so many veils concealing divine mysteries. Spiritual truth is hidden from all humankind except for the saints.'

One of the oldest Sufi treatises, written by Hujwīri, is called *The Lifting of the Veil,* in Arabic, *al-kashf,* a title adopted by many later writers.

Ibn al-Farid mentions 'veils of the shroud of the senses' (NICM p. 247). The Sufis regard being itself as a veil.

In Buddhism, the same veil which conceals pure Reality is Māyā. However, like the *shakti,* Māyā simultaneously veils and unveils, for, did it not veil the ultimate reality – the identity of the ego and the Self, of the *sich selbst* and of the Goddess – objective manifestation could not be perceived. In this context, the symbol deviates, since the veil ceases to be what prevents sight, but what allows it, by screening a light which, if unscreened, would blind – the light of Truth. This is the sense of the expression employed by Muslims that the face of God is veiled by seventy thousand curtains of light and darkness, without which everything on which he gazed would be burned up. The same reason caused Moses to veil his face when he addressed the Children of Israel. Muslims also say that God clothed his creatures 'with the veil of their names' since 'had he made manifest to them the knowledge of his power, they would have lost their senses and, had he revealed Reality to them, they would have died' (MASH pp. 699–700). (The veil of its name preserves the creature from direct sight which would make it faint away.) Similarly, sunlight has this twofold symbolic sense. It can be what reveals, but it can also, by excess of light, be what blinds. Thus the Thai say that the veil of daylight hides the stars, which are unveiled at nightfall (AVAS, BURA, CORT, EVAB, PHIL, GUEM, MASR, PALT, SOUN, SOUJ, VALI, WARK).

The secular power has sometimes appropriated this symbol to give itself the aura of holiness. This was true of the emperors of China, who always kept a veil between themselves and their visitors, whom they could see without themselves being seen. The same is true of the Caliphs, from the Umayyad dynasty onwards. Their chamberlains' duty included passing on the Caliphs' pronouncements during audiences and they bore the name of Hajib (curtain, or veil) because they were at once the persons who hid and revealed.

Ultimately, the veil may be regarded more as a means of communication than as an obstacle to it. Half-concealing, it invites fuller knowledge, as coquettes have known throughout the ages.

The symbol bears the same definition for hermeticism – what reveals itself through veiling, what conceals itself through unveiling.

Venus (see also APHRODITE; PLANET) The great importance which Central American civilizations attached to Venus and the Venusian cycle is well-known. In particular, both the Maya and the Aztecs used the planet to establish their calendars, as well as their cosmogony, both in any case being closely connected. The Aztecs computed Venusian years in groups of five, corresponding to eight solar years (SOUM). Venus stood for Quetzalcoatl, who died in the west and was restored to life in the east. In this reincarnation, the Plumed-Serpent God was depicted as an archer, feared as the spreader of disease, or as the death-god, his face covered in a death's-head mask. In this context, it must be remembered that this is one of the two aspects of the symbolic duality, death and rebirth, contained in the myth of Quetzalcoatl.

The movements of Venus, alternately rising in the east as the Morning Star and setting in the west as the Evening Star, have made it a basic symbol of death and rebirth. The two appearances of the planet, at either end of the day, explain why the Aztec god Quetzalcoatl may also be called 'Precious Twin' (SOUM, SOUA).

The association of Venus with the Sun through the similarity of their daily transits, sometimes deifies the planet as the Sun's messenger and an intermediary between the Sun and mankind. This is true of the Brazilian Gé Sherente Indians, who believe that the Sun has two messengers, Jupiter and Venus.

The Buryat regarded the planet as the guardian spirit of their horses. They made offerings to it in the Spring when they branded their foals, cutting the manes and tails of their horses. They also consecrated to it 'live horses which were not to be used for common purposes thereafter' (HARA p. 142). This tribe of nomadic pastoralists regarded Venus as the heavenly shepherd leading his flocks or herds of stars. The people of the Yenisei considered Venus 'the oldest star which guards all the others from harm'.

The ritual carrying-off of the Buryat bride was connected with the worship of Venus (HARA). In Yakut legend, she was a proud maiden who had the Pleiades as her lovers. The Kirghiz, like the original inhabitants of Asia Minor, believed that, as the Evening Star, Venus was daughter of the Moon (HARA p. 143).

The ancient Turks originally called Venus Arlig, the warrior, the man, then Star of Light (Lucifer) and later Tcholban (the Shining or Dazzling One) (ROUF).

Even in Sumerian times Venus was 'she who shows the way to the stars'. As goddess of evening she was the patroness of love and pleasure and as goddess of the morning she presided over 'battle and slaughter' (DHOB p. 68). She was the Moon's daughter and the Sun's sister and, since she appeared at dawn and dusk, it was only natural that she should be regarded as some sort of link between the deities of light and darkness. It was for this reason that, although she had the Sun as a brother, she had the Underworld goddess as a sister. Her kinship with the Sun – she was his twin sister – was the source of her warlike qualities and she was known as 'the Valiant One' and 'the Lady of Battles'. These derived from her role as morning star; but, in the role of evening star, the predominant influence was that of her mother, the Moon, and this made her the goddess of love and pleasure. Both Assyrian seals and paintings from the second millennium BC Palace of Mari show the lion as her attribute. Religious literature sometimes calls her 'the raging lion' or 'the sky-gods' lioness' (DHOB p. 71). As goddess of love, also known as 'she who loves pleasure and delight', her worship was associated with temple prostitution. Her myth contains a descent into the Underworld, which would explain the initiatory significance of Venusian symbolism. A Babylonian king called her 'she who at sunrise and sunset brings me good omens'. As she had done in Sumer, so in Assyria she appeared in dreams and foretold the outcome of wars. 'I am Ishtar of Arbela,' she is made to say to Asarhaddon in an oracle, 'Fear not! I go before and behind you.' Bow and arrows, symbols of sublimation, are among her attributes. In Assyria, she was 'Queen of Nineveh, she in whose lap sits Assurbanipal to suck from two of her breasts and to bury his head in two others' (DHOB p. 76). In a Babylonian liturgical text she is given the titles of 'Lady of Fate' and 'Queen of Lots' (DHOB p. 91n.).

In astrology, the planet Venus embodies sympathetic attraction, emotion, love, sympathy, harmony and gentleness. It is the planet of art and of sensory appreciation, of pleasure and pleasant things and, in the Middle Ages, it was called 'the Little Benefactor'. The sense of touch is one of its attributes, as well as all manifestations of the female nature, in luxury, fashion and personal adornment. Its Houses, that is, the signs of the Zodiac in which it is especially powerful – Taurus and Libra – are related respectively to the throat and breasts and to the curve of the hips, that is, with what is peculiar to the female figure.

From remote ages, Venus was the star of whispered confidences, and the chief of the heavenly beauties inspired lovers with the unalloyed impression which the gentle starlight leaves upon contemplative souls. Astrologers regard Venus as being partly linked to the emotions produced by physical attraction and love, which arise from that instinctive craving for physical contact which the baby has for its mother and which may develop into a sentimental altruism. The Venusian world of the human individual gathers into an emotional synergy of sensation, sensual feelings, instinctive attraction towards an object, intoxication, smiles, seduction, the exhilaration of pleasure, delight in the affinity and harmony of interchange and emotional community, as well as of those emotional states created by charm, beauty and grace. Furthermore, the goddess is presented at her most attractive in all mythologies and she is the only one whose advantages make her the rival of Aphrodite, patroness of marriage and consummate type of female beauty. Under her symbol, sheer pleasure in being alive rules the human heart in the Spring festival of sensual intoxication, as in the more spiritualized and refined pleasures of aesthetics. Her rule is that of tender kisses, of amorous longing and sensual encounter, of an appreciation of the beautiful, of gentleness, kindness and enjoyment as much as of loveliness. It is that of the peace of mind called happiness.

vertical axis A powerful symbol of elevation and progress in self-development.

Some psychotherapeutic techniques based upon the interpretation of dreams allot a privileged role, property and significance to the vertical axis. . . . On the one hand, the history of religion displays the frequency of ascensional imagery in certain ascetic practices and, on the other, both psychology and ethnography allow us to allot to the appearance of the vertical dimension the properties of a definite stage in the development of self-awareness.

(VIRI p. 36)

There are abundant examples from many different cultures of images of animals standing, like serpents, on their tails or, like lions and leopards, on their hind feet. In so far as they depict an upright stance, they are symbols of humans, since, according to Leroi-Gourhan, an upright stance is 'the first and most important criterion common to the human race as a whole and to its ancestors' (LERG pp. 33–4). A splendid low-relief from southern Mexico depicts a man crouched horizontally, his back arched and his chin sunk below his knees. Around his crouching figure is entwined a huge serpent rising up above his head. This is a symbol 'of human verticalization' (CHAS pp. 238, 255). It 'fittingly epitomizes the process of development by which one animal species is radically differentiated from another, the start of a process of standing upright which will ultimately produce the biped' and the stance of the human being. The standing serpent, like the plumed serpent, a symbol of the marriage of opposing forces, may perhaps be

an entity standing for the sudden hybridization of apparently irreconcilable species, an unexpected marriage of heavy matter clinging to the ground with a winged substance. . . . The reptile, every atom of its will-power focused upon an effort to transcend its condition, is the image by which is represented the advent of the human race, of beings endowed with senses which enable them to act in accordance with an invisible reality, far from the world of appearances.

Some vertical imagery in which the head is exaggeratedly large, appear to mark what Bachelard terms 'the slide from verticality to cerebrality'.

Vesta (Hestia) To the Romans Vesta personified the sacred fire which burned on the hearths of its citizens, as well as in the city itself. Vesta corresponds to the Greek Hestia and to some extent to the Hindu Agni. Hestia was courted by the gods, and in particular by the handsome Apollo and by Poseidon, but she repulsed all their advances and persuaded Zeus himself to protect her virginity.

Zeus granted her extraordinary honours. She was worshipped in the homes of all mortals and in the temples of all the gods. . . . Hestia never left Olympus. Just as the domestic hearth was the centre of the religious life of the home, so Hestia was the religious centre of the home of the gods. Because Hestia never left Olympus, she plays no part in legend. She remains an abstract principle, the Ideal of the hearth, rather than a personal deity.

(GRID p. 210)

In Rome she symbolized the demands of absolute purity. 'She presided', writes Jean Beaujeu,

over the conclusion of every act and event. In her hunger for purity, she protects the nursing mother but is not herself a fertility goddess. She was served by a college of ten virgins bound by the strictest embargoes (to break any of them was punished by death). Should any of them behave unchastely, she was buried alive in an underground vault. . . . Vesta was the goddess of the hearth and of fulfilment.

It is important to observe that all success, prosperity and victory was set beneath the seal of this absolute purity. The Vestal Virgins may, perhaps, have symbolized that continuous SACRIFICE through which constant innocence takes the place of continuous human sinning, or brings people protection and success (see VIRGINITY).

vestments See DRESS.

vine (see also WINE) The Children of Israel were surrounded by religions which regarded vines as sacred trees, if not divine, and the wine which they produced as the drink of the gods. A faint echo of these beliefs may be heard in the Old Testament (Judges 9: 32; Deuteronomy 32: 37ff.).

A later shift of emphasis made the Israelites regard the vine, like the olive, as one of the Messianic trees (Micah 4: 4; Zechariah 3: 10). Nor is it impossible that earlier tradition identified the vine with the Tree of Life in the Garden of Eden.

Thus from the very start vine symbolism appropriated extremely positive attributes.

In the first place the vine possessed and ensured life and what made life worth living – it was one of mankind's most prized possessions (1 Kings 21: 1ff.). A good wife was like a fruitful vine to her husband (Psalm 128: 3), while wisdom 'brought forth pleasant savour' like the vine (Ecclesiasticus 24: 17).

This develops quite naturally into the broadest strand of its symbolism. The Vine is Israel, seen as God's property in which he delights, from which he awaits the fruits and which he constantly tends (Isaiah 5: 7). However, the one who had so carefully tended it was disappointed because the 'noble vine . . . turned into the degenerate plant of a strange vine' (Jeremiah 2: 21). This is why the symbolism came to be transferred to the person of him who is the incarnation and the true replica of God's Chosen People, and the Messiah is compared with the vine.

Jesus proclaimed himself the true vine and warned that mankind, the separate branches, could not bear fruit unless they remained in him. Unless the individual did so, he or she was withered, cut off and cast into the fire (John 15: 1ff.).

In St Matthew's parable of the householder and the wicked husbandmen (21: 28–46), the vine stands for the Kingdom of God, originally entrusted to the Jews but now about to pass to other hands.

The symbolism of the vine was extended to every human soul. God was the man who planted the vine and who finally (Mark 12: 6) asked his son to visit his vineyard. Christ, taking Israel's place, in his turn will become comparable with a vine and his blood the wine of the New Covenant.

Mandaean writers use the word 'vine' not only to denote the Heaven-sent one, but also a whole series of beings from the upper world of light.

The vine is an important symbol, especially in respect of what it produces, wine, the image of knowledge. Hence it was undoubtedly no matter of chance that Noah, who ushered in a fresh cycle, was the first to plant the

vine. As we have observed, the Gospel-writers made the vine a symbol of
the Kingdom of God and its 'fruit' the Eucharist. Jesus is 'the true vine. I
take vine in its allegorical sense,' St Clement of Alexandria wrote (*Stromata*
1), 'as the Lord, the vine which we should till by means of the working of
our reason and of which we should eat the fruit.' The sap which rises in the
vine is the light of the spirit and the Father is the vine-dresser, at least in
those Gnostic concepts which set him apart from his vine, as the absolute
is set apart from the relative.

Iconographically, the TREE of Life is often depicted as a vine and this
meaning is corroborated by the terrifying description of the grape-harvest
in Revelation 14: 18–20:

And another angel came out from the altar, which had power over fire; and
cried with a loud cry to him that had the sharp sickle, saying, Thrust in thy sharp
sickle, and gather the clusters of the vine of the earth; for her grapes are fully
ripe. And the angel thrust in his sickle into the earth, and gathered the vine of
the earth, and cast it into the great winepress of the wrath of God. And the
winepress was trodden without the city, and blood came out of the winepress,
even unto the horse bridles, by the space of a thousand and six hundred
furlongs.

Cultivation of the vine was traditionally held to have been comparatively
late in Ancient Greece by comparison with corn cultivation. Thus it was not
the domain of some ancient goddess such as Demeter, but belonged to
Dionysos, whose worship acquired growing importance, associated as it was
with the knowledge of the mysteries of life after death. It was because
Dionysos was linked to the mysteries of death, which are also those of
rebirth and of knowledge, that the vine also became a funerary symbol, a
part which it continued to play in Christian symbolism (LAVD p. 1001).

Just as the vine was the plant kingdom's expression of immortality, so in
ancient tradition alcohol remained a symbol of eternal youth and of immortality. Both the French *eau de vie* and the Gaelic and Irish *uisgebeatha*
(whisky) mean 'water of life', while the Persian *māie-i-shebab* means 'beverage of youth' and the Sumerian *geshtin*, 'tree of life', and so on.

In the ancient Near East, the vine was identified with the 'herb of life'
and the Sumerian written sign for 'life' was usually a vine-leaf. The plant
was sacred to the Great Goddesses. The Mother Goddess was originally
called the Vine-stock Mother, or the Vine-stock Goddess.

The Mishna states that the Tree of the Knowledge of Good and Evil was
the vine.

The Mandaeans believed that wine was the physical form of light, wisdom and purity. The archetype of wine resided in the heavenly kingdom.
The archetypal vine consisted internally of water, while its leaves were
fashioned from the spirits of light and its nodes were seeds of light. The
vine was regarded as a cosmic tree, since its branches enfolded the Heavens
and its clusters of grapes were the stars.

Christian apocryphal writings are another channel through which the image
of the naked woman–vine was transmitted (ELIT p. 285).

violet Composed of equal proportions of RED and BLUE, violet is the colour of temperance, clarity of mind, deliberate action, of balance between

Heaven and Earth, senses and spirit, passion and reason, love and wisdom. The fourteenth major arcanum of the Tarot is known as TEMPERANCE and depicts an angel holding a vase in either hand, one red, the other blue, and ceaselessly pouring from one to the other a colourless liquid which is the water of life. This constant interchange of the chthonian red of the strength of impulse and celestial blue produces violet, although it is not shown on the Tarot. Thus the fourteenth major arcanum 'stands for perpetual regeneration through the ceaseless interflow of material energy' (RIJT p. 249).

If we take this interpretation a stage further we find that, in the circle of life, violet lies directly opposite GREEN. Thus it stands, not for the springtime passage from death into life, but for the autumnal passage from life into death, involution rather than evolution. Violet may well, in some respects, be the other side of green and, like it, be linked to the symbolism of the MOUTH. Violet, however, is the mouth which swallows and puts out the light, while green is the mouth which regurgitates and rekindles it. This explains why violet is the colour of secrecy since, behind it, the invisible mystery of reincarnation or at least of transformation takes place.

'This is why in medieval symbolic art Christ is depicted in a violet robe during his Passion' (PORS p. 234), that is to say, at a time when he had assumed fully his incarnation and when his sacrifice was to be wholly fulfilled, he wedded completely within himself the human, born of the Earth, which he was about to redeem, and the spiritual and celestial, to which he was about to return. The same symbolism causes the choirs of churches to be draped in violet on Good Friday. Prior to the Renaissance many gospelbooks, psalters and breviaries were written in letters of gold on violetcoloured parchment so that 'the reader had constantly before his eyes Revelation in letters of gold and Our Lord's Passion represented by the violet' (PORS p. 235).

Later, and as a result of the death symbolism of violet, in Western society the colour became that of mourning or of half-mourning. This more sharply conjures the notion of death not as a state, but as a phase.

Lastly, Portal quotes Winckelmann for the statement that Apollo's cloak was blue or violet, something which takes added importance from the thought of the kinship of this figure with that of Christ in late solar mythologies. Nor does the fact that violet was the colour of obedience and submissiveness contradict its association with Christ's Passion. Wallis Budge notes the Ancient Egyptian custom of hanging a violet stone round a child's neck to make it well-behaved and obedient (BUDA p. 326).

Violet is also the colour of appeasement, in which the blaze of red is softened. This is the meaning which should be attached to the bishop's violet vestments. He, unlike the mystic, has a duty to watch over his flock and must therefore moderate the heat of his passions – hence the colour of his vestment. Here again the colour is a definite emblem of temperance. With notable ingenuity, in the Far East the transition from red to violet is given entirely the opposite meaning. On a purely physical level it is taken to mean the transition from the active to the passive, from the *yang* to the *yin*. In Tantrism, ritual sexual intercourse between yogi takes place in a room with bluish-purple lighting because 'violet light stimulates the woman's sexual glands while red activates the man's' (AJMO p. 61).

viper Some Ancient Egyptian painters, symbolizing the transformations which the dead were to undergo from their shapes in this earthly life to the shapes into which they would be reborn in the other world, depicted them being swallowed by the jaws of a viper, wrapped in its stomach and expelled at its tail as SCARABS. Other paintings show the soul entering at the tail and expelled through the mouth. The viper, itself the bearer of a deadly poison, is conceived as an alembic (retort for distilling) and may play the part of the place or furnace in which these transformations occur. Maspéro suggests another explanation, in which the viper would symbolize the counterpart of the life of the gods. However, the transition of the souls of the dead through this counterpart would just as well make them ready for their new lives, in which they were to a degree deified. Once again the SERPENT is conceived as the agent of spiritual and physical change.

In dreams vipers derive from the unconscious and reveal impulses which have not been integrated into the conscious scale of values.

virginity (see also VESTA) The virginal state means the latent and unrevealed.

The Wisdom of Solomon alludes to the bird which hovered over the primordial waters – this relates to the TOHU-BOHU which was absence rather than confusion of form – and these virgin waters became fruitful, that is, possessed of life, thanks to this bird (the Holy Spirit, Wisdom or the Virgin) which brooded over them, revealed them and made them manifest.

The soul is also called virgin, when it is emptied. It becomes virgin and ready to receive divine seed in the sense in which Angelus Silesius wrote 'the soul which knows nothing and wills nothing . . . should this day become the bride of the eternal Bridegroom.' According to Master Eckhart, the virgin soul means the soul 'free from all external impressions and as malleable as before it was born'.

The virgin soul becomes the 'bride' in proportion as it receives the 'enlightening influx' of the Bridegroom. This causes Master Eckhart to write:

If man remained for ever virgin he would bear no fruit. To become fertile he must become woman. Woman? This is the noblest description one can give the soul and it is far nobler than 'virgin'. It is good that man should receive God into himself [*empfängt*] and in this receiving [*Empfänglichkeit*] he is virgin. But it is a better thing if God become fertile within him, for to become fertile by the gift received is to show thankfulness for that gift.

When the gift or fruit of divine influx takes shape within the man and reaches its fullness, the soul is raised to that highest level which denotes the state of the Mother of God. She gave birth to God in this world and became him to whom she had given birth.

The symbol of the Virgin, in her aspect of Mother of God or Theotokos, denotes the soul which God himself inhabits, self-conceiving within himself, for he alone is. The Virgin Mary stands for the soul made perfectly one, in which God himself becomes fertile. She is ever-virgin because she remains intact in respect of a fresh conception.

The Christian mystery, in which the divine child is born without human intervention, by this becomes akin to the myths of antiquity, describing the miraculous birth of the hero. The Virgin Mother of God symbolizes Earth directed heavenwards and thus becoming Earth transfigured, an Earth of light. Hence her role and her importance in Christian thought, as both the pattern and the bridge linking Heaven with Earth, the high with the low.

BLACK Madonnas symbolize virgin soil still to be fertilized and stress the passive aspect of virginity. At the close of the Middle Ages we may observe the popularity of blackness because of the dark colours of Byzantine icons.

The great female deity of the Celts – the equivalent of Minerva in Caesar's table of comparisons – possessed the two aspects of Virgin and Mother. In other words, her virginity was an essential prerequisite of her supremacy as a warrior and her maternal properties were of the essence of female godhead. After each birth the mother became a virgin once more. This is what happened to Dechtire, sister and bride of the god Lug, after each of the three times she conceived Cùchulainn. The Welsh king Math, son of Mathonwy, could not exist unless his feet were in the lap of a maiden, except only when he was prevented by the tumult of war. Such examples may also be compared with the frequent occurrence of companions to the Gaulish gods, of which the symbolism is undoubtedly identical. A Celtic goddess who bears several different names – Ana or Dana or Brigite in Ireland; Brigantia in Gaul; and so on – corresponds to the Classical Diana, duplicated in Rome by the Capitoline triad, her maternal aspect being Juno and her virginal Minerva-Pallas (OGAC 6: pp. 3–8).

In Islam, virginity is the unsullied light which shines upon the elect and in this role is known as the Virgin-Mother, 'the hour of life which is both the very first and the very last'. It is she who opens the doors of enlightenment and she who guides the mystic's journey to its goal. 'The Virgin of Light reveals to the elect the spiritual shape which is the New Man within him, by appointing herself his guide and leading him to the heights' (CORE 2: p. 321).

Virgo (23 August–22 September)   The sixth sign of the Zodiac, immediately preceding the autumnal equinox, is the symbol of harvest, work, manual dexterity and attention to detail. It is Mercury's second sign, in which he operates upon a lower, more terrestrial and practical level than in Gemini, which corresponds to the airy aspects of the Messenger of the Gods.

With Virgo we reach the end of the element Earth's cycle. Ahead lies the cold soil of Capricorn, ready for the Winter sowing, and behind the rich, dank, warm soil of Taurus, covered with greenery and the scents of Spring. Virgo displays soil scorched by Summer sunshine and with its nutritive properties exhausted. On it lie the reaped sheaves awaiting the thresher. The cycle of plant life ends with fresh, virgin soil awaiting the subsequent arrival of the sower. Hence the sign is depicted as a winged virgin bearing an ear or sheaf of corn. Mercury is the ruling planet. At harvest and threshing-time, when the produce is weighed and measured, we are in the realms of differentiation, categorization, of picking and choosing, wrapping in rules and regulations, confinement to bare essentials and of setting ourselves precise limits. Virginal differentiation more closely resembles the practice of a graphic style based upon the linear purity of abstract design. Sharp against this horizon stands the silhouette of a character who has an equivalent in the repressed anal complex of Freudian psychoanalysis. We are concerned with an overall disposition to retain and to control, along with self-control and self-discipline and a tendency towards economizing and meanness, to amassing, preserving and towards calculated delay. The character concerned is serious, conscientious to a fault, self-contained, sceptical, methodical, organized and attached to principles and to rules and regulations, sober and mindful of its duties as a respectable citizen, hard-working and always directed to what is difficult, drudging, thankless or painful, aiming above all to achieve a sense of security.

In Ancient Egypt, Virgo was the sign of Isis. As the sixth sign of the Zodiac it shares the symbolism of the number SIX and of the STAR OF DAVID. It pertains simultaneously to Fire and Water and symbolizes consciousness emerging from confusion, as well as the birth of the spirit.

V.I.T.R.I.O.L. These are the initials of the celebrated formula which encapsulated alchemical teaching – *Visita Interiorem Terrae Rectificando Invenies Operae Lapidem* – of which one translation might be: 'Go down into the bowels of the Earth, by distillation you will find the stone for the Work' (see ALCHEMY).

These initials form an initiatory password which also expresses the laws governing a process of transmutation which relates to 'the return of the individual to the deepest kernel of human personality. . . . It carries the sense of an instruction to descend to the deepest level of oneself to find that unbreakable kernel on which to build a fresh personality and a new individuality' (SERH p. 138).

Kurt Seligman provides a slightly different version of the initials and their meaning (SELM p. 110) – *Visita Interiora Terrae Rectificando Invenies Occultum Lapidem*, or 'Explore the inner things of Earth and by distillation you will find the hidden stone.' This expresses synthetically the different alchemical operations regarded from the different levels of transmutation, whether they be of metals or of the human being. In the latter case the symbolism goes rather deeper since it is a matter of setting aside the different degrees of unawareness, ignorance and prejudice and of rebuilding the self on the indestructible foundation of self-awareness, through which the individual may find the immanent and transformational power of God within him- or herself. Whichever of these two versions provides the better text and translation, their symbolism comes to the same thing.

void (see also EMPTINESS) To create a void within oneself in the symbolic sense given to the term by mystics and poets is to free oneself from the confused mass of mental images, desires and feelings; to escape from the wheel of fleeting lives; and to hunger for nothing but the absolute. This, according to Novalis, is 'the path which leads inwards', the way of true life. Jacques Maritain, as a philosopher, explains that 'when we speak of void, abolition, negation, stripping bare, we denote a reality in action, still and intensely a piece of life, the ultimate activation in which the void finds its fulfilment. . . . It is a form of energy, a supremely immanent action, the action which annihilates all activity.' It is the fruitional period – when a sense of enjoyment accompanies the action – of Self-experience. The Middle Path school of Buddhism holds that once voidness of discourse has been attained it provides an inexpungible experience of the Buddha's nature.

volcano See MOUNTAIN.

voyaging The real presence of God (*Shekinah*) was manifest upon the ARK of the Covenant, but *Shekinah* also means, literally, 'the Great Peace'. The RAINBOW which appeared above Noah's Ark also signified peace. Here we touch upon one of the basic aspects of voyaging as a means of achieving peace, the central state or Nirvana. Both the Ancient Egyptian *Book of the Dead* and the legends of the Chinese secret societies tell of a voyage which brings the traveller to the City of Peace or to the Market-place of Great Peace, while the Shankara speaks of crossing the Sea of Passions to reach Tranquillity. The Buddha is called the Great Mariner because he helps the traveller to the farther shore and across the ocean of life. Canonical Buddhist scriptures make the point that, after the crossing, the boat or raft should be abandoned, an idea similarly expressed by Master Eckhart. Tārā, the star, but also meaning 'that which causes to cross', sometimes takes a rudder or a boat as its emblem. St Peter's barque is a symbol of the Catholic Church and, because Christ is on it, it is the instrument of salvation. There is an echo of this in the nave (from Latin *navis*, ship) of a church, like the inverted hull of a boat and therefore to be regarded as the means of voyaging to Heaven. Before this the boat had been JANUS' emblem, since it could sail in either direction and was therefore a symbol of the god's two faces and twofold power. Nor should the countless voyages in quest of ISLANDS be forgotten, nor that of the Argonauts in search of the Golden Fleece – all were quests for the primordial spiritual centre or for immortality.

If the word 'arcane' – etymologically derived from *arca,* ark – suggests the mysteries over which Janus presided (the *Bhagavad Gītā* overtly assimilates boats to knowledge), his BOAT would seem to be related to the Sun-boat as well. Celtic art depicted a Sun-boat drawn by swans. The horse-headed Hindu Sun-gods, the Ashvins, sometimes have a boat as their emblem and it is depicted as a fertility symbol. According to the Shintō myth, casting Hiru-ko adrift in the Celestial Boat may well have some links to solar symbolism as well. The ocean voyaging undertaken by the Marquesas islanders seems to have been in quest for the Sun and they, like the Ancient Egyptians, believed that Sun-boats would take them voyaging after death. Manicheans used Sun- and Moon-boats to the same end and the theme of voyaging after death recurs in many other religions, as, for example, among the Thai. Once again it is a matter of escaping from cosmic limitations in search of immortality.

Additionally there was a widespread assimilation of the crescent Moon to the boat. This was especially overt among the Sumerians, whose celestial mariner was the Moon-god, the son of Enlil, the supreme deity. The water-god, Enki, who regulated the world, was also a mariner. In Japan, Prince Ninigi, the Sun-goddess's grandson and founder of the empire, also came down from Heaven in a boat and, in certain circumstances, a vision of his boat is a presage of wealth and good fortune (BENA, CHOO, COOH, CORT, DANA, GUEM, GUES, HERJ, HOUD, MASR, RENB, SAIR, SOUN, SOUL, VALA, VARG).

Vulcan See HEPHAISTOS.

vulture The Maya made the royal vulture, feeding on the entrails, a symbol of death (METS). However, the bird might well have been regarded as a regenerative agency for the life forces contained in decomposing matter and refuse of all sorts from the very fact that it lived off carrion and filth; in other words, as a cleanser or a sorcerer who ensures the cycle of renewal by transforming death into new life. This explains why, in their cosmological symbolism, the vulture was associated with water-signs. This is true of the Mayan calendar, where the vulture controls the 'precious storms' of the dry season, thus ensuring the renewal of plant life and becoming thereby one of the gods of plenty.

For the same reasons vultures were associated with celestial fire as a cleansing and fecundating element. In many South American Indian myths, the vulture is the first possessor of fire, which a Demiurge, generally helped by a toad, steals from him (METT, LEVC). In Black Africa, the Bambara take this symbolism to its ultimate limits on the mystic plane with the grade of initiates known as the 'Vultures'. The Kore 'vulture' is an initiate, who is dead to the profane world and who, cleansed and scorched by the ordeals of initiation, has penetrated the wisdom of the godhead. In public appearances of his confraternity, he takes the clown's part or, more especially, that of the child, for he is in fact new-born or rather reborn, but into the transcendental realms of God whose wisdom seems, to the eyes of the profane, like folly or innocence. Like a baby he crawls on the gound, eating whatever he finds, even including his own EXCREMENT. This is because he has conquered earthly death and has the power to transmute filth into Philosopher's Gold. He is called the wealthiest of men because he alone knows true gold. Lastly, in any comparison between grades of initiate and social station, he ranks with the woman who regularly bears children. Thus in Africa, as well as America, the vulture is a symbol of fertility and plenty on every level of wealth, both spiritual and material.

Nekhbet, the Ancient Egyptian vulture-goddess, protected childbirth according to folk belief, but the vulture is sometimes identified with Isis in the *Pyramid Texts*. The dead had to know the mysterious utterances of Isis which endowed them with life. 'Possession of the vulture's prayer will be a blessing to you in the land of a thousand fields.' At night and in darkness and death the vulture-goddess gives new life to the soul, which revives with the dawn. The vulture is also depicted on a hamper or BASKET, thus symbolizing conception within the womb.

In Ancient Egyptian art the vulture was often used to depict the power of the Mother-goddesses. Devouring corpses and restoring life, it symbolized the cycle of death and life in a ceaseless series of transmutations.

There is a very fine relief of Isis at the temple of Philae. The goddess is depicted in profile, seated upon a throne, her head enclosed, as if by a helmet, by the drooping wings of a great vulture, its head and tail sticking out before and behind, the whole surmounted by the lunar disk within in a pair of cow's horns curving like a lyre on either side. The goddess is naked to the waist and proffers a swollen breast as if to suckle a baby. This is a rare agglomeration of female symbols, personifying the birth-process throughout the universe, and one of the finest images of the eternal feminine.

In Greco-Roman tradition the vulture was a bird of augury. It was one of the birds sacred to Apollo because its flight, like that of swans, kites and ravens, provided omens. When, seated respectively upon the Aventine and Palatine hills, Remus and Romulus consulted the Heavens to determine where they should build their city, the former saw six vultures and the latter twelve and, accordingly, Rome was founded upon the spot where the omens had been most favourable.

vulva (see also MOUTH)   Euphemistically termed 'lovely big mother' by the Bambara, the vulva is the symbol of a gateway to secret wealth and hidden knowledge (ZAHB). Its symbolism is akin to that of springs, as well as to that of the mouth. It takes and gives, swallows the penis and regurgitates life, it marries opposites or, more accurately, it transmutes the one into the other, hence the mystery with which its charms are endowed, unlike the solar and diurnal male sexual organ. The Bambara also use the phrase 'to be strong and not to be strong' to denote the female sexual organs, which they compare with God in the following proverb: 'God is like a woman's sexual organs. He is the strong one, the powerful one, he is endurance. Yet at the same time he is temptation, he is greed and, lastly, he is surrender' (ZAHB p. 27). The Dogon and Bambara have evolved the symbolism of the vulva and of female sexual organs as a whole through the cosmogonic and ritual significance of the ANT-hill, which they regard as the world's vulva.

The castration-myth of the toothed vagina which is encountered wherever mankind and history intersect suffices to prove the power of fascination exerted upon men by this mysterious gateway both to life and to momentary death. One has only to look at Van Eyck's painting of Adam and Eve in the Ghent Altar to realize how deeply the history of our culture has been affected by this all-powerful questioning, that of the spirit faced by the mystery of life, that of culture faced by the secrets of nature. The one is Adam, whom the artist has been careful to depict with head half bent under the strain of thought, while opposite is Eve wriggling her hips and exposing her sex with a sort of untroubled shamelessness.

W

wagtail In Japanese myths of the beginning of things, the wagtail plays the part of a Demiurge, since it was from this bird that the primordial human pair, Izanagi and Izanami, learned the technique of sexual intercourse. It would doubtless be childish to interpret this purely on a realistic level, since the part played by the bird seems to have been analogous with that of the serpent in the Book of Genesis. It was simultaneously the one to reveal creative knowledge and the instrument whereby the subtle manifestation was transposed to the level of the coarse by revealing the individual to him- or herself.

The Ancient Greeks, too, linked the wagtail, the gift of Aphrodite, to love and magic potions, especially when the bird was tied to a rapidly rotating wheel, as in Pindar's description (*Pythian Odes* 4: 380–6) of how Aphrodite taught Jason the spell to remove Medea's respect for her parents. The wagtail might be taken as a symbol of love's enchantments.

wall Traditionally the wall or great wall was the enclosure which guarded and shut in a world to avoid the invasion of evil influences originating at some lower level. Walls had the disadvantage of restricting the realms which they enclosed, but the advantage of ensuring their defence while leaving the way open for the reception of heavenly influences.

Islamic esotericism is familiar with this symbolism, as is Hindu tradition. Such was the mountain ring formed by Lokāloka, the rock-wall which rings the cosmos at the centre of which Mount Meru rises. A deliberate expression of this is to be found in the outer walls encircling temples, and even more in the one encircling such a city as Angkor Thom which, as its inscriptions tell us, is 'a mountain of victory (*jayagiri*) with ramparts scraping the shining sky'.

It must be added that in our day cracks are supposed to have been made in this wall, which is doomed to collapse in the end and open the way to a torrent of diabolical influences. We no longer have Nu-kua to fill in the breaches with his five-coloured stones (COEA, CORM, GUER).

In Ancient Egypt the symbolic properties of a wall were based upon its height, since it bore the meaning of rising above ordinary levels. This relates it more to the symbolism of the vertical axis than to the horizontal plane. However, the building of fortresses means that the first sense was also present in the defence of frontiers. The White Wall separated Upper from Lower Egypt.

The famous Wailing Wall should perhaps be interpreted as a symbol of separation as well. This brings us to the most basic significance of the wall, as the separation of brethren in exile from those who remain at home. It has the property of marking the boundaries between nations, tribes and individuals, of marking the separation between families, between God and his creatures, between the ruler and his people and between the ego and the rest. Walls are interruptions to intercommunication with their twofold psychological repercussions – security which stifles and protection which imprisons. In this context, wall symbolism may be related to the passive and female aspect of that of the WOMB.

walnut In Greek tradition, the walnut was linked to the gift of prophecy. Worship was offered to Artemis Caryatis, beloved by Dionysos, endowed with the gift of second sight and changed into a walnut-tree which bore rich crops of nuts (GRID p. 126).

Some Irish glosses translate the name of the female allegory of Ireland, Eithne, as 'nut', assimilating a proper name to the common noun *eitne.* The etymology is baseless, being founded upon analogy, but it does inspire a concept similar to that of the Cosmic EGG, Ireland in fact being the macrocosm in miniature. In Ireland the hazel was also a fruit of knowledge (see NUT-TREE) (ROYD p. 246).

wand Like the STAFF, the wand is the symbol of authority and of second sight. Such powers might come from God, they might be magical and stolen from the heavenly powers, or they might be Devil-given, the magic wands of wizards, sorcerers or fairies. Without his wand, the seer would be unable to trace either on the ground the circle in which he stood to summon the spirits, or in the sky the square in which he would observe the flight of birds. Wands, especially those of hazel, used to be employed to dowse not only for wells, but also for mineral or other deposits. A magic wand was the attribute of Apollo's son, Asclepios (Aesculapius), the god of healing; and, according to Carnoy, his name means 'he who holds a magic wand'. The CADUCEUS, the symbol of healing, is no more than a magic wand round which a pair of SERPENTS are entwined, 'an echo of the very ancient TREE- and Earth-cults in the Aegean area, the latter closely connected with serpent-worship' (SECG p. 278). Again, it was a magic wand which Apollo promised to give Hermes (Mercury) in exchange for the lyre which the young god had just invented and constructed from a tortoise-shell and the sinews of a bull: 'a splendid staff of riches and wealth: it is of gold, with three branches, and will keep you scatheless, accomplishing every task, whether of words or deeds, that are good, which I claim to know through the utterance of Zeus' ('Homeric' Hymn to Hermes 529–32). Among the virtues possessed by this wonderful wand was the power to put humans to sleep and to waken them. 'The wand is so closely linked to the god [Hermes] in the shape of the *kerukeion,* that this herald's wand became the badge of the heroes and ambassadors who claimed the god's protection' (SECG p. 274).

The wand was the Celtic instrument of magic above all others and the symbol of the druids' power over the elements. The Ulster druid, Sencha, had only to wave his wand to silence utterly all those around him. However, it was more usual for the druid or *file* to touch a person with his wand and change the latter into some creature, generally a bird such as the swan, or a pig or wild boar. In the seven grades within the Irish bardic order, the doctor or *ollamh* was entitled to a golden wand, the *file* of the second rank to one of silver and the other grades to bronze wands. The heralds of the early Capetian line of French kings carried a holy wand which not only served as a badge of office but, above all, stood for their monarch's power (OGAC 16: pp. 231ff.; 14: pp. 339–40ff.).

Palomancy is the art of fortune telling by the use of small rods or wands and was not only practised throughout the East and in China, but in Germany as well. It was customary 'to strip the bark from one wand and to retain it on another, so that they could play the roles of heads and tails' or else to preselect one as the mark of a good and the other of an ill omen and then, 'when they fell, if one lay above the other the significance of the uppermost was the one accepted' (ENCD p. 112).

Rhabdomancy (foretelling the future using a stick), palomancy and dowsing undoubtedly all have the same distant ancestor for, since wands and staves all come from trees, their use on the human level must surely be that of the hand of God, since God merely had to touch something to give it shape or create it. Similarly, the magic wand will change something from its existing shape, as Circe's guests were changed into swine when she touched them with her wand, and the pumpkin from the kitchen-garden into Cinderella's splendid coach. The magic wand is the badge of an individual's power over material things when that power is derived from the superhuman.

In the Old Testament account (Numbers 17) of the budding of Aaron's rod, the rod itself symbolized a group and an individual with whom it was identified. When the rod budded, the family itself was regarded as prospering. Furthermore, once it had been distinguished by its budding, it symbolized God's choice and the authority invested in the family which he had chosen. This authority made the chosen person an intermediary between Jehovah and the Children of Israel. Their complaints would no longer rise up to God and consequently God would no longer punish their rebellion. The rod or wand symbolizes the mediation of the person to whom it belongs and who henceforth holds and carries it.

war (see also GAMES)   War has created in people's minds an image of the universal scourge and triumph of brute force, from antiquity to modern times with their enormous increase in the means of self-destruction; and yet it possesses highly important symbolic properties.

Ideally the ends of warfare are the destruction of evil and the restoration of peace, justice and harmony, both on the cosmic and social planes (especially true of Ancient China) and on the spiritual. It is the defensive manifestation of life itself. War was the task of the Kshatriyas, but in the battle of Kurukshōtra, as described by the *Bhagavad Gītā*, 'nobody killed and nobody was killed', since the battlefield was the Karmayoga, the struggle for the unification of being. Krishna was a Kshatriya, but so was the Buddha. Islam is much the same. The transition from 'minor to major holy war' is that from cosmic to internal equilibrium. The true 'conqueror' (*jina*) is the person who possesses peace of mind. The same symbolism may be discerned in the activities of the medieval military orders and especially the Templars, the conquest of the Holy Land not being differentiated, symbolically, from the *jina*. The *Mahābhārata* describes Vishnu as the all-conquering, but the forces against which he wars are the powers of destruction. The exploits of a Gesar de Ling in Tibet or the warlike ceremonial of the Yellow Turbans in Han Dynasty China had the sole aim of combating the power of evil demons. The legendary battles of Chinese secret societies, in which magic swords made of peach-wood were used, were battles undertaken by initiates 'to defeat Ts'ing and restore Ming' and, in fact, had as their objective the restoration of 'light' (*ming*). In both the mystic and cosmic sense of the term theirs was a war between light and darkness.

Boxing was taught in the initiatory centre of Chao-lin and some lodges possessed manuals of boxing, the similarity of sound between *Kiao-tse* and boxer being the basis of combat symbolism. The game of CHESS was another aspect of the warfare between light and darkness.

Even Buddhism, with its well-known pacifism, widely employs warrior symbols. The *Dhammapada* speaks of the Buddha as 'the warrior in shining armour', while Avalokitesvara entered the realms of the *asura* in the guise of a warrior. Here we are concerned with the forcible acquisition of the fruits of knowledge. If the Kingdom of Heaven belongs to those who take it by force, Buddhist violence is not the sole demesne of the Nichiren sect. 'Warriors, warriors we call ourselves', we may read in the *Anguttara-nikāya*. 'We fight for lofty virtue, higher effort and sublime wisdom and this is why we call ourselves warriors.' Victory over self and the honour of death in battle recall the gallantry of the Kshatriya as well of that of the Japanese samurai and the Sioux brave. The Buddha was a *jina* and this was also the title borne by the founder of Jainism. Inner struggle aims to condense the scattered world of appearance and illusion into the concentrated world of the single reality, the manifold into the one, disorder into order.

Warlike enthusiasm is expressed symbolically as rage and HEAT. Indra's warlike energy is *kratu*, but this is spiritual energy as well. Peace (*shānti*) is extinguishing the fire and it is also in relation to fire that ritual sacrifice is assimilated to the ritual of warfare. Furthermore, the sacrificial victim is pacified by death, pacification traditionally being a death to one's passions and to one's self. In the *Rāmāyana* the ritual performed by Parashurāma is the equivalent of a Vedic sacrifice. 'The offering of arrows is made by the bow', the army is the sacrificial fire and the enemy princes the sacrificial beasts. Taoism, too, was conscious of a liberation of the corpse through force of arms, which is directly related to the foregoing (COOH, DAVL, ELIY, GRIB, GRIH, MAST, MATM, SCHO).

When war is mentioned in traditional Christian writings, the term should also be understood in the sense of internal struggle.

Holy war is no external battle fought with real weapons, but a conflict which the individual wages within him- or herself, the inward confrontation of light and darkness. It takes place during the transition from ignorance to knowledge, hence the meaning of the phrase 'the whole armour of light' which St Paul uses.

It is a contradiction in terms and an abuse of the meaning of words to apply 'Holy War' to actual armed conflict. In tradition, no war of this sort is holy and to apply the term to the Crusades is wholly mistaken. The weapons and armour of the Holy War are of a spiritual order.

The Ojibwa Indians' preparations for war were no mere physical hardening but 'an introduction to the mystic life through self-denial'. Volunteers 'spent a year fasting in the solitude of the forest, seeking and obtaining visions', since 'war was regarded above all as a blood-libation', a 'sacred activity' (SERH pp. 160–1). Soustelle, too, makes a point of emphasizing the symbolic aspect of war. 'The warrior's normal lot was to offer victims in sacrifice to the gods and then himself to die upon the sacrificial stone. Thereafter he became one of the Sun's followers in Heaven' (SOUM p. 21).

warlock See under WITCH.

washerwoman In India, washerwomen are low-caste. Tantrism has, however, created in the washerwoman (*dhobī*) an important symbol, on the one hand by associating membership of a low caste with the sexual depravity requisite – whether or not symbolic – in the practice of certain rites and, on the other, by identifying her in some sense with undifferentiated *materia prima*. The coitus of sage and washerwoman, given such importance by Tantric writers, thus represents a *coincidentia oppositorum*, a marriage of opposites and a truly alchemical operation. The paradox is apparent rather than real if the washerwoman is associated with wisdom and if her 'dance' symbolizes the ascent of the *kundalinī*. The low-caste woman, Eliade explains, possesses the Tantric meaning of *nairātma* (non-being), or of *shūnya* (emptiness) in so far as she is liberated from any social attribute or qualification. She is polyvalent, something which must further bear some relation to the general symbolism of woman in her most elemental aspect (ELIY).

washing In the *Iliad* (1: 450) washing the hands was an act of ritual purification and, as in all religions, such ablutions were a preliminary to sacrifice. Ritual washing is a symbol of purification by WATER. Etymologically ablution means cleaning from the mud with which one is covered.

In the Gospels, when Pilate washed his hands it was, he thought, both to proclaim and to make himself free of all guilt and responsibility in a juridical decision which was both doubtful in itself and entailed fearful consequences. While such an action symbolizes a refusal of responsibility, it does not legitimate it.

As early as the time of the 'Homeric' Hymns, the notion had surfaced that mere washing is not enough to cleanse the conscience of moral guilt, purity of soul being a very different thing from cleanliness of skin. The latter is merely a symbol of the former since, 'so far as the wicked man is concerned, Ocean itself cannot wash the guilt from his soul.'

Irish writers often mention a king or lord going in the morning to wash in a well or spring. These ablutions were connected with the exercise of his kingly duties and it is possible that the symbolism is related to that of SPRINGS in general (CELT 15: p. 328).

Ablution allows the washer to absorb the virtues of the spring, the various properties of the waters being communicated to the person soaked in them. They cleanse, stimulate, heal and fecundate. Washing is a means of obtaining possession of the invisible powers of the waters.

wasp The mason wasp, which anaesthetizes the spiders on which its larvae will feed and which lives in close proximity to mankind, building its nests in the smoke-holes and on the walls of their huts, plays an important part in African animal mythology and symbolism. In Zambia, it is regarded as queen of all birds and reptiles and mistress of fire, which she acquired from God at the beginning of things so as to pass it on to mankind (FRAF p. 80). For the Bambara in Mali, the mason wasp is the badge of a higher grade of initiate, since it embodies the powers of sublimation, of transfiguration and of transmuting the profane into the sacred (ZAHV).

water The symbolic meanings of water may be reduced to three main areas. It is a source of life, a vehicle of cleansing and a centre of regeneration. These three themes are to be found in the most ancient traditions and they provide not only the most varied, but at the same time the most coherent series of combinations of images.

The undifferentiated mass of waters stand for the infinite nature of the possible, containing all that is potential, unshaped, the seed of seeds and all promises of evolution, as well as all threats of reabsorption. To immerse oneself in the waters and to re-emerge without having been utterly dissolved in them, except by dying a symbolic death, is to return to the well-springs and regain fresh strength from that vast reservoir of the potential. It is a passing phase of regression and disintegration which brings with it a progressive phase of reintegration and regeneration (see BATH; BAPTISM; INITIATION).

The *Rig-Veda* hymns the praises of the waters which bring life, strength and cleansing on both the spiritual and the physical planes:

Water, you are the ones who bring us the life force. Help us to find nourishment so that we may look upon great joy.... Waters yield your cure as an armour for my body, so that I may see the sun for a long time. Waters carry away all of this that has gone bad in me, either what I have done in malicious deceit or whatever lie I have sworn to.

(VEDR)

The variations upon these basic themes which different cultures provide, against a virtually identical background, will help us better to grasp and study the scope and nuances of the symbolism of water.

In Asia, water is the 'substantial' shape of manifestation, the origin of life, the element of bodily and spiritual regeneration and the symbol of fertility, purity, wisdom, grace and virtue. As a fluid, it tends towards dissolution, but in so far as it is homogeneous it tends to cohesion and concentration. As such, it might correspond to *sattva*; and since it always finds a lower level and flows towards the abyss its tendency is *tamas*, and since it stretches horizontally it tends also to *rajas*.

Water is *prakrti*, or *materia prima*; 'All was water' say the Hindu scriptures, while the Taoists say that 'the wide waters had no shores.' The World Egg, *Brahmānda*, hatched upon the surface of the waters, just as, in Genesis, the Breath or 'Spirit of God moved upon the face of the waters.' Water, say the Chinese, is *Wu-chi*, Chaos, primordial formlessness. The waters which stand for the full potential of manifestation are distinguished as the Upper Waters, which correspond to formless potentiality, while the Lower Waters correspond to the potentiality of form. The *Book of Enoch* was to translate this in terms of sexual opposites and iconographically it is often represented by the double spiral. The Lower Waters (potential of form) are supposed to be enclosed within a temple dedicated to the king of

the *nāga* at Lhasa. In India formless potential (Upper Waters) is represented by the APSARA (from *Ap*, 'water'). The notion of primordial waters
and of an ocean from which all things began is virtually universal. It is to
be found in Polynesia, and the peoples of southern Asia localize cosmic
power in water. This is often accompanied by the myth of the animal which
dived to the bottom, such as the wild boar of the Hindus, and brought a
scrap of mud to the surface, exposing the embryo of manifestation.

Water is the spring and channel of all life, so that sap is water and, in
some Tantric allegories, water stands for the breath of life, *prāna*. On the
physical plane, and because it is also the gift of Heaven, water is the universal
symbol of fertility and fecundity. In southern Vietnam the Montagnards
say that water from Heaven makes the rice; and they are, in addition, well
aware of the regenerative role of water, which they regard as a medicine
and beverage of immortality.

Water is as widespread an instrument of ritual purification. In this respect
WASHING plays an essential part from as far afield as Islam and Japan, via
the rites of the ancient Taoist Masters of the Holy Waters and not forgetting the Christian use of holy water. In India and southeast Asia statues of
the gods – and of the worshippers themselves – are regularly washed
(especially at New Year) as a rite both of cleansing and of regeneration.
Wen Tzu wrote that water by its very nature tended to purity, while Lao
Tzu taught that water was the emblem of the highest virtue. It was also a
Taoist symbol of wisdom for 'it is free from disputation'. It is also free and
unattached and flows with the slope of the ground. It is moderation as well,
since wine which is too strong should be mixed with water, even if the wine
is that of knowledge itself.

Water, as opposed to fire, is *yin*. It corresponds to the north, to cold, to
the Winter solstice, the kidneys, the colour black and to the trigram *K'an*,
the Abyssal. However, water is, in another way, linked to the thunderbolt,
which is fire. When Chinese alchemists talked of reducing something to
water this may be understood to mean a return to the primal and embryonic state, but they also said that this 'water' was fire; and thus alchemical
'ablution' may convey the sense of cleansing by fire. In Chinese internal
alchemy 'baths' and 'washings' might well be fire-based operations. Alchemical mercury, which is 'water', is sometimes described as 'fiery water'.

Lastly, we should observe that the ritual water employed in initiations in
Tibet is the symbol of the vows and promises made by the postulant.

In Jewish and Christian tradition, water in the first place symbolizes the
beginnings of creation. The Hebrew letter *men* (M) symbolizes tangible
water and this is the mother and womb. As the source of all things, water
makes manifest the transcendent and from this very fact should be regarded as a revelation of holiness.

Nevertheless, like all symbols, water can be regarded from two diametrically opposite points of view which are not, despite this, irreconcilable, and
this ambivalence occurs at all levels. Water is the source both of life and of
death, is creator and destroyer.

In the Old Testament WELLS in the desert and SPRINGS used by nomads are
so many joyous places where miracles may occur. Fundamental encounters
take place beside wells or springs and, like any holy place, the waterside

plays an extraordinary part. Here love comes into being and marriages are solemnized. The wanderings of the Children of Israel and the earthly pilgrimage of the human soul are intimately involved with external or internal contact with water, the latter becoming an oasis of light and peace.

Palestine was a land of springs and torrents. Jerusalem was lapped by the peaceful waters of Siloam. RIVERS were agents of God-given fertility, RAIN and DEW supplied their own fecundity and displayed God's goodness. Without water the nomad would have been doomed to a burning death under the Palestinian sun, so the water which he found in his wanderings was like manna: as it quenched his thirst it fed him too. This is why in prayer and supplication they asked for water, begging God to hear his servants and send rain and show them wells and springs. The laws of hospitality insisted that clean water should be given a guest so that his feet might be washed and his peaceful rest assured. The Old Testament celebrates the miraculous qualities of water and the New Testament accepted this inheritance and was to exploit it.

Jehovah was compared with Spring rains by Hosea (6: 3), with the dew which makes the flowers grow (14: 6), with the fresh water running from the mountains and with thirst-quenching streams. The righteous man is like a tree planted beside running water (Numbers 24: 6) and, in this context, water is regarded as a blessing. However, due acknowledgement should be made that it comes from God. Thus, according to Jeremiah (2: 13), in their unbelief the Children of Israel despised the Lord, forgot his promises and no longer looked upon him as the source of living waters. They built cisterns of their own, but these were cracked and the water leaked away. Jeremiah blamed the people for their treatment of God, the spring of living waters, mourning and saying that they would 'make their land desolate' (18: 16). Covenants with strange peoples are compared with the waters of the Nile and the Euphrates. The soul searches for its God as 'the hart panteth after the water brooks' (Psalm 42: 1). In this context, the soul is seen as parched and thirsty land; it awaits divine revelation, just as the parched land longs to drink in the rain (Deuteronomy 32: 2). Such symbolism, drawn from the deepest levels of Mediterranean experience, was to furnish Lorca with the theme of his tragedy, *Yerma*, the woman who is barren for want of a man just as the desert (*yermo*) is barren for want of rain.

It was perfectly natural for inhabitants of the Near East to regard water first and foremost as a sign and symbol of blessing, since water conditioned life itself. When Isaiah prophesied the new age, he spoke of 'streams in the desert' and the thirsty land becoming 'pools of water' (Isaiah 35: 6-7). St John talked the same language: 'the Lamb . . . shall lead them unto living fountains of waters' (Revelation 7: 17).

The Lord gives water to the Earth, but there is another and more mysterious water. This derives from Wisdom, which presided when the waters were created and took shape (Job 28: 25-6; Proverbs 3: 20; 8: 22, 24, 28-9; Ecclesiasticus 1: 2-4). This water dwells in the heart of the wise man and is like a well or spring (Proverbs 20: 5; Ecclesiasticus 21: 13). Its words are like a flowing brook (Proverbs 18: 4). 'The inner parts of the fool are like a broken vessel and he will hold no knowledge as long as he liveth' (Ecclesiasticus 21: 14). The Son of Sirach likens the Law (Torah) to Wisdom, because the Law pours out the waters of Wisdom. The Church Fathers regarded the Holy Spirit as being the fountain of the gift of wisdom which he poured into thirsty hearts. Medieval theologians took up this motif and applied an identical meaning to it. Thus Hugh of St Victor conceived of Wisdom as the possessor of waters in which it washed the soul.

Water became a symbol of the spiritual life and of the Spirit which God offered and which mankind often refused.

Jesus re-echoes this symbolism in his meeting with the woman of Samaria when he said (John 4: 14), 'whosoever drinketh of the water that I shall give him shall never thirst; but the water that I shall give him shall be in him a well of water springing up into everlasting life.'

Water, which was above all a symbol of life in the Old Testament, has become a symbol of the Spirit in the New.

Jesus Christ had revealed himself to the Woman of Samaria as Lord of the living waters, the well from which 'If any man thirst, let him come unto me and drink' (John 7: 37). Like Moses' rock, the water sprang from him and, on the Cross, the lance made blood and water flow from the wound in his side. Living waters flow from the Father, they are channelled through Christ's human nature or else through the gift of the Holy Spirit who, in the hymn for Pentecost, is *fons vivus* (a living fountain), *ignis caritatis* (the fire of love) and *Altissimi donum Dei* (the gift of the Most High God). St Athanasius explained the meaning of this teaching when he wrote: 'The Father is the spring, the Son is called the stream and we are said to drink the Spirit' (*Ad Serapionem* 1: 19). Water therefore partakes of eternity and whoever drinks of these living waters already shares eternal life (John 4: 13–14).

Running water, the water of life, stands out as a cosmogonic symbol. This is because it purifies, heals and rejuvenates whomever it leads to the eternal. According to St Gregory of Nyssa, wells hold still waters, 'but the Bridegroom's well is a well of running water. It has the depth of a well but flows like a stream', something not unrelated to our earlier reference to Lorca.

According to Tertullian, the Holy Spirit chose Water from all the elements and preferred it above the others because, from the very beginning, it seemed a perfect matter, simple and fertile and wholly translucent (*De baptismo* 3). It possessed of itself a cleansing property and for this further reason was regarded as holy: hence its use in ritual ablution, where its properties washed away all offences and all stain of guilt. The waters of baptism alone wash away sin, and baptism is only conferred once because it opens the way to a new state, that of the new person. This rejection of the old person, or rather death in a moment of time, may be compared with a FLOOD, for the latter symbolizes disappearance, washing away, the annihilation of one age and the appearance of a new one.

The cleansing properties possessed by water gave it the additional force of the power of redemption. Immersion was regenerative, it effected a rebirth in the sense of its being simultaneously alive and dead. Water wipes out what has gone before, since it restores the individual to a fresh condition. Immersion is like Christ's entombment. He came to life again after descending into the bowels of the Earth. Water is the symbol of regeneration and the waters of baptism lead explicitly to being 'born again' (John 3: 3–7). They are the means of initiation. *The Shepherd* of Hermas speaks of those 'who go down into the waters dead and come up again alive'. This is the symbolism of living waters and of the fountain of youth. Callistus reports St Ignatius of Antioch as saying that what he had within him were the waters which did and spoke. One might also remember that it was the Castalian Spring at Delphi which inspired the Pythoness.

Worship centres naturally upon springs and all places of pilgrimage have their wells and watercourses. Throughout the ages the Catholic Church has levelled its censures against the worship given to waters, but popular devotion has always respected the property of water as holy and able to make holy. However, pagan deviance and a return to superstitious practices always posed a threat and magic constantly watches for the opportunity of perverting what is holy in human imagination.

If the waters pre-existed creation, it is patently clear that they will be there for the new creation. The new being corresponds to the appearance of a fresh world.

In certain instances, as we observed at the beginning of this article, water can effect the workings of death. The 'great waters' foretold in the Old Testament are ordeals and the unleashing of the waters is the symbol of great calamities. Water can damage and destroy and tempests ravage the vineyards. Thus water possesses harmful powers and, in this case, it punishes sinners while the righteous have nothing to fear from the 'great waters'. The 'waters of death' affect only sinners and are turned into 'waters of life' for the benefit of the righteous. Like fire, water may be used as a trial by ordeal; the objects cast into it will be self-condemned, the water does not itself condemn.

Rain-water and sea-water symbolize the duality of the heights and the depths. One is fresh and the other salt. When clean, water is a symbol of life, cleansing and bringing into being (Ezekiel 36: 25); when bitter (Numbers 5: 18), it carries a curse with it. Rivers may be channels of blessing or shelter monsters. Rough water carries the meaning of evil and disorder. Isaiah compares the wicked with a stormy sea (57: 20).

Still waters convey a sense of peace and order (Psalm 23: 2). In Jewish folklore, the division which God made at the Creation of the Upper from the Lower Waters denotes the separation of the male from the female waters, symbolizing security and insecurity, male and female; this is, as we have stated, part of a universal symbolism.

Salt sea-water denotes bitterness of heart. Man, Richard of St Victor was to say, must pass through the waters of bitterness when he becomes aware of his own wretched state, but this 'holy bitterness' will be changed into joy (*De statu interioris hominis* 1: 10).

In Muslim tradition, too, water symbolizes many different things.

The Koran denotes that 'blessed water' which falls from Heaven as one of the signs of the godhead. The gardens of Paradise contain springs and streams of running water (for example, Koran 2: 25; 88: 12). Man himself was created from spreading water (Koran 86: 6).

The works of unbelievers are regarded as water by a thirsty man, but they are a mirage. They are like the dark depths of an ocean which successive waves obscure (Koran 24: 39–40). This present life is compared with waters which the wind scatters (Koran 18: 45).

In his commentaries upon Ibn al 'Arabī's *Fusūs*, Rūmī identifies the waters on which the throne of God stands (Koran 11: 9) with the breath of God the All-Merciful. When discussing the eternal manifestation of God, Rūmī says that 'the sea was covered with foam and in each bubble of foam something took shape, something assumed a form' (*Diwān*).

Jīlī uses a lump of ice, made of water, as a symbol for the universe. In this instance water is the *materia prima*.

In a more metaphysical sense, Rūmī uses the Ocean, its waters the divine essence, as a symbol of the divine foundations of the universe. This ocean fills all creation and its waves are creatures.

Furthermore, water symbolizes purity and is used as a means of cleansing. Ritual Muslim prayer can only be validly performed when the person praying has obtained ritual purity by a series of ablutions carried out with scrupulous attention to minutely prescribed rules.

Lastly, water symbolizes life, through the regenerative water of life which is to be found in darkness. The Sura of the Cavern (Koran 18: 61–3), describes how the FISH which was cast ashore at the meeting of two seas was restored to life when thrown back into the water. This symbolism is part of a motif of initiation, the Fountain of Immortality. The theme recurs constantly in Islamic mysticism, especially in Iran. The legends attached to Alexander the Great include the story of his setting out in search of the Spring of Life accompanied by his cook, Andras. One day when the latter was washing a dried fish in a spring, he found it coming back to life and he, too, discovered immortality. The spring lies in the Land of Darkness which may doubtless be compared with the symbolism of the unconscious, the female nature and *yin*.

In all other traditions throughout the world, water plays an equally primordial role which embraces the three themes which have already been stated, but with a particular emphasis upon the beginning of things. From the cosmogonic viewpoint, water embraces two antithetic combinations which should not be confused. Rain, the water which comes down from the sky, is a celestial semen which comes and makes the Earth fecund. It is therefore male and associated with heavenly fire. This is the water which Lorca summons in his tragedy, *Yerma*. On the other hand, primordial water, water nascent from Earth and the pale dawn, is female. In this instance the Earth is associated with the Moon, as a symbol of fecundation fulfilled; the Earth being gravid, the water emerges, so that now fertilization has taken place, germination can begin.

In both instances the water symbol contains that of BLOOD, but not the same blood in both cases, since blood itself partakes of a dual symbolism. Celestial blood is associated with the Sun and with fire, while menstrual blood is associated with Earth and the Moon. Behind this pair of opposites may be discerned the basic dualism of light and darkness.

The Aztecs called human blood, so essential for the Sun's daily regeneration, *chalchiuatl*, 'precious water', in other words green jade (SOUM). This brings us fairly and squarely back to the complementary qualities of the colours RED and GREEN. Water is the symbolic equivalent of red blood, the inner strength of green, since water carries in it the seed of life, corresponding to red, which causes the seasonal rebirth of the green Earth after Winter's death.

In Dogon cosmogony, too, the divine seed, water, the colour green, fertilizes the Earth to provide Heroes and Twins. These twins are born with human torsos, but are serpents from the waist downwards. They are green in colour (GRIE).

However, the Dogon and their neighbours the Bambara carry the notion of the water symbol, the fecundating life force, a stage further, since water, or divine seed, is also light and speech, the Word which makes flesh, of which the chief mythic avatar (embodiment) is the red copper SPIRAL. Yet water and speech only activate or manifest themselves, thus setting in motion the creation of the world, in the shape of 'moist' speech, in contrast with a twin half which remains outside the cycle of life made manifest and which the Dogon and Bambara call 'dry' water and 'dry' speech. These are expressions of ideas, that is, of potentiality, on the human as well as on the divine plane. All water was 'dry' before the Cosmic Egg took shape; within it the principle of moisture was born and this was the foundation from which the world sprang. However, when the almighty sky-god, Amma, created his double, Nommo, the god of 'moist' water and guide and principle of life made manifest, he (Amma) reserved for himself in the highest Heavens, outside the boundaries which he set for the universe, half these primordial waters, which remained 'dry'waters. Similarly, thought, which is speech unexpressed, is termed 'dry' speech since it only has potential properties and cannot beget. In the human microcosm it is the replica of primordial thought, the 'first speech' stolen from Amma by the spirit Yurugu before the creation of mankind. Zahan (ZAHD) regards this first speech, 'undifferentiated speech, without self-awareness', as corresponding to the unconscious. It is talking in dreams, speech over which humans have no control. Yurugu's avatar, the JACKAL, or pale fox, stole the first speech and therefore possesses the key to the unconscious and the invisible and, consequently, to the future which is no more than the time-component of the invisible. This is the reason why the most important Dogon system of divination is based upon questioning this animal.

It is interesting to observe that Yurugu is also associated with chthonian fire and with the Moon, which are universal symbols of the unconscious (PAUC, ZAHD, GAND).

Aztec funeral customs illustrate the basic division of all phenomena into two categories, controlled by the opposing symbols of fire and water, the moist and dry, in a quite remarkable way. Additionally, they show the analogy between this symbolic dualism and the notion of the primordial coitus of Heaven and Earth. 'All those who had been drowned or struck by lightning, along with lepers and those who had died of gout or dropsy, in other words, all those whom the rain- and water-gods had, as it were, marked out by removing them from the world' were buried. All others were cremated (SOUN p. 231).

This relationship between fire and water recurs in the funeral customs of the Celts. The lustral (purificatory) water which the druids used in their exorcisms was water in which 'a burning brand taken from the sacrificial fire had been extinguished. When there was a dead body within a house, a large pot was set at the doorway filled with lustral water brought from another house in which there was no dead body. All those who visited the house of mourning sprinkled themselves with this water when they left' (COLD p. 226).

Throughout Irish literature, water was an element which obeyed the druids, who had the power to loose or bind it. Thus King Cormac's evil druids bound the waters of Munster to reduce the inhabitants through thirst, and it was the druid Mog Ruith who loosed them. However, water was also, and by virtue of its lustral properties, above all the symbol of passive purity. It was the place and means of revelation for the bards who summoned it with incantation to obtain oracles. According to Strabo, the druids proclaimed that at the end of the world only the primordial elements, Fire and Water, would be left in control (LERD pp. 74–6).

The peoples of the North believed that the melt-water which flowed from the surface of the eternal ice-sheet during the very first springtime was the ancestor of all living things. Brought to life by the south wind, these waters gathered into the shape of a living body, that of the first giant, Ymir, from whom descended other giants, mankind and, to some extent, the gods themselves.

In his *Theogony* (131–3) Hesiod carefully distinguishes between the female element, water as protoplasm, the fresh, standing waters of lakes, and the male element, the foaming fecundating salt sea-water. '[Earth] bare also the fruitless deep with his raging swell, Pontus, without sweet union of love. But afterwards she lay with Heaven and bare deep-swirling Oceanus.' Hesiod links the distinction between barren and fecundating water to the interposition of love.

In many creation myths standing water occurs as the protoplasm of the Earth from which all life sprang. In some Turkic myths from central Asia, water was the mother of the horse. In Babylonian cosmogony, at the beginning of all things, before Heaven and Earth existed,

> from all eternity the primordial waters lay outstretched a single undifferentiated matter. From this mass two elemental principles emerged, Apsu and Tiamat. . . . Apsu was regarded as a male deity standing for the mass of fresh water on which the Earth floated. . . . Tiamat was none other than the sea, the abyss of salt water from which all creatures came.
>
> (SOUN p. 119)

Similarly Ancient Egyptian mythology generally depicts the creation as a mound of silt emerging from the waters. 'A great lotus came out of the primeval waters; . . . such was the cradle of the sun on the first morning' (POSD pp. 152, 53).

From these ancient symbols of water as the source of the fecundation of Earth and its inhabitants, we can turn to the psychoanalytic symbols of water as the source of the soul's fecundation, with rivers, streams and seas standing for the course of human existence and the fluctuation of desire and emotion. As in the case of EARTH, a distinction must be drawn symbolically between surface waters and the depths. Heroes' VOYAGINGS and wanderings on the face of the waters carry the sense of their being exposed to the dangers of life, which myths symbolize in the shape of monsters rising up out of the depths. The depths themselves thus become a symbol of the unconscious. Perversion also has its image in the mingling of water and earth (earthly desires) or in stagnant water which has lost its cleansing properties – silt, mud and MARSH-land. Frozen water – ice – is an expression of the extremes of stagnation, lack of warmth in the soul and an absence of that life-giving and creative emotion which is love. Frozen water is an image of total stagnation of the psyche, the dead soul.

(DIES pp. 38–9)

Water is the symbol of unconscious energy, the formless powers of the soul, of hidden and unrecognized motivation. Often in dreams, the dreamer may be 'sitting on a river-bank, FISHING. Water, symbol of what is still unconscious of itself, holds the contents of the soul which the fisherman tries to bring to the surface and which should be his food. The fish is a creature of the psyche' (AEPR pp. 151, 195).

waterfall Waterfalls are one of the basic motifs of Chinese landscape painting, from such painters of the T'ang Dynasty as Wu Tao-tzu and Wang Wei, to those of the Sung Dynasty. In basic pairings, the waterfall contrasts with the rock, MOUNTAIN and WATER, and *yin* and *yang*. The downward movement of the water alternates with the upward movement of the mountain, the dynamism of the waterfall with the static properties of the rock. It is, and this coincides with the teachings of Ch'an (Zen) Buddhism, the symbol of impermanence as opposed to changelessness. The waterfall persists as an entity, but is never the same. The Ancient Greek philosopher, Heraclitus, had already noted this in the phenomenon of the stream. Observing that in the same river it is never the same water flowing past, he provided the basis for the theories of the continuous evolution of beings and of the paradox of thought which claims to fix through rigid definition what is fluid. The drops of water which make up the waterfall are renewed each second, just like, according to Buddhism, the purely illusory components of manifestation.

The downward movement of the waterfall carries the same meaning as the downward direction of heavenly activity, deriving from the still centre, the Immutable, and displaying its infinite potentiality. Still water would provide the image of motionless latency from which all manifestations derive and to which they will ultimately return. Thus Wang Wei painted his waterfall with a hanging cloud of spray, a cloud which floats and from which water comes, the gleaming liquid spray passing and vanishing. Then in Japan, at Nikko, the splendid waterfall of Kegon derives from Lake Chuzenji and eventually flows into the sea by way of the River Daiya.

Waterfalls are also unharnessed elemental motion, the force-fields which one needs to master and control to one's spiritual benefit, something akin to the concerns of Tantrism. In other cultural areas, STREAMS and RIVERS carry a similar sense (BURA, GOVM, GRIV, GROA).

This symbol is also that of permanence of form despite change of content. Mme Liliane Brion-Guerry observes that by a species of inner vision 'beyond the natural appearance of the waterfall, its symbolic meaning may be discovered as an emblem of continuous motion, and emblem of the world in which the elements change ceaselessly while its shape remains the same.'

water-lily The Mayan hieroglyphic of the water-lily is the symbol of plenty and fertility, linked to soil and water, to the plant world and to the Underworld. It is often the symbolic hieroglyphic for the JAGUAR and the CROCODILE carrying the Earth on its back. It therefore gives expression to dark and powerful chthonian forces (THOH).

Water-lilies perform the same symbolic function for the Dogon in Mali. The water-lily is 'woman's milk' and has a relationship with throat and bosom. Nursing mothers are given water-lily leaves to eat, as are stock which have dropped their young. The mythic ram which impregnated the Sun came down to Earth on the rainbow and leaped into a pool covered with water-lilies shouting: 'The Earth is mine!'

The Ancient Egyptians regarded water-lilies as the loveliest of flowers. 'A great lotus came out of the primeval waters' on the first morning of creation to act as a cradle to the Sun, 'opening its flowers in the morning and closing them at evening. In this way the Egyptians visualized the creation of the world out of moisture' (POSD p. 152).

water-melon Because of the vast number of seeds which it contains, the water-melon is a fertility symbol. This is the reason why young married couples in Vietnam used to be given melon-seeds, together with oranges, which bore the same symbolic significance (DURV). In Ancient Greece the pomegranate seed played the same part as a fertility symbol (SEE DEMETER).

water- or wine-skin Chinese symbol of primordial Chaos, the water-skin epitomizes the undifferentiated animal since it has neither head nor 'opening' nor sense-organ. When, in the fable told by Chuang-tzu, his companions tried to cut seven holes in the water-skin of Chaos, one for each day of the week, the skin died, that is, it ceased to exist as something in its own right. This is the image of initiatory death and rebirth. In confirmation of this, Chu and Hu, who pierced the water-skin, are supposed to have been Lightning.

The dead and the criminal were sewn into skins and thus returned to Chaos. Hun-Tun, the water-skin of Chaos, was as red as fire and related to the BELLOWS of a forge, the latter being not only an image of the intermediary world but also a cosmogonic implement. Neverthless, the water-skin is a representation of Heaven. Wu-yi shot his arrows at it, but a thunderbolt came out of the heavenly water-skin and struck Wu-yi down. When Chu-sin – luckier, or perhaps more virtuous – struck the skin with the same weapons, down fell a rain of fecundating and regenerative blood (GRAD, GRAC).

waves In Greek legend, the Nereids, granddaughters of Oceanos, personified the countless waves of the sea. They were very beautiful and spent their time singing at their weaving and embroidery and swimming with the dolphins, trailing their long hair (GRID p. 314). Such images and activities derive from the way the waves weave and unweave their watery patterns to a solemn and soothing sea-music. The Nereids played no active part in mythology and, like them, waves symbolize the passive principle, the attitude of those who let themselves be borne away wherever the waves carry them. The waves may, however, be stirred to violence by external forces and their passivity is as dangerous as their uncontrolled activity. They stand for all the power of massive inertia.

Waves roused by the storm have been compared with dragons roused from the depths. In this instance, they symbolize the sudden inroads of the unconscious, another mass on the psychic plane, its inertia deceptive, spurred by instinctive impulses to attack the spirit, the vessel of the ego with reason at its helm.

Irish legend conjures up the 'ninth wave' and the term is used to define the limits of territorial waters. When the Goidels reached Ireland, at first they were repulsed by the magic of the druids of the Tuatha Dé Danann and they withdrew temporarily a ninth wave's distance from the shore. Waves, however, possessed religious and magical properties. Morann, son of the usurper Cairpre Cenncait (Cat's-head), was born deformed. His father's steward cast him into the sea, but when the ninth wave washed over him it gave him human shape and he began to speak. One of the sons of the goddess, or mythical character, Arianrhod (Silver Wheel) was called Dylan Eil Ton (Dylan, Son of the Wave). This goddess's symbolism is that of WATER, which is both the womb in which the individual takes shape and a source of life and purification (WINI 3: pp. 189–90; LEBI 4: *passim*).

As in the case of flames or clouds, to dive into the waves indicates a break with one's normal life-style, a radical change taking place in ideas, attitudes, behaviour and life itself. This symbolism should be compared with that of baptism, with its two phases of immersion and resurgence.

In the Old Testament waves symbolize particularly insidious mortal dangers of both the physical and moral order.

weapons Weapons are instruments intended to counter the monstrous and which become monsters in their turn. Forged to fight an enemy, they may be turned from their purpose and used to intimidate friends and neighbours. Similarly, fortifications may serve both as means to absorb the shock of invasion and as springboards for aggression. The ambivalence of weapons is that they may simultaneously symbolize the instruments of justice and of oppression, of defence and of conquest. However, whatever the circumstance, weapons provide the physical expression of will directed to a given end.

Some weapons were made by skilfully alloying metals or combining or alternating them. Agamemnon's arms and armour, as described by Homer, for example, were a careful blending of silver and gold. The most precious of metals were employed both for breastplate and shield, as well as for swords and other pieces of equipment. 'And about his shoulders he flung his sword, whereon gleamed studs of gold, while the scabbard about it was of silver, fitted with golden chains' (*Iliad* 11: 29–31). Since each metal possesses symbolic properties, it may be seen with what wealth of meaning each weapon may be endowed and with what magical powers one would attempt to invest it, remembering that BLACKSMITHS were supposed to be magicians. Arms identified their wearer and an exchange of weapons among the Ancient Greeks was a sign of friendship.

Dreaming of weapons betrays inner conflict and the shape of certain weapons defines the nature of that conflict. For example, 'psychoanalysts regard most weapons as sexual symbols. . . . The penis is most clearly denoted when pistols or revolvers occur in dreams as signs of psychological sexual tension' (AEPR p. 225).

In his Epistle to the Ephesians (6: 10–17), St Paul describes what might be called the Christian's panoply:

Finally, my brethren, be strong in the Lord, and in the power of his might. Put on the whole armour of God, that ye may be able to stand against the wiles of the devil. For we wrestle not against flesh and blood, but against principalities, against powers, against the rulers of the darkness of this world, against spiritual wickedness in high places. Wherefore take unto you the whole armour of God, that ye may be able to withstand in the evil day, and having done all, to stand. Stand therefore, having your loins girt about with truth, and having on the breastplate of righteousness. And your feet shod with the preparation of the gospel of peace; Above all, taking the shield of faith, wherewith ye shall be able to quench all the fiery darts of the wicked. And take the helmet of salvation, and the sword of the Spirit, which is the word of God.

Christian symbolism clearly appropriated these images to compile a list of correspondences in the Holy War and to evolve a sort of mystical manual of spiritual combat: the belt symbolizes truth and love; the breastplate, justice and purity; the boots, evangelical zeal, humility and perseverance; the shield, faith and the Cross; the sword, the word of God; the bow, prayer which is effective from a distance.

From this moral and spiritual point of view, weapons signify inner powers, virtue being nothing short of duties balanced under the control of the spirit.

Other lists of correspondences have been drawn up relating weapons to other different things, for example some weapons symbolize the four elements. The old-fashioned sling and the modern rifle, machine-gun, artillery piece, missile and rocket relate to the element Air; lances and chemical weapons, to the element Earth; swords and psychological weapons to the element Fire; tridents, to the element Water. A battle between sword and lance would stand for a battle between Earth and Fire; that between sling and trident, for a waterspout.

Furthermore, certain weapons symbolize certain offices. Club, staff and whip are the attributes of sovereign power; lance, sword, bow and arrows, attributes of the warrior; knife, dagger, dirk and boar-spear, attributes of the huntsman; and net and thunderbolt, attributes of the supreme deity.

In Jungian psychology, knives and daggers correspond to the dark zones of the ego and to the shadow, or unconscious part of the personality; lances to the anima, or female psychological tendencies in the male or the primitive unconscious; clubs, cudgels, nets and whips to the MANA; swords to the self (CIRD p. 349).

weasel In Irish tales from the Ulster cycle, King Conchobar's mother bears the name of Ness, or 'weasel'. Originally she was a warrior maiden; however, Ness may symbolize watchful love and, from a bad side, fickleness and falsehood. But this seems to contradict her initial stance as the fierce warrior.

It may well be that in the Middle Ages the Irish confused the symbolism of the weasel with that of the ERMINE (OGAC 11: pp. 56ff.; CHAB pp. 318–27).

weaving In Islamic tradition the weaver's loom symbolizes the structure and motion of the universe.

In North Africa, even in the most wretched hovels on the mountain plateaux, the mistress of the house owns a loom, a simple framework of a pair of wooden rollers supported by two uprights. . . . The upper roller is known as the heavenly roller and the lower one stands for the Earth. These four pieces of wood thus symbolize the entire universe.
Weaving is a work of creation and of bringing to birth. When the piece of cloth is finished, the weaver cuts the threads which hold it to the loom and, as she does so, pronounces the words of blessing uttered by the midwife when she severs the new-born baby's umbilical cord. It is as if weaving displayed in simple language the mysterious anatomy of the human race.

Servier, who describes the symbol so admirably, goes on to draw some comparisons:

The loom came from the East, a household object carried by successive waves of migrants from Asia to the Mediterranean. Did it bear a message from wise men, providing mankind in concrete terms with the earliest secrets of the knowledge of Being? Was it mere chance which made Plato have recourse to weaving for the symbol able to depict the world, the spindle, its weights divided into concentric circles representing the orbits of the planets?
(SERH pp. 65–6)

Cloth, THREAD, loom, SPINDLE and DISTAFF, whatever is used in spinning and weaving, all these are so many symbols of futurity. They are used to denote all that rules or intervenes in our fate. The Moon 'weaves' destiny and the spider, spinning its web, is an image of our fate. The Fates themselves were spinsters, weaving the threads of destiny, and they were Moon-deities, too. To weave is to create fresh shapes. 'For to weave is not merely to predestine (anthropologically), and to join together differing realities (cosmologically) but also to *create*, to make something of one's own substance as the spider does in spinning its web' (ELIT p. 181).
Countless goddesses and Great Goddesses hold spindles and distaffs and preside not only over birth, but over the course of time and the chain of cause and effect. In the Near East, examples of them are known going back to 2000 BC, amongst which we might mention the Great Goddess of the Hittites. Thus they were mistresses of time, of the span of human life, and sometimes were endowed with the harsh and pitiless lineaments of fate, the law which ordains the continuous and universal alteration of beings and from which the infinite varieties of form derive. The shimmering fabric of the world stands out against the background of human suffering. Spinsters and weaver-women perpetually open and close the cycles which affect individuals, nations and the cosmos itself.

week The days of the week have been restored to the symbolic setting of the number SEVEN. They comprise, as it were, a completeness, an epitome of space and time, a kind of developmental microcosm. The six working days have been regarded as orbiting, like planets, around the Sun, each of the days being assigned to one of the planets – Monday, to the Moon; Tuesday, to Mars; Wednesday, to Mercury; Thursday, to Jupiter; Friday, to Venus; Saturday, to Saturn; and Sunday, to the Sun. Activities appropriate to the astrological signs, as well as to the deities corresponding to the planets, seem to suit each day – planning, aggression, dealing, organizing, love, appraisal and rest.

weights and measures Weights and measures are both the means and symbol of accuracy, fair dealing, justice and harmony, whether regarded in respect of the individual and of society, or of knowledge, the emotions and action, in all their different forms.

Chinese tradition, especially, emphasizes the symbolic importance and interdependence of standard weights and measures since, as Granet observes, they determined not only size, but proportion, not only quantity, but quality as well. When he came to the throne, the exemplary virtues of the Emperor Chun were not simply displayed in, but caused by his standardization of weights and measures and the musical scale, thus establishing the framework for universal harmony (Chu-Ching 1: 2). When the Chou Emperor Wen came to the throne, 'he altered the weights and measures and determined the first day of the first month' (Ssu-ma Ch'ien, *Shih-chi* 4). It was apparently a matter of restoring imperial virtue after the decadence of the Yin Dynasty. The *Yu-ling* confirms that weights and measures and times and seasons had of necessity to correspond when it lays down that at each of the equinoxes 'weights and measures should be adjusted . . . containers standardized . . . weights on scales and measuring rods corrected.' This was because the equinoxes are, in fact, the points of balance in the cycle of the year and of *yin* and *yang*, so what better time could be chosen to check all weights and measures?

Correction of weights and measures by imperial authority could not but be arbitrary. Ssu-ma Ch'ien asserts that 'the sound of Yu the Great's voice was the standard for the musical scale and his body that for weight and measure.'

Granet thinks that from this we may infer that the height and weight of emperors and legendary heroes were always used during their reigns as the standard for weights and measures, which were thus regarded as displaying precisely their physical and moral qualities. Furthermore, were an inferior to alter them, it was regarded as rebellion, punishable by death (Li-Chi 3: 2).

What is quite extraordinary is that the standard for all weights and measures was sonic, the 'yellow [tubular] bell' or *huang-chung*, which when struck provided *kung*, the note which was the basis of the musical scale, being also the basis of all units of length. This, surely, was the most harmonious expression of world harmony and one which justified a regular verification of sound-effects.

We should add a note of caution in respect of the apparent rigidity of standards. During the period of the Warring Kingdoms, perfect imperial benevolence was to be found in the use of 'small' bushels for the collection of taxes and 'large' bushels for the distribution of imperial largesse in the form of grain (*Shih-chi* 46). This has an echo of the Gospel message and something like it is to be found in Luke 6: 38: 'For with the same measure that ye mete withal it shall be measured to you again.'

Measuring rods are, for their part, reminiscent of the 'golden reed' of Revelation 21: 15 used 'to measure the city . . . according to the measure of a man'. The measurements themselves were in symbolic numbers which bear little relationship to actual quantities; as Revelation 21: 17 continues, 'the measure of a man, that is, of the angel.' However, all that is measured, city, gates, setting and inhabitants, is to be understood in a symbolic sense. This is a fresh and fine example of the co-existence of the sacred and the profane in human speech and calculation (GRAC, GRAP).

well In all traditions wells are endowed with a sacred character. They actualize in a kind of epitome the three cosmic orders, Heaven, Earth and the Underworld, the three elements of Water, Earth and Air, and are a life-giving channel of communication. They themselves are a microcosm or

cosmic synthesis. They provide a channel of communication with the realm of the dead and the hollow echo which comes from their depths and the fleeting shimmer of rippling water deepen the mystery rather than make it clear. Looked at from bottom to top, a well is like some giant astronomical telescope pointed from the bowels of the Earth at the celestial pole. The whole forms a safety-ladder linking the three levels of the world.

(CHAS p. 152)

Wells are symbols of plenty and sources of life, especially to peoples – like the Children of Israel – for whom the existence of fresh water was quasi-miraculous. Jacob's Well, from which Jesus asked the Woman of Samaria to give him to drink, conveys the meaning of fresh water springing up – a draught of life and knowledge – as described in the article SPRING. De Saint-Martin interpreted Jethro's Well (*beur*), beside which Moses stopped, as a source of light (*ur*) and hence as a spiritual centre.

In the *Zohar*, a well fed by a stream symbolizes the marriage of man and woman. In Hebrew the word 'well' carries the meaning of 'woman' or 'bride' (ELIF p. 41).

Wells, furthermore, are symbols of secrecy and of dissimulation, especially of that of the truth, since Truth, as we know, comes naked out of the well. In the Far East wells are also symbols of the abyss of Hell.

The forty-eighth hexagram in the *I Ching* is called *tzing* (well). Commentators seem far too down-to-earth if all that they tell us is that 'a well which is not covered in and has a good supply of water is the emblem of sincerity and righteousness and a symbol of good fortune' (PHIL, SAIR, SOUP).

The image of the well of knowledge or truth ('truth is to be found at the bottom of a well') recurs in many esoteric tales. The Bambara, whose social structure and spiritual traditions invest their initiatory societies with immense importance, make wells symbols of knowledge, their copings being secrecy and their depths silence. The silence to which they refer is, naturally, that of contemplative wisdom, a higher stage in spiritual development and self-mastery in which speech sinks back and is absorbed into itself (ZAHB p. 150). Symbolizing knowledge, the well stands for the individual who has attained to that knowledge. This brings us back to the start of the article: if the well is a microcosm, it is the human being itself.

west See EAST.

whale The symbolism of the whale relates both to the 'Jaws of Darkness' and to the FISH. In India Vishnu's fish-avatar (incarnation) guided the ark over the waters of the Flood. In the myth of Jonah, the whale is the ARK itself and when the whale swallows Jonah, he enters into a time of darkness, intermediate between 'two states or modalities of existence' (Guénon). Jonah in the belly of the whale represents the 'death' which takes place during initiation. When he is vomited up, it represents resurrection and a new birth, as Islamic tradition shows particularly clearly. In fact *nūn*, the twenty-ninth letter of the Arabic alphabet, also means 'fish' and especially 'whale'. This is why the Prophet Jonah, Seyidna Yūnūs, is called Dhūn-Nūn. In the Kabbalah, the notion of a new birth, in the spiritual sense, is connected with the letter *nūn*.

The very shape of the Arabic letter – the lower half of a circle with a dot above indicating its centre – 'symbolizes Noah's Ark, floating on the waters'.

The semi-circle also stands for a chalice which might, in some circumstances, represent the womb. Viewed from this angle, that is, as the passive element in spiritual transformation, the whale in some sense stands for 'each personality to the degree that it contains the seed of immortality in its midst, symbolically represented by the heart.' In this context it is worth remembering the close relationship existing between the symbolism of the chalice and that of the heart.

Growth of the spiritual seed implies that the individual emerges from his or her separate state and from the cosmic environment to which he or she belongs, just as Jonah's return to life coincided with his emergence from the whale's belly. . . . This emergence was the equivalent of that of the individual who comes out of the CAVERN of initiation, its concavities represented equally explicitly by the semi-circular shape of the letter *nūn*.

(GUEN pp. 166–8)

The whale also crops up in the Koran (18) in the parable of Moses' journey, carrying with him a fish. Moses reached the meeting-place of two seas.

As he crossed the two seas and reached the point at which they met, the fish slipped out of Moses' hands and, regaining its native element, was restored to life again. The symbolism of the Arabic letter *nūn* and of the crescent shape which it forms in this context approaches in a peculiar way that of the cross, represented by the meeting of the two seas, and that of the fish, *ichthus*, the emblem of life which was also a mark of the resurrection in the eyes of the early Christians. It is certainly not a matter of chance that prayers for the dead consist of verses which mainly rhyme in 'n'.

(BAMC p. 141)

From the viewpoint of cosmogonic symbolism, Islamic tradition relates that once the Earth had been created, it floated on the waters. God sent down an angel who took the Earth on his shoulders. God then created a green rock to give him a firm footing and rested the latter upon the horns and back of a bull with forty thousand heads and hooves which stood upon a huge whale. (It was so huge that if the waters of all the seas were gathered together in one of its nostrils, they would be like a grain of mustard-seed in the desert.) As Tha'labi said: 'God created Nūn, the great whale.'

Given that the Earth rests on the angel, the angel on the rock, the rock on the bull, the bull on the whale, the whale on the waters, the waters on air and air on darkness, and that the whole structure depends upon the whale's movements, the Devil, Iblis, is supposed to have tempted the whale to rid itself of its burden and earthquakes are caused by the whale's wrigglings. The whale was, however, brought under control. 'God promptly sent a little creature down to the whale. It went into one of its nostrils and reached its brain. The great whale groaned and besought God who let the little creature out. However, it remained facing the whale and threatening to go in once again every time the whale was tempted to move about' (SOUS pp. 252–3).

The whale is therefore a bearer of the cosmos, a symbol of the Earth's foundations, like such other creatures as the ELEPHANT, TORTOISE and CROCODILE.

The whale plays a similar part in the initiation myths of Polynesia, Black Africa and Lapland to that in the myth of Jonah. Passing through the belly of a monster, often of a sea-monster, was sometimes specifically regarded as a descent into Hell. Whale-bones washed up on the coast of Vietnam were collected and used as cult-objects. The whale, as a sea-god, guided fishing-boats and saved sailors from shipwreck. Through simple extension, the whale-spirit could also be summoned to assist in the journey towards the abode of the immortals and, in this context, would seem to have played the part of a conductor of souls. This reminds us of the important place occupied by the whale in the Indian cultures of the west coast of Canada, among such peoples as the Kwakiutl, Haida, Tlingit and others, and especially of those famous masks with hinged jaws which can be opened to reveal a human face inside a whale or other monster. However it may be, the Vietnamese cult which we have just mentioned would seem to have been passed down from the Chams who, some traditions state, came from the sea and landed, like the whale, upon the coast of Annam. The south Asian tradition of gods cast ashore by the sea is also to be found in Japan. Nor should we forget that it was a miraculous whale which brought the Infant Saviour of the World to the Montagnards of southern Vietnam and freed them from evil.

Lastly, as symbol of the container and, depending upon what it holds, symbol of the buried treasure or sometimes of the impending misfortune as well, the whale always possesses the polyvalency of the unknown and unseen object within. The whale is the fountain of all the antagonistic interests which may spring into being. Then again, its egg-shaped bulk has been compared with two arcs of a circle welded together and which symbolize the upper and the lower worlds, Heaven and Earth.

wheat Wheat is above all else food, and not in Europe alone, since the ancient Chinese prayed to Hu-tsi, the Prince of Harvests, for wheat and barley. According to the *Chāndogya Upanishad*, wheat came from Water, just as Water came from Fire. Wheat, with wine and oil, was one of the ritual offerings of the Children of Israel and this Louis-Claude de Saint-Martin has translated into alchemical terms. Wheat was the passive substance, that is, mercury in the Great Work. It is also, he stressed, denoted by a Hebrew word which also means purity and has a root associated with ideas of choice (both passive and active), covenant and blessing. From these its ritual properties derive. Since it is a basic food-stuff, wheat carries the meaning of the food of immortality, which is another aspect of the Great Work. (See also RICE, which possessed a similar significance in China.)

One of the ceremonies of the Eleusinian Mysteries, however, brings out perfectly the basic symbolism of wheat. During a mystic drama commemorating the marriage of Zeus and Demeter, a grain of wheat was displayed, like the host in a monstrance, and contemplated in silence. Through the grain of wheat, those being initiated at the Greater Mysteries honoured Demeter, the fertility-goddess who initiated mortals into the mysteries of life. By silently displaying the grain, they conjured up the eternal cycle of the seasons, the return of harvest-time and the alternation of the death of the grain and its rebirth in the shape of the ear with its multitude of grains. Worshipping the goddess ensured the continuity of this cycle. The mother's womb and the womb of Earth have often been compared.

It seems certain that we should look for the religious significance of the ear of wheat in this feeling that there is a harmony between human and plant life, both being liable to similar vicissitudes. . . . Grains of wheat, the loveliest of the fruits of the Earth, when returned to the soil become the pledges of further ears of wheat.

(SECG p. 154)

In this context one might quote Aeschylus: 'Earth herself, that bringeth all things to birth, and having nurtured them receiveth their increase in turn' (*The Libation-bearers* 127–8). Or else Hesiod's noble prayer:

Pray to Zeus of the Earth and to pure Demeter to make Demeter's holy grain sound and heavy, when you first begin ploughing, when you hold in your hand the end of the plough-tail and bring down your stick on the backs of the oxen as they draw on the pole-bar by the yoke-straps. . . . In this way your corn-ears will bow to the ground with fullness.

(*Works and Days* 465–9, 473)

Recalling, as it does, the death and resurrection of the grain of wheat, the moving ceremony from the Greater Mysteries has been compared with the conjuring of the god who dies and is brought to life again which characterized the worship of the Dionysiac Mysteries. However, the second derives from the first. It is a reminder, too, that one of Osiris' emblems was the ear of wheat, 'symbol of his death and resurrection'. When, therefore, St John proclaims Christ's glorification, he has recourse to no symbol other than the grain of wheat: 'The hour is come that the Son of man should be glorified. Verily, verily, I say unto you, Except a corn of wheat fall into the ground and die, it abideth alone: but if it die, it bringeth forth much fruit. He that loveth his life shall lose it; and he that hateth his life in this world shall keep it unto life eternal' (John 12: 23–5).

In Ancient Greece and Rome, the priests sprinkled wheat or flour on the victims' heads before offering them in sacrifice. Perhaps this was to cast the seed of immortality or the promise of resurrection upon them.

The deep symbolism of the grain of wheat is perhaps rooted in something else which Jean Servier has noticed. The origin of wheat is utterly unknown, as is that of many other crop-plants such as barley, beans or maize. Cross-breeding can produce a wide variety of species and can improve their quality, but nobody has succeeded in creating wheat or maize or any one of the basic food-plants. Each different civilization regards the particular plant as essentially a gift of the gods linked to the gift of life itself. Demeter gave barley and sent out Triptolemus to spread the cultivation of wheat throughout the world. Xochiquetzal brought maize, while the Dogons' Blacksmith ancestor stole all the food-plants from Heaven to give them to mankind just as Prometheus gave them the fire of Heaven, and so on (SERH pp. 213–15). Wheat symbolizes the gift of life, the basic and primordial foodstuff which cannot be anything other than the gift of the gods.

wheel The wheel partakes of the perfection suggested by the CIRCLE, but with a degree of imperfection since it is related to the world to come, to continuous creation and hence to the contingent and the ephemeral. It symbolizes 'cycles, new beginnings and renewals' (CHAS p. 24). Nicholas of Cusa thought of the world as a wheel within a wheel or a SPHERE within a sphere.

Like the wing, the wheel is the preferred symbol 'of movement and of liberation from conditions of place and their correlative spiritual state' (CHAS p. 431).

In most traditions it is a solar symbol. Blazing wheels were carried to the hill-tops at the Summer solstice in torchlit processions and rolled down the mountainsides at the Winter solstice; wheels were carried on carts during festivals, wheels were carved on doors and gateways and existence itself was conceived as the Wheel of Life. Countless beliefs, spells and practices associated the wheel with the structure of solar myths (ELIT pp. 147–9).

In India, for example, 'the Seven harnessed the chariot to the solitary wheel: a solitary horse with a sevenfold name set in motion the wheel with the triple hub, the immortal wheel which nothing can stop and upon which all beings rest.' As with the Hindus, so with the Celts, the wheel was a cosmic as well as being a solar symbol. Mag Ruith was the *magus rotarum* or 'Wizard of the Wheels', and it was with the help of wheels that he uttered his druidical oracles. He was also 'Lord, Master of the Wheels and Grandson of the Monarch of the Universe'. He was the equivalent of the *Chakravartī*, he who sets the wheel in motion. In China, the man who possessed control of the wheel had the celestial empire in his power.

The consistent significance of this symbol in the majority of cultures would seem to be explained by its shape (spokes radiating from a hub) and its mobility. This shape caused the wheel to be regarded as a solar symbol. It was linked to Apollo as well as to thunderbolts and to the kindling of fire. The CHAKRA was one of Vishnu's attributes and it was an Aditya, or Sun. Nevertheless, the *chakra* is a DISC rather than a wheel. In Indian literature and art, wheels often have twelve spokes; this is the number of the Zodiac and of the solar cycle. The wheels of their chariots are essential features in any depiction of Sun, Moon or stars. Once again this is the result of the need to conjure the picture of the voyaging stars and their cyclical orbit. The thirty traditional spokes in the Chinese wheel (*Tao Te Ching* 2) are the sign of the lunar cycle (Granet).

The wheel stands out even more clearly as a symbol of the world, its hub being the still CENTRE, the First Cause, and its rim the manifestation which emanates from it by means of radiation. The spokes show the relationship between centre and circumference. The simplest form of wheel has four spokes displaying expansion to the four quarters of space as well as the fourfold rhythm of the Moon and the seasons. The six-spoked wheel re-echoes solar symbolism and is also reminiscent of the LABARUM. It may be considered as the horizontal projection of a six-armed CROSS. The most usual wheel has always been eight-spoked, as in the eight spatial orientations and the eight-petalled LOTUS with which it is identified. Both eight petals and eight spokes symbolize regeneration and renewal. The eight-spoked wheel is to be found from India, via Chaldea, to the Celtic world and it is also the arrangement of the eight Chinese trigrams. Although the Buddhist Wheel of Life has only six spokes, this is because only six classes of being (*loka*) exist, and if the wheel of *dharma* has eight spokes, this is because the Way comprises eight paths.

The cosmic significance of the wheel is given expression in Vedic literature. Its ceaseless turning is renewal. From it space and all the divisions of time were born. It is also the Rosicrucians' *Rota Mundi*. Only the centre of the cosmic wheel is motionless. This is the 'emptiness of the hub' which makes it turn (*Tao* 11), its navel (omphalos or *nabhi*). Within this centre stands the *Chakravartī*, 'he who makes the wheel revolve', the Buddha, Universal Man, the Ruler. The ancient rulers of Java and Angkor bore the title *Chakravartī*. This empty hub is the point at which celestial activity is deployed. The Ruler standing there is the only being who is unchanged in universal transformation (Chuang Tzu: 25). Another aspect of Chinese symbolism regarded the hub as Heaven and the rim as Earth, with Mankind the spoke which mediates between them. The Chinese noria (waterwheel), Chuang Tzu' potter's wheel, or St James's 'course of nature' (James 3: 6) are all expressions of the ceaseless whirlwind of manifestation from which release can only be obtained by transition from the circumference to the centre, by which is understood a RETURN to the centre of being.

The wheel which the Buddha set in motion was the Wheel of the Law (*dharma-chakra*). The law being that of human fate, there is no power able to reverse the direction in which the wheel revolves. Guénon judiciously compares it with the Western Wheel of Fortune. Hindus and Buddhists employ other symbols again. The wise man who obtains deliverance, says the *Sāmkhya*, is like the potter who has finished a pot: his life goes on, just as the potter's wheel continues to revolve under its own momentum. The *Visuddhimagga* teaches that life lasts the length of a thought, like the wheel which only touches the ground at one point on its rim. Nor should one forget that the Tibetan Buddhists' Wheel of Life, based yet again on the idea of ceaseless change, represents the multiple states of being successively. Tantrism also calls the 'subtle centres' wheels – or lotuses – because the current of the *kundalinī* runs through them like the axle through a wheel.

In Taoist inner alchemy, the purely conventional name of Wheel of the Law, or mill-wheel or noria, is given to the regressive motion of essence and of breath, which should bring them together in the furnace. In emblematic terms it describes a return from the periphery or circumference to the centre.

If one adds special cases, Devoucoux described the wheel as 'the image of Christian knowledge united with holiness'. The wheel is the emblem of St Catherine of Alexandria, the legendary Egyptian scholar saint who is patroness of Christian philosophers. The Celtic wheel of fire revolved in both directions alternately. This is a recurrence of the symbolism of the double SPIRAL (BELT, COOH, DEVA, ELIY, GOVM, GRAP, GRIF, GUEM, GUEC, GUET, GUES, BURA, MALA, SILI, VARG).

The wheel is a common motif in Celtic art. It is generally depicted in Gallo-Roman sculpture accompanying the Celtic Jupiter, usually known as Taranis, or the god with the wheel, or again as the snake-footed horseman. There are countless examples down to folk-level in the shape of terracotta and bronze figures and even charms. Because of the way it is depicted, most modern scholars have regarded the wheel as the equivalent of the thunderbolt, Jupiter's *fulmen*, in other words, as a solar symbol. Solar symbolism is not, however, the whole meaning of the wheel, which is also, and above all else, a representation of the world. For if one goes on to compare this with the Irish cosmic wheel of the mythic druid Mag Ruith (Lord of the Wheel), who was an avatar (incarnation) of the druid-god, the Dagda, the Celtic god with the wheel corresponds most exactly to the Hindu *Chakravartī*. He is at its centre, the motionless source of all motion, he being the axis of motion in which he takes no part since he is necessary to all things. A panel of the Gundestrup Cauldron depicts a man – a warrior, perhaps, or even the Lord of the Wheel – turning the Cosmic Wheel. Only the upper part of the god's body is displayed, with arms uplifted in prayer or in the symbolically impassive attitude of the First Cause from which all manifestation emanates. The wheel is also the symbol of change and the return of forms of being. A sword from Hallstatt in Austria depicts two youths, perhaps analogous with the Dioscuri, who are revolving a wheel and who must symbolize the alternation of day and night. Because it is like the circle, the wheel is also a celestial symbol and related to the notion of the centre.

Another geometrical figure often found in Celtic art of all periods is the roundel, and its symbolism parallels that of the wheel and the cross. The symbolism of the spiral is also very close to that of the wheel, and its alternating evolution and involution corresponds to the alchemists' *solve et coagula*.

The druid Mag Ruith's wheel was made of yew, a death-tree, and when it appears on Earth, it will mark the end of the world. Whoever sees it will go blind; whoever hears it will become deaf; and whoever touches it will die.

There is a Welsh goddess who appears in the Mabinogi of Math the son of Mathonwy, called Arianrhod, 'Silver Wheel'. She was the mother of two sons, one of whom, Dylan Eil Ton ('Son of the Wave'), immediately dived into the water in which he swam like a fish – this stands for a return to the First Cause – while the other, Llew, bore a name which corresponds to that of the Irish god, Lug. Featuring among the warlike 'ploys' of Cùchulainn was that of the wheel, in which the hero contorted his body into the shape of a wheel which rolled at enormous speed. Lastly, the root *roto* (wheel) frequently occurs in Gallic place-names such as Rotomagus, the modern Rouen.

In his *Celestial Hierarchy*, the Pseudo-Dionysius the Areopagite expiates upon the symbolism of the flaming wheels and winged wheels of which the Prophets spoke. Daniel, for example, describes his vision of the Ancient of Days and the Son of Man when the throne of the former 'was like the fiery flame, and his wheels as burning fire' (Daniel 7: 9).

Ezekiel for his part saw the wheels of the cherubim:

And it came to pass, that when he had commanded the man clothed with linen, saying, Take fire from between the wheels, from between the cherubims; then he went in, and stood beside the wheels. . . . And when I looked, behold the four wheels by the cherubims . . . and the appearance of the wheels was as the colour of a beryl stone. And as for their appearances, they four had one likeness, as if a wheel had been in the midst of a wheel. . . . As for the wheels, it was cried unto them in my hearing, O wheel [*galgal*] . . . And when the cherubims went, the wheels went by them: and when the cherubims lifted up their wings to mount up from the earth, the same wheels also turned not from beside them. When they stood, these stood; and when they were lifted up, these lifted up themselves also: for the spirit of the living creature was in them.

(Ezekiel 9: 6, 9–10, 13, 16–17)

The Neoplatonist theologian reveals the symbolic meaning of these wheels:

The wheels as being winged, advancing without turning and deviation, denote the power of their advancing energy within a straight and direct way, whilst their whole intellectual track is Divinely directed towards the same undeviating and direct way. But it is possible to interpret in another form the sacred description of the spiritual wheels, for the name Gel Gel, is given to them, as the theologian says. This shows, according to the Hebrew tongue, revolutions and revelations. For the Divine wheels of fire have revolutions by their perpetual motion around the Goodness itself; but revelations by the explanation of things hidden, and by the instruction of things on earth, and by the descending procession of the sublime illuminations to things below.

(PSEH 49–50)

In these scriptural passages therefore, the wheel symbolizes the unrolling of divine revelation. A further meaning is to be found in Ezekiel if we look at verse 12: 'And their whole body, and their backs, and their hands, and their wings, and the wheels, were full of eyes, even the wheels that they four had.'

The twofold image of wheels studded with eyes is an allegory, like star-eyes, which is intended to express the omniscience and omnipresence of the heavenly God. It conveys the clear meaning that nothing escapes the eye of God and that humans should pay him their respect.

And yet the wheel symbol was long lunar before becoming solar. Durand quotes Harding for the view that the sistrum carried by Isis or Diana stood for the lunar disc, 'heavenly Treasure of the Wheel', which appeared to the king on the day of the full Moon. 'The original significance borne by the wheel', Durand adds, 'was that of an emblem of the cycle of things to come, a magical epitome which enabled time to be controlled, that is, the future to be predicted' (DURS p. 348).

The wheel of the ZODIAC is a universal phenomenon with the meaning of the Wheel of Life. Later the Zodiac acquired solar significance, but originally it was lunar. Pre-Islamic Arabs called it 'Ishtar's Girdle' and the Babylonians 'the Houses of the Moon'.

In any case it was very late in time that the wheel acquired a solar meaning and this was when, for technical reasons, it was equipped with spokes. . . . Originally the zodiacal wheel, like that of the calendar, was a lunar wheel of solid wood reinforced with a square or triangle of timber pieces. This subdivided it internally and such divisions have numerological significance.

(DURS pp. 349–50)

Fulcanelli describes the alchemical significance of the wheel in these terms:

In the Middle Ages the central rose windows of cathedral porches were known as the *rota*, or wheel. Now 'wheel' is the alchemical hieroglyph for the time needed for the decoction of alchemical matter, and consequently for the process of decoction itself. The fire which the alchemist kept at a regular and constant temperature day and night during the course of this operation was for this reason called 'the fire of the wheel'. Nevertheless, in addition to the heat needed to dissolve the Philosopher's Stone, a second agent known as the Secret or Philosopher's Fire was required. And it was this fire, stimulated by ordinary fire, which made the wheel turn.

Fulcanelli next quotes an extract from a seventeenth-century alchemical treatise, *Traité de l'harmonie et constitution générale du vray sel*, by de Nuysement, which shows that this symbolic meaning given to the wheel is, as in Holy Scripture, that of the vehicle for the manifestation of power, which comes and goes between Heaven and Earth, marrying the sacred and the profane (FULC pp. 65–6).

To Jung and his school, 'the rose windows of the cathedrals . . . are representations of the Self of man transposed onto the cosmic plane' (Aniela Jaffé: JUNS pp. 241ff.). This is oneness in wholeness, and Jaffé, regarding the rose window as another form of MANDALA, adds that 'we may regard as mandalas the haloes of Christ and Christian saints in religious paintings.' In this context we revert to the symbolism of the cosmic centre and the mystic centre exemplified by the hub. Individuation takes place and balance is established when a two-way current is set up along the spokes from the centre to the circumference and from the circumference back to the centre. The wheel falls into the general category of emanation and return, symbols which give expression to the development of the universe and of the individual.

Wheel of Fortune While the Hermit points the individual down the path of a quest for solitude, the tenth major arcanum of the TAROT, the Wheel of Fortune, brings us back into the world and all its changes and chances. With the assistance of an image well-known in Classical antiquity and during the Middle Ages, it shows a flesh-coloured wheel standing clear of the ground on yellow wooden struts. Two strange creatures cling to either side of the wheel while a blue sphinx with a golden crown and red wings and holding a white sword sits on a narrow pedestal at its apex. The wheel has six spokes, red near the hub and white at the rim, and the whole is turned by a handle which is left in the undifferentiated colour, white. A monkey, head downwards, clings to the left side of the wheel. It wears a sort of skirt round its waist made up of three short, stiff pieces of material, the centre blue, the outer pieces red. On the right there is a yellow dog with a red tail, wearing a wide collar and a blue coat. It appears to be climbing towards the diabolically impassive sphinx. These two creatures have been regarded as the good spirit Hermanubis and the evil spirit Typhon. Be that as it may, the card's symbolism is linked to that which all traditions have given to the WHEEL. It stands for the alternations of good and ill fortune, chance and mischance, vicissitude, rising and the dangers of falling. In astrology it corresponds to the Tenth House, which represents social and professional status.

It is a solar symbol, the wheel of life and death following on one another's heels throughout the cosmos and, at a human level, perpetual mutability and eternal homecoming. 'Human life runs changeably onwards like the spokes of a chariot-wheel', Anacreon wrote. This motion of alternate elevation and depression is that of JUSTICE (eighth arcanum) itself as it tries to preserve a balance at all levels and does not hesitate to moderate successful creative achievement by destruction and death. The number of this arcanum (X) emphasizes this, lying as it does midway between the Chariot (VII) and Death (XIII).

The animal figures which revolve around the wheel of life may also be regarded as embodying the law of rebirth applied in so many traditions to those humans who in their lifetimes have failed to control their animal passions. In their rise and fall may be seen, too, that law of alternation, or even of compensation, which emerges from the history of mankind, of society and of the individual. From a more mystical viewpoint, the Wheel of Fortune is less an image of mere chance than of immanent justice.

wheelbarrow Mankind had long known the use of the wheelbarrow before a misunderstanding attributed this useful invention to Pascal.

The symbolism of the wheelbarrow derives from an overall view of the object regarded as an extension of the human arm and as a miniature farm-cart. In fact it symbolizes the enhancement of human strength in three different ways. The first is in intensity, since the two handles of the wheelbarrow form levers; the second in volume through the capacity of the barrow; and the third in freedom of movement, thanks to the wheel. From these differing viewpoints, a wheelbarrow is like a portion of the cosmic forces organized in the service of mankind. At the same time, however, it requires full responsibility from the human who may push it with greater or less enthusiasm, fill it with all sorts of different things and steer it in the wrong direction. Its balance also depends on the person holding the handles and it is just as easy to tip it over as it is to push it forward. In this context it might stand for fate with all its potential and all its ambivalence. It is the combined symbol of extracosmic powers (solar wheel, receptacle and arms providing the active principle) placed at the disposal of mankind; but these supplementary forces must of necessity be subject to human will and are merely the instruments of mankind. Mankind will be judged by the use to which it will have put this gift of energy.

Wheelbarrows are depicted in many legends, in which they play the role of instruments of fate. They may either be pushed along by a phantom in quest of the dying or carry a hidden treasure.

whip Symbol of judicial power and of the right to inflict punishment. In Ancient Egypt, statues of the god Min depicted him with the right arm bent at the elbow and raised so that 'the royal flail [or whip], salutary symbol of terror, floats mysteriously above his open hand.' But the god was also linked to fertility-cults and in fact Jean Yoyotte remarks that 'the other arm is slipped under his robe and in his hand he holds the divine phallus. . . . Such is the calm image in which the formidable divinity of the "bull which serves the cows" was incarnate, the life-giving master whose processions opened the harvest-season' (POSD p. 171).

Whips were also among the insignia of certain Ancient Greek deities such as Hecate, who used one to control the monsters of the Underworld, and the Erinnyes, who scourged the guilty, as well as of priests and civil dignitaries. In Zeus' shrine at Dodona the thongs of a whip held by the statue of a child struck a sacred cauldron when the wind blew, and the noise they made was regarded as the oracle of the god.

Whips are generally symbols of THUNDERBOLTS and they are also frequently found used for ritual FLAGELLATION by initiatory guilds with rain-making duties, such as the Bambara Kwore society (DIEB). It is significant that Kwore initiates use both whips and torches with which they scorch their bodies, thunderbolts being believed to bring rain.

Like the thunderbolt, the whip is also a symbol of creational energy and the part it plays in the Vedas is on the cosmic scale, transforming milk into the primordial food, butter. The APSARA came from the churning of the Sea of Milk, as did the seeds of life.

whirlwind Its helicoidal movement makes the whirlwind the symbol of evolution, but of an evolution beyond human control and directed by some higher power. It can have the twofold significance of down-draught or up-draught, of unstoppable regression or of accelerated progress. However, its violent nature marks it as an extraordinary interruption of the course of nature.

white Like its opposite colour, BLACK, white can stand at either end of the spectrum. Absolute in itself, with only the variations of mattness or gloss, it can signify either the absence of colour or the sum of all colours. Thus it is set sometimes at the start and sometimes at the finish of the daily round and of the manifested world, which endows it with ideal and asymptotic properties. However, the finish of life – the instant of death – is also the moment in which we cross the bridge between the visible and the invisible and is therefore another starting-point. White (*candidus* in Latin) is the colour of candidates, since candidates for public office in Ancient Rome wore white. Since it was one of the colours allotted to the cardinal points, most peoples usually made white the colour of both east and west, that is to say, those two distant and mysterious points at which the Sun is born and dies each day. In both instances white possesses the properties of a boundary, as do the ends of the endless lines of the horizon. It is the colour of 'passage' in the sense in which the word is used in 'rites of passage' and it is rightly the preferred colour for those rites through which changes in existence take place on the classic pattern of all initiation, through death and rebirth. The white of the west is the matt white of death, which absorbs the individual and inducts him or her into the cold, female lunar world. It is the herald of absence, nocturnal emptiness and the disappearance of consciousness and of daytime colours.

The white of the east is the white of returning and of the dawn, when the vault of Heaven can be seen once more, void of colour but rich with the potential of manifestation from which both microcosm and macrocosm have been recharged like electric batteries as they passed through the womb of darkness, the fountain of all energy. One sinks from gloss to matt; the other rises from matt to gloss. In themselves these two instants, these two whitenesses, are void, hanging between presence and absence, between Moon and Sun, between the two aspects of the sacred and its two sides. The whole of the symbolism of the colour white and of its ritual employment stems from this natural observation, from which all human cultures have constructed their philosophical and religious systems. A painter like Kandinsky, for whom the problems of colour were far more important than those of aesthetics, expresses the matter better than anyone else:

White, which is often regarded as a non-colour . . . is like the symbol of a world in which all colours, in so far as they are properties of physical substances, have vanished. . . . White acts upon our souls like absolute silence. . . . This silence is not something lifeless, but replete with life-potential. . . . It is a nothingness filled with childish happiness or, in better terms, a nothingness before birth, and before the beginning of all things. This perhaps was the sound emitted by the cold white Earth in the Ice Age.

One could hardly describe dawn better without actually mentioning it.

In all symbolic thought, death precedes life and all birth is rebirth. For this reason white was originally the colour of mourning, as is still the case in the Far East and as was for long the practice in Europe, especially at the court of the Kings of France.

In its unlucky aspect, glaring white is the opposite of RED. This white is the colour of vampires which thirst for the blood upon which the daytime world depends and which they lack. This white is the colour of shrouds, of apparitions and spectres and the colour – or rather the absence of colour – of Oberon, the Elf-king, the Alberich of the Nibelungen (DONM p. 184). It is the colour of ghosts, which explains that when the Bantu of southern Cameroon saw a white man for the first time, they called him an albino ghost (*Nango-Kon*). This made all the tribesfolk who encountered him run away until, assured that his intentions were peaceful, they all returned and pressed him for news of their dead relations since he had come from the kingdom of the dead. White, as Eliade observes, is often used in initiation rites as the colour of the first stage, the struggle with death. We should prefer to say that it is the colour of going to one's death, and this was indeed the significance of the Aztecs' making white the colour of the west. It is common knowledge that their religious thought was based upon the premiss that all human life and the cohesion of the universe itself depended upon the daily transit of the Sun, and the west, into which the Sun vanished, was called 'the House of Mists', standing for death, that is for entry into the invisible. Hence the warriors sacrificed each day to ensure the Sun's regeneration were led to the altar dressed in white cloaks (SOUM) and wearing white sandals (THOH) which insulated them from the Earth and sufficed to show that while no longer of this world they were not yet of the other. White, it was said, 'is the colour of the first steps their souls take before the warriors are sacrificed and depart' (SOUM). Similarly all the gods in the Aztec pantheon reported in myth to have been reborn after sacrifice wore white ornaments (SOUM).

The Pueblo Indians, however, make white the colour of the east, for the same reason, corroborated in that, in their thinking, the east comprehends notions of Autumn, the depths of the Earth and of religion (MULR p. 279, quoting Cushing and TALS).

In this sense, although white is the colour of the east, it is not a solar colour. It is quite unconnected with the colour of sunrise but is rather that of first light, that moment of utter void between day and night, when all reality is still bound up in a world of dreams, when the individual is numbed, suspended in a passive, hollow whiteness. For this reason it is the time for arrests, surprise attacks and executions. Traditionally the condemned person wears white, the garb of surrender and submission, like the white worn at First Communions and the dress worn by the bride when she goes to her marriage. Although this is called a wedding-dress, it is really the dress of someone going to her wedding. Once the wedding is over, white gives way to red, just as the first sign of day-break, on the backcloth of a first light as dull and neutral as a bed-sheet, the red planet, Venus, will appear. The whiteness is the spotless white of the operating table on which the surgeon's knife will soon make the red blood flow. White is the colour of purity, and originally it was not a positive colour showing that something had been undertaken, but a neutral, passive colour showing that something had yet to be fulfilled. This is certainly the original meaning of virginal whiteness and the reason why Christian ritual prescribes the burial of children in white shrouds decorated with white flowers.

In Black Africa where the rites of initiation determine the whole structure of society, young men who go into retreat after their circumcision smear their faces, and sometimes their whole bodies, a matt chalk-white. This is to show that for the time being they are outside the body of society; and on the day on which they re-enter it, now responsible adult males in the full sense of the term, their bodies are smeared with red instead of white. In Africa, too, as well as in New Guinea, widows, who are temporarily excluded from society, paint their faces white. At the same time in New Guinea they cut off one of their fingers. The symbolic significance of this mutilation is patent – they cut off the phallus which they once made stand erect during the second birth which was their marriage, to return to a state of latency. This is an image of a primordial, undifferentiated state, as white as the Cosmic Egg of the Orphic mystics, and thus their mourning places them in a state of awaiting a fresh awakening, for as one may see, this matt white is the whiteness of the womb and of motherhood, a spring which will flow at the touch of the magic wand. Out will gush the first of all liquid foods, milk, rich in unawakened dormant life, full of dreams, too, the milk the nursling sucks before he or she has opened an eye to the world of daylight, milk as white as lily or lotus. They, too, are images of the future, of awakening, rich in promise and potential. Milk is like the silvery light of the Moon, the planet which in the full is the archetype of woman's fertility, with its promise of plenty and of the dawn of day.

Thus a change gradually takes place and, as day follows night, the spirit will celebrate the splendour of a whiteness which is that of daylight, solar, positive and male. The white horses of Apollo, on which nobody can look without being dazzled, take the place of the white dream horse, Death's steed.

The positive qualities now acquired by white are also linked to the phenomenon of initiation. White is not the attribute of the postulant or candidate who walks to his death, but of the person who rises again, reborn and victorious from the ordeal. It is the robe of manhood, a symbol of the acceptance of responsibility, of the assumption and recognition of powers, of the fulfilment of a rebirth and of dedication. Early Christians called the initiatory rite of baptism 'Enlightenment' and the Pseudo-Dionysius the Areopagite describes what followed the making of the baptismal promises: 'Next, they throw garments, white as light over the initiated. For by his manly and Godlike insensibility to contrary passions, and by his persistent inclination towards the One, the unadorned is adorned, and the shapeless acquires shape, being made brilliant by a life entirely reflecting the light' (PSEN pp. 59–60).

The Celts reserved this 'positive' white for the priestly caste, and their druids dressed in white. Apart from the priests, only the king was allowed to wear white, since his duties were close to those of the priesthood, being a warrior entrusted with an extraordinary religious mission. King Nuada's symbolic metal was silver, a royal colour. Unless they were kings, all the characters in heroic literature dressed in white are druids or bards, members of the priestly caste. In Gaulish *vindo-s*, an adjective found in many different compound forms, conveys the meaning of 'white' and 'handsome'; in Middle Irish *find* means both 'white' and 'holy', the phrase *in drong find* denoting the angels in lives of the saints; while the Welsh *gwyn* and the Breton *gwenn* mean both 'white' and 'blessed' (LERD pp. 27–8).

In Japan, white haloes and white lotuses are associated with the Great Illuminator Buddha' hand-gesture of knowledge, in contrast with red and the gesture of concentration.

In its sense of daylight, white, the colour of initiation, becomes the colour of revelation, of grace and of the transfiguration which dazzles, awakening the intellect at the same time as it eludes its grasp. It is the colour of divine manifestation which remains around the heads of those who have known God. It takes the shape of a halo of light, the sum total of all colours. This triumphant white can only be seen on the mountain-tops.

And after six days Jesus taketh with him Peter, and James, and John, and leadeth them up into an high mountain apart by themselves: and he was transfigured before them. And his raiment became shining, exceeding white as snow; so as no fuller on earth can white them. And there appeared unto them Elias with Moses: and they were talking with Jesus.

(Mark 9: 2–4)

Elias (Elijah) is the lord of the life-principle symbolized by fire and his colour is red, while, in Islamic tradition, Moses is associated with the individual's heart of hearts and his colour is white, that hidden white of the inner light, the *sirr*, the hidden fundamental mystery of Sufi thought.

In Sufism the symbolic relationship between red and white also recurs. White is the essential colour of wisdom, which derives from the beginning of things and is the vocation lying before mankind. Red is the colour of the individual caught up in the darkness of this world and imprisoned in its bonds. Such is the individual upon earth,

a crimson-stained archangel. In truth I am white. I am a very old man, a sage whose essence is light.... But I was cast out, I too, into the Pit of Darkness.... Look at the sunrise and the sunset. There is an instant between them when the daylight side is whiteness and the night side is blackness, whence comes the crimson of the sunrise and the crimson of the sunset.

(CORE p. 247)

When solar, white becomes the symbol of fully expanded diurnal awareness, 'biting' into reality, and white teeth are regarded as a symbol of the intellect by the Bambara (ZAHD, ZAHB). It approximates to GOLD, which would explain why the two colours are associated in the papal flag proclaiming that the Christian God rules the Earth.

widow The word symbolically denotes Freemasonry, whose members are termed 'the Widow's children'. Hiram, the legendary founder of the Craft, was said (1 Kings 7: 14) to be 'the son of a widow', which is enough to explain the reference. However, it would also seem to relate especially to Isis, the widow of Osiris, that is to say, of the light, and hence to the search for the scattered remains of her dead husband. This quest is also that of the Mason who identifies himself with Horus, like him a 'Son of the Light'. The gathering-up of the scattered remains of Osiris (or of Purusha) corresponds to the re-creation of primordial oneness.

Reference might be made to the symbolism of the Greek goddess Hera, the widow, to the death of the Grand Master of the Templars, Jacques de Molay and even, if we are to believe Fabre d'Olivet, to the symbolism of the Hebrew word *vav*, but they all seem inconclusive. On the other hand, the 'widowhood' of Freemasonry, in respect of Templar tradition, might have some significance both from the doctrinal and the historic points of view (BOUM, GUES).

Use of the word by Masons and Templars, too, no doubt quite unconsciously, betrays the castrational sense with which everyday language and slang have invested the word. While in Victorian times 'the Widow' was slang for champagne (Veuve Clicquot), earlier generations had used the word for the gallows, a meaning it also had from as early as 1628 in France and one which was later applied to the guillotine.

wild celery This evergreen, aromatic, umbelliferous plant was used by the Ancient Greeks to crown the victors at the Isthmian Games. It symbolizes the happiness and triumph of youth. If it played an important role in funeral ceremonies, this was to show the state of eternal youth to which the dead person had just passed.

wilderness See DESERT.

willow   In the West, the external shape of the weeping willow evokes feelings of grief and associates it with death. Yet Hermas regarded the well-known vitality of the tree as making it a symbol of Divine Law. The survival of branches cut off and planted in the soil, the tree remaining undivided, illustrated a function of the observation of that Law. 'If these branches are planted in the ground and watered, many of them will come back to life again.' Furthermore, St Bernard compares the willow 'which is eternally green' with Our Lady.

These two latter interpretations are closely linked to Far Eastern willow symbolism, where it is, in fact, a symbol of immortality like the Freemasons' acacia. That is why the centre of the T'ien Ti Hui society's lodges, where the bushel-basket stands, is called 'the City of Willows' (*Mu Yang Cheng*). This city is an abode of immortality. In Tibet the willow clearly plays the part of the Tree of Life or 'central' tree, too, and this seems to have been the significance of the willows which used to grow in front of the shrine at Lhasa (Hummel). Willow branches also played an axial role in Uighur rites of circumambulation. One should note, if only for curiosity's sake, that the Taoist poet Hi Ch'ang worked at a FORGE beneath a willow planted in the middle of his courtyard, forges being symbolic means of communicating with Heaven. If the graves of mythical characters are dug in the shade of a willow tree, the meaning is equally clear. Lao Tzu loved to sit meditating under such a tree.

The willow is sometimes employed as the emblem of the Bodhisattva Avalokitesvara, regarded as the dispenser of fertility, in which role he equates with his Chinese female counterpart, Kuan Yin.

On the other hand, because it bears no fruit, the male willow is a symbol of purity. Lastly, we should observe that the swaying of its branches has made the tree an image of grace and shapely elegance, so that the comparison of a woman's body with a willow tree has become something of a cliché (GUET, HUMU, LECC, MASR, MAST, SOUD).

The willow was also a sacred tree for the Prairie Indians and a symbol of seasonal rebirth, while in western Russia the opposite was true. Here there is the proverb that to plant a willow is to prepare the spade to dig one's own grave (CATI, DALP). However, it is not stated whether the death which the willow foretells is conceived as a transition to the immortality which the tree symbolizes in other regions.

Additionally, willows possess a sacred and protective character and are associated with miraculous births. According to the Spartans, Diana was found in a willow-clump, and the Ancient Egyptians believed that Osiris enjoyed the same privilege, while Moses was found floating on the waters of the Nile in a willow basket. The leading role of the Logos or Word seems to have been symbolized both in East and West, in analogous ways, by the willow. A willow basket ensures protection (ALLA p. 58).

wind   There are a number of different aspects to wind symbolism. Because of its characteristic bluster it is a symbol of empty-headedness, fickleness and instability. It is also an elemental force belonging to the Titans, which speaks strongly enough for its blind violence.

On the other hand wind is synonymous with BREATH and consequently with the Spirit, a heaven-sent spiritual influx. This is why both the Book of Psalms and the Koran equate winds with angels as God's messengers. Wind even gives its name to the Holy Spirit. The Spirit of God moving across the face of the primordial waters is called *Ruah*, 'Wind', and it was a wind which brought the Apostles the tongues of fire of the Holy Spirit. In Hindu symbolism, the wind, personified as the god (Vāyu) is cosmic breath and the Word. It rules the 'subtle' world which lies between Heaven and Earth, the space which was filled by what the Chinese termed a breath, *k'i*. Vāyu imbues, shatters and cleanses, and is related to the points of the compass, which were generally speaking termed 'winds'. Hence Classical antiquity talked of the four winds and the Athenians built the eight-sided Tower of the Winds.

The Four Winds, furthermore, were related to the seasons, the elements and the 'humours' in a pattern subject to slight variation. In China, the eight winds corresponded to the eight trigrams.

In China, wind combined with water to denote geomancy, that is, in principle, the study of air currents together with those of water and earth in any given location (DANA, GUES, MUTC).

According to Hindu cosmogonic traditions contained in the Laws of Manu, wind was born of the spirit and engendered light:

Spurred on by the longing to create, the spirit . . . engendered space. Wind was born of the development of this ether . . . and was laden with all scents, pure, powerful and with tactile properties.

But, in its turn, light was born from the transformation of the wind, light which enlightens and with its radiance drives the darkness away, having dimensional properties.

(SOUN p. 350)

In Ancient Persia, in Zoroastrian tradition, wind played the part of world foundation and keeper of cosmic and moral balance. In the succession of creation 'the first of all created things was a drop of water.' Ormuz next created 'flaming fire and endowed it with the brightness of infinite light and its shape was that of welcoming flame. Lastly he made the wind in the shape of a young man, fifteen years old, who bears up water, plants, cattle, the righteous and all things' (SOUN p. 322).

In Islamic tradition, the wind has the task of confining the waters, but its substance, of cloud, air and countless wings, also imposes upon it the task of underpinning them. 'Then God made the Wind and gave it countless wings. He told it to carry the Water, which it did. The Throne, Avās, rested upon the Water and the Water rested upon the Wind.'

Ibn 'Abbās tells the same story:

Upon what did the Water rest? – Upon the back of the Wind, and when God wished to create living things, he gave the Wind power over the Water. And the Water swelled up in waves, and the waves were beaten into foam, and the Water gave forth vapours, and these vapours hung over the Water, and God named them *Samā* [that which is raised up], that is to say Heaven.

(SOUN p. 246)

In Biblical tradition, the winds are God's breath. God's breath brought order to the primordial TOHU-BOHU and brought to life the first man. Wind stirring the tree-tops heralded God's coming. Winds were also the instruments of God's power, bringing life, punishing and teaching. They were signs and carried messages like the angels. They were manifestations of a godhead which wished to communicate its feelings, were they of the gentlest kindness or of the most stormy wrath.

The Ancient Greeks pictured the winds as boisterous and rebellious deities shut up in the deep caverns of the Aeolian Islands. In addition to their king, Aeolus, they distinguished the north wind (Aquilon or Boreas), the south Wind (Auster), the east (and morning) wind (Eureus) and the west (or evening) wind (Zephyr). Each was iconographically distinct and depicted with its own especial attributes.

The 'Druid's Wind' was one aspect of the druids' power over the elements and was very closely related to breath as a vehicle for magic. When the Milesians, that is the Gaels, reached Ireland, the druids of the earlier occupiers, the Tuatha Dé Danann, drove their ships far away from the shore by means of a very violent Druid's Wind, recognizable because it did not blow above the height of the sails.

It would, however, be an exaggeration to call the manifestation of the godhead a god in its own right. Jean Servier rightly warns against such simplistic errors:

Often the inhabitants of the New World discovered by the West, like many mystics, used sensory comparison to make the infinite spirituality of this supreme Deity comprehensible. God was a breath, God was a wind. From this, ill-educated traders and missionaries who hoped to win over these grown-up children with promises of a material paradise, concluded that the Indians worshipped the wind and regarded it as God. Nothing could have been further from the truth.
(SERH p. 80)

When winds occur in dreams, they herald the imminence of some important event or change about to take place.

Spiritual energies are symbolized by a bright light or else, and this is less well known, by wind. When the storm gathers, one can foretell that there is a great movement of spirit or of spirits. From religious experience we know that the godhead may appear in the shape of a gentle breeze or of a great storm. It would seem that Orientals alone can understand the significance of the empty space in which the wind blows and which paradoxically they regard as a powerful symbol of energy.
(ALLA p. 200)

window In FREEMASONRY, the Tracing Boards of the Apprentice and Fellowcraft Mason depict three windows, covered with gratings, like the windows of the Temple of Jerusalem described in 1 Kings 6: 4. These three windows are said to correspond to east, south and west, the three 'stations' of the Sun. No window corresponds to the north, through which the Sun does not pass. This is to allow light to be received at these three stages and perhaps under three different modalities. The Apprentice stands to the north, so as to receive the greatest intensity of light through the southern window (BOUM, GUET).

In so far as it opens to air and light, the window symbolizes receptivity. If the window is round, the receptivity is the same as the eye's and that of consciousness. If it is square, it is terrestrial receptivity, in contrast with the gifts of Heaven.

wine (see also VINE) Apart from such highly individual interpretations as that of St Bernard, who linked it simply to 'fear and strength', wine is generally associated with BLOOD, as much from its colour as from the fact that it may be characterized as the essence of the grape. Consequently wine is the beverage of life or of immortality. Especially, but not exclusively, in Semitic tradition it is in addition the symbol of knowledge and of initiation, because of the INTOXICATION which it causes. In Taoism this intoxication is part and parcel of the virtues of wine.

In Ancient Greece, wine replaced the blood of Dionysos and represented the beverage of immortality. This, too, was the role it was given in Taoism, where it was subjected to long and complicated ritual preparation. In Chinese secret societies, rice wine was mixed with blood for their oath-taking and, as the communal drink, allowed members to reach 'the age of one hundred and ninety'. Such, too, is the significance of the chalice with the 'blood of Christ' in the Eucharist and prefigured in the sacrifice of Melchizedek. This brings us back, too, to the idea of sacrifice associated with the shedding of blood, a sacrifice which may at the same time be that of the abandonment of self-restraint associated with intoxication. The Children of Israel used wine as an element in their sacrifices, as did the Ancient Chinese, although in their case, it conveyed a different meaning as the essence of plant life.

Wine as the symbol of knowledge and initiation was no alien notion to the traditions which we have already mentioned and especially to the myths of Dionysos. India, too, presents us with an ambivalent symbolism in the myth of the churning of the Sea of Milk. Some commentators regard the *asura* as those who had not drunk wine (*surā*) while the *deva* were those who had agreed to drink it. The most discussed symbolism is that in the Song of Solomon (2: 4): 'He brought me to the banqueting house' (literally, 'house of wine'). Origen said that the wine was joy, the Holy Spirit and the Truth; St John of the Cross that it was 'God's wisdom in respect of the understanding; his love in respect of the will and his delights in respect of the memory.' To St Clement of Alexandria, wine was to bread what the contemplative life and gnosis were to the active life and to faith, while for Elias the Ecdosite, pure contemplation was 'the scented wine which makes those who drink it take leave of their senses', simple prayer being beginners' bread. Wine had the same attraction for Muslim mystics, Nabulusi calling it 'the drink of divine love', while in Sufism wine is the symbol of knowledge through initiation and this is the preserve of the few. Ibn 'Arabī called it 'knowledge of spiritual states' (BENA, CORM, DANA, PHIL, GUEM, KALL, MAST, SAIR, SCHC, SCHG).

In Old Testament tradition, wine was first and foremost a symbol of joy (Psalm 104: 14; Ecclesiastes 9: 7) and then, in more general terms, of all the gifts which God lavishes upon mankind (Genesis 27: 28).

Since wine was the drink of the gods in the religions which surrounded them (Deuteronomy 32: 37–8), it is understandable that the Children of Israel should have acknowledged its sacred properties and employed it in their worship (Exodus 29: 40, where the idea of the food of the godhead is still in evidence). Again, it is easy to understand why, because it was so closely linked with pagan worship, it should in certain circumstances have been prohibited. Jeremiah (35) mentions the sect of the Rechabites, who rejected wine among other signs of suspicious religious borrowings from these neighbours by the Israelites in their now settled state.

Because it carried with it intoxication, wine also became the symbol of the blindness with which God afflicted both individuals and peoples for their rebelliousness and lack of faith, the more severely to punish them (Jeremiah 25: 15ff., 27ff.). Sometimes through a process of symbolic shorthand, wine symbolizes God's wrath (Isaiah 51: 17; Revelation 9: 15).

In the New Testament, and especially in the writings of St John, the word is charged with a definite symbolic meaning, although it is not always easy to determine precisely what that meaning is. A case in point is the changing of water into wine at the marriage-feast at Cana (John 2): should we in fact follow early Christian commentators and take this as a symbol of the Eucharist?

Jesus at the Last Supper gives expression to a different symbolism with the words 'This is my blood of the new testament [covenant]' (Mark 14: 24), an allusion to the blood-sacrifice of the Old Covenant described in Exodus 24: 8. The comparison is explained by the phrase, in fact seldom used, that wine is the blood of the grape (Genesis 49: 11; Deuteronomy 32: 14). In post-Exilic times, blood may have been replaced by wine in sacrifices.

The motifs of vines, grape-harvests and wine which proliferate in funerary art show that the drink was regarded as a symbol of immortality. The influence of Dionysiac art is perfectly clear in the countless examples of these motifs. Pagan infection counted for much, no doubt, in Herod's innovative introduction of a golden vine into the Temple at Jerusalem (Josephus, *Jewish Antiquities* 15, 395; *Jewish Wars* 5, 210).

Islam employed the Bacchic symbolism of wine both in respect of the pleasures of the flesh and to denote mystical intoxication, just as praise of wine was to be found in the Song of Solomon, Classical mystery religions, the legend of the Grail and Christian worship. In Hebrew, the words 'wine' (*yain*) and 'mystery' (*sōd*) have the same numerical value – seventy. 'In Islam, the prohibition of wine-drinking adds still greater strength and scope to wine as a symbol' (DERV p. 120).

Sufis naturally interpreted in a mystical sense the verses of the Koran which say: 'and drink of a pure beverage shall their Lord give them' (76: 21) and 'choice wine shall be given them to quaff' (83: 25), as well as those which mention drinking, wine, chalices, springs and goblets (Koran 47: 16; 37: 44–66; 56: 18; 78: 34; 76: 5 and so on).

The great Persian mystic, Bāyazīd of Bisthām (d. 875), wrote: 'I am the drinker, the cup-bearer and the wine. In the world where all becomes One, all things are One.'

In his commentary for initiates upon Shabistarī's *Gulshan-i-Rāz* (The Rose-garden of Mystery), Lāhijī wrote that in this treatise of Sufi mysticism wine 'stands for love, ardent longing and spiritual intoxication'. Shabistarī himself wrote that 'wine, torchlight and beauty are manifestations of God.

Drink deep of the wine of annihilation. Drink the wine, for the cup is the face of the Friend.'

Ibn al-Fārid devoted his great poem *Khamrīya* (The Wine Ode) to the praise of wine, beginning it with: 'We drank to the memory of the Beloved a wine which intoxicated us before the vine itself was created.' Nabulusi, commenting on these words, wrote: 'Wine signifies the draught of Divine Love . . . for this love engenders intoxication and utter forgetfulness of all that exists in this world.' He added: 'This wine is the everlasting Love Divine which is to be seen in the manifestations of creation. . . . And this wine is light, too, the light which shines everywhere. And, again, it is the Wine of true Life and of the true vocation. All things have drunk of this wine' (DERV p. 126).

Jalāl-al-Dīn Rūmī, greatest of all Sufi mystic poets, writes in the same terms, alluding to the pre-existence of souls: 'Before a garden, a vine or a grape existed in this world, our souls were intoxicated with immortal wine.' Such symbolism is constant and, as constantly, is to be found the symbolism of the cup-bearer (God dispensing his grace, or the Master of mystical knowledge and so on) and of the tavern, which may denote the place where friends and confidants, that is to say those who share the same spiritual secrets, come together or, in an even more mystical sense, a centre of initiation. Of course this symbolism may also be employed to denote the pleasures of the flesh, as by Omar Khayyām and others.

Dionysos intoxicated his worshippers with wine, the bearer of joy. 'Wine, blood of the vine, in which they believed fire united with the principle of moistness and which alternately exalted and terrified their souls, was wonderfully fitted to symbolize the element of the godhead which the Ancients believed they saw displayed in the fruition of plant life' (SECG p. 290).

However, use of wine was 'forbidden in libations to the gods of the Underworld since it was the joy-bringing drink of the living. It was also forbidden to Mnemosyne and the Muses because it affects the memory. (These explanations are purely hypothetical.)' (LAVD p. 1013)

Wine is the symbol of hidden life and of secret and triumphant youth. Through this, and because of its red colour, it is a technicological reconditioning of the blood. The blood which the wine-press creates is the sign of a crushing victory over the bloodless flight of time . . . . The archetype of the sacred drink and of wine may be compared by mystics on a one-to-one basis with the sexual and maternal properties endowed in milk. In the childlike enjoyment of mystics, natural milk and artificial wine become one and the same.

(DURS p. 278)

Raki, the sacred drink of Anatolian Shi'ite sects, is called *arslan sütü* (lion's milk) in their secret language. As we know, Shi'ites regard the lion as a manifestation of Ali.

The Turkic and Tatar peoples of central Asia attribute the invention of intoxicants to the hero of the Flood. This hero is the patron of the dead, of drunkards and of small children.

The Bektashi word *dem* means 'wine', 'breath' and 'time'. The Pseudo-Dionysius the Areopagite compares God's teachings with wine, from their ability to reinvigorate.

Wines, nectars, meads and ambrosias all derive from the Heavens and are linked to celestial fire. In the Vedas, soma was brought by a solar bird, the eagle, to mankind. As the male drink above all others and an expression of fecundating and burning desire, it was associated with the horse in hymns. However, this glorification of manly strength, wholeheartedly linked to wine, brought with it the realization of an antagonistic duality of Heaven and Earth, resolved in intoxication at the same time as it was perceived.

In dreams, wine may be regarded as an element of the psyche possessing higher properties and related to a positive inner life. 'The soul appreciates the miracle of wine as a divine miracle of life – the transformation of what was terrestrial and plant into a spirit free from all bonds' (AEPR p. 167).

wings Wings are above all the symbol of flying, that is of weightlessness, dematerialization, release – whether of soul or spirit – and of transition to the subtle body. All traditions, whether Far Eastern, shamanistic, Muslim or Judeo-Christian, from East to West, agree on this point, for the flight of the soul and that of the shaman are both one and the same adventure in so far as they both predicate a freeing from the force of gravity, which alchemists expressed in the image of the eagle devouring the lion. In no tradition are wings there for the taking: they must be won at the cost of what is often a long and perilous lesson in initiation and purification. Here again, comparisons may be made between accounts left by shamans, those of great Christian or Sufi mystics and countless allegorical tales, among the most important of which are those of Hans Andersen. Contrary to popular belief, the wings of the saint in prayer are not a spiritual vision, as the belief in levitation bears witness.

Lightness and the ability to fly were properties of the Taoist Immortals and this was the way in which they were able to reach the Isles of the Immortals. The very etymology of the ideograms which denote them makes their power to rise into the air apparent. Their own especial diet made down or feathers grow on their bodies and their habits were sometimes akin to those of birds.

The term 'flight' has been universally applied to the soul in its aspiration towards a higher than human condition. This flight or escape from the body takes place through the crown of the head, according to a symbolism discussed under DOME. Apparently Taoism envisaged the flight of the 'subtle' body, which was none other than the 'Embryo of Immortality'.

Wings are also signs of the faculty of comprehension; as the *Brāhmana* puts it, 'He who understands has wings'; while the *Rig-Veda* says that the intellect is swifter than any bird. This is also why angels, actual, or symbolizing spiritual states, have wings.

Again, quite naturally, wings and feathers are related to Air, the subtle element above all others. Thanks to the feathers which grew from his arms, the heavenly architect Vishvakarma was enabled to complete his task as a Demiurge, as though with the bellows of a forge (COOH, ELIY, ELIM, GRIF, KALL, SILI).

In Christian tradition, wings signify light and airy motion and symbolize the *pneuma*, or Spirit. In the Old Testament they are a constant symbol of the spirituality or spiritualization of the beings provided with them, whether in human or animal shape. They relate to the godhead and to anything which may approach it after undergoing a transformation, such, for example, as the angels or the human soul. When wings are mentioned in relation to a bird, this most often concerns the dove, signifying the Holy Spirit. Because of its spiritualization, the soul itself possesses wings in the sense given to them in Psalm 55: 6: 'Oh that I had wings like a dove! for then would I fly away, and be at rest.' To have wings, therefore, is to leave earthly things behind and to attain to the heavenly.

The Church Fathers and mystics constantly employ the motif of wings, although they derive from Plato (*Phaedrus* 246). Holy Scripture speaks of the wings of God. They denote his blissful state and his incorruptibility. 'Hide me under the shadow of thy wings' (Psalm 17: 8); 'Therefore the children of men put their trust under the shadow of thy wings' (Psalm 36: 7). According to St Gregory of Nyssa, if God, the archetype, has wings, then the soul, created in his image, is also winged. While it may have lost its wings as a result of Original Sin, it has the power to regain them in the very tempo of its transformation. Through separating themselves from God, people lose their wings: when they return to him, they regain them. The more strongly winged the soul, the higher it can rise; and the Heaven to which it flies may be compared with a bottomless ABYSS. The soul can go on rising, since it can never reach Heaven in all its fullness. Like the wheel, wings are the normal symbol 'of movement away, of release from conditions of place, and of the entry into an appropriate spiritual state' (CHAS p. 431).

In general, then, wings will be an expression of rising to the sublime and of striving to transcend the human condition. They comprise the most characteristic attribute of the deified individual and of that person's attainment of the heights of Heaven. The symbolism of some images is transformed by the addition of wings. For example, serpents, signs of spiritual depravity, when winged become symbols of spiritualization and the godhead.

Together with sublimation, wings are the mark of release and of victory and are awarded to heroes who slay monsters or repulsive, savage, fabulous animals.

Hermes (Mercury) is well known for his winged heels, but Gaston Bachelard regards the 'heels which have become dynamic' as a symbol of the night traveller, that is of dreams of voyaging. This dynamic image which we experience is far more significant in terms of dream-reality than any pair of wings attached to the shoulders. 'Often dreams of beating wings are dreams of falling. To stifle our vertigo we flap our arms and this may make wings grow from our shoulders. But natural dream-flight, positive flight is what we do each night, it is no rhythmical flight, but duration of a leap forward, the swift creature of a moment which has become dynamic.' Bachelard goes on to compare winged heels with the shoes known as 'light feet' which Buddhist saints wore on their journeys through the air, and with the flying shoes in folk tales and with seven-league boots. 'The individual dreamer's powers of flight reside in his feet' he concludes. 'And so we shall allow our metapoetical researches to describe the wings which sprout from the heels as dream-wings' (BACS pp. 39–40). In this context the wing carries greater weight as a symbol of dynamism than as a symbol of spiritualization. When sprouting from the heel it does not necessarily imply a notion of sublimation, but rather of the release of our most important creative powers. Like the prophet, the poet has wings when he is inspired. (See also FLIGHT.)

winnowing-basket Because it was used to separate the good grain from dirt and chaff, the winnowing-basket was the symbol of choice. St John the Baptist, who went before, symbolically attributed its use to the one who would baptize with fire and the Spirit. 'Whose [winnowing-]fan is in his hand, and he will thoroughly purge his [threshing-]floor, and will gather the wheat into his garner; but the chaff he will burn with fire unquenchable' (Luke 3: 17).

The winnowing-basket or fan is the emblem of the distribution of rewards and punishments (Devoucoux), as well as that of initiation and of predestination.

In Hindu iconography, the winnowing-basket is the attribute of several ill-omened deities, among them Dhumāvat who personifies destitution and destruction. In this context the implement undoubtedly bears the sense of scattering, the act of throwing to the winds. It is also the attribute of Sītalā, the goddess of smallpox, who divides or separates death from life. She is said to have ears as big as winnowing-baskets and this is also a characteristic of the elephant-headed god Ganesha. Ganesha's ears winnow uncleanness, evil-speaking and wickedness, and thus open the way to knowledge and spiritual perfection (DANA, DEVA, MALA).

witch Jung regarded witches as a projection of the male *anima,* that is of the primitive female aspect which survives in the male unconscious. Witches give this detestable shadow a physical form of which they are unable to divest themselves and at the same time assume a formidable power. For women, witches are female versions of the scapegoat to which they transfer the darker side of their impulses (ADLJ p. 18), but this transference is in fact secret involvement in the imagined nature of witches. Until the dark forces of the unconscious are brought out into the daylight of knowledge, feeling and action, the witch will continue to live within us. She is the fruit of repression, embodying 'the desires, fears and other tendencies within our psyche which are incompatible with our egos, either because they are too infantile or for some other reason' (ADLJ p. 18). Jung noted that 'the anima . . . is often personified as a witch or a priestess' since women have stronger links with the forces of darkness and the spirit world (JUNS p. 177). The witch is the antithesis of the idealized image of womanhood.

Witches have been regarded from another angle as the deliberate perversion, under Christian influence, of priestesses, sibyls and female druidic wonder-workers. Unlike the initiates of Classical antiquity who joined the Visible to the Invisible and the human to the divine, they wore diabolical and hideous disguises, but the unconscious called up the fairy, of whom the witch, serving the Devil, came thereafter to be regarded simply as a caricature. As creatures of the unconscious, witches and fairies are ladies with a long history behind them, recorded in the psyche, and with a complicated development of personality transference which legend has shaped, clothed and brought to life as hostile characters (LOEF pp. 240–3).

Similarly the warlock or sorcerer is 'the manifestation of the irrational content of the psyche' (LOEF p. 31). External action and assistance will not free the victim from the grip of the sorcerer and from subjection to him. This can only be done by an inward change, which initially takes the form of a positive attitude to the unconscious, and by gradual integration into the conscious personality of all the elements emerging from the unconscious. The sorcerer is simply a symbol of undisciplined and untamed creative energy which may be unleashed against the interests of the ego, the family or the group. The warlock within, who has charge of 'the dark powers of the unconscious', knows how to use them and by their means to ensure his power over others. He can only be disarmed by making the same forces available to consciousness and by identifying the self with them through integration, instead of with the sorcerer by rejection.

Whether in Africa or in other parts of the world, sorcerers never pretend to be the animals, birds or reptiles on the masks which they wear, merely identifying themselves with the particular creature through a sort of symbolic kinship, all its strength coming from their own conviction and from the transference to them of the fears felt by those around them. Sorcerers are the antithesis of the idealized image of the father and the Demiurge. They are the aberrant forces of power, the nocturnal aspect of the shaman and medicine man, guardians of death as the latter are of life in the invisible world.

Grillot de Givry regarded warlocks and witches as the priests and priestesses of devil worship. They come into being in Christian countries through belief in the Devil preached by a Satanic Church. Hence the Christian Church takes black magic very seriously as a manifestation of Satan. 'The chief function of the sorcerer – as his name indicates – was to cast a *sors*, or spell, over those to whom, for some reason or another, he wished evil. He invoked the curse of Hell upon them as the priest called down the blessing of Heaven, and on this earth he was in complete rivalry with the ecclesiastical world' (GRIA p. 51). Alternatively the sorcerer by means of his alliance with the Devil filled his pockets or satisfied his private malice in opposition to the laws of God. Again, the sorcerer might practise all sorts of methods of divination, seeking out nature's secrets to obtain magical powers, yet again in contravention of Christian laws. The frontier between magic and science was, above all, determined by moral conscience and many saints, the forerunners of research scientists, were regarded as wizards superficially.

wizard See under WITCH above.

wolf The dog-wolf is synonymous with the savage in everyday English and the she-wolf with the depraved in everyday French, but the language of symbols, as one might suspect, gives these animals infinitely more complex meanings. This is the result, in the first place, of the fact that, as with all other symbolic vectors, they may be endowed with positive as well as with negative properties. The symbolism of the wolf would be regarded as positive from the fact that it can see in the dark. Hence it becomes a symbol of light, of the Sun, of the warrior and hero and of the mythic ancestor. This is the meaning attached to the beast in Scandinavia and among the Ancient

Greeks. To the first it was an attribute of Belen and to the latter of Lycian ('wolfish') Apollo.

The founder of the Chinese and Mongol dynasties was the Celestial Blue Wolf. Its strength and fighting abilities provided an allegory which the Turks carried down to the twentieth century, since Mustapha Kemal, who called himself Ataturk, 'Father of the Turks', was known to his followers as the Grey Wolf.

The Turkish people gathered round him and fought to regain their own identity, threatened by the decline of the Ottoman Empire. In so doing, they revived an ancient image, that of Genghis Khan's mythic ancestor, the blue wolf, a manifestation of the power of the light of Heaven (thunderbolt). Because it had mated with the white or yellow fawn, standing for the Earth, it gave his people a claim to have sprung from the sacred marriage of Heaven and Earth.

The Indians of the North American prairies seem to have attached the same symbolic meaning to this animal. The war-song of the Prairie Indians runs: 'A Lone Wolf I am . . . I roam in many places' (ALEC p. 189).

The Chinese also had a celestial wolf (the star Sirius) which was the watchman outside the Heavenly Palace (the Great Bear). Its polar character made them attribute the wolf to the north. It should be emphasized at this point that the watchman's role has replaced the animal's ferocious aspect and thus, in some areas of Japan, wolves are invoked to protect the people against other wild animals. This conjures up an image of exuberant strength expending itself in blind savagery.

The she-wolf which suckled Romulus and Remus was not solar and celestial, but terrestrial, not to say chthonian. Thus in both instances the animal remains linked to notions of fertility. In Turkic regions folk belief has preserved this heritage down to the present day. Among the Yakut in Siberia the most highly valued bezoar (a hard mass of material in the stomach) is that of the wolf, while in Anatolia, that is at the other end of the geographical range of the Altaic peoples, barren women still call upon the wolf so that they may bear children. In Kamchatka 'at the yearly October festival, an image of a wolf is made from straw and kept for a whole year so that the wolf can "marry" the young women in the village. A Samoyed legend is on record of a woman who lived in a cave with a wolf' (ROUF pp. 328–9).

This chthonian or infernal facet of the symbol forms another major aspect which appears to have remained predominant in European folklore. The story of Little Red Riding-Hood might be cited in evidence of this, but it merely re-echoes Greco-Latin mythology where Mormolyce, the wolf which suckled Acheron, was used to threaten children, just like 'the big, bad wolf' of today (GRID p. 303a). Similarly Hades, King of the Underworld, was dressed in a wolf-skin (KRAM p. 226), while the Etruscan deathgod was depicted with wolf's ears; and according to Diodorus Siculus, Osiris, too, was resurrected in the shape of a wolf 'to help his wife and son overcome his evil brother' (ibid.).

This was also the shape given to Lycaean Zeus, to whom human sacrifice to end droughts and other natural disasters was offered during the ages in which crop-magic ruled. Zeus then watered the fields with rain, made the fields fertile and ruled the winds (ELIT p. 78).

The Middle Ages generally depicted warlocks changing into wolves when they set off for their Sabbaths, while, on such occasions, witches wore wolf-skin garters (GRIA). In Spain, the wolf was the warlock's steed. Belief in lycanthropy (transformation into wolf form) and werewolves was current in Europe from Classical times, when Virgil mentions them, and only started to disappear slowly in the seventeenth century. They are one of the components of European folk belief and doubtless an aspect of the wood-spirits. According to Colin de Plancy, 'Bodin states brazenly that in 1542 one morning a hundred and fifty werewolves were to be seen in a square in Constantinople.'

This devourer symbolism is that of the MOUTH, the archetypal image of initiation, connected with the phenomena of the alternations of day and night and of life and death. The mouth devours and regurgitates. It is the initiator assuming, according to place, the shape of the most voracious creature in that particular area – wolf, JAGUAR, CROCODILE or other animal. In Scandinavian mythology the wolf is explicitly described as 'devouring the stars' (DURS p. 82) and bears comparison with the wolf which ate the quail in the *Rig-Veda*. If, as we have observed, the QUAIL is a symbol of light, the wolf's mouth is night, the cavern, the Underworld or the phase of cosmic *pralaya*. Release from the wolf's jaws is dawn, the light of initiation which follows a descent into the Underworld or *kalpa* (CHRC, DANA, DEVA, GUED, GUES, MALA, MASR, RESE, SOUN).

The giant wolf, Fenrir, was one of the most implacable enemies of the Norse gods. The dwarfs' magic was the only thing which could stop him in his tracks, by means of the magic ribbon which none could cut nor snap. In Ancient Egyptian mythology the great conductor of souls is called Anubis, 'he who goes about in the guise of a wild dog' and he was worshipped at Cynopolis as god of the Underworld (see JACKAL).

The jaws of the monstrous wolf which Marie Bonaparte mentions in her self-analysis as being associated with childhood fears consequent upon her mother's death, must remind us, Durand suggests, of Perrault's fairy-tales. 'What big teeth you have, Grandmother! There is therefore a very clear convergence between the bite of members of the dog family and fear of the destructive power of time. In this context Cronos is to be seen with the face of Anubis and of the monster which devours human time and even attacks the stars which measure time itself.'

Mention has already been made of the initiatory significance of this symbol, and it should be added that this gives the wolf, like the dog, a role as conductor of souls. An Algonquin myth shows the wolf in the guise of a brother of the Demiurge Menebuch, the great rabbit, ruling the kingdom of the dead, in the west (MULR p. 253). In Europe one of the wolf's recognized duties was that of conductor of souls. Evidence of this may be found in the words of a Romanian funerary song: 'the wolf knows the way through the forest and will bring you along a smooth path to the King's Son in Paradise.'

Lastly we would observe that the hell-wolf, and especially his mate personifying sexual lust, are among the obstacles along the path of the Muslim pilgrim to Mecca, and loom even larger on the road to Damascus, where they take on the proportions of beasts of the Apocalypse.

womb (see also EMBRYO; LINGAM; RETURN)   Womb symbolism is universally connected with manifestation, natural fertility and even with spiritual regeneration.

There is a widespread mythology of the Earth MOTHER, with an affinity to the womb, the Underworld, to CAVERNS and gorges. Mircea Eliade reminds us that the site of Delphi owes its name to the significance of *delphys* (womb). In other parts of the world springs are said to rise from the womb of Earth. Mines, too, are wombs from which obstetrically-related methods are used to extract minerals, embryos which have matured. Indian tradition held that precious stones grew in the rocks as in a womb. By assimilation, metal-workers' and enamellers' furnaces and the athanor of the alchemists carry the same significance.

The clearest and richest assimilation derives from the Vedas. The womb of the universe is *prakrti*, the Universal Substance which the *Bhagavad Gītā* identifies with Brahmā. 'To me great Brahmā is the womb in which I place the seed.' In the Purānas, this *yoni* is sometimes Vishnu, and the fecundator, Shiva. It is also Shiva's *shakti*, Parvatī. This is why the *yoni,* which it fertilizes, stands for the lingam, Shiva's emblem. Shiva's task of transformer also causes his assimilation to the womb of the universe.

Garbha (womb) was also the receptacle used to hold the sacrificial fire and, since it contained Agni, it contained the universe. The *cella* of the temple, identical with the 'cavern of the heart', was known as the *garbhagrha.* *Garbha* was also a word for stupa, but more specifically for the cavity containing the relics. These were called 'seeds' (*bijā*) and were like the kernels of immortality (*luz* or *sharīra*) which permit the individual to be reborn. Now, although the Vedic womb was the shapeless source of the manifested, it was also the abode of immortality, the central void in the cosmic wheel.

In the rites of the *dīkshā* the place in which the initiate is shut is known as the womb of his rebirth. From Europe to China alchemists quite explicitly envision the return to the womb as a prelude to regeneration and immortality. Residing in the womb is a timeless central state in which, Hindu writings insist, 'one has knowledge of all births.'

The nature of the embryo is, like Agni's, that of fire – it is radiant and can be seen within the mother's womb. The *Majjhima-nikāya* reports this of the Buddha; the Egyptians claimed it for the Sun, and there is a tradition that it was true of Christ, too.

The inverted triangle is the graphic symbol of the *yoni.* The three sides of this triangle are the three *guna* (concentration, dispersion and expansion) which are the basic modalities of nature. The Pythagoreans had a symbol similar to this triangle. Again, in Tantrism the *yoni* corresponds to the *mūladhārachakra,* the womb in which the *kundalinī* slumbers entwined around a lingam of light.

Because the Word *vāk* is the mother of knowledge, the seven vowels of the Sanskrit alphabet are still called the seven wombs, being the seven mothers of speech.

Titus Burckhardt has observed that in Arabic *rahīm* (womb) has the same root as one of the names of God, *ar-Rahmān*, 'the Compassionate'. It is by means of the Reality which this name expresses that the full potentiality of manifestation contained within the Divine Being is brought into existence. Hence *ar-rahmāniyah*, the compassionate bliss of God, may be conceived as the universal womb (BURA, BHAB, COOH, DANA, ELIY, ELIF, ELIM, JACG, JILH, KRAT, SECA, SILI).

A maternal symbol, similar, as we have said, to that of the cavern, it reflects, however, an especial need for tenderness and protection. When seen in adults' dreams it may be the sign of a regressive attitude, of a return to the womb, and of spiritual growth gravely restricted by serious emotional blockages.

While the womb offers protection, it also devours. The Mother is capable of a display of tyranny and cruelty. Of course she feeds her children, but there is the danger that she will keep them at an infantile level and restrict their spiritual growth, making them her puppets. In all mythologies, Mother-goddesses are depicted as despotic providers and overprotective and jealous mothers.

This negative property imparted to the symbol causes it to become a castrational image in the myth of the toothed vagina (see VULVA) which occurs in countless different cultures and which psychoanalysis has discovered to be universal. Doubtless the castrational aspect of the womb occurs because in it are located appetites and desires so voracious as to frighten anyone who does not dare to acknowledge his deep-seated animality.

wood First and foremost wood is matter and is in India the symbol of the universal substance, the *materia prima*. In Ancient Greece, *hyle*, which carries the meaning of primordial matter, literally means 'wood'.

In Ancient China, too, wood was one of the five elements which corresponded to the east and to Spring as well as to the trigram *Chen*, the breaking out of the manifestation and of nature. Plants sprout from the soil together with the thunder hidden in it. The *yang* awakens and begins its ascent.

In the Roman Catholic liturgy, 'wood' is synonymous with the tree of the Cross, as in the words of the Preface at masses of the Passion or of the Cross in the Roman Rite: 'so that . . . he that overcame by the tree, on the tree also might be overcome' (BURA, GRIF).

In Celtic tradition, wood and TREES partake of learning in all its shapes and aspects. The traditional Irish alphabet, ogham, was cut most frequently in wood and only carved in stone on grave monuments. There is complete homonymity between the words for 'learning' and 'wood' in all Celtic languages (Irish, *fid*; Welsh, *gwydd*; Breton, *gwez* (tree) and *gouez*, from the root *gouzout*, 'to know'). Unlike the Gaulish druids, the Irish seldom used oak, but more often yew, hazel or service-tree, literature rarely distinguishing between them. The HAZEL-nut was the fruit of wisdom and knowledge. Birch and apple also played a leading part in the symbolism of the Otherworld. Hazel-WANDS were generally used in magic; however, it was by cutting ogham letters on yew wands that the druid Dallan ('Little Blind Man') regained King Eochaid's wife, Etain, from the *sid* in which her first husband, the god Midir, had hidden her. Wood also played a considerable part in the casting of spells and to overcome Cùchulainn, who had resisted their magic, the children of Calatin enchanted plants and trees so that they changed into warriors armed for battle. The same legendary motif recurred in Cisalpine Gaul and Livy turned it into history in his account of the death of the ex-consul Postumius in 216 BC. The theme also occurs, inverted and taken in a good sense, in the strange Welsh poem attributed to Taliesin, *Kat Godeu*, 'The Battle of the Trees'. In Gaul trees often occur in the names of individuals and of such tribes as the Eburovices, Viducasses, Lemovices and so on (LERD pp. 67–72; CELT 7: *passim*; 15; OGAC 11: 1–10, 185–205).

In general terms, however, the symbolism of wood is constant – it possesses superhuman wisdom and knowledge.

As other peoples, so the Ancient Greeks and Romans dedicated woods, rather than wood, to different deities, and they symbolized the mysterious abode of the godhead. Each god had his especial wood and if he inspired reverential dread there, it was also a place where he was offered worship and prayer. The Romans could neither cut nor prune the trees in a sacred wood without preliminary and expiatory sacrifice. FORESTS and sacred groves were centres of life, reservoirs of refreshment, water and warmth, like a kind of womb, and hence were yet one more maternal symbol. They were the source of regeneration, often occurring in dreams with this significance and revealing the longing for security and renewal. They are a very forcible expression of the unconscious. Underwoods and deep forests of tall trees have also been compared with caverns and grottoes and this resemblance comes out in so many landscape paintings. All of which serves to confirm the symbolism of a vast and inexhaustible reservoir of life and mysterious knowledge. Even today the tradition of sacred groves, the preserve of initiation-societies, remains alive in many regions of Black Africa.

woodpecker In North America the Prairie Indians believed that the woodpecker averted such natural disasters as storm and lightning, hence its feathers were used in certain ritual ceremonies (ALEC p. 118). For the Pawnees, the bird was a symbol of security and an assurance of the continuity of life. They have a mythic story of the woodpecker arguing with the turkey as to which was entitled to be called protector of the human race. The turkey based her claims upon her prolificacy and the fact that no other bird laid so large a clutch of eggs as she. However, the woodpecker won the argument on the basis of that security which alone can ensure that life will go on. Admittedly she laid a smaller clutch but no predator could reach her nest in the hollow of a tree-trunk and when the birds left their nest they were sure to die of old age. The woodpecker was sensible and careful (FLEH).

The Semang Negrito regard the woodpecker as the culture-hero who first brought fire to mankind (SCHP p. 174).

In Ancient Greek and Roman tradition, the sight and the sound of a woodpecker hammering were taken as lucky omens by hunters. King Picus, too, famed for his powers of divination, was metamorphosed into a woodpecker and the bird was honoured as a prophet. It guided travellers on their way, and it was a woodpecker which flew with food to the cave in which Romulus and Remus lived as children. It was the bird sacred to Mars.

In all these traditions the woodpecker is regarded as the symbol of protection and of security. 'The woodpecker is undoubtedly a symbol of a return to the womb from the fact that it makes nest-holes in trees. This protective bird stands for re-entry within the mother, a liberating image of thought and desire born of introversion' (JUNG).

wood-sorrel (katabami) This plant, with its arrow-shaped leaves, is highly regarded in Japan as an expression of elegant simplicity and from the distant past has featured in the arms of the greatest Japanese families. One variety produces a single white flower at the end of its stem. Since this blossoms at Easter, country people call the plant Alleluia. It is, as it were, herald of the resurrection.

Despite its taste, like that of common sorrel bitter but refreshing, tonic and stimulant, the plant is also the symbol of comforting affection.

word The Dogon distinguish two sorts of words which they call 'dry' words and 'moist' words. The dry, or primordial, word was an attribute of the primeval Spirit, Amma, before he had begun the task of creation, and was undifferentiated speech, unaware of itself. It resides within mankind, but mankind does not know it. It has the potential property of divine thought, but at our microcosmic level is the unconscious.

'Moist' words germinated, like the principle of life itself, within the Cosmic Egg and they were the words given to mankind. They comprise audible sounds, regarded as one of the ways in which the procreative powers of the male are expressed, on a par with his semen. The word enters the woman's EAR – her other sexual organ – and then twines down into her womb to fertilize the seed and create the embryo. The word, in this same spiral form, is the light which descends on the Sun's rays to take physical shape in the Earth's womb as red copper. Moist words, like water, light, spirals and red copper, are simply one of the different manifestations – or meanings – of a basic symbol, the world made manifest, or of its lord, the water-god Nommo (GRIH).

The sum of Bambara mystical knowledge is contained in the symbolism of the numbers one to twenty-two and the Bambara regard the primordial oneness, one, as the figure of the Lord of the Word and of the Word itself. Within the same symbol, notions of chieftaincy, of the rights of primogeniture, of head and consciousness are all comprehended (DIEB). At another level and within a different context, a similar notion emerges from Jacob Boehme's view of the Word of God as being the life or motion of the godhead and containing all language, colour and virtue.

The notion of the fecundating word, carrying the seeds of creation and with its place in the dawn of that creation as the first manifestation of the godhead and pre-existence before any created form, is to be found in the cosmogonic concepts of many peoples. We have noted it in Africa, among the Dogon, and it recurs among the Guarani Indians of Paraguay who believed that God created speech as the foundation, before he gave physical form to water, fire, the Sun, to life-giving mists and lastly to the primordial Earth (CADG).

Many South American Indian tribes associate the Word with the principles of life and of immortality. This is especially true of the Taulipang who believe that the individual is endowed with five souls, of which only one reaches the other world after death. This is the soul which contains the Word and which leaves the body at regular intervals during sleep (METB).

Leenhardt records the Kanaka belief in New Caledonia that the word is an act, the very first act ever done. From this derives the terrifying power of the curse, traditionally regarded as the ultimate weapon, not because of the strength of the person uttering it since the individual has no intrinsic power, but because that act is the word of God or of the Totem invoked to cut the thread of life and annihilate the person cursed (LEEC p. 254).

In Biblical tradition,

> The Old Testament speaks of the Word of God, and of his wisdom, present with God before the world was made . . . ; by it all things were created; it is sent to earth to reveal the hidden designs of God; it returns to him with its work done. . . . For John, too, . . . the Word existed before the world in God . . . ; it has come on earth . . . ; being sent by the Father . . . to perform a task . . . namely, to deliver a message of salvation to the world . . . ; with its mission accomplished it returns to the Father. . . . The incarnation enabled the New Testament, and especially John, to see this separately and eternally existent Word-Wisdom as a person.
>
> (BIBJ John 1: 1; with full references to the relevant Biblical texts)

To Greek thinkers, Logos meant not only the word, phrase, speech, but also the reason and the intellect, ideas and the depths of a being's meaning, even divine thought itself. The Stoics regarded the word as the rationality immanent in the universal structure. Such notions were foundations for the speculations of the Church Fathers and of later theologians which over the centuries have evolved to analyse the teachings of Holy Scripture and especially the theology of the Word.

Notwithstanding differences of belief and dogma, generally speaking the word symbolizes the display of an intelligence in speech, in the nature of individuals and in the continuous creation of the universe. It is the individual's truth and light. This general and symbolic explanation in no sense runs counter to explicit belief in the Word of God and the Word made Flesh. In his treatise on *Divine Names*, the Pseudo-Dionysius the Areopagite laid the foundations for a synthesis in an especially pregnant section (PSEN p. 19). The word is the purest symbol of the manifestation of the individual, an individual capable of thought and of self-expression, or of the individual who is known to and communicates with another.

world The symbolism of the world, with its three levels, celestial, terrestrial and infernal, corresponds to the three levels of being or to the three modes of spiritual action. The inner life is thus projected into space in accordance with the general process of myth-making (see CONSTELLATION; PARADISE).

The location of these worlds in imaginary space is determined by their relationship with each other – the lower world lying beneath the upper world, the intermediate world lying between them. The words used to describe them and their arrangement in vertical order set these worlds within ascensional movement and dialectic and these emphasize their significance in terms of psyche and spirit. The intermediate world receives light from the upper world and the light stops there and goes down no further into the lower world. The intermediate world, however, only receives light to the degree to which it craves it, lays itself open to it or directs itself towards it. It is also liable to paths of darkness, those breaches in morality symbolized by rocky fissures, through which one slides into the Underworld.

Sometimes 'lower' simply denotes the Earth in relation to Heaven and not this Underworld. The lower world is an intermediate place of trial and inner transformation from which the spirit is intended to ascend but where it risks becoming depraved and perverted and falling into Hell.

The lower world is a phrase conveying the sense of movement, of ebb and flow, of repetition and of cycles. The individual eats only to become hungry again, drinks only to become thirsty, indulges in pleasure only to covet still more. All things are filled and emptied and suffer fresh satiety. This is why the unrighteous are said to walk round in circles, like donkeys rotating a millstone. It is in this sense that St Gregory of Nyssa compares the man involved in the cares of the world with the child building a sand-castle. The wind has only to blow or the sand to crumble and the castle falls down. Nevertheless, this motion can become a precious ally in the structure of human perfection and individual transformation. Human progress depends upon this continuous movement which governs humanity and becomes one of its assets.

(DAVS)

The lower world is a symbol of movement and the upper world one of eternal stillness.

The Ancient Egyptian concept of the lower world varies with religious belief: 'Sometimes the Egyptians saw it as a replica in reverse of this earth, with the sky inverted, the Nile and the sun. . . . At other times they imagined it as a vast expanse of water, where the night sun, after dying in the evening, recovered its powers of regeneration which had already enabled it to emerge at the time of the creation' (POSD p. 53). It was in this world of fields and marshes that the dead person travelled and worked. However, during the course of the millennia of Egyptian history, ideas on the nature of the other world underwent considerable change. Nonetheless they may be summarized as follows:

Daytime was reserved for quietly remaining in the tomb, with occasional excursions on earth. At night the dead man accompanied the sun on a subterranean journey to the other world, towing his boat and stopping on the way in the fields of Osiris. When the rays of dawn returned the sun to our world, the wandering soul flew in haste to his tomb to find shade and coolness in it.

(POSD p. 99)

The Ancient Greeks and Romans conceived of many paths linking this world with the Underworld, the realm of the living with that of the dead. The craters of volcanoes, fissures in the rocks down which streams vanished and the ends of the Earth were all believed to be such paths, while, at the other extreme, the peaks of high mountains communicated with Heaven. Furthermore, they conceived of a Heaven on several levels and an Underworld to match, the lowest level of which, Tartarus, was the prison of deposed deities. This Underworld (see HADES) was characterized by darkness, cold, fears, torments and an impoverished and spectral life, while light, warmth, joy and freedom reigned in Heaven. The Fortunate Isles, the abode of the blessed, and the Lands of the Hyperboreans were set aside for sages and heroes, images of a Heaven on a level lower than that of Olympian bliss reserved for the gods and for deified heroes. From Homer and Aristophanes to Virgil and Plutarch there are many descriptions of descents into the Underworld which bear witness to a strange fertility of imagined horrors and enjoyment in releasing a host of terrifying creations.

The Maya held the main attributes of the Underworld, home of the inner force of the Earth and of the aged Earth–Moon goddess, to be the water-lily, ear of maize, sea-shell, the colour black, the gods of the numbers five, seven and thirteen, the dog, the bone and the glyptic attributes in carvings of the death-god, the god of the number ten, with eyes and three dots or rings in a line scattered over his hair (THOH).

In the TAROT, the World, or the Crown of the Magi, is an expression of reward, of the crowning achievement, of the fulfilment of endeavour, ela-tion, success, enlightenment, public recognition and unforeseen good for-tune. In astrology it corresponds to the House. Gérard van Rijnberk identifies the World with the Wheel of Fortune (tenth major arcanum) because in some versions of the pack the woman is depicted standing upon a globe rather than surrounded by a garland, thus providing fresh arguments in favour of the relationship between the Tarot and the astrological Houses.

The World is the last numbered card in the Tarot and the twenty-first major arcanum, symbolizing growth brought to its full flowering since 'the Tarot is made up of groups of three and seven cards giving the number TWENTY-ONE the properties of the highest form of synthesis. It corresponds to the entire range of manifestation and hence with the World, the fruit of continuous creation' (WIRT p. 248).

A naked maiden, flesh coloured, with a veil thrown over her left shoulder and hanging down to and hiding her sexual organs, holding a wand in each hand – the JUGGLER held one in his left hand to catch the vital fluids – stands facing us at her full height. Her right foot rests on a narrow band of yellow earth, her left leg bent behind her right knee. (Both the EMPEROR and the HANGING MAN are shown in equivalent positions, the sign of the intention to concentrate one's strength.) The maiden is in the centre of a garland of long, narrow, black-veined leaves, successively blue, red and yellow. The ends are tied by a cruciform red knot. In the lower corners of the card are a flesh-coloured horse and a golden lion, and in the upper ones an eagle and an angel. These are generally described as the symbols of the four Evangelists, ignoring the fact that in his vision Ezekiel did not see a horse, but an ox (which was later made to correspond to St Luke). The better interpretation of this card is that they are symbols of the four elements, the horse for Earth, the lion for Fire, the eagle for Air and the angel, who appears to be carrying a cloud, for fecundating Water. They might also be symbols of the four points of the compass and of cosmic harmony, 'the eagle, the symbol of the east, of morning and of the vernal equinox; the lion, of the south and the Summer solstice; the ox [in this context the horse], of evening, the west and the autumnal equinox; the man [in this context the angel], of night, the south and the Winter solstice' (J. A. Vaillant in MARD p. 318).

On the psychological plane, the following explanation might be provided.

The horse is flesh-coloured and the only figure without a halo. Since, in the Tarot, this is the colour of the human, it would seem that flesh and blood without the halo of sublimation should in this context symbolize the individual human being in so far as he or she is the basis and starting-point for all spiritual development. The lion is yellow, a solar colour, but it has a flesh-coloured halo. We are still in a world comprising the physical and the spiritual, at the foot of the card, and yet the human dominates the bestial and the physical is on the road to spiritualization. The eagle in the right upper corner is golden-yellow like the lion, but has BLUE wings, reminding us of those worn by the Cupid on the sixth major arcanum (the LOVERS) and those of the DEVIL. These are the wings of the dark powers of the soul which can either be sublimated or turned in a harmful direction, depending upon the use to which we put our unconscious or our intuition. In this context the RED halo enlightens us since it symbolizes spirit controlling instinct. Lastly there is the angel, clothed in blue and white, with wings as red as his halo, clearly breaking clear of the border round the card. He will symbolize the Spirit, that highest quality which should motivate all action and be the fulfilment of all development. The red recurs at the foot, middle and top of the garland since the Spirit in its oneness is simultaneously the starting-point, the centre and the goal. The central figure has no halo, but the garland which surrounds her and on which she leans with her left hand is the almond-shaped mandorla (see ALMOND), the symbol of the marriage of Earth and Heaven, which may as easily surround the bodies of Our Lady or of Christ as it does Hindu deities. The woman herself is not standing still. The veil hanging from her shoulders looks wind-blown and her pose, balanced upon one foot, suggests movement, generator of matter; 'The World is in a whirl of movement, an endless dance in which nothing is still' (WIRT p. 248).

Thus the twenty-first major arcanum is simultaneously the sum of the world and of mankind – the world continuously created by the harmonious motion which keeps its elements in balance and mankind in its spiritual ascent. Thus depicted, the world is the symbol of structures which counterbalance one another, better expressed by Gilbert Durand as a structure of 'balancing antagonisms'.

worm Worms are symbols of life reborn from corruption and death. Thus, in a Chinese legend, the human race derived from the worms from the corpse of the primordial being, while in the Icelandic *Gylfaginning*, the gods commanded the worms within the corpse of the giant Ymir to assume human shape and human reason (HARA p. 82).

A similar myth recurs among the South American Cashihuana Indians; in it the first humans appeared after the flood from the bodies of the giants who had been the earlier inhabitants of the Earth (METS). (See also EXCREMENT.)

This concept would serve to confirm Jung's interpretation of the worm as symbolizing the destructive aspect of the libido, instead of its fecundating aspect. In the biological process, the worm marks the stage preceding dissolution and decomposition. In relation to the inorganic it points the way leading up from primordial energy to life; in relation to higher organisms, it is regression, or the initial and larval stage.

King Conchobar of Ulster was born clutching a worm in either hand. This motif may be compared with that of the serpents which Herakles (Hercules) strangled in his cradle, but such comparisons may be ill-founded. We are more probably concerned here with a transformation and a transition to a higher state, symbolized by the temporary larval state. This is true of the births of a number of characters in myth. Cùchulainn was born of the worm his mother, Dechtire, swallowed when drinking from a bronze goblet. The two bulls in the *Cattle Raid of Cooley* were born from the royal swineherds who were changed into worms and swallowed respectively by a cow from the north (Ulster) and a cow from the south (Connaught) (CHAB pp. 835–42; OGAC 12: p. 85; 17: pp. 363ff.).

In all these legends worms should be regarded as symbolizing the passage from Earth to light, from death to life and from a larval state to spiritual release.

Nevertheless, in dreams worms are interpreted as images of undesirable intruders who come to snatch away or destroy someone or something which you hold very dear (TEIR p. 98), or else mean that some physical situation turns to disaster (SEPR p. 278).

wormwood   As its Greek name (*apsinthios*, without sweetness) might imply, this aromatic plant symbolizes grief, mainly in the shape of bitterness, and in particular that grief caused by absence. However, even in Ancient Greece it was used to flavour wines and the Romans used it in an allegedly tonic drink for their athletes.

In the Book of Revelation, 'Wormwood' was the name of a star which flamed like a torch and which symbolized, in historic terms, the King of Babylon who was to lay Israel waste and, prophetically, Satan. 'And the third angel sounded, and there fell a great star from heaven, burning as it were a lamp, and it fell upon the third part of the rivers, and upon the fountains of waters; And the name of the star is called Wormwood: and the third part of the waters became wormwood; and many men died of the waters, because they were made bitter' (Revelation 8: 10–11).

Christian commentators interpret the fall of the star Wormwood as one of those cosmic catastrophes which will herald the Great Day of the Lord, that is, the end of the world and the Last Judgement. The fallen star will torment the inhabitants of Earth with a deadly bitterness, but what is peculiar is that this torment and these deaths will be the result of the waters turning bitter. If, at this point, one turns to the general symbolism of WATER, the primeval source of life, one is inclined to interpret this Wormwood as a disaster sent from Heaven to poison the very wells of life. One thinks of Hiroshima or of a nuclear explosion which would fill the waters with deadly radioactivity, or again of chemicals seeping into the water table through excessive use of pesticides and fertilizers in agriculture.

On an inner level and from the psychoanalytic viewpoint, Wormwood might be said to symbolize a perversion of the procreative drive, a poisoning of the springs, the waters made bitter.

Wotan (Odin)   The god with an insatiable appetite for more battles, greater power, more pleasure and more women, who sought to make his will the law governing all things and all creatures and who was ever bent upon absolute power, was the archetype of a Faust. He was also the god of the dead who quartered the battlefields to sacrifice fresh victims to the VALKYRIES. As a symbol of blind violence he travelled wrapped in a cloak of midnight blue, his face, with its single eye, concealed by a broad-brimmed hat. He always appeared when least expected. Wagner's interpretation created a more complex personality. The more it developed, the feeling of power fell prey to doubt, anxiety and despair. The development of the inner symbolism of Wotan's character reveals the internal contradictions of power, since not one of his achievements escaped the inexorable law of destruction and death. The god himself submitted to his fate, like nature omnipotent in creating life, but powerless to avoid death.

wrapping In China, the act of wrapping anything has always followed an unchanging rule which pays no regard to the shape of the object to be wrapped. The paper or other wrapping material is set before the packer, so that each corner is oriented upon one of the four points of the compass, while the object itself remains in the centre to provide the fifth point so dear to the Chinese, becoming the centre of the world and the object of almost holy attention. In this process there is no need of string and the parcel never comes undone. However, and above all, the object so wrapped acquires the properties of a small universe, the centre of care, attention and good wishes.

As we know, the art of wrapping parcels in Japan is something everybody practises, and with the greatest care and attention. European Christmas wrappings are nothing by comparison with the humblest Japanese parcel. According to Jean Barthes's thoughts on the subject, it is as if the object, as though concealed by the multiplicity of material, such as tissue paper, wrapping paper, boards and so on, ultimately loses all importance and might be described as having only symbolic value. It might be more accurate to say that wrapping, which is the gesture of giving in physical shape, in the end becomes a thought (BARS p. 60), behind which the contents of the parcel shrink to nothing. The symbolic contents – and hence the sum of what is signified that is hidden beneath the external appearance of the parcel – are only revealed or become apparent in the wrapping itself as it is untied, unwrapped and stripped away.

wren In Celtic symbolism the wren makes one of a pair with the raven, and the meaning of this dualism is linked to the pairings of druid and warrior and of boar and bear. Similarly, and in terms of popular etymology, symbolically the Irish word for wren (*drui*) is interpreted as 'druid among birds', while in Brythonic, the word denoting the bird is the strict linguistic counterpart of the Irish word for druid. The wren, therefore, corresponds to the priestly caste just as the raven corresponds to the warrior. Remains of these ancient traditions survive in a substantial body of Welsh folklore in which the wren is the King of the Birds. An old Welsh proverb says that death threatens anyone destroying a wren's nest, while in Brittany there is a 'song of the Wren' (OGAC 3: pp. 108–10; 12: pp. 49–67).

The North American Indian wren symbol is similar to the lark symbol in European folklore. Although the smallest and therefore the weakest of birds, it greets the Sun at dawn with a louder song than any other. The

Pawnee Indians call it the laughing bird and a very happy little bird (FLEH). It is curious that the Indians should call the bird 'happy', since the old Breton word for wren also meant 'happy'.

wrestling Depictions of wrestling and ceremonies involving real or mimic bouts derive from rites to stimulate the human procreative powers and the forces of plant life. 'The contests and fights which take place in so many places in the spring or at harvest time undoubtedly spring from the primitive notion that blows, contests, rough games between the sexes and so on, all stir up and increase the energies of the whole universe' (ELIT p. 320). These ritual bouts are replicas of immemorial archetypes and common to all religions. Jacob's wrestling with an angel may be interpreted in this light. Through his victory Jacob showed that he was the worthy source from which the Children of Israel and the members of the New Covenant could draw their energy. Ancient Egyptians, Assyrians, Babylonians and Hittites all staged mock bouts to represent the triumph of order over chaos. The Hittites, for example, 'as part of the feast of the New Year ... recounted and re-enacted the archetypal duel between Teshub the god of the weather and the serpent Iluyankash' (ELIT p. 400). Victory in a bout symbolized the creation of the world or participation in its continuing creation. From the inner viewpoint, creation is renewed or develops, symbolically, with every opponent overcome (see COSMOGONY).

Real or mimic wrestling bouts, like hunting or fishing exploits, were believed when successful to transfer to the victor a sort of magic power which was the pledge of victories to come. Similarly, the shadow-boxing which the modern contender practises to loosen up before a bout was originally intended to attract part of that magic power. The bout itself was the means of acquiring power, since the victor left the ring with an increase of strength. Ceremonial gestures and the sprinkling of salt are a prelude to any bout of traditional Japanese sumo-wrestling.

wrist The Bambara regard the wrist as the symbol of human skill, since it controls all manual work (ZAHB).

writing (see also LANGUAGE; LETTERS OF THE ALPHABET; NAME; SOUND) An ancient papyrus shows Thoth basing written letters upon portraits of the gods. From this, writing would seem to spring from what is holy, to be made in God's image and to be identified with mankind. It is the visible sign of the godhead in action, the manifestation of the Word. Some Muslim esotericists take the letters of the alphabet to be the very components of God's body. In India, Brahmā's SHAKTI, Sarasvatī, the goddess of speech, is also called the alphabet-goddess (Lipidevī), the letters being identified with the different parts of the body. The garland of fifty letters worn by the creator of manifestation, Brahmā, carries the same meaning. To read the letters in their alphabetical order is *anuloma*, development (*shrishti*), while to read them in reverse order is *viloma*, reintegration (*nivritti*).

The name of Almighty God is made up of FOUR letters for both Jews (JHVH) and Muslims (Hūwa: Allah), a fourfold determination of the Monad. Muslim gnosis relates these letters to the four elements, the four points of the compass and the four Angels of Glorification. One might, to all intents and purposes, join with de Saint-Martin in saying that these four letters express the properties and power of the godhead and that the full alphabet stands for the development of the Word (*anuloma*). Muslims conceive of the seven supreme letters as homologous with the Seven Intellects or Words of God. The twenty-eight letters of the full alphabet (twenty-eight being four times seven) are the complete individual, body and spirit as well as the Moon's twenty-eight Houses. Nevertheless, as Ibn 'Arabī explains, the Houses do not determine the letters, but vice versa. Furthermore, a whole structure of symbolism is based upon the fact that the Shahada (Muslim profession of faith) comprises four words, seven syllables and twelve letters. Creation is, in fact, envisioned as a book of which all created things are the letters. Furthermore, the 'Book of the World' expresses the oneness of God's primordial message, of which the sacred scriptures are merely partial translations. We should also observe that, as in Muslim esotericism, so in the Kabbalah, each letter corresponds to a number which thus determines the relationship between the elements of what is made manifest.

Naturally enough, such a view of the symbolism of the individual letters gives Holy Scripture a multiplicity of meanings. These meanings had a fixed hierarchy and Dante set their number at four. The Koran has seven. In fact, the gradual blurring of some of these meanings is not unconnected with the alteration of the shape of the writing itself. Those primitive ideograms, hieroglyphics, are translations of a divine and undoubtedly ritual language. Alterations to ideograms – especially apparent in China – removes this property. Furthermore, although the science of phonetic analogy was one familiar not only to the Chinese, but to the Hindus as well (*nirukta*), and even to Plato (there are suggestions of it in his *Cratylus*), as a valuable symbolic element it may easily tend to vagueness through apparent lack of logic. The study of language and even of grammar by a Patanjali or a Bhartrihari may turn it into what almost amounts to a spiritual exercise, a true piece of Yoga.

In India, both Hindus and Buddhists still make ritual use to a large extent of ideogram and lettering. They are employed diagrammatically, the 'roots' of Sanskrit letters alone being true YANTRA. Tantrism categorizes them as *tattvabīja* (syllable-seeds), that is, as what fixes the mantra in each of the individual's subtle centres. Similarly the symbolic letters of the *vajrayāna*, the *siddha*, stand for the Buddha and other holy persons and are incorporated on that basis into the mandala.

Mention too should be made of those many illiterates among the masters of spirituality, including Muhammad himself, the Zen Master, Hui Neng, and, nearer our own day, the great mystic, Rāmakrishna. Their illiteracy is the very opposite of ignorance, and symbolizes that instantaneous and intuitive perception of Divine Reality and release from enslavement to literalism and formality (AVAS, BEUA, CORT, LIOT, VACG).

While Chinese writing may be basically symbolic, this is because no sign is used to which no more than the properties of a sign may be attributed. The Chinese wanted every element of language – its sonority and graphic shape, its rhythms and meanings – to display the efficacy which belongs to symbols. By these means, expression is a figure of thought and this visual representation gives one the feeling that expression is not suggestion but actualization.

Thus it may be said that writing Chinese, like speaking it, is less a matter of following the requirements of a strictly intellectual order than of becoming concerned with the efficacity of speech and writing.

The virtues of this figurative writing, capable of expressing all levels of thought including even the most highly scientific, are that they allow words to assume their function of being activating forces.

The power of the written word is so strong in China that calligraphy takes precedence over painting. Wang Hsichi (321–79), the prince of calligraphers, had this to say about the art of writing: 'Each horizontal stroke is a mass of clouds in warlike array, each hook a bow bent with extraordinary strength. Every dot is a rock falling from a lofty mountain-top, each curl a copper hook, every curlicue an aged vine-branch and every free-flowing line, a runner ready to bound forward.'

The Ancient Egyptians employed various styles of writing. Hieroglyphics, sacred carvings, provided an inscriptional or monumental form of writing. Primarily it was based upon ideograms (images of ideas) but hieroglyphics also acted as letters.

The foundation of this system of writing was the combination in individual words of figurative and phonetic characters. In other words, hieroglyphics are drawings of different objects taken from the animal, vegetable and mineral worlds, from arts, crafts, etc., some of which express ideas and others sounds. These ideographic characters are classified as figurative or symbolic.

(PIED p. 262; see also POSD pp. 121–5)

The first category is self-explanatory, the second 'expresses abstract ideas which could only be shown by conventional or allegorical images. Thus war and battle were denoted by a pair of arms, one holding a shield and the other a spear' (ibid.). Thus Ancient Egyptian thought evolved from a substratum of symbols possessing higher properties than the merely conventional, being charged with magic forces and with a power to conjure them up. Hieratic writing was a simplified and abbreviated version of hieroglyphics and was used in papyri and in legal documents. It read from right to left, horizontally. Sacred scriptures alone continued to be written in hieroglyphics, in vertical lines like columns. Demotic writing derived from hieratic, but is extremely difficult to decipher. It was used especially in legal documents and for charms and spells as well (PIED p. 181). Lastly, there was a secret form of writing, basically phonetic in character, using homophony and puns, which can only be read by initiates or by those fortunate seekers who have successfully compared it with other forms of writing and unveiled the secrets of the characters which it uses.

All the documentary evidence which we possess relating to the Celtic world in the Classical period goes to show that the Celts both knew and used writing, without, however, attaching to it the importance which modern societies give it as a means of record-keeping and instruction. What has been written has, in fact, been made permanent for better or worse, without the possibility of alteration, while knowledge should be handed down and renewed by each generation. Writing was the province of Ogmios, the god with the chains, and possessed the highest magical properties. Furthermore, it carried with it serious sanctions, since a written curse possessed far more lasting effects than mere spoken or chanted spells. Ogham, the primitive Irish form of writing, was in any case so hard and difficult as to confine its use to short texts. Surviving examples are brief funerary inscriptions, nearly all of which simply comprise the name of the dead person.

Yet, despite all efforts to elevate writing into an image of God and a translation of the cosmos, even to deify it, writing may also be regarded as a debased form of speech. The history of writing only goes back for six thousand years and great masters such as the Buddha, Socrates and Jesus Christ left no written works. It symbolizes a loss of presence, for when writing comes in, speech goes out. It is an attempt to encapsulate spirit and inspiration and yet remains as a symbol of the missing spoken word. De Saussure, the founder of modern linguistics, rightly drew the line: 'Speech and writing are two systems of separate signs. The sole reason for the existence of the latter is to stand in place of the former.' Writing gives physical form to revelation, but it cuts the human links and replaces them by a universe of signs. To reactivate the revelation a speaking presence is required. 'You do not use a pen to write on the soul' said Joseph de Maistre. Jean Lacroix splendidly summarizes the symbolic properties of writing as opposed to speech as 'a secondary and dangerous attempt to take possession symbolically of the presence'.

Y

yantra The *yantra*, a geometric figure, is literally an aid or instrument and in Hinduism stands in purely linear and basically geometric terms for cosmic manifestation and the divine power. It is the graphic equivalent of the MANTRA, the mental prayer. Ritually their use is combined, the mantra, it is said, being the soul of the *yantra*.

The basic elements of the *yantra* – which may additionally comprise a third dimension which is not represented – are:

- triangle: with apex upright, being *purusha*, Shiva, Fire, lingam (phallus); inverted, *prakrti*, *shakti* (female energy), Water, *yoni* (womb); the centre is the undepicted dot, the *bindu*, undifferentiated Brahman, around which the opposite facing triangles revolve (the *shrīyantra* comprises four triangles with apexes upright, and five inverted);
- circles and lotus flowers, symbols of expansion in the intermediate world;
- the external square with gateways at the four points of the compass, symbol of the Earth;
- Sanskrit letters, their writing both 'fixing' the mantra and providing 'roots' in graphic shape (*mūla-yantra*).

In addition to the meanings to be drawn from combinations of these elements, the *yantra* possesses secret meanings and even powers consequent upon its being 'animated' ritually (AVAS, BENA, DANA, ELIY).

year The Latin for 'year' is *annus,* which some writers have compared with *anus* (ring) and then, by extension, with the cycle of the Zodiac. At New Year the Romans offered prayers to the goddess Anna Perenna (perhaps 'Ring, or Circle, of the Years'). The year is symbolized by the circle or cycle and its significance coincides with that of the ZODIAC. In accordance with the Greek representation of the OUROBOROS, the serpent chewing its own tail, one half white and the other black, astrologers divide the year into a spiritual, male hemisphere which runs from the autumnal to the vernal equinox and has as its mid-point the 'Gateway of the Gods', the Winter solstice, and a material, female hemisphere running from the vernal to the autumnal equinox with the Summer solstice, the 'Gateway of Mankind', as its mid-point (SERP).

In general terms, a year symbolizes the measurement of a complete cyclical process since, in fact, it contains its own ascendant and descendant, evolutionary and involutionary phases, its own seasons, and heralds the regular return of the same cycle. It is a cosmic cycle in miniature, and this is why its significance is not confined to the 365 days of the solar year, but relates to the whole cyclical structure. The addition of oneness (in the shape of the extra day in Leap Year every fourth year) symbolizes escape from the annual cycle and indeed from every cycle, in other words death and stillness or permanence and eternity.

Thus in those Irish mythical tales which endeavour, however clumsily, to translate the highest metaphysical concepts into comprehensible terms, a year and a day are a symbol of eternity. The exactly equivalent symbol is a day and a night, so that when the Dagda yields his home, the Bruig na Boind, for a day and a night to his son, Mac Oc, he yields it for all eternity. The oneness added is the opening which allows escape from the cycle and exit from the circle.

yellow Yellow is the hottest, the most expansive and the most burning of all colours in its intensity, violence and almost strident shrillness; or else it is as broad and as dazzling as a flow of molten metal, being hard to put out and always overflowing the limits within which one tries to confine it. The Sun's rays, searing the blue vault of Heaven, display the power of the gods of the Beyond, and in the Aztec pantheon, Huitzilopochtli, the Victorious Warrior, god of the midday Sun, was painted blue and yellow. Yellow, the glitter of gold, has the properties of a kratophany (manifestation of power), and in heraldry the pairing of or and azure [gold and blue] is the opposite to gules and vert [red and green], just as that which descends from above opposes that which ascends from below. The field on which they meet is the Earth's crust, our skin which goes yellow, too, at the approach of death.

In the pairing of blue and yellow, yellow is the male colour, the colour of light and of life, and can never be darkened. Kandinsky saw this clearly when he wrote that 'yellow tends so strongly to brightness that there can never be such a colour as dark yellow. It may therefore be stated that there is a very strong physical kinship between yellow and white' (KANS). Yellow is the vehicle of youth, strength and divine immortality. It is the colour of the gods. Anquetil says that Zoroaster's name means 'Glittering Golden Star, Freehanded, Living Star'. The Tibetan divine word, *om*, is qualified by *zere*, meaning 'golden' (PORS p. 68).

The glitter of gold sometimes becomes a two-way channel of communication, an intermediary between gods and mankind. Thus Frazer emphasizes that a golden knife was used in India for the most important horse-sacrifices 'because "gold is light" and "by means of the golden light the sacrificer also goes to the heavenly world"' (FRAG 11: p. 80 n. 3, quoting *The Sathapata-Brāhmana*).

In Mexican cosmology, golden yellow was the colour of the Earth's 'new' skin at the beginning of the rainy season, before it grew green once more. The colour is therefore associated with the mystery of renewal. For this reason the flayed god, Xipe Totec, Lord of the Spring Rains, was also the goldsmiths' god. During the Spring festivals his priests dressed in the yellow-painted skins of the victims sacrificed to placate this formidable deity (SOUM). Golden yellow was also an attribute of Mithras in Persia and of Apollo in Greece.

Since golden yellow is part of the divine essence, on Earth it became the attribute of the power of princes, kings and emperors and proclaimed the divine source of that power. The green bays of human hope were covered with the gold of divine power and the green palms of Christ's earthly sojourn were replaced by a golden halo when he returned to his Father. In Spain, on Palm Sunday, the faithful wave yellowed palms in cathedral closes.

Catholic priests, too, lead the dead towards eternal life against a back-cloth of yellow and gold. All conductors of the dead make use of gold to a greater or lesser degree. This was true of Mithras while, in Eastern tradition, hell-hounds, including the one in the Zend Avesta, have yellow eyes – all the better to see in the dark – and ears tinged with white and yellow. In Ancient Egyptian tomb-chambers the colour combination of blue and yellow was most usually employed to ensure the soul's survival, since gold stood for the colour of the Sun's flesh and that of the gods.

The discovery of yellow in the guise of eternal life in the chthonian world, brings us to the second symbolic aspect of the colour.

Because yellow was the colour of fertile soil, couples in Ancient China were advised that, to ensure that their marriage was fruitful 'and that *yin* and *yang* were fully harmonized, the hangings, pillows and sheets of the bridal bed should be woven from yellow gauze or silk' (VANG p. 342). However, this colour of the ripe crops of Summer gives advance notice of Autumn, when Earth is stripped bare and loses its cloak of greenery.

It also heralds decrepitude, old age and the approach of death, and ultimately yellow becomes a substitute for black. To the Tewa Pueblo Indians it is the colour of the west and for the Aztec and Zuni, that of north or south, as each associated one or the other direction with the Underworld (SOUM p. 63). In Buddhist Tantrism, yellow corresponds both to the 'centre-root' (*mulādhārachakra*) and to the element Earth, and to *Ratnasambhava*, whose light partakes of the nature of the Sun. To the Chinese, too, black and yellow were the colours of the north or of the underground abysses in which were the 'yellow springs' leading to the kingdom of the dead. This was because the souls which had gone down to the yellow springs, or the *yang* which had taken refuge there, longed for the renewal of the cycle which began with the Winter solstice. Although the essence of north and of the yellow springs is *yin*, they are also the source from which the *yang* is renewed. Furthermore, yellow was associated with black as its opposite and complement. When Chaos was differentiated, yellow was separated from black, and the polarization of the primordial undifferentiated state occurs in yellow and black as it does in *yang* and *yin*, round and square, active and passive (Li Tzu). According to the *I Ching*, yellow and black were the colours of the blood of the dragon-Demiurge. In this context we are concerned with a relative polarization of a primordial coagulation (CHOO, ELIF, GRAP, GRAR, GRIH).

In Chinese symbolism, yellow emerges from black as Earth emerged from the primeval waters. If yellow was the imperial colour in China, this was because the emperor stood at the centre of the universe, like the Sun in the centre of the Heavens.

When it collects at the level of this world, mid-way between the very high and the very low, yellow becomes no more than a perversion of the qualities of faith, intelligence and eternal life. Once the love of God is forgotten, it gives place to Satan's sulphurous influence, the image of overweening pride and of an intellect which will feed only upon itself. Yellow was associated with adultery since the sacred bonds of marriage had been snapped just as Satan (Lucifer) had snapped the bonds of divine love. The colour was originally associated with deception, as many other customs bear witness, such as that of painting the doors of traitors yellow in the sixteenth and seventeenth centuries to draw the attention of passers-by. The Lateran Council in 1215 ordered Jews to wear a yellow roundel on their clothes and the *Dictionnaire de Trevous* (1771) states that it was the French custom to smear bankrupts' houses yellow.

The traditions of the Peking Theatre bear equal witness to the reversal of the properties of yellow, its actors painting their faces in that colour as a mark of cruelty, deceit and cynicism, while painting their faces red to show honest and decent characters. Nevertheless, in this traditional theatre the costumes of princes and emperors – indicating the social status rather than the psychology of the characters – were yellow as well. This employment of yellow on the Chinese stage takes fully into account the ambivalence which makes it simultaneously the most godlike of all colours and yet, in Kandinsky's words, the most earthy.

This ambivalence recurs in Greek mythology. The golden apples from the Garden of the Hesperides were a symbol of love and concord which, despite their theft by Herakles (Hercules), remained the property of the garden of the gods. They were the true fruits of love since Gaia, Earth, had given them to Zeus and Hera as a wedding-present, and thus they were consecrated to the basic sacred marriage from which all creation sprang. However, the Apple of Discord, which was a cause of the Trojan War, was also a golden apple and the symbol of pride and jealousy. Greek mythology, again, brings together the two aspects of the symbol in the myth of Atalanta. Like the Roman Diana, this bloodthirsty virgin, while running a race against Hippomenes – whom, had she won the race, she had every intention of killing as she had her other unsuccessful suitors – yielded to an irresistible impulse of greed for the golden apples which the youth threw on the ground in her path. They caused her to lose the race and break her vows, but in so doing she discovered love.

Some peoples have tried to divide the symbol on the basis of mattness and glossiness, reminiscent of the symbolic distinction between matt and glossy WHITE, especially as it distinguishes the horses of the Underworld from those of Heaven. This is particularly true of Islam where 'golden yellow bore the meaning of wise and good counsel, and pale yellow that of treachery and deceit' (PORS p. 88).

The same distinction is to be found in heraldry, which gives yellow the properties of a metal (gold) rather than a tint.

yew-tree In the Celtic world, the yew was a funerary tree and in Ireland was sometimes used as a medium for ogham writing. Above all, however, in insular tradition it was the oldest of all trees. Its wood was also used on occasion for making shields and spears because it was so hard, and this denotes that it was a war symbol, as does the name of a young Irish warrior, Ibarsciath ('Yew-Shield'). This impression is further confirmed by the use of yew in some Gaulish tribal names, such as that of the Eburovices ('those who fight with the yew') who gave their name to Evreux in Normandy. Nevertheless the essential quality which provided the basic symbolism of the tree was the toxicity of its berries. Caesar quotes the example of the two vanquished Gaulish kings of the Eburoni who committed suicide by eating yew-berries. The wheel belonging to the mythical druid Mag Ruith (Wizard of the Wheels), was made of yew. It was an apocalyptic wheel. Lastly, Eochaid (*Ivocatus*, 'He who Fights the Yew') was one of the traditional names of the High Kings of Ireland (OGAC 11: pp. 39–42).

yin and yang (see also HEXAGRAM IN THE I CHING)   *Yin*, expressing the presence of clouds and dull weather, and *fu* (a hill or slope) make up the ideogram, *yin*; while *yang* comprises the same root, *fu*, together with *yang*, denoting the Sun risen over the horizon and its activities. Originally, there-fore, what was described were two sides of a valley, one in Sun and the other in shadow, and its study may have been one of the foundations of geomancy. By extension *yin* and *yang* denote the bright and dark faces of all things, their heavenly and earthly, positive and negative, male and fe-male aspects; in other words, they epitomize the twofold and complemen-tary character of the universe. *Yin* and *yang* exist only in relation the one with the other. They are inseparable and the rhythm of the world is the rhythm of their alternation. *I yin, i yang*, says the *Hi Tzu*: 'First a *yin* then a *yang* and then a *yin* and a *yang*.'

In the *I Ching*, *yin* is denoted by a broken line, – –; *yang* by a continuous line ——. They are combined to form trigrams and hexagrams. Three (or six) *yin* lines make up *K'un*, passive perfection, the Earth; three (or six) *yang* lines, *Ch'ien*, active perfection, Heaven. Heaven and Earth are the polarization of the primordial Monad, *T'ai Ki*, the Great Hinge. 'Out of One comes Two' says the *Tao* (ch. 42). The Monad is polarized and becomes settled in *yin* and *yang* in the process of cosmic manifestation and the splitting into two halves of the World Egg. 'I am One who becomes Two' says an Ancient Egyptian inscription. On the other hand, confining oneself to the realm of manifestation, *yang* and *yin* suggest respectively oneness and duality, the monad and dyad of the Pythagoreans, odd and even.

Yin–yang symbolism is expressed by a circle divided into two equal halves by a wavy line, one half white (*yang*) and the other black (*yin*), in which it is noticeable that the length of the dividing line equals half the external circumference of the circle and that hence the total perimeter of each half, of *yin* or *yang*, is equal in length to the total circumference of the circle. Such a diagram calls to mind the observation of the Kabbalist, Knor von Rosenroth: 'Heaven and Earth were joined in a mutual embrace.' The al-ternation and the fixed union of *yin* and *yang* is also expressed in the chess-board and in Shiva's simple fourfold mandala. Chou Tun-i's *T'ai Chi T'u* depicts them as three concentric rings split along their diametres into halves, alternately black and white. However, nothing can better express their dynamic and creative aspects (the five elements and the ten thousand be-ings), nor their interpretation, than the *yin–yang*. Once again it should be noted that the *yin* half bears a *yang* dot and the *yang* half a *yin* dot, a sign of their interdependence, the trace of light in darkness and of darkness in light. From the spiritual point of view, Schuon believes that this is a sign of 'the real Presence in the darkness of ignorance' and of individuality or of darkness in universality and the light of knowledge. The median line may stand for the track of an evolutionary spiral which expresses the symbolism of the *yin–yang* in terms of 'the cycle of individual destiny'. This is a minute fragment of a spiral, the two ends of the curve, its 'entrance' and 'exit', corresponding to birth and death.

In Japan *Jikkan* and *Jūnishi* correspond to the Chinese *yin* and *yang*. One should also mention a symbol very close to them, the *tomoe*, or rather *mitsu-tomoe*, Japanese but originating in Korea. It is an even more dynamic form of the revolving cycle, presenting cosmic tendencies in a triple form familiar to Hindus. It must also be observed that the Japanese *magatama* (imperial jewels) were shaped like a half *yin–yang*, close to that of the crescent Moon. In former times the *yin–yang* was related to the phases of the Moon. This was clearly connected with yet another aspect of cyclic development, but in this context seems of lesser importance since that night star, the Moon, was always *yin* in relation to the Sun (*yang*) (CHAT, GRAP, GUEC, GUER, HERS, LIOT, MATM, SCHS, WIEG, WILG, YUAC).

This symbol is the concentration of the deepest philosophy and one most characteristic of the Chinese spirit, which hardly feels the need to appeal to abstract notions of number, time, space, cause or harmony. To translate such notions, the Chinese have this concrete symbol which, along with the Tao, expresses the complete structure of the world and of the Spirit. For them there is no different spatial time-scale and they cannot conceive of it as independent of concrete activity. Human activity, be it manual or intellectual, cannot exist without time and space, just as time and space cannot be conceived without human activity.

They break down time into periods and space into areas and these periods and areas are qualified sometimes as *yin* and sometimes as *yang*, depending upon whether they are light or dark, good or evil, internal or external, hot or cold, male or female, open or closed, etc.

Yin and *yang* are the analysis and image of representations of space and time.

Early in its history China used places and times for religious purposes. These symbols then controlled liturgy and ceremonial as they controlled the arts of topography and chronology.

Although *yin* and *yang* stand for opposites, they never conflict, in absolute terms, because there is always a period of change lying between them and this allows for continuity. All things, individuals, times and spaces are at some stage *yin* and at another *yang*. At the same time all things partake of both through their future states and their dynamism with its potential for evolution and involution.

yoginī In the *Vajrayāna*, the *yoginī* symbolizes the CHAKRA and subtle channels which carry mental enlightenment (*bodhicitta*). This structure, which must be built mentally within the individual, comprises the body of the *yoginī* with whom the adept must identify. Tibetan iconography often depicts deities fused with their assistants. These persons coupled together denote that the Buddha state cannot be attained without the close marriage of Wisdom and Compassion, the subtle means specific to Tantrism and to EMPTINESS. Thus *bodhicitta*, or awareness of enlightenment, slumbering in the low *chakra*, is aroused and fated to rise until it reaches the thousand-petal lotus in the head. Thus the individual accomplishes within the self the marriage of male and female principles and recreates the primordial hermaphrodite.

yoke For reasons only too obvious, the yoke is the symbol of enslavement, oppression and confinement, and the Roman custom of making the vanquished pass under the yoke is self-explanatory. However, it takes a fresh dimension in Hindu thought. The Indo-European root, *yug*, from which the Latin word for yoke, *jugum*, is derived, finds a well-known application in the Sanskrit *Yoga*, which has the meaning effectively of uniting, linking and yoking together. It is by definition a system of meditation which aims to harmonize and to unify the individual so as to obtain self-awareness and ultimately the one true marriage, that of the soul with God and the manifestation with the First Cause (ELIY, GUEV, SILI).

Buzyges, who invented the yoke which allowed oxen to be controlled and harnessed, was also one of the earliest Athenian law-givers. Yokes symbolize discipline in two of its aspects: the first is chosen of one's own free will and leads to self-control, to inner unity and to oneness with God; the other is borne in a humiliating fashion (it is the dark aspect of the symbol) as in the famous case of the Caudine Forks. Here, a Roman army defeated by the Samnites was forced to crawl under a spear set horizontally over two others stuck into the ground, the *jugum ignominiosum*, the yoke of shame.

In Ancient Rome there was a place called Sororium Tigillum, the Sisterly Beam, under which murderers passed to expiate their crime. The first to do so was Horatius who had murdered his sister, Camilla, because she came out of the women's quarters and shamelessly proclaimed her grief for the enemy whom he had killed. This very ancient expiatory and purificatory custom was essential if the person concerned was to regain a place in society – you had to pass beneath the yoke. However, this ancestral use of the yoke implied more than mere submission to the city's laws. It was undoubtedly, as Beaujeu writes, 'a survival of the secret or artificial GATEWAYS through which the young man, once initiated, passed from the supernatural world in which he had undergone his ordeal into the everyday world.' It was thus truly the symbol of reintegration into society.

Z

zenith 'Zenith' ultimately derives from an Arabic word meaning 'the way of the head' and is the point where an imaginary vertical line rising above the observer cuts the celestial sphere above the horizon. It is the opposite of the nadir (itself derived from an Arabic word meaning 'opposite'), a point in the Heavens directly at the end of an imaginary line drawn from the observer's feet which runs right through the centre of the Earth and stretches to infinity.

The symbolism of both zenith and nadir derives directly from these definitions. The zenith marks the uppermost point on a WHEEL of which Earth is the hub, as though the hollow Chinese disc or *Pi* were set vertically against the horizon. The nadir marks its lowest point. In place of Earth, one might conceive a group, an individual or a psyche.

The relative opposition of zenith and nadir corresponds to the cycle of contraction and expansion of all forms of life which evolves over a period of time. The zenith marks the peak of the half-circle of expansion and therefore the start of the half-circle of contraction. On the other hand, the nadir marks the lowest point of the process of contraction and the start of the process of expansion. Furthermore the vertical is the accepted symbol of time and all manifestation unfolds in time. To pass from the zenith through the vault of Heaven would denote 'passing from life in time to life in eternity', passing from the finite to the infinite (SENZ p. 18). At the other end of the scale, passage from the nadir, at the lowest point of the involutive curve, would mark the deepest immersion in the thickest matter.

On the one hand, there is the road of materialization and on the intellectual level of conceptualization; on the other, that of spiritualization and intuition.

In so far as they relate to the Zodiac, Senard observes that

the nadir is set in the sign of Virgo, the element of Earth, but in which awareness of the divine has its birth, as symbolized by Virgo's complementary sign, Pisces, and from which begins a return to the boundless. In mythology and religion Virgo is always associated with the birth, or rather the rebirth, of the god who is the expression of Energy and Higher Consciousness. Virgo, like Pisces, is the house of Mercury, the messenger of the gods, and an intermediary and link between the gods themselves, that is Primordial Energies, and between gods and mortals. In Virgo, Mercury provides a link between the evolutive Energies in the lower or left-hand hemisphere and the involutive Energies in the right-hand or upper hemisphere.

(SENZ p. 18)

At the apex of the zenith it might be said that in the midst of life we are in death and at the lowest point of the nadir, that in the midst of death we are in life.

zero The numerical sign deriving from the Arabic word *sifra* (cipher) which, without having any value of its own, replaces the values missing in other numbers: it symbolizes the person without powers of his or her own who can only exercise delegated power.

'The Maya discovered the concept of zero and its use at least a thousand years before anything similar was known and used in Europe' (GIRP p. 318). Its representational shape was that of the SHELL or SNAIL and we know that the snail itself was a symbol of seasonal renewal. In the myths of the *Popol-Vuh*, zero corresponds to the moment when the Hero Maize-god was sacrificed by drowning in the river, and before he was born again to rise to Heaven and become the Sun. In the germination process of maize it corresponds to the moment which occurs as the seed disintegrates in the soil and before life manifests itself once more in the shape of the little maize-sprout emerging from the soil. This, then, is exactly in line with the traditions of European occultism, with the moment when polarization is reversed, the moment dividing the progressive hemisphere from the regressive hemisphere of the Zodiacal cycle. It may therefore be said that the great myth of the cycle of rebirth is epitomized by this symbolism of the Mayan zero. Through the womb symbolism of the shell, it is also related to foetal life.

In Mayan hieroglyphics, zero is represented by the SPIRAL, the closed infinite by the open infinite (THOH).

The Ancient Egyptians had no hieroglyphic to correspond to zero. 'There was no sign for nought but some scribes working with numbers thought of leaving a blank space where nought was intended to go' (POSD p. 161).

Symbolically their intuition was very accurate – zero is the pause in generation; like the Cosmic Egg, it is the symbol of complete potentiality.

It also symbolizes the object which has no properties of its own, but which confers properties upon others, as the zero placed to the right of a number multiplies it tenfold. It is thus linked with the initiatory significance of the Fool in the Tarot pack. This is the only one of the major arcana to be unnumbered, but it may either validate or annul other cards, according to its position or to the signs of addition or subtraction, multiplication or division which precede it.

Zeus (Jupiter) After the reigns of OURANOS (Uranus) and CRONOS, from whom he was descended, Zeus symbolizes the rule of the spirit. He was the regulator of the internal and external worlds and upon him depended the functioning of physical, social and moral laws. According to Mircea Eliade he was the 'archetype of the patriarchal head of the family' (ELIT p. 78).

The god of light, Homer calls him the sovereign and father of gods and men. Hesiod believed that from the third mythological generation onwards he presided over all celestial manifestation, while to Aeschylus, Zeus was Ether, Earth and Heaven. He was all things and set over all.

As the god who made the lightning flash he symbolized the spirit and the light of human intellect, god-given enlightenment and intuitive thought. He was the source of truth.

As the one who unleashed the thunderbolt, he symbolized God's anger, punishment, chastisement and outraged authority. He was the administrator of justice.

The dual effect of philosophical criticism and the purification of religious feelings caused great changes to the character of Zeus, from Homer's Olympian with his countless love affairs with goddesses and mortal women to the image of a sole and universal god. All that the name of Zeus symbolizes developed simultaneously. The way is long and the images varied from the almighty master of whim to the pure spirit. There can be no end to disagreement over the meaning of his symbol, as with that of all mythological characters, depending upon whether a particular stage in its development, an especial legend, a particular aspect of the godhead or level of analysis is taken as one's basis. The concept of Zeus as the supreme deity and as the

universal power evolved from its starting-point in the Homeric age to its finish among the Hellenistic philosophers and the concept of a single Providence. To the Stoics . . . Zeus was the symbol of the one God who personified the Cosmos. The laws of nature were the thoughts of Zeus. This is, however, the ultimate limit in the development of God and of one who escapes the bounds of mythology to enter theology and the history of philosophy.

(GRID p. 478)

The peak of this ascendancy of Zeus in the spirit of mankind is marked by Cleanthes' (331–232 BC) *Hymn to Zeus*.

Modern psychologists have set the seal of their disapproval upon certain attitudes in those who exercise leadership and this may be termed the Zeus complex. It is a tendency to monopolize all authority and to eliminate in others anything which might be seen as a display of independence, however rational and desirable. In this complex may be discerned the roots of an obvious feeling of intellectual and moral inferiority, and the need for a social compensation for this in authoritarian outbursts, as well as the fear of the subject that his or her rights and dignities are not being accorded due respect. This was the cause of Zeus' extreme sensitivity and liability to outbusts of calculated rage. Such attitudes demonstrate the persistent force of traditional mythology, which conflicts with modern management methods of open and productive communication between individuals and departments associated in the same enterprise and of in-depth training. In the end the Zeus complex comes into collision with these and its contradictions result in senseless decision-making. The over-authoritarian betrays a lack of reason.

ziggurat These Mesopotamian buildings were supposed to be the inspiration for the TOWER OF BABEL which, in Old Testament tradition, was the symbol of human pride attempting to make itself God's equal and thinking that it could mount to Heaven through purely material means. Ziggurats were built up in a series of three, five or seven increasingly narrow terraces linked by steep flights of stairs, the steps being as much as twenty-seven inches high and the towers themselves rising sometimes to the height of almost 300 feet. The seven terraces corresponded to the seven planetary Heavens and each was painted a different colour.

According to old Sumerian traditions . . . the 'Great Misfortune,' Saturn, was black. . . . [His step] was at the base, opposed to the highest degree, the gilded top of the tower where the sun resided. The second storey was white, the color of shining Jupiter; the third, brick-red, the colour of Mercury. Then followed blue for Venus, yellow for Mars, gray or silver for the moon. These colours boded good or evil.

(SELM p. 33)

In accordance with the Babylonians' own traditions, ziggurats had the symbolic properties of LADDERS and these gigantic towers were intended to make it easy for the gods to come down to Earth and for mortals to rise up towards Heaven. The ziggurat at Larsa bears the evocative name of 'The House of the Link between Heaven and Earth'. Sacrifice was offered upon their tops. They are also expressions of the enormous efforts of mankind to approach the godhead. When perverted, this effort reverts to deification of the human being him- or herself, intoxicated in the past by the magical and today by the technological methods employed to increase the powers of mankind. The quest for power takes the place of the search for God. The significance of contemporary Babel-building is the attempt to reach the apex of power. It completely inverts the original meaning of the ziggurat, which was the tree or axis linking the two centres, terrestrial and celestial.

The symbolism of the Mesopotamian ziggurat may be compared with that of the cosmic MOUNTAIN and with that of the temples built in the shape of mountains at Borobudur and Angkor and, hence, with that of the CENTRE of the world. 'When the pilgrim climbs [the temple or ziggurat],' writes Mircea Eliade, 'he is coming close to the centre of the world, and on its highest terrace he breaks through into another sphere, transcending profane, heterogeneous space, and entering a "pure earth"' (ELIT p. 376). By internalizing the symbol still further, it might be said that the ascent of the ziggurat corresponds to gradual spiritual cleansing until we reach the pure light of an inner space.

zither In the traditions of the Ural peoples the zither was made by a magician from various odds and ends; among them are often listed fish and animal bones, and animal hide and hair or fur. When Orpheus played upon it all nature was enraptured.

They use the phrase 'zither tune' to evoke bird-song.

The zither was an attribute of Terpsichore, the Muse of dancing who translated its tune into gesture to express the same emotions. It is also an attribute of Temperance, the virtue founded upon a sense of harmony, like music (TERS p. 99; see also LYRE).

Further, its shape is a symbol of the universe. Its strings correspond to the levels of the universe while its sound-box, open on one side and closed upon the other, like a tortoise shell, stands for the relationship between Earth and Heaven, like the flight of birds or the rapture induced by music (DAVR). The zither symbolizes the song of the universe in accordance with Pythagorean cosmology.

Zodiac (see also DECAN(ATE)) The Zodiac is simultaneously a symbol in its own right and a collection of individual symbols of which the significance varies with the changes in their interrelationship. Then, too, is has both the most highly concentrated and the most widely diffused meaning.

In all countries and in all ages studied by historical science, the Zodiac is to be found in almost exactly the same circular shape, with its twelve subdivisions, its twelve signs bearing the same names and its seven planets. In Babylon, Judaea, Ancient Egypt, Persia, India, Tibet, China, North and South America, Scandinavia, the Muslim lands and still many more, they knew the Zodiac and practised astrology. It is universally associated with the most important archaeological remains in the shape of steles and temples and places in which the mysteries were celebrated and initiations performed.

(SENZ p. 1)

The circle of the Zodiac is divided into twelve segments, twelve being the perfect number, which correspond to the twelve constellations. Four of these mark the strong points in the Sun's transit – Leo, Taurus, Aquarius and Scorpio. The culminating periods within the cycle, they fall between the Equinoxes (21 March; 21 September) and the Solstices (21 June; 21 December) and separate the seasons. 'They divide the circle of the Zodiac into four equal segments of 90° each.' The Zodiac is also the sum of cosmic, physiological and psychological symbols which illustrate and define the basic symbolism of the CIRCLE (CHAS pp. 21–2).

In astrology, Zodiac is the name given to a belt around the ecliptic in which move the planets and the wandering stars, which astrologers classify among the planets. The word is usually translated as 'animals' circle', although our Western Zodiac includes a woman (Virgo), a man (Aquarius) and children (Gemini) and the only wholly animal Zodiac is the Chinese. It is probable, therefore, that the word in general terms means 'constellation of living creatures'.

The Zodiac is the supreme example of a complete cycle. Each of its signs is an expression of a phase of development, described in the articles devoted to each.

ARIES ♈ = impulsion (on the cosmic level this is the primordial impulsion which comes before the 'dawning Brahman' or the birth of a universe);

TAURUS ♉ = effort, the build-up of the godhead or of the seed;

GEMINI ♊ = polarity (Hindu *Prakriti-Purusha*, or the separation of spirit and matter);

CANCER ♋ = passivity and attachment (on the cosmogonic level, the World Egg or the waters in which the seeds of the manifested world were deposited and over the face of which the Spirit of God moved);

LEO ♌ = life;

VIRGO ♍ = differentiation, phenomenalism;

LIBRA ♎ = sociability, the golden mean between opposing tendencies;

SCORPIO ♏ = fermentation, disintegration;

SAGITTARIUS ♐ = dualism of the instincts and higher aspirations (from the cosmogonic viewpoint, the return of the mortal to God);

CAPRICORN ♑ = elevation (Hindu *pralaya*, that is, death of the material universe);

AQUARIUS ♒ = transition to higher states;

PISCES ♓ = inner world (the Upper Waters in contrast with the Lower Waters of Cancer), transition to the original undifferentiated state.

The signs of the Zodiac may be divided in to four main groups, each one ruled by one of the powerful signs we have already mentioned. Senard summarizes their corresponding psychological states as follows (SENZ pp. 23ff.):

Pisces, Aries and Taurus comprise a group which corresponds to the mythological age of Ouranos (Uranus), one of undifferentiated biological effusion. It was the age 'of cosmic Principles and Energies which, from the human viewpoint, are expressed in the pre-rational instinctive character translated into the dominance of the unconscious, impulsiveness, sensuousness, and the predominance of the imaginative faculties.'

The second group comprises Gemini, Cancer and Leo and corresponds to the mythological age of Cronos, during which the expansive tendencies were halted in a period marked by a need to set in place, divide, classify and conceptualize, when a concern with structure overrode that for development. Senard so rightly calls it the grouping

of the principles of dissociation. Human beings separate from the primal, undifferentiated, group state. They become individualized, self-aware and then aware of the non-ego, of the sense of duality and of conceiving everything from the viewpoint of separate subject and object. The age is one of discernment and analysis and of conflicts between the opposites released by dissociation. Analytic intellect and rational consciousness predominate. Strongly developed self-awareness tends to egocentricify.

The third segment gathers Virgo, Libra and Scorpio together. It corresponds to the mythological age of Zeus, marked by a fresh expansion, but this time characterized by structure and hierarchy, in other words by harmonized development. It was the beginning of a climb towards the ZENITH, when suprarational consciousness and enlightenment started to burgeon. This is the phase 'of the principles of association expressed by the birth of right feeling and the quest for a balance between the psychological faculties as well as between the ego and the non-ego, the subjective and the objetive. Consciousness became aware of the manifestations of intuition.'

The last group of three comprises Sagittarius, Capricorn and Aquarius. It might be said that during this fourth age mythology gradually disappears and that its time is past as it makes way for mystical religion and, in particular, for Christian revelation and the Word made Flesh. According to Senard, it is the segment of

the principles of sublimation. Intuition becomes more and more the guide recognized and accepted by the individual on the path of return to the non-manifested. Guided by Beatrice, Dante ends his journey through the spheres in PARADISE (the ultimate day or light). Consciousness then freely functions outside the plane of what is manifested. Free from the chains of matter, time and space, it participates once more in the one and universal life, becoming interfused with the principle of creation. Supraconsciousness or omniscience becomes a reality.

This symbolism of biological and psychological development, acutely sensitive to the study of the relationship between the signs, can not only result in individual diagnosis, but in true psychological guidance.

In astrological terminology, zodiacal aspects apply to angular relationships between two planets or between two other factors in a horoscope, as for example the nodal point and the meridian or horizon. The principal aspects are: the conjunction, which, as its name implies, is the presence of stars (or other horoscopic factors) at the same point in the Heavens, where they intensify their influences and form a single whole, as husband and wife are made one flesh; the sextile, with an aspect of 60°, symbolizing a certain harmony and sympathy between the two factors in question; the square, with an aspect of 90°, an aspect of collision, tension and conflict between the two astral influences; the trine, with an aspect of 120°, creating the most harmonious, favourable and intimate sympathy between the two points in the sky; opposition, an aspect of 180°, emphasizing the most complete incompatibility of the two stars. In theory, opposition is shown as a double square, but some astrologers cast doubt upon its uniformly sinister and harmful nature. In fact there is a current tendency to substitute for 'benefic aspects' (sextile and trine) the term 'facilities and circumstances helpful to the individual' and for 'malefic aspects' (square and opposition), 'aspects denoting strong will, personal effort and struggle'. This was because the horoscopes of criminals (including the mass-murderer Landru) were found to contain a majority of benefic aspects, while those of people of the first rank (including the heroic Marshal Foch) were riddled with malefic aspects. Within the zodiacal circle, aspects make geometrical shapes which share the usual symbolism of TRIANGLE, SQUARE and HEXAGON.

Al-Iklīl – or Iklīl Al Jabbah (Crown of the Head) – is the Arabic name of the eighteenth station in the lunar Zodiac which some believe to be earlier than the twelve-sign solar Zodiac and which is a method of dividing the ecliptical belt into twenty-eight arcs, each of 12° 51' 26". Al-Iklīl lies between 25° 42' 53" of the sign of Libra and 8° 34' 183" of that of Scorpio. It would seem that the part which it played in astrology and its influence were especially strong in several traditions and are still so in several Eastern countries where this station is used as a guidemark. As we know, the common link between the lunar systems of the different traditions, Chinese, Hindu, Arabic, Persian and others, is the existence of stars which determine and set the boundaries of these twenty-eight stations and which are known in India as Jogatara. Although several lunar stations bear the same names as these stars, they cannot be in any sense confused or identified with them. In fact, as a result of the precession of the equinoxes most of these guidestars have been displaced and no longer even occupy the stations which bear their names. However, this in no sense alters the significance of the latter, since these lunar stations – like the solar Zodiac – were formed, in the astrologer's eyes, by the Moon's influence diffused along the paths of the solstices and equinoxes.

In India the name of this eighteenth station is Anurādha, meaning 'that which makes a circle, or a wheel, or is beautiful'. Its Hindu symbol is the PEACOCK displaying – perhaps the real reason for the wheel – although Poti provides it with the image of a platter laden wth rice, fruit, honey and flowers and making an offering to the gods. Collation of the different symbols associated with the lunar stations in different traditions, a study of their changes down the years and a critical examination of them have yet to be undertaken. They have some surprises in store for us and will doubtless provide us with the details of their original significance.

Bibliography

For ease of reference, the books are listed here by alphabetical order of their acronyms; for this reason, the authors' names do not follow strict alphabetical order, and books by the same author may occasionally be separated.

Biblical quotations are taken from the Authorized Version of the Bible; those from the Koran and from Dante's *Divina Commedia* are from Rodway's and Cary's translations respectively, and from Classical Greek and Latin authors from those provided by the Loeb Classical Library.

ADLJ   Adler, Gerhard, *Études de psychologie jungienne*, Geneva, 1957.
AEPR   Aeppli, Ernest, *Les rêves et leur interprétation*, Paris, 1951.
AFAN   Afanassiev, A. N., *Narodnye Rousskie Skazki* (Russian fairy-tales), 3 vols, reprint of 1855–63 edition, Moscow, 1957.
AIBL   Académie des Inscriptions et Belles-Lettres, *Comptes rendus*, Paris.
AINP   Ainaud, Juan, *Peintures romanes espagnoles*, Paris, 1962.
AJMO   Ajit, Mookerjee, *Tantra Asana*, Paris, 1971.
ALEC   Alexander, Hartley Burr, *The World's Rim: Great Mysteries of the North American Indians*, Lincoln (Nebraska), 1953.
ALLA   Alleau, René, *Aspects de l'alchimie traditionnelle*, Paris, 1953.
ALLB   Allmen, J. J. von, *Vocabulary of the Bible*, London, 1964.
ALLD   Alleau, René, *Encyclopédie de la divination*, Paris, 1965.
ALLH   Alleau, René, *History of Occult Sciences*, London, 1967.
ALLN   Allendy, René, *Le symbolisme des nombres*, Paris, 1948.
ALMT   Almquist, Kurt, 'Temple du cœur, temple du corps', in *Études traditionnelles* 378/9, Paris, 1963.
ALTA   *L'art ancien de l'Altaï*, Musée de l'Ermitage, Leningrad, 1958.
AMAG   *L'art magique* (compilation), Paris, 1957.
ANEI   *Anecdota from Irish Manuscripts*, 5 vols, Dublin, 1904–10.
ARBS   Arberry, A. J., *Sufism*, London, 1950.
ARCL   *Archiv für celtische Lexikographie*, 4 vols, Halle, 1898–1902.
ARNP   Arnold, T. W., *Painting in Islam*, Oxford, 1928.
ARNT   Arnold, P., *Le théâtre japonais*, Paris, 1957.
ARTF   *Histoire générale de l'art*, Paris, Flammarion, 1950.
ARTQ   *Histoire générale de l'art*, Paris, Quillet, 1938.
ARTT   Artaud, A., *Le théâtre et son double*, Paris, 1938.
ATLA   *Atlantis*, Paris, 1927–68.
ATTO   Attar, Farid-ud-Din, *The Conference of the Birds*, London, 1954.
AUBJ   Auboyer, J., 'De quelques jeux en Asie orientale', in *France-Asie* 87, Saigon, 1953.
AUBM   Aubert, Marcel, *La sculpture française au Moyen Age*, Paris, 1946.

AUBS   Auber, Abbé, *Histoire et théorie du symbolisme religieux*, 4 vols, Paris, 1884.

AUBT   Auboyer, J., *Le trône et son symbolisme dans l'Inde ancienne*, Paris, 1949.

AVAS   Avalon, A., *La puissance du serpent*, Lyon, 1959.

AVIH   Avila, Francisco de, *De Priscorum Huaruchiriensum Origine et Institutis*, Madrid, 1942.

BABM   Babelon, Jean, *Mayas d'hier et d'aujourd'hui*, Paris, 1967.

BACC   Bachelard, Gaston, *La flamme d'une chandelle*, Paris, 1961.

BACE   Bachelard, Gaston, *L'eau et les rêves, essai sur l'imagination de la matière*, Paris, 1942.

BACF   Bachelard, Gaston, *The Psychoanalysis of Fire*, translated by Alan C. M. Ross, London, 1964.

BACP   Bachelard, Gaston, *La poétique de l'espace*, Paris, 1957.

BACR   Bachelard, Gaston, *La terre et les rêveries du repos*, Paris, 1948. (reprinted 1965).

BACS   Bachelard, Gaston, *L'air et les songes*, Paris, 1948.

BACV   Bachelard, Gaston, *La terre et les rêveries de la volonté*, Paris, 1948.

BAJM   Bajov, P. P., *Malakhytovaïa Chkatoulka* (The Malachite Casket), 3 vols, Moscow, 1952.

BAMC   Bammate, Nadj Oud Din, 'La croix et le croissant', in *La Table Ronde*, Paris, décembre 1957.

BARH   Baruk, H., *Hebraic Civilisation and the Science of Man*, London, 1961.

BARS   Barthes, Roland, *The Empire of Signs*, London, 1983.

BAUA   Baumann, H. and Westermann, D., *Les peuples et les civilisations de l'Afrique*, Paris, 1948.

BAUO   Baudelaire, Ch., *Œuvres*, 2 vols, Paris, Gallimard, 1940.

BEAG   Beaujeu, J., Defradas, J., Le Bonniec, H., *Les Grecs et les Romains*, Paris, 1967.

BEAM   Beau, Georges, *La médecine chinoise*, Paris, 1965.

BECM   Becker, R. de, *The Understanding of Dreams*, London, 1968.

BEDM   Bedouin, J.-L., *Les masques*, Paris, 1941.

BEDT   Bédier, Joseph, *Le roman de Tristan et Iseut*, Paris, 1946.

BEGG   Béguin, Albert, *La quête du Saint Graal*, edited with introduction by Albert Béguin and Yves Bonnefoy, Paris, 1958.

BELT   Belpaire, B., *T'ang kien wen tse*, Paris, 1947–59.

BENA   Benoist, L., *L'art du monde*, Paris, 1941.

BENC   Benoist, L., *Regarde ou les clefs de l'art*, Paris, 1962.

BENE   Benoist, L., *L'ésotérisme*, Paris, 1965.

BENR   Benoit, Fernand, *L'art primitif méditerranéen de la vallée du Rhône*, Aix-en-Provence, 1955.

BERN   Berque, Jacques, 'A propos de l'art musulman', in *Normes et valeurs dans l'Islam contemporain*, Paris, 1966.

BETB   Bettelheim, Bruno, *Les blessures symboliques*, Paris, 1971.

BEUA   Beurdeley, M., *The Chinese Collector*, Rutland (Vermont) and Tokyo, 1966.

BEYD　　Beyer, Hermann, 'The Symbolic Meaning of the Dog in Ancient Mexico', in *America Antigua* X, Mexico, 1908.

BEYM　　Beyer, Hermann, *Mito y simbologia del Mexico antiguo*, tomo X, Mexico, 1965.

BHAB　　Bhattacharya, K., *Les religions brahmaniques dans l'ancien Cambodge*, Paris, 1961.

BIBJ　　*The Jerusalem Bible*, London, 1966.

BIBM　　*La Bible et son message*, Paris, November 1966.

BIRD　　Birge, John Kinsley, *The Bektashi Order of Dervisches*, London, 1937.

BLES　　Bley, P., Sagen der baininger auf Neupommern, Südsee, in *Antropos* IX, 1914.

BNMA　　Berdiaeff, Nicolas, *Un nouveau Moyen Age*, Paris, Plon, 1927.

BODT　　Bode, Wilhelm von, and Kühnel, Ernst, *Antique Rugs from the Near East*, translated by Charles Grant Ellis, Brunswick and Berlin, 1958.

BOEM　　Boehme, Jacob, *Mysterium magnum*, translated by N. Berdiaeff, 2 vols, Paris, 1945.

BOKT　　El Bokhari, *Les traditions islamiques*, translated by O. Houdas, Paris, 1914.

BORA　　Boratav, Pertev, *Aventures merveilleuses sous terre et ailleurs de Er-Töshtük le géant des steppes*, Paris, 1965.

BOTT　　*Botticelli*, Vienna and Paris, 1937.

BOUA　　Boulnois, J., *Le caducée et la symbolique dravidienne indoméditerranéenne, de l'arbre, de la pierre, du serpent et de la déesse-mère*, Paris, 1939.

BOUM　　Boucher, Jules, *La symbolique maçonnique*, 2nd edition, Paris, 1953.

BOUS　　Boullet, J., *Symbolisme sexuel, BIE* 5, Paris, 1961.

BREP　　Breuil, H., *Quatre cents siècles d'art pariétal*, Montignac, 1952.

BRIA　　Brion, Marcel, *Art abstrait*, Paris, 1956.

BRID　　Brion, Marcel, *Dürer*, London, 1960.

BRIF　　Brion, Marcel, *Art fantastique*, Paris, 1961.

BRIG　　Brion, Marcel, *Gœthe*, Paris, 1949.

BRIH　　Brion, Marcel, *L'âge d'or de la peinture hollandaise*, Brussels, 1964.

BRIO　　Brion, Marcel, *L'œil, l'esprit et la main du peintre*, Paris, 1966.

BRIP　　Brion, Marcel, *Romantic Art*, London, [1960].

BRIR　　Brion, Marcel, *L'Allemagne romantique*, 2 vols, Paris, 1962–3.

BRIV　　Brion, Marcel, *Leonardo da Vinci*, London, 1955.

BROT　　Bromwich, Rachel, *Trioedd Ynys Prydain*, Cardiff, 1963.

BUDA　　Budge, Sir E. A. Wallis, *Amulets and Superstitions*, London, 1930.

BUMN　　Buber, Martin, *Tales of the Rabbi Nachman*, New York, 1956.

BURA　　Burckhardt, Titus, *Art and Thought*, London, 1947.

BURD　　Burckhardt, Titus, *Introduction aux doctrines ésotériques de l'Islam*, Lyon, 1955.

BURE　　Burckhardt, Titus, *Le symbolisme du jeu des échecs*, Paris, 1954.

BURH　　Burckhardt, Titus, 'La genèse du temple hindou', in *Études traditionnelles*, Paris, juin, juillet, décembre 1953.

BURI   Burckhardt, Titus, ' "Je suis la porte", considérations sur l'icono-
        graphie des portails d'églises romanes', in *Études traditionnelles*
        308, Paris, 1953.
BURM   Burckhardt, Titus, 'Le masque sacré', in *Études traditionnelles*
        380, Paris, 1963.
BURN   Burckhardt, Titus, 'Nature sait surmonter nature', in *Études tradi-
        tionnelles* 281, Paris, 1950.
BURP   Burckhardt, Titus, *Principes et méthodes de l'art sacré*, Lyon,
        1958.
BURR   Burckhardt, Jacob, *The Civilization of the Renaissance in Italy*,
        translated by S. G. C. Middlemore, London, 1951.
BURS   Burckhardt, Titus, *Alchemy*, London, 1967.
BURT   Burckhardt, Titus, 'Commentaire succinct de la Table d'Émeraude',
        in *Études traditionnelles* 362, Paris, 1960.

CABM   Cabrera, Lydia, *El monte*, Havana, 1954.
CACL   Cachot de Girart, R., 'La luna y su personificación ornitomorfa
        en el arte chimu', in *Actas del 27° Congreso Internacionál de
        Americanistas, Lima, 1939*, vol. 1, Lima, 1940.
CADG   Cadogan, León, 'Mitologia en la zona guarani', in *Americana
        Indígena* XI, 3, Mexico, 1951.
CADV   Cadière, L., *Croyances et pratiques religieuses des Vietnamiens*,
        Saigon and Paris, 1957–8.
CAIJ   Caillois, Roger, *Man, Play, and Games*, New York, 1961.
CANA   Canseliet, Eugène, *L'alchimie*, Paris, 1964.
CAND   Canavaggio, Pierre, *Le dictionnaire des superstitions et des croy-
        ances populaires*, Verviers, 1977.
CARA   Cartier, Raymond, and Carone, Walter, *Archipel des hommes*,
        Paris, 1959.
CARH   Carcopino, Jérôme, *Études d'histoire chrétienne*, Paris, 1953.
CARL   Caroutch, Yvonne, *La licorne alchimique*, Paris, 1981.
CASN   Cassien-Bernard, Fr., *La Pa-Koua et l'origine des nombres*, Sai-
        gon, 1951.
CATI   Catlin, George, *Illustrations of the Manners and Customs of the
        North American Indians*, 2 vols, London, 1857.
CAZD   Cazeneuve, Jean, *Les dieux dansent à Cibola* (*le Shalato des indiens
        Zuñis*), Paris, 1957.
CAZJ   Cazelles, H., *Le jugement des morts en Israël*, in *Sources orientales*,
        vol. 4, Paris, 1961.
CELT   *Celticum*, annual supplement to *Ogam*.
CHAB   Charbonneau-Lassay, L., *Le bestiaire du Christ*, Bruges, 1940.
CHAD   Chapoutier, Fernand, *Les Dioscures au service d'une déesse*, Paris,
        1935.
CHAE   Charbonneau-Lassay, L., 'L'ésotérisme de quelques symboles géo-
        métriques chrétiens', in *Études traditionnelles* 346, Paris, 1958.
CHAG   Chamoux, F., *La civilisation grecque*, Paris, 1963.
CHAM   Champdor, Albert, *Le livre des morts*, Paris, 1963.
CHAS   Champeaux, G. de and Dom Sterckx, S. (O.S.B.), *Introduction
        au monde des symboles*, Paris, 1966.

CHAT   Chamfrault, A., *Traité de médecine chinoise*, Angoulême, 1957.
CHAV   Charbonneau-Lassay, L., 'La clef de voûte de Saint-Vincent de Mâcon', in *Études traditionnelles* 357, Paris, 1960.
CHIC   *Chefs-d'œuvre de l'art, de la Chine archaïque à l'Inde Moghole*, Paris, 1963.
CHOC   Chow Yi-Ching, *La philosophie morale dans le Néo-confucianisme*, Paris, 1953.
CHOM   Choisy, Maryse, *Moïse*, Geneva, 1966.
CHOO   Chochod, L., *Occultisme et magie en Extrême-Orient*, Paris, 1949.
CHRC   Christinger, R., 'La délivrance de la caille', in *Asiatisch Studien* 1–4, Bern, 1963.
CIRD   Cirlot, J. E., *A Dictionary of Symbols*, London, 1962.
CLAB   Claeys, J.-Y., 'Le culte de la baleine', in *France-Asie* 160/1, Saigon, 1959.
CLEE   Cles-Reden, Sibylle von, *The Hidden People*, London, 1955.
CLIM   Cline, Walter, *Mining and Metallurgy in Negro Africa*, Paris, 1937.
COEA   Coedes, G., *Pour mieux comprendre Angkor*, Paris, 1947.
COLD   Collin de Plancy, *Dictionnaire infernal*, Paris, 1863.
COLN   Collinet-Guérin, Marthe, *Histoire du nimbe*, Paris, 1961.
COMD   Combaz, G., 'Masques et dragons en Asie', in *Mélanges chinois et bouddhiques*, Brussels, 1945.
COOA   Coomaraswamy, Amanda K., 'The symbolism of archery', in *Ars Islamica* X, 1943.
COOD   Coomaraswamy, Amanda K., 'Symbolism of the Dome', *Indian Historical Quarterly*, Calcutta, 1938.
COOE   Coomaraswamy, Amanda K., 'Le symbolisme de l'épée', in *Études traditionelles*, janvier 1958, août 1974.
COOH   Coomaraswamy, Amanda K., *Hinduism and Buddhism*, New York, 1943.
COOI   Coomaraswamy, Amanda K., *Elements of Buddhist Iconography*, Harvard, 1935.
COOP   Coomaraswamy, Amanda K., with Horner, I. B., *The Living Thoughts of Gotama the Buddha*, London, 1948.
COOS   Coomaraswamy, Amanda K., 'Swayamâtrinnâ: Janua Coeli', in *Zalmoxis* II, 1939.
CORA   Corbin, H., *Avicenna and the Visionary Recital*, London, 1961.
CORD   Corswant, W., *A Dictionary of Life in Bible Times*, London, 1960.
CORE   Corbin, H., *En Islam iranien*, 4 vols, Paris, Gallimard, 1972.
CORF   Coral-Remusat, G. de, 'Animaux fantastiques de l'Indochine, de l'Inde et de la Chine', in *Bulletin de l'E.F.E.O.*, Hanoi, 1937.
CORH   See HAMC.
CORI   Corbin, H., *L'imagination créatrice dans le soufisme d'Ibn 'Arabi*, Paris, 1958.
CORJ   Corbin, H., *Le livre du glorieux Jâbir ibn Hayyân*, Zurich, 1950.
CORL   Corbin, H., *L'homme de lumière dans le soufisme iranien*, Paris, 1961.
CORM   Corberon, M. de, 'Le miroir des simples âmes', in *Études traditionelles* 322–49, Paris, 1955–8.

CORN   Corbin, H., Note sur *La duplication de l'autel*, par Molla Lutfi'l
        Maqtûl, Paris (see LUTD).
CORP   Corbin, H., *Histoire de la philosophie islamique*, Paris, 1964.
CORS   Corblet, Jules, *Vocabulaire des symboles*, Paris, 1877.
CORT   Corbin, H., *Trilogie ismaélienne*, Paris and Tehran, 1961.
COUL   Cougny, *Promenades au musée du Louvre*, Paris, 1888.
COUS   Coulet G., *Les sociétés secrètes en terre d'Annam*, Saigon, 1926.
CUMS   Cumont F., *Le symbolisme funéraire des Romains*, Paris, 1942.
CUNB   Cung Giu Nguyen, *Le fils de la baleine*, Paris, 1956.

DALP   Dal, V.-I., *Poslovitzy rousskogo narda* (Russian popular prov-
        erbs), Moscow, 1957, reprint of 1862 edition.
DAMS   Dam Bo (Fr Jacques Dournes), *Les populations montagnardes
        du Sud Indochinois*, Saigon, 1950.
DANA   Daniélou, Jean, *Advent*, translated by Rosemary Sheed, London,
        1950.
DANP   Daniélou, Jean, *Philon d'Alexandrie*, Paris, 1958.
DANS   Daniélou, Jean, *Primitive Christian Symbols*, London, 1964.
DANT   Daniélou, Jean, *The Theology of Jewish Christianity*, translated
        by John A. Baker, London, 1964.
DARS   Daremberg and Saglio, *Dictionnaire des antiquités grecques et
        romaines*, Paris, 1887.
DAUB   Daumal, R., *La grande beuverie*, Paris, 1958.
DAUE   Daumas, F., *La civilisation de l'Égypte pharaonique*, Paris, 1965.
DAUM   Daumal, R., *Mount Analogue*, London, 1959.
DAVL   David-Neel, A., *Initiations and Initiates in Tibet*, London, 1958.
DAVR   Davy, M.-M., *Initiation à la symbolique romane*, Paris, 1964.
DAVS   Davy, M.-M., *Un traité de la vie solitaire: lettre aux Frères du
        Mont-Dieu*, 2 vols, Paris, 1940–6.
DELC   Delebecque, Edouard, *Le cheval dans l'Iliade*, Paris, 1951.
DELH   Delcourt, Marie, *Hermaphrodite, mythes et rites de la fécondité*,
        Paris, 1958.
DELT   Delcamp, Edmond, *Le Tarot initiatique*, 11 fascicules, Maizières-
        les-Metz, 1962–5.
DEMG   Demargne, P., *Aegean Art*, London, 1964.
DEMM   Demieville, P., 'La montagne dans l'art littéraire chinois', in
        France-Asie 183, Paris, 1965.
DENJ   Deny, Jean, '70–72 chez les Turcs', in *Mélanges Massignon*, Da-
        mascus, 1956.
DENY   Dennet, R.-E., *Nigerian Studies, or the Religious and Political
        System of the Yoruba*, London, 1910.
DERI   Desvallées & Rivière, *Art populaire des pays de France*, Paris,
        1976.
DERS   Dermenghem, E., *Le culte des saints musulmans*, Paris, 1931.
DERV   Dermenghem, E., *L'éloge du vin*, Paris, 1931.
DESE   Desroches-Noblecourt, Christiane, *Egyptian Wallpaintings*, Lon-
        don, 1962.
DEVA   Devoucoux, Mgr., 'Études d'archéologie traditionnelle', in *Études
        traditionelles*, Paris, 1952–7.

DEVD   Devambez, P., *A Dictionary of Ancient Greek Civilisation* (with the assistance of R. Flacilière, P.-M. Schuhl and R. Martin), London, 1967.

DEVE   Devorepierre, *Dictionnaire encyclopédique*, Paris, 1860.

DEVP   Devambez, P., *Greek Painting*, London, 1965.

DHOB   Dhorme, Edouard, *Les religions de Babylonie et d'Assyrie*, Paris, 1949.

DICG   *Dictionnaire du gai parler*, Paris, 1980.

DICP   *Dictionnaire des personnages*, Paris, Bompiani, 1964.

DIDH   Didron, M., *Christian Iconography*, translated by E. J. Millington, 2 vols, London, 1851.

DIEB   Dieterlen, Germaine, *Essai sur la religion des Bambaras*, Paris, 1951.

DIED   Dieterlen, Germaine, 'Classification des végétaux chez les Dogons', in *Journal de la Société des Africanistes* XXII, Paris, 1952.

DIES   Diel, Paul, *Le symbolisme dans la mythologie grecque*, with Preface by G. Bachelard, new edition, Paris, 1966.

DIRK   Dirr, A., 'Der kaukasische Wild- und Jagdgott', in *Anthropos* XX, 1925.

DISA   Disselhoff, Hans-Dietrich, *Amérique précolombienne*, Paris, 1961.

DOND   Dontenville, Henri, *Les rites et récits de la mythologie française*, Paris, 1950.

DONM   Dontenville, Henri, *La mythologie française*, Paris, 1948.

DORH   Doresse, J., *Des hiéroglyphes à la croix*, Istanbul, 1960.

DORL   Doresse, J., *The Secret Books of the Egyptian Gnostics*, London, 1960.

DOUB   Dournes, J., 'La baleine et l'enfant sauveur', in *France-Asie* 79, Saigon, 1959.

DOUM   Doutte, E., *Magie et religion dans l'Afrique du Nord*, Algiers, 1909.

DROD   Droulers, Eugène, *Dictionnaire des attributs, allégories, emblèmes et symboles*, Turnhout, [1950].

DUMB   Dumézil, Georges, 'Un mythe relatif à la fermentation de la bière', in *Annuaire de l'École Pratique des Hautes Études* (5th section), Paris, 1936–7.

DUMH   Dumézil, Georges, *Le livre des héros, légendes sur les Nartes*, translated from the Ossetic with notes and introduction, Paris, 1965.

DUMI   Dumézil, Georges, *L'idéologie tripartite des Indo-Européens*, Brussels, 1958.

DUMS   Dumoutier, G., 'Le svastika et la roue solaire dans les symboles et les caractères chinois', in *Revue ethnographique*, 1885.

DUPE   Dupont-Sommer, A., *The Essene Writings from Qumran*, translated by G. Vermes, Oxford, 1961.

DURA   Durand-Lefebvre, Marie, *Art gallo-romain et sculpture romane*, Paris, 1937.

DURF   Durkheim, Émile, *The Elementary Forms of Religious Life*, London, 1915.

DURI   Durand, Gilbert, *L'imagination symbolique*, Paris, 1964.

DURS   Durand, Gilbert, *Les structures anthropologiques de l'imaginaire*, Paris, 1963.
DURV   Durand, M., *Imagerie populaire vietnamienne*, Paris, 1960.
DUSC   Dusson, H., *Les sociétés secrètes en Chine et en terre d'Annam*, Saigon, 1911.
DUSH   Dussaud, René, *Les religions des Hittites et des Hourrites, des Phéniciens et des Syriens*, Paris, 1949.

ECKT   Eckhart, *Traités et Sermons*, edited by Maurice de Gandillac, Paris, 1943.
EISB   Eissfeldt, O., *Der Bentel der Lebendigen*, Leipzig, 1960.
ELIC   Eliade, Mircea, *Shamanism*, translated by Willard R. Trask, London and New York, 1964.
ELIF   Eliade, Mircea, *The Forge and the Crucible*, translated by Stephen Corrin, London, [1962].
ELII   Eliade, Mircea, *Images and Symbols*, translated by Philip Mairet, London, 1961.
ELIM   Eliade, Mircea, *Méphistophélès et l'androgyne*, Paris, 1962.
ELIR   Eliade, Mircea, *Myths, Dreams and Mysteries*, London, 1960.
ELIT   Eliade, Mircea, *Patterns in Comparative Religion*, translated by Rosemary Sheed, London and New York, 1958.
ELIY   Eliade, Mircea, *Yoga*, London, 1958.
EMTR   Ernesto de Martino, *La terre des remords*, Paris, 1966.
ENCD   *Encyclopédie de la divination*, Paris, 1965.
ENCF   *Encyclopédie de la foi*, Paris, 1965.
ENCI   *Encyclopédie de l'Islam*, 5 vols, Paris, 1908–38.
ENCU   *Encyclopedia universalis*, Paris, 1975.
EPEM   Epes-Brown, J., 'Les miroirs chinois', in *Études traditionelles* 313, Paris, 1954.
EPET   Epes-Brown, J., 'L'art du tir à l'arc', in *Études traditionelles* 330, Paris, 1956.
ERAJ   *Eranos Jahrbuch*.
ERMR   Erman, Adolphe, *La religion des Égyptiens*, Paris, 1952.
ETUC   *Études celtiques*, Paris, 1936.
ETUP   'Polarité du symbole', *Études carmélitaines*, Paris, 1960.
ETUT   *Études traditionnelles*, Paris.
EVAB   Evans-Wentz, Dr. W.-Y., *The Tibetan Book of the Dead*, London, 1927.
EVAS   Evans-Pritchard, E., *Witchcraft, Oracles and Magic among the Azende*, Oxford, 1937.
EVDF   Evdokimov, Paul, *La femme et le salut du monde*, Paris, 1958.
EYTA   Evola, Julius, *Le yoga tantrique*, Paris, Fayard, 1971.

FAHD   Fahd, Toufic, *La divination arabe*, Leiden, 1966.
FAHN   Fahd, Toufic, 'La naissance du monde selon l'Islam', in *Sources orientales*, Paris, 1959.
FANO   Favre and November, *Color & Communication*, Zurich, 1979.
FARD   Fares, Bishr, *Essai sur l'esprit de la décoration islamique*, Cairo, 1952.

FAVS   Favre, B., *Les sociétés secrètes en Chine*, Paris, 1933.

FELM   Feline, Pierre, 'Arts maghrébins', in *L'Islam et l'Occident, Cahiers du Sud*, 1947.

FLEH   Fletcher, Alice, 'The Hako: a Pawne ceremony', in Bureau of American Ethnology 22nd Annual Report (1900–1901), Washington, 1904.

FLUC   Fludd, Robert, *Utriusque Cosmi Historia*, Oppenheim, 1619.

FORB   Forman, W. and B. and Dark, P., *Benin Art*, London, 1960.

FOUA   Fourche-Tiarko, J.-A. and Morlighem, H., 'Architecture et analogies des plans du monde d'après les conceptions des indigènes du Kasaï et d'autres régions', Institut royal colonial belge, *Bulletin des séances* IX, 3, Brussels, 1938.

FOUC   Fourche-Tiarko, J.-A., et Morlighem, H., *Les communications des indigènes du Kasaï avec les âmes des morts*, Institut royal colonial belge, Bruxelles, 1939.

FOUD   Fourche-Tiarko, J.-A., et Morlighem, H., *La danse de Tshishimbi chez les Lulua du Kasaï*, Institut royal colonial belge, Bruxelles, 1937.

FRAF   Frazer, J.-G., *Myths of the Origin of Fire*, London, 1930.

FRAG   Frazer, J.-G., *The Golden Bough, A Study in Magic and Religion*, 3rd edition, revised and enlarged, 12 vols, London, 1911–15.

FRAL   'Présence du royaume Lao', in *France-Asie*, Saigon, 1956.

FRCH   Chaboche, François-Xavier, *Vie et mystère des nombres*, Paris, 1976.

FRER   Freud, S., *Complete Works*.

FROA   Frobenius, Léo, *Mythologie de l'Atlantide*, translated by Dr. F. Gidon, Paris, 1949.

FROC   Frobenius, Léo, *Histoire de la civilisation africaine*, translated by Dr. H. Back and D. Ermont, Paris, 1936.

FULC   Fulcanelli, *Le mystère des cathédrales (et l'interprétation ésotérique des symboles hermétiques du grand œuvre)*, 3rd enlarged edition with three prefaces by E. Canseliet, Paris, 1964.

FUNP   Funck-Hellet, Ch., *De la proportion: l'équerre des maîtres d'œuvre*, Paris, 1951.

GALA   Gardet, Louis-Olivier Lacombe, *L'expérience du soi*, Paris, Desclées de Brouwer, 1981.

GAND   Ganay, S. de, *Les devises des Dogon*, Paris, 1941.

GANF   Ganshof, F.-L., *Feudalism*, London, 1952.

GARC   Garcilaso de la Vega (El Inca), *Comentarios reales de los Incas*, Buenos Aires, 1945.

GENT   Gennep, Arnold Van, in *Le tapis, un art fondamental*, Paris, 1949.

GEVH   Gevaert, Émile, *L'héraldique, son esprit, son langage et ses applications*, Bruxelles, 1923.

GEZH   Geza, Roheim, *Héros phalliques et symboles maternels*, Paris, 1970.

GHEO   Gheerbrant, Alain, *L'expédition Orénoque-Amazone*, Paris, 1952.

GHIP   Ghirsman, R., *Persia*, London, 1964.

GHIS   Ghirsman, R., *Iran*, London, 1962.

GHYN   Ghyka, Matila C., *Le nombre d'or*, 2 vols, Paris, 1931.

GHYP   Ghyka, Matila C., *Philosophie et mystique du nombre*, Paris, 1952.
GIEJ   Gieseler, Dr. G., 'Les symboles du jade dans le Taoïsme', in *Revue de l'histoire des religions*, Paris, 1932.
GIRD   Girault, Fr Louis, 'Essai sur la religion des Dagaras', in *Bulletin de l'Institut français d'Afrique Noire* XXI, série B, Dakar, 1959.
GIRP   Girard, Raphaël, *Le Popol-Vuh, histoire culturelle des Maya-Quiché*, Paris, 1954.
GIUP   Giuglaris, M., 'Les palais royaux de Séoul et leurs symboles', in *France-Asie* 81, Saigon, 1953.
GORH   Gorce, Maxime and Mortier, Raoul, *Histoire générale des religions*, 5 vols, Paris, 1948.
GOUL   Gourmont, Rémy de, *Le latin mystique. Les poètes de l'antiphonaire et la symbolique au Moyen Age*, Paris, 1913.
GOVM   Govinda, Lama Anagarika, *Les fondements de la mystique tibétaine*, Paris, 1960.
GOYO   *Goya, l'œuvre gravé*, Paris, 1948.
GRAB   Gray, Basil, *Persian Miniatures*, London, 1962.
GRAC   Granet, M., *Chinese Civilisation*, London, 1930.
GRAD   Granet, M., *Danses et légendes de la Chine ancienne*, 2 vols, Paris, 1926.
GRAF   Granet, M., *Festivals and Songs of Ancient China*, London, 1932.
GRAG   Gray, Basil, *Persian Painting*, London, 1947.
GRAH   Grabar, André and Nordenfalk, C. A. J., *Early Mediaeval Painting*, Lausanne, 1957.
GRAM   Graves, Robert, *Greek Myths*, London, 1958.
GRAO   *Les plus belles gravures du monde occidental*, Bibliothèque Nationale, Paris.
GRAP   Granet, M., *La pensée chinoise*, Paris, 1934.
GRAR   Granet, M., *La religion des Chinois*, Paris, 1951.
GREA   Grenier, Albert, *Manuel d'archéologie gallo-romaine*, IV/2, *Villes d'eau et sanctuaires de l'eau*, Paris, 1960.
GRIA   Grillot de Givry, *Witchcraft, Magic and Alchemy*, translated by J. Courtenay Locke, London, 1931.
GRIB   Griaule, Marcel, 'Note sur le couteau de circoncision des Bozo', in *Journal de la Société des Africanistes* XXVI, Paris, 1956.
GRIC   Grison, P., 'Coordonnées pour le site d'Angkor', in *Cahiers astrologiques* 119, Nice, 1965.
GRID   Grimal, Pierre, *Dictionnaire de la mythologie grecque et romaine*, with preface by Ch. Picard, 3rd corrected edition, Paris, 1963.
GRIE   Griaule, Marcel, *Conversations with Ogotommeli*, London, 1965.
GRIF   Grison, P., *Le traité de la fleur d'or du suprême un*, Paris, 1966.
GRIG   Griaule, Marcel and Dieterlen, G., *Signes graphiques soudanais*, Paris, 1951.
GRIH   Griaule, Marcel and Dieterlen, G., 'La harpe-luth des Dogons', in *Journal de la Société des Africanistes* XX, Paris, 1950.
GRII   Griaule, Marcel, 'L'image du monde au Soudan', in *Journal de la Société des Africanistes* XIX, Paris, 1949.
GRIJ   Grison, P., 'Notes sur le jade', in *Études traditionelles* 382, Paris, 1964.

GRIL   Grison, P., 'La légende des Hong', in *Études traditionelles* 377, Paris, 1963.

GRIM   Griaule, Marcel, *Masques Dogons*, Paris, 1938.

GRIN   Griaule, Marcel, 'Nouvelles remarques sur la harpe-luth des Dogons', in *Journal de la Société des Africanistes* XXIV, Paris, 1954.

GRIO   Grison, P., 'Le bouddhisme comme expérience spirituelle', in *Présence du bouddhisme*, Saigon, 1959.

GRIP   Griaule, Marcel and Dieterlen, G., *Le renard pâle*, vol. I: *Le mythe cosmogonique*, fasc. I: *La création du monde*, Paris, 1965.

GRIR   Grison P., 'Remarques sur le symbolisme angkorien', in *Études traditionelles* 356, Paris, 1959.

GRIS   Griaule, Marcel, *Symbolisme d'un temple totémique soudanais*, Rome, 1957.

GRIT   Grison, J.-L., 'Notes sur les trigrammes', in *Études traditionelles* 384/5, Paris, 1964.

GRIV   Grison, P., 'L'art de la vie et l'art du paysage', in *Trois estampes nouvelles sur le Japon*, Saigon, 1955.

GROA   Groslier, Bernard-Philippe, *Angkor*, London, 1957.

GROC   Grousset, R., *Chinese Art and Culture*, London, 1959.

GROD   Groddek, G. W., *La maladie, l'art et le symbole*, Paris, 1969.

GROE   Grousset, R., *L'art de l'Extrême-Orient*, Bern and Paris, 1950.

GROI   Grodecki, Louis, *L'Inde*, Paris, 1949.

GROM   Grodecki, Louis, *Symbolisme cosmique et monuments religieux*, Paris, 1953.

GUEA   Guénon, R., *Autorité spirituelle et pouvoir temporel*, Paris, 1929.

GUEC   Guénon, R., *Le symbolisme de la croix*, Paris, 1931.

GUED   Guénon, R., *L'ésotérisme de Dante*, Paris, 1925.

GUEE   Guénon, R., *Les états multiples de l'être*, Paris, 1957.

GUEI   Guénon, R., *Aperçus sur L'initiation*, Paris, 1946.

GUEM   Guénon, R., *Le roi du monde*, Paris, 1927.

GUEN   Guénon, R., 'The mysteries of the letter Nün', in *Artaud Thought*, London, 1947.

GUEO   Guénon, R., 'A propos des signes corporatifs et de leur sens originel', in *Études traditionelles* 291, Paris, 1951.

GUER   Guénon, R., *The Reign of Quantity and Signs of the Times*, London, 1953.

GUES   Guénon, R., *Symboles fondamentaux de la science sacrée*, Paris, 1962.

GUET   Guénon, R., *La grande triade*, Nancy, 1946.

GUEV   Guénon, R., *Man and his Becoming according to the Vedanta*, London, 1945.

GUIB   Guillet, J., *Thèmes bibliques*, Paris, 1950.

GUID   *Dictionnaire érotique*, Paris, 1978.

GUIO   Guiart, Jean, *The Arts of the South Pacific*, London, 1963.

GUTG   Guthrie, W., *The Greeks and their Gods*, London, 1950.

HADB   Hadewijch d'Anvers, *Écrits mystiques des Béguines*, Paris, 1954.

HAJC   Hajek, Lubor, *Chinese Art*, Prague, 1954.

HAMC   Hamidullah, M., *Le Coran*, annotated translation, Paris, 1955.

HAMK   Hampate Ba, Amadou, *Kaydara* (UNESCO paper).

HARA   Harva, Uno, *Les représentations religieuses des peuples altaïques*, translated from the German by Jean-Louis Perret, Paris, 1959.

HASE   Hastings, James, in *Encyclopaedia of religions and ethics*, 13 vols, Edinburgh and New York, 1908–21.

HAUM   Hautecœur, L., *Mystique et architecture*, Paris, 1954.

HAUV   Haulotte, E., *Symbolique du vêtement selon la Bible*, Paris, 1966.

HAVE   Havelock Ellis, H., *Erotic Symbolism*, New York, 1906.

HAYI   Hayek, M., *Le mystère d'Ismaël*, Paris, 1964.

HEHS   Hehaka, Sapa, *Les rites secrets des Indiens Sioux*, Paris, 1953.

HENI   Henry, Françoise, *L'art irlandais*, 3 vols, St-Léger-Vauban, 1963–4.

HENL   Hentze, C., *Mythes et symboles lunaires*, Antwerp, 1932.

HERA   Herbert, J., *Introduction à l'Asie*, Paris, 1960.

HERF   Herrigel, Gustyl, *La voie des fleurs*, Lyon, 1957.

HERJ   Herbert, J., *Les dieux nationaux du Japon*, Paris, 1965.

HERS   Herbert, J., *Aux sources du Japon: le Shintô*, Paris, 1964.

HERV   Herbert, J., *Les dix tableaux du domestiquage de la vache*, Lyon, 1960.

HERZ   Herrigel, E., *Zen in the Art of Archery*, London, 1953.

HOLA   Holdera, A., *Altceltischer Sprachschatz*, Leipzig, 1896–1922.

HOLK   Holas, Bohumil, *Le culte de Zie, éléments de la religion Kono (Haute-Guinée Française)*, Dakar, 1954.

HOLS   Holas, Bohumil, 'Fondements spirituels de la vie sociale Senoufo (région de Korhogo, Côte-d'Ivoire)', in *Journal de la Société des Africanistes* 26, Paris, 1956.

HOMC   Homer, *L'Odyssée, illustrée par la céramique grecque*, Paris, 1951.

HOMG   Homer, *L'Iliade, illustrée par la céramique grecque*, Paris, 1951.

HOPF   Hopkins, E. W., 'The Fountain of Youth', in *Journal of the American Oriental Society* 26, 1905.

HOUD   Houei Neng, *Discours et sermons*, Paris, 1963.

HPBA   *L'herméneutique permanente ou le buisson ardent* (joint authorship), Paris, Berg, 1981.

HUAB   Huart, Clément, *Traité des terms figurés relatifs à la description de la beauté par Sheref abd in Râmi*, Paris, 1875.

HUAH   Huart, Clément, *Textes persans relatifs à la secte des Houroufis*, London, 1909.

HUAN   Huart, Clément, *La poésie religieuse des Nosaïris* (reprinted from the *Journal asiatique*), Paris, 1880.

HUAS   Huart, Clément, *Notes prises pendant un voyage en Syrie* (reprinted from the *Journal asiatique*), Paris, 1879.

HUAV   Huart, P. et Durand, M., *Connaissance du Viêt-nam*, Hanoi, 1954.

HUGA   Hugues de Fouilloy, *De claustro animae, Meditativae orationes*, edited by M. M. Davy, Paris, 1934.

HUGD   Hughes, T. P., *A Dictionary of Islam*, London, 1896.

HUIA   Huisman, G., *Histoire générale de l'art*, Paris, 1938.

HUID   Huizinga, J., *The Waning of the Middle Ages*, London, 1955.

HUMU   Hummel, S., 'Die verschlossene Urflut in Stadt Hempel zu Lhasa
        und die Weiden vor dem Heiligtum', in *Kairos* 3/4, Salzburg,
        1964.
HUYA   Huyghe, R., *Art and the Spirit of Man*, London, 1962.
HUYD   Huyghe, R., *Dialogue avec le visible*, Paris, 1955.

IFHI   Ifrah, Georges, *Histoire universelle des chiffres*, Paris, 1981.
INDA   *Trésors d'art de l'Inde*, Petit Palais, Paris, 1960.

JACA   Jacquot, J., *Les théâtres d'Asie*, Paris, 1961.
JACC   Jacobi, Yolande, *Complexe, archétype, symbole,* translated by
        J. Chavy, with preface by C. G. Jung, Neuchâtel, 1961.
JACG   Jackson-Knight, W. F., *Cumaean Gates, A Reference of the Sixth
        Aeneid to Initiation Pattern*, Oxford, 1936.
JACT   Jacob, E., *Theology of the Old Testament*, London, 1958.
JAMM   James, E. O., *Myth and Ritual in the Ancient Near East*, London,
        1958.
JAPA   *L'art japonais à travers les siècles*, Musée national d'art moderne,
        Paris, 1958.
JAQJ   Jaquillard, P., 'Une découverte de l'Occident contemporain: le
        jade chinois de haute époque', in *Asiatische Studien*, 1/2, Bern,
        1962.
JARA   *Jardin des Arts*, Paris (77, 78, 80, 81, 94, 115).
JAUA   Jaubert, A., *La notion d'alliance dans le judaïsme*, Paris, 1963.
JEAD   Jeanmaire, H., *Dionysos, histoire du culte de Bacchus*, Paris, 1951.
JILH   Jili, Abd al Karîm al, *De l'homme universel*, Lyon and Algiers,
        1952.
JOBT   Jobe, Joseph, *The Art of Tapestry*, London, 1965.
JOIP   Joinet, Bernard, 'Psycho-pédagogie des symboles bibliques' (doc-
        toral thesis), Strasburg, 1966.
JUNA   Jung, C. G., *Psychology and Alchemy*, translated by R. F. C. Hull
        (*Collected Works* vol. 12), London, 1968.
JUNG   Jung, C. G., *La guérison psychologique*, Geneva, Librairie de
        l'Université, 1970.
JUNH   Jung, C. G., *L'homme à la découverte de son âme; structure et
        fonctionnement de l'inconscient* (preface and translation by R.
        Cahen-Salabelle), 2nd revised and enlarged edition, Geneva,
        1946.
JUNL   Jung, C. G., *Psychology of the Unconscious*, translated by Beatrice
        M. Hinkle, M.D., 6th impression, London, 1951.
JUNM   Jung, C. G., *Symbols of Transformation*, translated by R. F. C.
        Hull (*Collected Works* vol. 5), London, 1967.
JUNP   Jung, C. G., *Problèmes de l'âme moderne*, 1927.
JUNR   Jung, C. G., *Psychology and Religion*, translated by R. F. C. Hull
        (*Collected Works* vol. 11), London, [1969].
JUNS   Jung, C. G., *Man and his Symbols*, London, 1964.
JUNT   Jung, C. G., *Psychological Types*, H. G. Baynes's translation re-
        vised by R. F. C. Hull (*Collected Works*, vol. 6), London, 1971.
JUNV   Jung, C. G., *L'âme et la vie*, Paris, 1963.

KAKD   Kakouri, Katerina J., *Dionisiaka, Aspects of the Popular Thracian Religion of Today*, Athens, 1965.
KALE   Kalou, Rimpoche, *Enseignements bouddhiques tibétains*, Kagyu Dzong, 1975.
KALL   Kaltenmark, M., *Le Lie-sien tchouan*, Peking, 1953.
KALT   Kaltenmark, M., *Lao-Tseu et le taoïsme*, Paris, 1965.
KANS   Kandinsky, Wassily, *On the Spiritual in Art*, New York, 1946.
KEMR   Kemlin, J.-E., 'Les alliances chez`les Reungao', in *Bulletin de l'E.F.E.O.*, Hanoi, 1910.
KERA   Kersaint, Claire de, *La mystique des eaux sacrées dans l'antique Armor*, Paris, 1947.
KEYM   Keyserling, Count Hermann, *South American Meditations*, translated by Therese Duerr, London, 1932.
KHAB   Khatibi, *La blessure du nom propre*, Paris, 1974.
KNOS   Knorr de Rosenroth, *Le symbolisme des lettres hébraïques*, Paris, 1958.
KOPK   Kopczynska-Jaworska, Bronislawa, 'Das Hirtenwesen in den polnischen Karpaten', in *Ausgaben des Ungarischen Ethnographischen Museums*, Budapest, 1961.
KOPP   Koppers, Wilhelm, 'Pferdeopfer und Pferdekult des Indogermanen', in *Wiener Beiträge zur Kulturgeschichte und Linguistik*, IV, 1936.
KRAA   Kramrisch, Stella, *The Art of India*, London, 1954.
KRAM   Krappe, Alexandre H., *La genèse des mythes*, Paris, 1952.
KRAT   Kramrisch, Stella, *The Hindu Temple*, Calcutta, 1946.
KRIE   Krickeberg, Walter, *Ethnología de America*, Spanish translation by Pedro Hendrich, Mexico, Fondo de cultura economica, 1946.
KRIR   Krickeberg, Walter, 'Les religions des peuples civilisés de Mezo-Amerique', in *Religions amérindiennes*, translated from the German by L. Jospin, Paris, 1962.
KUCT   Kucharski, Paul, *Étude sur la doctrine pythagoricienne de la tétrade*, Paris (n.d.).

LACE   Lacan, J., *Écrits*, Paris, 1966.
LALM   Laloy, L., *Le rêve du millet jaune*, Paris, 1935.
LAME   Lambrino, *L'Égypte*, revue 'Encyclopédie par l'image', Paris, 1963.
LAMP   Lambsprinck, *La pierre philosophale*, reprinted Milan, 1971.
LANH   Landsberg (Herrade de), *Hortus Deliciarum*, Strasburg, 1899.
LANM   Lane, E. W., *Manners and Customs of the Modern Egyptians*, 2 vols, London, 1836.
LANN   Lane, E. W., *The Thousand and One Nights*, 3 vols, London, 1838–40.
LANS   Lanoé-Villène, G., *Le livre des symboles*, 6 vols, Bordeaux and Paris, 1926–35.
LAPV   Laplanche, J. and Pontalis, J.-B., *Vocabulaire de la psychanalyse*, Paris, 1967.
LATH   Latouche, Robert, *Le film de l'histoire médiévale*, Paris, 1959.
LAUA   Laude, Jean, *Les arts de l'Afrique Noire*, Paris, 1966.
LAUJ   Laufer, B., *Jade, a Study in Chinese Archeology and Religion*, Chicago, 1912.

LAVD   Lavedan, P., *Dictionnaire illustré de la mythologie et des antiquités grecques et romaines*, Paris, 1931.

LEBC   Lebrun, G., 'La chique de bétel', in *France-Asie* 36, Saigon, 1949.

LEBF   Lebeuf, J.-P., *L'habitation des Fali, montagnards du Cameroun septentrional, technologie, sociologie, mythologie, symbolisme*, Paris, 1961.

LEBI   *Lebor Gabala Erenn*, edited by R. A. S. Macalister, 5 vols, London, Irish Texts Society, 1938–56.

LEBM   Lebeuf, J. -P. et Mambeke-Boucher, B., *Un mythe de la création, Congo-Brazzaville*, Rome, 1964.

LECC   *Lectures chinoises* 1, Peking, 1945.

LECM   Leclercq, J., *Initiation aux auteurs monastiques du Moyen-Âge*, Paris, 1956.

LEEC   Leenhardt, M. *Notes d'ethnologie néo-calédonienne*, Paris, 1930.

LEER   Leeuw, G. van der, *Religion in Essence and Manifestation*, London, 1938.

LEHC   Lehmann-Nitsche, R., 'Coricancha, el templo del sol en el Cuzco y las imagenes de su altar mayor', in *Revista del Museo de La Plata* XXXVI, Buenos-Aires, 1928.

LEIA   Leiris, Michel, *L'Afrique fantôme*, Paris, 1934.

LEOV   Leon-Dufour, X., *Vocabulaire de théologie biblique*, Paris, 1962.

LERB   Lery, Jean de, *Histoire d'un voyage fait en la terre du Brésil*, Paris, 1880.

LERD   Leroux, Françoise, *Les Druides*, Paris, 1961.

LERG   Leroi-Gourhan, André, *Le geste et la parole*, Paris, 1964.

LERI   Leroux, Françoise, 'Les îles au Nord du Monde', in *Hommages à Albert Grenier*, II, Bruxelles, 1962.

LERM   Le Rouge, Gustave, *La mandragore magique*, Paris, 1912.

LERP   Leroi-Gourhan, André, *The Art of Prehistoric Man in Western Europe*, London, 1968.

LERR   Leroi-Gourhan, André, *Les racines du monde*, Paris, 1982.

LEVC   Lévi-Strauss, Claude, *The Raw and the Cooked*, translated by John and Doreen Weightman, London, 1969.

LEVD   Lévi-Strauss, Claude, *Du miel aux cendres*, Paris, 1966.

LEVM   Lévy-Bruhl, Lucien, *La mythologie primitive: le monde mythique des Australiens et des Papous*, Paris, 1963.

LEVS   Lévi-Strauss, Claude, *Le symbolisme cosmique dans la structure sociale et l'organisation cérémonielle de plusieurs populations nord et sud-américaines, le symbolisme cosmique des monuments religieux*, Rome, 1957.

LEVT   Lévi-Strauss, Claude, *Totemism*, translated by Rodney Needham, London, 1969.

LIOC   Lionnet, J., 'Les origines de la civilisation chinoise', in *Études traditionelles* 334, Paris, 1958.

LIOT   Lionnet, J., *Le Tao Te King*, Paris, 1962.

LITA   Lionel, Frédéric, *Le Tarot magique*, Monaco, 1980.

LOCD   Lo Duca, Giuseppe, *Dictionnaire de sexologie*, Paris, 1962.

LOEC   Loeffler-Delachaux, M., *Le cercle*, Geneva, 1947.

LOEF   Loeffler-Delachaux, M., *Le symbolisme des contes de fées*, Paris, 1949.

LOTL   Lot-Falck, E., *La lune, mythes et rites*, Paris, 1962.
LOTM   Loth, Joseph, *Les Mabinogion*, 2 vols, Paris, 1913.
LOUE   Louvre (Musée du), *Encyclopédie photographique de l'art*, 3 vols, Paris, 1936.
LOUP   Louis, René, 'Une coutume d'origine préhistorique: les combats sur les gués chez les Celtes et chez les Germains', in *Revue archéologique de l'Est* V, 1954.
LUEF   Lubac, Henri de, *L'éternel féminin*, Paris, Aubier, 1968.
LUTD   Lutfi'l Maqtul, *La duplication de l'autel*, translated into French with an introduction by Abdullah Adnar and Henry Corbin, Paris (n.d.).

MABG   *The Mabinogion*, translated by Lady Charlotte Guest; introduction by Rev. R. Williams, London, Everyman (n.d.).
MACC   Mackenzie, Finlay, *Chinese Art*, London, 1962.
MAEV   Maes, H., 'Les voyages fictifs dans la littérature japonaise à l'époque d'Edo', in *France-Asie* 182, Tokyo, 1964.
MAGE   Magnien, Victor, *Les mystères d'Eleusis (leur origine, le rituel de leurs initiations)*, Paris, 1950.
MAIR   Maiuri, Amedeo, *Roman Painting*, Geneva, 1953.
MALA   Mallmann, M.-T. de, *Les enseignements iconographiques de l'Agni Purâna*, Paris, 1963.
MALM   Malinowski, B., *The Sexual Life of Savages*, London, 1931.
MALW   Malory, Sir Thomas, *Works*, edited by Eugène Vinaver (Oxford Standard Authors), London, 1954.
MAND   Mannhardt, W., *Die Götter der deutschen und nordischen Völker*, Berlin, 1905.
MANG   Mannhardt, W., *Germanische Mythen*, Berlin, 1858.
MANW   Mannhardt, W., *Wald und Feldkulte*, 2nd edition, vol. 1, Berlin, 1904, vol. 2, Berlin, 1905.
MARA   Marques-Rivière, Jean, *Amulettes, talismans et pentacles dans les traditions orientales et occidentales*, with a preface by Paul Masson-Oursel, Paris, 1938.
MARD   Marques-Rivière, Jean, *Histoire des doctrines ésotériques*, Paris, 1950.
MARG   Marx, J., *La légende arthurienne et le Graal*, Paris, 1952.
MART   Marteau, Paul, *Le tarot de Marseille*, with a preface by Jean Paulhan and explanatory notes by Eugène Caslant, Paris, 1949.
MARV   Marcelin, Milo, *Mythologie vaudou*, 2 vols, Port-au-Prince, 1949–50.
MASA   Massignon, L., 'L'arabe, langue liturgique de l'Islam', in *Cahiers du Sud*, 1947.
MASC   Maspero, H., *Les religions chinoises*, Paris, 1950.
MASH   Massignon, L., *La Passion d'Al-Hallaj*, 2 vols, Paris, 1922.
MASI   Massignon, L., *L'âme de l'Iran*, Paris, 1951.
MASL   Massignon, L., *Essai sur les origines du lexique technique de la mystique musulmane*, Paris, 1922.
MASM   Massignon, L., *Mélanges*, 3 vols, Damascus, 1957.
MASN   Maspero, H., *Les procédés de 'nourrir le principe vital' dans la religion taoïste ancienne*, Paris, 1937.
MASP   Masse, H., *Croyances et coutumes persanes*, 2 vols, Paris, 1938.

MASR   Massignon, L., 'Les méthodes de réalisation artistique des peuples
        de l'Islam', in *Syria* 2, 1921.
MAST   Maspero, H., *Le Taoïsme*, Paris, 1950.
MATE   Matz, Friedrich, *Le monde égéen*, Paris, 1956.
MATM   Mat Gioi (A. de Pouvourville), *La voie métaphysique*, Paris, 1936.
MAUG   Maupoil, Bernard, *La géomancie à l'ancienne Côte des esclaves*,
        Paris, 1943.
MCPM   Meunier, Jacques, 'Grandes peurs et petits poissons', in *Le Monde*,
        26 July 1981.
MEAA   Means, P. A., *Ancient Civilisations of the Andes*, London, 1931.
MEDI   *Mediaeval and Modern Irish Series*, Dublin, 1933.
MEJP   Mejia Xesspe, Toribo, 'Mitologia del Norte Andino Peruano', in
        América Indigena XIII, 3, Mexico, 1952.
MEKE   Mekhitharean, Arpag, *Egyptian Painting*, Geneva, 1954.
MELN   Melikoff, Irène, 'Nombres symboliques dans la littérature épico-
        religieuse des Turcs d'Anatolie', in *Journal asiatique* CCL, 1962.
MENC   Menard, René, *Les carrelages historiques*, Paris, 1887.
MERF   Mercier, Paul, *The Fon of Dahomey*, London, 1954.
METB   Metraux, Alfred, 'Boy's Initiation Rites; Religion and Shaman-
        ism', in *Handbook of South American Indians*, vol. V, Wash-
        ington, 1949.
METC   Metz, René, *La consécration des vierges dans l'Église romaine*,
        Paris, 1954.
METD   Metraux, Alfred, 'El Dios supremo, los creadores y heroes cul-
        turales en la mitologia sudamericana', in *Americana Indígena*
        VI, Mexico, 1946.
METM   Metraux, Alfred, 'Mourning Rites and Burial Forms of the South
        American Indians', in *America Indígena* V–VII, 1, Mexico,
        1945–7.
METS   Metraux, Alfred, 'Ensayos de mitologia comparada sudamericana',
        in *America Indígena* VIII, 1, Mexico, 1948.
METT   Metraux, Alfred, *La religion des Tupinamba*, Paris, 1928.
METV   Metraux, Alfred, *Voodoo in Haiti*, London, 1959.
MEXA   *Mexique pré-colombien, art et style*, Paris, 1962.
MEXC   *Chefs-d'œuvre de l'art mexicain*, Paris, 1962.
MEYB   Meyer, Kuno and Nutt, Alfred, *The Voyage of Bran*, 2 vols, Lon-
        don, 1897.
MEYS   Meyerovitch, E., *Les songes et leur interprétation chez les Persans*,
        Paris, 1959.
MICA   *The Sculptures of Michael Angelo*, London, 1940.
MICP   *Le plafond de la Sixtine*, Paris, 1935.
MICS   Michaud, G., *Message poétique du symbolisme*, Paris, 1949.
MOKC   Mokri, Mohammed, *Le chasseur de Dieu et le mythe de Roi-aigle,
        texte établi, traduit et commenté avec une étude sur la chasse
        mystique et le temps cyclique, et des notes linguistiques*,
        Wiesbaden, 1967.
MOKP   Mokri, Mohammed, 'Le symbole de la perle dans le folklore
        persan', in *Journal asiatique* 463, 1960.
MONA   Monod-Herzen, G.-E., *L'alchimie méditerranéenne, ses origines
        et son but, la Table d'Émeraude*, Paris, 1963.

MORC   Morin, E., *Le cinéma*, Paris, 1960.

MORD   Morel, R., *Dictionnaire des superstitions*, Forcalquier, 1967.

MORR   Morenz, S., *La religion égyptienne*, Paris, 1962.

MOUJ   Mousset, P., *Le Japon*, Paris, 1960.

MUEP   Musée d'ethnographie de Genève, *La parure dans le monde*, Geneva, 1949.

MULR   Muller, Werner, 'Les religions des Indiens d'Amérique du Nord', in *Les religions amérindiennes*, translated from the German by L. Jospin, Paris, 1962.

MUSB   Mus, P., 'Barabudur, les origines du stûpa et la transmigration', in *Bulletin de l'E.F.E.O.*, Hanoi, 1932–4.

MUTC   Mutel, R., 'A propos de la clé de voûte mâconnaise au lion bibliophore', in *Études traditionelles* 358, Paris, 1960.

MUTG   Mutel, R., 'A propos des "graffites inconnus" de la chapelle du Martray à Loudun', in *Études traditionelles* 347, Paris, 1958.

MUTT   Mutel, R., *La Trinacria*, in *Études traditionelles* 319/20, Paris, 1954.

MVEA   Mveng, E., *L'art d'Afrique noire*, Paris, 1964.

MYFA   *The Myfyrian Archaeology of Wales*, Denbigh, 1870.

MYTF   *Mythologies des montagnes, des forêts et des îles*, general editor: P. Grimal, Paris, 1963.

MYTM   *Mythologies de la Méditerranée au Gange*, general editor: P. Grimal, Paris, 1963.

NAUM   Naumann, H., *Über Mikrophotographie und Yafisro, Instrumentenk*, 1934.

NGUA   Nguyen Van Huyen, *La civilisation annamite*, Hanoi, 1944.

NGUC   Nguyen Cong Huan, 'Le crapaud est l'oncle du Dieu du Ciel', in *France-Asie* 170, Tokyo, 1961.

NICH   Nicolas, Fr F.-I., 'Mythes et êtres mythiques de Haute-Volta', in *Bulletin de l'I.F.A.N.* XIV, 4, Dakar, 1952.

NICM   Nicholson, R. A., *Studies in Islamic Mysticism*, Cambridge, 1921.

NICO   Nicholas, Fr F.-I., 'Onomastique personnelle des l'Ela de Haute-Volta', in *Bulletin de l'I.F.A.N.* XV, 2, Dakar, 1953.

NICP   Nicholson, R. A., *The Idea of Personality in Sûfism*, Cambridge, 1923.

NICR   Nicholson, R. A., *The Mathnavi of Jalal ud Din Rumi*, edited from the oldest manuscripts available with critical notes, translation, and commentary, 8 vols, London, 1925–40.

OCUI   O'Curry, Eugene, *Manners and Customs of the Ancient Irish*, 3 vols, London, 1873.

OEIL   *L'œil*, Lausanne, nos 21, 29, 38, 40, 70, 82, 86, 108, 113.

OGAC   *Ogam – tradition celtique*, Rennes, 1948.

OGRJ   Ogrizek (and others), *Le Japon*, Paris, 1954.

OKAT   Okakura Kakuzo, *The Book of Tea*, London, 1919.

ORAI   O'Rahilly, T. F., *Early Irish History and Mythology*, Dublin, 1946.

ORMD   Ormesson, Jean d', *Dieu, sa vie, son œuvre*, Paris, 1980.

OUSI   Ouspensky, Leonid und Lossky, W., *Der Sinn der Ikonen*, Bern, 1952.

PALE   Pallotino, Massimo, *La peinture étrusque*, Geneva, 1952.
PALL   Pallis, Marco, *Peaks and Lamas*, London, 1939.
PALP   Palmade, Guy, *La psychothérapie*, Paris, 1961.
PALT   Pallis, Marco, 'Le voile du Temple', in *Études traditionelles* 384/5, Paris, 1964.
PAPT   Papus, *Le Tarot des Bohémiens*, Paris, 1889.
PARA   Parrot, André, *Nineveh and Babylon*, London, 1961.
PARI   Paret, Rudi, 'Symbolik des Islam', in *Symbolik des Religionen*, Stuttgart, 1958.
PARS   Parrot, André, *Sumer*, London, 1960.
PAUC   Paulme, Denise, 'La divination par les chacals chez les Dogon de Sanga', in *Journal de la Société des Africanistes* VI, Paris, 1937.
PAUM   Paulme, Denise, *La mère dévorante*, Paris, 1976.
PAYS   Payne Knight, R. and Wright, T., *Sexual Symbolism*, New York, 1957.
PCBC   Péret, Benjamin, *Le livre de Chilam Balam de Chumayel*, translation, Paris, Denoël, 1955.
PELC   Pelliot, Paul, *Mémoires sur les coutumes du Cambodge de Tcheou Ta-Kouan*, Paris, 1951.
PELG   Pellat, Ch., *Glossaire au Kitâb at-Tarbi watta-Wir de gahiz*.
PERC   Percheron, M., *La Chine*, Paris, 1936.
PERD   Pernety, Dom Antoine-Joseph, *Dictionnaire mytho-hermétique*, Paris, 1787; reprinted Paris, 1972.
    Philippe, Robert, *Les métamorphoses de l'humanité*, 8 vols, Paris:
PHIA   Philippe, Robert, *Les aventures*, 1967.
PHIB   Philippe, Robert, *La Barbarie*, 1966.
PHIC   Philippe, Robert, *Les cathédrales*, 1965.
PHID   Philippe, Robert, *Les découvertes*, 1966.
PHIG   Philippe, Robert, *La guerre sainte*, 1965.
PHIM   Philippe, Robert, *L'an mille*, 1964.
PHIR   Philippe, Robert, *Les renaissances*, 1966.
PHIU   Philippe, Robert, *L'universel*, 1967.
PHIL   *La petite philocalie de la prière du cœur*, translated by Jean Gouillard, Paris, 1953.
PICV   Picard, Max, *The Human Face*, London, 1931.
PIED   Pierret, Paul, *Dictionnaire d'archéologie égyptienne*, Paris, 1875.
PIEF   Piettre, A., 'Le thème de la "Fille du roi"', in *Études*, novembre 1964.
PIEP   Pierotti, Ermete, *Customs and Traditions of Palestine*, Cambridge, 1864.
PIRD   Pirot, L., *Supplément au dictionnaire de la Bible*, vol. 1, Paris, 1928.
PLAE   Planque, Michel, 'Eve', in *Dictionnaire de spiritualité*, Paris, 1937.
PLAI   *Plaisirs de France*, Paris, no. 196.
PLUV   Plummer, C., *Vitae Sanctorum Hiberniae*, 2 vols, Dublin, 1897.
PODE   Podolsky, E. and Carlson, Wade, *Erotic Symbolism*, New York, 1960.
POKE   Pokorny, Julius, *Indogermanisches etymologisches Wörterbuch*, Bern, 1954.
POPP   Pope, A., *A Survey of Persian Art*, Oxford, 1939.

PORA   Porée-Maspero E., *Étude sur les rites agraires des Cambodgiens*, Paris and The Hague, 1962.

PORP   Porot, Antoine, *Manuel alphabétique de psychiatrie*, Paris, 1952.

PORS   Portal, Frédéric, *Des couleurs symboliques dans l'Antiquité, le Moyen Age et les Temps Modernes*, Paris, 1837.

POSD   Posener, G., with the assistance of Serge Sauneron and Jean Yoyotte, *A Dictionary of Egyptian Civilization*, translated by Alix Macfarlane, London, 1962.

PRZP   Przyluski, J., *La princesse à l'odeur de poisson et la Nagi dans les traditions de l'Asie orientale*, Paris, 1925.

PSEH   Pseudo-Dionysius the Areopagite, *The Celestial and Ecclesiastical Hierarchies*, translated by Rev. John Parker, London, 1894.

PSEN   Pseudo-Dionysius the Areopagite, *The Divine Names*, translated by the Editors of the Shrine of Wisdom, Godalming (Surrey), 1957.

PSEO   Pseudo-Denys l'Aréopagite, *Œuvres complètes*, translated by Maurice de Gandillac, Paris, 1943.

PUEE   Puech, H.-C., *L'Évangile selon Thomas*, Paris, 1959.

RAMB   Ramos, A., *O Negro Brasileiro*, São Paulo, 1940.

RAMC   Ramos, A., *As Culturas Negras*, Rio de Janeiro, 1937.

RAMN   Ramnoux, Cl., *La nuit et les enfants de la nuit dans la tradition grecque*, Paris, 1959.

RANJ   Rank, Otto, *Don Juan, une étude sur le double*, Paris, 1932.

REAL   *Réalités*, Paris, janvier 1967.

REGR   *Revue des Études grecques*, Paris.

REID   Reichel-Dolmatoff, Gerardo, *Desana*, Bogota, 1968.

RELG   *Die Religion in Geschichte und Gegenwart*, 3rd edition, Tübingen, 1956–62.

RENB   Renondeau, G., *Le bouddhisme japonais*, Paris, 1965.

RESE   Restanque, E., 'L'enfant à la queue du loup', in *Études traditionelles* 360, Paris, 1960.

REVA   *Revue des Arts, Chefs-d'œuvre romans des musées de Province* 6, Paris, 1957.

REVC   *Revue celtique*, Paris, 1870–1934.

REYA   Reypens, L., 'L'âme chez saint Augustin', in *Dictionnaire de spiritualité*, Paris, 1937.

RICG   Richer, Jean, *Géographie sacrée du monde grec*, Paris, 1967.

RIEH   Riemschneider, Marguarate, *Le monde des Hittites*, Paris, 1955.

RIEP   Rieder, H.-R., *Le folklore des Peaux-Rouges, contes et légendes des premiers âges de la vie des Indiens*, Paris, 1952.

RIJT   Rijnberk, Gérard van, *Le tarot (histoire, iconographie, ésotérisme)*, Lyon, 1947.

RITS   Ritter, H., *Das Meer der Seele*, Leiden, 1955.

ROBG   Robertson, Martin, *Greek Painting*, Geneva, 1959.

RODL   Rodinson, Maxime, 'La lune', in *Sources orientales* V, Paris, 1962.

ROGG   Roger-Marx, Claude, *Graphic Art of the 19th Century*, London, 1963.

ROHP   Rohde, Erwin, *Psyche*, London, 1925.

ROMM   Roman, D., 'Remarques sur quelques symboles maçonniques', in
        Études traditionelles 282, Paris, 1951.
ROUF   Roux, Jean-Paul, *Faune et Flore sacrées dans les sociétés altaïques*,
        Paris, 1966.
ROUN   Roux, Cl.-H., *Quelques minorités ethniques du Nord Indochine*,
        Saigon, 1954.
ROWI   Rowe, J. H., 'Inca Culture', in *Handbook of South American
        Indians*, vol. II: *The Andean Civilisations*, Washington, 1946.
ROYD   *Royal Irish Academy Dictionary* (Contributions to a Dictionary
        of the Irish Language), Dublin, 1913.
ROYR   Royston Pike, E., *Encyclopaedia of Religion and Religions*, Lon-
        don, 1954.
RSHU   *Le rêve et les sociétés humaines* (compilation), Paris, 1967.
RUTE   Rutten, M., 'Emblèmes géométriques . . .', in *Revue d'histoire des
        sciences* 2, 1949.

SAIF   Saintyves, P., *Corpus du folklore préhistorique en France et dans
        les colonies françaises*, 3 vols, Paris, 1934–6.
SAIP   Sainte Fare Garnot, J., 'Le rôle du phénix en Égypte et en Grèce',
        in *Revue d'histoire des religions* CXXIX, nos 1, 2, 3, 1945.
SAIR   Saint Martin, L. Cl. de, *Tableau naturel des rapports qui existent
        entre Dieu, l'homme et l'Univers*, Rochefort-sur-Mer, 1946.
SAMG   Samivel (Paul Gayet-Tancrède), *Le soleil se lève en Grèce*, Paris,
        1959.
SCHC   Schuon, F., *L'œil du cœur*, Paris, 1950.
SCHD   Schuon, F., 'Le délivré et l'image divine', in *Études traditionelles*
        384/5, Paris, 1964.
SCHE   Schuon, F., 'Chamanisme peau rouge', in *Études traditionelles*
        378/9, Paris, 1963.
SCHF   Schuon, F., *Spiritual Perspectives and Human Facts*, London, 1954.
SCHG   Schuon, F., *Gnosis*, London, 1959.
SCHI   Schuon, F., *Images de l'esprit*, Paris, 1961.
SCHI   Schilder, Paul, *L'image du corps*, Paris, 1968.
SCHK   Scholem, G. G., *La Kabbale*, translated by Jean Boesse, Paris,
        1951.
SCHL   Schlegel, G., *Tian Ti Hwui, the Hung League or Heaven–Earth
        League*, Batavia, 1866.
SCHM   Schmidt, Albert-Maris, *La mandragore*, Paris, 1958.
SCHO   Scholem, G. G., *Les origines de la Kabbale*, translated by Jean
        Loevenson, Paris, 1966.
SCHP   Schebesta, Paul, *Les Pygmées*, Paris, 1940.
SCHR   Schuon, F., *Castes et races*, Lyon, 1957.
SCHS   Scholem, G. G., *On the Kabbalah and its Symbolism*, translated
        by Ralph Manheim, London, 1965.
SCHT   Schuon, F., 'Remarques sur le symbolisme du sablier', in *Études
        traditionelles* 393, Paris, 1966.
SCHU   Schuon, F., *The Transcendent Unity of Religions*, translated by
        Peter Townsend, London, 1953.
SECA   Seckel, Dietrich, *The Art of Buddhism*, London, 1964.

SECG   Sechan, Louis and Leveque, Pierre, *Les grandes divinités de la Grèce*, Paris, 1966.

SEGI   Segalen, V., *Les immémoriaux*, Paris, 1956.

SEGS   Segalen, V., *Stèles, peintures, équipées*, Paris, 1955.

SEJF   Sejourne, Laurette, *La simbólica del fuego*, reprinted from *Cuadernos americanos*, Mexico, 1964.

SEJQ   Sejourne, Laurette, 'L'univers du Quetzalcóatl', in *Nouvelles du Mexique* 33–4.

SELB   Seler, Eduard, *The Bat God of the Maya Race* (Smithsonian Institution, Bureau of American Ethnology, Bulletin 28), Washington, 1904.

SELM   Seligmann, Kurt, *The Mirror of Magic*, New York, 1948.

SENZ   Senard, M., *Le zodiaque, clef de l'ontologie appliquée à la psychologie*, Paris and Lausanne, 1948.

SERH   Servier, J., *L'homme et l'invisible*, Paris, 1964.

SERP   Servier, J., *Les portes de l'année*, Paris, 1962.

SILB   Silburn, L., *Le bouddhisme*, Paris, 1977.

SILI   Silburn, L., *Instant et cause*, Paris, 1955.

SKAG   *Skazki Narodov Severa* (Northern Siberian Folk-tales), Moscow and Leningrad, 1959.

SOLA   *Le soleil*, Zurich, Arthaud, 1961–2.

SOOL   Soothill, W. E., *The Hall of Light*, London, 1951.

SOUA   Soustelle, Jacques, *The Daily Life of the Aztecs*, translated by Patrick O'Brian, London, 1959.

SOUC   Soustelle, Jacques, 'Observations sur le symbolisme du nombre cinq chez les anciens Mexicains', in *Actes du XXVIIIᵉ congrès international des Américanistes*, Paris, 1947.

SOUD   *Sources orientales*, VI, *Les Danses sacrées*, Paris, 1963.

SOUJ   *Sources orientales*, IV, *Le jugement des morts*, Paris, 1961.

SOUL   *Sources orientales*, V, *La lune, mythes et rites*, Paris, 1962.

SOUM   Soustelle, Jacques, *La pensée cosmologique des anciens Mexicains*, Paris, 1940.

SOUN   *Sources orientales*, I, *La naissance du monde*, Paris, 1959.

SOUP   *Sources orientales*, III, *Les pèlerinages*, Paris, 1960.

SOUS   *Sources orientales*, II, *Les songes et leur interprétation*, Paris, 1959.

SOYS   Soymie, M., *Sources et sourciers en Chine*, Tokyo, 1961.

STEI   Stein, R. A., *La gueule du Makara*, Paris, 1977.

STEJ   Stein, Rolf, 'Jardins en miniature de l'Extrême-Orient, le monde en petit', in *Bulletin de l'E.F.E.O.*, Hanoi, 1943.

STOC   Stokes, Withley, *The Colloquy of the Two Sages*, Paris, 1905.

STOG   Stokes, Withley, *Three Irish Glossaries*, London, 1862.

SUSZ   Suzuki, Daisetz T., *Lectures on Zen Buddhism*, London, 1970ff.

SWAC   Swann, Peter, *The Art of China, Korea and Japan*, London, 1963.

SWAP   Swann, Peter, *La peinture chinoise*, Paris, 1958.

TALS   Talayesva, Don C., *Sun Chief*, edited by Leo W. Simmons, New Haven (Connecticut), 1942.

TARD   Tarsouli, G., *Delphes*, Athens, 1965.

TEGH   Tegnaeus, Harry, *Le héros civilisateur, contribution à l'étude ethno-
        logique de la religion et de la sociologie africaines*, Uppsala,
        1950.

TEIR   Teillard, Ania, *Le symbolisme du rêve*, Paris, 1948.

TERS   Tervarent, Guy de, *Attributs et symboles dans l'art profane, 1450–
        1600*, Geneva, 1959.

THAS   Thai-Van-Kiem, *Sengs et ginseng*, Saigon, 1953.

THEN   *Theologisches Wörterbuch zum Neuen Testament*, vol. I, Stutt-
        gart, 1933.

THIK   Thierry, S., *Les Khmers*, Paris, 1964.

THOH   Thompson, J. Eric S., *Maya Hieroglyphic Writing*, University of
        Oklahoma, reprinted 1960.

THOM   Thomas, L. V. and Luneau, René, *Les religions d'Afrique noire*,
        Paris, Fayard, 1969.

TODS   Todorov, Tzvetan, *Théories du symbole*, Paris, 1977.

TONT   Tondriau, Julien, *Objets tibétains de culte et de magie*, Brussels,
        1964.

TRIR   Trimborn, Hermann, *Religions du sud de l'Amérique centrale, du
        nord et du centre de la région andine*, in *Les religions Amérin-
        diennes*, translated from the German by L. Jospin, Paris, 1962.

TUCK   Tucci, Giuseppe, *Kamalila*, Paris, Nagel, 1974.

TUCR   Tucci, Giuseppe, *Ratilīlā*, Geneva, 1969.

TYAC   Tyan, E., *Le Califat*, Paris, 1954.

UNEC   *Le courrier de l'UNESCO*, Paris, juillet–août 1964.

URIB   *Uriburu*, Paris, 1978.

VACG   Vachot, Ch., *La guirlande des lettres*, Lyon, 1954.

VAJA   Vajda, Georges, *L'amour de Dieu dans la théologie juive du
        Moyen-Age*, Paris, 1957.

VALA   Valsan, M., 'Le triangle de l'androgyne et le monosyllabe "Om" ',
        in *Études traditionelles* 382, Paris, 1964.

VALC   Valentin, F. Basile, *Les douze clefs de la philosophie*, translated,
        with introduction, notes and interpretation of the illustrations
        by Eugène Canseliet, Paris, 1956.

VALD   Valsan, M., 'Le monosyllabe "Om" ', in *Études traditionelles*, mars–
        avril 1966.

VALH   Valsan, M., 'Le coffre d'Héraclius et la tradition du "Tabut"
        adamique', in *Études traditionelles* 374–5, Paris, 1962.

VALI   Valsan, M., 'L'initiation chrétienne', in *Études traditionelles* 389/
        90, Paris, 1965.

VANA   Van Lennep, J., *Art et alchimie*, Brussels, 1966.

VANG   Van Gulik, R., *La vie sexuelle dans la Chine ancienne*, Paris,
        1971.

VANS   Vandier, Jacques, *Egyptian Sculpture*, London, 1951.

VARG   Varagnac, A. et al., *L'art gaulois,* St-Léger-Vauban, 1956.

VASA   Vassel, J., 'Le dernier antre sibyllin', in *Études traditionelles* 316,
        Paris, 1954.

VEDR   *The Rig Veda, an Anthology*, selected, translated and annotated by Wendy Doniger O'Flaherty (Penguin Classics), London, 1981.

VERO   Verger, Pierre, *Notes sur le culte des Orisa et Vodun, à Bahia, la Baie de tous les Saints, au Brésil et à l'ancienne Côte des esclaves en Afrique*, Dakar, 1957.

VINO   Vinci, Leonardo da, *Tout l'œuvre peint*, Paris, 1950.

VIRI   Virel, André, *Histoire de notre image*, Geneva, 1965.

VIRS   Virel, André, 'Symbolique génétique et onirique' (unpublished: kindly made available by the author).

VUIO   Vuilleumier, R., 'Osée et les manuscrits', in *Revue de Qumran* I, 1958–9.

VUOB   Vuong Hong Sen, 'La chique de bétel et les pots à chaux anciens du Viet-Nam', in *Bulletin de la Société des Études Indochinoises*, Saigon, 1950.

VUOC   Vuong Hong Sen, 'Journal d'un collectionneur', in *France-Asie* 100–2, Saigon, 1954.

WARH   Ward, J. and Stirling, W., *The Hung Society or the Society of Heaven and Earth*, London, 1925.

WARK   Warrain, Fr., *La théodicée de la Kabbale*, Paris, 1949.

WENG   Wensinck, A.-J., *La pensée de Ghazzâli*, Paris, 1940.

WERS   Westermarck, E., *Ritual and Belief in Marocco*, 2 vols, London, 1926.

WHEA   Wheeler, Lady, *The Book of Archaeology*, London, 1957.

WHEI   Wheeler, Sir Mortimer, *Early India and Pakistan*, London, 1959.

WIEG   Wieger, Fr Léon, *Chinese Characters*, Hsien-Hsien, 1927.

WIET   Wieger, Fr Léon, *Les pères du système taoïste*, Leiden and Paris, 1950.

WILE   Williams, C. A. S., *Encyclopedia of Chinese Symbolism*, New York, 1960.

WILG   Wilhelm, Richard (translator), *The I Ching or Book of Changes*, London, 1951.

WINI   Windisch, Ernst, *Irische Texte*, 5 vols, Leipzig, 1880–1905.

WIRT   Wirth, Oswald, *Le tarot des imagiers du Moyen Age*, Paris, 1966.

WOLB   Wolff, Werner, *Changing Concepts of the Bible*, New York, 1951.

WOUS   Wou Tch'eng-Ngen, *Si yeou Ki*, Paris, 1957.

YAMB   Yamata, Kikou, *L'art du bouquet du Japon*, in *France-Asie* 137, Saigon, 1957.

YASJ   Yashiro, Yukio, *2000 Years of Japanese Art*, London, 1958.

YGEA   Yge, Claude d', *Nouvelle assemblée des philosophes chimiques, aperçus sur le grand œuvre des alchimistes*, preface by Eugène Canseliet, Paris, 1954.

YUAC   Yuan-Kuang and Canone, Ch., *Méthode pratique de civilisation chinoise par le Yi-King*, Paris, 1950.

ZAHB   Zahan, Dominique, *Sociétés d'initiation Bambara, Le N'Domo, le Kore*, Paris and The Hague, 1960.

ZAHC   Zahan, Dominique, *Les couleurs chez les Bambara du Soudan Français*, in *Notes Africaines* 50, Dakar, avril 1951.

ZAHD   Zahan, Dominique, 'Aperçu sur la pensée théogonique des Dogon', in *Cahiers internationaux de sociologie* VI, Paris, 1949.

ZAHV   Zahan, Dominique, *La dialectique du verbe chez les Bambara*, Paris and The Hague, 1963.

ZEIJ   Zeitlin, Salomon, 'Notes relatives au calendrier juif', in *Revue des études juives* 89, nos 177–8.

ZEIP   *Zeitschrift für celtische Philologie*, Halle-Tübingen, 1900.

ZERA   Zerries, Otto, 'Les religions des peuples archaïques de l'Amérique du Sud et des Antilles', in *Les religions amérindiennes*, translated from the German by L. Jospin, Paris, 1962.

ZWIC   Zwicker, J., *Fontes Historiae Religionis Celticae*, 3 vols, Berlin, 1934.